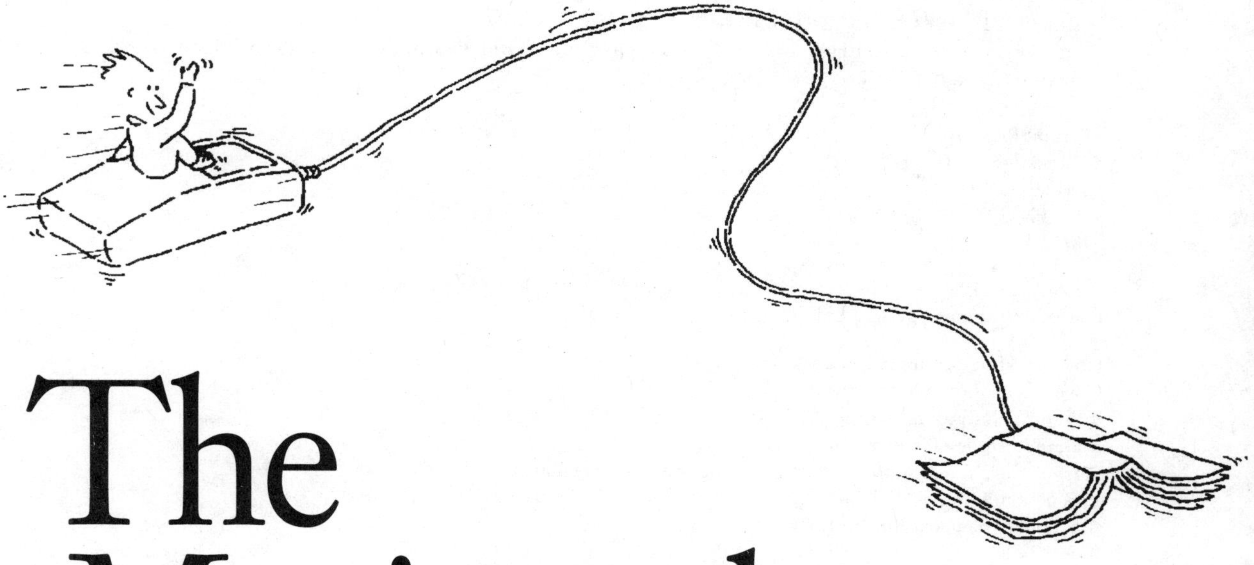

The Macintosh Bible

5TH EDITION

Edited by Darcy DiNucci, Elizabeth Castro, Aileen Abernathy, David Blatner, Connie Guglielmo, John Kadyk, Henry Norr, and Bob Weibel

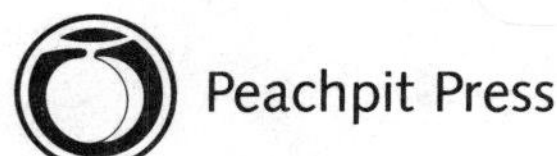

Peachpit Press

The Macintosh Bible, 5th Edition

Edited by Darcy DiNucci, Elizabeth Castro, Aileen Abernathy, David Blatner, Connie Guglielmo, John Kadyk, Henry Norr, and Bob Weibel

Peachpit Press, Inc.
2414 Sixth Street
Berkeley, CA 94710
510/548-4393
510/548-5991 (fax)

Cover and interior design: YO, San Francisco
Cover illustration: John Grimes
Technical illustrations: Laurie Wigham
Margin icons: Joe Crabtree, Art Parts
Copyediting: Tema Goodwin (lead), Eliot Bergson, John Hammett
Production: Proctor-Willenbacher
Art production management: Eliot Bergson
Index: Ty Koontz

Distribution
Peachpit Press books are distributed to the U.S. book trade by Publishers Group West, 4065 Hollis, P.O. Box 8843, Emeryville, CA 94609, phone: 800/788-3123 or 510/658-3453, fax: 510/658-1834. Peachpit books are also available from wholesalers throughout the U.S., including Baker & Taylor Books, Golden-Lee Book Distributors, and Ingram Book Company. Bookstores can also order using Wordstock or IBID (SAN 2028522). Resellers outside the book trade can contact Peachpit directly at 800/980-8999.

Library of Congress Cataloging-in-Publication Data
The Macintosh Bible / edited by Darcy DiNucci…[et al.].—5th ed.
p. cm.
Includes index.
ISBN 1-56609-140-3
1. Macintosh (Computer) I. DiNucci, Darcy.
QA76.8.M3M273 1994 94-30292
004.165—dc20 CIP

ISBN 1-56609-140-3

9 8 7 6 5 4 3 2 1

Printed on Recycled Paper

Printed and bound in the United States of America

Preface

BY Arthur Naiman

WHEN I FIRST CAME UP with the idea for the *Macintosh Bible* back in 1986, I told myself that editing and publishing it would take maybe 25% of my time, and that I'd be happy if it sold 50,000 copies.

Eight years and more than 800,000 copies later, I'm gratified by the book's success (to say the least). But I'm still reeling from the toll it took in my life—not 25% but 150% of my time, and even more when I was working on a new edition. So it was with great relief that I turned the editing and publishing of this Fifth Edition over to Peachpit Press and to the small army of Mac experts they assembled.

I've hardly seen a word of this edition, because I've been busy working on my new publishing company—Odonian Press. So far, most of Odonian's books have been in the Real Story series, which is based on a simple idea: political books don't have to be boring. Real Story books are short (about 100 pages), inexpensive ($5–$6) and written to be *read.*

People seem to appreciate those qualities, and have bought well over a hundred thousand copies. We even have a couple of bestsellers, both by Noam Chomsky: *What Uncle Sam Really Wants* and *The Prosperous Few and the Restless Many.* As I write this, we're working on a third Chomsky book, called *Secrets, Lies and Democracy.* Here's a list of our other titles:

- *The CIA's Greatest Hits* (each described in a couple of pages and accompanied by a cartoon)
- Gore Vidal's brilliantly written *Decline and Fall of the American Empire*
- Greenpeace's exposé of *Anti-environmental Organizations*
- two poignant and chilling country-specific books—*East Timor: Genocide in Paradise* and *Burma: the Next Killing Fields?*

- our "assassination trilogy"—*Who Killed JFK?*, *Who Killed Robert Kennedy?* and *Who Killed Martin Luther King?*
- and our only health title so far, *America's Favorite Drug: Coffee and Your Health*.

They're available wherever short, readable, nonboring books are sold. If you can't find them, or want to buy in quantity, please contact Odonian Press, Box 32375, Tucson AZ 85751 (602 296 4056 or 800 REAL STORY).

Well, that's about all I have to say. Thanks for your suggestions and support over the years. I've really loved the interaction and the feeling of being part of the Mac community. I only wish I'd had the time to answer all your cards and letters.

Whatever happens to each of us in the years to come, don't forget: This is the Mac. It's supposed to be *fun*.

Contents

Introduction

BY Darcy DiNucci

FOR EIGHT YEARS AND FOUR EDITIONS, Arthur Naiman and his team at Goldstein & Blair have made *The Macintosh Bible* the most popular book about the Mac. They cut through "old-age thinking," marketingspeak, and techtalk to let people know what's *really* important to know about the Mac. Now that Arthur's gone on to publish a whole new line of books, how can we carry on?

By doing the same thing again.

For this fifth edition, Peachpit Press has pulled together its own cast of Mac experts (including lots of familiar names from past versions) to update the *Bible*. In this edition, you'll find information on

- Power Macintoshes, the new generation of Macs based on the PowerPC processor
- the 500-series PowerBooks
- System 7.5, the new version of Apple's operating system
- the latest versions of important software, including Microsoft Works 4, Word 6, and Excel 5; and ClarisWorks 2 (including tips for using the new features)
- the latest in multimedia and CD-ROM technology
- getting onto the Internet with your Mac and a modem

and lots more.

To pull it all together, we divided the book's 25 chapters (plus four appendixes) among eight Mac experts—the editors of this edition. Then we asked those editors to pull together the most knowledgeable people they could find to compile information on the key things to know, the best products, and the hottest tips for each topic.

The Mac Bible Editors

Here are the editors of *The Macintosh Bible*, fifth edition. Look for their initials and opinions throughout the book.

Darcy DiNucci (DD), the project editor, has been writing and editing for computer publications, including *PC World*, *Macworld*, *NeXTWORLD*, *Publish*, and *MacWEEK*, since before the Mac was born. She now runs To the Point Publishing, a full-service publication-management company in San Francisco.

For this edition of the *Mac Bible*, Darcy's job was to make sure all the important topics were covered and explained clearly somewhere, by someone, and to put together a design and production team to turn it all into a book. She was also the primary editor on the chapters covering Working With the Macintosh, Fonts, and Sharing Files.

Elizabeth Castro (EC), the technical editor, fell in love with the Mac while living in Barcelona, where she founded Pagina Uno, a publishing house whose mission was to spread the Mac religion in Spain. She is the author of two books and a frequent contributor to the Spanish edition of *Macworld* magazine.

In addition to editing the chapters on Working with Words, Spreadsheets, Databases, and Utilities, as well as the appendixes on Where to Find Information and Buying Macs and Mac Products, Liz pulled together the initial outline for the book, read every chapter for technical accuracy, and contributed lots of hot tips culled from her years of playing and working with Macs.

Aileen Abernathy (AA) went from being a desktop publisher to writing about it for *MacUser* magazine. During her four years as senior editor, she covered electronic publishing and graphics as well as the really important stuff, such as games. She currently writes for *MacUser*, *MacWEEK*, *Publish*, and corporate clients. She edited the chapters on Graphics, Multimedia, and Games and Hobbies.

David Blatner (DB) is the coauthor of several books from Peachpit Press, including *Real World Scanning and Halftones*, *The QuarkXPress Book*, and *Silicon Mirage: The Art and Science of Virtual Reality*. He lectures around the world on desktop publishing topics and edited the chapter on Page Layout for this book.

Connie Guglielmo (CG), a former editor at *MacWEEK*, is now a freelance writer in San Francisco who covers technology for *MacWEEK*, *New Media*, *Wired*, and many other publications. When she's not working, she spends time with her three-year-old daughter, who loves to talk into the microphone on her PowerBook. She was responsible for covering Personal and Business Management, Integrated Software, Education and Reference, and Kids' Stuff for this edition.

John Kadyk (JK) remembers proofreading the two-page plan for the first *Mac Bible* at Won Thai restaurant in Berkeley in June 1986. He likes playing music and riding bikes when he's not writing, editing, or consulting about Macs. In this edition of the *Bible* (he's worked on all five), John oversaw (and wrote much of) the chapters on The Macintosh Family, System Software, and Basic Peripherals, as well as the appendix on Staying Healthy at the Mac.

Henry Norr (HN) is editor emeritus of *MacWEEK*; that means he used to be the editor. Now he writes a weekly column for the magazine, called "The Second Decade," about important issues facing Apple and its customers. His checkered past includes stints as a printer, machinist, community college teacher, researcher on Polish politics and Soviet economic history, and Mac trainer. Henry covered Memory, Storage, Preventing and Solving Problems, and Telecommunications for this edition of the *Bible*.

Bob Weibel (BW) bought his first computer, a 48K Apple II Plus, with money borrowed from his girlfriend, and he hasn't looked back. Versed in the Mac, the PC, and Unix workstations, Bob spent three years as writer and senior technical editor for *Publish* magazine, though you'll now find him covering a range of topics in the pages of *Macworld*, *PC World*, *MacWEEK*, *Photo District News*, and *PC/Computing*. He's coauthor, with Ted Nace and Robert C. Eckhardt, of *Desktop Publishing Secrets*, and coauthor, with David Blatner, of *The QuarkXPress Book*, *Windows Edition*, both published by Peachpit Press. Bob covered Printing and Networking for this book.

What to Look For

A look at this edition of the *Mac Bible* will show some major differences from—and lots of similarities to—earlier editions.

- **Who wrote what.** As always, you'll see the initials of the people who wrote each entry in the entry head. In this edition, the main contributors for each chapter are introduced on the table of contents page for that chapter.
- **Icons to help you find specific kinds of information.** As in earlier editions, you can use the margin icons to find hot tips, good features, and other kinds of information. A guide to the icons is provided on page xvi.

Products and Prices (DD)

We talk about lots of Macintosh products in this book, from the Mac models themselves to obscure shareware utilities: anything we think you might be interested in or might make your life easier (within our space constraints, of course). To make it easier to find these products, we've included contact information for all the products' manufacturers in Appendix D. To make it easy to get shareware or freeware that we recommend, Peachpit has compiled a set of floppy disks that contains many of them, available when you send the coupon in the back of this book and $10 to Peachpit Press.

When we recommend a product, we also list the manufacturer's suggested price, just for comparison shopping. When looking at those prices, remember that nobody *really* pays the list price for a piece of hardware or software. You can always get it cheaper—sometimes hundreds of dollars cheaper for some high-priced products—at almost any computer retailer, and especially by mail order. (Some tips on finding good dealers and good prices are included in Appendix C.) There are two exceptions to this rule. One is Apple equipment. At least when this book was written, Apple had the policy of not naming list prices but instead quoting an "ApplePrice," which is its estimate of what you would actually pay at a retailer. (Remember that when comparing prices on Apple and other equipment; the ApplePrice already includes the inevitable discount.) The other exception, of course, is shareware, which always costs the same (usually very low) price.

In keeping with *Mac Bible* tradition, we've rounded list prices up to the nearest logical figure, just to show those marketers that we're not fooled: *We* know that $39.95 is really $40.

- **Editors' polls.** A new feature of this edition is the editors' polls, which let you know what the *Mac Bible* editors think on topics of importance—like what's the best screensaver out there, or whether it really is important to have a color monitor.

Each editor had a pretty free hand in determining how to approach the topics he or she was responsible for. We just asked everybody to use the pages they were allotted to say the most important things about that topic they could think of. Generally, though, each chapter includes a basic introduction to the topic, pointers to any products you should know about in that category, and hot tips that should make your life easier. The chapter intros and tables of contents will give you an overview of what each editor decided to highlight.

We've included a *big* index and glossary in the back of the book. We try to explain Macintosh terms the first time they come up, but come on: Who knows what order you're going to read the book in, and we can't define every term *every* time. So if you hit a term you're not familiar with (well, a *Macintosh* term you're not familiar with), look it up in the glossary. And if you want to know more about any topic, turn to the index first. I bet you'll find what you're looking for.

Guide to the Icons

All those little icons in the margin of this book aren't just for show. They're there to help you find information you may be particularly interested in. (Okay, and for show, too; we especially like the skunk and the Grim Reaper.)

BARGAIN

Good is good, but good and cheap is even better.

CD-ROM

This labels products that come on CD-ROM, or information for people who use (or want) a CD-ROM drive.

HOT TIP

Every time you see this, you'll find out how to make your life a little easier. Sometimes, we have so many tips in a row (check out Part 2 of the book, where we describe lots of software) that we use just one of these icons for a whole bunch of tips and add a rule to show you how far the tips extend.

MAC BIBLE DISK

When you see this, the product we're talking about is included on the Mac Bible disks you can get from Peachpit. (See the coupon in the back of this book for more on how to get them.)

POWERBOOK

The information labeled with this icon should be particularly interesting to people who work on PowerBooks.

THINGS TO COME

Nobody can predict the future, but we try. (Since we're not afraid to be wrong, it's not a problem.)

BAD FEATURE

We haven't used this one a lot. Since space is short (yes, even in 1,100 pages), we've tended to focus more on recommending good products than panning the bad ones, but sometimes a big product does some really dumb stuff. This warns you.

GOOD FEATURE

On the other hand, this will help you find features you'll want to look for.

SYSTEM 7.5

This highlights new features you'll find in System 7.5, the system software version scheduled to be introduced just as this book went to press. The icon will lead you to the benefits of the new system in each area.

WARNING

You won't die—usually—if you ignore this icon, but you'll be a lot happier if you don't.

The (Mac Bible) Ten Commandments

1 *This is the Mac. It's supposed to be fun.*

For years, many businesspeople treated the Mac as a toy, while those of us who'd already had a bellyful of the deranged command structure of more primitive computers romped happily in the fields of Macintosh. Now the Mac has gotten some corporate acceptance and Windows has made the PC much more like the Mac. Both developments are basically good, but there's a risk that they'll engender a lifeless, "businesslike" homogenization of how personal computers relate to their users.

The rigid dichotomy between work and fun—and the acceptance of that dichotomy as inevitable and necessary—is, to quote The Firesign Theatre's Dr. "Happy" Harry Cox, "Old Age thinking." More clearly than any other computer, the Mac demonstrates that aesthetics enhance, rather than detract from, efficient work.

So don't let them turn the Mac into an expensive version of the PC, or the PC into a clumsy, bloodless imitation of the Mac. Demand fun as your birthright!

2 *Easy is hard.*

There's a macho attitude among some computer jocks (although certainly not among the best of them) that the harder something is to deal with, the more advanced it is. Actually, of course, it's very hard to make things easy. The more work you put into something, the less work the person who uses it has to do.

So if you find yourself beating your head against a wall erected by someone's laziness (or greed), look around for a different wall that someone else took the trouble to put a door in. And if anybody mocks what you're using as a toy, just smile and say, "Easy is hard. Hard is primitive."

3 *It's not your fault you're confused.*

Over the years, manuals have gotten better and programs are designed more sensibly than they used to be, but that's a little like saying how much nicer Himmler has been since his lobotomy. Often the problem is expertosis (the inability of experts in a given field to remember what it's like not to be an expert). Sometimes it's simple money-grubbing. In any case, the thing to remember is this:

If you're confused, it's not because you're stupid—it's because the people who designed that product, or wrote that manual, or rushed their employees so they couldn't do a good job, are stupid. Just make sure they, not you, pay for it.

4 *You can't do it all.*

Some experienced Mac users can make you feel like a loser because you're not up on the new products and techniques they're always discovering. But it's really just that you have different interests. Theirs is exploring the Mac and yours—if you're like most people—is simply using it.

Each approach has its virtues and neither is inherently superior to the other. So feel free to restrict yourself to a small number of Mac programs that you master and use intensively. Remember: You can't do it all—nobody can—so don't feel guilty about not trying.

5 *Make the Mac your own.*

There's never been a computer you could, as Omar put it, "remould...nearer to the Heart's Desire." So give yourself time to customize your Mac. Find the software you like best. Spend hours rearranging the desktop or the files on your disks. The more the Mac feels like your own creation, the more efficient and enjoyable your work on it will be.

Think of the Mac as your home. You wouldn't try to move every different piece of furniture in the world into your home, just because you could. You have furniture you feel comfortable with, appliances you need and use, decorations and toys that amuse you. Treat your Mac the same way.

A file saved is a file saved.

What shall it profit you if you create the greatest piece of work in the world but lose it because you forgot to save?

Despite how wonderfully easy it is to use, the Mac has as many traps and pitfalls as any other computer—maybe more. These don't have to be a problem, if you *save your work!* Of course it's a pain and it interrupts the flow of your thoughts, but that's nothing compared to what it feels like to lose work.

People are always telling you to save, as if it mattered to *them*. It's too bad saving has acquired this taint of moralism. Saving your work isn't something you *should* do because some authority tells you to. The appeal here is pure pleasure principle—you'll be a lot happier if you get in the habit.

Two, three, many backups.

Saving is only half the battle. Disks crash all the time. If you don't make regular backups, you may as well not save your work at all.

Combat the tragedy of the commons.

In English villages, the "commons" was a piece of land on which everyone could graze livestock. It's clearly in each villager's individual interest to graze as many head of, say, sheep on the commons as he or she can. Yet if all the villagers follow their own best interest, the commons gets grazed bare and all the sheep starve. This is called "the tragedy of the commons." It requires some social and environmental consciousness on the part of all the villagers, some long-range, unselfish thinking, to avoid the ecological catastrophe.

Just the same thing is true on the Mac. It's no big deal if one person doesn't pay for a shareware program, but if a lot of people don't, good shareware stops getting written. It's no big deal if one person copies a commercial program and uses it for free, but if a lot of people do that, software developers have trouble making money and start cutting corners. In both cases, slowly but surely, the commons becomes a barren patch of dirt.

9 *Allow for Murphy's Law (since you can't avoid it).*

Here's a piece of trivia few people know—the origin of Murphy's Law. In 1949, Captain Ed Murphy was an engineer working at Edwards Air Force Base in California. When a technician working in his lab miswired something, Murphy said, "If there's any way to do it wrong, he will." A co-worker of his, George E. Nichols, dubbed this Murphy's Law.

Murphy's Law has evolved into, "If anything can go wrong, it will," but it's interesting to note that it originally referred to incompetence, not to some sort of impersonal malevolence on the part of the cosmos.

In any case, things certainly do go wrong with distressing regularity. This happens less on the Mac than elsewhere, thanks to the care and dedication of its original designers. In fact, the Mac's ease of use can lull you into the dangerous delusion that Murphy's Law has been banished from its realm.

No sooner do you assume this than reality disabuses you of the notion—usually more abruptly than you'd like. It works sort of like the Greek concept of hubris: Pride—or, in this case, complaisance—goeth before a fall.

10 *That goes double for Sturgeon's Law.*

In the late '50s, Theodore Sturgeon (1918–1985) wrote a book-review column for a magazine called *Venture Science Fiction.* It was there he first enunciated Sturgeon's Law. "It's well known," he wrote (I'm paraphrasing), "that 90 percent of all science-fiction writing is crap. But then, 90 percent of *everything* is crap."

PART 1

The Mac Itself

Editors' Poll: What Makes a Mac a Mac?

AA: Attitude—the idea that you can actually enjoy working on a computer. You can have fun yet still be productive. I persuaded a friend to buy a Mac last fall, contradicting the sales pitch of a very PC-oriented salesman. He's so thrilled with it that he sent me a big thank-you bouquet for Valentine's Day!

DB: There's reasonable evidence that the Macintosh is not so much a computer as a religion. For those who like absolute truths, the Macintosh is a great machine for focusing one's attention. Of course, for those of us who live in the existential quagmire of relativism, the Macintosh is just one point on the wide spectrum of computing possibilities.

EC: A Mac is a Mac because you can explore as much as you want and you'll never break anything or destroy anything. There's always a Cancel button or some other familiar escape route at your fingertips. Macs don't bite.

DD: It's not the graphic interface; everyone's got that now. It's the Mac's insistence on an integrated and aesthetically elegant approach to everything it does, from its interface to its networking and, now, telecommunications. The Mac has always been the great communicator, both in its own interface and in the features it makes available to its users.

CG: It's that smiling face that greets you when you turn it on, the fact that you're able to change your desktop pattern and you're hard disk name anytime you want. (Last week my hard disk was Derybar, a lost island with buried treasure from a Sinbad the Sailor story. Before that it was Pemberley, an estate in a Jane Austen novel.) It's the whole idea that you don't have to be deadly serious just to get work done.

JK: The Mac is set up to work with you on human terms, rather than forcing you to work with it on computer terms. It's like the cockpit of a well-designed sports car, where all the controls and instruments the driver needs are within easy reach, so he or she can think about driving without wasting energy figuring out the vehicle.

HN: The Mac look and feel is what defines the platform in my mind. There are lots of other graphical user interfaces nowadays, and some of them have features I like, but the Mac has a consistency and elegance that none of the others can match. It's the Mac Toolbox— the set of system services built into ROM and the operating system—that makes this look and feel available to all applications. That's the real key to the system.

BW: Steve Jobs's vision of Macintosh entailed turning personal computers into true data-processing appliances with simplified controls, like Low, Medium, High—easier to use than some VCRs. And now Apple is pushing beyond the graphic user interface, for voice-activated interfaces and other methods of adapting the computer's power to the ways people actually approach their work.

1 Working With Your Mac

The Macintosh's graphical user interface is more than just good-looking: It's also designed to make working with a computer as easy as possible. And while some of these features have also been adopted by other operating systems on other personal computers, only the Mac has staked its business on being the best at them.

The Mac may be easier to use than any other computer in history, but that's not saying much. When you first sit down to use the Mac, you've got to memorize some rules, the same as with any computer. The difference on the Mac is that you need to learn those rules just once. You launch every program the same way, and you cut and paste text or graphics, save your work, and give commands the same way no matter what program you're using.

This chapter teaches the basic rules of working with a Macintosh. When you're finished, you should be able to find your way around the Finder (the Mac's desktop interface) and any Mac program. It starts with the very basics, so if you're already familiar with the Mac's interface, you can skip most of it. Even if you're an old hand at the Mac, though, turn to the tips at the end for some tricks you might not know about.

Contributors

Darcy DiNucci (DD) is the chapter editor.

Arthur Naiman (AN), John Kadyk (JK), Nancy E. Dunn (ND), Sharon Zardetto Aker (SA), Susan McCallister (SM), Charles Rubin (CR), Byron Brown (ByB), and **Karen Faria (KF)** were contributors to earlier editions of the *Macintosh Bible,* from which much of this chapter was taken.

Contents

The Macintosh Desktop (AN/JK/ND/SA/SM/CR/ByB/KF)

When you first turn on your Macintosh, you see a gray area with a few tiny pictures and symbols arranged on it. (If you don't see this, jump over to the box on page 7 titled "What to Do If Your Screen Doesn't Match the Pictures Shown Here.") What you're looking at is the Macintosh *Finder*. You never have to start the Finder yourself: The Macintosh opens it automatically when you start the computer. (In fact, we're only telling you this name for it because you will see it referred to that way sometimes.)

Since most of what you do on a Mac would be done on the top of a desk if you didn't have a computer, this area is also called the *desktop*, and many of the symbols you'll see there are in the form of objects you would use in an office. The desktop is the area in which you organize the contents of your hard disk, and from which you launch programs and open documents. In this section, we'll describe how to work with the items you see on the desktop.

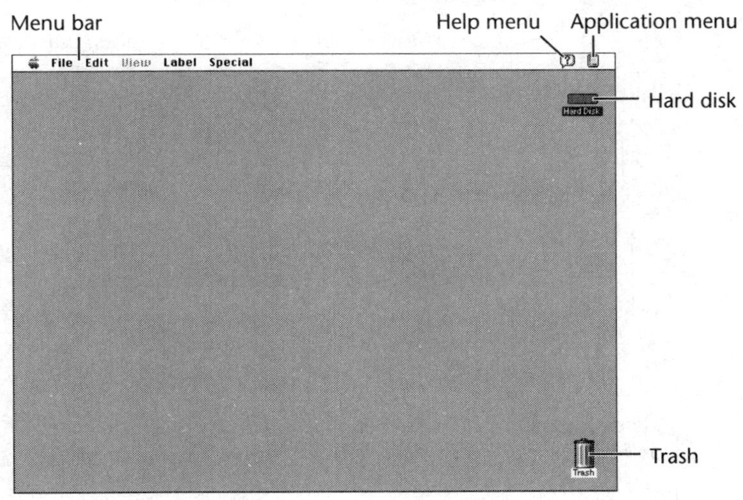

The Macintosh desktop is what you see when you first start the computer. From here, you can open programs and open, copy, and delete files.

The Graphical User Interface

The Mac's way of communicating with people is sometimes referred to as a *graphical user interface*. You control the computer by pointing at, moving, and manipulating little graphic symbols called *icons*. These icons stand for all the things you'll work with on your computer—disks, programs, documents, and so on.

Icons and What They Mean (AN/JK/ND/SA/SM/CR/ByB/KF/DD)

There's a different icon for each kind of information on the Mac. Here's a guide to the most common icons and a description of what they stand for.

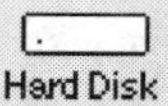

Disks are where you store your *files*. (A file is simply any collection of information saved under a single name on the computer.) They come in several varieties (described in Chapter 5), but the most common are hard disks and floppy disks, whose icons are shown here. The startup disk is in the upper-right corner of the desktop. Other disks that you add to your system, including floppies you insert, will line up under the startup disk at the right edge of the screen.

Programs are groups of instructions that tell the computer what to do. Each program has its own distinctive icon, with the name of the program written underneath.

Documents are like paper documents, but created with a program and stored on the computer. They usually have icons that look kind of like the icon for the program that made them (compare the icon here named "02.Power PC" with the one above for Microsoft Word, the program that created it). If the Mac can't tell what program created the document, it displays a generic, plain-paper icon, like the one called "READ ME FIRST!".

Folders hold groups of files—documents, programs, and so on. You use folders to organize your files. You can put folders within folders to your heart's content—whatever you need to organize your work and make it easy to find. You create folders using the New Folder command in the Finder's File menu.

Other icons stand for particular functions of Mac software. You just get to know what they are after seeing them again and again.

Two icons are always on your desktop: the icon for your *startup disk* (the disk that has the *system software* on it) and a trash can, where you put things you want to throw away. (System software is explained in Chapter 3.) Other icons will show up as you begin to work with the computer. The basic ones are described in the box above.

The Pointer and the Mouse

What you point at and manipulate icons *with* is called, with simple elegance, the *pointer*. When you're pointing at icons, the pointer takes the shape of a left-leaning arrow (↖). It can take other shapes, too, depending on what you're doing at the time (see the box "Pointer Shapes" on the next page).

The most important part of the pointer is the *hot spot*. That's the part of the pointer that needs to touch the item you're pointing at. On the arrow pointer, the hot spot is the tip. You're not really pointing at something unless the tip of the arrow is touching the object you're trying to point at.

What to Do If Your Screen Doesn't Match the Pictures Shown Here (DD)

If your screen contains more items than the ones shown in the illustration on page 5, don't worry. That could just mean that someone has left the desktop in a different order after they used it. The Macintosh desktop can be customized to the user's content. We'll tell you how to work with the items you see there as you read through this chapter.

If your desktop is missing the balloon with a question mark in the upper-right corner of the desktop, you're probably running System 6, an earlier version of the Mac's basic system software. (System software is described more fully in Chapter 3.) Some procedures are different in the two systems, but we'll be sure to tell you about them as we go along. (If you're running System 6, you also may be missing the icon in the top-right corner of the screen, labeled Application menu in the illustration on page 5.)

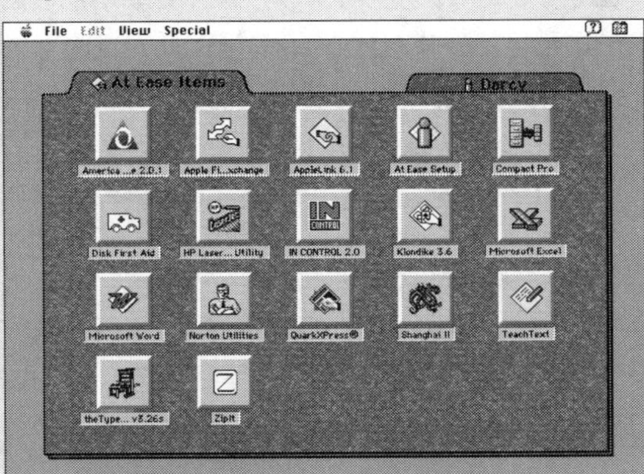

At Ease, which comes with Macintosh Performa models, uses this desktop.

If your screen looks like the illustration below, your computer is running At Ease, a program that comes with Performa Macintosh models and may be installed on other systems as well. (The different Macintosh models are described in Chapter 2.) At Ease is described at the end of this chapter. Even if you're running At Ease, though, you probably will also be using the Finder, and you will certainly be working with documents, which the rest of this chapter describes, so keep reading.

Pointer Shapes (AN/JK/DD)

The most common pointer icon is a left-leaning arrow (↖). When you're dealing with text, the pointer takes the shape of an *I-beam* (I). There are a whole slew of pointers for dealing with graphics, including [brush], [paint bucket], [spray can], [hand], and [lasso].

Sometimes the pointer turns into a wristwatch ([watch]). That means the Mac is busy carrying out a command or operation. In that case, you need to wait until it changes back to the pointer before you can do anything else.

You typically control the pointer with a *mouse*. (Other devices, like *trackballs*, are also used; you can read about trackballs in Chapter 6). When you roll the mouse around, the pointer moves in the same direction on the screen. You get so used to the mouse after a while, it begins to feel as if you're moving the pointer directly with your hand.

Here's a chance to clear up a very common problem beginners run into (we vividly remember the frustration ourselves): Often the mouse runs into something on the desk, or gets to the edge of the desk; if the pointer still isn't where you want it to be, what do you do?

The solution is simplicity itself. All you need to do to move the pointer further is *pick the mouse up* and put it down where you have more room to roll it in the direction you want. Aha!

Working With Icons on the Desktop

As we described in the box on page 6, there are lots of different kinds of icons. Although you'll find icons within programs as well as in the Finder, here we'll talk about working with the icons that represent programs, documents, folders, and other items on the desktop. In all the steps described here, you will use the basic mouse vocabulary: clicking, double-clicking, and dragging, described in the box on the next page.

Opening icons. You open a disk, folder, or document to see what's inside. You open a program to work with it. To open any item represented by an icon on the desktop, you double-click on its icon.

(You can also click once on the icon to select it, and then go up to the File menu and choose the Open command, but that's a whole lot more trouble than double-clicking. There's even a third possibility. You can also click on an icon

Clicking, Double-Clicking, and Dragging (DD)

Once you've pointed at something with the mouse, you use the mouse button to tell the Mac what you want to do with it. There are just three types of actions in the entire mouse vocabulary: clicking, double-clicking, and dragging.

Clicking. To click, you move the mouse pointer to the item you want to click on, then press and release the mouse button.

Double-clicking. Double-clicking means clicking the mouse button twice in rapid succession. (Be sure not to move the mouse between clicks or the Mac will interpret it as two separate clicks and not a double-click.)

Dragging. To drag, you start just as you would with a click: You move the pointer to the item you want to work with and press the mouse button. This time, though, *hold the button down* and move the mouse.

You'll use these mouse actions in various situations within the Finder and with other programs.

and hit ⌘O to open it. But why bother? In this case, double-clicking is so much easier.)

Hard Disk

You can tell an icon is open if it shows up as a grayed-out outline of itself. Look for its window on screen.

When you open a disk, folder, or document icon, the contents of that item appear in a window on screen. (You also get some great on-screen zooming effects as the icon opens.) When it's open, the icon itself turns into an outline of itself. If an icon's window is already open before you double-click on the icon, you won't see any zooming; that icon's window will just become *active*—move to the top of the screen and be ready for action.

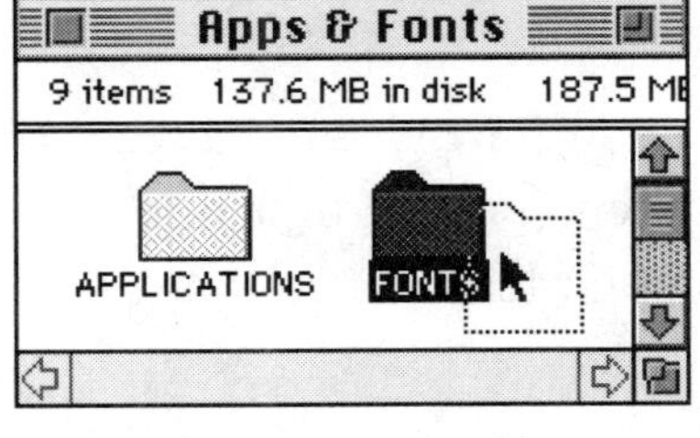

When you drag an icon, a "ghost" of the item sticks to the pointer until you release the mouse button, at which point the icon appears in the new location.

Moving icons. You can place icons anywhere on the desktop that you want them.

To move an icon, you simply drag it to its new position. You can move an icon to a new folder or disk by just dragging the icon over the icon of the folder or disk you want to copy it to, or into the open window of that folder or disk. (If you want to copy the icon to the new location rather than moving it, hold down the [Option] key as you drag. If the location you drag the icon to is on a different disk, the icon will automatically be copied, rather than moved.)

Renaming icons. One of the great pleasures of the Mac is being able to easily change the names of files and folders on the desktop whenever the whim strikes you. You do it by clicking directly on the icon's name (not on the picture part). When you do this, the name is highlighted and outlined. (If you miss the name and click on the picture, just press [Return] to select the name. In System 6, you can click anywhere on the icon and the name will just be highlighted, not outlined.) When the name is highlighted, you can type in a new name and press [Return] (or click outside the icon) to change it.

You edit icon names the way you edit text anywhere on the Mac—and this is as good a place as any to tell you about that. When you move the pointer over a highlighted icon name, it becomes an I-beam (I). Wherever you click the I-beam, a flashing bar called the *insertion point* appears, allowing you to start typing at that point, or to backspace over the characters behind it using the [Delete] key. If you press the mouse button and then drag the I-beam over a part of the name, you'll select it, which means you can then delete or type over that part.

When you see the I-beam pointer, you can use text-editing commands.

Click on an icon's name to select it. You can then change the name.

You can use any character but the colon (:) in an icon name, including spaces. The name can be up to 31 characters long.

WARNING

Two warnings about editing icon names. First, be careful about changing the names of files you haven't created yourself. For example, it's not a good idea to change the names of program files, font files, or system files because sometimes other programs look for those files by name.

Second, be sure the name of the icon is outlined before you start typing. If it's not, your typing will select another icon, rather than rename the first one. That's because in System 7 (not in System 6) typing the first letter of an icon's name is a shortcut for clicking on it.

Throwing out icons. When you want to delete a file, you just drag its icon to the Trash icon in the bottom right corner of the desktop.

In System 7, things don't get thrown out immediately; they stay in the Trash in case you change your mind. If you do change your mind, just double-click on the Trash icon to open the Trash window and drag the item back where it came from. (You can also click on it and choose Put Away from the File menu.)

When there's something in the Trash, it bulges (as in the illustration at left) to let you know it's not empty any more. When it gets emptied, it goes back to its normal, straight-sided shape (right).

To permanently get rid of whatever's in the Trash, use the Empty Trash command in the Special menu. (In System 6, the Trash is also emptied automatically under certain conditions—for example, when you remove a floppy disk that contains a file you've thrown away or when you turn off the computer. But in System 7, the Trash empties only when you tell it to.)

Ejecting floppy disks. There are several ways to remove a floppy disk, but the best way is to drag the floppy disk icon to the Trash. (Don't worry—nothing will be erased from the disk; it's just a way of telling the Mac you want to eject it.) You can also use the Eject Disk command on the Special menu, but if you do it that way, the Mac keeps a record of the ejected floppy and may later ask you to reinsert it—which can get to be a headache.

Sometimes the Mac won't let you eject a disk: You'll get an alert box that tells you that the disk couldn't be "put away" because it contains items that are in use. In that case, make sure all the files and programs on the disk are closed and try again.

Working With Windows

When you open a disk, folder, or document icon, the contents of that item will appear in a *window* like the one shown in the illustration on the next page. If you open a disk or folder icon, the window shows the files saved on that disk. What's a file? Simply any collection of information saved on the computer disk or in its memory. You can either create files yourself or—as in the case of programs, clip art, or other *software*—you can buy them.

In order to do anything with—or to—a window, it has to be active. You can have several windows open on screen at one time, but only one of them can be active.

A window is always active when it first opens. To make a window active, just click anywhere in the window. When windows overlap, the active window always appears on top of the stack.

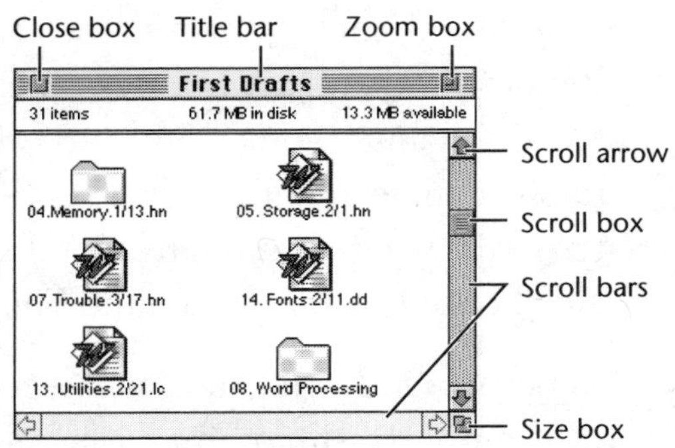

The contents of an icon always appear in a window. Every window has the same basic controls, described here.

Closing a window. To close a window, click in the little *close box* at the left end of the title bar. (You can also choose the Close command from the File menu or press ⌘W).

Move a window. You move a window by dragging it by its *title bar* (click anywhere in the title bar, then, holding the mouse button down, move the mouse to reposition the window).

Resizing a window. Drag the *size box* vertically, horizontally, or diagonally to manually resize a window. To automatically resize a window to show all of its contents (or as much as will fit on screen), click the *zoom box*. (In System 6, the window expands to fill the screen, not just to show the contents.) The next time you click the zoom box, the window goes back to its original size.

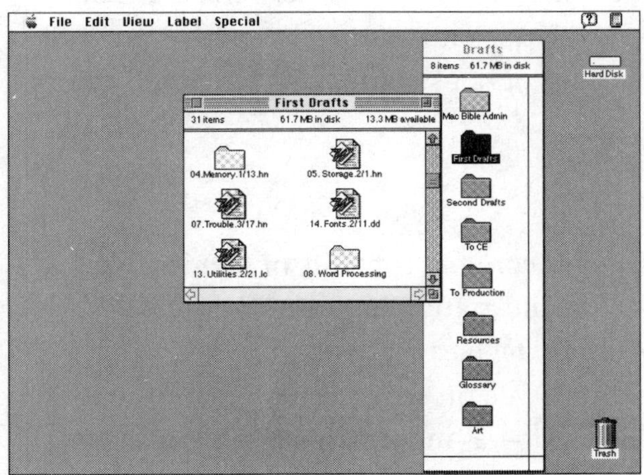

A window has to be active before you can do anything with it. To select a window (that is, to make it active), just click anywhere inside of it. When a window is active, it shows its scroll bars and other controls, and its title bar is filled in; when a window is not active, its title bar is white and the window name is dimmed.

Scrolling through the contents of a window. When the *scroll bars* in the active window are gray, that means there are items in it that aren't showing (or you haven't left enough space around the items that are showing). When the scroll bars in an active window are blank, that means everything is already displayed in the window. Sometimes one scroll bar is gray and the other is white (as in the window shown above)—it depends on where the missing information is located.

To bring hidden information into view, you can use the *scroll box*, the *scroll arrows*, or the gray area of the scroll bar itself:

- Drag the scroll box to move the contents of the window up or down.
- Click in the gray area below or above the scroll box to move one screenful at a time.
- Point to a scroll arrow and hold down the mouse button to scroll the window continuously until you let up the mouse button.

Changing the way files are displayed. Those big, colorful icons are great, but when you get a lot of files in a window, it's hard to keep them all on screen. The Finder's View menu lets you choose other options for viewing files. You can view them by small icon or by name in a number of arrangements (alphabetically by name, by the program that created them, by the date they were created, and so on). You'll learn how to use the View menu and other menus in the next section.

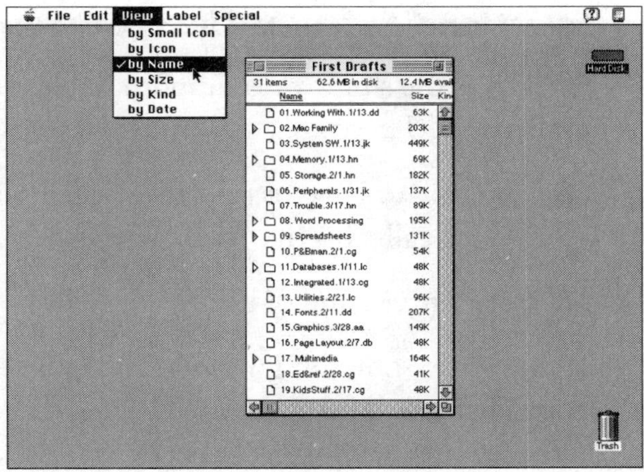

When you view a file window by name, as shown here, you can open the listed files and folders just as in an icon view—by double-clicking on the little icons. In System 7, you can also view the contents of a folder by clicking on the triangle next to the folder name to drop down a list of its contents.

Giving Commands (AN/JK/ND/SA/SM/CR/ByB/KF/DD)

There are lots of ways of telling the Mac what you want to do. So far, we've done things by manipulating icons on the desktop. In other cases, you use menu commands.

In the Finder, the Mac supplies two ways of giving menu commands: You can use the mouse to choose commands from the menu bar or, in many cases, you can use keyboard commands.

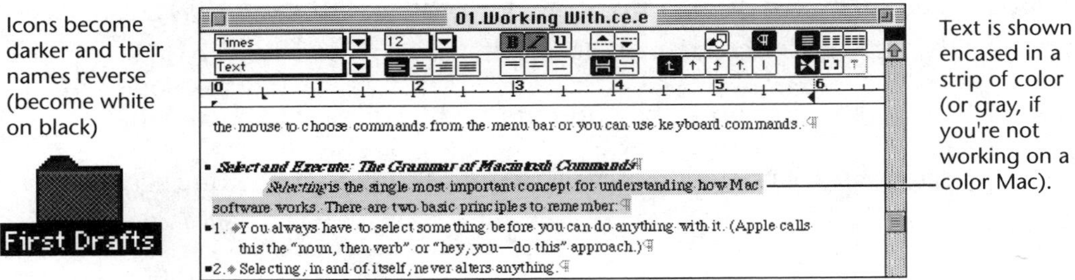

When an item is selected, it becomes highlighted.

Select and Execute: The Grammar of Macintosh Commands

Selecting is the single most important concept for understanding how Mac software works. There are two basic principles to remember:

1. You always have to select something before you can do anything with it. (Apple calls this the "noun, then verb" or "hey, you—do this" approach.)
2. Selecting, in and of itself, never alters anything.

Trying to do something when nothing is selected, or when something different from what you think is selected is selected, is the cause of 90 percent of the confusion people have when learning to use the Mac.

How exactly you select an item depends on the kind of item you're selecting. (Some general rules are presented in the box at right.) How do you tell if an item is selected? It's highlighted, as shown in the illustration above.

Using Menus

Across the top of the desktop you'll see a line of words. This is called the *menu bar*. The words you see (and the) are *menu titles*. If you put the pointer on a menu title and hold down the mouse button, a menu pops down over the desktop. Just as a menu at a restaurant is a list of things you can order, a menu on the Mac is a list of things you can order the computer to do.

Some menus are available whether you're in the Finder or another program. These are the menu (called the *Apple menu* since so few people can pronounce

Rules for Selecting (DD)

These rules for selecting text or objects apply in the Finder and in every Mac program.

Selecting icons

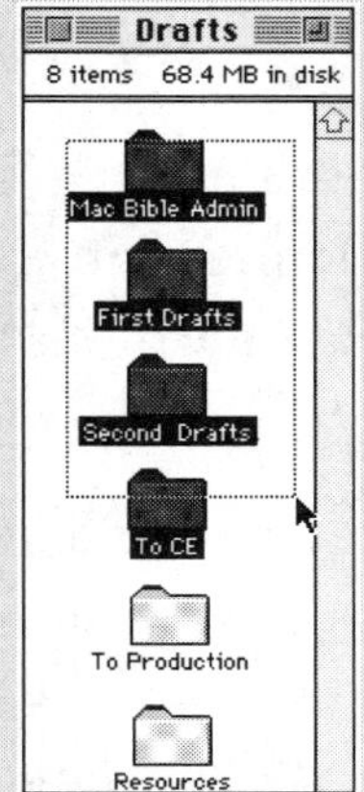

You can select a group of objects with a selection rectangle. Just drag the mouse diagonally across the area that includes the objects you want to select.

To select one: Click on it.

To select more than one:

- Press [Shift] as you click on objects after the first one.
- Drag a selection rectangle around it: Choose a location outside the border of an imaginary square that contains all the items and drag diagonally across the area. A dotted line will appear on screen around the area you're selecting. When all the items are enclosed, release the mouse button.

Selecting Text

To select a range of text:

- Place the I-beam pointer at the beginning of the text you want to select, press the mouse button, and drag to the end of the text. (You don't have to follow the line of text—just make a beeline for the end of the text you're selecting.)
- Click at the beginning of the text you want to select, and then press [Shift] while you click at the end of the range of text.

To select a single word: Double-click anywhere in the word.

Deselecting

To deselect everything: Click anywhere outside the selected area.

To deselect one object of a selected group: [Shift]-click on the item you want to deselect.

), the application menu, and System 7's Help menu (indicated by a balloon with a question mark). The rest of the menu bar may change when you launch a new program (though almost every program has a File menu and an Edit menu).

To select a command from a menu, keep the mouse button pressed down and slide the pointer down the menu. As you pass a command, that command will be *highlighted*—instead of appearing as black letters on a white background, it appears as white letters on a black background. When the command you want is highlighted (as New Folder is on the File menu in the illustration at right, you just release the mouse button to execute the command.

The File menu is what you see if you press the mouse button down while pointing at the word File in the menu bar.

If you slide the pointer down a menu and then decide not to choose any of its commands, you don't have to slide the pointer back to the top; just slide it off the side of the menu and let go of the mouse button.

As you can see, some of the commands in this menu are *dimmed* (their names are in gray, not black). This means you can't use them at the present time—if you slide the pointer past them, they won't highlight. If the command you want to use is dimmed, it could be because you've forgotten the first rule of the Macintosh: You've got to select the item you want to act on before giving a command.

A History of the Menu (AN/JK/ND/SA/SM/CR/ByB/KF/DD)

In the Mac's first several years, you could generally open only a single program at a time. The menu was made to hold programs, called *desk accessories* (sometimes called *DAs*), that you could open at any time. For example, you could open the Calculator DA and add up some figures while you were in a word processing program.

In System 7 (and under MultiFinder in System 6), you *can* open more than one program at a time, and switch between them as you wish. Programs that have been designated DAs now differ only very slightly from other programs. They're designed to be installed on the menu, but you can put them anywhere. Under System 7, the menu is used to hold any items you want to get to quickly. (See "The System Folder" in Chapter 3 for more details on how to customize your menu and other system features.)

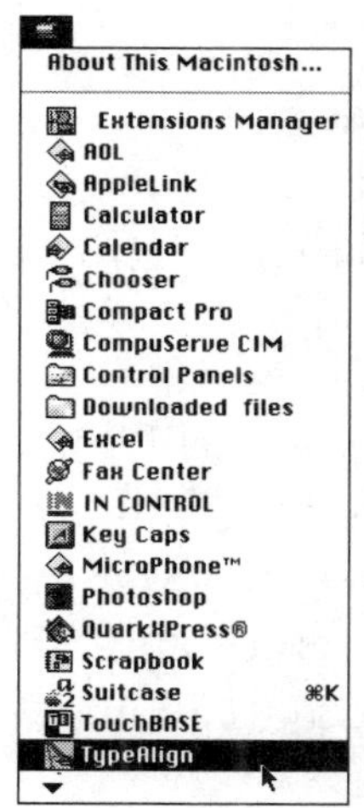

Sometimes a menu has so many commands on it that they run off the bottom of the screen. In that case, a downward-pointing triangle appears at the bottom of the part of the menu you can see (as on the menu shown here). Sliding the pointer past this triangle brings the additional menu items into view.

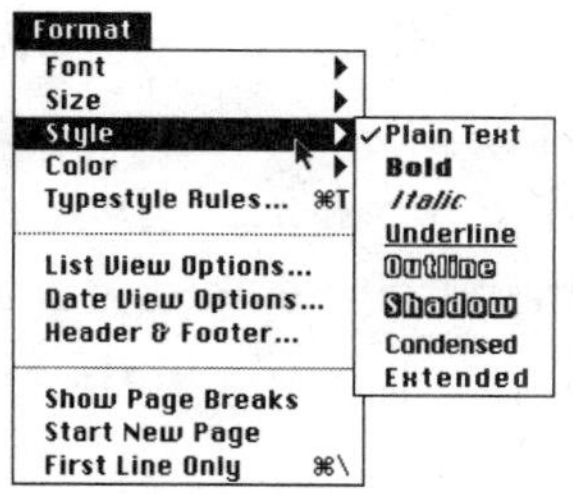

A right-pointing triangle to the right of a menu name means there's a submenu. The submenu appears when you highlight the command. To choose a command from the submenu, just slide the mouse over and down until the command you want is highlighted.

Check marks like the ones next to Plain Text on the Format menu in the illustration at left mean that the checked choices are currently in effect. For example, if you select Bold from the submenu and then reopen the menu, the Bold command will be checked, and whatever you have selected or whatever you type next will appear in bold.

Menu items that take check marks are called *toggles*—when they're off, choosing them turns them on, and when they're on, choosing them turns them off. There are also toggles that don't take check marks; instead, their names change to indicate what happens when they're selected. If you're using System 7, try choosing Hide Balloons from the Help menu for an example of this. After you've chosen it, the command changes to Show Balloons. (Of course, if someone had already used that command, it might have been on Hide Balloons when you started.)

Some menu items are followed by three dots (for example, the Typestyle Rules command in the Format menu shown above). That means that you will need to give more information before the command is executed. When you choose the command, a dialog box will appear. (Dialog boxes are described below.)

Keyboard Commands

Some commands have keyboard equivalents listed next to them on the menu—like ⌘ N next to the New Folder command on the File menu shown on page 16. This tells you that instead of moving the pointer up to the File menu, pressing the mouse button to make the menu pop down, going down the menu to the Open command, and then releasing the mouse button, you can simply hold down the ⌘ key and hit the N key to get the same result. (The ⌘ key, called the *Command key*, is in the bottom row of the keyboard, to the left of the

Modifier Keys

(AN/JK/ND/SA/SM/CR/ByB/KF/DD)

In this book, we use a special font to show the keys you press. Apple uses a different one in its menus, and the keys they indicate aren't always crystal clear. Here's a guide to the most common ones:

⇧ Shift

⌥ Option

^ Control

Spacebar; on some keyboards, it has no on it.) Many menu commands have keyboard equivalents. In most cases, the command equivalent is listed to the right of the menu name in the menu.

Keyboard commands are often simply the ⌘ key plus the first letter of the command name. Sometimes other *modifier keys*, such as Shift, Option, and sometimes Control are used with ⌘ to allow more options.

Dialog Boxes and Alerts

Choosing a command with an ellipsis after it (Open, for example, or Print) opens a *dialog box* (it's called that because the Mac is telling you something and asking for a response). A couple examples of dialog boxes are shown below.

You can move from one area of the dialog box to another either by using the mouse or by hitting Tab.

Dialog boxes have a number of different types of controls, shown in the illustrations below: text boxes, radio buttons, checkboxes, buttons, list boxes, and pop-up menus.

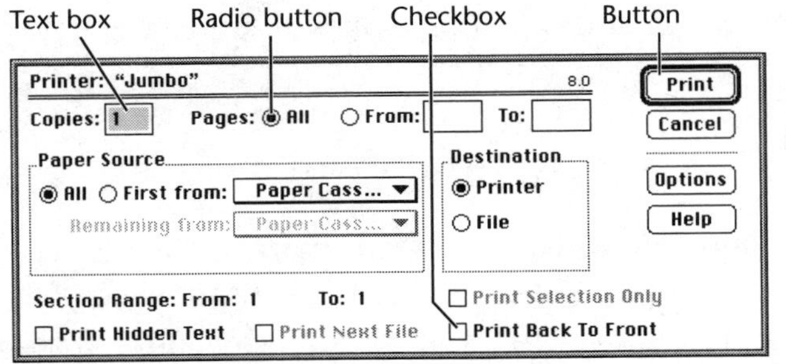

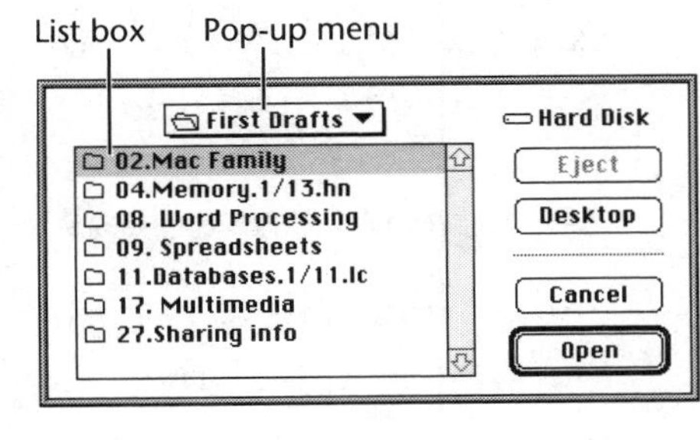

The Mac displays a dialog box when you choose a command that's followed by an ellipsis (...), meaning you'll need to supply extra information before the command is executed. At the left is an example of a Print dialog box, and at the right is an example of the Open dialog box (exactly how these dialog boxes look varies with the application you're in and other conditions).

Getting Help (AN/JK/ND/SA/SM/CR/ByB/KF/DD)

Anytime you can't figure out what's going on, you can turn to the Help menu (only in System 7). It appears next to the Applications menu on the right side of the menu bar; its icon has a question mark in it. Choose Show Balloons on the Help menu and, as you slide the pointer over items on the screen, balloons will pop up that briefly explain how whatever the pointer is on works. (How useful this is depends on how well the program's creators wrote the help; unfortunately, it's pretty useless in many cases, including in the Finder.) To get rid of the balloons, select Hide Balloons from the menu. Most newer programs, as well as the Finder, include Balloon Help.

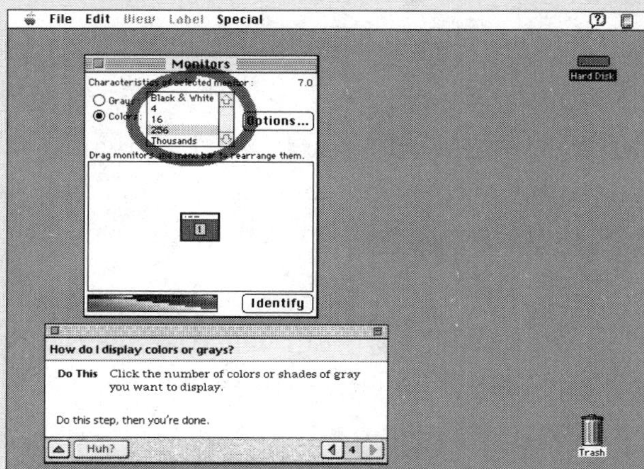

Apple Guide, Apple's new interactive help system, guides you through procedures step by step. Coach marks (like the circle you see here) show you just where to take the action described in the help window. Users can create custom Apple Guide help using AppleScript.

If you have the newest version of Apple's system software, System 7.5, you will also have another type of help, called *interactive help*, available. Interactive help offers a menu of actions you can ask for help with, and then it leads you through the process step by step.

The last command on the Help menu when you're in the Finder is Finder Shortcuts, which presents you with shortcuts for working in the Finder. Try them out once you feel at home with the Mac. (To get rid of the shortcuts window, click on its close box.)

Text boxes. When you see a *text box*, you just type in the information required. In the example, you would type in numbers, but sometimes you're asked for words.

Buttons. *Buttons* are rounded rectangles with commands inside them. When you click a button, the command is executed, just as if you'd selected a command from a menu. When a button is framed by a thicker border (like the Print button in the Print dialog box or the Open button in the Open dialog box), that means it's the *default* button—you can click it simply by hitting the Return or Enter key.

Radio buttons. *Radio buttons* are little circles with names next to them (like the circles to the left of Printer and File, and All and From in the Print dialog box at the bottom of the last page). When you click a radio button, it fills in (as with Printer and All). Like the preset buttons on a car radio, Mac radio buttons come in sets, and only one button in a set can be selected at a time (on the Mac, one radio button in each set *must* be selected at all times). When you click one radio button, the radio button in that set that was previously selected is automatically deselected.

Checkboxes. *Checkboxes* are used for lists of options that *aren't* mutually exclusive. All the checkboxes in a set can be selected or none can be. Clicking in a blank checkbox puts an *X* in it and turns it on. Clicking in it again turns it off.

List boxes. A *list box* (for example, the one in the Open dialog box shown in the illustrations on the next page) has a scrollable list from which you select your choice. You can open a file from this list by double-clicking the file name or by selecting it and then clicking the Open button on the right).

PlainTalk (DD)

PlainTalk is a system extension that lets you give voice commands to your Macintosh. (Who can use PlainTalk and its advantages and disadvantages are described more fully in Chapters 2 and 3.) Instead of using the mouse to move the pointer to the close box of the active window and clicking, you can just say, "Computer: Close." You can give many different kinds of commands this way, including any menu or dialog box command. You can also choose a name other than "Computer" for your Mac, if you want to get creative and not sound like Captain Picard.

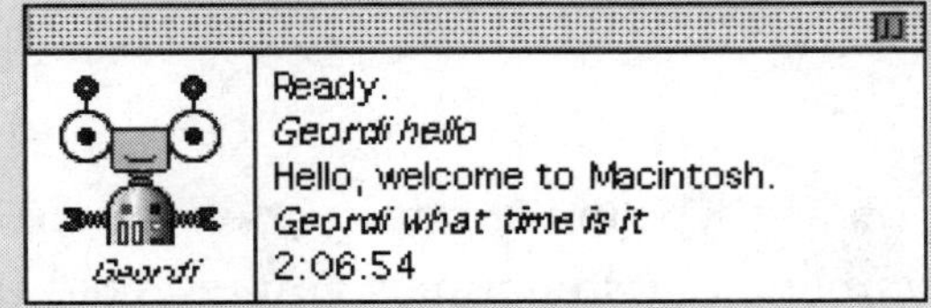

Geordi

Ready.
Geordi hello
Hello, welcome to Macintosh.
Geordi what time is it
2:06:54

Mac Bible editor Elizabeth Castro created a PlainTalk character named Geordi. The commands you speak to the computer are printed in italic in the PlainTalk box; the computer's replies are both spoken aloud and printed in plain text in the box.

If you're running PlainTalk and voice recognition is turned on, your opening screen won't look much different from the one shown at the beginning of this chapter. The only difference will be a small window at the bottom of your screen that has a little character and some notes about what's going on. By default the character is an ear, called Vincent (get it?), but you can choose from a half-dozen characters. When the computer is listening to you, the icon shows little sound waves in the direction of the character.

Pop-up menus. When you see a box with a drop shadow and a triangle beside the name, that's a *pop-up menu*. When you point to the box and press the mouse button, the menu drops down, and you choose an option from the menu just as you would with a pull-down menu: You drag to the one you want, and then release the mouse button.

If this is the folder you want to open a file from, click on that file's name in the file list and then click OK, or just double-click on the file name.

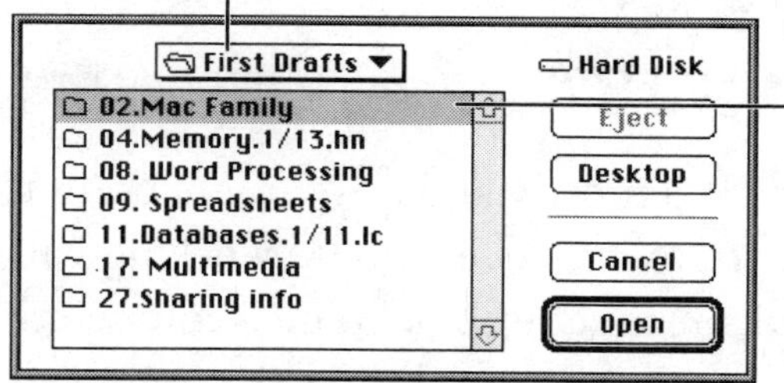

The file list shows the files in the last folder you opened or saved a file to.

If the document you want to open is in a different folder, point to the pop-up menu at the top of the file list to see a list of the folders that hold this one. They're shown in hierarchical order; that is, the folder that holds this one is just below it, the one that holds that is below that, and so on.

Drag the pointer to the name of the folder you want, or to the name of a folder that holds that folder. When you release the mouse button, the contents of that folder will show in the file list.

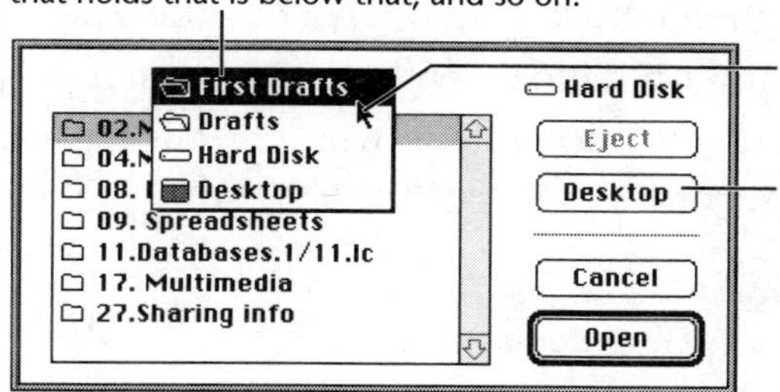

You can click Desktop to go straight to the highest level and start navigating from there.

How you navigate the Open and Save As dialog boxes is probably the single hardest part of the Mac interface for beginners to understand. Here's a guide. Don't worry, you'll get used to it.

The illustrations of the Open dialog box at right show an example of a pop-up menu that's a little tricky, but it's one you'll need to become familiar with. Instructions for using it are in the callouts to that illustration.

In System 7.5 and on Performa models, Macs can be set up so that some users' folders are off limits for saving and opening files. If that's the case on your computer, you may not be able to navigate to all the folders on your Mac, and you will need to save in the first folder shown in the dialog box's file list.

Executing your choices. When you're done making your selections, you just choose OK (or whatever the default button is) to execute your command. If you make a lot of selections in the dialog box and decide not to keep them, you can nullify all the changes you've made to all of them by clicking the Cancel button. (Typing ⌘. will usually give you the same result.)

Working With Documents

(AN/JK/ND/SA/SM/CR/ByB/KF/DD)

So far we've talked mostly about what you do in the Finder, but there are also common rules to follow when you're working with other programs. The rules you've learned so far about how to give commands still hold. Now we'll introduce you to some of the procedures and commands you will use to create documents with Macintosh programs.

Running Programs and Opening Files

As we mentioned before, you open a program just as you open anything else: by double-clicking on its icon. When you open a program by double-clicking on its icon, an empty document window appears on screen and the menu bar changes to show that program's own menus. (Sometimes, the program will display a dialog box for you to make choices in before it opens the document window.)

You can also open a program by opening a document that belongs to it. That way, the window that opens will contain the document you want to work on.

Exactly how you work on the document once it's open will depend on the rules of that program, but many of the rules will be the same ones you learned for working in the Finder. You'll select items and execute commands on them as you learned in "Giving Commands." If you're

The Launcher (DD)

With System 7.5 and Performa models, the Finder includes an extra feature, called the *Launcher,* that makes it easy to find and launch programs. The Launcher holds icons for any programs or files installed in a special folder, called the Launcher Items folder, inside your System Folder. You can launch any program or file by clicking *once* on its icon.

The Launcher adds a palette of program and file icons to your desktop.

You can move and close the Launcher window just like any other window (as described under "Working With Windows" in this chapter). If you've closed the Launcher, you can get it back by double-clicking on the Launcher icon at the right side of the desktop (on a Performa) or by choosing Launcher from the control panels in System 7.5.

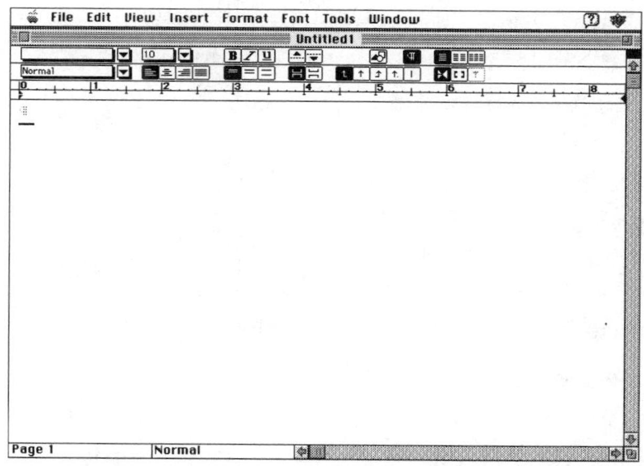

When you double-click on an application icon, the menu bar changes to show that application's menu choices, and a window for that application opens on screen. Sometimes the document window will have extra controls in it, like the Ruler and tool bar in this Microsoft Word window.

working with text, you'll use the same technique you used to rename an icon. You'll use buttons and pop-up menus just as you did in the dialog boxes we showed you.

Saving Documents

After you've worked on a document for a little while, it's crucial to save the changes you've made. Until you save a document, it exists only in the computer's memory and will disappear when you close the document or turn off the computer. (How memory works is described in Chapter 4.) When you save a document, it is copied from the computer's memory to disk, where it will be preserved even after the computer is turned off. Don't wait until you're finished working on a document to save it; instead, save every few minutes to guard against mishaps like a power failure or a computer problem that could cause you to lose the work you've done. (These accidents happen more often than you would expect.)

Almost every Macintosh program that can create documents includes a Save command in its File menu. The first time you save a new document, the Macintosh presents the Save As dialog box, allowing you to choose a name and location for the file. After a document has been saved once, choosing the Save command just saves the new version of the file over the previous version.

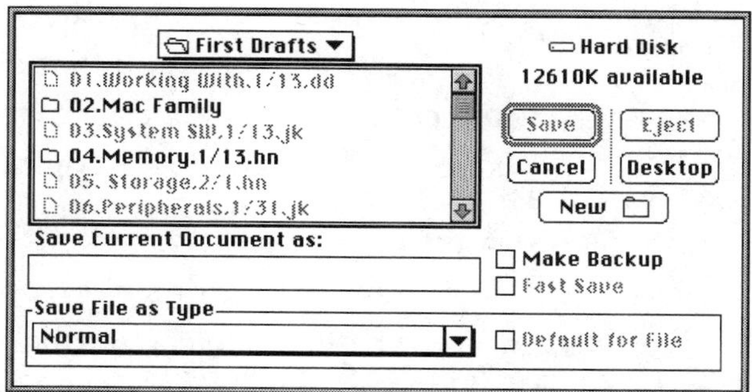

You type a name for your file in the Save As dialog box. You can also choose a new location for it using the pop-up menu as described for the Open dialog box on page 21.

If you want to preserve two versions of the document on the disk, you can choose the Save As command instead of Save. When you see the dialog box, you just type in a new name, and the new version will be saved on disk without overwriting the old one.

Cutting, Copying, and Pasting

One of the most elegant and useful tools on the Mac is the *Clipboard*—a temporary holding place for material that you *cut* or *copy* from one place so you can *paste* it in another. You can move or copy material from one place to another in a single document, or between two separate documents—even if the documents were created with different applications. You can cut or copy material of almost any length. Every Mac program has Cut, Copy, and Paste commands in its Edit menu.

Every program has an Edit menu with Cut, Copy, and Paste commands. The keyboard equivalents for those commands should also be the same in every program.

To remove something from its original place (either because you don't want to use it at all anymore or because you've decided to use it somewhere else instead), you select it and then use the Cut command. (The keyboard shortcut in every Mac program is the same: ⌘X.) Whatever you've selected disappears from its original location and is stored on the Clipboard. (The Finder and many other programs let you check the contents of the Clipboard by choosing Show Clipboard from the Edit menu.) Copy (⌘C) works the same way as Cut, except that the selected material stays in the original location in addition to moving to the Clipboard. Then, to place the cut or copied material in its new position, you select its new position and use the Paste command (⌘V).

If you just want to get rid of something, you can simply cut it and never paste it—it will disappear the next time you cut or copy. Or you can just hit the Delete key instead, and whatever's selected will disappear without even passing through the Clipboard. Another way to delete text is to select it and then just start typing—the new text replaces the old. That's a handy feature, but watch out: It's easy to accidentally delete something if you forget it's selected before you start your next task. If that happens, use the Undo command (see the box at right).

Things stay on the Clipboard until you copy something else, so you can paste the same thing many different places—as long as you remember not to cut or copy anything else in the interim. But remember, as soon as you cut or copy something else, the new material replaces the old on the Clipboard, and when you shut off the computer, the Clipboard's contents disappear.

Some programs offer another way to cut and paste information, called *drag and drop*. This lets users cut and paste without using the menu commands. After you select the material you want to cut or move, you point to the edge of the selection and simply drag it to its new location. Starting with System 7.5, Apple has built this capability into the system software, making this feature easy to implement for any programmers who want to include it in their programs, so expect to see more of it in the future.

The Undo Command (DD)

Most Mac programs have an Undo command in the Edit menu (⌘Z), which undoes the last thing you did. The first time you delete some text you want back, you'll immediately see what Undo is for. But be sure to use it right away; if you've done anything at all since the action you regret, you'll regret it forever. In many cases, Undo only works on the last action you completed (many programs are implementing "multiple undo" features that undo your last actions, one by one, for several steps back). After you've used Undo, the command in the Edit menu often changes to Redo: Using it again will undo your undo.

If the program you're using doesn't have a multiple undo feature but you really regret something you did a few steps back, there's often another option. Look for a Revert to Saved command in the File menu (some programs have it, some don't). Choosing that command returns your file to the last version you saved, discarding all your recent changes. If it's not there, you can just close the document without saving changes. When you open it again, it will be the old version.

Closing a Document

When you're ready to stop working on a document (at least for the time being), you have two choices. You can usually just close the document you're working on (leaving the program open) or quit the program (which closes the document automatically). You will find both commands (Close and Quit) in the File menu of the application. If you choose Close or Quit before you've saved all your changes, the Mac will display a dialog box asking if you really want to do that, giving you a last chance to save before closing or quitting.

In System 6, Mac beginners often get lost when they close the last document and are left with a blank screen with no icons on it. If you're using System 6, the thing to remember is that no desktop is completely blank—there's always the menu bar across the top. If you pop down various menus, you'll see that there are lots of things you can do. So here's something to remember—and it's a good tip for people using System 7, too: *When in doubt, explore the menu bar.*

HOT TIP

Switching Between Applications

In System 7 (and in System 6, if you're using MultiFinder) you can run more than one program at once; you don't need to quit one program before you open another. If you've got more than one program open, you can tell which one you're in by checking the icon at the far right of the menu bar (it stands for the Application menu). When you're in the Finder, the icon looks like a little Mac. When you're in another program, the icon changes to represent that program.

The Application menu lists the programs you have open. The active program has a check mark next to it. You can clean up your desktop by choosing Hide Others (to hide the windows of all nonactive programs) or Hide Finder (to hide the Finder icons).

The Application menu not only lets you quickly figure out what application is active, it lets you switch among the programs you have open. You just choose the program you want from the list. If the program you want isn't in the list, you'll have to open it from the Finder.

HOT TIP

There's another quick way to change between programs: Just click in a window belonging to the program you want to get to, or on the desktop if you want to get to the Finder.

Shutting Down

When you're done working and want to turn off the Mac, the first thing to do is get back to the Finder. Then choose Shut Down from the Special menu. Depending on what Mac you have, it'll either turn itself off, or tell you it's OK to turn it off.

It's very important to shut down properly, and not simply turn

The Four Principles

(AN/JK/ND/SA/SM/CR/ByB/KF)

Here's a recap of the most important principles to keep in mind when using the Mac:

- You have to select something before you can do something.
- By itself, selecting never alters anything.
- To open icons, double-click on them.
- When in doubt, explore the menu bar.

the computer off. Shutting down gives the Mac time to do a little housekeeping and make sure everything you think is stored on the disk really is stored there. But it's OK to chose Shut Down even if you have files open—the Mac will make sure everything is tidily put away before it closes down.

At Ease

(DD)

At Ease is a replacement for the Finder that comes with Performas. Unlike the Launcher, which also comes with every Performa, it's not installed automatically. You can also install At Ease on other types of Macs.

When At Ease is installed, most of the screen is taken up by a stack of giant file folders.

The front folder, called the Application folder, shows a palette of all the programs you can launch. As with the Launcher (described on page 22), you can launch programs by pointing at the program's icon and clicking the mouse button. Once a program is launched, it follows all the same rules it follows on a system without At Ease.

At Ease is designed so that whoever sets up the system can assign different levels of access to different users, so you may have to sign on before you even get to the At Ease desktop. While you use the Mac, At Ease may restrict you from saving or opening files in certain folders.

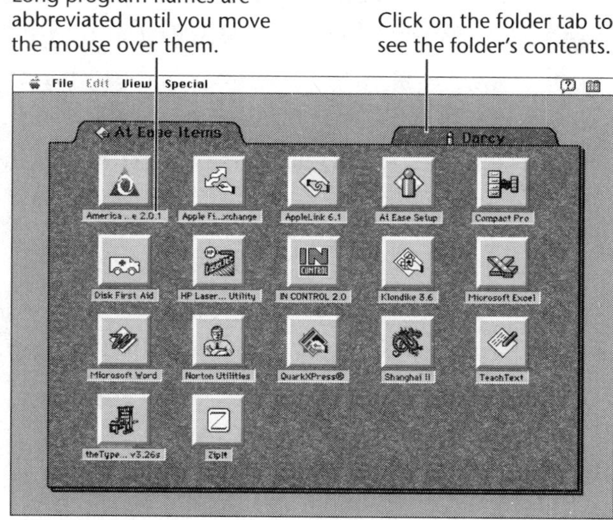

On the At Ease desktop, all your applications are in plain sight on the At Ease Items folder. Each user registered on the system also gets his or her own folder, where they can save their own documents.

Finder Tips

General Finder Tips

Finding out version numbers (JK). To find out the version number of the system software you're using:

1. Select the Finder from the Application menu (or just click anywhere on the desktop).
2. Select About This Macintosh from the menu.

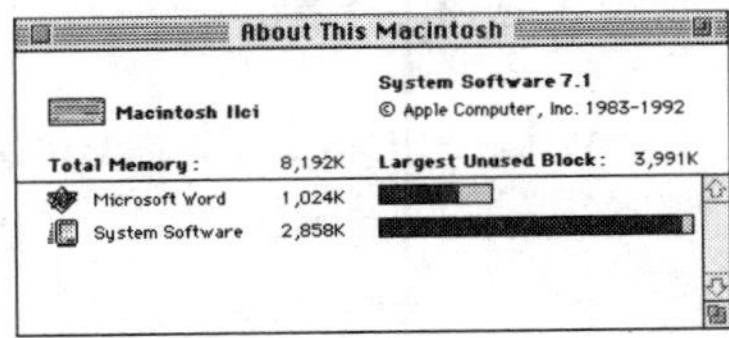

The System Software number is at the top right of the About This Macintosh window.

You can use this same method to find the version number of any program you're using. When you're in another program (not the Finder), the first command in the menu should read "About [name of program]." When you choose that command, a dialog box should appear with that information.

Finding out about files (DD). You can find out a lot of information about a file or any other item on the desktop, including how large it is, when it was created and modified, and other useful facts by selecting its icon and giving the Get Info command, either by choosing it from the Finder's File menu or by hitting ⌘I.

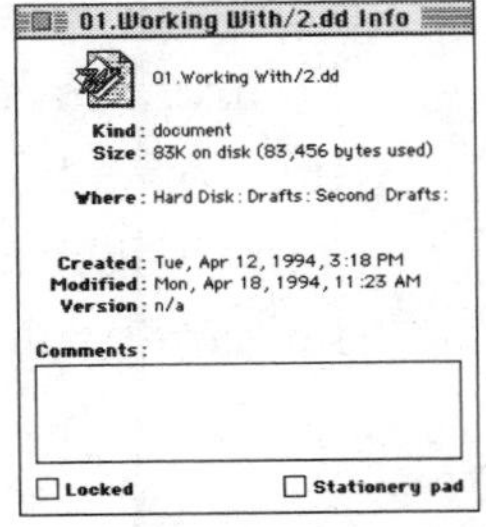

The Get Info box tells you basic information about a file. This is also where you can lock the file or make it read-only.

Locking files (SA/DC). To lock a file, select it on the desktop, and choose Get Info from the File menu (or hit ⌘I), and click the Locked checkbox in the box that appears. Locked files can't be deleted or modified. (You can use the Save As command to save an editable copy.)

To unlock the file, just click in the checkbox again.

On the desktop, it's easy to tell if a file is locked without opening the Get Info dialog box—if it's locked, you won't be able to select the icon's name for editing.

Alternate methods of ejecting floppies (SA/CR/AN). Generally, as we've said, the best way to eject a floppy disk is to drag it to the Trash. This erases the disk's directory from the Mac's memory. If you don't do it that way, a ghost of the disk icon is left on screen and the Mac will keep asking for the disk again when you try other file operations.

HOT TIP

Sometimes, however, it makes sense not to erase the Mac's memory of the disk. If you're going to be reinserting a disk soon, for example, leaving its ghost on the desktop when you eject it will save you time, because the Mac won't have to read the contents of the disk to create its windows all over again. Another reason to leave a disk ghost on the desktop (provided its window was left open) is if you're comparing its contents with another floppy's and you only have one floppy drive.

To leave a disk ghost on screen, you can eject the disk using the Eject command in the Finder's File menu. These keyboard shortcuts also do the job:

⌘E	Ejects the selected floppy (or floppies). This is the keyboard equivalent of the Eject command in the File menu.
Shift⌘1	Ejects the floppy in the (first) internal drive.
Shift⌘2	Ejects the floppy in the external (or second internal) drive.
Shift⌘0	Ejects the floppy in a second external drive.

A word of warning: Don't leave a floppy's ghost on the screen and then use the disk in another Mac; when you bring it back, the first Mac won't recognize it as the disk you ejected. In some situations, if you shut down your Mac or get a system bomb with a disk ghost on the screen, the floppy that it represents will be rendered unusable for any purpose, even for being erased!

If a disk won't eject (SA/CR/AN). Sometimes you'll drag a disk to the Trash and its ghost will remain on the desktop, or will bounce right back up to where it was. This often means there's a file open on the disk that you need to close. If you're sure there are no documents open on it, try closing any programs you were using with files on that disk; some programs (like TeachText) suffer from separation anxiety and won't let go of a document even after it's closed.

Escaping from disk-switching nightmares (Michael Bradley/SA/AN). If you have left a disk ghost on screen, you may get caught in an interminable disk-switching session (the kind that makes you want to scream at your Mac, "You

want that disk again? There's something sick about your obsession with that disk!"). If that happens, press ⌘. Sometimes you have to press it more than once and sometimes it won't work at all, but it's worth trying.

Canceling fast (AN/SA). In most places on the Mac, ⌘. will cancel what you're doing (printing, for example). It will also push the Cancel button in most dialog boxes. We've mentioned this shortcut elsewhere (because there are so many places where it works), but it's worth repeating (because there *are* so many places where it works). The Esc key also works, in most instances, as a substitute for ⌘.

Escaping from hang-ups (AN/ByB). In System 7, Option⌘Esc will usually free you from an application that's hung up, without your having to restart the computer. (This is almost reason enough to use System 7.)

Unfortunately, this only works if you can still use the mouse. That's because it opens a dialog box that asks you if you want to quit and lose all unsaved work, and you can't choose the Force Quit button (which is what you're going to want to do if you're hung) from the keyboard. The Force Quit button should have a double line around it, so you can select it by simply hitting Return, but it doesn't.

Selecting icons from the keyboard (JK/CR/EC). In System 7, you can find and select any file you want on the desktop or in its windows without having to hunt through a zillion icons with the mouse. Just select the window (or the desktop) and type the first few letters of the file's name. You can select items in Finder windows and on the desktop in alphabetical order by pressing Tab. (ShiftTab will select them in reverse alphabetical order.) You can also select the next item in one direction or another by pressing the arrow key that points in that direction.

The drag-launch (Nicholas Lavroff/JK). In System 7, you can open a document from the desktop by dragging its icon onto the icon of any application capable of opening it. This doesn't always work—if the application doesn't highlight when you drag the file over it, you will have to open the document from within the application. But it's useful if, say, you have a text file that you want to open with Word (you could even keep an alias of Word ready on the desktop for this very purpose. (Aliases are described in Chapter 3.)

Use [Option] to change move to copy (DD). When dragging icons to a new location, the icon will generally be *moved* if the new location is on the same disk as the old, or *copied* if the new location is on a different disk. To change the move to a copy, just hold [Option] while you drag the icon.

Turning off the Trash warning (CR). Normally, when you try to empty the Trash, the Mac will ask you if you're sure you want to do that. If you find this tiresome, you'll be happy to know that you can disable the warning. To do that, select the Trash icon, hit [⌘][I], and uncheck the Warn Before Emptying checkbox in the Get Info window that appears. If you like the warning in most circumstances but want to avoid it temporarily, just hold down the [Option] key when you empty the Trash.

In System 6, you get warnings when you drag applications or system software files to the Trash, and when you try to empty the Trash if it contains those items. To disable these warnings, hold down the [Option] key when you drag the items to the Trash or when you empty it.

The Trash and Desktop folders (CR). The Mac creates folders called Trash and Desktop Folder to store Trash contents or items placed directly on the desktop. They're normally invisible to the user, but you may see them on a disk you're sharing with someone else, or you may discover them while using a utility program like DiskTop. If you do see them, just leave them alone.

Restoring Clipboard contents (SA). If you cut or copy something and then realize you still need what was previously on the Clipboard, choose Undo (or hit [⌘][Z]). When it undoes the cut or copy, it also restores the Clipboard to its previous state.

Cutting and pasting PostScript (SA). To copy something from a PostScript program like Illustrator or FreeHand and paste it into a program that can't directly import PostScript material, hold down [Option] while you choose Copy from the Edit menu (or press [⌘][Option][C]). (You don't need to hold down [Option] when you paste.)

Accurate item counts in folders (CR/JK). In icon views, the line under a window's title will tell you how many items it contains, but it counts a folder and its contents as one item. The best way to find out how many items it *actually*

HOT TIP

contains, including files *within* folders, is to select it and choose Get Info (⌘I). (This only works in System 7; under System 6, Get Info doesn't count items within folders.)

Using labels (CR/JK). System 7 lets you attach labels to files and folders, so you can identify all the ones that belong to a particular project or that share some status the Mac wouldn't normally recognize. For example, people sharing a Mac can label their files with their own names to keep track of what belongs to whom. You can then sort files by label using the View menu.

To give a file or folder a label, select it in the Finder and then choose a name from the Label menu. If you've got a color monitor, each label has its own color, which also gets applied to the selected item. You can change the names and colors to whatever you want in the Labels control panel. (See Chapter 3 for more on control panels.)

Shortcuts in Open and Save As dialog boxes (SA/JK). Several keyboard shortcuts you can use in list boxes in Open and Save As dialog boxes are shown in the table at right.

To move	Use
To a different drive	⌘→
Up to the enclosing folder	⌘↑
Into the selected folder	⌘↓
Up and down through the list	↑ and ↓
To the bottom of the list	⌥

Here's another: In dialog boxes with list boxes, hitting a key selects the first folder or file name beginning with that character (or the next nearest character). If you type quickly, you can select a name by typing the first few letters of its name. (If you type slowly, each letter will be interpreted as a single letter and you'll keep jumping around the list.)

Working With Icons

Cleaning up windows and the desktop (CR/JK/SA). There's an invisible grid in icon-view windows and on the desktop that you can use to align your icons neatly. Use the Clean Up command on the Special menu to do the straightening. In its basic form, the command shuffles all the icons onto the nearest grid points, without changing the basic arrangement they were in. If you don't care about that arrangement, you can force the icons into neat rows and columns by holding down Option while you choose Clean Up.

If you hold down ⌘ while you drag a loose item, it'll snap to the nearest grid point when you release it. You can also use the checkboxes in the Views control panel to make icons automatically snap to a straight or staggered pattern along the grid.

Arranging icons by name, kind, and so on (JK/CR). You can sort items in icon views by any of the categories under the View menu, including the ones that normally give you list views (by Name, by Size, etc.).

With the window selected, choose the sort order you want from the View menu. Then go back and choose By Icon or By Small Icon. Lastly, hold down Option and choose the Clean Up command from the Special menu. It will read Clean Up by Name, or by whatever category you selected the first time, and will sort the icons in that order while it arranges them in rows and columns.

Changing icons (JK). In System 7, you can change the icon for any disk, file, or folder. First, use the Copy command to copy the graphic you want to use as an icon to the Clipboard. The go back to the Finder, select the item whose icon you want to change, and choose Get Info from the File menu (⌘I). Click on the item's icon (in the upper-left corner of the Get Info window) and a box will appear around it, then paste in a new icon (you can also copy the icon onto the Clipboard, if you want to paste it somewhere else).

You can also change an item's icon to a generic one for that type—a blank folder, document, and so on—by selecting the existing icon and hitting ⌘X.

Don't rename active files (JK/DD). Be careful to avoid moving or renaming files on the desktop while they're open in an application. That goes for the disks and folders that contain the files, too.

If you do, when you try to save the file, the application won't be able to find the folder it belongs in. It may present the Save As dialog box, even though the file's been saved. If that happens, you'll need to go ahead and save the file under a new name, and then delete the old file.

Managing Windows

Zooming to fill the screen (DD). In System 7, clicking a window's zoom box generally makes the window just large enough to show all of its contents. If you want it to fill the whole screen (leaving space for the disk and Trash icons on the right), you can, by holding down Option when you click the box.

Pop-down folder hierarchy (Nicholas Lavroff). If you've got a folder's window open on the desktop, there's an easy way to find out where it is in the hierarchy of folders on your disk. Just hold down ⌘ and click down on the window's name in the title bar. A pop-down menu will appear, showing all the folders that contain the open one. (This only works in an active window, so if the window you're interested in isn't active, you have to click on it first to make it active.)

First Drafts
Drafts
Hard Disk

31 items — 12.2 MB available

Name			Last Modified
01.Working With.1/13.dd			Mon, Jan 24, 1994, 5:12 PM
02.Mac Family	203K	folder	Mon, Mar 7, 1994, 5:15 PM
03.System SW.1/13.jk	449K	document	Wed, Apr 6, 1994, 12:50 PM
04.Memory.1/13.hn	69K	folder	Mon, Jan 31, 1994, 12:49 PM
05. Storage.2/1.hn	182K	document	Tue, Feb 15, 1994, 3:21 PM
06.Peripherals.1/31.jk	137K	document	Mon, Jan 31, 1994, 9:44 PM
07.Trouble.3/17.hn	89K	document	Thu, Mar 17, 1994, 11:24 AM
08. Word Processing	195K	folder	Mon, Feb 28, 1994, 11:21 AM
09. Spreadsheets	131K	folder	Tue, Mar 1, 1994, 3:04 PM
10.P&Bman.2/1.cg	54K	document	Tue, Feb 1, 1994, 1:50 PM

Holding ⌘ while you click on a directory window's title bar creates a pop-up menu showing the hierarchy of folders that holds the current one.

You can open any of the folders on the menu simply by selecting its name. If you hold down Option while you do this, the first window will close as the second one opens.

Automatic window closing with Option (AN/SA/JK). The Option key can help you keep your desktop from becoming cluttered with windows. Hold it down when you're double-clicking on an item in the Finder, and the window will close as the item you clicked on opens.

To close all the desktop windows at once, hold down Option while you close any window (by clicking in the close box or by using the ⌘W keyboard shortcut)—every other window on the desktop will close, too.

When you're switching between applications (including the Finder with the Application menu), holding down Option as you select the next application you're moving to will hide the windows of the application you're leaving.

Working in List Views

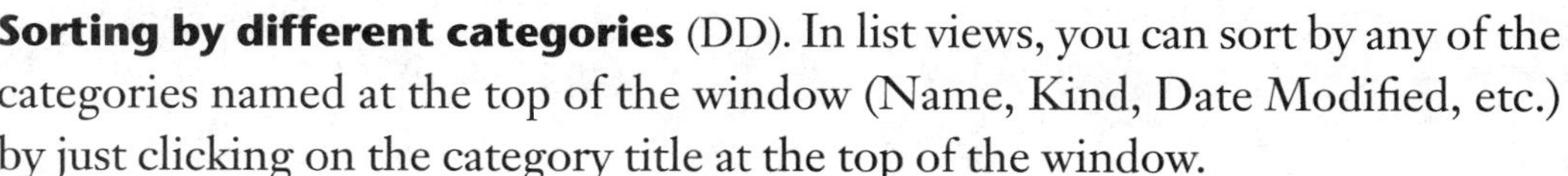

Sorting by different categories (DD). In list views, you can sort by any of the categories named at the top of the window (Name, Kind, Date Modified, etc.) by just clicking on the category title at the top of the window.

Multilevel outline views (JK). In System 7 list views, you can see a folder's contents by clicking the triangle next to it. If you want to also see all the levels—including the contents of folders in that folder—hold down Option as you click on the top-level triangle. (If you just click the triangle without holding down Option, the outline will disappear, but when you expand it again, all the contained folders will still be expanded.)

Using special characters to sort lists (SA/JK). File names are alphabetized both in list views on the desktop and in list boxes inside Open or Save dialog boxes. If you know the Mac's alphabetizing rules, you can force any document or folder you want to the top of any list by changing its name slightly.

Numbers come before letters, so *9* is sorted before *A*. Punctuation marks and other symbols are sorted before, after, or between the numbers and letters, according to their ASCII codes. The first 16 characters are shown in the box below. Putting any one of them in front of a file name will jump it to the top of the list, even ahead of numbers.

In System 6, you can use these symbols to keep *groups* of files together. For example, you might put an exclamation mark in front of the names of all documents relating to one project, and an asterisk in front of the names of documents relating to another project. (In System 7, it's easier just to assign labels to files that all relate to the same subject.)

Sorting Order of Special Characters (SA/JK)

In Finder lists, these characters will be sorted in the order they appear here, ahead of numbers and letters.

x ! " # $ % & '
( ) * + , - . /

Option characters (the ones you get by holding down Option or Shift Option when you type) may be sorted before, after, or between alphabetic characters, and the order is different in desktop windows than it is in list boxes inside dialog boxes. To make it easy on yourself, don't use option characters in file names.

Sorting numbered file names (SA). The Mac isn't very smart about sorting numbers—for example, 10 comes after 1 and before 2. If you want numbers to show up in numerical order, use a space or zero in front of the single digits, but none in front of the double digits:

Moving files into list-view windows (DC/JK/DD). Be careful when you drag a file to a window that's displayed in any list view. It's easy to accidentally select one of the folders when you point to the destination window, and then the file you're moving will be put inside that folder. You can have quite a time trying to find it after that.

To avoid this problem, drag the file to the part of the window just below the title bar (the rectangular space where the words Name, Size, Kind, and so on appear).

Automatic scrolling inside windows (JK/CR/EC). Windows in System 7 scroll automatically, so you don't have to resize them when you're moving a file from one place to another inside the same window. For example, if you want to move a file into a folder that's out of view in the same window, just drag the file to the edge of the window and the window will scroll in that direction.

The scrolling only works if you hold the pointer in the right spot, though. To scroll to the right or down, it has to be in the scroll bar on that side of the window. To scroll upward, hold it in the area below the title bar, where the column headings are. To scroll left, put the pointer close to the left border, inside the window.

System 6 Tips

Using MultiFinder (DD). You may not know that you can run several programs at once in System 6, just as you can in System 7; if you use MultiFinder, you can run as many programs at once as your memory will hold. The

Click MultiFinder only to start in MultiFinder when you restart your Mac.

If you have programs open when you choose Set Startup, you can tell the Mac to open them automatically on startup by clicking this radio button.

If you have selected items in the Finder when you choose Set Startup, you can open them automatically on startup by clicking this radio button.

Start up "Macintosh HD" with:
Finder MultiFinder
Upon startup, automatically open:
Selected Items
Opened Applications and DAs
MultiFinder Only
Cancel OK

To start MultiFinder, click the MultiFinder box in the Set Startup dialog box and restart your Mac.

most practical advantage is that you're able to do Finder operations—ejecting disks, finding files, and rearranging folders—without closing the application you're working in.

To use MultiFinder, choose Set Startup from the Special menu in the Finder and click one of the MultiFinder radio buttons in each set in the box that appears. (Your options are shown in the illustration on the previous page.)

You know if MultiFinder is active when you see an application icon in the top-right corner of your menu bar. To switch between running applications, click on that icon.

Switching to MultiFinder without restarting (SA). If you're running in Finder-only mode, you don't have to use Set Startup and restart the Mac to go into MultiFinder; instead, simply open the System Folder, hold down Option ⌘, and double-click on the MultiFinder icon. (If you do it this way, though, your Mac will start in Finder mode again next time you turn on the computer.)

When an empty folder isn't (SA/JK/AN). Just because there's a folder on your desktop named Empty folder doesn't mean there's nothing in it. Whenever you create a new folder (with the New Folder command) under System 6 or earlier, it appears with the name Empty folder. Remember that putting something in it doesn't change the name. (New folders in System 7 are named "untitled folder," which gets around this potential confusion.)

Editors' Poll: What's Your Favorite Thing About the Mac?

AA: Its Maciness. Its attitude that you can actually enjoy working on a computer. Its ease of learning and use, plug-and-play setup (unpack the box, plug in a couple of cables, and turn it on), and its superior graphics capabilities.

DB: My favorite thing about the Mac only exists in a few people's hearts anymore: It's the dream, the love, and the desire to do cool stuff. I'm sickened by Apple's corporate marketing strategies and highfalutin sales garbage. I fell in love with the computer next door, and when she grew up and moved to the big city I still held a place for her in my heart. But I know she'll never be the same.

EC: I think my favorite thing about the Mac is that it is generally consistent and logical. The same commands and keyboard combinations, and menus and dialog boxes, and icons and a million other things exist throughout the Mac world. Once you've learned a couple of programs, you've learned them all. And that means that instead of battling with an illogical, frustrating system, you can spend your time creating, experimenting, and playing.

DD: Two things. The first is that if I can't learn a program by just pulling down some menus and trying commands, I know something's wrong with the program, and not with me. The second thing is its customizability: Every few weeks, as the status of a project changes, I move my files and desktop into a new setup that works best for that phase.

CG: I've always enjoyed the fact that the original Mac team had a sense of fun. I interviewed Andy Hertzfeld [a member of the original design team and author of a lot of the first system software] a few years ago and he told me about how he designed the puzzle desk accessory. The powers-that-be told him that they couldn't ship it with the system because it took up too much space (at 7K). But Hertzfeld suspected that the real reason was that the DA wasn't "businesslike." So he went home and rewrote it and got it down to a ridiculously small number of bytes. The puzzle DA shipped with the Mac.

JK: Most of the time, you don't need a manual to use it.

HN: How crisp and neat the screens look.

BW: The best thing about the Mac is that I can forget it's there while I'm working. I'm paid to think, and since computers can't think, I don't want them getting in my way.

2 The Macintosh Family

Choosing a Mac can be a bewildering experience. It's no one-size-fits-all computer, and with more new models appearing each year (7 in '91, 15 in '92, 33 in '93…) and dozens of discontinued models on the used market, it can be hard to decide which is right for you. The good news (unless you're trying to sell a used Mac) is that each year's new Macs nearly always do more, work faster, and cost less than the ones introduced the previous year.

Features that were once special, like sound recording and the ability to plug a monitor directly into the Mac, have long since become standard on most models, and others, like Ethernet support, voice recognition, and even video recording, are becoming much more common. But for all their new features, Macs are still the easiest computers to set up and to use with networks, modems, printers, and monitors, and the basic way you use them hasn't changed.

This chapter explains what makes up a Mac, so you'll understand what makes one model different from another, and what makes the Power Macs so special. That should help you find the right new Mac or better understand the one you have.

Contributors

John Kadyk (JK) is the chapter editor.

David Hauer (DH) is a Macintosh consultant and BMUG helpline staffer. When that gets old, he plays notes, or writes them.

Ken Maki (KM) is a Mac consultant and the author of several computer books, including *Integrating Macs with Your PC Network* (Wiley).

Susan McCallister (SM) and **Arthur Naiman (AN)** edited previous editions of the *Mac Bible,* from which parts of this chapter were taken. Arthur also contributed a new entry to this chapter.

Contents

Branches of the Mac Family

The Mac family is currently divided into several branches: the *Power Macs, Quadras, LCs, Performas*, and *PowerBooks*. Each of these product lines includes several models, but there's some overlap between them. For example, the Quadra 605, the Performa 475, and the LC 475 are virtually identical, except for the names printed on the boxes, what you get with them, and the stores where you go to buy them.

This section describes each line, so you can decide whether one in particular suits your needs, or whether you'll want to investigate models in two or more of them. To find out more about a particular line, read its section later in this chapter. (If it's 1995 or later as you're reading this, much of the Power Mac section may apply to other branches' models as well.)

There are also scores of discontinued Mac models, many of which don't belong to any of these branches. For more on them, see the end of the chapter.

Power Macs and Quadras (JK)

Quadras and Power Macs are designed for businesses and home business users, and they tend to be the lines where Apple first introduces new high-end technologies like desktop video, voice recognition, or the ability to run PC software. The models at the top of these lines lead the Mac family in computing power

Macintosh: The Next Generation (DD/JK)

Apple's new PowerPC chip family was first introduced in the Power Mac line, but Apple intends to convert the other Mac lines over to it (and may have already started, depending on when you're reading this).

At this writing, the plan is to include PowerPC chips in some LC, Performa, and PowerBook models by early 1995, and to sell only PowerPC-based Macs by 1996. That doesn't mean that buying a non-PowerPC Mac is a mistake, though, because Apple and other companies plan to provide ways of upgrading most existing Macs to the new technology—see "Upgrading to PowerPC" at the end of this chapter for details. To get a better idea of the differences between these two generations of Macs, read the "Power Macs" section, later in this chapter.

and options for expansion (see "Expandability (Slots and Bays)" below); the ones at the bottom overlap with models in the LC and Performa lines.

The main difference between Quadras and Power Macs is in the type of processor chip they run on: Quadras use the 68040 chip—the high end of the same basic technology used in all Macs produced between 1984 and 1994—whereas Power Macs use the *PowerPC*, a new, more-powerful technology that Apple plans to include in all Macs by 1996 (see the box "Macintosh: The Next Generation," on the previous page, or for more on chip families, see the next section, "How Macs Differ Inside").

The Quadra and Power Mac lines overlap in both price and performance, but when Power Macs run software that's specially written for their PowerPC chip, they can be several times faster than Quadras. As more of this type of software becomes available, the Power Mac's advantages will become more apparent, and Power Macs will eventually displace Quadras. (Most Quadras can also be upgraded to the PowerPC—see "Upgrading to PowerPC" at the end of the chapter.)

AV Macs (JK)

The Quadra and Power Mac models whose names end in *AV* have special features, mostly related to audio (A), video (V), and communicating over phone lines. They can record and play back video and CD-quality stereo sound, making them well suited to people who design multimedia presentations, or those who like eperimenting with digital audio and video recording. If you buy a special adapter, an AV can also connect to a phone line and function as a speakerphone, answering machine, or fax modem. These features are further described in the "Support for Peripherals" section later in this chapter.

The audio capabilities also enable voice recognition, which lets you actually command your Mac through spoken words rather than the keyboard or mouse (AVs don't take dictation, though—see "Plain Talk" under "Enhancements" in Chapter 3 for more on voice recognition).

GOOD FEATURE

Apple appears to be trying to make these capabilities a more standard part of all Macs. So far, they've included the phone and audio capabilities on all Power Macs—all the AV models add are the video capabilities (although in either case, you still have to buy Apple's PlainTalk for Power Macintosh in order to use the voice recognition). The latest PowerBooks at this writing—the 520, 520c, 540, and 540c—can record and play CD-quality audio, but can't recognize speech.

The Mac vs. Windows (AN)

If you're wondering whether you screwed up by paying more for a Mac than you would have for a PC running Windows, Ron Lichty of Apple thinks you'll be interested in a recent study by the consulting firm Arthur D. Little. It found that Macintosh users finished a range of typical business computing tasks in roughly half the time it took Windows users. What's more, they did 85 percent of the tasks correctly, versus 43 percent for the Windows users.

In other words, with Windows, it took twice as long to work half as well. That's why Macs are worth the extra money. *[Printed copies of a brochure about the study are available from Starting Line at 800/825-2145, part number L00663/A.—JK]*

When you buy a Quadra or a Power Mac, you're paying only for the CPU itself—the box that contains the computing hardware. You then have to pick out your own software, monitor, keyboard, and other peripherals and buy them separately. Quadras and Power Macs are sold through computer stores and mail-order computer catalogs that have been authorized by Apple to support the computers they sell.

Performas (JK)

Performas are low- to medium-performance Macs that are packaged with everything you need to get started with your first computer, including a monitor, a keyboard, typical home-use software, and often a modem. (Sometimes the monitor is actually built into the computer itself.) They also come with a special version of the system software that helps novices avoid some of the mistakes common to new Mac users.

Performas are sold at consumer electronics outlets and appliance stores like Circuit City, Home Depot, and Sears.

LCs (JK)

LCs are similar to Performas but don't include the bundled peripherals and software. LCs are sold only to the students and faculty at schools and universities. LC models that have Performa counterparts use the same model number—for example, the LC 575 and the Performa 575 are the same computer.

PowerBooks (JK/DD)

The PowerBooks are portable, battery-operable Macs designed for people who need to work on the road, but they're popular with all kinds of other users who want the freedom to work where they want—in cafes, laundromats, or just another room of the house. They combine the computer, screen, keyboard, and trackball or trackpad into a compact package the size of a notebook, weighing from 4 to 7.5 pounds (depending on the model). They're popular as supplements to a desktop Mac, but many people like them well enough to use them as their only computer. At this writing, PowerBooks offer performance similar to the Performas and LCs, but they cost 1½ to 2½ times as much (depending primarily on the type of screen they have).

Workgroup Servers (JK)

Workgroup Servers are basically Quadras or Power Macs that have been souped up to work better as *servers*—Macs that provide a central location for resources accessed by a network of other Macs (like customer billing records at a mail-order company, for example). They're sold without monitors or keyboards, through the same outlets as Quadras, Power Macs, and PowerBooks.

How Macs Differ Inside

Aside from obvious features like built-in screens, differences between Mac models fall into three basic categories: *performance* (speed), built-in support for *peripherals* (like monitors, printers, scanners, and other devices), and *expandability* (the capacity to take add-on hardware later). Individual models can also come with different amounts of memory and storage and sometimes include other options that have a big effect on the price. The charts on pages 58–59 and 98–99 summarize the features of different Mac models. Here we'll explain why those features may or may not be important to you.

Performance

Performance—how fast the computer responds to commands from you and from software—is the single biggest factor in determining what makes one Mac better—and more expensive—than another. It depends a lot on what processor chip the Mac uses, although other factors—such as data paths, memory caches, coprocessors, and direct memory access—come into play as well.

The processor chip (JK/DH). The *processor chip* is the computer's brain: a small, flat, square piece of silicon containing thousands or millions of transistors, which are its brain cells. It's also called the *processor*, the *microprocessor*, the *CPU* (for central processing unit) or simply the *chip*—although the term chip is also used for components like RAM, which aren't processors. The processor does most of the Mac's actual computing work, but it's really just a slave to applications and system software, whose instructions it carries out.

There are two different families of processors used in Macs. Motorola's 68000 (or 68K) series—the 68000, 68020, 68030, and 68040—was built into all models produced until 1994 but are now gradually being replaced by the PowerPC chips made by IBM and Motorola.

The 68000 chip's name comes from the fact that it contains about 68,000 transistors, but the other 68K chips have many more transistors than their names would imply (the 68040, for example, has about 1.2 million). As you'd expect, the higher-numbered chips are faster and more advanced: In raw processing power, the 68020, 68030, and 68040 chips (abbreviated as '020, '030, and '040) correspond roughly to the 286, 386, and 486 chips made by Intel for PCs.

The 68LC040 (JK)

The 68LC040 is a less-expensive version of the 68040 chip. The two chips perform exactly alike except for certain unusual tasks that involve *floating-point calculations* (see "Coprocessors," on the next page). Since most people's computing doesn't involve this type of calculation, they can save money by getting a Mac with an 'LC040 chip instead a regular '040.

The PowerPC uses a different, more powerful design called *RISC*, which stands for reduced instruction set computer (the 68K chips use complex instruction set computer, or *CISC* technology). There are currently four types of PowerPC chips either being used or planned for the future: the 601 (the original PowerPC), the 603 (a low-power, low-cost version of the 601 for use in PowerBooks, LCs, and Performas), the 604 (a faster chip that should appear in Macs by mid-1995), and the 620 (the most powerful PowerPC that is currently planned).

More-Compatible '040s (JK)

Some old software won't work with the 68040 chip, but you can tell the 68040 to pretend it's a 68030 in the Cache Switch control panel. This lets you run '040-incompatible programs, but it slows down performance.

Clock speed (JK/DH). After the type of processor it runs on, the second most important factor in a Mac's performance is the speed the processor runs at. This speed—called the *clock speed* or *clock rate*—is determined by a vibrating quartz crystal, which acts like a pacemaker. Clock speed is measured in *megahertz*—millions of cycles per second (abbreviated MHz).

Clock speed is only useful as a measure of relative speed between processors of the same type: All other factors being equal, a Mac with a 68030 chip running at 33 MHz will be faster than one with a 25-MHz '030, but a Mac with a 68040 chip running at 25 MHz will be much faster than either of the '030 Macs.

Coprocessors (JK/DH/KM). A *coprocessor* is a secondary processor that specializes in a specific kind of computation, relieving the main processor of some work and speeding up the tasks it's specifically designed for. There are also secondary general-purpose processors that can technically be considered coprocessors (see "Upgrading Older Macs" later in this chapter), but in most discussions, "coprocessor" refers to a chip with a specialized function. A computer can have more than one coprocessor.

- **FPU.** The most common coprocessor used on 68K Macs is the math coprocessor, also called a *floating-point unit*, or *FPU*. The FPU doesn't really speed up the type of math most of us use in spreadsheets, adding up our monthly bills and such. But it greatly accelerates the kind of sophisticated calculations used in three-dimensional modeling, animation, financial analysis, scientific formulas, and computer-aided design.

  The Mac II contains a math coprocessor called the 68881, and many '030-based Macs come with its successor, the 68882, or can have one added. FPUs are built into the '040 and PowerPC chips, except the 68LC040. The 68LC040 chips can't take add-on FPUs, but you can get a shareware program called **SoftwareFPU** that, in most cases, will allow you to run programs that require one (although very slowly). (See the box on page 96 for more on SoftwareFPU.)

Motherboards, Logic Boards, and Daughterboards (JK)

Inside a Mac's case, you'll see what looks like a miniature city, in which the buildings are actually chips for things like RAM, ROM, and the processor, connected by tiny roads (which are really circuit traces). This is the *motherboard,* also called the *logic board,* which acts as the Mac's computing center and information switchyard. A *daughterboard* or *daughtercard* is a second, smaller board that attaches to either the motherboard or to an expansion card in one of the motherboard's slots. A daughterboard may contain a processor chip or perform some specialized function related to the board it's attached to.

- **DSP.** The '040-based AV Macs include a chip called the *DSP* (for digital signal processor) that some programs use to allow or expedite the processing of certain types of data (typically sounds or images, like video clips, scanned photographs, and digital recordings). To get the full benefit of the DSP, software has to be designed to take advantage of it.

  For example, there's a plug-in file available on on-line services called **AV DSP Power** that enables Adobe's Photoshop to use the DSP chip. With the plug-in, screen redraws and filters are from 10 percent to 300 percent faster, depending on factors like the amount of RAM in your Mac, its hard disk's speed, and the size of the image being processed.

The data bus (JK). Macs have an internal pathway—called the *data path* or *data bus*—for shuttling data around while they're working. The wider and faster this path is for a given processor and clock speed, the faster the Mac can handle tasks that require a lot of data transfer.

At this writing, all 68K-based Macs have a data path that's either 16 or 32 bits wide, while the Power Macs' data path is 64 bits wide. A Mac's data path usually runs at the same speed as its processor, but sometimes it's slower.

Memory caches (JK). A *memory cache* increases a Mac's performance by storing frequently used instructions in the processor itself, or in high-speed memory outside the processor, so it won't have to fetch them from regular RAM every time it needs them. Not many Macs have one: the Power Macs have a cache built into their processors (called a *Level 1* cache), and the IIci (later models only), IIvx, IIfx, Power Mac 8100, and the Workgroup Servers 95, 6150, 8150, and 9150 all come with external caches (called *secondary* or *Level 2* caches) installed in a slot on their motherboards.

Direct memory access (JK). Processors can spend a lot of time supervising the transfer of data between memory and hard drives, floppy drives, and other devices. Needless to say, that's time taken away from other things the processor could be doing. Some Macs—including the Power Macs, the AV Macs, and the Workgroup Server 95—have *direct memory access* (DMA) chips, which handle this processing, either for specific types of devices (e.g., disk drives) or for input and output *(I/O)* from all sources. This keeps I/O processes from slowing the Mac down overall.

Memory and Storage

Most of the Mac elements discussed in the surrounding sections—"Performance," "Support for Peripherals," and "Expandability (Slots and Bays)"—vary from model to model, but memory and storage can also vary within a given model. That's to say, once you've picked a particular Mac, you still usually get to choose how much memory and how big a hard disk you want in it, and you can often choose whether or not you want a CD-ROM drive. (Floppy drives are standard on all Macs except the PowerBook 100 and the Duos, to which you can add an external floppy drive.)

Memory/Storage in Model Names (JK)

Most Mac models are available with several different configurations of installed memory and hard disk space, which are sometimes indicated by a pair of numbers separated by a slash after a Mac's model name. The first number tells you how much memory is installed, and the second number tells you how big its hard drive is. For example, a PowerBook 180 8/120 has 8 megabytes of memory and a 120-megabyte hard drive. But don't confuse these numbers with Power Mac *model* names, which are also made up of two numbers separated by a slash (e.g., 6100/60). (We'll explain those when we talk about Power Macs later in this chapter.)

ROM (JK)

ROM stands for *read-only memory.* It's like software that's hard-wired into your Mac—basic, permanent information that tells it things like how to load up the operating system when you turn it on. As Macs evolve, new capabilities get added to their ROMs, like the ability to display colors (added long ago).

There are a few features (like color capability) that older Macs don't have built into their ROMs, but you can often make up for that by adding a file to your Mac's System Folder. In other cases, older Macs need a special file in order to use more recent system features: for example, some old Macs can't handle more than 8MB of memory because their ROMs aren't *32-bit clean* (i.e., they're not written to enable 32-bit addressing, which is required to access over 8MB of RAM). (For more on 32-bit addressing, see Chapter 4.)

Memory and hard disk sizes are measured in megabytes, and the more you can get of each, the better off you'll be. Most Macs come with less than you'll eventually want, but you can always add more later. *[Someone once told me that to stay up to date with the increases in software's requirements, you have to double your Mac's RAM and hard disk space every two years—looking back, he seems to have been exactly right.—JK]*

Everything you need to know about memory and storage is explained in Chapters 4 and 5. Here we'll just outline why they're important considerations.

Memory, a.k.a. RAM (JK/DH). A computer's *RAM* is the electronic working space it gives you to run programs and do your work in. (RAM stands for random-access memory, and is often just called memory.) Whenever the Mac is on, it keeps at least part of the system software and any opened programs and documents in memory. Physically, RAM takes the form of little black chips soldered onto your computer's motherboard and green cards (usually called *SIMMs*) installed in special slots; together, these function like quick-access storage bins for the tools and information the Mac's processor uses while it works.

The amount of RAM a Mac has determines how many files and applications you can have open at once, and how large they can be. Having more RAM can also keep your Mac from slowing down when you've got all those files open. All Macs come with some RAM built in, but you can buy and install more—how much more depends on the Mac.

Hard drives (JK). The *hard drive* or *hard disk* is the Mac's large, permanent storage area for all your applications, files, and system software (until you trash them). When you're working, the computer copies data it needs from the hard disk into RAM, where the data can be accessed and manipulated much more quickly.

Having a bigger hard drive means that you can keep more programs and files available. Almost all Macs come with a built-in (internal) hard drive, but it's easy to fill its capacity as you accumulate programs and documents over time; when that happens, you can add more room by replacing your drive with a bigger one or buying an external hard drive, which plugs into your Mac's SCSI port.

Floppy drives (JK). Floppy drives copy information to and from 3.5-inch floppy disks, those square plastic wafers with the sliding metal shutter at one end. Floppy disks store files and programs just like hard disks, but they hold much less and are noisier and slower to use. On the other hand, you can pop them in and out of the Mac easily, carry them anywhere, and use them in pretty much any Mac (provided it has the right kind of floppy drive).

Since 1990, all Macs except the PowerBook 100 and the Duos have come with a built-in floppy drive that can handle high-density (1.4MB) floppy disks. You can add an external floppy drive to any model that doesn't have one built in, and even some Macs with internal floppy drives allow you to add a second drive, either internally, externally, or both.

The old Mac 512Ke, Plus, Mac II, and some SE models' floppy drives can handle only double-sided double-density (800K) or single-sided, double-density (400K) disks; the ancient 128K and 512K models can only take 400K disks.

CD-ROM drives (JK). *CD-ROM* (compact disk, read-only memory) drives handle disks that look just like the audio CDs you use on stereos and that store as much data as a large hard disk (more than 600 megabytes). The difference is that you can't copy or save files onto a CD-ROM (at least not using an ordinary CD-ROM drive); you buy the disk with preinstalled files, like photos, graphics files, or encyclopedias.

Most CD-ROM drives can also play regular audio CDs, either through the Mac's speaker(s) or through headphones, and the drives built into current Macs are *Photo CD*–compatible, which means you can have a photo lab put your photos on disk, so you can modify them on screen, print copies, or paste them into documents. (For more on Photo CD, see Chapter 15.)

Support for Peripherals

A *peripheral* is any device that you set up to work with a computer. When a Mac *supports* a particular type of peripheral, that Mac is designed internally to work with that peripheral, and usually has a *port* or socket where you can plug one in without having to add any special adapter or interface. Types of support can vary—for example, some Macs support 21-inch monitors and some support only up to 17-inch monitors.

Monitor support (JK). Most current Macs have at least one port where you can plug in a monitor (some Power Macs have two). Apple has begun calling these *display ports*, but they're also sometimes called *monitor ports*, and in the past they were called *video ports*—which was fine until Apple introduced Macs with ports for connecting to camcorders, TVs, and VCRs (see "Motion Video," below). Unfortunately, Apple and others often still use the older term, so when you hear "video port" or "video support," you have to judge from context whether it's an actual video port or a display port that's being referred to.

The High-Density Display Port (JK)

The PowerPC-based Macs—and maybe others, by the time you read this—have a special, oversized display port called the *AV* or *high-density* port. The AV port is actually a combination monitor, ADB, sound, and video port that was designed for multimedia monitors like Apple's AudioVision 14 Display, which has built-in speakers, a microphone, and places to plug in a keyboard and other peripherals. You need a $30 adapter to connect any other monitor to an AV high-density display port.

Anyway, the size of the monitor you can hook up to a Mac and the richness of color it will display depends on which model it's connected to. Many Mac models allow you to upgrade the level of color displayed by increasing the amount of video RAM *(VRAM)* installed in the Mac. To use a larger monitor than your Mac will support, you have to buy a *display card*, which installs inside the Mac and gives you a separate port.

Modem Ports, Printer Ports, and GeoPorts (JK)

You can plug many devices into either a modem or printer port, but different Macs' ports allow different types of connections.

- On any Mac, the modem port can handle any *serial connections,* which connect the Mac to devices like label printers, inkjet printers, and modems. On AVs and Power Macs, the modem port also handles GeoPort connections, and on Power Macs it handles LocalTalk connections too (read on).
- On any Mac, the printer port can handle both serial connections and *LocalTalk connections,* which are how the computer hooks up to a network that's set up with LocalTalk cabling (see Chapter 23 for more on that). PostScript printers also require a LocalTalk connection to the Mac. On Power Macs and AVs, the printer port also handles GeoPort connections.
- The GeoPort is a type of printer port or modem port that allows voice or data connections to phone lines without a separate phone or modem (see "Phone and Fax Modem Features" below).

Except for the icon that labels it, there's usually no visible difference between the modem and printer ports, unless one of them is a GeoPort (which has nine holes instead of eight, but can still take eight-pin plugs). Any peripheral you buy will let you know what type of connection it requires, so you'll know which port to use.

The Power Macs and the discontinued IIsi, IIci, and Portable models use regular system memory for their monitor support. This can noticeably slow down performance on the older models because the memory is being shared between the monitor and whatever software is running on the Mac. With those models, it's sometimes worth getting a display card just to avoid the slowdown.

The Duos and some older Macs don't have any place to plug in an external monitor or install a display card, so you have to rely on their built-in screens or use a special adapter to attach an external monitor.

Networking (JK). There are two main types of cabling used for hooking up Macs into a network: *LocalTalk* and *Ethernet.* All Macs can connect to a LocalTalk network via their printer ports, and Power Macs can also connect to LocalTalk via their modem ports.

LocalTalk works fine for office e-mail and transferring small documents, but Ethernet works *much* faster. The additional speed is particularly helpful in situations where one or more Macs will be working across the network on files kept on another computer. Most current Macs have Ethernet ports, and it's getting nearly as easy and cheap to connect that way as it always has been to connect via LocalTalk, so Ethernet will probably take over as the main network system in use. For more info on networking, see Chapter 23.

THINGS TO COME

Sound and voice recognition (JK). All Macs have a built-in speaker, so they can beep at you when they want your attention and play the sounds that are part of many programs (games, especially). Some Macs (the 500-series LCs, Performas, and PowerBooks, in particular) have stereo speakers, so you don't miss out on the stereo sound on multimedia CD-ROMs, for example.

All Macs also have sound output ports, so you can connect headphones or external speakers; on most current models—except the LCs and Performas numbered below 475 and the PowerBook Duos—the output is in stereo.

All current models except the PowerBook Duos also have audio input ports where you can connect a microphone (a few models have mikes built-in, including the all-in-one LC, the Performa models, and some of the all-in-one PowerBooks). Most Macs at this writing can only handle mono input (the exceptions are the Power Macs, the AV Macs, and LCs and Performas numbered 550 or over).

GOOD FEATURE

On most Macs, the sound quality is about as good as what you get from an AM radio, but the AVs and Power Macs support CD-quality sound. That not only means you can record high-fidelity audio clips and get better-sounding playback through speakers or headphones, but it also means the Mac can "hear" well enough to take voice commands, if you get Apple's PlainTalk microphone and software (see "PlainTalk" in Chapter 3 for details).

For a chart showing the built-in sound capabilities of various Mac models, see Chapter 17.

GOOD FEATURE

Motion video (JK). The AV Macs have *video-in* ports that let you use the Mac screen as a monitor for a VCR or camcorder (so you're looking through the camcorder's lens via a window on the screen). You can also capture still

How to Read Your Ports (JK)

On a Mac's back panel is an array of *ports* (sockets) for hooking up all the other hardware that Macs are designed to work with. Depending on which model you've got, you'll have some or all of the following, and maybe even one or two rare ones we haven't listed.

This icon	**Appears above this port**	**Which is where you attach**
	Modem	A serial device, such as a modem or a non-PostScript printer; or on some Macs, a GeoPort Telecom Adapter or a LocalTalk connector
	Printer	A printer, LocalTalk connector, or serial device; or, on some Macs, a GeoPort Telecom Adapter
	SCSI	An external hard disk, CD-ROM or cartridge drive, scanner, or other SCSI device
	Ethernet	Ethernet network cabling
	Display	A monitor (one that your Mac is designed to support)
	ADB	A keyboard, mouse, trackball, or other ADB device
	Sound input	A microphone or other sound input plug
and	Left and right sound input	Patch cords from a stereo or other audio device (beware though: even though the inputs are stereo, some Macs mix them down to mono)
	Sound output	Headphones or speakers (with stereo miniplug)
IN or IN or	Video input	A camcorder or VCR that you want to record video from
OUT or OUT	Video output	A monitor or VCR that you want to display or record video onto
	Headphone	Stereo headphones (this unusual port shows up on the front panel of Macs that have it)
or	Floppy drive	An external floppy drive

images from the on-screen video, or record it to a movie file using VideoFusion's FusionRecorder, which comes with these models. You can use either composite (RCA) or S-video connectors, depending on which type your other equipment uses. The same Macs also have *video-out* ports, which let you display the Mac's screen image on a TV or record it on a VCR (you can use the same two types of connectors). So, for example, people who design animations and presentations can output them to videotape so they can be viewed virtually anywhere, without the need for a Macintosh. You can also display presentations—whether from tape or the Mac—on large TV screens, which are much cheaper than big-screen Mac monitors. But you can't display the Mac screen on both the computer monitor and a TV monitor at the same time.

Depending on the amount of VRAM installed and the size of the window, the AVs can display video at near-broadcast quality in up to 32,000 colors and can capture full-size *still* images in 16 million colors. But the Quadra models can only *record* video to small-frame QuickTime movies, at a jerky 10 or 14 frames per second (although if you record to memory instead of a hard disk, you can sometimes get up to 25 fps). The Power Mac AVs should handle this better, but no test results are available at this writing.

The AVs can handle video input in any of three formats: NTSC (the U.S. and Japanese standard), PAL (used by most of the rest of the world), or SECAM (French). They can output video in both NTSC and PAL formats.

Phone and fax modem features (JK). You can hook up a modem or fax modem to any Mac, but some models—the Quadra AVs and Power Macs, at this writing—can function as a speakerphone, an answering machine, or a 14.4Kbps fax modem, thanks to something called a *GeoPort.* The GeoPort isn't actually a separate port, but a special version of the modem port (and, on Power Macs, the printer port) that, with the help of Apple's $130 **GeoPort Telecom Adapter,** can connect the Mac to phone lines. (Be sure to get the right version of the adapter for your Mac.)

The Telecom Adapter comes with the software you need for all of this, including Jabra's Dialer software, which stores 20 names and numbers for speed dialing and allows you to use the voice recognition at the same time as the phone. (The ApplePhone software that came with the original Quadra AVs wouldn't allow

Just What You Need: A Videophone (JK)

The AV Macs' hardware makes them capable of *videoconferencing,* which lets callers using AVs and video cameras watch each other on screen while talking on the phone. You can't just set up a videoconference over an ordinary phone line, however (the huge load of voice and video data requires a special connection), so for most users, the AV videoconferencing connection will probably be limited to people connected over an Ethernet network. The AVs come with the software; you just have to buy the cameras and hook them up.

this, and Apple's modem software still doesn't.) If you like to type while you talk, Jabra's $170 **EarPhone** provides the headset and software necessary to use any Mac with a GeoPort as a hands-free telephone.

Expandability (Slots and Bays)

When one desktop Mac is bigger than another, it's usually because it's got extra room inside for installing internal drives (in addition to the ones that came with the computer) or *expansion cards.* Many people never have a need for such add-ons and can save money by getting a Mac without the extra *bays* (for drives) or *slots* (for cards) that larger Macs have.

Expansion slots (JK/DH). An *expansion slot* is a connector inside the Mac that lets you plug in a rectangular plastic *card* or *board* whose circuitry and components perform a special task, such as accelerating your computer or recording video clips onto its hard drive. The type and number of slots vary between Mac models (some don't have any). At this writing, there are two basic kinds: *processor-direct slots* (PDSs) and *NuBus* slots. Starting in late 1994, Apple plans to introduce Macs that use another, faster type of slot called the *PCI* (for Peripheral Component Interconnect).

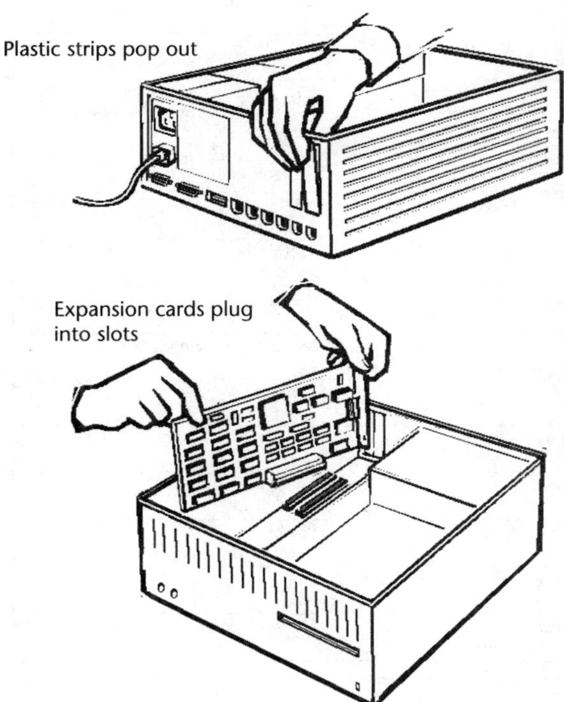

Expansion cards are often designed to connect to external devices, so slots usually line up with openings in the Mac's back panel (which are covered by removable plastic strips).

No Mac can take more than one PDS card, and installing one often blocks a NuBus slot. Processor-direct slots vary from model to model, so you have to be sure you're getting the right kind of PDS card for your Mac.

Peripheral Support on Mac Models (Through June 1994)

Model	ADB	Modem	Printer	SCSI	Sound-in	Sound-out	Ethernet	Monitor (maximum size)	Others
Desktop models									
Power Mac 6100	1	GeoPort, LocalTalk	GeoPort, LocalTalk	25-pin	Stereo	Stereo	Yes	Portrait or midsize	AV model adds second monitor port, video in and out
Power Mac 7100, 8100 and Power Mac AVs	1	GeoPort, LocalTalk	GeoPort, LocalTalk	25-pin	Stereo	Stereo	Yes	21"	AV model adds video in and out
Quadra 605	1	Serial	LocalTalk, serial	25-pin	Mono	Stereo	No	21"	
Quadra 610, 610 DOS Compatible, 650	2	Serial	LocalTalk, serial	25-pin	Mono	Stereo	Yes	21"	DOS card has monitor port, PC game port
Quadra 660AV, 840AV	1	GeoPort	LocalTalk, serial	25-pin	Stereo	Stereo	Yes	21"	S-video, composite video in and out
Quadra 700	2	Serial	LocalTalk, serial	25-pin	Mono	Stereo	Yes	21"	
Quadra 800	2	Serial	LocalTalk, serial	25-pin	Mono	Stereo	Yes	21"	
Quadra 900, 950	1	Serial	LocalTalk, serial	25-pin	Mono	Stereo	Yes	21"	RCA sound in (L&R, mixed to mono internally)
Performa 200	1	Serial	LocalTalk, serial	25-pin	Mono	Mono	No	None	Floppy
Performa 400, 405, 410, 430	1	Serial	LocalTalk, serial	25-pin	Mono	Mono	No	14"	
Performa 450, 460, 466, 467	1	Serial	LocalTalk, serial	25-pin	Mono	Mono	No	Portrait or midsize	
Performa 475, 476	1	Serial	LocalTalk, serial	25-pin	Mono	Stereo	No	21"	
Performa 550, 560	2	Serial	LocalTalk, serial	25-pin	Stereo	Stereo, headphone	No	None	Headphone
Performa 575, 577, 578	1	Serial	LocalTalk, serial	25-pin	Mono	Stereo	No	None	Headphone
Performa 600, 600CD	2	Serial	LocalTalk, serial	25-pin	Mono	Mono	No	14"	
LC, LC II	1	Serial	LocalTalk, serial	25-pin	Mono	Mono	No	14"	
LC III	1	Serial	LocalTalk, serial	25-pin	Mono	Mono	No	Portrait or midsize	
LC 475	1	Serial	LocalTalk, serial	25-pin	Mono	Stereo	No	21"	
LC 520, 550	2	Serial	LocalTalk, serial	25-pin	Mono	Stereo, headphone	No	None	Headphone
LC 575	1	Serial	LocalTalk, serial	25-pin	Mono	Stereo, headphone	No	None	Headphone
Macintosh TV	2	Serial	LocalTalk, serial	25-pin	RCA stereo	Headphone only	No	None	Video in (RCA and coaxial)
Workgroup Server 60, 80	2	Serial	LocalTalk, serial	25-pin	Mono	Stereo	Yes	21"	
Workgroup Server 95	1	Serial	LocalTalk, serial	25-pin	Mono	Stereo	Yes	21"	
Workgroup Server 6150, 8150	1	GeoPort, LocalTalk	GeoPort, LocalTalk	25-pin	Stereo	Stereo	Yes	Portrait or midsize	

Model	ADB	Modem	Printer	SCSI	Sound-in	Sound-out	Ethernet	Monitor (maximum size)	Others
Desktop models (continued)									
Workgroup Server 9150	1	GeoPort, LocalTalk	GeoPort, LocalTalk	25-pin	Stereo	Stereo	Yes	Portrait or midsize	
Centris 610, 650	2	Serial	LocalTalk, serial	25-pin	Mono	Stereo	Optional	21"	
II, IIx, IIfx	2	Serial	LocalTalk, serial	25-pin	None	Stereo	No	None	
IIci	2	Serial	LocalTalk, serial	25-pin	None	Stereo	No	Portrait (not 16" or 17")	Floppy
IIcx	2	Serial	LocalTalk, serial	25-pin	None	Stereo	No	None	Floppy
IIfx	2	Serial	LocalTalk, serial	25-pin	None	Stereo	No	None	
IIsi	1	Serial	LocalTalk, serial	25-pin	Mono	Stereo	No	Portrait (not 16" or 17")	Floppy
IIvi, IIvx	2	Serial	LocalTalk, serial	25-pin	Mono	Mono	No	14"	
IIx	2	Serial	LocalTalk, serial	25-pin	None	Stereo	No	None	
Classic	1	Serial	LocalTalk, serial	25-pin	None	Mono	No	None	Floppy
Classic II	1	Serial	LocalTalk, serial	25-pin	Mono	Mono	No	None	Floppy
Color Classic, Color Classic II	2	Serial	LocalTalk, serial	25-pin	Mono	Mono	No	None	
SE	2	Serial	LocalTalk, serial	25-pin	None	Mono	No	None	Floppy
SE/30	2	Serial	LocalTalk, serial	25-pin	None	Stereo	No	None	Floppy
Plus	None	Serial	LocalTalk, serial	25-pin	None	Mono	No	None	Floppy, keyboard, mouse
128K, 512K, 512Ke	None	Serial	LocalTalk, serial	none	None	Mono	No	None	Floppy, keyboard, mouse
Portable models									
Portable	1	Serial	LocalTalk, serial	25-pin	None	Stereo	No	RA	Floppy
PowerBook 100	1	None	Serial	30-pin	None	Mono	No	None	Floppy
PowerBook 140, 145, 145B, 170	1	Serial	LocalTalk, serial	30-pin	Mono	Stereo	No	None	
PowerBook 160, 165, 165c, 180, 180c	1	Serial	LocalTalk, serial	30-pin	Mono	Stereo	No	Portrait or midsize	
PowerBook 520, 520c, 540, 540c	1	None	LocalTalk, serial	30-pin	Mono	Stereo	yes	Portrait or midsize	
PowerBook Duo 210, 230, 250, 270c, 280, 280c	RA	None	LocalTalk, serial	RA	RA	RA	With Duo Dock	RA	Adapter or dock allows attachment of floppy drive
PowerBook Duo MiniDock	1	Serial	LocalTalk, serial	30-pin	Mono	Mono	No	Portrait or midsize	Floppy
PowerBook Duo Dock, Duo Dock II	1	Serial	LocalTalk, serial	30-pin	Mono	Mono	Duo Dock II only	Portrait or midsize	

RA = Requires adapter.

Which Mac for You? (JK)

Before you look for a Mac, think hard about what you will want to use it for, to make sure you don't close yourself off from some wonderful Mactivity that's only supported by certain models. But don't go spending hundreds of extra dollars for capabilities you're not sure you'll use, especially if they can be added later through upgrades.

Unfortunately, this book can't really steer you toward a particular model, because by the time it's printed, the market will have changed. Check with recent Mac magazines, knowledgeable friends, and user groups before you take the plunge.

HOT TIP

If you're on Ziffnet/Mac (available through CompuServe, which is described in Chapter 22) you can download a HyperCard stack called **"Which Mac Should I Buy?"** that will help you narrow down your choices. It's put together and updated regularly by Danny Goodman, a true Mac guru. For technical specs on all Mac models, past and present, two reliable sources are Harry Phillipo's beautifully designed **Mac History** chart (available from on-line services) and Mark Simmons's exhaustive and endlessly useful resource, **Mac Catalog,** which is available as a FileMaker Pro database or QuickTime slideshow from Ziffnet/Mac via CompuServe or from AppleLink or eWorld. (Both Mac History and Mac Catalog were used extensively in preparing this chapter.)

By contrast, you can add as many NuBus cards as your Mac has slots for (up to six on some models), and virtually any NuBus card will work in any Mac (space permitting—some Macs can't handle cards over 7 inches long).

Some Macs have a special processor-direct slot that can also take a NuBus card, if you get a special Apple-made adapter that's actually itself a card with a built-in NuBus slot. (Different models require different adapter cards, with ApplePrices ranging from $70 to $150. The IIsi has a slot that requires an adapter for either type of card—NuBus or PDS; both types of adapters include a math coprocessor, which the IIsi otherwise lacks.

In addition to these basic kinds of slots, some Macs contain special sorts of slots for adding memory, cache cards, internal modems, and so on. The AV Macs have something called the *DAV* (digital audio video) slot, which is designed to give direct access to their digital processing hardware. Boards that are designed for this slot can provide a big increase in performance in the handling of audio and video files.

Storage bays (JK). *Storage bays* are spaces inside the Mac for adding extra disk drives, in addition to the ones that come with the computer. There are two main sizes of bays, to match the two main sizes of drives: 3.5 inches (the standard size of floppy drives, hard drives, and some cartridge drives) and 5.25 inches (the size of CD-ROM drives, large hard disks, and some cartridge drives).

You don't need a storage bay to add one of these drives, though, because you can also hook up external drives to a Mac's SCSI port (floppy drives connect to the *floppy port*, on Macs that have one). You'll find extra bays in only a few models, such as the high-end Quadras and Power Macs (or in any Mac on which a CD-ROM drive is optional, if you don't get it with the CD-ROM drive).

Power Macs (JK)

The Power Mac line was launched in March 1994 as the first branch of the Mac family to be based on the new, more powerful PowerPC processor chip. Even though the PowerPC is completely different from the 68K processors used in all previous Macs, you use Power Macs the same way you use older models (Apple took pains to make it that way).

You can use most programs written for 68K-based Macs on a Power Mac, but they won't run much, if any, faster than they would on a high-end 68K Mac—in fact, they may run slower. To take advantage of the PowerPC chip's speed, you need software written specifically for it (called *native* PowerPC software). Again, this doesn't mean having to learn new and different programs from scratch—many of the most popular Mac programs will be available in Power Mac versions by the time you read this, and more will become available as time passes.

A given program may have separate installation disks for 68K Macs and Power Macs, or it may be installable in a *fat binary* version, which contains both 68K and Power Mac instructions, and uses whichever is appropriate for the Mac it's running on.

At this writing, only Power Macs have PowerPC processors, but eventually all Mac lines will be converted over to the PowerPC. So depending on when you're reading this, a lot of material may apply to some or all current PowerBooks, LCs, Performas, and Workgroup Servers as well.

The extra power of the PowerPC chip not only makes Power Macs run faster, it enables them to take on tasks that, on other Macs, are too slow to be practical—like running Windows programs—or require a special additional chip, like voice recognition.

The Power Macs running native software generally outperform Quadras, but whether they're one-and-a-half times as fast or eight times as fast varies a lot depending on what you're doing. Certain basic functions, like opening native files and applications, are always fast. Menus seem to pop down instantaneously, and using a paintbrush in graphics programs is more like the real thing because the screen keeps up with your brushstrokes. But some tasks will still only run at the pace of a midlevel Quadra, even within native applications.

The 68K Emulator (JK)

The 68K and PowerPC processor families each have their own language for communicating with software, and neither type of chip can, by itself, run programs written for the other type. So Apple built an interpreter (called an *emulator*) into the Power Macs' ROM, which translates instructions from 68K software for the PowerPC chip and interacts with 68K software the way a 68K processor would.

The result is that most 68K programs will run on a Power Mac, but only about as fast as they would on an '030- or '040-based Mac, because the translation slows things down. Also, since the emulator doesn't include an FPU, it won't let you run 68K programs that require one (unless you add the shareware control panel SoftwareFPU—and even then they'll only work slowly, if at all).

There's no formula for exactly how fast a given task in any program (68K or native) will run, but functions that use the Power Mac's blazingly fast FPU, QuickDraw (which calculates screen images), or QuickTime (a native version of which comes with Power Macs) should perform particularly well. Even 68K programs running in emulation can benefit from the Power Mac's native system software, particularly on jobs involving a lot of display calculations, like font changes or resizing graphics.

Overall, people who use native software for animation, rendering, CAD, image-editing, sophisticated math functions, illustration, page layout, and database management will get the biggest benefit

Acceleration by System Upgrade (JK)

The Power Macs come with a PowerPC version of System 7, but in fact, only part of the system software has been translated into PowerPC code.

With any Mac or system version, applications make heavy use of a part of the system called the *Toolbox,* a collection of prewritten routines that perform common tasks. According to Apple, programs only use a certain 20 percent or so of them 80 to 90 percent of the times that they access the Toolbox; so those are the routines Apple optimized for the PowerPC. The rest were left in 68K code, to be translated for later releases of the system. Consequently, if you upgrade a Power Mac's system software when new releases come out—and more of the system software has been converted to native PowerPC code—the computer should actually run faster.

(which is appropriate, since these are among the most notoriously demanding areas of computing).

Special Features on Power Macs

Power Macs have many features built-in that can be expensive options on other Macs—and some you can't get at all on other models.

Multiple monitor support. Except for the non-AV 6100, all Power Macs at this writing have two display ports, so you can connect two monitors at once—for example, a black-and-white one for text and a color one for games and graphics, or one for Mac programs and one for Windows programs.

GOOD FEATURE

On the Power Mac's back panel is a *high-density port,* which, at this writing, connects directly only to Apple's AV Display; to attach any other monitor, you'll need the $30 **Power Mac Display Adapter** (which comes free with the non-AV 6100, since you have no alternative to using it). This port supports mid- or portrait-size monitors, but not large (19- to 21-inch) monitors. It relies on the Power Mac's system memory rather than special VRAM—a setup that slows down operations on earlier Mac models, but shouldn't have a noticeable impact on the performance of Power Macs.

The non-AV 7100 and 8100 Power Macs also have a standard, 15-pin display port on an accelerated display card that comes preinstalled in their processor-

Acceleration by Cache Card (JK)

All the Power Macs at this writing—the 6100, 7100, 8100, and their AV versions—have a special slot where you can add a cache card, which dramatically speeds up many computing tasks. (The 8100 already has a 256K cache installed in the slot, but you can replace it with a 512K card.)

Reports say these cards are a very worthwhile investment: in speed tests in major Mac magazines, a 6100/60 with Apple's $300 **256K Cache Card** installed performed faster than a 7100/66 without one, and a 7100/66 got about 10 percent faster with the addition of the card. Overall, 68K software showed more improvement from the cache card than native PowerPC software did.

Mobius Technologies and Newer Technology may also have 512K and 1MB Power Mac cache cards available by the time you read this.

direct slot. This card redraws the screen faster than either of the other types of Power Mac monitor support, and it supports monitors up to 21 inches. Furthermore, its VRAM is upgradable, so your Mac can display more colors at once (up to 32,768 on the 7100, or 16.7 million on the 8100). For all these reasons, this port gives the best monitor support on the Power Macs.

The AV Power Macs have yet another standard monitor port, in the AV card installed in their processor-direct slot. Screen redraw from this port is the slowest, but it runs on 2 megs of VRAM (not upgradable), which allows it to support millions of colors on small and midsize monitors, and thousands of colors on monitors up to 21 inches.

Sound, phone, and fax modem features. Like the Quadra AVs and the 500-series PowerBooks, the Power Macs come with the ability to record and play back CD-quality stereo sound. If you buy Apple's **PlainTalk Microphone** ($30 ApplePrice), you can control your Power Mac by voice.

The Power Mac's modem and printer ports are extremely versatile: They're both GeoPorts, and both support LocalTalk, so either one will let you hook up to serial devices, networks, or—via Apple's Power Mac GeoPort Telecom Adapter—the phone line, for phone or fax modem communications (the Power Macs use a different adapter than the AVs).

AV models. The Power Mac AVs are the same as the basic models, except that they've got an AV card installed in their processor-direct slots (instead of the accelerated display card, on 7100s and 8100s). The Power Mac AV card provides a second display port and video-in and video-out ports, so you can view or record clips from a TV, VCR, or camcorder or use a TV monitor as a Mac display.

Careful With Those PDS Cards! (JK)

You can damage a Power Mac 7100 or 8100 if you remove the display or AV card that comes in its processor-direct slot, and then turn the Mac on without the card. Unfortunately, you pretty much have to take the PDS card out to install a cache card in a 7100, and you can't install memory in the 8100 without removing it. So if you make one of these upgrades, be sure you've put the card back in before you turn the Mac back on!

You'd think Apple would offer the AV card separately, so you could upgrade a regular Power Mac (and maybe get some credit for trading in its display card), but they're not planning to do that. So if you're choosing a Power Mac, be careful with your decision about whether to get the video feature.

Power Mac Model Names (JK)

Unlike many of the names Apple has given Macs in the past, the Power Mac models' names actually describe some of their essential characteristics.

In each name, the first digit indicates the type of box the computer is in (what Apple calls its "form factor"). The *6* in 6100 means that it uses the same flat, single-slot box as the Centris and Quadra 610 and the Centris and Quadra 660AV. The *7* in 7100 refers to the three-slot box used by the IIvx and the Centris and Quadra 650. The *8* in 8100 refers to the box used by the Quadra 800 and 840AV, which also has three slots, plus room for up to three additional drives in addition to the built-in floppy and hard drives. (All of these Power Macs are available with built-in CD-ROM drives as well.)

The second digit indicates the version of PowerPC chip the Mac uses: the 601 chip, in the case of the three models mentioned above (later Macs will be built around the 603, 604, and 620 chips). The numbers following the slash give you the clock speed (in MHz) that the Mac's processor chip runs at. At this writing, they're often left off, since none of the models is available with more than one chip speed.

The AV cards on the 7100 and 8100 AV Macs also include a DAV (digital audio video) slot like the ones in Quadra AVs, where you can add cards that extend the Power Mac's audio and video processing capabilities.

The ability to run PC software. Power Macs can run **SoftWindows**, a program from Insignia Solutions that lets you run DOS or Windows applications in a window on the Power Mac's desktop. No other Mac is powerful enough to do that. Insignia has also made PC emulators for 68K Macs, but they don't run Windows programs and are too slow to be useful unless you're desperate to run a PC program.

Don't Spread Windows Across Monitors (JK)

If you're using SoftWindows on a Mac with two monitors, don't position the Windows window so that it's split across the screens. Insignia Solutions says this really slows things down.

With SoftWindows, you can work in Mac and PC programs simultaneously and even cut and paste between the two environments. PC applications share the Mac's keyboard, mouse, hard disk, CD-ROM drive, and printer, and SoftWindows supports non-Mac network systems like Netware, LAN Manager, Windows for Workgroups, and TCP/IP. (Novell is also working on a PowerPC version of Netware, which won't require SoftWindows.)

SoftWindows has its drawbacks, too. Like Windows on the PC, it takes up a lot of memory—*9 megs* for version 1.0—so you'll need at least 16 megs in your Power Mac to run it, and if you're going to be using large programs simultaneously, you'll want even more. Also, version 1.0 emulates a 286 processor running Windows 3.1, and although it operates at the speed of a fast 386 or slow 486SX PC, that's still slow compared to what you'd get by buying a modern PC. And because it emulates a 286 processor, it can't run programs that require a 386, which includes many popular Windows programs.

At this writing, Insignia is working on a new version of SoftWindows that will emulate a 486 processor and should solve both the speed and compatibility issues; it may be available by the time you read this.

Editor's Poll: Are You Going to Upgrade to PowerPC Right Away?

AA: Nope; I'm happy with my souped-up IIci.

DB: I don't trust the first generation of anything. I'll wait a little while. Also, I bought my Quadra not so long ago, so I need to wait until I upgrade again.

EC: I am probably going to upgrade to the PowerPC within a year, after the dust has settled a little, and the first upgrade cards only cost half of what they did when they were released.

JK: No way. All my software is 68K and wouldn't run any faster on a Power Mac than it does on my Centris 650. I'll wait until Power Macs have gotten better and cheaper and there's Power Mac software I can't live without.

HN: I placed my order weeks before the rollout and got my machine (not from the dealer from whom I ordered it) a few days after the introduction. I love it!

All the Power Macs except the AVs are available in a configuration with SoftWindows preinstalled, or you can add it to any other Power Mac ($500 list)—provided you've got the minimum 16MB of RAM. (For other ways to run PC software on a Mac, see Chapter 25.)

Known Incompatibilities

Whenever you try to use old hardware and software with a new processor or operating system, a few areas of incompatibility crop up. Here's a list of problems we already know about. In general, calling a product's manufacturer is the best way to confirm a suspected incompatibility and get a reliable remedy.

- PDS cards designed for 68K Macs won't work on Power Macs.
- 68K programs that require an FPU won't work, because when they run on a Power Mac, they're handled by the emulator, which doesn't include an FPU. You can enable most of these programs to function by adding SoftwareFPU (a shareware utility described on page 96), but they'll work very slowly. A better solution is to upgrade to a PowerPC version of the program in question, since the PowerPC's FPU is one of its strongest features.

- Software written for the DSP chip in the Quadra AVs won't work, since the Power Macs don't have a DSP; they handle its functions with the PowerPC chip.
- Some programs work only with the Power Mac's Memory Manager control panel turned off (which also reduces overall performance by about 10 percent).
- A small number of programs won't work because they try to bypass the Mac's processor to work with other components directly—but since Power Macs have a different internal architecture than 68K Macs, the software may not find what it needs.

- Some 68K extensions have a serious impact on the performance of native applications, because they force the Power Mac to switch between the emulator and the PowerPC chip. (Old versions of After Dark, ATM, or Timbuktu can slow you down appreciably. Get rid of them or upgrade them to PowerPC versions as soon as they're available.)

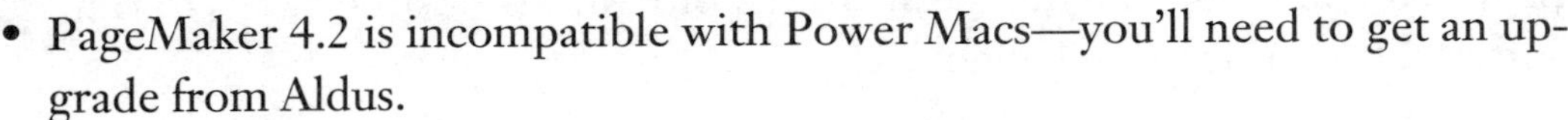

- PageMaker 4.2 is incompatible with Power Macs—you'll need to get an upgrade from Aldus.
- Third-party accelerated display cards may be incompatible with Power Macs or may run much slower unless you update their driver software and sometimes their ROM.
- Some older hard drives whose drivers don't support SCSI Manager 4.3 will slow down dramatically when used with a Power Mac. If you've got an old Apple drive, you can update its driver with HD SC Setup 7.3 or later, which comes with Power Macs. If you've got a non-Apple drive, call the manufacturer. Failing that, use a hard disk utility like La Cie's Silverlining 5.6, Casa Blanca Works' Drive7 3.0, or FWB's HD ToolKit 1.5 (later versions of these programs will work too). (For more on SCSI Manager 4.3 and hard disk drivers, see Chapter 5.)

Quadras

(JK)

Just as the Power Macs introduced the PowerPC chip, the Quadras introduced the 68040 chip, the second most powerful processor available on a Mac. Since then, the '040 has been built into the Performa, LC, PowerBook, and Workgroup Server lines as well (as the PowerPC will be too, soon), but the Quadra line still contains the most expandable, upgradable, forward-looking 68K Macs on the market. Quadras will be around for a little longer, but the Power Macs have taken over the lead at the cutting edge of Mac technology.

GOOD FEATURE

Apple designed the Power Macs around Quadra cases, so there's a direct upgrade path from the Quadra 610, 650, or 800 to the Power Mac 6100, 7100, or 8100, respectively. Some 68K-based LCs and Performas should soon be upgradable to a PowerPC chip, through a daughterboard or CPU transplant, but only Quadra models can be converted to actual Power Mac models.

Quadras are also the only current 68K Mac line that offers multiple NuBus slots and extra storage bays, on its midlevel and high-end models. At the low end, though, Quadras aren't much different from Performas and LCs, except in where they're sold and the extras that come with them. In fact, some models are built around identical computing hardware—the Quadra 605, LC 475, and Performa 475, for example.

The Quadras introduced built-in Ethernet (now standard on Power Macs and 500-series PowerBooks) and the AV features (discussed in the box "AV Macs" on page 43), some of which are now standard on Power Macs and are gradually being introduced to the other lines. Some Quadra models have also introduced improvements in the NuBus, SCSI, and memory technologies to enable the best possible performance, given the right peripherals.

The Quadra 600s are the desktop models, offering a range of performance and expandability that can cover the needs of most users working with 68K software, from the 605, with its single PDS slot and 25-MHz '040 chip, through the 33-MHz Quadra 650, which has three NuBus slots and a processor-direct slot. The "tower" models—the 840AV and 950—stand vertically and are better suited for work that demands extra capacity for various storage media—like color desktop publishing and multimedia production—and specialized processing functions, such as rendering. The 840AV, which is the fastest 68K Mac at this writing, is excellent for these tasks and for desktop audio and video production. The 950 (and the 900, which died in infancy at the birth of its stronger brother) are the ultimate in expandable tower Macs, with the most expansion slots (five) and space for additional drives (two or three) of any model except the Workgroup Server 95 and 9150, which are based on the same chassis.

LCs

(JK)

The original LC was introduced as the first low-cost Mac to include built-in support for a color monitor and a microphone for recording sounds. The current LC line still emphasizes affordability and multimedia, but it's now sold only to schools, colleges, and through campus-run stores, where you have to show a student or faculty ID to buy one.

The Mac TV

(JK)

The Macintosh TV is an all-in-one Mac like the LC 520, with a CD-ROM drive, a 14-inch color monitor, stereo speakers, and a TV tuner. To help it fit in with your stereo and VCR, the Mac TV and its keyboard and mouse are all colored consumer-electronics black.

It's a perfectly acceptable—but limited—Mac for typical, undemanding home or school uses: it runs on a 32-MHz 68030 processor, but its RAM is expandable to just 8 megs. There's a remote control for channel-surfing or playing audio CDs in the CD-ROM drive while you wait for your term paper to print out. It's also got jacks for hooking up either a VCR or cable TV, and you can capture single frames from the action on the screen to save as files on the Mac. The Mac TV is only sold through 250 or so U.S. retail outlets and the computer stores at college campuses.

The 68LC040-powered LC 475 and the discontinued LC, LC II, and LC III (which run on '020s and '030s) are small, flat computers without space for internal CD-ROM drives. The LC and LC II are fine for everyday computing tasks; the LC III is significantly faster than the earlier models, and the 475 is at least twice as fast as the LC III. However, none of this group comes standard with an FPU, which is required for some math and graphics programs, and you can't even add one to the LC 475.

The 500-series LCs all have a color monitor, stereo speakers, and a CD-ROM drive built right into the case, which makes them well suited for the

Built-in Screens

Model	Screen	Resolution	Colors/Grays	Notes
LC 520, 575	14-inch color	640 by 480	256/thousands	1
Performa 550, 560, 575, 577, 578	14-inch color	640 by 480	256/thousands	1
Macintosh TV	14-inch color	640 by 480	256	
Color Classic, Color Classic II	10-inch color	512 by 384	256/thousands	1
Compact Macs	9-inch B&W	512 by 342	B&W	2

Notes

1 These models require a VRAM upgrade to display thousands of colors.

2 All of these models except the SE/30 use regular system memory for video support; the SE/30 has 64K of internal VRAM.

wealth of multimedia CD-ROMs targeted for the education market. The 500-series LCs' all-in-one design also makes them easy to set up and to move from one desk, classroom, or computer lab to another. (What they don't have is a display port, so be sure you like the built-in screen before buying one of these.)

LCs are, at this writing, the least expandable line of desktop Macs; they each have a processor-direct slot, but none can handle a NuBus card, an extra internal drive, or more than 36 megs of RAM. But in raw processing power, current models overlap into the Quadras' range—only the Quadra 840AV's 40-MHz 68040 is faster than the LC 575's 33-MHz 68040. By early 1995, there should also be LCs based on the PowerPC 603 chip, and PowerPC upgrades should become available for earlier models, either from Apple or other companies (see "Upgrading to PowerPC" at the end of this chapter).

THINGS TO COME

Although the LC line doesn't offer AV models, by the time you read this there should be a more-expandable LC available that will let you use your monitor as a TV or record videoclips to disk by adding special low-cost cards that provide those functions.

To keep their prices down, many LCs don't come with system software installation disks or manuals (but then, if you've got a classroom full of Macs, these accoutrements tend to fill up shelves or wastebaskets pretty fast). If you need a set of manuals or system software, they're available as a separate purchase (currently about $50, but likely to go up when a new version comes out).

Performas

(JK)

The Performas are Apple's way of making Macs more accessible to the millions of American households that could really use Macs but so far haven't taken the plunge. They come prepackaged with a monitor, software, and everything you need to start computing (including an alternative, simplified interface). They're also easier to find than other Macs: They're sold through consumer electronics outlets and nationwide chain stores like Wal-Mart, where they sit alongside the VCRs, stereos, and other electronic gadgetry that have become standard in American homes.

Apple also makes it easy to get service on Performas. Users of other types of Macs are expected to get technical service from their dealers, but rather than asking dealers to support Performa users (who bought their Macs from the competition), Apple offers a year of toll-free phone support to Performa buyers—and when necessary, in-home service or pickup and delivery of equipment to be repaired at an Apple facility.

BARGAIN

For what you get, Performas are great buys—when you consider all the software and peripherals that come with the Performa package, they're lots cheaper than buying an identical LC or Quadra setup. On the other hand, if you were to do your own selecting, you might pick different software and equipment than Apple picks for you. Most of what the Performas include is good, but you probably won't use all of it, and the low-end Performa Display monitor is below many people's minimum standards for screen quality.

Bundled Software

The Performas' preinstalled software is selected for typical home uses: letter-writing, record-keeping, doing homework, and so on. At this writing, a typical collection includes ClarisWorks, Quicken, America Online, a software version of the American Heritage Dictionary, clip art, games, and more. Until System 7.5, the Performas had their own slightly different system software, including features designed to make applications more accessible and to protect the user from common pitfalls. These features are supposed to become options on all Macs, starting with System 7.5. (For more on those features, see Chapter 3.)

Performas also come with At Ease, which allows Mac owners to set their computers to accommodate multiple users who have varying levels of ability without jeopardizing valuable or private files. (See Chapter 3 for more on At Ease.)

Although Performas come with a lot of software installed on their hard disks, you don't get backup installation floppies for it in case your hard disk crashes. Instead, you get a pair of copy-to-floppy utilities called Apple Backup and Apple Restore, so you can make your own backups. (I've also heard that if you're stuck without any backups, Apple will send you the system software overnight.)

Performa/Other Mac Equivalents

Performa models	Other Mac models
200	Classic II
400, 405, **410**, 430	LC II
450	LC III
460, 466, 467	Like LC III, but with 33-MHz '030
475, 476	**LC 475, Quadra 605**
550, 560	**LC 550**
575, 577, 578	**LC 575**
600, 600CD	IIvx (but slower, since it lacks a 32K memory cache)

Models in bold are current at this writing.

Picking a Performa

Shopping around for a Performa can get very confusing because Apple gives slightly different model numbers to the same computer, depending on where it's sold and how it's configured. For example, the Performa 460, 466, and 467 are all the same computer, but the 460 has an 80-meg hard disk, while the 466 and 467 both have 160-meg hard disks. The only difference between the 466 and 467 is that the former is sold at Wal-Marts and the latter at Price Costcos.

The chart above should help eliminate some of that confusion by showing which groups of Performa models match what model in another Mac line.

As the chart shows, the Performas offer a slightly larger range of models than the LCs, including a choice of '030 or '040 chips in both the flat-box (400-series) and all-in-one, multimedia (500-series) body types. As with the LCs, any of these models will work fine for home uses, but the '040-based models (475, 476, 575, 577, and 578) are quite a bit faster than the others. If you're going to use mathematical, CAD, or other software that requires an FPU, steer clear of the 475 and 476.

Workgroup Servers

(JK)

You can use any Mac as a file server, but Apple has taken a few Quadra and Power Mac models and customized them with file-server software, adding hardware enhancements for particularly demanding networks and calling the results the Apple Workgroup Servers (AWS). (See the table below for their basic hardware equivalents.)

The AWS 60 and 80 are really just the Quadra 610 and the discontinued Quadra 800 with AppleShare. (AppleShare is described in Chapter 23.) The 95, on the other hand, is based on the Quadra 950 but runs on A/UX (Apple's Mac version of the Unix system software, which gives it the ability to execute more than one task at a time) and includes a special PDS card that lets it handle up to 14 external SCSI devices and 6 internal ones. The PDS card also speeds up the 95 with a 128K to 512K cache and direct memory access to SCSI devices like hard drives and backup drives.

Workgroup Server Hardware Equivalents

Workgroup Server	Quadra/Power Mac
60	Quadra 610
80	Quadra 800
95	Quadra 950 with PDS card
6150	Power Mac 6100 with 256K cache
8150	Power Mac 8100
9150	Body like Quadra 950 but with 80-MHz PPC 601 chip, 4 NuBus slots, 512K cache

The PowerPC-based models at this writing are the Workgroup Server 6150, 8150, and 9150, which are based on the same three Quadra body types but are built around the PowerPC 601 chip. The 68K version of AppleShare comes standard the 6150 but is optional on the other two models, which come with Retrospect Remote (described in Chapter 5) for backing up files.

THINGS TO COME

Until Apple comes out with a PowerPC version of AppleShare (expected sometime in 1995), the 6150, 8150, and 9150 should perform about at the level of the 68K-based servers (except that the AWS 95 will be faster, thanks to A/UX). In the meantime, Novell is working on a PowerPC version of its Netware, the industry-leading networking software.

If all this was Greek (or geek) to you, and you're interested in setting up a network, read Chapter 23. If you don't need to set up a large network, forget about it; these Macs aren't for you.

PowerBooks

(JK)

PowerBooks are portable Macs that weigh less than 7.5 pounds each and are small enough to fit into a briefcase or rest comfortably on your lap, but have computing power similar to that of Performa and LC models. They can run off rechargeable batteries or plug into the wall, so you can use them anywhere. They can all also accommodate an internal modem, so you can connect to the home office via AppleTalk Remote Access (discussed in Chapter 23) or log on to your on-line accounts. Not all models have built-in floppy drives, but those that don't can have one added externally. Instead of mice, PowerBooks have trackballs or *trackpads* (touch-sensitive pads that do the job of a trackball) in front of their keyboards.

The PowerBooks' main drawbacks compared to desktop models are their small screen size, limited expandability, and price-to-performance ratio. They've also generally lagged behind the desktop Macs in versatility and the adoption of new technologies. PowerBooks were the last Mac line to get the '040 chip, and there still aren't any '040-based models with an FPU. And although Apple has managed to fit a lot into their cases, don't expect to see PowerBooks with

PowerBook Models

The 100s (except the 100 itself)	The 200s	The 500s
The original PowerBooks, about 7 pounds with an all-in-one design, including a floppy drive and ports for peripherals.	The "Duos," 4 to 5 pounds, designed to plug into a "dock" that adds desktop features like disk drives and ports.	The second generation all-in-ones, 6.5 to 7.5 pounds.
Based on 68030 processors.	Based on 68030 and 68LC040 processors.	Based on the 68LC040 processor.
Use nickel-cadmium batteries.		Have a trackpad instead of a trackball and a fullsize keyboard with function keys.
RAM expandable to 8MB or 14MB.	RAM expandable to 24MB or 40MB.	RAM expandable to 36MB.
Keyboard 97percent of desktop size.	68040 models faster than 500s, thanks to 32-bit data bus.	Have an extra bay for a second battery or PDS card.
	Nickel metal-hydride batteries.	Stereo speakers and CD-quality sound.
	Keyboard 88 percent of desktop size.	Built-in Ethernet.
		Screens display more than most 100s and 200s.

Editors' Poll: Why Do You Need a PowerBook? Do You Have One?

AA: My new PeeBee 180 is a great go-anywhere tool for taking notes (in meetings, say), and writing articles in spare moments. As note-takers, they save a lot of time because I don't have to type up my illegible scribbles later on a desktop machine.

DB: My friend Steve proclaimed me the human on Earth "most needy of a PowerBook." I'm writing this in a hotel room 3,000 miles from my office, after writing several business letters on the airplane here, and I will work on another project next week at my folks' house (another 1,000 miles away).

EC: I can play Tetris in bed and write chapters of my books outside on the porch (with an extension cord), and mostly, sit in my favorite chair and write letters.

DD: As a freelancer working from my home, I take every opportunity to work in parks, cafes, and any location where I can see other humans. Right now, that only happens on the rare days when I'm editing on paper or can think of an excuse for a lunch meeting. I don't have a PowerBook yet, but...

CG: I bought my PowerBook so that I could work on stories while moving from room to room chasing my daughter (now 3), and also for working and staying in touch while on business trips.

JK: I don't *need* a PowerBook, but without one, I get tired of being chained to the desk all day every day. PowerBooks also have a more intimate feel than desktop Macs, and are just more fun to work on (I love my 180's screen and trackball). The PB has also come in handy when troubleshooting sick Macs at clients' offices.

HN: I have a 180. Having a PowerBook makes traveling for business a completely different experience from what it used to be, since AppleTalk Remote Access lets me be on the office net while I'm away, and I can get my e-mail and stuff from CIS and AppleLink and all the other damn services. I also use the PB a lot around the house, so I can work and still be part of the family in a way I can't be when I descend into my study to use my desktop machine.

an internal CD-ROM drive anytime soon. PowerBook keyboards have no numeric keypad, and some people are bothered by the smallish keys on 100- and 200-series models.

Still, you can't expect such computing power in such a convenient package without making some compromises, and once you get a PowerBook back to your desk, most current models can connect to typical desktop-Mac peripherals (like a large external monitor, CD-ROM drive, keyboard and mouse, or even, in some cases, expansion cards).

All-in-One vs. Dockable

At this writing, there are two basic types of PowerBooks: *all-in-ones* and *dockables.* We'll describe their basic physical differences below; for more on the different models, see the "PowerBook Models" table on page 75 and the "Comparing PowerBooks" section below.

All-in-ones. All-in-one PowerBooks (that includes the 500 series and the mostly discontinued 100 series) have most of the same features as a desktop Mac, including a built-in floppy drive and all the usual rear-panel ports for connecting to external devices. All-in-ones weigh 6.5 to 7.5 pounds (depending on the model and whether it has one or two batteries loaded), and measure just over 9 inches by 11 inches by 2 inches. The 500 series has a curvier, more ergonomic body design and is molded out of lighter-weight plastic.

The discontinued PowerBook 100 was a popular early model that's unique in several ways. Based on the 68000 processor, it has the regular set of ports but no floppy drive, uses a long-lasting lead-acid battery, weighs only about five pounds, and can run System 6 (all other models require System 7).

Dockables (Duos). The 200-series PowerBook Duos are slimmer and lighter than the all-in-ones (4 to 5 pounds, 8.5 inches by 11 inches by 1.5 inches), making them even easier to carry. But they lack floppy drives and most of the standard Mac ports; instead, they've got one port for connecting to a modem,

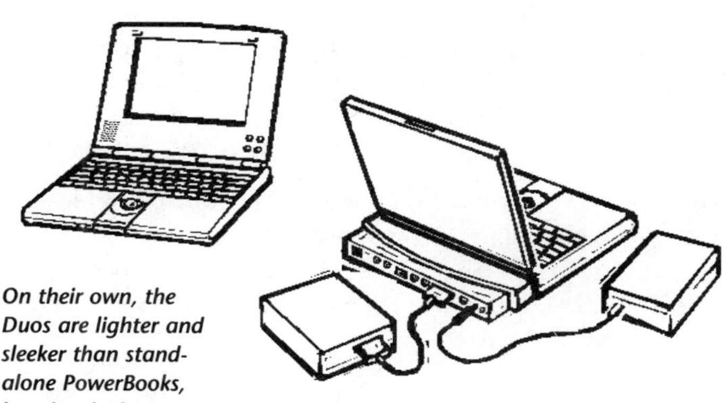

On their own, the Duos are lighter and sleeker than stand-alone PowerBooks, but they lack a floppy drive and the ability to connect to outside devices.

Plugged into one of the many available Mini-Docks, the Duos gain ports that can connect them to peripherals, including external floppy drives and 8-bit color monitors.

The Duo can also become part of a desktop computer when inserted into a full-size Duo Dock, which supplies a full range of ports, a floppy drive, NuBus slots, and support for 16-bit color.

printer, or LocalTalk network, and a 152-pin connector for hooking up to various types of *docks* (see the box below).

Which type is best? A Duo with Apple's MiniDock and an external floppy drive can do everything a regular PowerBook can, and weighs only a few ounces more. And unlike an all-in-one, a Duo lets you leave the dock and floppy drive at home when you don't need them.

But what about those times when you'll have an *unexpected* need for the floppy drive you left at home? To be on the safe side, you may end up lugging the extras around anyway, and if you're doing that, the all-in-one makes a much neater package.

On the other hand, for those who want their computer to be mobile *and* have access to NuBus expansion cards, the Duo/Duo Dock combination is cheaper than buying a desktop Mac *and* a PowerBook, and it eliminates the need to keep track of what files are on which computer, which computer's version of a file is the most current, and so on. The only problem is, if something happens to your Duo, you can't fall back on a Duo Dock the way you could on a real desktop computer.

Duo Docks

(JK)

Docks restore desktop-Mac capabilities to the Duo. The ultimate model, Apple's Duo Dock II, is basically a desktop Mac without a brain. The Duo slips into the Duo Dock like a videotape going into a VCR, providing the brain, and the pair becomes a desktop Mac, complete with the full range of standard Mac ports, an internal floppy drive, and spaces for an internal hard drive and two full-size NuBus cards. (The NuBus slots are horizontal, which makes them harder to access than on most Macs.)

The Duo Dock II has several features beyond the original Duo Dock, including an Ethernet port, a math coprocessor (optional on the original), a 32K memory cache, and enough room to handle the thicker, color Duo models (the older Duo Dock has to be upgraded with a new, higher top to handle them). The newer dock also supports monitors up to 21 inches (16 inches was the biggest the older one could manage).

If you don't need all the expansion capabilities of these big docks, you can also buy various mini-docks: smaller, portable adapters made by Apple, Newer, and other companies that let you hook a Duo up to floppy drives, hard disks, Ethernet networks, monitors, and other external devices.

Comparing PowerBooks

If you try out various PowerBook models, you'll immediately notice some striking differences—like screen quality, keyboard size, and whether there's a trackball or trackpad. But a lot of PowerBook features aren't so apparent, although some are at least as important as the obvious ones. This section gives you more detail on both types of features, to help you distinguish one model from another.

Screen quality. All PowerBooks have backlit LCD (liquid crystal display) screens, with controls for brightness and contrast, but they can be black and white, grayscale, or color, with several levels of quality in each category.

At this writing, color PowerBooks (whose names end in the letter *c*) are significantly more expensive (by $600–$1,500) than grayscale models. Grayscale models, in turn, are more expensive than black and whites, which seem to be being phased out of the PowerBook line.

The power-hungry screens on the first two color PowerBooks—the 165c and 180c—make those computers run hot and dramatically shorten the amount of time you can work on a single battery charge (later models don't have this drawback). But color screens are nicer to work on, and the screens of the 270c, 280c, and 540c can approach the photographic color quality of a desktop monitor displaying thousands of colors.

Whether monochrome or color, the overall quality of a particular PowerBook screen's image depends on which of two basic technologies it uses: *active matrix* or *passive matrix*.

On active-matrix screens, everything looks crisp, sharp, and solid and keeps looking that way even when seen from various angles and in different lighting conditions. The contrast is great, colors are brilliant, and some people (like me) prefer their overall quality to desktop monitors'.

On passive-matrix screens, the pointer and other objects sometimes look a bit washed-out and leave shadowy trails when you move them around. Worse, if you move the pointer fast, it sometimes *submarines*—that is, it disappears from the screen entirely until you stop moving it. Furthermore, passive-matrix screens are unreadable when viewed from an angle—which can be an advantage

PowerBook Screens

Model	Screen	Resolution	Grays/Colors
PowerBook 100	9-inch passive B&W	640 by 400	B&W
PowerBook 140, 145, 145B	9.8-inch passive B&W	640 by 400	B&W
PowerBook 160, 165	9.8-inch passive grayscale	640 by 400	16 grays
PowerBook 165c	8.9-inch passive color	640 by 400	256 colors
PowerBook 170	9.8-inch active B&W	640 by 400	B&W
PowerBook 180	9.8-inch active grayscale	640 by 400	16 grays
PowerBook 180c	8.4-inch active color	640 by 480	256 colors
PowerBook 520	9.5-inch passive grayscale	640 by 480	16 grays
PowerBook 520c	9.5-inch dual-scan passive color	640 by 480	256 colors
PowerBook 540	9.5-inch active grayscale	640 by 480	64 grays
PowerBook 540c	9.5-inch active color	640 by 480/ 640 by 400	256/ thousands*
PowerBook Duo 210, 230	9.1-inch grayscale	640 by 400	16 grays
PowerBook Duo 250, 280	9-inch active grayscale	640 by 400	16 grays
PowerBook Duo 270c, 280c	8.4-inch active color	640 by 480/ 640 by 400	256/ thousands*

* Color depth depends on screen resolution.

if you're trying to prevent snooping, but it's not so great if you're showing something to a group. Finally, color passive-matrix screens can look muddy, particularly on older models.

However, you pay a *lot* more for active-matrix PowerBooks (roughly $700 more for grayscale models and $1,600 more for color models), and the screen quality of passive-matrix models has improved. The faster processors help the screen keep up with what you're doing, and the 520c has introduced the *dual-scan* color screen, which redraws its top and bottom halves simultaneously, for twice the refresh rate, resulting in clearer, brighter colors at a reasonable price. If you still find yourself losing the pointer or I-beam on a passive-matrix screen, there are plenty of programs available that make them bigger and/or darker (many are described under "PowerBook Utilities" in Chapter 13).

Screen size. PowerBook screen sizes range between 8.4 inches and 9.8 inches (measured diagonally), but, as with desktop monitors, those measurements can be deceiving. It's a screen's resolution—measured in pixels—that determines how much information it will actually display, regardless of its physical size. For example, the 8.4-inch screens on the 180c, 270c, and 280c display just as much as most 14-inch monitors—640 pixels across by 480 vertically—things just look much smaller. By contrast, the 9.8-inch screens on the 140, 145, 145B, and 180 display only 640 by 400 pixels—one-sixth less information vertically—but at a more readable size. The 500-series PowerBooks offer a good compromise: 9.5-inch screens that display 640 by 480 pixels.

There's a trade-off between the number of pixels on a screen and the richness of color it can display, so the PowerBook 540c, 270c, and 280c let you switch down to 640 by 400 pixels in order to display thousands of colors, rather than the 256 colors you get when you're using them at 640 by 480 pixels.

External monitor support. You can hook an extra monitor to any of the 500-series PowerBooks or to the 160, 165, 165c, 180, or 180c, but the level of support varies from model to model. When attached to a dock, Duos can take an external monitor too. (The Peripheral Support chart on pages 58–59 shows the maximum monitor size each PowerBook can support.)

Maximum RAM. PowerBook RAM is more expensive than desktop computer RAM, and you can't upgrade incrementally by filling in a series of slots; the PowerBooks have just one memory upgrade slot, so if you install, say, a 4-meg upgrade and then end up needing even more RAM, you have to replace it, not just add to it. That means either trying to sell your original upgrade on the used market or throwing it away and losing whatever you spent for it ($150 or more).

So if you're going to expand your PowerBook's RAM, it's wise to get as big an upgrade as you can afford. This is particularly true if you're the kind of user who likes to keep up to date with the latest versions of software, work with multiple programs at once, or use graphics or desktop publishing software. Having a lot of RAM also enables you to set up a RAM disk, which conserves battery power and reduces time-consuming hard disk access (see Chapter 4 for more on memory and RAM disks).

Recent PowerBooks can handle much more RAM than previous models: Early models in the 100 series could only take 8 megs of RAM, while later models can take 14 megs; early Duos could take up to 24 megs, and current models take up to 40 megs; so far, the 500 series can take up to 36 megs.

Keyboards, trackballs, and trackpads. The keyboards on the 100- and 200-series PowerBooks are smaller than standard desktop keyboards, which takes a little getting used to. Some people with large hands find them hard to use. The Duos' keyboard is even smaller than the 100s', as is their marble-size trackball, but some people actually prefer the feel of their keys to the keys on standard PowerBooks.

Instead of a trackball, the 500 series has a *trackpad*, which uses an electric field to monitor your finger's movement across a little rectangle. The trackpad notices your finger's speed as well as the distance it travels, and it moves the pointer further when your finger moves faster. The trackpad is also supposed to be more accurate than a trackball, and *MacUser*'s editors tended to prefer it (it must be an acquired taste, because after a quick test-drive, I was glad to get back to my own PowerBook's trackball).

However, if you like having a click button above your trackthing (as the other PowerBooks' trackballs have), you'll be disappointed in the trackpad; it only has a single button, below the pad.

GOOD FEATURE

Expansion. A Duo in a Duo Dock is the most expandable PowerBook, but that's cheating, since then it's really a desktop Mac. The 500-series PowerBooks' second battery bay can alternatively take expansion cards: either PDS cards for things like wireless networking or AV-style video-in and video-out capabilities, or, with the help of Apple's $200 **PowerBook Expansion Module,** *PCMCIA* cards carrying tiny hard drives, modems, or other hardware. (The acronym PCMCIA stands for Personal Computer Memory Card International Association *[—or* People Can't Memorize Computer Industry Acronyms—*KM]*). There aren't any such PDS cards yet at this writing, but there are PCMCIA cards which were previously developed for use with PC notebook computers and PDAs like Apple's Newton.

SCSI connections. PowerBooks and Apple's Duo docks have a different type of SCSI port than other Macs and require a different type of cable or adapter to connect to SCSI devices. Several mail-order companies sell this type of adapter for about $30.

All PowerBooks except the 140, 145, 145B, and 170 also have a unique feature called *SCSI mode* that lets you use them as an external hard disk on another Mac. You set your PowerBook to SCSI mode in the PowerBook control panel, shut it down, and using Apple's **SCSI Disk Adapter** ($40 ApplePrice) and a SCSI cable, you connect it to the back of the other Mac. Then you restart both machines, and voilà: There's your PB's internal hard disk showing up as an icon on the other Mac's desktop.

With the help of the $50 **SCSI Doc** adapter from APS Technologies, you can use a standard SCSI system cable for either of the above types of SCSI connections (the adapter has a switch that lets you select which connection you want). (See Chapter 5 for more on SCSI devices.)

Microphones. All PowerBooks have built-in, monaural microphones except the 140, 145, and 170, which came with external mikes; the 145B, which came without a mike; and the 100, which doesn't support sound input.

Adjustable clock speed. Many PowerBooks allow you to extend the period you can work on one battery charge by reducing their processor's speed and restarting. (You make the adjustment in the PowerBook control panel.)

SCSI Mode, and Alternatives (JK)

SCSI mode can be worthwhile if you work on the same files on both a desktop Mac and a PowerBook and frequently go back and forth between them. It allows you to always work from the PowerBook's disk, so you can avoid having to move files you're working on between the computers (which can, in turn, result in duplicate files, and then confusion about which version is most current, or worse, work done on two separate files so that neither is fully current).

But for simply transferring files, it can be easier to just connect the two Macs with file sharing and a $15 ImageWriter II cable (or Ethernet, if both Macs support it); you can make the connection, see what's on both computers' disks, and transfer files, all without having to restart either Mac. For that matter, you can transfer files between the Macs on a floppy disk (1980s technology—horrors!). The transfer takes a bit longer, but unless the files are quite large, it shouldn't be a problem.

The Ins and Outs of PowerBook Batteries

PowerBook owners seem to be constantly seeking ways to work longer on a single battery charge, and an industry of third-party chargers, charge-prolonging utilities, and long-life batteries has sprung up in response. Nor has this obsession been lost on Apple, which has added better power-saving controls to the system software, designed the 500-series PowerBooks to hold two batteries, and seems to introduce a new, improved type of battery with nearly every new PowerBook release.

PowerBook Batteries

Model(s)	Charge (hours)	Battery type
100	2 to 4	Lead-acid
100 series (except 100)	2 to 3	Nickel-cadmium (NiCad)
165c,180c	1 to 2	Nickel-cadmium (NiCad)
PowerBook Duo 210, 230	2.5 to 4	Nickel metal-hydride (NiMH)
PowerBook Duo 270c, 280	2 to 4	Nickel metal-hydride (NiMH) type II
PowerBook Duo 250	2.5 to 6	Nickel metal-hydride (NiMH) type II
PowerBook Duo 280c	2 to 4	Nickel metal-hydride (NiMH) type III
500 series	Up to 3.5	PowerBook Intelligent Battery

There have been six different battery types so far, and they're not all interchangeable. The length of a given battery's charge depends not only on the type of battery, but on the PowerBook model it's being used in, the type and speed of its processor, the brightness of the screen, and how the computer's being used (activities that involve a lot of disk access drain batteries particularly quickly). In general, Apple's estimates of charge duration tend to be higher than what you'll actually get without taking steps to lower power consumption. This section will tell you a bit more about Apple's batteries, third-party alternatives, and ways you can make your batteries work longer on a single charge.

Battery types. Here are the different types of batteries used in PowerBooks at this writing:

- The *Intelligent Battery* comes with the 500-series PowerBooks. It uses a built-in processor chip to help the PowerBook manage its power needs more efficiently and provide a more accurate charge reading than you get using other battery types. It also recharges faster than earlier types.

- The *Type III* battery comes with the 280c and is supposed to last 15 percent longer than its predecessor, the Type II. Type IIIs work in other Duo models too, with the help of a System Enabler file that Apple packages with the batteries when sold separately ($100–$150).

- The *Type II* battery was introduced with the 250 and 270c, but comes with all other Duo models at this writing except the 280c. It offers a longer-lasting charge than the original Duo battery.

Don't Trust the Charge Symbol (JK)

There's a lightning-bolt symbol in the PowerBook's Battery desk accessory that's supposed to indicate that the battery is being charged. In fact, the symbol appears whenever the AC power adapter is plugged into the back of the PowerBook, whether or not it's carrying any juice to the battery. So to be sure your battery is recharging, check the Battery DA's "fuel gauge" after the adapter's been plugged in for a few minutes. (Or, if you use a PowerBook utility program, check its charging indicator.)

- The original Duos introduced Type I (though it was never called that) of the nickel metal-hydride (NiMH) composition used by all the subsequent types listed above. NiMH batteries last longer and recharge faster than the NiCad type used by the 100s.
- The nickel-cadmium (NiCad) batteries used by the 100s (except the 100 itself) have the shortest charge duration, and that duration gets shorter and shorter after many recharge cycles; to get the full charge back you have to let them run down *completely* and then fully recharge them. My ancient (1½-year-old) 180 runs down a charge in less than two hours, so I usually avoid battery hassles altogether by working in places where I can plug in; the cafés in my neighborhood have helped by installing outlets at nearly every table.

- The lead-acid battery used by the PowerBook 100 lasts longer than the NiCads, but it's the most dangerous to the environment when disposed of.

Sleep mode. PowerBooks go into a power-saving *sleep* mode when you leave them idle: The screen goes blank and the hard disk stops, but everything comes back on within a few seconds when you touch the keyboard. You can also put a PowerBook to sleep manually; in fact, that's the usual way to turn a PowerBook "off" (rather than shutting it down), because it comes back to life so quickly. Apple recommends shutting down before carrying a PowerBook around, but most people don't bother and don't suffer any consequences.

Switching batteries. The 500-series PowerBooks can hold two batteries at once and switch automatically to the second battery when the first runs down, doubling the length of time you can work at a stretch. (When you plug in a 500-series PowerBook, it charges both batteries at once, supposedly in just two hours of sleep mode or in four hours while the PowerBook's being used.)

The Duos let you swap batteries without shutting down (they have an extra lithium battery that lets you do this without losing your work). You can get an adapter for 100-series PowerBooks—the $20 **Memory Saver,** from Lind Electronics Design—that does the same thing by letting you plug a 9-volt battery into the power-cord socket while you change.

HOT TIP

Conserving energy on PowerBooks. You can work longer on one charge of a PowerBook's battery if you follow the suggestions in the Read Me file that comes with the computer. Here are some of those suggestions, plus a couple of our own:

- Keep the screen's brightness turned down.
- Keep AppleTalk turned off in the Chooser.
- Avoid using the hard disk by turning off virtual memory (if you've turned it on) and running your applications from a RAM disk (see Chapter 4 for more on both).
- Change the settings in the PowerBook control panel to maximum conservation, and if your PowerBook allows it, set the processor to a reduced speed.
- Whenever you take a short break, put the PowerBook to sleep.
- Get a PowerBook utility like Connectix's CPU or Symantec's Norton Essentials for the PowerBook, and adjust its settings for maximum battery conservation. (See Chapter 13 for more on these programs.)

WARNING

Use the PowerBook Battery Case (SM)

It's important to use the case Apple provides for the 100- and 200-series PowerBooks' batteries, because their contacts are prone to accidental shorting when they touch metal objects like keys or paper clips. A short could cause a fire or burns, and it's also likely to damage the battery, which is expensive to replace. (The 500 series' "Intelligent Batteries" have a built-in cover for their contacts.)

Alternative power sources. Several companies make external power packs that they say can provide up to nine hours of uninterrupted battery-powered work. Two of the more well-established at this writing are Technöggin and VST Power Systems, both of which make thin, long-life power packs that fit under your PowerBook and sell for under $200.

Other companies, including Lind Electronic Design and APS Technologies, make power adapters for under $100 that let you plug your PowerBook or Duo into a car's or boat's cigarette lighter.

Older Macs (JK)

Apple has released and discontinued a lot of Macs over the years. Many of them are still quite usable with today's software, and some (like the IIfx and Centris models) rival current models' performance. Even the oldest ones are still usable for simple tasks like word processing, if you don't need the latest versions of software (which usually require more RAM than older Macs can handle or run too slowly on Macs whose RAM capacity will accommodate them). Prices on new Macs have come way down, pushing used prices even lower. But don't assume that used prices are always bargains: It's hard for many Mac owners to accept how much their formerly expensive, state-of-the-art equipment has depreciated, so they'll often ask prices that are high, considering new Mac prices.

A used Mac can also save you a lot of money on software, if it comes with applications already installed on it. Often, current software's demands can overwhelm older CPUs, and the easiest way to get older, more appropriate software is to get it along with a used Mac. Earlier versions of applications are usually perfectly good, they just lack whatever features the manufacturer has since added to out-do the competition, or to get customers to buy upgrades.

BARGAIN

More detailed specifications for these computers are included in the charts in this chapter, but here's a rundown of the different groups of older models, along with the features they introduced.

128K, 512K, 512Ke

These first three Macs (introduced in January '84, September '84, and April '86, respectively) were named for the amount of memory they came with, which wasn't upgradable. They introduced the *compact* design used for several subsequent models, which includes a built-in 9-inch screen that's too small to show even the width of a letter-size page. With no fan and no hard disk, they're wonderfully silent except when accessing the floppy drive or giving alert sounds. The 128K and 512K came with 400K floppy drives; the 512Ke had an 800K drive instead. These Macs won't run most current software, but with vintage applications from the mid-'80s, they can still do the simple things they always did—elementary word-processing and basic graphics—albeit slowly.

Plus

The last silent, fanless model, the compact-design Plus (introduced in January '86) was the first Mac with an 800K floppy drive and a SCSI port, which allowed the addition of an external SCSI hard drive. It came with a full megabyte of memory, expandable to 4 megs, and can run some current software, but *very* slowly.

SE

Another compact, the SE (released in March '87) introduced the expansion slot, internal fan, and internal hard disk (though some models came with two floppy drives instead of a floppy and a hard drive). Models sold after August 1989 came with a 1.4MB floppy drive instead of the original SE's 800K drive. The SE also introduced the ADB connection used for current Mac keyboards and mice. It's got the same software and memory capabilities as the Plus.

The II's

Also introduced in March 1987, the Mac II was the first *modular* Mac—one with no screen built in, but with multiple expansion slots for adding video cards, networking cards, and so on. The original Mac II and two later models—the IIx (introduced September '88), and IIfx (March '90)—each have *six* slots, but you need to use one slot for a display card since there's no display port. The IIci (September '89) introduced the display port, the IIsi (October '90) added the ability to record sound, and the IIvx and its non-U.S. version, the IIvi (both October '92), introduced (along with the Performa 600CD) the internal CD-ROM drive. The models in the Mac II series range widely in performance, with the original Mac II at the bottom and the IIfx the most powerful '030-based Mac, at the top.

SE/30

The SE/30 (introduced January '89) was the first compact Mac to use the 68030 processor chip. With its 32-bit data bus, it's still the fastest compact Mac except the Color Classic II. With an FPU and RAM that's expandable to 128MB, it can easily handle most of today's software.

Portable

Before there were the 7-pound PowerBooks, there was the 15-pound Mac Portable (introduced September '89). The Portable has a similar, but much larger design, with a full-size keyboard and a trackball to the right of the keyboard. It has a beautiful active-matrix screen, but only a few late units came with backlighting. With RAM that's upgradable to 9MB, it can handle much of today's software, at speeds close to those of a Mac II (i.e., slow, but faster than an SE or Plus).

Classic and Classic II

The Classic replaced the SE in October 1991, but underneath its sleeker exterior, it's just a cheaper version of the same computer, without the SE's processor-direct slot. The Classic is marginally usable with today's software (i.e., not recommended). The Classic II used a much faster processor, and with RAM upgradable to 10 megs and an optional FPU, it's perfectly usable with most software, if a bit slower than the SE/30.

Color Classics

The Color Classic (introduced February '93) is a compact Mac with a color screen built into a slightly larger body, an LC processor-direct slot, and a slide-out motherboard that makes upgrades easy. It was replaced by the current Color Classic II (October '93), which runs considerably faster. Either Mac can handle most current software.

Centris 610 and 650

Named for their midlevel price and performance, the Centris 610 and 650 (introduced February '93) were the first mainstream, relatively affordable Macs based on the 68040 chip. Eight months later, the Centrises were given faster processors and renamed the Quadra 610 and 650. They're still competitive with today's 68K Macs. (The Quadra 660AV was also called a Centris when it was introduced in July 1993; it wasn't changed when it was renamed.)

Upgrading Older Macs (DH/JK)

If you already have a Mac but it has begun to feel inadequate for your needs, or if you've simply begun to covet your neighbor's computer, be aware that there are plenty of alternatives to buying a whole new Macintosh. They range from relatively simple incremental improvements like increasing RAM, getting a bigger hard drive, or installing an accelerated display card, through changing the machine into a different model via an official Apple motherboard swap, to special-purpose cards worth several times the value of the Mac itself (which can boost its performance to the level of a workstation computer).

But before you invest in a major upgrade, you should know that changing any given part won't necessarily make a Mac perform at the level of another Mac with that component. For example, a IIci with a 33-MHz 68040 accelerator isn't the equal of a Quadra 950, despite the fact that they're both running the same chip at the same speed; improvements in the later model's NuBus and SCSI transfer rates (among other things) give it the upper hand. Keep this sort of thing in mind when considering whether to upgrade your current Mac at all; frequently, the cost of the upgrade plus the resale value of the older machine can bring you within reach of a completely new Mac.

Upgrading to PowerPC

There are two main ways to upgrade to the PowerPC: by adding a card or by replacing your logic board. Apple has announced or released PowerPC processor upgrades for Macs with 68040 processors, mostly in the form of PDS cards. At this writing, it looks like upgrades for '030 Macs may come from companies other than Apple. In addition, Macs whose body types match one of the Power Mac or PowerPC-based Workgroup Server models' bodies can be fully

Editors' Poll: How Many Times Have You Upgraded Your Mac?

AA: Oh geez. Two Macs: SE (which I got in 1987) and IIci (1991). Two memory upgrades to the SE (I paid $150 per MB at one point!), two to the IIci. One hard disk each for the two machines.... An accelerator card for the IIci, plus a cache card. Um, that sounds like about eight or nine times, not counting peripherals like printers (two), CD-ROM drives (two), DAT drives (one), modems (a couple), an external floppy drive...

DB: I used a one-disk-drive 128K Mac for three years...and then was forced to get a second 400K disk drive. Then I bought an SE a year later, which got me through some tough times. I even designed and produced an entire magazine on that machine. Now I upgrade every year and a half. Regular as taking a bath!

EC: When I started my own company, I took a Mac II with me from my old job and later upgraded it to a IIfx. When I started working freelance and had to buy a Mac for myself, I upgraded again, to my current machine: a Quadra 660AV.

DD: After two years, I upgraded my SE with a Mobius 030 board and full-page monitor. Then I went to a IIci, which I upgraded to 8MB RAM when I bought it. I've since added a 340MB hard drive. Now it's time for an accelerator and about 16MB more RAM.

JK: Five times. After the 512Ke came a IIsi, then a PowerBook 180, whose memory I upgraded from 4MB to 8 megs. Then I replaced the IIsi with my current Centris 650, whose RAM I've increased from 8MB to 16MB. Then there are the peripherals: two modems, a scanner, a SyQuest drive, an ergonomic keyboard...

HN: I count nine CPU, memory, and accelerator upgrades. I have changed drives too many times to remember.

upgraded to that model through a logic board replacement. Several Macs can be upgraded either way, so you can choose one or the other, each of which has its advantages and disadvantages.

Upgrade cards. Apple's upgrade cards are much less expensive than their logic-board upgrades, and they leave your Mac's existing 68040 processor intact, so after the upgrade you can use either chip (you have to restart to switch between them). This flexibility is a big advantage if you're going to keep using 68K applications, since they'll often run faster on your old processor than on the upgrade card's 68K emulator.

This ability to switch is even more important if your 68K software uses a lot of floating-point math, since the 68K emulator in PowerPC upgrades won't support FPU calculations without the shareware control panel SoftwareFPU, which merely enables it to plod. (For more on SoftwareFPU, see the box on page 96.)

At this writing, Apple is shipping PowerPC upgrade cards for all Centris and Quadra models except the AVs and the 605. These cards run at twice the clock speed of whatever Mac you install them in. That sounds good, but it means their actual speeds are between 40 MHz and 66 MHz, whereas the slowest full-blown Power Mac at this writing runs at 60 MHz.

DayStar's PowerPC upgrade cards aren't paced by the Mac they're installed in, so rather than poking along at 50 MHz like some of Apple's upgrades, they run at 60 MHz or 80 MHz, and faster versions will probably be available by the time you read this. Furthermore, DayStar's own processors can be upgraded—unlike those on Apple's cards—and have other advantages, but they also cost more than twice as much as Apple's cards.

Choosing an Accelerator

(DH)

There are quite a few vendors currently selling accelerators, including DayStar, Newer, Sonnett, Mobius, and MicroMac, and new ones are constantly being introduced. So if you're in the market, try to get up-to-date information from Mac magazines or user groups.

Many accelerators come with, or can be upgraded with, additional memory, memory caches, FPUs, or other specialized acceleration. It's worth paying attention to such features, since they can have a significant impact on performance. For example, a memory cache can add another 50 percent or more to the speed of an '040 accelerator card but cost only about 20 percent of its price.

Speed differences between comparable accelerators from different manufacturers are likely to be slight. More important are the cards' compatibility and expandability, and the companies' customer support and trade-up policies. DayStar has the best reputation in most of those areas. Their accelerators are also the only ones that let you use Apple's virtual memory.

Find out whether there are known incompatibilities before you buy, particularly if you've got certain applications or hardware (like a sound or video card) that you can't do without. A money-back guarantee is the best protection against unpleasant surprises.

And as with all hardware purchases, there's also some value in choosing a company that's been around for a while: a five-year or lifetime warranty won't do you much good if the company goes under (as a number of accelerator manufacturers have done). (See Appendix C for more guidelines on buying Mac hardware and software.)

Cache Cards (DH)

As mentioned elsewhere, cache cards speed up the Mac by providing a small amount—typically 32K to 512K—of high-speed RAM, where the processor can quickly store and quickly access data while it's working. (Don't confuse these with DayStar's PowerCache cards, which are actually full-blown accelerators.)

Cache cards don't provide as big a speed-up as accelerators, but they're less expensive. The Power Macs, '040-based Macs, and the IIci, IIsi, and LC III all show significant performance improvement with the addition of a cache card. The Power Mac 8100 and later IIci's come with one already installed.

Other companies should also have PowerPC upgrades on the market by the time you read this, so shop around before you buy anything.

Logic board upgrades. Logic board upgrades typically involve getting an Apple dealer to move your old Mac's power supply and disk drives into the new computer. Upgrading to a full-fledged Power Mac model is more expensive than a card upgrade, and you lose your 68K processor, but you get all the additional features that come with Power Macs, including the GeoPorts, CD-quality sound recording and playback, support for two monitors (on most models), and (if you buy the PlainTalk microphone) voice recognition. If you swap up to an AV Power Mac, you also get video recording and playback.

Power Mac Logic Board Upgrades

68K Mac	Power Mac	Price
Centris or Quadra 610 or 660AV	6100/60 or 6100/60 AV	$1,000
Centris or Quadra 650, IIvx, IIvi, Performa 600 or 600CD	7100/66 or 7100/66 AV	$1,500
Quadra 800 or 840AV	8100/80 or 8100/80 AV	$1,900

A Speedier Processor

There are two main approaches to accelerating a Macintosh's processing abilities: 1) adding an accelerator card, which either supplants the original CPU with something faster or adds a specialized coprocessor that handles only certain specific tasks, or 2) increasing the clock speed of your current CPU.

CPU replacements. The replacement-CPU accelerators usually come in the form of cards that plug into a processor-direct slot or CPU socket (or, in some cases, clip onto the original CPU's legs) and supply a new processor that takes over all (or nearly all) the tasks that the original CPU would have handled.

At this writing, there are accelerators with '030 chips running as fast as 50 MHz and '040 chips running as fast as 40 MHz (the maximum speeds these chips were designed for). Some manufacturers are also working on accelerators built around Motorola's 68060 chip, which has never been used in a stock Mac model. These should perform somewhere between the speed of a fast '040 and a Power Mac running native software.

Coprocessors. Like the FPU built into many Macs, coprocessor accelerators step in only for a particular type of task that's particularly demanding of the main processor chip—noninteger math functions, Photoshop filters, and so on. Coprocessor accelerators specialize in one area and do that job much more efficiently than the original CPU would (though in most cases, they'll work only with applications that have been designed to use them). If your speed needs are that specific and there's an accelerator designed to meet them, this is definitely

The Multiheaded Mac (DH)

Some expansion cards set themselves up as completely independent CPUs, in effect giving you two (or more) computers that operate simultaneously in one box.

To add a second Mac to your first Mac's box, you need a **Radius Rocket** NuBus card with RocketShare software ($1,800–$2,000). The Rocket was originally designed to be an accelerator, but it works best when you configure it to work as a separate CPU. This approach is particularly well suited to situations where you want to assign specific, time-consuming processes—like rasterizing large graphics files, or long scanning jobs—to each processor.

But it's not for the faint of heart (or the thin of wallet): You have to set up the Rocket with its own RAM, hard disk (or partition of a drive), and system software, in addition to what your Mac already has. Also, the NuBus architecture leads to more compatibility problems than PDS cards have.

There are also expansion cards that let you add PC processors to your Mac—see Chapter 25 for more on them.

PowerBook Upgrades (JK/DH)

Screens

Apple sells active-matrix screens for the Duo 210 and 230, upgrading them to the Duo 250 or 270c. They're available only from Apple.

Processors

Apple has designed the 500-series PowerBooks to be upgradable to the PowerPC 603 chip, although the upgrades aren't available at this writing. The 500 series can also take expansion cards, so accelerator cards may become available for them. Apple makes upgrades for the 250 and 270c to convert them to the 280 and 280c, for $900 and $1,000, respectively.

the way to go. A YARC **Zuma** board ($3,600), for example, can accelerate CAD and 3-D rendering (in products it's compatible with) to speeds even a Mac with a very fast CPU accelerator won't be able to touch. (FPU upgrades are discussed separately below.)

CPU clock boosters. A few years back, some intrepid souls discovered that you could make a Mac IIsi run about as fast as a IIci by replacing its clock crystal with a faster one—a job that costs less than $10 in parts if you're good with soldering equipment. Now you can buy upgrades—through kits or mail-in services—that do the same thing for the IIsi and many other Macs, including the IIfx, Centrises, Quadras, and PowerBooks. Kits for the Power Macs are also being developed at this writing.

Such boosting depends on the fact that the processors in most of these Macs can handle a higher speed than they're rated for. Occasionally, a boosted processor won't work right; most upgrades allow the boost to be reversed in such cases, and the better kits include corrections for problems that can result from upgrades. The kits from Digital Eclipse (for PowerBooks, $380), can include replacement CPUs that have been tested at the new speed, while Newer Technologies' **Variable Speed Overdrives** (for the IIsi, IIfx, and Quadra 700, 900, and 950, $250) allow the user to fine-tune the oscillator speed until a stable level is reached. Such features help justify the cost of a kit, which is considerably higher than that of putting the upgrade together yourself.

Although the kits and services cost more than putting a boost together from scratch, you get more security from the packaged upgrades, many of which come with toll-free tech support lines and money-back guarantees. Most kits also provide a fan or *heat sink* (an attachment that conducts heat away from the processor) to keep the CPU cool at its new level of performance.

WARNING

CPU boosting generally provides more bang for the buck than other approaches to acceleration, doesn't use up any expansion slots, and, for some PowerBooks, constitutes the only acceleration option available. However, some problems have been reported, particularly in the areas of networking and video. And since it's not sanctioned by Apple, CPU boosting will void any remaining warranty (though some boosts can be removed without a trace).

Adding an FPU

Certain programs that handle sophisticated math functions, three-dimensional modeling, or high-end graphics perform dramatically better with an FPU, and some even require one to run. If you use this type of software but your Mac doesn't have an FPU, you can add one to many '020- and '030-based Macs for well under $100. Macs based on the FPU-less 68LC040 chip can't have one added, but some models let you replace the 'LC040 with a full-blown 68040 (these cost $250 or more). The chart on pages 98 and 99 shows which Mac models do and don't have FPUs built-in.

Apple provides FPU upgrades for the Duo Dock, the LC III, the Color Classic, and the IIsi (there's an FPU built into the adapter cards that are required to use the IIsi's expansion slot). You can also get FPU up-grades for earlier LCs (about $100) and many PowerBooks (about $230; $380 when combined with a CPU boost) from third-party vendors, including Dynamic Engineering, Digital Eclipse, and Shreve Systems.

SoftwareFPU (JK)

MAC BIBLE DISK

As a quick, cheap, but slow alternative to an actual FPU upgrade, you can get John Neil's $10 shareware control panel, SoftwareFPU. It will allow software that calls the 68K FPU to run, but very slowly, because it just routes the calls to the Mac's standard integer-based math system. At best, it's about 2½ times slower than a real FPU; at worst, it's about 20 times slower. Also, a bug in Apple's 68LC040 chip (not in SoftwareFPU) makes the program less than 100 percent reliable with machines based on that chip.

Adding Slots and Ports

Sometimes the speed of your computer isn't the problem, it's the lack of ports and slots for all the peripherals you want to add. Rather than getting a new, more expandable computer, you can just add the expansion capabilities.

Serial ports. If you need more than the two serial ports standard on most Macs (say, for example, you've got an external modem, a label printer, an inkjet printer, and a MIDI interface box), there are a couple of ways to accommodate all your devices. An external switching box like Momentum's $100 **Port Juggler** lets you connect several devices to one port—but you can still only use one at a time. If that's not good enough, you need something like Creative Solutions' **Hurdler** cards, which fit into a NuBus slot and give you two or four new serial ports that you can use all at once ($300 for two ports, $380 for four).

Expansion slots. A couple of products add NuBus or processor-direct slots to your Mac, either by modifying its case or providing a separate box with slots. DGR Technologies' **Max** and Sonnet Technologies' **Twin Slot LC** give an LC or LC II extra PDS slots and a 40-watt power supply for $200 to $350, and Second Wave has a whole line of products that expand PDS and NuBus options for many Macintosh models.

Hardware Specifications for Mac Models (Through June 1994)

Model	Life on the market	CPU chip/ speed (MHz)	FPU	Data bus width/speed	NuBus slots	Other slots	Maximum RAM	Notes
Desktop models								
Power Mac 6100/60, 6100/60 AV	3/94–	PPC 601/60	Yes	64/30	1	601 PDS, cache, DAV	72	1, 2
Power Mac 7100/66, 7100/66 AV	3/94–	PPC 601/66	Yes	64/33	3	Cache, DAV	136	2
Power Mac 8100/80, 8100/80 AV	3/94–	PPC 601/80	Yes	64/40	3	Cache, DAV	264	2
Quadra 605	10/93–	68LC040/25	None	32/20	None	LC III PDS	36	
Quadra 610, 610 DOS Compatible	10/93–	68LC040/25	None	32/20	1	'040 PDS	68	1, 3
Quadra 650	10/93–	68040/33	Yes	32/25	3	'040 PDS	136	
Quadra 660AV	7/93–	68040/25	Yes	32/20	1	'040 PDS, DAV	68	1, 3
Quadra 700	10/91–3/93	68040/25	Yes	32/16	2	'040 PDS	68	
Quadra 800	2/93–3/94	68040/33	Yes	32/32	3	'040 PDS	136	
Quadra 840AV	7/93–	68040/40	Yes	32/40	3	DAV	128	3
Quadra 900	10/91–5/92	68040/25	Yes	32/16	5	'040 PDS	256	
Quadra 950	5/92–	68040/33	Yes	32/25	5	'040 PDS	256	
Performa 200	9/92–10/93	68030/16	Optional	16/16	None	None	10	
Performa 400, 405, 410, 430	9/92–	68030/16	None	16/16	None	LC PDS	10	
Performa 450	4/93–10/93	68030/25	Optional	32/25	None	LC III PDS	36	
Performa 460, 466, 467	10/93–	68030/33	Optional	32/25	None	LC III PDS	36	
Performa 475, 476	10/93–	68LC040/25	None	32/25	None	LC III PDS	36	
Performa 550, 560	10/93–	68030/33	Optional	32/25	None	LC III PDS	36	
Performa 575, 577, 578	4/94–	68040/33	None	32/33	None	LC III PDS, comm	36	4
Performa 600, 600 CD	9/92–11/93	68030/32	Optional	32/16	3	Accelerator	68	5
LC	10/90–3/92	68020/16	None	16/16	None	LC PDS	10	
LC II	3/92–3/93	68030/16	None	16/16	None	LC PDS	10	
LC III	2/93–2/94	68030/25	Optional	32/25	None	LC III PDS	36	
LC 475	10/93–	68LC040/25	None	32/25	None	LC III PDS	36	
LC 520	6/93–2/94	68030/25	Optional	32/25	None	LC III PDS	36	
LC 550	2/94–	68030/33	Optional	32/33	None	LC III PDS	36	
LC 575	2/94–	68040/33	None	32/33	None	LC III PDS, comm	36	4
Macintosh TV	10/93–	68030/32	None	32/25	None	None	8	
Workgroup Server 60	3/93–	68040/25	Yes	32/20	1	'040 PDS	68	1, 3
Workgroup Server 80	3/93–	68040/33	Yes	32/32	3	'040 PDS	136	3
Workgroup Server 95	3/93–	68040/33	Yes	32/25	5	'040 PDS	256	3
Workgroup Server 6150	4/94–	PPC 601/60	Yes	64/30	1	601 PDS, cache	72	1
Workgroup Server 8150	4/94–	PPC 601/80	Yes	64/40	3	Cache	136	
Workgroup Server 9150	4/94–	PPC 601/80	Yes	64/40	5	Cache	264	
Centris 610	2/93–10/93	68LC040/20	None	32/20	1	'040 PDS	68	1
Centris 650	2/93–10/93	68040/25 or 68LC040/25	Optional	32/25	3	'040 PDS	132 or 136	
II	3/87–1/90	68020/16	Yes	32/16	6	None	68	6
IIx	9/88–10/90	68030/16	Yes	32/16	6	None	128	6

Model	Life on the market	CPU chip/ speed (MHz)	FPU	Data bus width/speed	NuBus slots	Other slots	Maximum RAM	Notes
Desktop models (continued)								
IIcx	3/89–3/91	68030/16	Yes	32/16	3	None	128	6
IIvi	10/92–2/93	68030/16	Optional	32/16	3	Accelerator	68	
IIsi	10/90–3/93	68030/20	Optional	32/20	1	IIsi PDS	65	1, 3
IIci	9/89–2/93	68030/25	Yes	32/25	3	Cache	128	
IIvx	10/92–10/93	68030/32	Yes	32/16	3	Accelerator	68	
IIfx	3/90–4/92	68030/40	Yes	32/40, 20	3	IIfx PDS	128	7
128K, 512K, 512Ke	1/84–9/87	68000/8	None	16/8	None	None		
Plus	1/86–10/90	68000/8	None	16/8	None	None	4	
SE	3/87–10/90	68000/8	None	16/8	None	SE PDS	4	
SE/30	1/89–10/91	68030/16	Yes	32/16	None	SE/30 PDS	128	6
Classic	10/90–9/92	68000/8	None	16/8	None	None	4	
Classic II	10/91–9/93	68030/16	Optional	16/16	None	None	10	
Color Classic	2/93–5/94	68030/16	Optional	16/16	None	LC PDS	10	
Color Classic II	10/93–?/94	68030/33	Optional	32/33	None	LC III PDS	36	5
Portable Models								
PowerBook 100	10/91–8/92	68000/16	None	16/16	None	None	8	
PowerBook 140	10/91–8/92	68030/16	None	32/16	None	None	8	
PowerBook 145, 145B	8/92–	68030/25	None	32/25	None	None	8	
PowerBook 160	10/92–8/93	68030/25	None	32/25	None	None	14	
PowerBook 165	2/93–	68030/33	None	32/33	None	None	14	
PowerBook 170	10/91–10/92	68030/25	Yes	32/25	None	None	8	
PowerBook 180, 165c, 180c	10/92–5/94	68030/33	Yes	32/33	None	None	14	
PowerBook Duo Dock, Duo Dock II	10/92–	n/a	Optional	n/a	2	None	n/a	
PowerBook Duo 210	10/92–10/93	68030/25	None	32/25	None	152-pin connector	24	
PowerBook Duo 230, 250	10/92–5/94	68030/33	None	32/33	None	152-pin connector	24	
PowerBook Duo 270c	10/93–5/94	68030/33	Yes	32/33	None	152-pin connector	32	
PowerBook Duo 280, 280c	5/94–	68LC040/33	None	32/33	None	152-pin connector	40	
PowerBook 520, 520c	5/94–	68LC040/25	None	16/25	None	PowerBook PDS	36	
PowerBook 540, 540c	5/94–	68LC040/33	None	16/33	None	PowerBook PDS	36	
Portable	9/89–10/91	68000/16	None	16/16	None	Portable PDS	9	

Notes

1 These Macs require a special adapter card in order to accept an expansion card.

2 DAV slot on AV models only.

3 Installing a PDS or DAV card in these Macs blocks one NuBus slot.

4 Communications slot, for installing inexpensive modem or Ethernet cards.

5 Discontinued date unknown.

6 Can't access over 8MB of RAM without MODE32 or 32-bit Enabler.

7 The IIfx's I/O bus runs at 20 MHz.

Editors' Poll: What Feature Are You Most Looking Forward to in System 7.5?

DD: As a concept, I really like the PowerTalk features: the ability to get all of your e-mail in a single In Box. That sure would have been handy on this *Bible* project. I'm also looking forward to QuickDraw GX: all those fine new fonts, and no more Print Monitor! (Of course, I'll need a big memory upgrade to take advantage of it.) Day to day, the clippings feature could be cool.

JK: I think the combination of AppleScript with the scriptable Finder could have the biggest impact, although most users will probably ignore its potential. I think QuickDraw GX will be the System 7.5 extension that brings the most important changes. But I have to admit, I look forward to all the convenient new interface treats (like the improved Find command, drag and drop, and so on) more than I do to any single new feature.

HN: WindowShade.

BW: Having network and telecom resources brought together under a single interface, via AOCE, will be a real boon to a lot of people in corporations.

System Software

When you first buy a computer, it's the hardware that gets all the attention. But what really makes the Mac what it is—an easy-to-use and highly customizable personal computer—is the *system software.* The system software creates the desktop, lets you organize your files in folders and windows, and gives you abilities, like cutting and pasting text and graphics, that work in virtually any Mac program.

Part of this basic software is written indelibly into your Mac's ROM; you never see it and can't modify it (short of buying a hardware upgrade). The rest comes in a collection of files and folders in your Mac's *System Folder,* to which you can add various enhancements. This chapter shows how recent system versions have improved on older ones, describes both the basic components and some of the major system enhancements available, and advises you on installing and modifying system software to get the most from your Mac.

Contributors

John Kadyk (JK) is the editor of this chapter.

Eric Apgar (EA) works at Apple's Internal Desktop Support group.

Arthur Naiman (AN), Sharon Zardetto Aker (SA), Charles Rubin (CR), Nicholas Lavroff (NL), and **Susan McCallister (SM)** all contributed to previous *Mac Bible* editions, from which parts of this chapter were taken.

Contents

System Versions

The Mac's system software has gone through many revisions over the years, each building on what came before it. (When you buy a new Mac, you get the latest version installed on its hard disk.) Modern Mac system history starts with System 7, which took a leap beyond its predecessor, System 6. The systems released prior to System 6 are out of use for the most part and aren't really worth discussing anymore.

Each of the two major system versions has evolved through several minor releases that fixed bugs, added features, and adapted the system for new Mac models: System 6 went from 6.0 through 6.0.8, and, at this writing, System 7.5 is about to be released. Like the system's evolution, the information in this section is cumulative; the features each version introduced have carried through subsequent versions, so what you read in the System 7 section applies equally to System 7.5.

> ### *Which System's on Your Mac?* (JK)
>
> To find out which system version your Mac is running, go to the Finder and select About This Macintosh (in System 7) or About The Finder (in System 6) from the menu.

About This Macintosh

Macintosh Centris650 — System Software 7.1 — © Apple Computer, Inc. 1983-1992

Total Memory: 16,384K — Largest Unused Block: 3,224K

Address Book	20K
America Online v...	800K
FileMaker Pro	1,800K
FindPro III 1.0.5	384K
Information Man...	1,024K
Microsoft Word	2,048K
Nisus® 3.4 Limit...	2,048K
SimpleText	512K
System Software	3,498K

The version of system software your Mac is running appears in the upper-right corner of the box you see when you choose About This Macintosh from the menu in the Finder.

Except where noted, assume this chapter (and this whole book) is referring to System 7 (although much of it applies System 6 too). Information that's specific to System 7.5 is indicated with an icon like the one next to this paragraph.

System 6 (JK/CR)

From the late 1980s until the middle of 1991, all new Macs came with System 6. Overall, it's simpler than System 7, but you can't customize it nearly as much, and it's not designed for the high-powered, memory-hungry software that's available today. On the other hand, both System 6 and applications that came out when it was current are small enough to allow you to work on older Macs with just 1MB of RAM, two floppy drives, and no hard disk!

Finder and MultiFinder. Unlike System 7, System 6 ordinarily allows only one application to run at a time, and it hides the desktop while you're running the program. To run multiple programs, you have to turn on MultiFinder, which comes with System 6, and your Mac needs at least 2MB of RAM (still just half of what System 7 requires). Without MultiFinder, you have to quit the program you're in whenever you want to open another application or even get back to the desktop. (See "System 6 Tips" in Chapter 1 for information on how to set up MultiFinder.)

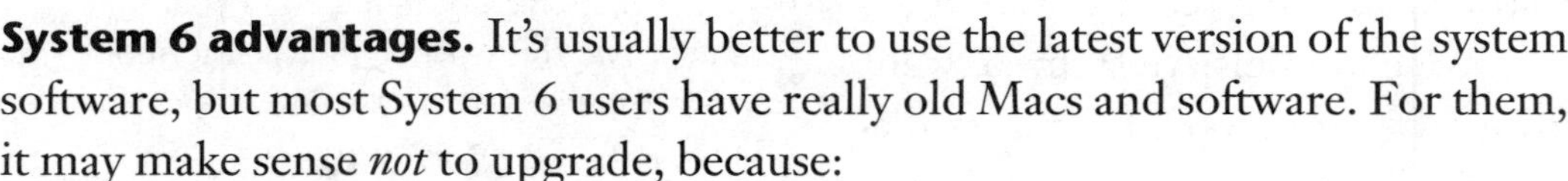

System 6 advantages. It's usually better to use the latest version of the system software, but most System 6 users have really old Macs and software. For them, it may make sense *not* to upgrade, because:

- System 7's memory and hard disk space requirements often exceed the capacities of older Macs, so their owners would have to buy expensive hardware upgrades to use it (see "System 7 Hardware Requirements," below).
- Older Mac programs (released before 1991) weren't written to take advantage of System 7 features like Apple events, Publish and Subscribe, and scripting (described below), so you won't get the full benefit of the upgrade unless you also upgrade your software.
- Not all older programs will work with System 7, particularly if its *32-bit addressing* or *virtual memory* features are turned on. (These are described more fully below and in Chapter 4.)

Early System 7

System 7.0, which introduced most of the features associated with System 7, was released in May 1991. Since then, System 7 has gone through several updates—some to add features to the basic system software (including 7.1 and 7.5), some that added features for the Performa line (7.0.1P and 7.1P), one that bundled high-end enhancements that Apple hadn't yet decided to include in the basic package (System 7 Pro), and a couple that just updated the basic system for new models (7.0.1 for the PowerBooks, Quadras, and Classic II; and 7.1.2 for the Power Macs).

Most of what was added in each of these versions will be included in a single basic system by the time you read this. But if you've got an earlier version, this section will describe what it has and what it might be missing.

Introduced with 7.0 (JK/CR/DD). Here's a quick guide to the major features and capabilities System 7 gives you over System 6. This list covers versions 7.0 and 7.0.1; later versions offer additional features and are covered in their own sections below.

- **Aliases.** You can create dummy icons for any disk, file, or folder. They let you keep the original buried several folders deep, or even on another networked Mac, and still access it from the desktop, the menu, or anywhere you decide to put the alias.
- **Stationery.** The Stationery option (in the Get Info window of every document) lets you turn any file into a template. Double-clicking on the original creates and opens a new, untitled copy of the document that you can use and modify without affecting the original.
- **An improved file finder.** The Finder's Find command gives you more ways to look for files than System 6's Find File desk accessory and fetches what it finds, rather than just locating it. (But System 6's and System 7.5's Find File DAs build lists of multiple finds, which some people prefer.)
- **File sharing.** Other Macs networked to yours can use files and folders on your hard disk, and vice versa. (For more on file sharing, see Chapter 23.)

- **More versatile menu.** You can put anything in System 7's menu—a file, a folder, even a shared item on another Mac. (System 6's menu was just for DAs.)
- **Easier font, sound, and DA installation.** To install these files in System 7, you just drag them onto your System Folder's icon. In System 6, you need a

Publish and Subscribe

(CR/JK)

Publish and Subscribe works like an automatic cut-and-paste feature, allowing you to link data in two files (or two places in one file) so that when you change it in one place it automatically changes in the other. When the information has to be transferred between files, the first file creates ("publishes") an intermediary file (an "edition") that contains the information; the second file then sets up a link ("subscribes") to the edition. From then on, updated data is automatically transferred through the edition from the first file to the second.

For example, if you write a weekly managers' report that includes a summary of changes in product inventory, you can have the warehouse manager publish a database's record of stock-level changes in an edition that your report subscribes to. The report then updates automatically.

special utility program, and the process is much more laborious. System 7 also lets you install DAs anywhere you want—not just on the menu, as in System 6—and open them by double-clicking on their icons.

- **Increased memory capacity.** Macs using System 6 can handle only 8MB of RAM; System 7 allows some Macs to use up to one *gigabyte* (1,024 megabytes) via 32-bit addressing (see Chapter 4).
- **Smarter memory handling.** System 7 uses more RAM, but it also handles memory allocation better, so you get fewer memory-related problems than in System 6.
- **Virtual memory.** You can increase your Mac's memory by using disk space as RAM. (For more about how this works, see Chapter 4.)
- **Support for TrueType fonts.** Apple's TrueType font format produces smooth characters in any size on the screen and on any printer. TrueType support and TrueType system fonts come with System 7, but you can get an extension that adds TrueType support to System 6.0.7 or 6.0.8 (see Chapter 14 for more on TrueType).
- **Support for Publish and Subscribe and Apple events.** Publish and Subscribe allows files to share data automatically (see the box "Publish and Subscribe," above). Apple events provide a way for applications to communicate with one another so that one application can invoke the features of another (see the box

"Apple Events and Interapplication Communication," below). They show up as special commands in applications that are designed to use them.

- **Help menu.** A new menu in the upper-right corner of the screen lets you turn on balloon help, giving you access to cartoon-style balloons containing helpful info that pop up wherever you move the pointer. balloon help works in the Finder and in other applications designed to support it.

- **New desktop features.** Various desktop features include labels for categorizing files, greater control over how files are displayed in windows, the ability to launch a file by dragging it onto an application icon, and the ability to display a folder's contents within the window that contains the folder.

Performa system software (JK). Before System 7.5, the Performas came with their own system versions (7.0.1P and 7.1P), which were just System 7 modified slightly to be easier for beginners to use. System 7.1P itself went through several modifications, 7.1P1 through 7.1P6, which included many bug fixes and

Apple Events and Interapplication Communication (JK/CR)

Apple events are part of Apple's overall scheme for enabling communication between applications (an Apple event is a command sent from one application to another). Apple events are an underlying technology through which AppleScript can control other applications, and through which applications that have been designed to take advantage of Apple events can control one another.

For example, you can use Word's Embedding feature to add an Excel spreadsheet to a memo you're writing in Word. Once the spreadsheet is embedded, it's part of the Word document, but you can modify it at any time using Excel: You just double-click on the spreadsheet, and it will open as an Excel file that you can work on with all the usual Excel commands (provided you have Excel installed on your Mac, of course). When you close the Excel window, the changes you made are transferred back to the Word document.

Apple events even work between Macs on a network, or over modem connections, provided that the Macs have Program Linking turned on in their Sharing Setup control panels. (Modem connections slow Apple events way down, so you'll need *at least* a 9,600-bps connection to make it worthwhile.)

At this writing, Apple is developing OpenDoc, a more powerful, seamless way of allowing multiple applications to work on a single document. (See the box on OpenDoc at the end of this section.)

THINGS TO COME

added a few new features, like a Shut Down DA on the menu and the ability to permanently change to your monitor's color-depth setting (earlier versions would always reset it to 256 colors at startup). System 7.5 took most of the Performa software's modifications and made them options you can select in the General Controls control panel on any Mac.

Some of the 7.5 options that were introduced by the Performa systems include the Launcher (described later in this chapter), default Applications and Documents folders, and the capability to automatically hide other programs' windows (the 7.5 option hides only the Finder's windows). The choice of fancy desktop patterns you get with System 7.5 also originated on the Performa systems. The Performas also come with At Ease software, which allows a Mac owner to replace the Finder with an even easier-to-use interface and to control access to programs and documents by people sharing the Mac (see "Enhancements," below, for more on At Ease).

Unlike most Macs, though, Performas don't come with system-installation disks; instead, you get a copy-to-floppy utility called Apple Backup & Restore, which allows you to create system-restoration disks by backing up your Mac's hard disk, as well as the rest of your files. (But if your hard disk crashes and you haven't backed up your system, I've heard that Apple will send you installation disks overnight.)

System 7.1 (JK). For people who create multilingual documents, the most important change System 7.1 brought was support for *WorldScript*, which lets multiple languages and multiple scripts coexist on the same system—even within a single document. With WorldScript, you don't need separate versions of applications or the system software for different languages, even for languages that use pictographs instead of character-based alphabets or that read from right to left. You just have to get the appropriate language kit(s) from Apple. Even without the language kits, 7.1 is more adaptable to international differences than prior versions, providing new control panels from which you can choose several means of expressing time, numbers, dates, and so on.

System 7.1 also made it much easier to handle fonts: Instead of keeping certain types of fonts in the System file and others in the Extensions folder, System 7.1 keeps all font types in a Fonts folder in the System Folder. Furthermore, font

suitcases you add to the Fonts folder stay intact, so it's easy to add and remove groups of fonts by keeping them together in suitcase files. (Previous systems needed utilities like Suitcase or MasterJuggler to access fonts in suitcase files.)

System 7.1 was also the first system designed to accommodate Mac models introduced after it was. Before 7.1, Apple had to release a new system version to accompany each release of new models, but System 7.1 has little files called Enablers, so later Macs could be retrofitted to use it. Apple then went hog-wild, introducing twice as many new models in 1993 as in the previous year, along with a raft of Enablers. (System 7.5 is slated to come with a universal Enabler, which will work for all Macs in release when 7.5 is introduced.)

System 7.1 also fixed some bugs in 7.0 and 7.0.1 and came bundled with the QuickTime multimedia system extension (see "Enhancements," below).

System 7 Pro (JK). System 7 Pro (a.k.a. System 7.1.1) was Apple's experiment with marketing two separate, concurrent versions of system software: It's a slightly modified System 7.1 bundled with QuickTime, AppleScript, and PowerTalk. (See "Enhancements," below, for more on each of these.) System 7 Pro increased confusion more than it increased sales, so starting with System 7.5, Apple went back to just one version of the system software, with the formerly "Pro" system enhancements included in it.

System 7.1.2 (JK). When the Power Macs were introduced, they came with System 7.1.2, a version of System 7.1 that was developed to work with their PowerPC hardware. System 7.1.2 also came with AppleScript and PC Exchange (described under "Enhancements," below), and added the following new features:

- SimpleText replaced TeachText, the generic text-and-graphics application that came with previous system versions (prior to System 7, TeachText handled only text). SimpleText supports multiple fonts, sizes, and styles within a document, can record and play back sounds, and can open more than one document at a time. If you've got PlainTalk, it can even read text files aloud. You can also get SimpleText by running System Update 3 on System 7.1 (see the box "Tune-Ups and System Updates," on the next page).

- The Graphing Calculator shows off the PowerPC's FPU by plotting math functions on a three-dimensional graph that rotates on screen.
- The Make Alias command got a keyboard shortcut: ⌘M.

Apple doesn't recommend installing 7.1.2 on a 68K Macintosh (although people have done so without complaints).

System 7.5 (JK/DD)

System 7.5, which should be available by the time you read this, brings together into one version the features and system extensions from System 7.1P, System 7 Pro, and the Power Mac system software. To these, it adds QuickDraw GX and a number of other new features and enhancements, including many new ways of handling files and data. (Because we wrote this before 7.5's release, some features and names may be slightly different than they appear here.)

If you're using an earlier system version and want a lot of what 7.5 has to offer, upgrading may be the cheapest (or only) way to get them, but if you're interested in only one or two of the new features or bundled enhancements, you may be able to save money by adding them (or equivalents) to your existing system (see the box "System 7.5 Envy" on page 117 and the "Enhancements" section later

Tune-Ups and System Updates (JK)

Apple periodically puts out *Tune-Ups* and *System Updates*—utilities you can get from Apple dealers, and sometimes on-line services and user groups—that fix bugs or enhance existing features. The improvements they bring are generally incorporated into the next release of the system itself.

For System 7.1 and System 7 Pro, there's **System Update 3**, which replaces the TeachText application with SimpleText, fixes several problems that could lead to crashes and corrupted files, and contains a slew of improvements to everything from the Mac's sound quality to the reliability of its disk drives. System Update 3 handles everything covered by earlier updates (System Update 2.0.1, Hardware System Update 2, and Hardware System Update 1).

For System 7.0 or 7.0.1, **Tune-Up 1.1.1** is essential: It removes some problems that occurred when working with low memory and fixes a bug that can make files and folders disappear. You can tell if it's installed by choosing About This Macintosh from the menu. If there's a • (bullet) next to the system-software version number, the Tune-Up is installed.

in this chapter). (You'll also save memory and disk space, which 7.5 consumes much more of than earlier systems.) But some of System 7.5's major features—like its scriptable Finder, new help system, and others—aren't available for earlier systems.

If you do install 7.5, you can keep its size to a minimum by using the Custom Install option (see "Custom Installing," below) and by not installing QuickDraw GX and PowerTalk if you don't need them. According to Apple, you can set up a no-frills version of System 7.5 on any Mac from the Plus on, as long it has at least 4MB of RAM. (Realistically, though, putting 7.5 on a Plus would be like putting a locomotive engine in a VW). If you'll be installing PowerTalk and QuickTime GX, the minimum configuration is an '020-or-better Mac with 8MB of RAM. On Power Macs, double the RAM requirements.

Where to Get System Upgrades (JK)

You used to be able to get system software for free from Apple dealers, user groups, and on-line services and make copies for friends and co-workers. If you're looking for a copy of System 7.0.1 or earlier, you can still probably get it free from some of these sources (user groups are probably the cheapest and easiest). But while system software is still included in the price of a new Mac, you have to pay to upgrade to each new version that comes out.

BARGAIN

Starting with System 7, Apple started selling upgrade kits, though you could still pass copies around. But since System 7.1 was introduced, system upgrades have become like any commercial software: You're supposed to buy one copy for each Mac, and you're not allowed to make copies for others. You can get them from the same places you get other Mac software (computer stores and mail-order companies) or direct from Apple.

Bundled enhancements. System 7.5 includes a number of major system enhancements, including QuickDraw GX, AppleScript, QuickTime, PowerTalk, PC Exchange, MacTCP, and Easy Open. Their benefits are described in the paragraphs that follow, and most are discussed more fully under "Enhancements," below. They are also discussed, in some cases, in other chapters of this book.

GOOD FEATURE

Better file access. System 7.5 takes further advantage of the menu's ability to offer quick access to files, folders, and commands. When you turn submenus on in the new Apple Menu Options control panel and select a folder on 7.5's

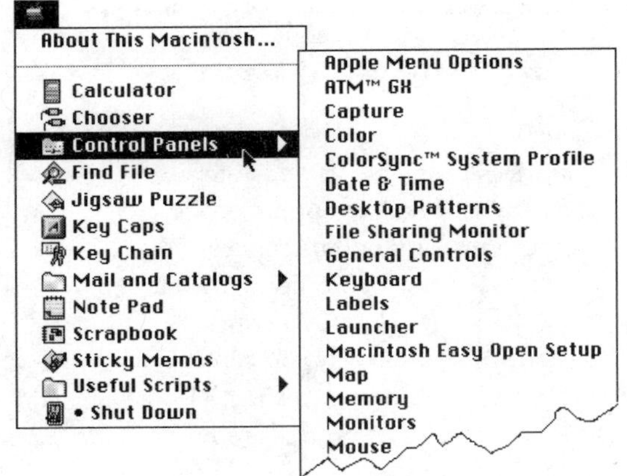

System 7.5's menu lets you access folder contents through submenus. It's also got a new Find File utility and folders that store recently used documents, programs, and networked items. At the bottom, there's a list of ready-made AppleScript scripts and a Shut Down command.

menu, a submenu appears on the right, from which you can select any item contained in the folder. If one of those items is itself a folder, it generates its own submenu when selected, and so on, up to five levels of menus. This lets you dig through to a particular file without having to open and sift through a lot of windows on the desktop.

The System 7.5 menu also includes folders for applications, documents, and networked items you've used recently, so you can reopen them quickly, without a lot of hunting.

Finally, there's a new Find File DA that combines features of System 7's Find command and System 6's Find File DA. The new Find File can search on more than one criterion at a time and builds a list of everything it finds matching the criteria. You can sort the list in the same ways you would a regular Finder window (by name, size, kind, date, etc.), and you can open or Get Info on items directly from the list.

Handling data scraps. System 7.5 introduced more and better ways of copying and storing bits of formatted text and graphics or taking quick notes, including the following:

System 7.5's new Drag and Drop capability lets you drag selected text or graphics from files to the desktop, where they become clippings that can be dragged into other files.

- Drag and Drop lets you drag formatted text or graphics from a document directly to another file or to the desktop. On the desktop, it appears as an icon called a *clipping*. When either the clipping or the data itself is dragged into another file, the original text or graphic will reappear there, complete with its original formatting (e.g., font, size, and style, if it's text)—provided the application you're using supports Drag and Drop, which will probably be true for most programs that come out after System 7.5. (If an application doesn't support Drag and Drop, you can still open a clipping with a double-click and copy its contents via the Clipboard—you'll lose formatting from the text, though.)

- Sticky Memos is a new DA that gives you an electronic equivalent to Post-its: little windows you can arrange to any size (the text automatically flows to the new margins) and format any way you choose. You can create several notes and set each one's text to a different font, size, and style. As with the real sticky notes, you can even choose different background colors.

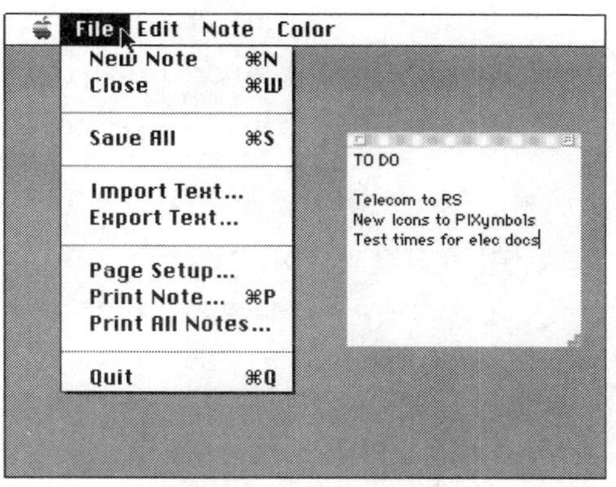

The Sticky Memos DA lets you add Post-it-like notes to your Mac's screen.

- 7.5's Scrapbook and Note Pad both support Drag and Drop. The new Note Pad can hold much more data (up to four large pages of text) and has new finding and printing capabilities.

File compatibility. System 7.5 bends over backwards to help you open files you don't have the creator application for—even if they're PC files on PC floppy disks—without losing their original formatting. PC Exchange (described in the "Enhancements" section, below) allows Macs to automatically read PC-formatted floppies. EasyOpen (described in Chapter 24) lists all the applications on your system that can open a file when you don't have the original application.

If you try to open a generic text or graphics file with earlier System 7 versions, the Mac offers to open it with TeachText. System 7.5 comes with the upgraded version of TeachText called SimpleText, which adds the ability to change the font, style, and size of text and to read text aloud on Macs that have the PlainTalk extension. Like TeachText, SimpleText also lets you create simple text files.

Working together. 7.5's bundled enhancements help Mac users collaborate with others, exchange formatted files, and connect with the vast sources of information available from the Internet and large institutional computers.

- PowerTalk makes it much easier to exchange files and messages with others by e-mail, fax, or local network without spending a lot of time on the mechanics of the exchange (see "PowerTalk" under "Enhancements," below, for details).

- QuickDraw GX enables Macs to save files in a format that can be viewed and printed from any other Mac that has QuickDraw GX, even if the second Mac doesn't have the file's original application or fonts (see Chapter 24 for details).

- MacTCP gives Mac users support for the TCP/IP protocol used for connecting to the Internet and communications with Unix systems at many universities and research institutions. (See Chapters 22 and 23 for more on how it's used.)

Automation. System 7.5's "scriptable" Finder lets you create scripts that automate Finder functions and commands within applications. The new Finder is also "recordable," meaning that AppleScript can watch you take a series of actions in the Finder and automatically generate a script to reproduce them. The scriptable Finder allows users to write much more powerful scripts than they could under previous systems. The AppleScript software (described under "Enhancements," below) also comes bundled with 7.5, so you've got all you need to use scripts or build simple ones.

GOOD FEATURE

To give you an idea what AppleScript can do, System 7.5 comes with several simple scripts, available from the menu, for doing things like putting an alias on the menu or turning file sharing on or off. The new Apple Guide help system (described under "Learning/Ease of Use," below) is also scriptable.

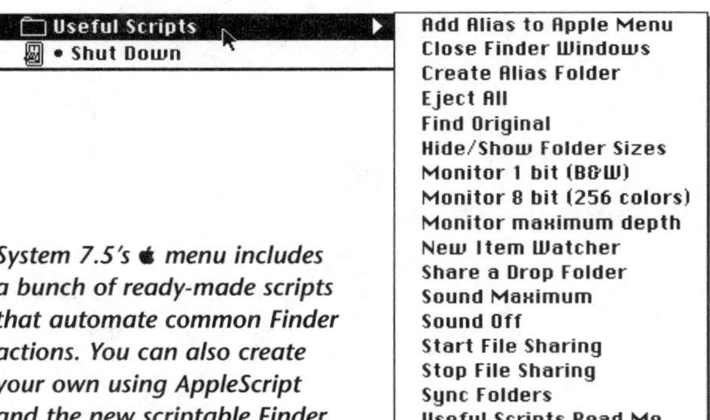

System 7.5's menu includes a bunch of ready-made scripts that automate common Finder actions. You can also create your own using AppleScript and the new scriptable Finder.

Fonts, graphics, and printing. These areas have been significantly improved by the release of QuickDraw GX, which comes with System 7.5. (Read about QuickDraw GX in the "Enhancements" section, below.) The functions of Adobe Type Manager (ATM), which lets Macs display and print PostScript fonts smoothly at any size, on any printer, have also been included with the system. (Adobe previously offered ATM to new Mac users for a small processing charge.) See Chapter 14 for more on GX fonts and ATM, Chapter 15 for more on QuickDraw GX's effect on graphics, and Chapter 21 for more on GX printing.

ColorSync, which also comes with System 7.5, helps different color devices—scanners, monitors, and printers—match their colors, preventing the expensive and time-consuming trial-and-error that's otherwise necessary to match colors between the screen and the printed page.

Learning/ease of use. System 7.5 builds in a couple of features from Performa systems that make the Mac easier for novices to use. It also introduces a new interactive, scriptable help system.

- *Apple Guide*, which shows up as a new Help command on the Help menu, teaches you how to do things by actually walking you through the process rather than just telling you in general terms how to do it. The computer draws "coachmarks" on the screen to help guide you (it's a little like watching John Madden draw diagrams of football plays on TV). At this writing, Apple Guide helps you only with the system software, but programs that come out after System 7.5 will probably offer built-in guidance, too (it could spare manufacturers a lot of tech-support calls). Businesses can also develop their own in-house guides using AppleScript and Apple's developer software, to avoid having to repeatedly teach standard procedures to new employees.

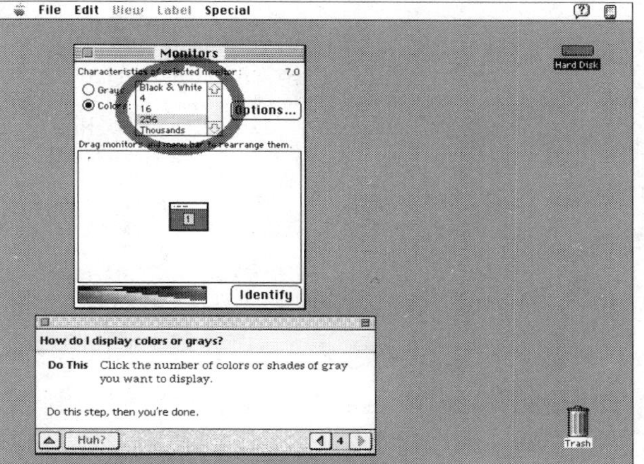

You tell Apple Guide what you want to do, and it shows you how—step by step.

- You can have the Mac automatically store any file you create in a special Documents folder on the desktop, to avoid accidentally losing files. (This is optional, and even if you've got the option turned on, you can always tell the Mac to save any given file somewhere else.)

- The Launcher, available before only on Performa systems, lets you collect programs and files in a special window, where they're displayed as large icons that you click on *once* to open.
- A Shut Down DA under the menu (also taken from the Performa system) lets you shut down your Mac from within an application, without having to go to the Finder first.

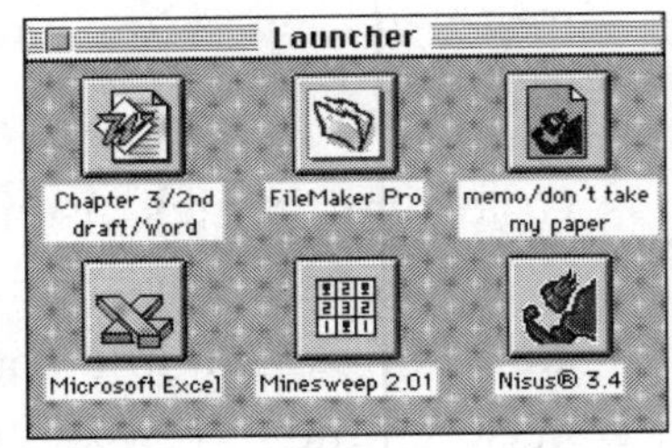

The Launcher arranges files and programs you select into a window. You can open the programs or files shown in the Launcher by clicking once on their icons.

Security and troubleshooting. System 7.5 gives you ways to protect the software on your computer and control over which extra files it loads when it starts up.

- You can lock your System and Applications folders to avoid accidental (or deliberate) deletion of your software.
- It includes Extensions Manager, a control panel that lets you control what system extensions, control panels, fonts, and other startup files the Mac loads when you turn it on. This is particularly useful when you're trying to troubleshoot problems or free up memory. It also allows different users on the same computer to set up their own sets of startup files.

Desktop niceties. You can reduce the clutter on your screen by setting desktop windows and icons to disappear automatically whenever you're using an application, via a new option in 7.5's General Controls control panel. A new control panel called WindowShade (based on a nearly identical shareware program) makes windows collapse into their title bars when you double-click on them.

You can choose your desktop pattern from a lot of exotic new textures, like coffee beans, turquoise water, or yellow straw. The menu bar now displays the time (and date, if you click on it) next to the Help menu.

The niceties are more than cosmetic, too—7.5 is also noticeably faster than 7.1 at copying files, launching files, switching applications, and displaying menus.

PowerBook features. A lot of new PowerBook features were released with the 500-series PowerBooks a few months before System 7.5 and were added to the

System 7.5 Envy

(JK)

There's a lot to admire in System 7.5, but if you just like some of its small-and-nifty features and don't want to upgrade your system, you can get some of them through shareware and commercial programs. If you're interested in more than one or two, however, you're probably better off forking over the cash for the 7.5 upgrade kit. (If you're worried about using up hard disk and RAM space, you don't have to install all the extras it includes.)

- MenuChoice and BeHierarchic (shareware) both give System 7 a hierarchical menu, and MenuChoice also keeps recently used items in a special folder. Lots of commercial software is also available to create a hierarchical menu (see Chapter 13).
- WindowShade, which collapses windows into their title bars, is available as shareware for System 7.
- PasteIt Notes (shareware) is very similar to the Sticky Memos DA.
- EasyPrint (shareware) gives you desktop printer icons that you can drop file icons on top of to print, just like QuickDraw GX.
- Find Pro III is nearly identical to 7.5's Find File DA, except that Find Pro III gives you more things to do with files it finds—including moving them, or making aliases or copies, directly from the "found" list. Unfortunately, Find Pro is only available from Ziffnet/Mac (accessible through CompuServe) or on-line services like AppleLink that post Ziffnet software (which isn't supposed to be shared).
- SuperClock! is an old-but-good shareware control panel that puts the time and date up on your menu bar.
- There's a freeware version of Extensions Manager that has the same name and does the same thing; there are also several commercial alternatives. (See Chapter 13 for more on those.)

new system. The PowerBook control panel does more of what third-party utilities like PowerBook Utilities from Connectix (see Chapter 13) have always done, like spinning down the hard disk during inactivity and automatically switching between high-performance mode and charge-conserving mode when the PowerBook switches between AC power and battery power. It also consolidates control over features such as screen dimming and *processor cycling* (which reduces the CPU chip's power consumption when it's not being used); but rather than having to adjust a lot of such settings individually, the user can still ignore them and use a slider bar to set the performance/conservation balance.

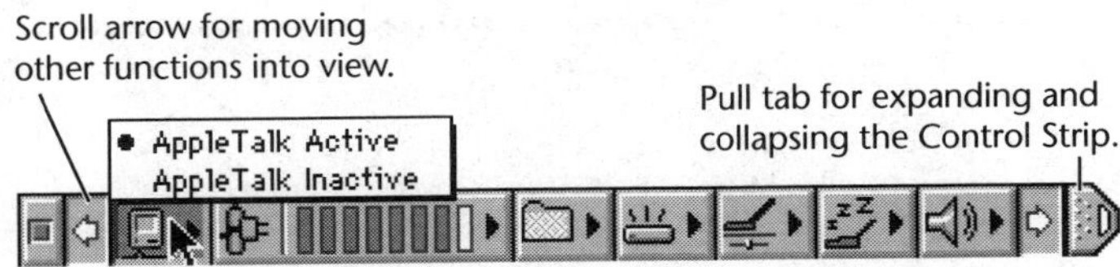

The Control Strip gives you easy access to the functions of the PowerBook control panel, plus control over the speaker volume, AppleTalk, file sharing, and more.

Since PowerBook users typically reconfigure their systems a lot to adjust to the different situations they find themselves in, Apple has created the Control Strip, a central, convenient way of accessing commonly used indicators and controls. The Control Strip is a tiny, collapsible ribbon that sits in a corner at the bottom of the screen; if you want to check the battery charge, turn file sharing or AppleTalk on or off, adjust the PowerBook's speaker volume, or use any feature of the PowerBook control panel, you just unscroll the strip and select the appropriate icon.

System 7.5 also includes PowerBook File Assistant (formerly sold separately), which synchronizes files between two hard disks. Synchronizing means hooking a PowerBook up to your desktop Mac—with file-sharing or SCSI mode—and updating designated folders on both computers with files from the other that are either new or more recent.

Support for telephone features. System 7.5 is designed to support third-party programs that integrate the phone with the Mac. Here are some ideas that may appear in future applications:

Unix and System 7 Together (JK)

The Unix operating system was developed for high-powered computers called minicomputers and workstations, and it's used extensively by universities and large organizations, public and private. There will soon be several ways for Mac owners to run Unix and Mac applications side by side on one computer.

The first (which has already existed for a long time) is A/UX, an implementation of Unix that lets the Finder and other Mac applications run concurrently with Unix programs on Macs. Development has also started on PowerOpen, a version of Unix for processors that will allow users to run Mac, PC, and Unix software not only on Power Macs but also on other RISC-based computers, like Sun SPARCstations and Hewlett-Packard and IBM machines.

In the meantime, Apple has released the *Macintosh Application Environment*, software that allows Mac applications to run under X Windows—a graphical user interface that runs on Sun and Hewlett-Packard machines, sharing the screen with Unix programs.

OpenDoc

(JK)

At this writing, Apple is revising the system software to support a revolutionary new document format called *OpenDoc,* which takes interapplication communication a step beyond what Apple events make possible. OpenDoc will allow you to use several applications to work on different types of data within a single document (called a *compound document* because of the multiple formats it contains). For example, a single OpenDoc document could contain graphics elements that you work on with an art program, text that you work on with a word processor, and video data that you edit with a video program. This way, parts of a document that would otherwise be separate files are kept together, where they can be edited in place. That eliminates the need to cut and paste between applications (perhaps losing formatting in the process) or to reimport a part into the main file every time it needs editing.

Apple also intends for OpenDoc to open the door for developers to create modular, customizable applications, to which specialized functions can be added as needed. Software developers will be able to focus their products on performing specific tasks rather than creating mammoth applications that try to do everything. But as with Apple events, OpenDoc will only work with applications that are written to support it.

- "virtual" telephones that let you place, answer, hold, and transfer calls on-screen
- receptionist programs that answer the phone and offer information or message-taking functions, according to caller input
- automatic call-out software for dunning past-due accounts

A more accommodating system. System 7.5 is better than earlier versions at handling the plethora of existing Mac models and supporting drive-intensive setups:

- It's the first system designed to support both Power Macs and 68K Macs. It also replaces the confusing array of System Enablers that came in 7.1's wake with a single universal Enabler for all Mac CPUs.
- It can accommodate storage devices of up to 4GB (the previous maximum was 2GB), improves disk performance on non-AV Macs, and is better at handling a large number of drives that are all mounted on one Mac.

Enhancements

Apple is always at work creating new capabilities for the Mac's system software. Sometimes these enhancements are released as part of a new version of the system software, and sometimes they're sold separately so you can add them to your existing system. Sometimes they come both ways.

Some of them—like QuickTime—don't do anything by themselves but rather create opportunities that other programs can take advantage of. They are generally included with any application that requires them. Others, like At Ease and PowerTalk, provide basic changes to your Mac's interface and are self-sufficient.

This section describes most of the major system enhancements available at this writing—the ones that Apple has chosen to bundle with the system software or certain lines of Macs. The enhancements listed here are available as separate products as well (except PowerTalk, which so far only comes with System 7 Pro and System 7.5). Other enhancements, as well as some of those mentioned here, are available as part of products that require them; they're described in the parts of this book that deal with their special capabilities.

AppleScript

(Ken Maki/JK)

People who have to perform routine tasks on a regular basis—weekly reports, daily file backups, hourly e-mail retrievals, and so on—can save a lot of time by having the Mac execute those tasks automatically. That's exactly what AppleScript makes possible.

Macro programs like CE Software's QuicKeys have been around for a long time, providing keyboard shortcuts for smaller tasks such as opening files and changing fonts. For more sophisticated scripting, users have turned to UserLand's Frontier. In 1993, Apple finally introduced its own sophisticated scripting software and then bundled it with the system software, starting with System 7 Pro and continuing with System 7.5. (System 7.5 is the first version that can take full advantage of AppleScript's potential, thanks to its scriptable Finder.)

You can use AppleScript, for example, to create a script to automatically prepare a weekly report by retrieving data over a network from database or spreadsheet files on colleagues' disks, copying it into the appropriate places in a word processing file, saving the new report, and e-mailing copies to a list of recipients. This whole series of tasks could be handled by one script, which you'd run by double-clicking on its icon. You can also use AppleScript for much simpler tasks—how you use it depends on your own needs and imagination.

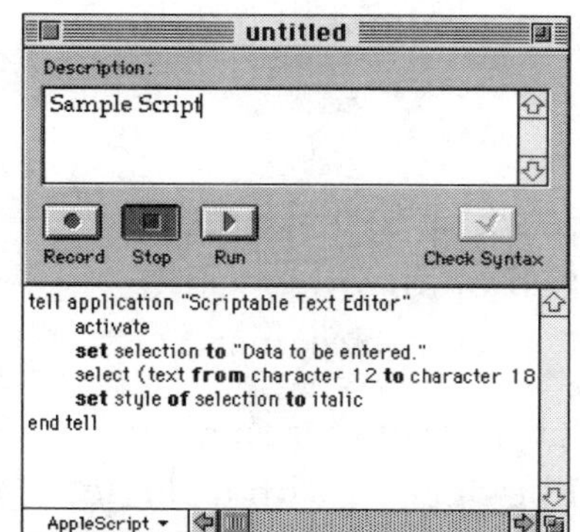

You write, edit, and test scripts in AppleScript's Script Editor program.

Scripts are created using the Script Editor application in one of two ways (or a combination of both): If your application is *recordable*, AppleScript can record your actions as you execute them and create a script to replay them. Or, with any application that is *Apple events–aware* (i.e., *scriptable*), you can write the script using AppleScript's programming language. When you use the recording method, the script you create shows up as written commands in the Script Editor, where you can modify them later. If you've programmed in HyperTalk—HyperCard's programming language—you'll find AppleScript commands familiar and easy to use.

GOOD FEATURE

A completed script can be saved on the menu or anywhere else that's handy, or as an application that you double-click on to run. If you design a stand-alone script to perform a particular activity on a file (such as compressing it with Compact Pro), you can run the script on any file by dragging the file's icon onto the script icon. (This type of script is called a "droplet.")

Mastering AppleScript takes time and practice, and simple shortcuts may be easier to create and execute with QuicKeys or Tempo II (described in Chapter 13). This is especially true since even scriptable applications often won't allow you to create scripts by recording, whereas QuicKeys and Tempo II can record macros in any application.

AppleScript, though, does allow more powerful, accurate scripting. For example, when you click a button in a dialog box, QuicKeys will remember *where* you clicked, but AppleScript remembers the *name* of the button; so even if the dialog box shows up in a different area of the screen, the script should still work. Also, scripts transcend the language of the computer they're run on—when you put a script written in English on a computer using KanjiTalk, it runs normally (the script itself is actually translated and can be edited in the new language).

As mentioned above, AppleScript comes with System 7.5, but it's also available as part of Apple's $190 *AppleScript Scripter's Kit*, which contains extra development tools, such as a custom interface designer. AppleScript requires System 7 to run, and on System 7.0 or 7.0.1, QuickTime version 1.5 or later must be installed.

At Ease (JK)

At Ease is a simplified version of the Finder that you can set up to make the Mac both easier to use and less vulnerable to getting messed up by other users. It comes with Performas but can also be bought separately to run on regular Macs.

To the user, a Mac running At Ease resembles the Launcher, in that they both present applications and documents as icons that can be opened with a single click. At Ease also makes all other windows and icons disappear when you're running an application. But At Ease takes a more comprehensive approach: As a Mac's owner (or administrator), you can set up At Ease to control how other people use your Mac, from using passwords to restrict access to controlling what applications they have access to and where they store their documents.

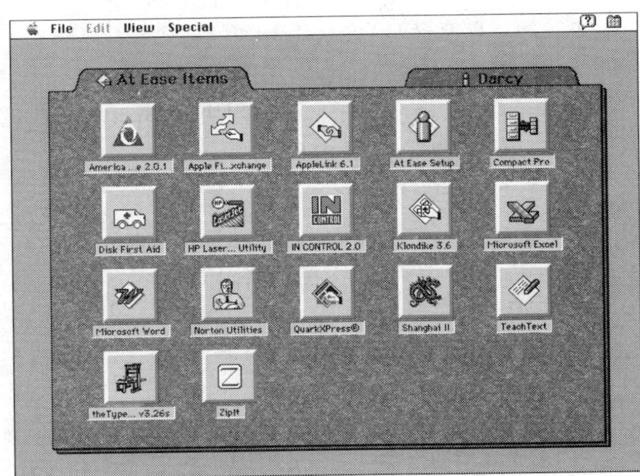

At Ease is a simplified—and restricted—environment that a Mac's owner can set up for other people using his or her computer.

For example, suppose your parents bought you a Performa to do your term papers on, but then suddenly they want to borrow it to write letters and prepare their taxes. You don't want your system to get cluttered with files they create, and you don't want them wasting time playing your computer games. Above all, you don't want them messing up your important files through their klutzy misuse of the computer.

By running the At Ease setup application, you create individual sets of privileges for Mom and Dad, so they can each access only the files, applications, and menu commands they need to get their work done (in fact, they won't even *see* the ones you haven't specified). You set it up so that the screen says *Hi, Mom/Dad* on startup. Whichever parent is using the Mac then selects his or her name, enters a password, and gets access to his or her own files and documents. To keep their files from showing up all over your hard drive, you can limit them to saving files only in their own personal folders or only to a floppy disk.

As you gain confidence in your parents' abilities and their respect for the computer, you can give them the option of using the regular Finder (they'll always have At Ease to retreat to when things get confusing). For Grandma, who can't read the fine print on icon labels, you can set At Ease to pronounce icon names when the mouse passes over them.

At Ease isn't a high-security system, though: Any user can select Go to At Ease Setup from the Special menu and turn At Ease off, so the Mac will start up with the Finder the next time it's turned on.

For situations in which you want more control, there's **At Ease for Workgroups**. The Workgroups version allows you to assign privileges to groups of users; gives you greater control over access to specific items on the , File, View, and Special menus; and allows for much greater security.

GOOD FEATURE

If you're a teacher in some fantasy classroom in which all the students have Macs on their desks, and they're all networked to your Mac, you can set up privileges for the entire class from your desk using At Ease for Workgroups. You can also have At Ease for Workgroups monitor how each student is using his or her computer—which programs and files, for how long, and so on. And since students love to beat the system in this kind of controlled environment, you can lock their hard disks so they can't circumvent At Ease by starting up with a floppy disk.

Bought separately, At Ease costs $60, and At Ease for Workgroups costs $300. Both versions require System 7.

PC Exchange (JK)

PC Exchange makes PC floppy disks show up as icons on the desktop, as if they were Mac disks, and lets you initialize high-density floppies in DOS format. It can also link PC file types to Mac applications, so you can open them by double-clicking as if they were Mac files. PC Exchange was included with the Performas starting with System 7.1P and with other Macs starting with System 7.1.2; PC Exchange requires System 7 and a Mac with a 1.4MB floppy drive (which has been standard on models since the later SEs). It costs $80 and is discussed further in Chapter 25.

SYSTEM 7.5

PlainTalk (JK/Michael Santiago/EC)

PlainTalk comes with the Quadra AVs, is available separately for the Power Macs, and has two parts. *Text-to-speech* enables applications that support it to read text aloud in a humanlike voice, while *voice recognition* works in conjunction with AppleScript to enable you to control your Mac by voice (to varying degrees, depending on the application's support of Apple events).

GOOD FEATURE

The text-to-speech feature gives you a choice of voices of varying quality. Although all of them sound like a computer talking, the high-quality voices' pronunciation is impressively close to human speech, complete with inflections around punctuation. PlainTalk is even smart enough to pronounce words and abbreviations differently depending on the context. For example, "Dr." is pronounced *doctor* when it's part of someone's name and *drive* when it's part of a street address. Similarly, *lead* is pronounced differently when used as a noun and as a verb. PlainTalk sometimes screws up, though—*read* often comes out as *red* when it should sound like *reed*.

The voice-recognition part of PlainTalk is designed to open files and activate menu commands, and you can also teach it special commands or set it to activate QuicKeys macros or AppleScript scripts. Any menu item in the application currently being used can be invoked using speech; in this limited sense, all applications support voice recognition. Applications that respond to Apple events can be more fully controlled by PlainTalk.

Unlike Articulate Systems' Voice Navigator (a third-party kit that gives you voice control over the Mac), you don't have to train PlainTalk to recognize your speech. By the same token, if your accent falls outside of the range of American accents it already knows, you can't teach it to understand you (although one tester found it responded well to his Catalan-inflected speech). Apple is working on versions of PlainTalk that will understand other accents and languages. In the meantime, Elizabeth Castro found that she could use the U.S. version with Spanish-language software if she pronounced the Spanish words phonetically in her "worst possible American accent."

But other users with U.S. software and American accents say they sometimes have to repeat commands several times before the computer responds, and when it does, there may be a long delay before the command is executed. The computer may even execute the wrong command or respond when you don't want it to, if you've got voice recognition on and are talking to someone in front of the computer.

The PlainTalk software includes a Speech Setup control panel to help reduce some of these problems; Speech Setup lets you set options like the computer's name (so it'll know when you're talking to it) and its listening sensitivity (so you can either make it more responsive or avoid accidentally triggering commands).

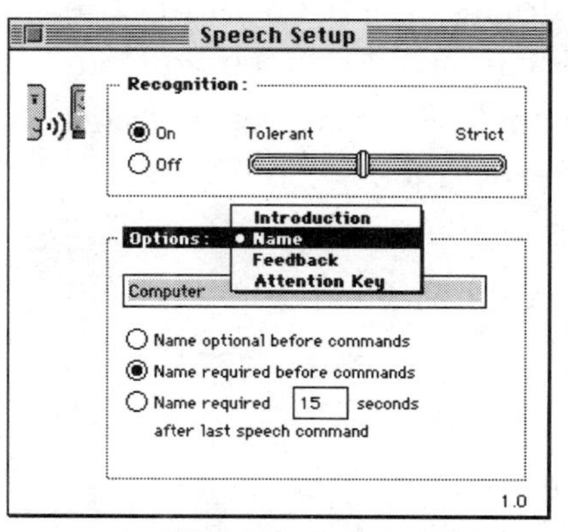

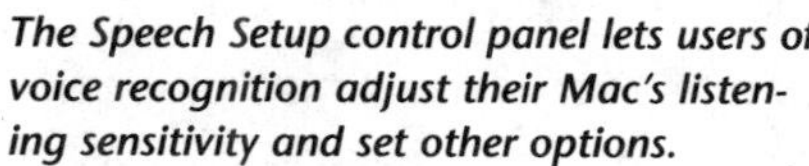

The Speech Setup control panel lets users of voice recognition adjust their Mac's listening sensitivity and set other options.

You can also improve the computer's response time and accuracy by using the Speech Macro Editor application to reduce the Mac's vocabulary and make voice recognition more tolerant. When you just use the Speech Setup control panel to increase PlainTalk's tolerance, it can do silly things like interpret the sound of a book page turning as someone saying *cut*.

When it's turned on, voice recognition consumes 2MB of memory, which some people find is too much to allow them to run other applications on '040-based AV Macs with only 8MB of RAM. Also, many current applications don't fully support voice recognition unless it's used in tandem with CE Software's QuicKeys.

The text-to-speech part of PlainTalk will work on any Mac with a 68020 processor or better (you probably need System 7, maybe 7.1, as well). Voice recognition works on fewer Macs—just the AVs and Power Macs, at this writing—and requires a special PlainTalk microphone ($30 Apple Price). PlainTalk is supposed to come with the AVs and Power Macs, but some shipped without it. You can get it by calling Apple at 800/SOS-APPL.

PowerTalk (JK)

GOOD FEATURE

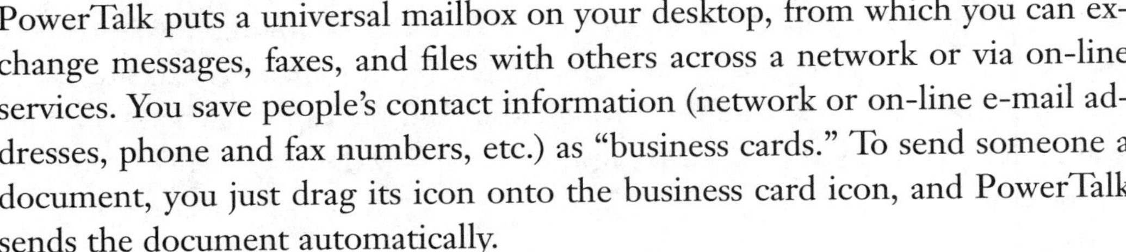
PowerTalk puts a universal mailbox on your desktop, from which you can exchange messages, faxes, and files with others across a network or via on-line services. You save people's contact information (network or on-line e-mail addresses, phone and fax numbers, etc.) as "business cards." To send someone a document, you just drag its icon onto the business card icon, and PowerTalk sends the document automatically.

PowerTalk also comes with its own e-mail system, called AppleMail, which doesn't require a server and allows messages to contain styled text, as well as images and video material, instead of just ordinary text.

Applications that support PowerTalk let you send documents from within the program by attaching an address window to the document, in which you can enter recipients' names, a message name, and even enclose other files by dragging their icons in from the desktop. PowerTalk keeps track of your contacts and the various network and on-line resources (such as file servers) at your disposal and categorizes them by means of connection (AppleTalk, phone, etc.) in lists stored in a Catalogs icon on the desktop. You can log onto a file server or address a message by pulling the appropriate name from these lists.

Since it's easy to undetectably alter e-mail files (compared to paper documents), PowerTalk comes with a security feature called DigiSign that users can attach to files they send. A recipient can verify a signed document's authenticity by clicking a button: If any attempt has been made to change the file, the verification message will show the "signature" as void. Apple means for the signature to be taken seriously—to get the signing software you have to fill out an application that includes a notary public's confirmation of your identity and send it to an outside agency (unless your company has a separate arrangement with Apple).

PowerTalk is available only as part of System 7 Pro and System 7.5. Large networks using PowerTalk can benefit from Apple's $1,000 **PowerShare Collaboration Server**. For more on PowerTalk, see Chapter 23.

QuickDraw GX

(JK)

QuickDraw GX, which is about to be released at this writing, makes big improvements to the way the Mac handles printing, graphics, fonts, and exchanges of formatted files between Macs. Programs that support QuickDraw GX can take advantage of all these features automatically. Here's a summary of some of the main benefits:

- New "intelligent" GX fonts adjust to context (with automatic ligatures, for example) and offer more styles and special characters. You'll also be able to adjust font weights, tracking, and other features in applications that haven't previously supported such powerful typographic control.
- QuickDraw GX adds graphics features previously available only with PostScript. For example, programs that support GX can make any graphic or text transparent and generate many other effects—like rotating and skewing.
- Macs with QuickDraw GX can save files in a format (the PDD or "portable digital document" format) that can be viewed and printed accurately from any other Mac that has QuickDraw GX, even if the second Mac doesn't have the file's original application or fonts. This makes it easy to e-mail documents to colleagues who may or may not have the same software you do, and it makes trips to the service bureau less nerve-racking.

GX also adds several capabilities for printing:

- Any printer can be shared on a network, not just AppleTalk printers.
- You can select printers in the Print dialog box rather than using the Chooser, or you can print a file from the Finder by dragging its icon onto the desktop icon of the printer you choose.
- You can easily preview, reschedule, and rearrange jobs waiting in a print queue by double-clicking the printer's icon (no more PrintMonitor!).

- You can customize print jobs from the Print dialog box (for example, by screening the word "draft" in the background on every page of an unfinished manuscript). Software developers can offer printer extensions that deliver other features accessed in this manner.
- You can mix page sizes in a single document. For example, for a subscription mailing, you could include a letter-size page for the sales pitch, an order card, an envelope to send the mailing in, and a smaller envelope for the reply all in one document.

QuickDraw GX requires System 7.1 or later and a Mac with an '020 processor or better (in other words, any recent model). No price is available at this writing, since the software hasn't been released yet. For more details on the features listed above, see Chapters 14, 15, 21, and 24.

QuickTime (JK)

QuickTime lets you cut and paste still or animated images, with or without sounds. For example, if you've got an AV Mac or a video digitizing board, you can record a video clip, paste it into a word processing file, and then send the file to a friend as a movie-letter. (Of course, your friend will also need QuickTime to play the movie back on his or her Mac.)

People often forget that QuickTime also lets you cut and paste sound and music clips in the same way. Version 2.0 supports MIDI (Musical Instrument Digital Interface) and has a built-in set of instrument sounds you can orchestrate. MIDI tracks take up much less disk space than audio recordings because they record instructions for performing a piece (like when to play what notes and how long to hold them) rather than actual sounds. QuickTime 2.0 will also support SMPTE (Society of Motion Picture and Television Engineers) time code, a multimedia industry standard for synchronizing multiple tracks of sound and video.

QuickTime requires System 6.0.7 or later and a Mac with an '020 processor or better. It comes with System 7.1 or later and with various third-party applications. Further details are discussed in Chapter 17.

The System Folder

(JK)

The System Folder contains the most important group of files on your Mac, including the System and the Finder, which the Mac needs in order to start up and run normally (the System file is described in its own entry below). Unless you're using System 6, most of the other files are organized into folders according to what they do.

In addition to the software that comes with the Mac, many applications keep files in the System Folder, and when you install software to go with a new external device (a scanner, printer, modem, or the like), that's usually where it goes.

Most of the System Folder's contents are there for the Mac, applications, and peripherals to use—you'll rarely work with them directly. But some files—the control panels, in particular—are there to help you customize your work environment, and several folders—the Apple Menu Items, Launcher Items, Speakable Items, and Startup Items folders—are there to give you quicker and easier access to almost any type of file.

Exactly which files and folders your System Folder contains depends on your system version, the Mac model you're using, and what software you've installed. Here are some of the files and folders you'll find, and how you can use some of them to customize your system:

- **The Apple Menu Items folder.** This folder stores everything that appears on the Mac's menu (with a few rare exceptions). Anything you put there—files, folders, applications, or aliases—will immediately show up in the menu, so you can get to it easily no matter what else you're doing.
- **The Clipboard file.** Where the Mac holds something you've cut or copied.
- **The Control Panels folder.** This folder stores utility programs that let you control how the Mac works. Control panels do things like set the volume level on the Mac's speaker, create a new desktop pattern, or establish file sharing with other networked Macs. There are many, many other control panels available—both commercially and as shareware—besides the ones that come with the Mac.

The Startup Disk (SA/AN)

When you turn on the Mac, it scans the various drives (including hard drives, CD-ROMs, floppies, cartridges, etc.) inside and attached to it, looking for a disk with a System Folder. When it finds one (normally it's the internal hard disk), that disk becomes the *startup disk*. Its system gets loaded into memory, and its icon appears at the upper-right corner of the Mac's screen.

Here's where the Mac looks for a startup disk first, then second, and so on:

1. the internal floppy drive
2. the second internal floppy drive (if there is one)
3. the external floppy drive (if there is one)
4. the disk specified in the Startup Disk control panel (called Startup Device in System 6)
5. the external serial (non-SCSI) hard disk
6. the internal hard disk (or any other device with a SCSI ID number of 0)
7. other SCSI devices (starting with ID number 6 and working its way down to 1)
8. after a 15-second wait, back to the internal floppy drive

HOT TIP

This sequence gives you several opportunities to preempt the normal, internal hard drive bootup. If you insert a floppy with a System and Finder on it, the Mac will boot off that instead. If you want the Mac to remove the internal hard drive from the startup sequence (an easy way to boot up from the CD-ROM drive), hold down Shift Option ⌘ Delete when you start up.

POWERBOOK

- **The Control Strip Modules folder.** This stores files that perform functions on the PowerBooks' control strip, on systems that have it.
- **"Disabled" folders.** These folders are created by extension-manager utilities, such as the Extensions Manager that comes with System 7.5, to hold files you want to temporarily exclude from the system.
- **The Extensions folder.** This stores *extensions*, which—you guessed it—extend your regular system software's capabilities by, say, enabling it to use a particular type of printer or display QuickTime movies. Extensions load into memory when you start up the Mac and run invisibly in the background.
- **The Fonts folder.** In System 7.1 and later versions, this folder stores the fonts (software that creates typefaces) you've installed in your System.

- **The Finder.** The Finder is the program that creates the Mac desktop, with its menus (, File, Edit, View, etc.) and Trash, disk, file, and folder icons. The desktop is described further in Chapter 1.
- **The Launcher Items folder.** This is where you put documents and programs that you want to have show up in the Launcher window.
- **The Preferences folder.** This folder stores the preferences files that keep track of the options you specify in the Finder and in applications—for example, what size icons you want next to file names in the Finder, or whether you prefer short or full menus in Word. (Unfortunately, lots of applications—especially older ones—ignore this folder and put their preferences files loose in the System Folder.)
- **The PrintMonitor Documents folder.** This is a holding place for temporary files the Mac creates when you print a document using background printing. This folder won't appear until you start using background printing.
- **The Scrapbook file.** The Scrapbook file stores the pictures, bits of text, sounds, and QuickTime movies you've pasted into the Scrapbook DA.
- **The Shutdown Items folder.** This is where you put files, programs, or scripts you want to open or run automatically after you select Shut Down from the menu or Special menu but before the Mac shuts off. For example, you could make a script that automatically backs up files you're working on and put it in this folder.

GOOD FEATURE

System Folders Before System 7.1 (JK)

With system versions before 7.1, the System Folder contains most of the same files and resources, as in later systems, but they're organized differently.

System 6 and earlier versions don't organize control panels, extensions, and other items into different folders. You can't install fonts and DAs in System 6 just by dragging them onto the System Folder icon; you need a special utility called Font/DA Mover, which installs them in the System file itself. (See "Using Font/DA Mover" on page 135.)

System 7.0 and 7.0.1 are like System 7.1, but without the Fonts folder; as with System 6, bit-mapped and TrueType fonts are kept in the System file. But you don't need Font/DA Mover, since the System 7 System file is a suitcase that opens when you double-click on it.

- **The Speakable Items folder.** On Macs that have voice-recognition capability, you put documents, programs, or scripts that you want to be able to open or run with voice commands into this folder.
- **The Startup Items folder.** This is where you put documents, programs, or scripts that you want the Mac to open automatically when it starts up. For example, you could install a script here that downloads your e-mail automatically when you turn on the Mac.
- **The System file.** The System file is the heart of the Mac's *operating system* (the software that controls a computer's basic operation); you can't run a Mac without it.
- **System Enablers.** Some Macs require one or more of these in order to start up under System 7.1 or 7.5.
- **Miscellaneous files and folders.** Other items you see in the System Folder are often resource files for other applications, placed there automatically by the program that uses them. You might also see temporary, or *temp* files, which sometimes become permanent, uselessly cluttering your System Folder.

System Software File Icons (JK)

Suitcase Files

Both the System file itself and the system font files are a special type of file called a *suitcase,* which is a bit like a folder—it opens a window on the desktop when you double-click on it. But unlike folders, suitcases contain only system *resources,* mini file entities of things like fonts, system beeps, and extra keyboard layouts that you can trade in and out of the System.

Control Panels

Under System 7, control panels—at least those that come with the system software—have their own kind of icon. It's a square with a little slider bar on the side or the bottom, like the one show here.

System Extensions

Apple's system extensions have their own type of icon, too—it looks like a puzzle piece.

The System File

(SA/Clair Whitmer)

The System file is the heart of the Mac system software; you can't run a Mac without it. Most of the information it contains consists of programming instructions that work hand-in-hand with the instructions in the Mac's *ROM* (read-only memory) chips on the computer's motherboard.

The System file is a suitcase file (see the box "System Software File Icons" on the previous page) that contains the system beeps and extra keyboard layouts that you can select in the Sound and Keyboard control panels. The System files for System 7.0 and 7.0.1 also contain certain types of fonts—see Chapter 14 for more on them.

Apple's DAs

(JK/DD)

The Mac comes with a small selection of *desk accessories*, or *DAs*: mini-applications specialized for quickie tasks you may need access to while you're using other applications. In System 7, DAs are usually installed in the Apple Menu Items folder, and you usually open them by selecting them from the menu. But you can also open them just like any other application by double-clicking on their icons. (In System 6, you can only open them from the menu, and you install them using the Font/DA Mover, as described below.)

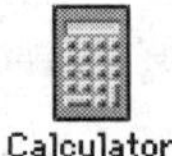

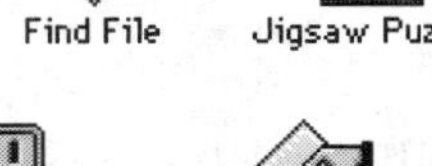

These desk accessories are all included with System 7.5. Most of them were included in earlier systems as well.

If you find that there are certain DAs you don't use much, take them out of the Apple Menu Items folder so they won't take up space on the menu (or consolidate them in a folder and put it on the menu, so they'll show up as just one item).

Control Panels

(AN/SA/NL/DD)

Choosing Control Panels from the menu opens the folder with that name in the System Folder, giving you access to a set of utilities that give you control over various aspects of the Mac. (You can also open control panels directly by opening the Control Panels folder and double-clicking on the individual icon.)

Types of Extensions (JK)

There are two main types of extensions: *system extensions* (also sometimes called *inits,* their name under System 6), and *Chooser extensions* (or, under System 6, *rdevs* for *Chooser devices*).

During startup, the Mac loads system extensions into memory, along with the system itself, directly extending its capabilities. (The little icons that pop up one by one along the bottom of the screen when you start your Mac show you what extensions and control panels are being loaded.) To work, system extensions have to load with the system, so you have to restart your Mac when you first install a new one.

Chooser extensions show up as icons you can select in the Chooser to set up connections through the Mac's modem and printer ports with networks or peripherals. There are also system extensions that help the Mac communicate with certain peripherals; both these types of external-device-related extensions are also called *drivers.*

The control panels are pretty self-explanatory, and when they're not, you can look them up in the manuals that come with the Mac. (If you haven't got a manual, use the Help menu.) See "Customizing Your System" in the "System Software Tips" section for some suggested control panel settings. Elsewhere in this book, we also describe how to use some control panels for certain tasks, such as adjusting your Mac's memory usage or setting up file sharing.

There are also many, many control panels created by commercial software developers other than Apple. Some of these are described in Chapter 13.

Adding to your system (CR/JK). You can add a new DA, font, extension, control panel, sound, or keyboard layout to your System at any time. In System 7, just drag its file onto the System Folder's icon; the Mac will automatically put the file where it belongs. (Be careful when installing sounds from sound-suitcase files: If you drag a sound suitcase onto the System Folder icon, it may be deleted, along with the sounds it contained. Instead, double-click on the suitcase icon to open its window and drag the sounds you want from inside it out onto the System Folder icon.

WARNING

If you want to add things to the System Folder without having them wind up in any of its subfolders, drag the files into the System Folder's open window instead of onto its icon.

System 6 doesn't organize system files into folders, but you install extensions, control panels, and printer fonts the same way—by dragging them to the System Folder. To install screen fonts and DAs, though, you need the Font/DA Mover utility that comes with the system software (see the next entry) or an alternative program such as Suitcase or Master Juggler (described in Chapter 14). To add sounds under System 6, you need a program like the shareware SoundMaster—or you can record your own, if you've got a IIsi or LC (which can run System 6 and come with microphones) or Farallon's MacRecorder microphone/software package. (Adding sounds is described in the "Sound" section of Chapter 17).

Using Font/DA Mover (JK)

Font/DA Mover is a utility for installing fonts and DAs in System 6 or for moving them between suitcase files. When you run the program, you get a dialog box like the one shown at right.

Select the Font or Desk Accessory button at the top of the box, depending on what you want to move. The program automatically displays those currently installed in the left-hand list box, but if you're not moving anything into or out of the system, click the Close button below the box and then click it again to open whatever file you do want to use (the button's name changes to Open after the first click).

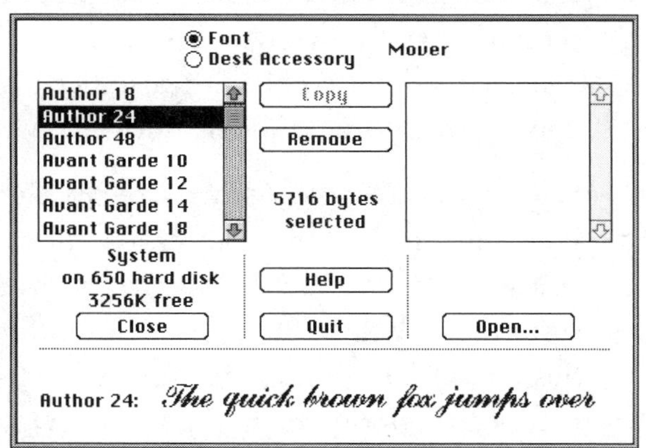

In System 6, you need Font/DA Mover (or an alternative, like Suitcase or MasterJuggler) to install DAs and fonts. (Font/DA Mover comes with the System.) Version 4.1 or later is also useful for moving fonts between suitcase files in System 7.

If you're moving items between files, click the button under the right-hand list box to open the other file (or to create a new one). Once it's open, select the items you want to move (you can Shift-click or drag through them to select more than one), click the Copy button, and they'll be copied to the file shown in the other box.

If you're removing items from a file, just select them and then click the Remove button.

Installing System Software

The system software comes preinstalled on new Macs' hard disks, but there are times when it's wise or necessary to install or reinstall system software yourself:

- when you upgrade to a new version
- after reformatting a hard drive
- to clean up file corruption (if you've been getting a lot of system errors)
- periodically, as routine maintenance

In most cases, all you have to do to install system software is double-click on the Installer icon on your system software disk and follow the instructions on the screens that follow. (At this writing, Performas, the PowerBook 145B, and some LCs don't come with Installer disks, so you have to restore a backed-up copy of the System Folder they came with.)

But if you want to control more closely what gets installed (to avoid swamping your hard disk with unnecessary files or to add only certain extensions), see "Custom Installing," below; if you want to clean up a potentially corrupted system, see "Clean Slate Installation (System 7)"; and if you're upgrading from System 6 to System 7, see "Preparing to Upgrade From System 6." Whenever you're considering upgrading to a new system (or any new software), you should first make sure your Mac meets the new software's requirements.

System 7 Hardware Requirements (JK/SM/CR)

To install System 7, you need a Mac with a SCSI hard disk and at least 4MB of RAM (8MB if you've got a Power Mac). If you're installing PowerTalk and QuickDraw GX, you'll need twice the RAM and at least a 68020-based Mac.

Judging from a prerelease version, you'll need anywhere from 7MB to 15MB or more of hard disk space to install System 7.5, *not* including the major enhancements—AppleScript, QuickDraw GX, and PowerTalk—which consume an additional 10MB or 12MB more. See "Custom Installing," below, for ways to keep these figures as small as possible. (Earlier systems require much less disk space.)

System 7 runs slowly on the Plus, SE, Portable, and the original Classic (but not the Color Classic or Classic II), so you may be better off sticking with System 6 on these machines. If you've got a Plus or an early-model SE (with an 800K floppy drive), be sure to get 800K installation disks. Only Macs with '030 (or faster) processors can use System 7's virtual memory and 32-bit addressing, which allow the Mac to access more than 8MB of RAM. (The only exception is the Mac II, which can be upgraded with a PMMU chip to use virtual memory.)

The Mac 128K, 512K, or 512Ke can be upgraded to run System 7, but it'd be wiser to buy a new Mac instead (or even a more recent used Mac), with System 7 and its manuals included in the price.

Preparing to Upgrade From System 6 (JK)

If you're upgrading from System 6 to System 7, there's a bit of special preparation you should do to minimize compatibility problems.

Check software compatibility. Run the Compatibility Checker (it's on the "Before You Install" disk). It scans all the software on your hard disk, tells you which items are potentially incompatible with System 7, and offers to put them in a folder called "May Not Work With System 7." If you choose to have "incompatible" programs isolated this way, feel free to try them out, one by one, after you complete the installation—in many cases, you'll find they work just fine with System 7, despite what the Checker says. If you find that a program you depend on could be incompatible with System 7, maybe you won't want to upgrade—at least until you're ready to upgrade your software.

Update your disk driver. You should also update your hard disk's driver before installing System 7 (especially if you plan to use virtual memory). If you have an Apple hard disk, just restart your Mac with the System 7 Disk Tools disk, run the HD SC Setup program, and click the Update button.

If you're using a third-party hard disk, you need to use the setup program that came with it, but there's a chance that it won't be System 7–compatible. If you're not sure, call the manufacturer to find out; if it isn't, the company should give you one that is.

Check for disk problems. Last, run the Disk First Aid program on the Disk Tools floppy. It will diagnose your drive for problems and, if there are any, repair them. If there are problems it *can't* repair, you should back up all your data, reformat your hard drive, and then restore its contents before you install System 7.

Clean Slate Installation (System 7) (JK/EA)

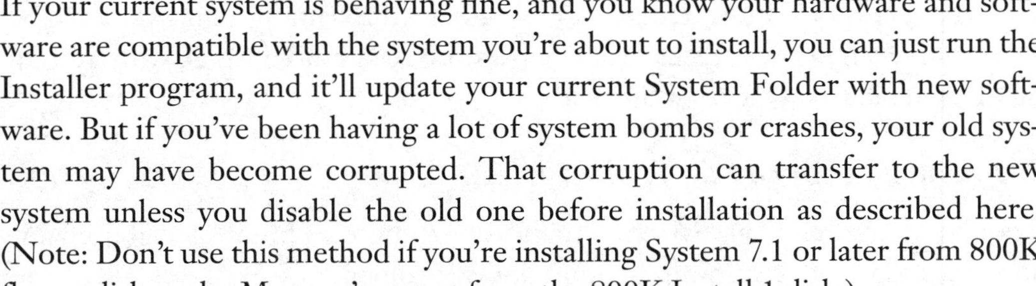

If your current system is behaving fine, and you know your hardware and software are compatible with the system you're about to install, you can just run the Installer program, and it'll update your current System Folder with new software. But if you've been having a lot of system bombs or crashes, your old system may have become corrupted. That corruption can transfer to the new system unless you disable the old one before installation as described here. (Note: Don't use this method if you're installing System 7.1 or later from 800K floppy disks—the Mac can't restart from the 800K Install 1 disk.)

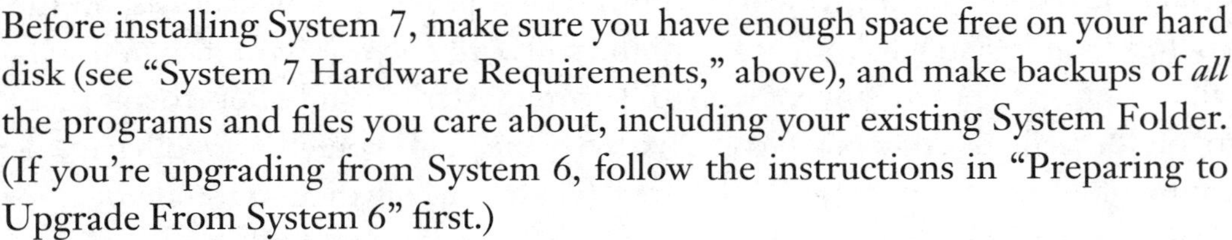

Before installing System 7, make sure you have enough space free on your hard disk (see "System 7 Hardware Requirements," above), and make backups of *all* the programs and files you care about, including your existing System Folder. (If you're upgrading from System 6, follow the instructions in "Preparing to Upgrade From System 6" first.)

Then proceed as follows:

1. Disable your old System Folder by dragging the Finder out of it (to the desktop, or somewhere you can retrieve it from if the installation fails). Then rename the folder "Old System Stuff" (or whatever), so a new System Folder can be created. Make sure there aren't any other System Folders on your disk; if there are, delete them. One way to check this is just to restart—you should get a blinking question mark after about ten seconds.

2. Restart your Mac and immediately insert the first installation disk into the floppy drive. Then run the Installer. Click the Easy Install button, or see "Custom Installing," below, for ways to avoid installing files you don't need.

3 When the Installer has finished, restart again, and you'll be running under the new system.

4 Drag all your non-Apple extensions, control panels, preferences files, and (if your old System was 7.1 or later) fonts from the Old System Stuff folder onto the new System Folder's icon—*not into its window*—being careful to avoid replacing files that already exist there. If you are managing your fonts, sounds, and DAs with a font/DA program like Suitcase (described in Chapter 14) and keeping them loose or in a differently named folder within the System Folder, drag them (or the folder you have kept them in) to your new System Folder's open window (not its icon), so they'll stay intact and the program can still access them.

Clean Slate Installation for System 6 (JK)

Just as with System 7, you can install System 6 over an existing System (6) Folder without losing any of its contents. But if your old System file was damaged, as often happens over time, that damage will probably remain in the newly installed system.

So before running the Installer, start up from the System Tools or System Startup floppy, drag your System file out of the System Folder and copy a fresh System file into it from the floppy. Next, *bless* your new system by holding down ⌘ Option and double-clicking on the Finder file. Then restart with the floppy and run the Installer. Lastly, use Font/DA Mover to copy any extra fonts and DAs from your old System file into the new one, and trash the old System file.

5 If you're upgrading from System 7.0.1 or earlier and had installed extra fonts, DAs, sounds, or keyboard layouts in your old System file, double-click on the System file icon. A window will open, allowing you to select such resources individually. Drag them from there onto the new System Folder icon.

6 Drag the Old System Stuff folder to the Trash.

7 If you just installed System 7.1, 7.1.1, or 7.1.2, you should run the **System Update 3** to get the best performance and reliability. Similarly, if you're installing System 7.0 or 7.0.1, run **Tune-Up 1.1.1** (the Tune-Up and Update are both available from Apple dealers; on-line services, user groups, and other such sources also carry the Tune-Up).

Custom Installing (JK)

When you run the Installer, the main dialog box gives you an option called Custom Install (or Customize), which allows you to specify exactly what system software gets added to your Mac. You can save a tremendous amount of disk space by installing only the system software for your Mac and by skipping any networking, printing, or other extras you don't need. (If you run Easy Install on a blank hard disk, you'll get 3.5MB of printer drivers alone, few if any of which you'll ever use!)

HOT TIP

Custom installing lets you decide whether you want features like file sharing, AppleGuide, and AppleScript (if the features are part of that system version). You can also choose whether to install a system that will work only on your Mac or on any Mac (the latter can take up much more space, but it's handy if the hard disk you're installing onto may be used by different models). You can select which printer drivers to install (there's no reason to install a dozen printer drivers if you've got only one printer).

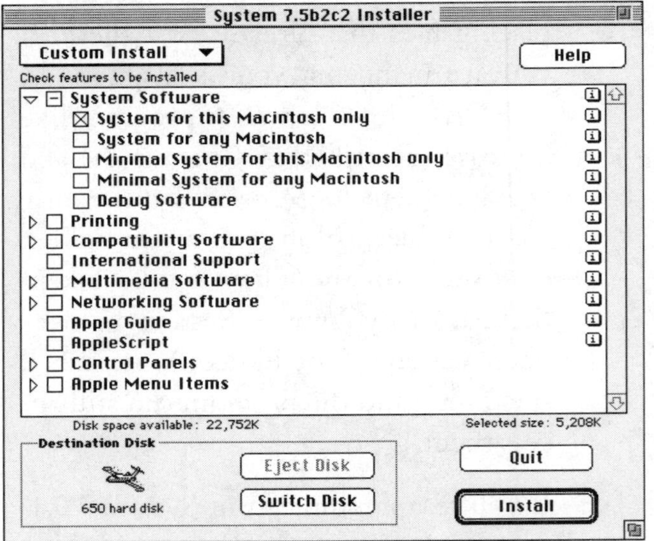

You can save a lot of disk space by using the Installer program's Custom Install option and choosing only the software you need.

If you change your mind in any of these areas, you can always go back later and install just the parts you skipped the first time around. Starting with System 7.5, the Custom Install window keeps a running tally of the disk space required for installation of the software you've selected next to a reading of the amount of space free on your hard disk.

Paring Down Your System Folder (SA/CR/JK)

Depending on how your system was installed, you may have a lot of fairly large files taking up space in your System Folder. If you've got plenty of room on your hard disk, this may not bother you, but otherwise you'll want to get rid of them. For example, if you don't have an ImageWriter or StyleWriter printer, you don't need their drivers in the Extensions folder. You can also toss special-purpose control panels and DAs such as CloseView, Easy Access, Map, Alarm Clock, Note Pad, and Puzzle if you won't be using them.

You can also remove the temporary files that applications sometimes leave in the System Folder, provided the program that created them isn't still running. (Well-mannered programs erase their temp files when you quit, but if you crash, the temp file will remain in the System Folder to help you recover your file.) Older versions of Word are notorious for leaving temp files around; they're named *Word temp 1, Word temp 2,* and so on (versions 5 and later put temp files in the Trash). PageMaker creates files called *PM001* and so on; FileMaker creates a *FileMaker temp* folder and puts its stuff in there.

System Software Tips

General

Creating a disk-space monitor (JK). The Views control panel's Show Disk Info in Header option keeps you aware of how much space is on your hard disk (information automatically supplied when you have windows set to view by icon). But you don't need this information in every window. Instead, just create a folder called Disk Space, set its window to display by icon, and put it in the Apple Menu Items folder. Then, whenever you want to know how much disk space you've got, select Disk Space from the menu and the window that opens will tell you.

Replace folder contents, not folders (SA/AN). If you drag a folder from one disk to another, and the destination disk already has a folder on it with the same name, the contents of the folder you're dragging completely replace the contents of the existing folder. This can be a big problem if the original folder (on the destination disk) contained files that the replacement folder doesn't.

To be safe, never replace a folder with a folder. Instead, work with folder *contents.* Open the folder you were going to drag, press ⌘A (for Select All), and drag all the items into the folder on the destination disk. If any of the files you drag have the same names as files already in the folder, you'll be asked if you want to replace them—but any additional files in the destination folder won't be touched.

Using stationery for templates (Michael Bradley/Dale Coleman/CR/JK). All applications have default settings for things like font and type size, ruler, print quality, spreadsheet size, and data format. Sometimes you can change the defaults, but often you can't. This means every new document will always start out formatted the standard way, whether you like it or not. If you don't like it, try using System 7's stationery feature to create templates of the formatting that you want.

A *template* is a document with a format that you use repeatedly—for example, one containing your letterhead, so you don't have to recreate the letterhead every time you want to write a letter. They're easy to make. First, open a new document and choose the formatting you want. When you're done, save the document with a name like Biz Ltr, Memo, or Standard Excel Template.

Then, on the desktop, select the document, hit ⌘I (for Get Info), and click the Stationery Pad checkbox in the window that appears. The next time you need to create a document with that formatting, open the template. The Mac will create a new, identical document, leaving the template untouched.

If you want to change the template, try opening it from within the application itself. If that doesn't work, select its icon in the Finder and uncheck the Stationery Pad checkbox in its Get Info window. Then open the template and modify it the way you would any document. After you've finished modifying it, be sure to check the Stationery Pad box again.

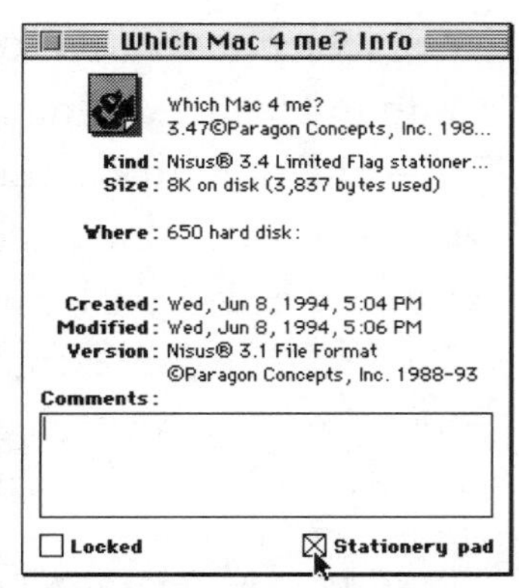

You can turn any document into a template from which the Mac can create new, identical documents by checking the Stationery Pad box in the Get Info window. (The Locked box is for documents that you want to protect from being changed.)

If you're using System 6, there's no stationery feature, but you can still make templates. Once you've made one, lock it with the Locked checkbox in the Get Info window, so you won't change it by mistake. When you open a template, use the Save As command immediately to create the new document. (Some applications also have an option for saving files as stationery inside the Save As dialog box.)

Running two systems (JK). It's usually not recommended to keep two systems on one hard drive, but that *is* a great way to try out a new system version without getting rid of the older one. (I worked that way for almost a year, switching back and forth between systems 6 and 7 without any problems.)

If you've got two hard drives, you can keep one system on each and switch between them using the Startup Disk control panel. Otherwise, you'll need **System Picker** and **Switcher** (both freeware programs) to tell your Mac which system to boot up from.

Before you install a second system, drag the System file out of your current System Folder and rename your System Folder (otherwise, your current system will be replaced).

Using Aliases

Making aliases (CR/JK/NL). You can make aliases (described under "Early System 7," above) of documents, applications, folders, even shared files on other computers. And since an alias isn't an actual copy, but just a remote control, it takes up only a couple of kilobytes on disk, even though it may represent a file or application that's several megs in size.

Making an alias is simple: You just select an item and then choose Make Alias from the File menu (or, in System 7.1.2 or 7.5, hit ⌘M). The alias will appear next to the original with its name in italics. You can then rename it or move it anywhere you want (the name stays in italics, though). You can move or rename the original, too, and the alias will usually keep track of where it went and what it's called. (Obviously, the original has to be somewhere accessible to your Mac, or it won't be able to open it.)

Since the menu is always accessible, many people put aliases there. Even the system software does that; the Control Panels command on the menu is nothing more than an alias for the Control Panels folder in the System Folder. (System 7.5 even comes with an AppleScript file that automatically installs, on the menu, an alias of anything you drag onto its icon.)

There are lots of ways to use aliases:

- You can't always keep applications out on the desktop or in your main hard disk window because they often demand folders of their own, containing dictionaries and other kinds of support files. But you can still access them easily through aliases. For example, you might have the Word application file inside a Word folder inside a Word Processing folder inside an Applications folder; but you can launch it without having to dig through all those folders by putting an alias of it on the menu or out on the desktop.
- What's good for applications is good for folders and documents, too. Keep aliases of letterhead and envelope templates right on the menu.
- If you like saving e-mail to a particular folder but the Save As dialog box always puts you in your on-line application's folder instead, put an alias of your e-mail folder there, and you won't have to navigate the list box every time you get a message.
- If you frequently go back and forth between two folders, put an alias of each inside the other.
- You can also make aliases for the Trash so that you don't have to hunt for it under open windows. Put Trash aliases inside any of the folders you use frequently. Then you can just drag files into the Trash alias when you're in that folder window.

Using aliases to mount shared disks (CR). Normally, to mount a shared disk or folder on your Mac, you have to open the Chooser, choose the AppleShare icon, select the server, type your name and password, click the OK button, select the shared item you want, click OK again, and then close the Chooser. But you can make an alias for a shared disk's icon that will store most of these steps and perform them automatically when you double-click on it.

First, mount the shared file as you normally would. Then select its icon on your desktop and choose Make Alias from the File menu. Then you can store the alias on the menu or anywhere you want. To mount the shared disk the next time, just double-click on the alias icon (or select the alias from the menu) and press Return (or click OK) in the dialog box that appears.

Using aliases to catalog files (NL). If you sometimes have trouble remembering which floppy disk or cartridge you've backed up a file onto, here's an easy way to catalog them. Make aliases of every file on every backup disk and put them in a folder on your hard disk (at just a couple of kilobytes per alias, they won't take up much room).

When you double-click on one of the aliases, the Mac will ask—by name—for the disk that contains it. (Be sure to physically label your backup disks with the same names they have on the desktop, or you still won't be able to find the right disk.)

Drag-and-drop file opening (JK/DD). It's handy to keep aliases of your favorite text and graphics applications out on the desktop so that you can use them (instead of TeachText or Simple Text) to open generic text and graphics files that you get. Just drag the file to the alias icon until the icon reverses and opens the file.

Customizing Your System

Opening files and running scripts automatically (JK). System 7 can run scripts or open files or programs automatically at startup or shutdown, if you add their icons to the Startup Items folder or Shutdown Items folder, respectively (the latter is available starting with System 7.5).

Speeding up name changes (JK/DD). If you're annoyed by how long it takes after you click on an icon's name before a frame appears around it—indicating that it's ready for editing—just move the mouse after you click and it'll be ready immediately. To reduce the delay that's built into the system, open the Mouse control panel and select the Double-Click Speed setting on the far right. That also sets the interval between clicking on a name and being allowed to change it. (There are also utilities, such as the shareware **Speedy Finder,** that do away with the delay.)

Customizing your system alert (NL/JK). On Macs that come with a microphone (or have one built-in, like the PowerBooks), you can record your own system alert sound. Just click the Add button and you'll get a set of controls like the ones on a tape recorder. Click the Record button, and start making noise.

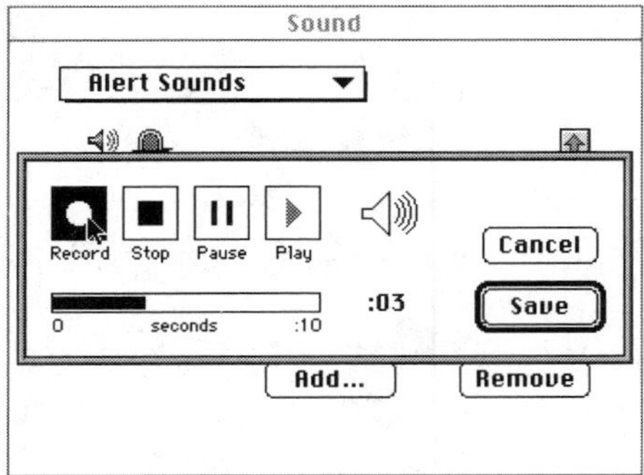

If your Mac has a microphone, you can record your own system alert using the Sound control panel.

You can also download sound files from on-line services and bulletin boards or buy them in commercial packages and add them to your system as beep sounds by dragging them to your System Folder icon. (If a sound is in a suitcase file, take it out first, since some systems delete the sound and suitcase when you try to install them this way.)

Silencing the Mac (AN/SA/EA). If you don't want to hear any system beeps, move the slider bar in the Sound control panel to 0; instead of making sounds, the Mac will flash the menu bar when it wants your attention. It will still play its chord when you start up or restart, though; to silence that sound, plug something into the audio-out port (labeled 🔊) on the Mac's back panel.

Blending your own highlight color (SA/NL/AN/JK). The Color control panel lets you change the color of window borders and the background that surrounds highlighted text. (You change the pattern of the desktop itself in the Desktop Patterns or General Controls control panels.) A list of colors appears on pop-up menus, and you can also mix your own highlight color.

To create a special color, select Other from the Highlight color pop-up menu. That opens the color wheel dialog box shown on the next page. (Yours may look somewhat different, depending on what system version you're using. It will also look less like the surface of the moon, because it will show colors instead of grayscale as in the illustration.) The wheel has a dot in it that shows the currently selected color. You can click anywhere in the wheel to move the dot, or you can drag it around.

To change the *hue* (the actual color), move around the circle. To decrease the *saturation* (the intensity of the color), move in toward the center of the circle.

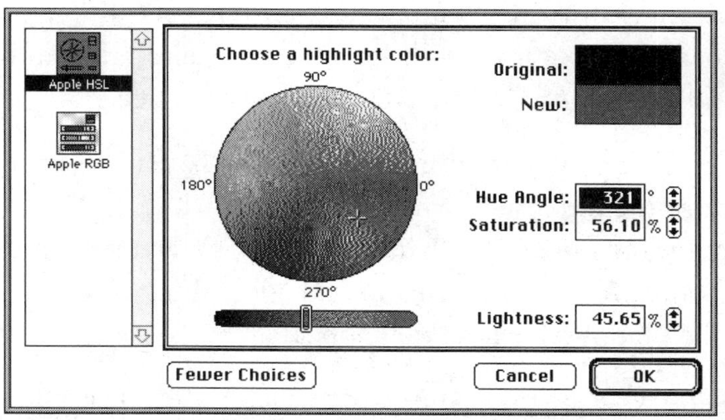

You can mix your own highlight color with the Color control panel's color wheel.

To change the *brightness*, use the scroll bar below the wheel. (When you move the scroll bar all the way to the left, you get black no matter what the hue or saturation is.)

In the upper-right corner is a two-toned square of color; the lower half of it shows the current color and the upper half the new color. Below that are numeric representations of the current color. You can work directly with them if you like, either by typing in new numbers or using the arrows.

Click OK when you have a color you like. Keep the color relatively light—selected text doesn't invert to white against a highlight color, so dark colors make selections unreadable.

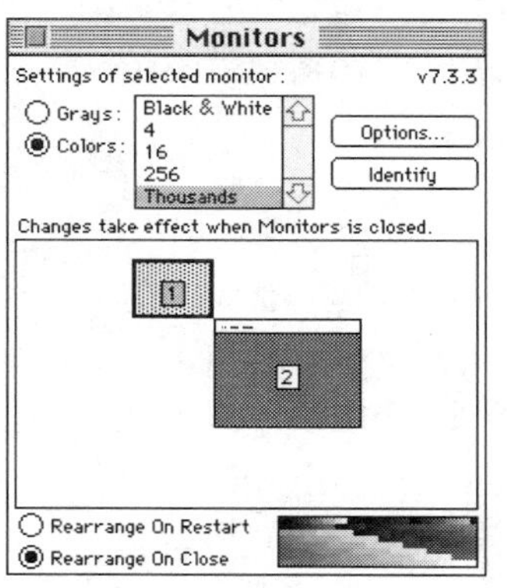

If you have multiple monitors, you show the Mac how you want their screens to intersect in the Monitors control panel. Positioning them in a diagonal relationship minimizes the problem of losing your cursor into the neighboring monitor.

Positioning extra monitors (AN). If you have more than one monitor connected to a Mac, the Monitors control panel lets you decide which one gets the menu bar and the desktop windows, and how you want the screens positioned in relation to each other. You can position them the way they really are on your desk, or any other way you want—as long as the squares that represent the monitors in the control panel are touching.

I use Monitor 1 only for color programs and usually leave it turned off. But the pointer still travels into the part of the desktop set aside for Monitor 1 (to get it not to do that, I'd have to actually remove Monitor 1's video card from my Mac). It's quite annoying to have the pointer keep disappearing into a black screen, so I position Monitor 1 so that it's just touching the least-used

corner of Monitor 2 (away from both scroll bars), as shown on the previous page. Amazingly, I still lose the pointer a fair amount, but less often than if I positioned Monitor 1's desktop anywhere else.

To change which monitor the menu bar shows up in, you just drag the miniature menu bar (shown at the top of Monitor 2 in the illustration) to the other monitor's icon. To change the Mac's startup monitor (the one that shows the Happy Mac and extension and control panel icons), hold down Option and drag the Happy Mac icon that appears.

The Mac assigns a number to each monitor; if you're not sure which screen is which, click the Identify button and the numbers will flash on the screens.

Keeping Finder windows small and fast (NL/AN/CR/JK). You can use the Views control panel to keep your Finder windows to a manageable size by minimizing the categories of file and folder information they show. The Show Version and Show Comments boxes come unchecked, and you should leave them that way. Most people rarely need this information, and if you do need it for a particular file, you can get it by selecting Get Info from the File menu.

Consider leaving the Show Label and Show Kind boxes unchecked as well; you'll be able to get a lot more information on your screen. There are much better ways to organize files than by labels, and you can get the kind information (telling which program created the document) with Get Info.

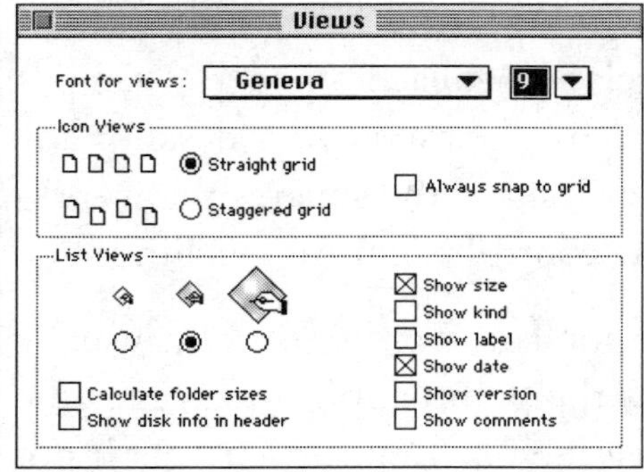

Checking fewer options in the Views control panel can help you keep desktop windows to a manageable size; choosing a lot of options can make the Mac sluggish when you're moving files and folders around.

If you're good at recognizing the different icons that applications give their documents, you can partially compensate for elimination of the Kind column in windows by selecting the middle-size file icon; then list-view windows will show a miniature of the file's actual icon rather than just a generic document or program icon.

Remember, though, that what you check in the Views control panel also determines what shows up on the View menu in the Finder. So, for example, if you want to be able to view files by date, you have to leave the Show Date box checked, even if you never look at that column in Finder windows—which is too bad, really, since that column is so wide.

You're also given the choice of having the Finder calculate and display folder sizes, but unless you need this information all the time, leave the box unchecked—it can really slow you down when you're moving or copying files.

System 6 Tips

Using the Control Panel (NL/JK). In System 6, control panels are called *cdevs* (for *c*ontrol panel *dev*ice*s*) and Control Panel is the name of the DA that lets you access them. When you select Control Panel from the menu, you get a window, like the one at right, with a scrolling list of icons displayed on the left side. When you click on an icon on this list, its controls appear in the area to the right.

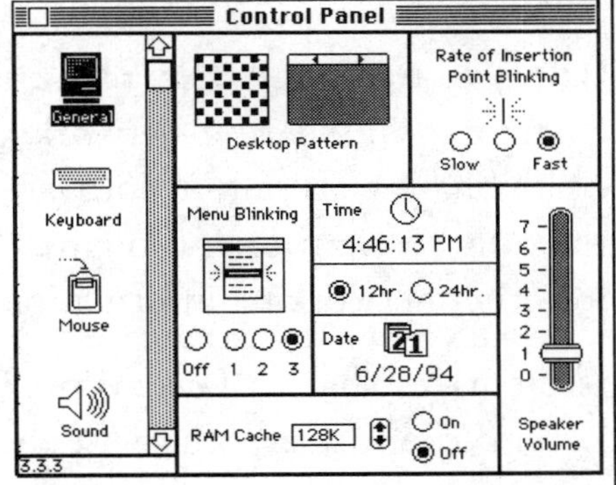

In System 6, all control panel utilities are in a single Control Panel box. To access new groups of controls, you click on the icons in the scrollable list at the left.

Because System 6 has fewer features than System 7, it has fewer control panels. System 6 includes the speaker volume and RAM cache controls in its General cdev, whereas System 7 handles them in its Sound and Memory control panels. Apart from these minor differences, though, cdevs/control panels work the same whether you're running System 6 or System 7.

Setting startup files in System 6 (CR). You can set your Mac to start with specific applications, folders, documents, or other items open. You use the Set Startup command in the desktop's Special menu (which also lets you set the Mac to start in the Finder or in MultiFinder). Here's how to use it:

- To start up in an application, select its icon on the desktop and then choose Set Startup. The dialog box that appears should indicate that that application is set to automatically open on startup. If you also choose to start up with MultiFinder, you can set documents or multiple applications to open in this way as well.

- To start up with a DA open, select it from the menu, choose Set Startup, and then click the Opened Applications and DAs button (but be aware that in doing so, you're also telling the Mac to automatically open whatever applications you're currently running).

If DA's disappear in MultiFinder (SA). If you just started using MultiFinder and find that there's little or nothing under your menu—or that you can't open anything that appears in the menu (all you get is a beep)—you need to put the DA Handler file into your System Folder. It's on the System Tools disk; just copy it over and restart your system.

Using 6 and 7 on the same network (CR/JK). Macs using System 6 and System 7 can share a network without any problems. System 6 Macs with AppleShare workstation software can even share the System 7 Macs' files (not the other way around, though). (See Chapter 23 for more on AppleShare and for other networking information.)

If the Macs share a LaserWriter, they must all have the same version of the LaserWriter driver; otherwise the printer will spend two minutes reinitializing every time it's used by a Mac with a different driver. Use the Installer on System 7's Printing disk to install the latest versions of the LaserWriter driver, Backgrounder, PrintMonitor, and other printing software on everyone's machines.

Memory

LIKE A PERSON, a computer with no memory would be helpless. Before your Mac can run a program or even display icons on the desktop, it has to load instructions into memory. Before you can edit a report, change the figures in a spreadsheet, or retouch an image, the Mac has to read the file into memory. And when you create a new document, it exists only in memory until you save it on disk.

The more memory you have available, and the more efficiently you use however much you have, the more you can do with your Mac: start up more programs, open bigger files, install more system extensions, look at more elaborate screensavers. And more memory makes many operations faster.

Fortunately, Macs are free of most of the arcane and archaic memory restrictions that bedevil users of DOS and DOS/Windows PCs. Unfortunately, the Mac memory story has become pretty convoluted in its own right. The aim of this chapter is to help you through this maze. You'll find out what memory is and what it does for you, how to determine how much you need, how to make the most of what you have, and how to add more if you need it.

Contributors

Henry Norr (HN) is the chapter editor.

Arthur Naiman (AN), Sharon Zardetto Aker (SA), and **Randy B. Singer (RS)** contributed to earlier editions of the *Macintosh Bible,* from which parts of this chapter were taken.

Contents

Memory Basics

Macs have several kinds of memory, but what people normally mean when they talk about a computer's memory is its *dynamic random access memory*, a term that's generally abbreviated to *DRAM* or just *RAM* for short. When the clerk at Sears, say, tells you the Performa 475 comes with 4 megabytes of memory, or when you try to open a scanned image in Adobe Photoshop and instead you get a dialog box informing you that there isn't enough memory, it's DRAM you're dealing with.

Physical Foundations (HN)

Physically, DRAM is made up of a bunch of silicon chips designed to serve as a temporary repository for digital information; inside these chips are thousands of microscopic switches, which the Mac turns on and off in particular patterns to represent words, numbers, pictures, sounds, and program code. This kind of memory is called *dynamic* because the Mac can change what's there at any time, adding, deleting, or moving information as it sees fit.

Most but not all Macs have some memory chips soldered onto their main logic board at the factory; the rest comes on small green plastic strips that plug into special slots on the logic board. You can add memory to the Mac by plugging in more of those cards (or replacing the old ones with new ones that have more memory capacity). Normally, these cards are called *SIMMs*, for *single in-line memory modules*, but PowerBooks and a few other models require different kinds of plug-in cards.

Memory vs. Storage (AN/Chris Allen/RS/HN)

The way computer systems store information bears some rough resemblance to the way we humans do. Broadly speaking, all the information available to us at any one time takes one of two forms: Some we have in mind—typically, important, recent, or frequently used information (plus, of course, an assortment of trivia). The rest is data we ourselves or others have stored away in more

The Many Flavors of Memory (HN)

It's common and convenient to call DRAM "RAM," but your Mac has other kinds of RAM that aren't D. All Macs, for example, have a small amount of what's called *parameter RAM,* or *PRAM,* where some basic hardware settings—like the speaker volume and other selections you make in the General Controls control panel—are stored; PRAM is maintained by a battery, so its contents will survive even when you shut down your Mac.

Some Macs also have *video RAM,* or *VRAM,* a special type of chip used to help display text and graphics on the screen; adding more lets you run a larger monitor, choose from among more colors, or both. High-performance Macs often have small amounts of *static RAM,* or *SRAM,* a kind of expensive, ultra-fast temporary memory. It's used in connection with processors so fast they'd be left twiddling their digital thumbs if they had to depend on standard DRAM to keep them supplied with instructions and data. Some PowerBooks even rely on something called *pseudo-static RAM.*

In addition, all Macs have another kind of memory that's not RAM at all: It's called *read-only memory (ROM)* because the Mac can read what's there but can't change, add, or subtract anything—ROM chips (generally known as ROMs) are designed to hold information permanently. Without its ROMs, a Mac wouldn't be much use. It wouldn't even start up, because code in the ROMs tells the machine what to do when you turn on the computer, and even if you could start the machine, it wouldn't be recognizable as a Mac because the chips also hold key instructions that the Mac operating system and Mac applications require.

permanent, if less accessible, forms—on paper, say. Before we can work with information of that second category—to include it in a report, for example—we have to read or review it so it's fresh in our minds; in effect, we move it into the first category.

In the case of computers, information in *memory* is analogous to what we have in our heads; information in *storage* is like what we have on file in our desks, file cabinets, libraries, and disks. The computer loads information—be it system software, application code, or data—into memory while it's in use. When it's not in use, that information is put in storage: on disks or tape. When you write a letter with your word processor or draw something in a graphics package, the new information you've created exists only in memory until you tell the computer, by giving the Save command, to put a copy in storage.

It's easy to confuse memory and storage. They're measured in the same units—bytes, kilobytes, megabytes, and so on (see "How Memory Is Measured" later in this section). There are gray areas that mix memory and storage, such as *RAM disks* and *virtual memory* (both discussed later in this chapter). And some people and manuals even refer to storage on disk as a form of memory.

Still, the basic distinction is fundamental: In memory, information is recorded electronically, by turning switches inside a silicon chip on and off; in storage it's saved magnetically on disks or tapes.

Two important practical differences flow from that technical one.

Volatility. Most kinds of RAM are *volatile:* Turn off the power and what was there is gone. Disk storage is non-volatile: You can shut down your drive, and your documents will still be there the next time you power up. If you've ever tripped over the power cord, had lightning knock out your electricity, or just suffered a system crash in the middle of a session on your Mac, you understand the distinction on more personal level: Barring serious damage to the disk, what you had previously saved to it will still be there, but work that was only in memory—what you did after the last time you saved—is gone for good.

Speed. Getting data to and from memory is much faster than writing or reading storage media. That's because storage devices involve moving mechanical parts, while the only things that move in memory chips are electrons.

How Come It Says I'm Out of Memory When There's Still Plenty of Room on My Hard Disk? (HN)

That's a question almost every new computer user poses sooner or later.

The fact is that the Mac, left to its own devices, is very clear about the distinction between storage and memory, and it won't substitute one for the other unless you give it some special instructions (described in the sections below on RAM disks and virtual memory). The processor in the machine can't work on information that's only on disk; it must first load that information into memory so it can have quick access to it. If there's no room in memory for the application you want to start up or the big document you're trying to open, all the disk space in the world won't help (unless you've set up virtual memory). And if, conversely, your hard disk is full, you can't save a file there, even if half your memory is free.

On a modern hard disk, the average access time—the time required, on average, to get to where data you're after is stored—is typically in the range of 10 to 20 *milliseconds* (thousandths of a second). That's a lot faster than most of us get around, but it's nothing compared to the speed of RAM: The DRAM chips in today's Macs respond in 60 to 80 *nanoseconds*, or millionths of a second.

How Memory Is Measured (AN/SA/RS/HN)

In the world of computers, memory, storage capacity, and data are all measured in the same units: bits, bytes, and multiples thereof. A *bit* (from "*bi*nary digi*t*") is the smallest unit of information. It can represent one of only two things—on or off, yes or no, zero or one. A *byte* is made up of 8 bits and thus lets you represent 2^8 (256) different pieces of information (00000000, 00000001, 00000011, and so on) in the *binary*, or *base 2*, numbering scheme that computers use.

A *kilobyte*, known familiarly as a *K* and sometimes written *Kbyte* or *KB*, equals 1,024 bytes. Since the prefix *kilo* means *thousand*, why 1024 bytes? Because computers, being binary-based, do things in multiples of two: 2, 4, 8, 16, 32, 64, 128, 256, 512, 1,024—a very familiar series of numbers if you've been around computers for a while.

Personal computer memory today is measured in *megabytes*. Usually called a *meg* and often abbreviated *Mbyte* or *MB*, a megabyte equals 1,024 kilobytes or 1,048,576 bytes (2^{20} bytes). Most Macs now come standard with 4 or 8 megs of RAM; depending on the model, you can boost your memory to as much as 256 megs. (The chart on pages 178–181 shows how much memory each kind of Mac can have, along with other details about the memory possibilities of different Mac models.)

Hard disk capacities, however, have already crossed into *gigabyte* (or *gig*, or *Gbyte*, or *GB)* range. That's 1,024 megs, more than a billion (2^{30}) bytes, or the equivalent of more than 2,600 of the 400K floppy disks used by early Macs. At this rate it won't be long before we reach the next plateau—the *terabyte*.

How Much Memory? (HN)

In theory, memory is one of those good things you can't really have too much of. But your Mac will set some limits for you, and so will your budget.

How Much Memory Do You Need?

How much memory you need depends, naturally, on lots of things: what Mac model you have, what system software and extensions you are running, what applications you use, and how many of them you want or need to keep open at once. In general, chances are you could use more memory than you think.

If you have an older Mac with only 1 or 2 megabytes and you are happy and productive with System 6 and the applications you got back then, there's no particular reason to spend your money on more memory.

But if you are running or planning to run 1990s software—applications, games, and most of all System 7—you really can't function effectively with less than 4 or 5 megabytes; after all, many users nowadays find the System alone taking up 2 megs or more, and it's common for today's major programs—and even many minor ones—to require at least that much.

In other words, on a 4-meg Mac, you'll be lucky if you can configure your system as you wish and run more than one or two programs at a time. If you want to use big programs like QuarkXPress and Adobe Photoshop, or have several programs open at once, you'll need 8 megs at a bare minimum.

And you don't want to run your Mac with its memory maxed out. Ideally, all software would handle low-memory situations gracefully, but that's far from reality: In my experience crashes are much more common when memory is tight. I like to leave at least a meg, preferably more, as a safety cushion.

A good rule of thumb, if you are buying a new Mac or considering a memory upgrade to your present setup, is to calculate how much RAM you think you're likely to need, and then see whether you can afford one and a half times or even twice as much. If you don't use it this year, you'll use it next year, and in the meantime it just might give your system an extra measure of stability.

24- and 32-Bit Addressing (HN)

To keep track of what's where in RAM, the Mac assigns each memory location a unique address. Originally, it used *24-bit addressing,* which simply means the addresses could be no more than 24 bits long. In the binary system, that comes out to roughly 16.77 million addresses. But the Mac reserved half of those addresses for other purposes, such as tracking information in ROM and on NuBus cards. That left only about 8 million addresses for RAM locations—hence an 8MB limit on available memory.

When the Mac was first designed, in the early 1980s, that seemed like plenty, but it soon became clear that Mac developers and Mac users would eventually demand access to more memory. So in the late '80s Apple began switching its own ROMs and system software over to *32-bit addressing* and urging Mac developers to do likewise. With 32 bits of address information, the available address space jumps to 4GB, of which 1GB is now set aside for memory.

32-Bit Clean

But the transition raised some problems. The Mac has always worked with information organized in blocks 32 bits long, but since only 24 bits were used in memory addresses, developers—including Apple's own software engineers—often used the remaining 8 bits for other kinds of information. If the Mac tried to read all 32 bits as an address, it would be steered in a very wrong direction, and crashes would result.

Software that properly used all 32 bits for addressing is known, in AppleSpeak, as *32-bit clean*. To work in 32-bit mode—to have access to more than 8MB of memory—your software (including the software stored in the ROMs of your Mac) must be 32-bit clean. Systems prior to System 7 and the ROMs in most Mac models developed in the 1980s were not 32-bit clean, which is why they couldn't normally handle more than 8MB; many applications and utilities from that era were also unclean, which is why they crash if you run them on a newer system using 32-bit addressing.

To preserve compatibility with old software, Apple left 24-bit addressing as the Mac's default mode for several years after it had cleaned up its own act, but it enabled System 7 users with clean ROMs to switch to 32-bit mode via the Memory control panel. By now, however, virtually all current software is 32-bit clean, so switching isn't ordinarily a big problem. In fact, in the Centris/Quadra 660AV, the Quadra 840AV, and the Power Macs, 32-bit addressing is mandatory (you don't have a choice), and that will no doubt be the situation with future Macs.

Cleaning Dirty ROMs

Even owners of the older Mac II models and the SE/30 now have access to more than 8 megs of RAM, despite their "dirty" ROMs. The problem was solved first with a free software patch called **MODE32,** which was developed by Connectix Corp. Under pressure from owners of these machines, Apple acquired the rights to MODE32 and began distributing it free. The company has since released its own equivalent software, called the **32-bit**

Enabler, but users have reported numerous compatibility problems with it. If you've got an SE/30 or one of those older Mac II models, and you need access to more than 8 megs, MODE32 remains your best bet. Both programs are widely available from user groups, online services, and savvy dealers.

Note that 32-bit memory addressing has nothing to do with another kind of 32-bit mode you are likely to hear about and maybe use: 32-bit Color QuickDraw (the "millions of colors" option available on some Macs, described in Chapter 15). All they have in common are similar names and binary mathematics.

Granted, you might be able to save some money if you wait and buy the extra RAM next year, since per-megabyte prices for RAM generally decline over the years. But they've been declining relatively slowly (and sometimes even rising) over the last few years: The previous edition of this book, published in 1992, gave $35 per megabyte as the typical mail-order price at the time. If you had postponed a RAM purchase then in hopes of declining prices, you'd still be waiting, and you wouldn't have had use of the extra RAM all this time.

How Much Memory Can You Have?

No matter what Mac model you have, there's a built-in limit on how much memory you can install. You can't add extra memory at all to the original 128K Mac or to the 512K or 512K Enhanced models (unless you get some unauthorized modifications made to your hardware). And the Plus, the SE, and the original Classic are limited to a maximum of 4MB of RAM.

Early Mac II models, such as the II, IIx, and IIcx, as well as the closely related SE/30, had the hardware to handle lots more memory, but System 6 and code in the machines' ROMs imposed an effective limit of 8 megabytes. With System 7 and some special software patches to fix the ROM problems (see the box on 24- and 32-bit addressing on these two pages), you can now install much more generous amounts of RAM in those models. (In the case of the original Mac II, however, you'll need to add a special memory management chip and get special SIMMs.)

The ROMs in newer Macs theoretically support up to a gigabyte of RAM—more than anyone could afford and, with current RAM chips, more than would fit in any desktop box. That means the main limiting factor nowadays is the number of SIMM slots Apple builds into each model. Most current desktop models allow much more memory than most users need, but the range varies widely. While the Quadra 650, for example, can handle up to 136MB of RAM, the 605 has only one SIMM slot, which can hold up to 32MB on top of the 4 megs soldered to the logic board.

PowerBook memory capacities are also limited by space—there simply isn't room for a lot of extra chips inside the notebooks' cramped cases. (See the box "Adding Memory to PowerBooks," later in this chapter.)

If you are shopping for a new Mac and expect to use memory-intensive programs such as Adobe Photoshop, or you're hoping to hold on to your new purchase for many years, it makes sense to give some consideration to differences in maximum memory when picking out a model, even though you are not planning to add extra memory immediately. Although 36 megs may sound like a lot now, that's what most people thought about 4 megs back in the days of the Mac Plus.

A summary of how much memory each Mac model can handle is supplied in the chart on pages 178–181.

Virtual Memory (HN)

Virtual memory, as its name implies, isn't real memory—it's hard disk space that's used as temporary memory. In effect, VM (as techies call it) enables your machine to work as if, or anyway *almost* as if, it had more RAM than it really does, so you can open more programs and larger files.

Virtual memory software comes free with System 7. All you have to do to turn it on is click a few buttons in the Memory control panel and reboot. But as this section will show, it's got significant downsides as well as upsides. For many people, it may be better to use one of the memory-stretching utilities described under "Managing Your Memory," below.)

Turn virtual memory on and off by clicking one of these radio buttons.

If you have more than one hard disk on your system, choose the disk you want to use.

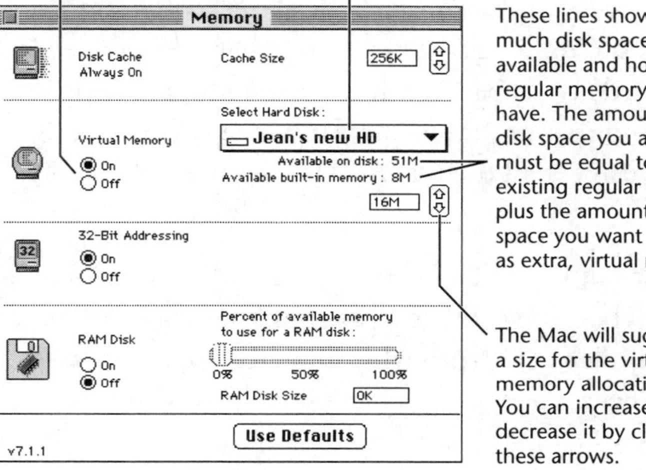

These lines show how much disk space is available and how much regular memory you have. The amount of disk space you allocate must be equal to the existing regular memory plus the amount of space you want to use as extra, virtual memory.

The Mac will suggest a size for the virtual memory allocation. You can increase it or decrease it by clicking these arrows.

You tell your Mac to use virtual memory by turning it on and typing the amount of disk space to set aside in the Memory control panel.

Pros and Cons

The main good thing about VM is that it gives you the functional equivalent of extra RAM for much less than the real thing. That's because disk capacity is so much cheaper than real memory—as little as a dollar per meg, as of early 1994, versus $35 to $40 a meg for RAM.

The downsides are several: VM can slow down your Mac appreciably, especially if you don't use it carefully. It can also eat up a lot of disk space: Apple's implementation requires that you set aside space on disk equal to the *total* amount of memory you want—including your real RAM—not just the extra virtual memory. And you can't use VM on Macs with 68000 processors (such as the Plus, SE, Classic, Portable, or PowerBook 100) or on 68020-based Macs, such as the LC and LC II and stock Mac IIs, which lack a special chip called a *paged memory-management unit* (PMMU). Apple's VM software won't work on most accelerator cards for these older machines, either, but Connectix offers an alternative called **Compact Virtual** ($100), which does work with most accelerators and even comes bundled with many of them.

Setting Up Virtual Memory

VM can slow your Mac down not only because hard disks are always slower than RAM, but also because there's a lot of extra reading and writing of the disk when the Mac has to *page*, or swap, data between it and memory. To minimize these problems, be sure to designate your fastest drive (if you have several online) as the location for the VM storage file.

Conventional wisdom (and Apple manuals) holds that performance suffers if you try to expand total memory to more than twice your actual RAM—in other words, if your Mac has 8MB of real RAM, for example, don't set total memory to more than 16MB. The experts at Connectix, however, call that a misconception—they contend that there's little overhead involved in keeping many programs open in the background, and that no serious performance issues arise as long as each of your applications can get all the real RAM it requires when you bring it to the foreground.

My own experience seems to bear out what Connectix says. You do suffer some delay during "context switches" (when you activate a program that's been in the background). But you'd have a similar delay (probably a longer one, in fact) if the application you want hadn't been open and you launched it directly from disk.

Serious slowdowns are likely, though, if you use VM to load an application so large it won't fit in real memory, even if it's the only one you are running. In that situation, the program may have to stop its operations frequently to exchange data between RAM and the swap file on disk—a real drag on performance.

Managing Your Memory (HN)

You probably don't think much about how your Mac uses memory, and ordinarily there's no reason you should. But if you find yourself unable to open as many programs as you think you should be able to, or if your programs are crashing or telling you they don't have sufficient memory, knowing what's going on back there can sometimes help you solve the problem.

How the Mac Divvies Up Its RAM

Some of your RAM is consumed by the Mac operating system; the rest is available for applications.

What the system takes is called the *system heap*. Its size depends on many factors, including the version of the system you are running; the extensions, cards, and other add-ons you've installed; and the size of the Disk Cache setting in the Memory control panel. (The disk cache setting is described under "The Memory Control Panel Cache," below.)

What's left over after all that is called the *application heap*. As you launch programs you want to work with, each lays claim to a chunk of the application heap, on a first-come, first-served basis, and programs don't give up what they've claimed until you quit.

About This Macintosh...

To see where your RAM is going, go to the Finder and choose About This Macintosh from the menu. In addition to detailing how much total memory is available and the size of the largest unused block of memory (see the illustration below), this screen shows with numbers and bar graphs how much memory the system and open applications have claimed. The filled-in part of each bar represents the proportion of the reserved memory actually in use.

This screen can be a useful tool for tuning and troubleshooting your system. If you find that an application's bar has a lot of unfilled white space—more than a third of the bar's total length, say—when you are using the program in your normal way (typical number and complexity of documents open, typical range of features in use), it may be taking more memory than it really needs. Conversely, if an application's bar is almost entirely filled, it's running low on free memory—a condition that can cause crashes.

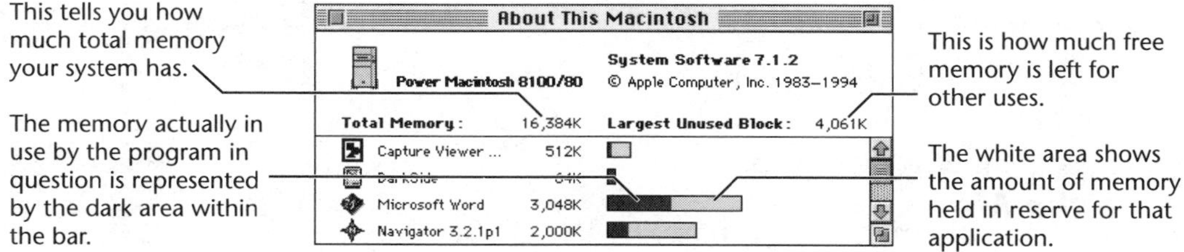

The screen you get by selecting About This Macintosh from the menu can help you understand where your RAM is going. It forms a bar chart that shows how much memory has been allocated to the system and each open application.

Changing Applications' Memory Usage

How much RAM a program normally takes is determined by information provided by the developer and stored inside a part of the program called the *SIZE resource*. But if your analysis of About This Macintosh suggests that some programs should be taking more or less RAM, you can easily change these settings.

To do this, close the program (if it's open). Then click on the program's icon on the desktop, and press Cmd I or choose Get Info from the Finder's File menu. In the lower-right corner of the Get Info box that then appears you will see a box called Memory Requirements containing (under System 7.1) three items: suggested size, minimum size, and preferred size. The first is the developer's advice about how much RAM the program needs. The second is the minimum the program requires; if that much isn't available, you won't be able to launch the program. The third item determines how much memory the program will grab if it can. (System 6 has just one "application memory size" field, and System 7.0 doesn't display the "minimum" field.)

WARNING

You can control how much memory your applications use by editing the values in the minimum and preferred fields. My advice is to never reduce the minimum value at all: Doing so would only increase the risk of poor performance and crashes. I'd also hesitate before setting the preferred amount to less than the developer's suggestion, even if About This Macintosh shows some memory going to waste (represented by white space within the bar). If, however, the preferred value is far above the suggested size, and you consistently see a lot of white space in the bar when you're using the program normally, you should be able to reduce the preferred setting safely, thus freeing up some memory for other programs.

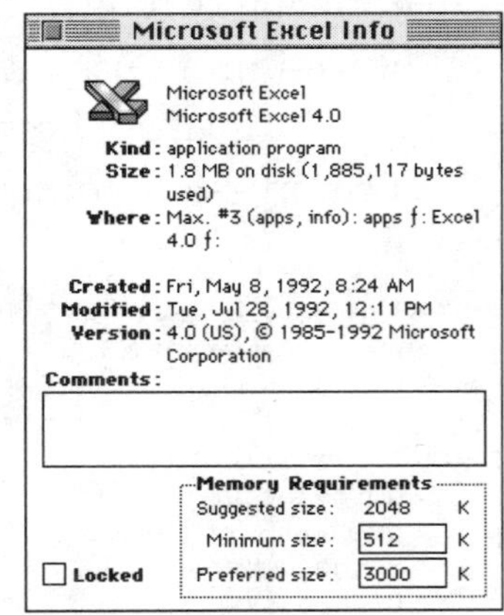

Selecting an application and then choosing the Get Info command brings up a box where you can specify the minimum and preferred amount of memory that should be set aside for that application next time it is opened

HOT TIP

If you've got the memory to spare, however, it's often a good idea to increase the settings. I routinely increase both the preferred and minimum memory sizes for each new program I install by about 25 percent. In some cases that's probably an unnecessary extravagance, but in my experience it tends to reduce the number of crashes I suffer, and I'm willing to sacrifice some RAM in the interest of stability.

Don't Let the System Take It All!

No matter how you slice it, System 7 needs a good bit of RAM—usually at least 2 megabytes, and up to 6MB in System 7.5. But if you want to preserve as much as possible for applications, here are several things to check:

- **The Disk Cache setting in the Memory control panel.** The disk cache is a section of your system heap the Mac operating system sets aside for holding (caching) information you've recently read from disk, so it can be retrieved quickly if it's needed again (how this works is described under "The Memory Control Panel Cache," below). If you prefer to have the RAM free for other purposes, you can reduce the cache setting.
- **The RAM Disk setting in the Memory control panel.** Memory set aside for a RAM disk (described under "RAM Disks," below) reduces the amount available for applications. (It is counted as part of the system's memory allocation in About This Macintosh.) If you are not using your RAM disk, shut it off and reboot so you can use the memory for other things.

Why Won't My Program Open When About This Macintosh Says I Have Enough Free Memory? (HN)

Occasionally, if you've opened and closed several applications, you may find yourself unable to open another program, even though you think you should have enough RAM available for it. That's usually because of a condition called *memory fragmentation,* which can leave parts of your free memory inaccessible.

Suppose you start a session with 4MB of memory free. You open a program that takes 1MB, then another that takes 2MB, then a third that takes the remaining 1MB. After working for a while you close the first and third applications. That leaves you with a total of 2MB free, but in two separate 1MB chunks, separated by the 2MB allocated to the application that's still open.

If you should now try to open a fourth program, one that requires 2MB of RAM, you'll run smack into a "not enough memory" dialog because the Mac requires a contiguous block of memory for each application.

The only solution I know of is to close the 2MB application, so you're back to having 4MB of memory free. Then you should be able to reopen that program, plus the second 2MB application that wouldn't open earlier.

- **The amount of memory you're devoting to extensions.** Unfortunately, the Mac alone doesn't give you that information, and neither do the developers of most extensions. But most of the leading commercial and shareware extension managers—utilities that let you monitor and control the loading of extensions—provide information on the amount of memory each extension requests as it loads. (Extension managers are described in Chapter 13.) Another option is **TattleTech,** a utility from Decision Maker's Software that reports detailed information about all aspects of your system. It's "goodcauseware" (the author, John Mancino, asks you to make a donation to a nonprofit organization of your choice), and it's excellent. Each extension might not take up a lot of memory, but taken together, they add up.

MAC BIBLE DISK

- **The number of fonts you are using.** How many fonts you are using can have an effect on the amount of memory your system consumes (see Chapter 14 for more on how to handle them).

Invest in a Memory-Management Utility

Two innovative utilities that appeared in late 1993 and early 1994—Jump Development Group's **OptiMem** and Connectix's **RAM Doubler**—introduced new ways to get more out of Mac memory. The two programs use different techniques, but each makes it possible to keep more applications and documents open without investing in more RAM or setting aside disk space for virtual memory.

GOOD FEATURE

OptiMem. Jump's OptiMem ($130) does its thing essentially by preventing applications from hogging more memory than they are actually using. It does this by intervening when a program is launching, and allocating it only the minimum amount of memory it needs to start up. (It uses the minimum setting displayed in System 7.1's Get Info window, except in cases where Jump has found in real-life testing that a higher amount is necessary.)

The memory thus saved is put in a special dynamic reserve and doled out in the form of small supplementary allocations to applications when they have actual need for it; when the operation that required the additional memory is over, the memory is returned to the central pool until it is needed again. The total memory listed in About This Macintosh doesn't change, but more programs can be open because the amount of RAM each reserves is reduced.

According to Jump, OptiMem works with any Mac but requires System 7.

RAM Doubler. With Connectix's RAM Doubler ($100), applications get the same memory allocation they would ordinarily get—when possible, the amount specified in the Get Info box's Preferred Size field. What's different is that the Mac system sees twice as much total memory as actual installed RAM. Most of the time, RAM Doubler produces the extra effective memory by shuffling the contents of RAM—essentially, it looks for RAM claimed but not actually used by applications in the background (the white parts of applications' bars in About This Macintosh) and temporarily gives that RAM to the program in the foreground. If that's not sufficient, RAM Doubler uses data compression techniques to compact the contents of RAM; only if that's still not enough does it swap memory contents to disk.

RAM Doubler is compatible with System 6.0.5 and up, but it requires an '030- or '040-based Mac or a Mac II with an add-on paged memory-management unit. Because RAM Doubler depends on the CPU to execute its on-the-fly compression and decompression algorithms, it works best on fast Macs. (A version that runs on Power Macintoshes should be out by the time you read this.)

Which one's best? Between the two programs, I'd say go for RAM Doubler if you have the right hardware. Connectix seems to know more about Mac memory than anyone, even Apple, and it shows: The program couldn't be simpler to install (one click and a reboot are all that's required). There's a slight performance penalty, but it's virtually unnoticeable most of the time on Macs with at least 8MB of real RAM. (Like VM, though, it's not a solution if you want to open one large application that wouldn't fit in your regular RAM.)

If you have an older Mac that won't run RAM Doubler, OptiMem is worth considering, but it's more complicated, it doesn't work with some applications, and its developers had to do a lot of special tweaking to get it to work with others; be sure to check that it works with your main programs before you invest in it, and if you do install it, stay in touch with Jump so you'll know about the frequent updates.

Using Memory to Improve Performance (HN)

If you are fortunate enough to have a surplus of memory and you're looking for a little extra performance, there are several ways you can use some of the former to add to the latter.

The Memory Control Panel Cache

Because RAM is speedier than any disk, your Mac should work faster when it can get the data it needs from memory instead of storage. That's why Apple built a *disk cache* (sometimes known also as a *RAM cache*) into the Mac operating system.

The cache is a portion of your Mac's memory set aside to hold information you have recently read from disk. How does this help performance? The answer is that, statistically speaking, there's a significant probability that data you've just read from disk will be needed again soon. That's not always true, of course, but it's true often enough to make the cache worthwhile. Under System 7 you can't even shut it off (though you can control how much RAM it gets).

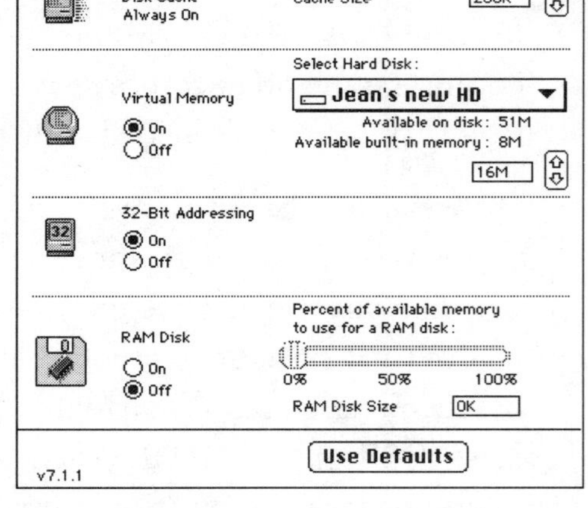

You can control the size of the built-in disk cache in the Mac's Memory control panel. System 7's Memory control panel is shown here; in System 6, you can also turn the cache (then called the "RAM cache") on and off. (The Memory control panel may look slightly different on your computer—its settings vary according to the hardware you have installed.)

The problem is that Apple's caching algorithms are not very efficient, so the disk cache provides only a slight performance boost, at best. And the larger the cache, the longer it takes to search it, so more time goes to waste when there's a *miss* (the desired data isn't there), and it takes longer to find it even when it is there.

> ### *Caches and Caches* (HN)
>
> The disk cache you manage from the Memory control panel probably isn't the only cache in your Mac. The 68030 and '040 processors, plus the PowerPC, have small caches built right into the chip. On some systems there is also a *secondary* or *Level 2 cache*—a bunch of high-speed static RAM on a card plugged into the logic board. The Mac IIci had a special slot for a cache card, and Apple eventually made such slots standard. The Power Macintoshes can also accommodate cache cards, and one comes standard with the Power Mac 8100/80. On top of that, many hard drives have their own cache memory built in.
>
> These caches are all different from the Memory control panel cache, but they all work on the same principle: All are designed to boost performance by holding data temporarily in some nearby, high-speed repository so it can be retrieved without going back to the slower sources from which it originally came.

The optimal point depends on your work habits and the software you're using, but most users find that a setting of 96K or 128K works best; some argue for 256K. Higher amounts slow performance, so you should reset it even if you have RAM to burn.

HOT TIP

It's especially important to set the cache to the minimum level if you're using Adobe's Photoshop, because interactions between the disk cache and Photoshop's own built-in virtual memory system can cause serious delays.

Alternate Caches

Some hard disk drivers implement their own caching schemes, and they do a better job than Apple does. (Hard disk drivers and what they do are described in Chapter 5.) **Spot On** from MacPeak Research and version 3 of **Drive7** from CasaBlanca Works let you turn on caching and choose among several configuration options in their control panels.

It's hard to know just how much good all this does, but in my experience it provides a small but perceptible performance boost. Competitors also seem to see something in the technology. At the time of this writing several said they intend to add caching to future versions of their driver packages.

RAM Disks

Another way to use memory to improve performance is to create a RAM disk—a chunk of RAM formatted so that the Finder sees it as a disk volume and can read and write files on it. There are two principal advantages to RAM disks and several disadvantages.

The advantages:

- **Speed.** Because all transactions on a RAM disk happen at electronic rather than mechanical speeds, they're much faster than similar operations on any physical disk. Many telecommunications users in particular find that downloading files to a RAM disk before moving them to a more permanent home can speed file transfers and thus reduce on-line charges.

- **Power savings.** On a PowerBook, if you can get all the system, application, and data files you are actively using into memory (either on a RAM disk or in the remaining main memory), you'll no longer need to access the PowerBook hard drive—you can let it spin down or even, if you've made the RAM disk the startup volume, unmount the real disk altogether by throwing its icon in the Trash. Since spinning drives require constant power, this technique can prolong battery life appreciably: By unmounting the drive in a PowerBook 170 and relying entirely on a RAM disk, I once made it from San Francisco to Atlanta on one battery. (A PowerBook with a sleeping drive is refreshingly quiet, too.)

The disadvantages:

- **Volatility.** The overriding problem with RAM disks is that they last only as long as the power is on. If it's cut off—by a power failure, an inadvertent shutdown, or a run-down battery—your work is gone for good. Several RAM disk programs, however, deal with this problem by automatically backing up your files to the hard disk.

- **Hassle.** Once you save a file to a hard disk, it should be there every time you turn on your system and mount that volume. In the case of RAM disks, you have to load files onto the disk every time you create one. There are several programs that can automate the process, but it still takes time. (On a PowerBook you can minimize this problem by letting your system sleep instead of shutting it down when you are not using it; RAM disks survive system sleep.)

- **Large RAM requirements.** To make a RAM disk big enough to hold an application (to say nothing of a System Folder!), you need to dedicate a lot of memory to it—memory that will no longer be available for any other purpose, such as opening applications. And if you copy an application to the RAM disk and then open it, you are devoting two large chunks of memory to it. Unfortunately, it's precisely where the advantages of a RAM disk are most compelling—on a PowerBook—that RAM is most limited and most expensive.

If all of this adds up to something worth trying, there is now a wide selection of utilities for creating and managing RAM disks.

The Memory control panel RAM Disk. Most recent Mac desktop and notebook models let you create and configure a RAM disk via—surprise!—the Memory control panel. (You have to restart before the new disk will appear on the desktop.)

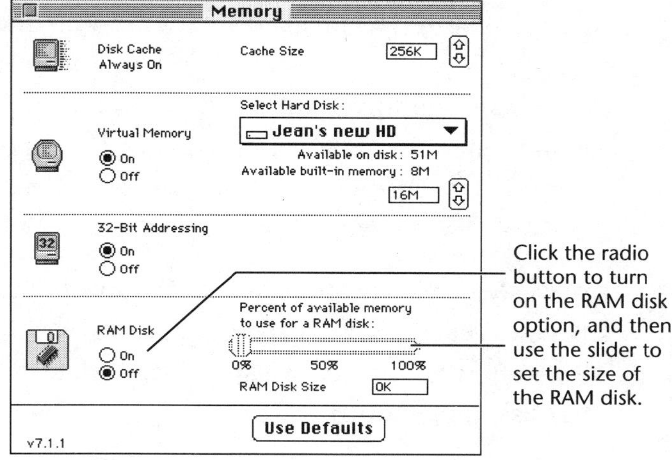

If you have a recent Mac model, one pane of the Memory control panel lets you set up a RAM disk, which will appear after you restart your machine.

The Apple software is missing two valuable features other RAM disk programs offer: automatic loading of preselected files when the disk is created and automatic backup to less ephemeral media. You can, however, add these capabilities by using other utilities in conjunction with or as an alternative to the Apple RAM disk software.

RamDisk+. A popular $35 shareware RAM disk program by Roger Bates, **RamDisk+** can automatically load files you have preselected onto the RAM disk at boot-up and copy new or modified files back to the hard disk folder they came from at user-defined intervals. Because the program can create its own RAM disk, it can be used on machines where Apple's software can't, and if you're running with 24-bit addressing, RamDisk+ can even use memory the Finder can't see. If, on the other hand, you create a RAM disk with the Memory control panel and then restart with the RamDisk+ extension also loading, the latter will provide its file-loading and backup services for the Apple-created volume. (It's even smart enough not to try creating a second RAM volume itself.)

Atticus RAMDiskSaver. Atticus RAMDiskSaver, a $70 utility from Atticus Software, was designed specifically to work with RAM disks created with the Memory control panel. It can be set to back up files on the RAM disk either to a special folder or to their original location when you shut down, on command or at regular intervals; thereafter, it can reload the same files onto the Apple RAM disk at startup.

Maxima. Connectix's $100 entry in the RAM disk category also creates its own RAM disk and provides automatic backup and loading, and it, too, can utilize excess memory otherwise invisible in 24-bit mode. (In addition, it can extend the system memory limit in 24-bit mode from 8MB to as much as 14MB and use the remaining RAM as a RAM disk.) **Maxima 3.0,** a new version under development at this writing, adds an on-the-fly compression feature to increase the RAM disk's effective capacity.

MAC BIBLE DISK

AppDisk. A $15, System 7–only shareware utility from Mark Adams, **AppDisk** lets you create a RAM disk at any time, without rebooting. It also provides an auto-save function (curiously, it saves data from the RAM disk right into the AppDisk application).

Adding More Memory

(HN)

The earliest Macs, back in 1984 and 1985, had their meager memory soldered to their logic boards and no slots for adding more. Fortunately, Apple came to its senses before too long, and since 1986 almost every new Mac has had slots that make it easy to add more memory.

Except in the case of the Mac Portable, PowerBooks, and some versions of the original Mac Classic (all of which require specially designed memory cards), adding memory means plugging in extra SIMMs.

All About SIMMs

SIMMs generally measure about 1 by 4 inches, in most cases they hold eight RAM chips, and for some reason they are always green.

It would be nice if you could just walk into a dealer or pick up the phone and order a generic SIMM anytime you wanted to put more RAM in your Mac. Dream on. The bad news is that SIMMs come in hundreds of varieties, and only one or two will work on your Mac.

RAM Speed (HN)

Though the rate of change has been slow by computer-industry standards, RAM chips have grown steadily faster over the years as manufacturing techniques have improved and system designers have searched for ways to keep speedy processors supplied with data. The Plus and the SE used memory that poked along at 150 nanoseconds; the Quadra 840AV needs RAM rated at 60 nanoseconds. (Remember, fewer is faster.)

If you are buying add-on RAM, you (or the vendor you are buying from) need to know the speed your Mac requires—RAM that's too slow will make your system unreliable. Buying memory that's faster than your system requires doesn't do any harm—as long as you don't install it in the same bank with slower memory—but neither will it improve your Mac's performance.

You can narrow things down by excluding PC SIMMs, which usually have a ninth chip for something called parity (cleverly designed to crash your system if a passing cosmic ray or some other electronic quirk happens to mess up your memory). These *parity SIMMs* will fit in Mac SIMM slots, and some Mac owners have successfully used them, but there's really no percentage in trying.

But even among Mac SIMMs there are dozens of variables: chip density (from 256 kilo*bits* to 16 mega*bits*, for now), total SIMM capacity (from 256 kilo*bytes* to 32 mega*bytes*), pin count (30 on older Macs, 72 on new ones, 64 on the oddball Mac IIfx), and memory speed (from 150 nanoseconds on the Plus and SE down to 60 nanoseconds on the Quadra 840AV).

Even if you've identified the type of SIMM you need, you can't just buy one and add it to whatever memory you already have: There's a complex set of rules about what amounts of total memory each Mac model will support, whether and how you can combine different capacities in the same Mac, and, in Macs with several banks of SIMM sockets, which to fill first.

In short, it's a mess, and there's really no way and no reason for anyone except memory vendors to try to keep it straight. The only rational strategy is to deal with vendors who know the Mac well, check to make sure they have a money-back, no-hassle guarantee, tell them exactly what Mac model you have, and hope and pray they'll sell you the right SIMMs. If you want to bone up a little first, though, take a gander at the memory configurations chart on pages 178–181.

Buying Memory

SIMMs are available from most of the same sources as other computer equipment, and with the same caveats: Storefront computer dealers usually have the highest prices; discount electronics outlets and the computer superstores that have sprung up in most metropolitan areas generally come next; and mail-order vendors normally have the lowest prices. (See Appendix C for more on buying Mac-related hardware and software.)

Adding Memory to PowerBooks (HN)

Boosting the memory in Apple's notebook models presents some special problems. RAM for PowerBooks tends to be more expensive than for desktop Macs, since the notebooks require lower-power chips and specially designed memory expansion cards rather than standard SIMMs. To compound the problem, the design seems to change with each new model. Apple makes its specs available to selected outside manufacturers, but sometimes not in final form until just before or even after new models are released; the manufacturer then has to design the card and find sources for the necessary components.

For all these reasons, RAM expansion cards for new PowerBook models are often scarce and expensive when the machines first ship. Several times third-party RAM vendors, unable to get adequate supplies of Apple-spec components (because Apple is taking everything available), have come out with alternative technologies. Sometimes they work fine, but there have been cases where vendors have had to stop shipments and make changes in their cards after problems cropped up.

I don't ordinarily advise people to buy memory from Apple, because it usually costs too much, but if you are buying a brand-new notebook, consider ordering it with a full complement of RAM, or else plan to wait a few months while the dust settles (and prices come down) before buying from a third party.

Fortunately, relief is on the way. The latest PowerBooks, following the example of Apple's Newton MessagePad and many PC laptops, have a new type of slot that makes it much easier to install extra memory (as well as tiny hard disks, modems, or other add-ons). Without even opening the case, you can just slide a credit-card-shaped circuit board into the system. It's known as a PCMCIA slot, because it's based on a standard set by an industry group called the Personal Computer Memory Card International Association, but computer industry wags have come up with lots of alternative interpretations of the name—my favorite is People Can't Memorize Computer Industry Acronyms.

Before you hit the phones, arm yourself with a little knowledge about current prices. The best way to do so is to find a recent copy of *MacWEEK*, the Mac newsweekly, and check the ads. (I work at *MacWEEK*, so my biases are obvious, but most people in the industry agree that the publication's back pages have become the marketplace where prices on Mac memory and peripherals are set.) If you can't find a copy of *MacWEEK* (it's not available on newsstands), look in the monthlies, *Macworld* or *MacUser*, for phone numbers, but call for current prices. They change fast.

Among the mail-order vendors, the differences in quality and service seem smaller than they used to be, and nowadays most major suppliers are knowledgeable about the Mac; the suggestions that follow are by no means exclusive. But when I have to buy RAM, the first place I call is Technology Works (a.k.a. TechWorks) in Austin, Texas, because it meets all my criteria: Prices are good (though generally not the very lowest); the products are first-class; the people are deeply committed to the Mac; the company provides a 30-day money-back guarantee, lifetime warranty, and toll-free tech support; and it's big enough to give me confidence it'll be around long enough to make those promises meaningful.

GOOD FEATURE

Among the alternatives, The Chip Merchant in San Diego is generally reputed to have the lowest prices, and despite some problems in the past, service is now said to be good. Newer Technology in Wichita, Kansas, has somewhat higher prices, but it's a pioneer on the capacity and performance frontier and generally among the first to market with reliable support for new Apple products. Other well-regarded suppliers include Microtech International of East Haven, Connecticut, and The LLB Company of Bellevue, Washington.

BARGAIN

Can You Install It Yourself?

Installing SIMMs in most Macs is not too difficult, but it can be tricky until you've learned the ropes, and there's some risk involved: A slip of the hand and you could snap off some little piece of plastic—next thing you know you'll be faced with a bill for a new logic board. I've installed Mac memory many times, but I've never once done it without breaking into a nervous sweat. I've found Mac SEs and PowerBooks particularly hairy, just because space is so tight.

There's no shame in paying someone to do the job for you, any more than in paying a mechanic to do routine maintenance on your car. That said, you can save some money and acquire a little sense of mastery over the technology if you do it yourself. A few pointers:

- Make sure you have good instructions and read them over before you start. Major RAM suppliers usually provide illustrated installation guides; some offer instructional videos.
- Don't try to do the job on a cluttered desk. Set up an unencumbered workspace with room for all the parts you have to remove.
- Don't start unless you know you have plenty of time available. You sweat more if you're watching the clock.

- You need unusual tools to open the cases of compact Macs and PowerBooks, and you won't get far if you don't have them. You'll a need long-shafted Torx T-15 screwdriver for compact Macs such as the Plus, SE, or Classic; Torx T-8 and T-10 screwdrivers for PowerBook 100-series models; and a T-8 to add RAM to a PowerBook Duo. Your RAM vendor should be able to supply the tools you need, or you can find them at automotive parts stores.
- You should use an antistatic mat and wear an antistatic bracelet while working inside the machine. (I don't, but I *should*.)
- Be sure to unplug your system before opening it. If you're operating on a PowerBook, make sure it's fully shut down, not just sleeping. Remove the battery, too, and then wait several minutes before starting to work.

Finding Out More

As you've undoubtedly figured out by now, the Mac memory story is pretty complicated. Connectix Corp., in addition to developing a whole series of useful, memory-related utilities, has done the Macintosh community a major service by producing a comprehensive handbook on the subject called the *Macintosh Memory Guide*. It contains a detailed history of Mac memory, along with tables detailing everything you need to know about memory options and requirements for all Mac models past and present.

Where Did All My New Memory Go? (HN)

With the latest Mac models you don't have to do anything special to take advantage of any amount of memory your Mac can handle. But with older machines there is a small but easily overlooked extra step required: opening the Memory control panel, clicking on one radio button to switch from 24-bit addressing to 32-bit addressing, and restarting your Mac.

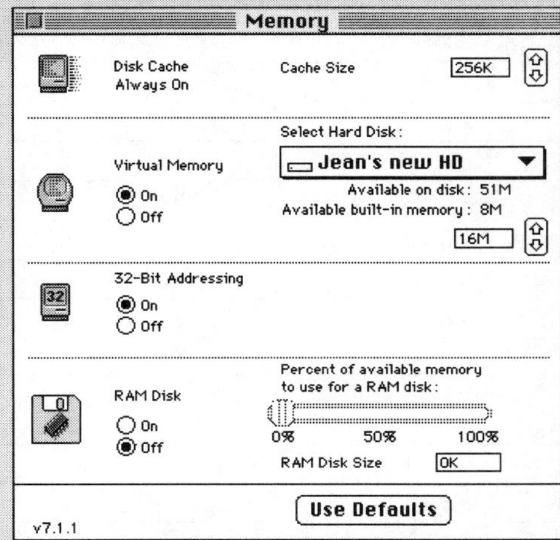

After increasing your memory to more than 8MB, you may need to change your system's memory use by turning on 32-bit addressing in the Memory control panel. If 32-bit addressing is off, the Mac can address only 8MB of memory, no matter how much you actually have installed.

The way Macs used to keep track of what was in memory, 24-bit addressing imposes a limit of 8MB on system memory, regardless of how much is installed. Switching to 32-bit mode removes that limit. (For more on 24- and 32-bit addressing, see the box on page 158.)

If your older Mac came with 8 or fewer megs of RAM, it is probably set to run in 24-bit mode. If you forget to change it, you can spend $300 for another 8 megs, install it, and find that you don't have any more memory available than before. (If you are in 24-bit mode, About This Macintosh depicts any installed memory beyond 8 megs as part of what the Mac System takes up.)

Connectix used to give the booklet away free. Now it only distributes and updates it in electronic form, via user groups and on-line services. But if you prefer hard copy, you can get an up-to-date version of much of the same material in booklet form from Technology Works, the memory vendor mentioned above. Ask for the *Memory Solutions Guide.*

Another information resource along the same lines is *SimmStack*, a HyperCard stack developed and regularly updated by Apple's Mark Hansen. It, too, is available free from on-line services and user groups.

Memory Configurations for Different Mac Models

Mac Model	RAM soldered on (MB)	SIMM slots	Possible SIMM Sizes (MB)	Possible RAM Configs (MB)	RAM Speed	Notes
128*	128K	0	N/A	128K	N/A	
512K/512Ke*	512K	0	N/A	512K	N/A	
Plus*	0	4	256K,1	1,2.5,4	150ns	1,4
SE*	0	4	256K,1	1,2,2.5,4	150ns	1,4
SE/30*	0	8	256K,1, 4	1,2,4,5,8,16,17,20,32	120ns	4
Classic*	1	2	256K,1	1,2,2.5,4	150ns	1,2
Classic II	2	2	1,2,4	2,4,6,10	100ns	3
Color Classic	4	2	1,2,4	4,6,8,10	100ns	3
LC*	2	2	1,2,4	2,4,6,10	100ns	3
LC II*	4	2	1,2,4	2,6,8,10	100ns	3,8
LC III, Performa 450	4	1	1,2,4, 8, 16,32	4,5,6,8,12, 20, 36	80 ns	3, 18
Performa 200*	2	2	1,2,4	2,4,6,10	100ns	3
Performa 400*, 405*, 430*	4	2	1,2,4	2,6,8,10	100ns	3,8
Performa 475, 476	4	1	4,8,16,36	4,8,12,20,36	80ns	
Performa 600*	4	4	256K,1, 2, 4, 16	4,5,8,12,20, 68	80ns	3,10
Performa 550	4	1	1,2,4, 8, 16, 32	4,5,6,8,12, 20, 36	80 ns	
II*	0	8	256K,1,4	1,2,4,5,8,17,20	120ns	1,4,5,6,7
IIx*	0	8	256K,1, 4	1,2,4,5,8,16,17,20,32	120ns	1,4,5,6,7
IIcx*	0	8	256K,1,4	1,2,4,5,8,16,17,20,32	120ns	4
IIci*	0	8	256K,512K,1,2, 4	1,2,3,4,5,6,8, 9,10,12, 16,17,80ns	80ns	3
IIfx*	0	8	1,4	4,8,16,20,32	80ns	3,9
IIsi*	1	4	256K,512K,1,2,4	1,2,3,5,9,17	100ns	3
IIvi*	4	4	256K,1,2,4,16	4,5,8,12,20,68	80ns	3,10
IIvx*	4	4	256K,1,2,4,16	4,5,8,12,20,68	80ns	3,10
Centris 610*, Quadra 610, AWS 60	4	2	4,8,16, 32	4,8,12,20,36,40,44, 52,68	80ns	3,18
Centris 650*, Quadra 650	8	4	4,8,16,32	4,8,12,16,20,24,28,32, 36,40, 44,48,52,56,60, 64,68,72,76,80, 84,88, 92, 96, 100, 104, 108, 112, 116, 120, 132	80ns	19
Centris 660AV	4	2	4,8,16,32	4,8,12,20,36,68	70ns	3,18
Quadra 605	4	1	4,8,16,36	4,8,12,20,36	80ns	
Quadra 700*	4	4	1,4	4,8,20	80ns	3
Quadra 900*	0	16	1,4	4,8,12,16,20,24,28,32, 36,40,48,52,64	80ns	3

* Product no longer being produced by Apple.

Notes

1 Third-party 1MB SIMMs with only two chips are incompatible with these computers. Apple two-chip 1MB SIMMs may be found, however, in the SE/30, IIci, IIsi, LC and Quadra 950.

2 The Classic has 1MB of RAM soldered to its logic board. Additional RAM requires an expansion card. Apple's Macintosh Classic 1MB Memory Expansion Card has 1MB of additional RAM and two SIMM connectors.

3 These systems have 32-bit-clean ROMs. Computers with 32-bit-clean ROMs can take advantage of more than 8MB of physical RAM under System 7.

4 The ROMs in these systems are not 32-bit-clean, but with the 32-Bit System Enabler under System 7.1 or MODE32 with versions of System 7 prior to 7.1, they can run in 32-bit mode and can take advantage of more than 8MB of physical RAM.

5 The Mac II and IIx require special 4MB SIMMs. Be sure to specify your Macintosh model when ordering these SIMMs and make certain the vendor is aware of the difference. The Mac II requires the Macintosh II FDHD Upgrade to use 4MB SIMMs.

6 To take advantage of more than 8MB of physical RAM, the Macintosh II must have a PMMU installed and the 32-Bit System Enabler (or MODE32 with versions of System 7 prior to 7.1).

7 The Macintosh II won't start up if you install 4MB SIMMs in bank A. Install 4MB SIMMs in bank B, and use 256K or 1MB SIMMs in bank A.

8 These systems can address a maximum of 10MB of RAM. When the SIMM slots are filled with 4MB SIMMs, the lower 2MB of DRAM on the logic board can't be addressed.

9 The IIfx requires 64-pin SIMMs.

10 Only eight-chip 16MBx1 SIMMs have been tested on the Mac IIvi and IIvx.

11 The Macintosh Portable has 1MB of RAM soldered to the main logic board. You can add more RAM using an expansion card, which can have from 1MB to 4MB of RAM or, in the case of the backlit Portable, 1MB to 3MB of RAM.

12 If the processor-direct slot (PDS) is used for other peripherals, the maximum RAM is 5MB for the Portable and 4MB for the backlit version.

13 The PowerBook 100 has 2MB of pseudostatic RAM on the main logic board and one expansion slot. Additional RAM requires a RAM expansion card.

14 The PowerBook 140, 145, and 170 have 2MB of pseudostatic RAM on the main logic board and one expansion slot.

15 The PowerBook 145B, 160, 165c, 180, and 180c have 4MB of pseudostatic RAM on the main logic board and one expansion slot.

Memory Configurations for Different Mac Models (continued)

Mac Model	RAM soldered on (MB)	SIMM slots	Possible SIMM Sizes (MB)	Possible RAM Configs (MB)	RAM Speed	Notes
Quadra 950, AWS 95	0	16	1,4	4,8,12,16,20,24,28,32, 36,40,48,52,64	80ns	3
Quadra 800*, AWS 80	8	4	4,8,16, 32	8,12,16,20,24,28,32, 36,40,44,48,52,56,60, 64,68,72,76,80,84,88, 92,96,104,108,112, 120,136	60ns	19
Quadra 840AV	0	4	4,8,16,32	8,16,32,64,128	60ns	3,18
Power Mac 6100/60	8	2	4, 8, 16,32	8,16, 24, 40, 72	80ns	21
Power Mac 6100/60AV	8	2	4, 8, 16,32	8,16, 24, 40, 72	80ns	21
Power Mac 7100/66	8	4	4, 8, 16,32	8, 16, 24, 32, 40, 56, 72, 80, 88, 104, 136	80ns	21
Power Mac 7100/66AV	8	4	4, 8, 16,32	8, 16, 24, 32, 40, 56, 72, 80, 88, 104, 136	80ns	21
Power Mac 8100/80	8	8	4, 8, 16,32	8,16,24,32,40,48, 56, 64, 72,80,88,96, 104,112.120,136,144, 152,160,168,176,184, 192, 200, 208, 216, 224, 232, 264	80ns	21
Power Mac 8100/80AV	8	8	4, 8, 16, 32	8, 16, 24, 32, 40,48, 56, 64, 72, 80,88,96, 104, 112. 120,136,144, 152, 160, 168,176,184, 192, 200, 208, 216, 224, 232, 264	80ns	21
Portable*	1	N/A	N/A	1,2,3,4,5,6,7,8,9	100ns	4,11,12
Portable* (backlit)	1	N/A	N/A	1,2,3,4,5,6,7,8	100ns	4,11,12
PowerBook 100*	2	N/A	N/A	2,4,6,8	100ns	3,13
PowerBook 140*,145*	2	N/A	N/A	2,4,6,8	100ns	3,14
PowerBook 145B	4	N/A	N/A	4,6,8	100ns	3,15
PowerBook 170*	2	N/A	N/A	2,4,6,8	100ns	3,14
PowerBook 160*	4	N/A	N/A	4,6,8,10,12,14	100ns	3,15
PowerBook 165*	4	N/A	N/A	4,6,8,10,12,14	100ns	3,15
PowerBook 165c*	4	N/A	N/A	4,6,8,10,12,14	85 or100ns	3,15,16
PowerBook 180*	4	N/A	N/A	4,6,8,10,12,14	85 or100ns	3,15,16
PowerBook 180c*	4	N/A	N/A	4,6,8,10,12,14	85 or100ns	3,15,16
PowerBook Duo 210*	4	N/A	N/A	4,6,8,10,12,16,24	70ns or 85	3,17
PowerBook Duo 230*	4	N/A	N/A	4,6,8,10,12,16,24	70ns	3,17
PowerBook Duo 250	4	N/A	N/A	4,6,8,10,12,16,24	70ns	3,17
PowerBook Duo 270	4	N/A	N/A	4,6,8,10,12,16,24,32	70ns	3,1*

* Product no longer being produced by Apple.

Notes (continued from page 179)

16 For the PowerBook 165c, 180, and 180c, we suggest 85ns pseudostatic RAM. Use of 100ns pseudostatic RAM results in a performance decrease of approximately 5 to 10 percent.

17 The PowerBook Duo 210 and 230 have 4MB of low-power DRAM on the main logic board and one expansion slot.

18 These systems use 32-bit wide, 72-pin SIMMs (fast-paged mode) not previously used in Macintosh computers.

19 These systems use "memory interleaving" when SIMM pairs are used (for example: two 8MB SIMMs). This can improve performance 5 to 10 percent. The Centris 610, Centris 650, and Quadra 800 have flexible memory systems, meaning that any supported SIMM size can go into any SIMM socket in any order, and they can run with partially populated banks. They don't support 1MB, 2MB, or 64MB 72-pin SIMMs.

20 Some early Centris models had only 4MB of RAM soldered on the logic board. Those units cannot be configured to hold 96, 112, or 120MB of RAM.

21 Power Macs use 32-bit, 72-pin SIMMs, and they must be installed in pairs of equal capacity.

Editors' Poll: What Kind of Mac Do You Use as Your Primary Workstation? How Much Memory and Storage?

AA: A Mac IIci, and after three years I still love it. (It does help to have a 24-bit accelerator card, a RAM cache, and so on.) I've got 20MB of RAM, for those Photoshop-PageMaker-Word-TouchBase-CompuServe days, and 600MB of storage. (Data files, like *Mac Bible* chapters, are on Pippin, my internal 80MB disk; applications and art files are on Goliath, the external 529MB drive.)

DB: I use my 128K Mac for a hatrack, my SE as a QuickMail server for the office, and I'm sending my IIsi to my folks so they can learn how to use a Macintosh. Now I'm using a Quadra 650 for most of my work, and on the road I use a PowerBook 170. Because I do a lot of work with desktop publishing, I need the power of the 650, and I've also added some cards like a SuperMac Thunder II to speed up my Photoshop work. I've got 24MB of RAM, but now I wonder when I'll be able to afford 64. I've got a 400MB hard drive, a 120MB drive, a SyQuest 44 with 15 cartridges, and a handful of 128MB magneto-opticals. And I'm running out of space.

EC: Centris 660AV with 16MB of memory (which seems like enough to me, although my Photoshop-loving husband wishes we had more). I've got a 500MB hard drive and an 88MB SyQuest with about 30 cartridges.

DD: A IIci 8/80, with a 230MB external hard drive and a 44MB Syquest on the old SCSI chain.

CG: I spend equal time working on a Power Book 160 (4/80) and a Mac IIci with a 14-inch Apple monitor, 17MB of RAM, an extended keyboard, a 210MB internal hard disk, a 105MB external hard disk, and a 2,400-baud external modem.

JK: Centris 650 with 16MB of RAM and a 230MB hard drive.

HN: I've got a Power Mac 8100/80. I've got 16MB of memory and two 1-gig drives for storage.

BW: Currently, I'm using a IIsi with 6MB (I really should have double that).

5 Storage

If you're like most computer users, you aren't much more interested in computer storage than in bookcases. Like shelves, after all, hard drives, floppies, CD-ROM drives, and tape backup units don't actually do much—they just provide a place to leave the files you've created and collected when you're not using them.

In fact, though, nothing is more critical to the performance and reliability of your computer system than your storage devices. If your drive is slow, you'll be staring at the wristwatch pointer and twiddling your thumbs when you should be working or having fun. If your hard disk crashes, it can take hours or years of your work with it, and if you haven't taken the necessary precautions, you may never get those files back. Problems like those can make you rue the day you ever heard of high technology.

No one can guarantee that you'll never have such hassles. But this chapter aims to improve your odds, by providing background information and tips that help you manage your storage devices effectively and prepare for the worst.

Contributors

Henry Norr (HN) is the chapter editor.

Randy B. Singer (RS) is a practicing attorney and an Apple Legal Fellow. He writes for *Law Office Computing* and *Law Technology Product News,* runs a Macintosh user group for attorneys, and hosts the yearly MACLO (Macintosh in the Law Office) show.

Arthur Naiman (AN) and **Sharon Zardeatto Aker (SA)** were editors of previous editions of *The Macintosh Bible,* from which parts of this chapter were taken.

Contents

How Disks Work

(AN/SA/RS/Susan McCallister/HN)

The most common Mac storage technologies, including hard disks, floppies, tape, and most other removable media, are magnetic; that is, bits of data are recorded by changing the magnetic polarity of small areas on the surface of the storage media.

Magnetic media consist of an iron-oxide coating on a *substrate*, or foundation layer. In the case of floppy disks, the substrate is...well...floppy. It's a flexible plastic similar to recording tape. Inside the rectangular, hard plastic case, it's doughnut-shaped—round with a hole in the center.

With hard disks, the substrate is usually made of aluminum. Typically, a hard drive actually has several separate disks, or platters, stacked on top of each other and enclosed, together with a motor to spin them, in a sealed metal case.

On both kinds of drives, read/write heads store data by giving bits of the iron-oxide coating a positive or negative magnetic charge, to correspond to the 1's and 0's of digital data; they read the data by checking to see what the charges are.

Since iron oxide is what rust is made of, you can think of the contents of magnetic media as stories written in rust with a magnet. (With *The Macintosh Bible*, you don't get just information—you get poetry.)

Modern floppy drives are double-sided—the drive has heads that read and write data on both sides of the media. Hard drives have a pair of read/write heads for each platter. The heads are mounted on arms in much the same way that needles are mounted on the tone arms of record turntables, and they move in toward the center or out toward the edge as the disk spins.

Floppy drives rotate the disk at 300 r.p.m.; in a hard disk the platters spins at anywhere from 3,600 r.p.m. to 7,200 r.p.m. (no wonder it feels faster to work from a hard drive). While the read/write heads of floppy disk drives actually touch the disk, in hard drives they float over the platters on a cushion of air that's thinner than a human hair. The tolerance is so fine that the smallest dust particle can spell disaster. That's why hard disks are sealed.

Along with the mechanism itself, Macintosh hard drives, whether internal or external, have a *controller board*—the electronics that control the drive and manage its communications with the Mac. External drives also include a fan, connectors, a power supply (a device that converts the 110-volt AC from your wall socket into the lower-voltage DC power the drive motor requires) and, of course, the outer case.

Bits and Bytes (HN)

Storage is measured in the same units used for memory. A bit is one piece of information—on/off, yes/no, 1/0, +/–. A byte is made up of 8 bits, and the units we generally measure storage in—kilobytes, megabytes, and gigabytes—are multiples of that. Each unit is about 1,000 (actually 1,024) times the last: A kilobyte is 1,024 bytes, a megabyte is 1,024 kilobytes, and a gigabyte is 1,024 megabytes.

In recent years several technologies that use light as well as magnetism in the process of reading and writing data have also become common on the Mac. For a description of how they work see "Removable Media" and "CD-ROM," later in this chapter.

Formatting Disks (HN)

Every writable disk—floppy, hard, removable, or optical—has to go through a one-time setup process before you can use it on a Mac. This operation is known as *initializing* or *formatting* the disk. (Technically speaking, these terms refer to separate parts of the process, but for most purposes they're interchangeable.)

Instructions for formatting floppies are built into the Mac. Whenever you insert an unformatted (or otherwise unreadable) floppy, the machine will ask if you want it initialized. If you select an already-formatted floppy disk in the Finder and choose Erase Disk from the Special menu, the floppy will be reformatted.

Hard drives are usually shipped preformatted, but if you have to reformat, or if you want to format an optical disk or other removable media, you'll need to launch a special formatting application. (In the case of a hard drive, the Finder's Erase Disk command just erases the data on the disk; it doesn't reformat the media.) Apple's formatter, Apple HD SC Setup, comes with the Mac, but it works only with Apple-brand drives; third-party hardware vendors include utilities they've developed themselves or licensed from others. Several developers also sell retail packages that can format drives regardless of brand (see "Upgrading Your Formatter and Driver" later in this chapter).

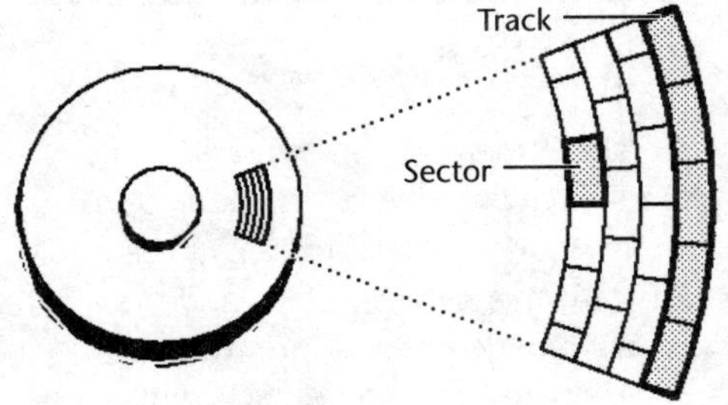

Sectors on floppies and standard hard disks hold 512 bytes (half a K); floppies have 80 tracks per side (on hard disks that number varies). The 1.4MB drives in all recent Macs, known as SuperDrives, have 18 sectors on each track. PCs use a similar floppy disk format.

Formatting the media organizes it to receive information. If you think of a new disk as a blank sheet of paper, formatting is like drawing a grid that covers the surface with boxes to put data in. What results is like graph paper, except that since disks are round, they have *tracks* (rings around the disk) and *sectors* (divisions within a track) instead of columns and rows.

Most hard disk formatting utilities (HD SC Setup is an exception) give you the option of dividing the disk into several *partitions*, or logical *volumes*—portions of one physical disk that are set up so the Mac will treat them as if they were separate disks. (For more on partitioning disks, see "Getting the Most Out of Your Hard Drive" later in this chapter.)

Directories and Desktop Files (HN)

When a disk is initialized, part of it is set aside for *directories*, where the Mac creates and looks up records about the name, size, and location of every file and folder on the disk.

These directories are critical: If they get corrupted, as they easily can, you could lose access to your data, even if it's actually stored safely on the disk.

Initializing also creates special invisible Desktop files; in System 6 there's only one, but System 7 has two: Desktop DB and Desktop DF. They store icons, the size and location of open windows, how the contents of windows are displayed (by Icon, Name, etc.), the Get Info information for every file, and so on.

Disk Drivers (HN)

To tell it how to read and write any disk, the Mac needs a kind of software called a *driver*. A driver for Apple floppy drives is built into the Mac's ROMs, so it doesn't have to be kept on each disk. On hard disks and removable cartridges (not including CD-ROMs), the driver software is installed by the formatter in a special section of the disk. One of the first things the Mac does when you start it up—during what's known as the *boot-up* process—is to go to that location on each drive it finds and load the driver into memory.

Ordinarily you don't have to pay attention to your hard disk driver; it should just do its thing automatically. (In fact, you can't even see it on your disk, even with programs that show files invisible from the Finder.) But remember that it's there, because in some circumstances you can save yourself a lot of trouble by reinstalling or updating it. (See Chapter 7 on troubleshooting and the section on SyQuest cartridges later in this chapter for some examples.)

Connecting External Drives to the Mac (HN)

When Apple in the mid-1980s went looking for a way to connect hard disks to the Mac, it settled on a then-obscure industry standard known as the Small Computer Systems Interface, which is abbreviated to *SCSI*, pronounced "scuzzy." (A now-defunct company called LoDOWN Corp. used to make specialized peripherals called "write once, read many" drives. They gave their Mac version my all-time favorite product name: the LoDOWN SCSI WORM drive. It sounded to me like something the good guy would call the bad guy in a classic cowboy movie.)

Aside from dockless Duos, every new Mac since 1986 has had a SCSI port (connector), and, except for floppy drives, virtually all Mac storage devices use SCSI to exchange data with the Mac. (So do most Mac scanners, many printers, and a host of other peripherals.)

You can *daisy chain* (connect in series) up to seven devices to one SCSI port; if you want to attempt to attach more peripherals than that, you can buy an expansion card that gives your machine a second SCSI channel or "bus," or you can get one of the high-end Macs, such as the Quadra 950 or the Power Mac 8100/80, that have two SCSI buses built in. The ins and outs of dealing with SCSI are described under "Riding the SCSI Bus," later in this chapter.

Over the next few years, Apple is planning to gradually replace SCSI with a new peripheral-expansion bus it calls *FireWire*. The new standard promises numerous advantages over SCSI: It's supposed to be capable of transferring data more than twice as fast as SCSI on a Quadra or Power Mac (and planned future enhancements will make it several times faster still). It will use smaller, cheaper cables and eliminate most of the hassles involved with connecting multiple peripherals via SCSI (see "Riding the SCSI Bus," below). On top of all that, it includes special provisions for real-time audio and video—you'll be able to connect a video camera to the FireWire bus and see the picture on the Mac screen.

Dealing With Floppy Disks

Almost everyone has to deal with floppies sometime. New software usually comes on floppies, and they remain a convenient medium for moving files between your computer and someone else's.

400K, 800K, and 1.4MB Disks (HN)

The earliest Macs had 400K floppy drives. (That seems small now, but at the time, PC disks held only 360K.) The second generation, starting with the Mac Plus, used *double-sided, double-density* disks, with a capacity of up to 800K. In 1988 Apple introduced the *SuperDrive*, a drive that can read and write 1.4MB *high-density disks*, 800K disks, and 720K or 1.4MB disks formatted for PCs.

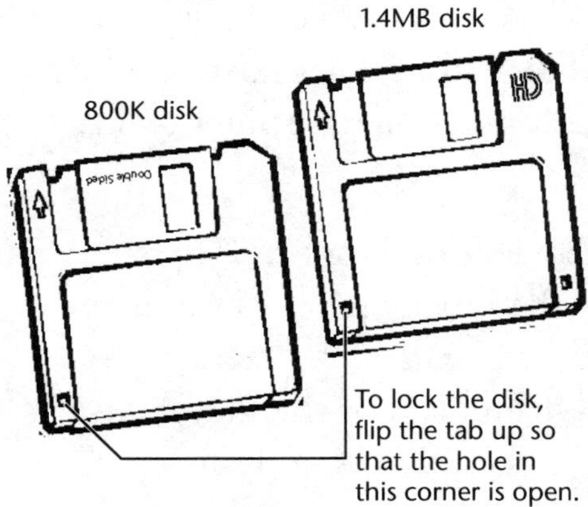

You can usually tell a 1.4MB floppy disk at a glance by looking for a small hole in the upper-left corner and the notation "HD" on the plastic case.

Typically, 1.4MB disks cost a bit less on a per-megabyte basis. Assuming you have a high-density drive, there's generally no reason to buy the lower-capacity disks unless you need to distribute data to users who don't have a SuperDrive. *[I disagree: Many times I need to send 50K (or 500K) files to other people. Why spend the extra money on a high-density disk that goes mostly unused? Also, I don't like to jam nonrelated items on disks just to use up all the space. In those cases, I can often fit all the items related to one topic on a double-density disk, again saving the more expensive high-density disks for larger files.—EC]*

Locking Disks and Files (SA/RS/AN)

To lock, or write-protect, a disk so nothing on it can be changed or erased accidentally, simply slide the little tab in the upper-right corner so that the square hole is open. It's a good idea to lock the master disks you get with new applications and system software. In the Finder, locked disks have a padlock in the upper-left corner of their directory windows.

Formatting Floppy Disks (SA/AN/RS/HN)

The first time you insert a new floppy disk into your drive, you'll get a dialog box that reads "This disk is unreadable: Do you want to initialize it?" If you click OK, you'll get a series of dialog boxes leading you through the process (see the illustrations at left).

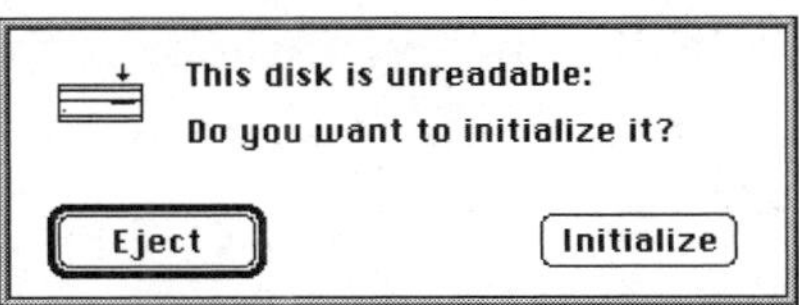

You'll see this dialog box when you insert an unformatted floppy or one that has been damaged.

Sometimes when you insert a floppy that you know is already formatted, you get the same dialog box or one that begins, "This is not a Macintosh disk." Several things can cause this problem: The disk may be damaged; the drive may be dirty or out of alignment; or you may have inserted a high-density disk formatted for 1.4MB in an 800K drive.

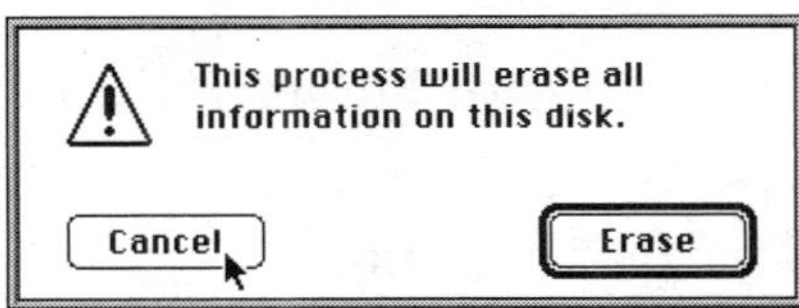

The next dialog box gives you a chance to turn back, warning you that proceeding will erase the disk.

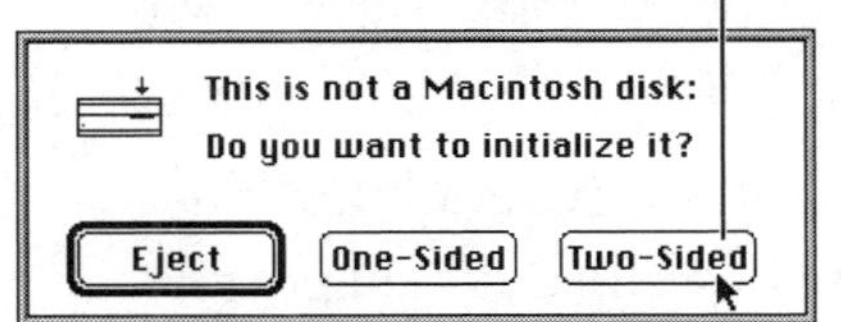

You'll see this dialog box only if the disk you inserted is a double-density (not high-density) disk.

In either case, think twice before you click OK to initialize the disk, because any information already on the disk will be truly erased (wiped clean, not merely removed from the directory), and file-recovery utilities won't be able to find it.

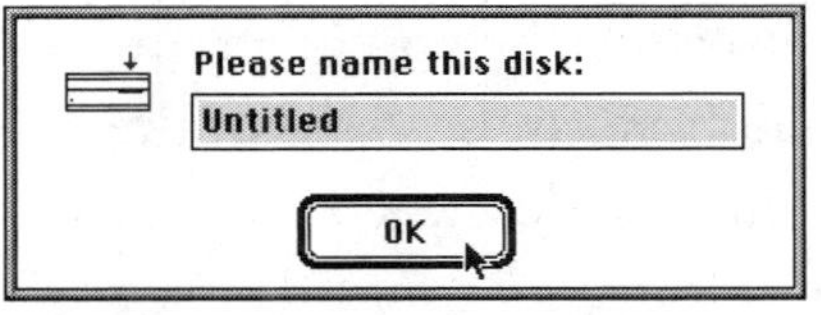

Next you'll get a chance to name the disk. If you don't type another name, the disk will be named "Untitled," but you might want to pick something more descriptive. You can change the name later if you wish.

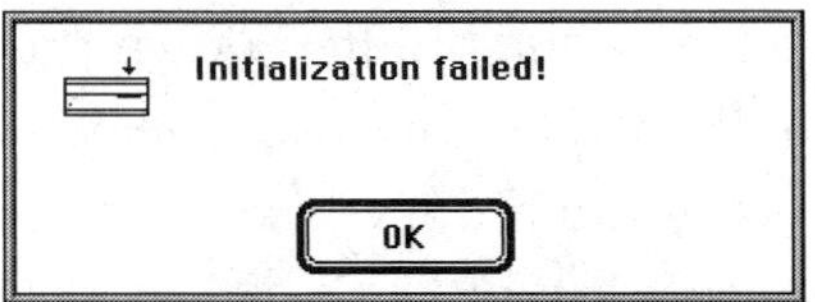

If you see this dialog box, there's some physical problem with the disk or drive. If you see it, throw out that disk and start over.

If the contents of the disk are important to you, click Eject and then try the methods described in the next entry, "Unreadable Floppies."

You can use floppy disks over and over. When you're ready to reuse one, it's a good idea to reinitialize the disk (using the Special menu's Erase Disk command) rather than just dragging the old contents to the Trash. Erasing the disk reinitializes it and causes the Mac to check the entire disk. If it finds any bad blocks—problem areas—it will mark them so the drive won't try to write data to them; if there are problems the Mac thinks it can't deal with, it will report that initialization failed. Then the prudent thing to do is throw the disk away and try another.

Unreadable Floppies (HN)

If your Mac tells you it can't read a floppy, don't panic—the odds that you can recover the data on it are generally pretty good, if you have the tools.

At the first sign of problems with a floppy disk, the Mac offers to initialize it. Don't let it; click Eject instead. Then write-protect the disk (with the sliding plastic tab) so it can't be damaged further as you try to recover its contents.

Once it's protected, try reading it in another Mac—often the alignment of the heads in two floppy drives is just different enough to make a disk that's unreadable in one drive readable in another. If the disk was last used in a Mac other than yours, try that drive in particular, if it's nearby. If another drive can read the data, copy it to the hard drive and then to a new floppy.

If that doesn't work, try a data-recovery application—they generally produce good results with floppies. (Data-recovery utilities are described in Chapter 7.)

Floppy Disk Jams (HN)

When a floppy disk does not eject, you can often get it out by restarting your system while holding down the mouse button or by inserting the end of an unfolded paper clip (use a heavy-duty one) into the small hole to the right of the disk slot. Even if you can see the back edge of the disk just inside the slot, do not try to yank out the disk with pliers or another tool. Doing so could damage your disk drive heads or pull the metal shutter off the disk. Instead, you'll have to have the drive serviced.

Sometimes the metal shutter on a floppy disk starts to lift up from the plastic surface of the disk. If that happens, the safest course is to copy the contents of the disk and throw it away, because it may jam in the drive sometime soon.

Many floppy jams are caused by the distinctly low-tech problem of labels coming unglued. This seems to be a problem particularly with disks used for commercial software distribution. Check the short side of the label before you insert a floppy. If it is loose, lift it off the disk and either restick it or cut it off.

Caring for Your Floppy Drive (HN)

Dust and oxide residue from the recording media can accumulate inside the drive and cause disk errors. Several times when I have started to get frequent "This disk is unreadable" messages, cleaning my drive with a disk-cleaning kit solved the problem. Kits are sold by computer and office-supply dealers. There are several brands, but 3M's **Head Cleaning Diskette Kit** (around $10) is the only such product certified by Apple for use with SuperDrives. If your environment is dusty or smoky, or if you're just the fastidious type, do a preventive cleaning every few months.

A $60 package called **DriveTech** from MicroMat Computer Systems combines the 3M cleaning materials with software described as "drive diagnostics." It's got a wizzy graphical interface and it runs read and write tests, but it doesn't actually give you any diagnostic information—the tests are all pass/fail. When I ran them on a drive that was causing problems, it passed all the tests but continued to give me grief, so the whole exercise didn't do me much good.

Airport X-ray Machines (HN)

Many people persist in believing that airport security systems can wipe out the data on floppies, but there's little scientific basis for this fear and tons of real-life experience to the contrary. If there's any danger at all, the experts say, it's not from the X-rays used to look inside your bags but from magnets in the conveyor-belt drive system. Unless the machine is old and way out of adjustment, though, there should be no problem.

In any case, whenever you travel, it's always a good idea to leave a backup of any valuable files at home.

Choosing a Hard Drive

For several years all new Macs have had internal hard drives preinstalled, so buying a Mac means buying one of the drives Apple offers, like it or not. (Apple doesn't manufacture its own drives; like other Mac storage vendors, it buys the drive mechanisms it resells from one of the handful of actual drive manufacturers.)

Apple never offers the biggest and fastest drives on the market, but it usually picks solid, middle-of-the-road performers, and many Mac owners are content to stick with the original drive for the life of their computer. On the other hand, hard drives have a way of filling up fast, and many users find themselves in the market for a second drive, or a bigger replacement, sooner than they anticipated.

With scores of vendors in the Mac storage business, and each offering dozens of options, choosing a drive can be a daunting task. Fortunately, you have to go out of your way to buy a bad drive these days: If you shop from an established vendor and choose a mechanism from a well-known manufacturer, chances are you'll wind up satisfied. But if you want to get the most for your money, it pays to consider the lay of the land before making a choice.

Sizes and Shapes (HN)

From the user's point of view, the variable that most obviously distinguishes one drive from another is capacity—80MB, 230MB, 1GB, and so on. But drives are also commonly categorized by two physical dimensions: the diameter of the platters inside and the height of the whole sealed mechanism. Together, these dimensions are the basis for size standards that make units from different manufacturers interchangeable. Call them "form factors" if you want to sound like a computer-industry insider.

(This is all pretty complicated, but it's something you might need to understand if you ever expect to shop for a new hard drive to install inside your Mac; if not, skip the rest of this section.)

The earliest hard drives for desktop computers were called "full-height 5.25-inch drives." Their platters were 5.25 inches in diameter and the mechanism was 3.2 inches high, a standard agreed to by drive manufacturers and used in designing the drive bays of the first personal computers; today only a few very high capacity drives (such as 650MB and 1.3GB magneto-optical drives) are built in this shape, and they don't fit inside most Mac models.

By the mid-1980s, as computer manufacturers learned to pack more data onto fewer platters, they began to introduce "half-height" 5.25-inch drives, 1.6 inches high. That size now survives mainly in removable-cartridge devices such as CD-ROM drives and 44MB and 88MB SyQuest drives. New hard drives today are mostly 3.5 or 2.5 inches in platter diameter: The former are used in most desktop computers, while the latter are designed for notebook computers such as PowerBooks.

Most 3.5-inch drives are 1.6 inches high, but some are only 1 inch high. The latter, called "low-profile," are the only kind that fit in some Macs, such as the LC series and its Performa cousins. The 2.5-inch drives come in several heights, but they are identified by their actual height in millimeters. (Don't ask me why they mix inches and millimeters.)

Internal vs. External Hard Disks (AN/RS/HN)

An *external* drive is one that comes in its own box and plugs into the Mac via a SCSI cable. An *internal* hard disk is one that's mounted inside the Mac itself. Internal drives use the Mac's fan and power supply, and they don't require a case, so they're typically $100 to $200 cheaper than the equivalent external hard disk. They take up no desk space, they don't need a power outlet, and you don't have to lug a separate piece of equipment around when you're moving your Mac.

But there are also several disadvantages to internal drives and advantages to externals. An internal drive makes your Mac heavier. Servicing or replacing the drive requires taking the computer apart or taking the whole thing to a dealer. If you are going to work at different Macs from time to time, it's a hell of a lot easier to bring along an external drive than to schlep the whole Mac (unless, of course, you have a PowerBook...). And if you trade in your Mac for a newer

When Does 250 Megabytes Equal 230 Megabytes? (HN)

The grid lines laid down on a disk when you format it take up space. Even more is set aside for directories, the driver, and the map used to identify different partitions. Altogether, these elements can fill something on the order of 5 percent or more of your disk space, even before you start loading system software, applications, or documents. The total original capacity of a drive is called its "unformatted capacity"; what's left after initialization is called the "formatted capacity."

Most Mac storage vendors nowadays advertise the formatted capacity of their drives, but some talk in terms of unformatted capacity. One vendor's 250-meg drive may not actually hold any more of your data than another's 230-meg drive if the first figure means unformatted and the second formatted.

model, it's easier to reconnect an external drive to the new computer than to worry about transferring an internal one (if it will even fit) or its data.

There's no appreciable performance difference between internal and external versions of the same drive mechanism using the same driver, even if the external cable is longer than the internal one—the time it takes the data to move down a cable is negligible.

Drive Speed (HN)

There's no single index for measuring the performance of hard drives. If you care about maximum speed, you need to pay attention to several variables and weight them differently depending on your Mac and what you do with it.

Seek and access times. The simplest variable is *average seek time* or *average access time*. Both are measured in *milliseconds* (thousandths of a second, abbreviated *ms*), and, basically, both measure the same thing: how long it takes your drive to get to the data you want. Technically, average seek time is how long it takes the heads to move to the desired track; nowadays, it's usually somewhere between 8 and 20 ms. Average access time is the sum of that figure plus an additional, smaller amount (normally about 6 or 8 ms) for latency, the average wait for the desired sector to come around under the heads once they get to the right track. (The odds that the right sector will be arriving just as the heads reach the track are slim.)

Unfortunately, many vendors are sloppy and inconsistent in their use of these terms; some will even tell you they mean the same thing. If milliseconds matter to you, be sure you're using the same standard when comparing products: A drive with an average *access* time of 15 ms is actually faster than one with an average *seek* time of 12 ms.

Are such distinctions even noticeable? I can't tell the difference between a drive with an average seek time of 10 ms and one where the figure is 12 or even 15 ms. On the other hand, any of those drives feels considerably more responsive than one with a seek time of, say, 25 ms.

Throughput or transfer rate. *Data transfer rate* is a measure of how fast a drive can deliver data to the Mac once it gets to the sectors it's looking for. The transfer rate is counted in megabytes per second (or sometimes, just to confuse things, mega*bits* per second). Today's drives usually have transfer rates between around 1.5 and 4 megabytes per second.

If you deal mostly with small files or database records, transfer rate is less important than seek or access time, because your drive will spend more time getting to the data you need than transferring it to the Mac. When you open a letter created in Word, say, or look up a customer's record in a FileMaker database, you don't read in large amounts of data, so even large differences in actual transfer rate have negligible consequences. But if you work with large scanned images in Adobe Photoshop, for example, or big QuarkXPress layouts, or giant QuickTime files, transfers actually take whole seconds, so differences in the transfer rate matter—much more than a difference of a few thousandths of a second in seek or access time.

Note also that there's a difference between *burst* transfer rates and *sustained* transfer rates. The former measures how fast a drive can pump out a small amount of data loaded into memory buffers on the drive controller; the latter is how fast it can deliver larger amounts, even after the buffers are empty. Burst rates are much higher, so some vendors focus on those, but for most purposes the sustained rate is more important.

Portable Drives: Data to Go (HN)

If you need a Mac in two places—at home and at work, say, or in two offices you use at different times—a PowerBook is a great solution, especially a Duo: Set up a dock or minidock at one or both ends, stuff the 4-pound notebook in your bag when you leave, and you're in business.

But what if you already have desktop Macs at both sites?

The cheapest and easiest solution, of course, is just to carry the files you need on floppies. But even high-density disks don't seem as big as they used to, and you may soon find yourself carrying a whole pocketful. Besides, that approach invites version-control problems: Imagine spending much of your weekend polishing up a report, and then discovering when you get to work on Monday that the floppy you thought it was on contains only last Friday's rough draft...

Another strategy is setting up matching removable-media drives (described later in this chapter) at both locations—just store the files you need on the cartridge and work on them at either place. But that can get expensive, and it doesn't give you much flexibility, because you can use that data only where there's a compatible drive.

So you might want to consider another approach: a portable hard drive. Here are several possibilities.

Small Standard Drives

Many storage vendors offer 3.5- or 2.5-inch mechanisms in floppy-drive-size cases. Some even offer battery packs for use with PowerBooks on the road.

Liberty Systems specializes in tiny drives: It offers hard drives in a variety of capacities in amazingly small cases. They aren't cheap, and the smallest units don't have fans—an omission that could reduce reliability over time. But they are very popular among Apple employees, among others.

Before you choose a standard drive, check to find out if the power supply is built in—you don't want to carry one of those bulky black bricks every day.

Pocket Drives

One of the top Mac storage vendors, La Cie (pronounced *lah-SEE*), packages 2.5-inch drives in tiny cases; these **PocketDrives** weigh only 10 ounces and truly fit in a shirt pocket. At this writing, choices range from a 40MB unit priced at $240 to a 256MB version for $450. I've used an 80MB PocketDrive for years to carry work between my home and my office, and it's been great for me.

You do need a special connector for these drives, so they're best suited for use in places you're at regularly—it's not good form to mess with your host's SCSI chain when you're just visiting. I got an extra connector, so I can leave one plugged in at home and the other at work. I also got two of the optional external power supplies, because I couldn't always get the drive to mount on my Mac IIfx when I relied on the default power source (a little cable that grabs some juice from the ADB port). All that added up to some extra hassle and expenditure, but once I got it set up, it's been absolutely reliable.

Other vendors now offer similar cases, but La Cie's design is elegant, and you get the company's excellent Silverlining utility software.

PowerBook Leftovers

Because many PowerBook owners eventually outgrow their original built-in hard drive and replace it with a higher-capacity model, it's not hard to find users or dealers who have slightly used 2.5-inch mechanisms on their hands. It's also not hard to find external cases for these drives—APS and many other drive vendors sell them, as does Casa Blanca Works, publisher of the Drive7 formatting program (see the box "Upgrading Your Formatter and Driver," on page 214). Pick up a surplus mechanism, order a case, put the two together (it's simple), and you've got a portable drive for a pittance.

BARGAIN

And no matter how fast your drive can deliver data, it won't do you much good unless your Mac can receive the information at the same speed. The SCSI ports on most pre-Quadra Macs couldn't handle more than about 1 to 1.5MB per second (the IIci got up to about 2MB per second), so drives with faster transfer capabilities didn't do you much good. Centris, Quadra, and Power Mac models, however, have improved SCSI systems that can handle about 4MB per second, so drives that are slower than that can become a bottleneck.

Spindle speed. The standard *spindle speed*—the rate at which a hard drive's platters rotate—used to be 3,600 r.p.m., but in the last few years drive manufacturers have begun delivering drives that spin at 4,500, 5,400, even 7,200 r.p.m. The extra rotation speed reduces latency, but its main value is to boost sustained transfer rates: The faster the disks are spinning, the faster the drive should be able to read in all the data it's after. You'll notice the difference mainly with big files.

If you are concerned about noise in your work environment, make sure your vendor offers a money-back guarantee before you order a high-spindle-speed drive. Some of them give off a high-pitched whine that drives some users crazy.

SCSI-2: Should You Care? (HN)

The industry committee that defined the original SCSI standard, operating under the auspices of the American National Standards Institute, followed it up with a clearer, cleaner, and more complete (and much longer) specification known as *SCSI-2*. The revision made a host of technical changes, and it defined two high-performance extensions to the original spec: *Fast SCSI,* a mode that allows data to be transferred to or from disks in bursts of up to 10MB per second, compared with a maximum of 5MB with regular ("slow") SCSI; and *Wide SCSI,* a mode that doubles the width of the SCSI bus (so it can transfer 16 bits at a time instead of 8) and thus boosts maximum throughput to 20MB per second.

Almost all new hard drives are advertised as "SCSI-2 devices" or "SCSI-2 compatible." But don't be fooled: Such a device isn't necessarily going to perform any better for you than one with no such label.

It's not that the vendors aren't telling the truth; let's assume they are. It's just that most of the changes in SCSI-2 don't make any perceptible difference in performance. And the two that might—Fast SCSI and Wide SCSI—don't work on most Macs! (One of the two SCSI ports on the Power Mac 8100 does support Fast SCSI, and other high-end models may do so in the future.) Even most third-party SCSI adapters for the Mac (cards that plug into the NuBus or a processor-direct slot and provide enhanced SCSI circuitry) don't support Fast mode, though some of the most recent cards do.

Reliability (HN)

No matter how fast a drive may be, you don't want it if it's not reliable. A good warranty might enable you to get the drive replaced eventually, but even that won't protect you against the hassles you'll have to go through first.

Fortunately, today's hard drives are much less likely to experience hardware failures than those built even a few years back.

Drive mechanism manufacturers measure the durability of their drives in terms of "mean time between failures," or MTBF—the number of power-on hours a drive will, on average, last before some component gives out. For most new drives the figure runs from around 200,000 hours to 800,000 hours.

Now, that first figure comes out to almost 23 years and the second to more than 91 years, so it's safe to say that these claims are not based on actual field experience—they're derived by running a bunch of drives simultaneously in a lab and somehow extrapolating from the rate of breakdown during the test period. Even though statisticians say the technique is legitimate, I personally have trouble accepting the idea that running a hundred drives for a year tells us much about what's likely to happen when you run any one of them for 100 years, or even three years.

Still, MTBF probably means something, at least as an indicator of relative reliability, so it's worth considering when you are choosing a product. But try to supplement it with reviews in Mac publications and first-hand reports from users (check with your local user group or favorite on-line service).

Keep Your Radio Waves to Yourself (HN)

Storage devices, like many other kinds of electrical equipment, generate radio-frequency interference (RFI). In an effort to ensure that such equipment doesn't disrupt radio and TV reception in surrounding homes and offices, the Federal Communications Commission established standards and certification procedures for "computing devices." Basically, every computer and peripheral marketed to the general public must pass a battery of tests at an approved lab before the agency will grant it "Class B" certification; until it does so, and the vendor adds a sticker to that effect, the device can't legally be sold through normal channels. (Check the fine print on the bottom of your mouse and on the inside front pages of your hardware manual; you should see an FCC ID number and a reference to compliance with Part 15 of the FCC rules.)

Most storage devices that reach the market carry the required sticker, but if you look closely, it's not hard to find a drive without a sticker. Enforcement is spotty at best, and some vendors consider the whole system an example of wasteful overregulation—they say even devices that don't meet the Class B standard cause no problems in real life.

But I've personally seen drives cause problems with TV reception, and there are occasional reports of interference with emergency communications networks. Besides, the regulations are the law of the land, and they're backed by criminal penalties—not only the manufacturer, but also the reseller and even you the user of an unapproved unit could theoretically be fined or sent to jail. (That's not likely to happen, of course—even the most egregious violations usually result in nothing more than a slap on the vendor's wrist.)

If you do discover that a storage device you've just picked up lacks an FCC sticker, I'd suggest contacting the vendor and requesting a replacement unit with the proper approvals. If the vendor can't or won't provide that, I'd demand my money back. Remember, the law is unambiguously on your side.

Noise Level (HN)

If you are buying a drive to use at home or in a private office, be sure to ask about noise levels (a function of both the drive mechanism and the case design). Decibel levels you wouldn't notice in a large office could drive you crazy at home.

Removable Media (HN)

If you are in the market for a second drive, it might make sense to consider a *removable-media* drive—a SyQuest, Bernoulli, magneto-optical, or floptical drive. These very different storage technologies have one thing in common: They all put your data on cartridges that can be easily removed and replaced. That means you can lock up the data if you are worried about security, carry it with you to a service bureau, mail it to a client, or simply put it aside while you work on something else. And it means you can expand your total storage capacity just by adding more cartridges—in many cases a much more economical approach than buying more and more hard drives.

Another generic name for all these devices is *removable-cartridge drives.* Some people call them plain removables, but that term can be confusing because it's also applied to a much less common and more expensive type of device in which the whole drive mechanism—not just the recording media—can be removed. (If you want to be literal about it, floppy drives as well as tape-backup units are removable-media devices, but the term is usually not applied to either of those technologies.)

SyQuest Drives

SyQuest drives (or just SyQuests, in everyday usage) were the first popular removable-media devices on the Mac, and they remain the most common. They are so named because they all incorporate mechanisms manufactured by one company, SyQuest Technology, but virtually every vendor that sells any Mac storage products sells them.

The technology is close to that of ordinary hard drives, except that there's only one platter and it's encased in a plastic cartridge. When you insert the cartridge, a metal shutter (like those on floppy disks) opens up to give the read/write heads access to the recording surface. Because SyQuest drives are based on hard drive technology, their performance is almost as good. That makes them the fastest removable-media system, though the latest Bernoulli drives (described below) come close.

The original SyQuests for the Mac used 5.25-inch cartridges usually described as having a capacity of 44MB (though in fact the capacity of a formatted cartridge was closer to 41 or 42MB). Those cartridges remain a de facto standard in the prepress business. But now SyQuest also makes drives that use 5.25-inch cartridges with formatted capacities of 88MB and 200MB, and it has added 3.5-inch versions with cartridge capacities of 105MB and 270MB. All of these are usually sold as external drives, but some vendors also offer internal versions that fit into many recent Mac models.

THINGS TO COME

SyQuest also makes 1.8-inch versions of its drives. They come on the credit-card-size expansion cards that plug into what are known as PCMCIA slots (see Chapter 2). Newtons and many non-Apple laptops already have such slots, and new PowerBooks and eventually some desktop Macs will, too.

Pursuing the old Gillette razor strategy, SyQuest prices its mechanisms low and makes its money on cartridges. The drives still cost more than standard hard drives of similar capacity, but they are among the cheapest removable-media solutions. As this was written, mail-order prices ranged from a low of $200 for a 44MB internal to around $650 to $700 for a 270MB external unit. Cartridge prices range from $60 to $100.

Among the various SyQuest models, the 3.5-inch units (especially the 270MB drive) are the fastest and, on a per-megabyte basis, cheapest; they are the best bet if you are buying for only personal use or for exchanging data with others who have a similar drive.

But if you plan to use the cartridges to carry your images or layouts to a service bureau, you should go with a 5.25-inch unit, because the 5.25-inch drives installed in most such operations can't read the smaller cartridges. Among the

Are SyQuests Reliable? (HN)

In the early days many users of SyQuest drives encountered a variety of problems: The drives were sometimes flaky (especially low-cost implementations that lacked proper internal shielding), cartridges were easily corrupted or damaged (be sure to throw the disk icon in the trash and let the drive spin down before you try to remove a cartridge), and you couldn't count on being able to interchange cartridges among different SyQuest drives, because the various vendors' drivers were incompatible.

Most of those problems, however, seem to be fixed in the newer models; the 88- and 200MB 5.25-inch units are much more reliable than the original model, and the 3.5-inch drives are more reliable still. And SyQuest has promoted a software standard that makes most cartridges interchangeable, regardless of the driver.

In general, SyQuest drives will probably never be quite as reliable as fixed hard drives, because movability adds some extra strains and risks. But if you need removable media, and you take normal precautions (including regular backups, of course), don't let out-of-date horror stories deter you from buying a SyQuest.

5.25-inch alternatives, the 200MB version offers the best performance. Although it costs the most in absolute dollars, it's cheaper per megabyte. And it can read and (slowly) write 44MB and 88MB cartridges. (The larger-capacity drives have to make three passes to write over a lower-capacity cart.)

Bernoulli Drives

SyQuest's arch rival is Iomega Corp., which calls its removable-media drives *Bernoulli* boxes. These devices, marketed mostly by Iomega itself, are not actually hard drives—the medium inside the cartridges they use is floppy—but in capacity and performance they're more like hard disks than floppies.

So far, all Bernoulli drives are in the 5.25-inch size, but recent versions of the drive can accommodate cartridges with a variety of capacities, from 35MB to 150MB; higher capacities are, as always, under development. The original Bernoulli boxes were noisy, slow, and, most of all, expensive; Iomega didn't share SyQuest's strategy of pricing the mechanisms low and marketing them through other vendors. But the latest Bernoulli models are fairly quiet and fast, and the company has finally decided to make them more or less competitive with SyQuests in price.

In a Bernoulli cartridge the disk floats on a cushion of air as it spins, making the media immune to the head crashes (physical contact between the head and media) that can ruin a standard hard disk or SyQuest cartridge; if something goes wrong, the Bernoulli media falls away from the heads, instead of the heads falling on the media. On the other side of the ledger, Bernoulli drives have some problems of their own, such as media wear and tear, which makes regular head cleaning necessary.

Comparing Removable Media

Disk	Capacity
Floppy	1.4MB
Floptical	21.5MB
Bernoulli cartridge	35MB–150MB
SyQuest 5.25-inch cartridge	44MB–200MB
SyQuest 3.5-inch cartridge	105MB–270MB
5.25-inch magneto optical	650MB–1.3GB
3.5-inch magneto-optical	128MB–256MB

The main disadvantage of the Bernoulli drives, from a Mac point of view, is that they are less common than SyQuests. If you need to send large amounts of data to a service bureau or any other company that depends on the Mac, you should check in advance, but you can almost assume they'll have a 5.25-inch SyQuest drive on hand; the odds that they'll have a Bernoulli, a 3.5-inch SyQuest, or a magneto-optical drive are much slimmer.

Magneto-Opticals

Magneto-optical (MO) drives—also known as erasable optical drives—read and write 5.25-inch or 3.5-inch removable disks enclosed in a hard plastic case. They look a bit like floppies, but in terms of capacity and speed, they're more like hard disks. The media inside consists of a rigid plastic or glass substrate coated by several kinds of metallic alloy, in layers. One of the characteristics of the coating is that its polarity can be changed only at very high temperatures. When you write data to an MO disk, a laser heats a tiny spot on the media to about 150° C, at which point the polarity of that spot can be changed by an electromagnet located underneath it. Areas of the surface with different polarities reflect light differently, and that's how the laser reads the information.

Some industry observers once expected magneto-optical drives to replace ordinary hard disks as the norm in desktop storage. (One of them was Apple founder Steve Jobs, who designed an MO drive and no hard drive into the original NeXT computer.) It hasn't happened, and now doesn't seem likely to. But the technology has won a following, especially in the graphics and publishing fields, mainly because it combines removability with high capacities.

First-generation MO drives used 5.25-inch cartridges, and most used a standard format that allowed up to 650MB of data per cartridge (325MB per side—you have to flip them over). Drives using the Maxoptix Tahiti mechanism, however, could always hold a full gigabyte. And the latest drives from all vendors support a 1.3GB standard format (650MB per side).

The original drives were painfully slow, but the new ones alleviate that problem. The fastest of them, from the companies Pinnacle Micro and Alphatronix, are almost as fast as a midrange hard drive. What they don't solve is the cost problem: Most 5.25-inch MO drives still cost between $3,000 and $4,000 (although several Mac vendors do market a 5.25-inch Sharp mechanism that holds 650MB per cartridge for around $2,000). Cartridges cost $200 to $300—not bad if you need to archive gigs of data in an easily readable format.

In recent years, 3.5-inch MO drives using cartridges only a little thicker than a floppy have appeared on the market. The most common capacity currently is 128MB per (single-sided) cartridge, but new models holding 230MB on similar carts have begun to appear. The drives are available from many Mac storage vendors, at prices ranging from $800 to $1,400; extra carts are around $30 to $50. Performance levels are in the hard disk range, but barely—access times and transfer rates are about what you'd have expected from a decent hard drive six or eight years ago.

That's too slow to make a good primary working drive, but it's not bad as a place to put files and projects you don't require regularly—those you open up occasionally or might need for reference or reuse in the future. Since the cartridges show up on your desktop just like a hard disk and the files are stored in standard format, it's easy to open them from the MO or drag them to your hard disk; you don't have to run a special program to retrieve the file, as you ordinarily do if you use a tape drive for backup (tape drives are discussed under "Backing Up," below).

If SyQuest and Iomega were still stuck in the under-100MB range, 3.5-inch MOs would have a lot of appeal. As it stands, MO's only advantage is a slight savings in media cost; new SyQuest and Bernoulli systems are cheaper and faster.

Flopticals

Floptical drives are so called because they use a combination of floppy and optical technologies. They store 21MB of data on 3.5-inch removable disks that look just like standard floppies. The key to their higher capacity is a series of optical *servo* tracks—concentric circles etched onto the media during manufacturing—which make it possible to position the head far more precisely than the guidance system used in ordinary floppy drives is able to do. Performance is better than a regular floppy but worse than any hard drive.

If you don't have a SuperDrive yet and you've finally decided you need one, a SCSI floptical drive makes sense, since it can read and write standard 1.4MB disks and doesn't cost a whole lot more than a regular Mac 1.4MB drive. But if what you're after is extra storage space, forget flopticals—you can get a SyQuest with much greater capacity and better performance for less.

CD-ROM

(HN)

A few years ago *CD-ROM* (compact disk, read-only memory) drives were a specialty item mainly used in libraries; today they are well on the way to becoming standard equipment in desktop Macs, especially in the home and school markets.

A CD-ROM drive (sometimes called a *player*) isn't essential to the functioning of your computer in the way that a hard drive and a floppy drive are; if you are just using your machine for things like word processing, spreadsheets, and communications, you can get along fine without one. But if you hope to take advantage of the increasing wealth of multimedia reference and entertainment titles available on the Mac, you're missing the boat if you don't equip your system with this third kind of drive.

What's It For?

The beauty of CD-ROM is large capacity at low cost: The disks can hold up to about 600MB of data—more than 400 floppies' worth—yet they cost only a dollar or two to manufacture in volume.

Editors' Poll: Do You Have a CD-ROM Drive?

AA: Yes, because more and more of the stuff I need/want—clip art, photography, fonts, cool games, educational software—is on CD-ROM, and it's only going to grow as a distribution medium.

DB: I have a CD-ROM drive on my machine because I'm living in the '90s. I know of several people who are still living in the '70s and they don't have a CD-ROM drive. Look: Friends don't let friends drive without CD-ROM.

EC: I have an internal CD-ROM drive, but I didn't always. Apple kept sending me their developer CDs, but since I didn't have a drive, I couldn't read them. It was awful. And I kept getting more and more catalogs that described all this neat-looking software. I don't buy many disks, and I don't have time to look at even the ones I have, but at least now I can.

DD: Nope. Never could think of a reason why I needed one, though now I'm being tempted by the font collections distributed on CD-ROM; it's often a lot cheaper to buy fonts that way.

CG: The number of kids' titles, not to mention reference and educational stuff, that's published on CD-ROM discs makes it a necessity as far as I'm concerned. Watching my daughter play with Just Grandma and Me and The AmandaStories was enough to convince me.

JK: I have one so that I can take advantage of the huge amounts of software and information that come on Apple's developer CDs. I've used multimedia CDs too, but in general I'd prefer a good video or a trip to the movie theater.

HN: Yep. I use it mainly to get stuff from the disk Apple mails to developers every month.

BW: I haven't been able to justify buying one. I spend almost no recreational time on computers.

That makes them an ideal medium for products that involve quantities of data so vast they can't practically be distributed on floppies and stored on your hard disk: games and encyclopedias that incorporate lots of graphics, music, and video; collections of high-resolution images; ZIP code directories; research databases; and technical manuals. Even with things that do have to be installed on your hard disk before you can use them—system software, development tools, and major applications—it's cheaper, easier, and better for the environment to use a single CD instead of a mountain of floppies for distribution, installation, and archiving. (For more on what's available on CD-ROM, look for the CD-ROM icon throughout this book.)

CD-ROM Hardware: What to Look For

As their name suggests, CD-ROM drives read disks that look just like standard audio CDs. (The "-ROM" is supposed to distinguish the computer kind from the music kind, even though both varieties are actually read-only.) The technologies are so similar that most CD-ROM drives can play audio CDs, too. In both cases, the 5-inch disks are usually made of rigid plastic coated with a metal alloy. Information is stored on these disks in the form of tiny dents or pits, which reflect light differently from the nondented portions. CD and CD-ROM drives read the disks by shining a laser beam on the surface and interpreting the pattern of reflection.

CD-ROM drives connect to the Mac via the SCSI port. Drives can be installed internally in most recent Macs (except PowerBooks, the Quadra 605, and other small-case Macs), or you can hook up an external box. As with hard drives, each approach has its pros and cons: Internal mechanisms cost less and take up no disk space; external drives are easier to move around.

Up-to-date CD-ROM drives can read *Photo CD* disks, a format developed by Kodak for storing digitized photographs; most drives offer *multisession* Photo CD support, meaning that they can read all the images on a disk even if they were recorded on the disk at different times. You can get your family photos developed on disk, so you can use programs such as Adobe Photoshop to retouch them. If you're a graphic designer, you can take advantage of stock photo collections in Photo CD format. There's no significant price premium for a drive with Photo CD capability, so you don't have anything to lose by getting it, and it just might come in handy some day.

Until recently, CD-ROM drives have required you to place the disk you wanted to play in a *caddie*—a plastic box that resembles the jewel boxes audio CDs come in but that has a metal shutter like a floppy drive. Many newer drives, however, have a built-in motorized tray that makes caddies unnecessary—just place the disk in the tray, give it a nudge, and the tray will slide into the machine. It's a much simpler, more elegant solution than trying to find a caddie every time you want to play a new disk. Other things being equal, go for a drive that has a tray.

Brand Names

Over the years, most Apple-brand storage products have been mediocre at best; people bought them because they came with the Mac, not because of their merits.

That's not the case with Apple's recent CD-ROM drives, the CD 300 and its successor, the CD 300 Plus. They offer excellent performance (as CD players go), they support multisession Photo CDs, and they come with good software for playing audio CDs and manipulating Photo CD images. And in its efforts to establish the Mac as the leading platform for multimedia, Apple has set surprisingly low prices.

Some Toshiba and top-of-the-line NEC mechanisms may be a tad faster; NEC's low-end drives are cheaper (and slower); and many users report satisfaction with Plextor (formerly Texel) drives. But on the whole, when it comes to CD-ROM, there's no reason not to buy Apple.

CD-ROM Drivers and Accelerators

As CD-ROM has increased in popularity, numerous CD-ROM utility software packages—Casa Blanca Works' **DriveCD** ($80), CharisMac Engineering's **CD AllCache** ($70), FWB's **CD-ROM ToolKit** ($80), MacPeak Research's **Spot CD** ($70), and Optical Access International's **Universal Access CD SuperCache** ($125)—have appeared on the market.

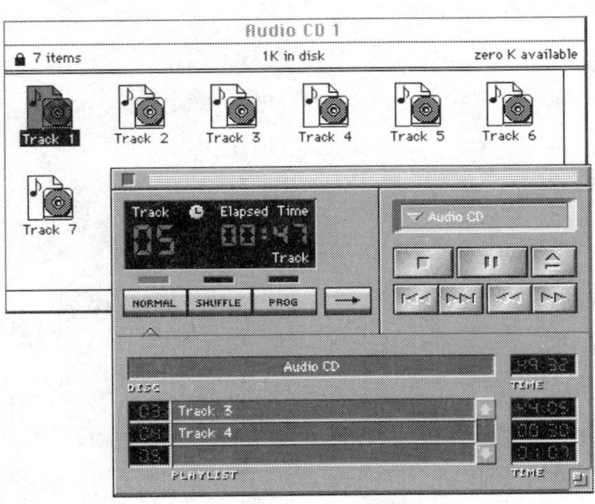

Make sure any CD-ROM drive you are considering comes with Mac software, including software that will let you control the playing of audio CDs from the Mac. Shown here is the AppleCD Audio player. Audio CD cuts show up on the desktop as if they were Mac files (background).

These packages have several functions. First, they are universal drivers, enabling you to use CD-ROM drives from almost any manufacturer (as long as they are made for SCSI) on the Mac. If you have a non-Apple CD-ROM drive with software that isn't up to date and reliable, you are probably

Standard, Double, and Triple Speeds (HN)

CD-ROM technology is intrinsically slow: Access times and data transfer rates are more like those of floppies than hard disks. As of this writing, state-of-the-art drives offer average access times of 200 to 300 ms.

In terms of transfer rate, for years CD-ROM drives were limited to a transfer rate of 150K per second, the standard set for music CDs. But a few years ago manufacturers figured out a way to make their drives spin twice as fast and thus deliver twice the throughput (300 to 330K per second); they drop back to standard speeds for audio disks.

These double-speed drives are now the industry standard. (Single-speed drives are still available, and they are somewhat cheaper than the newer models, but unless you plan to use your drive mainly to play audio CDs, I wouldn't go near a single-speed unit.)

Several manufacturers have taken the same idea a step or two further: At this writing Pioneer markets a quadruple-speed CD player, and NEC has triple- and quadruple-speed units; other manufacturers are likely to follow. The faster spindle speeds do make copying files faster, but current games and other programs played directly from the CD don't benefit appreciably. That won't happen until the software is rewritten to take advantage of the extra speed. Someday quadruple-speed or faster drives may be standard, but for now they don't seem to be worth the extra cost.

better off investing in one of these commercial packages than trying to squeeze an update out of the drive vendor.

GOOD FEATURE

Second, most of the packages include a desk accessory or other software that enables you to play audio CD disks on CD-ROM drives. (Apple's CD-ROM software includes a DA that does this job nicely, but the software that comes with some third-party drives doesn't deliver audio support.)

Third, all of the utilities listed above, as well as **SpeedyCD,** a $60 control panel from ShirtPocket Software, attempt to make CD-ROM usage faster by caching—copying—information from the CD drive, which is slow, to your hard disk, which is faster, or in some cases to memory, which is very fast. They can make permanent copies of CD directories on your hard disk, then direct the Mac to use the copies instead of the originals when you click on the disk's icon on the Mac desktop. Creating these cached directories takes some extra time, but they definitely make navigating the disk faster.

CharisMac Engineering's CD AllCache is one of several CD-ROM driver packages that use caching in an attempt to speed performance. The buttons in the lower row automatically configure the cache to the optimal settings for specific types of disks.

Several of the utilities also give you the option of caching the CD's contents, as well as its directories. This can make using the disk considerably faster under some circumstances.

Don't expect any of these utilities to make your CD-ROM drive feel fast by hard drive standards—no software can completely overcome the fundamental limitations of the hardware. But if you spend a lot of time working with CD-ROM disks, even a modest speed-up may be worth the price.

Among these programs, I've had the best luck with CharisMac's CD AllCache and Casa Blanca Works' DriveCD. The former comes with cache options specially preconfigured for different types of CDs and in some cases for specific titles. The latter has a simpler, cleaner interface, and it not only caches data you've already used but also reads ahead to load nearby sectors into the cache in case you go on to read them.

Choosing a Good Brand (HN)

Almost all storage vendors get their drive mechanisms from the same few manufacturers: Quantum, Seagate, Conner Peripherals, Maxtor, Micropolis, Fujitsu, Digital Equipment Corp. (DEC), and, yes, IBM. All these manufacturers provide high-quality drives, so it may not appear to make much difference where you buy, and price may seem to be the only consideration. Wrong. Sure, the mechanism is the single most important variable in a storage product. But between two drives with the same mechanism, the bundled driver and utility software and, in the case of external drives, the quality of the other components, such as the fan, power supply, case, connectors, cables, and shielding, can make a huge difference in performance and reliability. And even if the hardware and software are identical, warranties, service, support, and stability vary widely from vendor to vendor.

The Formatter and Driver

Whether or not they ship their drives preformatted, nearly all Mac storage vendors include a formatting utility. For most users the software that comes with their drive is good enough, whatever it is. But the various packages do differ, in features as well as performance and reliability. Most utilities, for instance, let you partition a drive into separate volumes (find out why under "Getting the Most Out of Your Hard Drive," below), but not all let you password-protect a volume (require a password before the volume can be opened), and an even smaller number give you the option of having your files automatically encrypted (so no one but you can read them, even if someone else gets access to the disk). Some utilities make you run a special application to mount a new drive on the desktop, while others offer a more convenient control panel. Some programs also provide extensive diagnostic and benchmarking tools.

The quality of the driver can also make a real difference in the performance you can get out of a given disk. FWB's Hammer drives, for instance, regularly come out at or near the top in performance benchmarks, not because FWB hardware is much different from its competitors', but because FWB's drivers are superior.

You can always upgrade your driver if you don't like the one you got with your drive (see "Upgrading Your Formatter and Driver" on the next page), but if the driver is important to you, you can get some of the best software for free with the right brand of drive.

Recommended Drive Vendors

I won't try to recommend specific mechanisms because they change too fast. But generally speaking Quantum drives tend to be among the best in relatively low capacities (500MB or less)—they don't break any performance records, but they're usually reasonably quick, quiet, and reliable. In the mid range (500MB to 1.2GB), Quantum, Seagate, and DEC make good drives. At higher capacities, Seagate, with its Elite and Barracuda lines, has been the dominant supplier in the Mac market, but Quantum is coming on strong, DEC and Fujitsu have their fans, and many multimedia users recommend Micropolis's AV drives, which are specially designed to ensure good performance with long sound and video files.

Upgrading Your Formatter and Driver (HN)

If your current driver is lacking some features you'd like, or if you just want to try to squeeze some extra performance out of your drive, you can buy a new formatter/driver separately.

FWB's $200 **Hard Disk ToolKit** is the Rolls-Royce, or maybe the Ferrari, of the category, but for most people it's overkill—more modules and options than you can shake a floppy at. (If you're interested in learning more about storage technologies, though, the 190-page manual is a fabulous resource.) A "Personal Edition," minus the manual and some of the advanced features, is $80.

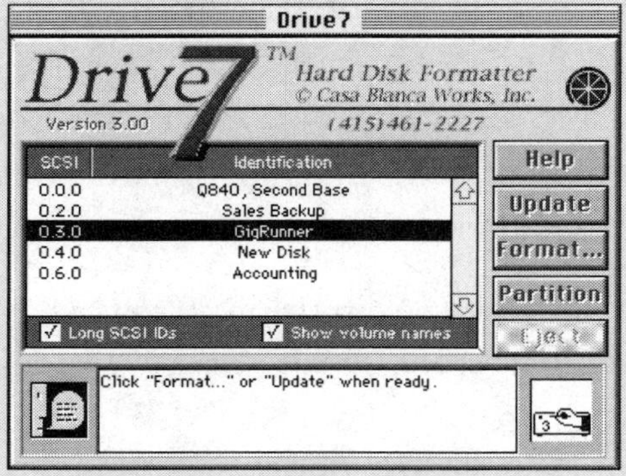

Casa Blanca Works' Drive7 has carved out a niche as a reliable and easy-to-use formatting package that works with virtually all hard drives.

Most of the other good disk utilities (except MicroNet's) are also available to anyone. La Cie offers its venerable **Silverlining** package for $150 (note, though, that the company's policy of charging for most updates, even small ones, has drawn some fire on the bulletin boards). **Anubis** from CharisMac Engineering ($130) and **SCSI Director Pro** from Transoft ($100) are among the other full-featured alternatives. MacPeak Research's $100 **Spot On** isn't as well known, but it offers a RAM-caching feature that can give your drive an extra lift. (See Chapter 4 for more on RAM caching.)

For ease of use, **Drive7** from Casa Blanca Works ($80) has long been the champ, and the latest version also provides high-performance features such as caching. (Apple has even licensed the underlying code used in Drive7 for incorporation into a future version of Apple HD SC Setup.)

Software Architects' **FormatterOne Pro** ($50) is another dependable and inexpensive choice, while the same company's **FormatterFive** ($200) lets you create DOS partitions so you can share a disk or cartridge with a PC. Software Architects also offers several special-purpose versions of its formatter: **MultiBus Manager** ($95) works on souped-up systems with multiple SCSI cards, while **Formatter5 Pro** ($500) works with Scitex volumes and other disk formats used in prepress operations.

As to brands and vendors, two of the largest and most respected in the mail-order category are APS Technologies and La Cie. APS offers a wider variety of storage products and accessories, its prices are excellent (though rarely the very lowest), and its products are solid and well made. It provides a toll-free support number, which is staffed by knowledgeable, friendly people (and an adequate number of them). The company is celebrated for near-heroic feats of service and repair.

GOOD FEATURE

La Cie was bought by Quantum a few years ago and now specializes in the parent company's mechanisms (though it also markets tape drives, removable-media devices, and other peripherals from other manufacturers). Like APS, La Cie provides good prices, solid if not chart-topping performance, and attractive and innovative case designs. La Cie drives come with a superior utility (Silverlining), but the company's record for service isn't as distinguished as APS's—some customers have complained that it charges too much for Silverlining updates, its support lines aren't toll-free, and its phone system seems to get overwhelmed every few years.

At the high end, MicroNet and FWB are regularly on the leading edge in performance. Both also provide good support, but MicroNet has a better record for regularly updating its utility and getting new versions out to users promptly and without hassle.

There are many other fine companies in the Mac storage market, so don't take these as exclusive recommendations. Just remember how dependent on your hard drive you're likely to become, buy from a vendor you have reason to believe is worthy of your trust, and hope the company doesn't change.

Dodging the Wreckage (HN)

The Mac storage market is a rough-and-tumble one, marked by tough competition, rapidly changing technologies, and razor-thin margins. So it's not surprising that many one-time leaders have fallen by the wayside. GCC, the original Mac hard drive company, has all but abandoned the storage field, as has PCPC, another early leader. SuperMac, which rose to prominence with its pioneering SCSI drives, long ago shut down its storage division. Meanwhile, a succession of once-high-flying mail-order vendors—Jasmine, Maxcess, Crate, and Ehman, among others—have crashed and burned, leaving their customers to make their way through the wreckage.

Bottom line: Things change fast in this industry, so look before you leap, even if you think you know where you're going. And remember that it may not pay to spring for the lowest price.

Getting the Most Out of Your Hard Drive

Ordinarily, you shouldn't have to think about your hard drive—just turn it on and it should do its thing. But to get all the performance and capacity you paid for, you do need to pay some attention to setup and maintenance.

The Interleave Ratio (HN)

Because older Macs couldn't digest data as fast as it could be read off even the relatively slow hard disks of those days, you had to tell your formatting software to go through some special tricks to give the Mac a little time to catch up between each bit it read from the disk. If you didn't give the machine regular breathers, it would essentially choke on the data coming off the disk, and that would make it even slower than if it did take the rests. (I'm simplifying grossly, but you get the idea.)

This process was called setting the *interleave ratio*, or just the interleave. The Mac Plus required an interleave ratio of 3:1; for the SE, the Classic, and the PowerBook 100, the requisite ratio is 2:1.

All recent Macs, however, have been able to handle a 1:1 ratio, which makes performance much better. Most formatters now suggest or automatically utilize the optimal ratio, so you shouldn't have to think about the issue at all—if you confront a choice, just leave it at 1:1 unless you are working on one of those old models.

Partitioning Your Hard Drive (HN)

Not too long ago I found my 300MB hard disk packed almost to the gills, so I went out and picked up a refurbished 1GB drive. (As a computer writer and editor, I save more files than money.) I hooked up the new drive and copied all the files on the old drive to it. Suddenly the disk had less than 400MB free—the data that filled "only" 300MB on the old drive took up more than 600MB on the new one.

How could that happen? The secret lies in an obscure technical concept known as the *allocation block*. The Mac file system divides up the disk space it has to keep track of on each volume into these units. For technical reasons, it can deal with a maximum of 65,536 of them per disk. That means their size varies, depending on the size of the disk: On a hard drive that holds less than 60MB, each allocation block occupies 1K; on an 80MB drive, they're each 1.5K; on a 300MB drive, they're 5K each; and so on, all the way up to 32K on 2GB drives.

Now, the Mac permits only one file in an allocation block—no cohabitation allowed. So if the file is small but the allocation block is big, the rest of the allocation block goes to waste. And if the file has both a resource fork and a data fork, as many Mac files do, each fork of each file gets its own allocation block.

My drive had tens of thousands of small text files. On the 300MB drive, each took up at least 5K of disk space, even though they were actually smaller than that; on the 1GB drive, the same small files each occupied 16K of space! The 30,000 files that filled about 150MB on the old drive took up almost half a gigabyte on the new one.

That's the main reason people *partition* big drives—as I did as soon as I realized what was going on. Partitioning means dividing a single physical disk into two or more logical volumes—separate sections that look to the Mac, in most respects, like completely separate disks. Each volume can have its own 65,536 allocation blocks, and since the size of the volume is smaller, the size of each block will be smaller, too.

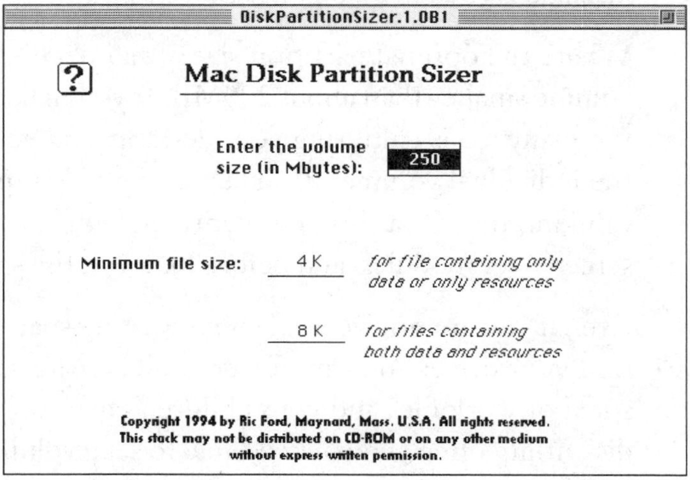

Disk Partition Sizer, a nifty HyperCard stack by Ric Ford, can help you figure out whether it's worthwhile to partition your drive and, if so, how to divide it up. Just type in the size of the partition you are considering, and the stack will return the minimum amount of space each file will take up.

By dividing my drive into four volumes of 250MB each, I reduced the allocation block size from 16K to 4K. In my case that meant much more efficient use of the space: A 3K text file would waste only the 1K remaining in its allocation block, instead of leaving 13K empty out of a 16K allocation block.

If your drive is smaller than, say, 300MB, the space savings probably won't justify partitioning. Likewise, if you mostly have big files, partitioning is not necessary: Since big files are spread over many allocation blocks, and all but the last are completely filled, the percentage of your capacity going to waste will be small. But since the average size of new hard disks gets bigger every year, while the 65,536 number doesn't change, more and more users are running into the problem of wasted space. *[Another solution I recently experimented with, since I too have lots of little files (3 or 4K taking up a minimum of 8K) was to compress huge groups of them into a single archive, with Compact Pro (or StuffIt). Then the savings is twofold.—EC]*

HOT TIP

Fortunately, most disk utilities now give you the option to partition. Apple's doesn't, which is one good reason to consider buying a commercial formatting package if you have a big drive.

What's the optimal partition size? It all depends, but I usually don't make any volume smaller than about 200MB. If you make too many volumes, you'll have too many icons cluttering your desktop, and you are apt to run out of space on the individual volumes. (I once made a 50MB partition for my System Folder, thinking that I was leaving plenty of room to grow. Then I started collecting screensaver modules, and before I knew it the space was all gone.)

Even if you are not worried about wasting space, there may be reasons to partition your drive: You can, for example, create separate partitions for your personal or work files and your children's games. Depending on the options your disk utility offers, you may be able to set a volume not to automount (appear on the desktop automatically) at bootup, but only when you explicitly call it up; for even stronger protection, some formatters let you require anyone trying to mount your volume to enter a password.

Setting Up a Folder Hierarchy (AN/RS/HN)

Keeping your hard disk well organized will not only make it easier for you to find things, it will also speed up your system's performance. That's because folders with hundreds of items take much longer to open, both on the desktop and from an application's Open or Save As dialog box. It's better to group your files in multiple folders and subfolders—folders nested within folders—than to toss them all in a few bulging folders. As a very rough rule of thumb, if you've got more than 20 items in a folder, it's time to think about making a subfolder. (Unfortunately, you can't do that with the special reserved folders System 7 creates, such as the Control Panels or Preferences folders.)

Fighting Fragmentation (HN)

When you save a new file—a word processing document, say—the program will probably tell your Mac not only to store what you've already written, but also to set aside some extra space on adjoining sectors in case you decide to add more to the file later. When you save a second file, the Mac will jump over the reserved empty space before creating the new file.

But suppose the first file is the opening scene of your new novel, while the second file is a short letter to a publisher summarizing your plot. Once you've fired off the note, you go back to your novel and write some more, and before you know it, the space the Mac left for that file is full. The next time you save, the system will look in the adjoining sectors, but they're already occupied by the letter. So it will have to find some other location on the disk for the rest of your file.

By the time the Great American Novel is complete, it might be saved on disk in dozens of segments, or fragments, even though it's all one file; assuming you are also saving some other files as you go along, they'll take up the spaces between the fragments of your novel. That means that when you open the file and scroll through it, the read/write heads on your disk will have to jump around from place to place on the disk to assemble the whole file. And that takes much longer than reading a file of the same size that's all in one contiguous area.

The problem is called *fragmentation*, and if it gets bad enough, it can slow the performance of your drive perceptibly. You can get rid of it by backing up your files, erasing your drive, and restoring the original data, but chances are there are other things you'd rather be doing than backing up, reformatting, and restoring your hard disk. So utility software developers have invented a kind of program that deals with the fragmentation problem for you, with no reformatting required. The programs are called *defragmenters* or *optimizers* (because they optimize disk performance). They work by analyzing your disk and then, using memory and the empty spots on your disk as temporary storage, shuffling fragments of files around until each forms a neat, contiguous whole.

The best of the bunch is Alsoft's **DiskExpress II,** which lists for $90 by itself or for $130 as part of the company's **Alsoft Power Utilities** collection. DiskExpress can do its thing on command or whenever your Mac is sitting idle, any time or during hours you specify. (I set it to work between 4 and 6 in the morning.) Besides defragmenting, it can track what files you use most often and group them at the most accessible parts of the disk. Altogether, it's a great tool for the compulsive hard disk jockey.

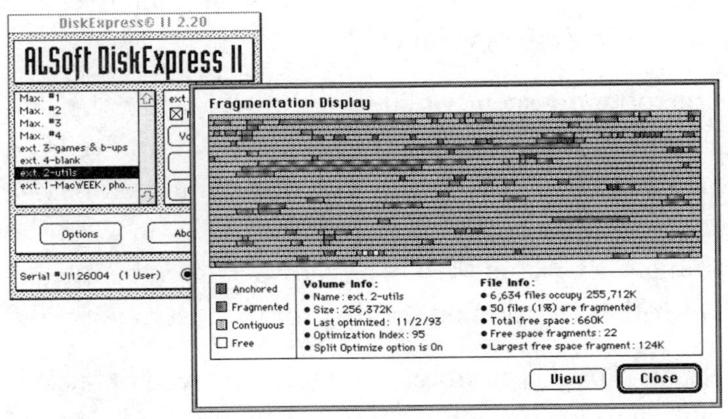

Alsoft's DiskExpress II can optimize your disk when your Mac is idle. The control panel includes a button that brings up a map and statistics showing the degree of fragmentation on any mounted volume. The second-darkest shade of gray represents files that are fragmented.

If you're not in that league but might wish to tune up your drive once or twice a year, you'll find simpler optimizers in the leading data-recovery packages: Symantec's Norton Utilities and Public Utilities and Central Point Software's MacTools. Data-recovery packages are discussed in Chapter 7. (As I wrote this, Symantec was making plans to acquire Central Point Software, so if you can't find MacTools under the Central Point name, it may be a Symantec product.) Owning one of these packages is a good precaution anyway; the optimizers are an extra bonus. (There's also an optimization command in La Cie's Silverlining disk formatter.)

All of the optimization programs take precautions to ensure your disk won't be scrambled if there's a crash or a power outage during the defragmentation process. But it's always a good idea to make sure you have an up-to-date backup before letting an optimizer loose. (Take it from me—I once lost a 150MB drive that wasn't backed up to an errant optimizer. That one's no longer on the market…)

Riding the SCSI Bus

SCSI is the standard *bus*, or electrical communications channel, for connecting storage devices and other peripherals to the Mac. It usually works reasonably well if you follow its rules and you have only one or two devices plugged in. But add any more than that and odds are you'll run into problems; if you didn't know any better, you might think you were dealing with a PC, not a Mac.

Below are some guidelines for dealing with issues that may come up, but one of SCSI's perverse charms is that no set of rules always works: All too often a "legal" setup won't work, and breaking the rules will fix it. Even the experts call it "voodoo" (or worse). Your guiding principle should be "Whatever works."

A word of caution: Never change any SCSI settings, or plug or unplug any SCSI cables, without powering down all the devices on the chain. Some people do it and get away with it, but they're risking expensive hardware damage.

SCSI Connectors (HN)

There's no single standard for SCSI connectors and cables. Most Macs have 25-pin *DB-25* SCSI connectors, but PowerBooks use a variant called *HDI-30* because it's smaller (even though it has 30 pins instead of 25). HDI-30 cables in turn come in two forms, depending on whether you want to connect your notebook to a peripheral or to another Mac. Most peripheral devices have *DB-50* (50-pin) connectors, so the most common kind of Mac-to-peripheral cable is

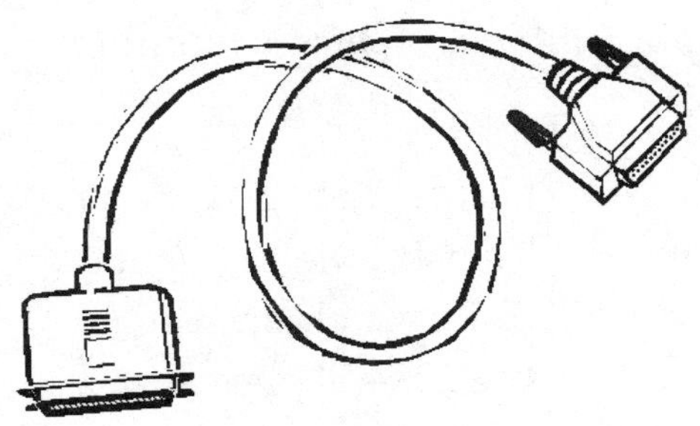

SCSI cables are the ones with long flat connectors at each end. Most have 25 pins at one end and 25 or 50 pins on the other, but other configurations are also common. Check the number of holes in the SCSI port of the peripheral you want to attach before buying your cable.

called a *DB25-to-DB50* cable; Apple calls it a *system cable*. But some SCSI devices have 25-pin connectors, and some recent ones use a newer, smaller 50-pin connector design called *microSCSI* or *microD*. And add-on cards that support Wide SCSI have a 68-pin connector known for some reason as a *P connector*.

Cable Quality (RS/HN)

The quality of your cables can make the difference between constant hassles and a bus that hums along smoothly. It may seem silly to spend $40 or $50 for a few feet of wire, but if you are building a complex SCSI chain, this is not the place to economize—especially if you are working with one of the Macs noted for its SCSI sensitivities, such as the Quadra AV models and the Power Macs. Look for *double-shielded* cables—they're thick and heavy because they have lots of shielding around the separate wires inside the cable to minimize the possibility of signals on one line generating noise on another. And gold-plated connectors are recommended.

GOOD FEATURE

The cables Apple sells are of pretty good quality, and some peripheral vendors supply good cables. But few if any match the extra-high-quality cables offered by a small company called Berkeley Data Access. It offers old-fashioned personal service and very reasonable prices. The only catch is that the minimum order is four cables. A new competitor in the field, Granite Digital, charges much higher prices but does accept small orders.

[Berkeley Data Access has a large scrapbook of testimonials from customers attesting to the fact that simply using its high-quality cables can cure the most vexing of SCSI problems. On top of that, the company sells the cables for much less than others might sell them for (and they would be worth the higher price!). If you don't need four cables yourself, get your friends to pool their orders with yours.—RS]

SCSI Cable Lengths (HN)

If your SCSI chain is too long, signals may be too weak to be received clearly and you are likely to experience a variety of problems. Theoretically, the chain can extend up to 7 meters (about 23 feet), measured from your computer to the last device in a SCSI chain, including all internal ribbon cables. But Apple recommends a maximum of 6 meters (about 20 feet), while many vendors say 5 meters. A general rule: The shorter, the better.

If you must push the length limit, you may be able to improve performance and reliability with PLI's **QuickBooster,** a $100 device that amplifies SCSI signals so they'll reach distant devices without retries.

As for the length of individual cables, that's one of the murkiest areas in the black art of SCSI. Some people have problems with long cables; still others have trouble with very short ones (about 18 inches is the shortest generally available). Some people say all your cables should be the same length, but there's no theoretical reason that should be true. If you have a variety of cables on hand, try them and see what happens—remember, whatever works. But if you are buying new cables, you might as well stick to the middle ground: 3-foot lengths.

Termination (HN)

The electrical signals that race up and down your SCSI cables generate electrical echoes, or *noise.* If they're not suppressed, these reflections can be strong enough to confuse devices on the bus, which think they are signals but can't interpret them. That can cause an array of problems, including slowdowns, data errors, drives refusing to appear on the desktop, and crashes.

That's why you need *terminators,* or resistors, at either end of the SCSI chain. Terminators can be internal (attached inside a device) or external (plugged into one of the device's SCSI ports).They require a small amount of electrical power—termination power—which is supposed to be, but is not always, provided by the SCSI device. The rules for termination vary according to the Mac model you've got.

Active Terminators (HN)

A useful feature in some new drives, and one well worth looking for, is *active termination*—a terminator that automatically turns itself on when needed and off when not needed. La Cie offers this feature in many of its drives, including the Joule family, its nifty new line of stackable drives. APS Technologies has built a patent-pending implementation it calls DATerm (for digital active termination) into its SR 2000 line of cases for external drives. According to APS, these devices not only turn termination on and off but also smooth out several kinds of electrical fluctuations on the SCSI bus, thus improving both reliability and performance.

APS also offers a separate, external version of DATerm under the name **SCSI Sentry.** It offers diagnostic LED lights, and because you can connect it to a wall outlet, it enables you to place a device that doesn't provide termination power last on your SCSI chain. At $100 it's not cheap, but some users—particularly people with very elaborate SCSI chains and users of Macs with very fast SCSI circuitry, such as the Quadra AV models and the Power Macs—say it's the only thing that's gotten the goblins off their bus.

Granite Digital offers a somewhat similar add-on called the **SCSIVue Active Diagnostic Terminator.** It lacks the external power option, but it's cheaper: Prices for versions that fit common connectors range from $50 to $80. And Berkeley Data Access sells an end-of-chain active terminator for only $28 and one with a pass-through connector (so it can go in the middle of a chain if necessary) for $38, but remember that you have to order at least three other items at the same time.

For most Macs. Generally speaking—here's one of those rules that usually works—the first and last devices on the SCSI chain should be terminated. The first device is the Mac: If you have an internal hard drive, it should be terminated (if it's a factory-installed drive, or if it's dealer-installed and your dealer is worthy of your business, it will come with terminators). If you don't have an internal drive, most Macs require a special terminator for the internal SCSI port. (If you normally have an internal drive but have to remove it for servicing, say, don't forget to have your dealer add termination.)

The last device—the one at the other end of the SCSI chain—should also be terminated. In between—normally—the other devices on the chain should *not* be terminated. If you have a device with internal termination, put it at the end of the chain, if that's convenient; if not, or if you have more than one internally terminated device, you or a technician will probably have to remove the terminating resistor from one of them.

The Mac Plus. Because the Mac Plus has no internal SCSI connector, your first external device (the one closest to the Mac) is considered the first device and should be terminated, as should the last device on the chain. If you have only one drive on the chain, it should be terminated.

The Mac IIfx. The Mac IIfx follows the general rules above, but it requires a special terminator at the end of the chain. It's black, and Apple calls it the SCSI Terminator II. One should have come with your IIfx.

PowerBooks. PowerBooks are something else again. Hard-drive-equipped PowerBooks have a small internal terminator, but if you are connecting external devices, Apple recommends adding two more terminators: One should go between the HDI-30 cable attached to your PowerBook and the first device. If only one external device is connected, the other should go on the device's unoccupied SCSI port; if there are several, the terminator should go on the last device in the chain.

If you are planning to connect a PowerBook to a desktop Mac in *SCSI disk mode*—setting up the PowerBook's hard drive to function as an external drive attached to your desktop machine—the termination rules are hopelessly complicated. Fortunately, they are very clearly illustrated in Apple's PowerBook manuals. Check there.

Turn 'em On or Take 'em Off (HN)

Power up all devices that are currently attached to your SCSI chain before you turn on your Mac. In some cases that's not strictly necessary—your system will work fine even when one or more devices are off. But more often than not, a device with no power can cause problems for others. If you really don't plan to use it in a session, consider removing it from the chain next time you power down.

Conversely, when you are shutting down, leave your peripherals on until you have safely shut down and shut off the Mac itself. Turning a device off while the Mac and other peripherals are on could cause a damaging power surge.

SCSIProbe (HN)

If I could have only one software utility to help me manage my SCSI chain, I'd take SCSIProbe, a freeware control panel written by Apple engineer Robert Polic. (It's now officially sponsored by SyQuest Technology, which puts its name in the control panel, but it's still available from user groups and on-line services.)

SCSIProbe-3.5sq

SCSIProbe 3.5sq

ID	Type	Vendor	Product	Version
0	DISK	CDC	94171-9	5841
1	DISK	QUANTUM	GO80S	5.34
2				
3				
4	TAPE	ARCHIVE	Python 25501-XXX	2.39
5				
6	DISK	IMPRIMIS	94601-15	0477
7	CPU	APPLE	MACINTOSH IIfx	$067C

Update | Mount | Options...

SyQuest TECHNOLOGY

SCSIProbe provides useful information about each device on your chain. But its real value lies in the Mount and Options buttons. The former brings to the desktop any device that's on the chain but didn't appear when you first booted up—a SyQuest cartridge you've just inserted, for example. The Options button provides, among other things, an easy way to load during the same session cartridges that have different drivers.

SCSI ID Numbers (Michael Bradley/SA/AN/Chris Allen/HN)

A SCSI chain can contain seven devices plus the Mac. Each device on the chain gets its own SCSI ID number (also known as an *address*), from 0 to 6. The Mac itself is always assigned ID number 7; an internal hard disk (if there is one) normally gets number 0. Otherwise, ID numbering has no necessary relationship to the physical order of the devices on the chain.

Most external SCSI devices provide switches that make it easy to change the ID number. Before you add a new peripheral to your system, check the numbers and, with all devices powered off, make the changes necessary to eliminate any conflicts. The stakes are real: If any two devices on the chain have the same ID, your system will crash, and you may even wipe out data on one or more hard disks.

SCSI number switches are almost always tiny and in the back of the drive (and therefore hard to get to). If you put the ID number on a sticker or spot of masking tape on the front of each device, though, you can see at a glance which numbers are used by which devices and which are free. (You can also determine the SCSI ID of any device with your disk formatting software or with SCSIProbe, an invaluable freeware device-management utility described in the box above.)

SCSI Troubleshooting (HN)

SCSI problems can cause a variety of symptoms, ranging from inability to boot your system or use some of your peripherals to sporadic, unpredictable crashes or data corruption. Symptoms like those can also be caused by software problems, however, so before you tackle the harder hardware question, it's generally a good idea to see if a software fix can resolve the situation. See if the problems persist when you boot up with extensions disabled, when you reinstall your system software, or when you zap your parameter RAM—see Chapter 7 for more on all these procedures.

If that doesn't work, here are some variables to consider and manipulate.

- First, if you've just added a new device, power down, take it off the chain, and try again. If everything else works normally, you know the problem is with the newcomer or its relationships with its neighbors. Likewise, if there's a very old device on the chain, or one you know to have SCSI problems, take it away next and see what happens.

SCSI Manager 4.3 (HN)

The component of the Macintosh operating system that handles SCSI transfers—the SCSI Manager—used to be pretty dumb: It could deal with only one device at a time, and while it was waiting for a drive to complete a task, it tied up the whole Mac. In 1993 Apple finally came up with an improved version, called **SCSI Manager 4.3.** It's built into the ROMs of AV and Power Macs, and it's likely to be in future models, too; eventually, Apple may release a version for older Centris and Quadra Macs.

The main virtue of the new SCSI Manager is that it is *asynchronous*—it doesn't keep the CPU tied up while it is working, and it can assign jobs, like reading or writing some data, to one drive while another is working on a previous assignment. When disk drivers, the operating system, and applications are rewritten to support such features, SCSI Manager 4.3 could bring some needed improvement to Mac input/output performance.

In the short run, however, it doesn't do much good. In fact, it can actually slow things down appreciably if you hook up a drive with a driver that is not SCSI Manager 4.3–savvy. By the time you read this, most drivers should have been updated, but if you've had a drive for a while and you want to use it with a new Mac, you should update the driver or reformat with a new utility. Check with your drive vendor or drive utility publisher.

- If those steps don't isolate the problem, power everything down, disconnect the SCSI cable attached to the Mac, and try again. If you've still got a problem, it's probably not a SCSI issue but one that involves system software or drivers. If you can boot up normally with no SCSI connection, you have confirmed your suspicions that the problem lies somewhere on the chain.
- Vary anything and everything (as long as the power is off when you are changing things). Swap cables, reverse the order of the devices on the chain, add an extra terminator, or take one away. If you can stand it, make these changes one at a time, rebooting and testing after each change. You can save time by rebooting with the Shift key down, or (better yet) setting your extension manager to skip all, so you won't have to wait for extensions to load. It will take time, but at least you can tell what variable has produced a change.
- Some combinations of devices (particularly if an older SyQuest drive or a scanner is involved) simply never work well, no matter how you organize things. In such cases, you have no choice but to remove one of the conflicting devices from your SCSI chain, at least temporarily, in order to use the other.

Backing Up (HN)

According to an ancient saying, there are two kinds of computer users: those who've had a hard disk crash and those who are about to. All computer storage devices, for now and for the foreseeable future, are inherently unreliable—they're susceptible to directory corruption, electrical glitches, and mechanical breakdown. And don't forget the risk of human error: Almost everyone who has used a computer for any length of time has at one time or another inadvertently trashed some important file.

Nevertheless, most computer users don't bother to back up their data—they just don't think about it, or they decide it's not worth the hassle, or they say they'll get to it later. It's your choice, of course, but remember the bottom line: If you don't have a good—i.e., recent and complete—backup, the odds are great that sooner or later you will lose documents that are important to you.

If you do decide to make backups, you need to choose backup media, software, and a strategy.

Backup Media

Having an extra hard disk is the fastest and easiest choice—you can simply drag files and folders to it to make a backup, and back again if you need to restore. But this approach also has clear disadvantages: Doubling your disk capacity is expensive, and the second drive is as vulnerable to breakdown, fire, or theft as the first.

Floppies are the other obvious choice, and on the face of it the most economical, since you already have the drive. But you should factor in the cost of your time, since backing up to floppies requires near-constant attention over at least several hours (depending, obviously, on the size of your backup). In an era when 160 or 230 megs are standard and gigabyte drives are common, floppies just won't do for full backups. They remain a good choice for quick backups of a select group of critical files—your tax return, say, or your dissertation.

The other choices are removable cartridges and tape. Using removable media—Bernoulli, SyQuest, or magneto-optical disks—offers many of the advantages of using an extra hard disk: You can back up and restore directly from the Finder, and you have the added advantages of expandability (if you run out of space, just get another cartridge) and portability (you can easily take a cartridge offsite for safekeeping).

The only real disadvantage of these options is the cost of media. A 230MB drive, for example, will need at least six 44MB or three 88MB SyQuest carts for a single backup—that's at least $300 right there; if you want the added security of duplicate copies, or your drive is bigger than that, media costs go up proportionately. And if you want to preserve archives of files no longer on your disk—copies you keep in reserve in case you ever need them again for reference, recycling, or updating—along with backups of your current files, the expense can go through the roof.

That leaves tape. In many ways it's the most un-Mac-like medium, since you can't ordinarily mount tape drives on your desktop, and you have to run special software to copy or restore your files or even to see what's on a tape. And the drives aren't exactly cheap: At this writing the least expensive digital audio tape (DAT) drives—the most common type of tape backup unit on the Mac—are about $800, while those with the latest technology (called *DDS-2 drives*) start at $1,400.

But tape has one huge advantage: The cost per megabyte is practically infinitesimal. With DAT, you can put anywhere from 1 to 4 gigs of data, depending on tape length and whether the drive supports compression, on a tape that costs about $15; if you buy one of the latest models, using the DDS-2 standard, you can put 8 or 10GB on one $35 tape.

(There are many other kinds of tape drives, most of them cheaper than DAT. But even the cheapest cost $450 or more, the tapes are usually more expensive than DAT cartridges, and, most important, you won't find many Mac users running any of those devices, so support can be hard to come by. If money is the issue, I recommend saving up until you can afford a DAT drive. I did, and I've never regretted it.)

DeskTape (HN)

You can't ordinarily mount a tape on the Mac desktop, but there are a couple of software products that make this trick possible. The outstanding entry in this small category is **DeskTape**, from Optima Technology. Used in conjunction with a DAT drive (or with another, more expensive tape technology known as *8mm*), this $300 utility lets you treat a tape as if it were a 2GB hard drive. It's not fast enough for launching applications, but it's great for files you don't use most of the time but like to keep handy. And because it's on the desktop, it makes ad hoc backup of critical files a breeze—just drag them over.

Backup Software

If you are using a tape drive, you have only a couple of choices for backup software, and if you're like most other Mac tape users, you'll end up choosing Dantz Development's **Retrospect** ($250 retail, but bundled free with many tape drives). It (alone) supports almost every backup medium known to humankind, it offers an amazing array of features, it's exceptionally well supported, and though it's not exactly uncomplicated, version 2.0 provides an appealing interface and simplifies things enough so it's not hard to get done what you need to. Besides, it probably came bundled with your tape drive, since almost every vendor includes it. (If you are on a network, you can get a version called

Retrospect Remote and have every drive on the net automatically backed up over the network at night.)

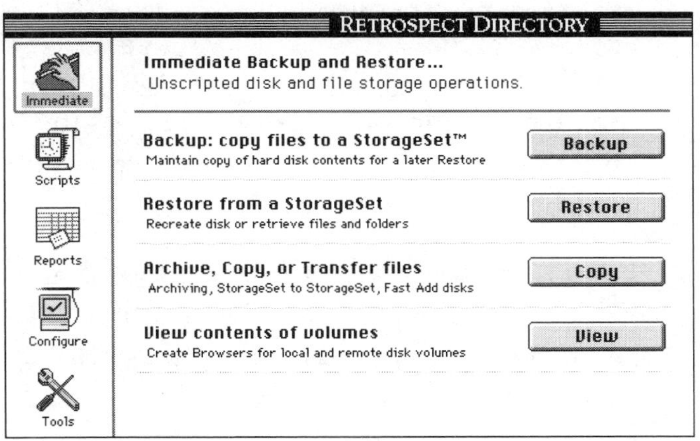

Dantz Development's Retrospect has long been the de facto standard software for backing up with Mac tape drives. With version 2 (shown here), it's even become reasonably easy to use.

If you are using any media you can mount on the desktop—floppies, hard disks, or cartridges—you don't need anything except the Finder to make copies. But you'll probably want to do *incremental backups*—backups that encompass only the files that have been created or modified since the last backup—between more time-consuming full backups of everything on your disk, and for that purpose (among others) a good backup utility makes life much simpler.

If you've already invested in a data-recovery utility like MacTools or Norton Utilities (covered in Chapter 7), you already own a backup utility. These programs are OK, but they—especially MacTools' CP Backup—can be pretty hard to use. Many users, once they get serious about backup, invest in a specialized utility. In this category, too, the best-sellers come from Dantz: **DiskFit Direct** ($50) is the easiest to use, while **DiskFit Pro** ($125) offers more features. **Redux Deluxe** ($80) from Inline Software is another popular choice.

Other utilities lurk in the background, always ready to back up your files on command, on a schedule you set, or automatically at shutdown. Recent entries include **SafeDeposit** ($190) from Dayna Communications and **FileDuo** ($150) from ASD Software.

Alternatively, with a little ingenuity you can create your own automatic backup system out of other popular utilities, such as CE Software's QuicKeys (optionally in conjunction with DiskTop, now published by PrairieSoft) or No Hands Software's Magnet. (See Chapter 13 for more on QuicKeys, DiskTop, and Magnet.) If you are into scripting, you can also create automatic backup scripts using Apple events with AppleScript or UserLand Software's Frontier.

Backup Strategies

The best way to get yourself to back up is to make it a routine that demands little if any effort or attention. Many of the backup utilities have a scheduling option, so all you have to do is set up the program and make sure media are available.

I don't do that (why not? I don't know), but I do leave my DAT drive on my SCSI chain almost all the time, and I keep two tapes, Odd and Even, close at hand. When I'm winding up a serious work session, I fire up Retrospect, pop in a tape (Odd or Even depending on the date), and let her fly. With two recent backups, I'm pretty well protected even if one tape should get damaged or corrupted. (I've had several tapes go bad over the years.)

If your backup software has a verification option, as Retrospect does, turn it on. That way the software will read back every file it's backed up and check it against the original to make sure the copy is accurate. It can double the time required to complete a backup, but it's worth it. (Besides, the sensible way to do a backup is to start it at the end of your computing day or schedule it to start automatically during the night. That way, who cares if it takes a few extra hours?)

However diligent you are in making incremental backups, it's a good idea to do a new full backup from time to time.

And it's plain common sense (though I don't do it) to keep a backup offsite, to protect you from such threats as fire or theft.

Basic Peripherals

To operate your Mac, you need a few essential pieces of equipment besides the computer itself. You need *input devices* (a keyboard and a mouse, generally) to control the computer with, and a monitor or screen to see what you're doing (and so the computer can communicate back to you).

Scanners aren't *essential* to operating your Mac, but they're getting more popular for the average user, and...well we couldn't decide where else in the book to put them, so they're covered here, too.

With some Macs (the Performas, PowerBooks, and all-in-one models) a monitor and sometimes a keyboard are included with your computer (or built right into it). If you buy another kind of Mac, or even if you're just thinking of upgrading, or you just want to consider your options (how about a trackball instead of that mouse?), this chapter will give you the lay of the land.

Contributors

John Kadyk (JK) is the chapter editor.

Scott Aronian (ScA) operates Brøderbund Software's digital video facility, and prior to 1994 he could proudly name and describe every Mac model.

Brad Bunnin (BB), principal author of *The Writer's Legal Companion,* is an attorney who practices literary law.

Andreu Cabré (AC) is a Catalan designer living in Northampton, Massachusetts, who writes poetry, paints, and is a fan of Barcelona's soccer team.

John Grimes (JG) is a cartoonist whose works include a book called *Reality Check* (Tenspeed Press) and the cover of this book.

Joe Matazzoni (JM), a former *Macworld* editor, writes about desktop publishing and interactive media.

Randy B. Singer (RS) is a practicing attorney, an Apple legal fellow, and a contributor to *Law Technology Product News* and *Law Office Computing.*

Arthur Naiman (AN), Sharon Zardetto Aker (SA), and **Susan McCallister (SM)** edited earlier editions of *The Macintosh Bible,* from which sections of this chapter were taken.

Contents

Monitors

Not all monitors are made alike, and more than any other piece of your Mac's equipment, your monitor will define how you think of your computer. Your choice will define whether you see your work in black and white or have a choice of millions of colors, and the quality of the screen may determine whether you start getting a headache after an hour or work comfortably all day. In this section, we'll describe what to look for in a Mac monitor, how to find out whether the monitor you want will work with your computer, and run through some of the many choices on the market.

Finding What You Need

This section outlines the points to consider in determining what kind of monitor you're looking for.

Monochrome or color? (JK/BB/AN). This decision really only applies to full-page and two-page monitors, since no one seems to make small or mid-size monochrome monitors anymore (although you may be able to find a nice used Apple 12-inch).

Monochrome, which means *one color*, includes both black-and-white and *grayscale* monitors, which can display black, white, and shades of gray. (Many people call all monochrome monitors black and white, as if they were TVs, but the ones sold nowadays are more often grayscale. For more on this difference, see "Richness of Colors or Grays" below.

The computer industry tries to make you feel that you *must* have a color monitor (and, in fact, some games won't work on monochrome monitors). But monochrome monitors have certain practical advantages, the biggest being that text and figures look crisper and better on them. It's harder for color monitors to create a crisp, solid image, because each *pixel* (picture element, or dot) on their screens is composed of three tiny dots—red, green, and blue—that your eyes merge into a single, colored dot.

Editors' Poll: Do You Need Color on Your Mac?

AA: I personally do, 'cause I do lots of color graphics, design colorful publications, play colorful games, and so forth. I also think color is a great visual cue in apps and in the Finder. Color coding folders and files in the Finder, for example, makes for faster visual searches.

DB: Yes, on my office publishing system I need color. However, most of the work I do on my PowerBook is in black and white.

EC: Yes, I need color for creating graphics and illustrations, for playing with video (if I ever get around to it), for layout, and for games. Oh yeah, and my favorite screensaver doesn't run without color either.

DD: No, most of the time I don't. I mostly do writing and page layout of one-color projects. The only time I really *used* color was to design my company brochure; then it was fun to see the second color on screen. It sure makes Shanghai more fun, though.

CG: I actually do need a color system because a lot of kids' software requires color. Since I do word processing most of the time, color isn't really a necessity, but it's a nicety.

JK: No, but it sure is nice. I didn't have a color monitor until just recently, and I still just use the monochrome for almost all my work because it's larger and I like it better for black-and-white text.

HN: No, but the world is colorful and I really like having color on my computer.

BW: Color makes the Mac interface more pleasant to use.

As beautiful as color is, most of us spend the bulk of our computer time using word processors, spreadsheets, databases, checkbook programs, and the like, where color doesn't matter much. Also, scrolling (and other forms of screen response) takes longer with color images than with black-and-white ones (this is true of grayscale images, too). Finally, a color monitor takes up more desk space and costs more than a monochrome one of the same size (though they're much more affordable than in the past). *[They also throw out more radiation, if you're worried about that. (Reasons you might be are described in Appendix A, "Staying Healthy at the Mac.")—DD]*

So if you're mostly going to use your Mac for the typical text-and-figures purposes mentioned above, and not for graphic arts programs, games, clip art, or other color-intensive applications, consider getting a monochrome display.

Monitor sizes (JK/BB). Most monitors fall into one of four basic size categories, based on their shape and diagonal screen measurement.

- Small (12-inch to 15-inch) monitors are fine for typical home uses: writing letters, using personal accounting software, playing games, and so on.
- Mid-size (16-inch or 17-inch) monitors allow you to display quite a bit more, but they're not quite tall enough to show the full length of a letter-size page with margins, or wide enough to show two adjacent pages.
- Full-page or *portrait* monitors (15-inch, but shaped differently than "small" 15-inch monitors) are designed to show a full letter-size page, with a little room next to it to leave the disk and Trash icons showing. The word portrait indicates the monitor's tall, rectangular shape (the term landscape is sometimes used to describe the shorter, wider shape of ordinary monitors).
- Two-page (19-inch to 21-inch) monitors display two full letter-size pages side by side, so they're great for desktop publishers. They're also useful for graphic artists and people who make large spreadsheets or who keep a lot of documents open at once.

Pixels and resolution (JK). Don't attach too much importance to a screen's physical size (it rarely matches the actual image area anyway). What matters more is how much information fits onto the screen, which isn't directly related to the screen measurement.

The image you see on a Mac's screen is made up of many tiny dots called *pixels*. The amount of information that fits on a screen depends on how many pixels it displays, which is called the screen's *resolution*. For example, Apple's standard resolution for small external monitors is 640 pixels across the screen and 480 from top to bottom; for mid-size monitors, it's 832 by 624; for portrait monitors, it's 640 by 870; and for large monitors, it's 1,024 by 768 or 1,152 by 870.

When you set a mid-size monitor to a resolution of 1,152 by 870, you're putting a lot more pixels in the same area, so the monitor uses smaller pixels, and everything on the screen looks smaller. The size of the pixels used at a

Standard Pixel Measurements for Different Screen Sizes

Monitor size	Standard resolution (width by height)
12-inch to 15-inch	640 by 480
16-inch to 17-inch	832 by 624
portrait	640 by 870
19-inch to 21-inch	1,024 by 768 or 1,152 by 870

given resolution is measured in pixels per inch, usually expressed as *dpi* (for *dots per inch*).

Monitors of the same general size and pixel dimensions often have different dpi because they have different-size image areas. Macs are designed so that a 72-dpi screen displays at actual size; a one-inch line on the screen will print out as a one-inch line on paper.

GOOD FEATURE

Many monitors can be set up to display at any of several different resolutions—depending on the capabilities of the Mac they're hooked up to—so you either cram more information onto the screen or blow everything up to a more readable size. Such monitors are called *multisync* or *multiscan* monitors and can usually be used with PCs as well as Macs. You generally need to get a special adapter plug from the monitor's manufacturer—usually for free or cheaply—to make a particular resolution work, but if you've installed a display card, you should be able to make the switch in the Monitors control panel. Apple and NEC make software that allows their multiscan monitors to make the switch without even restarting.

HOT TIP

Using PC Monitors With Macs

(Michael Santiago/JK)

Color or monochrome VGA monitors—the type that PCs normally use—work with all current modular Macs and most PowerBooks—all you need is an adapter (a little doo-hickey that fits between the end of the video cable and the Mac). Some monitor manufacturers supply them to their Mac customers, or you can get one for about $25 from James Engineering. Ordinarily, VGA and SVGA monitors run at slow refresh rates (60 Hz and 56 Hz, respectively), which can make their screens look flickery; but some adapters (like the MacComp series from James) will bring the rate up to Apple's standards. (Refresh rates are described under "Image Quality" in this section.)

Be sure the adapter you get is intended for your model of Macintosh and will give your monitor the correct screen resolution. You also may need to adjust the sync setting on the monitor (particularly if you notice a green look to the screen when it's turned on).

Richness of colors or grays (JK/AN/SA/ SM/Mac Kenny). On black-and-white monitors, each pixel can be either black or white. What looks like gray—the standard desktop pattern, for example—is actually made up of alternating black and white dots. On grayscale monitors, however, each pixel can be black, white, or a shade of gray. On color monitors, each pixel can be black, white, or any of over 16.7 million colors, including grays—an image of almost photographic quality. You select which level of color you want in the Monitors control panel (see the box "Setting Levels of Gray or Color" on the next page).

Number of Colors With Different Bit Depths

Bits per pixel	Number of available colors or shades
1	2 (black and white)
8	256
16	32,000
24	16.7 million

The richness of the color palette available with a given Mac and monitor setup is called its *bit depth*, which refers to the number of bits of the Mac's memory assigned to each pixel. One-bit color gives you just black and white; 8-bit gives you 256 colors or shades of gray; 16-bit gives you over 32,000 colors or shades of gray; and 24-bit gives you over 16.7 million.

The bigger the monitor, the more pixels it has, and the more memory is required for a given bit depth. The number of colors you can actually get out of your machine depends on the video capabilities of your Mac. So, for example, a Mac's built-in video support may be able to put 32,000 different colors or grays at once on a 16-inch screen, but only 256 at once on a 21-inch screen, because it has so many more pixels. With a 24-bit display card installed, the same Mac can produce 16.7 million colors on either of those monitors.

Video support, display cards, and acceleration (JK). Most Macs sold nowadays have some level of built-in video support, which means that you can connect a monitor directly to the Mac's video port. But the level of support varies quite a bit between models, so don't assume you'll be able to plug any monitor into any Mac. Generally, the more recent and expensive the Mac model, the more kinds of monitors it will support; see Chapter 2 for a partial list of which Macs support which monitors.

Setting Levels of Gray or Color (JK/SA/SM)

When you first hook up a new color monitor, you may be chagrined to find that everything's in black and white. To make it show colors, just select the Colors button in the Monitors control panel and then choose how many colors to display from the box to the right (only the ones your Mac or display card can handle will show up). By the same token, you can turn a color monitor into a grayscale one by clicking the Grays button and then choosing from the list box.

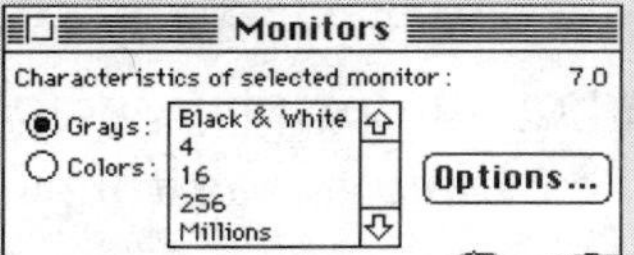

The Monitors control panel is where you switch between black and white, grayscale, and color, and where you select the levels of color or gray.

If your monitor is set to display a lot of colors or grays, you may find that scrolling (and other forms of screen response) seem sluggish. To speed things up, choose a smaller number of colors or grays, or choose Black & White (or invest in an accelerator card…or a faster Mac).

On some Macs, you can expand the video support by buying a VRAM upgrade (see Chapter 2 for more on VRAM), which will allow you to hook up a larger monitor or get more colors on the same monitor. Otherwise, you'll have to buy a *display card* (which plugs into one of your Mac's expansion slots) or, if your Mac doesn't have a slot, get a display interface box that plugs into your Mac's SCSI port. The last surviving two interface boxes I found were Radius's $200 **PowerView** and MicroMac's **SCSIview** ($300 for monochrome, $400 for 8-bit color), both of which support a huge variety of external monitors, including two-page displays.

If you work with large, full-color (24-bit) images, you may find that it takes forever for the screen to redraw whenever you make a change or even drag an image a couple of inches. If that's the case, you'll probably want to invest in a display card that includes *graphics acceleration.* Some graphics accelerator cards can make changes appear several times faster than they would without acceleration, but they can also cost several times the price of a regular display card. (See the box "The Need For Speed" in Chapter 15 for more on graphics accelerators.)

Image quality (JK/AN/BB). A monitor's *refresh rate*—how often it redraws the image on the screen—helps determine how steady and solid the image looks.

(Don't confuse the refresh rate with the screen's ability to keep up with the mouse when you move a graphic around on the screen, though; the latter depends on the speed of the Mac and its graphics acceleration, if it has any.)

The refresh rate is measured in *hertz* (times per second)—abbreviated *Hz*. If a screen refreshes too slowly, you get *flicker* (also called *strobe*). The larger the screen, the more flicker is likely to bother you, so larger monitors usually have higher refresh rates. (Actually, the refresh rate is linked to the monitor's resolution, so a given monitor can have different refresh rates depending on which resolution is in effect.)

Monitors that plug into the Mac's video port have to operate at the refresh rate that the Mac produces, which depends, in turn, on the type and resolution of the monitor connected to it. Generally, any monitor that's connected to the Mac's video port and operates at a resolution of 640 by 480 pixels has to run at 67 Hz; if the resolution is any higher, it has to run at 75 Hz. The main exceptions are VGA monitors and SVGA monitors, which were developed for PCs but can run on most current Macs and are often cheaper than Mac monitors. On the Mac they can run as low as 60 Hz or even 56 Hz, although some Macs let you increase the refresh rate of SVGA monitors up to 70 Hz or 72 Hz in the Monitors control panel (press the Options button).

Peripheral vision is particularly sensitive to flicker, so if you're in doubt about a screen, turn away from it and see how it looks out of the side of your eye.

A Video Card, Not a Video Card (JK)

For a long time, the term *video card* meant just one thing—an expansion card that you put in your Mac to connect it to a monitor. Now there are video digitizer cards, which can record clips from videotape, and other video cards that help your Mac display full-motion video on the screen. So in this chapter we'll say *display card* when we mean the kind of video card that drives the monitor and has nothing to do with desktop video—as in QuickTime and television.

Several other factors contribute to image quality. *Dot pitch*, which is the distance between individual dots of phosphor on the screen, affects the overall clarity of the image. Generally, anything below .30mm is acceptable, and most Mac monitors fall within that range. With color monitors, sharpness depends partly on the ability of the display tube to focus the three color beams to hit the right spots on the screen (this is

Evaluation Checklist

(AN/BB)

Monitors are a lot like speakers—you can look at technical specs all day long, but the only way to buy speakers is to listen to them, and the only way to buy monitors is to see them in action, ideally side by side. What you're looking for is a crisp, high-contrast, rock-solid image—one that isn't washed-out or fuzzy, doesn't waver or flicker, and isn't distorted around the edges. Getting that is more important than any other consideration, and worth paying more for.

Remember—you're going to be staring at the screen for *thousands* of hours, and anything less than a great image will really drive you nuts. Skimping on the quality of your monitor is like buying an uncomfortable bed—whatever you save won't be worth it in the long run.

[Monitor reviews in magazines (and books like this) can be helpful, but they're no substitute for seeing first-hand what you intend to buy. You can usually trust that a magazine's top pick will be a good monitor, but I've had experiences that have directly contradicted what I've read.—JK]

Here's a checklist of things to look for when you've got a monitor in front of you:

- Is the screen image sharp? Trust your eyes.
- Is the screen big enough so that you don't have to scroll constantly? Some monitors let you change the resolution to get more on the screen, but that often makes text too small to read comfortably.
- Do you have room to view the screen from a comfortable distance? This is especially important for very big screens (and older monitors—those that aren't MPR II–compliant—which you should sit an arm's length away from in order to minimize your exposure to ELF and VLF emissions).
- Is the screen image distorted? Look for a lack of symmetry, and for lines that should be straight but aren't. (Some monitors have adjustments that let you correct distortion.)
- Does the image flicker when you're at a proper viewing distance?
- Are controls easy to reach and use?
- Does the screen display's color spectrum please you? You may have noticed that some brands of color film look redder or yellower than reality, while others are bluer or greener. The color balance of monitors varies the same way. Is there a way to change the color balance if you want to? For example, can you match screen color to a particular color in a 35mm slide?

GOOD FEATURE

called *convergence*, and a few monitors let you adjust for it—a very good feature). *Distortion* refers to a screen's tendency to misrepresent shapes—to display straight lines as bowed, for example. It's often most noticeable at the edges and corners of the screen, and it's more common on large monitors than small ones.

Emissions and MPR II (JK). Monitors produce electromagnetic emissions—called *ELF* and *VLF* (extremely low frequency and very low frequency) radiation—that, according to some research, may increase your risk of cancer (for more on this subject, see Appendix A). There's no conclusive evidence that the risk exists, and no level of exposure that has been determined to be safe, so the U.S. government doesn't regulate monitors in this area. The Swedish government has produced a set of low-emissions guidelines called MPR II, and most current monitors adhere to their standards. If you wonder whether a monitor you're considering meets the Swedish guidelines, just ask; most that do will advertise it.

Energy Star (JK). In an effort to cut down on energy consumption, the Clinton administration set up the Energy Star program. Energy Star requires that all computer equipment sold to the U.S. government drop its power consumption below 30 watts when it's not being used.

Equipment manufacturers don't want to be excluded from selling to the Feds (they're the world's biggest customer, after all, accounting for 10 percent of all computer equipment sales in the United States), so most of them are changing their products to meet the standards. As a result, a lot of hardware is being designed to automatically go into a low-power mode or turn itself off when it's not being used.

For example, Energy Star–compliant monitors from Apple, NEC, and Radius all have a screen-saver-like feature that not only dims their screen, but reduces their power consumption by 50 to 85 percent if you stop using the Mac for a given length of time. To bring one of these monitors back up to full power, you just move the mouse or hit any key.

Monochrome Portrait Monitors

Timing prevented us from comparing these portrait monitors side by side, but all of the models below are good and have been around for awhile. The only argument would be over which is the most outstanding (Susan likes the Apple and Brad prefers the Mirror). Color portrait monitors are discussed on page 248.

Apple Portrait Display (SM). This grayscale monitor ($710 ApplePrice) comes the closest I've seen to the crisp, bright image on the old compact Mac's 9-inch screen. The screen is very flat and the image is crystal-clear and rich with contrast. It's really a pleasure to look at every day. *[This monitor's main disadvantage (besides the price) is that it doesn't come on a tilt-and-swivel stand, like most others.—JK]*

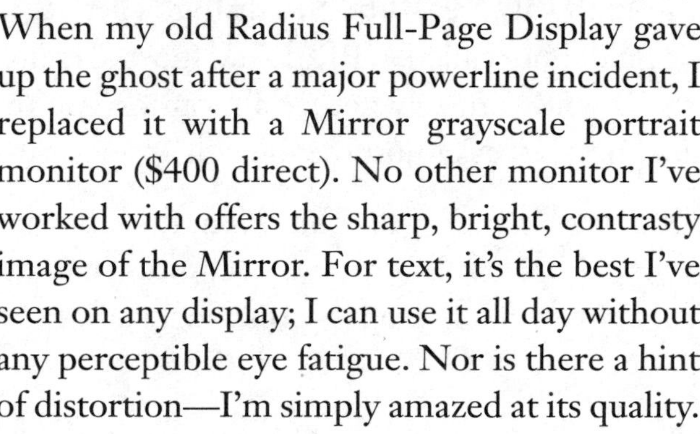

Mirror Monochrome Portrait Monitor (BB). When my old Radius Full-Page Display gave up the ghost after a major powerline incident, I replaced it with a Mirror grayscale portrait monitor ($400 direct). No other monitor I've worked with offers the sharp, bright, contrasty image of the Mirror. For text, it's the best I've seen on any display; I can use it all day without any perceptible eye fatigue. Nor is there a hint of distortion—I'm simply amazed at its quality.

About the Monitor Reviews (JK)

We reviewed several monitors in each category, based on their success in magazine reviews and in retail sales, and then wrote reviews of our top choices. In some cases, companies were skipped (for example, those that were changing their product lines as we went to press). The monitors we did review certainly aren't the only ones worth considering; if you find something else you like, your opinion is worth as much as what's written here.

If your Mac doesn't have a video port that will support the monitor, you can get the monitor with an 8-bit grayscale display card for $520 (the manual, which is well written and well illustrated, makes installation simple). The monitor also comes with software that can increase the type size of menus and includes a no-frills screen saver.

Radius Full-Page Display GS and Radius Pivot Monitor (JK/AN). The Radius **Full-Page Display GS** ($600 list, $400 mail order) is a high-quality grayscale portrait monitor that powers down when it's not being used and comes with Radius's overnight-replacement warranty (see the box "Radius and NEC Service" on page 248).

The **Radius Pivot** is similar in quality, but it's designed to accommodate wide documents by pivoting from vertical to horizontal. When you move from, say, a letter to a spreadsheet, you just tip the monitor over onto its side. It takes just a moment for the image to re-form in the new configuration.

The Pivot currently lists for $700, and you'll need a display card to get the horizontal orientation to work on the Quadras 660AV and 840AV. There's also a color Pivot, which is described below.

Monochrome Two-Page Displays (JK)

Since many current Macs' video ports support these large monitors, they're effectively less expensive than when you had to buy both the monitor and a $400 display card. Most of the models on the market nowadays look pretty good.

SuperMac and **RasterOps** make very nice, almost identical 21-inch grayscale monitors, both using the same Hitachi tube ($1,200 and $1,300, respectively). Radius makes a 20-incher ($1,000) and a 21-incher ($1,200): Both display 1,152 by 870 pixels, but the 20-inch screen has tiny pixels (82 dpi) compared to those of the 21-inch screen (74 dpi). Mirror and Mobius both make very usable, inexpensive 19-inch monitors for about $700. If your Mac doesn't have a video port, both companies make a black-and-white versions that come with a display card. At this writing, the Mirror combo costs $750 and the Mobius set $800.

Small Color Monitors (BB/JK)

Most people opt for small color monitors—they're reasonably priced, yet they have the advantages of color. The choices described here are the leaders in the field, in the order of our preference.

NEC MultiSync 3FGe. NEC's **MultiSync 3FGe** ($600) is the best small monitor in the group we looked at. The screen quality is superb: bright enough for use in well-lighted rooms, with good contrast, sharp, clear lines, and no visible flicker or distortion. Images are markedly smooth and grain-free, and colors are natural, neutral, and life-like. Black and white text is brilliant and easy to read.

In addition to the standard brightness and contrast controls, the 3FGe has knobs for adjusting horizontal and vertical size, centering, and distortion, and for manual *degaussing*, which resets the screen's color adjustments. (Multiscan monitors like this one need size and centering controls to adapt to the variety of computers and boards they connect to.)

Older Monitors and Display Cards (JK)

Monitors designed to work with a specific display card, as many early monitors were, won't work if you plug them into a modern Mac's video port. Watch out for this problem if you're buying a used monitor. Look out for flicker, too, because these older monitors didn't conform to Apple's standard refresh rates.

Although it's priced in the range of other 14-inch monitors, the 15-inch 3FGe is sized squarely between the small and mid-size categories. In fact, things look oversized at the normal small-monitor resolution of 640 by 480, because the pixels are a chunky 63 dpi. But if you increase the 3FGe's resolution to 832 by 624 (which is normal for 16- and 17-inch monitors), you can fit much more on the screen, and images are still a very readable 77 dpi (so, in effect, you're getting a mid-size monitor for about the price of a small one). NEC's DPI on the Fly software lets you switch between the monitor's various resolutions from the Monitors control panel, without having to switch cables and adapters.

GOOD FEATURE

The 3FGe meets Sweden's MPR II emissions limits and comes with a three-year warranty. Its manual is clear, complete, and organized so that new users can easily find and understand the information they need.

NEC also makes a cheaper, lower-quality 15-inch monitor called the **3V** ($500), and a more expensive one called the **4FGe** ($655). The 4FGe uses the same tube as the 3FGe, but it provides a way to adjust color balance, is Energy Star–compliant, and can be taken up to a resolution of 1,024 by 768 pixels. It uses digital push-button controls, which are a little harder to use than the simple knobs on the 3FGe.

Apple Macintosh Color Display. Apple's **Macintosh Color Display** ($445 ApplePrice) is very much like previous small Apple monitors: compact, high-

HOT TIP

Getting the Green Off the Screen (JK)

Some VGA monitors, including Apple's discontinued Basic Color Monitor, often show an overly green screen color when connected to some Centris and Quadra models. To fix this problem with the Apple monitor, you can get a Basic Color Monitor system extension from Apple dealers. On non-Apple monitors, also check for a *sync* switch; you may be able to de-green your screen by changing its position.

The extension should always work with Apple's monitor, but it may cause some non-Apple monitors to go blank. If that happens, you need to remove it. Here's how:

1. Start or restart the Mac with [⌘] [Option] [P] [R] held down.
2. After you've heard the startup chime *twice,* release those keys and hold down [Shift].
3. Drag the Basic Color Monitor extension from your Extensions folder to the Trash.

AudioVision 14 Display (JK/Ken Maki)

Apple's **AudioVision 14 Display** ($650 ApplePrice) follows the multimedia theme of many recent Macs. It was designed for use with AV Macs, but it can work with any model that supports an external monitor. It uses the same picture tube as the Apple Macintosh Color Display, but includes 2.5-inch stereo speakers, a built-in microphone, volume and recording controls, and a set of special ports.

On the side of the monitor are ports for attaching external speakers, headphones, a CD-ROM drive, an audio CD or tape player, and a keyboard or mouse. There's also an S-video–in port, so you can use the AV 14 as a monitor for a camcorder or VCR. The AV's video cable has a special connector that's designed to feed all these various inputs back to one port on the back of the Mac. But at this writing, only the Power Macs have the kind of port that can handle it; with all other Macs, you have to use an adapter that awkwardly splits the sound, video, and ADB signals back into separate plugs.

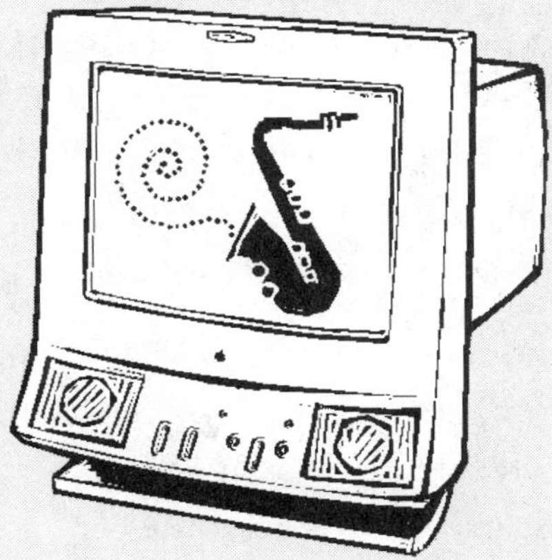

Apple's AV 14 Display has a built-in microphone, stereo speakers, and ports for plugging in a CD- or tape-player and a VCR as well as Mac peripherals.

Unfortunately, the AV monitor has had a number of problems (enough, in fact, that Apple has a special section for it on its 800 SOS-APPL tech support line). For example, the settings in its special sound and video control panels are complicated and not intuitively arranged, and you have to change them depending on how you're using the monitor. Also, the position of its microphone and speakers leads to feedback when the monitor is being used as a speakerphone on an AV Mac, so you have to use an external microphone or set of headphones.

Still, the AV 14 is a good-quality monitor (better and more neutral-colored than the Macintosh Color Display), and it performs many AV functions well, if you can avoid its rough spots.

quality, and simple to set up and use. The manual is less informative than that of other monitors, but there's little you'll need to know. Front-mounted user controls are limited to contrast and brightness (other controls are hidden behind a panel in back and are intended for technicians only).

Apple's image quality, which used to be the best available, has been surpassed by NEC's, but it's still very good. Sharpness and contrast are above average, brightness and contrast are high, and there's no distortion. Colors are strong, smooth, and cool, with a gray-green cast. Black-and-white text is soft, but whites are clear. Apple meets the Swedish emissions standards and offers a one-year warranty.

The Macintosh Color Display is less expensive and less bulky on the desktop than the NEC 3FGe. But it's limited to one resolution—640 by 480—so you can't set the screen to display more material, as you can with most third-party monitors.

Color Portrait Monitors (BB)

The $800 **Mirror Color Portrait Monitor** and the $1,000 **Radius Precision-Color Pivot Monitor** are both portrait monitors, but, like the grayscale Pivot monitor described above, the Color Pivot can also turn sideways so its long side is horizontal. When plugged into a Mac's video port, the Pivot has a resolution of 624 by 832—the standard resolution for mid-size monitors but less than the Mirror's standard full-page resolution of 640 by 870. However, you can get full-page or two-page resolutions from the Pivot using Radius' PrecisionColor interface cards: the 8XJ ($600, for full-page) and the 24XK ($1,000, for two-page).

GOOD FEATURE

Both monitors offer good image quality, with moderate contrast and brightness and muted colors. The Mirror's colors have a cool, greenish cast to them, but its text looks better than the Pivot's, and it's $200 cheaper. In fact, if I were buying *any* color monitor, I'd buy the Mirror—for its price, for its black-and-white text quality, and for its portrait orientation. But I don't need accurate colors in my work, which is mostly writing, nor do I often work with spreadsheets. If I did, I'd buy the NEC 3FGe for its better price and image quality, rather than the Pivot or another portrait monitor.

Both monitors come with a full complement of controls: brightness, contrast, size, centering, distortion, and degaussing. Both have one-year warranties, but only the Radius meets Swedish emissions standards.

Radius and NEC Service (JK)

GOOD FEATURE

Radius and NEC both offer exceptional warranty coverage. When you call them with a problem that they decide is a hardware defect, they'll send you a replacement monitor overnight. Radius will actually go so far as to send someone out to install the new monitor for you.

Medium-Size Color Monitors

Not only are 16- and 17-inch color monitors bigger in screen size, but they are also bigger in *footprint* (the space they take up on the desktop), weight, and bulk than the 14-inchers, and they cost two or three times as much, although they display less than twice as much information. And despite the fact that they generally offer more controls over color and image, their image quality usually isn't as good as that of the smaller monitors. But if you need one, here are a few recommendations.

NEC MultiSync 5FGe (BB). Even the $1,045 **NEC MultiSync 5FGe,** the best of the group we looked at, doesn't meet the high standards set by its little brother, the 3FGe. Still, its color quality is excellent, and black-and-white text is contrasty and relatively sharp. The two NEC monitors share the same clean and functional design, fine manual, and three-year warranty. Like the 4FGe, the 5FGe uses push-button controls to manage brightness, contrast, size, centering, distortion, and color-matching functions.

Sony Mulitiscan 17se (BB). My second favorite among the 17-inchers was the $1,500 **Sony Multiscan17se.** The monitor's contrast, brightness, and overall image quality are average. Sharpness is better than average but not as good as the NEC's. Colors are muted but neutral. Geometry and color controls are sophisticated, even extending to hue and saturation. Black-and-white text is average. One special feature sets the monitor apart: It goes into a power-saving mode to reduce energy consumption. The 17se comes with a one-year comprehensive warranty, and the tube itself is covered for two.

Apple Multiple Scan 17 Display (JK). As we were going to press, Apple discontinued its 16-inch monitor and introduced the **Multiple Scan 17** ($1,070 Apple Price) as its replacement. We weren't able to get one in time for review, but if its screen is as beautiful as the old 16-inch monitor's, the Multiple Scan 17 should be worthy of consideration. Even more so than its predecessor, in fact: The new monitor supports three resolutions and includes software that lets you switch between them without restarting. Besides the usual brightness, contrast, and centering controls, it's got an adjustment for color accuracy, and it complies with Energy Star specifications and MPR II emissions guidelines. Like the other monitors listed here, it works with PCs too, but unlike the others, it doesn't require an adapter to work with the Mac—instead, an adapter is provided for using it with PCs. Apple's warranty is just a year, though.

Large Color Monitors (JK/BB)

We haven't reviewed large color monitors because most users don't need them. If you do, you should gather information from recent magazine reviews and the experiences of desktop publishing service bureaus, user groups, and anyone you may know who does a lot of computer graphics, before deciding what to get.

You can now buy 19-, 20-, and 21-inch color monitors for under $2,000, but unless you have a high-end Mac (one of the top Quadra or PowerMac models), you'll have to spend several hundred dollars more on a VRAM upgrade or a display card to get decent color richness. If you have an older Mac, it probably won't support this size monitor at all, so you'll have to buy a display card to use it at its intended resolution.

Buy a 20-inch monitor only if you genuinely need the large screen and have a place to put it; you'll find its presence overwhelming unless you can sit well back from it. (That's hard to do with a monitor that's almost 20 inches deep—there's not much desk space left for your keyboard.) *[These monstrosities dominate whatever room they're in; it's like putting a dishwasher on top of your desk.—JK]*

Keyboards

When you buy a modular Mac, the keyboard usually isn't included. Most people will automatically buy an Apple keyboard, even though there are plenty of others on the market that might suit a particular person's purposes much better. Here are some hints on what to look for and which products supply it.

Evaluating Keyboards (JK)

Keyboards may seem generic, but there are plenty of differences to consider. To do a worthwhile comparison, use the information here to think about what you want. Then find a keyboard (in the following sections or in a store or catalog)

Editors' Poll: Do You Ever Really Use the Numeric Keypad on Your Keyboard?

AA: Constantly!! I use it to navigate in MS Word (left, right, page down, previous editing location, etc.) and to play games such as Super Tetris.

DB: In Microsoft Word I use it to move around my document. In QuarkXPress I've assigned style sheets to each key. Mostly I use it to add up things in Excel or the Calculator.

EC: Through no fault of my great typing teacher, Mr. Berkman, I never learned how to type the numbers in the regular keyboard without moving my fingers off the keys, and the numeric keypad is a lot faster. I also sometimes use it to navigate around in Word or PM.

DD: I was about to say no, but then I did my taxes this weekend and was really happy to have it there.

CG: Whenever I use the calculator DA I use the numeric keyboard (which is to say, not all that much).

JK: Yes! Anytime I enter a phone number in my address book or use the calculator DA. Even though I'm not really a ten-key typist, it's *much* faster and easier to use than the numbers above the letter keys.

HN: I use the keypad occasionally when entering numbers in a spreadsheet or calculator.

BW: Come to think of it, No. I took typing in high school, and skipped accounting.

that seems to offer that. If you can, try it out, or get a money-back guarantee when you buy it; you won't really be able to judge its performance until you've used it at your own Mac for awhile.

- **Key feel.** Every keyboard has a slightly different feel. Do you prefer a hard, solid keystroke or a softer, mushier one? You'll need to do some hands-on testing to decide.

- **Ergonomics.** Using a keyboard a lot can also put you at risk for various injuries, some of which can become permanent disabilities (see Appendix A for more on this). If you're constantly typing, you should seriously consider getting one of the specially-built keyboards coming onto the market that are designed to avoid the main causes of these injuries.

- **The numeric keypad.** Most keyboards come with a numeric keypad, or at least have an option to add one. The keypad saves a huge amount of time for people who enter numbers a lot and can touch-type the ten-key layout. For people who don't use it, the keypad is just an obstacle on their hand's way to the mouse.

You can also assign other functions to the keypad, though. If you hit the Clear key in Word, the numbers become controls for moving the insertion point up or down or to the start or end of a line (when you hit Clear again, they go back to being number keys). If a disability prevents you from being able to use the mouse, you can use the Easy Access control panel to make its number keys move the pointer.

- **Function keys and other controls.** Apple's extended and adjustable keyboards, and many third-party keyboards, include function keys, which some programs (Microsoft Word and Excel, for example) use as shortcuts for standard commands. You can also use macro programs like QuicKeys (described in Chapter 13) to assign any function you want to these keys. Some keyboards, like Apple's Adjustable Keyboard, have special buttons that control the volume on the Mac's speaker and start and stop sound recordings.
- **Built-in trackballs.** Some keyboards have trackballs built in, which saves you the expense of buying one separately. But don't assume the keyboard's trackball will work the same way as others you've used—I've tried some that are virtually unusable (see the TrakPro review below).
- **Key arrangement.** Some keyboards have ⌘, Option, and Ctrl keys on both sides of the Spacebar, or other unique layouts you may find very convenient or very annoying. Again, it's ideal to try before you buy, or at least get a money-back guarantee.

Standard and Extended Keyboards (AN/BB/JK)

Most people buy one of Apple's two basic, tried-and-true keyboards: the 81-key Apple Keyboard or the 105-key Apple Extended Keyboard, which has a row of fifteen function keys (including Undo, Cut, Copy, and Paste), a cluster of command keys—Home, End, Page Up, Page Down, Help, and ⌦ (forward delete)—and extra ⌘, Option, and Control keys to the right of the Spacebar. Arthur can't stand the planklike size of the extended keyboard, but many people like it.

A number of companies besides Apple make extended keyboards. DataDesk was one of the first; Brad finds its $170 **101E** lighter yet more satisfying to the touch than Apple's or other companies' boards. It has a set of modifier keys at both ends of the Spacebar, which some will find convenient. John likes the solid, positive tactile feel of Key Tronic's keyboards, but he had some compatibility problems with its TrakPro model (see the review below).

Ergonomic Keyboards

As we mentioned above, heavy keyboard use can put you at risk for some very serious and permanent injuries (to find out more, read Appendix A). People are concerned enough over this issue to look for products that will protect rather than harm them, and companies are beginning to develop keyboards for this new market. Here are the main two models available for the Mac.

Apple Adjustable Keyboard (JK). If you want a keyboard that's more comfortable than ordinary models, the Apple **Adjustable Keyboard** ($145 ApplePrice) is the least expensive alternative you'll find, and although it's not as thoroughly ergonomic as the Kinesis reviewed below, it may be all you need.

It's got two basic improvements over ordinary keyboards:

- It supports your hands with comfortably curved, sloping palm rests that attach to the front of the keyboard.

- It's hinged at the top so you can split it down the middle. You can adjust the angle of the split to match the angle at which your hands approach the keyboard, so there's no sideways bend at the wrist. (The straight-line arrangement of ordinary keyboards forces your hands to bend outward, which can be a factor in keyboard-related injuries.)

I found typing on the adjustable keyboard so much easier, more comfortable, and more relaxed than on Apple's standard keyboard that I ordered one as soon as the loaner had to go back to Apple.

The numeric keypad is separate, with its own palmrest, and includes the function keys and other extras found on the extended keyboard. It can be attached to either side of the main keyboard, or left off entirely. The main keyboard has handy extra buttons for controlling the Mac's sound and for recording, if your Mac has a microphone.

The only thing I really didn't like about the-adjustable keyboard was the loose, tab-in-slot way the palmrests hook up to the keyboard. If you lift the keyboard, they come off, so if you have to move it around much, you'll be frustrated trying to constantly reattach those loose pieces of plastic. Other users may be annoyed at the amount of desk space the keyboard takes up, particularly if you include the numeric keypad. But for straight typing, I thought the keyboard was great, and it's actually cheaper than Apple's Extended Keyboard.

The Adjustable Keyboard splits down the middle so your wrists won't have to bend sideways, and it includes detachable palmrests.

Kinesis Ergonomic Keyboard (RS). When you first see the Kinesis keyboard ($500, Kinesis) it looks like a piece of modern sculpture. It's actually a QWERTY keyboard that's been redesigned to correct the awkward postures that can lead to repetitive stress injuries. According to independent studies cited by Kinesis and glowing early reports from users, it really works. In fact, it even helps you to sit in the correct posture, resulting in fewer backaches!

The Kinesis separates left- and right-hand keys and arranges them in "bowls" to let the hands rest in a natural position.

The Kinesis's left- and right-hand keys are set in two concave bowls that are separated by several inches of empty surface, so that your arms project straight forward to the keyboard rather than angling in from the sides. The keys are arranged so that your thumbs are higher than the rest of your hand, and palms face each other slightly. The result is that your hands and arms remain in a natural position while using the keyboard, and very little finger movement is necessary to push down each key.

Some keys have been relocated, so you do have to do a little relearning, but the keyboard also has a built-in ability to be remapped. The numeric keypad is embedded in the right keyset, so you don't have to take your hand off the keyboard to use it. Overall, the Kinesis is no bigger than Apple's Extended Keyboard, despite its built-in PowerBook-style palm supports.

Using the Kinesis requires much less effort than does a standard keyboard. I highly recommend that you try one, even if you don't (yet) suffer from any kind of repetitive stress injury.

Keyboards With Trackballs (JK)

I was initially attracted to the **TrakPro** ($250, Key Tronic) because it has a trackball built into the right end of the keyboard. I always liked the way the trackball is integrated with the keyboard on PowerBooks and the Mac Portable, and this looked like a similar arrangement for desktop Macs. Unfortunately, it's not.

The trackball has the main clicking buttons at the top of the ball, so you can't roll with your fingers and click with your thumb. Instead, you have to either click with one finger while rolling with the other or use both hands to operate the ball, either of which is very awkward. There *are* buttons below the ball that you can program to be clickers, but they're small, uncomfortable, and offer a lot of resistance to being pushed.

It also bothered me that the TrakPro has no built-in arrow keys. Instead, it's got page control keys that you can make function as arrow keys, but you have to assign them that function every time you turn on the computer. I had further problems when I hooked up a mouse to the keyboard: After restarting, the pointer would sometimes freeze, or its motion would be too slow (and not fixable using the Mouse control panel).

On the other hand, I very much liked the solid feel of the keys themselves. If Key Tronic could eliminate the problems I've mentioned, the TrakPro could be a great keyboard, instead of a good idea that didn't come off right.

The **TrackBoard** ($130, MicroMachines) wasn't available at the time of this writing, but it should be when you read this. In a picture of a prototype, the TrackBoard's trackball looks more like the one on the PowerBooks (and, for those who remember, even more like the one on the Mac Portable). It's got a thumb bar below the ball for clicking, and two buttons above the ball for double-clicking and dragging. The TrackBoard has function keys, but a numerical keypad is optional.

Non-English Keyboards (JK)

Apple makes standard and extended keyboards for all the major Western European languages, plus Japanese, Korean, Russian, Persian, Hebrew, Greek, Turkish, Icelandic, Finnish, and Flemish. To use them properly, you need the corresponding version of the system software. You can order both the keyboard and the system software through Apple dealers.

A Chord Keyboard (Caleb Clark)

The **BAT Personal Keyboard** (from Infogrip) is a seven-button keyboard that lets you type one-handed: there's one key for each of your four fingers and three for your thumb. You hit combinations ("chords") of the seven keys to produce all the various keyboard characters. For example, the chord for the letter *g* is the middle thumb and ring finger keys pushed down simultaneously.

Standard keyboards are faster than the BAT for straight typing, but the BAT is convenient for things like layout or text editing, because you can keep one hand on the keyboard and one on the mouse, and never look away from the screen. I put the BAT to the left of my standard keyboard so I can type on either one according to the situation, and it works great.

The BAT has a palmrest and ergonomically designed keys, and it didn't take that long to learn. You can get a left- or right-handed BAT for $300, or buy both for $500 and use them together.

Mice and Other Pointing Devices

Mice are one of the Mac's great innovations. They give you much more direct control over what's on the screen than any keyboard could. The mouse controls the pointer, which gives you the ability to select objects on the screen and control cursors in word processors, paintbrushes in art programs, and paddles in shuffleboard games.

Mice

There's nothing wrong with the mouse that came with your Mac, but you may someday have to replace it, or there may be a substitute that would better fit the way you use your Mac. For example, some mice and trackballs have extra buttons that lock down for dragging objects, or for other purposes that you can assign. Here are several alternative mice you might consider.

Editors' Poll: Do You Ever Use a Pointing Device Other Than a Mouse?

AA: Nope, although I wish I had a Wacom pressure-sensitive digitizing tablet.

DB: I have a trackball and a pen-based tablet. I don't love trackballs, but I'm learning to like them more than mice, and they take up much less desk space (I put mine right next to my keyboard on a pull-out keyboard tray so that I don't have to extend my arm too far). I'm just getting used to the tablet, but I think I'm going to like it a lot in the not-too-distant future.

EC: No, I usually use a mouse (or trackball on my PowerBook), but if I were a graphic artist, I'd buy a pressure-sensitive pen in a second. Less than a second.

DD: Never tried one.

CG: No.

HN: I *never* use a mouse, always a trackball.

JK: Nope.

BW: I've used pressure-sensitive digitizing tablets, especially with Fractal Design Painter. Obviously, they're great for drawing and painting, but clumsy when it comes to using menus.

Ergonomic Mice (RS). The top of Logitech's **MouseMan** ($120) is molded to fit your palm (there are different versions for right and left hands). MouseMan has three buttons—one for clicking and two that can be programmed to issue frequently used commands. *[I find three buttons uncomfortable and confusing, as do most people (according to research Apple did before deciding on its one-button mouse).—AN]* You can adjust the resolution to up to four times that of Apple's mouse (400 dpi vs. 100 dpi); this lets you move the pointer more quickly, which is especially handy on larger monitors.

If you have an older Mac with an older mouse, and you like the idea of ergonomic but don't want to spring for a new mouse, a kit called **Mouse Topper** ($20, Contour Designs) lets you put a new top on your old mouse that will make it as comfortable as the ergonomic models. The converted mouse is rounded and wider in the area that fits in your palm, and it has a much larger and easier-to-use button.

A cordless mouse (AN). I've often found the cord on my mouse getting in my way as I make the big, sweeping arm movements so typical of people with my particular constellation of neurological defects. Perhaps you have the same problem. The solution is a cordless mouse that transmits its motion to the Mac with an infrared beam, like Z-Nix's **SuperMouse** ($110). When you're not using it, you place it in a cradle on your desk to recharge it.

A mini-mouse (RS). At first glance, the **Gulliver** ($70, Appoint) looks a like the heel from a small boy's dress shoe. Actually, it's a miniature mouse that's ideal for use with PowerBooks. It's small enough to pack in a laptop tote bag and requires less space to use than an ordinary mouse (which helps, since you never know where you'll be breaking out the PowerBook). It isn't as comfortable as a full-size mouse, but if you have a PowerBook and only a real mouse will do for you, you might want to check out the Gulliver.

Mouse Pads (JK/RS)

If you have a fairly smooth desk (but not *too* smooth) and your keyboard isn't constantly surrounded with papers, sticky food residue, and other desk clutter, you probably don't need a mouse pad. But having one helps keep an area clear for the mouse and gives it a good surface to roll on. *[But watch out for those slick, hard plastic pads (often with some company's logo or other advertising on them). Using one of them is like trying to run a 100-yard dash on a track covered with ball bearings.—RS]*

Fixing a Jerky, Rough-Rolling Mouse (SA/SM/AN/RS/JK)

Over time, gunk builds up on the rollers inside a mouse, making it feel rough and causing the pointer to skip jerkily around the screen. Luckily, there's an easy way to fix it.

Remove the ring at the bottom of the mouse by turning it (or sliding it, on some older mice) and drop the ball out into your palm. Then, using a penknife or pencil eraser, scrape or rub off the track of crud that you'll see on the rollers inside. Wipe the ball with a cloth, and put the mouse back together. *[This little chore is really worth the time it takes. The difference between a gunky, rough mouse and a clean, smooth mouse is astounding.—JK]*

For a quicker, easier way to clean your mouse, there's a $15 kit from Curtis that's the epitome of simple yet elegant design. You put a drop or two of cleaning fluid onto a Velcro-covered ball that's resting on a Velcro pad, then put the mouse (with its regular ball removed) over the Velcro-covered ball and roll it around. It's easy, it's hygienic and...it's fun. *[And it's a waste of money. Just follow the directions above.—RS] [It's not a waste of money if you're taking care of 15 to 20 Macs and cleaning a mouse once or twice a week. It's much faster and easier to use the kit.—JK]*

Trackballs (BB)

Trackballs are like upside-down mice. You roll a ball in a stationary holder, rather than sliding a box across the desk, so they require less desk space than mice (and some people just like 'em better). Trackballs also control the pointer more precisely than a mouse does (which is particularly important for graphics). They all have at least two buttons: one that's like a normal mouse button, and one that can lock in the down position so you can drag objects or menus without holding the button down with your finger.

The Stingray. The **Stingray** ($130, CoStar) has a small ball that's easy to control; its two buttons take the form of a pair of sloping wings, which surround the ball. They're so sensitive you have to be careful not to click them accidentally. You can alter pointer speed and select which button you want to use as the normal click and which as the click-lock—a boon to lefties. *[I like the Stingray's ball, but its huge buttons leave you no place to rest your fingers without risking an accidental click. They look stylish and justify the trackball's name, but I prefer a flat, even surface when I'm trying to click.—JK]*

TurboMouse. TurboMouse ($170, Kensington) is the best-known (and most expensive) trackball; year after year, Mac magazines give it top review ratings and "Best of" awards. Still, I prefer the Stingray, because it felt better under my hand.

The TurboMouse's ball is much larger and heavier than other trackballs', so it has more inertia, and there's a touch of grain or resistance, unlike the ultra-smooth Stingray and PowerBook balls. The two buttons' position, size, and feel are excellent. They require enough pressure to keep you from accidentally clicking (a problem with the Stingray), without making you aware of a need to press hard.

The TurboMouse's new software has a lot of fancy features. For example, you can select spots on the screen and make the pointer jump to them by clicking both TurboMouse buttons and rolling the ball in the right direction. But some of these features seem like overkill; I want my pointing device to be simple, precise, reliable, and absolutely second nature to use. Furthermore, the manual is poorly organized and poorly written.

BAD FEATURE

[I don't mind the excessive features, but I just don't find the TurboMouse to be comfortable. Kensington touts its "large, comfortable ball," but if you're resting your hand on a desk in front of the TurboMouse, your hand has to bend sharply upward at the wrist, which is uncomfortable and ergonomically dangerous. Kensington seems to realize this, because it now makes a special foam pad to elevate the wrist, but it's still awkward compared to using the PowerBooks' built-in trackball.—JK]

Thumbelina. Thumbelina ($70, Appoint) is a tiny (1½-inch square) hand-held trackball that fits comfortably in your palm. It's designed for giving presentations in which you use the mouse a lot but the keyboard not much, if at all. Instead of having to stay sitting at or bent over a desk, you can sit or stand where you're comfortable and control the Mac with Thumbelina (her cord is nearly six feet long).

The correlation between ball and pointer movement is pleasingly precise. Thumbelina is comfortable and has three well-positioned buttons with sensible functions: One is the click button, another gives you click-lock, and a third toggles the mouse speed up or down so you can get across the screen fast or move slowly and precisely.

[I think Thumbelina is marvelous, but when I tried two of them on a PowerBook 180, neither worked, although all other ADB devices did. Appoint says no other 180 users have reported this problem.—JK]

TrakMate. Key Tronic's **TrakMate** ($150) is based on a great idea. It's a wrist rest for your keyboard that has a built-in trackball. The wrist rest *is* great—it has a soft but firm springboardlike feel and is comfortable to work with for long periods. I didn't particularly like the trackball, though. Like the TrakPro keyboard reviewed earlier, the TrakMate's ball is designed to be rolled with one thumb, and its keys are positioned to be clicked with the other. If you work this way, you may love the TrakMate, but I like to operate trackballs with one hand, rolling with the fingers and clicking with the thumb, and the TrakMate won't allow that.

BAD FEATURE

TrackMan. As we were going to press, Logitech was about to release a new, ergonomic version of its $140 **TrackMan** trackball, with three buttons at the end of a large, curved palm rest, and the trackball off to the side for your thumb to use.

THINGS TO COME

Pen Input

(RS)

Pen input devices are electronic versions of the tools we use to put ink on paper. They're well suited to graphics programs. The ones we looked at use either a roller (like a ball-point pen) or a special tablet to communicate their movement to the Mac.

MousePen Pro. The **MousePen Pro** ($70, Appoint) is one of those inventions that you look at and say, Why didn't I think of that? It's small, light, and shaped like a pen with a small ball at the end; you move the pointer by rolling the ball around on almost any surface—from a sheet of paper to your pants leg.

POWERBOOK

The MousePen is great to use with a PowerBook if you don't like the built-in trackball; you can put a Post-it on the handrest area below the keyboard to serve as a sort of mouse pad for it. It's also a natural for drawing or painting—although it's not as good as the graphics tablets described later in this section (it doesn't respond to pressure and it's not as precise).

Appoint also makes less-expensive ($40), more playful versions of the MousePen: the **Jurassic Mouse,** which looks and feels like a little dinosaur; the **Cray-on Mouse,** which looks like a Crayola crayon; and the **Barbie Mouse.**

Mac HandWriter. Mac HandWriter ($200, Communication Intelligence) is a stylus/tablet combo that, unlike the tablets described below, is designed more for editing text than illustrations.

Like Apple's hand-held Newton MessagePad, it can recognize your handwriting and change it to type. Unlike the Newton, though, the HandWriter requires you to print letters (no cursive) on a horizontal line. This isn't easy, since the tablet is unlined and your writing doesn't show up on the tablet itself. The HandWriter's recognition wasn't completely accurate, but it improved when I turned down the speed of recognition in the accompanying control panel.

GOOD FEATURE

The HandWriter is better at editing existing text. For example, you can delete a word by drawing a backslash through it, and other gestures do things like inserting spaces or carriage returns. The HandWriter's pen has a little button that acts like a Cmd key—when you push it while writing a particular letter, it's equivalent to typing the corresponding command from the keyboard. The tablet also provides an interface that can be used within any application and includes floating windows of tools and shortcuts similar to the button bars in Word and Word Perfect.

The HandWriter is worth considering as an editing tool or as a nontypist's alternative to dictation or hunt-and-peck typing. But personally, I think it's worth the price just to fool around in a graphics program like ColorIt. *[The stylus feels more like a paintbrush than a mouse does, but serious artists will be happier with the pressure-sensitive tablets described below.—JK]*

Pressure-Sensitive Tablets

(AC)

Pressure-sensitive tablets let you imitate traditional painting media, like brushes or charcoal, by changing the thickness, color, or opacity of a line in proportion to the pressure you apply with the stylus as you draw. A good tablet can recognize at least 120 pressure levels (although a lot of software still can recognize only 60). A stylus should also be light, cordless, and responsive. Many styluses offer buttons to which you can assign specific functions.

Some tablets also let you trace images placed under a transparent sheet of plastic, control the ratio between the active area of the tablet and the screen area where you want to draw, and create macros, which can be activated by the menu strips or stylus button.

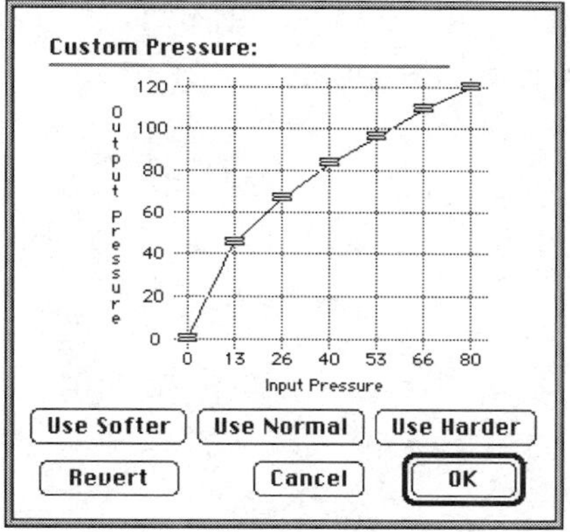

The Wacom ArtZ's Custom Pressure Curve lets you adjust the tablet's sensitivity at different pressure levels.

Wacom ArtZ tablets. Wacom, the industry leader for some time, has introduced the **ArtZ** tablets ($440 for the 6- by 8-inch tablet), which can interpret as many as 120 pressure levels. Their stylish, featherweight stylus has a single button to which you can assign different functions and macros.

The best thing about the ArtZ tablets is that you can completely customize the performance of the stylus and the tablet, and save different sets of preferences for each program you work with, so you don't have to waste time switching them back and forth. My favorite adjustment is the Custom Pressure Curve, which lets you control the tablet's response to different pressure levels, so you can, for example, obtain a softer and more sensitive "brush."

CalComp DrawingSlate. The **CalComp DrawingSlate's** cordless, battery-charged stylus is easy to use, and although it's a little heavier than the Wacom's, the stylus is really responsive, and the tip has a great feel to it. The stylus has two buttons for defining actions or commands that, together with the 18-function menu on the tablet, make DrawingSlate a useful tool for working with macros.

GOOD FEATURE

DrawingSlate's ADB cable lets you connect both the mouse and the tablet simultaneously, which really helps when you can't reach certain zones of the screen with the stylus. Its reasonable price ($400 for the 6- by 9-inch tablet) and great quality make it a serious competitor for the better-known Wacom tablets. Maybe the weakest point of the DrawingSlate is that you can't control the 120 input/output pressure levels with any precision.

GOOD FEATURE

BAD FEATURE

SummaSketch FX. The stylus that comes with Summagraphics' **SummaSketch FX** ($650 for the 12- by 12-inch tablet, which is the smallest) has the best tip. It's got an elastic and springy touch to it that makes double-clicking as easy as pie and painting a pleasure. Its triangular-shaped body is not very comfortable, although it minimizes the chances of your dropping the pen. It has a couple of buttons that are used as mouse buttons. Unfortunately, the documentation that comes with the tablet isn't very good, and its installation is tedious and confusing. It comes with three separate cables (which is a drag, except for my cats) and an ADB box, which makes the tablet a pain. Its mapping capabilities (which determine what area of the screen is controlled by the tablet) are limited and not very intuitive, except for one control that lets you adjust the speed of the cursor.

Kurta XGT. The **Kurta XGT** tablets ($425 for the 6- by 8-inch tablet) offer up to 256 pressure levels. The stylus is big and heavy, but if that doesn't bother you (I wonder if Picasso was ever bothered by heavy brushes?), then they are a good choice. They only offer a few restricted mapping capabilities, but on the positive side, Kurta's software has an interesting template feature that's useful for creating layout guides and grids.

Scanners

Scanners are devices that convert images—typically photographs or other artwork—into digital form so they can be stored and manipulated by computers. When used in conjunction with *OCR (optical character recognition)* software, they can also convert a page of text into an editable document on your computer.

Mac-compatible scanners range in price from a few hundred dollars to a hundred *thousand* dollars. The ones under $10,000 are great for jobs that don't require precise detail or color reproduction, but they can't compete with high-end equipment when it comes to demanding jobs like color photographs in slick publications.

There are more than a hundred scanners on the market today. The models change frequently and there are often variations even between one individual unit and another. So in addition to the reviews of particular models in the next section, we've explained, in general terms, what to look for when evaluating scanners.

How Scanners Work

(JM)

During scanning, light is reflected off (or passed through) the artwork and focused onto *CCDs (charge-coupled devices*—basically, light sensors) that convert the light energy to electricity. Color scanners use colored filters (or sometimes a prism) to read red, green, and blue values separately, and then combine the three single-color scans to yield a full-color image. Though the principle is the same for all scanners, units differ in how many readings per inch they take (the scanner's *resolution*), how much color information they capture at each reading (the scanner's *bit depth*), whether they take separate passes of the light source to read the red, green, and blue values (three-pass scanners) or take all the readings in a single pass (minimizing the chance for misregistration and speeding up the scanning process), and the quality of the scanning software that comes with the machine.

Bit depth (JM). One-bit scanners read all sample points as either black or white. There aren't very many of these around anymore. Most people use 8-bit grayscale scanners (for 256 shades of gray) or 24-bit color scanners (256 shades each of red, green, and blue, for a total of more than 16 million colors).

Some scanners read 36 or 48 bits of information at each sample point, even though their final product is a 24-bit file. Doing this reduces the amount of *noise* (inaccurate data) that CCDs inherently produce. (The less noise there is in relation to total data collected, the more usable information the scanner can deliver.)

Line Art, Halftones, and Resolution (JM/DD/JK)

The resolution you want depends on what you're scanning. If it's *line art* (i.e., words or drawings in black and white, with no grays), you want a resolution that matches that of the printer you'll use (for laser printers, usually 300 dpi or 600 dpi). *[You can usually get a better final result by using a scanner's optical resolution and blowing the result up in Photoshop than you can by using the scanner's enhanced resolution, although the latter saves time.—ScA]*

If you're scanning a photograph or another image with a lifelike variation of colors or shades of gray (called *continuous-tone* art), you'll normally end up printing your scan as a *halftone,* which creates the illusion of an even shift between colors or grays using ink or toner dots of different sizes or densities.

Halftone resolution is measured in *lines per inch (lpi),* an arcane measurement that harkens back to photographic methods. Basically, the more lines per inch, the smaller the dot size and the better-looking the image. The standard for newspaper quality is 65 lpi; for general lithographic uses, it's 133 to 150 lpi.

As a rule of thumb, you should scan at a resolution of at least 120 percent of the line screen you'll use for printing. So if you need a 150-line halftone, scan at 180 dpi or more. You can increase the sharpness of your image by increasing the dpi you scan at, up to about 200 percent (300 dpi for a 150-line screen, say); beyond that, you get diminishing returns. If your scans are destined to appear on computer screens, the same rule of thumb applies, but use the monitor's resolution (usually 72 to 75 dpi) instead of the halftone screen's.

When you scale an image up, you reduce the resolution correspondingly (doubling it, for example, cuts its resolution in half). This is where most people come up against the limitations of their devices. For example, if you have a 300-dpi scanner and want to output a 150-line halftone from a 35mm slide at a scan-to-output ratio at 150 percent, the printed image can only be about 2 inches by 1.4 inches.

This extra information doesn't go to waste. A common problem when you alter scans is that you lose information—if you brighten colors, for example, you might lose image detail. But when you scan 48 bits, you can tell the scanner to digitally convert only the brightest 16 million colors, say, so that its final 24-bit image contains the best information.

Resolution (JM/AN). A scanner's resolution refers to the number of sample points per inch it's capable of capturing (often expressed as *dpi,* although *spi* is more accurate). Some scanners are also rated in terms of *total resolution,* the maximum number of points they can sample. To compare these two figures, divide the total resolution by each dimension of your intended output, then average the two figures. For example, a scanner whose total resolution is 2,000 by 3,000 dots can output a 5-inch by 7-inch image at a resolution of about 415 dpi (2,000/5 = 400; 3,000/7 = 428.6; (400+428.6)/2 = 414.3).

Types of Scanners

(JM)

There are three major types of scanners:

- *Hand-held scanners* literally roll across the artwork. They're small and relatively inexpensive, but they only scan in strips of about four inches wide. Some come with software that lets you piece together multiple scans to build a larger image, but that process is annoying and imprecise. Also, images are often distorted, because it's impossible to roll a hand-held scanner without wavering or changing speed.
- *Flatbed scanners* operate like photocopiers; you place the artwork on a glass surface, and a scan head and light source move across it under the glass. Flatbeds can scan almost anything that has at least one flat side, even a slab of marble. Most of them can't scan transparencies or slides, but a growing number of manufacturers offer attachments for that purpose. All flatbeds will scan up to at least 8½ by 11 inches, and some go up to 11 by 17 inches.

OCR

(JM)

Nowadays, most scanners can use *OCR* programs, which recognize the letters on a scanned page of text and store them as actual characters, editable in a word processing (or other text-handling) program. Make sure any scanner you buy lets you scan from within the OCR software you want to use; otherwise you'll have to scan a page, save it as a graphic, and then open it with your OCR software. OCR really isn't worth getting involved with unless you're going to be digitizing lots of documents. And if you're going to be digitizing lots of documents, you'll want a scanner that's fast. (For more on OCR software, see Chapter 8.)

Bit depth is irrelevant for OCR, since you'll be scanning in 1-bit (black-and-white) mode anyway. And the standard flatbed resolution of 300 dpi is more than enough.

Some scanners pull pages through a series of rollers. This means you can't scan books (or anything else that you can't tear into single sheets) and the rollers have a tendency to mangle documents. Flatbeds are by far the best choice; the same problems that limit hand-held devices for image scanning make them a pain for reading documents.

- As their name suggests, *transparency scanners* scan transparent materials. (*Slide scanners* might be a more appropriate term, since units that can scan transparencies larger than 35mm tend to cost over $20,000.)

Evaluating Scanners (JM)

Evaluating scanners is easy if your scanned images will only be displayed on the screen; just do some test scans and compare the results on a monitor like the one you'll be using. The best images to use for tests contain fine detail and a mix of bright and muted colors; a human face is ideal, since small tonal shifts can make it look totally wrong.

If your scanned images will be printed out, don't try to evaluate them on a screen. Scans that look dull on a screen may actually contain better data for printing than those that look bright and colorful. It usually isn't possible to make a scan and then print it on the output device you're planning to use, but you can at least avoid some of the most obvious and common problems by making a few test scans and analyzing them with Photoshop's Levels chart (other image-editing programs have similar capabilities).

First, make sure that the values in the chart don't continue off the scale, and that the chart has no gaps in it; either may be a sign that the scanner is making brightness and contrast corrections you didn't ask for, or that it can't read pure black or pure white. (With color images, you'll probably have to look at the red, green, and blue levels separately to see the gaps.)

In the chart below, the values spill off the ends of the graph and there are gaps—both indications that data has been automatically adjusted. In the chart on the next page, the values fit within the scanner's range, and the output of this scan will contain more image detail.

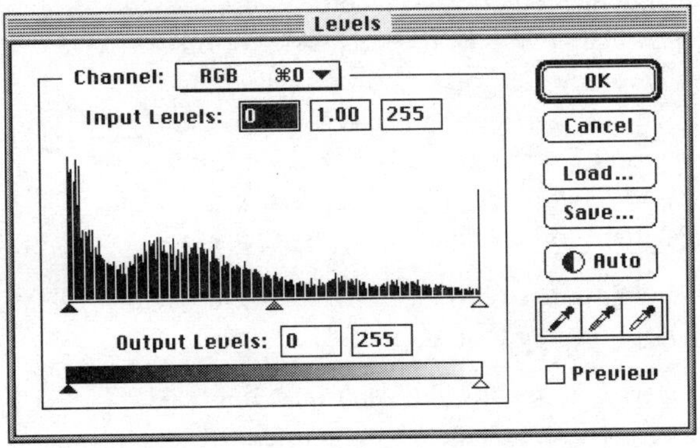

The gaps in the chart and values extending beyond the chart's range mean this auto-adjusted scan won't look as good as it could.

Next, look for excessive noise (this test works best with images that have dark areas in them). You do this by moving the light gray (middle) triangle (it's just above the space after Output Levels in the windows shown here). As the dark areas of the picture lighten up, check them for streaking and random mottling. There will always be some noise, but if you try a few different scanners, you'll quickly see how they vary.

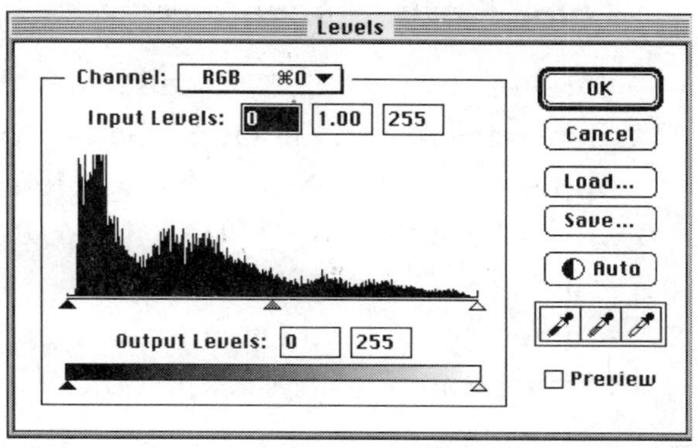

This scan will contain more detail; the values fit within the chart's range.

To test the sharpness of color scanners, scan a piece of line art or text that's printed on very glossy stock (imagesetter output works well), then zoom in until you see the pixels. The black edges should have a faint, colored halo about two pixels wide. If the halo is more like a rainbow four or five pixels wide, the scanner isn't registering the red, green, and blue layers properly.

In the end, the quality of your scans will depend just as much on your skill in processing them as on how good a scanner you used. Just about every scan needs to be brightened and sharpened in software, and no scanner program can take the place of a good image-editing program like Photoshop (which comes bundled with many scanners). Also remember that, for most people, differences in quality won't matter as much as differences in convenience. Small color imbalances probably won't bother you if you're producing newsletters, but a slow scanner will annoy you every time you use it. Check out our speed test results, below, or those in one of the Mac magazines.

The scanner should provide a Photoshop plug-in or some other software that enables you to scan directly into your image-editing package. Since all scans need correction, most people find this the most convenient way to work; but for even more convenience, check out Ofoto from Light Source, which automates the correction process and comes with Apple's Color OneScanner (reviewed below).

Color Flatbed Scanners (ScA)

We chose five scanners for this review, based on their popularity (to see whether there was a reason for it) and their success in other independent evaluations: the **Apple Color OneScanner**, the **Hewlett-Packard ScanJet IIcx**, the **Mirror MirrorScan 800**, the **UMAX UC630**, and the **UMAX UC840**. For the test, I scanned an 8.5- by 11.6-inch image in 24-bit color at 72 dpi and evaluated the scanners based on their speed and output quality. All the scanners have 8.5- by 14-inch scanning areas, except the Mirror, whose surface is 8.5 by 11.6 inches.

GOOD FEATURE

Color OneScanner. If you find the details of color scanning overwhelming, you'll appreciate Apple's Color OneScanner ($1,060 ApplePrice). Its excellent manual includes a clear explanation of color reproduction, and it comes with Light Source's excellent Ofoto software, which can automate the entire scanning and correction process. (But it's one of the few scanners that doesn't come with some version of Photoshop.) The Color One is a one-pass scanner (meaning that it scans the original just once, rather than once each for red, green, and blue) with an optical resolution of 300 by 300 dpi, and enhanced resolution of 1,200 by 1,200 dpi.

The Color One completed the test scan very quickly: A preview took 40 seconds and a full scan took only 45 seconds. But when using Ofoto to automatically analyze the original image, make any adjustments, and then give you its final scan, the process can take from five to seven minutes (although the results are excellent). An experienced user could get similar results from the 45-second manual scan with a couple of minutes' work in Photoshop.

The uncorrected test scan's overall image quality was as good as the Mirror's, but slightly below that of the HP IIcx and the UMAX models (all discussed below). Its sharpness was acceptable—about the same as the UMAX 630's—but the other scanners did better. Grays were perfectly neutral (i.e., untinted by any color) and tonal range was good. Dark areas didn't retain all of the original's details, but they were free from the grainy noise that is common in low-cost scanners. Color saturation was only average, but greens and blues were very true to the original (the reds less so).

ScanJet IIcx. The Hewlett-Packard ScanJet IIcx ($1,180) offers excellent performance for the price—it produced both the fastest and the best-quality test scan of this group. Its single-pass engine has an optical resolution of 400 by 400 dpi, with enhanced resolution of 1,600 by 1,600 dpi.

I was amazed by the IIcx's speed. Previews took only 15 seconds, and the test scan took just 31 seconds, making the IIcx by far the fastest desktop scanner I've ever used. The output was also the sharpest of the scanners I tested, slightly sharper than the UMAX 840. Even so, there were jaggies on the IIcx's scans that made the edges of lines look slightly rough when enlarged.

After a few small postscan adjustments, dark grays were neutral, but medium and light shades carried progressively warmer tinges of color (i.e., yellow and red crept in). Oranges, reds, and yellows were very saturated, and greens and blues were the most accurate of the scanners in this review. Tonal range was also the best tested, if only by a slight margin. Details showed up well in lighter shades and dark tones were very good, showing very little noise.

One of the IIcx's few weaknesses is its software. Instead of giving direct access to the scanner from within Photoshop, like other scanners, the HP's driver links Photoshop to a separate DeskScan II application. When you start a scan from Photoshop, there's a pause of 15 to 30 seconds before the DeskScan interface appears and previewing or scanning can start. I found this delay intolerably long and unfortunate considering the speed of the scanner itself. The wait must be endured before every scan, even if you've just done one; the only workaround I found was to scan directly from DeskScan, then open the resulting file in Photoshop to make adjustments.

For OCR users, the IIcx has new built-in technology that's supposed to help OCR software recognize small and unusual type.

MirrorScan 800 Plus. The MirrorScan 800 Plus ($1,100 direct, from DTP Direct) is easy to use and comes well equipped with software (including both Photoshop and Olduvai's Read-It Pro OCR software), but it's very slow, has a substandard scanning area, and produces unspectacular output.

The Mirror has an optical resolution of 400 by 800 dpi, with enhanced resolution of 800 by 800 dpi. At 8.5 by 11.6 inches, its scan area is slightly smaller than that of most scanners. The 800 Plus is a three-pass scanner, so it's slow—far slower, in fact, than all the other scanners in this review. Previews aren't too bad at 40 seconds, but the test scan took four minutes (although, oddly, a 300-dpi scan of the same size took only 90 seconds longer).

BAD FEATURE

The scanner's Photoshop plug-in includes a prescan gamma adjustment, which helps you control contrast within the tonal range of the scanner's output. (The HP IIcx was the only other scanner in this review whose software offers this adjustment.) The manual does a poor job of explaining how to use the plug-in, but with a little practice you can find gamma settings that can greatly improve the quality of your scans.

The test scan looked about as sharp as the UMAX 840's but not as crisp as the HP IIcx's. Medium and light grays were neutral, with a shift toward blue in the darker shades. Uncorrected, the image was generally dark and the colors were dull rather than saturated. After a little lightening, the overall image quality got as good as the Apple's but with less color purity than the UMAXes' and less highlight detail than the HP IIcx's.

UMAX UC630 and UMAX UC840. The UMAX UC630 ($845) and UC840 ($1,175) also have three-pass engines. The 630 has an optical resolution of 300 by 600 dpi and an enhanced resolution of 600 by 600 dpi; the corresponding numbers for the 840 are 400 by 800 dpi and 800 by 800 dpi. The 630 comes with Photoshop LE (Limited Edition—an abridged version of the program) and PhotoFlash, Apple's software that includes tools for enhancing images, browsing through collections of scans, and placing images into documents. The 840 comes with the full version of Photoshop.

Both machines completed previews in 30 seconds and the test scan in 2 minutes, 45 seconds, which is a respectable speed for three-pass scanners, but both scanners' uncorrected scans looked dark and low in contrast. Grays were neutral on the 840 and slightly warm on the 630. The 630's scan showed about the same (limited) level of detail in dark tones as Apple's scan. The 840's dark tones showed more detail—almost as much the HP IIcx's.

Although both UMAX scanners' uncorrected scans looked bad, adjustments made using Photoshop's Levels commands brought forth color purity and overall image quality that were close to those of HP IIcx's output. These Photoshop adjustments take a little extra time, but all the scans in this review benefited from them to some extent.

Conclusions. The Apple scanner is a good choice for users who want good scans without the hassle of having to make their own adjustments and who don't need a copy of Photoshop—although if money's not an issue, you can get the same convenience with the HP and UMAX scanners by buying a copy of a LightSource's **Ofoto 2** ($400). For most other users, the HP ScanJet IIcx wins for its speed and output quality, despite the annoying delay when scanning from within Photoshop. If you can't afford the HP, but you can afford to wait a little longer for your scans, consider the UMAX 630. At least at press time, it had the cheaper price. Since prices are always changing, though, comparison-shop when you're ready to buy.

Hand-Held Scanners

(JG)

As mentioned above, hand-held scanners have major drawbacks: They only scan in strips of about four inches wide, and it's hard to do a good job of patching these strips together. Because human hands and arms aren't as precise as a track-mounted scanning head, the resulting image is often distorted. *[I've seen a plastic scanning tray with a track-mounted trolley for hand-held scanners in some obscure catalog, but I can't say how well it would work.—JK]*

BARGAIN

But if jazzing up correspondence or simple flyers is all you're after, then a four-inch hand-held grayscale scanner might be the better alternative to a $1,000 flatbed. Here are a couple, but there are others on the market.

LightningScan 400. As hand-held scanners go, Thunderware's **LightningScan 400** ($500) and **LightningScan Pro 256** ($650) are hard to beat. Cleverly numbered to confuse, both models scan at up to 400 dpi. For the extra $150 or so (less at street prices), the Pro 256 generates 256 shades of gray rather than 32 (neither does color). If you want to scan photos, that's not a bad investment.

ThunderWorks' software allows both models to mate side-by-side four-inch scans, and they both come with Olduvai's Read-It! OCR software.

ScanMan 32. ScanMan 32 ($500, Logitech) worked just fine on small pieces of line art—the 300-dpi output on a LaserWriter was surprisingly crisp and clear. Scans of photos ranged from acceptable to disappointing and revealed the problems of outputting more shades of gray than were actually scanned (ScanMan interpolates the difference).

Like Thunderware's scanners, ScanMan can blend side-by-side scans together, but you have to scan *absolutely* straight and parallel for scans to match up. To help you do that, you can tape a straightedge to the table or spend $30 for a specially designed plastic guide (it should be included in the package, but it isn't).

7 Preventing and Solving Problems

NO MATTER HOW CAREFUL YOU ARE with your Macintosh, something will go wrong eventually.

Even users who run strictly factory-issue hardware and plain vanilla software—current versions of a handful of mainstream applications and a System Folder that hasn't changed since Apple's Installer got through with it—occasionally find that their hard disk won't boot up, their cursor won't move, or double-clicking a document won't open its application. And the more you expand and customize your system—by installing cards, attaching peripherals, and loading extensions and other doohickies—the higher the odds that you'll face these or other problems.

The aim of this chapter is, first of all, to prescribe some preventive medicine—habits and precautions, involving both your hardware and your software, that should reduce the risk of problems. Then we survey common maladies and what to do about them, focusing particularly on procedures for recovering data from crashed disks and deleted files. Finally, we review some of the tools and resources you can utilize to diagnose and treat problems.

Contributors

Henry Norr (HN) is the chapter editor.

John Kadyk (JK), another editor for this edition of the *Mac Bible*, wrote a lot of material in this chapter as well as for earlier editions, from which parts of the text were taken.

Contents

Preventive Medicine: Hardware

Good housekeeping and a few painless precautions can help keep your hardware fit and trim for years to come.

Keep It Cool and Clean (JK/HN/Lauren Antonoff)

Heat can shorten the life span of electronic equipment, so keep your hardware away from direct sunlight and appliances that generate heat. Make sure the vents on the top, rear, or sides of the case aren't blocked by papers, peripherals, or anything else. And don't smoke in front of your Mac.

When dust builds up inside Macs, it makes a little blanket that traps the heat generated by the computer's electronic components. If you open a Mac and see a lot of dust, don't just leave it there—take the case outside and blow into it (then turn your face away to avoid the rising cloud). If that doesn't get everything clean, pick up a can of compressed air (just a few bucks at Radio Shack and camera stores) and give your Mac a good blast. *[The fans in some desktop Macs suck more dust into the case than would otherwise end up there—one argument (besides saving electricity) for turning the computer off when it's not being used.—JK]*

Dust covers are a common accessory, and they may do a little good, especially if you leave your machine idle for long periods. But since most dust is drawn in while the computer is in use, don't count on a cover as a complete solution.

Warding Off Electrical Threats

Electricity is your Mac's lifeblood, but if it arrives in the wrong form and quantities, it can damage virtually all the components in your Mac—in some cases beyond repair.

Get a surge protector (AN/JK/HN/Lauren Antonoff). A sudden spike in the electrical current from a wall socket can damage any electrical appliance. Macs are supposed to have some surge protection built-in, but as an extra precaution add a *surge protector* (a power strip with a buffer to protect your equipment if the voltage suddenly changes). Plug your peripherals into the surge protector, too—they're at least as vulnerable as the Mac.

Send It UPS (JK/HN)

If your computer suddenly loses power (due to a blackout, someone tripping over your power cord, or whatever), you'll lose any work you haven't saved. Beyond that, some types of documents (database files, for example) can get so badly damaged that they can't be recovered.

To guard against this danger, some computer owners get an *uninterruptible power supply (UPS),* a device that instantly switches to battery power if the electrical current stops flowing. They're not designed to keep you running indefinitely, but at a minimum they give you enough time to finish what you're doing and shut down your computer safely.

A UPS can cost quite a bit, depending on capacity—the cheapest we've seen lists for $140, while the most expensive units can cost thousands of dollars. Unless you are in a location where power is generally unreliable, the investment may not make sense for the individual user—just remember to save your work frequently. On the other hand, if your business depends on a network database, for example, it might be a good idea to get one for your server. One UPS maker, American Power Conversion, even offers a Mac program called PowerChute, which notifies other Macs on a network of an impending shutdown when the server kicks over to the UPS. Of course, that assumes that the other machines still have power.

Surge protectors are particularly important if you live in an area where blackouts are common (due to thunderstorms or whatever), because there's generally a power surge when electricity returns after a blackout. If you don't have a surge protector, immediately unplug your Mac and all peripherals whenever the power goes out, so the equipment will be safe when the juice comes back on.

Panamax and Best Power Technology are two leading manufacturers of surge protectors. Their products can withstand much stronger spikes than most of the surge protectors sold in hardware and discount stores—just as a Bentley will protect you better than a cheaper car. Panamax even warranties your own computer equipment—not just the surge protector—against damage by lightning!

GOOD FEATURE

[I have a client who had the main power feed to his house go down during a tree-removal operation. Several devices not connected to Panamax surge protectors were fried. One Panamax surge protector was toasted, but no equipment protected by a Panamax surge protector was damaged, and the company replaced the fried unit. After talking to Panamax representatives, I'm fully convinced that they stand behind their warranty.—Ken Maki]

Pull the plug before lightning strikes (C.J. Weigand). A surge protector may not be good enough during a thunderstorm, because lightning can arc across open contacts and do extensive damage to your equipment. So if it's thunderstorm season where you live, get in the habit of pulling the plug out of the wall whenever you shut down your system for any length of time. If you have a modem connected to your Mac, also unplug the incoming telephone line or disconnect the cable; your computer can be zapped just as easily by lightning striking your telephone line.

Discharge static (Larry Pina). In the middle of a dry New England winter, just walking across the room can build up a terrific static charge, especially around synthetic fabrics, rubber-soled shoes, and wall-to-wall carpeting. Under these conditions, touching anything connected to an electrical ground results in a painful shock. The static charge can be so bad that it even triggers an instant lockup (on the computer, not you).

One solution is to use a surge suppressor with an integral static-draining touch pad. A company called Systems Control offers several models under the name **MacGard**; prices start at $60. When you tap it, you hear the same crackling noise that's normally associated with a painful shock, but the discharge is much slower and completely painless. You can then touch your Mac safely. MacGard also offers superior surge protection—in lab tests I ran, it outperformed several units costing twice as much.

Power down before unplugging peripherals (HN). Turn the power off—not just to the Mac, but to every device attached to it—before plugging in or unplugging SCSI cables; otherwise you might cause a short that could damage the Mac or drive. It can be a pain if you have to change your hardware configuration regularly, and some daredevils don't bother—but they're putting their Macs and peripherals at risk.

The same goes for Apple Desktop Bus (ADB) cables. Even though the cables that go to your mouse and keyboard carry only a small amount of power, unplugging one can blow a fuse on some Mac logic boards. I know—I fried a Mac II (at the beginning of one of the busiest weeks of the year for me) by disconnecting a keyboard.

Ground yourself while working in the box (JK). Even routine static electricity—the kind you can get walking around the house—can be strong enough to damage electronic components, so be sure you discharge yourself before handling expansion cards or SIMMs or doing anything else under the Mac's hood. You can also buy grounding straps that you attach to yourself at one end and to a grounded object at the other. If your Mac is plugged into a grounded, three-hole outlet—and it should be—you can ground yourself to its power supply (the big metal box inside the Mac, where the power cords plug in). If you don't have a grounding strap, touch the power supply periodically while you work to dissipate any charge that's built up.

Shut It Off or Leave It Running? (JK/HN)

There are plenty of reasons to turn your Mac equipment off when you're not using it (e.g., conserving energy, eliminating the noise caused by the fans, reducing the risk of problems caused by power glitches). But for the longevity of the equipment, most serious users and technicians seem to agree that it's better to leave it on, unless you are going to be away for several days or longer. (Some people recommend leaving everything on no matter how long you'll be gone.) When equipment is turned on, the electronic components warm up and expand; when it's turned off, they cool down and contract. This causes stress that can eventually wear them out.

Likewise, the motor in your hard disk has to generate extra torque (which means extra stress) to spin up the platters from a standing start; once it's already spinning, keeping it going is a breeze. Besides, when a drive is spinning, it's safe from *stiction*—a condition in which the heads in effect get stuck on the surface of the platters. Internal or external, drives are happier if they stay on and spinning all the time; leaving the equipment on avoids these stressful changes.

The exception to the rule, most people agree, concerns the monitor: The benefits of turning it off when you leave (saving tube life and electricity and, in air-conditioned offices, eliminating a heat source) outweigh the costs in stress on the circuitry.

[I make it a habit to leave my Mac on, but I turn off my monitor at night. For years I've been asking for someone to tell me what the cutoff point is: If I'm leaving for a half-

hour lunch, should I shut if off? How about a two-hour meeting? Unfortunately, I've never been able to get a straight answer. My own rule of thumb is that if I'll be gone an hour, I turn it off. But your guess is as good as mine.—HN]

[I, on the other hand, always turn off everything at night. I can't stand the hum of the disk drive and fan. Besides, if my system were always on, I'd always be working. So far, no troubles. I've heard that the notion that turning equipment on and off is bad for it dates from earlier days when computers and peripherals were much more fragile.—DD]

Many new monitors come with software that automatically puts them into an energy-saving low-power mode when your system has been idle for a specified period. Apple's Energy Saver control panel, for example, will power down compatible monitors after 15, 30, 45, or 60 minutes of system inactivity. If your monitor comes with such software, use it—it saves almost as much electricity as flipping the switch.

Macs on the Move

Macs are pretty sturdy machines, but with the partial exception of PowerBooks, they're not designed for rough treatment. When you do have to move your Mac around, some special precautions are in order.

Don't move drives while they're on (JK). Hard drives contain read/write heads moving back and forth less than a hair's breadth away from furiously spinning platters. Delicately written onto the surface of those platters are your Mac's system software, applications, and files. The moral: Handle hard drives carefully. PowerBook drives are designed to withstand a considerable amount of shock, so you can safely move your notebook around a room or use it in a moving car, for example, while it's spinning. But if you're on a bumpy road or in some other situation in which sudden sharp movements might occur, it's safest to shut the machine down or put it to sleep. In the case of a desktop drive (or a Mac containing one), shut down before moving your equipment.

Shipping your Mac (JK/Paul Blood). Save the boxes and cardboard or Styrofoam packing that your Mac equipment came in (if it's not already too late). If you ever need to ship any of it anywhere, you'll want the box the manufacturer designed to give it a safe ride. There are places that will custom-build a box for you, but they may charge you $80 to $90 for the service. Besides that, you may void your warranty if you ship equipment in a box other than the one the manufacturer created for it (so you're both increasing the risk of damage and eliminating your remedy if something does get damaged).

The problem with shipping a Mac in its original box is that the box lets everyone know that a valuable computer is inside. A solution recommended in the previous edition of this book is pulling the box apart, then reassembling it inside out. Unfortunately, that may not be such a good idea. Reader Lynne Colley wrote to report that if a Mac shipped this way gets damaged, the shipping company can refuse to compensate you on the grounds that you used a "weakened box." As an alternative, Lynne suggests simply packing the original box inside another box.

Carrying a PowerBook (JK). PowerBooks don't have handles, but they fit conveniently into most briefcases, shoulder bags, and small backpacks, and as long as you don't forget what's in there and start flinging the bag around, there's no reason to buy a special carrying case. On the other hand, if it cramps your style to be that cautious and preoccupied, or if your regular bags tend to fill up with crumbs and paper clips, a separate case might be a good idea. There are plenty on the market, with varying levels of protection (from plain canvas to foam-lined hard cases) and space for accessories (from slots for a few floppies to special compartments for a power adapter, spare batteries, and even a printer). You can get a close look at a couple of brands at most computer stores or a see pictures of many more alternatives in the catalogs of the big mail-order Mac outlets.

Plugging into foreign wall sockets (JK). Many Macs can take either the 110-volt power that comes out of wall sockets in the U.S. and Japan or the 220-volt power used by Europeans and Australians. All you need is an adapter to make your plug fit into the socket of the country you're visiting. Be careful, though: Before you leave, find out for sure what the country's voltage level is and what your Mac can handle, and remember that electrical service can be pretty unstable in some countries.

Mac peripherals like monitors can often handle different levels of power, too—again, just be sure you know before you plug in.

Preventive Medicine: Software and Data Files (HN)

Software-caused problems cost Mac users far more wasted time, lost data, and general hassle than hardware failures. We can't immunize you against bugs and incompatibilities—they seem to be inevitable at this stage of technological evolution. But in the software arena as in hardware, sticking to some simple safe-computing practices can help keep the glitches to a minimum.

Use the Installer

Installing new system software or a major application used to be a matter of dragging a few icons to your hard disk; today it commonly involves copying scores of files, decompressing them and placing them in special locations, moving or removing older software, or even copying a new resource into an existing

Reversing the Damage (HN)

To my mind, the worst thing about installers is that developers rarely tell you, either onscreen or in the manual, exactly what they do. That make it hard to undo the damage if you later decide to toss out the program.

Apple's Installer, which is also used by most third-party companies, is capable of removing what it installed—provided that the developer writes the necessary script. Unfortunately, too few developers do so, but you can always try this: Hold down the Option key and see whether the Install button turns into a Remove button. If it doesn't work in the main screen, click on Customize, select one or more specific items, then press Option again and see if you can remove them.

Installers that give few choices and little information infuriate me. Aside from the concrete problem of preventing removal, they violate one of the defining principles of the Mac, articulated a decade ago in Apple's Human Interface Guidelines: The user should be in control. An Easy Install option is fine for those who want it, but the rest of us should have additional choices—and everyone should have information.

Fortunately, version 4 of the Apple Installer offers more user options than previous versions did, and several other developers now offer competing installers that also put the user in control. But it's still up to developers to license one of these products and take good advantage of its capabilities. If you find programs that still don't give you the control you want over the installation process, contact the developers and give them a piece of your mind.

file. If you try to do it manually, there's a good chance you'll mess up. Many problems users encounter can be traced back to some misstep in this complex process.

That's why it's important to use the *installer programs* that now come not only with Apple's system software but also with most applications and even many utility packages. These installers carry out scripts written by the developer that specify exactly what files need to be placed where, sometimes depending on the type of Mac involved.

Granted, installers can be a pain: They tend to clutter up your disk unnecessarily (who needs another copy of TeachText, and what the hell is A/ROSE for?) and put programs on the startup volume when you want them on your applications volume, or at the top level of your disk when you want them inside a folder.

Still, it's better to let the installer do its thing; you can experiment later, if you wish, with eliminating files you think you don't need or moving things to different locations.

System Folders: One's Enough, but a Backup's Handy

Press ⌘F in the Finder and search on your startup disk for *system folder*—how many copies do you find? If you only find one, you're in good shape. If there's more than one on your startup disk, you're asking for trouble: A multiplicity of System Folders on one volume can cause system software and applications to get confused and sometimes crash. (It also explains why users can't find some newly installed font or control panel after rebooting: They put it in the wrong System Folder!)

How did all those System Folders get there, anyway? Usually it's an unintended consequence of copying floppies to your hard disk. Say you want to copy an application from the floppy, but instead of opening up its window and selecting the relevant files you just drag the floppy icon to your hard disk. You end up with a new folder having the same name as the floppy, and if the floppy has a System Folder on it, you'll get an extra one of those too.

If you have some disk space to spare, it's not a bad idea to keep an extra, up-to-date copy of your System and Finder (or even your whole System Folder)

Changing Startup Disks (HN)

Under some circumstances you may want to keep more than one system around—you may, for example, have to keep a copy of System 6 available so you can use some old software that crashes under System 7. There's little risk in doing so, as long as you keep the System Folders on separate disks. When you need to change startup systems, open the Startup Disk control panel, select the disk you want to be the startup volume, and restart. (That doesn't work on the Mac Plus.)

Alternatively, you can select (or *bless)* the System Folder that you want with a handy freeware application called **System Picker.** If you want to change startup disks at boot time, install Startup Manager, the extension-management component in Now Software's **Now Utilities** (described in Chapter 13), or a freeware extension called **System Switcher**—either one will give you a choice among startup volumes if you hold down a specified key during bootup.

If you keep System Folders in several partitions on the same physical disk, you'll need to use System Picker, System Switcher, or Startup Manager to control which folder will be blessed. The Startup Disk control panel lets you highlight a particular volume on the disk you choose, but that's an illusion: When you restart, the Mac will boot from one of the volumes on the indicated disk—but not necessarily the volume you've highlighted.

on-line—if your main system gets corrupted, switching to the backup is easier than doing a complete reinstall. If you choose to keep a backup installed, though, either keep it on a separate hard disk (see the box above) or compress the backup with a utility such as StuffIt, DiskDoubler, or Compact Pro; that way, there's no danger that it could be confused for the active system, and it won't take up so much space. (If your original system software gets badly damaged, boot from a floppy, decompress the backup, throw away the damaged original, and reboot.)

Keep Your Extensions Under Control

By making it easy to install control panels and system extensions (known in the System 6 era as "inits"), Apple gave users a terrific way to customize their systems and new features but also opened a Pandora's box: Extensions are the single most common cause of instability in the Mac environment.

It's not just that some (commercial as well as shareware and freeware) extensions are poorly written and tested—even well-behaved extensions can be problematic under certain circumstances. That's because all of them occupy memory that might otherwise be available for other uses, and because they make changes that other developers could not necessarily foresee. (Sometimes two extensions even try to modify the same aspect of the system in different ways—then you could have some real problems.)

Some conservative users, overbearing managers, and self-centered tech-support staffers have their own solution to this issue: Don't install any extensions, or at least none that are not Apple-standard. Like abstinence in other areas of life, this approach does allow you to avoid some problems, but it also means denying yourself a lot of pleasure and opportunity. Instead, my recommendation is safe computing: If you know what the dangers are and take prudent precautions, you can reduce your risk to acceptable levels and find your way out of any problems that do arise. Here are some guidelines.

Be discriminating. A simple rule: The more extensions you install, the greater the chance of incompatibility among them or with other programs. Don't add an extension just because it exists or sounds cool. Make sure it delivers real value. That doesn't mean never adding things that are just fun, such as funky sounds or desktop decorations—after all, fun's a value, too. But remember that there are always trade-offs, so use your judgment.

If you have a Power Mac, pay special attention. Some extensions written before the new machines appeared slip code designed for 68K processors into areas of the operating system that Apple has rewritten in PowerPC code. In most cases they'll run, and most of the time they won't do any harm, but in some situations they can slow down your Power Mac appreciably. The biggest offenders are Adobe Type Manager 3.6.1 and earlier and After Dark 2 and earlier.

Add new extensions one at a time. Don't download a half-dozen extensions and dump them all at once into your System Folder—it'll make debugging much more complicated if problems do arise. Add one extension, reboot, and try out your commonly used or most-sensitive applications to make sure everything's in order. Then go back and repeat the procedure with the next extension you want to add.

Use an extension manager. You can manage your control panels and extensions manually (by dragging them in and out of their special folders and then rebooting), but like most jobs, this one is a lot easier if you have a tool specialized for the task. Fortunately, there are now several extension-management utilities. My current favorite is Casady & Greene's **Conflict Catcher II** ($80) because of its diagnostic capabilities (see the box "An Automated Conflict Catcher" on page 301), but Now's Startup Manager, Inline Software's INIT Picker, and others also work very well. (Some extension managers are reviewed in Chapter 13). And if you don't want to spend money, just use Ricardo Batista's **Extensions Manager,** which is distributed free and included with System 7.5. It doesn't have quite all of the features its commercial competitors have, but it's much more than you might expect from a freebie.

SYSTEM 7.5

The main point is to install one of these programs, even if you don't often reconfigure your extensions lineup. It won't cause any harm if you don't use it, and it will save you a lot of grief if trouble ever arises.

Be cautious about reordering. One of the standard techniques for managing extensions is to change their loading order: Sometimes extension B will cause a crash if A is already in memory, but they'll both be happy if B goes first. Most of the extension-management utilities now let you change the order by dragging items around, or you can do it yourself by adding a letter, punctuation mark, or space in front of a file's normal name.

Personally, I'm wary of this approach. Not because it doesn't work—it often does—but it can make your System Folder an even more confusing place than it was before: Files no longer appear in the order you'd expect in list views, and extension combinations that previously worked fine may no longer. (Even developers who test their products thoroughly aren't likely to test every conceivable loading order.)

If trouble arises, be heartless. You can't always have your cake and eat it too. If two extensions you like don't get along reliably, don't just load both and keep your fingers crossed: Pick the one you value most and toss the other. (If you want one most of the time but another on special occasions, reconfigure and reboot. The leading extension managers all allow you to make sets of extensions you can select at bootup, often just by holding down a key as the machine starts up.)

Know Your System

If you ever need to get tech support from a vendor or friend, the person trying to help you may well want to know details about your Mac configuration, including both hardware specifications (model number, processor speed, total memory, installed cards, etc.) and software particulars (system version, names and version numbers of the applications you use, the extensions and control panels you have installed, and so on).

You can gather all this yourself and put it in a notebook, but it's much easier to have the Mac do its own inventory. If you own Now Utilities (described in Chapter 13), you can use the Now Profiler application to collect such information. The most thorough program of this kind, though, is a freeware utility called **TattleTech** (formerly TattleTale).

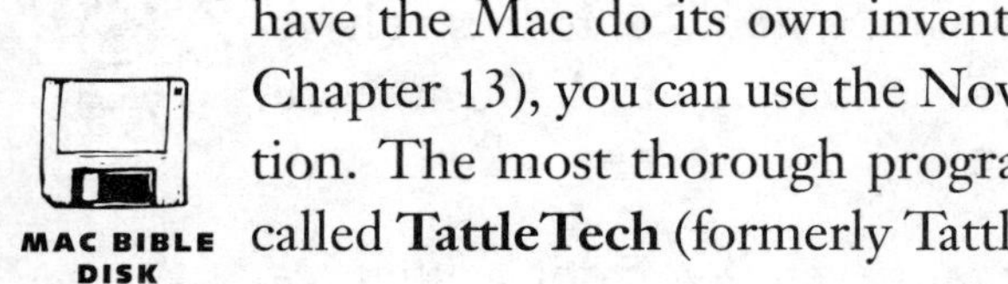

Whichever you use, have it gather the information and print out a report. Then file it away, so you'll have access to the information even if your computer is down. Remember to update the profile from time to time as your system changes—recently added files are quite likely to be the culprits when new problems arise.

Use the Shut Down Command

Always shut down by selecting Shut Down from the Special menu in the Finder. On Mac models that then tell you to shut them off with the switch, the command might seem like a pointless extra step. But it's not: It tells the Mac to do some small but important housekeeping chores, including saving the contents of the disk cache (see Chapter 5) to disk. If you just flip the switch, you may lose that data and even, conceivably, damage some open files. Besides, it won't really save you any time: The next time you start up, the Mac will see that it wasn't shut down properly, so it will start checking out your disks to make sure everything is in order—a process that eats up much more time than using the Shut Down command in the first place.

Tune Up Your System

When it finds significant bugs and performance problems in the Mac system, Apple sometimes releases interim fixes pending the next update of the system as

The Disk Check Bug (HN)

If you do shut off the power without using the Shut Down command—or if you had no choice and had to reboot because your Mac crashed or froze up—you may find only a blinking question mark on your screen the next time you try to start up. Or you may be able to boot up only to have the Finder tell you that one of your other volumes is "not a Macintosh disk."

Sometimes these problems are a result of real damage to the *boot blocks*—the section of the disk that the Mac reads when you first start it. But sometimes there's nothing at all wrong with the disk, and the blinking question mark or the dialog box is a result of a bug in the checking routine—the *Disk Check*—that the Mac goes through when you restart after an improper shutdown.

The bug only shows up under some very particular circumstances that have to do with the size of the disk or partition and the number of fragmented files on it, but it's a big bother if you happen to get bitten. You can ordinarily get your disk back by using some of the techniques discussed under "The Blinking Question Mark" in the "When Trouble Strikes" section later in this chapter, but they all take time, and there's always some risk that those techniques won't work—so you're better off trying to root out the problem completely.

One way is to use an optimizer regularly to *defragment* your disks. (Such utilities are included in Norton Utilities and Mac Tools, whose antivirus and data-recovery functions also come in handy for troubleshooting, as described later in this chapter.) But you can also get an estimate of how likely it is that your disk will be susceptible to the problem by running **Disk Bug Checker,** a free utility developed by Central Point Software and available through on-line services and user groups. If it reports that your disk is in serious jeopardy, it's worth your while to back up the data and reformat the disk with slightly different partition sizes. After reformatting, run Disk Bug Checker again to make sure your new partitioning scheme is safer. (See Chapter 5 for more on partitioning hard disks.)

a whole. In the days of System 7.0 and 7.0.1, these updates were called *System 7 Tune-Ups;* more recently, Apple has collected its fixes on disks known as Hardware, Software, or System *Updates*.

In most cases the problems fixed by these patches have been relatively minor and/or obscure. But some are significant. System 7, for example, brought out an old bug in the Mac file system that under some conditions could cause files to disappear off the Mac desktop. (They'd be there for a while, and you could locate them with the Find command, but you couldn't see them in the Finder.) Version 1.1.1 of the System 7 Tune-Up prevented the bug from devouring additional files, though it didn't bring back items already lost. (Version 7.1 or later of Apple's Disk First Aid attempts to reverse the damage.)

If you are running System 7.0 or 7.0.1 (the last version of the system Apple made available free of charge), you should definitely install the Tune-Up. If you have one of those system versions and are not sure whether you have the Tune-Up, check the About This Macintosh dialog box (under the menu in the Finder); if it shows a bullet (•) in the system number, you are already protected; if not, get the Tune-Up from your dealer or user group. (Better yet, upgrade to System 7.1, which has the fix built in.)

In general, it's a good idea to stay informed about such system updates. Unfortunately, Apple doesn't notify its customers even about serious problems, so the burden is on you to keep in touch via on-line services, a user group, or Mac magazines.

Give Your Programs Enough Memory

After extension conflicts, shortages of memory are probably the biggest source of instability on the Mac: The less free RAM available, the greater the risk of a crash or freeze. And that rule holds for individual applications as well as the whole system. Each program you launch gets a certain memory *allocation* or *partition*, and if you fill that up, you could have problems even if there's plenty of memory lying idle on your system—the Mac doesn't normally redistribute memory dynamically among applications.

Here are some guidelines for minimizing memory-related risks.

Increase the preferred and minimum memory settings of your applications. Developers generally don't want their products perceived as memory hogs, so they tend to set the minimum and preferred memory amounts (the data the system uses to allocate memory to a program when you launch it) to levels that may be too low for real-life use. You can give your programs a safety cushion by increasing these amounts: Simply go to the Finder, select the program's icon (when it's not running), and press Cmd I or select Get Info from the File menu. Under current versions of the system you can change Preferred and Minimum values. Hit Enter or just close the Get Info window, and the new numbers will be saved and used the next time you launch the program.

As a rule of thumb, I normally increase both values for every new program I install—usually by about 25 percent. That means I can't keep as many programs open as I could otherwise, but I'm glad to make that sacrifice in order to avoid crashes.

Keep an eye on About This Macintosh. The About This Macintosh box (which you can get to from the menu when you are in the Finder) is a convenient source of information about memory usage, and it's worth watching if you are encountering otherwise inexplicable problems. It will tell you the total amount of memory available, the largest unused block, and the amount allocated to the system and each open application. Pay special attention to the bars next to each application listed: The length of the bar represents the size of the program's memory partition; the darker, filled-in section represents how much of that memory is actually in use at that moment.

Don't worry if the System Software bar is almost completely filled—that's normal under System 7, and the system should be able to get more memory if it needs to (so long as some remains free). But if one of your applications regularly fills up its bar, it's a good idea (especially if you've experienced crashes in that program) to quit from it and use Get Info to increase its allocation before reopening it. (Conversely, if there's a large amount of "white space" in an application's bar when you are using it in a normal way, you could experiment with reducing its Preferred setting.)

Get more memory, real or virtual. If very little free memory is available anywhere, try closing an application or two or turn on virtual memory (in the Memory control panel) and reboot. If you are in this situation frequently, pick up a copy of **RAM Doubler** from Connectix if your Mac has a PowerPC, a 68040, a 68030 or a 68020 processor with an added *paged memory management unit;* or get Jump Development's **OptiMem** if you have an older model. Both programs will let you keep more programs open without the performance penalty entailed with Apple's virtual memory. (See Chapter 4 for more on virtual memory and on RAM Doubler and OptiMem.)

Of course, the best way to avoid tight-memory problems, if your budget permits and your Mac has the capacity, is to install more real RAM.

Install SCSIProbe

If you ever have any external drives connected to your Mac, one of the smartest and easiest steps you can take to prepare yourself in case of SCSI troubles (such as external drives that are AWOL when you boot up your Mac) is to install a control panel called **SCSIProbe**. Written by Robert Polic and now underwritten by SyQuest Technologies (the company that makes removable-media hard drive mechanisms), it's free from user groups and on-line services.

This 30K gem has several useful functions. It identifies all the devices on the SCSI chain by name, type, and SCSI ID number; if a device isn't listed, it's not communicating at all with your Mac. The info is nice, but what's most useful is the Mount button: If you click it, it will attempt to mount any connected device that isn't already on your desktop. On many occasions it has mounted drives for me that otherwise refused to appear.

GOOD FEATURE

SCSIProbe is especially valuable if you have a SyQuest drive and use cartridges formatted with different programs, because it can mount almost any cartridge, even if the cartridge wasn't in the drive when you started up the machine.

Get and Use an Antivirus Utility

Because the threat of viruses has received so much publicity, many users are quick to suspect infection if they encounter unexplained difficulties. Actually, though, the odds that your problem was caused by a virus are very slim. Although early viruses such as nVIR and WDEF spread quite widely, the Mac community became much more alert and effective at protecting itself, and no recent infection has gotten very far.

Still, the threat is real enough to justify taking precautions, which means installing an antivirus utility and keeping it up to date as new viruses appear. Symantec's **SAM** ($100), DataWatch's **Virex** ($100), and Central Point **Anti-Virus for Macintosh** (available separately for $70 or as part of the $150 **MacTools**) all include applications to scan your disk for viruses as well as extensions that try to protect against new infections. All three companies make it easy to update their software when a new virus is discovered.

The other popular choice—and the one I use, even though I have all the available commercial packages—is **Disinfectant.** Developed and maintained as a public service by John Norstad, it's available through user groups, on-line services, and bulletin boards. The program is simple but effective: It includes a command to install a protective extension, it has superb documentation covering the whole virus problem built into the application, and it is updated by Norstad and his team as fast as any commercial developer when new threats are discovered. The only downside to Disinfectant is that (as of this writing) it has no update mechanism, so if you are getting it by modem, you have to download a whole new copy each time a new virus surfaces.

Many journalists, computer novices, and corporate-computing managers seem to think that free and shareware programs downloaded from bulletin boards are the principal means by which viruses spread. Nothing could be farther from the truth, despite a handful of well-publicized incidents—on-line libraries are almost always virus-free because their operators have every incentive to check their files closely. The main danger of infection today comes from places where computers are accessible to the public, with school and college computing laboratories highest on the list. (Service bureaus and stores that let customers copy shareware or system software used to be big problems too, but by now most have cleaned up their act.)

Get a Data-Recovery Package

There's a special category of utility software designed to help users avoid or recover from problems that can cause the loss of data. The leaders in the field are Central Point Software's **MacTools** and Symantec's **Norton Utilities for Macintosh** (both $150). Norton version 3 will incorporate Public Utilities, a former competitor Symantec added to its list when it acquired Fifth Generation Systems. (Symantec recently bought Central Point too, but for now MacTools remains on the market.)

While exact features vary, all of these packages have several capabilities in common. They all include modules that will check the directory structures on your disks for corruption and attempt to repair them if possible; they all have undelete functions, enabling you, in many cases, to recover files that have been emptied from the trash; and they all include *optimizers* that can improve disk performance by ensuring that your files are all stored in one piece rather than as fragments scattered around your disk. The latest versions include extensions that can check your disks in the background when your Mac is idle and warn you if they detect problems.

Obviously, none of these programs can spare you from true hardware failures. They usually can't repair individual files that have become corrupted, and even certain kinds of directory damage may be too much for them. Some of their procedures are very time-consuming—things you'd do only when you're desperate. In short, they're not magic, and they're no substitute for keeping an up-to-date backup of your data.

But in many cases the utility programs can detect and repair damage before it's caused you to lose data. And if your disk has already crashed, they can *sometimes* enable you to get some or all of your files back. When they work, they can save you the hassle that reformatting your disks and restoring your data from a backup involves. They can also recover recent files that you might not have yet backed up. And their undelete functions are very handy—there's not much that makes you feel worse than inadvertently throwing away an important file.

All in all, getting one of these programs is a good investment if you make heavy use of your computer. Just don't let it lull you into complacency about backing up.

If you choose not to invest in a commercial data-recovery program, at least be sure to keep copies of Apple's **Disk First Aid** (version 7.2 or later) handy. It doesn't pretend to address all the issues covered by its retail rivals, but it can fix many of the most frequent forms of directory corruption. (Older versions of Disk First Aid solved only a very limited set of problems, leading some users to dismiss it as rarely worth the trouble. Version 7.2 or later, however, addresses a wider range of problems. It's also got a much better interface.)

Keep a Good Set of Emergency Tools Handy

Many problems that could cost you hours of work and anxiety—and even lead to the loss of all your files—can be fixed in a matter of minutes if you have the proper tools available. Prepare a set of disks for use in emergencies, write-protect them (by sliding the plastic tab in the upper-right corner of each floppy so you can see through the hole), and don't let them get lost amid all your other floppies—put them in a special place where you'll be sure to find them should trouble strike. Your tool set should include all of the following (even though you won't be able to fit them all on one disk).

A bootable floppy. If your hard disk won't start up your Mac because the system software on it is damaged, there's still a good chance you can get access to your files—and start the work of repairing the system on the hard disk—by booting your system from a floppy. If you got a set of Apple floppies with your machine, you can always use the original Disk Tools disk as your emergency disk; just make sure it's locked, so it doesn't accidentally get damaged.

Better yet, prepare your own emergency disk in advance and set it aside in case of need. First copy your Disk Tools floppy to your hard drive, then drag the floppy's icon to the trash. Next, insert a new or freshly initialized disk and name it something like Emergency Disk. Drag the contents of the Disk Tools disk from your hard disk to the new floppy. Then comes the tricky part: Double-click on the Emergency Disk icon, then on the System Folder icon it contains. Drag the System and Finder icons from the System Folder window to the Emergency Disk window. Release the mouse, then drag the same System and Finder icons back into the System Folder window. That may seem like going around in circles, but it gets the Mac to write boot blocks on the floppy, making it a bootable disk. (A miniature Mac should now appear on the icon of the System Folder of the Emergency Disk.) Then copy SCSIProbe to the floppy.

If you don't have a Disk Tools disk, you can make your own equivalent. Insert a new or freshly initialized disk and name it something like Emergency Disk. Copy the System file, the Finder, SCSIProbe, and (if you have a recent Mac) the *System Enabler* from your hard disk's system folder to the Emergency Disk. (Enablers are special files containing system software specific to a particular Mac model. Your machine won't boot without it.) Then drag the System, Finder, SCSIProbe, and Enabler icons from the Emergency Disk's main window to the System Folder you just created. (The miniature Mac icon should now appear on the System Folder icon.) If there's any room left, add a copy of Apple's Disk First Aid utility.

Whether you copy Apple's Disk Tools floppy or prepare an original emergency disk, test it in advance to make sure it will really boot your Mac: Shut down your machine, insert the Emergency Disk, then restart—the Mac should start up from the floppy. If it does, lock the disk, label it, and set it aside to be ready in case of emergency. (Just don't forget where you put it.)

A complete set of system installation disks. Use copies of the system floppies that came with your Mac or the disks you used the last time you upgraded to a new system version. (If your Mac came with a CD-ROM drive, you can use Apple's system CD instead.)

A copy of your disk-formatting software. If your hard disk fails to boot, it could be a result of damage to the driver software on the disk. Most disk formatters enable you to reinstall or update the driver. If you can run the formatter from a floppy, you may be able to recover the hard disk quickly.

HOT TIP

If you can fit the formatter on a bootable system floppy, do so; it will save you a lot of floppy-disk swapping. (For the same reason, if you have multiple hard disks, keep a copy of the formatter on each volume.)

A disk-recovery utility. Recovery programs like Norton Utilities, Public Utilities, and MacTools (see above) all come with emergency boot disks containing a stripped-down system and a disk-repair application. Make sure *before you need it* that the disk will actually boot your Mac. Recent models require recent system software, plus an enabler. If that software wasn't available when your recovery utility was last updated, or if it simply wouldn't fit, your emergency boot disk won't get you out of your emergency.

Central Point Software's MacTools 3 or later will build an emergency disk for you from your System Folder. If you are using a different data-recovery package and the emergency disk that came with it doesn't boot your Mac, contact the utility's publisher for advice.

When Trouble Strikes

No matter how conscientiously you've maintained your hardware and how careful you've been about software installation and usage, trouble is bound to strike occasionally. This section details some common problems and what you can do about them.

The Sad Mac and the Chimes of Death (HN)

If you power up your Mac and instead of the familiar boing you hear a strange sequence of chords and a frowning Mac icon (known as the *Sad Mac*) appears when you normally see a smiling one, you may well have a hardware problem requiring a service technician's attention. But that's not a foregone conclusion. Before you call the dealer, there are several steps you can take.

1. Shut the machine off, check all your cables (especially SCSI), and try powering up again.
2. If that doesn't work, insert a system floppy and start again.
3. If that doesn't work, and you have SCSI devices attached, shut the machine and all SCSI devices off, disconnect the SCSI cable from the back of your Mac, and reboot.
4. If that doesn't work, it might be time to call for help, but if you are even a little comfortable working with hardware, try shutting everything off, opening up your Mac, grounding yourself (by putting on an antistatic strap or at least touching the power supply), then checking to make sure that all cards and SIMMs are *seated* properly—that is, that they don't seem loose in their slots. Then put everything back together and try again.

If you still get the chimes and the Sad Mac, call your dealer or service provider.

(The codes that appear under the Sad Mac, as well as the sequence of chords you hear, are supposed to give some clue to the nature of the problem. But you pretty much have to be a trained technician to read these entrails.)

The Blinking Question Mark (HN)

A blinking question mark indicates that the Mac has passed its initial self-tests but can't boot up because it hasn't found a disk with *boot blocks* (special areas, set aside when you install a valid System Folder on a volume, that hold critical start-up information) and a working system. If you have external devices on your SCSI chain, make sure they are turned on. If that's not the problem, shut everything down and check the cables. If that does no good, try booting with a system floppy.

If you can boot from a floppy. If you can get your Mac to start from a floppy, cross your fingers and hope your hard disk(s) appear on the desktop (it may take a long time). If not, and if you have SCSIProbe or a similar utility on the floppy, check whether it can see and mount your external drives. If that doesn't work, try version 7.2 or later of Apple's Disk First Aid utility (if it's not on your hard disk, look on Apple's system CD or Disk Tools floppy). If the program finds your disk and identifies a problem it can fix, let it. Then reboot.

If Disk First Aid doesn't solve the problem, run the formatting utility you originally used on the hard disk; if it sees the disk, find and use the command that lets you reinstall or update the driver. Then quit the program and try rebooting.

If you see your hard drives. If you can get access to your hard drives after booting from a floppy, the first thing you should do is copy (to another floppy, a file server, or an external hard drive) any critical files that aren't already backed up. (That will undoubtedly help you proceed more calmly through the remaining steps).

Next, find the System Folder on your startup volume and drag the System and Finder files out of it to the root directory of the disk (the window that opens when you double-click on the disk icon) or to another folder outside the System Folder. Close the System Folder's window, then drag the System and Finder icons back into it. As noted above, this isn't pointless fiddling; moving the System and Finder will make the Mac update the volume's boot blocks, and that in itself is sometimes enough to make it bootable again. Restart and see.

Reinstalling System Software (HN)

If your Mac won't boot up or is acting erratically, you may be able to cure it by replacing your system software with a clean version.

If you have a compressed backup copy of your System Folder, the process is easy: Give your current System Folder a new name (I call it "ex-System Folder") and drag the System and Finder files out of it into the Trash.

Then decompress your backup System Folder. Drag the System and Finder files out of the new System Folder to another location on the disk, then back into the folder they came from. This forces the Mac to update the disk's boot blocks and to "bless" the new folder as the volume's primary System folder.)

If you don't have a backup of an up-to-date System Folder (or if your backup is *so* up-to-date that it carries the same corruption as the version you just threw away), you'll need to boot from a set of Apple system floppies (the ones that came with your Mac or a newer set) or from the Apple CD-ROM that came with your drive. Then run the Installer.

Using the Installer correctly can be a little trickier than it seems, because it doesn't recognize many kinds of corruption. If it finds System and Finder files already present in a valid System Folder, it may update them (if it's installing a newer version) or just leave them alone. Either way, the damage you are trying to get rid of may remain.

To make sure you get a clean version of the system software when you reinstall it, follow the procedure given in Chapter 3 under "Clean Slate Installation (System 7)" in the "Installing System Software" section. That will ensure that the Installer creates virgin, uncorrupted copies of all the required files from scratch. When copying your extra resources from the old System Folder after reinstalling the system, don't copy over old Preference files—they could be corrupted. (Most programs will create new Preference files if needed; at worst you'll have to redo some settings.)

If that doesn't work, follow the same steps listed in the section above: Ask Disk First Aid to check and (if necessary and possible) repair your boot volume; also try reinstalling your hard disk driver with the utility you use to format your hard drive. If none of those measures gets the drive to boot properly, it's time to reinstall the System Folder on your startup volume.

Don't be complacent. If any of these tricks get your hard disk to boot again, give thanks but don't stop there. Something made the problem occur, and it's highly likely to strike again, so you should take appropriate steps. If you haven't already reinstalled the system, do so now. Update your backup and back up new files frequently, at least until you are sure you've fixed the problem.

Crashes During Bootup (HN)

If you see the happy Mac and the Welcome to Macintosh dialog box, but the machine crashes before the desktop appears, try rebooting with the Shift key held down. Under System 7 that will disable all extensions (including control panels that have init resources in them).

If you still can't complete the boot-up process, you very likely have some kind of system corruption. Boot from your system floppies or the system CD-ROM that came with your Mac. (If you are booting from the CD, press Cmd Shift Option Del to bypass the the internal hard disk and boot from the CD.) Then reinstall your system software, following the directions on the previous page.

If that doesn't work, try booting again from a floppy or CD, going to the Preferences folder inside your startup disk's System Folder, and throwing away the Finder Preferences file. Or try rebuilding the desktop and zapping the PRAM (see the box on page 303).

If you can boot successfully with extensions disabled, you've pretty well established that the problem involves bugs or incompatibilities among your extensions.

Isolating extension problems. Tracking down extension problems is a major pastime for Mac users who like to customize and enhance their systems. When you have 15, 20, or even 50 extensions loading—each of them making a variety of modifications to the standard Mac environment—it can be a challenge to determine just which one is causing crashes. But several techniques can make the hunt easier.

One is to use an extension manager (described above and in Chapter 13)—don't be without one if you are running more than, say, a half-dozen extensions. In addition to giving you easy ways to turn individual items on or off, the better extension managers take note of crashes that occur while extensions are loading; the next time you boot up they will (if you have this feature activated) disable the last extension to load before the crash on the previous startup attempt, on the theory that it's most likely to have caused the problem. If you can boot smoothly with that extension turned off, you've already identified the source of the problem, though you can't tell without further testing whether that extension alone is causing the problem or whether it's due to some interaction with one or more of the extensions that loaded ahead of it.

If your extension manager doesn't solve the problem for you, try disabling the extension you added most recently—if things used to be stable but aren't any longer, there's reason to suspect the newcomer.

The binary method. The real challenge comes when crashes are caused not by a single extension but by an interaction among two or more. Many users and even some experts and tech-support personnel will tell you this situation requires you to disable all extensions, then reactivate one and reboot, reactivate one more and reboot, and so on, ad nauseam, until you have found the conflict.

HOT TIP

Nonsense—this approach takes forever! A much more rational and faster approach is called the *binary method*: Disable the first half of your extensions. If the problem persists, you know it's caused by one or more items on the second half of your list, and you don't have to worry (for now) about testing those in the first half; if the problem is cured, you've traced it to something on the first half of the list, and you can stop worrying about those in the second half. In other words, you've effectively put half your extensions through testing in just one launch.

Once you've identified the half containing the culprit, shut off half of that group and reboot. If the problem persists, shut off half of the remainder. And so on.

When the problem disappears, you know it's likely to have been caused, at least in part, by one of the extensions in the last group you disabled. Turn half the items in that group back on, but disable *all* your

An Automated Conflict Catcher (HN)

GOOD FEATURE

Conflict Catcher II, Casady and Greene's $80 extension manager, can automate the binary testing process for you. When you use its test mode, it disables half your extensions, reboots, and asks if the problem persists. Depending on your answer, it will try another group and ask again. It's nothing you couldn't do yourself, but the program chews through the problem with impressive speed and determination. In most cases it can finger the culprit(s) in just a few minutes.

It's an excellent extension manager in other ways too (described in Chapter 13). Highly recommended.

other extensions. Then work through the small group until you have identified the individual extension that's causing the problem.

It sounds cumbersome and time-consuming, and it is—just not nearly as cumbersome and time-consuming as testing your extensions individually.

When Programs Don't Work (HN)

If a utility or application doesn't work normally, first reboot with your extensions turned off and see if the problem goes away. If it does, you know you have a conflict, and you should use one of the methods described above to isolate it. If the problem persists when the extensions are off, either the program in question or its Preferences file may be damaged. Open the Preferences folder in your System Folder (it's a little like lifting up a big rock in the woods—you'll likely be amazed at how much is going on in there), throw out the problem program's preferences file, then try the program again. If that doesn't solve the problem, throw away the whole program (including all standard associated files) and reinstall it from your master disks.

Corrupted Files (HN)

At times you may get a message that one of your files is corrupted when you try to open it with the application that created it or another that should be able to read its format. There are several tricks you can try:

- Duplicate the file in the Finder and try to open the copy.
- If the file in question is a Microsoft Word or Excel file, the FileFix module from Central Point's MacTools may be able to fix it. Many databases and some other applications also come with special utilities to repair damaged files.
- Abbott Systems' **CanOpener** ($125) can extract text, PICT images, icons, and sounds from files of almost any format, including many damaged files. You can read and copy the recovered resources right in CanOpener, or you can save and open them with another program. The file may not look the way it did in its native application, but at least you can recover some of its main contents.

When the Desktop Doesn't Work Properly (HN)

If some of your files have lost their usual icons in favor of generic document and application icons, or if you double-click on a document icon and get a message that the application that created it can't be found even though you know it's around, it's time to rebuild the desktop—the invisible files in which the Mac stores information about your files, including icons, comments from the Get Info box, and the application to be launched when you double-click on the document.

The standard procedure for rebuilding the desktop is to hold down the [Cmd] and [Option] keys during bootup. (You actually need to hold the keys down only near the end of the bootup process, after extensions are loaded.) The Mac will then ask you if you really want to rebuild the desktop, reminding you that doing so will wipe out any Get Info comments that may be associated with files on the disk. (If you need to preserve the comments, you can do so with the shareware utility **CommentKeeper** or with SuperComments, part of Atticus Software's **Super 7 Utilities,** described in Chapter 13).

MAC BIBLE DISK

Zapping the PRAM (HN)

Another time-honored folk remedy for Mac ills is *zapping the PRAM*—clearing the *parameter RAM*, a small area of memory in which the Mac stores settings such as the preferences you select in the General Controls and Sounds control panels. (It's nonvolatile memory, kept alive by battery, so these settings survive when the Mac is shut down).

Just how the PRAM gets corrupted and what effects this has is something of a mystery, but clearing it can sometimes cure a variety of otherwise inexplicable problems. The only cost is that you'll have to reset the Apple control panels the way you want them.

To zap the PRAM under System 7, hold down [⌘][Option][P][R] as you boot up. (It's also a good stretching exercise for your fingers.)

If you have several hard disks or partitions that appear when you start up, the Mac will ask you about rebuilding the desktop for each volume in succession. You see only one desktop, but you've got a separate desktop files on each disk or partition.

The [⌘][Option] combination cleans out the desktop files, but it does not completely replace them with new ones. For that reason, corruption in the file can sometimes survive the rebuilding process. If you suspect this is happening or just want to be careful, you can completely delete the Desktop files yourself—that will force the Finder to create brand new ones. To do so, use a utility that lets you see invisible files, such as ResEdit or DiskTop. Find the files named Desktop DB and Desktop DF in the top-level directory of your disk and move them to the trash.

An easier way to accomplish the same result is to use one of two free utilities: **TechTool**, a simple application that does nothing but delete the desktop or zap the PRAM (see the box on page 303); or **Desktop Reset**, an extension that does the same thing when you press the ⌘ Option combination at bootup.

Of Dust and Drives (JK/HN)

Dust can gum up floppy drives to the point that they no longer eject disks properly or can't read them. If you see the message "This is not a Macintosh disk. Do you want to initialize it?" when you insert a floppy that you know perfectly well is a Mac disk, you might have a serious problem with the disk, but there's a pretty good chance you just need to do a little housekeeping.

You can sometimes blow the dust out of a floppy drive yourself, but you may just end up blowing the dust further into the drive mechanism. A Mac repair shop can disassemble your floppy drive, clean and lube it, and align the read/write heads to make it work like a new drive.

[Before taking the drive in for repair, which is bound to be expensive, try your luck with a floppy-drive cleaning kit (available from most computer stores and mail-order outlets). There's been some controversy about these kits—some people say they do more harm than good. But if you get the kit manufactured by 3M (it's marketed by a number of companies), you should be OK—it's been endorsed by Apple for cleaning SuperDrives. On several occasions it's done wonders for flaky floppy drives on my machines.—HN]

IIsi and LC Sound, Light, and Fan Blackouts (JK)

On Mac IIsi's and LCs, the speaker, fan, and green disk-access light (the light on the case that flickers when the Mac is accessing an internal hard drive) sometimes conk out—intermittently or permanently. That's because they get their power and signals through little metal tabs that press against contacts on the logic board, and both the tabs and/or contacts get corroded.

You'll probably notice a dead speaker pretty quickly—there'll be no startup chord, no alert sounds while you work, and no other signals. You may not notice if the disk-access light goes out, but who cares? The fan is the one to look out for. If you keep working without it—particularly in a hot environment—you run the risk of overheating your Mac's logic board and having to replace it.

This is an expensive repair, so be aware of the sound your si's or LC's fan usually makes. If you turn it on and it's quieter than usual, check with your hand that it's pumping air out the back. If not, shut it down. You can try to fix the problem yourself by cleaning the contacts on the logic board, but if that doesn't work, take the machine in for repair.

Diagnostic Tools

(HN)

Several vendors—now including Apple—offer utilities designed to help you test and monitor the performance of your Mac system and identify problems. They're not magic, but they could save you hours of troubleshooting.

Hardware Diagnostics

My favorite among these diagnostic programs is **Peace of Mind** ($150), now published by Diagsoft: It's got a nice graphical interface and a very thorough suite of tests. In expert mode it gives you complete control over which tests it will run and displays detailed information about the results it gets. Version 2 (not out at this writing) is supposed to include a feature that enables you to dial the publisher automatically for technical assistance.

Another popular diagnostic program is Micromat's **MacEKG** ($150), but I never found it as useful as Peace of Mind.

The latest player in this arena is Apple. The company has provided a limited directory-diagnostic and repair program—Disk First Aid—as standard equipment for many years. A few years back the company began shipping a more comprehensive diagnostic tool called MacCheck with some Performas and PowerBooks. And now Apple sells a still broader program called **Apple Personal Diagnostics** ($130). Its features aren't unique—most are available in one or another competing program—but the combination is: At least at this writing, no other package combines hardware diagnostics and speed tests with directory checking and repair.

If you have a Power Mac, check with the vendor before investing money or time in any of these programs. At press time none of them—even Apple's own Apple Personal Diagnostics—worked on the new models.

Help!

Several companies (starting with Apple) have tried to deliver programs designed to help users identify possible software-compatibility problems. Only one such offering—Teknosys's **Help!**—has survived and been updated regularly. Using what the company calls a "knowledgebase" that has been carefully collected and verified with the assistance of scores of users and vendors, it surveys the user's Mac and looks for conflicts, obsolete versions, improper installations, and other problems; in each case it not only names the problem but also suggests a solution. It generates attractive reports and even simulates different Macs, so you can figure out which of your software is likely to have problems if you upgrade to, say, a Power Mac.

The full version, with all reporting and simulation features, lists for $150, while subscriptions to knowledgebase updates range from $40 to $75. But for $50 you can get a Personal Edition, and for another $25 you get two semiannual knowledgebase updates. A multiuser network version starts at $520 for 25 users.

No program like this can ever be absolutely complete and up to date, but Help! can be very helpful, especially if you don't feel like spending hours every week burrowing through the on-line backwoods looking for similar information (and trying to figure out how much of what you see there is actually true).

PART

Macintosh Software

Editors' Poll: What Programs Do You Use All the Time?

AA: Top two: MS Word (surprise) and TouchBase. Both are customized to a fare-thee-well. I take care of my finances with Quicken (which makes my accountant happy), my faxing with FAXstf (I have a fax modem), my on-line work with CompuServe Information Manager, and my Mac management with Disinfectant, Norton Utilities, and Retrospect. In my writing and graphics work, I use Photoshop and PageMaker, Excel (as a glorified table- and list-maker, rarely as an actual number-cruncher), StuffIt Deluxe (file compression), and MacEnvelope (for printing envelope labels that include my logo and return address). I also swear by several utilities, especially Now Utilities (in particular I *love* NowMenus, Startup Manager, and SuperBoomerang), ATM, Capture (for screen shots), and, of course, After Dark.

DB: I use QuarkXPress, Microsoft Word, MasterJuggler, Navigator (for CompuServe access), and TouchBase Pro every day except Sunday (when I don't go into the office...well, usually I don't).

EC: Word, QuicKeys, CIM and AOL, PageMaker, and Compact Pro. However, my Programs folder is 100MB, and that's only after I copied most of my stuff to SyQuests. There are a lot of programs I use only once in a while (generally, right after I take them off my hard disk).

DD: Word all the time; Excel for schedules and status sheets, TouchBase for my telephone numbers, and, since I've been working on the *Bible,* CompuServe Information Manager is open whenever my computer is on so that I can write an e-mail message as soon as I think of something I need to tell an editor.

CG: I spend 97 percent of my time working in Microsoft Word.

JK: Nisus, Word, Excel, FileMaker Pro, Compact Pro, various telecom programs.

HN: Word, Computer Select, Navigator, AppleLink, AOL, MicroPhone, QuickDEX, Now Up-to-Date, ARA, ARACommander, Eudora, VersaTerm-Link, TCP/Connect II, QuickMail, loads of utilities. Retrospect, Capture, Excel.

BW: As a writer and small-time publisher I use Word, PageMaker, and QuarkXPress. I also use the QuickLink telecommunication program that came with my MDS fax modem.

Working With Words

THE MOST BASIC TOOL for working with text is the *word processor*. The term conjures up visions of word baloney, complete with nitrates and nitrites, but what a word processor really does, as you probably know, is let you write and then change your mind about what you've written, reordering the words and paragraphs, changing their fonts and styles, and then adding more. In the first section, we'll tell you what to look out for in word processors.

Next, we'll tell you about spelling and hyphenation dictionaries, grammar checkers, thesauruses, and writing guides that help you perfect your text.

Sometimes the problem is not how to get your text on the page, but simply what to put on the page. The section on the new crop of brainstorming programs shows how software can help you get your ideas on paper.

If the text is already printed, what you need is an OCR program to read it into your Mac. These are described before the final section of word processing tips.

Contributors

Elizabeth Castro (EC) is the chapter editor.

Lofty Becker (LB) teaches law and serves as an assistant sysop on the MAUG(R) CompuServe forums.

Rick Casreen (RC) is a writer, the source of The Pelorian Press, and consultant for Yes Computers of Noho, Massachusetts.

Kristi Coale (KC) has held staff editing positions at *InfoWorld* and *MacUser* and now freelances for *MacWEEK, MacUser,* and other magazines.

Charles Seiter (CS) is a writer, chemist, and contributing editor to *Macworld.*

Randy B. Singer (RS) is a practicing attorney and Apple Legal Fellow who leads user groups for attorneys who use the Mac. It took him three years to learn most of the features in Microsoft Word; now he's working on WordPerfect.

Arthur Naiman (AN), Sharon Zardetto Aker (SA), Susan McCallister (SM), Nancy E. Dunn (ND), Dale Coleman (DC), and **Paul Hoffman (PH)** contributed to earlier versions of the *Mac Bible,* from which parts of this chapter were taken.

Contents

Word Processors

Putting words onto a screen instead of down on paper changes the way you write. Most people in their pre–word processor stage say, "I could never write with a word processor, I just use it to type the final draft. I need to feel connected to the page with a pen." But once you get started, the pen is quickly forgotten as the word processor helps you be more flexible in your writing and concentrate on your ideas.

For example, because a word processor lets you insert a couple more words (or paragraphs or whatever) in something you've already written, you can work on getting your thoughts down and not worry about getting them in the perfect order right from the beginning. A word processor lets you do as many drafts as you need, from the first brainstorm to the last spelling check. Instead of spending your time typing each draft, a word processor lets you keep what was good and just work on the new parts. And if you ever make a mistake, just find it and get rid of it—and print out a new copy.

What to Look for in a Word Processor (EC)

A word processor's basic functions are to let you enter, edit, and format text. To do that job well, most word processors let you:

- change fonts, font sizes, and character styles
- change the margins
- add headers and footers
- check your spelling
- count your words
- preview your document on screen

In addition, there are a few features that only some word processors have, and in fact, only some people need. Those are discussed below.

Multiple undo. Nisus was one of the first programs to expand on the Mac's most beloved command, Undo, by letting you go back more than one step. Version 6 of Word finally includes multiple undo, as do many other non–word processor programs, but WordPerfect 3 and WriteNow still do not.

Macros. Macros let you complete a number of actions with a single keystroke. Suppose that after many years of typing on a typewriter you've never kicked the two-spaces-after-the-period habit. You might want to create a macro that replaces double spaces with singles. You can create macros with Nisus, WordPerfect, and Word.

Page layout and graphics. In line with the "one program to do everything syndrome," some word processors provide features normally found in page layout and in graphics programs, such as dividing text into columns, creating and placing images in a document and wrapping text around them, or drawing and cropping images. If you need these extras, make sure they're not too watered down to be of use.

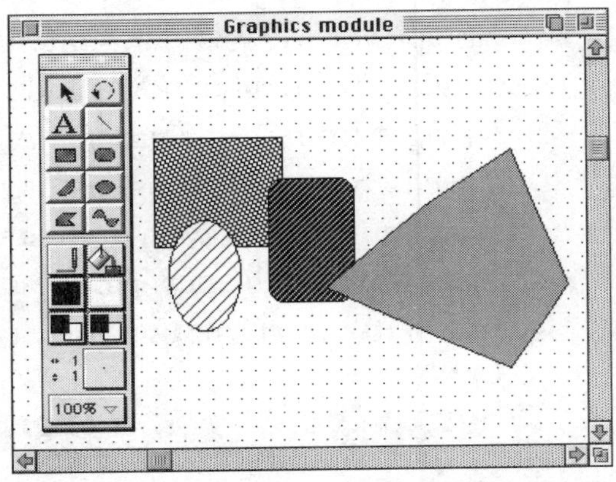

WordPerfect's Graphics module lets you create and fill basic forms, insert graphics from other programs, and group and align objects.

Outlining. Helping you put your thoughts in order is what outlining is all about. Although there are whole programs dedicated to the task (see "Brainstorming," later in this chapter), some word processors let you outline your document right within the same program.

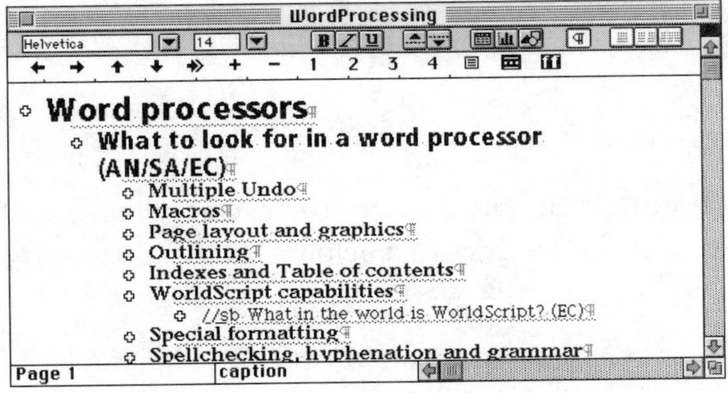

Word's outlining is one of its least known but most useful features. Applying levels automatically applies the corresponding styles.

Generating indexes and tables of contents. If you are writing anything longer than ten pages, you will need at least a table of contents and perhaps an index as well. Creating a table of contents or an index involves tagging the words or paragraphs that should be included. The program then compiles the file, complete with the proper page numbers.

WorldScript capabilities. If you write in languages other than English or with alphabets other than the Roman one, be on the lookout for word processors that support the language or alphabet you use. Nisus, for example, supports 19 languages, 11 of them with non-Roman alphabets, and includes dictionaries and WorldScript compatibility for each of them. (See the box below for more on WorldScript.

Special formatting. Apart from the basic bold, most word processors offer some specialized formatting tools that let you more easily create tables, mathematical equations, footnotes or end notes, and other hard-to-format text.

Checking spelling, hyphenation, and grammar. Word processors can also make sure you put the correct number of *m*'s in *committee*, break the word *mis-hits* in the correct spot, and help you decide between *effect* and *affect*, just to give a few examples. Spelling checkers should be fast and accurate and have a large dictionary; hyphenation dictionaries should place hyphens all at once or in individual words, as you desire; and grammar checkers should be fully customizable so that you can skip the parts you deem unnecessary. If you're not satisfied with your word processor's checkers, there are several stand-alone applications that can do the trick. See "Spelling Checkers" later in this chapter.

What in the World Is WorldScript? (EC)

The Mac has been able to write in different languages and different alphabets for quite some time. That's nothing new. What WorldScript does is allow the Mac to support double-byte languages (like Japanese and Chinese), while, for programmers, it standardizes the use of different alphabets with *scripts*. This means that you can use more than one alphabet with the same system software.

For the user, however, this is a lot less than it seems. Although WorldScript is built into Apple's System software from version 7.1 on, to actually type something in a foreign alphabet, you'll need one of Apple's Language Kits (the **Japanese Language Kit** goes for about $250 retail) and a program that supports WorldScript, like Nisus or WordPerfect.

Time-savers and other little helpers. The current crop of word processors has button bars and extra rulers to help you get to the commands more easily. They also feature commands like Word Count, Auto Save, and Auto Backup.

PowerBook specials. PowerBook users will appreciate a number of features designed especially for them in most major word processors. First, there is generally a special mini-installation procedure for PowerBooks to save space on disk. Second, many word processors offer battery indicators and clocks in their info bars and fattened cursors and cursor finders to combat "submarining."

Import/export to other formats. Most word processors allow you save your documents in a variety of formats so that you can use your text with other programs. Generally, you don't need to save text any special way if its destination is a page layout program. If you want to use it with another word processing program, it's probably best to save it in that word processor's native format, although the target word processor may be able to open the document directly. As a last resort, or if you want to import your document into a database or spreadsheet program, save the document in *text only* format. All formatting will be lost, but you'll be able to read the document from virtually any other program.

Styles. A *style* is a collection of paragraph and character formats that you can apply in one fell swoop to selected text. They were introduced to the Mac by Microsoft Word and are probably that program's best feature.

The great thing about styles is that when you change their definition, every paragraph tagged with that style will also change automatically. This makes changing the formatting of an entire document as simple as changing the definitions of a few styles.

There are two basic kinds of styles: *character styles* and *paragraph styles*. Character styles generally include text attributes such as bold and italics, type size, font, and color and can be applied to any amount of text, from one letter to a whole word or sentence. Paragraph styles include the same attributes as character styles, as well as leading, space after and before a paragraph, justification, and other paragraph-based attributes. Paragraph styles may be applied only to an entire paragraph (or paragraphs).

Styles and Style Sheets (AN/EC)

It's really a pain how Microsoft appropriates words that already have meanings, like *style,* and assigns them new, contradictory meanings.

At the beginning of Mac history, a style was something like bold or italic that you applied to a word or two. Microsoft, however, in version 3 of Word, came up with an inspired idea: Make a named collection of styles (like Frutiger, bold, 10 points, with 12-point leading) that you can apply to a paragraph all at once.

It was a great idea. The only problem is that they called the collection of styles a *style*. Then, Aldus followed Microsoft's lead by calling their styles *styles*, but went one better by calling their collections of styles *style sheets*. Quark didn't want to be outdone, so they called their styles *style sheets*.

So. A collection of styles is a style. A collections of styles is a style sheet. And a collection of style sheets is also a style sheet. No wonder so few people use them.

Styles may also be based on one another, allowing you to change all the styles in your document just by changing the primary style. You may indicate which style should be applied automatically to the next paragraph, which may save you time by letting you format as you write.

Choosing a Word Processor

Word processors are the programs most people use most often, so choosing one isn't a decision to be made lightly. Several reviews follow this entry, but you might want to also check out the reviews in Macintosh magazines (and read the ads, too).

Word 6 (EC). **Microsoft Word** ($500) is probably the most widely used program for the Macintosh, although few people would call it the most popular. While its excellent treatment of styles and practically excessively complete set of commands and options have made it the choice for many, Microsoft's size and arrogance, coupled with Word's inconsistent and complicated user interface make its followers somewhat lukewarm in their praises. Version 6 adds some important and clever innovations, but it fails to make them easy to use.

Word 6's best new feature is AutoFormat, which magically applies styles to a document so that recalcitrant users can finally take advantage of styles.

AutoFormat looks at each paragraph and decides if it is a heading or body text by its length. Users may (if they *really* want to) review the changes made by the AutoFormat command or change the style definitions.

Word's new ghostwriters, AutoText and AutoCorrect (which replace the now defunct Glossary), are a great idea. AutoCorrect automatically replaces typos like *teh* with *the*. Or you can define an AutoCorrect entry to automatically type out *Worldwide Institute for Research and Investigation* when you type the simpler *wwi*. AutoText completes the same function but requires you to click a button to activate it. The idea is that you use AutoCorrect for everyday instant replacements and AutoText for more unusual tasks, like inserting a graphic or table.

Word's help system has improved tenfold. What used to be a sketchy and annoyingly small help window has now blossomed into a two-window system, with step-by-step instructions and some demos and examples. Word also provides a system of *wizards* that walk you through the process of creating a memo or a report. Finally, Word offers a "Tip a day": Each time you open Word, a

Getting What You Need (EC)

What you look for in a word processor should depend on what you plan to use it for. If you need to write a doctoral thesis, footnotes will be up high on your list of priorities. If you are a writer or translator, you will need a word count feature. If you write manuals, outlining and styles will help you out a lot. Try to get what you need without paying for a lot of features you'll never use. The table below matches up some features with some uses. It's a start on your shopping list, at least.

If you write	Look for
Thesis/term papers	Footnotes
Manuals	Styles, outlining, index and table of contents
Translations	Word count, spelling checkers
Grant proposals	Import/export with spreadsheet program
Fiction	Multiple undo, word count, spelling checker
Invoices	Tables, easy-to-use tabs
Commercial correspondence	Spelling checker, templates
Pamphlets or newsletters	Incorporation of graphics, multiple columns

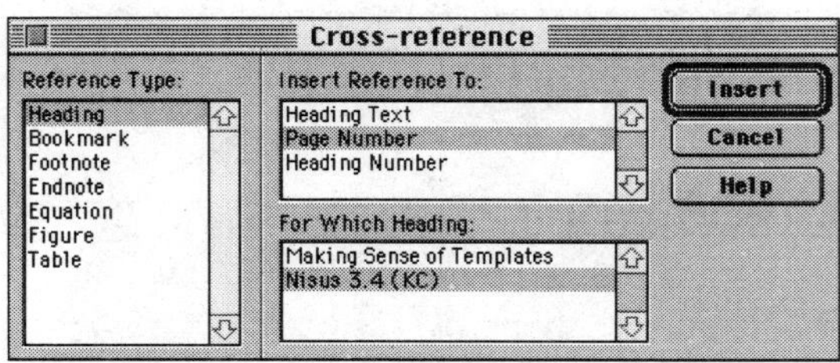

Microsoft Word's Cross-reference feature allows you to create dynamic references to different sections of your document.

new tip will appear on the screen. If you get tired of seeing them, clear the Show Tips at Startup checkbox at the bottom of the screen.

Word has also added several features that had begun to crop up in the competition: character styles, zoom in, revision marks, multiple undo, and drop caps. Word's graphics capabilities have improved substantially; you can now group, resize, and even add captions to your graphics within Word. Unfortunately, all the added features have made Word an unwieldy beast. It takes up almost 17MB on your hard disk and is as slow as molasses in January.

If you write long documents and need to make references to other sections, tables, or figures, Word's cross-referencing feature will save you a lot of time. Instead of typing *For more information, see Chapter 6, Steps to a Perfect Romance*, you'll just type *For more information, see Chapter* and then tell Word which Chapter number and heading you want to refer to. It will fill in the chapter number and the heading text and change the reference if you change the text later.

Word has a new system of templates (which are kind of like document styles) in which you can store macros, styles and other formatting, graphics, text, and customized menus and toolbars. You can create new documents from any of your templates, create global templates that affect all new documents, or automatically update existing documents according to a common template in order to keep them consistent.

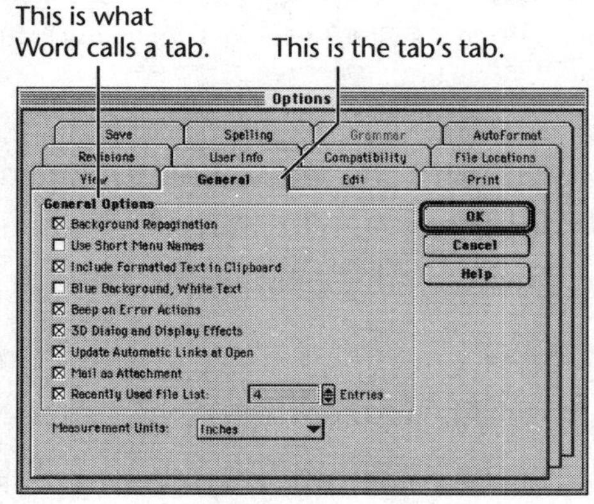

Microsoft Word's uses a new sort of dialog box, which Microsoft calls a tab.

Because Word 6 has so many features, Microsoft decided to create a new sort of dialog box, which it calls a *tab*. Actually, the tab is the part you click, and the part that changes looks a bit like an index card, except that each one is practically smothered

Editors' Poll: What One Feature Would You Change in Microsoft Word if You Could?

AA: The date format that Word uses in the header when you click the Date icon. I hate that it spells out the entire date: "March 29, 1994." Until version 5.0, it inserted "3/29/94." I hate it so much that I made a workaround: I put the "print date short" glossary item (with a keyboard shortcut) in my Work menu and I insert *that* in the header/footer instead.

DB: I'd pull out 80 percent of the features and make it a lean, mean, word processing machine. As it is, it's a bloated pig of a program, and I'd switch to something else in a minute if I could find any other program that handled style sheet and worked with QuarkXPress and PageMaker as well as Word does.

EC: I would make it easier to add columns and rows to tables. Tables are great, but they are ridiculously difficult to change once you've set them up. From what I've seen, WriteNow and MacWrite do them a lot better.

DD: I *really* hate the way Word flies in the face of Apple's interface standards and makes you do things when a dialog box is open that you should never be able to do. I understand it will be different in Word 6, but in Word 5, say you want to import a style sheet from another document. You open the Styles dialog box and then, *with the dialog box still open,* choose Open from the File menu. I can do this every day, and I still often stare at that dialog box and think, What do I do now? before I remember to look in the menus. Another example: When you want to add a keyboard command in the Commands dialog box, Word presents you with an *alert* box (the kind where usually all you can do click OK), and you're supposed to type your keyboard command with that box showing. It's just against all the well-learned rules that make the Mac easy to use.

CG: That's a book.

BW: It's always bugged me that Microsoft has given the ugliest, most useless formats to the outline styles (heading 1, heading 2, and so on). Why? Why?

with buttons, checkboxes, pop-up menus, and lists. Why Microsoft chose to call this a "tab" when we finally started to understand what a real tab is, I can hardly begin to fathom.

Next on my hit list are Word's toolbars. Word's options are available as little buttons with darling, incomprehensible icons on ten different toolbars that you can view, hide, turn into floating palettes, or customize. Maybe someday I'll learn what each one means, but I doubt it. To confound things, some buttons give an immediate response, while others make a dialog box appear. There's no way to tell the difference, so it discourages typical Macintosh exploring. One nice new feature shows the name of the option only if you leave the cursor over the button for a few seconds. That way, you get help if you need it but won't be distracted when you don't.

But what bugs me most about Word is how it thumbs its proverbial nose at consistency—both with its own and with other programs' interfaces. For example, when you drag and drop, you press [⌘] to copy (instead of [Option], as is used in almost all drawing programs as well as the Finder). When you want to resize a graphic proportionately in Word's regular window, you press [Shift] and drag a corner handle; if you are in Word's Graphics window and press [Shift] while you drag a corner handle, you will *crop* the image. Basic Mac interface rules are ignored. And Microsoft insists on changing the default keyboard combinations with every version update.

These may seem like minor aggravations, but they are really important. They take away your confidence and initiative, since you're never quite sure what's going to happen. Even though Microsoft Word 6 can do everything except chop tomatoes, I'd like it a lot better if it acted like a real Mac program by letting me take advantage of what I already know and not assuming that I want to learn everything from scratch.

WordPerfect 3.0 (RS). For years users have had a love/hate relationship with Microsoft Word and its amazingly complete but, shall we say, "well concealed" features. Although Word users say they'd switch if they had the chance—and with **WordPerfect 3.0** ($500, WordPerfect Corp.) they have an excellent alternative—those same users are somewhat reluctant to scale the learning curve of a new word processor. Well, I personally have made the switch and want to tell you that not only is the switch easy, but WordPerfect is a much friendlier and more powerful word processor than Word. At this writing, WordPerfect is the premier word processor for the Macintosh. At this writing, it's also the only one available in a native version for PowerPC Macintoshes.

WordPerfect's new button bars (similar to Word's standard toolbar) are completely customizable. There are three standard button bars, but you can create your own with any of WP's 300 functions and then place it on any border of the screen.

The rulers (which appear only at the top of the page and may not be customized), display the options for layout, font, styles, table, list, merge, and mailer options, making them instantly accessible and eliminating the need to hunt through menus.

You'll find an excellent feature at the bottom of the screen: WordPerfect's status bar. Its help feature instantly and unobtrusively tells you what the button that you're pointing at is for, although it doesn't work with menus and dialog boxes (hopefully this will be implemented in the future). The status bar can also give you information about the time, date, current page number, the status of caps lock and number lock, and your battery charge, if you are using a PowerBook.

WordPerfect has a bunch of endearing features. First, it's noticeably faster than Word. There is a preview feature that lets you see the contents of a document in a small window before opening it so that you can be sure it is the document that you want. Like Word, it offers drag-and-drop editing capability (addictive once you've tried it, much more intuitive than cut and paste). You can have WordPerfect automatically back up the document you are working on, and you can have it show a vertical line that projects down from a tab or margin mark when choosing a new setting for one of these (a great aid for getting things lined up). You can even have WordPerfect automatically compress documents when saving them—another great feature for PowerBook users—and the compression is actually on a par with the best stand-alone compression utilities!

The grammar checker Grammatik (see below) integrated into WordPerfect is about as useful as any other grammar checker (that is, it is only useful if you have a ton of time to spend using it, weeding out things that have been incorrectly flagged and trying to understand some of the more arcane suggestions). WordPerfect's table creation ability is not only easier to use than Word's, but you can enter simple mathematical equations inside of these tables, giving you basic spreadsheet abilities right inside WordPerfect. WordPerfect's graphics capabilities are also very powerful, offering full color capability and nice page layout functions. In fact, if you have WordPerfect, you really don't need an integrated program (described in Chapter 12); WordPerfect is a better choice if you need heavy-duty word processing capabilities.

WordPerfect allows you to work in three virtual layers. Draw Overlay is the layer above your normal working layer, and Watermark is the bottom layer. Watermarks, which are things like "DRAFT" printed in large light grey letters diagonally across your document, are a royal pain to implement in Word but a pure joy in WordPerfect; as are overlayed graphics or editors' notes. You can use both overlays and watermarks simultaneously in WordPerfect.

WordPerfect can automatically create tables of contents, tables of authorities (great for attorneys, like myself), sidebars, indexes, and many other types of lists. You can also do separate end notes and footnotes. As you can imagine, these features make WordPerfect a delight for scientific, technical, and professional writing, as well as for writers of books and newsletters.

WordPerfect is the only word processor to fully implement all of Apple's advanced technologies: QuickTime, Apple events, PowerTalk, AppleScript (and Frontier), and WorldScript. WordPerfect also has a powerful yet easy-to-use macro language.

Problems? OK, there are a few. Although the style sheets in WordPerfect are very powerful and easy to use, they work differently than Word's and so may be a little hard to get used to at first (they were for me). WordPerfect has only very basic importing and exporting capabilities; although it can save to and import from Word, it cannot read or create WordPerfect 6 for DOS files. (WordPerfect says it may license DataViz translators, described in Chapter 24, to solve this problem.) WordPerfect's outlining features are no match for Word's. Still, I'm sold.

Nisus 3.4 (KC). **Nisus** ($400) is the first "large" word processor I have ever liked, partly because the folks at Paragon Concepts paid attention to some smaller, albeit very important, details. Where other programs might let you blithely print a document on the wrong size paper, Nisus will offer you a Page Setup dialog box before letting you continue on to the Print dialog box. And if you decide you really do want to print on that size paper, just click Print Anyway. Nisus gives you the choice.

Nisus has some very strong formatting and editing capabilities. You can make discontiguous selections of text, handy for producing newsletters and resumes

or any document that has several different styles and text sizes. I like the ability to name the different rulers you may use in a single document. This facilitates the copying of different rulers, and thus formats, between paragraphs; you just place your cursor by the paragraph you want to format and select the desired ruler from the ruler pull-down menu.

One thing Nisus does better than Word is search for text. Text search in Nisus is augmented by a Catalog window, which is similar to the standard Open dialog box. But the Catalog lets you copy file lists into Nisus windows, and, with the help of an Add To Search List macro, lets you search for text in files that are located in different folders. Another thing Nisus has over Word is its thesaurus—it makes the one Microsoft uses look woefully inadequate.

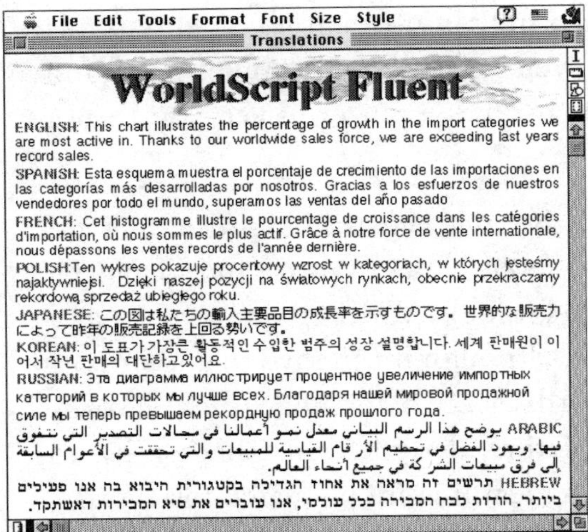

Nisus supports 19 languages and lets you combine two or more on the same page with a minimum of grief.

Nisus's WorldScript support is particularly strong. Not only can you type in double-byte (Japanese, Chinese), right-to-left (Arabic, Hebrew), Roman (English, Spanish, and so on), and Eastern European and Cyrillic languages (e.g., Russian and Polish), but you can also find and manipulate text. This may sound like a simple task, but a quick thought to tables, right-aligned and left-aligned text, tabs, and other direction-sensitive formatting will convince you otherwise. Nisus makes it easy.

But Nisus isn't without its problems. It has always been a memory-based word processor, meaning that all open documents are stored in RAM. Nisus did this to make the program fast at scrolling, typing, and saving—which it is, even when you elect to display everything in PostScript. However, it makes working with large documents a hassle. I broke the memory barrier a few times when Nisus was the only application running and four documents (one of which was 350K) were open while I was doing a lengthy find/replace. It is a shame that a memory-based word processor has so many functions, such as multiple clipboards and unlimited undos, that are also a drain on RAM.

Mini–Text Editors

(LB/RC)

Text editor is a term used for word processors that work with plain ASCII text. The good text editors will open text files faster than most word processors (some of which insist on converting the files to their own format before displaying them), and the best include tools that make common manipulations, such as stripping line feeds, quick and easy.

McSink

Many Macintosh users fell in love with Dave McWherter's shareware **McSink** desk accessory ($35) and followed it to the commercial version—**Vantage** ($100), from Baseline. It will do almost anything legal to a plain-text file—inserting and removing line prefixes, zapping control characters, balancing parentheses, you name it. It works like a flash with any size file as long as RAM's available. Unhappily, Baseline hasn't done much to update it, and it's a little long in the tooth today.

BBEdit

BBEdit Lite is the free, stripped down version of Rich Siegel's **BBEdit,** a "bare bones" text editor for programmers. The name no longer fits the product; even the free version will do many of the most useful manipulations found in Vantage, and it will also convert those special Mac characters (curly quotes, em dashes) that will cause trouble if you're planning to send a text file to a non-Mac user. BBEdit Lite's rock solid and slick as a greased pig, one of the greatest bargains in the computer world. Programmers, or those wanting extra power, can upgrade to BBEdit for $50, but the Lite version's faster, and if it does all you want, go for it.

Tex-Edit and SaintEdit

Tex-Edit is a public-domain editor (even the source code's public domain, so if you want to hack it, you can). We mention it here because it's one of the few programs supporting Apple's new Speech Manager, so you can get your Mac to read text to you. Tex-Edit is limited to 32K files (just like TeachText or SimpleText), but it can read any part of a document, so you can even work through a megabyte-size file in small chunks. Another good choice for Speech Manager support is Craig Marciniak's **SaintEdit** ($10 shareware), which will read almost any size text file (if there's enough RAM). SaintEdit also lets you set your preferred text and window color. For some reason, however, the author has limited SaintEdit to displaying in its own, custom fonts.

Eliza

Eliza is a fast little text editor that is great for manipulating text that rides on the Internet. It strips or adds carriage returns and line feeds, converts tabs, trashes foreign control characters, and stupefies smart quotes. Plus, it has one feature no other word processor is likely to add. Eliza will psychoanalyze you. Choose Start Interview from the Eliza menu and your computer, verging on malpractice, will challenge you with all the classic Freudian accusations. Granted she's generally lame, unlikely to make you sane, but she occasionally offers a humorous diversion in a friendly, masochistic kind of way. Eliza is freeware, available from most on-line systems and user groups.

I also wish that the Windows tool—for now a pop-up menu under the Tools menu—would become its own menu and that the items it listed were my open windows. It would be a little more consistent with other word processors like Word and WriteNow.

Still, Nisus gets my vote for the best "large" word processor because it offers so many features without intimidating a user.

WriteNow (KC). **WriteNow** ($250, SoftKey International) has been my word processor of choice for a number of years, and what endears it to me most is its svelteness—it takes up a mere 595K of RAM—particularly since I use a PowerBook as my desktop computer. So it should come as no surprise that my favorite feature in the new version (4.0) is part of the PowerBook Extras. I have been lazy about finding one of those utilities that keep track of your cursor on the screen. But now I don't need to worry about it anymore since one of the Extras is a Large Text Cursor.

WriteNow is fast and easy to use, yet it's undaunted by a three-column layout.

The PowerBook Extras also make battery use more efficient. It will save an active document and store open documents in RAM instead of continually going to the hard disk, a function that drains battery life. The trade-off is that (as with Nisus) you could run into problems working with large documents. Fortunately, you can turn this feature off.

Version 4.0 lets you add tables to your documents and convert tab-delimited tables into the new WriteNow table format. Tables are easily created and edited, thanks to a tool palette that lets you click on buttons to add or delete columns and rows, and you can adjust row height and column width on screen by pulling on the borders with the pointer. Another welcome feature is the ability to insert PICT, EPS, and MacPaint graphics into a document. Working with graphics in previous versions meant pasting them in from the Clipboard (and converting them to PICT) with no real ability to perform minor editing. Now users can resize, crop, and reposition graphics.

What should be a relief for WriteNow loyalists is that the program is basically the same, even though it has changed owners (T/Maker used to sell the package). It's the same program that years ago let you add and copy rulers throughout a document—and it's also the same program that only in the last two years added style sheets to its feature set. The biggest relief for me is knowing that it still has its great thesaurus—equaled only by the one included in Nisus (which I'll swear is the same one).

MacWrite Pro (LB). MacWrite has always been the easiest word processor to learn and use, but for a long time it lagged in features. The new version, **MacWrite Pro 1.5** ($250, from Claris) includes not only the standard wordsmith's tool kit (dictionary, thesaurus) but also a powerful set of formatting tools so elegantly implemented that you'll actually use the features, not just have them. For example, most word processors support kerning, but how many people really use it? MacWrite Pro can kern automatically. As one would expect from a Claris product, it supports PowerTalk and includes a good suite of scriptable events for AppleScript. (For more on PowerTalk and AppleScript, see Chapter 3.)

MacWrite Pro's basic orientation is a page, and what you see is precisely what prints (except for QuickTime movies, which always print the first frame). Columns (equal or variable width) and tables are a breeze, though the table can't cross page boundaries. Fonts, sizes, and character or paragraph styles can be selected from a menu or a windoid.

When you write by hand you can go anywhere on the page—scribble in the margins or put a headline at the top or a special bit of text anywhere you like. In

A Couple of MacWrite Tips (LB)

MacWrite Pro is so easy to use that it's hard to find useful tips, but here's one: if you hold down the ⌘ key while the splash screen's displaying, you'll get an Open dialog instead of a blank new document. Another: If you routinely work with different sets of preferences, standard fonts, and styles, just save each one in a Stationery document and open the relevant one instead of resetting the options manually.

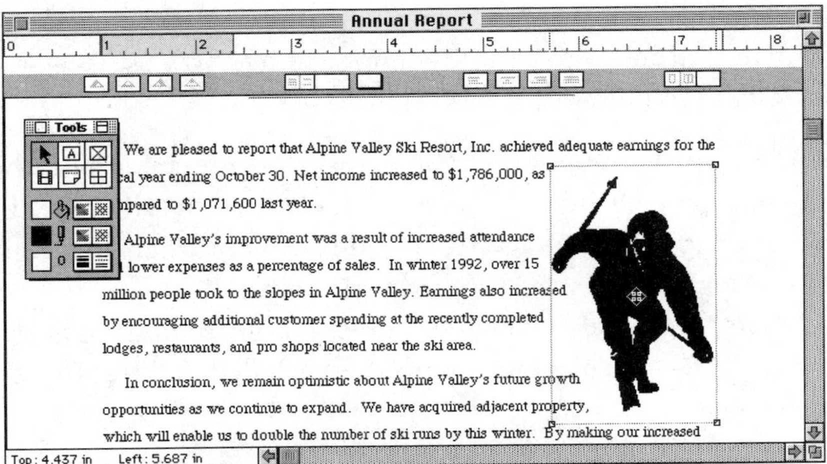

MacWrite lets you create "frames" that you can place anywhere on the page. You can also place tables, QuickTime movies, and electronic sticky notes and move them about as needed.

most word processors, placing that text (or picture) just where it should be is an exercise in frustration. MacWrite, once again, does this right. Headers and footers show up in the right spot. Add a footnote, and you're typing at the bottom of the page. For anything else, just insert a "frame" (which can contain text, a table, graphics, or even a QuickTime movie) and drag it where you want. In each case, ⌘ Return brings you back to where you were in the main text. MacWrite Pro supports the "editable graphic objects" (EGO) standard, so if you use dedicated equation editors such as MathType or Expressionist to create mathematical equations in your MacWrite documents, you can double-click an equation to open the relevant editor.

For all its ease of use, MacWrite Pro still lacks features some want in a word processor. It will create a table of contents but not an index, and there's no outliner or macro facility (although AppleScript users can script most anything). If you don't like the keybaord shortcuts, too bad: You still can't customize them. And if you regularly deal with large plain-text files, you'll want to get a specialized text-file editor, since MacWrite Pro insists on translating those files to its own format, taking time in the process.

Still, the current version of MacWrite Pro is an impressive tool, particularly strong in ease of use and formatting power. It's nice to see this old standby back in the competition.

Writing Aids

(RC)

Every writer struggles with spelling, word choice, and grammar. We all make typos. We all periodically scratch holes in our heads searching for just the right word to use. And we all occasionally become so enamored with what looks like sparkling prose that we forget the simple rules of good sentence construction.

The most familiar books on my desk are a 90,000-word dictionary, *Roget's International Thesaurus*, and *The Chicago Manual of Style*. Something similar to all three of these indispensable references is available to you from your keyboard. The question is this: Do you want a dictionary designed by the team that built your word processor? If you say "Yes, that makes sense," then you're an idealist. Like food processors, word processors are meant to blend the concoction, rather than provide the raw ingredients.

Look closely at old Microsoft Word, the acknowledged granddaddy of Mac word processors, and you'll notice a toothless thesaurus, a spelling checker that limps, and a grammar checker with a pigheaded scowl and a paddle aimed at your butt. Every time you click ⌘L, an idiot dialog box says, "Loading Spelling Dictionaries," and then you wait. This is Microsoft's "improved" spelling checker. I long ago lightened the beast by trashing the spelling, thesaurus, and grammar modules (you'll find them in the Word Commands folder).

Replace them all. Go for a lightning-fast spelling checker, an enormous thesaurus that cross-references with a dictionary, and a grammar checker that works while you eat lunch and then presents an annotated analysis upon your return. Of course, if your writing load is light, don't bother. Most word processors provide adequate tools for these tasks, but once you experience the more powerful writing aids, you'll understand why I'm so rude to Word.

Spelling Checkers

Get a spelling checker that discreetly follows your typing, politely asks if you'd like a correction, and then instantly makes the change. The warning signal can be any system beep sound, so on a Mac with a microphone, use a recording of a loved one softly saying your name and you may actually enjoy your mistakes. If you don't like the "interactive" approach, "batch check" a selection or an entire document at lightning-fast speed while accessing a dictionary large enough to know all but the most arcane corners of your vocabulary. You can add words to a small dictionary, but your checks will be faster if it doesn't have to frequently ask you about unknown words.

After a batch check, you can see an analysis of your document. Get a count of characters, syllables, words, sentences, and paragraphs. With a couple clicks I can know exactly how much Peachpit Press is paying me for this paragraph!

Examine a spelling checker's grammar tools before investing in a high-end grammar checker. Most stand-alone spelling checkers look for the more common usage mistakes: incorrect capitalization, hyphenation errors, double punctuation, and double words (like "the the").

Never entirely trust a spelling checker. Grammar checkers may ask you about your use of *two* when you meant to use *too* or *to,* but spelling checkers are not that smart. For maximum protection, you should always proofread a printed version of a document. I don't know why this works, but it does! Perhaps our eyes become mesmerized by the screen and can therefore more easily find errors on the soothing texture of the printed page, but it's probably just looking at the document in a different form that lets you see things you didn't previously catch.

Spelling Coach Professional. Spelling Coach Professional ($200, Deneba) comes as close as any spelling checker to doing it all. Batch check selections or let Coach Pro watch for errors while you type. A pop-up menu gives you options for correct spellings, and if none seems appropriate, you can ask for phonetic guesses. If that doesn't get you to a correct spelling, request the alphabetic list and glance through a table of likely words. Coach Pro includes a 95,000-word spelling dictionary and legal, technical, and medical supplements that can bring it up to 188,000 words total. You also get an 85,000-word dictionary with definitions, and if that isn't enough for you (am I sounding like a late-night commercial yet?), Coach Pro also includes the great Big Thesaurus (described under "Thesauruses," below).

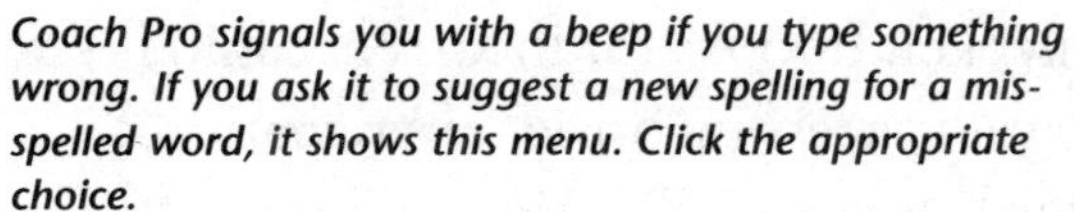

Coach Pro signals you with a beep if you type something wrong. If you ask it to suggest a new spelling for a misspelled word, it shows this menu. Click the appropriate choice.

Coach Pro lets you decide whether you want its dictionaries loaded into RAM or accessed from the hard disk. The RAM option speeds up checking and can also reduce the need for PowerBooks to spin up hard disks every time the dictionary is needed.

The program starts you out with all its hot keys unconfigured. Go to the Coach Pro menu and select Preferences. Click the Edit Hot Keys button and then assign hot keys for the five most useful commands. Use the Control key as a modifier, because it's unused by most other programs, and spelling checkers need to be available everywhere without conflicting with other commands.

Sometimes Coach Pro doesn't recognize a program, and you'll notice its menu icon doesn't appear in the menu bar. Click the "interactive" hot key to add the Coach menu and "teach" it to always load with that program.

Coach Pro is fast and reliable, but I do have one complaint. When you check a word that turns out to be correct, Coach Pro doesn't say "correct"; instead, it makes you paste the correct word over itself. Even though it's fast, that's still a waste of time.

Thunder 7. This is the only program that rivals Coach Pro, and if it had a definition dictionary, I would probably throw Coach Pro away. With interactive and batch checking, a "large thesaurus," and a speedy and smooth interface, **Thunder 7** ($100, Baseline) is a pleasure to use. The batch-checking dialog box is a little too button-dependent, though. The buttons are cute, but I prefer Coach's Hot Key options.

The Thunder 7 package includes lots of writing tools, among them thesaurus and glossary tools, each described in their respective categories, below. Another impressive extra is GhostWriter. This tiny tool will automatically save a copy of all your keystrokes, allowing you to reconstruct lost work after a system crash or power failure.

Lookup. Lookup ($40, Working Software) is a fast and elegant little interactive DA spelling checker. It will check a highlighted selection, but only one word at a time—a major limitation. For more power, use the program with its bigger companion checker Spellswell (described below). It can share Spellswell's 93,000 word dictionary, or use its own.

Spellswell. Spellswell ($75, also from Working Software) is more than a spelling checker but not quite a grammar checker. It looks for incorrect capitalization, missing apostrophes, missing or extra spaces, incorrect abbreviations, and double words. It also looks for "poor word choices." The Word Choice option will explain the difference between "among" and "between" or prompt you to choose among "can't," "cant," and "Kant." Most of Spellswell's checks are optional, so every time you write "two" it doesn't have to ask you again and again if you really mean "too." Word Choice was the first feature I turned off.

Two Special Tools (EC)

Two of my favorite word processing tools have no category: these are **Sonar Bookends,** an index and table-of-contents creator from Virginia Systems ($130), and **DocuComp II,** an ingenious tool from MasterSoft ($180) that tells you exactly what the differences are between two versions of a document.

Sonar Bookends goes about creating indexes in a unique way: You can either have it search your entire document and pick out all the words that appear ten times or less, or you can make a list and tell it to find on which pages those words appear. In my opinion only the second option makes sense, and as long as your words are somewhat unique, you'll be happy with Sonar's results. Sonar Bookends also includes an Addition and an Xtension for creating indexes and tables of contents in PageMaker and Quark, respectively.

DocuComp is an essential program for anyone who works with various versions of a document. The program compares any two documents and then shows on screen or in printed form exactly what text has been added, deleted, or moved. Many lawyers, for example, use DocuComp to make sure that the changes they have specified, and only those changes, have been made in a contract or agreement. Editors can use the program to see which changes have been made (and which have been ignored) in a manuscript before the book goes to press.

Grammar School

No one I know likes grammar checkers. Writers loathe editors, computer and human, and anyone who has tried a computer grammar checker complains about frequently inappropriate or incorrect advice. Mood swings can approach insanity when you use the interactive mode, in which you plod through criticism after criticism, endlessly clicking the Ignore button. Computers are simply not smart enough to navigate through the aesthetics of language (not yet), and few of us have the patience for tedious machine-suggested corrections and uncomfortable program interfaces.

Grammar checkers can be useful, but it helps to understand the nature of this two-headed beast. Grammar checkers are really grammar and style checkers. If you are learning English grammar for the first time, a computer is an excellent tool for identifying abuse of the rules. Style is another matter. Do you start sentences with "There" or "It" too often? Are all your sentences long and complex? These are simple style considerations. Analysis becomes more complicated when you switch from checking a business letter to examining the structure of a short story intended for junior high school students.

All grammar checkers allow you to customize search parameters. In addition to turning individual rules off and on, a good grammar checker lets you choose an analysis scheme, or a "filter set," for different types of documents (fiction, technical, business, legal, newsletters, academic papers, proposals, and so on). Considerations that may vary include passive voice, split infinitives, colloquialisms and slang, sentence length, use of technical terms, prepositions at the end of a sentence, and more.

The analysis can be interactive (make changes one by one while the checker looks on), or annotative (examine a marked-up copy of the document). A summary analysis is also provided that will give you statistics on word, sentence, and paragraph count, suggested grammar and style changes, and results from various readability tests (general readability is determined by sentence length and the average number of syllables per word).

Most checkers can read documents from popular word processors and then make changes that retain the document's format (indents, character styles, and so on). In some cases, however, you might have to save a document with a different format in order for the checker to even read it. If you are not using Microsoft Word or WordPerfect, or if you want to analyze the text in a program other than a word processor, it's a good idea to check compatibility with the manufacturer.

Writing is an art, not a science. Don't let a grammar checker bully you. Give a piece of your writing a full-blown examination to discover what areas the checker finds as weaknesses, and then decide if you agree. After a few tests you should start to customize the checker's settings. Make it ignore "whatever be total rad, man" if you consider clichés with nonstandard modifiers and subject-verb disagreement part of your personal style.

The top three grammar checkers have all borrowed features from one another in their present incarnations. Here are the differences that remain.

RightWriter. RightWriter ($50, Que Software) highlights the text in question and then prompts you to either make changes or move on to the next selection. The Next button, however, is the window's "default" button. It has a dark line around it, meaning that you should be able to just hit the Return key to activate it, but you can't. Hitting Return replaces the highlighted selection with a paragraph return. The selected text is entirely lost because there's no Undo for this action! The only way to get your selection back is to close the document and not save changes. Aside from this glaring error and the minor inconvenience that the program doesn't check for spelling, RightWriter offers powerful style analysis, well-designed filter sets, and an excellent on-screen help module.

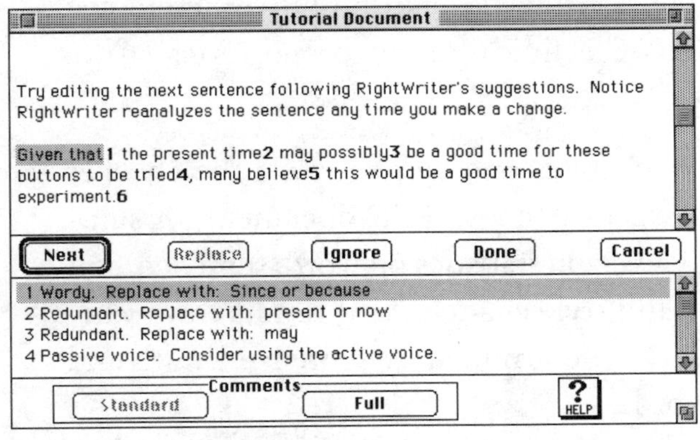

RightWriter can check your documents in batch mode or while you watch (as shown here).

Correct Grammar. Serious grammarians will appreciate Correct Grammar's 135,000-word spelling dictionary and that the program lets you write your own grammar or style rules to "conform to a corporate or personal standard." The program can share Microsoft Word's User dictionary, but it does not check Word documents that have been "fast saved." A tutorial button gives you rule explanations, and a Help button turns System 7 balloon help off or on. The balloons describe the function of the program, and this two-level help system is nice once you get used to it. As for that huge dictionary…the manual states that Correct Grammar is "based on the expertise of the publishers of the *American Heritage Dictionary*." I'd like to put that sentence through a BS checker. **Correct Grammar** is available from SoftKey International for $100 and comes included with WriteNow 4 (described earlier in this chapter).

Grammatik. Included with WordPerfect 3 and available in its Tools menu, Grammatik 5 for the Macintosh reads over your document and alerts you to errors in style, grammar, and spelling. It has a good help system with clear examples and explanations. Unfortunately, the theory is not as good as the practice, and, as is often the case with grammar checkers, what Grammatik considers an error is not always what you might consider an error. If you are tired of hearing about a certain kind of mistake, choose Ignore Class. Unless you've already got WordPerfect, Correct Grammar is a better choice.

Thesauruses

I lust after an accurate computer version of *Roget's International*, still the best thesaurus available. With an eye toward simplicity (and perhaps avoiding litigation), all computer thesauruses seem naked to me without a device similar to *Roget's* great association index. Listing words similar in concept to your chosen word, the index takes up almost half of *Roget's* thesaurus and provides an invaluable brainstorming tool. The better computer thesauruses give you a window showing various meanings of a word followed by paragraphs of synonyms and antonyms and related, compared, and contrasted words.

In an unscientific test I looked up several words in different thesauruses. Alternatives for the word *big* illustrate the results. The Microsoft Word thesaurus gave me 9 meaning groups with a total of 60 synonyms. Thunder 7 offered 8 meaning groups with 233 suggestions. Big Thesaurus presented 10 meaning groups with 273 alternatives. Leafing through *Roget's* pages gave me 16 meaning groups and 262 words and phrases, but *Roget's* also provided an additional 56 cross-references to such terms as *big cheese*, *bighearted*, and *big time*.

GOOD FEATURE

Big Thesaurus. This is one of the fastest and most seamlessly designed utilities in any category. A Big Thesaurus menu automatically appears in all your programs. Highlight a word, and a keystroke (or a menu click) will instantly open the thesaurus window. You can easily open additional windows for any words you see in the first window. This multiple-window scheme comes close to *Roget's* index in that when several windows are arranged to be simultaneously visible, glancing from one to the other increases your chances of finding just what you need. An automatic window arranger would be a nice addition. **Big Thesaurus** can be bought separately ($100, Deneba) or as part of Spelling Coach Professional.

Thunder 7. Baseline says that the thesaurus in **Thunder 7** ($100, Baseline) can display 1.4 million words selected from a 40,000-word list of "entry points." Suspiciously, this is the same number Big Thesaurus claims to display, and yet Thunder's lists never seem as big as Big Thes's. Even so, it's big enough to satisfy anyone but a fiction writer. Like the rest of Thunder 7's features (see the entries under "Spelling Checkers" and "Glossary Tools"), the thesaurus is fast and trouble-free. In both Thunder and Big Thesaurus, double-clicking on any word in the list will paste the word into your document.

Glossary Tools

I first encountered glossaries in Microsoft Word 3, in which typing ⌘ Del and then my initials instantly pasted my full name and address at the insertion point. Glossary entries in Word can be an image (like a company logo) or any length and format of text. Two glossary programs (and Word 6) have taken the glossary concept to its next logical step. Without the need for a ⌘-key prefix, type any preconfigured abbreviation and your full entry is instantly typed for you.

MagicTypist. MagicTypist ($130, Olduvai) comes preconfigured with a host of magic guesses that cause your menu bar to flash distractingly. You can ignore the flash and keep typing, but if you're a slow or even medium-fast typist, a dialog box appears with magic suggestions. Keep typing and the box automatically disappears, but the flash and box can play real havoc with your concentration. Even though you can partially turn this feature off, anyone who really knows how to type will want to spend some time removing a lot of the magic suggestions from the control panel.

MagicTypist automatically learns words that you type that are not in its dictionary. It then tries to type the word for you before you get halfway through. This is a surprise that often made me smile and say, "How did you know that word?" Just as often, however, I was pissed that I was interrupted.

Thunder 7. Glossary control in Thunder 7 is not as intuitive as in MagicTypist, but maybe you don't want it to be. I like the idea that you must teach Thunder 7 all its entries except for the preconfigured date and time abbreviations.

HOT TIP

When teaching Thunder 7 an entry with carriage returns (like your name and address), you can't use the Return key in the Glossary dialog box because it operates the box's default button. Instead, when you get to the end of a line you must type Option J. This will appear as a delta symbol and will show up in your document as a carriage return.

Writing Guides

The Chicago Manual of Style serves as the most popular comprehensive guide for writing correctly. The less comprehensive but more poetic *The Elements of Style* by Strunk and White is the classic tiny book that because of its size probably gets used more often. Do you need something similar on your computer? If you still like the feel of a real book and already own one of the above classics, save your money. It's nice to have a style guide open on your desk while your document is visible on the screen. If you need a style guide on a regular basis to conform to corporate or government standards, than the speed of an on-line guide may be a worthwhile advantage.

Correct Writing. Correct Writing ($30, SoftKey International) gives you a choice of a DA or a HyperCard reference for style and grammar rules. The interface is boring, but the information is extensive and easy to search through.

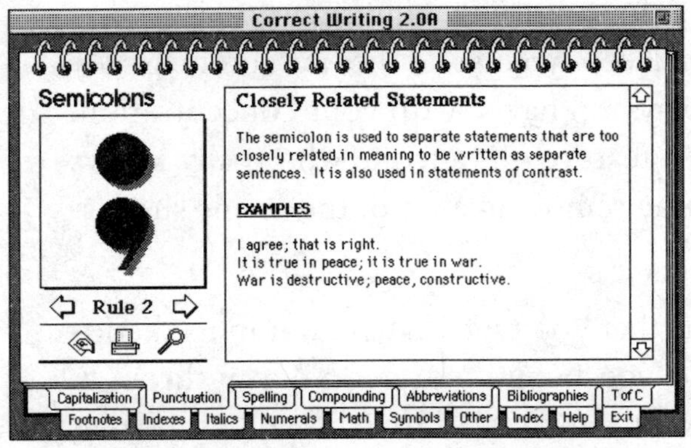

Correct Writing offers a writing guide in an easy-to-use HyperCard stack.

Unlike my *Chicago Manual*, Correct Writing offers some suggestions for writing on a computer. For example, in reading about proper usage of an ellipsis, you are told the keyboard shortcut for making one. Be careful though—they tell you it's Option : when actually it's Option ; (of course, that is the same key, just with or without the Shift key).

Brainstorming

(RC)

Sometimes it's not the right word or spelling you need when you sit down to write, it's the right idea. When I'm stuck for a specific word, I hot-key Big Thesaurus (from Deneba Software, described under "Thesauruses," above) and browse through lists of related and contrasting words. Reverse dictionaries, which generate root concepts from two or three user-supplied ideas, also stimulate my imagination. When I'm really stuck for an idea, however, I simply open a window and write. I let my ideas flow and eventually my mind begins to make connections, seemingly on its own. The more analytical left-brained approach would have me methodically generating lists of logical questions that, once answered, would present an outline of the relevant neighborhood pictured on an emerging brain map. Of course, there is also the "no-brain" approach. Periodically leave the computer. Go in the kitchen and eat a banana. Do nothing for a while. Experts say that inspiration fills a vacuum.

The software described below falls into two categories, both of which are meant to fire up your imagination. Either the program carries an interactive database of suggestive ideas or inspirational concepts, or it simply gives you an inspiring window within which to visualize your own ideas. Corkboard and

Inspiration provide friendly environments; you supply the ideas. To sell these as "brainstorming tools" is a little like when freeze-dried food was invented. People started selling Instant Water. The directions said, "Just add water." IdeaFisher does not give you the friendliest of environments, but it does give you the water in the form of a huge database of phrases. Synchronicity and Creative Whack Pack are both friendly, but they are also philosophically rich enough that they are nearly able to "think" along with you.

Corkboard

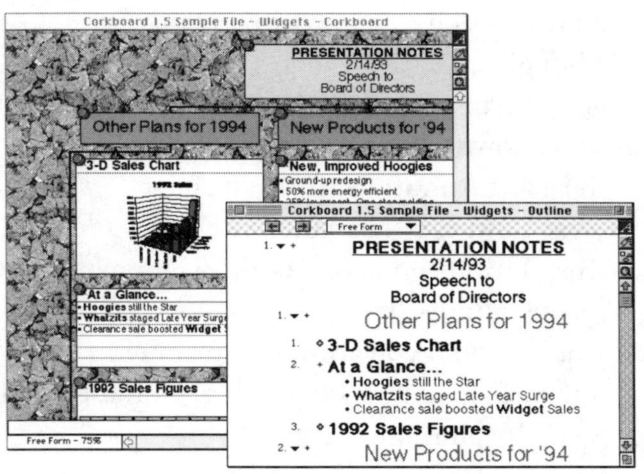

Corkboard has you put your ideas on index cards that you can then rearrange as you need to. Convert the corkboard into an outline at any time.

Pinning index cards onto a corkboard is a common brainstorming technique for many writers. Write ideas on cards, pin them on the board, and then move the cards around the board as the ideas begin to sequence themselves into an appropriate order. The expansive space of the corkboard lets you arrange a lot of cards into any formation. Unfortunately, your computer screen isn't as large as the wall of your office, but MacToolkit's **Corkboard** ($300) largely overcomes this limitation through creative manipulation tools. Shrink the cards, click them into rows, attach secondary cards to primary cards. If you're feeling left-brained, switch to a text-based outline view, make changes, and find your cards appropriately rearranged when you return to the corkboard. A moderately sized thesaurus plus good use of color and graphics makes Corkboard fertile ground for developing a strategy. Turn the "virtual" into reality by printing out your cards and pinning them on the wall behind your computer. Use Corkboard as your idea library and source for new cards.

Inspiration

Take away the square index cards of Corkboard, replace them with any shapes you like, add connecting lines, and ta-da—flow charts! I started with a cloud-shaped box, typed in my main idea, and then with successive clicks (or keystrokes), I soon had a screen full of clouds, each labeled with related thoughts. (Use [⌘]-click or press [Enter] to instantly create a new idea in its own cloud.) As with Corkboard, **Inspiration** ($300, Inspiration Software) lets you switch to a text-based outline of your diagram. With Inspiration, however, both diagrams and outlines easily become slick visual presentations. Use the handy templates for memos, letters, and five types of charts, and if you are a busy planner needing word processing, simple page layouts, chart drawing, and a right-brained planning tool, you may find you only need Inspiration.

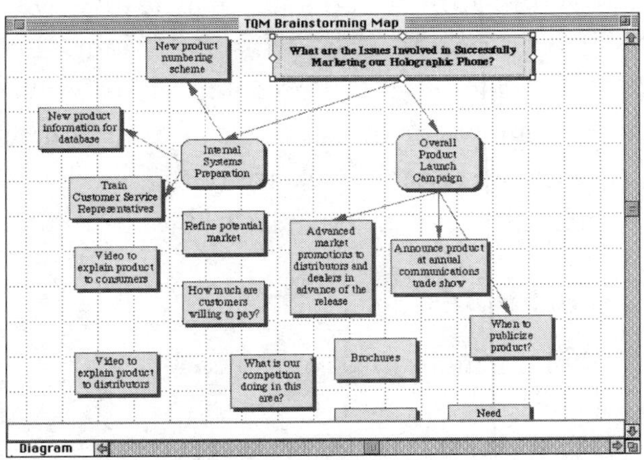

Inspiration lets you brainstorm in diagram style. Once you've finished, you can convert the diagram into an outline.

IdeaFisher

Combining thousands of idea-provoking questions and nearly six megs of words and phrases, **IdeaFisher** ($200, Fisher Idea Systems) is like having Commander Data as your brainstorming partner (OK! OK! So Data has a bigger brain!). The questions (the QuestionBank) help you clarify the issue at hand. The words and phrases (the IdeaBank) stimulate your imagination and help you make associations among ideas.

Suppose you're designing a promotional campaign, writing a story, inventing a new product, or trying to solve a problem. Open up the appropriate QuestionBank and let IdeaFisher grill you for ideas. The questions are not numbered, so you don't feel the pressure of having to answer every one, but I still wrinkle my nose at the sight of anything resembling a test. I prefer to turn directly to the IdeaBank and browse. The interface, basically multiple windows

HOT TIP

with lists of categories and words, is intimidating at first. Here's a suggestion: The program starts up with a window called Idea Notepad. This is where you store all the interesting words and phrases you find. Open Idea Words and Phrases on the IdeaBank menu. Click OK in the first window that opens. (This is the Alphabetical Index. For now, as long as you're on the right word, just click OK whenever it pops up.) From this point on, highlight any entry that looks relevant, then press ⌘E or the Enter key (not the Return key). This will put the entry on your Idea Notepad. Double-clicking will take you to another window filled with related words, phrases, or categories. As you collect and collect, continually think about how these ideas relate to your goal. Solutions will pop into your head. This is the touchy-feely world of the intellect.

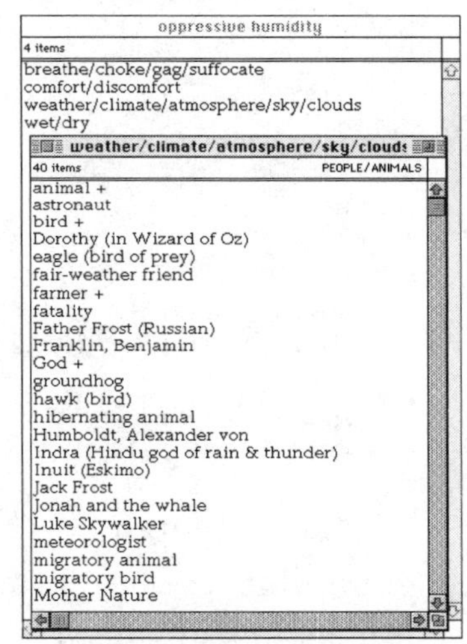

IdeaFisher poses a series of questions to get the juices flowing. After answering as many or as few as you like, use the lists of categories and words to help you brainstorm ideas.

The concept behind IdeaFisher is simple and yet subtly astounding. If, however, you've collected pages of ideas and still haven't had your creative breakthrough, follow the manual's suggestion: "Sometimes the perfect solution will occur after you have stopped working with the program. The process of concentration, coupled with the variety of idea prompts, can stimulate the subconscious and, later, a perfect solution pops into mind." Which is, after all, the "no-brain" approach.

Creative Whack Pack

Reminiscent of the ancient Chinese *Book of Changes* (see "Synchronicity" below), the 64 "suggestion cards" of **Creative Whack Pack** ($30, Interactive Creativity Software) lead you to reconsider a problem or issue from a new, inspired point of view. Type in your issue and then click to receive your cards. All of the cards offer solid inspirational suggestions, along with a picture and a short, well-chosen story. With quotes from sages like Leonardo da Vinci and Lao-Tzu, the cards push you to look at your issue in a new light, consider a new technique, offer advice on decision making, or "whack" you with a suggestion for a helpful activity. Simplicity, humor, and wisdom come together to make the

First, Creative Whack Pack shows you one of the cards with the caption.

Creative Whack Pack

See the Obvious

"Only the most foolish of mice would hide in a cat's ear," says designer Scott Love, "but only the wisest of cats would think to look there." Don't miss the obvious. What are you overlooking? What's the most obvious thing you can do? What resources and solutions are right in front of you?

After a few seconds, the card is flipped over and the story is revealed.

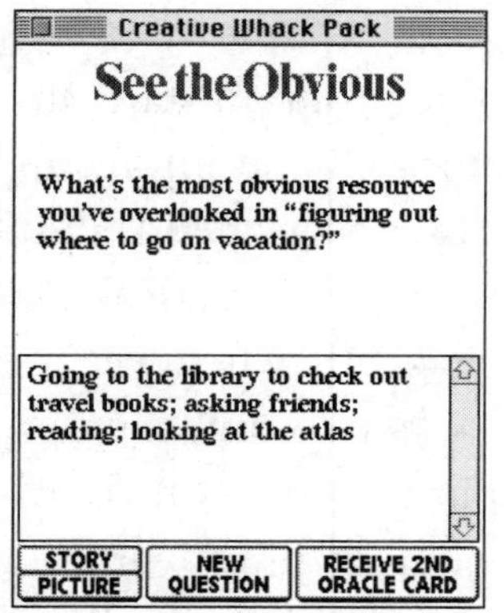

A few seconds later, Creative Whack Pack relates the story to the problem you're trying to solve (in this case "figuring out where to go on vacation").

Creative Whack Pack a rewarding brainstorming tool. Bring the Whack Pack to a planning meeting and you'll likely get a raise. Ask a frivolous question with a group of friends and suddenly you have a party game.

The documentation is thorough in explaining the philosophy behind the program, but it's slim in technical advice. That's OK, though, because the only thing you really need to know is how to load the program onto your hard disk.

Synchronicity

Swiss psychiatrist Carl Jung invented the term "synchronicity" to help explain his concept of a collective unconscious that connects all events in the world. Visionary Software uses the term as a title for a computer version of what many consider the oldest book in the world, the Chinese *I Ching*, or *Book of Changes*. The *I Ching* is an oracle that gives advice based on an ancient technique astoundingly compatible with modern theories in physics and mathematics.

Pose a question to **Synchronicity** ($50, Visionary Software) about an issue that concerns you. Tapping on the keyboard replicates the ancient process of dividing yarrow sticks or throwing coins. Based on a mathematical/philosophical construct too complex to describe here, the answer you receive presents relevant advice from Chinese philosophy. Five thousand years of Chinese leaders "brainstorming" with the *I Ching* is an endorsement more convincing than anything I could write. Purists may resent the venerable book's transformation into high-tech, but the divination technique is sound, and the translation of the ancient text is surprisingly well written for modern times.

OCR Software (CS)

Optical character recognition (OCR) software lets you scan a printed document or fax and translate it into a file that you can modify with your word processor. In theory, you simply take a page from a magazine (for example), scan it to get an image file, and let the OCR software interpret it into text. OCR saves you from typing in the text manually and offers a compact solution to storing fax images or piles of paper copies.

Your results, however, will depend heavily on the quality of the original image. Most OCR programs recognize letters by a scheme called *feature analysis*, looking for loops and stems and other topological features of characters (the idea is to be able to read many different fonts with a single technique). In a blurry document in which letters run together, the technique is usually baffled; in very light documents, breaks in letters also defeat the recognition process.

OCR works best on copy printed at 600 dpi or above, is still usable for 300 dpi, but pretty much falls apart at 200 dpi. Although some programs provide smoothing and contrast utilities, if you have to spend half an hour tweaking a scanned image—faxes are notoriously borderline cases—you often are better off setting your fingers to the keyboard right from the start. Here's the gruesome truth: Accuracy of 96 percent sounds pretty good, but it means a mistake in just about every text line. You can spend lots of time editing (even with a spelling checker) a file that was read 98 percent correctly.

One of the bright lights on the OCR horizon is the use of grayscale information, which, when processing letters, appears to be the best way around the "breaks and blurs" problem mentioned above. Other techniques, which were basically well known a few years ago but were too computation-intensive to be practical on a humble Mac II, have started to appear in mainstream OCR products. In fact, OCR is an area in which real progress has been made in the last 18 months—even if you can get along indefinitely with Excel 4 instead of 5, you won't be happy with older OCR software, even as a gift.

OCR programs fall into two categories: fairly expensive professional software, worth having if you're facing a big job (hundreds of pages), and software that's worse than useless. Here, we're only going to discuss products that are worth investigating.

OmniPage Professional

Caere Software's **OmniPage Professional** was the first choice for OCR even in earlier versions. With the latest release (5.0), Caere has addressed three key problems. First, the program can now use grayscale information from a scan to improve accuracy on less-than-perfect documents (it supports every scanner you're likely to encounter). Second, it can improve the quality of received or scanned faxes by guessing at missing fax codes (a fax transmission is actually a series of on/off codes of different lengths, and it's possible to "reconstruct" degraded faxes somewhat by experimenting with the most likely codes). Finally, the new product includes phrase-level language analysis and statistical analysis of three-letter groups to push reading levels past 99 percent. This version of OmniPage actually does work the way people have been led to expect OCR software to work.

GOOD FEATURE

OmniPage Professional ($700) tends to give better results than its companion product from Caere, **OmniPage Direct** ($300); OmniPage Direct has, as you would expect, a smaller feature set, but it also has a somewhat detuned statistical processing agent.

If you have large collections of documents generated in the same font, OmniPage Professional's training feature can make significant accuracy improvements. On three standard Mac fonts (Geneva, Times, and Chicago) at 600 dpi, trained accuracy is essentially 100 percent. Ambitious users can, with a bit of programming, manage automatic operation of OmniPage Professional from within word processing or other applications with OmniPage Pro's Apple events hooks.

TypeReader

TypeReader ($700) from ExperVision has a snappy, no-nonsense interface and the best documentation of any OCR product, with tips for optimizing the output of each type of popular scanner. In tests, it runs a very close second to OmniPage Professional, in fact edging it out on typed documents and good-quality faxes.

TypeReader lacks the ability to rotate scans, which means you can't work with text documents printed in landscape mode unless you use an image editor like Adobe's Photoshop to rotate the scan file first. If you have lots of scanned documents, you won't want to do this.

WordScan and WordScan Plus

These generally competent programs ($300 for **WordScan**, $600 for **WordScan Plus**) from Calera Recognition Systems offer many interface convenience features, and their overall accuracy on key documents rates just behind the Caere products. They're quite good at certain dot-matrix scans, so they're worth a look if you're trying to scan and read older computer-generated documents.

WordScan Plus has additional nice touches, such as a pop-up verifier window that flags likely errors in an easy-to-see, moving text box, and movable "job separators" that delimit document sections and save them to separate files.

TextPert

TextPert ($700) from CTA has a special set of strengths. The program supports an awesome array of foreign alphabets, and it has special facilities for dealing with tables and spreadsheets, so you may find it a first pick for some financial applications. For plain old text documents, it isn't as accurate as Caere's OmniPage Direct, though, and it costs more.

General Word Processing Tips

Two basic word processing rules (SA/AN). No matter what program you're using, here are a couple of basic rules to follow:

- Only hit the Return key at the end of paragraphs, not at the end of each line.
- Don't use spaces to align words horizontally; they won't line up straight on paper, even if they look straight on the screen. Instead, use tabs to create columns, the Center command (or whatever it's called in the program you're using) to center text, and margin or indent settings to move text in from the margins.

Apply the most-used style first (EC). If you've got to format a big, or even medium-size, document from scratch, first apply the style that you use most to the entire document. Then you can concentrate on formatting just the headings. In Word, after you apply the first style, you can use the Repeat command (⌘Y) to format the rest.

Keeping only some of the local formatting (EC). Imagine that someone (not you, of course) has littered your text with unwanted boldface. If you eliminate all the local formatting, you'll lose the italics that you want to keep. But there's a clever little trick that will let you keep some of the local formatting and rid yourself of the parts you don't want: Change the style's definition so that it includes the local formatting *you don't want*. Then change it back. Your unwanted local formatting will have disappeared, and what you want will stay put.

Em dashes, en dashes, and hyphens (AN). *Em dash* is the technical name for what people normally just call a dash—there's one right there. (It gets its name from the fact that it's more or less the same width as a capital *M*.)

An *en dash* is half the length of an em dash and is used to indicate ranges of numbers (1926–66) or as a minus sign. (It gets its name from the fact that it's more or less the same width as a lowercase *n*.)

Hyphens are shorter than either. Here's a comparison of the three:

em dash —

en dash –

hyphen -

On the Mac, you get an em dash with Option Shift -, and you get an en dash by holding down Option -.

The option space (AN). The option space character (generated by holding down the Option key while pressing Spacebar) has two unique features. The first is that it's always a hard (or nonbreaking) space—which means that if it falls at the end of a line, it won't break; instead, it will drag the word before it down to the next line, along with the word after it. This is useful when you want to keep phrases like WW II and J. B. S. Haldane all on the same line, but it can make for a very uneven right margin (or, if your text is justified, for lines with very loose spacing).

The second feature is that, in some fonts, the option space is wider than a regular space (but narrower than two).

Smart quotes (SA). If your word processing program doesn't automatically give you left- and right-leaning (" and ") quotation marks (also called *curly quotes* or *smart quotes*), and if you're not using a separate smart-quotes utility, you can use your word processor's find-and-replace function to substitute curly quotes for all your straight quotes (' and ").

To do that, you have to assume that every open (or leading) quotation mark will be preceded by a space—which is almost always the case. (Close, or trailing, quotation marks aren't necessarily followed by a space, since the next character may be a punctuation mark—or, in programs like Word, a paragraph marker.) Given that assumption, you just replace every instance of the straight quotation mark that's preceded by a space with an open quotation mark (Option [). Then replace every remaining instance of the straight quotation mark with a close quote (Option Shift [).

Dumb quotes (C. J. Weigand). Using smart-quotes utilities can be annoying, because backspacing over or selecting a quote or apostrophe and then retyping it can leave it facing the wrong direction. I prefer the "dumb quote" approach.

Using QuicKeys (from CE Software, described in Chapter 13), I reassign the curly apostrophe (') to the straight apostrophe key and the curly quotes (" ") to the left and right braces keys ({ and }, i.e., Shift[and Shift]). That way I'm always sure of typing the correct symbol. If I ever need to type a straight apostrophe or braces, all I have to do is temporarily turn QuicKeys off (which you do by hitting ⌘Option.).

[C.J. converted me to this approach, but I did him one better—I assigned the curly quotes to the unshifted [and] keys to make them even easier to get to. I found relearning the new key positions virtually effortless, even though I'd been touch-typing on the old key positions for almost 30 years.

While I was at it, I made Shift, and Shift. print out as , and . instead of as < and >. I moved < and > to the \ key and moved [and] to where the braces { and } normally are (Shift[and Shift]). I even thought of getting rid of the letter Z, since I hardly ever use it. But then I thought, zees may be fooleesh. So I relented and decided to let Z stay.—AN]

Low-rent glossary substitutes (DC/AN). Many word processors don't have glossaries (often-used words, phrases, paragraphs, or even graphics that you can recall with a keystroke and paste into your document). But there's an easy and obvious way around that:

Just use two or three unique characters as abbreviations for the longer text. For example, you might type *tmb* every time you want the phrase *The Macintosh Bible* to appear. Then, when you've finished entering your text, just before you check the spelling in the document, you do a global search for *tmb* and replace it with *The Macintosh Bible* everywhere it appears in the document. Some people find this technique of using abbreviations more convenient than permanently setting up glossaries.

[But remember to check the Whole Word option when doing this kind of global change. I forgot to when changing all the RW's *after entries in Chapter 17 to the full name,* Rich Wolfson, *and wound up with dozens of* LaseRich Wolfsonriter's, *several* otheRich Wolfsonise's *and one* straightfoRich Wolfsonard.*—SA]*

Text markers (DC). Some word processors have a specific function that lets you mark places in a document so you can return to them later. But it's easy enough to do that in any program simply by inserting unique characters (like ##1, ##2 and so on, or any other combination of characters that wouldn't appear in normal text). Then you just use the Find command to move to these points in your document quickly.

Removing returns from imported documents (DC/PH). Sometimes when you transfer a document created on another computer into your word processor, you'll find carriage returns at the end of each line. (You may need to select a special command to show the carriage-return symbols.) Since most word processors use carriage returns only to mark the ends of paragraphs, you'll need to remove all the ones that fall elsewhere. Here's how to do that:

Select the entire document. Now choose Replace from the Edit menu and change each occurrence of two carriage returns (in Word type *^p^p*) to some unique characters that don't appear anywhere in the document, such as ##. Click the Replace All button.

Next, choose Replace again and change each occurrence of a single carriage return to a single space. Click the Replace All button. Now choose Replace for a third time and change each occurrence of ## (or whatever you're using) to a single carriage return. Again, click on the Replace All button. All the carriage returns in your document should now be at the ends of paragraphs.

Microsoft Word Tips

All of these tips work in Word version 6. Some may also work in earlier versions.

General Word Tips

Making sense of Word's new tabs (EC). Word has implemented a new sort of dialog box in Word 6 called a *tab*. Actually, the tabs are what you click on to get an index card–like dialog box to appear, but Microsoft merrily uses the word *tab* to refer to both the index card and the tab that you click on to make it appear.

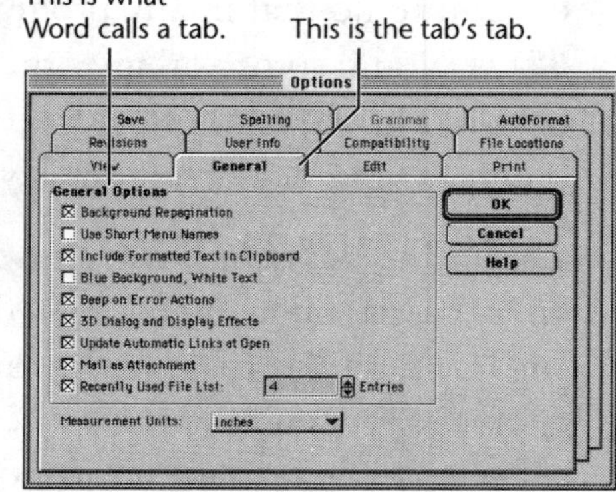

Word's General tab is roughly equivalent to anyone else's General Preferences dialog box.

To get to the options cards (which is what we'll call them), you generally have to select Options from the Tools menu and then click the name of the options that you want to modify (what you click on is a tab). In the tips, that process will be summarized by something like "select This Option in the General options card," instead of "select This Option in the General tab, which you got by selecting Options in the Tools menu and clicking on the General tab."

Creating a new document (EC). You wouldn't think that you'd need a tip to create a new document, but that's what you get with a 17MB word processor. If you select New from the File menu, you'll get a dialog box that lets you pick what template you want to base your new document on. If you click New (or press ⌘N) on the standard toolbar, Word will just quietly open a new document and not ask so many questions about it.

Using shortcut menus (EC). One of Word's cool new features is the shortcut menu. You hold down ⌘Option and click, and depending on what you've got selected, you get a special menu with the options you need.

Documentation for the blind (EC). If you need nonprinted documentation, you can find Microsoft software documentation on audiocassettes and floppy disks from Recording for the Blind (800/221-4792).

The footnote window (SA/PH). To review or edit text in the footnote window, press [Shift] while you drag the split bar, or press [⌘][Option][Shift][S]. To close the footnote window, drag the split bar to the top or bottom of the window, or press [⌘][Option][S].

You don't have to close the footnote window after typing text into it. You can just click in the main part of the window to continue working on your document, or hit [⌘][Option][Z] or [0] (zero) on the keypad (to place the insertion point immediately after the footnote reference mark in the main document).

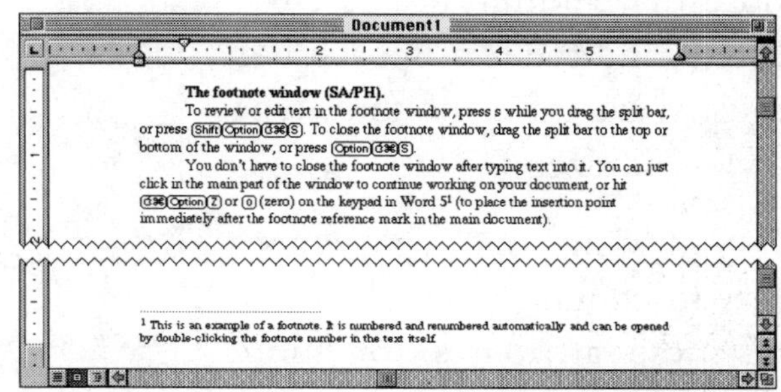

When you create a footnote, Word opens a separate window in which you type the information.

Annotations (EC). If you need to make comments about a document to a colleague (or to yourself), you might try to style your text in a special way or set it in 48-point Times, but the easiest way is to create "annotations." Place the cursor where you want to place the note, and then select Annotation from the Insert menu. You'll be able to enter your comments in the bottom pane of the window (or in a separate window in Word 5). Your initials (if they appear in the User Info options card) will appear next to your comments.

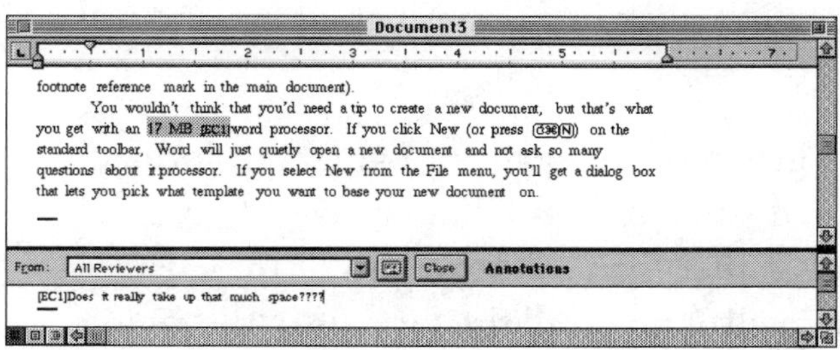

Word's Annotation feature helps workgroup members communicate with each other about specific parts of a document.

The real trick is this: When you place the cursor in an annotation, Word highlights but does not select the text in the document, allowing you to comment on the text without replacing it. To really select the text, press [Option][F11].

Supercharging Replace (PH/ ND/EC/DD). In Word 5 and 6, you can search for and replace text in specific fonts, type styles, and sizes. You can even search for any text with a given font, type style, or size, or for a particular style from the document's Style sheet. So, for example, you can search for all 11-point Optima plain text and change it to 10-point Dom Casual italic.

There are still a few limits. The Find What and Replace With boxes have a limit of 255 characters, and the text in each box must share the same font, type style, and size.

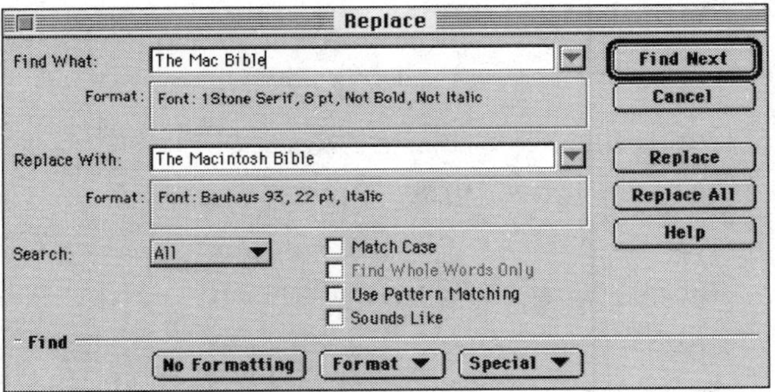

You can use Word's pop-up menus in the Find and Replace dialog box to search for line breaks or tabs or to paste in something you've copied from the document itself.

If you want the replacement text to contain more than one of these attributes (or more than 255 characters), type and format the text as you wish it to appear, and then copy it. Then select Clipboard Contents from the Replace With Special menu (or type ^*c*, that is, Shift 6 and then C).

You can also look for (or replace text with) special characters—like paragraph returns, spaces, or tabs—by selecting them from the Special menu. You can also select regular text or special characters or a combination of both, copy your selection, and paste it into the Find What or Replace With boxes.

The Repeat command (SA/PH/EC). The Repeat command (⌘Y) repeats the last command, your last edit, or the last thing you typed. For example, if you've just applied a style to a paragraph, you can click in another paragraph and use Repeat to apply the style there too.

If you want to use Repeat to apply a group of character or paragraph formats (bold, outline, and italic, say, or justified, indented, and double-spaced), use the Character and Paragraph dialog boxes rather than the keyboard or the Format menu. That way the Repeat command will apply to all the formats in the dialog box, instead of just the last one you applied.

The old keyboard combination for the Repeat command was ⌘A. From version 5 on, it was changed to ⌘Y to accommodate the new Select All command. But you can select all by triple clicking in the selection bar, so if you want, change the Repeat command back to ⌘A, where it's much easier to get at. *[It really bugs me when they change keyboard combinations on me. Seems like I finally commit one to memory when they decide to make it do something completely different.—EC]*

Finding again (SA/PH). To find another occurrence of the word, phrase, or format you last searched for, you don't have to open the Find or Change dialog boxes again—just press ⌘ Option A, or use the = key on the numeric keypad.

Combining this with the general Repeat command (⌘Y) lets you search for something, apply a format to it, and then search for the next occurrence, all from the keyboard and without using dialog boxes. *[If you've changed Repeat back to ⌘A, it's easier still.—EC]*

Searching for case (EC). If you are searching with the Match Case option checked in the Find or Replace dialog boxes, you should be aware that you may not find text that has been formatted with the All Caps or Small Caps options. This is because these two options do not actually change the text (as does the Change Case command); instead, they simply change the outward appearance of the text.

Selecting and Navigating in Word

Moving stuff around (EC). Word invented *drag and drop*, the ability to select a word or paragraph and then (with the pointer facing to the left), simply move it to a new location. No cutting, no pasting, and it leaves your Clipboard alone. If you want to *drag and copy*, hold down the ⌘ key while you drag.

There's one special use for it: When you're outlining, you can't drag (to promote or demote) more than one heading of the same level at the same time...that is, unless you use drag and drop.

Here's an added move trick: To move a paragraph up or down, select it and hit Option Shift ↑ or Option Shift ↓.

HOT TIP

The selection bar (AN/EC). You can select rows of text quickly by putting your pointer in the selection bar—a narrow, invisible column to the left of your text. (You know you're in it because the pointer changes from an I-beam to a right-pointing arrow). When you see that arrow, you can click once to select the line the pointer is next to, double-click to select a paragraph, and triple-click to select the entire document.

Toggling window sizes (SA). There are four ways you can toggle between the size and shape window you've created and one that fills the whole screen:

- Click on the zoom box (at the right end of the title bar).
- Double-click on the title bar itself.
- Double-click on the size box in the lower-right corner.
- Press ⌘ Option].

Window splitting (SA). Word lets you view your documents in three ways: outline view, normal view, and page layout view. You can also view part of your document in one view and part in another, or two noncontiguous parts of your document in the same view. Just split your windows by dragging the black box in the right scroll bar. Or press ⌘ Option S for the same effect. (The command works as a toggle, so you can use it to put the window back together as well.) You can also double-click the black box to split or reconstitute a window.

Double-click here to toggle between split windows and one window.

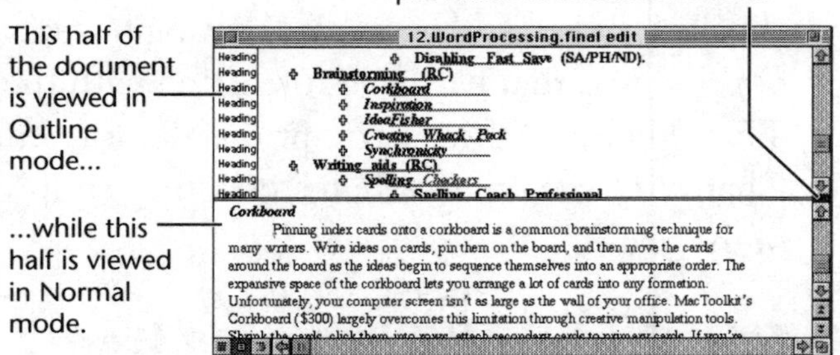

You can divide a window in two to see two different pieces of one document. Each piece can be viewed in a different way.

Navigating backward (RS). ⌘ Option Z moves you to the last position of the insertion point; in Word 5, the 0 (zero) on the numeric keypad does the same thing. Say you're typing and see a mistake. You can go to the mistake and correct it, then press the keypad 0 or ⌘ Option Z to jump right back to where you were. (Word remembers your last four positions, so you can use these keypad commands for complicated sets of jumps around your document.)

HOT TIP

Basic selection commands (SA/ND/EC). Word offers several selection shortcuts, as shown in the table below.

And, of course, as with virtually all Mac programs—you can select any amount of text either by dragging across it or by clicking at one point and then [Shift]-clicking at another.

To select	Do this
A word	Double-click anywhere in it
A sentence	[⌘]-click anywhere in it
A line	Click in the selection bar
A paragraph	Double-click in the selection bar
The entire document	[⌘]-click in the selection bar, press [⌘][A], or triple-click in the selection bar

You can also select text by combining the [Shift] key with the arrow keys.

Using [Option] to select (SA/PH/ND). Holding down the [Option] key as you drag lets you select any rectangular area of the screen. This is a great way to select individual columns, as shown at right.

◆	1992◆	1993◆	1994
Peas◆	200◆	245◆	276
Carrots◆	125◆	150◆	120
Beans◆	300◆	350◆	780

You can select a column in Word, even if it's not part of a table, by holding down the [Option] key and dragging.

In earlier versions of Word, if you wanted to delete an [Option]-key selection, you had to cut it ([⌘][X])—you couldn't use [Delete]. (The Mac would just beep at you if you tried.) In Word 6, you can use [⌘][X] or [Delete].

Note that if any part of a graphic is selected this way, the entire graphic is affected by the deletion or formatting.

Special deletes (SA). As you no doubt know, the [Delete] key erases the character to the left of the insertion point, and you can also use it to delete whatever amount of text you've selected. But Word has other delete commands as well:

- [⌘][Option][F] erases the character to the right of the insertion point (only in Word 5). If you have an extended keyboard, the [⌦] key does the same thing in both Word 5 and 6.
- [⌘][Delete] deletes the previous word—or, if you're in the middle of a word, everything from the insertion point to the beginning of the word. (In Word 5 use [⌘][Option][Delete]).

- ⌘ Option G deletes the next word—or, if you're in the middle of a word, everything from the insertion point to the end of the word.

Scanning a long document (SA). When you switch to Outline mode, only the first line of each paragraph in your document is displayed. This makes it very easy to skim through a long document when you're looking for something. (If you see whole paragraphs, click the Show First Line Only button.) Unfortunately, only body text is abbreviated in this way, not long headings.

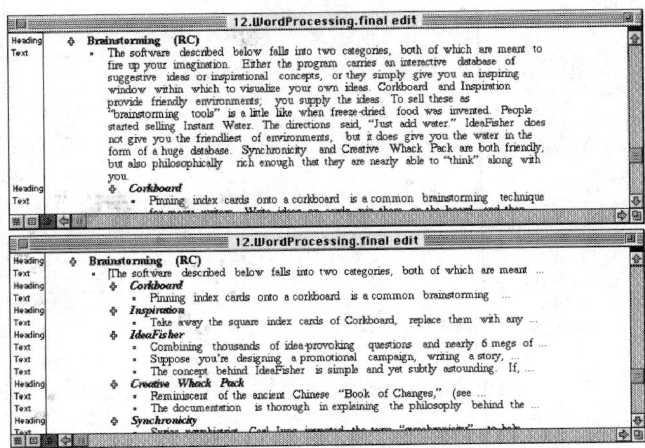

Click the Show First Line Only button in Outline view to show only the first line of your body text.

Using Formatting and Styles in Word

Get Word to do your styles (EC). If you can't stand the thought of figuring out what styles are but wish your documents looked just a little bit classier, try selecting AutoFormat from the Format menu. Word will apply styles as it sees fit and won't bother you much about it. You can review the changes if you're really interested and even change the style definitions if you want to, but if you prefer not to know, nobody will be the wiser.

Telling character from paragraph styles (EC). Word combines both the character and paragraph styles in a single menu. How do you tell them apart? Paragraph styles are in bold and character styles are not.

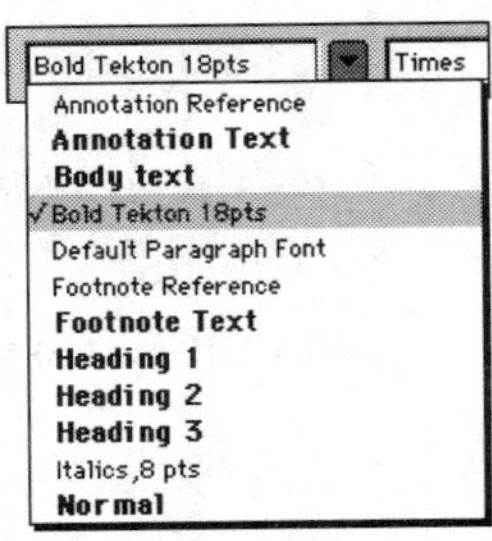

In Word 6's Style menu, character styles are shown in plain text and paragraph styles are shown in bold.

Use outlining to apply your styles (EC). Word's outlining is probably one of its least well known features, but it does two things extremely well. First, when you promote or demote levels in outline view, Word automatically applies the corresponding heading styles to your text. Second, it uses that information if you later wish to create a table of contents. You can change the style definitions that Word uses (which are hideous), but just don't touch the names: heading 1, heading 2, and so on.

Applying styles from the keyboard (EC). You've always been able to apply styles from the keyboard by pressing ⌘Shift S and then typing the first few letters of the style in the status bar in the lower-left side of Word's window. In version 6, ⌘Shift S takes you directly to the Style menu, where you again must type the first few letters of the style to apply it to the selected text. Word 6 also lets you use the arrow keys to go through the styles once you are in the Style menu.

Speedy bullets (EC). Are you still typing your bullets (or dashes) by hand? Well, you're done. From version 5 on, Word lets you select your text, and then click the Bullets button on the Formatting toolbar. In version 6, if you prefer numbers, click the Numbering button. You won't be able to select the bullets (or numbers) once they're formatted, so to get rid of them, click the corresponding button a second time.

Picking the best style names (EC). Just when you think life kind of makes sense, Word comes at you with a really goofy feature, like style names that can be up to 253 characters long. You could use this whole paragraph as a style name, although you'd spend more time typing its name than you did thinking it up!

This is one of those times you growl and then ignore Word's intriguing interface: Give your styles short descriptive names. Then, preface the name with a unique 2-letter abbreviation and a space; an example might be "bt Body text." Now to apply the style, you just have to type 2 letters instead of 9 (or 253). Make sure you make the abbreviation lowercase; style names are case sensitive, and you don't want to waste your time fussing with the Shift key.

Printing your style definitions (EC). If you want to make sure that you have defined your styles correctly, say, according to your designer's specifications, you can print a list of the styles by selecting Print in the File menu and selecting Styles in the Print pop-up menu in the lower-left corner of the dialog box. (In Word 5 and earlier, open the Style dialog box and select Print from the File menu.)

Displaying your style names (EC). If you would like to see the style names to the left of your document as you format it, enter a number larger than 0 in the Style Area Width box in the View Options card. To hide the style names, change this value to 0.

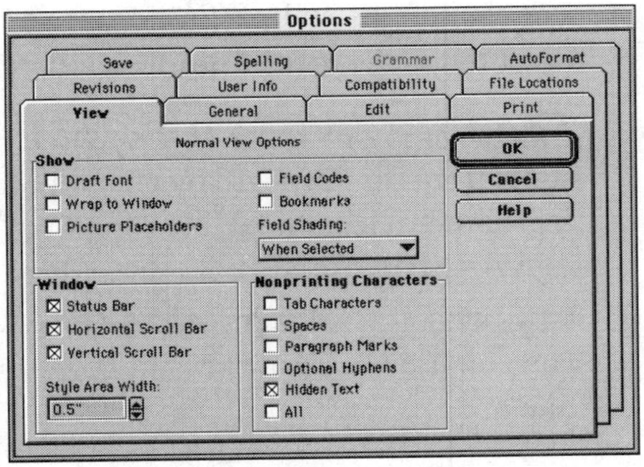

Enter a number larger than 0 in the Style Area Width box in the View Options card to view the name of the style next to each paragraph.

Creating default styles (SA/PH/SM/EC). There are default styles that Word always uses, like the Normal style and those used for automatic page numbers and index entries. You can change their definitions and add new defaults of your own.

Why should you want to add your own defaults? Because nondefault style sheets are stored with the document in which they were created. So if you create a style for one document and forget to define it as a default, you'll have to import it into each document you want to use it in.

To make a style a default, just click the Add To Template box in the New Style dialog box and then click OK.

Changing default styles (SA/PH/SM/EC). Modifying default styles is easy. Just select All Styles (it's a button in Word 5's Style dialog box and an option in the List pop-up menu in the lower-left corner of Word 6's) and then double-click the style you want to change. (In Word 5 and earlier, the names of the default Styles have a bullet in front of them.)

Prime candidates for changes are:

- the Normal Style (the default for a new document)
- page number (used for the automatic page number)
- line number (used when you want the lines of your document numbered)

Page number and line number are based on the Normal Style, so if you change Normal to 10-point Times, the page numbers and line numbers will also be in that font and size.

Remember to click the Add to Template box in the Modify or New Style dialog box so that you will be able to use the new default styles with the new documents you create.

Retroactive default styles (SA/EC). When you change the definition of a default style, paragraphs defined as that style automatically reflect the changes—but only in the current document and future ones. A preexisting document using that style normally will not show the changes—unless you either open the document, Select All, and paste it into a new, empty window or import the new style sheet into it (see the next entry for how to do that).

To make sure that the documents based on a common template maintain consistent styles, select Templates in the File menu and then click the Automatically Update Document Styles checkbox in the Templates and Add-Ins dialog box that appears. When you open a document, the template's styles will override any styles with the same name and any extra styles will be copied to the new document. Any styles found in the document that are not part of the template will be left unchanged.

Moving styles from one document to another (EC). Remember the Font/DA Mover? Well, Microsoft has created a style mover for Word 6 that works almost exactly the same way (of course it would be too easy to call it that; instead, it's called the Style *Organizer*). At any rate, it's an easy way to copy or move styles from one document or template to another.

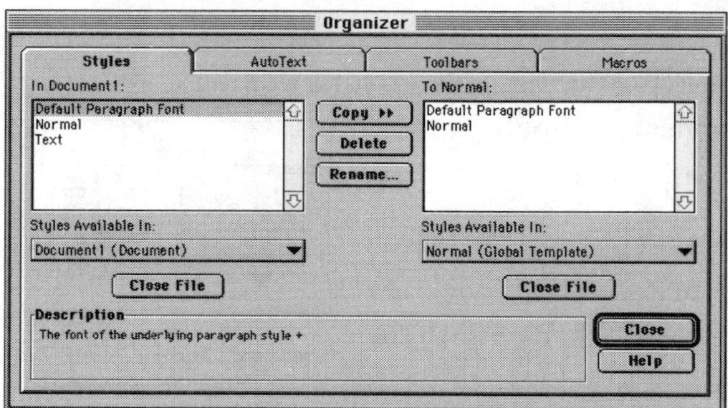

Word's Style Organizer bears a striking resemblance to the Font/DA Mover. Just click on the style you wish to copy to the new document and then click Copy.

If you want to copy just one style from one open document to another, the fastest way is to copy the ¶ symbol from the

desired paragraph and paste it into the new document. The style will be automatically copied to the Style dialog box. However, if a style with the same name already exists in the new document, the original style will remain unchanged.

In earlier versions of Word, copying styles from one document to another is much less intuitive. You open the Styles dialog box and then select Open from the File menu (which you wouldn't expect to be able to get to). Then select the file from which you want to copy the styles.

Next Style override (SA). This tip doesn't work in Word 6, but it's so good we left it in. When you define a style to have a Next Style, pressing [Return] to start a new paragraph switches to that next style. When you want to stay in the current Style, you can override the Next Style option by pressing [⌘][Return] instead.

Leading control (SA/PH). To control leading (line spacing) in Word, go to the Paragraph dialog box (the keyboard shortcut was [⌘][M] in Word 5, but Word 6 has no keyboard shortcut), select Exactly under Line Spacing, and then type the number of points of leading you want into the Line box. You don't need to type *pt* or anything after the number; Word knows you mean points if you don't specify inches or anything else.

So, for example, if you want to print out text 11/13 (11-point type on 13-point leading), you first select the text, then go to the Character dialog box and type 11 in the Size box, then go to the Paragraph dialog box, choose Exactly, and type 13 in the Line box.

Copying character formats (SA/EC). You can copy existing combinations of character formats (font, size, and styles) and apply them to existing text or at the insertion point, so they affect whatever you type next.

With Word 6, select the original text and then click the Format Painter button. When the cursor changes into the Format Painter icon with an I-beam, click on the text where you want to copy the formatting.

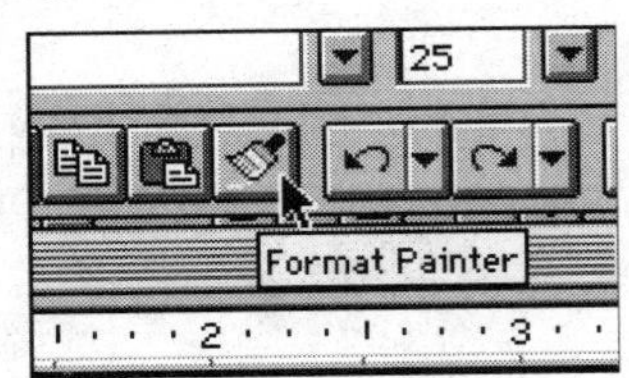

Use Word's Format Painter button to "grab" the format of one piece of text and apply that format to another piece of text.

If you double-click the Format Painter button, you'll be able to apply the formatting to as many other paragraphs as you wish. Press Esc when you're finished.

With earlier versions of Word, try this:

1 Select some text formatted the way you want and press ⌘ Option V. The words Format To appear in the status box (in the lower-left corner of the window).

2 Select the text you want the formats applied to. (This second selection is underlined rather than highlighted.)

3 Press Return or Enter.

4 Continue typing if you wish.

Soft and hard hyphens (SA/EC). Word gives you a choice of three different kinds of hyphens. Regular hyphens are what you get when you hit the - key; they're always displayed, and the words they connect split when the hyphen falls at the end of a line.

A soft hyphen (also called a discretionary hyphen) is printed only when it falls at the end of a line (and the letters it connects are split). If the soft hyphen doesn't divide a word, you'll only be able to see it on screen if you have chosen the Show ¶ option (in the toolbar or from the View menu in Word 5), in which case it will appear as a hyphen with a tiny dot underneath it. To enter a soft hyphen, type ⌘ -.

A hard hyphen (also called a nonbreaking hyphen) is always displayed, but it won't let the words it connects be split across two lines. To enter hard hyphens, type ⌘ Shift -.

If the keyboard combinations given here do not work for you, someone may have changed them (including Microsoft!). To find out how to enter a soft or hard hyphen, open Microsoft Word Help from the Help menu and search for Hyphenation in the list. If Word were a normal program, you'd open the Customize window and select the command, but since you'll find them (or not find them) in a very peculiar order in Word 6, it's rather a waste of time.

HOT TIP

Embedding TrueType fonts (EC). If you want to send a document with TrueType fonts to a colleague but are not sure whether she has the fonts you used, you can *embed* the fonts so that she can read and print the document correctly. Just check Embed TrueType Fonts in the Save options card.

Using the ruler (SA/PH). There are two triangular markers at the left end of Word's ruler. The bottom one controls the left margin and the top one controls the indentation of the first line. If you drag the bottom marker (the margin), the top one (the indent) moves with it, but the top marker can move separately—that's how you change the distance between the two.

Move the top triangle to set the indent for the first line of text...

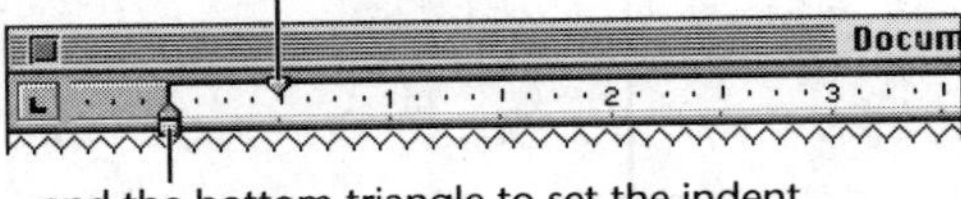

...and the bottom triangle to set the indent for the second and subsequent lines of text.

Word 6's ruler looks a bit different but works essentially the same as in earlier versions.

(You can move the bottom marker separately as well, by holding down the Shift key while you drag it.)

If you want to set a margin or indent to the left of the zero mark on the ruler, just slide the marker to the left; after an initial hesitation, the window scrolls so you can get to the negative numbers. (To scroll to the left of the zero mark without moving anything on the ruler, just hold the Shift key down while using the left scroll arrow at the bottom of the window.)

The default unit on the ruler is inches, but you can change it with the General window of the Preferences command (on the Edit menu). To change the default tab stops, use the Document command and type the new distance you want in the Default Tab Stops box.

Tab tricks (SA). When you have a series of tabs on the ruler, moving one tab doesn't affect the others—unless you hold down Shift, in which case all the tabs to the right of the one you're dragging move together. This is very useful when you have tabbed columns set up and want to shift them all, but unfortunately it only works in Word 5.

For Word 6 users, hold down the Option key while you drag a tab to see its precise distance from the left and right margins.

Using Graphics in Word

Saving space (EC). A Word document in which you place many illustrations may balloon in size. To keep it svelte, you can just *link* the graphic to the original document by clicking the Link To File box and clearing the Save Picture In Document box when you select the illustration to place. (You select it with the Picture command in the Insert menu.) The disadvantage is the loss of speed, since Word will need to consult the original illustration for viewing and printing.

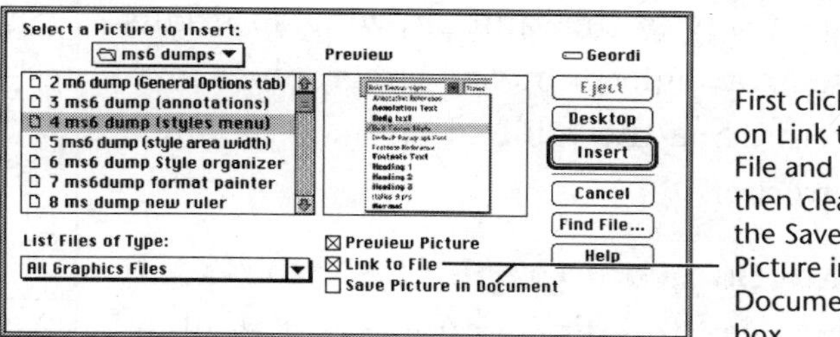

You can cut down on file sizes by saving links to graphics, rather than the graphics themselves, with a document.

Quicker scrolling (EC). If you find that you could go out for coffee between clicks as you scroll through a document, you may want to temporarily replace your illustrations with placeholders (click Picture Placeholders under Show in the View options card). You'll be able to scroll much more quickly, and the illustrations will print as usual.

Quick printing (EC). If your graphics take their sweet time coming out of the printer and you just need to proof the text, check the Draft Output box in the Print options card. Your document will print a lot faster—but without graphics.

Resizing graphics (EC). In typical Microsoft style, Word uses some standard and some nonstandard (and contradictory) commands for resizing graphics. See the table below.

Action	**With the drawing tools hidden**	**With the drawing tools showing**
Drag side, top, or bottom handle	To resize in that direction	To resize in that direction
Drag corner handle	To resize proportionately	To resize in that direction
Shift and drag a corner	To crop	To resize proportionately
Press ⌘	No effect	To resize from center

Restoring a graphic (EC). If you make changes to a graphic's size (in Page view), you can restore the original size by selecting Picture in the Format menu and then clicking the Reset button.

Typical drawing shortcuts (EC). Word uses many of the same drawing shortcuts used throughout most Mac graphics programs. See the table at right for a quick refresher.

Do this	To
Hold down [Shift] while drawing	Constrain to perfect squares and circles
Double-click	Complete free-form objects
Press [Esc]	Cancel drawing or complete free-form objects
[Backspace] or [Delete]	Delete last line segment or selected object
Press [⌘]	Draw from the center
Double-click on a tool	Lock on that tool for more than one action
Press [Option] while dragging	Copy selection to new location

Choosing your graphics editor (EC). If you need to edit a graphic, just double-click it. Word automatically assumes that you want to use its drawing tools to make the changes and will open a new window for you. If it's an object-oriented graphic, Word will let you make changes, and if it's a bit map, you'll be able to add to the graphic or change its size.

But that's not the tip. If you want to use *another* program to edit your graphics, you can set that program as the default (with the Picture Editor menu in the Edit options card). Then when you double-click a graphic, Word will launch that program automatically (as long as you have enough memory).

Reshaping free-form shapes (EC). If you create a free-form shape and then click on it, you select the whole shape, as if it were grouped. To move the individual anchor points, which Word in its infinite desire to re-create terminology calls *vertices*, click the Reshape button in the Drawing toolbar. Then drag those babies where you want them to go.

To add a new vertex, hold down [⌘] while you click on the line where you want it to go. To get rid of an existing vertex, hold down [⌘] while you click on it.

Rotating text (EC). Even though Word has a Rotate command, it won't let you rotate text. If you have a text box selected when you click Rotate, the box rotates and leaves the text behind. Seems pretty bogus to me. To get around that, create the text in an external graphics program, input it, and then rotate away. Alternatively, you can copy the text as a picture, using ⌘Shift D, and then paste it in and rotate it.

The invisible grid (EC). You can use Word's invisible grid to help align objects in the drawing area. But if you hate grids like I do, you'll be happy to hear that you can turn it off by clicking the Snap To Grid button in the Drawing toolbar and then clearing the Snap To Grid checkbox in the dialog box that appears. To get rid of the grid temporarily (or to bring it back if you've banished it), hold down ⌘ while you drag. (Hallelujah, Word follows the standard; this is the same way that grids are activated and deactivated in the Finder and in FileMaker.)

Labeling pictures the easy way (EC). If you want to create labels, or *callouts*, to describe the different parts of an illustration, don't use regular text and laboriously draw lines back and forth. Instead, click the Callout button, position the pointer where you want the indicator line to start, and then drag to where you want to write the text. A box will appear in which you can enter and format the text.

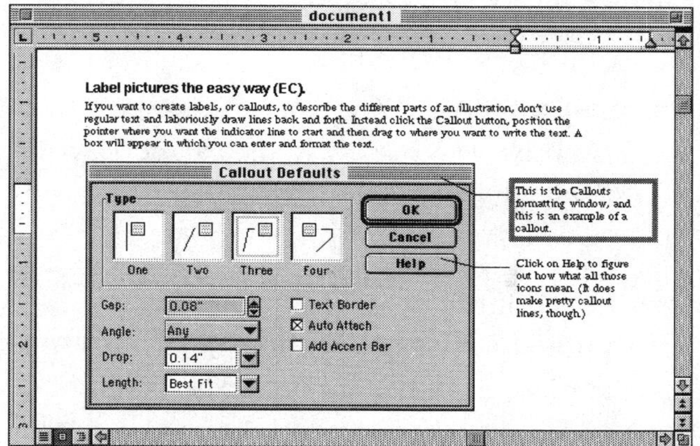

Word's Callout button makes it easy to link text with a specific area of an illustration.

Creating a watermark (EC). If you want a graphic to appear in the background of your page (say, the word *draft*, for a lawyer's brief), you'll need to click the Send Behind Text button. If you want to place an imported graphic or text behind the text in your document, you'll have to place it in a text box in the drawing area and then click the Send Behind Text option.

If you want the watermark to appear on every page, place it in a header or footer. Position it where you want; it doesn't necessarily have to go at the top or bottom of the page.

Keeping captions with graphics (EC). The best way to keep a caption with a graphic is to select them both and frame them together by selecting Frame from the Insert menu.

If you want to add a caption to an existing graphic that is already framed, position the cursor inside the graphic and press Enter (or select Caption from the Insert menu). Then type.

You can also set up dynamic cross-references to these captions, which will, for example, keep track of what page Table 1 is on.

Stylish frames (EC). If you use frames a lot, create a style defined as a frame. Then select your text and format it with the appropriate style and you're all done.

Resizing a frame (EC). You can change a frame's size in the Frame dialog box, but it's much easier to switch to Page Layout view and then drag the frame's boundaries that show up in the rulers.

Working With Columns and Tables in Word

Combining different numbers of columns (EC). If you want only part of your document to be laid out in two columns, you'll have to divide it into sections (select Break from the Insert menu). Then place the cursor in the section that you want to format in two columns, and press the Columns button. Each section must have the same number and same size columns throughout, but you can create as many sections as you need.

Creating a banner headline (EC). You could use the technique described in the previous tip to create a banner headline—one that is centered and goes from margin to margin—by typing the headline text at the top of the left column, pressing Enter, selecting the headline, clicking the Columns button, and dragging to select a single column. Center and format the headline as desired.

Creating uneven columns (EC). When you drag the column markers on the ruler, you don't just change one column, you change them all. How do you create two columns that have different widths? You have to open the Columns dialog box and check Left or Right for the automatic settings, or click Two or

Three Columns and then uncheck Equal Column Width below. Finish off by entering the widths you want for your columns. Now when you drag the column markers in the ruler, you'll only affect that one column.

Adding lines between columns (EC). OK, this isn't really a trick, but since you might spend a while using the Borders command or some such thing to place lines between your columns, I'll give you this hint: Use the Line Between option in the Columns dialog box.

Creating column breaks (EC). If you want text to appear at the top of the column, use a column break: Place the cursor before the text and press [⌘][Shift][Enter].

Adjust for double indenting (EC). If your columns seem narrower (or wider) than they should be, check that your columns don't have extra formatting such as indents.

Using tabs inside tables (EC). Since the [Tab] key will take you to the next cell in a table, how do you enter a tab in a table? Well, if you're doing it a lot, you probably need another column. But for just once in a while, try [Option][Tab].

Selecting and editing tables (PH/EC). Word 6 finally has a decent way to select parts of tables. To select one cell, place the cursor just *inside* its left border and click. To select a row, place the cursor just *outside* its left border and click. Selecting columns hasn't changed; place the cursor just above the column until it turns into a downward-pointing arrow. You can drag and drop columns and rows and use [⌘] to copy as you drag, but don't try to copy or paste the normal way—it doesn't work.

Although Word makes adding rows to the end of tables easy (just put the insertion point in the last cell and press [Tab]), inserting rows in the middle or removing rows and columns is a pain—you have to use the Table Layout command from the Format menu and then make the appropriate choices.

If you edit tables much, you'll be happy to see that Word 6 has a new button for inserting cells, rows, and columns (depending on what you've got selected). What do you select to add a column on the end of your table? All of the end-of-row marks.

Since Word still makes you go through a dialog box to delete cells, rows, or columns, you might want to add keyboard shortcuts if you do a lot of table editing.

Word does let you select a whole row (click the little box to the left of it) and then move it to a new location with drag and drop. (Don't cut and paste, it won't work like you expect.) If you hold down ⌘ (not Option, which would be too similar to standard Mac interface design for the folks at Microsoft), you'll place a *copy* of the selected row or column.

Using the Word Dictionary

Checking words in the dictionary (EC). Word lets you look up words that you don't know how to spell by letting you use an asterisk in place of the letters you're not sure of. For example, if you want to look up *receive*, but can't remember that *i* comes before *e*, and all that, then enter *rec*ve* in the Spelling dialog box. All the words that begin with *rec* and end with *ve* will appear, and you'll be able to pick *receive* from among them.

Excluding words from the dictionary (EC). There are several words with two correct spellings, like *color* and *colour*, *gray* and *grey*, and many more. If you want Word to flag any of these words, you have to enter them in the Exclude dictionary, which is a kind of anti-dictionary: Word will question any word it contains, even if it is part of another dictionary.

Working With AutoText and AutoCorrect in Word

Ghostwriting with Word (EC). Make sure you don't define AutoCorrect entries with real words; since Word automatically replaces the word with the AutoCorrect definition, you'll never be able to use that word again in your text! For example, to have Word enter *The Macintosh Bible, 5th edition*, I created an AutoCorrect definition called *tmb*. Every time I type *tmb*, Word changes it into *The Macintosh Bible, 5th edition*. If I used the word *Bible* as the name, I wouldn't be able to type *Mac Bible* without Word changing it into *Mac The Macintosh Bible, 5th edition.*

And don't limit your AutoCorrect definitions to text. You can have Word introduce graphics, tables, or whole paragraphs as you type (see the next tip). If you don't want Word to insert things automatically, use AutoText instead.

AutoCorrect graphics and formatted text (EC). To include graphics or formatted text in your AutoCorrect definitions, select the item before opening the AutoCorrect dialog box, and it will automatically appear in the With box. Check Plain Text or Formatted Text as desired and enter the name, or trigger, that you wish to use to have Word type out the selection. Remember not to use real words as triggers; you won't ever be able to type them without Word replacing them with their AutoCorrect definition.

Unusual AutoText entries (SA/PH). The AutoText feature (formally the Glossary) can store anything that you can select in the document. Here are some entries that may not have occurred to you but that can be quite useful:

- **Graphics.** You could, for example, automatically insert a logo or letterhead.
- **Section breaks.** All the section definitions (number of columns, page-number position, and so on) are stored in the section-break symbol (a double line that runs across the page). Keeping them in the collection of AutoText entries lets you apply section-formatting options quickly.
- **Character format combinations.** To do this, select a single character with a variety of formats—14-point Times bold italic, for example—and store it in the AutoText box. When you retrieve it, hit Shift← to select it and then type whatever you want—the new typing will have the retrieved format. (If you have Word 6, it's probably easier to use a character style.)
- **Paragraph formats.** First press ⌘J (or choose Show ¶ from the View menu *[this is the one that used to be ⌘Y—EC]*). Then select a paragraph marker (¶) and open the Glossary window. (Why retrieve paragraph formats from the Glossary instead of using a style sheet? Because the style sheet includes character formatting, and sometimes you won't want that.)
- **Tables.** Create tables with the number and size of rows and columns you need, and store them in the Glossary for quick retrieval.

Editors' Poll: Do You Always Upgrade Your Software When a New Version Is Released?

AA: Yes, if it's stuff I use every day in my work and has new features I need. For instance, I got FAXstf 3.0 right away. Other times, no. To wit: I'm a fanatical TouchBase user, but I still haven't upgraded to TB Pro because I hate the new interface with its multipage layouts; the current version does most everything I want (except for the bug that corrupts the Comments field).

DB: I have so much software sitting about my office, I'd need a 4D database just to keep track of what needs to be upgraded. In fact, I'm embarrassed to admit that I often don't even register many of my programs, so I sometimes don't know when an upgrade is available. I wish I did, though. Maybe that'll be my New Year's resolution.

CG: Sure, and I also still believe in Santa Claus. Anyone who has had anything to do with technology knows that people who latch onto new, just-released, first iterations of hardware or software are not early adopters—they're crazy fools with a death wish.

DD: Hardly ever. Often I'm upset at the new version, usually for adding much more than I need, at a great cost of memory and hard disk space. I don't need all that stuff. Sometimes, though, I need to upgrade because I need to be using the same version others in the field are using to make sure we can keep exchanging files. Don't even get me started on that…

JK: Not immediately; I usually upgrade when I start craving the newer version's features, from using them on someone else's machine or hearing a lot about them. But I still keep a copy of Word 4 on my PowerBook because it boots up quicker and takes up less space in memory and on the hard drive than the current version.

HN: I usually upgrade promptly, but not always. I check out new stuff ASAP, but hold off on installing it and using it regularly if I know of or have reason to suspect reliability problems or incompatibilities with other software I value (depending, of course, on how appealing the new features of the upgrade are). I'm particularly conservative in the area of telecommunications. I stuck with Red Ryder, then White Knight, for years after they had fallen behind the feature curve, relative to the competition, because they did what I needed and the capabilities added to the newer revisions weren't of any value to me.

BW: I'm timid about immediately diving on a new major rev, generally waiting for the fabled X.0.1 maintenance release. I don't have the time or inclination to beta test products for which I've paid good, hard-earned money. If the old rev is serving adequately I don't risk my deadlines by changing horses in midstream.

Spreadsheets

The first software package for the personal computer, VisiCalc, was a spreadsheet program. It became wildly successful and made people realize that perhaps there was a money in selling software. Twenty years later, spreadsheets have grown up quite a bit. Not content to just add and subtract, they can now solve complex financial analysis problems, create three-dimensional graphs, and generate automatic monthly reports. We'll tell you just what you can expect from today's spreadsheets and give you a new collection of tips for the Macintosh's most popular spreadsheet, Excel.

Contributors

Elizabeth Castro (EC) is the chapter editor.

Marty Sobin (MS) provides Excel and FileMaker Pro training and consulting when he isn't studying the stock market, playing squash, collecting cookie jars and Pez dispensers, or watching his four-year-old son.

Arthur Naiman (AN), Sharon Zardetto Aker (SA) and **Susan McCallister (SM)** wrote and edited earlier editions of *The Macintosh Bible,* from which parts of this chapter were taken.

Contents

Who Needs a Spreadsheet?

If you climb to the base camp of Mount Fuji, you'll be rewarded with an amazing view. For most people, that's enough. Only a few will put on their crampons and ropes and oxygen bottles and make the hike to the summit. Working with spreadsheets, though perhaps not so beautiful, is quite similar. A short trek to the base camp of sums and tables may be sufficient for most, while only a few will undertake the arduous trip to macros, financial analysis, and three-dimensional charts.

Spreadsheet Base Camp (SA/AN/SM)

A spreadsheet is a grid of *cells* (little boxes) that are arranged in (horizontal) rows and (vertical) columns. (The term *spreadsheet* is used both for the software and for the grid of data you create with it, though sometimes the grid is also called a *worksheet*.) You put numbers in the cells and tell the spreadsheet to perform mathematical operations on them.

Let's say you create a column that represents your monthly budget, with the first cell for rent or mortgage, the next for utilities, the next for food, and so on. Then you put twelve of those columns next to each other, one for each month of the year. Such a spreadsheet can calculate your budget for each month (the total of each column) and how much you spent—or plan to spend—in any given category in the course of a year (the total of each row). You can also have a total calculated for all categories in the entire year, and averages for categories or months.

The great strength of spreadsheets is that if you change a number in one spot, every other number that depends on it is recalculated automatically. So if you change the utility cost for May (when your lover will be in Italy and you'll be making many long, passionate international phone calls), the total for May will change, and so will the yearly total for utilities, the yearly total for all categories, the average monthly budget, and any other calculations you've set up.

That's the key to the spreadsheet's "what-if" capability—you can change a number or two and see what effect it has. For example, you can figure out how

This table was formatted with Excel's AutoFormat tool and the Colorful 2 option.

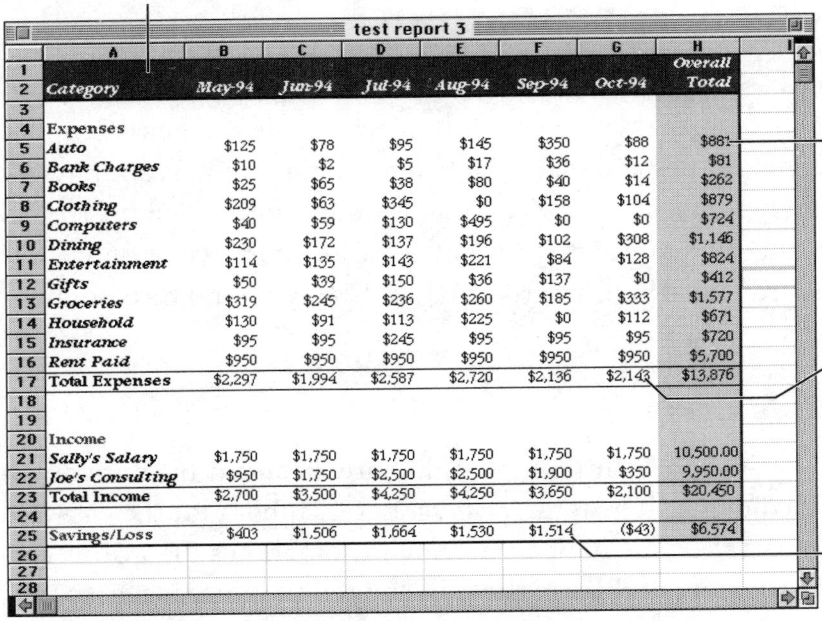

test report 3

	A	B	C	D	E	F	G	H
1								*Overall*
2	*Category*	*May-94*	*Jun-94*	*Jul-94*	*Aug-94*	*Sep-94*	*Oct-94*	*Total*
3								
4	Expenses							
5	*Auto*	$125	$78	$95	$145	$350	$88	$881
6	*Bank Charges*	$10	$2	$5	$17	$36	$12	$81
7	*Books*	$25	$65	$38	$80	$40	$14	$262
8	*Clothing*	$209	$63	$345	$0	$158	$104	$879
9	*Computers*	$40	$59	$130	$495	$0	$0	$724
10	*Dining*	$230	$172	$137	$196	$102	$308	$1,146
11	*Entertainment*	$114	$135	$143	$221	$84	$128	$824
12	*Gifts*	$50	$39	$150	$36	$137	$0	$412
13	*Groceries*	$319	$245	$236	$260	$185	$333	$1,577
14	*Household*	$130	$91	$113	$225	$0	$112	$671
15	*Insurance*	$95	$95	$245	$95	$95	$95	$720
16	*Rent Paid*	$950	$950	$950	$950	$950	$950	$5,700
17	Total Expenses	$2,297	$1,994	$2,587	$2,720	$2,136	$2,143	$13,876
18								
19								
20	Income							
21	*Sally's Salary*	$1,750	$1,750	$1,750	$1,750	$1,750	$1,750	10,500.00
22	*Joe's Consulting*	$950	$1,750	$2,500	$2,500	$1,900	$350	9,950.00
23	Total Income	$2,700	$3,500	$4,250	$4,250	$3,650	$2,100	$20,450
24								
25	Savings/Loss	$403	$1,506	$1,664	$1,530	$1,514	($43)	$6,574
26								
27								
28								

The Savings/Loss value is made up of formulas that subtract each value in row 17 from the corresponding value in row 23. For example, the formula for this cell is =F23–F17.

Here we use a similar formula, =SUM(G5:G16), to add the columns of numbers.

The Savings/Loss value is made up of formulas that subtract each value in row 17 from the corresponding value in row 23. For example, the formula for this cell is =F23–F17.

A simple spreadsheet might sum up monthly expenses and income. (Microsoft Excel is shown here.)

large a mortgage you can afford at various rates of interest, or how much profit you'll make if you sell 1,000, 5,000 or 10,000 units of a product.

Spreadsheets have other uses as well. Since you can put text as well as numbers in cells, spreadsheets provide an easy way to lay out complicated tables, even if you don't have them do any calculations. And most spreadsheets can also create charts, which can be very useful, since numbers are more easily understood when presented graphically.

The Spreadsheet Summit (MS)

As you've seen, this rectangular grid of cells is a simple, useful tool. But use your imagination—and some less-obvious features—and its possibilities extend to sophisticated data analysis and presentation. For an example of some more advanced uses, let's look at a day in the life of Bob, a large company's Excel guru.

9 a.m.: Worksheet consolidation. The director of marketing calls to say he is analyzing sales by individual salesperson and by the company's various selling regions. He maintains a separate worksheet for each region with the different salespeople's monthly figures. He wants to combine the totals from the individual worksheets onto a single worksheet. Bob suggests using the Consolidate command to create a new worksheet with the summarized information from the various worksheets.

9:30 a.m.: Financial functions. The planning department is reviewing plans for future projects and wants to compare the projected profits of specific projects in order to choose the best ones. Bob suggests several financial functions, built into Excel, that let users calculate present and future cash flows and rates of return. Once the people in the planning department do these calculations, they can rank the projects by rate of return using the Sort command.

10:30 a.m.: Function macro creation; charting. The sales department calls Bob with a couple of questions. First, can Bob automate the calculation process to let a data entry clerk easily and quickly enter data into cells on a worksheet and have the proper sales commission automatically appear in other cells? Bob suggests creating a function macro—a custom function that completes calculations not available with the regular set of Excel functions. The data entry person doesn't need to know the details of the calculation—he just enters in the sales data and presses Return. Bob prepares the COMMISSION function macro and saves it in Add-in format in the Excel Startup folder (so that it will load whenever the user launches Excel). Now the COMMISSION function can be used like any other built-in function.

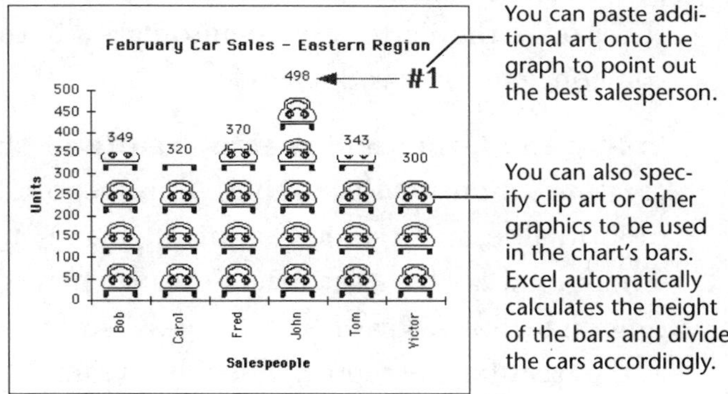

Excel can quickly chart spreadsheet information in a number of chart formats, such as the bar chart shown here.

Next, the sales manager wants to graphically display monthly sales figures so that the best salesperson's result stands out. After Bob shows Excel's numerous chart options, the sales manager decides that a column chart with monthly figures for each salesperson will show the information she wants. She also wants a big #1 with an arrow pointing to the best performance. Bob does this by pasting a picture onto the chart and drawing an arrow using Excel's drawing tools. Now there is no question who had the month's best sales figures. As Bob starts to go back to his office, the sales manager makes one additional request. She would like to make the chart more interesting by changing the chart columns into a stack of cars to represent the product being sold. Bob quickly formats the chart with a clip art image of a car.

1:00 p.m.: LOOKUP function; linking worksheets. The people in the inventory department call to ask whether they can type a product code into a cell and get the corresponding product name, cost, and selling price to appear in adjacent cells. Bob explains how to set up a worksheet with product codes and product information and then use the LOOKUP function with another worksheet (e.g., the Parts List) to automatically retrieve desired information when someone enters a product code.

1:30 p.m.: Command macro creation. The billing department needs help creating a monthly Receivables Aging report. Since the format is the same each month, Bob suggests a Command macro to automate the report creation. Though he can have the macro create a new worksheet and do detailed formatting on it, Bob knows it's easier and faster to use a previously created template as the basis for the report. Then, he creates a macro that

1. opens up the report template
2. requests an "as of" date for the report
3. activates a document listing customer sales and payments
4. finds the first sale for which full payment hasn't been received
5. compares the sale date (corresponding to the selected balance) to the report date, to see whether it is 30, 60, or 90 days past due, then places the desired information in the proper location on the report template
6. finds the next sale for which payment hasn't been received
7. repeats steps 4 and 5 until all sales are processed
8. saves the report with the "as of" date in the title

The billing manager is happy. In the future, when he needs to prepare a Receivables Aging report, he will just run the macro.

4:00 p.m.: Using the Solver command for "what-if" analyses. The accounting department calls with an emergency. They have until the end of the day to decide whether to accept a special fleet order for 1,000 cars at a price 10 percent less than normal. The company is already producing at near capacity and must determine if there is enough profit at the lower selling price to cover the higher costs of overtime pay and placing additional plant operations on-line.

There may be a number of units less than the full order that will maximize total profits. Bob uses the accounting department worksheets that contain profit calculation formulas. Using Excel's Solver command, he determines the number of units that gives the maximum profit within the constraints of labor and plant costs. He shows the accounting department that for the maximum profit the company should limit the sale to 450 cars.

A macro sheet is identical to a regular worksheet, but instead of numbers and formulas, it contains commands (and sometimes, descriptions of those commands).

Column A contains the actual commands that the macro will perform, one after the other.

Column B contains a brief explanation of what each line does.

Receivables Aging Macro

	A	B
1	**RECEIVABLES AGING MACRO (a)**	Macro Title and "Run" Shortcut Letter
2	=OPEN("Receivables Aging Template")	Opens Receivables Aging Template
3	=INPUT("Please enter date to make the report as of:",)	Displays Dialog Box requesting report "as of" date
4	=FORMULA(A3,'Receivables Aging Template'!ReportDate)	Enters "as of" date onto Receivables Aging Template
5	=FORMULA.GOTO('Customer Sales and Payments'!$G$3)	Selects starting point for obtaining data
6	=SET.NAME("NextRow",0)	Helps macro choose starting row to enter data
7		
8	=FOR("Counter",0,COUNTA('Customer Sales and Payments'!$B:$B)-2,1)	Begins loop that finds data and places it in report
9	=IF(SELECTION()>0,,GOTO(A18))	Checks to see whether cell contains positive balance
10	=SELECTION()	Temporary storage of Balance Outstanding
11	=OFFSET(SELECTION(),0,-6,)	Temporary storage of Sale Date
12	=OFFSET(SELECTION(),0,-5,)	Temporary storage of Customer
13	=OFFSET(SELECTION(),0,-4,)	Temporary storage of Invoice Number
14	=IF(A3-$A$11-15>=90,FORMULA($A$10,OFFSET('Receivables Aging Templat	Checks whether data is current or # of days past due
15	=FORMULA($A$12,OFFSET('Receivables Aging Template'!$A$12,NextRow,0))	Places descriptive data in appropriate cell
16	=FORMULA($A$13,OFFSET('Receivables Aging Template'!$B$12,NextRow,0))	Places descriptive data in appropriate cell
17	=SET.NAME("NextRow",NextRow+1)	Designates next row to enter data
18	=SELECT("r[1]c")	Selects next Balance Outstanding amount
19	=NEXT()	End point of loop
20		
21	=ACTIVATE("Receivables Aging Template")	Makes the report the active worksheet
22	=SAVE.AS("Receivables Aging."&A3,1)	Saves report with "as of" date in title
23	=RETURN()	Ends macro

5:00 p.m.: Still more ways to use Excel. It's time to go home. Bob didn't get any calls today for help with statistical data analysis using Excel's specialized functions, or outlining, which would allow a user to automatically hide rows and columns and summarize data on a worksheet. He was especially sorry that he didn't get any requests for database analysis, because Excel 5.0 greatly improves database handling and summarizing with a tool called the Data Pivot.

Few companies can afford to have a Bob on their payrolls to work on Excel all the time. Yet the individual data analysis and presentation needs mentioned above happen often, even in small businesses. It pays for the average user to make the effort to learn how to use a spreadsheet program for data analysis and presentation.

Other spreadsheet programs do not do everything that Excel does (and conversely, some do things that Excel doesn't). However, all major Macintosh spreadsheet programs provide a way to place and summarize information in cells, draw charts, and create macros.

Choosing a Spreadsheet

Microsoft claims that Excel 5 is the *best* spreadsheet for the Macintosh, but I think that's rather like saying that Apple makes the best Macintoshes. Of course it's true, but until there's real competition, I think it says rather more about their marketing clout than their product's excellence. If you want an industrial-strength spreadsheet, Excel is indeed the only game in town, but if you intend to stay mostly at the base camp, with occasional forays into tougher territory, some of the less ambitious entries are worth a look.

Microsoft Excel (EC)

Since its early versions, Excel has offered many important features: macros, formatting, notes on cells, access to every command from the keyboard, outlining, and much more. Perhaps the most striking difference in the latest version, **Excel 5** ($500), is that each document is now made up of 16 worksheets. (The group is called a *workbook*.) This makes it easy to organize all the information in one document, without having to put it all into one worksheet. Unfortunately, the added scroll bar and sheet tabs at the bottom of the window take up precious monitor space.

Version 5 also lets you edit the contents of a cell right in the cell—which means no more trips to the formula bar. Also, since you can select a portion of a cell, you can format it independently of the rest of the contents; you can, for example, put just one word of a title in italics instead of the whole thing. However, there's still only one level of Undo.

Excel 5, like Word 6, adopts Microsoft's latest alternative to dialog boxes, the new system of *tabs*, or option cards. Tab is a confusing term since the options are not actually contained on the tabs, but rather on the cards that they are attached to. At any rate, you can click on the tabs to see the plethora of options that Microsoft Excel 5 now offers.

GOOD FEATURE

I love Excel's new Auditing toolbar, an ingenious tool for analyzing spreadsheets and figuring out which formulas are based on which values. You can view (and then hide) tracer arrows that graphically point to a cell's precedents and descendants. The Notes button is now found on the Auditing toolbar.

Excel 5 also has a new Scenario Manager that lets you look at different possibilities in a "what-if" situation and then print them all at once. The PivotTable Wizard helps you chart cross-table data and then extract exactly what you need.

BAD FEATURE

Excel, like its cousin Word, has an AutoFormat tool that converts plain tables into formatted beauties. Unfortunately it doesn't use styles to make the change, so it's a real pain to make even a small change in the formatting.

Finally, perhaps one of the simpler tools will be the one to warm most Excel users' hearts: The AutoSum button now works on more than one cell at once and can also calculate grand totals. (See the Excel tips at the end of this chapter for more on how it works.)

Excel is a complete spreadsheet program whose advanced features have no rival in the Macintosh world. It's also demanding on your computer's storage and memory (requiring 8MB of storage and 2MB of RAM), as well as on your pocketbook. If your needs or resources are more limited, read on.

Ready-Made Spreadsheets (EC)

Several companies offer spreadsheet templates that you can use even if you haven't figured out how to use every function in your spreadsheet program. You simply enter the information in the spaces provided and the rest is done for you. Freemyers Design offers the A–Z Forms Templates for Macintosh, and Heizer Software has a complete catalog, from tax forms templates to invoicing. Although these spreadsheets are almost always in Excel format, you can often open them with other spreadsheet software.

What Ever Happened to... (EC)

Perhaps Excel's earliest and best competition came from Full Impact, a powerful spreadsheet from Ashton-Tate that disappeared when Ashton-Tate was eaten up by Borland International in 1991. Wingz, from Informix, despite an expensive promotional campaign, came and went quietly during 1991. Claris brought out Resolve in 1992 but bowed out shortly thereafter. Probably Lotus 1-2-3, which was able to secure 10 percent of the market in its heyday, was Excel's most important challenger. With 14 million users on the PC, Lotus had the name recognition, the user base, and the resources to make a lasting impression. And although the Mac version of Lotus 1-2-3 got rave reviews, Lotus says it will not continue to upgrade the product past version 1.1. Who's next?

Integrated Software (EC)

Although Microsoft is clearly the spreadsheet king, the spreadsheets included in integrated software packages like ClarisWorks and Microsoft Works are nothing to be sneezed at. They include basic spreadsheet capabilities, a limited set of functions, formatting, and two-dimensional charting. Take a look at Chapter 12, Integrated Software, for more information.

Biplane (EC)

Who's afraid of the big, bad wolf? Not **Biplane,** the fast, light spreadsheet from Night Diamonds Software ($60). Biplane fits on one 800K disk and takes up only 500K RAM, which makes it ideal for PowerBook users. Although it doesn't let you customize to the nines or outline, its 102 built-in functions and eight chart formats allow you to do practically everything you need. And Biplane can read and save Excel 4 files.

MacCalc (SA)

This gem of a program fills the bill for lots of personal spreadsheet users. It has no charting capabilities and its worksheets are small (999 rows by 124 columns) compared to Excel's (16,384 rows by 256 columns). It lets you assign different fonts, styles, and even notes to cells—all for just $140 list. If you need a basic spreadsheet program but have no use for the other modules in an integrated program, Bravo Technologies' **MacCalc** is the answer.

Microsoft Excel Tips

All of these tips work with Excel 5. Many also work with earlier versions.

General

Dividing spreadsheets logically (EC). If you use only one worksheet for several areas of data, place the second area below and to the right of the first (in a diagonal line). If you later need to add columns or rows to the first area, the second area will remain unaffected.

Open worksheets automatically (EC). If you generally work with the same worksheets, place them in folder called Excel Startup Folder (5) in the Preferences folder in the System folder. (Whew.) Every time you open Excel, these worksheets will open automatically.

Getting used to Excel 5 (EC). If you just started to get the hang of Excel 4 and want to make the change to version 5 gradually, select the Microsoft Excel 4.0 Menus in the General options card. You can use the menus that you're accustomed to, and Excel 5 will interpret your choice in terms of what's available for the new version. When you're ready to use the options in Excel 5 that aren't part of Excel 4, you can deselect the option.

Windows vs. Macintosh (EC). Microsoft has created just one manual for both Excel for Macintosh and Excel for Windows. Although the programs are practically identical, there are some options available only for Windows users. Keep that in mind as you read the manual.

Second, the keyboard shortcuts are slightly different. In general, what is [Control] in Windows is [⌘] in Macintosh, and what is [Alt] in Windows is [Option] in Macintosh. ([Shift] is [Shift], around the globe.) Generally, but not always, the manual points out which keys are used with which type of computer.

What do those cute little buttons mean? (EC). Icons are great, but like many other things, only in moderation. Microsoft has filled its programs with icons that are sometimes hard to distinguish.

To cheat, select Show Balloons in the Help menu and point to the button in question.

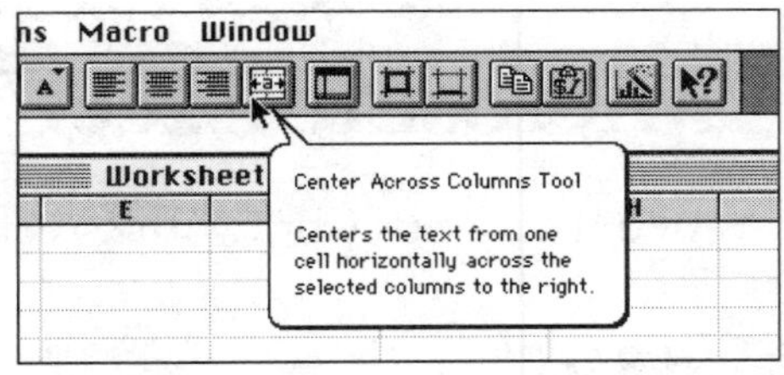

If you can't remember what an icon is for, select Show Balloons in the Help menu and point to the button in question.

Taking advantage of the Tip Wizard (EC). While you're working with Excel, it watches you and gives you the opportunity to find out if there is a simpler way to achieve your objective. When it has a suggestion to make, a light bulb appears in the button bar. Click it if you want to see the suggestion, or ignore it if you've already had enough suggestions that day.

Quick previews (EC). Since the top left corner of your worksheet is the part that is shown in the preview window in Excel's Find File dialog box, this is a perfect spot to put information about what the worksheet does. To see the preview, select Preview in the View dialog box.

Treating numbers like words (EC).There are times when you'd like Excel to just leave your numbers alone and not format them. Imagine that you're entering a list of part numbers or postal codes. The last thing you need is Excel lopping off your leading zeros or trying to interpret your text. The best solution is to select the area and then add an @ sign in front of the number. (@ tells Excel to treat the number as text.) You can also precede the number with an apostrophe to have Excel treat it as text. Watch out, though: When numbers are treated as text, you cannot perform calculations on them.

A bouquet of Excel shortcuts (SA/Bob Umlas/MS).

- ⌘Y repeats the last thing you did. This is especially useful for repeating something you did in a dialog box, without having to open the dialog box again.
- ⌘U activates the formula bar and places the insertion point at the end of the data there.
- There are three ways to cancel any change in the formula bar: clicking on the X icon to the left of it, or hitting ⌘. or Esc.

- The Calculate Now command on the Options menu affects all open spreadsheets, but if you hold down [Shift] before you open the menu, only the current spreadsheet is recalculated.

Selecting and Moving

Edit directly in the cell (EC). If you want to change the contents of a cell directly in the cell (without having to point at the formula bar), double-click the cell.

Moving a cell (EC). You can drag a cell by its border to move it to a new location. Hold down [Shift] to insert it between other cells. Hold down [Option] to copy it to the new location. Hold down [Shift] and [Option] to insert it and copy it.

Navigating from the keyboard (EC). You can use the keyboard to move around your document. Here are the keyboard shortcuts you might need:

Left, right, down, or up	[←][→][↓][↑]
Up or down one window	[Pg Up][Pg Dn]
To the beginning of the row	[Home]
To the beginning of the sheet	[Cmd][Home]
To the last cell containing data on the sheet	[⌘][End]
To next sheet	[Option][←] or [Option][→] or [⌘][Pg Up] or [⌘][Pg Dn]
From pane to pane	[F6]

Moving and copying sheets (EC). You can move a sheet by selecting its tab and dragging it to a new location—even in another workbook (just make sure the tabs are visible in both workbooks). If you want to move the sheets to a new workbook, drag them outside the workbook window and release the mouse button. Add the [Option] key to those actions, and you'll *copy* one or more sheets inside a workbook to another workbook, or to a new workbook.

Shortcuts for inserting columns and rows (SA/AN/EC). There are faster ways than the Insert command to insert a row or column.

- ⌘I inserts a new row above, or a new column to the left of, the selected one.
- Option-clicking on a row number inserts a new row above that row, and Option-clicking on a column letter inserts a new column to the left of that column.
- Option-clicking in a cell inserts a new cell above it.
- Shift Option-clicking the leftmost or bottommost cell in a selection inserts, above or to the left, as many cells as there were selected.

Creating new sheets (EC). When you open a new workbook in Excel 5, Excel automatically creates 16 sheets. You can change this setting by modifying the number in the Sheets In New Workbook box in the General options card. If you want to insert new sheets in an existing workbook, choose Worksheet from the Insert menu, or press Shift F11. To delete a sheet, click its name tab and press Delete.

Renaming sheets (EC). You can change the name of a worksheet by selecting Sheet in the Format menu, but it's much easier to double-click the little tab at the bottom of the sheet. The Rename dialog box will appear, and you can enter the new name.

Entering Data and Formulas

Entering the same info in several cells (EC). If you want to enter the same data (perhaps a constant) into several cells, select the cells, type the info, and then press Control Return. For more complicated or after-the-fact fills, read the next entry.

Filling cells (EC). Excel's AutoFill feature lets you enter data into several cells at once. Generally, you enter that data into the first cell and then drag the fill box (that teeny square in the lower-right corner of the cell) to the last cell desired. If you want Excel to recognize a series (5, 10, 15, etc.), enter the data in the first two or three cells, and then drag the fill handle. You can also double-click the fill box to fill in the series—Excel will look at the adjacent cells to decide how far the series should extend.

Sales	Jan-94	Feb-94	Mar-94	Apr-94
Peas	$125	$244	$150	$256
Carrots	$250	$260	$285	$350
Broccoli	$120	$150	$199	$325
Squash	$240	$221	$180	$125
Totals	$735			

The Fill box

Sales	Jan-94	Feb-94	Mar-94	Apr-94
Peas	$125	$244	$150	$256
Carrots	$250	$260	$285	$350
Broccoli	$120	$150	$199	$325
Squash	$240	$221	$180	$125
Totals	$735	$875	$814	$1,056

Excel adds these formulas automatically.

Double click the fill box...and Excel will look at the contents of the adjoining cells to see how far it should carry the series.

Excel automatically increments some values, like Jan and Qtr1, but it doesn't automatically increment individual numbers. If you want Excel to increment those values it normally leaves alone, or leave alone those values it normally increments, press Control while you drag the fill handle.

If you often type the same list—say the list of departments in your company—you can create a custom list so that after you type the first division, you can use the fill box to fill in the rest. To create a new list, click New on the Custom Lists options card.

Entering fractions (EC). If you type *1/2* into a cell, Excel will think you mean January 2 of the current year, even if that cell is not formatted as a date. To make Excel understand you're talking about the fraction one-half, type *0 1/2*.

Quick time (EC). You can enter the current time in an Excel cell by pressing ⌘-. To enter today's date, press ⌘;.

Watch that punctuation! (EC). If you're having trouble with a formula, check whether you've used one of the following punctuation marks and symbols incorrectly:

Parentheses — If you type a number in an Excel cell between parentheses, Excel understands that the number is negative. If you use parentheses in a formula, Excel will calculate the contents of the parentheses before completing the formula.

Commas — Since Excel uses commas to separate arguments in a formula, you should not use them to separate the thousands in a number in a formula.

Dollar signs — Since Excel understands that the dollar sign designates absolute references, you shouldn't use it to indicate dollars and cents. Instead, you can format the number so that the value shows in dollars and cents, if you wish.

Displaying formulas (EC). If you're working on a particularly vexing spreadsheet, it's often helpful to be able to quickly see which formulas do what and where they come from. Press [⌘] + apostrophe to view the formulas on screen. Press it again to see the resulting values. You can see where a formula comes from by displaying the precedents and descendants.

Looking at both values and formulas (MS/SA/AN). There's an easy way to simultaneously view the formulas in your spreadsheet and the values that result from them. Choose New Window from the Window menu, format the second window that opens to display formulas, and format the window you were working on to display values. Then just display both windows side by side.

Those Darned Error Messages (EC)

Until Excel's error messages are a little more descriptive, here's a table that should help you decipher them:

#DIV/0!	Your formula is trying to divide by zero, which is not allowed.
#N/A	There is a value that is not available for some reason.
#NAME?	You've used a name (say, of a range) that Excel doesn't recognize; if you're not using ranges, this message almost always means that you've misspelled a function name.
#NULL!	Specifies an invalid intersection of two areas, that is, an empty set.
#NUM!	Uses a number incorrectly.
#REF!	Refers to a cell that is not valid. This usually happens when you cut or move a cell. To avoid this error, use ranges instead of direct cell references.
#VALUE!	Uses an incorrect argument or operand (check your formula for extra or missing commas and parentheses and that all your functions are spelled correctly).
#####	This isn't really an error, it just means that the result is too long to fit in the column. Double-click the right border of the column to adjust.

Using a comma as a placeholder (EC). If you are using a function with several arguments and want to leave one blank, insert a comma in its place. Otherwise, Excel will have a fit and think you've forgotten to give it some vital information.

Using constants in your formulas (EC). If you want to use certain constants in your formulas, you can set off an area in the top left corner of your worksheet to hold those values and then use absolute references to that area in your formulas.

If you prefer to have those constants hidden from view, you can create invisible named constants with the Name command on the Insert Menu. First, choose Define. Then type in the name under Names in Workbook and the definition under Refers To. You can use this named constant in your formulas the same way you use named ranges.

Using AutoSum (EC). AutoSum is that button with the Σ—a sigma, to you Greek fans—the symbol that mathematicians use to denote a *sum*. Excel uses it for sums too; select a cell at the bottom of a list of numbers and then click the AutoSum button, and Excel will create a sum formula for you. Press Return if it selects the range correctly.

AutoSum has been improved with version 5. Here are a couple of neat tricks:

Select more than one cell (in your totals row) and click AutoSum to calculate the sum for all of them at once. If you prefer, you can select the cells you want to total and then click AutoSum—Excel will add the cells in the appropriate row.

To sum both rows and columns at the same time, select a range that includes the rows and columns that you want to sum, along with the row and column that will contain the sums. Then click the AutoSum button.

Before

Sales	Jan-94	Feb-94	Mar-94	Apr-94	Totals
Peas	$125	$244	$150	$256	
Carrots	$250	$260	$285	$350	
Broccoli	$120	$150	$199	$325	
Squash	$240	$221	$180	$125	
Totals					

After

Sales	Jan-94	Feb-94	Mar-94	Apr-94	Totals
Peas	$125	$244	$150	$256	$775
Carrots	$250	$260	$285	$350	$1,145
Broccoli	$120	$150	$199	$325	$794
Squash	$240	$221	$180	$125	$766
Totals	$735	$875	$814	$1,056	$3,480

Select the rows and columns that you want to sum, along with the row and column that will contain the sums, and Excel will calculate the sum formulas in both directions.

Before

Sales	Jan-94	Feb-94	Mar-94	Apr-94
Peas	$125	$244	$150	$256
Carrots	$250	$260	$285	$350
Broccoli	$120	$150	$199	$325
Squash	$240	$221	$180	$125
Vegetables	$735	$875	$814	$1,056
Blueberries	$750	$725	$780	$950
Peaches	$245	$275	$240	$295
Apples	$125	$130	$185	$150
Fruits	$1,120	$1,130	$1,205	$1,395
Grand Total				

After

Sales	Jan-94	Feb-94	Mar-94	Apr-94
Peas	$125	$244	$150	$256
Carrots	$250	$260	$285	$350
Broccoli	$120	$150	$199	$325
Squash	$240	$221	$180	$125
Vegetables	$735	$875	$814	$1,056
Blueberries	$750	$725	$780	$950
Peaches	$245	$275	$240	$295
Apples	$125	$130	$185	$150
Fruits	$1,120	$1,130	$1,205	$1,395
Grand Total	$1,855	$2,005	$2,019	$2,451

If your tables contain subtotal data (like the Vegetables and Fruits subtotal lines in this example), the AutoSum tool is smart enough to add up just those values to arrive at the correct grand total.

If you have already entered sum formulas within the area that you wish to sum, AutoSum will calculate the grand totals correctly and won't add the subtotals together with the individual numbers.

Getting a hand while you're entering a formula (EC). If you get stuck while entering a formula and need help, press [Ctrl][A] after typing the function name. The Formula Wizard will appear and will explain which arguments are needed and what the formula does.

If you just want to paste the names of the arguments, press [Ctrl][Shift][A] after typing the function name.

Checking the spelling of functions (MS). If you type the name of a function in the formula bar rather than using the Paste Function command, you run the risk of misspelling it. The trick is to type the name in lowercase letters. Correct function names are converted to all caps when you hit [Return] or [Enter], so if a lowercase name doesn't convert to all caps, you know it's wrong.

Calculating part of a formula (MS/SM). You can calculate part of a formula by selecting it and hitting [⌘][=]. That part is immediately converted to a value. If you want the value to remain, hit [Return] or edit it further first. If you only want a sneak preview of that part of the formula, cancel the calculation (by hitting [⌘][.], [⌘][Z], or [Esc], or by selecting Undo Typing from the Edit menu) before you do anything else, and it will return to its original state.

From relative to absolute (EC). If you've already entered a cell reference in a formula and want to change the reference type (relative, absolute, or mixed), you can type the dollar signs where needed or select the cell reference and press ⌘T until Excel places the dollar signs where you want them.

Using ranges (EC). You probably know what a regular range reference looks like: a couple of cell references divided by a colon. For example, A3:D7 means all of the cells from A3 to D7. It's a great way to select a whole column or block of cells at once.

If you use a comma to separate the cell references (for example, A3,D7), Excel understands that you want A3 and D7 but not the cells in between. If you put a space between two references, Excel determines the intersection; A3 D7 would generate the NULL! response, since there is no cell that is both A3 and D7. However, A3:D3 B2:B4 would select B3, since that cell is common to both ranges. (See "The great intersecting ranges trick," below.)

To reference a range or cell in a different worksheet in the same workbook, simply precede the cell reference with the name of the sheet and an exclamation point, Sales92!A3:D7.

Now that I've told you all this, you should know that the easiest way to refer to a set of cells is to give them a name you won't forget, such as Profits, Zipcodes, or whatever. Simply select the cells and then type a new name in the Reference area to the left of the formula box. Now you can use that name in other formulas to refer to the selected cells.

The great intersecting ranges trick (EC). Intersecting ranges always seem just a tad too complicated, but here's a great use for them. Imagine that you have built the following worksheet:

The range *Jan-94* refers to cells C7:C9, *Feb-94* refers to cells D7:D9, and so on.

If you enter *Mar-94 Profits* in any cell on the worksheet, the value returned will be the intersection of the two ranges, in this case, the value of cell E9: $3,000.

Similarly, the range *Sales* refers to cells C7:F7, *Expenses* refers to cells C8:F8, and so on.

	Jan-94	Feb-94	Mar-94	Apr-94	Totals
Sales	$485,000	$258,000	$253,000	$385,000	$1,381,000
Expenses	$250,000	$275,000	$250,000	$325,000	$1,100,000
Profits	$235,000	($17,000)	$3,000	$60,000	$281,000

You can use the column and row titles to name your ranges.

Now select the entire table, choose Name from the Insert menu, and click Create. This creates named ranges for each column and row. Now type into any empty cell *Mar-94 Profits* (that's a *space* between Mar-94 and Profits) and Excel will perform the *intersection* of the Mar-94 and Profits ranges—the cell that is common to both ranges, which, miracle of miracles, is exactly the cell that contains the profits you had in March. Nifty, huh?

Using the range pop-up menu (EC). To the left of the formula entry box, you'll find the Name box. To select a range, type it in this box, or select it from the pop-down menu.

Notes about notes (Bob Umlas/SA/AN/EC). Excel lets you attach notes to cells, to help you remember what you were thinking of when you wrote the formula (sort of like comments in a program). To attach a note window to the cell you're in, use the Note command on the Formula menu or press Shift⌘N.

Once a cell has a note, you will see a small red dot in the cell's upper-right corner. Double-click a cell with a note to see its note. You can hide the little red dots by clearing the Note Indicator check box in the View Options card.

Pressing Return closes the Notes dialog box. To move down a line within it, use Option Return. When the Notes window is open, you can scroll your spreadsheet in the background—but only if the insertion point is in the Cell and not if it's in the Note!

Shift⌘O selects all the cells in the spreadsheet that have notes. To review them, choose Show Info and Arrange All (both are on the Windows menu). Click on the spreadsheet window and use Return to jump from one cell to the next. As you do, the notes you made will be displayed in the Info window.

You can also print your notes. Select the Notes checkbox in the Sheet Options card in the Page Setup dialog box. Check Row and Column Headings to print the cell references along with the notes.

Formatting

Adjusting column widths and row heights (EC). If there is not enough room to display the contents of a cell, Excel will display a series of number signs (#####). You can adjust the width of a column or the height of a row with the

Column and Row options in the Format menu. But why bother? Just double-click the right border of the column or the lower border of the row to adjust the cell sizes to automatically fit in the contents.

Making more columns fit (EC). One of the things that really gets on my nerves is long titles above relatively narrow numbers. You want to see several columns on the page, and those long titles really screw you up. Your first option is to try wrapping the text (select Alignment from the Format menu and Wrap text in the Alignment dialog box).

	Midwestern	Eastern	Southern	Pacific Rim	Northeastern	Southwestern	Totals
Sales	$485	$258	$253	$385	$425	$465	$2,271
Expenses	$250	$275	$250	$325	$350	$425	$1,875
Profits	$235	($17)	$3	$60	$ 75	$ 40	$396

If your column titles are too long, either abbreviate them or set them vertically with the Alignment dialog box.

If that doesn't work as you'd like, try rotating the text 90 degrees (in the Orientation area of the Alignment dialog box). Although the titles will be slightly harder to read, you'll be able to fit many more columns on a page, and on a screen.

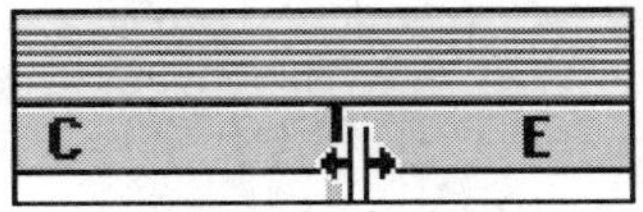

Place the pointer between the two columns until it turns into a double-lined pointer, and then drag to reveal the hidden column.

Hiding rows, columns, and individual cells (EC). Sometimes you don't want to display all the information you have. The easiest way to hide a column or row is to drag its right or bottom border until it coincides with that of the previous column or row. To reveal the hidden data, place the cursor at the border of the column or row until it changes into a double-lined pointer and then drag.

If you want to hide a single cell, format it with three semicolons. Its contents will be visible in the formula bar when the cell is active, but it will not print.

Use text boxes to point out important data (EC). If you want to call attention to one part of your data, use a text box. Click the Text box button and then drag the mouse to draw a box on the sheet. You can format the text as needed and then rotate it to point to the desired area. This is a great way to explain where your data came from. You can link a text box to

File Edit Formula Format Data Op
Normal
A2 1245000

	A	B	C
1	Mary's Salary		
2			
3			
4			
5			

Enter ;;; in the Code box of the Number Format dialog box to make the cell's contents invisible.

a particular cell by selecting the text box, clicking the formula bar, typing an equal sign, clicking the cell you want to link to, and then pressing Return. When you move the cell, the text box will be moved with it.

Charts and Graphics

Creating a separate chart sheet (EC). You can create a chart right on the same sheet as the data it comes from, but if you prefer to have the chart on its own sheet, select the data and then press F11.

Selecting hidden objects in a group (EC). Whereas in most drawing and desktop publishing programs you use ⌘ to cycle through the layers in a drawing, in Excel you must use the arrow keys. (As usual with Microsoft products, the possibilities are there, you just have to learn how to use them from scratch.)

Hiding graphics to speed scrolling (EC). You can temporarily hide the charts and graphics in an Excel spreadsheet to speed up printing and scrolling. Use ⌘6 to move through the three options.

Creating a chart from rectangular data (EC). If you're trying to create a chart from a table, make sure that the top left cell—which is usually empty—is also selected. Excel gets nervous and will create very strange charts if you don't give it rectangular data with which to work. This is especially important if you are selecting nonadjacent cells.

Modifying charts (EC). To change a chart's formatting or type, double-click the chart and then select the appropriate option. Once a chart is activated in this way, you can select the different elements of the chart with the arrow keys. Press Esc to deselect the chart.

To change a chart's size or location, click it once and then resize, move, or delete it.

Where page breaks start their work (EC). The easiest way to designate what should print is to select what you want to print and then select Set Print Area in the Option menu. If you prefer setting page breaks, remember that the break occurs so that the selected cell will be at the top left of the new page (not the bottom right of the last page).

10 Personal & Business Management

WHEN IT COMES RIGHT DOWN TO IT, managing your life and your business is about getting access to the right information when you need it, in a form that is instantly usable. Welcome to personal and business management software, designed to help you manage, among other things, your time, your schedule, your projects, your workload, your money, and your personal and business contacts.

A lot of those tasks belong to a relatively new genre of software called *personal information managers*, or PIMs. They combine the functionality of address books, calendars, schedulers, and to-do lists, among other things.

For financial management, there are a number of accounting packages for the Macintosh, including Quicken, a personal accounting program that is ranked among the best-selling software of all time. We've divided this category into software that makes sense for individuals and for small businesses.

And for managing aspects of your personal legal information, you'll also find prepackaged forms that ask only for your time and input.

Get to it!

Contributors

Connie Guglielmo (CG) is the chapter editor.

Scott Beamer (SB) has written a book and numerous articles on business software.

Rochelle Garner (RG), a former executive editor of *MacWEEK* and *Corporate Computing,* is now a freelance writer based in San Carlos, California. She has been writing about technology in business for the past 12 years and continues to keep track of her deadlines despite the number of PIMs now installed on her PowerBook.

Arthur Naiman (AN) edited the last four editions of *The Macintosh Bible,* from which parts of this chapter were taken.

Contents

Managing Time and Contacts (RG)

Until recently, programs lumped under the rubric of personal information managers (also known as PIMs) consisted of a hodgepodge of little programs. Your choices fell into these categories:

- address books, which were basically electronic versions of your Rolodex
- calendars, which allowed you to view a month or an entire year, fully color-coded so you could visualize upcoming project deadlines, meetings, appointments, and important family events (not to mention your dental checkup)
- to-do lists, which took the concept of the old bulleted list on paper to new heights by allowing you to, among other things, rank the priority of things to do and remind you with visual and audio alerts when it was time to do something

In recent years, though, PIMs have grown. Now a single program is designed to tackle the all-encompassing job of keeping track of your working life.

Take address books. For the most part, these handy electronic card files have been superseded by a new genre of PIM software called *contact managers*. Not content to simply track names and numbers, contact managers are true databases that let you organize, sort, and arrange every person in your life by whatever criteria you choose. Most also let you write letters, create faxes, and print on a variety of envelopes and labels. No wonder, then, that many people consider contact managers their most important software.

Calendar programs also have assumed larger roles—scheduling and reminding you of weekly meetings, appointments, and to-do items.

The latest twist in PIMs, though, is a merging of contact managers with schedulers that have been linked with System 7's Publish and Subscribe feature to automatically update and attach shared information. So when your calendar tells you that you've promised to have a conference call with Wilma and Fred on Friday, a mouse click not only finds their phone number but also dials the number for you.

GOOD FEATURE

Try Before You Buy

PIMs are supposed to simplify your life. But with a product definition like that, just what are you supposed to look for? With calendars, you want views you can read without eye strain, to-do lists you can set up without poring over a manual, and events you can reschedule in less time than it took to find out that your meeting's been changed. Contact managers? If you manage lots of names, you'll definitely want different ways to categorize and view the people in your life.

When it comes to PIMs, feature lists are practically irrelevant. It's not what these products do that counts, but how they do it. The reasons are twofold: First, the current features war means that practically every product offers variations on a theme. Does your calendar display multiday projects with banners across the days? You bet. But the real question is what you have to go through to put that banner where you want it.

The second reason is that the "personal" in personal information manager should be taken seriously. A series of steps that will seem annoying to some are the height of simplicity to others. You've heard the adage, "try before you buy"? Well, if you don't try out these products—really run them through their paces—there's a good chance you'll be disappointed. We turn to these programs to make sense of our disordered lives. To do that, though, they must work seamlessly with the way we think.

Your Choices

The PIMs described here—the most popular in the market according to the editors at the major Mac magazines—range in price from $80 and $350 and from simple address-book managers to programs designed to help you define your life and goals.

DateBook Pro and TouchBase Pro. Aldus's Consumer Division (now part of Adobe) sells the industry's top calendar/datebook duo, **DateBook Pro** and **TouchBase Pro,** available together for $150 or separately for $80 each. Each unit is strong on its own, and together they're unbeatable. The problem? Such power doesn't come for free: Expect to spend a lot of time with the manuals before getting down to work with these two.

DateBook Pro lets you slice, dice, and mince your days into bite-size chunks. And since DateBook Pro runs on a network, you can let your already over-stressed assistant (if you're lucky enough to have one) manage your day.

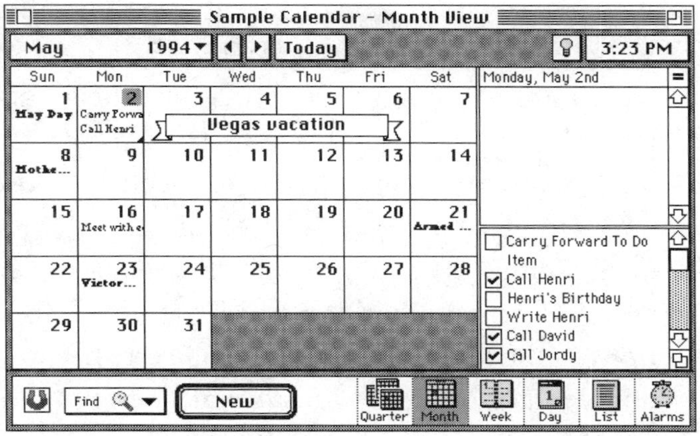

DateBook Pro's calendar shows at a glance how many meetings you've booked and projects you've got due on a monthly, weekly, daily, and even hourly basis.

Naturally, DateBook Pro provides alarms, reminders, to-do lists, and a calendar. But unlike other programs, DateBook Pro manages your day as if it were a fine piece of art to be crafted and molded. For instance, its "busyness" feature lets you see at a glance which parts of your day (morning, midday, afternoon) are swamped with meetings or deadlines and which have room for one more meeting. The *Gantt chart* (a visual representation of a project) is attractive, but it has some drawbacks. For one, it will display only Events (a day's occurrence with a beginning and an end) but not to-do items—and only in Day and Week views. That's not terribly useful for projects that, for example, involve research for two weeks, three days of writing, and then a deadline—with milestones in between. (More on Gantt charts and a description of some programs that create them better are described in the box on page 404.) Still, this mother of all datebooks is outstanding for people whose days are action-packed and who need help over the network to keep their lives in check. Now you just have to find the time to learn the program.

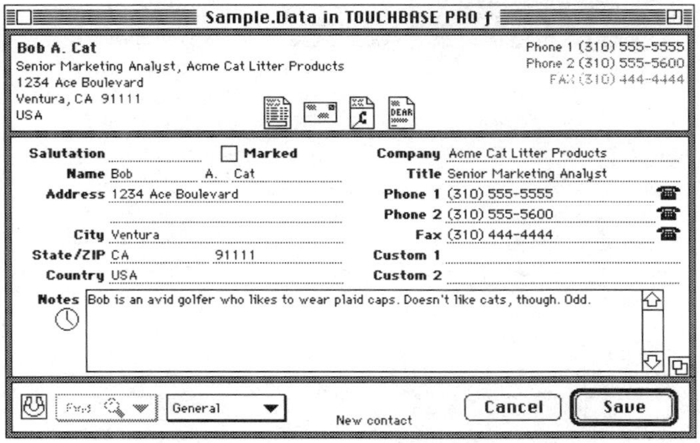

TouchBase Pro provides an elegant interface for its electronic Rolodex. From within each Rolodex-style card, you can also create a fax cover sheet or compose a letter with address and salutation in place. Everything is just a mouse click away.

TouchBase Pro is an elegant electronic Rolodex. Unlike some other contact managers, it has a fairly rigid structure for entering information—names, numbers, and addresses must be entered in their respective fields. But it does provide a handy way to search for contacts. From within each contact's Rolodex-style "card," you can create a fax cover sheet; compose a letter (with address and salutation in place before you type); dial the phone; maintain a phone call log; and print a range of envelopes, labels, and address books. Built-in shortcuts let you enter information via pop-up or pop-down lists, or simply by typing abbreviations—TouchBase Pro fills in the rest. If you've got DateBook Pro, a simple double-click brings up a history of all events and to-do items associated with the person you're looking up. When used on Macs equipped with System 7, the Pro twins link and update each other.

GOOD FEATURE

GOOD FEATURE

Arrange. This program ($350 from Common Knowledge) is a graphically elegant program that suggests bare-bones simplicity. Don't be fooled. On top of the usual assortment of contact management features (including call tracking, multiple contact lists, and a plethora of ways to filter and sort those contacts), as well as calendars and schedulers that are linked (automatically), it comes with other goodies. These include a Grabber, which lets you capture information from other applications as well as from on-line services, e-mail, and CD-

U.S. Government

Name	Phone	Fax
Federal Information Center	(800) 726-4995	
President Bill Clinton	(202) 456-1414	
Hillary Rodham Clinton	(202) 456-6266	
Vice President Al Gore	(202) 456-2326	
Mike Espy - Agriculture	(202) 720-2791	(202) 720-2166
Ron Brown - Commerce	(202) 482-4901	(202) 482-4901
Les Aspin - Defense	(703) 697-5737	
Richard Riley - Education	(202) 401-1576	(202) 401-3130
Hazel O'Leary - Energy	(202) 586-5575	(202) 586-0834
Carol Browner - EPA	(202) 260-2080	(202) 260-6257
Donna Shalala - Health	(202) 690-6867	(202) 690-6608
Henry Cisneros - HUD	(202) 708-1420	
Bruce Babbitt - Interior	(202) 208-6416	(202) 208-6956
Robert Reich - Labor	(202) 219-7316	(202) 219-8699
Warren Christopher - State	(202) 647-6575	(202) 647-7120
Janet Reno - Attorney General	(202) 514-2007	(202) 514-5331
Fredrico Pena - Transportation	(202) 366-5580	
Lloyd Benston - Treasury	(202) 622-2960	(202) 622-1999

Arrange doesn't feel like a database for nothing. It's built around a database, allowing you to create records for each of your projects, including descriptions, categories, and lists of people (of course, stored in the program's contact list) who will be working with you on the project. You can also assign a priority level to each project.

ROMs; file synchronization for PowerBook users who need to reconcile files on the road with those back at home or in the office; and the ability to launch files and applications from outside the program. Over a network, Arrange lets users link to documents stored on a server, marks who last had their hands on a networked document, and shares information over an e-mail system (it supports most of the popular e-mail systems, described in Chapter 23).

Here's the catch: The database that drives Arrange is both the program's strength and its weakness. Everything about Arrange screams "database," from its infinitely customizable fields and topics, to its interface, up through the manual. Common Knowledge even offers a developer's tool kit for crafting custom database applications. But don't expect to turn this puppy into a show dog without some training. Yours, that is. Still, if you already understand databases—or are at least willing to invest some sizable up-front effort—you can arrange Arrange in whatever way suits your fancy.

Dynodex is a simple-to-use contact manager that includes templates for writing short memos and letters. Of course, the address information on the letter can easily be culled from the contact manager.

Dynodex. With **Dynodex** ($60), Portfolio Software merged simplicity and graphical elegance to create a beautiful little contact manager. No manual is necessary—its intuitive icons are complemented nicely by Dynodex's on-screen help. It also includes three formats for short memos and letters, and it tries to anticipate commonly typed words—filling in CA when you type C in the State field, for example. Definitely a nice touch. (Unless, of course, you live in Connecticut or Colorado, in which case you can select the appropriate state from the pop-up list.) There's also a new control panel device, called Dynofind, that lets you look up information in multiple Dynodex files without running the Dynodex software.

The interface has three dimensions, and not just for show: Press Option while clicking on any raised box, and up pops a list of commonly used words and abbreviations for that field. For instance, if you click on the Title box with Option pressed, you'll see a list of titles such as President, Engineer, and Vice President. Click on the Edit option in every pop-up menu to add and delete shortcuts. Type *p*, and the word "president" instantly appears. Portfolio promises a calendar in the summer or fall of 1994 that will link to Dynodex.

FirstThingsFirst Proactive. Imagine a cross between a calendar and an outliner that lets you jot down thoughts, ideas, and goals. You've just envisioned **FirstThingsFirst Proactive** from Visionary Software ($149)—a weird hybrid of appointment keeper and thought organizer. The core of the program is a full-featured outliner that lets you develop your ideas and plans (I really need a better handle on expenses), name your goals (reduce costs for next month), and then develop related tactics to meet them (buy less Scotch tape). Then, when you're ready to put deadlines to those goals, you can drag the pertinent item over to the calendar. It's odd, but it works.

While the outliner is this program's main attraction, the calendar is no afterthought. In fact, you can create as many interconnected calendars as you can think of, if that will help you organize your day. (Maybe a special calendar for when to add chemicals to your hot tub, even.) What's more, you can schedule events, set up reminders—just about everything that you can do in every other calendar program. And because Proactive can run over a network, you can even distribute a calendar that delegates tasks to someone else.

In Control. Attain's entry, **In Control** ($130), is the ultimate to-do list manager, making changing or adding or deleting anything easy: As the commercial says, Just do it. It's a dream to figure out, easy to format, and attractively laid out. You can immediately start filling out lists of things to do, places to go, and dates on which those things must be accomplished. The resulting lists can then be displayed automatically in the program's calendar. Moving tasks to different days of the month is just a matter of drag and drop—from the list view onto the calendar or from one day to another. And it's all made even simpler by a remarkably easy-to-understand manual. With the latest version, In Control 3, Attain has extended that ease to managing simple projects: Its to-do list lets you track events

Project Managers: The Real Story (RG)

Do you ever get the feeling that a simple scheduler can't handle all the tasks involved in your important project? Do you contemplate using a project manager instead? Well, maybe you should, but proceed with caution. Project managers—programs such as Micro Planning International's **X-Pert**, Lucas Management Systems' **Artemis Schedule Publisher**, and Welcom's **OpenPlan**—are big, complex programs intended for managing huge numbers of people and tasks.

How huge? Welcom's OpenPlan ($4,200 for the single-user version), for example, was an invaluable tool for managing construction of the now-defunct Supercolliding Superconductor.

Artemis—another major name in project management—is a big supplier to the aerospace industry. You'll find its mainframe, VAX, PC, and Mac versions of Schedule Publisher ($2,000) used throughout the Space Shuttle project.

Project Scheduler 5 ($700), from Scitor; **Manager** ($700), from Micro Planning International; **Project** ($700), from Microsoft; and **MacProject II** ($600), from Claris, are all intended for less-daunting tasks—like building a house. And it's possible that one of these programs will, in fact, offer the kind of resource management (resources in this arena are defined as people and material) you need for that Excedrin-size project. But don't expect to just pick up and run with the program—not even with the acknowledged ease-of-use leader, MacProject II.

That's because project management is a complex discipline in its own right, developed by the U.S. Navy in the early 1950s to help build the Polaris submarine. Think about that for a minute: The discipline grew out of the government, never known for taking the easy approach to anything. And that discipline is the foundation for all these programs. So don't blame the product if it seems obtuse in its approach to project management. Its philosophical foundation started off that way.

that have a date but not a set time when they must be done. Its daily schedule displays a handy little graph of your day's activities—with bars showing your most heavily booked times. It also has an integrated calendar with daily, weekly, and monthly views, with a nice implementation of banners that don't obliterate text you've already typed in. And through its use of Apple events, In Control works directly with FileMaker Pro databases—eliminating duplicate databases for you FileMaker Pro users who, for instance, may have been using your customer database as your contact list. Like Arrange, InfoDepot, and many other programs in this arena, In Control lets you link information to other documents or applications. Time to update Fred's employee evaluation? Just click on the linked word processed document and it's on your screen. Now get to work.

GOOD FEATURE

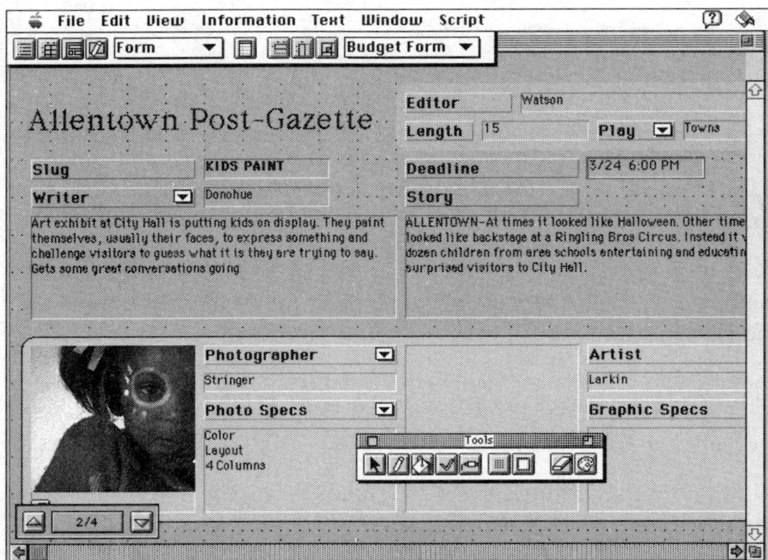

InfoDepot is being tested by the Gannett Newspaper Group as a story-tracking program that would allow editors to assign reporters, photographers, and deadlines to each story. The key is that the program presents the editor with a visual look at who's working on what and what status the story has; because it's tied into other programs via Apple events, that status is constantly updated.

InfoDepot. Think of **InfoDepot** (formerly FairWitness, $300), from Chena Software, as a kind of information overseer. In many ways, InfoDepot is for the professional whose job *is* time management. People just wanting to organize their appointments and to-do lists would probably find this program overkill.

The program starts you off in outline view, letting you put down ideas, events, and things to do or manage in a kind of free-form fashion. From there, you can transform that view into a timeline, an assortment of tables, or a form of your own design. But that's just the beginning. The neat part about InfoDepot is its support of Apple events; InfoDepot can automatically link and update other Apple event–aware applications, including the Aldus and Now bundles, Microsoft Excel, QuarkXPress, PageMaker, and WordPerfect. On the simplest level, that means you develop an outline of things to do in InfoDepot, and then reach out to other calendar- and contact-managers that you might prefer. It also means that InfoDepot can be set up to stretch well beyond the personal information category. The Gannett Newspaper Group, for instance, is testing InfoDepot as its story-tracking program. Click on an image of a photograph, and InfoDepot takes the photo editor to the actual electronic image. (Apple events and how they can be used are described in Chapter 3.)

InfoDepot takes some getting used to, since it does things in a way that isn't immediately obvious. (Example: When in table mode, you can click your mouse outside a column to create a new column.) But it does have some nice features. Just set up a column for dates, then type in a string à la *1/17; 1/24*. Hit Return and those numbers automatically transform into *January 17, 1994 to January 24, 1994*. That date string will automatically place itself on an InfoDepot calendar or in a calendar from Aldus or Now. Everything works over the network, allowing users to share and make changes to the same documents.

InTouch and DateView. You want simple? The venerable little address book from Advanced Software, **InTouch** ($100), fits that description. You bring up the old-style address book from the menu. That approach buys you speed—for quickly calling up that phone number you need while working on your research report. What you see when you call up InTouch is a Rolodex-size screen that now, with version 2.0.8, sports a colorful, immediately graspable interface for working with names and addresses. InTouch lets you type in free-form information, an approach that's comfortable to use, although it poses problems if you want to export your information into another program that uses fields.

Beyond the address book, it also sports a handy search facility, a calendar reminder, a phone dialer, and a print facility set up for a variety of envelopes. With its built-in Snap printing utility, you can print envelopes and labels from your word processor without first having to launch InTouch.

Until earlier this year, InTouch was one of the last stand-alone address books on the market. Now, though, InTouch has an appointment and to-do list companion—**DateView 1.0** ($100), which works with InTouch or by itself.

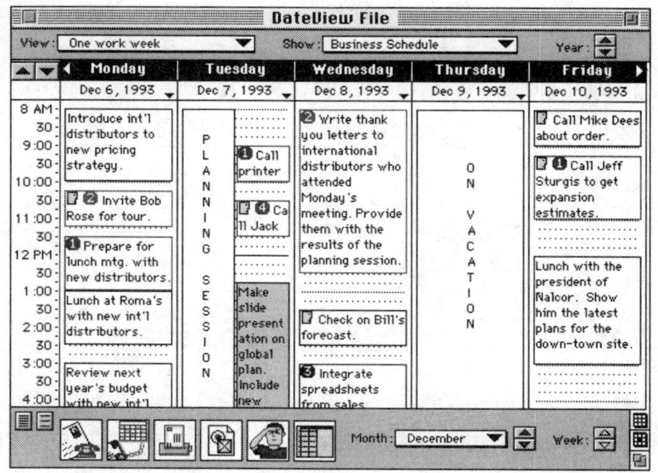

DateView is a simple and easy-to-use appointment book and to-do list companion to InTouch. Need to look at your schedule for the week ahead? DateView's got it for you, day by day.

As with InTouch, figuring out DateView is simplicity itself. Buttons and dialog boxes are self-explanatory. Create events by double-clicking on a day or by clicking and dragging to the displayed beginning and end times. Reschedule events just by grabbing and dragging. And like the other offerings that pair contact and appointment managers, InTouch and DateView share and update mutual information over System 7.

Unfortunately, DateView comes off as a decidedly wimpy relative to its hefty calendar competition. It doesn't have a zillion ways to change fonts, format layouts, or cut up your day. What it does offer is a fast way to call up and peruse your week's schedule so you can return to the task at hand.

GOOD FEATURE

Now Contact and Now Up-to-Date. Entering information in **Now Contact** ($100) from Now Software is a simple matter of tabbing through different fields. Once you enter information, you can decide how the program will arrange and display it. One nice feature with Now Contact: You can edit information while in List view (nearly every program has one—which lists and sorts all your contact files—but few programs let you modify contact information from that view). Later, you can scan lists of your different contacts, organized by category. There's also a bare-bones word processor for drafting form letters and faxes, and a document logger that lists all correspondence for each contact. Perhaps the best part of Now Contact is QuickContact, a pull-down menu (added to the Finder) that shows your most-often-called contacts and phone numbers. It's available at any time from any app.

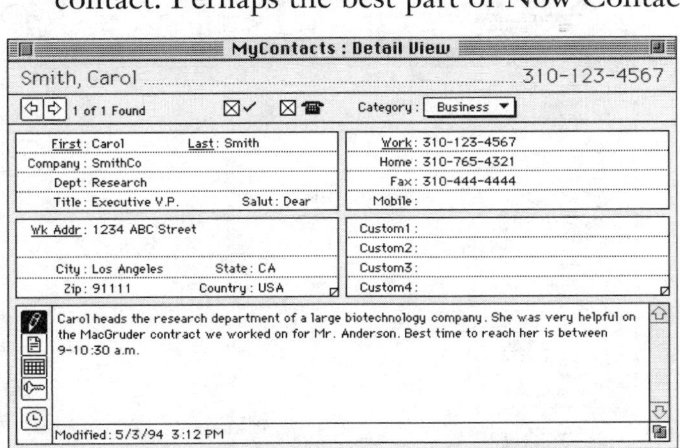

Now Contact gives you instant access to your contacts; simply click on a contact in the List view and up pops a Rolodex-style card with complete details.

But while Now Contact is a pretty good contact manager, its real strength is its integration with **Now Up-to-Date** ($100). Like the Aldus Pro twins, the Now bundle ($150) links to form a serious information manager. With both programs on your hard disk or network server, for instance, you can see all events and to-do items for each person on your contact list. You can even create new Events in Now Up-to-Date from within Now Contact. Both programs are server-based (they can be accessed by anyone on your network), opening up schedules and contacts to your work group or small office.

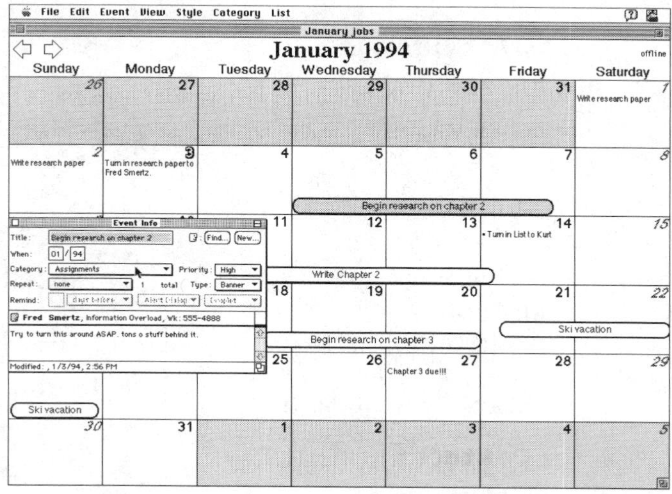

Want to set aside a few days to work on a special project? Putting a banner across a few days in your calendar to remind you when you need to work on that project is a breeze with Now Up-to-Date. Of course, a mouse click brings up a window with complete project details in case you look at the calendar and forget what the project is all about.

While powerful, Now Up-to-Date offers fewer options for dissecting your day than does Aldus DateBook Pro, its closest rival. But from its beautifully laid out calendars to its color-coded to-do lists, Now Up-to-Date really does everything you'd want from an appointment program. Events can be set to recur with a dizzying range of frequencies (from every day to the first Wednesday of each month). To-do items can be scheduled for specific days or whenever you get around to them, and items can be sorted and organized according to a variety of categories.

Now Up-to-Date is an absolute breeze to learn and use. Unlike Aldus's Pro twins, you don't have to be tied to the manual to find your way around. You can quickly add to-do's, events, and holidays to the calendar just by typing. Want a banner across several days? ⌘B does the trick—then just grab and stretch to fit. And if an event or to-do involves someone in your Contact database, just double-click on the item in the calendar, tell who in Contacts should be associated with that task, and attach it. If you want to parse your days, weeks, and months into a million facets, turn to Aldus DateBook Pro. If you want a more limited set of features that you don't have to be a pro to learn, you'll find Now Up-to-Date more your style.

GOOD FEATURE

Gantt Charts

(RG)

When an a appointment keeper/calendar does too little, and a project manager does too much, you might find that a Gantt chart program is just right. These programs include Varcon Systems' **Great Gantt!** ($200), Mainstay's **MacSchedule Plus** ($400), AEC Software's **FastTrack Schedule** ($280), and Micro Planning International's **KeyPlan** ($400).

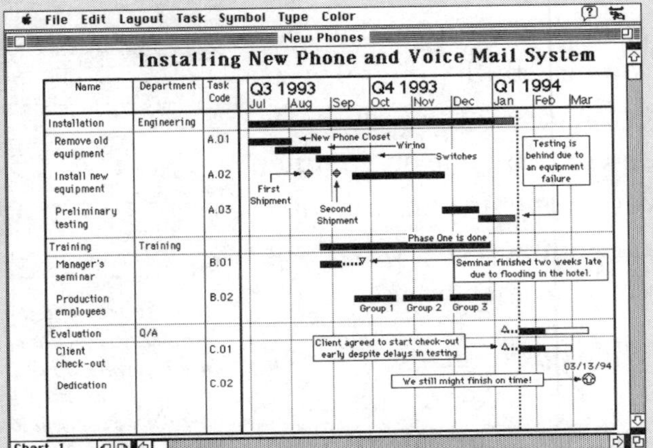

Gantt charts, such as this one created by Great Gantt!, are essentially visual timelines that show you important deadlines and milestones for the projects you're working on.

Gantt charts are essentially timelines that show you important milestones, as well as those important task dependencies. They give you an instant view of the project status. Of course, to be useful, you must constantly update the programs—otherwise you're working with yesterday's news.

Unlike full-blown project managers—which can track virtually unlimited numbers of calendars, people, and tasks— these programs are aimed at people managing smaller projects, with up to maybe 30 tasks. They are also much simpler to grasp and use than their heavy-duty counterparts. Within them, you can define start and finish dates, define dependencies (task B requires the completion of task D, for instance), and see important milestones.

What distinguishes these programs from the simple schedulers listed in the PIM marketplace is their ability to show you how the project is going and whether you'll make your deadline.

If you need to manage projects in addition to managing your busy day, consider adding one of these Gantt makers to your management arsenal.

Rae Assist. For PowerBook owners whose workaday lives depend on the Filofax, you have a friend in **Rae Assist** ($200). In fact, Rae Technology pushes that day-minder metaphor throughout its program. Every page, every form, every calendar looks like an electronic facsimile of those pervasive little binders. Like its leather-bound brethren, Rae Assist is set up to keep track of business and personal contacts; handle to-do lists and projects; and help plan your activities by the day, week, or month. Its electronic foundation lets you link people and companies to projects, as well as categorize each lead and customer.

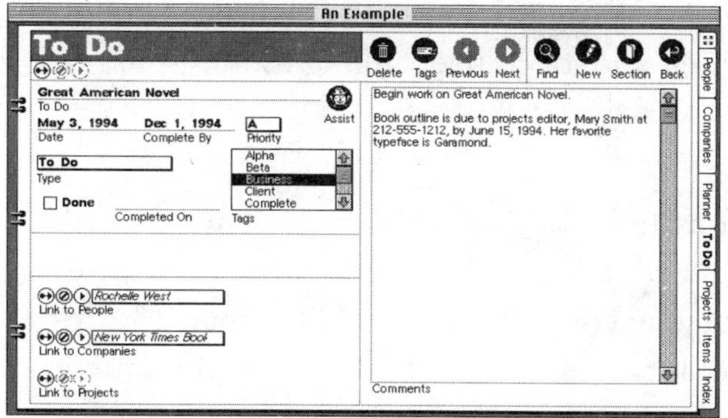

Rae Assist mimics the look of paper-based leather-bound binders that we're so used to carrying around. The contact manager presents information in a simple and easy-to-read interface.

Rae Assist's drawbacks stem from an interface that manages to stress ease of use over simplicity. Case in point: With every item you enter, you must first click New, and when you're finished, click OK. It's annoying. Worse, there's no sense of being able to reach in to organize the information the way you want it. The simple act of jotting down projects, to-do lists, and names requires more patience than I possess. (It doesn't help that Assist makes a mechanical "clunk" sound when you switch views.)

Managing Your Money

Financial management applications run the gamut from low-cost programs, designed to automate your checkbook and help you prepare your taxes, to multimodule integrated applications, for managing the books of companies ranging in size from mom-and-pop stores to large corporations.

Personal accounting programs, designed to help individual users get a grip on their personal expenses, generally rely on a very simple interface (usually a check or check register). Once entered and categorized, information can be retrieved and viewed in a variety of ways. Every time you write a check, for instance, you can assign it a category (such as food, rent, or entertainment). With a few clicks, you will see how much you've spent on food that month, for a few months, or for the year to date.

The small-business programs are the next step up, based on the double-entry accounting system of debits and credits and offering more sophisticated account-tracking and reporting capabilities, including balance sheets, profit and loss statements, and amortization schedules.

The programs selected and described here were chosen after sifting through product reviews in the major magazines, and, of course, talking to lots of users.

Personal Accounting

With just a little bit of time and effort (and a relatively small outlay of cash), you'll be able to get your finances in order using one of the programs in this category. Don't let the low prices fool you; you'll find a myriad of fancy features here—from tools for budget planning to creating and analyzing investment portfolios.

BARGAIN

Quicken (SB/CG). **Quicken** ($70), a checkbook program from Intuit, gets high marks for ease of use. The screen looks just like a check. Quicken keeps all your accounts—checking, savings, credit cards, loans, investments, and cash—in a single file. The program prints checks (on standardized check forms you can buy from Intuit), pays bills, updates your register, and reconciles your bank account. (When your account doesn't reconcile, the program offers to make an entry of the difference so it will reconcile next time. You decide if that's a good practice or not.)

GOOD FEATURE

Version 4 adds QuickFill, a feature designed to simplify data entry. As you start typing an entry for a transaction, Quicken does a quick search to see if it matches a transaction you've entered before and automatically fills in the rest of the text for you. Improved 2-D and 3-D graphs give you a quick overview of your income and expenses. As you record a transaction, identify what it was for—groceries, phone, utilities, new software—and the program tracks your spending and creates graphs showing you visually how your money is being spent. You can also create graphs showing your net worth and your budget plan versus actual income and expenses.

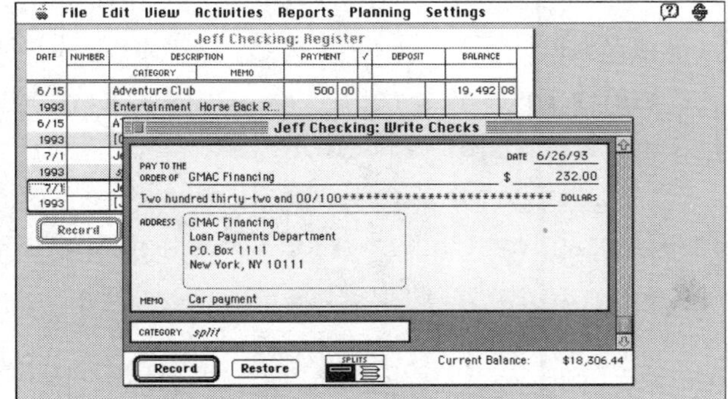

Perhaps one of the reasons that Quicken is one of the best-selling packages of all time is because the personal financial manager is so simple to use. Entering information is as easy as writing a check.

Version 4 also offers a slew of features for tracking investments, including things like stocks, bonds, mutual funds, CDs, and IRAs, and for creating reports showing you the status of your portfolio. There's even a feature for importing stock prices from Prodigy's QuoteTrack on-line stock-information service. (See Chapter 22 for more on Prodigy and other on-line services.) Loan amortization tools allow you to calculate changes in principal and interest as you make payments, and create payment schedules. Quicken also allows you to export data to spreadsheet and tax programs.

Keeping Up On All Accounts (CG)

Like every other category of Mac software, there are new entries in the accounting market on an ongoing basis. One way to get a handle on the range of programs available is to contact the Macintosh Accounting Consortium (MAC), a nonprofit organization sponsored by Apple, major software developers, and a network of consultants and CPAs who use these programs. The consortium will provide you with product information as well as make recommendations on products. If nothing else, MAC is a good place to start gathering product literature. Based in Campbell, California, MAC can be reached by phone at 408/366-8330 or by fax at 408/364-1662. You can also reach them via AppleLink at MACACCT.

MacMoney (CG). Survivor Software's **MacMoney** 4 ($80) is also a low-cost and easy-to-use record keeper and financial management program geared toward individuals. You enter data in a window resembling, yes, a check, and you can also print checks using the program. MacMoney tracks bank accounts, credit cards, cash, assets, liabilities, income, and expenses. It has an optional budgeting feature and Plans Menu for planning loan, savings, and retirement strategies.

You'll also find elaborate reports; the capability to categorize your accounts, expenses, and income into 1,000 categories (things like entertainment, mortgage, food, and gifts) that are easily accessed from a scrollable window; and support for exporting data as a tab-delimited text file to spreadsheets, databases, and other programs.

If you have a home-based or small business and really don't want to make the leap into small-business accounting programs, Survivor offers an $80 add-on module, called InvoicIt 1.41, that adds invoice and accounts-receivable functionality to MacMoney. InvoicIt can handle up to 2,000 clients with name, address, telephone, billing terms, and year-to-date totals for each account.

Managing Your Money (SB). Both Quicken and MacMoney do a better job of managing your checkbook than **Managing Your Money** ($40) from MECA Software. What made MYM different from its competitors was its tools for managing stock portfolios and planning and tracking life insurance needs, retirements savings, kids' college funds, and taxes, but both Quicken and MacMoney now offer similar features.

With MYM, you have to spend a lot of time learning the program and entering your financial statistics. Most users probably never get modules in operation and are haunted by their vows to enter more data "next weekend." Once you get MYM up and running, though, all the parts work together well. For instance, if you sell some stock, entering the sale in your portfolio also updates the balance of your checking account, your net worth, and your tax files.

The clearly written manual and extensive on-screen help make the program fairly easy to use. And you can also get the CheckFree electronic bill-paying service as a built-in option.

MYOB Accounting (SB/CG). MYOB (which stands for Mind Your Own Business) is a low-cost integrated application that offers general ledger, accounts receivable and accounts payable, inventory, and checkbook modules. Although

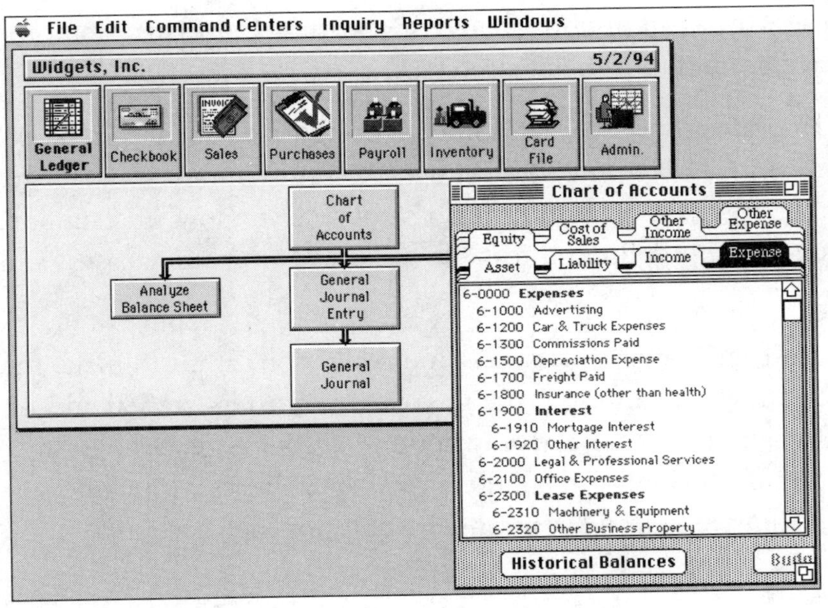

For small-business owners who want a program that's easy to set up and use, MYOB is a good choice. Entering financial information is simple and straightforward, with electronic invoices, for instance, that look like the invoices you're used to seeing.

Best!Ware (formerly Teleware) designed the program specifically for small-business owners, it can be used for personal financial management and is considered a Quicken competitor. Two versions are available: **MYOB Accounting** ($100), and **MYOB Accounting with Payroll** ($200) for, obviously, small businesses with employees.

MYOB is a good choice for people who don't know much about keeping books and don't particularly want to learn. The manual even offers three ways to set up, for users who have different expectations: those who are starting a new business and want to do things right, those who are migrating from some other way of doing books (another program or doing books by hand), and those who want a quick-and-dirty start (rather like an electronic checkbook), with the option to later expand their use of the program.

MYOB offers a card file that automatically keeps track of customer, vendor, and employee information, and it can serve as an electronic phone and address book with auto dial. The to-do list automatically alerts you to overdue receivables, payables discounts about to expire, and inventory items that need to be reordered. As if that's not enough, MYOB also automatically prompts you to make recurring payments, such as your rent, on a timely basis. All in all, it's one of the easiest small-business accounting packages to set up and use.

MacInTax Tax Planner (SB/CG). An overwhelming favorite since its introduction in 1985, **MacInTax** ($80), from Intuit, helped define tax planning on the Macintosh. The easy-to-use program, continually updated to reflect changes in tax law, helps you fill out your tax forms. To simplify the whole process of putting your financial information in digital form, Intuit provides good on-line help, and a feature called "The EasyStep Interviewing Systems" guides you through the process of setting up your tax forms. You can import financial data from Quicken into the program, which should save you some typing time if all goes well.

On screen, you see an exact replica of the paper tax forms, but there's an important difference: The forms do calculations for you, and they're linked so that a figure you input (or that is calculated) on one form automatically appears where you need it on other forms (and changes if the first figure changes). With the W-4 withholding allowance calculator, you can determine how much you need to withhold from your earnings so that you don't end up owing money at the end of the year. The estimated tax calculator computes your estimated tax payment based on the IRS's 1040 form. The 1040ES and W-4 forms are IRS-approved and can be printed and submitted as tax documents. (For another $50, you can buy Intuit's MacInTax State Supplements, which provide tax forms for individual states.)

If you dread figuring out your taxes and filling out tax forms, MacInTax may be for you. Although you still have to enter the financial information in your 1040, at least the program does all the calculations for you.

Not everyone may need tax software. If your tax situation is very simple, it may take longer to install MacInTax than to do your returns by hand. However, if you're interested in doing "what-if" tax scenarios for periods up to five years, or if you want to see the difference in dollars between submitting "married filing jointly" and "married filing separately" statements, or if you have a fair number of entries on Schedules A, C, D, or E, you're a good candidate for MacInTax.

Small Business

Keeping a good set of books can sometimes make the difference between survival and failure for a small business. Remember, though, that someone has to be responsible for learning the software, setting it up, and using it on an ongoing basis. There's also no benefit in having the data in electronic form and generating lots of reports if no one uses the reports to make informed management decisions.

Small-business accounting packages are aimed at companies that have to keep track of the finances and costs associated with a few employees and numerous suppliers and clients. These applications provide the kinds of reports that investors, banks, and, of course, the IRS require of businesses, including comprehensive balance sheets, profit & loss (P&L) statements, tax and benefit calculations for employees, client records (including billing and receivables), inventory reports, cost of goods sold, and the like. You'll also find that the functionality needed to do these tasks is relegated to various modules, which are designed to work in an integrated and seamless environment (changes in one module for one account are reflected in the account records in other modules when necessary). Most companies offer free demo versions of their programs, allowing you a chance to see what you're getting yourself and your staff into ahead of time—something to take advantage of. If you don't take the time to investigate first, it could end up costing you time and money later on.

Peachtree Accounting 2.0 (SB/CG). **Peachtree** is a solid small-business accounting package, modestly priced at $170, that boasts an installed base of nearly one million businesses. Its modules include General Ledger, Accounts Receivable, Accounts Payable, Payroll, Inventory, Job Costing, Bank Reconciliation, Purchase Order, Budgeting, and Custom Forms Design. All the modules are integrated, meaning that information entered or changed in any module is automatically updated in all the other modules. The program is designed to handle companies of all shapes and sizes, supporting an unlimited number of transactions, customers, vendors, accounts, items, jobs, and employees. It also includes an interactive HyperCard tutorial, an on-line accounting basics textbook and glossary, and many handy checklists that help with initial setup and routines such as closing.

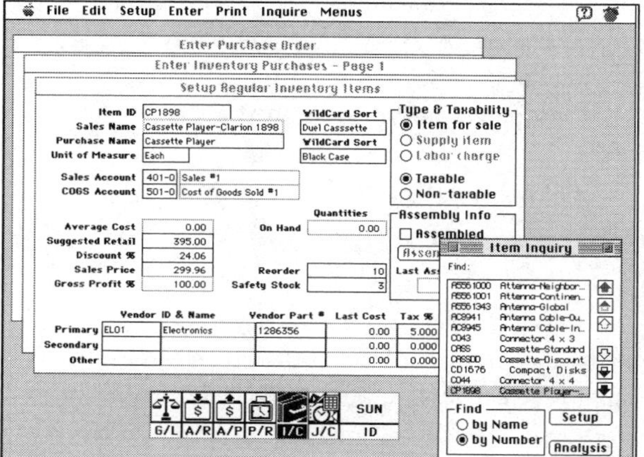

One of the most popular small-business accounting packages on the Mac, PeachTree integrates a variety of modules for tracking your business. Entries are straightforward, and an interactive HyperCard tutorial provides you with on-line accounting basics.

Each accounting period can be open, closed, or locked. A locked period can be viewed with all transaction detail, but it can't be edited; this prevents accidental changes to the wrong period. The program also offers multilevel password security to protect your business information.

MultiLedger and Payroll (SB). CheckMark Software's **MultiLedger** is the small- to medium-size-business package that accountants prefer. For them, it's straightforward and elemental, but if you aren't an accountant, its professional accounting practices may be somewhat opaque.

For $400, you get General Ledger, Accounts Receivable, Accounts Payable, and Inventory modules; a multiuser version is available for $700. CheckMark also publishes the highly respected **Payroll** (priced at $300), a payroll system for managing salaried and/or hourly employees that can be used by itself or as a module within MultiLedger.

The program is rather conservative—each month must be closed (although adjustments can be made to any month in the current year). While it provides a wide variety of reports, the reports can't be customized. And screens have a plain-Jane look, though pop-up menus speed data entry. The bottom line: MultiLedger is a good choice for those confident about keeping books.

The High Road (CG)

Many small-business managers decide they don't have the time or expertise to thoroughly research which accounting package would be best for them, so, saying they want "the best," they ask for recommendations from dealers or consultants. Or they ask their accountant (who probably doesn't use a Mac). In either case, the answer is likely to be one of the multimodule, sophisticated packages. But a high-end accounting system makes sense only for those who have industrial-strength needs—a networked environment, thousands of transactions per month, and two or more full-time employees working on the books. Get the picture?

Some of the names you'll come across in this category include **A4** ($2,000 to $6,000), from Softek Design; **FlexWare** ($700 per module), from Manzanita Software Systems; and **Connected Accounting** ($1,000), from EveryWare Development.

One of the best-selling, high-end packages, and a name you're likely to hear over and over from the professionals, is **Great Plains Accounting** from Great Plains Software. Great Plains has more modules than probably any other Mac accounting system (modules range in price from $500 to $1,000). What it doesn't have is a great Mac interface. The company has sold a Mac version of its PC product for years, but it still looks and acts like an MS-DOS program.

Legal Help

(AN/CG)

Nolo Press, publisher of a variety of self-help law books, also offers a host of software applications designed to help you get your legal life in order. **WillMaker 5** ($50), for instance, comes with a book giving background information on the various choices that you will face when making a will. Or you can just let yourself be walked through the program and only consult the book when you want. When you're done, WillMaker prints out a will that's a legal document in any state except Louisiana (whose laws are based on the Napoleonic Code rather than English common law). WillMaker costs a small fraction of what a lawyer will charge to draw up a will for you, or of what the probate court will extract as tribute if you're foolish enough to die intestate (without a will).

Nolo also offers **Living Trust** ($56), which is estate-planning software. It helps you create a living trust, which lets you will property to people without having to go through probate. The program has enough flexibility to accommodate life's complexities (different assets, for example, can have different custodians and beneficiaries). You can't preview a trust document until you have completed all the steps of the program, though you'll find it's fairly easy to edit a completed version before you print and sign it. Living Trust comes with on-line help and a comprehensive manual; it pays to study the manual or you might make a mistake that could invalidate your efforts. Conveying property properly can be tricky, so you probably should have an attorney review the living trust you produce. But even if you do consult an attorney, the software should save you money and educate and inform you about the entire process of managing your estate.

Organizing your personal records isn't something you plan a weekend around, but like making a will, it's something worth doing. To help you get your financial, legal, and personal information in order, Nolo offers a useful product called **Personal RecordKeeper** ($30). The program has more than 200 categories and subcategories to organize and store information. For instance, you can compute your net worth and create inventories of all your insured property (just remember to take the disk with you in case of a fire). You can also protect your records with a password and print all or selected records.

Editors' Poll: Have You Ever Used Apple Events Scripting to Tie Applications Together?

AA: If you mean AppleScript, no. If you mean have I taken advantage of Apple events, yes. PageMaker uses Apple events to supply hot links to FreeHand and other programs. So does Fetch, TouchBase Pro (if I ever install it), and a bunch of other programs.

DB: I think Apple events scripting is one of the coolest features to come out in a long time, and I think that Apple is doing a really poor job of promoting it. Yes, it's programming, but it's so easy and so powerful! I'm using it to script QuarkXPress and FileMaker Pro together. Next I'm going to create little stand-alone applications using the FrontMost utility that comes with AppleScript 1.1. It lets you make buttons and pop-down menus and so on. Very impressive work.

EC: I think AppleScript is cool. I've never learned to program, but it seems like I could use AppleScript to create my own programs, or to make the programs I have do exactly what I want, sort of the next step up from QuicKeys. I just bought *The Tao of AppleScript* from BMUG and plan to do some summer reading...

DD: I'm not a real tinkerer: I mean, I haven't even tried QuicKeys yet.

JK: No, I don't. I've never had enough of an ongoing need for this kind of linkage to make it worthwhile to set up.

HN: No, but once the scriptable Finder arrives, I expect to see a lot of neat utility functions appearing as scripts.

BW: Currently, my projects vary too greatly, but if I found myself performing ongoing, repetitive computing tasks that incorporate predictable stages, I'd AppleScript the hell out of them.

Databases

ONE OF THE NICEST PARTS ABOUT having a Mac is that you can make it do all the things that *you* hate to do. Databases are a perfect example: You may hate filing, but ask your Mac to put your collection of 15,246 baseball cards in order of each player's average RBI over the last ten years and you'll make its day.

In this chapter, we'll show you how databases organize information, from fields and records, to reports and mailing labels. We'll also give you a rundown on the most popular software available so that you can decide which database manager is right for you. Finally, at the end of the chapter you'll find a whole new collection of tips and tricks (mostly for FileMaker) so that you can get the most out of your database.

Contributors

Elizabeth Castro (EC) is the chapter editor.

Robert Lauriston (RL) is a computer journalist based in San Francisco who has been using FileMaker since 1987.

Jonathan Oski (JO) is vice president, manager of network and technology planning at BOT Financial Corporation in Boston. He is also a contributing editor for *MacWEEK*.

Arthur Naiman (AN), John Kadyk (JK), Sharon Zardetto Aker (SA), and **Susan McCallister (SM)** were all major contributors to earlier versions of the *Macintosh Bible,* from which parts of this chapter were taken.

Contents

What Is a Database?

A database organizes information by dividing it up into smaller, labeled pieces. An address book might be divided into names, addresses, and phone numbers; a checkbook into check numbers, payees, and amounts; a dictionary into entry words, types of speech, and definitions. A computer can use these labels to help it quickly sift through huge amounts of data, perhaps in order to find a certain name (or check number or entry word) or to list clients by ZIP code (or some other criteria).

The database managers described in this chapter allow you to organize information in your own way or organize a kind of information that is not covered by an already-existing program. Some examples of home-grown databases are recipe books and videocassette catalogs, but many people also create contact managers, checkbook registers, and accounting programs.

Databases, Databases, and Databases (EC)

The address book, checkbook, and dictionary that I mentioned above are all *database files*—groups of information divided into labeled pieces. You create, manipulate, and view database files with a *database application*, such as Now Contact or Quicken. You can also create custom database applications (I have one called "Biblebase") with a *database manager* like FileMaker Pro, 4th Dimension, or Omnis7. The tricky part is that most people refer to all three—database files, database applications, and database managers—simply as *databases*.

Furthermore, the line between database files and database applications is very thin indeed. So thin that the two may even be embodied in the same icon on the desktop. Take my Biblebase database application, for example. I created it with FileMaker Pro to hold all of my contact information for this project. The database file is the *information*, that is, the names and addresses themselves. The database application is the way that I have set up *how to enter and process that information*. Both are contained in the icon Biblebase.

Stand-alone database applications like Now Contact or Quicken, usually marketed not as databases but as "information managers" of one kind or another, are

FileMaker Pro is a database manager; Recipes includes the database application and the database file in one icon.

4D First is a database manager, Music Collection is the database application, and Music Collection.data is the database file.

perfect for people who don't want to design the system but would rather just enter the information. (Personal information managers were described in detail in the previous chapter.)

What Can You Do With a Database Application? (EC)

Of course, word processors and spreadsheets can also hold information such as names and addresses, recipes, or glossaries. Why would you want to use a database application to organize that information? The answer lies in the way information is stored in a database. Each piece of information is labeled, perhaps as a "first name" or "check number" or "ingredient." This labeling allows the database to access and manipulate the data very quickly, which in turn allows you to consult individual parts of your data, order it, and then output portions of it (or the whole thing).

Storing information in an electronic database lets you see the same information in a number of ways, selected and ordered according to your current needs. For example, suppose you have a list of names and addresses. A database will allow you to order (that

Spreadsheets vs. Databases (EC)

Spreadsheets and databases are two similar ways of looking at information and, in fact, can perform many of the same functions. Each row of a spreadsheet contains a collection of pieces of information, each with its own label (the column label). You can think of columns as *fields* and rows as *records*. (If you don't know what fields and records are, don't worry, we'll explain them later in "Parts of a Database File.")

And although you can create a database file with a spreadsheet program and can search and sort without problem, you will be severely limited with respect to reports, entry forms, and other types of specialized layouts.

On the other hand, you can use a database as a spreadsheet, keeping track of monthly and yearly totals, for example, but you will have limited means of charting and creating "what-if" scenarios, a spreadsheet's most powerful feature.

is, *sort*) the list by last name, in order to create a printed phone directory, and later by ZIP code, to print labels for a bulk mailing. You can also quickly find the portions of your data you want to work with, say, all of your clients in the Northeast, or all those that haven't ordered in the last six months. These tasks would be much more difficult with a static list in a word processor.

Parts of a Database File (SA/AN/SM/JK)

Here are some basic terms you need to know when using a database program. To help make them clearer, we'll compare each with a concrete, real-world example that you're undoubtedly familiar with—a Rolodex file.

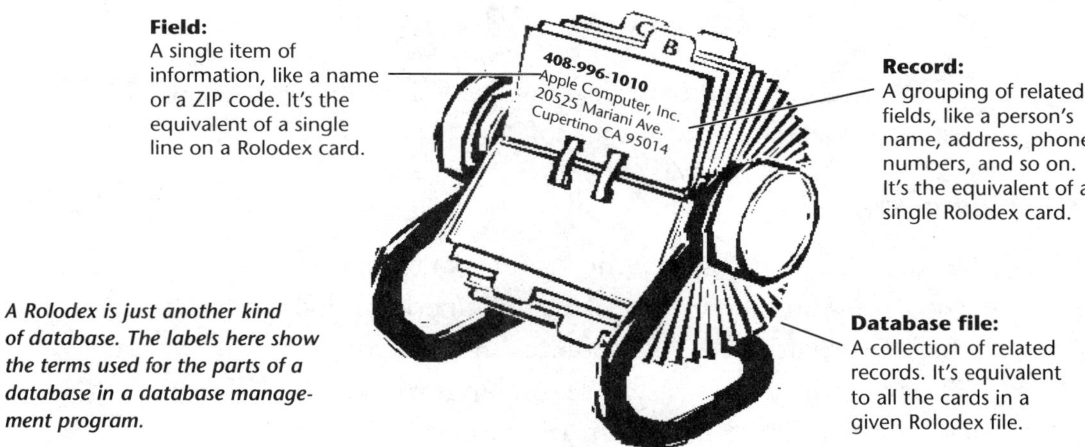

A Rolodex is just another kind of database. The labels here show the terms used for the parts of a database in a database management program.

Flat-File vs. Relational (EC)

The main difference between the two major kinds of database programs—*flat-file* and *relational*—is the way they share information. Suppose you have a database to do your invoicing. In order for the name and address of your client to appear on your invoice, there will have to be a link between the Clients file and the Invoices file.

In a flat-file database, you will create fields in the Invoices file in which to *copy* the information from the Clients file, using a *lookup function*. You can automate the copying process, but it is important to realize that the information now resides in two separate places. Changing the information in one file will not automatically update it in the other.

In a relational database, the information in the Clients file is not copied but, instead, a link is created—usually with a key word like an ID number—that connects the Clients information to the invoice. Whenever you look at or print the invoice, the program consults the Clients file and displays the latest information available. In addition, when you look in the Clients file, you can list what invoices have been made to that client. Finally, if the Invoices file is linked to other files, like Products, Payments, or whatever, the client information is automatically linked to those files as well.

Choosing a Database Manager

In this section, we'll review the two leading flat-file database managers and one easy-to-use relational database manager.

FileMaker Pro

(SA/JK/SM/AN/EC/Charles Rubin)

FileMaker ($400, Claris) has been the flat-file database of choice for Mac users ever since the program first came out in 1985, perhaps due to its clever use of *lookups*, which have since been incorporated into the competition. FileMaker is like a good strategy game: It's easy to learn, but it will keep you interested for a long time. This means it lets you start right away, but it can still perform relatively complex database tasks.

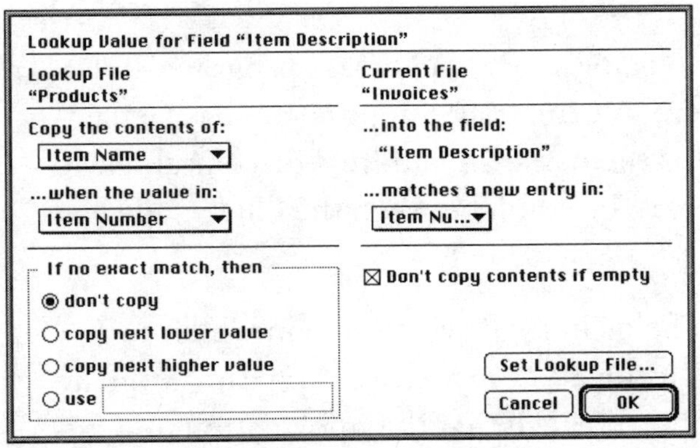

FileMaker makes even complicated features like lookup functions easy to use.

The newest scripting features, added to version 2.1, expand FileMaker's powers even further. A script may contain almost any command in FileMaker's menus and may be defined to act on a specific field, file, or layout, or to pause and wait for user input. You can also send (or receive) Apple events in order to share information with files created with other software or to take advantage of features in another program (like using QuicKeys to dial the number in your Telephone field through your modem). Finally you can assign scripts to buttons, making them easy to get to and use.

Perhaps one of FileMaker's best features is the ease with which you can design views or *layouts*. You use MacDraw-like graphics tools (and the same keyboard shortcuts) to design data entry windows, lists, reports, mailing labels, and form letters. Adding frames and rules in various colors and thicknesses helps to divide the layouts visually and makes the information easier to enter and understand.

You can generate a wealth of reports with FileMaker, once you've conquered the rather difficult concepts of "parts" and "summaries." Unfortunately, many users never do. Hopefully, the next version of FileMaker will include a QuickReport function like 4D First's or a CrossTabs function like Panorama's.

In addition to Text, Number, Date, Time, Calculation, and Summary fields, you can also create Picture/Sound fields in your FileMaker database. FileMaker is clever enough to save only one copy of each picture, sound, or QuickTime movie on the hard disk and then refer to it when necessary, saving time and disk space.

Most flat-file databases are made to be used by one person, but FileMaker Pro has strong multiuser features. You can share a file with any number of people on a network (even if you don't have AppleShare or System 7), and you can assign passwords to different users to control their access to various layouts or fields.

To sum up: Unless you need a fully relational database, FileMaker is a very good choice. It is chock-full of features that even beginners will be able to sink their teeth into.

Panorama (JK/AN/EC/Byron Brown)

Panorama ($400, ProVue) is a flat-file database with lookup capabilities and a useful feature, called Clairvoyance, that is a great help in entering data. If what you're typing matches data in existing records, Clairvoyance finishes the entry for you. (If it guesses wrong, you can just continue typing over the guess.) You can even use Clairvoyance with lookup fields, which is especially helpful for entering ID codes from less-active clients.

POWERBOOK

Panorama keeps your entire database file in RAM, which makes it very fast—and ideal for PowerBook users, since battery use is kept to a minimum. On the other hand, if you plan to create very large databases, you'll have to make sure you have enough RAM to open them. Panorama's size on disk, a mere 584K, will make cramped PowerBook users even happier. And the documents it creates are typically two to three times smaller than the equivalent files in FileMaker.

Invoices:XTABS:Sales per City

	Nov 90	Dec 90	Jan 91	Feb 91	TOTAL
Grass Valley	980.93	479.04	721.96	938.42	3,120.35
Nevada City	192.11	802.31	194.25	373.94	1,562.61
Sacramento	215.20	114.95	469.38	297.70	1,097.23
Smartville	308.31	12.34	62.90	145.90	529.45
Roseville	125.13	270.80	64.00	49.94	509.87
Truckee	129.03	99.02	169.80		397.85
Auburn		290.98	9.98		300.96
Strawberry Valley	84.51	56.15	82.42	53.55	276.63
West Sacramento	34.17		89.09	150.05	273.31
Keddie	14.96	11.33	62.02	136.61	224.92
Rough And Ready	37.22	15.38	137.14		189.74
Dutch Flat		159.71		18.36	178.07
Colfax	56.48		114.66		171.14
Volcano			73.84		73.84
Yuba City			27.69		27.69
•**TOTAL**	**2,178.05**	**2,312.01**	**2,279.13**	**2,164.47**	**8,933.66**

Panorama's CrossTabs feature helps you quickly analyze numerical data in spreadsheet fashion, comparing rows and columns.

Panorama's macro language, PanTalk, lets you assign keyboard shortcuts to any command or sequence of commands. You can completely customize your windows, menus, and dialog boxes. In addition, you can use the macro recorder to watch you as you work and remember your actions for later.

Panorama's CrossTabs feature, which compares two sets of data in spreadsheet fashion, and its automatic Graph function are ideal for analyzing numerical data. And Panorama offers advanced drawing features like magnification, pixel-accurate drawing, and a wide selection of tools.

If you plan to work from a PowerBook or are especially worried about speed, Panorama is the right choice.

4D First (EC)

BARGAIN

For a truly relational database at a reasonable price, try **4D First** ($300, ACI US). Designed as an entry-level database with many automatic features, 4D First is a pared-down version of 4th Dimension (see the box on page 424) that can stand on its own or be used as a run-time version to open 4D files. This means that you can not only use the hundreds of 4D database templates that are already available, but you can also create new database applications as you need them.

Although 4D First is slightly more difficult to learn than a flat-file database such as FileMaker or Panorama, the relational strength and automated features it offers may be worth the trouble. For example, 4D First automatically creates input and output layouts, and its QuickReport and Graph features make analyzing your information easier than with FileMaker.

4D First's general interface and design tools are not nearly as Macintosh-like as they should be. Everyday keyboard shortcuts such as Shift for restraining or Option for copying simply don't work. The Search dialog box doesn't let you tab from one area to another or select fields with the arrow keys. On the other hand, 4D First lets you view the database application while you're designing it, saving you endless trips back and forth to make sure your modifications have worked as you hoped.

4D First has two nice features that help you prepare your database for other users. First, you can add balloon help to the fields in a layout. If you (or your data entry operator) forget what goes in a field, simply activate balloon help and point to the field with the mouse. Second, you can create a whole set of custom menus for your users so that they have access to all the commands (and only those commands) that you want them to.

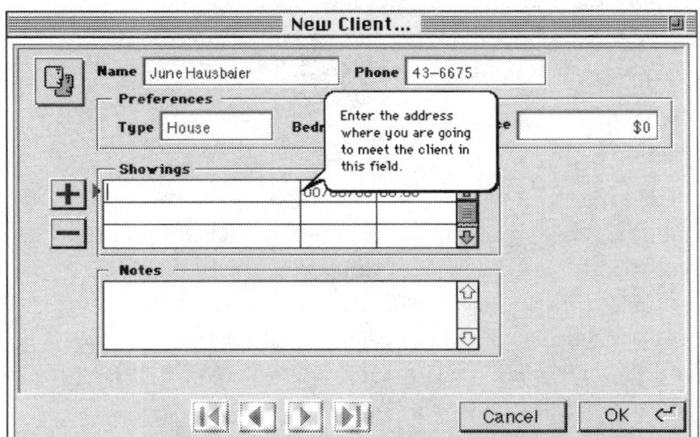

You can add your own balloon help to any field in any 4D First layout, to help remind you or your data entry operators what and how information should be entered in each field.

Finally, if you ever need a really powerful database, you can upgrade directly to 4th Dimension, and from there to a Sybase or an Oracle system. And every database you've developed so far will still work.

If You Need a Programmable Database Manager (JO/RL)

As Robert constantly tells embarrassed new computer users, there's no such thing as a wrong question. However, there *are* questions that let you know something's wrong. One of the worst goes something like this: "We need to buy a relational database. Which one is best?"

Why does this question mean something's wrong? If you *really* needed to buy a relational database manager, you'd already have a strong opinion about which was best—because you'd be an experienced database programmer.

Learning to program a high-end database is a serious undertaking, comparable to learning to program in Pascal or Basic. You can't learn to design database applications by messing around with 4D, FoxPro, or Helix, any more than you can learn to write C programs by using a compiler. If you want to learn database programming, you'll either need to take classes or spend many hours studying books.

Here we give you an idea of the strengths and weaknesses of the most popular high-end databases so you'll know which class to take!

4th Dimension
4D ($900, ACI US) is probably the most widely known of the Macintosh relational database products. The big sister of 4D First, ACI's easy-to-use relational database product, 4th Dimension, or 4D, gives the developer the most control over the user interface, with a full programming language. 4D can be used to develop a variety of applications ranging from single user to departmental and, when coupled with database server products like 4D Server, enterprisewide database applications.

Helix Express
Helix Express ($450, Helix) is probably the most unconventional of the bunch due to the method it uses to create database applications. Where most relational database development systems rely on procedural languages, Helix Express has taken a more visually oriented approach to creating applications—relying on tiles that you fill in with the appropriate building blocks. There is no code per se to a Helix application. Its proponents insist that it allows you to create applications much more quickly and intuitively. Helix is great for database neophytes, though it takes some getting used to if you're accustomed to the "old way. "

FoxPro

Microsoft's FoxPro is worthy of consideration by virtue of the vast number of dBase and FoxBase applications that can be used with it. This includes a number of mature, vertical-market applications written for Intel-based PCs. In addition, FoxPro for the Mac, unlike Helix and 4D, allows you to create applications that can be transferred to and from Macintosh, DOS, and Windows platforms without a lot of hassle. And at least while FoxPro is being introduced, you may be able to find it for under $100, as Microsoft attempts to grab a share of the market.

Omnis7

Finally, Blyth's Omnis7 is more a professional application-development system than a relational database product. Though you can create stand-alone applications with Omnis7, its hefty price tag of close to $3,700 (for the development system) puts it beyond the reach of many database hobbyists and budding developers. It, too, excels in the creation of cross-platform database applications. Omnis7 applications are unique in that both Macintosh and Windows users can share the same program and data files. This makes it the best product for creating applications that will be used in environments where a mix of PCs and Macs are found.

Working With a Database Manager (EC)

Work with a database manager is generally divided into two parts: designing the database application and using the application to enter and view the information.

Creating a Database Application

When you create your own database application, it is up to you to decide how to divide up the information, how it will be entered, and how it will be output. If this is done carefully and well, entering and using the information should be easy tasks, requiring very little training.

Defining fields. The fields in a database serve to divide the information up into smaller pieces so that the database can sift through the information more efficiently. You should create a field for each category of information—that is, each piece of information that will be similar among many records but different in some way from the rest of the information within the record.

The classic example is a Last Name field. In an address database, all your records will have one, and the last name is clearly distinguishable from the other information in the record (Street, ZIP code, Telephone, and so on).

Should You Do It Yourself, Buy a Canned Application, or Hire a Programmer? (RL)

For simple tasks like address books and recipe collections, it's fairly easy to make your own applications using FileMaker Pro or Panorama. For more complex tasks, like tracking inventory, accounts receivable, and payroll for a business, however, the DIY approach may be crazy, since even professional database developers may need weeks or months to create such complex applications.

When a job's too big to do yourself, the main decision is whether to buy an off-the-shelf application for the task (such as Great Plains for accounting), or hire a developer to build a custom database application. If you can find a canned application that meets your needs, it's likely to be a lot less expensive than a custom job. On the other hand, it may not do exactly what you want, and you may end up having to figure out workarounds for those limitations. Ask other people in your line of business what applications they use and how satisfied they are, or check trade publications for ads. Check out the vendors' on-line support forums on CompuServe and America Online to get an idea of the problems their users might be facing.

If you *can't* find an appropriate off-the-shelf solution, check the same sources for referrals to database programmers. You want to find people who understand not just programming but also the needs of your particular business. Before hiring anyone, check their references carefully. It's best to choose a programmer or company with a long history of customer satisfaction. Make sure your developers fully document their work, including extensive comments in the database code itself so that you are not dependent on them for any necessary future modifications.

Another example might be the Kind field in a Recipe database. Each recipe will be of a certain kind (say, Dessert, Main Course, Appetizer, etc.), and this information is clearly different from the other fields (Ingredients, Directions, Prep Time, Cooking Time, etc.).

Creating layouts. The second step in creating your own database application is designing layouts. You should create different layouts for different purposes: one for data entry, one for viewing lists on screen, one for mailing labels, one for the annual sales report, and so on. You'll have to decide which fields to put in each layout and where to place them. You will often put field labels next to the fields so that you can remember what information is contained (or needs to be contained) in each field.

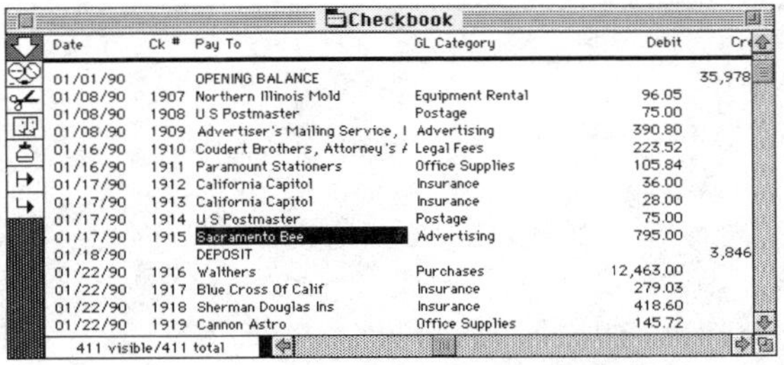

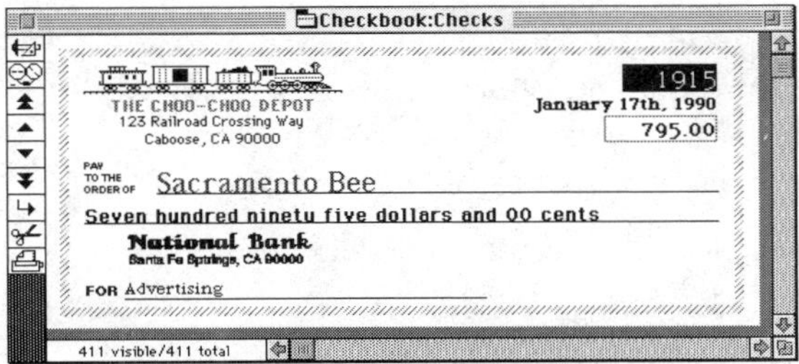

Different layouts present the same information (or parts of the same information) in different ways. Information viewed in a check register layout (top) looks completely different when viewed as an individual check.

Creating layouts is quite similar to using a graphics program; it involves dragging elements around the screen, making them bigger and smaller, drawing lines and aligning objects (constantly). It is important that your database manager be flexible and easy to use.

Using a Database Application

Once you've defined your fields and created the layouts, you can begin to enter information, search or sort the information that the database contains, and output it in practically any way you need.

Entering information. Of all the tasks involved with databases, actually entering the information is by far the easiest—and the dullest. You simply create a new record and start typing. When you have filled in the information for one record, you create a new record and start again. Most databases save your data automatically each time you create a new record.

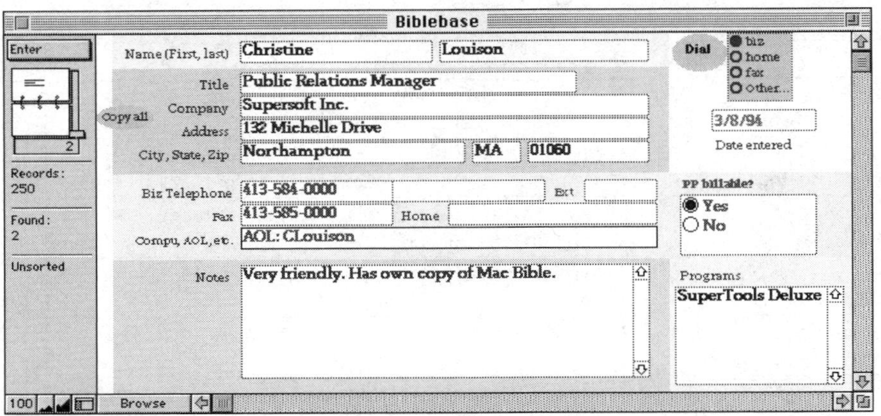

To enter data in a database file, simply click on a field (the white spaces in this example) and type away. Hit the Tab *key to move to the next field.*

Database Templates (EC)

If your heart doesn't skip a beat at the thought of calculated fields, procedures, and subtotals, but you'd still like to be able to take advantage of a database, consider letting someone else set up your application. The PIMs discussed in Chapter 10 are ready-to-use database applications that keep track of names and addresses, meetings, and to-do lists. You can't modify their structure, but if you're just looking for a contact manager or an address book, you probably won't need to.

A more flexible solution is to buy a *database template*—a database application that someone has already created with your database manager. Sometimes the application includes a database file that already holds information you can use or add to; other times you simply enter your own data. In most cases, you can modify the application, adding fields and layouts.

BARGAIN

If you have a limited budget, try finding freeware or shareware templates on-line. Claris, for example, offers a FileMaker forum on America Online (Keyword: Claris) that is chock-full of database templates. There's one that catalogs baseball cards and one that tracks deductible gas mileage. There's even one with over 40,000 U.S. postal codes and their corresponding cities and states, which you can use to automate your data entry.

There are developer associations for almost every database program, where you can find out about templates for your program. For FileMaker database templates, call the Claris Software Alliance (408/727-8227). For Panorama templates, contact ProVue (714/892-8199). There are more than 1,200 4D developers; call ACI US for a catalog (408/252-4444).

(Many database managers come with a few templates included with the software, and though they might be useful for looking at and getting a feel for the program, I haven't found them very useful in "real life.")

Database templates created with FileMaker Pro tend to be for home and small-business use and usually cost less than $500. Here's a sampling:

Name	**Price**	**Description**
BizBasics Working Solutionz Software	$400	Tracks sales orders, work orders, invoices, products and services, inventory, employees and shipping
FireForms Richard Carlton Consulting	$100	Automates various tedious forms that must be routinely written by the California Department of Forestry and Fire
Hoops Joe Huber and Associates	$50	Allows a basketball coach to keep and print team, player, and opponent statistics
MemberTracker Creative Software Solutions	$130	Records membership status, personal data, and meeting attendance
Party/Event Planner Graphic Imaginations-GIP	$30	Tracks invitations, RSVPs, seating assignments, gifts, and more
TrialMaker TrailMaker Software	$300	Allows litigators to store information as it is gathered from sources during the preparation of a trial and then generate fact summaries, lists of witnesses, law and evidence summaries, marked exhibit lists, and much more

Database templates developed with 4th Dimension (which can also be used, but not modified, with 4D First) tend to be aimed at larger businesses and often cost upwards of $5,000. Here are some of the more unusual (and less expensive) offerings:

Name	Price	Description
BizBasics Working Solutionz Software	$400	Tracks sales orders, work orders, invoices, products and services, inventory, employees, and shipping
Curator of Birds AuiComp Macintosh Solutions	$700	Provides complete histories of individual birds, pairs, and colonies upon which systematic evaluation of procedures, bloodlines, etc., are to be based
Grass Roots Lobbying Advanced Laser Graphics	$2,500	Gives complete legislator biographical data, including committee and subcommittee membership (complete mail merge included)
MacParish Hoffmann Software	$600	Maintains complete demographic records of all families and family members in a church as well as their involvement in church ministries and activities
Motorcycle Maniacs ISIS International	$900	Maintains inventory, outside-source searching, shipping information, payment, credit, collection, and other information about motorcycles and motorcycle repair
Pulley Designer Footprints	$1,000	Calculates optimum pulley-shaft size, sizes all associated components, creates a bill of materials, and produces a dimensioned engineering arrangement drawing
Resource Scheduler Desert Sky Software	$800	Schedules rooms and other limited resources and invoices customers for usage. Also tracks items needed, such as AV equipment, special setup requirements, and food

Many database managers allow you to import information from word processors, spreadsheets, and other databases so that you can keep the typing to a minimum. The original information must be divided into fields (usually by commas or tabs) and records (generally with returns) so that the database knows where to put each piece of information.

Sorting. All databases allow you to put your records in order, according to the criteria you give it. For example you can sort your address database by last name (or by ZIP code, or by ZIP code *and* last name). Sort your recipe file by ingredients (or prep time needed, or category). In addition to using any criteria (or combination of criteria), you can usually sort in ascending, descending, or in a custom order (like high, medium, and then low).

Searching. Searching lets you instantly find a client after entering his or her ID code, or find all of the recipes that use, say, fresh salmon *and* heavy cream. Searching yields all the records that satisfy all or part of the given criteria, depending on the logical operators used.

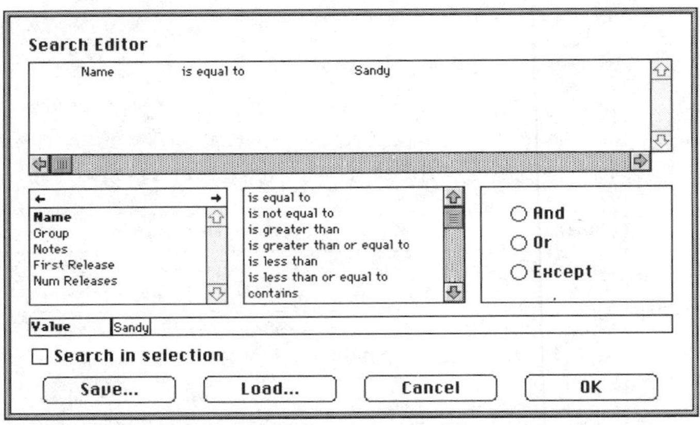

4D First presents a somewhat intimidating, though complete, dialog box with which to define the search. (It also lets you use the same method as FileMaker, though it's not shown here.)

Outputting data. The simplest way to output data is to show it on your screen. For example, you might search for an individual record to view or modify the information it contains on screen.

FileMaker's Search "dialog box" looks exactly like the same layout in Browse view. You type the information you're looking for in the appropriate field and click Find.

Databases are especially useful because they allow you to output your data on paper in almost any way you can imagine (and can create a layout for). You can create mailing labels, directories, monthly summaries, individual charts and histories, form letters, and any number of custom lists and reports.

Summary reports are one of the more complicated but more powerful features of a database. (Ain't that always the case?) For example, you can list your baseball cards by Card Type and then by Year, and then have the database calculate the value of each year's collection.

Using macros or scripts. Most database managers let you create *macros* or *scripts* to speed up and automate your work. For example, to create your monthly mailing labels, suppose you search for all your active clients, put them in order of ZIP code and last name, and then output them with a layout called

Mailing Labels. You can create a macro with the name "Print monthly mailing" to perform all of these steps automatically. The next time you need to print your mailing labels, just choose Print Monthly Mailing from the appropriate menu.

Database Tips

Database Design

Use all the data entry control available (EC). Almost all databases offer some help in keeping your data as accurate and consistent as possible. Use data entry control options to let you select values from a list, mark checkboxes or radio buttons, automatically enter data, restrict data to a certain value or range, or insist that a field contain at least something.

Different layouts for different uses (EC). Even if your monitor is so big it touches both sides of your room, you shouldn't try and put every single field in each layout. Instead, create a different layout for each use: one for data entry, one for creating a phone book printout, one for address labels, and so on.

If you do have many fields in a layout, use background color (or gray shades) to distinguish different areas.

Formatting ZIP code and telephone fields (SA/AN/EC). Make sure your ZIP code and telephone fields are set up to treat entries as text and not as numbers. A numeric ZIP code field will strip the leading zero from 07461 and may perform a subtraction on 07461-8976. FileMaker actually ignores any nonnumeric characters you may have entered, such as hyphens and parentheses, but it is nice enough to leave them where they are. You can even display them, as long as you haven't changed the Number format of the field.

Formatting ZIP codes and telephone numbers as text fields also makes it easier to find a group based on the first few numbers. If you search for 9 in a ZIP code field formatted as text, you'll get all those that *begin* with a 9 (a good piece of the West Coast). If you search for 9 in a ZIP code field formatted as a number, you'll get all those ZIP codes that are *equal* to 9, which wouldn't yield you very many.

Duplicate files before working on them (Steve Michel). It's good practice to keep at least two copies of any database file, and three of any active one. But if you're too lazy to do that, at least do yourself the favor of duplicating a database file before launching the application to work on it. Most databases keep their files on disk and automatically save changes to them while you work. So the file you had on disk when you began to work is not the file you'll return to when you're done.

Annotating databases (Steve Michel/EC). It's easy to forget what a particular report, sort, or calculation is supposed to do—it's hard to explain very much in a two- or three-word layout title. I have one file I use at least three times a week, but recently when I went to make some changes to it, I lost a couple of hours' work because I couldn't remember what each layout was for and how it worked.

Some programs let you add comments directly to a layout (select Form Comments in the Setup menu in Panorama and create Balloon help for fields in 4D First), but even if they don't, you can still get around the problem. If the program allows you to include nonprintable text (like FileMaker does), you can put a detailed note formatted in that way right on the form itself.

FileMaker Tips

Getting around (EC). You can use the keyboard shortcut ⌘Tab to go to the next record, search petition, layout, or page, or ⌘Shift Tab to go to the previous one.

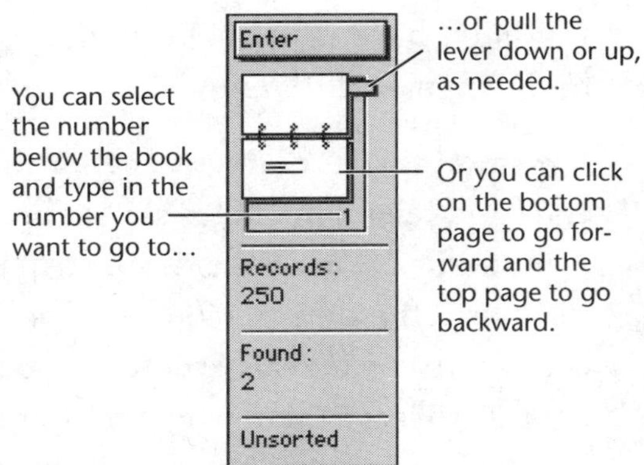

Use FileMaker's "little book" to pass through the records, search requests, or pages in Preview mode.

The number below the little book, in the upper-left part of the window, tells you how many records (or search petitions, layouts, or preview pages) you have created. Go directly to the record you need by selecting the number and typing the appropriate one. This is an especially good trick in Preview mode when you know what page you want to go to.

Assets
☒ Tall
☐ Dark
☐ Handsome
☒ Intelligent
☐ Rich
☒ Funny
☐ Other…

Use checkboxes when you want to be able to select more than one option.

Sex: ● F ○ M

Use radio buttons when you want to be limited to one choice or another.

Selecting from a list of values (SA/SM/EC).When a field is formatted to display a set of values, either in a list or with checkboxes or radio buttons, you can use the ↑, ↓, ←, and → keys to move through the values, or you can type the first few letters of the word you want. Then hit Return (not Enter) to accept the entry. The moral of the story? Set up your lists so that each value begins with a different letter, and don't ever use pop-up menus—they can't be accessed from the keyboard but are identical to lists in every other way.

With radio buttons and checkboxes you can *deselect* an already-marked option in the same way—typing the first letter and then pressing Return.

If you're trying to *find* something based on a radio button or checkbox, you won't be able to use Return to select or deselect a value since Return would activate the search. In this case, you'll have to (gasp!) click the box manually.

The choice between radio buttons and checkboxes directly affects data entry. Use radio buttons when you want to be able to choose only *one* of the options. Use checkboxes when you might want to select *more than one*.

Choosing "none of the above" (EC). FileMaker version 2.1 lets you add an "Other" option to pop-up menus, checkboxes, and radio buttons (select Field Format and then check Include "Other…" Item). However, if you format your field as a pop-up list, you don't need an Other option. Simply press Enter or Esc instead of selecting a value from the list, or press Delete if you've already selected something, and type a new value or leave it blank.

Bypassing the Delete alert (SA/JK). When you use Delete Record to remove a record from your file, FileMaker asks you if you're sure you want to delete it. This is a normal Mac touch—giving you a chance to change your mind before an irreversible operation is performed. But if you're *sure* you want to delete the record, Option⌘E will avoid the dialog box.

Looking for empties (and nonempties) (EC). The best way to find empty fields is by typing an equal sign (=) in the field in Find mode. To find nonempty fields, type an equal sign in the field, check the Omit box, and then click Find.

On the other hand, the fastest way to find empty *records* is to sort your file in order of a field that should never be empty—like a client's name. All the empty records will appear at the top of the list.

Eliminating duplicate records (EC). First and foremost, *don't* use the duplicate operator to look for duplicates. Because of the way FileMaker creates its index, by analyzing each individual word of a field, it would flag *Claris Corporation* and *Microsoft Corporation* as duplicates, but not *MS Corp* and *Microsoft Corporation.*

Zip	Address	Lastname	Name	Company
01042	2317 W. River Boulevard	Matheson	Bill	Matheson Consulting
01042	542 W. River Blvd.	Miller	James	MicroBiz USA
01060	132 Michelle Drive		Christie	Supersoft
01060	132 Michelle Drive	Louison	Christine	Supersoft Inc.
01060	46 Main St.	Miller	James	TechStar Products

By sorting your database in order of ZIP code and then address and viewing them in list form, you can quickly find, and then eliminate, the duplicate records. (Note that the two James Millers are not duplicates, and this method helps to keep that clear.)

A good way to find and eliminate duplicates in an address database is to order your data by ZIP code, street address, and name, in that order. View them as a list. The real duplicates are those that are at the same address, with *almost* the same name but not quite. You'll be able to identify and get rid of them quickly.

Ask for a little and you'll get a lot (EC). You're Ronald Reagan and you're looking up your old friend, the former leader of the Soviet Union, in your database. You know his name is Gorbachoff or Gorbichef, or something like that. Don't tax yourself, just search for "Gorb." Any name that begins with those letters will appear in the found set. Even if you know how to spell it, you should search for as little as possible. This saves you the trouble of entering more than is necessary, and it gives you a better chance of finding the information, even if *it* was entered incorrectly.

Special pastes (EC). You can save a lot of time by using FileMaker's special paste functions.

Current date	⌘-
Current time	⌘;
Contents of field in last record	⌘ + apostrophe
Current user name	Shift ⌘N
From the index	⌘I

Holding on to a tool (EC). Generally, after you use a tool in Layout mode, it switches automatically to the pointer. FileMaker has always let you hang on to a tool indefinitely by double-clicking to select it. If you want tools to be blocked with a single click, check "Always block layout tools" in the General Preferences dialog.

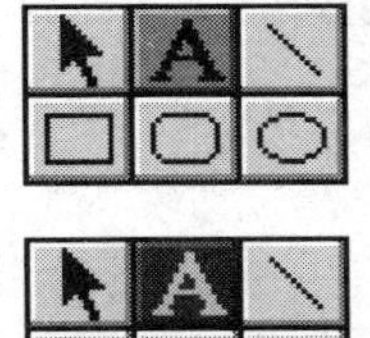

Click once on a tool to use it once and then go back to the pointer. Double-click on a tool if you want to use it more than once in a row. (Its colors will be inverted to show that you've "locked" on to it.)

Fast sizing and styling in layouts (SA/JK). Create a copy of any object on a layout by holding down Option and dragging. This is a fast way to create text labels with the same fonts, size, and style—just make several copies and then edit the text.

When you drag a single *field* this way, you get a dialog box that lets you choose which field you want to appear in the new spot—it doesn't have to be the one you moved. This is an easy way to add new fields to a layout, with the same size and attributes.

Dotted lines and fat radio buttons (EC). You can create dotted lines by selecting a zigzag line pattern. They're great for separating subsummaries.

You can make your radio buttons and checkboxes stand out more by changing their line thickness and color.

542 W. River Blvd.	Amherst	MA	01042
132 Michelle Drive	Northampton	MA	01060
46 Main St.	Northampton	MA	01060
Total Number of Clients in Massachusetts: 47			

Create a dashed line by selecting a 2- or 3-point-wide line with a zigzag pattern.

If you're using big type, use big, fat, colored radio buttons. Make them thicker by adjusting the line width. Color them by choosing a line color (not a fill color).

Paid? All Part None

Paid? All Part None

You can use FileMaker's line patterns and widths to add color to your buttons and boxes.

Command selecting (EC). Press ⌘ while selecting and anything the selection marquee touches will fall into its grip. Without ⌘ you will have to completely enclose the objects you wish to select.

More selecting tricks (EC). Click any one of the tools before choosing Select All to select all the objects created with that tool.

Select one field, press Option, and then choose Select All to select all the fields of the same type (all the text fields, all the date fields, etc.).

HOT TIP

Restraining yourself in one or more directions (EC). You probably know that if you hold down [Shift] while resizing an object or field, your movement is restricted to just one direction: horizontal or vertical.

If you hold down [Option], your movement is restricted in both directions, and the object becomes a perfect square or circle.

Overriding grids and magnets (SA). To move something in a layout grid without the movement being affected by the grid or the magnetized T-squares, you don't have to turn them off—just hold down [⌘] while dragging.

A database with moving parts (EC). You can delete any empty parts (that's Part with a capital *P*, as in Body, Footer, etc.) in a layout by dragging the bottom border up to the next part or by selecting the part's tag and pressing [Delete].

If the part contains any objects or fields, hold down [Option] to drag the bottom border past the objects or fields without deleting them, or select the part and press [Option][Delete] to delete the part and anything it contains.

You can change a part's identity by double-clicking its tag and selecting a different part type. This won't affect its contents.

Get rid of the body (EC). I wish there were space to talk at length about FileMaker reports. You can do some really amazing things. Here's one little tip to whet your appetite: When you're creating summary reports—say, to count up your baseball cards and check how much the collection is worth—don't forget that you don't need a body. The body contains information about each card (say, Mike Schmidt, Philadelphia Phillies, 1972–1978, .255) that may distract you from the totals that the report is designed to show (like the fact that your Topps collection is worth $26,457).

Total value for Boston Red Sox	$0.20
Total value for Kansas City Royals	$0.75
Total value for New York Mets	$1.90
Total value for New York Yankees	$3.65
Total value for Oakland A's	$2.75
Total value for 1979	**$9.25**

If your list is designed to give subtotals and grand totals, get rid of the body so that the individual records do not distract you from the big picture. In this body-less report, there are two subsummary parts, a header and a footer. (In this example, the subsummary parts are defined to print "below.")

Cheat sheets (EC). Since FileMaker lets you create these incredible scripts, you don't have to remember how to sort, search, or print your report. But how do you remember what it was for? Write a short description at the top of the report, format it in red, and then select "Do not print the selected objects" from the Slide objects dialog box (select Slide Objects in the Arrange menu). And no, Virginia, nobody knows why they put this option in the Slide Objects dialog box.

Copying layouts (EC). Technically, you can't copy a layout from one File-Maker Pro database to another. The best way to take advantage of an existing FileMaker database, with all its fields, layouts, and scripts, is to clone it, and then adapt it as needed. (Select Save a Copy in the File menu.)

You can, however, copy a layout, including all text, fields, lines, and other illustrations (but not page or column size), as long as the database into which you want to paste the information already has definitions for the fields you wish to copy. How? Believe it or not, just copy and paste.

Relookup of just some of the records (SA/EC). If you've changed information in a file that's used as a lookup (say, you've updated names and addresses that are looked up by your invoicing file), the Relookup command in the Edit menu can update all, some, or just one of your records.

To update all your records, choose Find All in the Select menu, place the cursor in the lookup field and select Relookup. If you want to update a group of records, select those records with the Find command before using the Relookup command.

To force an update for only the current record, move to the field that does the lookup. Make a minor change to it—say, add a space and then delete it. When you move out of the lookup field, the "new" information in it will force a lookup and the rest of the record will be updated.

Searching and sorting repeating fields (SA/EC). FileMaker's special repeating field option (which gives you multiple entries in a single field) is great, but it's sometimes also confusing. For example, if you sort by a repeating field, only its first entry is sorted on. But if you search for something in a repeated field, all its lines are searched.

The only way to sort a repeating field is by importing the records to a clone of the original file and selecting Add New Records and Splitting Them Into

Separate Records when appropriate. (This is the first step in creating an inventory file.)

Creating automatic serial numbers with letters (EC). If the serial numbers in your company happen to start with a letter, you can still get FileMaker to fill the information in automatically, by combining an Auto-enter serial number with your code.

Create a field called Autonumber, checking the Auto-enter Serial Number option in the Options dialog box. Create a field called Code for your code. Use a pop-up list if you have a couple of different codes.

Then create a calculated field (Coded Serial, not to be confused with Sugar Coded Serial), that adds the two together, perhaps with a hyphen to separate them visually:

Coded Serial = Code & "–" & Autonumber

If you are adding serial numbers to a group of records that are already in the database, use the Replace With Serial Numbers option (Select Replace in the Edit menu), which is new to version 2.1.

Checking for length (EC). When entering names and addresses into your database, your assistant often puts in the first three digits of the ZIP code but sometimes forgets to look up the rest. You want to check and make sure each record in your database has a five- or nine-digit ZIP code. Create a field (Ziplength) with the following formula:

Ziplength = Length (Zip code)

Now search the Ziplength field, omitting all those records with five or ten (nine digits plus a hyphen) characters. You'll immediately find which ZIP codes have been entered incompletely. Sort the records you find in order of State, City, and then Address, pull out the ZIP code directory, and hand it to that assistant!

Integrated Software

IF YOU'RE LOOKING FOR THE EQUIVALENT of the Vegematic among Macintosh applications—one program that does it all—integrated software is it. All the programs described in this chapter package together, under one application icon, some combination of the basic software tools most people use day to day. These tools include a word processor, page layout tools, a spreadsheet, a database, drawing tools, and a communications program.

We'll spell out why you might choose an integrated application instead of investing in several separate, specialized applications. You'll find out who's who in the market and get a quick overview of which combination of tools each program offers.

If you've already bought one of the two most popular integrated applications on the Macintosh, ClarisWorks or Microsoft Works, check out our list of word processing, database, spreadsheet, communications, and drawing tips, tricks, and shortcuts that should help you get the most out of those programs.

Contributors

Connie Guglielmo (CG) is the chapter editor.

Charles Rubin (CR) has written more than 20 books, including the best-selling *Macintosh Bible "What Do I Do Now?" Book* (Peachpit Press); the *Macintosh Bible Guides to ClarisWorks, FileMaker Pro,* and *System 7.1* (all from Peachpit Press); and *Running Microsoft Works for the Apple Macintosh* (Microsoft Press).

Carolyn Said (CS), a senior editor with *MacWEEK,* spent many hours on the phone with the product managers at Claris and Microsoft to master the subtleties of integrated software.

Contents

Getting the Works (CG)

Integrated applications offer one-stop shopping to Macintosh users who may not want or need separate specialized applications for some of the basics. The basics we're talking about (each of which is usually called a *module* in integrated applications) are word processing, database management, spreadsheets, telecommunications, and drawing. All of the programs in this category (which are descendants of the granddaddy of integrated software, AppleWorks for the Apple II computer) combine a word processor with some of these other tools.

Integrated applications offer several advantages over a collection of individual programs:

- **Price.** These programs range in price from $250 to $300; you don't have to be a financial wizard to figure out that buying an integrated application is less expensive than buying a stand-alone word processor, drawing program, spreadsheet, and so on.

- **Program size.** If you want or need to keep the number of applications on your hard disk to a minimum, then having one application rather than several saves you space (an integrated application may be ideal if you have a PowerBook or Duo and want to pack a lot of functionality in limited hard disk space).

- **Integration.** Because all the tools or modules are integrated, sharing data between each of the modules and moving among the modules is, for the most part, a snap.

The trade-off is that these programs offer a limited set of features compared to the stand-alone applications. Yes, the basics are here, but if you need to automate your accounts receivable department or plan to write a textbook complete with footnotes and indexes, then you may need the more specialized features the stand-alone applications offer.

Choosing an Integrated Package (CS)

Which program you choose will depend on the combination of basic modules you need (the chart below shows what features the leading integrated packages offer). There are clear market leaders in this category: ClarisWorks (which was bundled free with Apple's Performa Macs) and Microsoft Works are ranked as the two best-selling integrated programs for the Mac. What does that mean to you? Well, in addition to the comfort of knowing your choice is backed by the opinions of thousands of other users, it means there's extensive support available for both products, including books, training services, libraries of macros—and the tips at the end of this chapter.

GOOD FEATURE

Although Microsoft Works owned this category for years, ClarisWorks, introduced in 1991, has leaped ahead in popularity in the past two years. In fact, ClarisWorks was the best-selling business application for much of 1993, a tribute to its elegant integration, fully featured modules, and trim application size. Microsoft floundered badly with a pallid Works 3 release in 1992, but it is now fighting back with a major rewrite, Works 4, which should begin shipping in mid-1994.

At a Glance: What Integrated Programs Offer (CG)

	Word processing	Spreadsheet	Database	Communications	Drawing	Painting	Page layout	Other
ClarisWorks 2	•	•	•	•	•	•	some	
Microsoft Works 4	•	•	•	•	•	•	some	address book,calendar
WordPerfect Works	•	•	•	•	•	•	some	
GreatWorks 2	•	•	•	•	•	•	some	outliner
RagTime 4			•	•		•	•	SQL links
HandiWorks		•	•			•	•	phone book

ClarisWorks was the only integrated package at press time to have a native version for Power Macintoshes. Feature for feature, the PowerPC version is identical to the version for Macs built on the Motorola 68000 family of chips, but it runs much faster due to the improved performance capabilities offered by the PowerPC processor. The makers of Microsoft Works, WordPerfect Works, and RagTime and HandiWorks also say they plan versions of their programs (described below) for the new PowerPC processor; those versions are expected to ship sometime in 1994.

ClarisWorks (CS)

ClarisWorks 2 ($300) gets high marks for integration. All of its modules can be called from a single page; you don't have to quit one module and start another—a definite speed advantage. For example, you simply drag a rectangle onto the page to drop a graphic into a word processing document; the tools and menus immediately change to reflect that you are now drawing. ClarisWorks also has many advanced features, like an option for creating slide shows, Bézier drawing tools similar to what you'd find in a high-end illustration program, a huge thesaurus (more than 600,000 words), a fast spell checker, built-in macro capabilities, more than 100 built-in spreadsheet functions, automated log-on scripts for popular on-line services, and more than 20 file translators (the more translators you have, the easier it is to share files with people who use other programs).

The Shortcuts palette offers 150 different shortcuts that give you one-click access to commonly used features. The palette is context-sensitive, meaning it will only show the icons appropriate to the environment you're working in. The palette is also editable; you can include the shortcuts you want and exclude those you don't want, and you can make your own 16-color icons.

Claris also has one of the best reputations in the business for on-line support. The ClarisWorks support forum on America Online is a thing of beauty, offering a complete Tech Info database. You can also post questions for the tech support folks; they'll respond on the same day, sometimes within the hour.

ClarisWorks lets you anchor blocks of text and graphics to particular locations on a page, move them around, and link them. This means that, with a little practice, you can substitute ClarisWorks for a page layout program (at least for documents of about five pages or less; for longer documents, it's not worth the trouble). If you had to pick one piece of software to stay with for years, ClarisWorks offers a great combination of tools in a well-integrated environment.

Microsoft Works (CS)

By the time you read this, Microsoft will have shipped **Works 4** ($250), which addresses some major problems with the previous version. In fact, some users of Works 3 "backtracked" to version 2 because they preferred the way some of the features in that version worked. Works 4 integrates its modules using Microsoft's Object Linking and Embedding (OLE) 2.0 technology. This approach works well; you simply click a button and draw a rectangle to, say, insert a spreadsheet in a word processor. You can then edit the embedded object by double-clicking it, and you can also embed objects from other OLE programs within Works. (OLE is Microsoft's version of the same type of technology Apple is introducing with OpenDoc, described in Chapter 3.)

Microsoft beefed up the software with plenty of new features, such as a slide show; a tool for creating tables; an equation editor for editing equations with mathematical symbols and subscripts; an AutoSum button for calculating totals automatically; multilevel database sorting for doing complex searches; and drag-and-drop editing, which lets you move or copy a selection by just dragging it to the desired location. It ships with a selection of clip art and a Gallery for organizing clip art images, and it now comes with about 36 file-conversion filters.

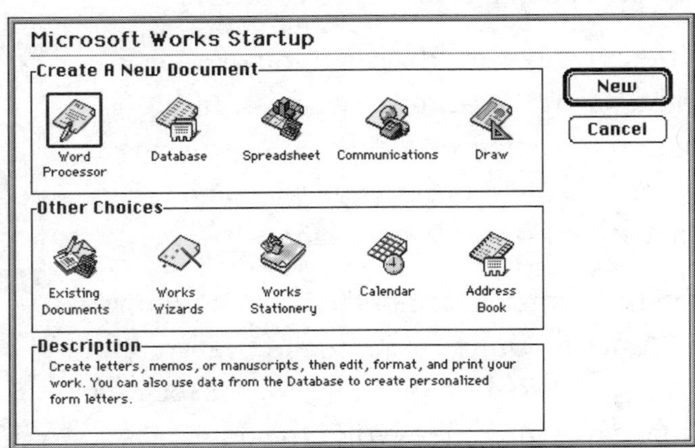

To choose a module in Microsoft Works 4, you click on an option in the opening dialog box. Because all the modules are integrated, it's easy to share data among the word processing, database, spreadsheet, and drawing modules and to make sure that changes made to information in one module are reflected in the others.

Works 4 also adds a new calendar and address book, as well as new paint tools supporting gradient fills, rotation, filters for creating special graphics effects, and support for Adobe

Photoshop plug-in tools and filters (described in Chapter 15). Microsoft's WordArt feature includes TrueType fonts and provides tools for different shadow effects, shapes, and text and line rotations. You can also use WordArt to create fancy headlines and banners.

Works 4 offers some features that simplify common tasks such as writing letters, generating reports, and designing newsletters. A feature called WorksWizards helps create documents such as greeting cards and newsletters by posing simple questions that users answer. Almost 40 AutoStart templates (called "stationery documents" in Works) provide a quick starting point for creating different types of documents (such as a Grade Book, Cash Flow Projection, and Home Inventory) designed for teachers, business users, and home users.

GreatWorks (CS)

Symantec Corp.'s **GreatWorks 2** ($300) is the most System 7–savvy integrated package. While other programs also use Apple's Publish and Subscribe technology, GreatWorks' implementation lets you make automatic copy-and-paste links between different GreatWorks documents. Users I've talked to say this is somewhat clunky because you're going through as many steps as you would to publish and subscribe between separate programs; unlike the other programs in this category, which offer seamless (and in most cases automatic) integration between modules, there is no integration advantage. GreatWorks also has a long list of file translators.

If GreatWorks' modules aren't as smoothly integrated as those in ClarisWorks or the new Microsoft Works, many of its modules are strong as individual applications. Its paint module is a pretty fair color paint program its own right. (It supports 8-bit painting, offering up to 256 colors in its color palette.) And the word processing module offers outlining functions, which is particularly useful for preparing long documents or presentations.

WordPerfect Works (CS)

WordPerfect Works ($250; formerly BeagleWorks from Beagle Bros. Software) also uses Apple's Publish and Subscribe technology to integrate its modules. From any module, you can double-click on data created in another module to edit it; the appropriate toolbar and menus automatically appear. The program also has a floating toolbar common to all modules.

The word processing module is strong, supporting paragraph styles, irregular text wrap, and mail merge. The draw and paint modules, on the other hand, are limited, offering only a few text colors and no gradients (smooth transitions from one color to another). The spreadsheet module is decent, and the buttons for commonly used functions are nice, but the database is poorly designed and cumbersome to use.

WordPerfect says version 2 will ship in 1994 for about $150, a $100 price reduction. None of the new features had been determined at press time.

RagTime and HandiWorks (CS)

By virtue of price, intention, and execution, MacVONK's **RagTime** doesn't really belong in the "works" category. At $600, it costs more than twice as much as the other integrated packages, and since it lacks a database and draw/paint modules, it's not really comparable to them. RagTime is most appropriate for people who need its heavy-duty page layout features and links to heavy-duty SQL databases. (For more on RagTime's uses as a page layout program, see Chapter 16.)

But RagTime was a pioneering attempt (it hit the market in the mid-1980s) by a European company to merge spreadsheet, word processor, and page layout functions, and from RagTime, HandiWorks was born. **HandiWorks** ($175) is a trimmed-down version of RagTime, with a word processor, spreadsheet, and basic drawing and page layout tools, that also sports a phone book module and a good list of file translators for reading in data from a variety of other Mac programs.

Unfortunately, neither program has kept pace with the competition. But by the time you read this, a complete rewrite called RagTime 4 should be out. According to MacVONK, a page laid out with RagTime 4 will be able to contain objects of all types, such as spreadsheets and graphics, which will remain fully editable and *live linked* to the original files (live linked means that any changes made in the original files are automatically updated in any documents those files are placed in). Version 4 should also add such features as support for AppleScript, enhancements to business graphs, automatic table-of-contents generation, and better drawing tools. One of RagTime's strengths is that it supports links to other programs; for example, you can buy software to connect it to a SQL database or to Claris's FileMaker Pro. Its layout features are also strong, and the new version's object-oriented approach promises smooth integration.

At press time, MacVONK had not decided if it would also release a new version of HandiWorks based on RagTime 4.

ClarisWorks Tips

General

Saving memory (CR). ClarisWorks runs in as little as one megabyte (under System 6) or two megabytes (under System 7) of memory, but you can run short of memory during long communications sessions or when using the paint program. Here are a few ways to maximize memory when using these document types:

- Use the Communications preference option to change from an unlimited scrollback area to one of a small fixed size, and use the Capture Text command to store communications data in a file on your disk instead of in memory.
- To free up more memory for paint documents, use the Resolution & Depth command to set the pixel depth to Black & White, 4 colors, or 16 colors, instead of using thousands or millions of colors.
- Since ClarisWorks' Paint module demands a lot of memory, Claris recommends increasing memory allocation to at least 2,048K before using it.

Recycle macro keys (CS). If you create lots of macros and find yourself running out of macro keys, try assigning macros to specific ClarisWorks document types instead of creating macros that work everywhere. For example, you could use ⌘ Option 2 to double-space a word processor document, and use the same keys

to choose a fixed number format with two decimal places in the spreadsheet. Just be sure to check the document type you want in the Record Macro dialog box as you define each macro.

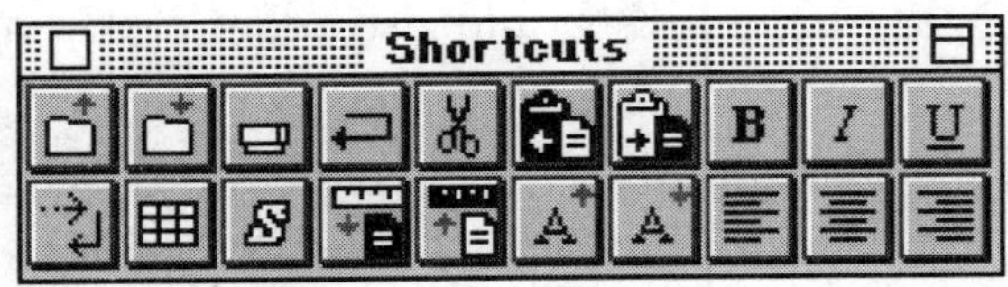

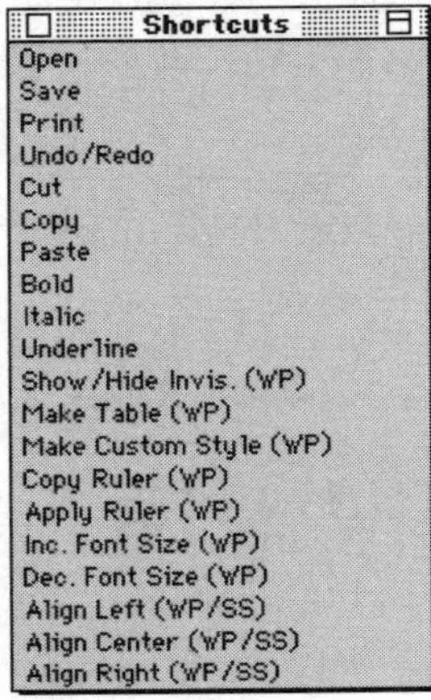

ClarisWorks' Shortcuts palette (top) gives you access to commonly used functions, represented by icons, with one mouse click. In case you can't remember what each button on the Shortcuts palette does, you can view the Shortcuts palette as names instead (left).

Which shortcut is which? (CR). If you can't remember what each button on the Shortcuts palette does, you can display the shortcuts as names instead of icons. Just change the Palettes Preferences to Show Names. To find out what one specific button does, choose Edit Shortcuts, click the button in the dialog box, and look in the Description area.

Wrapping text around a graphic (CS). You can wrap text around a graphic even when you're not in the word processing program. Turn Frame Links on for the frame with your text. ClarisWorks will wrap text around graphics that were created with the drawing tools or pasted in PICT format. If you need to wrap around other objects (e.g., bit-mapped graphics, EPS files, and so on), draw a borderless white object that is slightly larger than your graphic and move it behind the pasted-in graphic (using Send to Back).

Fast help (CS). The on-screen Help system tries to guess what you need information about when you call it up with ⌘?, but it's often wrong. Click the asterisk button to go right to the index and select the topic you need help with from there.

Creating predefined formats (CS). You can create predefined document formats such as a fax cover sheet, standard memo, or presentation. The format will have all the type styles and other formatting you've defined. Do a Save As and select Stationery on the pop-down menu. This will save a template with your formatting; you can then select it whenever you create a new document.

Creating slide presentations (CS). A nice feature in ClarisWorks is the ability to create on-screen slide presentations. There are several different ways to do this; in fact, any environment in ClarisWorks can be turned into a slide presentation. Some of the less obvious ways to do this include:

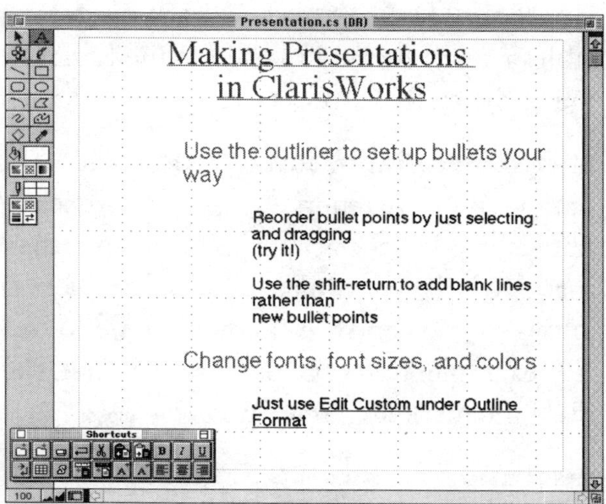

This presentation was set up in ClarisWorks' draw module by inserting text frames in Outline view.

- From the Draw program, insert text frames. Switch them to Outline view. Use the custom Outline format to define the fonts, sizes, and styles for each level in your presentation. (You can have multiple levels, so, for example, the first level could be 36-point Times bold; the second level 30-point Times Italic, and so on.)
- From the Database program, set up a Database layout with a title and a few bullet points. You can then enter data to create a very quick presentation.

Creating default formats (CS). You can create a default document for each of the programs; then every time you open that module it will automatically default to your predefined formatting. To do this, create a Stationery document and, for the word processor, name it *ClarisWorks WP Options* (for the draw module, substitute *DR;* for the paint module, *PT;* for the database module, *DB;* for the spreadsheet module, *SS;* and for the communications module, *CM*). In ClarisWorks 2, you must keep these documents inside the Stationery folder; in ClarisWorks 1, keep them in the ClarisWorks folder.

Word Processing

Define character styles by example (CR). You can name custom character styles and apply them by choosing the Define Styles command and selecting options in the Define Styles dialog box. But if you want to name a style that already exists in your document, it's faster to select a character that has that style before

you choose Define Styles. When you select a character, that character's style options are preselected in the Define Styles dialog box, and all you have to do is name the style. Faster yet, use the Outlined S shortcut in the Shortcuts palette.

Faster merging in form letters (CR). If you know the names of fields whose data you want to merge in a word processor document, you can type the field names inside special merge markers rather than using the Mail Merge command. ClarisWorks merges data from field names specified inside the markers « and » so you can type the field name to be merged enclosed in these markers. For example, to merge data from a FirstName field, type *«FirstName»*. To produce the marker characters, press Option \ (for «) and Shift Option \ (for »).

Inserting graphics (CS). There are two ways to bring in graphics:

- If the cursor is an I-beam and you have a blinking insertion point in your document, Pasting will bring in the graphic as a (usually) large character in the line with the previous characters.
- If you select Show Tools and select the graphic tool (the arrow) and then Paste, your graphic will appear as a completely separate object above the text. Inserting or changing text will not affect its position. If you have ClarisWorks 2, you could then choose Text Wrap and wrap the text around your graphic.

The second option is preferable if you're trying to do any kind of page layout; use the first option if you want to make sure the graphic stays tied to a particular text section.

Printing envelopes (CS). Under the Page Setup dialog, you can select a pop-up list for various envelope formats. The Envelope—Center Fed and the Envelope—Edge Fed selections simplify specifying an envelope layout.

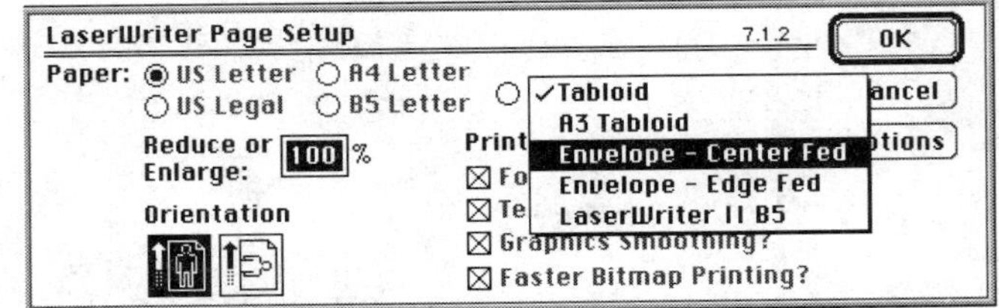

ClarisWorks offers preformatted envelope formats from a pop-up menu in the Page Setup dialog box.

Or you can make a template that works with envelopes of certain sizes. You can then use it over and over with just a few keystrokes.

- Open a new Drawing/Graphics document. Use Page Set Up in the File menu and select Envelope.
- Drag out a Text frame and type in an address for testing. Place it in the bottom-right quadrant. (You could also include another frame for a return address on the upper left, and yet another for a graphic.)
- When all is working, leave three Xs where your address was and save the file as a Stationery document in the menu Items folder (in System 7).
- To use it, select the name and address in your letter and copy it to the Clipboard. Open the Envelope Template in the menu. Then just double-click the three Xs, paste, and print!

Toggling invisible characters on and off (CS). ⌘; will toggle invisible characters, such as paragraph and return symbols, on or off.

Creating tables (CS). Instead of using the table tool, you can easily create a table in a word processing document by using spreadsheet frames. Like a graphic, the table can be free-floating (easily moved around within the document) or tied to a specific section of text.

Paint and Draw

Selecting images precisely without the lasso (CR). Using the lasso tool is the most common way to select an image without selecting white space around it. But you can do the same thing more quickly by holding down the ⌘ key while dragging the selection rectangle around the image(s) you want to select. To select all the images on a document without any white space around them, double-click on the selection rectangle tool while holding down the ⌘ key.

Using a draw document for page layout (CR). It might seem best to use the word processor for newsletters, but creating text frames in a Draw document gives you much more flexibility about how you arrange blocks of text and graphics on a page. Once you've created text frames, you can link them (so text flows from one frame to another in the same story). And, since frames are objects, you

HOT TIP

can select them and use the draw document's alignment commands to precisely line up columns and graphics.

Using draw documents for multi-page printing (CR). Paint documents in ClarisWorks can be only one page long. To create a multi-page paint document, open a draw document and add the number of pages you want, then create one or more paint frames on each page.

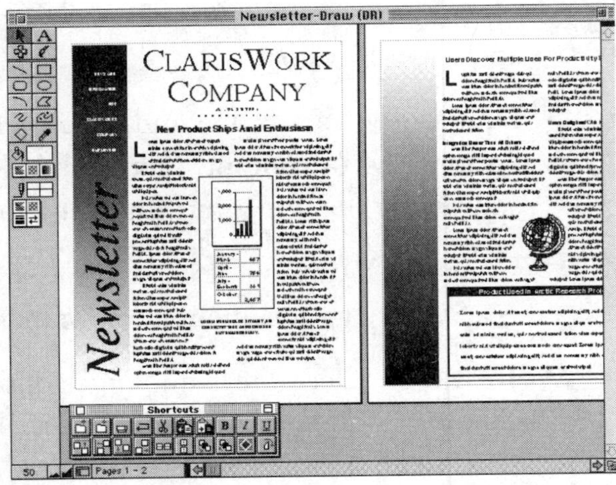

You can use text frames in a ClarisWorks draw document to create page layouts.

Spreadsheet

Saving paper (CS). Before printing your spreadsheet, drag through to select just the range you want printed, select Print Range under the Options menu, and click OK. At this point, it's helpful to select Page View under View to see how it will print out. Since you can keep working in this view, you can adjust the column widths so pages break the way you want them to.

Making big chart changes (CR). If the chart formatting options in the spreadsheet aren't flexible enough for you, copy the chart to a draw document, select it, and then use the Ungroup Picture command to break up the chart into its components. After you use Ungroup Picture, you can select different chart elements like the legend or a group of bars, and then use the Ungroup command to break up elements further. For example, you could ungroup a series of bars to select and change the fill pattern in one bar. Unfortunately, once you paste a chart into a draw document, it becomes unlinked from the original spreadsheet, so make sure the chart shows exactly the data you want before modifying it in a draw document.

Inserting multiple rows or columns (CR). The Insert Cells command in the spreadsheet takes a while to work, and using it repeatedly to insert several rows or columns seems particularly slow. You can speed things up by selecting as many rows or columns as you want to insert and then using the Insert Cells command. ClarisWorks will then insert as many rows or columns as you have selected.

Moving data between databases and spreadsheets (CS). You can move data from a database to a spreadsheet—or vice versa—by selecting all of the records (by using that command in the Edit menu) and copying that data into a new spreadsheet. You can go the other direction as well, but you'll need to re-create the field names and definitions.

Shortcuts for formatting spreadsheets for presentations (CS). After you put data in a spreadsheet, you can do a lot to dress it up and format it exactly the way you want. In the Shortcuts palette you can access commands to automatically size rows and columns, turn on and off row and column headers, and specify whether grid lines should be solid or dashed, for example. Since it's still a spreadsheet, you can also make a chart out of it.

Database

Creating forms (CS). The database program is your best bet for creating forms with ClarisWorks. In addition to allowing you to print out the form, this will let you enter the data for each form into a separate record in your database so that if you want to sort or do any database analysis, your data is already entered. To create forms, go into a new layout and drag to create a large text frame. Type in the "background" of your form, and then create a field for each fill-in blank and drag each field box into place. Switch back to Browse mode, and you're ready to enter data.

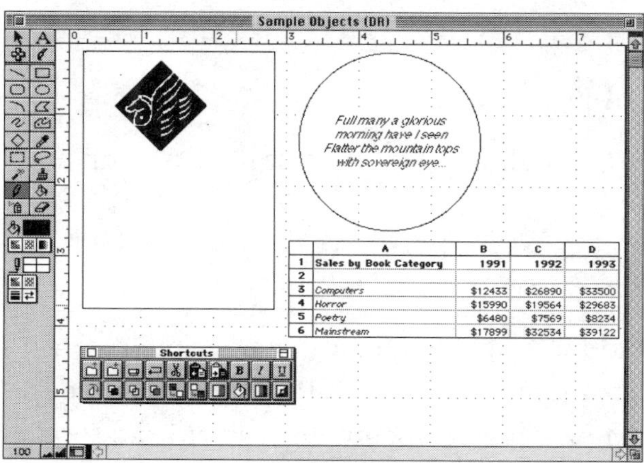

For better-looking spreadsheets, suitable for presentations, use the Shortcuts palette to turn grids on and off and to automatically size rows and columns. You can also insert graphics and text balloons.

Setting up labels (CS). When setting up labels, getting fields to line up next to each other can be tricky. Say you have two fields: First and Last. You'd like Last to

HOT TIP

slide next to First when it prints. Three things must be true: the *tops* of the fields must be exactly lined up (use 400% view so you can see what you're doing, or use the Align Objects command in the Arrange menu), the fields can be very close but they *cannot* touch, and the height of the fields cannot increase as you go from left to right.

Communications

Capturing sessions (CS). Capturing information in a session is most reliably done with Capture Data rather than by saving the Comm document itself. Saving the Comm document is best used only to retain the settings (phone number, etc.) for calling a particular service or bulletin board. To keep the file small, save it before using it. Note that ClarisWorks 1 defaults to screen capture (saving everything that you type and that appears on the screen), whereas ClarisWorks 2 defaults to port capture (saving every byte of information coming from the time you contact the service). Check Preferences under the Edit menu to confirm which is being used.

Minding your macros (CS). Never use more than one Macro Wait command within a macro, that is, if you want things to go smoothly. To maximize reliability, select Record Pauses when creating the macro.

Microsoft Works Tips

These tips are for Microsoft Works 4, though many of them will also work in Works 3.

General

HOT TIP

Embedding objects (CS). You can add a graphic, spreadsheet, or table to a document without ever leaving the word processor (actually, the same holds true for any document—not just word processing documents). From the tool palette select the appropriate tool by clicking on it, and then draw out a rectangle where you would like the object to appear in your document. The appropriate tools for the object you have chosen will appear. To edit that object later, simply double-click on it. Using the same steps, you can add any number of OLE 2.0 objects, including a Microsoft Excel spreadsheet or chart, a Microsoft Word document, WordArt, ClipArt, or Equation Editor.

Fast searches in Address Book (CS). If you type a name in the word processor and then open the Address Book, the name will automatically appear in the Match Records dialog box, ready to be matched to a record in the database.

Opening multiple documents as one Workspace (CR). If you regularly work with two or more Works documents at a time, you can save the documents as a set, called a Workspace, so they're easier to open. Just open all the documents you need to work with (a database file and a form letter, for example), and then use the Save Workspace command on the File menu to save the documents with a project name. Works creates a workspace "document." The next time you double-click on the workspace document, all the documents saved with it will open at the same time.

Getting to balloon help (CS). Hold down Shift ⌘ Option to get instant access to Balloon Help for descriptions of the items on the toolbar and palette.

Word Processing

Zooming (CS). Formatting changes and alignment of graphics and text will be a lot easier to see if you zoom in on your document. It can be magnified up to 800 percent using the magnifying glass buttons on the ribbon, or zoom to a particular percentage by clicking on the down arrow at the bottom of the window. The percentage will show next to the arrow.

Automatic entry of search text (CS). To speed search and replace, select text before you bring up the Find or Replace command (both on the Search menu). The selected text is automatically entered into the Find What text box.

Speed spell checking (CR). You can make Works' spell checker run a little faster by resetting some of the standard spelling options. First, choose the Spelling command from the Document menu and click the Options button. Then, click the Ignore Words In All Caps and Ignore Words With Digits boxes (so an X appears in each of them). If you don't need Works to help you with alternate spellings, click the Always Suggest box to remove the X from it—it takes extra time for Works to look up and display alternate spellings.

HOT TIP

Faster access to the thesaurus (CR). You can use Works' built-in thesaurus to find synonyms whenever you want, not just when you select a word in a document. Just choose the Thesaurus command from the Document menu, type the word whose synonyms you want to look up into the With box, and click the Look Up button.

Paint and Draw

Resizing paint frames (CS). While resizing a paint frame (with the frame handles), hold down the ⌘ key. This resizes the frame without scaling (and distorting) the contents.

Making a discontiguous selection (CS). If you need to change the colors, for instance, in some but not all parts of an image, you can select several different (discontiguous) sections of a paint frame by holding the Shift key down while using the selection tool.

Selecting colors (CS). Hold down the ⌘ key and click on the paint selection with the wand tool to select all occurrences of a particular color throughout an image.

Rotating text (CS). You can rotate text created in the Draw tool by any degree by clicking on the Rotate Text button on the toolbar and selecting the number of degrees for rotation.

Rearranging pages (CS). Instead of using Copy, Cut, and Paste to move pages of text in a Draw document, you can easily rearrange pages by dragging and dropping them in the Page Sorter. This view shows all the pages in a Draw document side by side in a thumbnail preview. Select Views from the View menu and drag to choose Page Sorter.

Creating master slide elements (CS). Use the Master Slide feature to automatically insert a graphic or title onto all slides in a presentation. Access the Master Slide through the toolbar, or in the Format menu select Master Slide Attributes. In the View menu, scroll to Views.

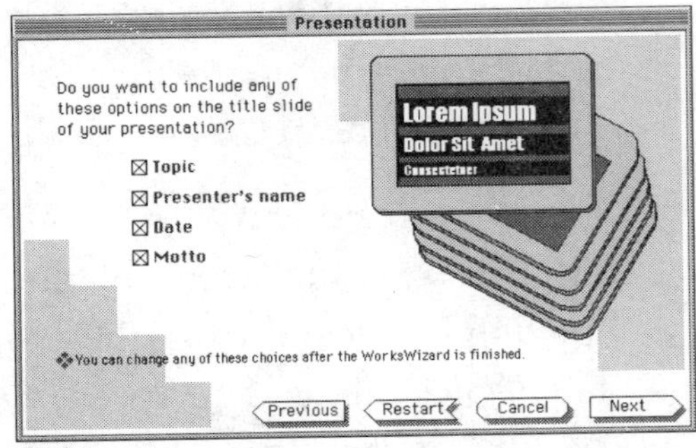

When creating a slide-show presentation, use the Master Slide feature to place elements, such as your name or logo, on every slide.

Working along straight lines (CR). You can force Works to draw straight lines at 45- or 90-degree angles by holding down Shift as you draw with the Straight Line tool. To move an object along a straight 45- or 90-degree line, select the object and hold down Shift as you drag it.

Embellishing lines with arrows (CR). You can add an arrow to one or both ends of any straight line you draw in Works. To move an arrow from one end of a line to the other, just flip the line around: Select the line, choose Rotate from the Draw menu, click the Horizontal Flip and Vertical Flip checkboxes, and then click the OK button.

Creating identical columns (CS/CR). Instead of trying to re-create similar-size columns one a time (and then spending time trying to align them), you can create multiple (one, two, three, or four), identically sized columns by clicking on the New Columns button (in Works 4) on the Column tool in the floating tool palette. After you've selected the number of columns you want, drag out a rectangle on the page and Works will automatically create the desired number of equally sized columns within that rectangle.

To create a group of identical columns in Works 3, make one column the size you want, select it, duplicate it, and then drag the duplicate to the proper location. This is much faster than trying to draw identical columns from scratch.

Spreadsheet

Selecting areas to be printed (CS). If you have more than a single cell selected in the spreadsheet when you choose the Print command, Works will print the range you have selected, not the entire spreadsheet.

Moving spreadsheet cells in groups (CR). By taking advantage of the drag-and-drop functionality added in Works 4, you can move a range of cells faster and more easily than you can with the Move command: Simply select a range of cells, click near the edge of the selection when the cursor becomes a pointer, and then drag the selection to the desired new location. To move a group of cells from one place to another in Works 3, select the cells, hold down ⌘ and Option at the same time, and click on the upper-right cell in the area where you want the selection to move.

Using ranges in formulas (CR). After you begin a formula, you can specify a range of cells by simply holding down the mouse button and dragging the mouse pointer across a group of cells. As you do this, the range address appears in the formula.

Getting to cell notes (CR). Cell notes are incredibly handy for inserting back-up or explanatory information about numbers in your spreadsheets. To open a cell note quickly, hold down the ⌘ key and double-click on the cell whose note you want to display.

Creating new charts (CR). Instead of using the New Chart command to make a chart, select the data you want in the chart, click the Chart tool in the tool palette, and then hold down the mouse button as you drag an outline where you want the chart to appear. When you release the mouse button, the chart will be drawn inside the outline.

Handling charts (CR). Having a lot of charts can clutter up your spreadsheet. To neaten things up, resize all your charts so they're about an inch square and move them all to one blank area of your document. When you need to view or print one of the charts, resize it and move it to its own separate page.

Database

Record counting (CS). You can automatically count the number of records in a field by creating a "serialized" field. To do that, choose Field from the Insert menu and click on Serialized in the dialog box that appears.

Preformatted labels (CS). If you've always found label-making cumbersome, you'll be happy to know that Works contains database forms for 22 of the most common Avery label formats. To access them, choose Form from the Insert menu. In the resulting dialog box, click on Label, and then select whichever label type you want.

Printing records (CS). Use the Mark Records for Printing option (in the Tools menu) to print records that can't be filtered. For instance, if the printer mis-prints a few labels (or you put them on the wrong envelope), you can mark those records to be reprinted.

Creating new fields (CR). When you're in Design view and need to add a new field to your file, hold down ⌘ and then press the mouse button to drag out an outline where you want the field to appear. When you release the mouse button, the New Field dialog box will appear, and you can then type a name for the new field. (In Works 3, oddly enough, you don't have to hold down the ⌘ key).

Changing field names and formats (CR). The fastest way to make field-name or format changes is to double-click anywhere on the field in List or Design view. This brings up a Field Format dialog box in which you can change the field name or format. In Works 3, changing the field name and its format requires that you go to two different dialog boxes: You'll need to double-click on the field's name to display the Field Name dialog box and double-click on the field's data space to display the Field Format dialog box.

Entering data in a form (CR). When you enter data on a Data view form, the selection moves from one field to another in the order in which you added fields to the form. In Works 4, to change the tab order all you have to do is choose Tab Order from the Format menu. In other versions, make a new form and add the fields in the tab order you want.

Communications

Automatic sign-on (CS). Microsoft Works will record your sign-ons to automatically log onto commonly used services. To record a sign-on sequence, select Sign-On from the Tools menu and then select Record from the submenu. When you finish your recording, you will be prompted to name your sign-on sequence and save it. In future communications sessions, you can simply select Play and your script name, and Works will automatically sign onto the service.

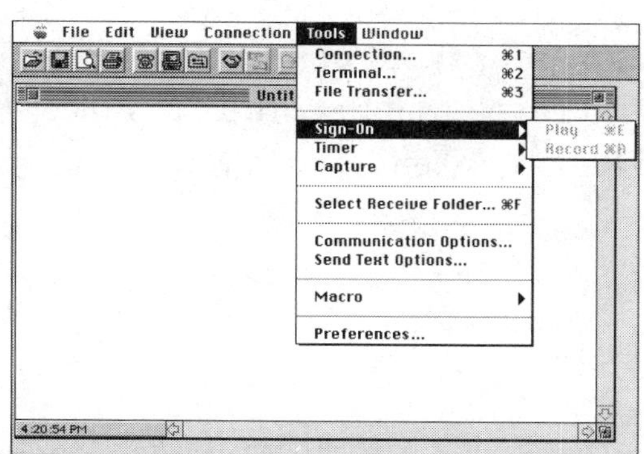

If you use on-line services a lot, you might find it easier to record and save the sign-on sequence. When you need to sign on, just chose Play and the program executes the sign-on script for you—including dialing the number, entering your name and password, and even going directly to your favorite on-line forum.

Tracking time and costs (CS). Works now has a timer that will keep track of time spent on-line and the charges for the session. Make sure to reset the timer and charges log whenever you begin a new session; you can also reset the timer at any time.

Faster communications (CR). It takes forever to close a communications document when you have Works set to use an overflow area. To speed up communications documents, choose Preferences and click None in the Overflow Area Size box, and then click the Always Capture Text option.

Continuing to work during file transfers (CR). Works can maintain a connection during a long file transfer even if you activate another Works document. Just start sending or receiving, and then switch to the other document and continue working. When the file transfer is complete, Works will beep twice to let you know so that you can return to your communications document.

Calendar

Changing appointments (CS). Move appointments quickly by using drag and drop (instead of deleting and retyping the information). Select the appointment to be moved, hold down the mouse button as you move the selected text to the new location, and then release the mouse button to move the appointment.

Keeping track of To Do items for individual projects (CS). Display all the To Do items for a particular project by assigning each item a key word (such as Report, Meeting, etc.), which you can then sort on.

13

Utilities

A UTILITY USED TO BE a program that didn't create its own documents but, instead, expanded the capacity of other programs. Although some utilities now create their own documents, their main purpose—helping another program (or the System)—remains. Common early utilities were file finders, spell checkers, and memory adjusters. Now, thanks to the efforts of countless hackers and shareware authors, you can find a timesaving utility for practically every task on the Mac, from changing the number of colors displayed on your monitor to seeing when the sun will rise tomorrow morning in Calcutta.

Contributors

Elizabeth Castro (EC) is the chapter editor.

Rick Casreen (RC) is a writer, the source of The Pelorian Press, consultant for Yes Computers of Noho, Massachusetts, and infamous for the phrase, "Everything in moderation is usually not enough."

Kristi Coale (KC) has held staff editing positions at *InfoWorld* and *MacUser* and now freelances for *MacWEEK*, *MacUser*, and other magazines.

Raines Cohen (RaC) grew up near Boston but went to Berkeley in 1984 to help start the international users group, BMUG. He worked on the staff at *MacWEEK* for five years and co-authored *Hayden's PowerBook Power Book*.

Ken Maki (KM) is a Macintosh consultant and an author. He lives in Portland, Oregon, where he volunteers time to the Portland Macintosh Users Group and writes Macintosh books for John Wiley and Sons.

Contents

A Tool for Every Job

Since this book has a finite number of pages, we can't mention each and every utility, or even every category of utilities: There are just too many. You'll find discussions of some important utilities in other chapters. Memory management utilities are discussed in Chapter 4, "Memory." Look for a guide to backup, recovery, and virus detection in Chapter 5, "Storage." And font-management utilities are covered in Chapter 14, "Fonts." In this chapter, we've limited ourselves to commercial utilities in a few general-interest categories that you won't find covered elsewhere.

What Do They Do? (EC)

If there's something about the Mac's interface that bothers you—the folder icons seem a little boring, you want to be able to work on other things while you're copying a disk, you don't want to have to answer all those questions every time you format a disk—there's probably an inexpensive utility that will fix it for you. Likewise if there's a task you find cumbersome, like sorting out which files are the most current between your PowerBook and your office computer. And doubtless there are utilities that do things you never would have dreamed of asking for—like one that adds Tarzan swinging from your menu.

Shareware Utilities (DD)

MAC BIBLE DISK

We didn't have room to cover even a fraction of the great shareware utilities cooked up by public-minded programmers, but it would be a shame to miss out on them. Many of the shareware and freeware utilities mentioned in this book are included on the *Mac Bible Software Disks* (see the card at the back of this book for information on how to get them), but these and many others are also easy to get through on-line services and user groups. (See Appendix C for more on those sources.) On America Online alone, there are over 5,000 shareware and freeware Macintosh utilities to choose from. While shareware utilities are sometimes not as rigorously tested and well supported as the commercial offerings, they are often of high quality and well worth a test drive.

The Power of Utilities

Here is a rundown of the main types of utilities discussed in this chapter.

Type	Function
Extension manager	Controls which extensions and control panels are active, to avoid conflicts (which cause bombs)
Utility collection	Generally includes three or four of those described in this table, along with a few extras
File finder	Locates files on your hard disk that match a given name, type, date created, or other specification
Text retrieval	Locates files that contain text that you specify
Synchronization	Keeps versions of files on different Macs (often a home PowerBook and an office desktop model) in sync
Compression	Reduces file sizes
Security	Protects files, folders, or an entire hard disk from prying eyes
PowerBook utility package	Package specially designed for PowerBook tasks such as monitoring battery and hard-disk use and finding elusive cursors, among other things. Often includes a clock.
Desktop tools	Souped up versions of tools already in the Mac system (clocks, scrapbooks, and calculators are covered here)
Macro utility	Lets you create keyboard shortcuts to execute a given command or sequence of commands
Desktop diversion	Changes the desktop pattern, icons, and cursors, or adds amusing characters to the desktop
Screensaver	Protects the monitor from "burn in" by periodically changing the image on the screen (say from Mickey to Goofy)
Screen capture	Takes a snapshot (or movie) of your screen so you can use it in a manual or boast about your latest high score in Tetris
Resource editing	Lets you customize the interface of Mac software by changing the text in menus and dialog boxes, the color and shape of icons, and other attributes

What They Do That They Shouldn't (EC)

A utility may either be an application (including a desk accessory), an extension, or a control panel (and sometimes a combination of two of these). Since extensions and control panels may take up a bit of the System memory heap and occasionally rewrite parts of the System in order to work correctly, they often conflict with other extensions and control panels using the same stretch of memory, creating a system hang in the process. Applications, on the other hand, manage their memory independently and do not affect the System, thereby causing fewer problems.

Unfortunately, the vast majority of the utilities on the market are extensions and control panels (you expected that, didn't you?). When you boot up your average Mac, a parade of icons marches across the screen, showing you what is being loaded into your System. Aside from the possible conflicts that may occur, this takes time; restarting a Mac that has 10 or 15 extensions may take several minutes longer than starting a Mac that has just one or two.

What's Init for You? (EC)

Back in the days of System 6, all the files that loaded at startup, including system extensions, utility extensions, printer drivers, and control panels were called *inits*. Now each type of file gets its own name, although they're often referred to generically as extensions. Control panels are also sometimes called *cdevs*, for control panel *dev*ice. And Chooser extensions (generally printer drivers), are sometimes called *rdevs*, from Choose*r* *dev*ice.

So, if you can choose between two utilities, and one is an extension or control panel and the other is a stand-alone application, choose the application. And when a utility application includes an extension as an addition to the program, you might decide to use just the application.

How Can You Tell if a Utility Is an Application? (EC)

There are several ways to tell whether a utility is an application or an extension.

Application	Extension or control panel
You can double-click its icon to open it, and (almost always) see a File and Edit menu when you do.	When you double-click it, you see the message "This file adds functionality to your Macintosh" (if it's an extension), or (if it's a control panel), a small window will open but you generally won't see either a File or Edit menu.
When open, you see the utility's icon in the Application menu (on the upper right corner of the screen).	When open, the utility's icon does not show in the Application menu.
You can install it anywhere on the Mac (including the Startup Items folder in the System folder).	You must install it in the Extensions folder, in the Control Panels folder, or in the System folder itself.
No icon appears during bootup.	An icon may or may not appear during bootup.

Extension Managers (EC)

If extension managers lived in a monarchy, they would be the king. While they are utilities themselves, their main goal is to organize and control all the other utilities (their subjects).

Sorting Out Extension Conflicts

Extension managers help to solve conflicts at startup by letting you define which files should load and in which order. You can also define sets of extensions and control panels for individual projects or tasks and then press a key at bootup to load only that set, thus saving time. Most programs also offer reporting options that tell you which extensions and control panels are installed and how much memory they are using.

Choosing an Extension Manager

You have four principal choices when selecting an extension manager. As in many utilities categories, there is a high-quality freeware program, as well as several commercial ones that have a few more extras.

EM's main window is very similar to windows in other extension managers. You click on an extension or control panel to add it to the active list.

Extensions Manager. One of the best extension managers is simply named **Extensions Manager,** or EM for short. Developed by Ricardo Batista, an engineer at Apple, it was later released as freeware and can be found on BBSs and through user groups. It is a no-frills package that does the basics well, even letting you activate (or deactivate) fonts and startup items (in the Startup Items folder), although you can't change their loading order. The only way to have a set load automatically at reboot, however, is to choose the set from the EM control panel before closing down—and if you can remember to do this, you're a lot better organized than I am. Version 3.0 of Extensions Manager is included in System 7.5.

Conflict Catcher. If you are having problems with your extensions but don't know which one is the culprit, try **Conflict Catcher II** ($80, Casady & Greene). Conflict Catcher can change the loading order of extensions and assign keys to sets to invoke them at startup. Conflict Catcher has one more advantage: a special detective system that helps you sleuth out which extension may be causing problems by enabling and disabling the extensions in controlled groups.

GOOD FEATURE

InitPicker. If you wish to define various sets of extensions that you can invoke at startup according to the task at hand, **InitPicker** ($70, Inline Design) is the best option. Although it can't enable or disable fonts, I found its interface, and especially its system for defining sets of extensions, the easiest and clearest to use.

Now Startup Manager. Startup Manager is one of the components of **Now Utilities** (see "Utility Collections," below), and like the other extension managers mentioned here, it can create sets of extensions, change their loading order, and enable and disable each one individually. Now's Startup Manager has one special feature: It lets you change the startup *disk* (as well as the extensions you want to load) even after your Mac has started to boot up—just press the Spacebar when you see Welcome to Macintosh and then select the startup disk in the pop-up menu.

GOOD FEATURE

Tips for a Quick Startup (EC)

HOT TIP

- Does your fax modem only ring when your computer is turned off or hung? Do you sit there tensely urging your 27 extensions to load as fast as they can so that your Mac can boot up and answer the phone? Mine does, and I do. The solution is to create an extension set with just the fax-modem software extensions. Then, if you need to reboot quickly to answer a fax, you can press the corresponding key, reboot, answer the fax, and then reboot with the complete set of extensions at your leisure.
- Most extension managers will let you open them up before the startup process begins so that you can change the configuration after a bomb. For Now Startup Manager and Conflict Catcher, hold down the Spacebar while booting up; with InitPicker, hold down the ⌘ key.
- If you want to restart your Mac without a single extension or extension manager, hold down the Shift key until the Welcome to Macintosh sign appears. To keep just your startup items (in the Startup Items folder) from opening, hold down the Shift key after your inits load but before you reach the desktop.

Utility Collections

Since utilities tend to be small programs, many software developers package several of them together. We've divided the main utilities packages into general-purpose and PowerBook utilities.

General Purpose (EC)

It's practically impossible to compare utility collections, since most of them include disparate combinations of programs. Instead, we'll explain what each collection contains, and if it's worth your trouble.

Minor Utilities You'll Find in Many Collections (EC)

There are common elements in many different utilities collections. Here's a quick description of the minor utilities that often form part of a collection. The most important ones are discussed elsewhere in this chapter and in other chapters in this book.

Type	Function
Hierarchical menu	Adds submenus to the Apple menu that give you access to the contents of folders (or folders inside folders)
Custom or WYSIWYG menus	Shows Font menus with the fonts they name or in the sizes and/or color you choose
Automatic save	Saves your work after a particular amount of time or number of keystrokes
Disk diagnostics (system analysis)	Gives a full breakdown of the state of your computer system, from chips to monitors to extensions
Control panel management	Lets you change monitor bit depth, printers, time, and/or colors from a menu in the Finder instead of with the control panel (or Chooser)
Launchers	Quickly opens commonly or recently opened applications, documents, or control panels without making you sift through the Finder
Key Caps or Key Finder	Helps you find what keyboard combination is necessary to produce lesser-known symbols such as accented characters
Disk-use indicator	Gives visual feedback when the computer is accessing information on disk

Keeping Items in the Launch Menus (EC)

Now's launch menus change to reflect the documents and applications that you use the most. To make sure an item stays on one of Now's launch menus even if you don't select it very often, press the Spacebar while selecting the item with the mouse. The item will be underlined, and when you release the mouse, it will move to the top of the list and stay there until you tell it to move (by selecting it once again with the Spacebar held down).

Now Utilities. Now Software's **Now Utilities** ($130) includes a scrapbook organizer and clipboard editor, hierarchical and WYSIWYG menus, an extension manager, a file finder, an automatic save function, and a system analyzer. The installation was quick and easy and didn't conflict with anything already in my bursting System Folder.

Now's file finder, SuperBoomerang, was surprisingly clever at figuring out what I wanted and when, but it was too slow (on my Centris 660 with a 500MB hard disk to search) to be worth using. The extension manager is very good and the scrapbook organizer is the best I've seen (they are described in more detail in the sections covering similar utilities later in this chapter). Now Menus' hierarchical menus let you choose options from control panels without opening them. It also tacks on two more menus to each side of the menu bar: one of recently used applications and the other of recently used documents.

Connectix Desktop Utilities. Connectix Desktop Utilities (CDU) from Connectix ($100) provides keyboard shortcuts, a cursor locator, control panel management, desktop beautifiers, file synchronization, limited security, and a screen dimmer. CDU is something of a jack of all trades and master of none: It includes many utilities, but none is particularly spectacular. The screensaver only dims the screen (no fun pictures here); the security system can be overridden by booting from a floppy, and you can't customize the desktop beautifying schemes (except for the background picture).

CDU does, however, have one option that I haven't found in any other utilities package: hide background applications (in the AppManager). It will automatically hide each application as you open the next, keeping your desktop free of clutter. Also handy is its Keyboard Power feature, which lets you choose any menu or dialog box option from the keyboard by typing one of the letters in its name (usually the first letter, but CDU underlines it so you know). The synchronization module (EasySync) is described with other synchronization tools later in this chapter.

WizTools. **WizTools** ($130, ASD Software) has so many utilities in its collection that its hard to remember them all. It has a color-depth switcher, special tools for the Finder, a keystroke recorder, a file/program launcher, simple macros, PowerBook tools, hierarchical menus, backup and synchronization tools, a world clock, and a "mailbox folder" (that signals you when something has been added, say, via System 7 file sharing). I fell in love with WizTools because of PopUpFolder—hold down the Control key (or whichever modifier you choose) and click a folder on the desktop to see—and get to—its contents.

WizTools also lets you add a Quit command to the Finder to free up memory, view the items on the desktop in small icon view, and add an International menu for switching between keyboards. Its division of the Empty Trash command into disk drives is ideal when you only want to empty the trash of one disk or the other, and the Mailbox folder is a perfect way to set up a simple mail system with System 7. (A mini tip: If you're looking for a time-zone map, click the WizTools logo in the control panel and then click the Customer Support button.)

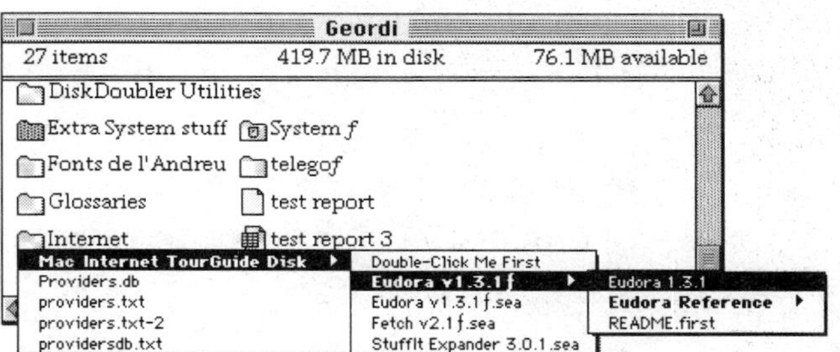

With WizTools' PopUpFolder, click on a folder in the desktop with a modifier key held down to reveal the contents of that folder. This means you can select items several layers down without leaving a trail of open windows behind you.

Norton Utilities. Symantec's **Norton Utilities** ($150) includes great backup and data protection tools (see Chapters 5 and 7, respectively, for more information on those), but it also includes encryption tools as well as several general system enhancements: a file finder, a Key Caps substitute, hot keys for the Open and Save dialog boxes, a disk-use indicator, and for System 6 users, a way to customize the desktop that is somewhat similar to System 7's View control panel. Consult the respective sections in this chapter for more information about the encryption and file-finder modules.

Alsoft Power Utilities. The **Alsoft Power Utilities** package ($130, Alsoft) includes a wide variety of utilities, the most important of which are a font manager (MasterJuggler, described in Chapter 14) and disk optimizing, partitioning, and diagnostics (described in Chapter 5). It also includes a couple of smaller system enhancements, including a disk-activity indicator, hierarchical menus, and a screen dimmer.

Magnet. **Magnet** ($130) is a unique, intuitive tool from No Hands Software that is designed to perform automatic backups, synchronization, and file searches. Most of its modules are described in other sections of this chapter.

Super 7 Utilities. **Super 7 Utilities** ($100, Atticus) turns your regular menus into tear-off menus that you can position anywhere on your screen and supplies a printer menu, an alias trasher, a sound manager, and a comments manager (for the Get Info window), as well as a file finder that I was unable to make work on my Mac. I love break-off menus, and Super 7's work quite well, and being able to choose a printer from a menu in the Finder instead of the slower-than-molasses Chooser is always a welcome respite. But are two-sevenths of the product really worth the price tag?

HAM

(EC)

This little utility with the strange name from Inline Design ($80) lets you set up a group of programs and documents that you can launch with a single keystroke. **HAM** also remembers how you left your Mac before shutdown and automatically opens each document so you can pick up where you left off. HAM stands for Hierarchical Apple Menu, and it is probably the best hierarchical-menu utility you can find. Besides converting the Apple menu in a veritable tree of folders, it lets you reorder items in the Apple menu without changing their names and remembers what you've opened most recently.

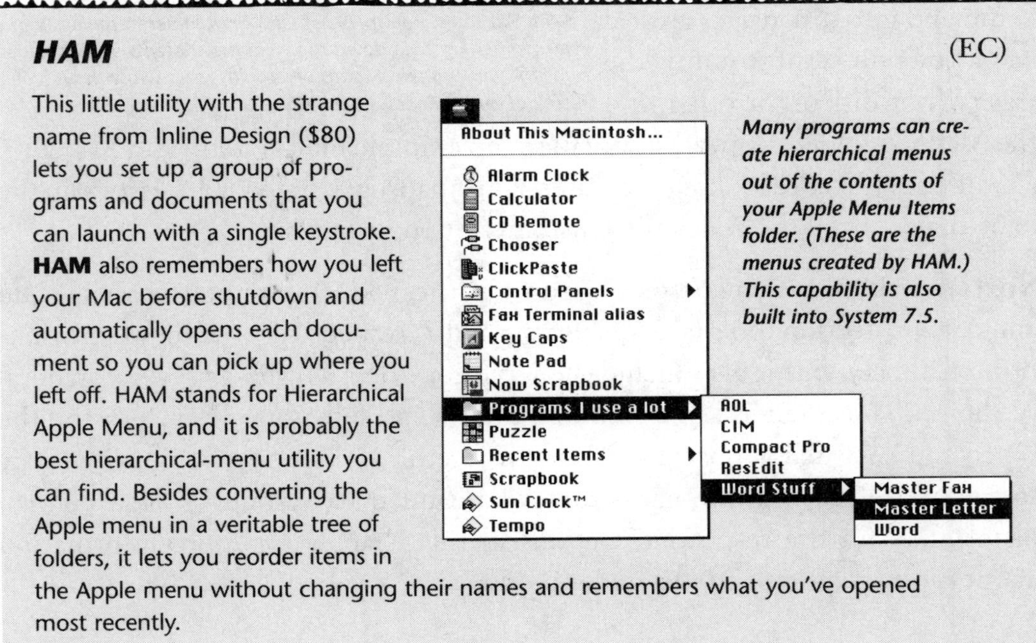

Many programs can create hierarchical menus out of the contents of your Apple Menu Items folder. (These are the menus created by HAM.) This capability is also built into System 7.5.

Square One (EC)

SquareOne (Binary Software, $75) is a little program with one mission—launching programs—that it completes well. Imagine making aliases of all your most commonly used programs and then pasting them onto a little card so they won't get lost. Square One simplifies the process and then makes the palette readily available whenever you need it. If all you want is a program launcher, Square One is a good place to start.

Square One lets you create a floating palette with your most-often-used programs, in any shape you wish.

PowerBook Utilities (RC)

Dare I say it? PowerBooks are like the stereotypical jock—powerful but not very bright. Apple gave us power in a small box but left it up to software developers to add the brains. The best of the bad Apple examples is the puny Battery program that floats on your desktop like an anemic traffic hazard. (Some of this changes with the 500-series PowerBooks and System 7.5, as described in the box on the next page.) An ideal tool for battery health should be accurate, unobtrusive, and smart enough to control the power consumption it monitors. Fortunately, four products accomplish this and other desirable management tasks. The question then is how to choose among the four.

The four general utility PowerBook programs we looked at track the charge level of your battery and allow for a variety of settings to control power consumption. All four are serial-port-aware, meaning they won't let your PowerBook fall into sleep mode while communicating with other computers. They all offer the minimum in security measures, just enough to keep your files safe from the eyes of the mildly unscrupulous curious idler. And all of them offer solutions to the problem of cursor *submarining*, which is when the cursor

Going Mobile With 7.5 (EC)

New software introduced with the 500-series PowerBooks and included with version 7.5 of Apple's system software includes many of the utilities offered in the commercial programs reviewed here. One of its principal features is a customizable Control Strip that can be moved around on the screen and adapted to fit the user's needs. It allows you to monitor battery usage, file sharing, hard disk spin, sound settings, video mirroring, and AppleTalk. The PowerBook Assistant also synchronizes files between the PowerBook and a desktop Mac, either manually or automatically, making sure you've always got the most up-to-date documents where you need them. Finally, you can set up your PowerBook to automatically send queued documents to a printer, once you're connected to one.

"submerges" or disappears form view when moving because some PowerBook screens (any except the active-matrix screens) cannot keep up with the speed of the cursor.

Power consumption is controlled by turning off or down various power-hungry components after a user-specified period of inactivity. You can trust your power management utility to turn off the backlight, rest the processor, spin down the hard disk, or put your precious PowerBook to sleep. Spinning down the hard disk while working in a program that doesn't regularly access the hard disk will save power and give you more time on your current battery charge (you can hear the disk drive spinning when a program is accessing the hard disk).

But maybe you don't want to wait for the hard disk to spin back up again every time you need it. You don't want to lose performance just to gain a little extra battery time. Perhaps you don't want it to spin down at all when you're plugged into an AC outlet. It's not difficult to learn to adjust the various "timeout" controls, and all these programs let you set separate timeouts for battery versus AC use.

All of the four programs reviewed here have lost any major bugs that may have once plagued them, so my preference for The Norton Essentials for PowerBook is based on its interface, and the other factor that will occupy the rest of this section—the extra features that the four software companies determined would round out the ideal PowerBook utility package. Read all four product reviews for descriptions of the tantalizing extras offered in different combinations in each of these programs. For a quick comparison, check out the chart at right.

The Power in PowerBook Utilities

(RC)

Many PowerBook utility collections have similar features, but their quality varies from product to product. Here's a guide to what's where and how good it is.

	PBTools	Power To Go	CPU	Norton
Airport ease	○	●	○	●
Caps Lock help	●	○	•	●
Cursor finder	•	•	●	●
Custom cursors	•	•	•	●
Discharge help	●	●	●	○
File compression	○	•	○	○
File sync	○	○	•	●
Hot keys	•	•	●	•
Menu autodrop	○	●	●	○
Processor speed shift	○	●	●	○
Remaps arrow keys	●	○	●	○
Screensaver	●	●	●	○
Security	•	●	•	•
User sets	○	●	●	○

○ Not available • There, but could be better ● Present and generally delightful

PBTools. A serious geekhead workplace lurks beneath **PBTools'** appealing simplicity of design. One control panel offers easy access to battery analysis, security, and power and sleep adjustment. A compact menu-bar icon displays more information than seems possible in such a tiny space. With a glance you can check the battery-charge level, AC connection, hard disk spin, and AppleTalk and Caps Lock status.

Enter battery nerdhood with PBTools' PowerWatch station. Use adjustable graphs and diagnostic logs to track voltage thresholds, charge/discharge curves, and other health matters for up to four different batteries. Deep Discharge Battery easily reconditions nickel cadmium batteries. Logic doesn't seem to dictate how any of the four software companies made their choices on the extras

they includeds, but I like PBTools' key remapper: While pressing the Control key, you can use the arrow keys as Page Down, Home, Page Up, and End keys. PBTools is by Inline Software and retails for $100.

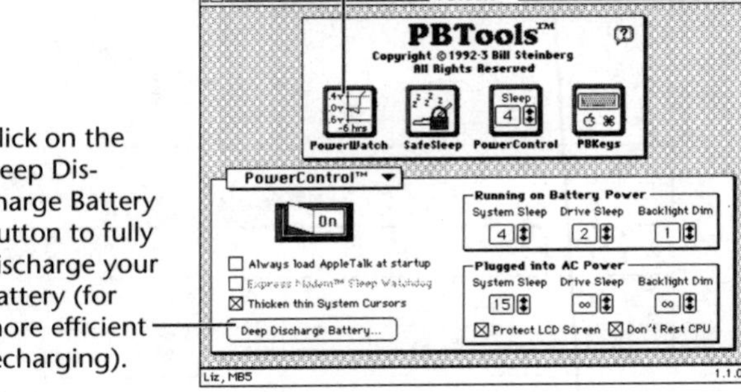

Just one of PB Tools' four settings windows, the PowerControl window lets you set the timeouts for system sleep, drive sleep, and other power-saving features.

Power To Go. You might easily argue that **Power To Go** ($100, Claris) offers too many extra features, especially while you watch its installer place files in seven different locations on your hard disk, but the real problem is that its many features aren't well coordinated. Take the included SpaceSaver file compression program (developed by Aladdin, makers of StuffIt). It may be a great program on its own, but you can't access it from any other module, and you can't even get tech support for it from Claris!

Luckily, Claris didn't forget about the normal PowerBook concerns. Among many well-designed features, Power To Go lets you create what I call User Sets. Configure one set of timeouts and settings for yourself and another for your spouse, or create different work environments for office and home. If you can't bear the idea of adding one more item to your menu bar, you'll appreciate Power To Go's user-configurable floating palette. Design the palette to show only the battery charge level or lengthen the palette to include a variety of indicators plus a sleep button and a travel clock. The clock can display as many cities as you want. A hot key will pop the palette off and on the screen. Menus pop down without a click (although they won't pop back up until you click elsewhere). Password security in Power To Go is the strongest of all four programs because it can't be defeated by simply starting up with the extensions turned off.

Connectix PowerBook Utilities. Connectix PowerBook Utilities, also called CPU ($100), vies with Norton Essentials for the position of most-recommended PowerBook utility, perhaps because the others haven't been around as long. CPU is loaded with features, and it gives you a choice as to how cluttered with

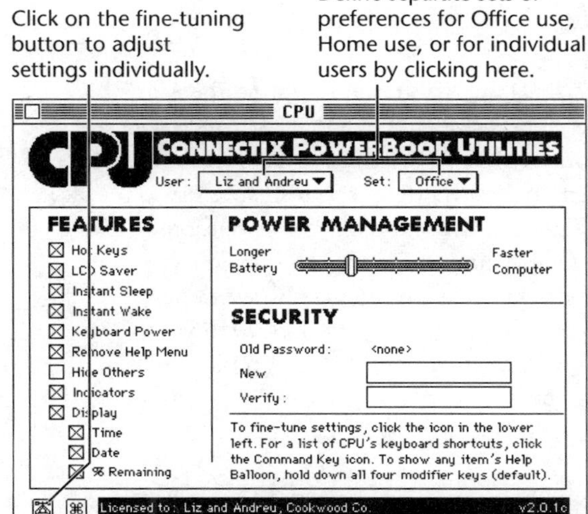

CPU has a general control panel (shown here) as well as a fine-tuning control panel for each group of settings.

various power indicators you want your menu bar to be. Like Power To Go, CPU gives you menus that drop without a click—a nice feature because the trackball makes you use two fingers to press and drag. Unlike Power To Go, CPU's menus disappear without a click (and correctly so) if you take the mouse away from the menu without selecting an option.

CPU also includes Keyboard Power: Use key combinations to select menu items and buttons in dialog boxes. Get used to Keyboard Power and you'll wonder how you did without it! CPU addresses a major PowerBook concern with the inclusion of EasySync, a file synchronization extension (synchronization software is described under "File Synchronization," below).

The Norton Essentials for PowerBook. With my particular work habits and my PowerBook Duo, I don't need discharge help, processor-speed shifting, or the few other features missing from **Norton Essentials for PowerBook** ($130). Norton has its own appeal, based on well thought-out features, such as its file synchronization, but I especially like it because it does the basic power management work effectively, and I'm a sucker for clever gadgets, of which Norton has its share.

Caps Lock control makes decidedly "up and down" sounds when the key is activated. You can free up menu space by making the balloon help icon disappear. Select from a variety of battery gauge types, from "gas tank" to percentage figures. Power Cursor allows you to customize all of the five common cursor shapes, and it's the only program of the four that lets you fatten the arrow cursor. If you sometimes lose your cursor, Norton's cursor locator is quite an entertaining beacon.

Going Through Airport Security (RC)

Both Power To Go and Norton Essentials provide special hot keys for interrupting the Mac's long startup sequence and then shutting down very quickly after showing airport security personnel that your PowerBook isn't hiding a collapsible Uzi. PBTools has to be applauded, however, for not encumbering its program with yet another module, and instead offering a couple of strategies. "Hold down the Shift key at startup, bypassing all your extensions. There's no need to irritate the people behind you while you wait for all your system extensions to load." Of course, the only person you irritate is yourself. Everyone else walks past you. Walk with them by using the second strategy. Arrive at the X-ray machine with your PowerBook in sleep mode. Startup from sleep is very fast. Use a sleep hot key to put the little guy back to sleep instantly, and stroll off to your gate.

GOOD FEATURE

Finally, Norton allows you to define different settings for different programs. You can have Norton automatically turn off the hard disk timeout for a program like Word, for instance, that frequently accesses the hard disk.

Compression

Anyone with a hard disk stuffed to the gills is faced with the same problem: finding more disk space. An inexpensive alternative to buying another hard disk is to purchase a compression program.

What Is Compression? (KC)

Compression is the act of making a file smaller. It is common to hear how a compression package will increase your disk size, but that's just marketing hype; the *files* get smaller, the disk stays the same size. Compression software comes in two flavors: *file-level* and *driver-level.*

File-level packages offer numerous choices as to how the package will work for you. Compression in file-level programs can either be initiated immediately or set up for a later time when the Mac is not in use: a specific hour, at shutdown, or after a specified period of idleness. Some packages also let you set up a "sleep" corner, a place where you can move your cursor to activate the compression scheme.

You have fewer such choices with a driver-level utility. Driver-level utilities compress your entire hard disk at installation. You may have some choice as to how the program will compress your disk—faster versus tighter—but, mostly, the choice is limited to installing or not installing these programs.

Whether file- or disk-level, these packages use *lossless compression*, meaning that files retain all of their information after compression. You can compact and then extract a file as many times as you need to, and you will always have exactly the same file. *Lossy compression*, on the other hand, is employed by utilities that perform JPEG compression and other such methods used in compacting video files, for example, where some information is lost during compression.

It is not necessary to compress your whole hard disk, of course. You may wish to compress only one file, say, to send it more quickly to a friend via CompuServe, or a group of files that you don't work with very often, in order to save disk space.

Since file level and driver level packages work so differently, we will discuss them separately.

File-Level Packages (KC)

A file-level compression package lets you select individual files, folders, or groups of files and folders to compact. Several features are becoming quite common among these programs:

- choosing between compressing your files quickly (and compressing less) or compressing to save more space (and taking more time)
- selecting files by their labels, types, prefixes or suffixes, and among a list of applications for inclusion or exclusion from compression
- creating some form of a *self-extracting archive* (which can be recomposed without the compression software)
- determining the amount and type of idle time that needs to occur to activate idle-time compression
- translating files compressed in a variety of compression formats, not just the program's own

- adding passwords to restrict access to compressed files
- compressing documents directly from the Finder using a special menu added next to the Special menu, or by drag and drop
- segmenting large files into pieces (to fit them on floppy disks, for example)

StuffIt Deluxe (KC/EC). Even if **StuffIt Deluxe 3.0.7** (Aladdin Systems, $120) weren't the most powerful compression program for the Mac, which it is, it would still be the sentimental favorite: first, for having been around so long, and second, because it started out as a shareware program written by high school student Raymond Lau. Its age is something of an advantage: The majority of the files you find on-line have been compressed—and, more important, can be decompressed—with StuffIt.

HOT TIP

StuffIt compresses your files—either manually with the main program or automatically with the included SpaceSaver module when your Mac is idle—in *archives*, separate documents that may contain any number of your original files. As with other programs, you can segment the archives into two or more pieces, say, to fit on floppy disks. The ingenious View option lets you peek at text and PICTs inside your compressed files. And you can protect your archives from inquiring minds with encryption and a password. One quick tip: In the main StuffIt window, hold down the ⌘ key to make Add the default button, the one that Return or Enter will activate.

Tips for Using Self-Extracting Archives (DD/EC)

HOT TIP

- Often, older versions of compression software cannot read files that have been compressed with newer versions of compression software. If you're not sure whether the recipient will be able to open the file, make it a *self-extracting archive,* which can decompress itself.
- A self-extracting archive is actually an application, and it uses memory like any other application. If you get an "insufficient memory" message when you double-click on a self-extracting archive, give it more memory (with the Get Info box).
- If you are compressing a very small document (say, under 25K), it usually doesn't make sense to make it self-extracting. That is because compression programs add from 18K to 25K of instructions onto the file so it knows how to decompress itself. Instead, use a program that you know the recipient has, or send the file uncompressed.

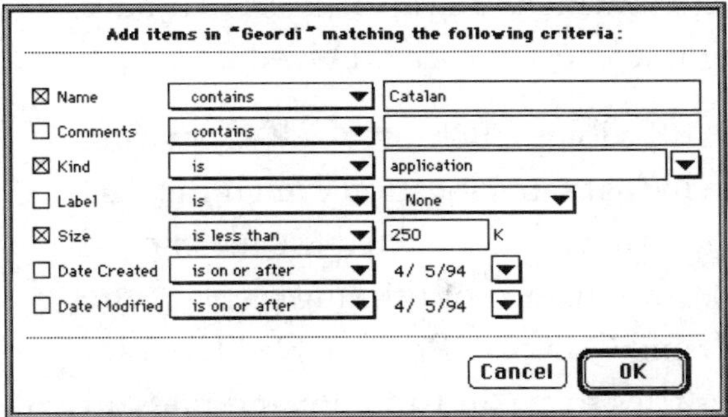

StuffIt lets you add files to an archive according to the criteria you set. (You can also look for them yourself, if you prefer.)

StuffIt's Magic Menu, which appears next to the Special menu in the Finder, and its drag-and-drop compression let you compress files right from the desktop. MagicMenu also includes a set of scripts that can automate such operations as Stuff and Mail, where a file is automatically stuffed and then enclosed in a QuickMail or Microsoft Mail document and sent from the Finder.

StuffIt's completeness comes at a price—it costs almost twice as much as DiskDoubler (see below) and occupies 2MB on your hard disk. A shareware version, StuffIt Lite ($25), limits you to stuffing and unstuffing but may be all you need. The automatic compression module, SpaceSaver, can also be purchased separately for $60.

Now Compress (KC). **Now Compress 1.0.1** ($100, Now Software) offers a lot of the features of StuffIt Deluxe without overwhelming you. The program gives you several ways to run the compression utilities depending on your preference for using menus, keyboard equivalents, or a control panel. Under System 7, you can even compress, expand, and archive files by dragging the file to one of three icons: Compress Now, Expand Now, or Archive Now. And it lets you segment an archive to make it fit on several floppies.

Now Compress is fast, and it can work automatically or on call. Unfortunately, it cannot decompress StuffIt archives, although since the software for many online services, such as America Online, offers automatic decompression of StuffIt files, this may not be a problem.

DiskDoubler (KC/EC). What I most like about **DiskDoubler** ($60, Symantec) is that you can choose from among four different compression methods ranging from the fastest compression/decompression to the tightest compression. If you're unsure which method you should use, the program offers two additional options that look at a file and guess which of the four methods would offer the smallest compression in the shortest amount of time. The program also comes with a small set of tools like DD Verify/Repair, which can repair disks that have not been accessed for months—something not unusual with archived files.

BAD FEATURE

Liz has always found DiskDoubler a bit inflexible: Click on a self-extracting archive and it will generally expand the file in that same location even if the disk is already full (it depends on whether the person who compacted the file clicked the Prompt When Expanding check box). And instead of offering to place the expanded file in another location (as StuffIt and Compact Pro do), DiskDoubler just gives up. Similarly, when DiskDoubler tries to expand an item and finds an existing item in the same location with the same name, it doesn't let you choose between replacing the file or skipping the expansion, it simply shuts itself off.

MAC BIBLE DISK

Compact Pro (EC). My personal favorite in this field is **Compact Pro,** a shareware program by Bill Goodman. Although it is neither automatic nor has a Finder menu, Compact Pro's main program can compress and expand, add passwords, and split large files with the best of them. Compact Pro is fast and reliable and worth every one of the $25 it costs.

More Disk Space (KC). **More Disk Space** ($100, Alysis) gives you a lot of flexibility in how you can compress your files, but it doesn't distinguish itself much from the other programs mentioned here except for its operation along a network. Network administrators will be happy to know that MDS can be installed onto other Macs on the network from a central location. MDS can also be set up on a server to automatically compress files that are added to it.

Driver-Level Compression (KC)

Driver-level compression utilities are supposedly easier to use than file-level packages because they compress your entire disk as part of the installation process and carry out expansion and recompression without any user intervention. All files remain compressed and are decompressed only when the Mac reads them from the disk.

WARNING

Use caution when using driver-level compression utilities. They replace your Mac's hard disk driver, which controls how the Mac and all its applications handle files. Before installing any driver-level utility you should make sure your hard disk is completely backed up.

Stacker. I am not a fan of disk-level compression packages, but if I were to use one, it would be **Stacker 1.0** ($150, Stac Electronics). Stacker is the least intrusive of these disk-level utilities, since it merely attaches itself to your existing disk driver instead of replacing it. As with other disk-level programs, Stacker includes a checker utility that examines the data structures of your hard disk to make sure they are in order and offers to repair them if it finds a problem. It also lets you use other programs like Disk First Aid and Norton Utilities.

eDisk and TimesTwo. Alysis's **eDisk** ($150) and Golden Triangle's **TimesTwo** ($150) are much more intrusive than Stacker, and I don't recommend either one. Both replace your hard disk's driver, and in the case of eDisk, it must erase your hard disk in the process. This means that you have to spend time reinstalling your system software and applications once the disk is compressed. In the case of TimesTwo, the program partitions your disk into one that is a Macintosh disk and another that is a TimesTwo disk. So, in a sense it is reformatting your disk, but it is not erasing your files. Should you want to remove TimesTwo from your disk, however, you will be stuck with restoring all of your files and applications because it will reformat your drive.

BAD FEATURE

Security

(KM)

Unfortunately, we live in a world where everyone must be concerned about security. Quite simply, there will be times when you want to safeguard your data and keep your information from falling into the wrong hands.

Many screensaver programs offer a low amount of security: You can define a password that must be entered to exit the screensaver and see what was on the screen. This may be useful for short-term antisnooper prevention, but a would-be prowler will only need to restart the Mac with the Shift key held down to override this limited security system.

Levels of Security

As with all things Macintosh, there are several different ways to secure your data, each of which may be available separately or as part of a larger software package.

Invisible files. The simplest method for securing data is to make the folder or file invisible. This can be done quickly using a utility such as ResEdit or DiskTop (both discussed in this chapter). Invisible files and folders can no longer be seen in the Finder, but they are visible from the open dialog box of some applications. This is a very simple means of security and will deter only the laziest prowler.

Locked folders. For a little more security, try a utility that can lock a folder. The contents of a locked folder cannot be accessed without a password, but the information in the folder is not encrypted. This is a very good method for keeping people from browsing through your data while keeping it available for you.

Data encryption. The next level of security is to use a simple data encryption program that requires a password. Encryption programs secure your data by scrambling the information and unscrambling it when you provide the proper password. Basic encryption programs are generally secure; only someone who is very knowledgeable and determined could get to your data once it's been encrypted.

There are several data encryption methods, but the most secure is called DES, which stands for *Data Encryption Standard*. DES was established by the National Bureau of Standards (an arm of the National Security Agency) and is supposedly impossible to break unless you possess the encryption key, that is, the password. (See the box on the next page, however, for the other side of the story.)

Locked hard disks. The final way to secure your data is to lock your hard disk so only you or someone with the password can access its data. With utilities that lock a hard drive, your data remains, but the drive cannot be accessed without the password. The more secure programs can also encrypt the drive's data.

Security Choices

Since many software companies develop more than one package to address different security needs, we've grouped the following reviews by developer.

FileGuard and TrashGuard. ASD Software makes a couple of security packages called **FileGuard** ($250) and **TrashGuard** ($80). FileGuard is a comprehensive security package that provides disk-, folder-, and file-level security. It

Big Brother May Be Watching You (KM)

If you think that DES encryption is secure, think again. Developed by the NSA (National Security Agency), many believe the code was written to be broken, at least by NSA agents. Bell scientist Michael Wiener introduced a paper at Crypto93 (a conference for cryptographers) describing a microprocessor chip that will enable the NSA to break any message encrypted with DES in two minutes.

There is, however, a solution called Pretty Good Privacy (PGP), a *public key cryptography* application. Our government and others are unhappy about the existence of this program because when you use MacPGP to encrypt a message, it is unbreakable—or as close as you can get without spending a whole lot of money to decipher it.

MacPGP is freeware, but you will have to search for it because anyone who posts it on a bulletin board risks being prosecuted by the federal government for violations of export law or sued by PKP, a company that holds the patent on some of the technology used in PGP. Despite the opposition, MacPGP will be available from Viacrypt in Phoenix, Arizona, as a commercial program sometime around the end of the summer. If you want secure communications that are truly private (remember the right to privacy?), then MacPGP is the only option.

will automatically encrypt your data as it is saved to the hard disk. You can also use it to prevent files from being copied off your hard drive. For Macs that are used by several people, you can set up a security system that allows access using an AppleShare-like privilege setup.

TrashGuard is a simple utility that completely erases a file when it is placed in the trash. The space the file occupied is overwritten, making it unrecoverable.

CryptoMatic, FolderBolt Pro, NightWatch, MacSave, and QuickLock. Kent Marsh makes a family of security products that can be used to lock up your hard drive, encrypt files, lock folders, and prevent casual access to your Macintosh.

All of the Kent Marsh products are developed with the idea that you should only purchase the product that provides the level of security you need. Yet each of the products is made to work with the others to provide a complete security system. One of the unique features of the Kent Marsh system is the use of an Administrator's disk, which will allow access to your data even if you forget your password. The Administrator disk or program that comes with your Kent

Marsh product will work on your machine only; someone else with a Kent Marsh Administrator disk cannot gain access to your data.

NightWatch II ($160) is Kent Marsh's hard disk security software. It does not encrypt files, but it does prevent access to your hard drive. Access to the hard disk can be gained with a password or with a key disk. NightWatch II also includes a security screensaver that prevents someone from accessing open files on your Mac when you leave it unattended.

FolderBolt Pro ($130) is used to manage access to folders. You can determine the level of access someone has to your folders by making them read-only, write-only, or completely locked. FolderBolt also lets you lock the trash (in System 7) so only someone with the password can delete files.

CryptoMatic ($100) is a complete encryption package that lets you use a variety of encryption standards to encrypt files or folders. If you have to send a file to someone else, you can create a self-deciphering file that the recipient can open without the CryptoMatic extension—as long as he or she has the proper password. In addition to encrypting files, CryptoMatic also allows you to securely erase files so that they are unrecoverable—even with data recovery software like the Norton Utilities.

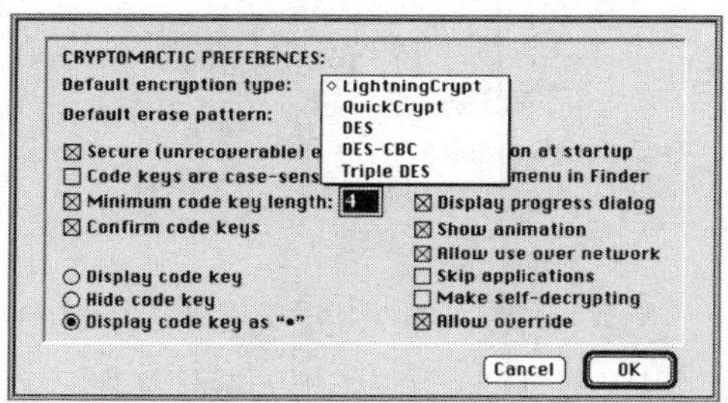

CryptoMatic gives you a wide variety of security options in its Preferences dialog box.

QuickLock ($30) is a screensaver that prevents others from using your Mac without the proper password. In addition to preventing someone from accessing your data, QuickLock can be set to periodically ask for a password even while the computer is in use, acting as a timed sentinel.

AME. Access Managed Environment, or AME ($280, Casady & Greene), is a multilevel security package providing varying levels of access to different users and an automatic user log. AME offers disk-, folder-, or file-level security and can even be set up to reject floppy disks so that nothing can be copied from your disk. AME includes a secure delete feature so that trashed files cannot be recovered.

Problems With Security Software (KM)

The problem with encryption and data protection is that your data will only be as secure as your password. If your password is easy to guess, or if you've written it down next to your computer (don't laugh, I've seen it happen), your data is not secure, regardless of the encryption method. Also, if you forget your password or if your drive should crash, retrieving your information will be almost impossible. Keep an unencrypted backup in a secure place such as a safety deposit box.

Finally, if you are installing disk-level security, then the boot blocks of the hard drive will be modified by the program, making recovery of any files next to impossible. Make backups before you install the software.

AME is very comprehensive, providing tools for almost every security need. It can even be used to prevent desktop modification and setup—ideal for multi-user access where each user has his or her own secure folder. With AME's tracking features you can also delete files that belong to specific users. AME can also be used in an AppleShare environment to restrict access to AppleShare volumes or other AppleTalk devices.

Critical warning! Do not use any hard disk utility programs or update the hard disk drivers on a drive protected by AME. Doing so will destroy the data on your hard drive or cause your hard disk to crash.

DiskLock. Symantec's **DiskLock** ($190) is a general-purpose security package. that includes hard disk locking, an activity log for tracking user access, a folder lock, and file-encryption capabilities. It also has a built-in screensaver to prevent unauthorized access while you are away from the Mac. DiskLock is a good choice for comprehensive security.

CDU and CPU. The multipurpose packages **Connectix Desktop Utilities** (CDU) and **Connectix PowerBook Utilities** (CPU) provide security features for your Macintosh along with a suite of other features (see "Utility Collections," above). Each of these packages has hard disk locking and screensaver features that require a password for access to the Mac.

File Synchronization (KM)

POWERBOOK

What do you do if you have two hard drives and you want each drive to have the same data files? One option is to open up each folder and compare the files one by one, but it'll take you a long, long time. (System 7.5 offers file synchronization, but only through its PowerBook File Assistant. See the box "Going Mobile With 7.5" on page 474 for more details.) Synchronization utilities come to your rescue and update files on two disks quickly and automatically.

How Synchronization Works

Synchronization utilities operate by comparing two folders (or hard drives), named, say, Office Stuff and Home Stuff, and reconciling the contents of each. First, the program checks each file's name and modification date in Office Stuff and then looks to see if a similar file already exists in Home Stuff. If no such file exists, the program copies it over automatically. If the file with the same name *does* exist, the program checks to see which file is more recent. Depending on how you've configured the program, it may copy the more recent version into the appropriate folder (whether it be Office Stuff or Home Stuff) or ask you which version you want to keep.

Getting in Sync

When you go shopping for a synchronization utility, one of the features you'll want is a *merge* function. Performing a merge means moving the files from Home Stuff to Office Stuff, for example, but not the reverse. The merge capability is important when you have more files on a desktop Mac than on your PowerBook and you only want the new files you've created moved to the desktop Mac.

Magnet. Magnet ($130, No Hands Software) is a full-featured file organization utility that not only synchronizes your files but is also useful in managing all of your files. Of all the programs listed here, Magnet is probably the most powerful, due to its built-in find capabilities, which can be used in conjunction with its backup and synchronize tools (see the description of those features under "Finding Files" later in this chapter). Also, it can automatically mount an AppleShare volume and perform a scheduled synchronize, backup, or merge. (See Chapter 23 for more on AppleShare.)

Twins (WizTools). WizTools' set of System 7 utilities (see page 471) contains a very complete synchronization tool called Twins. You can schedule when Twins will perform its task and use scripts to control what is backed up or synchronized. It is an impressive utility.

EasySync (CPU and CDU). EasySync is included with both Connectix utilities collections, **CPU** and **CDU** (see a more complete description under "Utility Collections," above). It is an efficient utility that lets you quickly synchronize folders from the desktop. When you move a file or folder into a folder that contains an item with the same name, you will be asked if you want to synchronize, merge, replace, or cancel the copy or move. You can also create predefined merge or synchronization templates for future use.

File Runner. File Runner ($100, MBS Technologies) can be used for backups in addition to file synchronization. With File Runner you create specification documents that tell File Runner which files to back up or synchronize. Unfortunately, File Runner does not have a file merge option.

Inline Sync. Inline Sync ($130, Inline Software) has a unique system that lets you link the folders and files you want to keep synchronized. The links are automatically maintained, and they make it easy to schedule updates. Inline Sync's intuitive interface makes the synchronization process easier than with some of the other packages.

PowerMerge. PowerMerge ($130, Leader Technologies) is specifically made for reconciling files on a PowerBook with those on a desktop computer. Although it is not as feature-rich as some of the other utilities, PowerMerge does have the most complete manual. The current version does not have an automatic or timed synchronization capability.

Finding Files

The Finder, that program that represents the contents of your hard disk in the form of a desktop with folders and files, gets its name from the fact that it was supposed to help you find things. Early versions of the Finder, ironically enough, had no Find command at all—the user was the *real* finder. Later, a desk accessory was added to the system software that showed a little man running around finding your stuff. He was useful but not particularly powerful, and soon there were many utilities on the market designed to sift through your hard disk in more ways than you can imagine, as we describe below. For those of you who depend solely on Apple's System software, you'll be happy to know that System 7.5's Find command has been greatly improved (also discussed below).

File Finders (EC)

As hard disks get bigger and bigger, more files burrow their way down into the depths of your folder organization—or is that disorganization? (OK, so I had the same problem with smaller hard disks, but it's a great excuse!) The solution to finding those errant files is the *file finder*, which will search using criteria such as the file's name, creation date, modification date, and other basic external information. Some advanced file finders include the ability to search for text *inside* the document, although they don't do it as well as the dedicated packages, which are described in the next section, "Text Retrieval."

System 7.5's Find command is really an alias that points back to the Find File desk accessory that's automatically installed in the Apple menu. At first glance it looks quite similar to the Find command offered by System 7.1, but it offers two important improvements. First, there are more criteria to base a search on, and, perhaps more important, you can base a search on more than one criterion at a time. This means you can search for those files that begin with *Bible* and that were also modified after June 6, 1994, for example, something that was not possible under System 7.1. Second, Find File displays all of the files that match your criteria in a scroll window so that you can quickly choose the one you want and either open it, print it, get info about it, or open the folder that contains it.

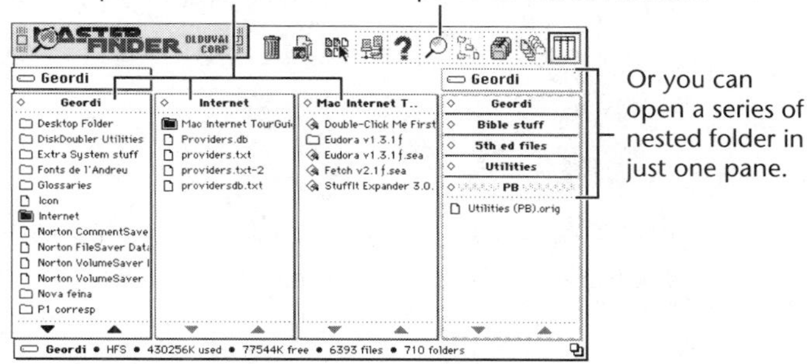

MasterFinder is a great substitute for the Finder's own Find command.

MasterFinder. This great little utility does everything a little better than the Finder itself and is so easy to use that you don't mind adding a new program to your repertoire. And it's fast! In an unscientific test on my 500MB hard disk, **MasterFinder** ($150, Olduvai) took only 4 seconds to find a set of files, while the System 7.1's Find command and DiskTop (described below) took 20 and 60 seconds, respectively. MasterFinder remembers where you've been, includes a launcher menu for often-used applications and documents, and automatically shrinks to a mini-window when you switch to another application.

GOOD FEATURE

Magnet. **Magnet** ($130, No Hands Software) can search for files based on practically any criteria (including limited text-content searches) and is just as fast as MasterFinder. It also has one important advantage over the others discussed here: You can define "triggered" sets so that Magnet automatically starts up at the specified time (or after the specified action), searches with the specified criteria, and then copies, moves, or creates aliases of the files it finds, even if they're on a remote server. These features make it a great backup and synchronization program as well as an excellent file finder.

GOOD FEATURE

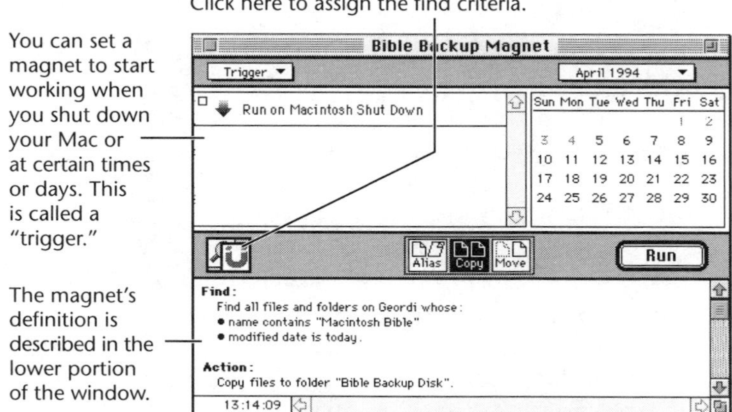

Magnet first asks you to define a search and then lets you move, copy, or create aliases of the files found, either manually or at a "trigger." Shown here is an example of a backup magnet—it searches for all the documents in my current project that have been modified today and then copies the files to an external disk at shutdown.

One last thing I can't help but add: Magnet's way of helping you find documents created by a certain application—giving you a scroll box of applications to choose from—is the right way to solve the problem. Never again will I have to remember Microsoft Word's file type code (WBDN? WBND? WDNB?).

DiskTop. DiskTop ($100, PrairieSoft) used to be the best Finder substitute around. Unfortunately, DiskTop seems to have been neglected by CE Software, and its new owner, PrairieSoft, has yet to make any marked improvements, even with version 4.5, released in January 1994.

Fast Find (Norton Utilities). Fast Find (the file finder included with **Norton Utilities**, described above under "Utility Collections") is not nearly as fast as MasterFinder, but it has a few special options you might like. You can quickly view a document's text contents to see if it is the one you're looking for (click the magnifying glass icon), and there is an icon editor hidden in the Get Info box (double-click the item's icon in the Fast Find window).

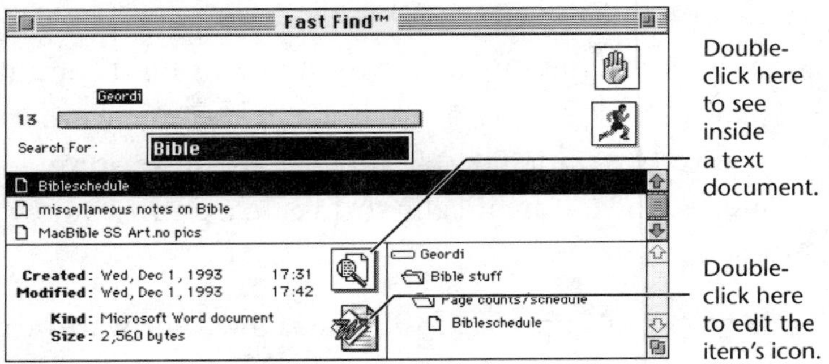

Fast Find is not the fastest file finder, but it has two special features: an icon editor and a text document "peeker."

Text Retrieval (KC)

The basic function of a text-retrieval package is to find a document stored anywhere on your system by searching the text that it contains. To do that job well, most text retrieval packages will let you:

- search for part of a word, a word, or a string of words
- select a disk or specific folder to search
- add other information to a search, such as the creation date of a file, and use Boolean operators (see "Winnowing Those Files" on page 514)
- save your search criteria for use in later searches

- use your Mac for something else while it searches for your text in the background
- create and maintain an updated index of the files and folders on your disk, to expedite file searches
- read the contents of found files from within the search program
- search over a network

Alki Seek. If it weren't for the fact that this program doesn't generate an index and doesn't search in the background, I'd tell you that **Seek 2.1** ($40, Alki Software) was the best search package available for individual users. I have a soft spot for this program because it has so many ways to narrow down a search—without bogging down the user in the process.

The strongest feature of Seek is its "banter box." With so many options available for building a search string, this box is a necessity. It answers the question, "What was I looking for again?" by giving you a plain English description of what you had set up as your search criteria.

Seek has a very elegant interface. The majority of the program's operations are handled in two main windows—one to set up a search and one to show the results. The search window has icons representing the different criteria you can select to define your search, and Seek lets you search for files and folders by location, date, size, and application as well as by content.

OnLocation. Despite its weak search criteria, **OnLocation 2.0.1** ($130, On Technology) is the best search tool available on the Mac, mainly because of its speed (it creates indexes) and its ability to work in the background.

OnLocation's search criteria are paltry at best. The program offers text searching with the Boolean operators AND and OR as well as a half-hearted wildcard search—it can match the root of a word to find related files. I harp on the lack of search criteria so much because OnLocation has the potential of returning a daunting list of files—particularly since it can work over a network and search remote volumes.

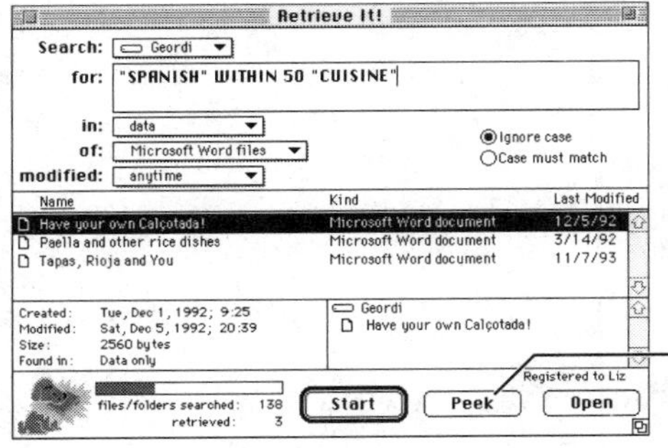

Click on Peek to see the contents of the document in context to make sure it's the document you want.

Retrieve It! offers the best qualifiers, including proximity and Boolean operators.

RetrieveIt! RetrieveIt! **1.0** ($90, Claris) uses Boolean operators and a couple of other qualifiers to help you find what you need. RetrieveIt! has numerous proximity operators, letting you look for words before or after other words, for instance. You can search several volumes, and you can look for files according to when they were created and modified and by which application. Like Seek, RetrieveIt! is best suited for searches through small amounts of data, since it does not create an index. If you do wind up in a long search, however, you can send RetrieveIt! to work in the background.

To me, the nicest feature of this package is that you can stop a search in progress, which is particularly useful if a search is taking too long and you wish to modify your criteria. Just the same, I'd have a hard time choosing it over Seek, since RetrieveIt! costs more.

Winnowing Those Files (KC)

Although they're supposed to simplify your computing life, text-retrieval programs can give you a headache by returning with never-ending lists of files containing your designated text. To help save time, retrieval programs offer search criteria to help pare down the number of files the program will search and return.

Boolean and Proximity Operators

Most text-retrieval programs have Boolean operators—words like AND, OR, and NOT—that you place between words and text strings in your search. Other programs, such as RetrieveIt!, offer a more extensive set of operators, including proximity descriptions that let you zoom in on text. So, for example, a search for *Spanish Within 50 Cuisine* will return only those documents that contain the words *Spanish* and *cuisine* if they appear within 50 words of each other.

Wild Cards

Some programs, such as Seek, let you use wild cards instead of some of the letters of a word to help you find words you don't know the spelling of or to look for several related words at a time. For example, you could type something like *tech** and the program could return files containing the words *technology, technique,* or *Technicolor.*

FetchIt. FetchIt 3.0, from CRA Z Software ($40), is an extension that enhances the functions of the standard Save and Open dialog boxes by installing a pop-up menu containing several functions—most notably text retrieval.

FetchIt's Look 'Fer command lets you search for text strings in files in a given folder (and only in that folder) and is smart enough to automatically narrow the scope of the search to files the active program can read. A successful Look 'Fer will bring along a Context Window that shows you the part of the file where FetchIt found the match. The utility also lets you continue your search with Look 'Fer Next, which picks up where Look 'Fer left off, using the same criteria.

FetchIt also includes other utilities, such as Find, which looks for text in file and folder names. FetchIt also lets you change disks and rename, delete, copy, and move files and folders—all from within an application.

Desktop Tools

Never content to just accept things straight out of the box, the programmers behind the software in this section offer souped up versions of the tools that are included with Apple's system software.

Scrapbooks (EC)

In 1984, Apple's Clipboard was revolutionary. It let you copy and then paste as many times as you wanted. But once you copied or cut another item, the first disappeared forever. Apple's Scrapbook was designed as a safe place to store those images and text that you might want to place from day to day, but still, you could only have one Scrapbook. Several developers have improved on both Apple's Clipboard and its Scrapbook. If you do a lot of copying and pasting, they may be worth your while.

KopyKat. KopyKat (CRA Z Software, $90) lets you copy up to ten items and store them in temporary clipboards. Paste the last item copied with ⌘V as usual, or hold down ⌘Option and click to have a pop-up menu appear with

GOOD FEATURE

each of the items currently stored. The best thing about KopyKat is that you don't even notice you're using it—it is fast and works exactly like the regular System (with the Option key added). One minor problem: In Microsoft Word, KopyKat doesn't copy and paste formats correctly. (If you want to drive your cats really cra-z, click the CRA Z logo in the control panel a few times. My cat, Cookie, came running into my office, convinced I was hiding a renegade cat inside my Mac.)

ClickPaste. ClickPaste ($100, Mainstay) lets you paste text, images, sounds, and other items from a pop-up menu that appears on the screen when you press any two modifier keys. This Scrapbook substitute stores the items in a fol-der right on your desktop, making it easy to organize them in a way that helps you find them later. Putting new text, PICT files, or sounds within Click-Paste's reach is just a question of putting them in the ClickPaste folder. For more-complex copies, such as EPS or PageMaker files, you use the Save Clipboard command in ClickPaste's pop-up menu.

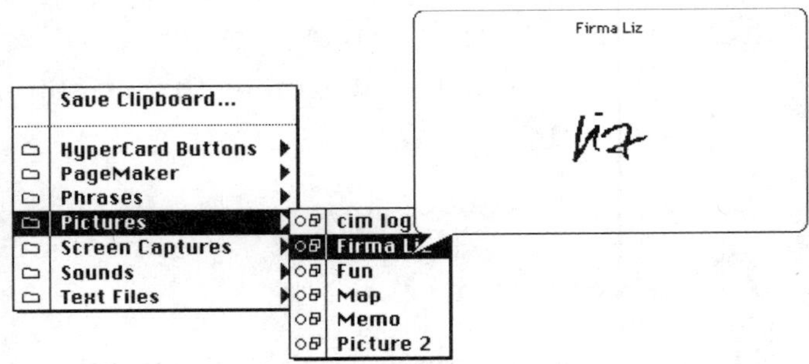

Press the two user-assigned modifier keys (I use Ctrl Option) and click to make the ClickPaste menu appear. Then select the item you wish to paste from the submenus. If you have selected Show Balloons in the ClickPaste desk accessory panel, you will see a preview of each object you can paste.

BAD FEATURE

MultiClip. MultiClip ($150, Olduvai) tries to do so much more than the simpler KopyKat (or the still simpler Clipboard from Apple) that it loses the most important battle: transparency. Each time you copy, the Mac goes "brrrrrrr-rrrrrrrrrrrrrrrrrz." It only takes a few seconds, but more seconds than I'm willing to wait. It's just not worth it.

Now Scrapbook. Slightly less immediate, but much more powerful, is Now Scrapbook (part of the Now Utilities package described under "Utility Collections," above). You must open Now Scrapbook (it's an application) to access its images, but once you do, you'll be greeted with three different ways to view your images; the ability to import and export Paint, EPS, PICT, TIFF, sound, text, and QuickTime files; and a clean interface that you can mouse around in without looking at the manual. Now Scrapbook has a superb printing feature, which lets you print catalogs of your scrapbooks, either in full size or in miniature.

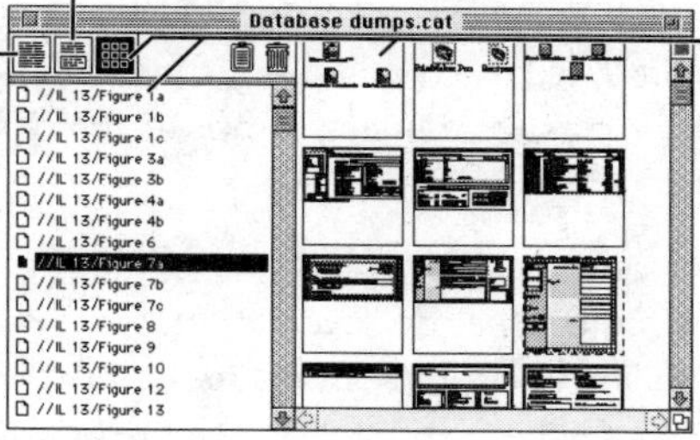

The Individual With Keywords view button offers a text box in which you can type notes or categories to help you find images later.

Click on the Individual View button to see each item in the Scrapbook individually, at full size.

Miniatures View shows reduced-size images and a scroll list of names.

The Now Scrapbook window gives you three ways to view the items in a catalog.

Macros

(EC)

A macro program lets you assign a keyboard combination to one or more actions or commands. ⌘S (to save) and ⌘Q (to quit) are probably the most famous built-in macros on the Mac, but they barely scratch the tip of the macro iceberg. Imagine opening any program or document, choosing a printer, choosing any command in any menu or dialog box, or setting up a series of actions to perform—like applying Photoshop's Sharpen filter to every file in a folder—all with a single keystroke. Macros let you do all this and more.

QuicKeys. I've used CE Software's **QuicKeys** ($170) macro-creating control panel for years to generate "dumb quotes" and to create keyboard equivalents for menu commands. It's performed flawlessly, and I've gotten so I can barely work without it (as I realized when I upgraded my system software and didn't have a compatible version of QuicKeys for a few days).

I found earlier versions of QuicKeys a bit complex and hard to use, but the current version, QuicKeys 3.0, is pretty intuitive. I don't doubt that there are more powerful macro programs around, but I don't use ten percent of QuicKeys' power and neither will most Mac users.

QuicKeys 3.0 has a whole slew of extensions, which let you, say, dial your telephone through your modem or select a printer from the Chooser. It also supports Apple events and AppleScript (described in Chapter 3).

Editors' Poll: What's Your Favorite QuicKeys Shortcut?

DB: I use it in every application. For instance, I often have to do mind-numbing tasks in Microsoft Word, such as adding a bullet to 50 different paragraphs in a list. I just make a QuicKey that adds a bullet, jumps to the next paragraph, adds another bullet, and so on.

EC: There're so many. At work I used to have a shortcut for changing from one printer to another, and then to the fax modem. But my favorite QuicKeys are those that I set up for a specific project that do several things in a sequence. Like, select a line, erase the first word, style the line in Headline 1, go to the next line, make the first word bold, and then move the cursor to the beginning of the next paragraph, where I start typing.

JK: The three I use most often open my address book and change fonts and font sizes.

HN: Mostly I use QuicKeys for simple text strings, but I guess my favorite is a sequence that changes AppleLink from my personal account to the *MacWEEK* account. Switching involves resetting a couple of obscure things in dialog boxes, so it was a big pain. I was very pleased with myself when I got it automated.

GOOD FEATURE

Tempo II Plus. Tempo II Plus ($180, Affinity Microsystems) is the most powerful macro utility you can get (short of AppleScript or UserLand's Frontier, which are more like programming environments). One of the most important benefits it has over QuicKeys is that it is interactive—it can assess the contents of a field in a database, the codes that precede paragraphs, or part of a file's name in order to decide what action it should perform next.

For example, suppose you want to sharpen a group of Photoshop files. You'll need to open each one, apply the filter, gaze off into space as the filter is applied, save the document, and open the next one. Since Tempo can choose files by name, you can have Tempo process each file sequentially, while you either find something better to do or just gaze off into space the *entire* time.

Tempo has an incredible array of "Externals." You can use them in a macro to check how much free space you have on disk, assign and use variables, find out how long a particular string is, repeat a macro a given number of times, and much more. You can automate practically any Mac function with Tempo.

TempoEZ. If all you want to do is assign keyboard shortcuts to a few menu commands and programs, you'll find all you need in **TempoEZ** ($80, Affinity Microsystems), the scaled-down version of Tempo II Plus, discussed above. TempoEZ also lets you play more complicated macros created with Tempo II Plus.

Clocks

There are probably 50 different clocks that you can place in varying locations on your Mac desktop, from the menu bar, to a floating clock, to part of a screensaver. Unless you have System 7.5, with its built-in clock that appears in the menu bar, you should know about the two described here.

SuperClock! (Chris Allen). **SuperClock!** is a control panel that puts a small clock on the right side of your menu bar. It has a number of customizable features, including a timer with an alarm and the ability to sound on the hour. SuperClock! was written by Steve Christenson and is freeware—but if you like the program and want to pay something for it, Steve asks that you send a donation to Packard Children's Hospital at Stanford. System 7.5's clock was based on SuperClock!.

Sun Clock (EC). If you'd like to know at what time the sun will rise in Calcutta (as I promised at the beginning of this chapter) try out **Sun Clock** (Palo Alto Software, $40), the program that shows where the sun is shining (or would be

Remembering the Reminder (EC)

One of the trickiest things about macro programs is remembering which keyboard combination you've assigned to which action. Using a mnemonic system (P for PageMaker, Q for Quark) is only the beginning. Try to use the modifier keys (Control, ⌘, Option, and Shift) as consistently as possible. Perhaps you'd use ⌘ for simple operations within a program (in line with the keyboard combinations already in use in most programs) and Control for Mac-wide actions like opening programs or documents. Second, don't define a shortcut for every single action; you won't be able to remember each one's keyboard combination. If you need to consult a macro template or "quick reference guide" on screen, you might as well select the command from the menu.

shining, if it weren't covered by clouds) throughout the world. It seems kind of silly, but if you do business (or pleasure) with people in other time zones, you can see in an instant if it's the right time to call, without having to add and subtract time zones.

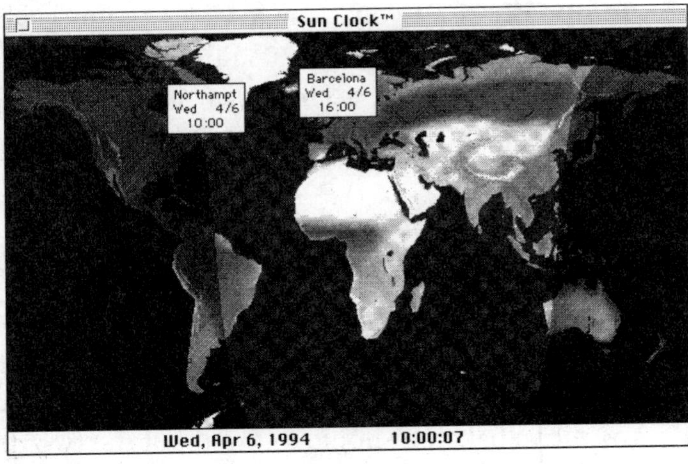

Sun Clock shows you where the sun is shining throughout the world.

Calculators (RaC)

While Apple's Calculator, preinstalled on your Apple menu, works just fine for the basics, several developers offer souped-up alternatives. When you go to buy one, evaluate carefully which one matches your style of data entry (conventional or reverse-Polish notation) and provides the features you need without taking over your screen. Many of the calculators described below include a Print command.

Calculator Construction Set. Dubl-Click Software's versatile **Calculator Construction Set** ($100) has been around for years, and its longevity may largely be attributed to its flexibility: You can create your own custom calculators with a toolbox similar to those found in a painting program. CCS contains emulations of popular scientific and business calculators (such as those from Hewlett-Packard and Texas Instruments), but you can modify them with no

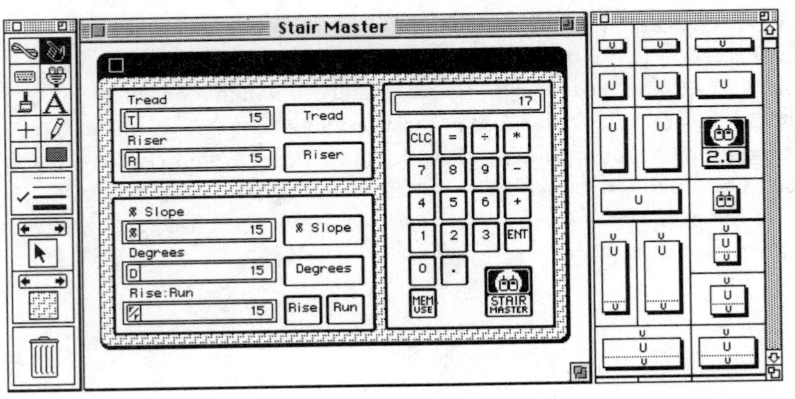

Dubl-Click's Calculator Construction Set lets you build your own calculator, without programming.

programming or create your own task-specific calculators to run within the program or as stand-alone applications.

CAL. Thought I Could went more than a little beyond the realm of ordinary calculators when it created **CAL** ($80), the talking calculator and calendar. On Macs that support PlainTalk, Apple's speech-recognition software, you can simply tell it what to do. On all Macs, it can read out both the numbers you enter and the results, helping you verify data entry without looking at the screen. It also sports an animated, scrollable, printable, selectable, copyable, exportable, and importable electronic tape, user-configurable buttons, scientific functions, and a built-in calendar with reminders!

GOOD FEATURE

zCalc. Pixel City's new scientific calculator ($70) supports reverse-Polish and regular notation, pop-up grids with scientific functions, 100 user-labeled data storage registers, a stack, and hexadecimal calculations. **zCalc** includes a unit converter; statistics functions; a financial calculator; and PixelProbe, which measures color settings at any screen location. Graphic artists could take advantage of the latter feature to pick up or determine colors—the scientific way.

CalcuPad. Tuesday Software's **CalcuPad** ($30) can save and print its calculations as documents. The application takes a unique approach: first you enter the calculations, and then the program returns the results, spreadsheet-style. The program includes 63 arithmetic, math, conversion, logical operation, and programming functions. You can customize the math symbols and use different languages, such as C programming, to operate the calculator.

Screen Capture

Have you ever wanted to take a snapshot of what's on your Mac? Perhaps you want to show someone how beautifully you've organized your hard disk, or prove that you really did score 25,413 in Tetris. One of the most peculiar features of the Mac is that it has a built-in "camera" for just this purpose. Hold down [⌘][Shift][3] and you'll create a document titled Picture 1 (or 2 or 3…) in the main level of your hard disk.

HOT TIP

If you double-click the file, you'll be able to open it with TeachText, which, surprisingly, will let you crop the picture. Just click and drag with the cross-hair to select the portion you want to save and then select Copy. You won't be able to paste the image directly in a TeachText file (since it won't accept pasted PICTs), but you can paste it into the Scrapbook (on the Apple menu) or in most drawing, layout, and even some word processing programs.

If you're looking for more sophisticated screen capture, read on.

GOOD FEATURE

Exposure Pro (EC). The best screen capture program, without reservation, is **Exposure Pro** ($140, Baseline Publishing). If you've ever spent long hours cropping and cleaning up the edges of dialog boxes and menus, you'll quickly agree that Exposure Pro's automatic clean-up commands are worth their weight in gold. Just click a button and the active window or menu appears pristine before you, ready to save. In fact, Exposure Pro has a whole slew of graphic-editing options, including lines and frames of differing weights, shades, and colors and a text tool so that you can fake menu items and sample text on the fly.

Exposure Pro lets you save your screendumps in PICT or paint format, either in a separate file (with a default name that you set) or directly to the clipboard or scrapbook of your choice. For the grand finale, Exposure Pro's manual is complete, and it's full of keyboard shortcuts. If you need to create more than one screendump, this program's for you.

WARNING

The readme file on Exposure Pro's installation disk says that if you upgrade your system with the Apple System Installer while Exposure Pro is installed, your Mac will lock up during startup and "the only fix" is to reformat your drive. You'd think the competition had written that note! Although it's true that Exposure Pro won't work until you reformat the drive, you can boot up safely holding down the Shift key and won't have lost a thing. I know. It happened to me. (The better solution is to temporarily remove Exposure Pro from the System folder before you upgrade the system software.)

GOOD FEATURE

Capture (EC). Holding a respectable second in the screen-capture Olympics is **Capture** ($130, Mainstay). In fact, Capture boasts three features that are missing from Exposure Pro. First, it lets you save screendumps in two different TIFF formats. Second, it has a clever repeat feature that lets you capture exactly the same area as the previous dump. If you want to create a series of shots that illustrate the changes in a specific area or window of the screen, this option will save you the trouble of selecting and cropping each image. Finally, Capture has a timer that lets you take a shot without holding down any keys. This is the only way I could ever have taken the shots of screensavers later in this chapter (since screensaver images disappear when you type the keyboard shortcut to shoot the image).

Spectator and CameraMan (Michael Murie). Ever need to show others how to do something on the Mac but can't make a personal appearance? How about a training video or a product demo? Use **CameraMan** ($150, Vision Software) or **Spectator** ($150, Baseline Publishing) to capture your on-screen activity as a QuickTime movie, and send it instead. Both utilities let you add narration (a sound track) while watching the movie, and CameraMan Edit (my favorite) even lets you adjust the placement of sounds by clicking and dragging.

Both programs are constrained by the Mac's performance and the amount of information being captured. For best results, use 8-bit color (or less) and limit the capture area to half the screen. You will still get fewer than 10 frames per second (4 is typical), so work slowly and deliberately when recording—move the cursor, pause, and then perform the action.

Desktop Diversions

"The desire to add purely aesthetic enhancements to the desktop is either a measure of a higher order of civilization or a neurotic compulsion to keep busy even when we're doing nothing."—Rasa Peloria

Why not add aesthetic improvements, even whimsical ones, to your workplace? Our real desks (the ones with legs and a wooden desktop that your Mac sits on) would be less than comfortable without a colorful sheet of blotter paper, a handsome pen holder, a nicely framed photo of the spouse and kids, and tasteful artwork hanging on a nearby wall. So go ahead and make the Mac desktop into a personalized mural, animate the icons on your menu bar, turn the mouse cursor into a spinning globe, and when you insert a disk, have your Mac respond, "Ahhhh, I needed that!"

Screensavers (EC/AN)

Most computer monitors (like most TVs) use cathode ray tubes. They're coated on the inside with phosphor that glows when a beam of electrons hits it, creating the image on the screen. Leaving the same image on the screen for a long period of time can exhaust the phosphor in certain areas, causing it to shine less brightly, or not at all. That's where *screensavers* (also called *screen blankers)* come in.

Screensavers keep track of how long it's been since you hit a key or the mouse button and automatically black out or change the image on the screen after a certain amount of time (which you specify), and they continue changing it so that no single image gets burned in. Hitting any key or moving the mouse brings back the image that was there before the screensaver kicked in.

After Dark

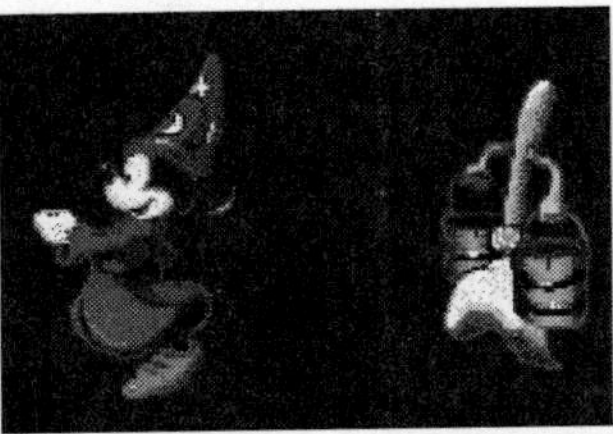

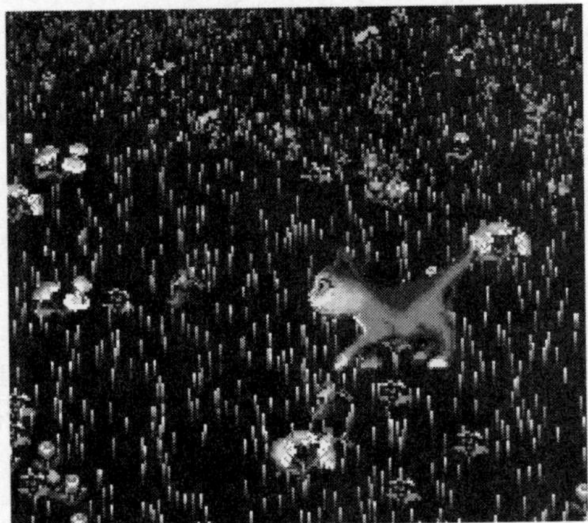

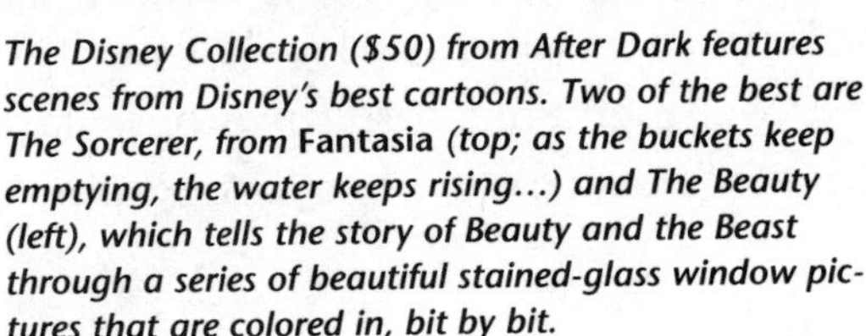

The Disney Collection ($50) from After Dark features scenes from Disney's best cartoons. Two of the best are The Sorcerer, from Fantasia *(top; as the buckets keep emptying, the water keeps rising…) and The Beauty (left), which tells the story of Beauty and the Beast through a series of beautiful stained-glass window pictures that are colored in, bit by bit.*

In addition to having the most varied collection of modules, the best animation, and the largest collection of shareware add-ons, After Dark also lets you combine modules. Here, for example, we have Boris the cat (the first module) in the Meadow (the second module). Bucolic, ain't it?

Bliss Saver

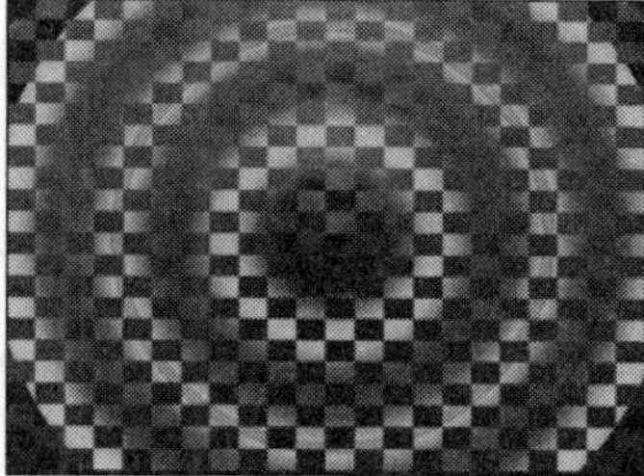

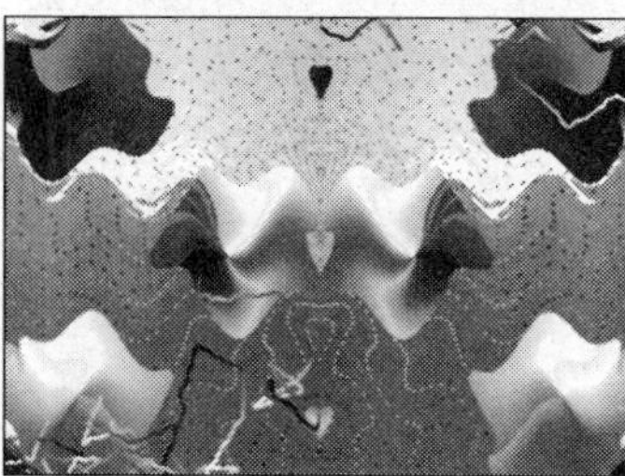

Showing screen shots of Bliss Saver's writhing, fluid screensavers is like trying to describe a symphony by playing a single B flat. You can change the colors, waveforms, and shapes from the keyboard as the screensa ver "plays" to make your own "compositions." This is one of the best screensavers I've seen in a long time ($50, Imaja).

Pyro

Pyro ($40, Symantec) was one of the first screensavers, and it remains one of the plainest. One of the modules I like best is Clock, shown here. Most of the remaining Pyro modules are inferior knockoffs of the competition.

Hot Jots

Want to leave yourself a couple of Post-its without sticking them to the outside of your Mac? Hot Jots ($45, Component Software) is the perfect choice.

Wallpaper

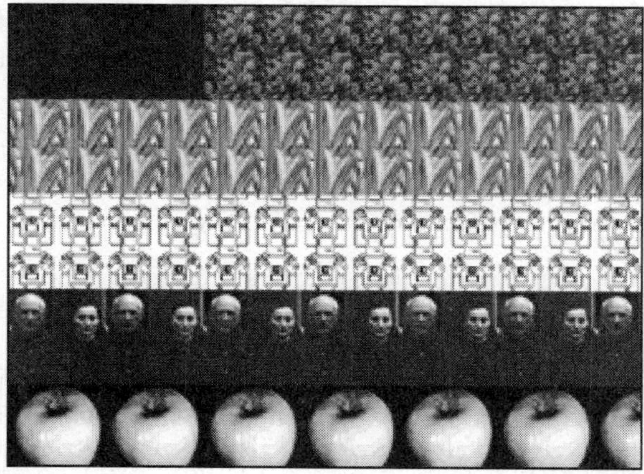

The Wallpaper in the Dark program ($60, Thought I Could) is a great way to show off all your Wallpaper samples at once. It lets you combine varying sizes of swatches of wallpaper in horizontal or vertical bands or individual squares.

Snoopy Screen Saver

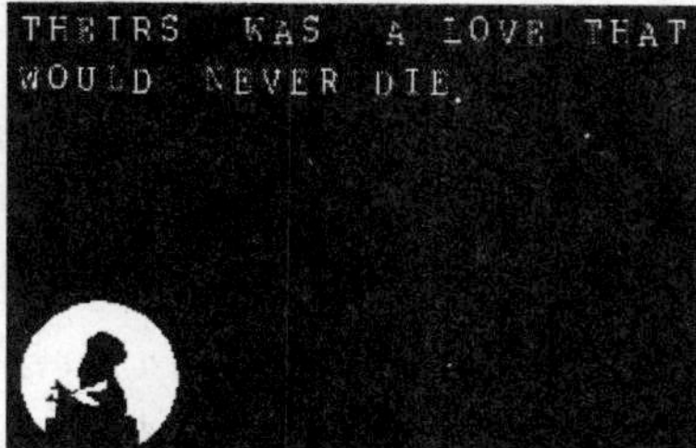

Image Smith depends too much on the charm of the Peanuts gang to pull off The Snoopy Screen Saver ($50). The drawings are true Schulz, but the animation is shoddy, the music is choppy, and there are way too few modules.

You can turn most screensavers on immediately—the "sleep now" feature—by moving the pointer to a particular corner of the screen, which is useful when you're working on something you don't want everybody to see. And you can temporarily turn most screensavers off as well—the "never sleep" feature—by moving the pointer to a different corner of the screen, which you might want to do if you needed to watch something on the screen but weren't going to touch your keyboard or mouse for a while.

In the old days, most screensavers disrupted printer or modem activity. Modern screensavers are more respectful, and they either adjust themselves automatically to make sure other activities proceed as normal or let you do it.

Just as Greek drama arose out of religious choruses, so a whole new art form is rising out of the pedestrian task of protecting the phosphor on monitors. There are times when I sit hypnotized by my screensaver, unable to move the mouse to get back to work. And I'm sure the best is yet to come.

Rather than explain how cute Boris (After Dark's cat) is and what Bliss Saver does, I'll just show you (see the illustrations on the prevous two pages).

Interior Decoration (RC)

The Macintosh system uses an 8- by 8-pixel square that, when tiled (repeated again and again), forms a seamless pattern across the desktop. The 8-by-8 restriction, however, limits the creativity of the overall effect. Increase the square to 128 by 128, and you may not even notice the repetition. The larger format, and the addition of more colors (Apple's General Controls control Panel allows only eight colors at a time), creates impressive backgrounds that can simulate the rich warm feeling of marble, wood, rice paper, a field of clover, or a pool of water. Desktop pattern programmers seem to feel that some people want to be rudely distracted by their desktops, so you could also make your desktop look like plastic, dirt, a pool of coffee beans or jelly beans, or some eye-bending optical illusion that can fry the cerebral cortex in about two seconds. Any pattern program you use will likely have one or two patterns that you love, and dozens more that are just fun to see on your screen. All of them allow for importing another program's patterns or selecting from among the several shareware pattern collections that are available.

Wallpaper, Chameleon, and Screenscapes. **Wallpaper** ($60, Thought I Could) has to be my favorite pattern program, even though I fell in love with a pattern called Artbeats Agean that comes with **Chameleon** ($60, Logical Solutions), and another pattern called Raking Nightmare from **Screenscapes** ($45, Kiwi Software). All three programs include more patterns than normal people can look at in one sitting, plus pattern editors that let you modify existing patterns or make your own from scratch (or by sampling and tiling anything you find interesting on your desktop). Chameleon's patterns tend to be conservative, which means you will probably find more that you'll want to use. (The desktop is supposed to be in the background, isn't it?)

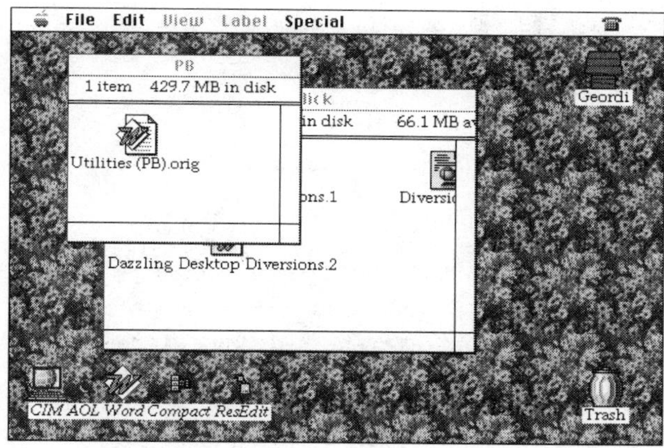

Desktop patterns can be distracting or soothing, depending on the tastes of the viewer. Most programs let you change patterns automatically with each bootup.

Wallpaper offers a lot of soothing patterns as well, but you can also choose from a fantastic array of animals, mazes, famous faces, flags, and more. Check out but never use their Patterns from Hell; those fill your screen with a host of phantom arrow pointers, folders, or trash cans!. Screenscapes offers a variety of styles, but adds an artistic polish with patterns that have a hand-painted feel. The big extra from Wallpaper is a screensaver called Wallpaper in the Dark, which runs a slide show of patterns when your computer sleeps and will also run After Dark modules (although, for some unknown reason, not the Star Trek collection).

GOOD FEATURE

Chameleon and Screenscapes are applications that act once on the system and then quit, which means they do their thing without hogging memory or risking system conflicts. Wallpaper works the same way, unless you want to use its randomizing feature, which changes the desktop pattern you're greeted with every morning. Then it has to sit in the System Folder and function as a control panel. Screenscapes rotates patterns without mucking with the system.

Enhancers You Already Own (RC)

Some customizing effects are available without the addition of any new software.

New Desktop Patterns

Use the General Controls control panel to choose a new desktop pattern or create your own. System 7.5 includes some patterns that are more interesting than those offered with earlier versions of the system software, but it doesn't let you create your own anymore, and that really bites.

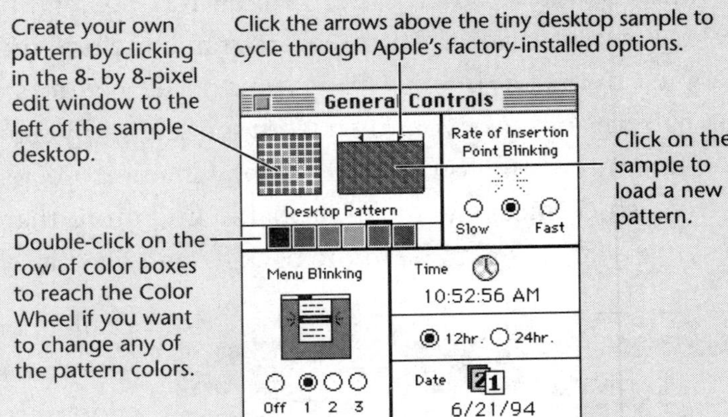

In System 7.1 and earlier, you can edit your desktop pattern in the General Controls control panel.

A New System Beep

If you get tired of having your Mac signal you with the normal "beep," open the Sound control panel and select a different sound as your system alert. If you don't like the sounds provided and your Mac has a microphone, click on Add and create your own. You can also buy collections of sounds, copy them to the System Folder, and then choose them from the Sound control panel.

New Icons

In System 7, you can easily replace or modify the icon of any element on the desktop. Simply select the item, choose Get Info from the File menu, and then click on the icon in the upper-left corner. Then you can paste in a new icon from the Clipboard, copy that icon to a new location, or cut the current icon to revert to the default icon.

Page procedures Info

Page procedures

Kind: Microsoft Word document
Size: 6K on disk (3,584 bytes used)

Where: Apps & Fonts:

Created: Sat, Jun 11, 1994, 12:56 PM
Modified: Thu, Jun 16, 1994, 11:12 AM
Version: n/a

Comments:

Locked   Stationery pad

To copy an icon, open the Get Info box, select the icon, and choose Copy from the Edit menu (⌘C). To replace an item's icon, you select the icon and paste one from the Clipboard.

You can also design a new icon with any paint program and then paste it into the item's Get Info window. For best results, make sure that the entire icon will fit in the Get Info window's icon box (a 32- by 32-pixel square). System 7 will take any oversized icon image and try to make it fit, but it will usually smoosh it into unrecognizability. Also, make the outer edges of your new icon black (or any dark color). Light colors on the edge of an icon often get lost in the transfer process.

Desktop Textures and Before Dark. Desktop Textures and Before Dark are two solid shareware applications that don't have pattern editors but do let you choose patterns from an easy-to-access list—an excellent feature none of the commercial programs offer. Also, both shareware programs have easy-to-find ways to virginize your system and return your General Controls control panel back to normal (see the box "Back to Square One," above). I even used Before Dark's fast virginizer to repair my system after Now Fun! ate my system colors. (Now Fun! has an easy way to restore system colors, but it's not well documented in the manual.)

Back to Square One (RC)

Pattern programs usually rewrite the system code to install a new pattern. If the new pattern is larger than Apple's eight color 8- by 8-pixel standard (and most good patterns are), then the new pattern will erase the eight color boxes normally available in your General Controls control panel. All three programs address this effect in the back of their manuals and show you how to get your color boxes back if you want to stop using the program.

Icon Editors (RC)

Each icon you see on your screen is actually a family of eight icons. Every icon has two color versions (16 and 256 colors), a black-and-white version, and a mask to highlight the icon when it's selected and to blacken it completely when it's open. These four versions come in both small and regular icon sizes. When you make an icon from scratch in a paint program, you end up pasting only one regular-size version into the Get Info window, and the Finder approximates the rest. Icon editors allow you to custom-design *all* the members of the family. You can modify any existing icon or easily create new ones. Icon editors should also allow you to maintain icon libraries and simplify the process of replacing one icon with another.

Icon 7, I Like Icon, and Icon Mania. The cost of an icon editor may seem prohibitive considering the tiny piece of art you get out of it, but hand-crafted icons can look like little jewels on your desktop. The three commercial icon editors currently available have similar editing features but different approaches to operating. **I Like Icon** ($60, Baseline Publishing) and **Icon Mania!** ($70, Dubl-Click Software) are applications. Simply drag an icon onto the I Like Icon's application icon and the program launches, bringing you directly to the

Welcome To "Your" Macintosh (RC)

I've learned to live with the little, overly cute Mac happy face as the first thing that greets me every time I turn on my computer, but that boring gray "Welcome to Macintosh" screen has no place in my gallery of computer art. I'm not even sure the grammar is correct. You can easily replace that opening screen if you have any one of a number of paint programs that can save documents in the StartupScreen format—Canvas and SuperPaint come to mind, and some utility programs, such as GIFConverter (shareware) can also save documents as StartupScreens. Check the options in your paint program's Save or Save As dialog box. Name the new document "StartupScreen" (capital S in Screen, and no space between the words) and simply drag it to your System Folder.

edit window. Icon Mania! opens like a regular program and presents you with a handy three-column window. The first column displays icon libraries. The second column displays the icons on your computer, and the third column is a pasteboard for temporary storage while you're working. Double-click on any icon to reach the edit window. **Icon 7** ($80, Inline Design) is a system extension. Open any icon's Get Info window and double-click on the icon's picture to open Icon 7's editor.

Icon 7 gives you a seamlessly integrated way of operating, and even though I loathe to add any more extensions to my System Folder, I like Icon 7's overall simpler approach to editing, and its text tool (it's nice to be able to emblazon a folder with a big letter or a short word). I Like Icon has some better traditional painting features (a paintbrush with variable line widths, for example), but because icons are so small I end up doing most of my painting with just the pencil and paint bucket (fill) tools. I Like Icon lets you make animated icons, but even though they're fun to watch once or twice, they soon become tiresome.

GOOD FEATURE

Icon Mania blows away the competition by integrating icon selection, editing, and library storage into an easy-to-navigate single-window display. Like Adobe's Photoshop, Icon Mania lets you create thumbnail icons of any graphic file. You can even select just a part of the file to be the representative icon. My favorite Icon Mania feature is its ability to customize the system's default icons. New Folders and Alert Icons can be enhanced, and you can choose from 30 new Trash icon styles or make your own. Now when I throw away a file, Ronald Reagan pops out of the trash can with the lid on his head.

All three programs come with icon libraries. I Like Icon has the more extensive and imaginative collection—surprising, because Inline, the maker of Icon 7, produces a variety of great games populated by a host of icon-size characters. In fact, many of the little plants and creatures from Inline's game Darwin's Dilemma are included in Icon 7's library. Icon Mania! has the best variety in its well-organized libraries, including custom folders for most of your favorite programs, as well as celebrity, classic art, and business icons.

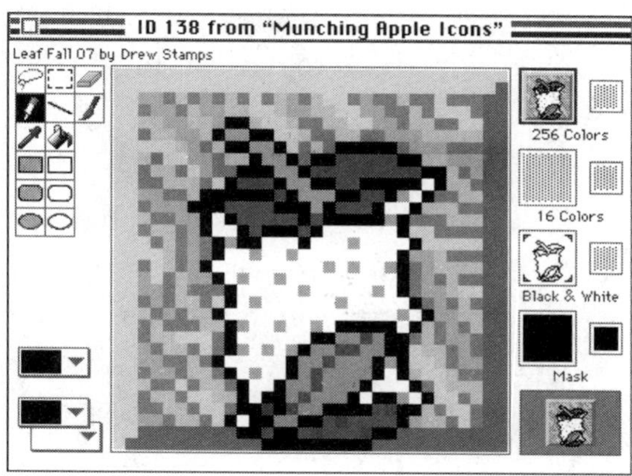

The I Like Icon icon editor offers a lot of painting tools, but it might be overkill: The icons are so small that you do all your editing with the pencil tool anyway.

IconBoss and iContraption. Check out the shareware editors **IconBOSS** and **iContraption** for a cheaper introduction to creating icon art, although neither program is as slick and trouble-free as its commercial cousins.

Icon Collections. **Icon Gallery** ($60, Component Software) is a commercial collection that grew out of Icon Factory, a utility created for adding icons to HyperCard stacks. The 850 icons in the collection were a little too cute for my taste, and because they are all created by one two-person art team, they all seem too similar. *(I was dazzled by the collection! The icons are well-crafted, make good use of color, and are really useful. I didn't find them cutesy or repetitive.—EC)* At this writing, Component was preparing to release volume 2 of the Icon Gallery.

Icon Antics (RC)

Here's a cool little trick for monitors running 16 colors (PowerBook owners take note). When an icon is selected, its black-and-white version is displayed. Using an icon editor, select an icon showing a person's face. Change the black-and-white version of the face to show a different expression. With some creative mouse clicks you can raise the eyebrows, open the mouth, even flare the nostrils. Now when you click once on the new icon, the selected version will look quite surprised!

Many shareware icon collections are available on-line, but the quality of the artwork varies greatly. I've seen a version of *Star Trek*'s Mr. Data that looks no different than Barbie's Ken, but I've also seen renditions of the Simpsons and Fred Flintstone that are as bright and appealing as the stars themselves.

Total Makeovers (RC)

Change the colors of everything: menu bar, windows, text, scroll bars, buttons. Then change the design of all those elements: round corners, emboss, add double arrows on your scroll bars, even make your Mac look like an IBM PC if you're feeling particularly perverse. Then customize or even animate all your cursors (perhaps turn the wristwatch cursor into a spinning Earth). Change the desktop pattern, and then make your Mac respond with a wacky sound every time you insert a disk or restart. Dubl-Click, the makers of ClickChange, used to describe this process as "taking your Finder to a party."

ClickChange's desktop decorating schemes are centralized in one control panel.

ClickChange and Now Fun! If you are planning on totally redecorating your Mac, it's probably not a bad idea to reduce the chance of system conflicts by having one program make all the changes. **ClickChange** ($90, Dubl-Click Software) and **Now Fun!** ($70, Now Software) can do all the tricks described above, plus more. Now Fun! follows ClickChange's lead in most respects and offers a valid alternative to ClickChange's well-designed customizing. ClickChange offers a menu-bar clock, substitutes icons for menu titles on your menu bar, and gives you a handy way to shrink open windows to show just their title bars (a feature also included in System 7.5 with its Window Shade control panel). Now Fun! includes a screensaver module.

Aside from these differences, the two programs vary greatly only in how they deal with changing the desktop pattern. ClickChange gives you a system tweaker similar to the one found in Chameleon or Wallpaper. Now Fun! lets you place one or more pictures on your desktop. You can crop, resize, and tile the graphics to cover the entire desktop or place several pictures in different places at the same time.

The screensaver in Now Fun! seems like a cheap knock-off of After Dark, but it does have one great module. With VoiceWaker you can walk up to your sleeping Mac and wake it up by nonchalantly saying something like "Screen, please." (Your Mac must have a microphone.) That impressed my friends who thought they had seen everything.

Neither program adequately addresses the issue of losing system color control from Apple's General Controls control panel after you make color changes. Virginize your system with these programs by clicking on "System Default," "Standard," or "Factory-issue" settings in the various control panel windows.

And Now for Something Completely Different (RC)

A couple of decorator utilities defy categorization. They're weird and they're fun, but don't expect them to boost your production.

UnderWare. The most verbal fun I've had this week was calling up Bit Jugglers and saying to their tech support guy, "I have a technical question about UnderWare." **UnderWare** ($60) is two programs in one—a screensaver and something Bit Jugglers calls the Dynamic Desktop. After a user-definable period of time (usually just a few seconds), your desktop comes alive with a great variety of animated events. Unlike with a screensaver, your open windows in applications remain unaltered so that you can keep working.

UnderWare creates scenes right on your desktop, while you're working.

My favorites include Billy Bounce, a little guy who bounces in three dimensions inside your monitor, periodically smacking up against the inside of your screen; Jindak the wizard, ready to cast a spell; and Robber, a little crook who breaks through your desktop and reappears later with your processor chip in his hands and the computer police hot on his trail. You may tire of UnderWare rather

Shareware Desktop Toys (RC)

The following is my list of great shareware toys for the desktop.

Aurora. As in ClickChange or Now Fun!, add color to every part of your desktop.

Eyeballs. Eyes in the menu bar follow the cursor.

FolderPICT. Open a folder, and instead of icons, view a picture of your choice.

Fun House. Opens a goofy fun house "mirror" on your screen.

Globe. A tiny application puts a beautiful spinning globe on your desktop.

Invisible Clock. A female voice automatically announces the time.

Melt. Double-click to melt the entire image on your screen.

Momentum. Laws of physics make your windows glide around the desktop.

MultiDog. A ghost dog runs around your icons.

Sound Extracter. Make system sounds out of the sounds imbedded in any program.

Soundmaster. Assign system sounds to accompany Finder actions.

SpinNit. Windows spin into view when you open icons.

TailDragger. The arrow cursor turns in the direction it's moving.

quickly, and not everyone has room for the 5.5 megs of space the 26 desktop dynamos require (you can always remove the ones you don't use), but UnderWare gets my vote as the best new addition to the world of desktop procrastination.

Star Wars Visual Clips. Instead of Darth Vader merely saying "Yes, Master" when you command your Mac to empty the trash (a trick possible with Soundmaster, described in the box "Shareware Desktop Toys" at left), you can watch a QuickTime movie of old Darth himself being polite. **VisualClips Featuring Video-Beep** ($60, Sound Source Unlimited) lets you assign clips from the original *Star Wars* movie to your system beep, disk insert, restart, hourly chime, and eight other Finder actions. The full-color clips appear in a tiny window that pops into view just long enough to display the clip. The sound quality is wonderful, and the image quality, although a bit grainy, is far superior to most QuickTime clips I've seen. Expect to use more than 12 megs of disk space if you want to store all 32 clips. Also, this program could really use an installer. It takes a good half hour to load.

Resource Editing

(EC)

One of the nicest things about Macintosh software, and something that sets it apart from most PC software, is that the code that makes the program run is separated from the interface that's presented to the user—the dialog boxes, alerts, menus, options, icons, pictures, sounds, and so on, collectively known as *resources*. That means you don't have to be a programmer to futz around with the interface; all you need is a resource editor.

There are two good resource editors available for the Mac: Apple's **ResEdit** and Mathemaesthetics' excellent **Resorcerer.** Although both programs can do the job, Resorcerer offers many time-saving options that programmers will love. Resorcerer can find and replace text in resources, decompile the text in resources for spell checking or printing, and it has a great icon editor, just for starters. Resorcerer is also more stable, more flexible, and generally more powerful.

Unfortunately, the difference in price—ResEdit is freeware, while Resorcerer costs a binary $256—makes ResEdit the only choice for most home editors.

Used incorrectly, ResEdit or Resorcerer can make your program (or your system) inoperable. Make sure you *always* work on a copy, and in the case of system resources, make sure you have a disk you can boot up your Mac with, in case you damage the installed System.

ResEdit's Potential

You can change (or just copy) resources from practically any application (including desk accessories), extension, control panel, or other nondocument file. A few programs, most notably those from Microsoft, cannot be looked at or tinkered with. (Spoilsports.) Remember that you are working with other people's creations. Any changes you make to copyrighted software are theoretically illegal—at the very least, don't distribute the modified software. Here's a list of some things you can do.

Change the text. Personalize your programs and the System itself by changing menu commands, keyboard shortcuts, dialog text, and even alerts.

Grab pictures and sounds. Open a program with ResEdit to copy out its icons, pictures, or sounds for use in any other program or as a decoration. Use the Scrapbook to store any interesting items you find (including sounds); paste them later wherever you want.

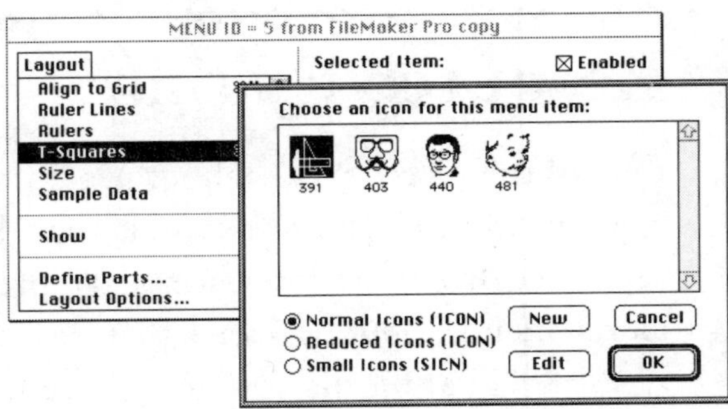

Add a little life to your menus with icons. Select Choose icon from the Menu menu to make the dialog box appear as shown here. Then select New and either create your own icon or paste one in (the one selected is from Icon Gallery).

Use Get Info. If you have an "orphaned" document on your Mac—one with a generic icon—and you want to know what program it was created with, open ResEdit and use the Get Info command in the File menu. It will tell you the Type and Creator of the document, which will often clue you in to which kind of program you'll be able to use to open the document.

Take advantage of your big screen. If you've got a big screen, you probably get awfully tired of every program that is designed for the old nine-incher of the Mac Plus. With ResEdit, you can make scroll boxes longer and scratch palettes bigger—to give just two examples—to take advantage of the added space.

In regular FileMaker, you can only see 10 fields at a time in the Define Fields dialog box. Make the scroll box a little bigger in ResEdit as shown here (DITL, DLOG 5000) and you can fit 18, or as many as you've got room for on your screen. (Then make the calculation box bigger!)

Remap the keyboard. Open the System file and hold down the Option key while you drag out the "U.S. System 6" keyboard file. A copy will be placed where you leave the pointer. Open this file with ResEdit and check out the KCHR resource. You can remap your key- board by dragging letters to the desired location on the keyboard in the lower part of the screen. Once you're done, change the resource's name, save the file, and drag it to the System Folder. Then use the Keyboard control panel to select the new keyboard layout.

Three Steps to Happy ResEditing

If you follow these three steps (along with general Mac hygiene, like regular saves and backups) you should be able to modify your resources without fear.

1. **Always, but always, work on a copy.** I've already said this, but it bears repeating: Never work on your sole copy of a program or the System. Instead, make a copy of the program and make changes to *it*. It is quite easy to damage a file so that it will never run again, and unless you have a clean copy, you will have lost it forever.
2. **Be careful what you touch.** You'll find dialog box contents in DITL, with the window size and title in a corresponding DLOG or ALRT. Menus are in MENU and CMNU, and often in STR#, where you'll also find other text used in dialog boxes. Look for icons in icl8, ICON, ics4, and so on. Pictures are in PICT. Cursors are in CURS. You'll find some stray buttons in CNTL. You generally won't have much reason to touch anything else, and you probably shouldn't.
3. **Don't create, just modify.** Don't erase anything and don't create anything: You should only modify what's already there. Generally, you should stick to cosmetic changes—modifying a button's text, size, color, and shape is fine; changing it from a button to a checkbox will probably cause the program to hang.

ResEdit Tips

HOT TIP

Jumping around. Since ⌘O is used to open files, ResEdit lets you use Return and Enter to open practically everything else. Try it while you have a resource item selected in a list, or while you have a button selected in a dialog box, just to name a few spots. You can use ⌘W to close, and the arrow keys to move up and down the lists. You can also type in a resource item number (or a name if it has one) to jump to that resource item.

Use the Get Resource Info command. Many programmers don't bother to name their resources. When you open a resource type, you may just see the number and size. You can give a resource item a name (or a *better* name), to help you find it later. Simply press ⌘I and type in a name. When you close the Info box, the name will appear in the list. You can change an item's name without problem, but don't touch anything else in the window; the ID number and type should not be modified. (On rare occasions, and almost never with DITL, DLOG, MENU, or STR# resources, a resource item name is used as text in the program itself. Changing the resource item's name will change the text in the software.)

Aligning. If you're really picky about aligning things, which most people who bother with ResEdit usually are, you'll find that entering values in the Top, Bottom, Left, and Right boxes is the fastest way to align items. The numbers entered refer to the number of pixels from the given edge. The arrow keys also work nicely for moving one pixel at a time.

Hidden objects. Sometimes you'll find that various objects are piled up one on top of another in a DITL. To see all the objects in a dialog box, hold down the Option key. Each item's ID number will be revealed. To select an object that's below another, use the Select Item Number command in the DITL menu, enter the appropriate number, and press Enter.

14

Fonts

IT MIGHT NOT BE TOO MUCH TO SAY that fonts made the Mac what it is today. In addition to its graphical user interface, what really delighted the Mac's first users was that they could create something on a computer that didn't look like it came from a computer. The Mac's first typefaces, limited as they were, were far better than anything anyone had seen before on the desktop. People soon learned that the typefaces they used for a document had a big impact on the way it was received. And fonts made the Mac *fun.*

The Mac took that promising beginning even further when it adopted PostScript in its first LaserWriter, and desktop publishing was born. Desktop publishing made the Mac respectable and brought it into a lot of offices. And today, it's still the fonts—in a number, quality, and variety that the first Mac users never dreamed of—that can make people really passionate about their Macs. Now, as Apple introduces QuickDraw GX, type on the Mac enters a whole new dimension, as designers dream up animated fonts and other surprises.

In this chapter, we'll talk first about the technology of Macintosh fonts, then get into the fine points of using them. If you need help with type terminology, there's a quick-reference guide on page 555.

Contributors

Darcy DiNucci (DD) is the chapter editor.

James Felici (JF) writes about fonts and publishing technology from (where else?) Fontès, France, which is about a half hour north of Béziers and 20 minutes east of St. Genie de Fontedit. He's a contributing editor and ex-Managing Editor of *Publish* magazine. His books include *The Desktop Style Guide* (Bantam/ITC).

Erfert Fenton (EF) writes about fonts and graphics for *Macworld* and other magazines. She's also the author of *The Macintosh Font Book* (Peachpit Press).

Alastair Johnston (AJ) has taught typography and graphic design for more than 20 years at U.C. Berkeley, Mills College, and other institutions of higher education. He is also a partner in Poltroon Press, a letterpress printing and publishing company in Berkeley.

Contents

Kathleen Tinkel (KT) is a writer/designer who set her first type on a pre-WWII Varityper that she found in a closet at her high school. Today, as a journalist,, Kathleen covers desktop graphic design and typography for *Step-by-Step Electronic Design,* publishes the newsletter *MacPrePress,* writes about computers and the graphic arts for numerous publications, and hosts the type forum on CompuServe.

Arthur Naiman (AN), Sharon Zardetto Aker (SA), and **Nancy E. Dunn (ND)** contributed to earlier versions of *The Macintosh Bible*, from which parts of this chapter were taken.

What Is a Font, Anyway? (JF)

Glad you asked. Alphabets come in different designs: skinny, fat, formal, casual, ghastly, and gorgeous. An alphabet (accompanied by a slug of numbers, punctuation marks, and so on) with a particular design is called a *typeface*. A *font* on the Mac is a jumble of computer code that creates text in a specific typeface, say Times or Helvetica.

A typeface and a font are not the same thing, any more than a cookie and a cookie cutter are the same thing. So when you want to set some type in a specific typeface, you choose the corresponding font, and your Mac will make the letters and numbers you type appear in that typeface.

When you see a printed page then, you can say "What typeface is that?" or "What font did you use to make that?" But you can't say "What font is that?" because the font is in your computer, not on the page.

The next term you need to learn is *font family*, which is a group of typefaces that are designed with similar features so they'll look good together on the page. Like most families, font families all go by a single family name (such as Times or Helvetica). A typical font family consists of four members: a regular version (usually used for text) plus a heavier bold version, a slanted italic version, and a bold-italic version. When you're shopping for a font, then, you normally get a disk containing four of them, one for each typeface in the family.

But font families, like human families, come in all different sizes. The Helvetica family, for example, contains over 50 members, varying by degrees of boldness and character width, among other features. On the other hand, some typefaces are one of a kind, woeful orphans with no family to call their own.

With these three bits of type jargon—*fonts*, *typefaces*, and *font families*—under our belts, we can wade into the wild world of Mac typography.

How the Mac Uses Fonts (DD/JF)

As the Mac has grown up, its techniques for handling fonts and type have gotten slicker and more sophisticated. Font technology has followed suit. There are now at least four kinds of Mac fonts out there—four distinct font formats, each with its own way of digitally encoding how letters should be drawn on your screen and on your pages. It can get a little confusing, but it's not as bad as it sounds. A little history will help sort out the story.

Bit-Mapped Fonts

When the Mac was introduced in January 1984, it had just one font format. It used *bit-mapped fonts* to display type on screen and to print to the only available Mac printer, the ImageWriter. The Macintosh screen and the ImageWriter both had the same resolution—72 dots per inch—and bit-mapped fonts were built to match them.

A Mac font consisted of a set of 72-dpi dot-by-dot drawings of each letter in a typeface. A printed ImageWriter page, then, was essentially a dot-for-dot replication of what you saw on screen, so the font that created your screen type also created your printed type.

Manhattan 12

Manhattan 24

For bit-mapped fonts to be really readable, a separate 72-dpi font must exist for each size you'll be using. If the right size isn't installed, the Mac will stretch the installed size to compensate. The example shows the difference between the screen versions of Manhattan at 12 points (for which a font is installed) and at 24 points (for which it's not).

But because the position of each dot was predefined in the font, you needed a separate font for every size of type you wanted to create. If you requested a type size that wasn't installed, the Mac would just stretch or squash letters from an existing font—adding or subtracting bits here and there—which tended to produced some odd and very hard-to-read shapes.

These days, 72-dpi bit-mapped fonts for printing are still available from only a couple of sources (most notably Dubl-Click Software, with its World Class Fonts line). For the most part, it's an outmoded format, superceded by the formats we'll talk about next.

Fonts Everyone Has (DD)

As of this writing, 20 fonts come with System 7. Your Mac only needs three of these—Chicago, Geneva, and Monaco—which it uses for the text that appears in dialog boxes, menus, and so forth. The others are a few basic fonts for use in documents. All of them are loaded into your System Folder automatically when you install your system software, where they're available to any application you use on your Mac. These could be all the fonts you'll ever need. But you probably wouldn't be reading this chapter if you were that kind of person.

Here's a description of the fonts you get with System 7—the fonts every Mac owners has.

Fonts you need to have installed so that your system works properly:

Geneva	Geneva is the font normally used for file and folder names on the Mac desktop. It started out as a bit-mapped version of the classic sans serif typeface Helvetica.
Chicago	You look at Chicago so often on menus, in the titles of windows, and in dialog boxes, that it's easy to forget how gorgeous it is. (That's only fitting, since it's named after the Garden City, where virtually all the streets are tree-lined and where the lake front, fringed with parks and beaches, stretches for 30 miles.)
Monaco	A problem with a *monospaced* font like Monaco (in which all the letters are exactly the same width) is that when it's made bold, letters in small sizes—especially *m's* and *w's*—look like blobs on the screen. You'll spot it here and there in dialog boxes and other parts of the Mac interface.

Basic Fonts, included because everyone needs a serif, a sans-serif, and a couple of special-purpose fonts before they feel like getting out of bed in the morning:

Times	Times is the standard, boring serif typeface that everyone tells you to use if you don't want to go out on a limb and pick another. It's used a lot, mostly because it's built into the system.
Helvetica	Helvetica is the standard, boring sans-serif typeface.
Courier	Courier is an excellent choice if you want to make your laser printer look like a typewriter. (What were these people *thinking* of?)
Σψμβολ	That is, Symbol, supplies Greek characters, math symbols, and other characters you might need to supplement your other fonts, such as primes for inch and foot marks (′ ″), and playing card suits (♥ ♦ ♣ ♠) for typesetting your bridge column.

New York	New York was the Mac's original serif font, created to complement the sans-serif Geneva. Bigelow and Holmes radically redesigned it in creating the TrueType version. TrueType New York's large x-height and lively variation in stroke weight capture the Big Apple's energy, making it a classy alternative to the sedate Times, on which it was originally based.
Palatino	Classy, elegant, readable Palatino was designed by a titan of 20th-century typography, Hermann Zapf.

GX fonts you get with System 7.5:

SYSTEM 7.5

Apple Chancery	This calligraphic italic type was included by Apple to show off TrueType GX's skills in automatically substituting alternative characters. This font contains over 1,000 characters (you get four alternates for just about every character).
Tekton +	Tekton, a font created by designer David Siegel to mimic architects' hand lettering, is one of Adobe's most popular fonts. This GX version provides ligatures, fractions, small caps, and all the programmable behavior of GX fonts (described on page 530). Only the regular weight is included with the system.
Hoefler Text	Designed by Jonathan Hoefler, this is an elegant text face family with beautiful modeling and a distinctly Old World style. Hoefler describes his creation as a marriage between the design styles of Garamond and Kis. The complete Hoefler character set numbers over 500 characters.
Skia	Skia is a thoroughly modern sans-serif design created by Matthew Carter. From the single Skia font you can generate weights from light to black and widths from narrow to extended—and anything in-between.

PostScript

Almost exactly one year after the Mac debuted, Apple introduced the LaserWriter printer and Adobe System's new *PostScript* font format. The LaserWriter and its 300-dpi resolution not only produced beautiful pages, it also changed the relationship between the Mac and its printer. Instead of simply passing off its screen images for printing, the Mac now passed off files (written

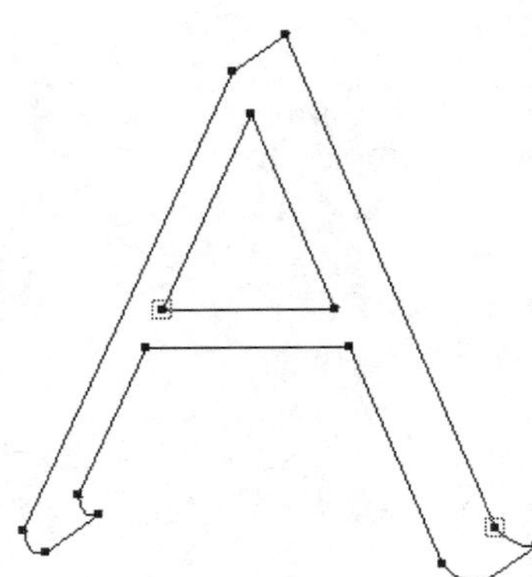

TrueType and PostScript fonts are outline fonts: The font information describes the shape of the letter, which can be scaled to any size and output at any resolution.

in the PostScript programming language) that were reinterpreted by yet another computer inside the LaserWriter, a computer that rebuilt the images at 300-dpi resolution.

PostScript fonts broke the link between screen resolution and printer resolution. The Mac still used 72-dpi bit-mapped fonts to create the type on screen, but when you sent the file to the printer, the Mac substituted matching PostScript fonts for use on the page. Instead of storing images of letters as distinct patterns of dots, PostScript fonts stored those images as mathematically described outlines—electronic stencils that could be scaled to any size and then "colored in" by a printer imaging at any resolution. To do the required computations, you needed a *PostScript interpreter*—a computer inside the printer—a feature that makes PostScript printers relatively expensive.

SYSTEM 7.5

The practical effect of this for Mac owners (in addition to getting snappier-looking print) was that now they had to reckon with two kinds of fonts—72-dpi *screen fonts* plus resolution-independent *printer fonts* (also sometimes called *outline fonts*). This created (and still creates to this day) a lot of confusion. Only with System 7.5 and QuickDraw GX is the need for bit-mapped screen fonts for PostScript fonts finally eliminated (see "QuickDraw GX and GX Fonts," below). With earlier systems, the only way for your Mac to make a PostScript font available to your applications is for you to install a corresponding bit-mapped screen font.

PostScript Type 1 and PostScript Type 3 fonts. A few PostScript fonts were included with the LaserWriter, but soon Adobe (in conjunction with Linotype Corporation) began producing PostScript fonts in large numbers. Adobe created its PostScript fonts in a high-quality format known as *Type 1*. For a fee, font manufacturers could license the technology.

At the same time, Adobe released the recipe for a similar but not-quite-as-good format called PostScript *Type 3*, which other type makers could use to produce their own PostScript fonts without paying a licensing fee. (Type 2, by the way,

PC Font Formats (DD)

IBM-compatible PCs can use both TrueType and PostScript fonts. But PC TrueType and PostScript fonts are actually different from Macintosh TrueType and PostScript fonts. If you are using a PC as well as a Mac, you need to convert your Mac fonts to PC format before you use them on the PC (or vice versa) using a utility such as Ares Software's FontMonger or FontHopper, or Altsys's Metamorphosis Pro. (FontMonger and Metamorphosis Pro, which also provide other font-editing features, are described on page 574.) *[For converting PC TrueType fonts to Mac TrueType fonts, I recommend* ***TT Converter,*** *a shareware program you can get on any on-line service. TT Converter just changes the headers on the files so they can be used by the Mac, the simplest and least-intrusive way to make the conversion.—KT]*

was a short-lived format that never really made it into circulation.) Type 3 fonts didn't have *hinting*, special instructions that optimize the characters for low-resolution printing and display, and Type 3 fonts tended to look lumpy and unclear at laser printer resolutions.

After Adobe released the Type 1 recipe in 1991, however, the Type 3 format was pretty much dropped, and everyone began making all their PostScript fonts in the Type 1 format. By that time, though, there were already hundreds of thousands of Type 3 fonts in circulation, and most of them are still around today (fonts don't wear out very fast).

Adobe Type Manager. In 1989, Adobe announced **Adobe Type Manager** (ATM), which turned the Mac into its own PostScript interpreter for type. With ATM, when you set type in a size for which you don't have a bit-mapped screen font installed, you don't get those nasty lumpy letters on screen; you see much smoother shapes, much closer to what you get from a PostScript printer. The catch is that ATM works only with PostScript Type 1 fonts, not Type 3 fonts.

Janson 48

Janson 48

The top example shows what 48-point Janson looks like on screen without ATM (the 12-point bit-mapped screen font has simply been quadrupled in size). The bottom example shows what it looks like with ATM installed. Quite a difference, eh?

ATM also interprets type for printers, making it possible to get better-quality type out of cheaper (non-PostScript) printers. In this scenario, when you hit Print, ATM will create images of all the type on the page at

300 dpi (or whatever the resolution of the printer is) and pass the images on to the printer. You get PostScript type without the expense of a PostScript printer.

In System 7.5, ATM is installed right along with the system software. If you have an earlier system, you can get ATM for $60 from Adobe (or free with many other Adobe products).

Multiple Master fonts. In 1991, Adobe introduced a variation on Type 1 fonts called *Multiple Master fonts*. A Multiple Master font, as the name implies, is several fonts in one. A single font, for example, could contain master outlines for a very thin version and a very fat version of the same typeface design. You can then build new fonts for custom typefaces by creating blends between the two extremes. A single Multiple Master font can have several such "design axes." In addition to light and bold, it could have narrow and wide versions, upright and slanted versions, or serif and sans-serif versions. You can blend these features as you wish to create an infinite number custom instances of the font.

You can manipulate type in some similar ways using page layout and graphics programs, but a custom Multiple Master font has the advantage of being an interpolation between two versions created by the typeface's designer—you're never far from what the designer intended. The Multiple Master font generator (the program that actually builds the new fonts for you) adjusts the proportions of the letterforms appropriately for the size and weight you've specified, with larger openings inside the letters in small sizes, or thinner lines in large sizes, for example.

Unfortunately, Multiple Master fonts are difficult to create, which has made them fairly rare and rather costly.

TrueType

Also in 1991, in an attempt to wrest control of type away from Adobe, Apple introduced a new font format called *TrueType*. Like PostScript fonts, TrueType fonts use outlines that can be interpreted for any size and any resolution, on screen or for a printer. And like PostScript fonts with ATM, TrueType doesn't need an interpreter in the printer; for TrueType, the interpretation is done by the Mac's own system software. Unlike PostScript fonts, though, TrueType

Synthetic Fonts (DD/JF)

The newest trend in font formats is a concept called *synthetic fonts,* a concept being pioneered by Ares Software with its FontChameleon (described on page 574), and by ElseWare, with its Font Works software, which at press time was announced only for the Windows platform (although there were some indications that it would be brought to the Mac soon).

Both of these synthetic-font technologies rely on a sort of master proto-font outline that can be pulled and stretched in any direction according to external font descriptors: instructions that come from you, your application, or your operating system. For the user, this means a big reduction in the hard disk space required to hold fonts. FontChameleon, for example, uses a single outline that can be instructed to assume the form of almost any typeface that uses standard letter forms (in other words, not specialty faces such as a longhand script face or a black letter face). The instruction sets are only 5K to 6K in size, and you can create the fonts you want on demand, almost instantaneously. Font Works uses highly abstract font descriptions of 5K or so that can be elaborated ("inflated," so to speak) into fully formed fonts in the blink of an eye. With such technologies, your system will be able to create the fonts you need when you need them, dump them when you don't, and not have them cluttering up the place in the meantime.

FontChameleon also lets you customize its font descriptors—the instructions that give the outlines their shape—allowing you to build custom fonts by changing the x-height, weight, and other factors of the basic typefaces they've built into the product. In principle, a TrueType GX font should be capable of similar variability, if the typeface designer builds in the instructions to define how the face should appear at different weights, x-heights, character widths, and so forth. (These terms are defined on page 555.)

But synthetic-font variations can't match the quality of hand-designed typefaces. Even if the font carries very elaborate instructions for how it should appear after it's been altered, there's no substitute for having a good designer supervise the formation of each shape and curve of each character.

For those who send electronic documents, this technology can be quite a boon. When these products are installed, you can send an electronic file to your colleagues without worrying whether they have the fonts—the fonts can be generated automatically as they're needed.

fonts have never needed screen fonts to operate on a Mac, which has made them easier to install and manage.

TrueType runs automatically on Macs with System 7. Mac owners running System 6.0.5 or later can use TrueType fonts if they add a TrueType system extension to their System Folder. (Apple does not sell the extension directly, but it is included with some QuickDraw printers such as the StyleWriter II.)

For typophiles, TrueType offers some sophisticated capabilities that potentially place it a cut above the PostScript format. We say *potentially* because most of these Epicurean features are strictly optional and don't always find their way into the TrueType fonts you buy. But TrueType fonts are theoretically capable of crisper resolution at low resolutions (such as on screen) and are built to take advantage of the Line Layout Manager feature of System 7.5, which can provide more professional-looking typesetting in heretofore typographically inept applications such as word processors and spreadsheets.

Almost every font manufacturer now sells its fonts in both TrueType and PostScript Type 1 formats (Adobe, of course, sticks strictly to PostScript), and this has made things more complicated for font users. (More about the problems in choosing one font format over the other, or in using both, are described under "Do You Have to Choose?" below.) Ironically, TrueType hasn't been very successful on the Mac—its real success has come on IBM PC compatibles running Windows, which also uses the format.

QuickDraw GX and GX Fonts

The next shoe is dropping right about the time this book is going to press. Apple has just started shipping *QuickDraw GX*, a system extension that changes (among other things) the way the Mac handles fonts, and it clears the way for a whole new font format: *GX fonts*. QuickDraw GX will be included with System 7.5 and with some products, such as GX fonts, that require it (the developer must license GX from Apple). You need at least System 7.1 to run it.

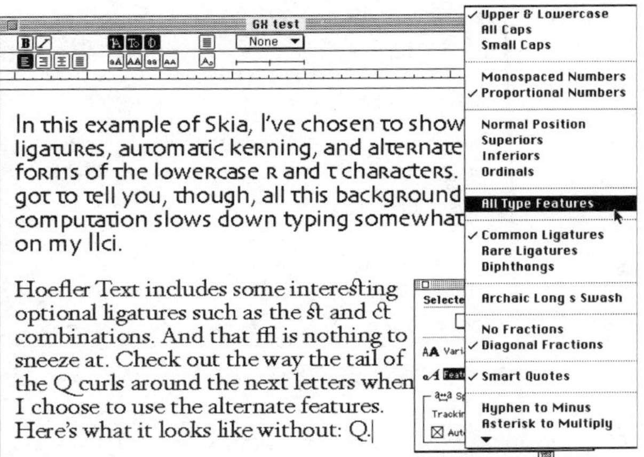

This screen shows some of the special typographic features built into two of the GX fonts that ship with System 7.5: Skia and Hoefler Text. In order to access such capabilities, you must have an application that recognizes them. At press time, there were none (GX wasn't yet released), so here we used GXWrite, an application Apple built specially to show off GX features.

GX fonts can include conditional instructions that allow fonts to decide for themselves when to use alternate characters—or even to change their shapes at programmed intervals. GX fonts will come in both PostScript and TrueType formats.

Much like Multiple Master fonts, GX fonts can use their programmability to vary design features of the font. Shown here are variations on Crank, a GX font created by David Berlow of The Font Bureau. You would select the variation of the font you want to use in a particular case by selecting it from a menu such as the one shown in the illustration on the previous page.

One important effect of QuickDraw GX is that it puts PostScript and TrueType fonts on equal footing in the Mac's operating system. Like TrueType fonts, PostScript GX fonts will be recognized directly by the Mac, so you'll no longer need to load the bit-mapped versions of the fonts into the system. You'll install and use TrueType and PostScript GX fonts just like you use TrueType fonts—just drag the font suitcase onto the System Folder icon. The only difference will come when you print. At that point, the printer driver will send TrueType fonts to the Mac's QuickDraw interpreter, while PostScript fonts will be sent to ATM or to the printer's PostScript interpreter.

This all sounds like sweetness and light, but there will be some rough edges during the transition to font utopia. For example, if you use the QuickDraw GX extension with a pre-7.5 version of the System, you'll have to "enable" PostScript fonts for GX using a special utility—the Type 1 Enabler—that Adobe provides along with the GX extension. (The Enabler basically adds some whoosis to the whatsis so the thingamajig doesn't blow a gasket and your fonts will work.) When you install System 7.5, all the PostScript fonts in your System Folder are automatically enabled for QuickDraw GX. GX will exact a cost in system memory, as well; you'll need about two extra megs of RAM if you plan to use it; Apple recommends a minimum of 8MB.

GX's programmability can also be used to animate fonts. Here we show an example from a Font Bureau GX font called Zylos. The bicyclist is a single character from the font; the GX programming causes the character to move across the screen, the cyclist pedaling all the way. Such animated fonts might be used for on-screen or video presentations.

GX and the Future of Fonts (DD)

As this book goes to press, it's unclear exactly how important QuickDraw GX will be for fonts. (It also has important effects on printing and in graphics in general, as described in Chapters 21 and 15, respectively.) Anyone who buys a new Mac after System 7.5 is released will have it automatically. Others will need to upgrade, either by buying the new system software from Apple or by getting the GX extension along with a product, such as a GX font, that uses it. At this writing, Adobe, Bitstream, and Linotype-Hell had all introduced GX font designs.

GX allows amazing new capabilities in fonts, such as those shown in the illustrations on the previous pages. Since GX fonts can contain up to 16,000 characters (up from 256 in earlier TrueType and PostScript formats), they can contain designed fractions, true small capitals (as opposed to the mutant dwarfs created by the Small Caps option in the Style menu), and other characters you needed an expert set for before. And because these typographic niceties are included at the system level, they will be available in any program that supports GX.

Judging from past experience with Apple system-software upgrades, though, a lot of people who already have computers won't be upgrading right away, and that means there are going to be a lot of people out there for a long time who are running their Macs without GX. Because not everyone will need or value the special features GX fonts can offer, and because building those features into a font takes a lot of trouble, GX's typographic features will probably be reserved for a fairly small and relatively expensive category of fonts.

There's also the question of application support. Users can get access to all those features only through applications that support the technology, and at press time, it was unclear whether biggies—Quark and PageMaker—were going to sign on, although a dark horse in the page layout sweepstakes—Ready, Set, Go—had pledged to support it.

Does It Matter Which Format You Use?

There's no argument that TrueType and PostScript fonts provide better-quality printed output than do bit-mapped fonts. Which of the two outline formats is better, however, is a source of much controversy. But if you judge the quality of a font format by the type you see on the page, there's little debate: Both formats are capable of producing great-quality type at any output resolution.

If you're not using QuickDraw GX, TrueType has an edge in simplicity. TrueType fonts require you to install only one file, compared to PostScript's two. And if you use PostScript fonts, you'll also need to get Adobe Type

Manager to see clear screen type at all sizes and to get good quality type from non-PostScript printers.

On the other hand, for jobs that will be printed on high-resolution imagesetters, PostScript has the advantage. Because it had such a long head start on TrueType, PostScript became the standard for use in professional publishing applications. The result is that imagesetters have built-in PostScript interpreters. On those machines, printing using TrueType fonts can be very slow, because all the image processing has to be done by the Mac, in software—the TrueType image-processing program can't take full advantage of the PostScript computer. Most service bureaus, then, won't let you near their imagesetters with a TrueType font, although this is changing slowly.

A final problem with TrueType is that can't use TrueType fonts at all if you're running a System version earlier than 6.0.5, or if you're using 6.0.5 or 6.0.7 but don't have the TrueType extension.

Do You Have to Choose?

Most people end up with a variety of font formats in their systems because they tend to shop for specific typefaces, that is, specific designs, regardless of format. Even if you opt for PostScript as a standard (perhaps because most of your work is eventually output to PostScript imagesetters), you usually end up with a few TrueType fonts, if only because Apple's basic TrueType and bit-mapped fonts are installed automatically each time you install or reinstall your system.

This generally causes a problem only when you have PostScript and TrueType versions of the same typeface installed. The Mac has built-in methods for choosing between font versions at print time (described under "Fonts and Printing," later in this chapter), which could result in your ending up with one version of the font when you expected the other. This could produce unexpected line endings or other untoward changes in your printed pages. In some cases, the printer can get so confused it doesn't print anything at all.

The best advice is to pick one font format to work with and stick with it—it just reduces confusion. If you do mix font formats, try not to have different versions of the same typeface installed. (If you buy a font that supplies both TrueType and PostScript versions on the disk, copy just one onto your system.) The greatest confusion will arise with the most common typefaces—the ones supplied with the system (including Times, Helvetica, Courier, and Symbol) and the ones built into most PostScript printers (which are often supplied with Adobe Type Manager).

Font Files

When you open a font disk, you may be greeted by an alarming array and variety of icons and files. Because each font format is handled differently by your Mac, each kind of font requires a different set of font files, and each vendor may organize its fonts differently on the disks it provides. The following is a guide to what you're looking at on a font disk, and what to do with it all.

Buy 'em by the Family (JF)

As discussed above, fonts generally come grouped in families, variations on a basic typeface design that are meant to be used together. There will usually be four: a plain (used for text), an italic or oblique, a bold, and a bold italic or bold oblique. The name of the plain, text version is usually also the name of the family. When you buy a disk of Bodoni fonts, then, you can expect to find Bodoni, Bodoni Italic, Bodoni Bold, and Bodoni Bold Italic. But, as pointed out above, some typefaces have very extended families, with dozens of members.

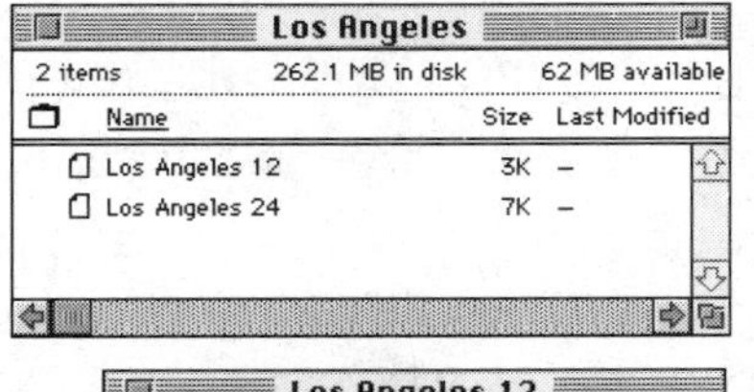

Bit-mapped fonts come in a single suitcase (top), which opens to reveal separate files for a different sizes (top left). If you click on a font file, you can see a sample of the typeface at that size (bottom left).

What You See Is What You Bought (JF/DD)

The kinds of font files you get and the way they are arranged on the disk depends on their font format and the way the vendor has chosen to serve them up. Here, arranged by font format, are all the files (with their various icons) that you might find on a font disk and all of the guises in which they may appear.

Bit-mapped fonts. If you buy a bit-mapped font, you'll probably get a single suitcase, which holds various sizes of the font. Its name will simply be the name of the typeface family. Alternatively, you might get a number of suitcases, one for each member of the family.

TrueType and PostScript GX fonts. TrueType and PostScript GX fonts are usually packed into a single suitcase that includes the outline fonts and may include some bit-mapped screen fonts as well (see the illustration above right).

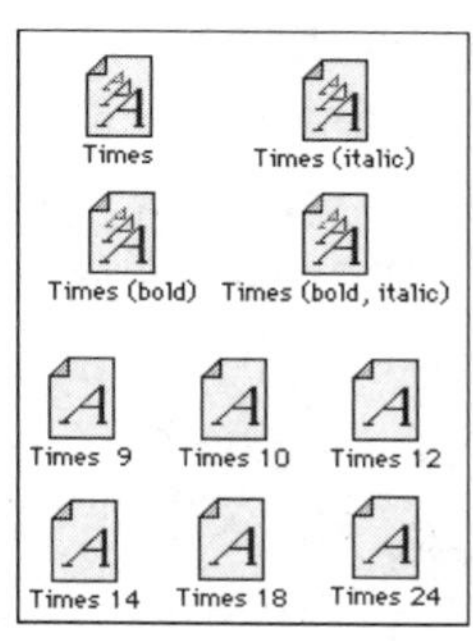

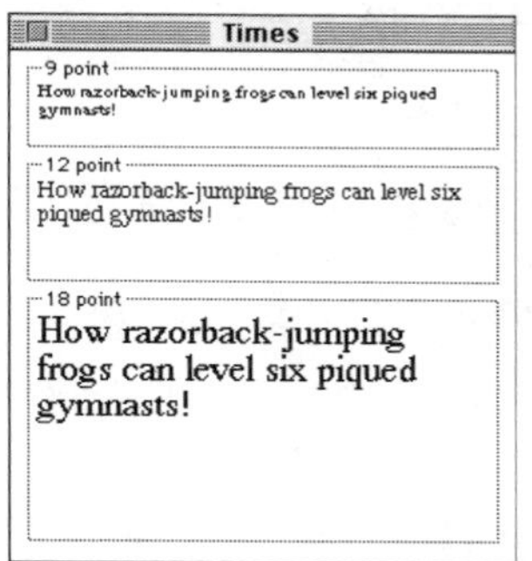

TrueType fonts also come in single suitcases, but when you open it (top left), the suitcase includes outline fonts (marked with a set of receding A's) as well as (usually) bit-mapped fonts for different sizes. Clicking on the icon of a TrueType font file reveals samples of the typeface in several sizes (bottom left).

PostScript fonts. If you buy PostScript fonts, you usually get an outline font file for each family member, plus a suitcase containing bit-mapped screen fonts in various sizes. You may also get one or more folders of things called AFM files. For the most part, you can ignore the AFM files—just leave them on the disk they came on. If an application needs them (it's rare), the program's documentation will tell you so and will tell you where to put them in your system.

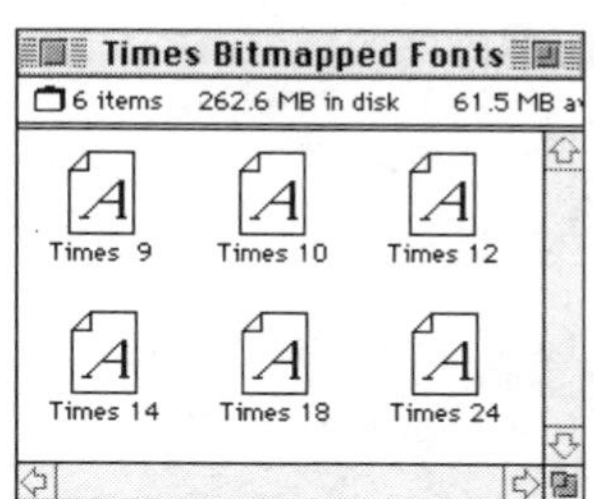

PostScript font disks usually contain three different types of files (top left): bit-mapped screen fonts (in the suitcase), printer fonts (shown here with Adobe's striped logo), and a folder of AFM (Adobe Font Metrics) files. Double-clicking on the suitcase file would show the screen fonts it holds, and clicking on one of those would show a sample of the typeface in that size, as for the bit-mapped font shown on the opposite page.

PostScript font files may be arranged in a number of different ways. Some vendors put all the PostScript fonts in one folder and all the bit-mapped screen fonts in another. Some leave them all loose on disk. Some put the bit-mapped fonts in a suitcase, some don't.

If you're looking at your files in icon view (as shown in the illustration), also note that PostScript printer font icons may look different than the ones shown here. Adobe's icon is shown, but font makers often use their own icon designs for their printer fonts (see the box "Printer Font Icons" at right.)

Printer Font Icons (DD)

Font makers usually create their own distinctive icons for their printer fonts (a sampling is shown below). If you can't interpret the icon, you can always select the icon and choose Get Info to see whose font it is.

Suitcase Files (JF/DD)

In System 6 and earlier versions, all bit-mapped fonts had to be packed in suitcases for the System to recognize them. Since System 7, you don't need suitcases anymore—they're just a housekeeping convenience. In either system version, you can use them to package screen fonts or TrueType fonts into a neat family bundle. Likewise, you can stuff into a single suitcase a set of fonts you always use together, such as those for your monthly budget report.

With System 7, it doesn't make any difference whether font files are in a suitcase when you get them, or how they're arranged. You can pack and repack them to your heart's content.

With System 6 (which uses suitcases only for bit-mapped fonts), you create, open, pack, and unpack suitcases with the Font/DA mover, as described under "Installing Your Fonts," below. In System 7, it's easier; suitcases act just like folders. You can double-click on them to open them, and you can add files to them by dragging a file icon onto them in the Finder. Since Apple doesn't ship Font/DA Mover with System 7, though, you'll need a program like Suitcase or Master Juggler (described below) to create new suitcases or, as Robin Williams suggests in her book *How to Boss Your Fonts Around* (Peachpit Press), you can recycle your suitcases: Just duplicate an existing suitcase (select the suitcase icon in the Finder and press ⌘D), empty out the duplicate (by double-clicking on it and dragging its contents to the Trash), repack it with the fonts you want there, and rename it.

HOT TIP

Installing Your Fonts (DD)

How you install fonts on your Mac depends on what System version you have: The technique seems to have changed with every System update in the recent past.

Installing Fonts in System 6

If you're using System 6, you load fonts directly into your System file using a utility called the Font/DA Mover that came with your system software. It's interface is pretty straightforward, as illustrated below. The fonts you install with Font/DA Mover won't be available for use until you restart your Mac.

In the case of PostScript fonts, Font/DA mover installs only bit-mapped screen fonts, which your applications will use in building your documents; your PostScript printer fonts go *loose* in the System Folder. (Make sure they're not in folders, or they won't be found at printing time.) Unless you're using Adobe Type Manager, you won't need the PostScript printer fonts until it's time to print.

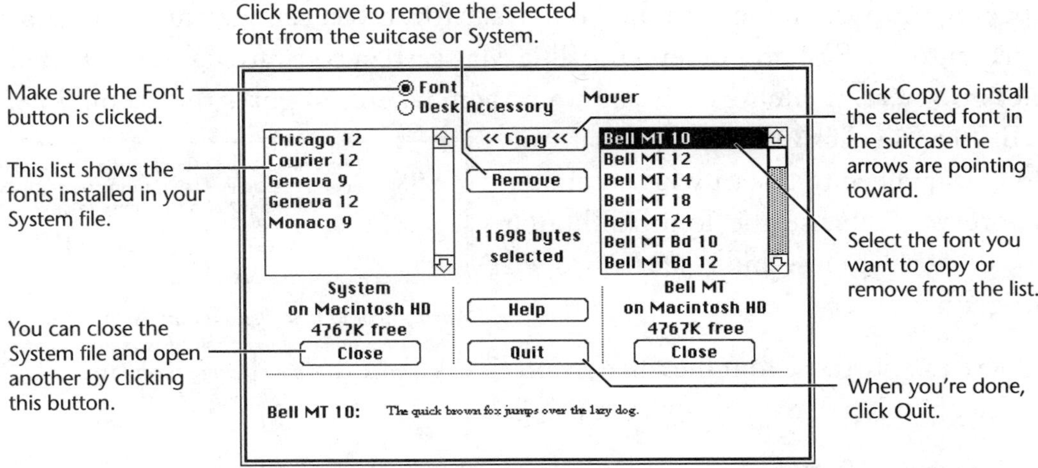

When you open Font/DA Mover, the fonts already installed in your System Folder are displayed in the box at left. You open the new font suitcase with the Open button at the right, select the font you want to install, and click Install.

Why Do We Still Need Bit-Mapped Fonts? (JF)

In Macs without QuickDraw GX, the system will only work with PostScript fonts if bit-mapped screen fonts for those fonts have been installed. In those Macs, the system still looks for the bit-mapped fonts to determine which fonts are available for use. But why are bit maps included with PostScript GX and TrueType fonts? Two reasons:

- It's quicker for the Mac to use the ready-made bit maps on screen than it is to ask TrueType or ATM to create screen type from the outline printer fonts. Also (and more importantly), below about 16 points, the bit-mapped screen fonts are more legible than type generated from outlines (they're hand-drawn, so they just look better). Bit-mapped screen fonts are simply easier on the eyes, which can mean a lot after a long day of gazing into the screen.

HOT TIP

- If a document created with TrueType fonts finds itself in an environment that lacks those fonts (a PostScript printer, for example, or a different Mac), PostScript fonts representing the same typefaces can be substituted for them. Sometimes, however, line endings and layouts may change when this font substitution occurs *unless* the Mac that created the document was using bit-mapped screen fonts. Why? Don't ask (the answer is a techno-nightmare). Just use the TrueType screen fonts if you've got them—it's cheap insurance.

Installing Fonts in System 7

Installing and managing fonts has gotten a lot easier with System 7. Instead of opening the System file with the Font/DA Mover, you can now just drag your fonts onto the System Folder icon. The Mac system software figures out what files go where, politely asks if you want them where it figures they should be, and after you click OK, it just does it. You don't even need to restart your computer before you can use the fonts (although you do need to close and restart any open programs).

When you drag font files onto the System Folder, the system determines where each file should go but asks your permission before placing them there.

Where exactly those font files go depends on what version of System 7 you're using:

- In System 7.0, the bit-mapped fonts go into the System file itself, while the outline fonts go into the Extensions folder. To de-install a font, you simply drag the font icon out of the Extensions folder and put it somewhere else (a Fonts folder outside of the System Folder is a logical option). To de-install a bit-mapped screen font, you open the System file (by double-clicking on it) and then drag out all the screen fonts for the face you want to get rid of.

- In System 7.1 and 7.5, things get simpler yet: All font files go in a single Fonts folder inside the System Folder.

When installing fonts in System 7, it's best to drag the files onto the System Folder icon and let the Mac take care of stowing the fonts in their proper place. Alternatively, you can drag the font files right into the Fonts folder. But if you just drag them into the open System Folder window, the Mac will simply copy them there, trusting (in all its innocence) that you know what you want.

How Many Screen Fonts Do You Really Need? (JF/KT)

There are lots of opinions on how many sizes of screen fonts you should install with PostScript fonts, and whether you need to install them at all with GX or TrueType fonts. Here's a sample:

Jim suggests installing all your screen fonts, at least for sizes below 16 points: *Since screen fonts munch very little hard disk space, and they consume virtually no memory, there's no reason not to use them. Do your eyes a favor.*

Kathleen agrees: *If you do most of your work in a word processing or similar application that doesn't support zooming, you need to work with type in its actual size. At 10 and 12 points, a well-made bit map is still easier to read on screen than the image of a letter cooked up by ATM or TrueType.* She goes on, however, to state exceptions to the rule: *If you're working in applications that allow you to magnify text for editing, you'll rarely be using the screen fonts anyway, so giving good disk space to what is actually a random set of sizes is a waste.*

Kathleen also discards the italic screen fonts: *When working with Adobe's own PostScript fonts, ATM converts italics from the printer outlines whether the screen version is present or not, so italic screen fonts are excess baggage.* She recommends keeping the bold screen fonts, though, especially for faces that come in more than two weights, because when choosing typeface weights from the Style menu, it's not always obvious which weights are derived from which other screen fonts (see "Using Font Styles," later in this chapter).

If you have a relatively slow system like a Mac Plus or an SE, keeping your screen fonts installed may speed up your system, since the Mac won't spend its energy using ATM or TrueType to generate screen type for the installed sizes. On faster systems, the slowdown may be barely noticeable.

Managing Your Fonts

Installing fonts in the ways described above is easy enough, but depending on how many fonts you have, loading all of them directly into your system can start slowing you down. For one thing, every font you install takes up a small, but perhaps significant, amount of memory. The larger your system grows, the less memory you have to run programs, and because every time you launch a program it has to take inventory of all those fonts, your Mac will be slower starting up, slower opening programs, and slower executing some commands. And another thing: If your system is full of fonts you rarely use, you're probably wasting a lot of time scrolling through mile-long font menus to get to the one or two you fonts you generally want.

In either case, it's time to start thinking about managing your fonts.

Slimming down your suitcases (DD). One way to simplify your font menus and pare down the amount of memory your fonts use is to be more selective about what font files you install. Dragging all the icons on a new font disk over the System Folder will install every file on the disk, but you may not need them all.

If you're using TrueType fonts or PostScript fonts with QuickDraw GX, you don't need to install the bit-mapped fonts at all (but see the box "Why Do We Still Need Bit-Mapped Fonts?" on page 538). If you're using PostScript fonts with ATM, you need to install just one screen font for each typeface (any size will do, so pick the smallest). ATM will use the printer fonts (which you *do* need to have available) to create type for the screen and for non-PostScript printers. That's the technical minimum. For opinions on the *optimal* minimum, see the box "How Many Screen Fonts Do You Really Need?" on the previous page.

Using Suitcase and Master Juggler (DD). If your font library contains more than about 20 font families, it's likely that you don't actually need all those fonts at the same time. So why not offload a few of them? If you do, both you and your Mac will be able to work more efficiently. Two all-purpose font-management programs have made themselves almost indispensable for people who use a lot of fonts, letting you pop files in and out of your system in a trice.

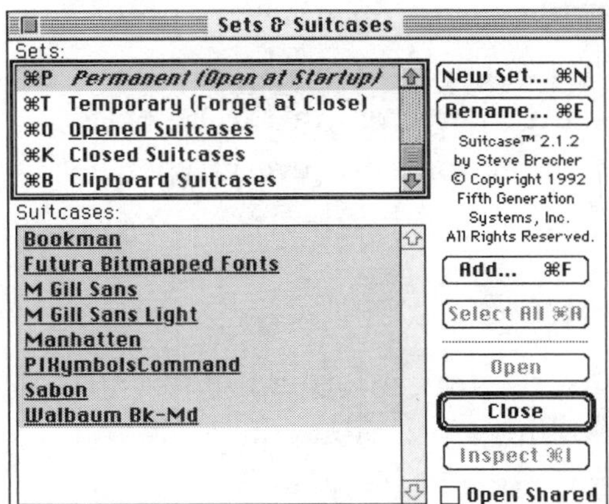

In Suitcase from Symantec, you can create separate sets of fonts for each publication you're working on and open all the fonts in the set with a single click.

Suitcase ($70), from Symantec, and **MasterJuggler** ($80), from Alsoft, both let you easily install and de-install fonts through a desk accessory (there's no need to run back to the Finder). Both also include a lot of other handy font-management tools, such as utilities that let you check font numbers (fonts with identical internal ID numbers can confuse some stupider programs—see "Solving Font Problems," later in this chapter), compress your font files, and perform other useful chores. Both programs offer similar capabilities, but Suitcase has an extra that can prove invaluable: It lets you divide your fonts into sets for individual projects, allowing you, for example, to open at once all the fonts need for a newsletter. This feature alone makes up for the program's rather confusing interface.

Of course, System 7's easy-in, easy-out method of font installation makes it a snap to both install fonts when you need them and de-install them when you don't—without a separate program. (Tips on how to manage this are supplied under "Font Tips" at the end of this chapter.) The main drawback of working this way is that you have to retreat to the Finder to perform your font swapping.

Fonts and Printing (JF)

Whether you print using PostScript or TrueType, fonts play the same role: They supply character outlines used to create printable text. Generally, documents don't really *contain* any fonts—they simply call for particular fonts to be used and describe how the text should be sized and positioned. (The exception: There are some pure PostScript files, which you can use to deliver your documents to off-site printing services that don't have your fonts in-house. For details on that, see "Using Service Bureaus" in Chapter 21.)

You can create a document perfectly well using only bit-mapped screen fonts—your application needs to know only how much space the letters take up (information stored in the screen fonts), not what the characters in the typeface actually look like. But at printing time, the printer fonts for every typeface called for in a document have to be available.

PostScript Printing vs. QuickDraw Printing

Whether you use PostScript or TrueType fonts, the font information in your document must be *interpreted*, that is, rendered into a printable image. If you print using QuickDraw, this image processing is done inside your Mac, while PostScript printers use their own built-in image-processing computer. If you're printing with PostScript fonts on a QuickDraw printer, ATM does the interpreting inside your Mac. (ATM is described on page 527; the difference between PostScript and QuickDraw printers is described in Chapter 21.)

In either case, the interpreter has to have access to the fonts you used to create the original page. This is simple for QuickDraw printing, because everything is done in your Mac. The entire image of each page is assembled there and passed to the printer, which needs very little in the way of brain power to reproduce the page image being spoon-fed to it by your Mac.

But when printing with PostScript, you may need to get fonts from your Mac into the printer—a process called *downloading*—where the printer's on-board computer can get to them. (Downloading is described in more detail below.)

Not all fonts need to be downloaded to the printer, because PostScript printers always come with some *resident fonts*—fonts built into the printer's ROM. This is usually a set referred to as the *LaserWriter 35*, shown in the box at right. Every PostScript printer has at least the Times, Helvetica, Courier, and Symbol fonts built in, to provide a common set of fonts that all PostScript users can share, regardless of which program or printer they use. You can also attach a hard disk to some PostScript printers for permanently storing large numbers of fonts, in effect adding to the number of resident fonts.

The LaserWriter 35: Fonts Almost Everybody Has (DD)

Most PostScript printers come with a set of PostScript typefaces, often referred to as the "LaserWriter 35" (they first appeared together in Apple's LaserWriter Plus), built into their ROMs (the printer manufacturers usually also provide the bit-mapped versions of these fonts on disk for loading into your operating system). They're also available as part of Adobe's **Type Basics** pack ($200). Except for Symbol, Zapf Chancery, and Zapf Dingbats, all these fonts come in full, four-member families, including plain, bold, italic, and bold-italic versions (that's why they add up to 35 instead of the 11 shown here).

PostScript Versions of Basic System Fonts

Courier
Helvetica
Palatino
Symbol (Σψμβολ)
Times

Additional Fonts

ITC Avant Garde Gothic
ITC Bookman
Helvetica Narrow
New Century Schoolbook
ITC Zapf Chancery
☆✳✣ ✺❁❒❄

Automatic PostScript Font Downloading (JK/JF)

When you click OK in the Print dialog box, the Mac calls down to the PostScript printer, "Yo, file coming! You got Palatino down there?" The printer, consulting its list of built-in fonts, might answer, "Always! Send that file!" Whereupon the Mac might say, "You got Frutiger, too?" and get the answer, "Never heard of it; send it down." In which case the Mac downloads Frutiger to the printer, where it's stored in memory. It takes about 15 seconds to download a font.

This Mac/printer dialogue and downloading continues until all the necessary fonts are in the printer (in which case your pages print), or until the printer runs out of memory (in which case the printer freaks out, sends an error message to the Mac, and quits in a huff).

This way of getting the fonts you need into the printer is called *automatic downloading*, and fonts sent to the printer this way stay in the printer's memory only until the document has been printed, after which the fonts are dropped to make room for those in the next print job.

Automatic downloading is the easiest way to handle fonts because you don't do anything special—just choose Print. It's also the logical strategy for a workgroup that uses many different fonts—one person's downloaded fonts are automatically cleared out to make room for those needed by a comrade's job.

Off-Site Printing (JF)

If you create files for printing elsewhere, you need to make sure that the remote site has all the fonts your job needs. With professional service bureaus, this is usually not a problem, because they maintain up-to-date font libraries. To be safe, though, send a list of all the fonts you've used, including their full names, manufacturers, and formats (TrueType, TrueType GX, PostScript, or PostScript GX).

If the people you're sending your files to don't have the necessary fonts (down to the right manufacturer and format), you've got a problem. It's a violation of your software licensing agreement (you did *buy* your fonts, didn't you?) to give copies of fonts to anyone else unless you stop using them yourself for the duration of the loan and also get those fonts back without leaving any copies behind.

There are two ways to get around this. The first is to mutter "Take a hike, capitalist running dogs" and send the fonts anyway. This makes you a criminal. A more acceptable approach is to create Encapsulated PostScript (EPS) versions of your files, embedding the fonts needed to print them. (Instructions for doing this are in Chapter 21.) Many font vendors' licensing agreements, however, also prohibit this (Adobe and Linotype-Hell are exceptions).

Typesetting shouldn't create moral challenges, but there you are. I'm sure you'll do the right thing.

If you use the same fonts over and over again, though, it's a waste of time to have them downloaded and deleted every time you print. It's smarter to download the fonts so they stay resident in memory, a process called *manual* or *permanent downloading*.

Manually Downloading PostScript Fonts (JF)

Manual downloading copies fonts into the printer's memory so they stay there "permanently" (until the printer is turned off). You manually download fonts with a special program, such as Apple's LaserWriter Font Utility (included with the System) or Adobe's Downloader (free with Adobe fonts). If your printer has a hard disk attached, these programs can also copy your fonts permanently onto it, where they'll stay until you erase them.

The benefit of manual downloading is that your pages print faster because you download the fonts just once (in the morning, say, when you start your printer), not every time you print. Manual downloading also helps your printer pack fonts more efficiently into memory. (Tips for manually downloading fonts are included in Chapter 21 under "Laser Printer Tips.")

The Case of the Missing Font (JF)

The Mac and PostScript printer have a fixed routine when it comes to finding the fonts they need to print a page. Here's how the search proceeds:

1. check the printer's ROM (where built-in fonts are kept)
2. check the printer's RAM (which temporarily stores downloaded fonts)
3. check the printer's hard disk (if it's got one)
4. check the Mac's System Folder

If your system doesn't find the required PostScript font in any of those places, the Mac will look for an equivalent TrueType font in the System Folder.

But what happens when your printer or Mac can't find a font it needs for printing? One of two things:

- it will use the screen font to print lumpy-looking screen-resolution type
- it will substitute another font, usually Courier, which is so ugly you can't miss the substitution

If you're using Adobe's Super ATM (described in Chapter 24), the program will create a substitute for the missing font using a generic Multiple Master serif or sans-serif typeface. The substitute won't look exactly the same as the missing font, but at least it will have the correct character widths (also know as *font metrics*) so that your layout will be preserved, with all original line endings intact.

Special Characters and Specialty Fonts

With the fabulous variety of fonts and styles on the Mac, you can get text to look just about any way you want it to. But what if your imagination—or your business—extends further than the Latin alphabet? Not to worry; the wide, wide world of fonts has something for everyone, and the special characters you need are often lurking right in the fonts you already own.

The Standard Special Characters (AN/SA/JK)

There are some characters on computer keyboards you won't find on typewriter keyboards—the backslash (\), the vertical bar (|), the less-than and greater-than signs (< and >), and so on. But when people talk about special characters on the Mac, they mean ones that aren't shown on the keyboard at all. Some fonts have idiosyncratic special characters of their own, but there's a set of standard special characters that nearly all fonts share. No bit-mapped font contains all of them—Geneva and Chicago seem to have the most—but most outline fonts have the full set.

The diagrams at right show where they appear on the keyboard under System 7 (some of them are different under earlier system versions).

To get one of these special characters, you hold down the Option key (with or without the Shift key) while pressing another key. (Note that on some Mac keyboards the Option key is labeled Alt.)

Let's say you want to type: *Hein, mec! Parlez-vous français?* To get the special character ç in *français*, you hold down Option while hitting C. To get certain other special characters, you have to hold down the Shift key as well. For example, if you hit Shift Option C you get an uppercase Ç instead of a lowercase one. (In this case, the two characters are related,

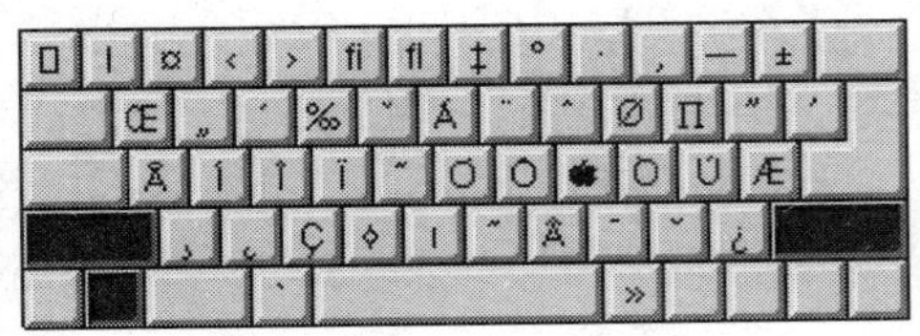

Almost any font will have the special characters shown here, mapped to these positions on the keyboard. The top illustration shows the characters you get when you press the Option *key. The bottom one shows the characters available with* Shift Option.

but sometimes the Option and Shift Option characters have nothing to do with each other.)

Other characters (mainly accented ones) require a three-keystroke sequence. For example, to set the acute accent in *café*, you hold down Option, type E, and voilà! You see absolutely nothing! But release Option and hit E again, and the accented character will appear. The Option-whatever keystroke combo tells the Mac to get the accent, and the next single keystroke tells it what letter to put it over. This same two-step technique works for creating characters topped with a dieresis (¨), accent grave (`), caret (ˆ), or tilde (˜).

Mnemonics for Special Characters (SA/AN/JK)

Understanding why certain special characters are placed on certain keys can help you remember where they are. (If the logic isn't obvious, look for a connection that means something to you.) The bullet (•) and the degree symbol (°) resemble the asterisk; all three are on the * key. The dagger (†), which you get with Option T, looks like a *T*. The diamond (◊) and the square-root symbol (√), both of which incorporate the V shape, are on the V key.

The copyright symbol can't be on the C key, since ç and Ç are already there, but its shape is similar to a G and that's the key you'll find it on. The ellipsis (…), which has three dots, is on the same key as the colon (:), which has two. Other easy connections are π and ∏ on P, ® on R, µ (mu) on M, ¢ on the dollar sign, and ¥ (the yen sign) on Y.

Expert Sets (EF)

Expert sets, or *expert collections*, are companion fonts for certain typefaces that provide special characters such as small caps, fractions, old-style numbers (the kind that dip below the baseline), and ornate alternate letters. Unfortunately, they exist for only a handful of fonts. The larger character sets allowed by TrueType GX will do away with the need for expert sets; all variant characters can be included in the main font. But it's not clear how you'll be able to get at them all unless Apple adds some additional access keys beyond the Option/Alt and ⌘ keys.

Pictorial and Decorative Fonts (DD)

Fonts aren't limited to letters and numbers, either. There has recently been an explosion of *pictorial fonts*, which assign images to the different keys of your keyboard. They're available from almost any font vendor, and several font designers, such as Judith Sutcliffe at Electric Typographer, specialize in such fun and decorative images. A sampling of them is supplied on page 566 and 567.

Foreign-Language and Special-Purpose Fonts (DD)

Some fonts are made just to supply those characters that the standard Latin alphabet fonts don't include. These include foreign-language fonts, such as Kanji, Arabic, Cyrillic, and other non-Latin alphabets, and *pi fonts* that include such utility characters as mathematical symbols, map-making symbols, musical notation, credit card logos, and other useful and decorative shapes. A sampler of special-purpose and foreign-language fonts is supplied on pages 568 and 569.

Finding the Character You Need

It's often hard to remember which key combination to hit to produce the character you need, or even whether the font you're using has that character. There are a couple of handy programs that you can use to quickly find what you need.

Key Caps (AN/SA/EF/JK/DD). Key Caps is a desk accessory included in the system software of every Macintosh. You'll find it in your menu.

When you choose Key Caps, the Mac displays a representation of a keyboard and puts a new menu title, Key Caps, at the right end of the menu bar. The keyboard shows what characters are mapped to what keys on the keyboard. In the Key Caps menu, you can choose which font you want to look at.

When you hold down the Shift key, Key Caps darkens the Shift keys on its display and shows you the characters available on the keyboard when you press Shift. When you hold down Option, it displays a keyboard like the one shown at left. System 7's version also shows which keys give you accents that you can apply to other letters (they're outlined in gray).When you hit one of those keys, the display changes to show which letters you can apply the selected accent to (they're outlined in black).

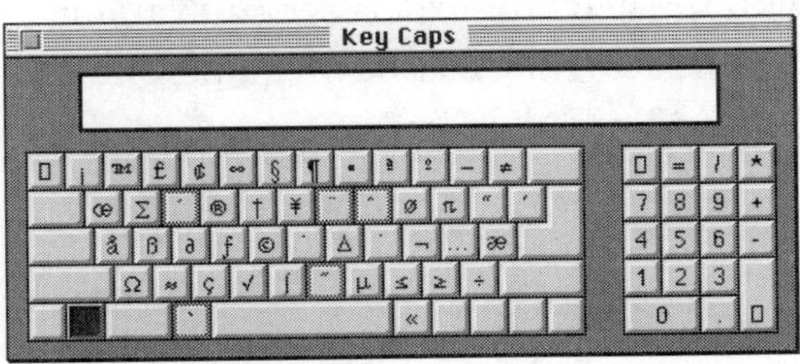

The Key Caps display shows which characters are mapped to which keys on the keyboard. (This display shows what you'll get with the Option key pressed in the Adobe's PostScript Janson font.) The keys outlined in gray are accent keys.

You can enter text in the sample text area at the top of the display by typing on your real keyboard or by clicking on keys in the Key Caps window. You can cut or copy this text from Key Caps into any document. (It won't appear in the font you chose in Key Caps, but it's easy enough to change the font once you're back in your document.) If you need a string of special characters, it's usually easier to type them in Key Caps, copy them to your document, and then change the font, than it is to remember where each symbol is on the keyboard and type them directly into your document.

> ***The Missing-Character Box*** (AN/SA/JK)
>
> When a font doesn't have a given special character, it will produce the *missing-character box* (as shown, for instance, on the Enter key in the Key Caps illustration on the previous page) when you type the character. The missing-character box will only print on dot-matrix printers (which get their letter images directly from the screen), not on laser printers.

Other ways to do the same thing (ND/DD). Key Caps is handy, but it's not the perfect answer to the problem. When you need a character but don't know which keys to press to produce it, do you want to labor to decode a little picture of the keyboard layout? No! You just want to find the character right away.

Günther Blaschek's freeware PopChar puts a display like this at the top of your screen when you touch a hot spot on your menu bar. You just click on a character to insert it in your document. The keystroke you would use to get the character is shown in the upper-right corner.

Our favorite tool for this job is a nifty freeware control panel from Günther Blaschek called **PopChar**. Once installed, PopChar inserts a tiny hot spot on the menu bar. When you want to find a special character, you point to that spot and an array showing every character in the current font appears at the top of your screen. Drag the pointer to the character you want, let go of the mouse button, and the character is automatically inserted into your document. If you don't want to insert it directly in the open file, drag the pointer below the character box, and "More…" appears in the top right. Click there to turn the box into a window with an area into which your chosen characters are placed.

You might also already have utilities that act as Key Cap substitutes. In Microsoft Word, you can call up an array of all the Macintosh characters by pressing [⌘][Option][Q]. As with PopChar, clicking on a character inserts it into your document. Dubl-Click Software packages **BigCaps,** another Key Caps–like utility, with its World Class Fonts. If you have Norton Utilities (described in Chapter 13), you've got a little utility, called KeyFinder, that shows all the characters in a font, but it doesn't insert them into your document when you click on them. If you already have one of these utilities, give 'em a try.

Using Font Styles

From the beginning, the Mac included not only different fonts but different ways you could style them. Like its font formats, though, the Mac's styles have come a long way since then, resulting in (as usual) both more possibilities and more confusion for users.

The Mac's Basic Styles (KT/AN/EF)

The bit-mapped fonts that the first Macs came with were drawn in just one style—the plain (roman) style—at each size. To add variety to these fonts you used an application's Style menu. To get Geneva Bold, you selected the Geneva typeface, styled it Bold, and then the Mac mathematically rendered the new version by applying a formula like "increase the width 20 percent" (to create a bold face) or "slant right 12 degrees" (to create an italic).

The early Style menus offered at least these styles: Plain, Bold, Italic, Bold Italic, Outline, and Shadow, so any font could thus be rendered in 16 possible variations (including combinations of two or more styles). In addition, some applications added other styles, such as Strikethru, Underline, and Condensed.

✓Plain Text
Bold
Italic
Underline
Outline
Shadow
Condensed
Extended

Most Macintosh applications will include a set of styles, like these, that you can apply to your text, regardless of what styles are included in the font family. If the appropriate font style is not installed (or if the font is not properly linked), the Mac will create the style by applying a mathematical formula to the basic font specs.

How Styles Should Work

(KT/DD)

When Adobe introduced PostScript outline fonts, things became more sophisticated. Most PostScript typeface families consist of a number of fonts, each one representing a distinct design, differing from its cousins in terms of weight, character width, slant, and other features. This means that the type designer, and not the computer, makes the decisions about how much bolder than a plain (or roman) typeface its bold style should be, and the italic isn't just a slanted roman, but a true italic typeface. As described under "What Is a Font, Anyway?" at the beginning of this chapter, most typeface families consist of at least four different font files—different ones for the plain (or roman), italic, bold, and bold-italic styles. TrueType fonts have followed suit, providing different outline fonts for each basic style (although they're often rolled together into a single suitcase).

When Adobe introduced its PostScript fonts, it *linked* its family font styles so they worked like the Mac's native fonts. In other words, you get the same result whether you select Helvetica and style it as Bold or choose the Helvetica Bold font.

The Outline and Shadow effects, though, are still added by the Mac—they're not part of the font. And for this reason, the rendering isn't always successful, and results vary from printer to printer. Shadow effects printed on a high-resolution imagesetter, for example, typically appear so faint that they're almost invisible—if they appear at all.

To complicate matters, not all font families have their styles internally linked. When working with such a group of fonts, choosing italic, for instance, will just add a slant to the roman style. The only way you can tell whether the face is correctly linked or not is by comparing the printed results of the two methods—what you see on the screen won't necessarily appear on the printed page.

Applying Styles

(KT)

So assuming the members of your font family are correctly linked, should you apply your styles using the Style menu (or its keyboard shortcuts) or by choosing a specific font? I personally think you should use the Style menu, for a couple of reasons.

Reasons to use the Style menus. First, it makes your files using PostScript fonts more portable—using the explicitly named fonts means that anyone you send your files to (including a service bureau) must have screen fonts for all the family members installed as well. If you use the Mac's styles, it doesn't make any difference how the recipient's Mac is set up, as long as the screen font for the "plain" version is installed and the printer fonts are available. (Of course, all output services should always keep screen fonts for all their typefaces installed as a matter of course, but you can't count on that.)

Font Style Shorthand (SA/EF/AN)

The weight or style of a typeface supplied by a particular font is often indicated by initials preceding the font name. Here are some of the initials you're likely to see, and what they stand for:

B	bold	*L*	light
Bk	book	*N*	narrow
Blk	black	*O*	oblique
C	condensed	*P*	poster
D	demibold	*S*	semi
E	extended	*Sl*	slanted
H	heavy	*U*	ultra
I	italic	*X*	extra

Sometimes you'll see them in combination—*XBO*, for example, stands for *extra bold oblique*.

Another advantage to using menu styles is that it makes changing typefaces easier. If you used Garamond for a job and then decided to reset it in Caslon, all you'd have to do is change all the text to Caslon, and all the Garamond bolds and italics would automatically be changed to Caslon bolds and italics.

Reasons to apply individual styles. There are conditions, though, under which applying styles via the menu can cause problems. The first is when a font has more than the four styles listed in the Style menu. Take Helvetica, for example. If you style Helvetica to be Bold, you'll get Helvetica Bold. But what do you get if you Style Helvetica Light to be Bold? Logically, you might think that you'd get the version of Helvetica that was one step bolder, namely Helvetica Regular. Wrong! You actually get Helvetica Black (which is bolder than Helvetica Bold). This is because font makers have had to cram styles actually designed as "light," "thin," "medium," "heavy," or "extrabold" into two arbitrary Mac weight categories: Regular and Bold. In large typeface families, it's impossible to predict which font is linked stylistically to which other fonts.

Organizing the Font Menu (SA/EF/AN/DD)

If you have large font families installed on your Mac, the first thing you notice when you go to the font menu is how *messy* it is. Because the letters that indicate the font's style are often placed in front of the font name, and since the fonts are alphabetized in the menu, the different members of a single typeface family can be strewn all through the list.

Before: The letters in front of some font names that specify their weights or styles make a mess of your type menu, spreading the different members of a single typeface family (such as Futura in this example) throughout the menu and making style names hard to read.

There are two ways to avoid this: The first is to use a system extension such as **Adobe Type Reunion** ($65), Dubl-Click Software's **MenuFonts** ($70), or Eastgate System's **Fontina** ($70), which reorganize your font menu so that all the members of a font family appear under a single submenu named for that family.

The other solution is to "harmonize" your fonts using Font Harmony, a utility that comes with **Suitcase** from Fifth Generation Systems. (Suitcase is described on page 541.) Once your fonts are harmonized, you'll see only the typeface name in the font menu. You get the bold, italic, and bold-italic styles by using keyboard shortcuts or the Style menu.

Which program you use is a matter of preference. If you don't like the effect you get with one of the system extensions, you can just remove the extension from your system to put everything back to normal. But "harmonizing" your fonts is for keeps: to pull them apart again, you'll need to reinstall all your fonts.

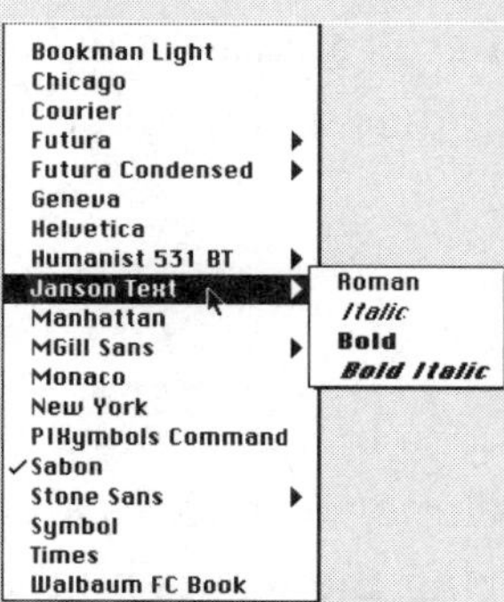

Adobe Type Reunion is a no-nonsense fix—it just organizes the menu, putting all the members of a single family in a submenu under the family name.

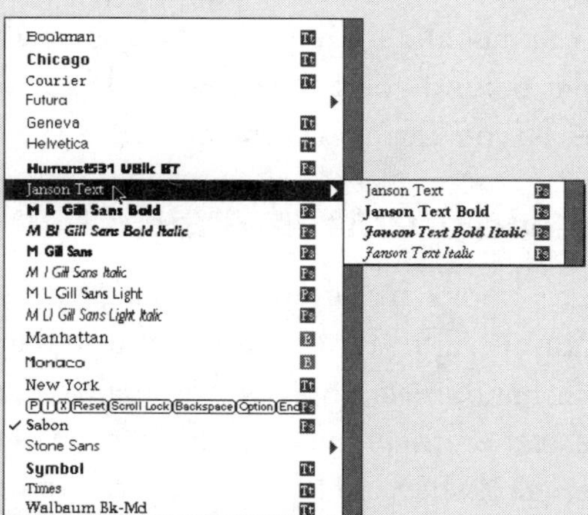

MenuFonts goes a step further, putting the font names in the typefaces they name and indicating whether the font is TrueType, PostScript, or bit-mapped.

You should also watch out for cases where a style is applied to a font already designed with that style—for example, bolding a bold face or italicizing an italic. This can easily happen when, for example, you've set all your italics by selecting a specific italic font, and then at the last minute you've gone through and changed the basic font to the italic style via a search-and-replace operation. The results are generally pretty ugly— if bold characters are large enough, you may even see two images superimposed, and all the italics will seem too inclined. Most font manufacturers design their fonts so you can't inadvertently create double bolds or double italics, but because it takes an extra programming step, many smaller font producers don't do it.

Typesetting Basics

(AJ/DD)

Working from the Style menu is just the beginning of what you can do to style type. Macintosh software that's designed to work with type (word processing, page layout, and graphics programs) usually offers lots of features that let you precisely control the look of type on the page. There are two important things to remember about using these controls: 1) the default settings aren't necessarily the best for every situation, and 2) to badly apply these programs' controls over tracking, word and letterspacing, and leading can be worse than not adjusting them at all. To get you off on the right foot, here's a crash course in the principles behind good typesetting. (If you are unfamiliar with the terms used here, see "Type Terms" on the next page).

Basic Concept: The Ideational Unit

Children's books are often set in large sizes of type. Why? Not because kids have poor eyesight. It's because children read words letter by letter. Adults, on the other hand, read whole words at a time, recognizing the words by their silhouette rather than by examining each letter. These letter clusters (called *ideational units*) have to fit together well in order to be easily legible. The best-quality fonts are designed with the proper letter fit to create smooth, easy-to-read ideational units.

Type Terms

(AJ)

When choosing and using fonts, you'll run into terminology that may be unfamiliar. Here's a guide to the basic vocabulary of typography:

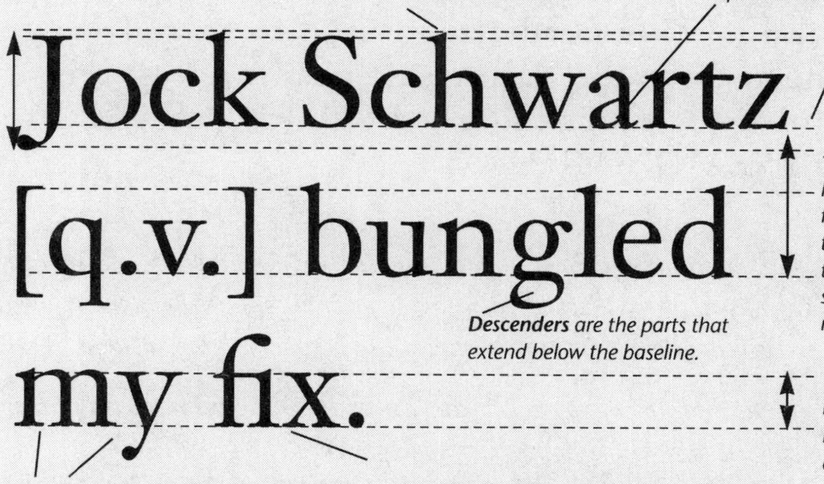

Type size *is measured from the top of the ascenders to the bottom of the descenders. It is measured in units called points. (There are 72 points per inch.)*

Ascenders *are the parts of lowercase letters that extend above the x-height.*

Counters *are the open spaces inside letters.*

Jock Schwartz

The ***baseline*** *is an imaginary line the letters sit on.*

[q.v.] bungled

The space from line to line, usually measured from one baseline to the next, is know as the ***leading.*** *Like type size, it is generally measured in* ***points.***

Descenders *are the parts that extend below the baseline.*

my fix.

The ***x-height*** *is the height of a lowercase letter, without any ascenders or descenders.*

Serifs *are the small strokes that finish the ends of letters. Typefaces without serifs are called* ***sans serif*** *typefaces.*

A ***ligature*** *is a character that ties together two or more letters that otherwise don't set well together. The fi ligature, shown here, prevents the dot of the i from overlapping the hook of the f.*

Tracking

For the reasons stated above, you should never idly tinker with the letterspacing of the typefaces you are using, a setting controlled by the "tracking" feature in most applications. Jamming letters together or spreading them apart to fill a justified line are common errors that impede legibility and usually ruin the appearance of the page. Another typographic crime is trying to get the type to fit a predetermined space by manipulating it in a drawing program such as FreeHand or altering its character widths in programs such as PageMaker or QuarkXPress. A smarter alternative is to choose a different size type or a different typeface.

Tracking too tight

Now is the time for all good men to come to the aid of the party. Yes, we're having a party, and you are cordially invited to attend. To get here: Take the Valley exit heading west and follow the signs marked SIMPKINS PARTY to SEMIRAMIS WAY.

Tracking too loose

Now is the time for all good men to come to the aid of the party. Yes, we're having a party, and you are cordially invited to attend. To get here: Take the Valley exit heading west and follow the signs marked SIMPKINS PARTY to SEMIRAMIS WAY.

[That said, I've got to speak up for the tracking control in at least one situation: Sometimes the only way to fit that last word onto a page is to change the tracking by just a hair—maybe -2 percent. It's not even noticeable, and it saves a lot of trouble.—DD]

[Altering tracking has another purpose, too: It's a useful and legitimate way to overcome a basic typographic optical illusion: that type appears to be more loosely spaced the larger its point size. In the days of metal type, we had different versions of typefaces for use in large display *sizes, and these faces had a much closer fit to compensate for this apparent looseness. These days, when proper titling faces are still a rarity, we have to make due in display settings with faces that have been designed to space correctly at text sizes. The solution? Tighten the tracking as point size increases, starting at about 18-point, and continue tightening progressively in larger sizes; at 72-point, tracking can be tightened by 10 percent or more in many faces.—JF]*

Leading

The space between lines of type—called *leading* (pronounced *ledding*) by typesetters and in page layout programs and called *line spacing* in some word processors—is often automatically set at 120 percent of the type size. (For 10-point type, for instance, the leading would be set at 12 points.) While this setting may work fairly well in a lot of cases, its often worth experimenting with to determine what looks best for the typeface and line length you're using. Typefaces

Now is the time for all good men to come to the aid of the party. Yes, we're having a party, and you are cordially invited to attend. To get here: Take the Valley exit heading west and follow the signs marked SIMPKINS PARTY to SEMIRAMIS WAY.

No extra leading: 14-point type on 14 points leading (14/14)

Now is the time for all good men to come to the aid of the party. Yes, we're having a party, and you are cordially invited to attend. To get here: Take the Valley exit heading west and follow the signs marked SIMPKINS PARTY to SEMIRAMIS WAY.

Three points leading: 14-point type on 17 points leading (14/17)

with small x-heights (and longer ascenders and descenders) generally need less leading than do faces with comparatively large x-heights, and pages with short lines of text need less leading than do pages with long lines. (The white space between lines serves as a highway for your eyes to follow when moving from the right-hand margin back to the left.)

HOT TIP

Justified or Ragged Right?

People often consider a justified right margin (making all the lines exactly the same length, as in this book) the hallmark of professionally typeset text, probably because this feature was all but impossible to achieve with a typewriter. The truth is, though, that when you ask your Mac to justify your type it has no choice but to mess with the spaces between the letters or between the words in each line, making for inconsistent spacing that can make reading a chore. Many word processing and page layout programs allow you to control the maximum and minimum amounts you'll allow the program to stretch or compress the spaces, but the best amount is none at all. Remember, then, that if you must justify the right margin, you'll need to spend some time adjusting line breaks—and even rewriting sentences if necessary—to get your lines to set smoothly, with consistent-looking spacing.

Kerning

Kerning is the act of adjusting the spacing between individual letters. This makes up for the fact that the letterspacing built into the font just can't work with every possible letter pair. Some fonts have built in tables of *kerning pairs*—pairs of letters that require special letterspacing adjustments—but the software you use must also be sophisticated enough to put those adjustments into effect. (Most page layout programs are.) In addition, most page layout and graphics programs offer features that let you manually kern pairs of letters individually.

Manual kerning must be done carefully: It's possible to kern too much as well as too little. And once you start kerning, it's hard to stop, because changing the fit of one pair of letters changes the relative relationships of everything else on the line. The best rule is to kern only when the line appears unsightly, when there are eye-catching gaps between letters, or when pairs of letters appear pinched together. It's also important to proof your hand-kerning work on a high-resolution printout; it's hard to judge kerning on screen.

Letterspacing

Letterspacing is loose tracking taken to the extreme: spreading letters apart to improve the airflow between them. It's another fine art that requires diligence and an experienced eye to practice effectively. Letterspacing is most useful when you're working with lines in all capitals, because capital letters were really designed to be set with lowercase letters and not with all other capitals. Most programs let you space out letters in tiny increments: You just keep pushing or pulling until the line looks right. As with kerning, the time to employ letterspacing is when the line just looks wrong without it, and it always takes a few tries to get it just right. *[And remember to make your word spaces big enough in letterspaced lines—in widely spaced text, they often have to be exaggerated to stand out sufficiently.—JF]*

Neither kerned nor letterspaced	SEMIRAMIS WAY
Kerned and letterspaced	SEMIRAMIS WAY

Buying Fonts

(KT/EF)

You can buy fonts from a dizzying variety of sources. Any given font is usually available directly from the manufacturer or from any number of retailers who have licensed it from its original maker. Software discounters such as CompUSA, MacConnection, MacWarehouse, Egghead, and The MacZone all sell fonts, and so do some office supply stores. (In fact, I saw PC font packages at a Price Costco last summer. Can coin machines at airports be far behind?) You can even download fonts from a new commercial service on CompuServe. You can find the names of vendors in books like this one, in design and computer magazines, or by word of mouth from your friends.

Shareware Fonts (DD)

Almost every bulletin board service—CompuServe, America Online, and others—has a desktop publishing forum that features hundreds of shareware or freeware fonts. These are usually rather goofy designs created by nonprofessional designers, just for the fun of it, but the work of some serious type-hounds is also available there. Download the font, and if you like it and want to use it, send the creator the asked-for fee, anything from a fan letter to $15 or so. The quality of these fonts ranges from down-and-dirty to pretty impressive.

What sometimes makes things confusing is that a company you tend to identify as a font maker—Adobe for instance—also licenses fonts from other sources. The thing to remember is that just because you buy a font from Adobe (or Linotype-Hell or Monotype) doesn't make it an Adobe (or Linotype-Hell or Monotype) font. All of these companies, and many more, license each others' fonts (though not all sell them at the same prices). We're also seeing a new phenomenon: font vendors, such as Precision Type, that make no fonts of their own but sell (usually at a low price) only fonts licensed from others.

How do you find out what typefaces each vendor offers? For starters, you can contact font vendors and ask for their catalogs. If you want to see font samples from many companies, combined with articles on various facets of typography, we'd suggest three publications. ***x-height*** is a quarterly newsletter/catalog ($18 per year) from FontHaus. ***U&lc,*** ITC's quarterly journal ($14 per year), just celebrated its 20th anniversary. ITC also publishes ***The ITC Directory of New Typefaces,*** specimen pages of new faces from leading foundries and designers

($190 including quarterly updates). The *Directory*'s three-ring-binder format allows you to insert updates, and an index helps you locate faces by category, name, or designer (See Appendix D for information on how to contact these companies.)

In addition to selling fonts singly, most of the major manufacturers offer package deals that significantly reduce the cost per font. Adobe sells its Type Basics pack (the 35 basic PostScript printer fonts described on page 543, plus 30 more faces "specially chosen to complement the 35 printer fonts") for $200. Adobe's Value Pack, including 30 text, script, decorative, and display faces, sells for just $60, which works out to a couple dollars per font. And those are the list prices: You can get these packages and similar ones from other vendors through mail-order companies for about 40 percent less.

Adobe, Monotype, Agfa, and the other vendors with large libraries also offer their entire libraries on CD-ROM. The CD itself is available for a nominal cost, and most of the fonts are unavailable until you call the manufacturer with your credit card number. In return, the vendor tells you the secret codes that unlock the fonts you want. Most of the font vendors offer bargains to customers who buy fonts this way, charging $25 or so for fonts that may normally retail for $100 or more. Most also offer unlocked CDs, giving you access to an entire library on your desktop. The price leader at press time was the Bitstream CD offered by Precision Type, delivering 1,085 top-quality fonts for $1,090. Other font libraries, such as FontHaus and URW, offer their entire libraries for as little as 20 cents per font.

Ares and ElseWare, with their synthetic font technologies, have a new twist on font sales. Their programs each create more than 200 fonts from compact font descriptors, so you buy a whole library of fonts when you buy the software. (See the box "Synthetic Fonts" on page 529 for more on these programs.)

On the following pages, we've pulled together a small sampling of fonts in four different categories: text fonts, display fonts, pictorial fonts, and special purpose fonts. They should at least give you a taste of what's out there. Happy hunting.

Font Sampler: Text Fonts

(AJ)

A good text font should be basically invisible. If you read a book all the way through and don't notice the typeface, the typographer has done a good job. If, however, you keep noticing a weird *g* or odd swash capitals, your mind wanders and the author loses his or her grip on your attention.

That's not to say that text types are boring. In fact, they're some of most beautiful typefaces around, and without getting in the way, an appropriate text face can impart an appropriate character to the text. For short copy such as advertisements, you can afford to get a little more allusive and experimental with the text type.

Text fonts can be divided into several categories, based on the historical period in which their basic design emerged. A flexible font library should include one or more from each category to accommodate all kinds of work.

Old Style

Sabon (Linotype-Hell/Monotype, various prices), designed by Jan Tschichold in 1966, is a quiet and refined version of the classic Garamond model.

Adobe Garamond ($275, expert set $185) is an excellent example of Old Style type that's a little lighter and appears slightly smaller than Sabon.

Old Style types begin with the romans of Francesco Griffo, cut for Aldus Manutius in Venice in the late 1490s. Griffo refined earlier models by increasing the contrast between vertical and horizontal strokes, reducing the height of the capitals, straightening the crossbar in the eye of the *e*, and substituting round dots (like that over an *i*) for diamond-shaped ones. The Old Style model was perfected in France by the mid-16th century by two men: Claude Garamond and Robert Granjon.

Dutch Old Style

Kis (Bitstream, $50 per weight) is a condensed and tight-fitting version of Kis Janson.

Monotype's Ehrhardt ($160), redrawn in 1937, is a condensed type, more interesting than its Janson.

Dutch Old Style began when Christopher Plantin hired Granjon to design a type that would be more economical to print with. To make the type sturdier, the face was made bolder. To fit more on a page, Granjon shortened the descenders and condensed the type somewhat. Then, because the tiny counters of the more-condensed *e* and *a* tended to fill with ink, he enlarged them. Dutch Old Style types make good workmanlike text faces. (This book is set in Adobe's Janson Text, a classic of Dutch Old Style.

Transitional

Monotype's Bell ($160, expert set $105) is an elegant choice as a basic text type that also looks great in large, display sizes.

ATF Bulmer (Bitstream, $50 per weight) has contrast that points the way to modern types.

Transitional types were inspired by the Rococo copper-engraved lettering popular in the 18th century. The French were first to lighten type and restore some of its calligraphic modeling. This group of types has high contrast and a primarily vertical stress (that is, the narrow parts of letter strokes in characters such as *o* and *e* are at the top and bottom of the letter, not off-center, as is the case with Old Style typefaces).

Modern

Walbaum is a German type that is lighter, wider, more curvaceous, and more readable than most moderns. The Berthold version (licensed by various vendors) is less severe than others.

Designed to reflect improvements in type cutting and printing technology, including smoother paper, modern types are generally hard on the eyes, having a strong vertical emphasis with marked contrast between thick and thin portions of the letters, and thin hairline serifs. Bodoni is the best-known example of this style.

Sans-Serif

Paul Renner's Futura (Elsner + Flake via FontHaus, $40 per weight, or Fundición Tipografica Neufville via Adobe, $275 for three styles) is a clean, modern type that never gets tired and works well in all its weights and styles.

Gill Sans (Monotype, $240 for the text weights) is a humanist type with a bit more personality than Futura.

Hans Ed Meier's Syntax (Linotype-Hell, $40 per weight) is another family group with great flexibility and readability.

Although any book on typography will tell you that sans-serif typefaces are difficult to read for long stretches, they are increasingly popular for setting text. The best of them (like the faces shown here) have a lot of variations for setting work that requires different levels of headings and different kinds of emphasis.

Ahistoric Faces

Electra (Linotype-Hell, $40 per weight) is an elegant type from W.A. Dwiggins with an understated calligraphic quality.

Eric Gill's Joanna (Linotype-Hell, $40 per weight) is his greatest typeface. Its slab serifs make it appear flashy and angular in large sizes. (Also available in Adobe's Value Pack for $40.)

Bitstream Charter ($50 per style), designed by Matthew Carter, is a quiet type, constructed to be legible in extreme variations of weight.

Swift (Elsner + Flake via FontHaus, $290 for the family or $60 per weight) designed by Gerard Unger in 1985 for newspaper work, has a chiseled look, condensed capitals, and a large x-height.

Many 20th-century designers have devised faces that have no particular historic model in mind. Eric Gill, Jan Van Krimpen, and W.A. Dwiggins produced many wonderful types around mid-century that are still popular. Contemporary designers such as Gerard Unger, Matthew Carter, and Sumner Stone are also producing enduring models.

Fancy Text

Cochin (created by Monotype in 1917, digitized by Matthew Carter in 1977 for Linotype-Hell, $90 from Adobe) manages to look simultaneously like an engraved type from the Rococo period and an Art Deco face from the early 20th century.

Michael Harvey's 1990 Ellington (Monotype, $290) has the consummate confidence and control one would expect from a stonecutter. Its bold weights are also very distinctive.

Koch Antiqua (Alphabets, $70 per weight from FontHaus) or Eva-Antiqua (shown here), based on Koch's Eve (from Spiece Graphics via FontHaus, $60 per weight) are recent re-creations of types cut in Germany in the 1920s that show the heritage of pen-drawn lettering.

Some text faces are a little too fancy for book work but have great appeal for dust jackets or display work. Texts shorter than books, like greeting cards, announcements, even works of poetry, could use one of these fancier types. You could also use these in headings to contrast with a more sober text type.

Font Sampler: Display Fonts (AJ)

These are types designed to be used at large sizes to break up blocks of text and grab your attention. They range from quiet, enlarged versions of text types to the wildest faces a type designer can dream up.The strong personalities of display faces can instantly bring a sense of a time and place. Remember, the more personality a typeface has, the less versatile it will be—but the more appropriate for some specialized use.

The traditional categories are decorated, engraved, script, slab serif, and sans serif. When building a library, it's good to have some reliable standbys (like the Smaragd shown here) as well as some more goofy ones (like the Xavier Black or Ad Lib).

Smaragd (Linotype-Hell)

SEE THE TREASURES OF ROME

Gudrun Zapf von Hesse's Smaragd, from Linotype-Hell ($40), is a classy, all-caps in-line face, the subtlest kind of decorated type, which features a white line inside the stroke, making the type appear incised. From here the "decorated" category branches out to letterforms made out of other things, like cactus, banana peel, Band-Aids, whatever.

Poetica (Adobe Systems)

The Pleasure of Your Company

As a rule, scripts are hard to read and should be restricted to short bursts of text. Sometimes script capitals used with a text face can create a nice effect. Adobe's Poetica ($275, $185 for the expert sets), shown here, is a beautiful calligraphic face with lots of variant forms.

Egiziano Classic Black (FontHaus)

15 Men on a Dead Man's Chest

Dennis Ortiz-Lopez's Egiziano Classic Black, from FontHaus ($60), is one of the best re-creations of a historic slab serif: a style based on geometric letter shapes with bold flat serifs grafted on. The style, which was popular in the late 19th century, can sometimes be extremely dull and heavy.

Bernhard Gothic (Spiece Graphics via FontHaus)

Fly to New York

Spiece Graphics' Bernhard Gothic, from FontHaus ($70 for one weight, $40 for additional weights), is an elegant sans serif dating from the 1920s. It has unusual variant characters, including swash italics and a Greek *e* and works well at all weights.

Xavier Black (Castle Systems)

RHUMBA TO CUGAT'S ORCHESTRA

The wacky Xavier Black, from Castle Systems, is a type you'll want to use for display work at least once. It comes by itself for $50.

Ad Lib (Bitstream)

Phil Silvers as Bilko

ATF's goofy Ad Lib ($50, Bitstream) looks something like Ben Shahn's lettering for "What's My Line?" It is extremely informal and very evocative of the fifties (it dates from '61).

Goudy Stout (Castle Systems)

BEWARE OF THE BULL

Fred Goudy claims that his Goudy Stout ($50, Castle Systems) was a typographic lapse, but I think it's one of his best types. This all-caps face looks like it was conceived after a night of drinking and tango-dancing.

Berthold Lo-Type (Adobe Systems)

Serenade in Ragtime

Berthold Lo-Type (Adobe, $190) is a quirky German poster letterform from the turn of the century. Some very unusual characters, like the *f, g,* and *t,* add to its charm. Its quirky details are best appreciated at large sizes. The Adobe package has several weights and styles.

Willow (Adobe Systems)

Wanted! Dead or Alive!

Willow is a highly condensed type, a member of Adobe's best-selling Wood Types package ($185). (They're called wood types because they're based on late 19th Century American typefaces, which were carved from wood rather than forged in metal.

Font Sampler: Decorative and Pictorial Fonts (EF)

Pictorial fonts can be practical (pictures of credit cards, telephones, or cut-on-the-dotted-line scissors to use in ads), silly (kids' drawings or wacky birds), or simply ornamental (borders, fleurons, and other decorative elements). The following samples show just a few of the dozens of pictorial fonts available. (We didn't have the space to show a complete character set for every font, but the sample characters will give you the flavor of each.)

Adobe Wood Type Ornaments 2 (Adobe Systems)

Adobe's Wood Type Ornaments collections provide lots of old-fashioned ornaments. This font is included in the Adobe Type Basics package, which offers 65 fonts for $198, or sold with the Adobe Wood Type package for $185.

Adobe offers other pictorial fonts as well, including the popular Zapf Dingbats font (one of the LaserWriter 35 illustrated on page 543), in the Plus Pack, as well as fonts containing audio symbols, map symbols, ornaments, and yet more dingbats.

Credit Cards (Agfa)

If your business welcomes popular credit cards, you'll find this font handy for creating ads, menus, and the like. It costs $50 from Agfa.

Other pictorial fonts from Agfa illustrate astrology, animals, borders, ornaments, business, communications, games, sports, medicine, military, music, transportation, TV listings, logos, dingbats, and symbols.

DingBRATS (DS Design)

These dingbats from some of America's youngest type designers are a refreshing change of pace. The font includes 100 charming drawings by kids for $55.

Tommy's Type (The Electric Typographer)

Electric Typographer Judith Sutcliffe based this playful line o' type on some lettering sent to her by Santa Barbara historian Walker A. Tompkins ($45, includes Catastrophe, a font made up of cats). Other pictorial fonts from The Electric Typographer depict masks and petroglyphs.

Birds (FontHaus)

This antic aviary ($50) is just the thing for adding a spot of whimsy to a document. I like a font that makes me laugh.

FrankenFont (Handcraftedfonts Company)

Now you can create your own people without all the muss and fuss of stealing body parts from graveyards. FrankenFont ($65) consists of 74 parts that can be combined to make 1,000 human figures; each figure is assembled by typing a three-character combination.

Vine Leaves, Volume 1 (Lanston Type Co.)

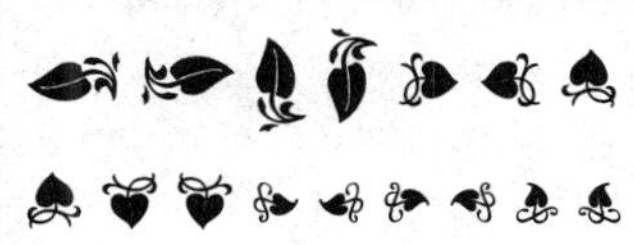

The Lanston Type Company has brought many classic faces from Goudy, Caslon, and other respected designers into the digital age. To augment these traditional faces, Lanston offers old-style borders, initial caps, and ornaments, including the 128 vine leaves in this font ($75).

Organics (Letraset)

Letraset's Fontek Design Fonts series ($90 per font, $350 for six fonts) offers several pictorial fonts in a variety of styles, inspired by everything from woodcuts to paper cutouts. (Note: Although Letraset has improved the font's performance, placing too many of the intricate Organics on a page might hang up a printer with less than 4MB of memory.)

Linotype Game Pi (Linotype-Hell)

This set of game fonts ($145) includes chess, checkers, dice, dominoes, and playing cards (French and English styles).

Other pictorial fonts from Linotype-Hell include dingbats, ornaments, maps, warnings, audio symbols, holiday motifs, astrology symbols, and borders.

Font Sampler: Special-Purpose Fonts (EF)

Macintosh fonts aren't limited to the Latin alphabet. If you speak a non-European language, chances are you can find a font for that language. For that matter, Mac fonts aren't even limited to words; you can find fonts for the languages of music, mathematics, and other symbolic systems. This section presents samples of several special-purpose fonts along with information on where to look for others (see Appendix D for company addresses and phone numbers). Because of space constraints, we haven't shown the complete character set for each font.

MathFont Series (Automated Graphics)

$\frac{7}{9}$ $\frac{3}{4}+\frac{2}{5}$

$\frac{x+5a}{2a^2}$ $\frac{29}{42}$

This font is specially designed for setting elementary-level math equations. Numbers and symbols are overlaid on a grid (which disappears when you print the font), so you position and type characters on the grid lines, rather than manually adjusting the numbers to create equations.

If you're not setting mathematical equations but just need fractions that match a particular font, try one of Adobe's Expert Collections (extensions to selected fonts, which include fractions and other special characters) or Adobe's New Century Schoolbook/Helvetica Fractions.

Petrucci (CodaMusic Technologies)

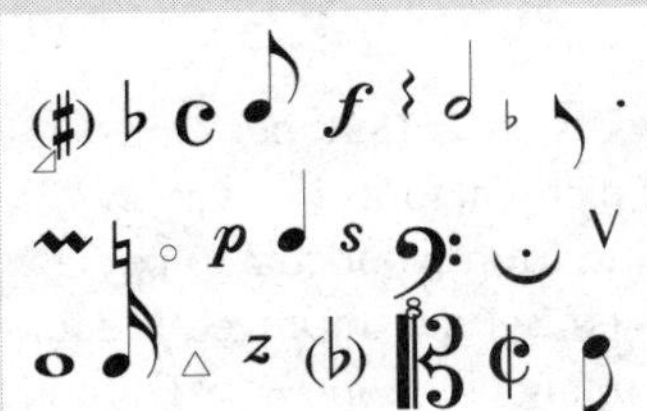

Petrucci includes basic music notation symbols. Other fonts available from The CodaMusic Font Series are Seville (guitar-chord symbols), Newport (jazz and percussion symbols), Midicom (symbols for MIDI data and events), and Rameau (theory and composition symbols). The fonts sell for $70 apiece.

Torah Sans Script (Font World)

פ ף צ ץ ק ר ש ת
ך ל מ ם נ ן ס ע
ג ד ה ו ז ח ט י כ
לכ ץ צ ץ ק ר ב

Font World doesn't simply offer Hebrew fonts; it offers hundreds of Hebrew fonts in a variety of styles. The company's designers have created 36 custom faces that are being used to typeset a new edition of the Talmud (which has been photographically reproduced until now). Font World provides many other fonts as well, including Arabic, Cyrillic, Georgian, Greek, Thai, Vietnamese, and many Western European and Central<None>/Eastern European languages ($100 to $400).

Cyrillic (Linguist's Software)

аАбБвВгГдД
еЕёЁ}{зЗиИ
йЙкКлЛмМ

Linguist's Software offers many language fonts, including Cyrillic (shown here), Arabic, Cambodian, Coptic, Georgian, Greek, Gujarati, Hebrew, Hindi, Inuit, Korean, Laotian, Persian, Punjabi, Thai, Tibetan, and Vietnamese. (Prices range from $80 to $200 per font.)

Stone Phonetic (Adobe Systems)

a ɐ ɑ ɒ æ ʌ b ɓ
β ʙ c ƈ ç ɕ t ȼ d
ð ɖ ɗ ʤ đ d z

Adobe's Stone Phonetic ($185) provides the symbols and diacritical marks for the International Phonetic Alphabet (IPA), which represents the sounds of a wide number of languages (or 'l{˜gwKDes, phonetically speaking). The font comes in a serif and a sans-serif version.

DruScott and Custom Handwriting Fonts (Lazy Dog Foundry)

Why write when
you can type
with DruScott?

Remember the days when letters were written by hand? Yyou can revive that quaint custom without abandoning your trusty word processor—just order a custom font made from your own handwriting from Lazy Dog. Depending on how many characters you want (you can probably live without most of the characters invoked by [Option] or [Shift][Option]), the font will run you between $200 and $500. (Signature Software will also make a custom font from your handwriting, for $80 to $500 per font.)

If your handwriting isn't worth immortalizing, you might consider buying one of Lazy Dog's prefab handwriting fonts ($100 each). The DruScott font is shown here.

TF Crossword (Treacyfaces)

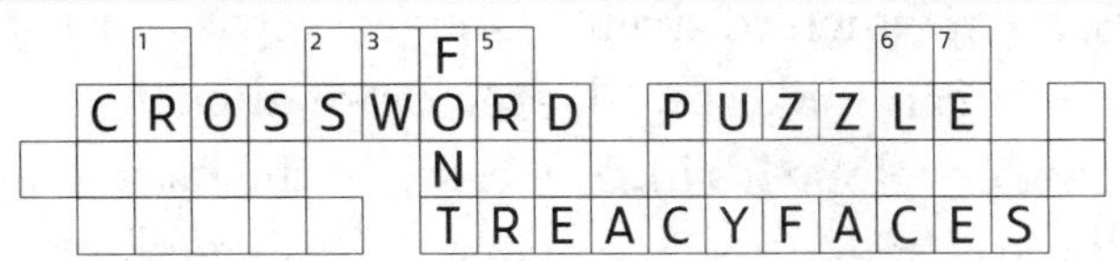

Create your own crossword puzzle (with or without the solution) with this clever font.

Creating Special Typographic Effects

There are lots of ways to get type to do crazy things. The PostScript outline format uses the same Bézier curves that create PostScript graphics in such programs as Aldus FreeHand and Adobe Illustrator. You can import your type into such graphics programs and stretch it, bind it to a path, or otherwise distort it. Programs specifically designed to manipulate type do a whole lot more (and more easily, too), as the following programs demonstrate.

TypeAlign (DD)

TypeAlign ($100, Adobe) lets you place type along paths of any shape, kern it, shape it, and add colors and some special effects to it, all from an inexpensive and easy-to-use desk accessory. A special "snapshot" feature lets you make TypeAlign's window transparent, so you can design your typographic creation right on the background it will be pasted into. TypeAlign creations can be exported into other documents as EPS, PICT, or Illustrator files.

Type Align is a desk accessory that lets you quickly position type along unusual baselines and then kern, letterspace, and color your creation.

TypeStyler (EF)

TypeStyler ($220, Brøderbund) lets you get right to work (or play) with a library of 35 shapes (called *envelopes*) in which to stretch, squeeze, twist, or rotate PostScript or TrueType fonts. You can make text larger or smaller, fatter, or skinnier by changing the size of the envelope it's in. You can edit the basic shapes in the library by dragging handles to change a shape's curves. Reshaped text can be printed from TypeStyler or exported to a graphics program.

The newest version at press time, TypeStyler 2.0, adds support for 24-bit color, spot color separations, and trapping. (These terms are described more fully in Chapter 16.) Version 2.0 also provides more precise control over reshaping text envelopes, offering two sets of handles (rather than one) for editing curves, and it provides a feature called Letter Fusion, which turns the letters in a word into a single fused object, so you can apply effects (a color blend, for example) across the entire object rather than just to individual letters.

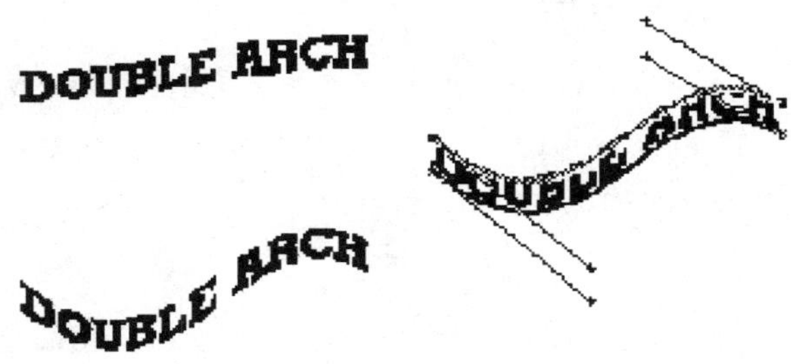

TypeStyler's "envelopes" let you push and pull type into new shapes. The new version supports color separations and trapping.

Effects Specialist (EF)

Rather than providing shapes, **Effects Specialist** ($200, Postcraft International) comes with a library of 120 special effects you can apply to PostScript fonts. They range from the mundane (outlining characters or adding a drop shadow), to the exotic (a chrome finish, text on a musical staff, text in a spiral shape), to the bizarre (text made out of railroad tracks, run over by tire treads, or filled with piano keys). You tailor them by specifying qualities such as character color (or gray shade), outline shade and width, character fill pattern, and shadow angle.

Although many of the effects are wacky enough to make the underlying text downright unreadable, I had a lot of fun playing with them (one of my favorites is Shaky). Effects Specialist also offers effects with names like Earthquake, Crash, Cracked, Split, Tumble, Twist, Vibrate, Knock Out, Panes, and Fire. (The fact that Postcraft's offices and warehouse are only a few miles from the epicenter of the big Northridge earthquake makes me a little nervous about its other effects—Hydro, Windy, Bunker, and Glow.)

Shaky, Crash, and Fireworks are just three of the 120 effects you can apply to type with Effects Specialist.

LetraStudio (EF)

Like TypeStyler, Letraset's **LetraStudio** ($250) lets you place TrueType or PostScript text into "envelopes" of various shapes. You can reshape an envelope to get the effect you want on a particular selection of text and save the modified envelope for later use.

You can also embellish text with color graphics or artwork imported from Illustrator or FreeHand, and LetraStudio's effects can be applied to these graphics as well. LetraStudio provides a limited set of drawing tools (including a line, a circle, and a rectangle); for more complex work, you can paste your text effect into a graphics program and work on it there.

StrataType 3d (EF)

StrataType 3d ($200, Strata) transforms PostScript or TrueType text into 3-D shapes, letting you then add textures (marble, wood, chrome, or ones you create yourself from scanned PICT images), adjust the size and shape of beveled edges, position text (on an arc or in a circle, for example), rotate letters, set a vanishing point, add a background, and position a light source. Then you sit back while the program renders the image.

You can save the image as a PICT, TIFF, or EPS file and transfer it to a graphics application or page layout program. (Note: StrataType 3d does some hefty calculations for rendering, so 8MB of RAM is suggested.)

Pixar Typestry 2 (EF)

Like StrataType 3d, **Typestry** ($300, Pixar) converts characters from PostScript or TrueType fonts into three-dimensional objects, allowing you to add textures (glass, gold, marble, and so on), adjust lighting (19 light sources are available), rotate your creations, and apply other effects.

It's the "other effects" that make Typestry stand out. For example, you can animate a block of text (either as a series of frames or as a QuickTime movie), making it spin, scroll, or zoom toward the viewer, for example, complete with professional effects such as motion blur. My favorite command is Particle Physics, which lets you specify just how a letter will blow to smithereens.

Typestry specializes in 3-D shapes and animations, letting you add textures and lighting effects.

GOOD FEATURE

Typestry 2 is not only impressive, but it's fun to use as well. For example, to create the effect at left—a frame from a Typestry animation—I typed a letter from Caustic Biomorph, one of my PostScript fonts; selected the Moldy Cue Ball texture (which resides in the Floofy folder, of course); and chose the Sky background. Then I activated the Particle Generator and tweaked controls such as Particle Life Span and Ejection Speed. Finally, I used the program's animation module to produce a puff of spores from the greenish letter. But don't worry—Typestry lets you create beautiful effects, too. (Note: Like StrataType 3d, Pixar Typestry has a big appetite for memory—Pixar suggests at least 8MB.)

LogoMotion

(Ben Long)

LogoMotion (Specular, $150) is the type program to use for quickly producing simple animations. LogoMotion's simple Gouraud shading results in less realistic images than Typestry or StrataType, but it allows you to quickly create animations of extruded and lathed type. LogoMotion can also morph one 3-D shape into another over time.

Designing, Editing, and Customizing Fonts

The programs described here let you customize your fonts in a variety of ways. Some let you translate fonts into new formats, for use on PCs or in illustration programs. Others let you add characters to existing fonts, remap your keyboard, or add graphics to your fonts. Yet others let you redesign the fonts you already have or make your own fonts from scratch. (These are the same programs used by many professional type designers to create commercial fonts.)

Metamorphosis Professional (KT/EF)

Metamorphosis Professional (or Meta Pro, as it's familiarly called) from Altsys ($150) converts fonts to and from common Mac and PC (and Nextstep) formats. It will also open many older Type 3 fonts, enabling you to convert them to Type 1 fonts. Metamorphosis also has the useful ability to fetch outline data from certain PostScript printer ROMs and hard disks (for modifying fonts that aren't even in your Mac). It also lets you convert font outlines into PICT or EPS graphic outlines so you can treat characters as graphic elements in programs like Canvas, FreeHand, or Illustrator.

FontMonger (EF/KT)

FontMonger ($150, Ares Software) is even more versatile than Metamorphosis Pro (as long as you don't need to convert a PostScript Type 3 font). Besides the standard Mac and PC TrueType and Type 1 formats, it will open fonts in Nimbus Q, Intellifont, Corel, and LaserMaster formats.

One of FontMonger's main uses is in adding characters to a font. Say you're writing a scientific paper in Palatino and you find yourself frequently needing certain Greek letters from the Symbol font. Rather than constantly switching between the two fonts, you can add the Symbol characters you need to Palatino and then type both the text and symbols from your new combination font.

FontMonger can alter characters in any font to create fractions, small caps, superscripts, subscripts, and narrow, wide, or slanted characters. Of course, these algorithmic alterations won't look as good as characters created by a living, breathing type designer, but if you don't happen to have a type designer lying around, this is an excellent alternative. FontMonger can also import Illustrator or FreeHand artwork into a font or change the positions of the characters on the keyboard.

FontChameleon (DD)

Ares Software's new **FontChameleon** ($300) doesn't let you wreak havoc on your own fonts. Instead, it provides raw data from which you can create new fonts that are variations on a host of classic type styles (200 are included). When you're satisfied with the results, you build your creations into new TrueType or

PostScript Type 1 fonts. Once you've picked a base font to work with, you simply manipulate sliders to change attributes such as the weight, width, slant, and x-height of the font along a continuous scale. FontChameleon moves from the sublime to the ridiculous with its last slider: It lets you blend between two typefaces. Why? I dunno.

FontChameleon includes raw data for 200 fonts, which you can build into TrueType or PostScript Type 1 fonts as you need them, customizing their designs along the way.

Fontographer (SA/KT)

Fontographer ($500, Altsys) lets you create your own PostScript or TrueType fonts, letter by letter. If you don't want to start drawing from scratch, Fontographer offers many automatic creation tools (including autotracing of printed or hand-drawn artwork) or allows you to import an existing font and modify the character outlines individually or en masse.

With the current version (4.0.4), you can create Multiple Master fonts, interpolate between weights or other features of two separate fonts, automatically clean up extra Bézier control points (often the result of autotracing), and accept input from pressure-sensitive graphics tablets to create calligraphic fonts. It also offers excellent automated production tools for adjusting font metrics (which define the way the characters fit together), hinting (to make the type clear and readable on the screen and on low-resolution printers), and building extensive kerning tables.

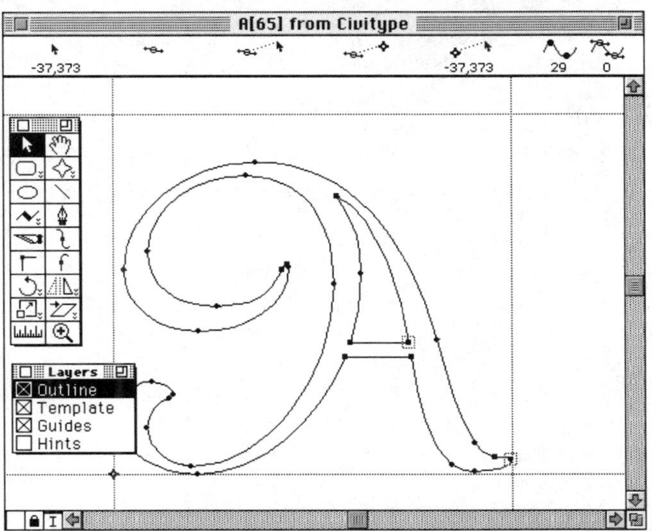

Fontographer's editing window (shown here), lets you change the shape of individual letters using Bézier curves. Its professional-level features include tools for hinting and creating Multiple Master fonts.

FontStudio (KT)

Like Fontographer, Letraset's **FontStudio** ($500) lets you import and alter existing font outlines or draw new fonts from scratch (in either PostScript or TrueType format). It can also save characters as PostScript graphics for modification in Illustrator or FreeHand.

GOOD FEATURE

Although it's gone a long time without an update, FontStudio still works, and it has a few advantages over Fontographer. It allows you, for instance, to create anti-aliased grayscale screen fonts, which use pixels of varying brightness to give them fuzzy edges, paradoxically making them easier to read. FontStudio also helps make the mysteries of font hinting understandable through a slick visual interface.

Ikarus-M (KT)

Ikarus-M ($600, URW) is the new Mac version of a font-building program that was used by professional font designers long before the Mac made the scene. It's for people who are really serious about commercial font production and are willing to spend some time learning its rules.

In contrast to the Bézier curve editing used by Fontographer and FontStudio, Ikarus-M relies on a carefully drawn paper-based design with data points marked out in advance and entered by means of a digitizing tablet. Alternatively, you can use the autotracing companion tool (Linus-M) for handling automatic input of scanned images ($350, or Ikarus and Linus together for $900). Because one person can lay out the points, and another, less-skilled person can enter them into the computer, Ikarus is an excellent tool for big production environments.

Solving Font Problems (DD/KT)

Let's be honest: Fonts are bound to cause you some trouble. Constant loading, unloading, and reloading of resources from lots of different manufacturers into your precious system is bound to cause some funny business once in a while. The problems are rarely insoluble, usually consisting of getting one typeface when you want another. Careful font management is the answer to most of them. (For a good, no-nonsense guide to that, look for *How to Boss Your Fonts Around* by Robin Williams, from Peachpit Press. In the meantime, take a peek at the "Font Tips" section at the end of this chapter.)

The following is a summary of the font problems we've run across most often, along with advice on how to solve them. We'll start with the easy ones.

Where's My Font? (SA/AN/JK)

Sometimes you know you have a font installed, but it doesn't appear in the Font menu. The first thing to do is not to be so sure of yourself—double-check to see that the font is really installed correctly (this is the most common source of the problem). Remember that in Mac systems prior to System 7, fonts you install don't appear in the Font menu until after you've restarted the computer.

If you're using Suitcase or Master Juggler (described on page 541), fonts may not appear in the menu as expected because you opened the suitcase file the font is in *after* you launched the application you're using. If that's not the case, the problem may arise because you have different fonts with the same ID number (described below) in separate open suitcases.

Bit-Mappy Fonts When Printing (DD)

Sometimes you'll get output that looks almost right, but the characters in certain typefaces look a little shaky—jagged around the edges, bearing an eerie resemblance to screen type. This problem typically happens when you're using PostScript fonts, and it usually means that your system had the proper screen fonts on hand, but it couldn't find the corresponding printer fonts. In that case, your Mac will often simply copy the bit-mapped version of the type from your screen onto your printed page.

To solve the problem, just make sure the printer fonts are installed correctly before you try printing again. Remember that fonts from different manufacturers (or in different formats) may have identical names, so you can have a Bodoni screen font from one manufacturer and a Bodoni printer font from another manufacturer, and they may not work together.

Font ID Conflicts (KT)

When the Mac was first introduced, with its impressive collection of 11 bit-mapped fonts, Apple allowed for a total of 256 different ID numbers to identify all the fonts on the Mac. The Mac System and existing Mac applications used these ID numbers (rather than the fonts' actual names) to specify fonts in the documents you created. Apple reserved the first 128 of these numbers for its own use, anticipating that there would never be more than 128 Macintosh fonts from other vendors. Since there are tens of thousands of fonts out there today, this was, in fact, an underestimate.

You can guess what happened next: As fonts proliferated, many of them appeared with the same font ID numbers. The result was that a trip to the font menu was like a spin of the roulette wheel.

To solve the problem, Apple introduced a new numbering system in 1988. It replaced its old FONT resource (a gob of code deep inside the font) with a new one called NFNT (for "new font"), which allowed 16,000 different numbers (still not enough to provide each font with a unique number, but enough to reduce the odds of someone using two identically numbered fonts at the same time). Apple also assigned a range of font numbers to each font developer and started asking Mac application developers to have their programs ask for the font by name instead of ID number. For their part, font manufacturers settled on unique naming conventions for their fonts.

ID conflicts still exist, but they're much rarer, and if you use Suitcase or Master Juggler, those programs will automatically (and temporarily) renumber your fonts as you call for them if their ID numbers conflict with those of other fonts that are in use.

What happens more often are conflicts *on screen*, conflicts between numbers for maybe just one size and one style of a screen font. Even when the screen display is wrong, however, your printout should be fine. (You can usually get rid of this problem by reinstalling your fonts.)

It Looks Like the Right Typeface, But My Layout Has Changed

(DD/KT)

Many fonts are published by more than one company; Brush Script, for example, is available from seven publishers. Not all font names are trademarked, however, so although fonts with the same name may look a lot alike, they're not always identical. When you print your documents on someone else's system (say at a service bureau), you've got to be sure your fonts not only have the same name but that they are also from the same manufacturer.

This is further complicated by the fact that fonts from a single *manufacturer* may be sold by different *vendors* under their own labels. Companies that cross-license each others' fonts may not be selling exactly the same font. When you're telling an output service what fonts you've used in the documents you're sending them, give them the name of the typeface, the name of the vendor, and the creation date, if available. (You can get this by selecting the printer font file in the Finder and choosing Get Info from the File menu.)

Printed pages sporting the wrong version of the right font can be hard to spot, unless you're an ace typographer. You may notice, though, that the line breaks of the new output may be different from those on a proof print you created on your own printer, or that the type looks more crowded or more loose than in your original version.

The only way to be really safe is to bring copies of your own fonts to the service bureau or other printing site. There, we've said it. (See the box "Off-Site Printing" earlier in this chapter to learn the legal lowdown on this kind of criminal caper.)

Surprise Bit Maps (JF)

Even though you've installed ATM and your fonts are all properly installed, you can still end up with crude bit-mapped type on screen. Why? Because you're using an old Type 3 PostScript font, which doesn't work with ATM. This may not be apparent at smaller point sizes, especially if you have a full set of bit-mapped screen fonts installed, but it becomes dreadfully apparent at larger sizes. For this same reason, avoid using Type 3 fonts if you're using ATM to drive a non-PostScript printer—you'll wind up with the same ghastly type on the page as you see on the screen.

Font Tips

Never rename printer fonts (SA/EF). Screen fonts can be renamed in programs such as Fontographer or ResEdit. You might want to do this if there's a particular font you want at the top of the menu for quicker access, or if you find the regular font name hard to remember. If you rename the screen font, the right printer font will still be found when you go to print. If you rename a printer font, though, it won't be found, and you'll get crummy, bit-mapped type on your printed pages.

Managing fonts without Suitcase (DD). System 7.1's easy-in, easy-out method of font installation makes font handling a breeze. Just create a folder on your hard disk outside your System Folder and store all your less commonly used fonts there. (Put each family in its own folder to make things easy on yourself.) Then, when you need a font, open your fonts folder, grab the icons you need, and drag them over the System Folder icon—the system will put them where they belong. When you don't need a font any longer, open the Fonts folder inside your System Folder and drag out the fonts you want to de-install (remembering, of course, that you can't do this when any application programs are open), and pop them back into their storage folder.

When you install them, your fonts show up in your Font menu right away, although you'll have to quit any open applications and open them again before they become accessible there.

Create font sets with suitcases (DD). Using System 7, you don't need to pack your TrueType fonts and screen fonts in suitcases at all, but it sure makes life easier. Packing all the members of a single font family into a single suitcase lets you install all the files with a single mouse click (if you're using Suitcase or Master Juggler) or with a single drag-and-drop (if you're not). It also cleans up your font folders.

But there's no need to stop there. Say you've got a set of fonts that you always use together—you bought them specifically to use in a newsletter project you do, or you just always like to use Sabon with Futura. Packing those screen fonts into a single suitcase lets you move and install the whole set easily.

Another reason to pack those suitcases is to override the limit on the number of fonts you can have installed at one time. You can have only 128 screen-font files or suitcases installed at once, but each of those suitcases can have up to 256 screen fonts in it, raising the limit to a number sufficient to sate the appetite of the most voracious font monster.

Use ATM's font caching (KT). ATM uses a caching system for the screen type images it derives from printer font outlines—once it draws a letter in a particular size, it stores that image in memory so it can simply copy it rather than redraw it the next time it's called for. ATM is perceptibly slower when it has to draw a character in a new typeface and a new size for the first time.

You can define the size of this memory cache in the ATM control panel. If your cache is too small, characters already drawn will be dumped to make room for new ones, which defeats the purpose of having a cache in the first place. Adobe recommends allotting about 50K for every font you expect to be using at any one time. The size of your cache should be relative to the number of fonts you use as well as the amount of memory your system has. You don't want to boost the size of the cache higher than necessary, because the space it sets aside for caching fonts will not be available for your other applications.

When working with service bureaus, provide your screen fonts (KT). Even when you and your service bureau seem to be using the same fonts, you could still run into trouble with incompatible versions. Font companies often upgrade their font libraries by adding extra kern pairs, tweaking designs, or updating to current technology standards, leaving multiple versions of the same fonts in most font libraries. To ensure that you and your service bureau are using *exactly* the same font, provide a suitcase holding all your screen fonts along with your job. This, by the way, is perfectly legal. It's the distribution of *printer* fonts that the font companies worry about.

Using TrueType fonts with service bureaus (KT). TrueType fonts will defer to corresponding PostScript Type 1 fonts under many circumstances. If you're sending a file to the printer that has Type 1 fonts in ROM (Times Roman, Helvetica, Symbol, and Courier are in virtually all PostScript printers, including imagesetters), there is no way to print the TrueType versions of those faces. If it is imperative that you output in TrueType and the work isn't set in any of the printer's ROM faces, you'll need to supply the fonts to the service bureau and advise them to remove all traces of any PostScript version of the same face from the hard disk of their imagesetter before attempting to print your job.

Don't bury your fonts (KT). Fonts included in EPS files often create problems, especially EPS files created in QuarkXPress or PageMaker and then included in another document. Manually downloading the font solves the problem, but if a font is buried two levels deep (within an EPS file that is in turn part of another EPS file), all bets are off. (See the next tip for another alternative.)

Outlining fonts (KT). If you're creating an EPS file in a drawing program such as Illustrator or FreeHand, it's tempting to convert font characters to editable outlines. If you do this, there will be no problem printing the shape (which has become a simple drawing and is no longer part of a font that needs to be fed to the printer), but it may also wreak havoc on the type. PostScript uses a fill routine that allows the edges of the drawing to be softened, which may blur the fine details of a letterform. This option is reasonable for some typefaces with simpler design features, though, especially bold sans-serif faces.

15

Graphics

From its first programs, MacPaint and MacDraw, to today's photo-realistic 3-D images, the Mac has always dazzled us with its graphics prowess. You can see evidence of the Mac's digital artistry everywhere you look: magazine ads, product packaging, posters, audio CDs, technical schematics, book covers, even TV commercials and hit movies.

While a computer graphics program won't automatically make you an artist, it *will* let you do things that are time-consuming, expensive, or even impossible with traditional tools. With the appropriate software, you can easily draw infinite variations on a design, test different color schemes for a business logo, make an eye-catching chart for a presentation, adjust the sharpness and contrast in a scanned photograph, or create a 3-D mock-up of your latest invention.

Whether you're a first-time artist, business presenter, or professional designer, there's a graphics package to meet your needs. In this chapter, we'll show you the different kinds of graphics you can create on the Mac, help you pick the right applications, and reveal some tricks for getting the most out of your favorite programs.

Contributors

Aileen Abernathy (AA) is the chapter editor.

Ben Long (BL), the major contributor to this chapter, uses his Macintosh to illustrate books, create interactive multimedia applications, and write for *MacWEEK*.

Shelley Cryan (SC) writes frequently for computer publications such as *MacUser* and *Byte* from New York.

Erfert Fenton (EF) is a *Macworld* contributing editor specializing in fonts and graphics.

Deke McClelland (DM) is a contributing editor to *Macworld* and the author of books on Canvas, Illustrator, FreeHand, and Photoshop.

Kirsten Parkinson (KP) is a senior writer at *MacWEEK*, where she specializes in graphics software.

Gregory Wasson (GW) covers desktop publishing and graphics for several publications and is the author of *MacUser Guide to Shareware* (Ziff-Davis Press).

Arthur Naiman (AN) and **Sharon Zardetto Aker (SA)** edited past editions of the *Mac Bible*, from which parts of this chapter were taken.

Contents

Graphics Overview (AA)

Graphics programs for the Mac fall into three basic categories:

- *Paint* programs create images made up of different-colored *pixels* (picture elements). Each pixel is described by one or more data bits, so paint images are referred to as *bit-mapped graphics*. You can create digital paintings from scratch or scan images (such as photographs) and save them as bit-mapped graphics. Paint programs can often be identified by their names: DeskPaint, PixelPaint, Painter.

- *Draw* programs treat each item you create as a discrete object, rather than as a collection of pixels, so their drawings are called *object-oriented graphics*. Some draw programs are based on PostScript, allowing you to create images that look great printed at any size on a PostScript printer. There are specialized draw programs for charting and *CAD* (computer-aided design). As with paint programs, some draw programs have revealing names: Expert Draw, IntelliDraw, Cricket Draw.

- *3-D* graphics programs let you simulate a three-dimensional image on your two-dimensional computer screen. When you move and rotate 3-D objects, they look and behave like objects in the real world.

- *Animation* software adds motion to images created in paint, draw, or 3-D graphics programs.

Some programs—such as SuperPaint, artWorks, Canvas, and ClarisDraw—provide both draw and paint tools, and many 3-D and presentation programs offer animation capabilities. But no matter what type of graphics program you use, the resulting artwork will be one of two types: bit-mapped or object-oriented. If you do much graphics work, you'll probably want programs for producing both types of graphics, as they have different strengths and weaknesses.

Bit-Mapped Images

The Mac stores bit-mapped graphics (also called *raster* images) as a map, or grid, of pixels, with each pixel identified by its location and color value. Painting

The Need for Speed (AA/BL)

If you plan to work with 24-bit images, 3-D graphics, or animation, you'll need a fast Mac, lots of RAM, a capacious hard disk, and a 24-bit display. If time is money, you'll also want to boost the computer's performance with a graphics accelerator board, particularly if you don't have a Power Mac. There are two basic types of graphics accelerators: QuickDraw boards (also called *accelerated video cards*), which speed up screen redraws, and DSP (digital signal processor) cards, which ramp up certain processor-intensive operations.

QuickDraw Acceleration

A QuickDraw accelerator speeds up display tasks such as scrolling and zooming—particularly important if you're working in 24-bit color and/or on a large monitor. (The acceleration isn't limited to graphics—you'll also be able to scroll through a spreadsheet or word processing document much faster.) Prices vary, depending on the Mac model, monitor size, screen resolution (pixels per inch), and accelerator features. If your monitor is 16 inches or smaller, Radius's $600 **PrecisionColor Pro 24XP** is a good buy. If cost isn't a factor, however, and you want superfast screen redraws and goodies such as high resolution, CMYK acceleration, and an on-board DSP chip, SuperMac's **Thunder II GX•1360** ($3,300) is the way to go.

BARGAIN

DSP Acceleration

The most time-consuming part of graphics work isn't screen redraw, however, it's the number-crunching routines used in special-effects filters, image resizing and rotation, JPEG decompression, and color-mode changes. Happily, DSP accelerators are tailor-made for those operations. Painter and Photoshop can use the DSP chips in AV Macs to boost performance, but don't despair if an AV Mac isn't in your future. DayStar Digital, Radius, and SuperMac offer DSP accelerators that make specific operations five to ten times faster on other Macs. SuperMac's $500 **ThunderStorm for Adobe Photoshop** is arguably the best (and most economical) choice. At this writing, DSP accelerators are available only for Photoshop, although the optimized filters bundled with the cards will work in most programs that accept Photoshop plug-ins (see "Plug-In Power" on page 594). Some 3-D packages also can use specialized accelerator boards to rev up the rendering process; see the "Three-Dimensional Graphics" section later in this chapter.

Power Macs

For the ultimate speed boost, however, get a Power Mac. A graphics application running in native mode on a Power Mac performs two to six times faster, on average, than it does on an '040 Mac such as the Quadra 800. And that's overall, not just for specific operations. Accordingly, companies are racing to upgrade their paint, draw, 3-D, and multimedia programs for the Power Macs. Many of the heavyweights mentioned in this chapter and in Chapter 17—Painter, Photoshop, Illustrator, FreeHand, ClarisImpact, Canvas, DeltaGraph, and more—should have Power Mac versions available as you read this. The increased computing power also will allow companies to add features to Power Mac programs that were not practical before. For example, look for more 3-D programs to offer motion blurs and the ability to paint textures directly onto objects.

THINGS TO COME

on a bit-mapped canvas is like painting on a real one: Whatever color or image you place on the canvas replaces what was there before, and the new image becomes a permanent part of the canvas and is no longer editable as an individual element. You can't easily change the shape of a curve, for example, because the Mac doesn't think of it as a curve, just a collection of pixels. The bit-mapped nature of a digital painting or a scanned photo can cause problems when you move, resize, or rotate it. When you select and move part of a bit map, you rip pixels from one location and put them somewhere else, leaving a hole behind. Enlarging or rotating a bit map can cause a bad case of the *jaggies*—a blocky, stair-stepped look.

Bit maps

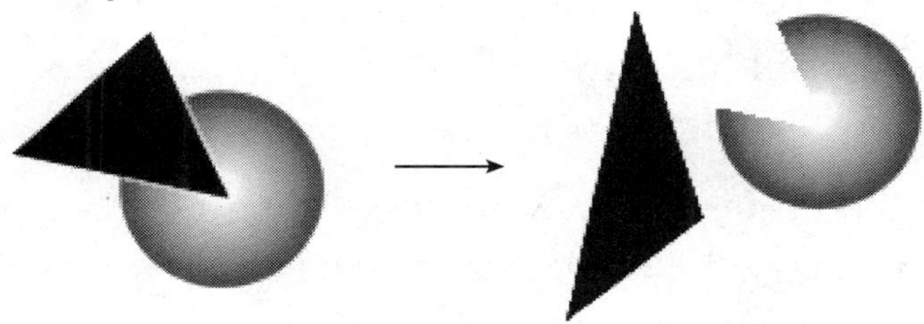

A bit-mapped image is a mosaic of pixels in fixed locations. Moving a bit-mapped shape means ripping out pixels, leaving a hole behind. Enlarging and distorting the shape accentuates its jaggedness.

Objects

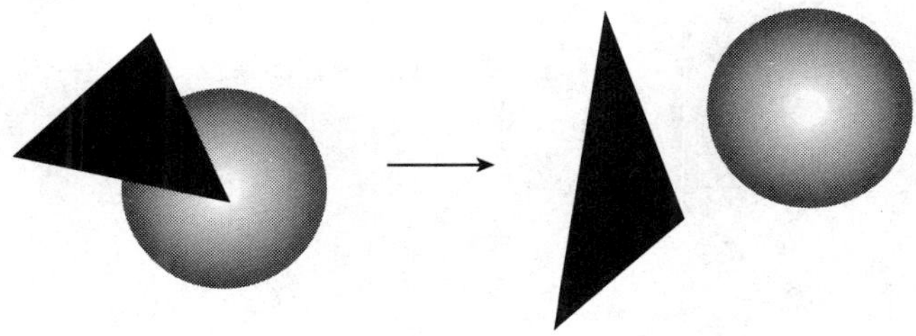

In contrast, each element of an object-oriented graphic remains a discrete entity, so you can move the shape without affecting other parts of the image. And no matter what editing changes you make, the shape retains its crisp appearance.

When you print a bit map, the printer reproduces the image exactly as it's stored. An image saved at a resolution of 72 dpi (dots per inch) will be rough around the edges compared to a 300-dpi graphic. But each image will look the same whether it's printed on a 300-dpi laser printer or a 1,200-dpi imagesetter, because a bit map never varies from the resolution specified within the painting program.

GOOD FEATURE

Bit-mapped graphics do have one key advantage, however: You can edit the image pixel by pixel. This makes them a perfect medium for retouching scanned images and lets you achieve painterly effects that mimic those of natural media.

Object-Oriented Graphics

Object-oriented graphics (sometimes called *vector* graphics) store information about an image as a series of mathematical equations. This data can be encoded either in *QuickDraw* (the Mac's native graphics language) or in *PostScript* (Adobe's page description language).

Object-oriented images are easy to edit because each object remains a discrete entity. You can select any object—a circle, say—at any time and change its line width, fill, color, or transparency. Enlarge, reduce, rotate, or reshape an object, and it retains its crisp appearance. Moreover, you can move objects around in a drawing as if each were on a separate, transparent sheet. Stack and hide objects as necessary—the obscured parts won't be erased as with bit-mapped graphics. (Some newer paint programs offer similar features. See "Painting With Layers" on page 599.)

When you output an object-oriented image, the program tells the printer, "a rectangle, two inches wide and one inch tall," and lets the printer render the image at the best possible resolution. Thus, unlike bit maps, object-oriented graphics are *resolution-independent.* A drawing printed on a 1,200-dpi imagesetter looks far superior to the same image output on a 300-dpi laser printer.

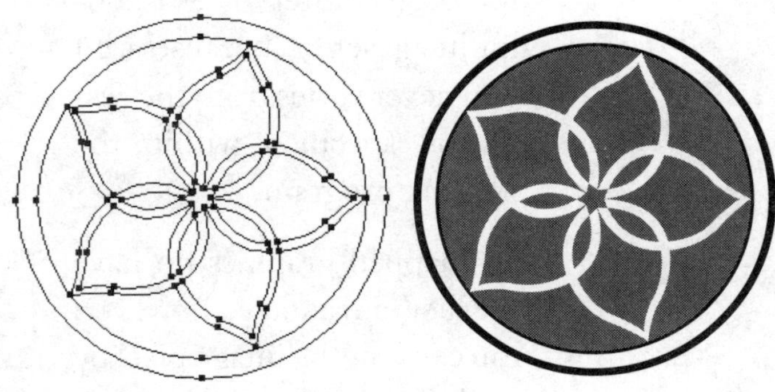

An object-oriented graphic is composed of mathematically defined paths and drawing instructions. The object prints at the highest resolution available, so its lines and fills always look sharp and smooth.

Object-oriented graphics are excellent choices for detailed work such as logos, maps, diagrams, and technical illustrations. Because of their clean, sharp appearance, however, these images often scream "computer generated" and don't have the naturalistic look of traditional media such as paints and pencils.

Graphics File Formats (AA)

Every graphics program saves files in its native format, which may or may not coincide with one of the basic file formats used to transfer images among programs. For instance, Photoshop defaults to its proprietary Photoshop format, and to open its images in another program you must save them in a format such as TIFF. (See Chapter 24 for more on sharing graphics and other files among programs.) Most graphics programs can open and save files in several formats. (Some can even read PC graphics formats such as BMP or PCX.) Here are the graphics file formats you're most likely to encounter.

- *Paint* is the oldest and most limited format, holding only black-and-white bit maps at 72 dpi. Paint files (file type PNTG) are limited to 8 by 10 inches.
- *TIFF* (tag image file format) files are also bit maps, but they can be any size, resolution, or color depth. TIFF is the most versatile, reliable, and widely supported bit-mapped format and is the standard format for saving scanned images. The format does have several variations, however, which means that occasionally an application may have trouble opening a TIFF file created by another program.
- *PICT* files are sometimes called *metafiles* because they can contain both bit maps and QuickDraw-based objects. PICT is the standard format for graphics that are cut or copied to the Clipboard and for drawings that won't be output on PostScript printers. This format is ideal for on-screen presentations, but page layout programs sometimes have problems with PICT files.
- *EPS* (encapsulated PostScript) files are the standard way of storing high-resolution PostScript illustrations. An EPS file usually has two parts: a PostScript (text) description that tells a PostScript printer how to output the resolution-independent image, and (optionally) a bit-mapped PICT image for on-screen previews. (An EPS file without a PICT preview is usually displayed as a gray rectangle.) EPS files generally can't be edited, even by the program that created them (Illustrator files are exceptions).
- *JPEG* (Joint Photographic Experts Group) is a sophisticated technique for compressing full-color bit maps. A 24-bit image saved in JPEG format can be reduced to about 1/20th of its original size with no apparent image degradation.
- *PICS*, the standard format for animations, is essentially a collection of bit-mapped PICT images in sequential order, much like movie frames.
- *DXF* (drawing interchange format) is the standard file-exchange format for 3-D and CAD programs.

Painting

Paint programs can be loosely divided into two categories: painting and image-editing. This division is becoming increasingly blurred as each assumes more features of the other, yet they still have distinct differences.

- *Painting* programs are primarily for creating original artwork from scratch. They offer tools for creating primitive shapes (such as circles, rectangles, and polygons), paint buckets (for coloring objects), lots of brushes and pencils, and *natural-media* effects (such as watercolors, chalks, and paper textures).
- *Image-editing* applications make it easy to clean up and alter preexisting images, such as those captured with a scanner or digital camera. Instead of tools for making circles and squares, image editors provide tools for color correction and contrast adjustment, sharpening and smudging, and eye-catching special effects.

The Tools (BL/AA)

Painting and image-editing applications do have many features in common—such as selection marquees, erasers, and paint buckets—but each has specialized tools to call its own.

Painting. In addition to the painting tools shown in the tool palette at the top of the next page, look for the following features, many of which are also found in image-editing programs:

- image distortions, such as resize, rotate, flip, and skew.
- fill patterns, which you can customize or apply as-is to any area of an image.
- custom color palettes, for saving special colors you want to use for particular jobs.
- multiple levels of undo, so you can backtrack to earlier stages of an image—otherwise a difficult maneuver in paint programs.

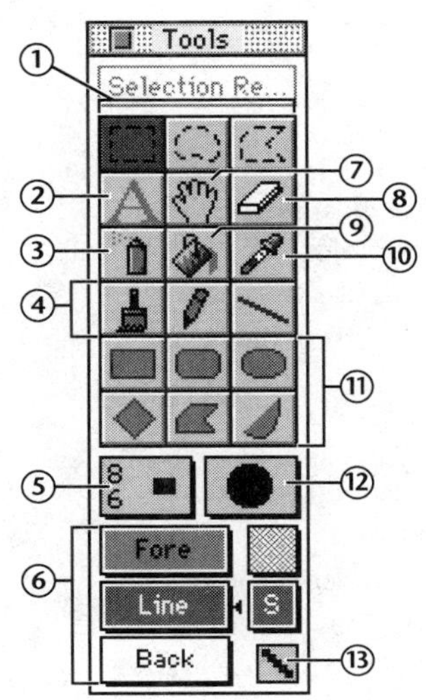

1. Selection tools, for selecting parts of an image
2. Text tool, for adding bit-mapped text
3. Spray can, for creating airbrush effects
4. Brush, pencil, and line tools, for freehand painting
5. Line-width control, with separate indicators for horizontal and vertical width
6. Color and pattern pop-up palettes, for specifying colors and patterns for the foreground, background, and lines
7. Grabber hand, for navigating around an image
8. Eraser, for erasing parts of an image
9. Paint bucket, for filling a selected area with a color or pattern
10. Eyedropper, for picking up a specific color from an image
11. Graphic primitives, for creating rectangles, circles, polygons, and curves
12. Brush-shape selector, for specifying the size and shape of brushes
13. Anti-aliasing control, for smoothing lines created with other tools

BrushStrokes' tool palette resembles that of most paint programs.

- natural-media tools that emulate oils, watercolor, chalk, paper textures, and other traditional media and let you adjust parameters such as brush size, opacity, and number of brush hairs. Many programs support pressure-sensitive digitizing tablets, which provide an even more realistic painting experience (those are described in Chapter 6).

- anti-aliased tools for combatting the *jaggies*, the stair-stepped look you get when you draw a diagonal or curved line in a bit-mapped image. *Anti-aliasing* is a process that blends the colors of adjacent pixels to minimize these rough edges. When you paint with an anti-aliased brush, for example, the edges of your strokes are automatically blurred to produce smooth lines. Some programs also let you anti-alias (or *feather*) the edges of a selection so you can paste one image into another without unnatural-looking sharp edges. (If your program doesn't have anti-aliased tools, you can smooth away the jaggies after the fact with Ray Dream's $130 **JAG II** utility.)

GOOD FEATURE

- variable resolution, so you can print artwork with a resolution higher than the on-screen 72 dpi. Many programs can save bit-mapped images at any resolution, ensuring sharp, crisp output even when you send files to a high-resolution printer or imagesetter.

Color, Color, Everywhere (AA)

In choosing a graphics program, color depth is no longer a major factor. The era of 8-bit color—which limited graphics to 256 colors and prevented us from creating photorealistic images—is (almost) gone. Today even entry-level programs offer 24-bit color, allowing us to work with millions of colors and produce images ranging from photographs to drawings with smooth blends. (Sometimes 24-bit color is called 32-bit color, which is actually more accurate. Those extra eight bits per pixel don't give you more colors; they're reserved for special operations such as masking or transparency effects.)

Color management—the consistent matching of color from scanner to screen to printer—remains a persistent problem, however. Many companies, from Apple to Kodak, offer color-management strategies, but if you use Photoshop or QuarkXPress, one of the best (and cheapest) solutions is **EfiColor Works** ($200, Electronics for Imaging). This system-level software has direct hooks into the two programs, allowing you to achieve accurate image colors across a wide range of scanners, monitors, and output devices.

Still working with shades of gray? No worries. Graphics programs work just as well with black-and-white or grayscale images, and your color artwork will print fine in grayscale.

Image editing. Image-editing programs are famous for letting you alter reality—literally changing a zebra's stripes, for example, or creating the ultimate paparazzi shot, say, Madonna out on the town with Burt Reynolds. They offer specialized selection tools that let you isolate part of an image based on its color, shape, or texture, then alter those attributes or move the selected element to another location. These tools also make it easy to create *composite* images—combining two or more images into a single seamless graphic.

Besides the image-editing tools shown in the tool palette at the top of the next page, look for:

- color-correction controls, which let you adjust the hues, saturation, brightness, and contrast of images—particularly useful for tweaking colors and fine-tuning shadows and highlights in scanned images.
- support for scanner drivers (usually in the form of Photoshop plug-ins), so you can scan images directly into the program.
- special-effects filters and/or support for Photoshop plug-ins (see "Plug-In Power" on page 594). Filters let you enhance or transform an entire image,

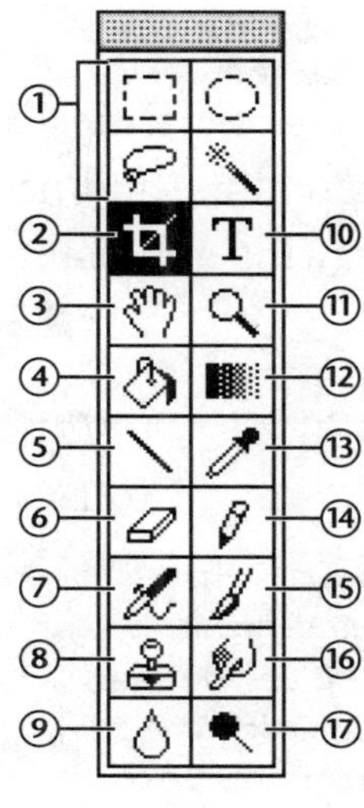

1. Selection tools, including marquee, ellipse, lasso (freehand selections), and magic wand (selects areas with similar color values)
2. Cropping tool, for changing the size of an image
3. Grabber hand, for scrolling an image in the window
4. Paint bucket, for filling selected areas with colors or patterns
5. Line tool, for painting straight lines
6. Eraser, for changing pixels to the background color (usually white)
7. Airbrush, for painting a diffuse spray of the current color
8. Rubber stamp, for cloning parts of an image and placing exact copies elsewhere
9. Sharpen/blur (water drop) tool, for sharpening or diffusing part of an image
10. Type tool, for entering bit-mapped text
11. Zoom tool (magnifying glass), for magnifying or reducing an image's size on screen
12. Gradient tool, for making blends between two tints or color
13. Eyedropper, for selecting a specific color in an image
14. Pencil, for adding single pixels or painting freehand lines
15. Paintbrush, for painting soft-edged (anti-aliased) strokes of variable opacity
16. Smudge (fingertip) tool, for smearing painted areas
17. Dodge/burn tool, for lightening or darkening part of an image

Most image-editing programs have tools similar to those found in Photoshop, shown here.

or just selected areas, with a couple of mouse clicks. With the right filter, you can sharpen a subject's facial features, emboss your corporate logo, despeckle (remove dust and dirt) from a scanned photo, or make the photo look like a watercolor painting.

- masking features, which let you isolate part of an image and apply color changes, filters, or other effects to that area alone. Conversely, you can use a mask to protect an area from changes applied to the rest of an image. At its simplest level, a mask works like a stencil: Some parts are opaque, others are transparent. Several programs provide 8-bit masks (also called *alpha channels*), which have 256 gray levels that let you vary the degree of mask transparency to create subtle gradations and shadings or to seamlessly composite one image with another.

GOOD FEATURE

- color-separation capabilities, for professional output of color images. The program should automatically separate image files into the four process colors (cyan, magenta, yellow, black) used in printing.

Choosing a Paint Program

Painting packages range from simple programs for general users to artistically inclined applications that let you imitate real-world oils, watercolors, and papers. There are even one-stop programs that provide both drawing and painting tools.

Plug-In Power

(AA/BL)

If your paint program doesn't have that fancy-schmancy special effect you want, chances are you can find it among the plethora of Photoshop plug-ins. Adobe's plug-in architecture, originally developed for Photoshop, has become a de facto industry standard and nearly every paint and image-editing program—as well as some 3-D packages and QuickTime editors—lets you add capabilities via Photoshop plug-ins. The list includes SuperPaint, Color It!, PhotoFlash, Painter, PixelPaint Pro3, Canvas, StrataVision 3d, and Premiere. Just pop the plug-in files into the appropriate folder, and your program's menus will sprout new scanner drivers, export capabilities (such as JPEG compression), or special-effects filters. The list of Photoshop plug-ins is too extensive to cover, but here are some highlights.

If you're looking for nifty special effects, **Kai's Power Tools 2** ($200, HSC Software) is a sophisticated package that can generate endless streams of textures, gradients, and fractals. Volume 1 of Aldus's **Gallery Effects** series ($100 to $200 each) is easier to use and offers a good selection of filters that simulate traditional media, including Graphic Pen, Watercolor, and Smudge Stick. (The package includes a stand-alone utility in case you don't have a program that supports plug-ins.) Also take a gander at **Paint Alchemy** ($100, Xaos Tools), which uses a unique paintbrush technology to transform an image into organic-looking brush strokes.

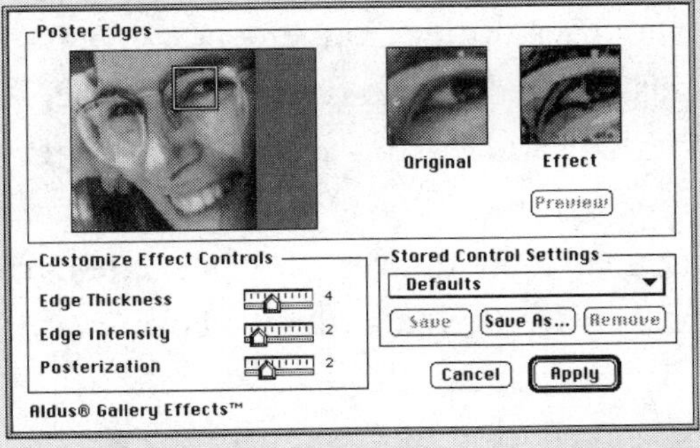

You can easily turn a photo into a painting with Gallery Effects, a Photoshop plug-in that provides natural-media filters such as the Poster Edges effect shown here.

Two other plug-ins worth consideration are PhotoMatic and PicturePress. **PhotoMatic** ($230, DayStar Digital) lets you automate almost any task (or series of tasks) in Photoshop by recording your activities as an Apple events script. You can then run the script on individual images or batch-process entire folders of images—even over a network. **PicturePress** ($100, Storm Technology) uses JPEG compression to reduce bit-mapped images to a fraction of their original size, saving vast amounts of storage space and network transmission time.

Budget offerings (AA). Thanks to the popularity of home-based color Macs, the low-end paint market is booming, with at least half a dozen programs in the under-$100 range. All offer the basic complement of painting tools and features—plus a few extra fillips—and work well in black-and-white and low-memory situations, making them good choices for PowerBook and monochrome Mac users.

Expert Color Paint ($50, Expert Software) combines simplicity with a well-rounded tool set, including a magic wand, brightness/contrast controls, anti-aliasing, and simple special effects (Blur, Sharpen, Invert). You can define custom tool sets and color palettes, and it offers multiple undos—a feature conspicuously missing in Photoshop. Another long-time favorite is Zedcor's **DeskPaint,** always bundled with its companion product, DeskDraw (see the "Drawing" section, below). For a mere $30 (if you order directly from Zedcor), you get features similar to those in Expert Color Paint, albeit with a less elegant interface. DeskPaint has some nice special effects (such as Oil Painting and Mosaic), simple masks, and *autotracing*, which lets you convert a bit-mapped graphic into an object-oriented one. Version 4 of Zedcor's dynamic duo, due in fall 1994 for $100, is a major overhaul that adds capabilities such as image cataloging and support for QuickDraw GX, scanners, and Photoshop plug-ins.

If you'd like to mix fun with practicality, get **Prism** ($60, Delta Tao), the successor to the whimsically named, critically acclaimed Color MacCheese. It invites playful exploration with a water drop (for blurring), paint roller (for gradients), rake (for scattering pixels—say, to make a tree look more realistically leafy), and snowflake and tree tools (for instant doilies or fractal forests). Best of all, though, is the transmogrifier, which sprays color change, adding texture to solid colors. On the downside, Prism can't handle TIFF files.

BrushStrokes (AA). If you're new to computers and digital painting—or just want an elegant, full-featured program at an entry-level price—Claris's **BrushStrokes** is a good bet. Trampling all over the memory of MacPaint (Claris's previous budget paint program), BrushStrokes has an astonishing array of features for $140, including gradients, some clever selection tools, and simple masking. Its attractive, easy-to-navigate interface is supplemented by an impressive on-line help system (the manuals are good, too). Handy feedback

Paint/Draw Combos (EF)

There are two inexpensive programs that provide both paint and draw tools in a single package: the perennially popular SuperPaint and its upstart competitor, artWorks. Both offer niceties such as autotracing, QuickTime compatibility, and proprietary plug-in architectures for adding new capabilities, as well as support for Photoshop plug-ins. (For details on autotracing, Bézier curves, and other drawing features, see the "Drawing" section, later in this chapter.)

SuperPaint ($100, Aldus Consumer Division) implements drawing and painting as two overlapping layers; while you see both layers at once, you work in only one at a time. The paint tools include a copy brush that lets you paint with a selected portion of an image (similar to Photoshop's rubber stamp tool). The draw layer provides autotracing, gradient fills and textures, and custom lines and rulers, but it lacks a Bézier curve tool (although you can convert objects into editable Bézier curves). Version 3.5 supports scanner drivers and pressure-sensitive tablets, which work well with pressure-sensitive tools such as a calligraphy brush, charcoal, and a variable-size eraser. SuperPaint's performance is sluggish, however, and despite many upgrades, it still doesn't support the TIFF or EPS formats, and the zoom tool retains an annoying bug: Enlarged drawings display jagged lines rather than smooth shapes.

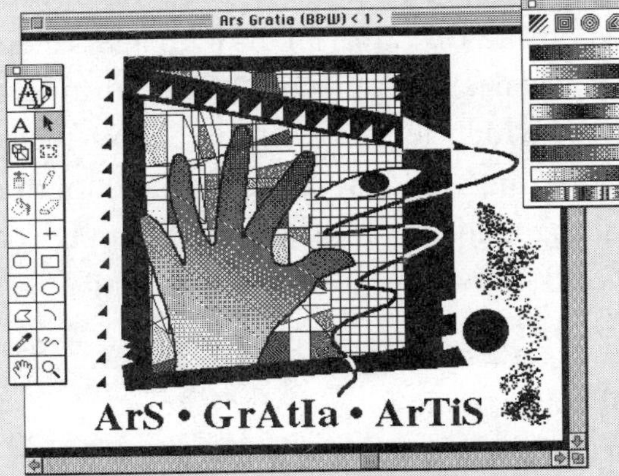

SuperPaint provides both paint and draw tools in a single program. In this image, for example, the text, pencil, eye, and gradient-filled hand were created with drawing tools, while the background patterns and airbrush effects were added in the paint layer.

Deneba's **artWorks** ($150) is the younger sibling of Canvas (a combo program that's weighted toward the drawing side; see the "Drawing" section, below. Accordingly, it has many similar tools and capabilities—and the same complex interface. While it may not be as easy to learn as SuperPaint, artWorks does have features—anti-aliasing and a Bézier curve tool, for example—the former doesn't offer.

artWorks also provides constant access to both paint and draw tools, rather than making you move back and forth between layers. artWorks supports unlimited document layers, which may contain both draw and paint objects and can be hidden or rearranged at will. Its bag of tricks also includes an Alignment command, the ability to blend from one shape to another, and a variety of plug-in tools (such as a three-color airbrush).

features take the guesswork out of painting: Preview windows let you see the results of filters before you apply them; the Tools palette shows current color and line settings; and when you use a brush, the cursor changes to reflect the

BrushStrokes packs a lot of power for a budget paint program. Here, the toucan is being tweaked with the Brightness/Contrast controls (a feature borrowed from image editors), which include a handy preview window and on-line help. All image elements are from BrushStrokes' bundled clip art collection.

color and brush shape you've selected. Furthermore, when you save custom tool settings, they appear as thumbnail icons in a special palette for one-click retrieval—a novel approach.

Painter (BL/AA). Fractal Design defined natural-media painting (digitally speaking) with its flagship product, Painter. A must-have program for experienced or would-be digital artists, **Painter 2** ($400) gives you a palette of pencils, charcoals, chalks, inks, oils, crayons, markers, and other specialized tools that mimic the characteristics of their real-world counterparts. Its digital dyes bleed, spill, and absorb just like real paints. Papers reveal their textures when you draw or paint on them, strokes show brush bristles, and watercolors stay smearable until told to dry.

GOOD FEATURE

You can paint on a blank canvas or turn an existing image (a scanned photo, say) into an Impressionist painting or pencil drawing (among many possibilities). You can edit the tools—perhaps altering the shape and angle of a brush tip—and there are predefined brush-es that imitate the styles of Van Gogh (multi-colored strokes) and Seurat (patterns of dots). Painter does have a fairly complex interface, however, and its natural-media tools fairly scream for a digitizing tablet, because it can translate pen pressure into color opacity, stroke width, and other attributes.

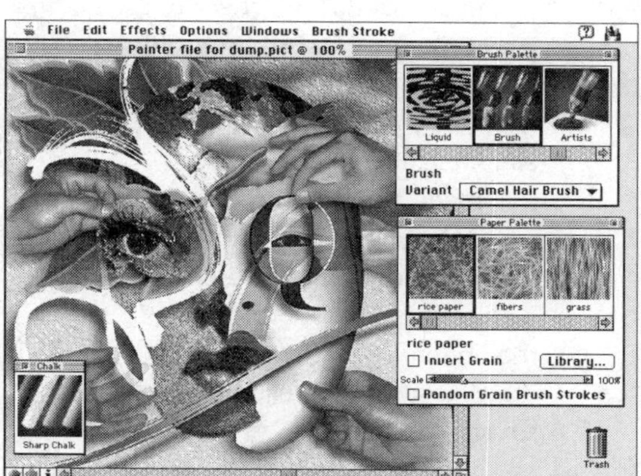

Artist Glenn Matsui used Painter, the natural-media wonder, to create this arresting image. Painter's watercolors, chalks, and other tools mimic their real-world counterparts, down to their ability to interact with digital papers, brushes, and inks. You can minimize screen clutter by tearing off just the tools you need.

Despite cribbing by its competitors, Painter still has features you can't find anywhere else. Its liquid-media tools, for example, let you create glass distortions and marbling effects. You can use its lighting controls, which resemble those found in 3-D programs and photography studios, to produce effects such as billboard or splash lighting. Painter also moves in on Photoshop's turf with a range of image-processing features, from posterization and blurs to sophisticated masking capabilities (called *friskets*). Painter can't draw geometric shapes, such as circles and rectangles, but you can import EPS images created elsewhere.

As if all this weren't enough, for another $150 you can get **PainterX2**, an add-on that endows Painter with unlimited floating selections (see "Painting With Layers," on the opposite page). The X2 extension can store floating selections

Artists in Training (AA)

Perhaps you don't just want to *use* a paint program, you actually want to *learn* to paint (or draw). A digital tutor does have advantages over traditional media: Making and matching colors is easier, you don't have to wait for oils to dry, there's nothing to spill, and you can delete mistakes without ruining the rest of your masterpiece.

If this appeals to you (or to a young acquaintance), check out Fractal Design's **Dabbler** ($100) or Delta Tao's **Apprentice** ($60). The programs have several similarities, including natural-media tools (pencil, chalk, oils), the ability to create original artwork or draw over reference pictures (such as photos), and the option to play back your drawing sessions stroke by stroke.

Dabbler's learn-to-paint tools are organized into four "drawers." Click on one, such as Papers (shown here), to see its contents. You can place frequently used tools on the front of the drawer for easy access.

Dabbler's simple interface may seem a bit precious to adults, but it's the more polished program, with a greater variety of painting tools as well as paper textures (both borrowed from big brother Painter). Precreated brush variants let you mimic artists such as Seurat and Monet, and it supplies animated drawing lessons and a how-to-draw manual from Walter Foster Publishing, a leading purveyor of art-instruction books.

Painting With Layers (BL/AA)

The latest advance in painting programs is the concept of object-oriented editing—the ability to manipulate bit-mapped images as if they were objects in a drawing program. Instead of a single digital canvas, you turn pieces of a painting into layers (à la FreeHand or Canvas), allowing you to select and manipulate them at will.

Collage lets you import and manipulate bit-mapped images as if they were objects in a drawing program. You can move, resize, or rotate any element at any time or apply special effects. The Element palette lets you change the layering of image elements by repositioning them in the list.

Say, for example, you import a scanned photo of a cat into a picture of a cozy cottage. Instead of the cat becoming a permanent part of the underlying painting as soon as you deselect it, you make it a discrete layer. Now you can reselect it at any time, perhaps to resize it and add a shadow. Then, by shuffling the image layers, you can place the crouching cat behind some flowerpots. All this, in a *painting* program.

Specular International created **Collage** ($350) specifically to composite photos and other images into seamless collages. So, while it lacks painting and image-editing tools, Collage offers excellent masking features and object-oriented handling of imported graphics. And because you work with a 72-dpi screen proxy for each image, Collage is faster than working with large, high-resolution files. PainterX2, PixelPaint Pro3, and Photoshop 3 also offer object-oriented editing; see their write-ups elsewhere in this section.

in a library (for dragging into any document), and it also gives you the ability to create custom color palettes within Painter. Version 3 of Painter, due out in fall 1994, will have a new interface that integrates the X2 extension plus a raft of new features, such as the ability to make QuickTime animations. Finally, if you're still viewing the Mac world in black and white, note that Fractal also offers **Sketcher,** an $80 grayscale version of Painter.

PixelPaint Pro3 (BL). If you want natural-media and image-editing tools in a single package, consider **PixelPaint Pro3** ($380, Pixel Resources). Besides supplying many (but not all) of the capabilities of those two genres—from an Impressionist brush and paper textures to contrast and brightness controls—PixelPaint has a few tricks of its own. It's the only painting program, for

example, with built-in floating layers for object-oriented editing (for more on this capability, see "Painting With Layers," above) and support for Apple events scripting, allowing you to automate tasks such as applying filters or color corrections.

PixelPaint also has an unusual half-drawing/half-painting mode called Wet Paint that provides an easy way to paint specific shapes. As in a drawing program, you can create lines, curves, and shapes by clicking and dragging out objects. Once you've shaped an object to your liking, PixelPaint strokes it with the selected paint tool. If the resulting brush stroke doesn't look quite right, you can reshape the path and stroke it again. On the downside, PixelPaint can't handle 8-bit images, multiple undos, CMYK editing, or EPS images.

Image Editors

In the image-editing arena, Photoshop is king. If you don't have a royal budget or the hardware to spare, however, there *are* alternatives.

Photoshop (AA/BL). The Cadillac of image editors and a swell paint program to boot, Adobe's **Photoshop 2.5** is the standard against which other programs are judged. Considering the program's scope, its interface is straightforward and it has nearly every tool and function you could possibly wish for.

Most tools have a variety of options, such as opacity, anti-aliasing, and pressure sensitivity. You can, for example, create a brush with up to 999 pixels and define its shape, angle, and softness. The pen tool lets you create precise selection areas by tracing them with Bézier curves (see the "Drawing" section, below), but the magic-wand tool is a wimp compared to its elegant counterparts in Color It! and Painter. (Sing along now: A Shift-click here and a Shift-click there, here a click, there a click, everywhere a click, click.)

Photoshop's powerful image-editing tools include the rubber stamp, which lets you clone a piece of an image. It works like a brush, but instead of painting with a color, you select part of the image (say, a parrot) and paint with that. You define the size and shape of the rubber stamp via the Brushes palette, shown here.

Photoshop's tools for readying images for four-color (CMYK) printing are superb, ranging from the ability to edit in CMYK mode to the creation of custom color palettes. The Variations dialog box lets you visually adjust color and brightness by comparing thumbnail images—great for novice color users—and you can correct the exposure of specific image areas with the dodge (lighten) and burn (darken) tools.

Sophisticated 8-bit masking features let you work with multiple alpha channels (masks) to create complex composites and special effects. The Quick Mask mode simplifies the process of making a single mask—look Ma, no alpha channels. And, of course, Photoshop has the most robust set of image filters available, ranging from Gaussian Blur and Unsharp Mask to Emboss, Pointillize, and Shear. If you still aren't satisfied, Adobe's plug-in architecture lets you choose from a smorgasbord of third-party filters (see "Plug-In Power" on page 594). Version 3, due in summer 1994, will support multiple layers (see "Painting With Layers" on page 599) and let you apply lighting effects to images.

Photoshop can directly operate most scanners via plug-in drivers, and it's renowned for the variety of file formats it imports and exports, including JPEG (compressed images), BMP and PCX (PC-side formats), DCS (preseparated images for placement in QuarkXPress), and Kodak's Photo CD format (see the box "Photo CD" on the next page). Photoshop also offers extensive control over output. It's the only program that generates duotones, tritones, and quadtones, and it also lets you adjust the resolution, edit color separation tables, control ink coverage, and more.

All this power has a price: $900 to be exact (the street price is around $600). You also need at least 8MB of RAM to run Photoshop effectively, and it prefers more. Even with a RAM glut, some operations, such as special-effects filters, take time to apply. Fortunately, Adobe provides special plug-ins that boost performance on AVs and Power Macs, and some hardware companies offer Photoshop accelerator boards that speed up processor-intensive operations (see "The Need for Speed," on page 586).

If Photoshop's price and features seem a tad overwhelming, consider getting Adobe's **Audition** package instead. For $250 Audition supplies Limited Editions of both Photoshop and Premiere (Adobe's video-editing software), plus a

Photo CD

(AA)

Maybe you've heard the hype: Eastman Kodak's *Photo CD* technology is a fast, inexpensive way to create and access digital photos. Just drop off a roll of 35mm film at a Photo CD outlet—anywhere from the corner drugstore to a professional photo lab—and a few days later you get back a CD-ROM containing high-quality scans of all your photographs (including those unfocused shots of your feet). The cost? About $1 per image.

For once, it's all true. Photo CD—Kodak's way of ensuring its longevity in a future filmless society—is a great way to get pictures into the computer. You don't have to own a scanner or pay a service bureau $40 apiece to scan your photos, because Photo CD does a fine job of capturing the color and detail of the original images. (To find a Photo CD outlet near you, call 800/242-2424, ext. 36.) Each image is stored on the disc in five different resolutions, from a thumbnail-size preview to an 18MB scan suitable for high-resolution magazine work. (The larger images are compressed.) Each Photo CD holds about 100 images; if a disc isn't full, you can take it back with your next roll of film and have more images added. You also can put previously developed slides and negatives on a Photo CD for under $2 per image—a great way to archive favorite photos, as CD-ROM is a more permanent medium than film.

If you have a Photo CD–compatible CD-ROM drive and appropriate software, you can view electronic thumbnails of the images, open the image files, edit them just like any other digital photograph, save them in other formats (such as PICT or TIFF), and place them into page layouts or presentations. Hardware-wise, you need a color Mac with 8MB of RAM and a *multisession* CD-ROM XA drive such as the AppleCD 300. (Other companies, including NEC and Toshiba, also offer compatible drives.) On the software side, a few programs—including Photoshop 2.5, PageMaker 5, Painter 2, TeachText 7.1, and image-cataloging utilities such as Fetch and Shoebox—can directly open or import the Photo CD format. Kodak naturally offers several means of handling Photo CD images, including **Photo CD Access Plus** ($50), a utility that can rotate and crop images and convert them to other file formats.

With the right system software, however, you can access Photo CD images without *any* special programs. All you need are System 7, QuickTime 1.5 and its accompanying Apple Photo Access extension, and version 4.0.1 of Apple's CD-ROM drivers (Foreign File Access and so forth). When you insert a Photo CD disc, the system software automatically does some magic that lets you see and open each resolution of each image as if it were a PICT file. This means you can import the images into any program that supports PICT files or drag an image from the CD-ROM onto your hard disk for later use. (The pseudo-PICT files even have color icons of the images.) The system software also creates a Slide Show file and viewer utility, which lets you browse the images within a QuickTime movie frame.

CD-ROM of stock photos and movies. **Photoshop LE** doesn't provide high-end features such as color separations and CMYK editing, but you get most of the features and flavor of the full version, and you can always upgrade later.

Color It! (AA). MicroFrontier's **Color It! 3** is essentially a poor man's Photoshop. This $150 program provides a plethora of versatile tools for painting and image retouching, including 8-bit masking, customizable settings (for things like brush size, opacity, and anti-aliasing), numerous filters (it also supports Photoshop plug-ins), and CMYK separations. Moreover, it has two features Photoshop should implement: 16 levels of undo and a dynamite magic wand tool, which makes it easy both to select like-colored image areas and to remove unwanted portions from the selection range. Unfortunately, Color It! is unduly difficult to learn and use, a situation not remedied by its poor documentation.

PhotoFlash (Neil McManus). Apple's $280 **PhotoFlash** was developed for folks who need nothing more than a quick-and-easy way to scan an image, clean it up, and place it in a page-layout program. PhotoFlash lets you capture an image with a Photoshop scanner plug-in, straighten it, sharpen or blur it, change its color depth, and save it in a number of formats. If you're feeling rambunctious, you can remove dust and scratches, apply Photoshop plug-in filters or use Apple events scripting to automate tasks such as processing multiple images or placing them in QuarkXPress or PageMaker.

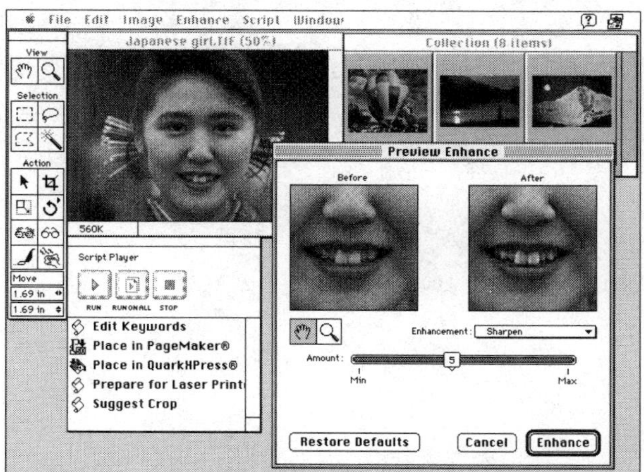

PhotoFlash is an easy-to-use utility that lets you quickly scan images and perform basic clean-up chores such as sharpening. You can store images in a rudimentary catalog (top right) or use Apple events scripts to place them directly into a page layout (lower left).

PhotoFlash comes with an integrated browser for cataloging and retrieving images, but you can't save separate collections of images (everything is lumped into one unwieldy library). Its lame browser notwithstanding, PhotoFlash is so elegant I found myself grumbling when a touch-up task forced me to open Photoshop. (For a look at

Managing Your Media (AA)

The Mac's graphics bounty does have a downside: Trying to track hundreds (or thousands) of images scattered across hard disks, floppies, CD-ROMs, and SyQuest cartridges can be a major time-waster. The solution? A media-cataloging program—a specialized database that lets you create a master catalog of all your graphics, no matter what their format or location. A single catalog can hold 32,000 images or more; each cataloged image is represented by a thumbnail-size preview (which is linked to the original file) and identifying text. Using filenames, keywords, or other criteria, you can quickly find and retrieve graphics ranging from EPS illustrations to scanned photographs to QuickTime movies.

For individual users, Aldus's **Fetch** ($150 single user, $300 multiuser), **Cumulus PowerLite** ($200, Canto Software), and **Multi-Ad Search** ($250, Multi-Ad Services) are all good choices. They have excellent features, catalog a wide variety of file formats, and let you place cataloged images directly into PageMaker and QuarkXPress documents—with Cumulus, you simply drag and drop images from a catalog directly into a page layout. If you work with Photo CD images, both Fetch and Eastman Kodak's **Shoebox** ($140) provide special support features.

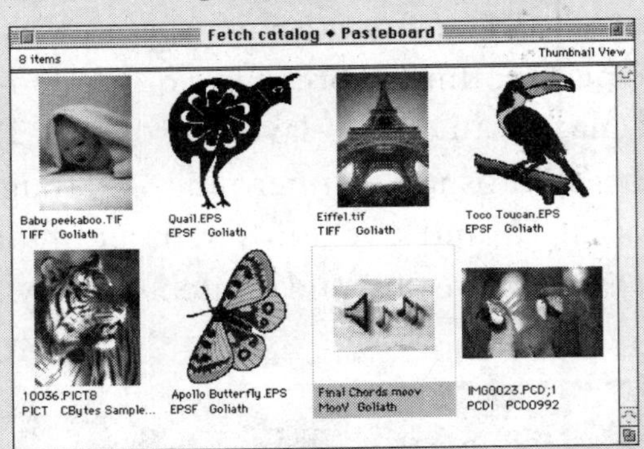

A media-cataloging utility such as Fetch lets you quickly find, view, and retrieve graphics.

GOOD FEATURE

If you're managing graphics over a network, however, get Canto Software's **Cumulus PowerPro.** This client/server database is easy to use and—best of all—*fast,* even on a busy network. It can automatically catalog files dropped into designated folders and lets you automate tasks with Apple events scripting. Pricing starts at $1,500 for five users.

full-fledged image-cataloging programs, see the box "Managing Your Media," above).

General Paint Tips

These tips should work in most paint and image-editing programs and in the painting components of programs such as SuperPaint, Canvas, HyperCard, and ClarisWorks. Some will even work in draw programs. But remember: Life has no guarantees.

Tool palette shortcuts (AN/SA/AA). Double-clicking on icons in the tool palette usually produces some handy shortcuts. For examples, see the chart at right.

Double-click on	To
[selection rectangle] or [lasso]	Select the entire window
[eraser]	Erase the entire window
[paintbrush]	Bring up a palette for changing brush size and shape
[pencil]	Zoom to 8x magnification (or back to normal view)

Preselect your tools (AA). Be sure to choose all the parameters—color, pattern, line width, brush size, and so on—you want *before* you begin painting. Unlike a draw program, you can't change your mind about these things after the fact; your only choice is to undo or delete the area and start over.

Shift effects (AN/SA). Holding down Shift while you use a tool usually constrains its movement and forces shapes to be of equal length and width. See the chart at right for some examples of its actions.

Shift +	Lets you
[paintbrush]	Paint straight horizontal or vertical brush strokes
[pencil]	Draw straight horizontal or vertical lines
[hand]	Shift the window contents horizontally or vertically
[eraser]	Erase in straight horizontal or vertical swipes
[rectangle] or [selection rectangle]	Create squares (instead of rectangles)
[oval]	Create circles (instead of ovals)

Lasso tricks (AA/AN). The lasso tool lets you select an irregularly shaped area (such as a flower) by tracing around it. (Sometimes you can select an object simply by double-clicking it with the lasso.) In many programs, you can choose whether the lassoed selection will shrink to exclude any surrounding background (the same is often true for the selection rectangle). Some programs, such as BrushStrokes and SuperPaint, let you opt to exclude all background areas—such as the interior of an *O*—from a selection; this is often called the *transparent* or *X-ray mode*.

Note that you don't have to draw a complete loop with the lasso to select an area. The program will automatically close the loop with a straight line between where you start and end the lasso drag.

HOT TIP

Eraser alternatives (AN/AA). The eraser deletes parts of an image, changing erased areas to the background color (usually white). Here are three other ways you can erase bit-mapped artwork:

- To quickly erase large areas, use a selection tool (the selection rectangle or lasso, for example), then hit Delete.
- Use the paintbrush—in any convenient size and shape—to paint over the desired area with white paint (or whatever the background color is).
- For detailed, pixel-by-pixel erasing, go to a magnified view and use the pencil with white paint (or the background color).

Preventing paint bucket spills (AA). When you fill a selected area using the paint bucket, it fills the *entire* contiguous area. This can produce unexpected results if there's a pixel or two missing from the border of a supposedly enclosed shape. The paint will spill out through the gap into the surrounding area. If this happens to you, immediately choose Undo, then locate the gap in the outline and use the pencil to close it up.

Duplicating an image (SA/AN/AA). The easiest way to copy an image isn't the cut-and-paste routine. Nope, all you have to do is press Option while dragging a selected area. Instead of moving the original image, you'll peel away an exact copy. If you also hold down ⌘, you'll leave a trail of images behind as you drag the selection. The more slowly you drag, the more copies there'll be. Holding down Shift as well (which means ⌘ Option Shift in total) keeps the dragged copies in a straight line. In some programs, you can adjust the spacing between copies by changing the current line width.

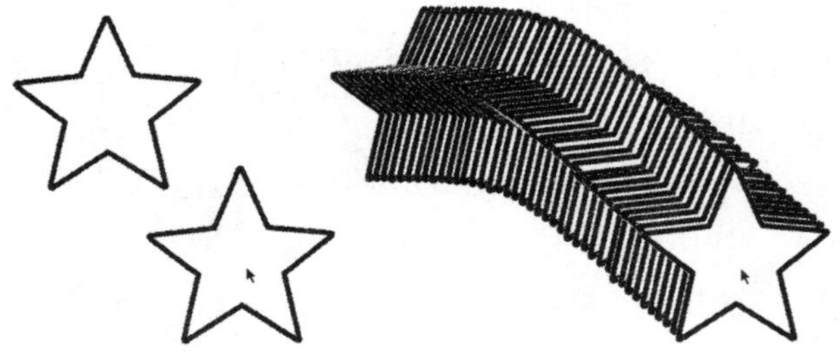

In most graphics programs, you can clone an image by pressing Option and dragging (left). If you hold down ⌘ as well, you'll leave a trail of images (right).

Resizing bit-mapped images (AA). Enlarging a bit-mapped image is generally a Bad Thing, because the image deteriorates into a jaggy mess. Instead, make the original image as large as possible, then scale it *down* to whatever size you

Shareware Extras (GW)

Most of this chapter covers commercial software, but on-line services and user groups also offer a variety of shareware (and freeware) graphics programs. If you aren't ready to ante up for a commercial paint program, for example, the freebie **ColourPaint** provides a color alternative with simple MacPaint-like tools. Stuck with a monochrome Mac? The black-and-white **LightningPaint** ($14) has the painting basics plus some mondo cool tools (spiral, starburst) and special effects (fish-eye lens, gradients). **NIH Image,** a freeware image-editing program, rivals some commercial programs. It was created for use with medical scans and X-rays, but you can easily use it for more artistic pursuits. I've also been dazzled by the freeware **MandelTV,** an entertaining DA that generates Mandelbrot fractals and saves them as PICT files.

On the drawing side, **DesignerDraw** (free) comes in handy if you need to produce simple organization or flow charts. Like some commercial products, it preserves line connections if you drag linked text boxes around. **AppleDraw** ($30) has most of MacDraw's tools and is a good choice for basic drawing tasks, such as logos, although it doesn't have the oomph for sophisticated illustrations.

There are also a few nifty utilities that can enhance your graphics experience. **Super Ruler** ($10) is a clever DA that displays a vertical or horizontal ruler on-screen. It's great for page-layout measurements in word processors that lack vertical rulers. Creating perfect gradient fills with smooth transitions between colors is something of an art; the $5 **Blender DA** calculates the minimum number of steps you need to specify in programs such as Illustrator or FreeHand to attain that perfect smoothness. And if you have a lot of graphics to keep track of, **ImageCatalog** (free) lets you organize, annotate, and access PICT, TIFF, MacPaint, and some EPS graphics.

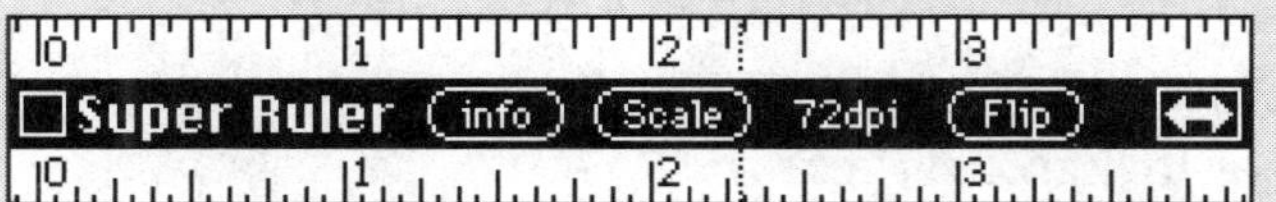

You can quickly measure columns of copy with Super Ruler, a shareware utility that displays this ruler horizontally or vertically.

need. Reducing the size of a bit map effectively increases the resolution, thus improving its appearance. For optimum results, use a multiple of the original size—half or one-fourth the size, for example. (This approach is mandatory if you insist on enlarging the image.) Here are four ways to resize a bit map:

- Select the image, hold down Shift, and drag to shrink the image proportionally. This works in most programs, including page layout and presentation documents.

HOT TIP

- Import the full-size image into a draw program (or the drawing component of a combination program) and reduce it there. This will minimize the loss of detail, particularly if there's text in the image.
- Boost the image's resolution in a program such as Photoshop. When you increase the resolution—say, from 72 dpi to 300 dpi—the image size will shrink proportionally.
- Open the Page Setup dialog box (File menu) and change the Reduce or Enlarge percentage to less than 100. The on-screen image won't change, but when you select Print, the image—along with everything else on the page—will be scaled down to the specified size. (Remember to return the percentage to 100 when you're finished.)

Global nudge commands (SA/AN/AA). Every graphics (and page layout) program should let you move selected objects pixel by pixel (called *nudging*). But if yours doesn't, here's how to make your own nudge commands that will work in any program—paint, draw, page layout, you name it.

You need the Easy Access control panel in your Control Panels folder. (If it's not there, install it from your original system disks and restart the Mac.) Press [⌘][Shift][Clear] to activate one of its handiest features, Mouse Keys. Tap [0] on the numeric keypad twice to lock down the mouse button. Now you can use [2], [4], [6], and [8] on the keypad to move any selected object down, left, right, or up one pixel at a time. (Press the keypad's [.] twice to release the mouse button and press [⌘][Shift][Clear] to turn off Mouse Keys.)

Photoshop Tips

Most of these Photoshop 2.5 tricks work in earlier versions as well. For the ultimate in tips and techniques, get *The Photoshop Wow! Book* ($35, Peachpit Press).

HOT TIP

Changing views (EC). Photoshop has several shortcuts for zooming in and out. Double-click the zoom tool to see an image in 1:1 view (one image pixel is equal to one screen pixel). Keep in mind that the 1:1 view may not correspond to the image's actual dimensions. For example, if the image resolution is higher than the screen resolution (typically 72 dpi), the image will appear larger on screen than it actually is.

To instantly zoom part of an image to fill the screen, use the zoom tool to drag out a selection rectangle around the area you want to magnify.

Some viewing shortcuts don't use the zoom tool. Double-click the grabber hand, for example, to make the image fit in the window. To change the magnification and simultaneously change the window size, press ⌘+ or ⌘-. To zoom in or out while you're using another tool, press ⌘Spacebar or Option Spacebar and click in the window.

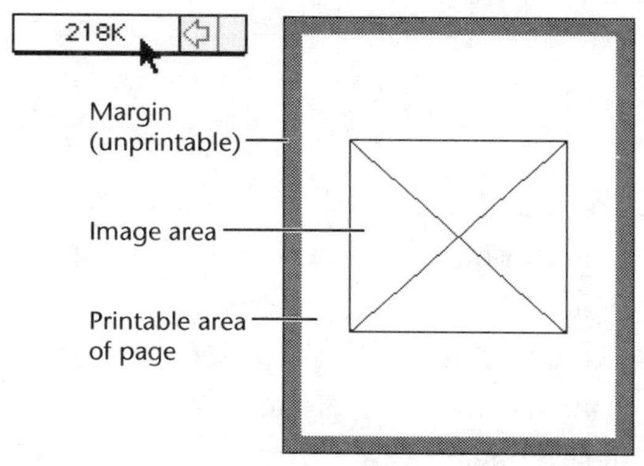


```
     Width:  493 pixels (7.145 inches)
    Height:  452 pixels (6.551 inches)
  Channels:    1 (Grayscale)
Resolution:   69 pixels/inch
```

In Photoshop, clicking on a window's file-size indicator (top left) brings up a page preview (middle) that shows you whether your image will fit on the printed page. Option-click to see other pertinent image details (bottom).

Quick page previews (AA). The file-size indicator at the lower left of a window has two pop-up screens of document details. Click and hold on the indicator to see a page preview that shows your image size relative to the printable page area. Depending on the options selected in the Page Setup dialog box, you may also see registration marks, labels, and other elements. Option-click to see data about the image's dimensions, resolution, and color channels.

Precision editing (EC/AA). Each tool has a cursor that looks like its icon. While cute, these cursors don't lend themselves to precision editing. If you want to know exactly where the paint bucket will drop its load, you can change the cursor into a crosshair by pressing Caps Lock. This trick works for all the tools, including the magic wand and rubber stamp. (Press Caps Lock again to restore the original cursor.)

Multiple views (AA). The New Window command (Window menu) lets you create one or more duplicate windows for an image. You can change the magnification and channel information for each window independently, giving you different simultaneous views of your artwork. Whatever editing changes you make in one window show up instantly in the other(s).

HOT TIP

Fine-tuning selections (EC/AA). Photoshop's selection tools (the selection rectangle and lasso) are more robust than those in most paint programs. You can eliminate part of a selection, for example, by pressing ⌘ while dragging with the desired selection tool. Shift-dragging adds to a selection, even if it's in another part of the image. You can make a polygonal (straight-sided) selection area with the lasso by holding down Option and clicking at the desired corner points. You move a selection by dragging it, of course, but you can move just the selection marquee instead if you hold down ⌘ Option as you drag. Choosing Inverse from the Select menu switches the selected and unselected parts of the image—particularly handy since it's sometimes easier to first select the areas you *don't* want to change.

The Grow and Similar commands (Select menu) let you extend a selection based on color values. The color range they add depends on the tolerance value specified in the Magic Wand Options dialog box (double-click the magic wand icon to open it). The Grow command adds areas adjacent to the selected area that have similar color values. The Similar command enlarges the selection by including all areas in the image that are similar in color.

Hiding the palettes (EC). Tired of the toolbox and other palettes obscuring your handiwork? Press Tab to hide them all. Pressing Tab again will make them reappear.

Selecting colors (EC/AA). The eyedropper tool lets you select a color in the image that you want to be the foreground or background color. Normally, a click with the eyedropper changes the foreground color. If you hold down Option while clicking, however, the eyedropper will change the background color instead.

If you're using another tool, you can change the foreground color on the fly by pressing Option. This turns the current tool into the eyedropper. Click the color you want to use, let go of Option, and continue painting using the newly selected color.

Fast fills (EC). You don't have to use the Fill command or the paint bucket to paint a selected area with the foreground color. Just press Option Delete. To fill a selection with the background color, press Delete.

Dialog box shortcuts (EC). In several of the image-correction dialog boxes—including Levels, Curves, Color Balance, Brightness/Contrast, Hue/Saturation, and Posterize—a Reset button will appear if you press Option. By clicking Reset, you can restore the original image settings without having to close the dialog box with the Cancel button.

You can also reposition the image with these dialog boxes open by using keyboard shortcuts. You can zoom in or out with ⌘ Spacebar or Option Spacebar, and press Spacebar to move around with the grabber.

Magic eraser (AA/BL). The Revert command (File menu) lets you undo all changes made to an image since the last time you saved it. But if you hold down Option as you drag the eraser, you'll restore just the underlying area to its previously saved condition.

Ready-Made Patterns and Textures (AA)

Need a nice marble background for a book cover? How about some knotty pine for a 3-D model or fabric swatches for an architectural rendering? Numerous companies offer packages of predesigned patterns and textures that you can use in artwork and presentations or wrap onto the surfaces of 3-D objects. Most are 24-bit images in PICT or TIFF format and will *tile* seamlessly, meaning that if the image isn't large enough to fill the area, it repeats itself without showing any joints.

Form and Function provides everything from paper and bricks to shrubbery and jelly beans in its **Wraptures** series ($130 each on CD-ROM). **Fresco** ($200 on CD-ROM, Xaos Tools) offers classy abstract designs, while Pixar's $300 **One Twenty Eight** CD-ROM has photographic textures and Artbeats' **Marble & Granite** collection ($350 on CD-ROM) includes beveled buttons and mortises, seamless tiles, and bump maps for 3-D renderings (see "Three-Dimensional Graphics" later in this chapter).

If you want to try your hand at texturing, check out **Pattern Workshop** ($50, Micro-Frontier), a Photoshop plug-in that lets you edit its 160 premade patterns or make your own. Another plug-in, **Terrazzo** ($200, Xaos Tools), provides 17 symmetry effects for turning any section of a bit-mapped image into a tilable texture, while Specular's $200 **TextureScape** program generates seamless, high-resolution textures from EPS images created in Illustrator or FreeHand. The latter two programs let you add complexity to a texture by adjusting properties such as gloss, transparency, bumpiness, and color. TextureScape also has sophisticated lighting controls and can animate textures over time.

HOT TIP

You can use the magic eraser to give an image a hand-colored look. Open (or save) a color image, then convert it to black and white by choosing Grayscale from the Mode menu. Then select RGB Color to switch back to color mode for editing. Now you can use the magic eraser to paint the original color back onto selected areas.

Controlling letter spacing (AA). Working with text in Photoshop can be difficult, since the characters are just a collection of bit maps, but here's a quick way to adjust the spacing between individual letters (called *kerning*). Type some text, and while the type tool is still active, press ⌘. The cursor will turn into the lasso. Now you can deselect any of the letters by circling them, then use the arrow keys to push the remaining letters closer to (or farther from) the deselected ones. By doing this several times, you can precisely control letter spacing. (Alternatively, you can press ⌘ Shift and drag the lasso around the letters you want to remain selected.)

Filter previews (AA). Photoshop 2.5 has an undocumented checkbox that lets you turn on (or off) wireframe and thumbnail previews for nine distortion filters, including Pinch, Spherize, Twirl, and Zigzag. To reach the checkbox, hold down Option and select any of the distortion filters' names from the list under About Plug-in (menu). Now whenever you use one of the filters, its dialog box will let you preview the effect before you apply it. (In version 2.5.1, the default setting is to show the previews.)

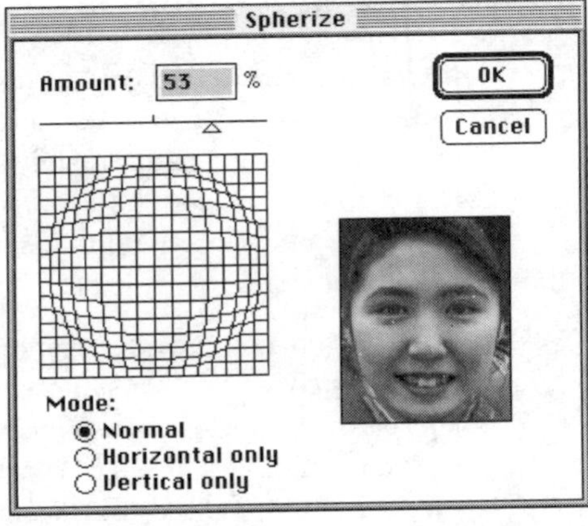

An undocumented feature in Photoshop lets you turn on (or off) previews in several of its filter dialog boxes.

Applying filters to individual channels (BL). You can achieve some interesting, subtle effects by using a filter on individual color channels rather than on the entire image. For example, try applying the Noise filter separately to each channel—R (red), then G (green), then B (blue)—in an RGB document. (You can selectively edit channels via the Channels palette.) Rather than the grainy, colorful noise you get by applying Noise to the entire RGB image, you'll get a film-grain-like effect.

Drawing

Paint and draw applications have been doing some feature swapping lately, but a drawing program, with its underlying object-orientedness, is still your best bet for the following types of graphics:

- finely detailed drawings with precise dimensions, such as technical illustrations and architectural renderings
- artwork that needs to be changed frequently
- illustrations with lots of text and/or type manipulations
- maps, diagrams, and charts

Tools of the Trade (BL/AA)

All draw programs offer tools for creating geometric shapes (rectangles, ovals, polygons), straight lines, arcs, freehand shapes, and text. They let you scale, measure, group, and align objects to create precise drawings, and they supply color controls for adding sophisticated shading and blends. Note that although draw programs have some features (such as rectangle and line tools) that seem similar to those in found paint programs, functionally they're quite different. A

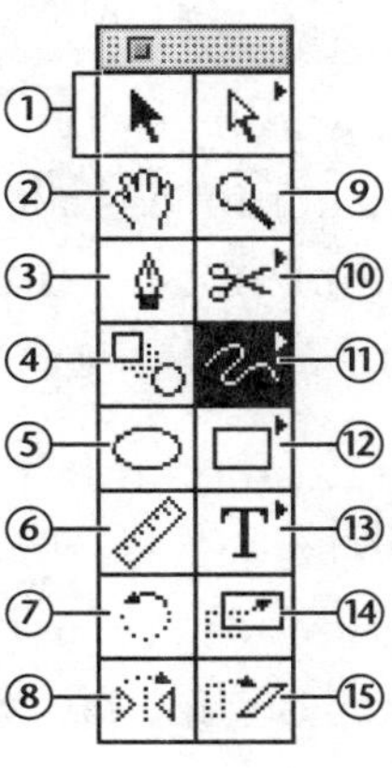

1. Selection tools, for selecting an entire object or just one segment
2. Grabber hand, for scrolling an image in the window
3. Pen, for drawing straight lines and Bézier curves
4. Blend tool, for creating graduated blends between two colors or shapes
5. Oval, for drawing circles and ovals
6. Measuring tool, for measuring the distance between two points
7. Rotation tool, for rotating objects around a fixed point
8. Reflection tool, for mirroring an object across an axis
9. Magnifying glass, for zooming in and out
10. Scissors, for splitting a line or curve into two pieces
11. Freehand tool, for drawing irregular lines
12. Rectangle, for making rectangles and squares
13. Type tool, for entering fully editable text
14. Scale tool, for resizing an object
15. Shear tool, for shearing or skewing an object

Illustrator's tool palette contains tools common to most draw programs.

rectangle drawn in DeskDraw remains a fully selectable and editable object, while one painted in DeskPaint becomes an uneditable part of the underlying bit-mapped painting.

The tool palette on the previous page shows typical drawing tools. Top-notch illustration programs also offer the following features:

- **Precise drawing controls,** including rulers, grids, and the ability to numerically specify an object's dimensions.

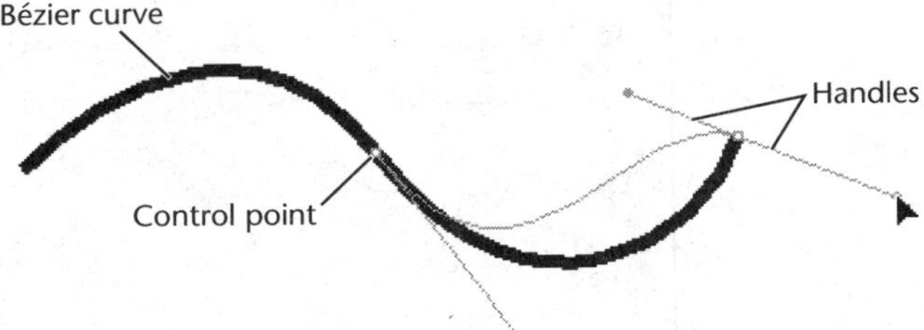

You draw a Bézier curve by clicking to establish a starting point, then clicking elsewhere and dragging to shape the curve. Each click creates a new curve segment. The orientation and length of the two handles attached to each control point determine the curve's slope and size (curviness). In this case, by pulling the right handle down, we're pushing the curve up.

- **A Bézier-curve tool,** which lets you easily create and edit complex curves. Bézier curves contain straight or curved line segments connected by control points. By moving these points or their attached handles, you can individually adjust the shape of each line segment.

- **Object-management controls,** including reordering, alignment, grouping, and locking. Move Forward and Move Backward commands are essential when you're dealing with objects stacked on top of each other. Alignment controls let you align and/or distribute objects along a particular axis. A grouping command helps you organize complex illustrations by allowing you to link several items—all the pieces of a bicycle, say—so you can move, scale, rotate, and copy them as a single object. Lock and Hide commands let you make selected objects uneditable so you don't accidentally edit them.

- **Layering controls,** which let you segregate parts of an illustration on different levels, or layers, that behave like transparent overlays. With layers, you can work on one part of a complex illustration without disturbing other parts. If you're drawing a map, for example, you could put the roads on one layer, the towns on another, geographic features on a third layer, and text on a fourth. That way, when you need to add a road, you don't have to worry about accidentally obliterating a town or filling in a lake. You also can shuffle the layer order and selectively turn layers on and off—you could hide every layer but the one you're working on, or just print selected layers.

- **Good text handling.** All draw programs let you enter and edit text just like a word processor. Most provide formatting controls such as kerning, leading, alignment, and tabs. Because generating special type effects is a popular use for draw programs, you can often add automatic drop shadows and fill characters with colors or blends, as well as stretch, rotate, skew, or bind text to a path (such as a curve).
- **Autotracing,** which lets you convert font characters or bit-mapped graphics into outlines that can be reshaped and edited just like any other object.
- **Strong color controls.** Most programs let you create custom colors, tints, and gradients. Some provide palettes for spot-color systems such as Pantone and TruMatch, and/or let you assign colors using percentages of CMYK (cyan, magenta, yellow, black) or HLS (hue, lightness, saturation) instead of the default RGB (red, green, blue) mode.
- **Color-separation capabilities.** If you're doing high-end color work, you'll want to separate images into their CMYK components before going to press.

Drawing Partners

After ten years, Claris has discontinued the hugely popular MacDraw, the Mac's first drawing program. But have no fear: There are plenty of candidates to take its place—from drawing programs aimed at generalists to those for professional illustrators—including MacDraw's successor, ClarisDraw.

Drawing on the cheap (EF). If you're more concerned about the potential dent in your bank account than sheer number of features, consider **Expert Draw** or **DeskDraw.** Expert Draw ($50, Expert Software) offers the drawing basics, plus advanced goodies such as unlimited drawing layers (memory permitting), object libraries, text on a path, and the ability to blend one shape into another. Its main drawbacks are the lack of a Bézier-curve tool and autotracing, and it's not quite as simple to use as Zedcor's DeskDraw ($30, bundled with DeskPaint). DeskDraw is a reliable, no-frills program that retains the simplicity and compactness of its original incarnation as a desk accessory. *[System 6 users*

QuickDraw vs. PostScript

(AA)

Drawing programs are based either on QuickDraw (the Mac's native graphics language) or PostScript (Adobe's page description language). Traditionally, business users favor QuickDraw-based programs, while professional illustrators prefer PostScript. QuickDraw programs are more numerous, less expensive, and easier to learn and use. QuickDraw images can be printed on more (and less-expensive) printers, and no matter how complex the drawing, you never get output errors.

PostScript-based programs, on the other hand, can manipulate images in ways that are difficult (or impossible) in QuickDraw. PostScript is famous for producing sophisticated illustrations with fine lines (called *paths*), complex curves, seamless blends, special text effects, rotation, skewing, and transparency effects. PostScript illustrations are infinitely scalable, but for best results they must be output on a PostScript-compatible printer—and if a drawing is too complex (too many blends, for instance), it may not print at all. At this writing, there are four programs that offer PostScript features: the two heavyweights, FreeHand and Illustrator, plus CA-Cricket Draw III and Canvas (a polyglot program that also supports QuickDraw).

The wind may have shifted by the time you read this, however, thanks to the release of QuickDraw GX, Apple's next-generation imaging technology that will expand the Mac's built-in support for graphics, fonts, color management, and printing. A full-blown page description language, QuickDraw GX should bring many of PostScript's traditional strengths to every graphics program that supports it. For example, the QuickDraw GX extension will add system-level support for rotation, scaling, skewing, and image transparency. The new font architecture will allow any application to provide typographic capabilities such as kerning, tracking, fractions, and ligatures. And unlike PostScript, QuickDraw GX lets you output these complex images on a wide variety of printers, even inexpensive models. If you have an older Mac, however, you may miss out on QuickDraw GX—Apple recommends running it on at least an '030 machine with 8MB of RAM.

can still install the DA.—AA] It doesn't have drawing layers, though, and you can't mix smooth curves and sharp angles in a freehand shape. On the plus side, DeskDraw's easy to learn—and you can't beat the price.

Both programs have companion painting products, or for a bit more money you can get SuperPaint or artWorks, which provide drawing and painting tools in a single package. (For details on all these programs, see "Painting," earlier in this chapter.)

Business graphics (KP/Carolyn Said/SC). There's a relatively new subcategory of drawing programs that targets the general business user, who's presumably more interested in producing organization charts than fancy gradient fills. If this sounds like you, check out **IntelliDraw 2** ($100, Aldus Consumer Division) or **ClarisDraw** ($400, Claris). The programs have many things in common, including "intelligent" tools that simplify the creation of business graphics such as forms, floor plans, maps, and diagrams. Their object-linking features let you easily control the relationships between objects, including shape, size, alignment, distribution, and drop shadows. For example, if you enlarge one object in a linked group, the other objects also grow. Move one, and the others follow. And connector lines stay attached when objects are moved—a handy feature if you're making family trees or org charts.

GOOD FEATURE

Both programs provide substantial libraries of templates and clip art, allowing you to assemble drawings quickly. You can also save your own drawings into the libraries for future use. A nifty shortcut: You can drag and drop objects across document windows or from the library palette into a drawing, avoiding cut and paste entirely. Their shared-features repertoire also includes good text handling, some arty extras (such as gradient fills and text-on-a-path), basic slideshow capabilities (with QuickTime support), and file compatibility with their Windows versions.

GOOD FEATURE

The programs aren't complete clones, however. ClarisDraw, the successor to the MacDraw dynasty, is the more versatile player, providing basic painting and image-editing tools (not unlike SuperPaint) and simple page layout features (linked text frames, text wrap, style sheets). And yes, you can import documents created in MacDraw II or Pro. IntelliDraw, on the other hand, offers the cleverly named symmetrigon tool, which mirrors whatever you draw (making it

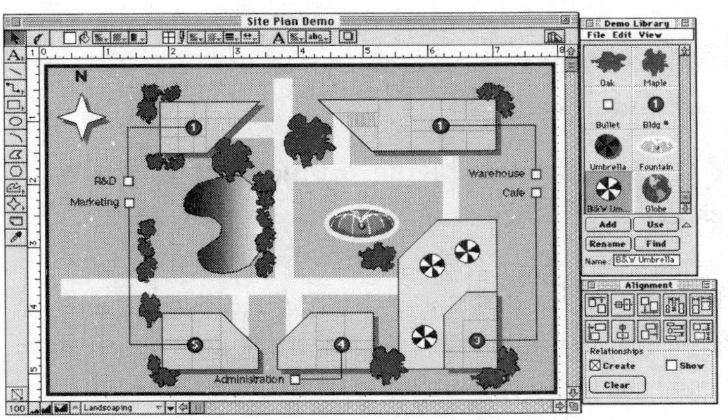

ClarisDraw is aimed at folks who mainly do bread-and-butter drawings such as floor plans, forms, and organization charts. It provides easy access to tools and numerous built-in drawing aids. For example, its SmartSymbol libraries (upper right) contain thousands of precreated images, which you can drag and drop into your drawings, and the SmartAlign palette (lower right) simplifies object alignment.

easy to create symmetrical shapes), and special effects such as 3-D perspective and warping.

For an even *more* business-oriented approach, try **ClarisImpact** ($400, Claris). This hybrid drawing/presentation package provides specialized tools for drawing seven common business graphics: graphs, tables, org charts, time lines, flow charts, network diagrams, and calendars. To create any of those, you simply select the appropriate tool and drag out a selection rectangle. A dialog box asks you for details, such as the number of levels in an organization chart. Then ClarisImpact draws the graphic, complete with text placeholders that you replace with your own information. With its integrated word processing and slideshow capabilities, the program resembles its sibling ClarisWorks (see Chapter 12), allowing you to complete many projects without ever leaving the program.

CA-Cricket Draw III (KP/AA). Way back when, Cricket Draw was the first PostScript drawing program for the Mac. While it has long since been eclipsed by Illustrator and FreeHand, the current incarnation—which Computer Associates has cleverly named **CA-Cricket Draw III 2.0**—still offers solid drawing capabilities, plus a few unique features, for $130.

Cricket Draw's tools are Bézier-based, so every object (even rectangles and circles) can be ungrouped and edited as Bézier curves. You can create simulated 3-D objects with its extrude tool—this produces particularly cool effects with gradient-filled type—and the Tweening command lets you blend one object into another in more complex ways than in FreeHand or Illustrator. Cricket Draw has a wealth of text-handling features, from tabs and kerning to a spelling checker and text-on-a-curve. There are some nifty PostScript special effects, such as fountain fills, and you can directly edit a document's PostScript code. Unfortunately, Cricket Draw also has some serious shortcomings. For instance, it's the only major program without drawing layers.

BAD FEATURE

Canvas (DM). No one can accuse Canvas of lying dormant. If the folks at Deneba so much as *smell* a feature in another program, they glom it. As a result, **Canvas 3.5** ($400) has enough drawing, painting, PostScript, text, special-effects, and printing capabilities to satisfy just about anyone—indeed, it's often called the Swiss Army knife of graphics programs—and it looks *great* on features-comparison lists, even surpassing FreeHand and Illustrator.

Graph-ically Speaking (SC)

Many drawing, presentation, and spreadsheet programs offer decent graphing capabilities, but sometimes decent isn't enough. Maybe you need a less-common chart type (histograms, anyone?). Or you'd like more control over formatting and labeling. You might want to graph a complex mathematical function, or fit a curve to a set of points. If so, you need a dedicated graphing program, which lets you import data in a variety of formats (or directly type the data in spreadsheetlike cells), tweak the chart's appearance till you're satisfied, and export the finished graph in PICT or EPS format for use in your favorite word processor, spreadsheet, or presentation program.

Name a chart type, and **DeltaGraph Pro 3** ($200, DeltaPoint) is likely to have it, plus a dozen others you've never heard of (but someone else uses constantly). In all, it has 57 graphing options, including 3-D, pie, pictograph, bubble, spider, and high-low-open-close. If that sounds overwhelming, there's a Chart Advisor to help you pick and create the appropriate graph for your needs. The interface can be a bit confusing, but it offers a plethora of customization options—from color to imported graphics—and over 40 mathematical and statistical functions. DeltaGraph Pro can even turn your finished graphs into a slide show, complete with transition effects.

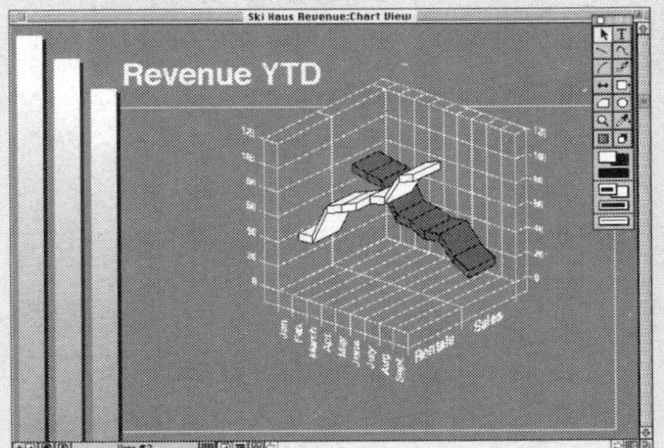

DeltaGraph Pro offers the ultimate in chart design, with 57 chart types, extensive customizing options, and decent presentation features.

For a quick and easy way to generate basic, respectable-looking graphs, consider **CA-Cricket Graph III 1.5** ($130, Computer Associates). It lacks DeltaGraph's multitude of graph types (it has just ten, and none are 3-D) and presentation features, but it's a solid program that requires only 1.5MB of RAM, half of what DeltaGraph needs. If you need sophisticated data analysis, **KaleidaGraph 3** ($250, Synergy Software) offers chart types and mathematical functions aimed at scientists, engineers, and financial analysts.

Technical illustrators and architects appreciate its precision-drawing tools, multiple overlapping layers, and ability to add dimensions and labels to drawings. Its robust text handling—from kerning and style sheets to a spelling checker and multiple columns—make it suitable for short page layout jobs. Special effects include an envelope tool that lets you distort objects as if they were reflected in a funhouse mirror. When applied to text, you can generate type effects previously available only in dedicated logo editors such as Letraset's LetraStudio (see

Chapter 14). In addition, Canvas has Bézier curves, compound paths, "smart" connector lines, pressure-sensitive pens and brushes, slide shows, color separations...the list goes on and on (and on).

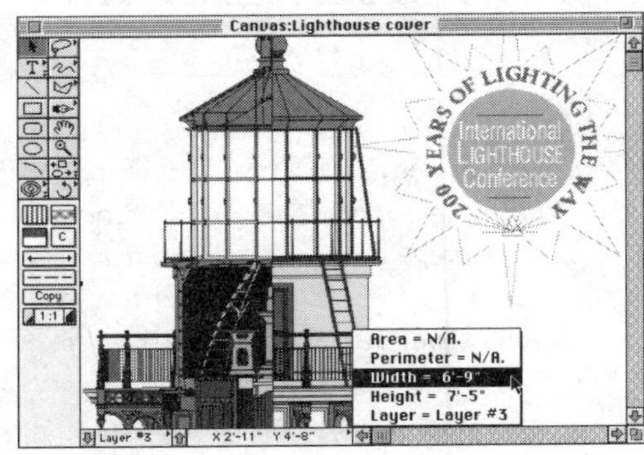

Like its competitors, Canvas can produce technical drawings and perform a variety of type tricks, but its dimensioning capabilities give you a precision normally found in CAD packages. For example, you can attach dimensioning data to a selected object using the Information Manager's pop-up menu.

BAD FEATURE

This treasure trove of features comes at a cost: Canvas is complicated to learn and use, with tools tucked in weird places, and it is occasionally slow and a tad buggy. Because some tools are provided as plug-ins, you can simplify things a bit by not loading them, but personally I prefer a program with fewer bells and whistles and an interface I can navigate without scrambling for the (unwieldy) manual.

Illustrator and FreeHand (BL/AA). Adobe's **Illustrator** and Aldus's **FreeHand** sit astride the Mac drawing world. Both are powerful PostScript-based programs that let you do seemingly magical things with illustrations. They cost the same ($600 list; about $400 by mail order) and require the same level of hardware (an '020 CPU, 8MB of RAM, and System 7). So which should you choose? Although each has a fanatical following, in truth the programs are so evenly matched that they differ only in small details. If you have a CD-ROM drive, though, Illustrator 5.5 is a particularly good deal because it includes a CD-ROM containing tutorials and tips, 180 PostScript fonts, and clip art. But whichever program you buy, expect to spend some time learning to use it effectively.

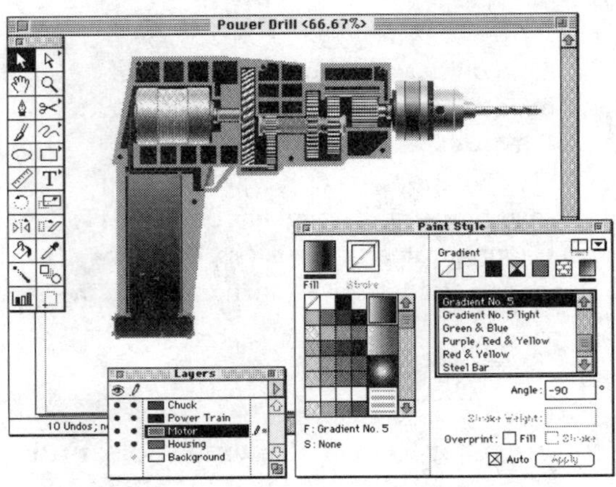

Illustrator's Layers palette lets you view or hide pieces of an image (the background is hidden here), select a layer for editing (we're editing the Motor layer), and rearrange layers by changing their order in the list. The shading on the chuck, drill bit, and motor was created by filling shapes with gradient fills using the Paint Style palette.

These PostScript powerhouses can produce complex, detailed illustrations with smooth curves and subtle blends that print at the highest resolution available on a PostScript printer or imagesetter. The current versions remedy previous competitive differences, providing drawing layers, multiple undos, excellent color controls, gradient fills, robust text-handling features, column and tab controls for creating tables, special effects (rotate, skew, text on a path, and so on), pressure-sensitive pen tools, and editing in preview (WYSIWYG) mode in both programs. Their cool compound-path tools make it easy to split and combine shapes. You can create new shapes by cutting pieces out of existing ones (the background will show through the holes), or add several shapes together to make a new object.

That said, there are a *few* differences. Illustrator uses fewer tools to do the same jobs; for instance, it has one tool for creating both lines and curves, while FreeHand has several. Illustrator 5.5 has better charting options, a plug-in technology that lets you add new filters and features (no, these aren't Photoshop-compatible plug-ins), and the ability to import, edit, and produce the PDF files used by Adobe's Acrobat software (see Chapter 24). Unlike its competitor, however, Illustrator still can't import TIFF or JPEG files.

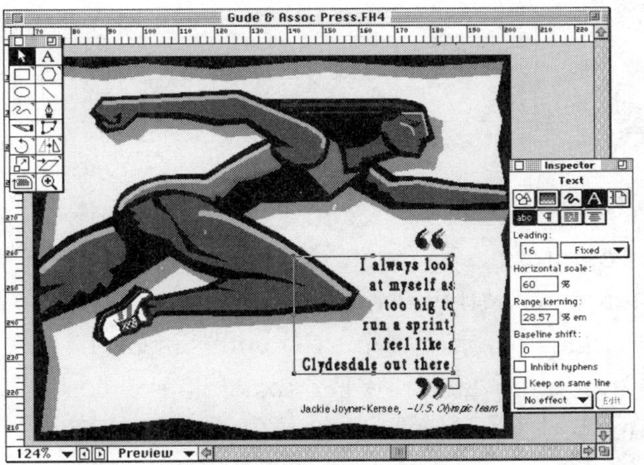

FreeHand's Inspector palette is a one-stop location for changing the attributes of any element. To switch from text attributes (some of which are shown here) to those for objects or fills, you just click the appropriate button. The natural-looking brush strokes in this image were created using the freehand tool with a variable-stroke setting and a pressure-sensitive drawing tablet.

FreeHand 4 lets you apply colors simply by dragging them from a color palette and dropping them onto an object, and it has multipage capabilities that—combined with text tricks such as column balancing, paragraph formatting, and copyfitting—actually surpass PageMaker for small-document design. You can, for instance, create pages of different dimensions, so you can create an entire set of related documents (business cards, envelopes, stationery) in a single FreeHand file.

Footnote: At press time, Adobe and Aldus had announced plans to merge. Adobe (which is, in reality, acquiring Aldus) says it will support both programs, but it's a good bet FreeHand won't get the same attention as home-grown Illustrator. Realizing this, FreeHand's developer, Altsys, is trying to grab the program back from "its most feared competitor." Keep your fingers crossed.

General Draw Tips

These tips should work in most programs, but there's no accounting for programmer idiosyncrasies. Also see "General Paint Tips," above, for more shortcuts that work in draw programs.

Shift effects (AN/SA/AA). As with paint programs, holding down Shift while you use a drawing tool usually acts as a constraint. For example, to force an object (or group of objects) to move only horizontally or vertically, hold down Shift while you drag them. (See the chart at right.)

Shift +	Lets you
╲	Draw lines that are horizontal, vertical, or diagonal (45°)
□	Create squares (instead of rectangles)
⬭	Create circles (instead of ovals)
➤	Resize a selected object proportionally

Drawing from the center (EC/AA). Shapes such as □ and ⬭ are normally drawn from one edge to the other. If you press Option while dragging, however, you can draw the shape from the center instead (this also works in Photoshop). This is especially useful for drawing circles that you want to center around a particular object. (Exception: ClarisDraw and MacDraw Pro make you click a special icon to switch between drawing modes.) Sometimes, pressing Option Shift will both draw from the center and constrain tools (see "Shift Effects," above).

Faster screen redraws (AA/BL). Color, blends, and lots of layers can really slow down screen redraws, especially in PostScript programs. To speed things up, work in black and white as much as possible, use the outline (as opposed to preview) mode if one's available, and hide any layers you don't need to see. If you're using custom blends (made by blending one shape into another), put them in their own layer and turn it off whenever possible. And Illustrator users, take note: If a screen redraw in Preview mode is taking too long, you can interrupt it with ⌘-, which returns you to outline mode.

Pasting EPS images into other programs (AA). Many programs, such as word processors, can't directly import EPS images. But you can still get PostScript images into these programs with this clever workaround: Select the illustration in your draw program and hold down Option while choosing the Copy or Cut command. This copies the PICT screen image as well as the internal PostScript data to the Clipboard. When you paste the graphic, the receiving program thinks it's a PICT image and accepts it. Since the pasted graphic retains all the PostScript data, however, it will print as a PostScript image.

Turning text into outlines (AA). Most programs let you make text any color you want, but you can't add gradients or other special effects to the letters. The solution: Convert the letters into editable outlines, which you can then fill with

Cool Tools (BL)

Illustrator, FreeHand, and Canvas can perform almost any drawing trick you might need. Sometimes, however, a specialized utility still does the job better. For example, all three programs offer *autotracing* tools, which let you turn bit-mapped images into object-oriented line art. They're fine for occasional use, but if you have a library of drawings or blueprints you'd like to scan and convert to EPS line art, spend $200 on Adobe's **Streamline 3,** an autotracing utility that's fast, simple to use, and more accurate in its renderings.

Streamline can generate editable PostScript artwork from photographs, sketches, and illustrations, whether they're in color or black and white. You can scan artwork directly into Streamline and use its drawing and image-editing tools to clean up images before and after tracing. The program can posterize traced images and automatically fill in up to 256 colors or 16 grays, then save them as Illustrator, FreeHand, PICT, or DXF files.

Some drawing programs offer *extrude* tools, which let you create simulated 3-D objects (turning, say, a circle into a cylinder), but they're no match for Adobe's **Dimensions** ($200) or Ray Dream's **addDepth** ($150). Both utilities can take 2-D illustrations generated in drawing programs and give them a third dimension, complete with realistic perspective, shading, and highlights. They also have drawing tools for creating 2-D artwork from scratch. addDepth is faster and simpler to use, letting you extrude text and objects with a minimum of fuss. Dimensions offers *lathing* (spinning an outline around a central axis) as well as extruding, so it can produce more complex 3-D artwork (such as bottles).

Dimensions and addDepth let you move and rotate the resulting 3-D objects in 3-D space, add lights and specify surface colors, and save the finished 3-D artwork in formats editable (if you so desire) in Illustrator or FreeHand. You can also map artwork onto 3-D objects—an invaluable feature for package design. For example, you could create a 3-D soft-drink bottle in Dimensions and then wrap a FreeHand-generated label around it.

gradients. Since the letters are now drawing objects, you can also change their shapes—great for creating custom logos—or paste pictures inside them. The approach to converting text into outlines varies from program to program. ClarisDraw, Canvas, Illustrator, and FreeHand have specific commands; after converting the text, remember to ungroup it before editing individual letters. In other programs you have to be more circuitous, for example, first autotracing text in DeskPaint and then bringing the outlines into DeskDraw.

By turning text into editable outlines, you can change the letter shapes and fill them with gradients, just as you would any other object.

Editing EPS files (AA). An EPS file generally can't be edited after it's created; you usually can't even open it by double-clicking the file icon. The image can be imported into a page layout or other document and resized, rotated, and cropped, but you can't edit the actual contents—a recipe for disaster if you later need to change something. (Illustrator and FreeHand are exceptions; they can open and edit their own EPS files. Photoshop also can open EPS files, but converts them into bit-mapped images.) To avoid problems, be sure to also save the image in the program's native file format. For instance, if you create a drawing in Canvas and save it in EPS format, save it as a Canvas document as well. That way you'll always be able to edit the original image, which can then be reexported as an EPS file.

Publish and Subscribe to yourself (AA). Most draw programs have Publish and Subscribe features, which can greatly streamline chores like designing business cards or tickets. All you have to do is make the original item, publish it, and then subscribe to it enough times to fill a page. Now you have a bunch of linked copies within the same document so that whenever you change the original design, the copies are all updated automatically. (See Chapter 3 for more on Publish and Subscribe.)

Canvas Tips

Canvas is so feature-rich that we could fill this book with tips on it alone. But we'll restrain ourselves to these essential how-to's for versions 3 and 3.5.

Turning off unnecessary tools (David Pogue/AA). Canvas takes up a lot of disk space and memory. Fortunately, you can save some memory by not loading tools you don't need. Just press Spacebar while the program is starting up; this brings up the ToolPicker, which displays a list of external tools that you can turn off (or on). If you're in the middle of a project and discover you need a tool that's deactivated, version 3.5's Tool Loader lets you activate it while Canvas is running.

Tool shortcuts (AA). Canvas normally switches back to the graphics selection tool (↖) after each object you draw. To keep using another, hold down ⌘ and keep drawing. To disable the automatic selection tool, click the Retain Selected Tool checkbox in the General Preferences dialog box.

You can use keyboard shortcuts to switch temporarily to other tools. To access the grabber, hold down Spacebar. For the dropper, press Option`. For the text tool, it's ⌘OptionT. And no matter what tool you're using, you can quickly magnify an object by holding down OptionTab and clicking. To zoom out, press OptionShiftTab while you click.

Many tools in the toolbox have a pop-up menu that you access by pressing the relevant icon. The text tool actually has three palettes. Normally you see a list of text styles. ⌘-click the icon, however, and you'll get a pop-up list of fonts. Shift-click for a list of font sizes.

Double-click for quick editing (David Pogue/AA). While a single click selects an object, double-clicking usually places you into editing mode. For example, no matter what tool you're using (even the graphics selection tool), double-clicking on a text block will switch you to text-editing mode. (To return to the previous tool, hit Return.) Double-clicking on polygons, Bézier curves, 3-D objects, and parallel lines also puts them into editing mode. Double-clicking other objects, such as rectangles, brings up the Object Specifications dialog box.

HOT TIP

Using different Prefs files (AA/DM). Canvas lets you switch between multiple Prefs files, which can save loads of time on document setup. You could use one set of preference settings for business forms, for example, and another for technical drawings. You can save customized settings to a new Prefs file by choosing Save As, selecting Canvas Prefs from the dialog box's pop-up menu, and giving the file a new name. To choose a different Prefs file for a new document, use the Open command. To switch Prefs files on startup, hold down [Shift] until Canvas asks you to locate the file you want to use; you can restore all settings to the original defaults (ignoring the current Canvas Prefs file) by clicking the No Prefs button.

FreeHand and Illustrator Tips

The tips in this section work in FreeHand 4 and Illustrator 5.5, and most work in earlier versions as well.

HOT TIP

Changing tools (BL). The most-used tools in Illustrator and FreeHand are the graphics selection tool, the grabber for moving the page around on screen, and the magnifying glass (zoom tool). Happily, you can temporarily switch to these tools at any time by pressing the keys shown at right in either program.

To get	Press
↖	[⌘]
✋	[Spacebar]
🔍+	[⌘] [Spacebar]
🔍−	[⌘] [Option] [Spacebar]

If you have the magnifying glass selected, holding down [Option] changes the plus sign (enlarge) to a minus sign (reduce). To zoom an area by an arbitrary amount, use the magnifier to drag a selection rectangle around it.

Nudging objects (BL/AA). You can move objects in 1-point increments by selecting them and pressing the appropriate arrow keys ([↑] [↓] [←] [→]). (A *point* is a graphic-arts and typographic measurement that equals about 1⁄72 inch.) You can adjust the nudge distance in either program's Preferences dialog box. To adjust the spacing between text characters—two letters or entire sentences—select the text and hold down [Option] while pressing [←] (tighten) or [→] (loosen). This is a great way to tweak type to fill a certain width.

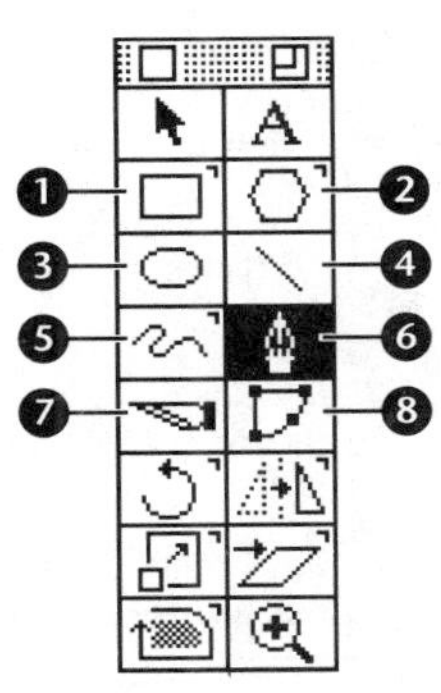

You can select many of FreeHand's tools by pressing a number on the keyboard or numeric keypad.

FreeHand shortcuts (SA/BL/AA). You can quickly switch to any of FreeHand's basic shape tools by pressing a number key (see the illustration at left). These keyboard commands work even if you've hidden the tool palette to save screen space.

And don't forget that you can select a small object that's lying behind a larger one by holding down Control while you click on it. On a similar note, you don't have to ungroup a set of objects to select one of its members. Just Option-click on the item you want to edit. You can combine these two tricks: Control Option-click selects one member of a group that's hidden behind other objects.

Editing basic shapes (SA/AA). When you draw a simple shape (such as a rectangle, oval, or polygon), you've actually drawn a series of lines and curves that are automatically grouped. Both FreeHand and Illustrator let you ungroup the object and edit its component parts. For instance, to quickly create a perfect half-circle, use the oval tool to draw a circle (press Shift to keep it round).

Then, if you're in FreeHand, choose the Ungroup command (⌘U). Four points will appear on the circle. Using the knife tool, Shift-click two opposite points and then deselect everything. Select the half of the circle you don't want and hit Delete.

In Illustrator, choose the direct-selection tool (hollow arrow) and either Shift-click or drag out a selection marquee to select the two quadrants of the circle you don't want. Hit Delete and you're left with a half-circle.

Text on a path (SA/AA). FreeHand and Illustrator let you bind text to a path (line), which means you can place text on curves, create borders made up of dingbat characters, or do whatever else strikes your fancy. In Illustrator, the type size changes automatically when you resize a path, but resizing a path in FreeHand normally changes only the path, not the font size. If you want the text to be resized as well, use the Group command to group the text to the path.

Painting shortcuts in Illustrator (BL/AA). The paint bucket and eyedropper let you copy Illustrator's fill and stroke attributes from one object to others. To customize which attributes the eyedropper picks up and the paint bucket applies, double-click on either tool icon to bring up their Options dialog box. While drawing, you can toggle between the two tools by pressing Option, which makes it easy to grab colors from one area to fill another. You also can change the cursors for the paint bucket and paintbrush into crosshairs for precision editing by pressing Caps Lock.

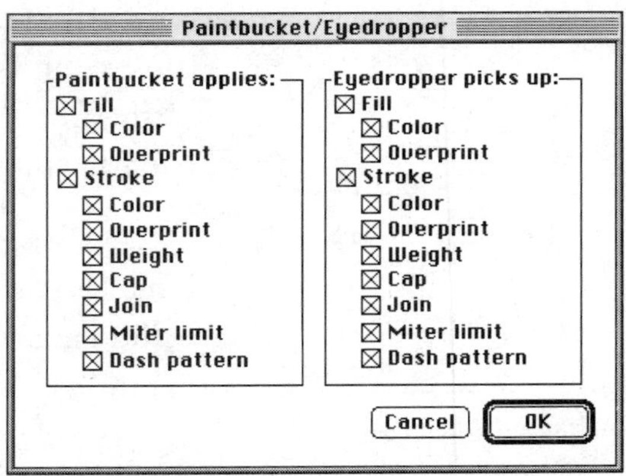

You can use Illustrator's paint tools to copy fill and stroke attributes from one object to another. This dialog box lets you specify which attributes the eyedropper picks up and the paint bucket applies.

Quick transformations in FreeHand (SA/AA). Trying to get the right effect when you're rotating, scaling, or skewing an object with the mouse is often a case of trial and error. For faster, more accurate results, choose a transformation tool and Option-click on the desired object. The Transform palette will open, allowing you to specify exactly the parameters you want.

Blends vs. gradients (AA/BL). You can create smooth color shadings using either blends or graduated fills (gradients), but there are important differences between the two. A *graduated* fill is a linear or radial transition between two or more colors. *Blends* are actually a series of objects that produce a smooth progression between two colors or shapes (or both at once)—say, from a red star to a blue square. Because the component elements can gradually change shape as well as color, you should always use blends to make color fills that follow the contours of an object. Blends also make fewer demands on the computer and printer than do graduated fills, so use blends when possible to save time and memory.

Another reason to use blends instead of fills is if you want to import the illustration into Photoshop. Photoshop can't import Illustrator 5's gradient fills, but if you choose Save As in Illustrator and then select Illustrator 3 from the Compatibility pop-up menu, Illustrator converts all gradients into blends, which Photoshop can handle.

You can use simple shapes filled with blends to create 3-D buttons. For the illusion to work, the blends must progress in the directions shown here.

Simple 3-D shapes (BL). You can create basic 3-D buttons and objects with FreeHand and Illustrator's blend tools. This effect works best with circles, although it works to a lesser degree with any shape. Draw a circle, then draw a smaller circle inside it. Fill the outer circle with a graduated fill that goes from a light color at the top to a dark color at the bottom. Fill the inner circle with a gradient of the same colors going in the opposite direction. (Make sure the small circle is on top of the large circle.) Voilà—the illusion of 3-D.

Illustrator's handy helpers (EC/AA). Here are two more neat things to know:

- Just as in page-layout programs, you can drag guide lines out from the rulers to help you position objects and text. If you press Option while dragging a guide, it will flip from vertical to horizontal (or vice versa). To move a guide once you've dropped it (if it's locked), hold down Control Shift and then drag it. Wish you could have a diagonal guide? It's easy: Just select the guide, then rotate or skew it with the appropriate tool.
- You can choose what's displayed in the status line (lower left of the window) via its pop-up menu. The choices include current tool, amount of free memory, and number of remaining undos. Hold down Option while you click on the status line to access some *really* weird stuff, including a pair of eyeballs that will watch your cursor's movements.

Turn arrowheads into icons with FreeHand (BL). Unlike Illustrator, Free-Hand lets you create arrowheads from scratch if you don't like the predefined line endings. The Arrowhead editor also has an unintended side benefit: It's a great storehouse for simple objects such as symbols and icons. Turn a frequently used icon into an arrowhead and it's always accessible for use in any illustration.

HOT TIP

To create a new arrowhead-cum-icon:

- Draw an object as a single path and copy it to the Clipboard.
- Select the path icon in the Inspector palette, and then choose New from the Arrowheads drop-down menu.
- In the Arrowhead editor dialog box, click the Paste In button to insert the object as an arrowhead.
- Scale and position the object, and then click the New button to save it as an arrowhead.

To use your "arrowhead," click a single point with the pen tool and then select the arrowhead style. To resize it, just change the line width.

Transparent colors in FreeHand (AA). FreeHand 4 has a great undocumented feature: the ability to create transparent colors—that is, when two colors overlap, you can make the top one appear transparent. All you have to do is select two overlapping colored objects, hold down Option and choose the Intersect command from the Path Operations submenu (Arrange menu). Ta da! A Transparency dialog box appears. Move its slider to change the topmost color's degree of opacity. When you click OK, FreeHand creates a new object that's the same size and shape as the overlapping area and contains the new color you just created—which gives you the illusion of transparency. (This effect only works with flat color fills. You can't make lines and graduated fills transparent or see them through other objects.)

Three-Dimensional Graphics

Part drawing, part painting, and part CAD, three-dimensional graphics software gives you an illustration tool that's radically different from conventional paint or draw programs. Although they're represented on a two-dimensional computer screen, 3-D graphics behave like objects in the real world. If you rotate them, you see the back of them, and if you move them, you see what's behind them. What's more, when you move and rotate 3-D objects, the computer automatically handles the redrawing of such things as lighting, shadows, and perspective.

Three-dimensional graphics are ideal for a range of uses. Illustrators and animators can create photorealistic illustrations. Designers can do comprehensive drawings of proposed products and packaging. Engineers and architects can visualize products and buildings, even to the point of simulating walkthroughs and substituting construction materials (how would that wall look with wood paneling instead of stucco?). Three-dimensional graphics can even help educators teach children about an eclipse.

If you're interested in exploring the world of 3-D graphics, be forewarned: Rendering photorealistic 3-D images takes practice, and you'll spend a lot of time twiddling your thumbs. Even a Quadra 950 packed with RAM can take hours to render a photorealistic 3-D picture, which may be many megabytes in size. The good news: With a Mac and off-the-shelf software, you can produce high-quality 3-D artwork that would have been impossible ten years ago on *any* computer. For optimum performance, you need at least a 68030-class Mac, 12MB of RAM (preferably 24MB), and *lots* of hard disk space.

The Components of 3-D

Creating a 3-D graphic has five basic steps: modeling, texturing, scene building, rendering, and (optionally) animation. Not every 3-D program does all of these things. Some packages are just modelers, some are just renderers, and some do everything except animation. Here's an overview of the components, followed by a look at how different products implement them.

Modeling (BL). The first step in 3-D graphics is to create the objects. In 3-D, everything in your scene is an object. If you're modeling a boat floating down a river, then the boat (and each of its component parts) is an object. So are the water, river banks, trees, and clouds.

Modeling tools let you create *primitives* (basic shapes such as a sphere or cube) or add a third dimension to a 2-D outline via *extrusion* (extending the outline into three dimensions) or *lathing* (spinning the outline around a central axis). Some modelers also have special warping tools that let you stretch the model's "skin" to create more curvy, organic shapes.

Most 3-D programs display a model as a *wireframe*—you only see the lines connecting the object's vertices (sort of complex chicken wire). A few modelers, such as auto•des•sys's form•Z (a professional-level program described below), let you work with solid forms rather than hollow skeletons. This means you can actually sculpt an object: Chip away at a sphere to slowly reshape it into a face.

You can save your models in a variety of formats, but if you want to transport images to other modeling programs (to take advantage of their unique strengths, perhaps), be sure your 3-D program supports the DXF file format. DXF doesn't retain features such as linking and joint information, but it's the only universal format for importing and exporting 3-D images.

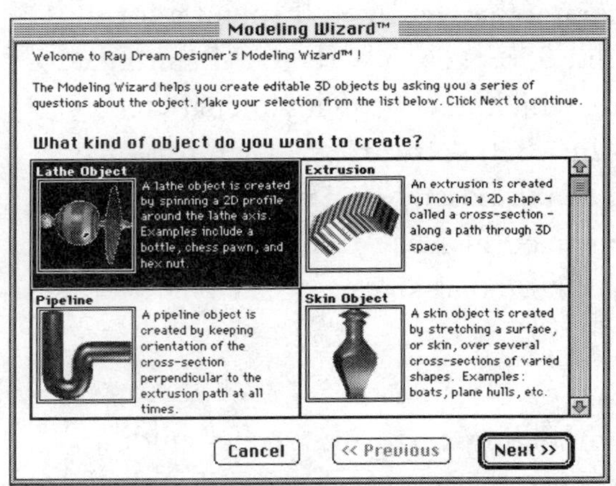

If you're a novice modeler, Ray Dream Designer's Modeling Wizard can lead you through the process of creating 3-D shapes (even complex ones). Once you've described the object you want to build, the Wizard creates it for you.

Texturing (BL). OK, you have a wireframe boat floating down a wireframe river amongst wireframe trees. Hardly photorealistic. To remedy this, you assign surface attributes (textures) to each object. For instance, you might stipulate that the boat's hull is fiberglass, the river is full of water, and the tree trunks are made of (you guessed it) wood. Assigning textures doesn't actually make the wireframe boat *look* like wood; that happens later, during the *rendering* process.

Most 3-D packages come with predefined textures—everything from granite and oak to handmade paper and reptile hide. You can also use textures from clip art collections (see "Ready-Made Patterns and Textures" on page 611) or create your own using a scanner (digitize a chunk of marble, perhaps) or paint program. Some 3-D programs even let you import QuickTime movies and place them on an object's surface.

Whatever texture you use, note that wood doesn't look like wood just because of its color. It also needs that woody texture: the grain, dents, and abrasions. To get that look and feel, 3-D programs supply a second set of images, called *bump*

Calling All CADs (AA/BL)

The high-end drawing arena is called *CAD (computer-aided design).* Primarily used by engineers, architects, and designers, CAD packages are renowned for their finely detailed drawings, high degree of precision, and steep learning curves. They supply specialized tools that let you easily create complex objects such as walls, wiring, plumbing, and circuitry. Most provide precise numerical control (called *dimensioning*) over their drawing tools, intelligent cursors (which provide constant feedback on their location and relationship to other objects), symbol and object libraries (doors, windows, cabinets, furniture, and so forth), and support for PICT and DXF files (the latter being the standard file-exchange format for CAD and 3-D programs).

CAD is generally divided into 2-D (lower-end programs used to draft blueprints and diagrams), and 3-D (high-end packages for producing complex models). If you're interested in 2-D CAD, **Blueprint** ($300, Diehl Graphsoft) is a general-purpose drafting tool that offers that unbeatable combination: excellent performance and a good price. **MacDraft** ($450, Innovative Data Design) is easier to use, albeit more expensive. **PowerDraw** ($800, Engineered Software) costs twice as much and has a frustrating interface, but it's the most versatile of the bunch, thanks to its specialized plug-in tools and Pascal-based programming language.

BARGAIN

Three-dimensional CAD programs offer even more sophisticated tools, including, of course, 3-D modeling. You'll find programming languages (for creating custom tools and applications), support for databases and spreadsheets (for generating cost estimates and shopping lists), and the ability to see your designs from various viewpoints (such as elevation or perspective). Autodesk's **AutoCAD** ($3,750) is the industry standard, offering solid-modeling capabilities that are ideal for designing engines and other mechanical contraptions. Ashlar's **Vellum** (2-D version, $2,500; 3-D version, $3,000) has an innovative, easy-to-use interface, while **MiniCad** ($800, Diehl Graphsoft) is the bargain buy, with a feature set that goes head-to-head with AutoCAD. If you need a super-specialized architectural package, we recommend **ArchiCAD** ($4,450, Graphisoft).

Want to put your ideas in perspective without spending a fortune in time and cash on a high-end program? The hottest area of CAD software is 3-D visualization, popularly called *walkthroughs.* A walkthrough program lets you create a model, such as a house, and then navigate through it simply by dragging the mouse. They're cheaper and easier to use than AutoCAD and its brethren, and although most don't offer sophisticated texturing or lighting, walkthroughs do provide a good feel for spatial design and are useful tools for client presentations. Virtus's **WalkThrough Pro** ($400) is the leader in this category, combining ease of use with fast rendering, texture mapping (add wallpaper and carpeting, say, or show a QuickTime movie on a wall), and furniture libraries. Another good choice is SketchTech's **UpFRONT** ($300), which provides excellent modeling tools and robust import/export capabilities, although its interface takes time to master.

GOOD FEATURE

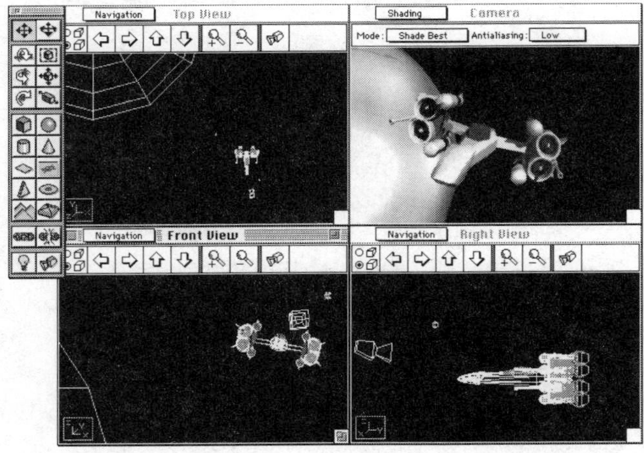

To help you position and light your 3-D models, Infini-D provides four views of the scene: top, front, and right, as well as from the viewpoint of your virtual camera. You can reposition objects by dragging them in any of the four views.

maps, that you also apply to the model's surface. The bump map tells the program which parts of a texture are higher or lower (bumpier) than other parts.

Scene building (BL). Key elements in creating realistic 3-D scenes are positioning and lighting the models and choosing your vantage point (called the *camera*). Packages for 3-D graphics offer different options for lights and cameras. Lighting choices might include Distant (mimics sunlight), Point (radiates light in all directions, like a light bulb), Spotlight (casts a cone of light onto a particular area), and colored filters. With your virtual camera you can pan, zoom, and (sometimes) switch lenses (to wide-angle, telephoto, or fish-eye).

Rendering (BL/AA). After you take a snapshot of the final scene with your virtual camera, the program will *render* (draw) the final image, adding the specified textures, shadows, reflections, and highlights to your wireframes. The renderer may also let you add effects such as depth of field or fog to blur parts of the scene that are farther away. You can render an image at various quality levels, each of which has benefits and trade-offs, so be sure your renderer supports the approach you need. *Phong shading*, for example, can create good-looking images in a reasonable amount of time, but you can't use it to make your boat cast reflections in the river. For that, you need a renderer that can perform *ray tracing*, a much slower process.

Textures, shadows, and other attributes are added to 3-D models during the rendering process. Here, a wireframe model created in Sketch is being rendered using the program's excellent ray-tracing technique.

The Ultimate Renderer (BL)

If you're serious about 3-D graphics, investigate Pixar's **MacRenderMan** (bundled with Showplace for $500, or $400 on CD-ROM). As its name implies, RenderMan is a rendering-only application, but it can achieve a photorealism that no other program can touch—and Pixar has the Oscar to prove it. If you've seen *Jurassic Park, Terminator 2,* or *The Abyss,* you've seen RenderMan's rendering techniques, called *procedural shaders,* in action. Procedural shaders are little programs that define the way light should interact with a model's surface, allowing you to generate effects ranging from stretching, flexing dinosaur skin to flowing liquid-metal cyborgs.

GOOD FEATURE

RenderMan is an application-independent, stand-alone rendering system—in fact, it works much like a PostScript printer driver. You select its renderers from the Chooser, and it uses a language, RIB (RenderMan Interface Bytestream), that's essentially PostScript for 3-D images. Several 3-D applications provide RenderMan support, including Macromedia Three-D, Swivel 3D Professional, Presenter Professional, and Pixar's own Showplace and Typestry. These programs let you apply RenderMan shaders to your 3-D models, then send the finished scene (as a RIB file) to RenderMan for output.

Because rendering the finished 3-D image can take hours (even days), you'll probably first want to do a faster, low-quality rendering to preview the scene. Three-dimensional packages also employ several strategies to speed up the rendering process. If you're on a network, several companies provide software that lets you distribute rendering tasks across several Macs; of course, each computer must have enough RAM and disk space, as well as the software. Some programs, such as Infini-D, MacRenderMan and Presenter Professional, support YARC Systems' **Zuma** board, a $3,000 RISC-based accelerator that can render images up to ten times as fast as a Quadra 950. The most economical option, however, might be to buy a Power Mac.

HOT TIP

Another way to speed up rendering is to turn off anti-aliasing, one of the most time-consuming parts of the rendering process. You can then run the finished image through Ray Dream's **JAG II**, a $130 anti-aliasing utility that smooths away rough edges in mere minutes.

Once your image is rendered, you could have a 3-D scene that's almost indistinguishable from a photograph. The completed picture can be saved as a PICT or

TIFF file, which you can then place in another program or open in an image-editing program for further touch-ups.

Animation (BL/AA). Creating three-dimensional graphics has one other, optional step: After you've built and textured your models, but before you render them, some programs let you add animation. To animate 3-D objects, you define key points in space that the objects will move through. The software then draws (or *tweens*) the in-between points to create continuous movement. Good animation software provides powerful tools for defining motion paths (Bézier curves, for example), the ability to animate an object's attributes (size, scale, texture, and so on) as well as its position, and good lighting and rendering capabilities. Optional features include motion blurs, morphing, and automatic banking and smoothing controls, which create more realistic motion when an object rounds a corner. (For more details, see "Animation," later in this chapter.) VIDI's Presenter Professional even lets you attach sounds to objects and generate acoustic effects as they move. For example, you could assign a whistle sound to a train model and place a microphone in the scene beside the tracks. As the train approaches and passes the microphone, the sound will change automatically.

Once your paths and motions are defined, it's time to render the final graphic. But remember: If your Mac requires ten minutes to render a single frame, it will take four hours to render *one second* of 24-frame-per-second animation!

Choosing a 3-D Package (BL)

As with categories of software, picking a 3-D program depends on what you want to accomplish (and what you can afford). There are excellent 3-D packages available at every price level, but if you're really *really* serious about 3-D, you're probably going to want several programs, because each 3-D program does one or two things very well or has a unique feature.

GOOD FEATURE

Entry level. An excellent starting point for the novice 3-D user, **Ray Dream Designer** (Ray Dream, $350) provides full-featured modeling and rendering—perfect for still images—but lacks an animation module. The program's Modeling Wizard lets beginning modelers easily build complex models out of simple shapes, and it has a few features 3-D veterans will appreciate. For example, it's the only program that lets you paint pictures, colors, and textures directly onto your models.

If all you want to do is create 3-D type or flying logos, **LogoMotion, StrataType**, and **Typestry** are inexpensive programs specifically designed to turn text into 3-D objects and, if you like, add special effects or animation. See Chapter 14 for details.

Midrange. If you have $700, you can choose between two popular 3-D programs, Strata's **StrataVision 3d** and Specular International's **Infini-D**. Both of these all-in-one solutions provide modeling, rendering, and animation, making them good starting points for 3-D, but they also offer enough power to do professional-quality work. StrataVision shines in modeling and rendering, while Infini-D has a more intuitive interface and better animation features, including automatic banking, smoothing, and velocity controls. Pixar's **Showplace** ($500, bundled with MacRenderMan) has reasonable scene-building and texturing features, but it's really a glorified front end for RenderMan (see "The Ultimate Renderer" on page 635).

Another $700 option is Alias Research's **Sketch!**, one of the best modelers in any price range. Besides its simple-to-learn interface and powerful tools for creating just about any shape, Sketch! also has one of the best ray-tracing renderers out there. If you're creating still images (it has no animation module)—particularly smooth, curvy, organic shapes—Sketch! is a bargain.

High end. If you're looking for a professional-level 3-D package, the best value is Strata's $1,500 **StudioPro,** which combines powerful, intuitive modeling and rendering with an excellent animation interface. The renderer has natural-media effects such as chalk and watercolor, giving you traditional-looking artwork in full 3-D. Animation effects include Explode and Atomize (for those *Lawnmower Man* jobs), and the plug-in architecture lets you add more capabilities, such as cloud generation or morphing. (For an example of the realistic results you can produce with StrataVision 3d and StudioPro, check out Myst, an awesome game reviewed in Chapter 20.)

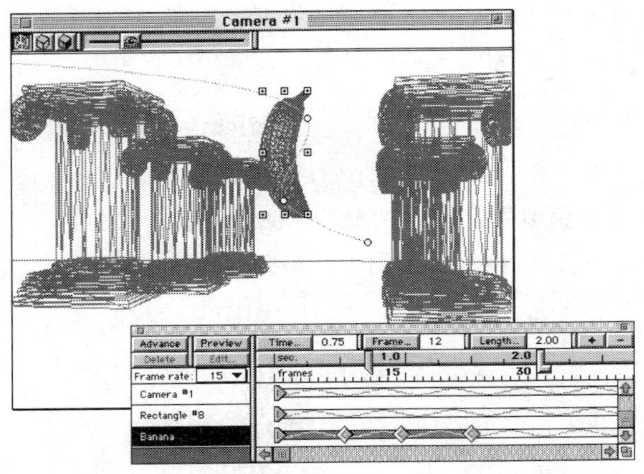

StudioPro has an excellent animation component, allowing you to create movies of 3-D objects moving, spinning, and flying. In this image, a banana is being "flown" through a scene of marble columns. Using the Animation palette, we're defining the path (the curved line) we want the banana to take by specifying key frames (the white circles) and time intervals. StudioPro will use a tweening process to generate the intervening frames.

VIDI's **Presenter Professional** ($2,000) is an excellent modeler, renderer, and animator. Its powerful sculpting tools and MacRenderMan support make it an ideal choice for professional illustrators, and, as mentioned, it's the only program that can generate sound effects based on object movement. A $1,200 sibling, **ModelerPro,** offers Presenter Pro's modeling power minus its rendering and animation modules. If you want to try your hand at solid modeling, get auto•des•sys's **form•Z** ($1,500), which has a great modeler and is easy to use.

Animation

An animation creates the illusion of motion by displaying, in rapid succession, a series of pictures (called *frames*) in which an image's position changes incrementally from one frame to the next. In *flipbook* or *card-based* animation, each frame is drawn from scratch. But since the background and other elements may not change for many frames, it's more efficient to draw each element on a separate transparent layer, called a *cel* (short for celluloid, the traditional animation medium), and only redraw those elements that change from one frame to the next.

Digital Animation (BL)

Many Mac-based animation programs imitate traditional techniques. You draw *key frames*, which show the background and characters at specific points in a scene, then define the paths the characters will take during the scene. When you're done, the software draws the intervening frames—*tweening*—to create the illusion of continuous movement.

Most animations are more complex than simply moving a shape along a path, however. If you want to animate a bird flying through the air, it's not enough to show the bird moving forward—you must show its wings flapping as well. Consequently, most programs let you assign a series of pictures—one for each wing position of the flying bird, say—to a path. The finished animation will play the images in sequence along the predefined path.

Some 3-D animation programs also can mimic film and video's tendency to blur moving objects. Study a video of a moving car, for example, and you'll see that the car is slightly blurred in each frame. In a traditional animation, however, the car would be perfectly clear in each frame, an effect called *strobing*. Programs that offer motion blurs can blur each frame based on the direction that objects are moving, producing more realistic-looking animations.

GOOD FEATURE

Programs usually save animations as PICS or QuickTime files, allowing you to use them in other applications that support those formats. PICS is the standard format for animations. QuickTime is increasingly popular, however, because it's supported by so many applications, always plays animations at the correct speed (even on slower computers), and has an Animation compressor that reduces file sizes. (For more on QuickTime's capabilities, see Chapter 17.)

While the Mac is a great tool for creating and editing animations, it isn't necessarily the optimum playback device, because it can't always get the frames onto the screen fast enough. At less than 15 frames per second, an animation will flicker. To watch animations at higher frame rates, you'll need lots of RAM and a fast Mac (either a Power Mac or one with an accelerator card). If you want to output animations on film or videotape, you'll need specialized hardware and software; see "High-End Video" in Chapter 17 for details.

Animation in Action (BL)

There are few stand-alone animation programs because most animations are created as part of videos, multimedia presentations, or 3-D graphics sequences. No matter where you find it, however, animation software can be divided into three general categories: frame-based, warping and morphing, and 3-D.

Frame-based animation. This approach most closely resembles the traditional techniques described above. Good software will have powerful paint tools (for drawing the elements in your key frames), tweening controls, and QuickTime support for output. In addition, look for an easy-to-use interface for creating and sequencing cels, as well as the ability to map out your characters' motions both over time and in relation to each other (does one character pass in front of or behind another, for example).

Animation Works ($200, Gold Disk) is one of the few programs that does nothing *but* generate animation. It has path-based animation tools for defining characters as well as *onionskinning* (the ability to trace a previous frame to create a new frame), and it is ideal if you already have multimedia or video-editing software and simply need to create animations to include in presentations or videos.

Macromedia Director ($1,200, Macromedia) is the program most commonly used for serious animation work on the Mac. If your needs are less hard-core, consider **Cinemation** ($500, Vividus), an animation-based presentation program; **MotionPaint**, part of Motion Works' $250 Multimedia Utilities package; or **ADDmotion II** ($95, Motion Works), which lets you create animations within HyperCard. For more details on these products, see "Presentations" in Chapter 17.

Morphing and warping. *Morphing* is the smooth transformation of one shape into another, like a pop star turning into a panther. *Warping* lets you stretch and distort an image as if it were made of digital Silly Putty. The increasing popularity of these special effects is partly due to the excellent morphing software now available on the Mac. For product details, see the "Video" section of Chapter 17.

Three-dimensional animation. Three-dimensional animation has been used to create everything from the dinosaurs in *Jurassic Park* to opening titles for the SuperBowl. Adding a third dimension to animation can produce more realistic results than a 2-D approach; for instance, you can usually create motion blurs and add shadows and reflections that shift with movement. To do 3-D animation, you generally need a 3-D graphics program. To get the scoop on features and products, see the "Three-Dimensional Graphics" section, above.

Clip Art

(AA)

If you don't have the time, talent, or software to create graphics from scratch, take heart: There are literally tens of thousands of predesigned images—from simple line art to full-color photographs—that you can use, royalty-free, in your publications and presentations.

If you can imagine it, there's probably clip art to cover it. Subject matter ranges from the commonplace (people, sports, business, holidays, nature, flags, transportation, food, logos, borders, backgrounds) to the specialized (medical, military, teddy bears). Some packages cover a range of subject matter; others focus on a single topic, such as maps. You likewise can choose from a variety of illustration styles, from contemporary and high-tech artwork to art deco, digital woodcuts, and Celtic designs.

Clip art comes in both bit-mapped and object-oriented file formats (TIFF, PICT, EPS), and many companies now supply color images, which also look and print just fine in black and white. The resolutions of bit-mapped images range from 72 dpi (suitable for newsletters and on-screen presentations) to 300 dpi (magazines, posters, ads). CD-ROM collections are increasingly popular because they hold more images (640MB worth) and are more convenient than piles of floppies. Due to their file sizes, stock-photography collections are available only on CD-ROM.

You can plop clip art images into your documents as-is, or you can open them in a draw or paint program and edit them to meet your needs. (EPS images are usually Illustrator files, so you can edit them.) Delete unwanted elements, select and use just one piece of an image, add or change colors—it's up to you.

A sampling of the many companies, subjects, and drawing styles available in the clip art realm is shown on the next three pages. You can also get clip art from on-line services and user groups, although it's often of lesser quality.

Clip Art Sampler

ARRO International
Series: ARROglyphs
Packages: Environment (left), $150; Wildlife (right), $70
Formats: EPS, TIFF

3G Graphics
Series: Images With Impact
Packages: Places & Faces (left), Accents & Borders 2 (right), $130 each; 6-volume series $500 on CD-ROM
Formats: EPS, PICT

Creative Media Services
Package: Megatoons Part II, $150
Formats: TIFF

C.A.R.
Series: Clipables
Packages: Clipables (left), $250; Statements (right), $130
Formats: EPS

Dream Maker Software
Series: Cliptures; MacGallery
Packages: Cliptures 4: World Flags (left), $90; MacGallery V: Holidays and Special Occasions (right), $50
Formats: EPS (Cliptures), Paint (MacGallery)

DS Design
Series: KidBAG
Package: Art by Kids, $80
Formats: EPS, TIFF

Image Club Graphics
Series: DigitArt
Packages: Celebrity Caricatures (left), $70; Sports & Leisure (right), $100; 30-volume series $800 on CD-ROM
Formats: EPS

Metro ImageBase
Packages: Metro Food CD (left), $80; Metro ImageBase on CD (right), $150
Formats: EPS, TIFF

PhotoDisc
Series: PhotoDisc
Packages: Business and Industry (left), Retro Americana (right), $300 each
Formats: TIFF, PICT, JPEG

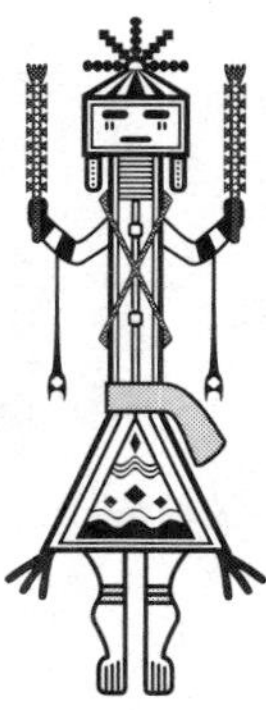

RT Computer Graphics
Package: Santa Fe Collection, $180
Formats: EPS

Totem Graphics
Series: Totem Color Clip Art
Packages: Fish (left), Domestic Animals (right), $40 each; 18-volume series $395 on CD-ROM
Formats: EPS

T/Maker Company
Series: ClickArt
Packages: Beastly Funnies (left), $50; Studio: Business Art (right), $100
Formats: EPS, PICT

Clip Art Sampler (continued)

Cartesia Software
Series: MapArt
Packages: Countries & Continents (left), U.S. States (right), $180 each; four-volume series $3280 on CD-ROM
Formats: EPS, PICT

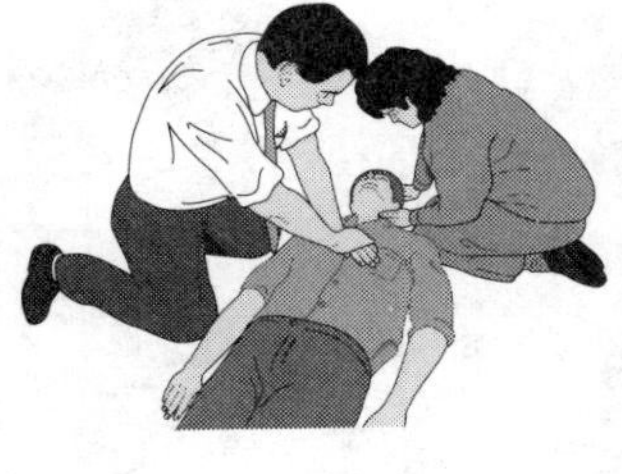

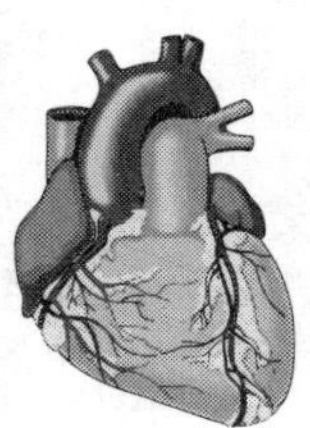

TechPool Studios
Series: LifeART
Packages: Emergency (left), $200; Super Anatomy I (right), $230
Formats: EPS, PICT

16 Page Layout

If you think of constructing a document in terms of constructing a building, then a page layout program is the construction site, and its palette of text and graphics tools would be the hammers and saws you use to shape the pieces and knock them together. Instead of cement, I-beams, and sheet rock, you're working with electronic fonts, graphics, lines, and colors.

Word processing programs handle text (with some graphics handling tossed into the best ones), and graphics programs handle pictures (though they usually include some basic text tools, too), but page layout programs are designed to handle all the elements of a document. The tools of a page layout program are designed to help you combine text, graphics, and colors in ways limited only by your imagination.

Although the most sophisticated page layout programs can handle any professional-level task they're handed, including fine typographic adjustments and color separation for offset printing, page layout programs aren't just for professional designers. Some of the most popular programs make the task of building a page as easy as dropping your own text and pictures into ready-made layouts. In this chapter, we'll talk about how to choose a page layout application that suits your needs.

Contributors

David Blatner (DB) is the chapter editor.

Randy Anderson (RA) is a Macintosh trainer and consultant in the Seattle area specializing in Multi-Ad Creator and electronic publishing.

Steve Roth (SR) is a contributing editor for *Macworld* magazine and the coauthor of several books, including *Real World Scanning and Halftones* and *Real World PageMaker* (both from Peachpit Press).

Contents

Page Layout and Desktop Publishing (DB)

Desktop publishing—the ability to lay out documents for print on a personal computer—was born in 1985, when Aldus introduced PageMaker, the first page layout program. Before that, all type for publication was set photo-mechanically at professional type shops and returned to the designer in long strips that would be cut apart and pasted on boards, which were, in turn, photographed to make film for the printing plates. As the layout evolved, the type might be reset repeatedly—sometimes at great expense. When the layout was finished, the columns of type were glued onto sheets of cardboard marked with the page dimensions—a laborious, time-consuming task.

Page layout programs changed publishing forever. Now you simply construct your document on screen, then print it out on a laser printer or imagesetter to create your final pages. No more gluing paper strips, no more messing with wax

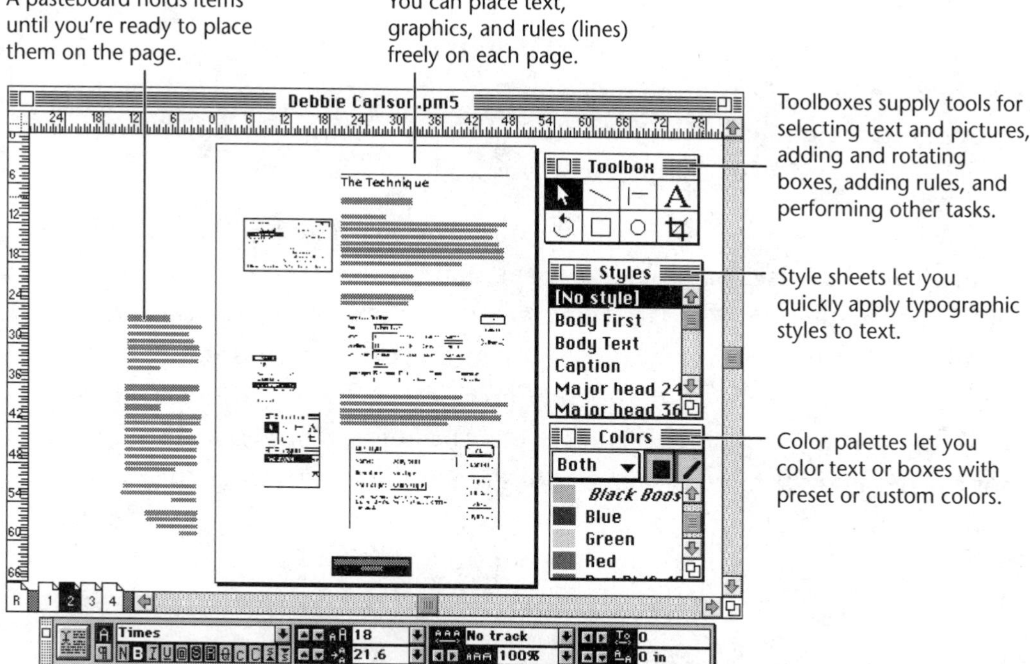

A page layout program provides tools for placing and manipulating words, pictures, and text on a page. PageMaker version 5 is shown here.

or rubber cement and T-squares. Professional-level publishing tools are no longer locked in type shops manned by a guild of specialized workers. They're right in your Mac, ready to be wielded by any designer, or editor, or anyone who cares to learn to use a program.

The Right Tool for the Job (DB)

Having lots of tools available makes work easier—if you know what to do with them. But if you don't, they just get in the way (and could even be dangerous!). If you're building a shack in the backyard, you don't need the most expensive, precision-tuned, highest-grade tools to get the job done. It's the same with page layout software. If you're putting together the company or church newsletter, you probably don't need to use the same tools as someone who's creating an ad for *Vogue* magazine or laying out a 300-page book on Renaissance art. A less expensive and easier-to-use program may do just fine.

You can think of page layout programs in three categories: design-based, suitable for commercial or graphic design use (fine carpentry); document-based, for long, often technical documents (the Trump Tower); and low-end, for small businesses or home use (that toolshed you've been wanting).

The low-end, economy packages typically cost less than $300 and are suitable for much of the basic page layout that's done today. You can easily put text, graphics, and rules on your pages and move them around. The next level—document-based applications—are ideal for businesses handling long, text-heavy documents. If you work doing documentation for Boeing or General Motors, there's a good chance that this is what you should be using. The designer page layout programs often don't handle long documents as well as the document-based programs, and they leave out some of the simpler or low-end features of the economy programs. In their place, you get high-end tools for working with color, printing, and typography.

We'll discuss each of these categories in more detail, as well as why you'd want to use them, below.

Designer Page Layout

The first programs most people think about when you say "desktop publishing" are **Aldus PageMaker** and **QuarkXPress.** They're the primary competitors in the designer version of the "battle of the stars," although we'll see later why there are also plenty of reasons to use other programs.

In this section we'll first take a hard look at QuarkXPress and PageMaker—how they're different and why you'd want to use one or the other—and then we'll look at a lesser-known program that has a lot of potential, Multi-Ad Creator.

If You're Not a Designer

(C.J. Weigand)

Having a page layout program won't make you a good designer any more than having a saw and a hammer will make you a good carpenter. When you're just getting started with page layout, the temptation is to try every trick in the book. Here, as in most of life, however, moderation may be best. The following are a few general design guidelines I've found useful:

- Mixing more than three typefaces or styles on a page is something a professional designer will do only rarely.
- Use color to set your publications apart from others, but don't be gaudy. Spot color tastefully applied might be all you need to catch a reader's eye. And in a market where color predominates, the absence of color can also be used to good effect.
- Leave plenty of white space to balance your compositions. A cluttered page is likely to be overlooked as being too "busy" to spend time with.
- Organize you message around a dominant visual element. A single large headline or graphic can help to focus your readers' attention; several will probably confuse them.
- Use subheads to break up your text and sustain interest. You can also separate large blocks of text by using well-placed pull quotes. Set them in a different font or type style from the main text.
- Additional emphasis can be given to text and graphics by accenting them with boxes or frames. Drop caps can further heighten interest but should be used sparingly.
- Design facing pages together. Two pages that look great separately can clash terribly when placed next to each other.
- Above all, be consistent. Consistency lends credibility to your message.

QuarkXPress vs. PageMaker (DB/SR)

We consistently hear rumblings about how either PageMaker or QuarkXPress is so much better or easier to learn than the other. The truth (at least the way we see it) is that this is balderdash. QuarkXPress and PageMaker used to play leapfrog regularly, with each new version jumping way ahead of its competition. Over the past few years, though, the two programs have evened out somewhat and they're now in a state of semiequilibrium. The latest versions of both (PageMaker 5.0 and Quark 3.3) let you add text, graphics, and rules to documents of any length. Both offer an amazing array of sophisticated typography, graphics, and color tools that can meet the most exacting professional standards.

GOOD FEATURE

Perhaps the biggest difference people note is that QuarkXPress has text and picture boxes, while PageMaker doesn't. We maintain that this, too, isn't quite true: PageMaker has boxes—they're just invisible! Click on a picture or block of text and you can clearly see its bounding box. Both programs have floating palettes that let you control objects on the page; both programs let you style

Editors' Poll: Which Is Better, PageMaker or Quark?

AA: PageMaker! This one of those religious issues (you tend to stick with the faith you were weaned on). For high-end users, QuarkXPress had the upper hand for a few years, but now the playing field's level. For non-high-enders, PageMaker is easier to learn and use. I love being able to load a story or picture into PageMaker's cursor and just put it anywhere I want, drawing out the "box" and placing the element at the same time.

DB: I usually don't follow trends, but when almost every major newspaper and magazine in North America uses QuarkXPress, it's hard to argue with them. I side with XPress, though I think PageMaker is more useful for some things, like indexing.

EC: PageMaker, by a long shot. I hate Quark's text and image boxes and I hate its inflexibility. PageMaker lets me do exactly what I want, in the quintessential Mac way: Just click on it and move it around. Make it bigger, make it smaller, change its color, whatever. It's completely intuitive. For me, using Quark is a punishment.

DD: To be fair, I haven't used PageMaker since about 1986. When I tried it then, though, I was really upset at some of the crazy ways it handled text. I turned to Quark, found everything I wanted, and have never looked back.

BW: I would sooner have to choose between Allah and Jehovah. I use both, depending on the project. Often, a single layout requirement will dictate which way I go.

text and offer very precise typography; and both programs enable you to create flyers, magazines, books, newsletters, and newspapers. So next time someone tells you "this one is better than that one," just walk away. Neither is inherently better. The one you choose depends more on which program has the one feature you can't do without.

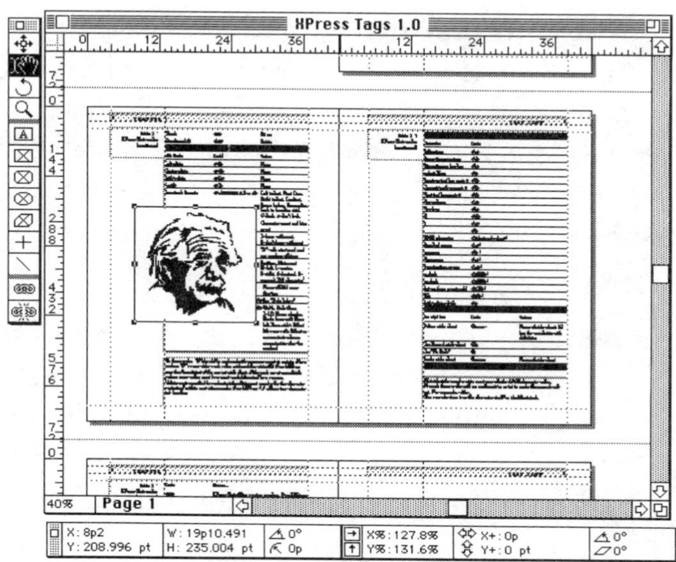

In QuarkXPress, you first create a text or picture box, either on the page or on the pasteboard area surrounding each page. You can then modify the boxes and import text and graphics into them.

That said, though, there actually are significant differences between the two programs. Because talking about how the two programs are the same doesn't really get us anywhere, we'll focus here on the sometimes subtle, sometimes obvious ways the two programs differ.

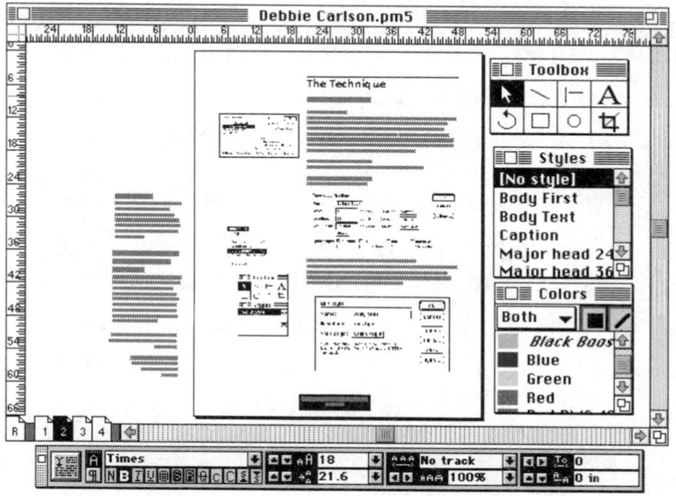

In PageMaker, graphics and text are placed directly on the page or pasteboard instead of inside boxes.

Warning: These two programs are made for professional designers, and the discussion here may seem pretty esoteric—even like gibberish—to the uninitiated. We've tried to explain terms as we use them here, but if you're in above your head, keep reading. You may feel more at home with the low-end packages described later in the chapter.

The workspace. In QuarkXPress you can see as many pages at once as will fit in the window, and each page or spread has its own pasteboard (an area you can use to temporarily store elements you haven't placed yet). In PageMaker, you view one spread at a time, and the pasteboard is common to all pages. Each program also has a Library palette for storing items common to a number of pages, which you can use as a document-wide—or even a multi-document-wide—pasteboard.

Building pages. Quark-XPress pages consist of text and picture boxes (plus rules)—you draw a box and then fill it with text or a graphic. PageMaker page elements seem to be different but are actually quite similar. You don't have to create picture or text boxes before you add pictures or text in PageMaker, an approach that some people think makes PageMaker simpler and more intuitive.

GOOD FEATURE

XPress's text-box approach allows for multiple-column text boxes; you change the number of columns in a dialog box, and the text reflows accordingly—a tiresome task in PageMaker.

GOOD FEATURE

Templates. PageMaker's templates are ingenious little scripts that create publications (including style sheets) based on dialog box selections (page size, label template, etc.). Surprisingly, XPress's few in-the-box templates are for special purposes and lack style sheets (preset text formats), so they aren't of much use.

Palettes, tools, and controls. Both programs have a floating palette that lets you precisely modify elements on your page, such as object placement, text formatting, picture formatting, and so on. PageMaker's Control Palette has leapfrogged XPress's Measurements Palette, offering more flexible control, in addition to both character *and* paragraph text formatting (yes—paragraph styles are available from the palette).

Both programs let you create libraries of objects, images, and text. However, in PageMaker's Library Palette you can search by keyword, description, and author name, and you can import libraries from Aldus Fetch, an image-archiving program (see Chapter 15). XPress's Library doesn't provide the searching (you can only select by the items' names), but you can have multiple libraries open.

Color: The Final Frontier (DB/DD)

One of the most important differences between the designer-level page layout programs and the others is the ability to handle color for offset printing (printing on a printing press rather than a desktop color printer). Here is a guide to some of the issues.

Color Separation
On a printing press, each color is printed separately. To create color for printing, a page layout program must be able to separate the colors onto separate pages for output. Those separations are usually printed to film, from which the different printing plates can be made.

Spot vs. Process Color
How the colors are separated depends on whether they will be printed with *process color* or *spot color.* Spot color is printed with an ink of the specified color, in a single pass through the press, and is generally used when the document includes just one or two colors, for decoration. You typically choose spot colors out of a swatch book, such as a Pantone Matching System (PMS) book, and some page layout programs include on-line versions of the Pantone and other color matching system palettes for easy color specification.

With process color, all colors are created by printing the image with different tints of four colors: cyan, magenta, yellow, and black (CMYK). Process color is more economical to use when the piece you're printing includes more than four colors, and it is always used to print color photographs.

Trapping
When paper is flying through the printing press, it often gets misregistered, and each color isn't printed exactly where it should be. This can cause gaps at the edges between colors where the white paper shows through (read: "really ugly"). *Trapping* is the process of slightly overlapping colors at their edges so that when misregistration occurs, there won't be an ugly gap. This is an area that even the best page layout programs haven't really mastered yet. Even though some programs (like QuarkXPress) let you trap from within the program, the best solution is often to have the service bureau that outputs the job take care of the trapping for you.

Pages and master pages. In XPress you can view and scroll through multiple spreads (and spreads can include more than two pages), drag pages between documents, view thumbnails, and easily rearrange page order (this is possible—though very slow—with PageMaker's Sort Pages Addition (see the box "XTensions and Additions," below). Also, QuarkXPress offers 127 master spreads per document, compared to PageMaker's one. Each master page can be a template for a type of page in your document. For instance, your table of contents can be based on a TOC master page, your opening spread can be based on

GOOD FEATURE

XTensions and Additions (DB/SR)

Both PageMaker and QuarkXPress let you add functionality by adding plug-in modules (PageMaker uses "Additions," XPress uses "XTensions"). Some of these modules are free (PageMaker comes with a whole mess of them), though most cost between $20 and $300. Some specialized XTensions cost even more than the program itself. (You can get a catalog of XTensions, as well as the XTensions themselves, from XChange, a Colorado-based cooperative.)

Although similar on the surface, Aldus Additions are ultimately less powerful than Quark XTensions. Some XTensions fundamentally change XPress's feature set (for instance, SketchPad, which adds full drawing tools—including Bézier curves and putting text on a curve). With some well-implemented exceptions, Additions are often more like sophisticated macros à la QuicKeys, but with dialog boxes. For example, the Bullets and Numbering Addition simply sets indents and types characters, with no real intelligence.

This discrepancy is partly due to the paucity of third-party Additions developers (PageMaker started using Additions only a year or so ago; Quark had a head start of several years). But it's also due to PageMaker's underlying technology for Additions, which doesn't give programmers the flexibility that Quark does with its XTensions. Additions all reside in a big list on the Additions menu, for instance, while XTensions can add to or modify any menu or dialog box.

the Opening Spread master page, and so on. You can edit master items on document pages in XPress, and control whether they're replaced when you apply a different master page to a document page.

Measurements, rulers, and guides. In almost every instance, XPress offers finer measurement increments than does PageMaker—often ludicrously fine. However, more important, in QuarkXPress you can use arithmetic operators (+, -, /, and *) and mixed measurement systems (3p5+1cm, for instance) in all the palettes' dialog boxes. In PageMaker you can use only + and –, and those only in the Control Palette, and you can't mix measurement systems.

On the other hand, in PageMaker you can specify a custom vertical ruler increment, and objects and guides will snap to ruler increments—both great when you're working with grids based on leading.

GOOD FEATURE

Long documents. If you spend much time producing longer, text-intensive documents, PageMaker is the hands-down choice in this category (see also "Handling Long Documents: FrameMaker," later in this chapter). It gives more options for importing and appending styles, and its style sheets don't wipe out local formatting as easily as XPress's do. It also creates tables of contents for multiple documents, renumbers pages for multiple consecutive documents, and it has the best indexing system I have ever seen. QuarkXPress can create indexes and tables of contents with an XTension (which will cost you another $100 or so), but not as elegantly as PageMaker.

Objects and object relationships. With QuarkXPress's box-oriented approach, you can create oval and polygonal graphic containers. PageMaker only supports cropping pictures with rectangles. (If you want a polygon in PageMaker, you have to draw it in an illustration program and import it.) XPress's other object formatting features—especially graduated fills—put it well ahead of PageMaker in this category. XPress also creates editable wraps around irregular shapes—such as circles or pictures—automatically. In PageMaker you have to create and resize irregular text wraps manually.

QuarkXPress's Group command groups items so that they act as a unit when you move or otherwise manipulate them. PageMaker groups items via an Addition, converting the objects to EPS (slowly—it can take more than 30 seconds to group two objects on a Quadra 650). Ungrouping the text and graphic items is possible (which is sort of amazing, when you stop and think that they're EPS files), but grouping eradicates text wrap settings and breaks links (permanently) between threaded text blocks. Plus, you can't edit items within the group, as you can with XPress. And, to top it all off, color objects in PageMaker get turned into black and white unless you have a color printer selected in the Print dialog box when you run the group addition.

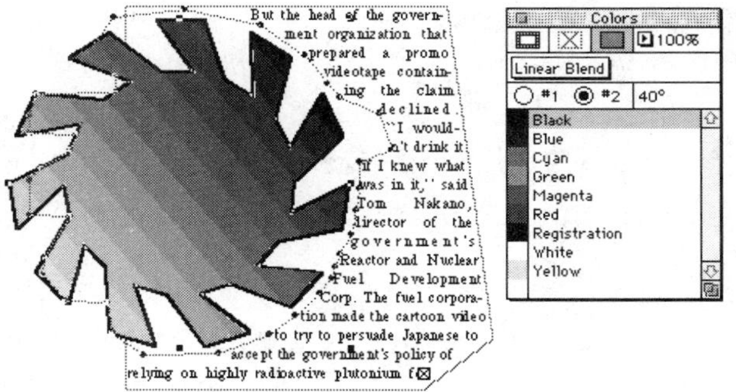

QuarkXPress's ability to create graduated blends, polygons, and manual text around polygons make it a powerful design tool.

PageMaker's inability to automatically align items (a feature available in MacDraw since 1985) is just plain ridiculous. XPress provides comprehensive controls for aligning objects or distributing them evenly across a space.

On the other hand, PageMaker has the added benefit of letting you wrap text on both sides of a picture; QuarkXPress doesn't.

Anchored objects. Anchoring boxes (also known as "inline graphics") is a way to attach graphics and/or blocks of text to a certain spot in the text so that they flow along with the text as changes are made. The way QuarkXPress handles its boxes means you can use inline text boxes in addition to inline graphics (which PageMaker also supports). In XPress you can automatically align anchored boxes to either the baseline or the cap height, which you can't manage as easily with PageMaker.

Word processing. While XPress's word processing feature list looks more impressive on the surface, PageMaker's Story Editor—a pop-up window displaying text in an easy-to-read format—makes editing much faster and more convenient. It opens a separate text window in which you can make your changes without waiting for the text to reflow with each new line. Both programs insert curly quotes for you while you're typing, but XPress offers five methods for different languages.

Both programs offer reasonable filters for importing and exporting text to and from Mac word processors, but PageMaker also includes filters for PC word processors. The XPress Tags filter is great for transferring and manipulating fully formatted text using straight text coding. It's far superior to PageMaker's Smart ASCII and Rich Text Format (RTF) filters.

Typography. QuarkXPress has long been known as a typographic powerhouse, but the truth is that both programs are quite powerful and impressive in this department. On the other hand, there are a few niggling little points that drive us crazy. Drop caps, for example. QuarkXPress's drop cap feature is easy and powerful. PageMaker comes with a crude Addition for creating drop caps that has two big problems: line-ending hyphens disappear, and if you edit the paragraph, line breaks get all messed up.

And, while QuarkXPress has the lead in kerning ability (PageMaker has a relatively coarse kerning increment), PageMaker definitely pulls ahead in tracking. It provides five editable tracking levels per font, applicable on the paragraph level. XPress offers one editable track per font, applicable on the document level.

QuarkXPress has a bunch of other cool typographic features, too. For instance, the Indent to Here character (type ⌘\) indents the rest of the paragraph to the Indent character's position. And the (wonderful) automatic ligature generation replaces fi and fl characters with ligatures (like those shown here), breaking them into separate characters when letterspacing increases beyond a specified amount. See Chapter 14, "Fonts," for more on tracking, kerning, and ligatures.)

Windows versions. Both programs are available on the (shudder!) Windows platform, and both let you move documents between the two platforms relatively easily. And, although there are some issues surrounding consistency of fonts and graphics, most of the problems have fortunately been worked out.

Support. Both Quark and Aldus offer 90 days of free support (but you pay for the call). Quark starts the clock when you register the product, but Aldus only starts counting after your first call, and unlike Quark, Aldus also offers another 30 days of free support after you upgrade. After your time runs out, Quark offers a single month of tech support for $25, and Aldus offers a 900 line ($15 per call). Both companies also offer a year of tech support—for a price: $150 per year for Quark, $100 for PageMaker. Aldus also offers a few extras under the one-year plan: It picks up the toll charges, sends you minor program updates automatically, and gives you a 25 percent discount on major upgrades. Under Aldus's $179 Premier plan, you get the year of toll-free support and a 40 percent discount on upgrades.

Quark sends you its helpful *XPressions* newsletter only if you pony up for the one-year plan. You get the really great *Aldus Magazine* for free, as soon as you register your copy of PageMaker.

Which one's for you? There's no doubt about it: You can produce consummately professional publications of almost any type with either PageMaker or QuarkXPress. The differences lie in how easily you can produce those documents.

And Keep an Eye Out For... (DB)

THINGS TO COME

Just before I finished this chapter, I saw two programs that I had to at least mention here: **Viva Press Professional** and **3B2**. These are both dark horses, could-be contenders in the high-end page layout market. Viva Press Professional (VPP) is from TechWare in Germany and at the time of this writing is only being distributed in the United States by Interpress Technologies in New York. 3B2 is from Advent in the U.K., and is distributed in the U.S. by XyVision. Both handle color separations, tables of contents, index generation, and object grouping—in some cases better than any other program.

GOOD FEATURE

VPP has all the makings of strong competition for PageMaker and QuarkXPress. It uses palettes for document pages, style sheets, and object formatting like other programs. However, it also has some really innovative features, such as aliases (objects or pages that are linked to other objects or pages; change the original, and all the aliases change, too), object guides (any object can be a guide), and Bézier curve drawing tools. You can impose your pages for printing directly in the program and create style sheets for pictures, lines, paragraphs, and even words or characters (most other programs only let you create paragraph styles).

As of this writing (mid-'94) Viva Press Professional is clearly a 1.0 program with a lot of room to improve. However, if TechWare continues to upgrade its product regularly, there's little doubt that you'll be hearing more about this program.

If you come from a traditional typesetting background, you should take a serious look at Advent/XyVision's 3B2. This program is a feature-packed powerhouse, but the user interface is horrendously complicated (of course, like everything, once you get familiar with it, it's not so bad). It's especially powerful for longer documents (see "Handling Long Documents: FrameMaker," below). In fact, perhaps the best reason to work with 3B2 is its cross-platform compatibility with PCs (there's a DOS—not Windows—version) and Unix systems.

There have been several good programs from overseas that failed in the United States, but their failures are typically the result of marketing and distribution problems. Whether these two can cut it remains to be seen.

For longer and more text-intensive documents, PageMaker's superior style sheets and book tools give it the edge. For more design-intensive work (brochures, ads, fliers), XPress's grouping, locking, alignment, and distribution tools make it a better choice. In its latest version, PageMaker handles color EPS files and the mechanics of color separation better (making it a good choice for production work), while XPress has EfiColor color management (a plus for design work and if you want to separate RGB files directly).

Multi-Ad Creator

(RA)

If your needs go beyond laying out single-page designs, you can skip this section entirely. On the other hand, if you'd love to have the ultimate single-page design and layout program, read on. **Multi-Ad Creator** (from Multi-Ad Services, $1000) is probably the best-kept secret in professional Macintosh publishing software. While it's used by a zillion newspapers, magazines, and in-house ad departments, Multi-Ad's marketing is so bad that most people still don't know about this very cool program.

GOOD FEATURE

Multi-Ad Creator is clearly designed to make ads, but you could make any one-page piece with it. Let's look at some of the features (I can only touch on my personal favorites for lack of space). First of all, importing graphics is a snap, either with a command key shortcut—no special bounding boxes needed—or by grabbing them from a floating palette that lists files. You can easily make 1-bit TIFFs transparent or colorized. Then, you can make an automask for any imported image—quickly blocking out areas of an image you don't want to see or act upon with a command. Multi-Ad creator also has an automask feature that can trace areas in an image automatically.

Multi-Ad Creator can handle only single pages, but boy, can it handle those. It includes some of the best graphics and file-handling tools of any page layout program available.

Integrated Page Layout for Businesses: RagTime (DB)

RagTime, a page layout program in an integrated package, made a big hit in Europe, but for some reason Americans never got too interested in it. I don't know why, because it's really a pretty cool program that more people should know about.

RagTime is not really design-oriented—it gives you little control over typography and color—and at a list price of $600 it doesn't fit into the home-business or economical-package category. It's not really designed for long, text-heavy documents, either. It's really a business page layout program, suitable for interoffice memoranda, notices to investors, or even a business newsletter.

RagTime lets you create spreadsheets, graphs, pictures, and text on the same page, without ever leaving the program. Then you can link them all together. For example, you might have a spreadsheet on one page that lists inventory prices and cost of sales figures. Then you could link those numbers to the text on another page so that when you change the spreadsheet, the numbers in the text would also change. Same thing goes for the dynamic graphs. In fact, you can even link text to a spreadsheet in another document on your hard drive.

Because RagTime is not well known, you often have to get information about it directly from its North American distributor in Canada, MacVONK (what a name!). (Ragtime is also covered as an integrated package in Chapter 12.)

If you don't like how the mask turned out, you can use the Edit Mask floating palette; it contains sophisticated pen tools like FreeHand and Illustrator. You can even mask an image with a polygon or a starburst (Multi-Ad Creator's Starburst tool has no peer, even among drawing programs).

But wait—there's more! If you can't find your linked graphics on disk, you can tell the program to go find them for you. Or, you could use the accompanying program, Multi-Ad Search. This database lets you keep all your graphics and Multi-Ad Creator documents organized—a must if you're surrounded by thousands of files. You can use Search's thumbnail images to find something, or, even better, you can use its sophisticated searching features.

GOOD FEATURE

Text handling is incredibly powerful. Especially so are Multi-Ad Creator's style sheets. They are beyond—far beyond—anything you've ever seen, including not only character styles, but also algorithmic styles ("the first line of the paragraph should be in Helvetica, then change to Palatino; put a Zapf Dingbats bullet at the beginning of the paragraph;" and so on).

Multi-Ad Creator's printing and color control is also high end, giving you precise control over color separations. Perhaps best of all, you can export your entire ad (or just a portion of it) as an EPS or DCS (separated EPS) file so that you can bring it into your larger multipage layout program.

Trying to describe all of Multi-Ad Creator's features in a piece this long is just plain cruel. Instead, if this is something that might make your life better, try a demo version (just write to Multi-Ad at the address in Appendix D).

Handling Long Documents: FrameMaker

(DB/SR)

If you're not trying to create a fancy design but rather are attempting to present a lot of content (text and graphics) in a straightforward form, you probably want to look into a document-based program. On the Mac, this category belongs to **FrameMaker,** from Frame Technology.

If you've struggled with long documents in Microsoft Word, PageMaker, or QuarkXPress, you'll find FrameMaker a joy to use. You can use it for short documents and brochures, but it's not really designed for that. It's set up for documents that have a pretty consistent layout from page to page. It can handle graphics and rules, but it doesn't have the typographic and graphics-oriented bells and whistles that PageMaker or QuarkXPress have.

For long but relatively simple documents like technical manuals or in-house guides, you really need something more like an exalted word processor than a page layout program. FrameMaker fits the bill. At $800 it does a *lot* more than Word, but using it feels more like word processing than page layout: Its talents are geared more toward handling words than pictures.

FrameMaker's built-in word processor has an excellent spelling checker, extensive find-and-replace features, automatic index and table of contents generation, footnotes, and so on. FrameMaker has the best table-handling of any Mac program I've seen, plus unique features like automatic cross-referencing and conditional text (that is, *insert if...*, which lets you include or exclude certain text and different versions of a document, if, for example, you're doing documentation for a product that has two slightly different versions). It's also got a very impressive equation editor, for doing things like math texts.

GOOD FEATURE

Also, because FrameMaker is available on so many different platforms—including Windows—it's also great for large corporations that need to move documents around among Macs, PCs, and Unix-based systems. You can even use a Reader utility to read FrameMaker files over networks or on CD-ROMs.

Once you've learned the program, it's easy to use, and it's also well documented in a reference guide. The information is not organized well for *learning* the program, though. And, unfortunately, I haven't yet found a good book on FrameMaker to recommend to beginners.

"It's the Economy, Stupid" (DB/SR)

In the industry, we tend to call this last type of page layout program "low-end," but perhaps a better term would simply be "inexpensive," because these applications are often incredibly powerful and up to many everyday page layout tasks. Let's take a quick look at each of these programs and why you might want to consider using them.

Ready, Set, Go!

We've always thought that the arguments people get into over whether PageMaker or QuarkXPress is better are rather silly. Ultimately, it becomes sort of a religious preference. But we didn't know the extent of religious preference until we met people who use **Ready, Set, Go!** This impressive page layout program has appeared under two names: Ready, Set, Go! and

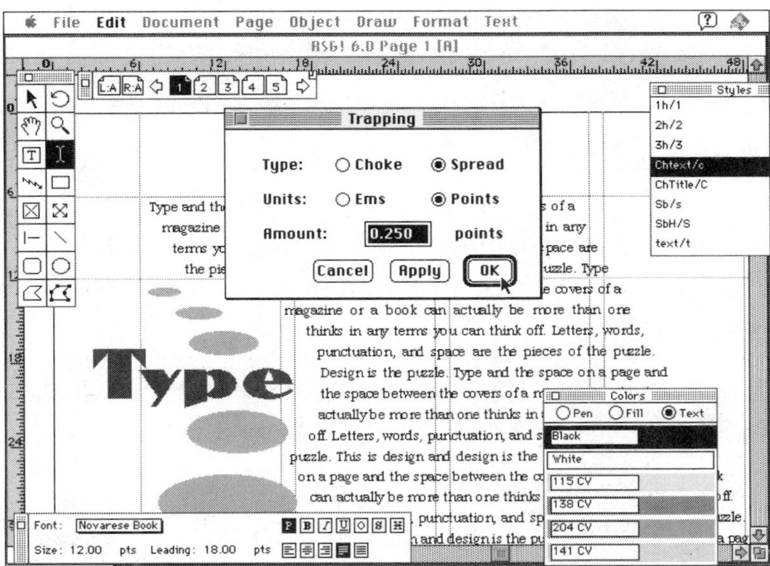

Ready, Set, Go! offers a full complement of designer page layout tools at an economy price.

DesignStudio. Letraset sold it for awhile, but now Manhattan Graphics—the original developers—have taken the product back.

Users of Ready, Set, Go! appear to be incredibly happy with it, but I can't tell whether it's because they love the program or they're happy that they got such a powerful program for such a low price. In fact, Ready, Set, Go! offers almost all the functionality of PageMaker or QuarkXPress but at only half the price (it retails for only $400, and if you have a previous version of the program you can upgrade for between $70 and $90, depending on which version you own).

RSG is customizable in a number of ways. If you want a pasteboard, you can have it; if you want a toolbar, you can get one. The word processing features are great (many people write documents within RSG instead of a word processor), and the graphics capabilities are strong. You can rotate, scale, and crop graphics and text in various ways, and then make the text run around a picture automatically. You can even make text boxes in strange shapes.

Manhattan Graphics implemented style sheets in RSG on a character level but not on a paragraph level, which makes using them somewhat nonintuitive if you're used to programs such as Microsoft Word, PageMaker, or QuarkXPress. Plus, they've included a very powerful tab feature (though it's rather difficult to figure out, and the documentation doesn't help much). Then there are the bells and whistles, such as gradient fills and QuickTime support. RSG also handles

GOOD FEATURE

color very well; you can do separations of both process and spot colors. RSG also offers free technical support on a toll-free line (if you're calling from the United States), so if you're stumped they can probably help you quickly and cheaply.

Perhaps the biggest problem with the program is that it's not supported by consultants, service bureaus, and trainers as widely as is PageMaker or QuarkXPress. Service bureaus are often not familiar with it, so they don't like supporting it; training is difficult to find; and even finding other users to talk about the program with can be a chore.

Ready, Set, Go! is clearly not a perfect program, but there's no doubt that if you're making magazines, brochures, or newsletters on a budget, it's one you should look at.

PublishIt! Easy (SR/DB)

Many people refer to **PublishIt! Easy** (TimeWorks, $200) as the Swiss Army knife of desktop publishing, and since it includes robust tools for page layout, text editing, drawing, and painting, that moniker is appropriate.

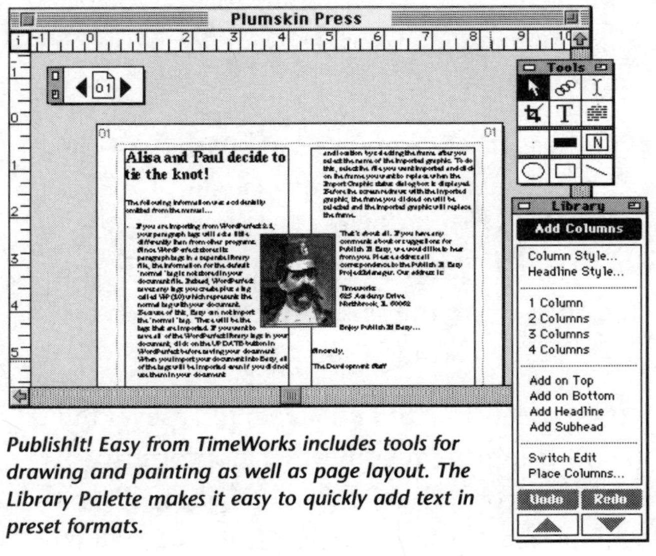

PublishIt! Easy from TimeWorks includes tools for drawing and painting as well as page layout. The Library Palette makes it easy to quickly add text in preset formats.

There's good text editing (including a relatively robust Find/Change), spell-checking, and even a thesaurus. Text formatting includes most of the controls that casual users need, plus some nice extras, such as automatic and manual kerning (only in full-point increments). Although hyphenation is a batch process—you have to select the text you want hyphenated and use the Insert Hyphens command—it's quite speedy and pretty smart.

PublishIt! Easy's tools for offset printing are not powerful: Color options are limited, and color separation is nowhere to be found.

More than anything, Publish-It! Easy stands out for its interactiveness. It's great for casual users who often find themselves trying things out on the page. As you resize a text frame, for instance, the text reflows inside the frame interactively—it doesn't wait for you to release the mouse button (very cool). Most of its dialog boxes let you see the results of your changes before you click OK in close the box. And several palettes make it easy to get at the profuse number of tools.

So what's wrong with PublishIt! Easy? Not a whole lot, especially considering the low (and often heavily discounted) price. There are limitations—like its restriction to integral point sizes—that aren't a great problem for general business or home users, but some other things are more than annoying. For instance, there are no style sheets (something we use every day).

One of the great things about this program is how small it is. The whole thing weighs in at under 300K on disk (plus space for the dictionary, thesaurus, and so on). This makes it not only easy to use even on a pared-down system, but also quite fast to run. This program is more than enough to keep most nonprofessional page makers very happy.

Aldus Home Publisher (SR/DB)

When Aldus Corporation—the creators of PageMaker—bought Silicon Beach Software a few years ago, one of the properties the company picked up was a page layout program called **Personal Press,** designed for beginning and occasional page makers. Now, Aldus has bundled Personal Press along with a bunch of templates, TrueType fonts, clip art, and "specialty" paper—in a package called **Aldus Home Publisher** for $50.

One notable interface innovation is Personal Press's use of proxies. Almost every dialog box lets you see a representation of the changes you're making on the actual text or graphic you're working on, so you can try things out before you click OK. Another innovation is the facility for placing Notes that contain the date, time, and any remarks you want to pass on to your workgroup cohorts. You can hide or show the Notes and print them out as well.

There are other cool features, too, like an Equals tool that makes two objects the same size and shape, and a Replicate function with options for replicating a page element a given number of times.

Text is handled relatively well—you can either type directly on the page or import text into a text box—and there's a well-designed spelling checker and thesaurus to polish your prose. On the other hand, the type formatting controls are rudimentary, which is perhaps to be expected in a low-end page layout program. You can specify a number of typographic settings, but there's no automatic kerning, which would be an obvious way to help novice users create good-looking publications.

And although you can apply a wide variety of line and fill patterns, you can't specify a simple percentage tint or a line thickness smaller than 1 point, which almost guarantees that publications will look amateurish.

Personal Press's AutoCreate feature is designed to let novices build documents quickly based on the provided templates. A separate manual describes the templates ("you need four stories and three graphics for this newsletter"), and you just choose the text and graphics to fill the boxes. Personal Press then builds the publication, pulling the files into the template. The templates have one key flaw, however: They don't include style sheets (and even if they did, style sheets in Personal Press don't include paragraph formats). So once you've flowed the text in, you're on your own for spec'ing the type.

If I were choosing between Aldus Home Publisher and PublishIt! Easy, I would definitely opt for the latter. PublishIt! Easy may not have style sheets or come with clip art and paper samples, but it's generally easier to use and has a more snazzy design.

Books and Magazines (DB)

No one ever learns all this desktop publishing stuff by themselves. Hiring a consultant, a trainer, or attending classes is usually my first recommendation. But there are two problems with that tack. First, classes take time and money (sometimes lots of both). Second, your teacher can't be there for you at 11 p.m. on the night before your deadline. So here's a list of just a few publications that you might find helpful when you need an all-night consultant.

Books

Roger Parker's *Looking Good in Print* ($25, Ventana) does a good job of covering design essentials, offers help in selecting typefaces, and provides hints for effective use of the tools of the trade. Lots of graphics make it a quick read.

The 208 pages of *Gray Book* ($25, Ventana) are crammed with clear, detailed, and relatively sophisticated discussions of contrast, lighting, shading, scanning, and many other important topics for people working in black and white. Plus it contains lots of terrific illustrations.

Real World PageMaker ($28, Random House) was originally written by Steve Roth and Olav Martin Kvern, and the newest edition added Bruce Fraser to the list. This is the first must-have book if you're using PageMaker. It covers *why* PageMaker works the way it does, more than simply how.

Robin Williams's renowned *PageMaker Easy Reference Guide* is being updated (with the help of Barbara Sikora) for PageMaker 5 and renamed *Peachpit's PageMaker 5 Companion (Peachpit Press, $35).* The last version of this book was packed with every tidbit you'd ever need to know about PageMaker. The new version should also be a must-have.

I'm a little biased about *The QuarkXPress Book* ($30, Peachpit Press) because I wrote it. However, I really do think it's the best reference book on QuarkXPress out there, and Quark agrees with me—they even use it to train their technical support staff!

I also wrote the *Desktop Publisher's Survival Kit* ($23, Peachpit Press), which covers a lot of the material that you already have in your hands (plus even more) and focuses on the essential information you need to know to be efficient in desktop publishing.

Magazines

Publish is the most well-known desktop publishing magazine, though I often find it less useful than others. It's the kind of magazine that you can usually pick one or two gems out of every issue, making it worth the subscription price.

If you own and register any Aldus product, you already have a subscription to *Aldus Magazine*. This little monthly is packed with goodies, from basic information to power-user tips and tricks. Unfortunately, it only talks about Aldus products, such as PageMaker and FreeHand.

ThePage is a handsome almost-monthly newsletter from The Cobb Group that does a good job of covering the field. However, at $70 per year, the subscription price is a bit steep.

PageMaker and QuarkXPress Tips

Seeing what you're moving (DB). When you drag something in QuarkXPress or PageMaker, what you see is an outline of the item; when you stop dragging and let go of the mouse, the item itself appears in the new position. But when you're trying to align something carefully, that just isn't good enough. However, if you hold down the mouse button for about half a second (until the cursor flashes once), you can actually see the object move instead of just a box.

Grabber hands (DB). One of the coolest subtle features of both PageMaker and QuarkXPress is the grabber hand. Instead of clicking on the scroll bars all the time to move around your document, hold down the Option key while clicking and dragging somewhere on your page. A little hand icon appears and moves your page in the direction that you're dragging. This seems like a really little feature, but it speeds up life a lot!

Selecting through objects (Byron Brown). When you have elements lying on top of one another, you often need to click through one to get to the object below. In PageMaker, you can Cmd-click to grab though the top item. In QuarkXPress, you use Cmd Option Shift-click. In either program, the first time you click you move one layer down, the second time you move another layer down, and so on. Once a buried item is selected, you can bring it to the top using Bring to Front, or you can move it out of the way by giving it a different origin in the Measurements/Control palette. In QuarkXPress, you can then press the F5 key for Bring to Front and Shift F5 for Send to Back; Option F5 is Bring Forward a layer, and Shift Option F5 is Send Backward a layer.

Copying paragraph formats (DB). In QuarkXPress you can copy all the paragraph attributes of one paragraph to another by first putting the cursor in the new paragraph (the one you want to copy *to*), then Shift Option-clicking on the old one (the paragraph you want to copy *from*). Tabs, indents, and even style sheets are copied.

Shrinking PageMaker files (SA/AN). PageMaker files get bigger as you work on them. That's because the program *appends* changes to the existing file when you save, rather than replacing it with the new, edited version. You can often cut the size of a PageMaker file in half (or more) by choosing Save As instead of Save from the File menu. When you Save As with the same file name, the old file is completely replaced by the current one, ridding yourself of all those old appendages and reducing the file size.

Returning from the Story Editor (EC). To enter the Story Editor in PageMaker, triple click any text block or press ⌘E.

The way in which you leave the Story Editor determines what you see when you get back to layout view. If you type ⌘W or click the close box to leave the Story Editor, you'll return to the page you were in when you entered the Story Editor, that is, the page you see behind the Story Editor window. But if you select Edit Layout from the Edit menu, you'll go to the place in the layout that contains the insertion point.

Viewing the whole pasteboard (EC). If you want to see the whole page at one time, you select Fit in Window from the View menu of either PageMaker or QuarkXPress. However, if you want to see the whole page, the spread, and even the surrounding pasteboard, you can hold down a modifier key while selecting Fit in Window. In PageMaker you hold down Shift; in QuarkXPress, you hold down Option.

Finding and changing more than one character style (EC). Did you know that in PageMaker you can look for more than one character style (bold, italic, etc.) at a time using the Find dialog box? Just select the first style and then select the second. When you let go of the mouse button, you'll see one of the styles with a plus sign, indicating that there is more than one style selected. To deselect either style without deselecting all of them, click it. To deselect all of the styles, select Any from the pop-up menu.

Automatically deselecting objects (DB). You can deselect any object or objects in QuarkXPress 3.3 by pressing Tab when the Item tool is selected. I find this really helpful, especially when you're zoomed in and you can't find a blank spot on the page to click on. In PageMaker, there's no auto-deselect command,

but you can do the same thing by typing ⌘ Spacebar, which switches to the Pointer tool and deselects everything.

Moving files between platforms (DB). If you need to move either graphic files or documents between the Macintosh and Windows, you should typically use the lowest common denominators for everything. That means, use PC EPS and TIFF files (most graphic programs on the Macintosh can write them). And all your file names should be eight-dot-three (eight letters or numbers, followed by a period, followed by a three-letter extension). For example, you could use 8LTRBLUS.TXT.

17 Multimedia

MULTIMEDIA—THAT SEDUCTIVE BLENDING of graphics, sound, video, animation, and text—isn't just a buzzword anymore. The reality is all around us, in attention-grabbing business presentations, in interactive kiosks at shopping malls, in the latest CD-ROM games, and in electronic encyclopedias that take us on guided tours of the Louvre or teach us about Mozart's music.

Multimedia isn't just the domain of high-end professionals, either. A plethora of Mac-based software lets even fledgling computer users take advantage of multimedia's promise. Businesses can produce on-screen slide shows, complete with sound and video, and computer-based training systems. Schools can use multimedia tools for class projects and interactive learning applications. Individuals can create concert-quality music performances and digital home movies.

In this chapter, we'll explore three key components of multimedia: sound, music, and video. Then we'll look at the latest in presentation programs and authoring tools, which let you pull all the pieces together into a multimedia extravaganza.

Contributors

Aileen Abernathy (AA) is the chapter editor.

Christopher Breen (CB) is a San Francisco Bay Area musician by night. By day he's a contributing editor to *MacUser*.

Shelley Cryan (SC) runs a consulting business in New York and writes frequently about presentation software for computer publications.

Michael Feerer (MF), an award-winning architect and Mac consultant based in the Pacific Northwest, is the author of *Premiere with a Passion* (Peachpit Press), a guide to Adobe Premiere.

Michael D. Murie (MM), a multimedia consultant based in Massachusetts, is the author of *The QuickTime Handbook* and *Macintosh Multimedia Workshop,* both published by Hayden Books.

Contents

The Multimedia Machine (AA)

"I'm glad to be out of that bag!"

The Macintosh has come a long way since those words were uttered by the 128K Mac during its introduction. But even in 1984, the Mac had some of the primary ingredients of that as-yet-uncoined term, multimedia. With its first sentence, the Mac showed off its built-in sound chip and internal speaker. (It had an external speaker jack, too.) The first Mac also provided graphics capabilities, albeit only in black and white. It took a few years for the Mac's multimedia personality to be fully realized, but the die was cast.

Fulfilling the Promise

Over the past ten years and innumerable Mac models, Apple has continued to add multimedia features to the basic Macintosh hardware and system software. No matter which model you have, you've got sound and graphics features that set the Mac apart from DOS-based machines, plus plug-and-play access to additional hardware. The current high-end Macs offer CD-quality sound, and the AV models add video-capture hardware. Here's a guide to the multimedia features you already have in your Mac.

Sound. Every Mac model can record and play 8-bit mono sound. AV Macs, Power Macs, and the 500-series PowerBooks support 16-bit stereo input and output. Owners of older Macs (the IIfx and earlier) must input audio through the serial port using additional hardware, but current Mac models have built-in recording capabilities (an audio input jack and/or a microphone). If you have System 6.0.7 or greater, you don't even need extra software to record (*digitize*) sound; the Sound control panel has (limited) recording capabilities. (For a complete list of the sound options for various models, see "The Mac's Built-In Sound Capabilities" on page 682. The AV Macs have more sophisticated sound (and video) recording capabilities, thanks to their FusionRecorder software.

Graphics. Photorealistic color images, 3-D graphics, and animation require more processor power than the early Macs could deliver (not to mention a color monitor). Apple addressed this problem with the Mac II family and 32-bit QuickDraw. The Mac II and its siblings supplied better performance, color capabilities, more memory, and a larger storage capacity (essential for those huge graphics files), plus expansion slots for the accelerators, video display cards, and digitizer boards we'd need. Then 32-bit QuickDraw (later incorporated into System 7) brought 16 million colors to the desktop and supported the special effects used in photo-retouching and multimedia applications.

Multimedia software. Apple's next contribution was HyperCard, arguably the Mac's first multimedia application. Originally bundled with every Mac, HyperCard let you combine text, graphics, sound, and interactivity (via programmable buttons) in on-screen presentations. Unfortunately, today's Macs only come with a run-time version, the HyperCard Player; if you want to create new presentations, you must buy the full version.

In 1991 Apple supplied the final ingredient of multimedia—video support—in the guise of QuickTime. This system-level support for video, audio, and graphics enables anyone with at least an '020-class machine to make and play movies (with soundtracks!).

Video. The AV Macs come with everything you need to record video. Using the digitizing hardware built into an AV machine, you can capture and display 16-bit digital audio and video without having to buy separate digitizing boards. Just plug an audio or video source (such as a camcorder, VCR, or videodisc player) into the AV's video ports, fire up the bundled FusionRecorder software, and start recording. The AV Macs also have a DSP (digital signal processor) chip, which provides huge performance gains for processor-intensive operations such as the special effects used in graphics and video applications. (The Power Macs build the functions of the DSP into the CPU.)

The AV Monitor (AA)

Apple's AV monitor, which can be used with any Mac that supports an external monitor, is the only Apple hardware that can play true stereo. In fact, the AudioVision 14 Display is a multimedia powerhouse all by itself: It has two bass-reflex speakers, a built-in microphone, audio in and out ports, and a video port for hooking up a camcorder or VCR. If it had a CPU we wouldn't need a Mac! (See Chapter 6 for more on the AV monitor.)

Clip Media (AA/CB/SC)

You don't have to be an artist, video producer, or musician to put together professional-looking multimedia presentations. Dozens of companies offer royalty-free collections of clip art, photography, movies, and sounds. If you have $400 and a CD-ROM drive, Volume 1 (Business and Technology) of Macromedia's **ClipMedia** series can supply almost everything you need for a complete multimedia experience: movies, animations, graphics, sound effects, music, backgrounds, and buttons. **WraptureReels** ($130 on CD-ROM, Form and Function) is an excellent disc of broadcast-quality animated textures and backgrounds (such as clouds, waves, and fire), while **Backgrounds for Multimedia** 1 and 2 (Artbeats, $230 and $290 on CD-ROM) provide tasteful backdrops. For more art and photography options, see "Clip Art" in Chapter 15.

As for prepackaged sound libraries, our favorites include the officially licensed ***Star Trek, Star Wars,*** and ***2001: A Space Odyssey*** collections from Sound Source Unlimited ($60 each, floppy disks); **Sound Library 2000**, a $50 CD-ROM of sound effects from Wayzata Technology; and **A Zillion Sounds**—actually, more like 2,000 sounds ($25 on CD-ROM, BeachWare).

Finally, for multimedia presentations requiring a little license-free background music, try **Killer Tracks,** three CD-ROMs tailored for sales, training, and education (Killer Tracks, $70 each or $175 for the set). Other good musical choices include **Clip Tunes** ($200 on CD-ROM, Digidesign) and **MusicBytes** ($100 on CD-ROM, Prosonus), which offers tunes performed by famous musicians such as Jeff "Skunk" Baxter of Steely Dan and Doobie Brothers fame.

What Else Do You Need?

The Mac's native hardware and software provide the foundation for building a multimedia system of any complexity. Your experimentation with the Mac's multimedia features might be limited to adding a QuickTime movie to your Startup Folder or adding voice annotation to your e-mail. With a presentation program and some clip media (see the box above), you could build and present a whiz-bang sales pitch or quarterly report. As you'll see in the following sections, the possibilities are limited only by your ambition.

Besides tools related to your specific interests (the sound, music, video, presentation, and authoring products described below), you'll probably want a few other gadgets. First and foremost, buy all the memory and storage you can afford. These days even mainstream presentation programs such as Persuasion and PowerPoint want an '020 Mac with 5MB to 8MB of RAM, and audio and video files are notorious storage hogs, requiring capacious hard drives. And you'll need a color monitor, of course, preferably with a 24-bit accelerator board.

Also give serious consideration to a CD-ROM drive. More and more companies are taking advantage of the 640MB capacity of CD-ROM discs to distribute their software—in fact, it's about the only way you can buy collections of movie or sound clips. There are several speedy, reasonably priced drives on the market, or you can get the attractively priced **AppleCD Multimedia Kit** ($630, Apple), which includes Apple's excellent AppleCD 300 CD-ROM drive, a pair of AppleDesign Powered Speakers, and several CD-ROM titles.

Sound

(CB)

To really put the *multi* into multimedia, a presentation must stimulate more than the optic nerve. These days, sound on the Macintosh encompasses everything from digitized laughter to a dedicated QuickTime audio track to 16-bit, CD-quality audio recording and editing systems. Every user—from multimedia novice to professional producer—can easily add sound to presentations and applications by exploiting the Mac's native sound capabilities, coupled with such tools as sound-editing applications, microphones, digital audio boards, and CD-ROM drives.

Digital Sound

The Mac records and stores sound digitally. Digital recording is like making a movie, but instead of taking a series of photos that become frames in a moving picture, you're taking *samples* (audio snapshots) of a sound wave at regular intervals and translating them into numbers for storage on the computer. When played back at the same rate, the samples reproduce the original sound.

The number of samples taken per second is called the *sampling rate*. The higher the sampling rate, the greater the accuracy of the recording and the better it'll sound when played back. Digital sound files can be 8-bit or 16-bit and may be either mono (one channel) or stereo (two discrete channels).

The difference between 8- and 16-bit sound is similar to the difference between 8- and 16-bit color: It's a matter of resolution. The 256 colors used in an 8-bit color palette can't represent an object in a truly realistic way, whereas the 65,536 colors used in 16-bit images can approach photographic quality. This principle also applies to sound. An 8-bit sound sample is broken down into 256 parts that represent the sound wave; a 16-bit sound sample is represented by 65,536 parts. Sure, you can tell the 8-bit sound coming out of your Mac represents a saxophone, but the low resolution won't fool you into thinking Branford Marsalis is tootling in your ear.

The 8-bit sound chip in most Macs (all but the AVs and Power Macs) can record or play back up to 22,254 samples per second (abbreviated as 22 kHz), which yields sound quality comparable to an AM radio. The Mac also can record sound at 11 kHz, but this lower sampling rate is generally reserved for narration or for situations where file size is crucial.

Sound Manager 3 (CB)

Sound may be an integral part of the Mac experience, but that doesn't mean it's always well implemented. For example, the Mac II family has a stereo speaker jack, but the machines only play the left channel of stereo sound through the internal speaker (the IIsi is an exception). And the LC II and many Performa models only play mono sound, period, from both the speaker jack and the internal speaker. (For a complete list of the Mac's sound options, see "The Mac's Built-In Sound Capabilities" on page 682.)

Happily, the Sound Manager 3 extension addresses some of these inequities. It mixes stereo sound to mono and shoves it through the internal speakers of Macs with mono-only capabilities, and it plays both channels of stereo sound on the LC II and Performas. Sound Manager 3 also provides other audio goodies:

- It plays 16-bit sounds through Apple's 8-bit audio chip. (Sound Manager converts the sound to 8-bit files for playback.)
- It plays 16-bit sounds at their full fidelity through a 16-bit audio card.
- It takes on the sound chores of QuickTime, allowing movies with soundtracks to play back at a higher frame rate. (QuickTime becomes less choppy.)

The Sound Manager 3 package (which includes version 8 of the Sound control panel) is freely available on-line and is often included with audio-hip games and CD-ROMs. To use it properly, you also need System 7 and QuickTime 1.5 (or greater).

If you have an AV Mac, Power Mac, or 16-bit audio board (see "Affordable 16-bit sound cards" in this section), the Mac can handle sampling rates of 44.1 kHz (the standard for audio CDs) and 48 kHz (the standard for digital audio tape [DAT]). The higher sampling rates better preserve the live sound's pitch and dynamic range (loudness) and virtually eliminate distortion.

Of course, the higher the sampling rate, the larger the file size. One minute of 22-kHz sound takes up about 1.2MB of hard disk space, and a minute of 16-bit, 44.1-kHz stereo audio requires 10.5MB. Some applications let you compress sound files, but while this makes your files substantially smaller, the sound quality suffers enormously. Due to these constraints, it's a good idea to use 8-bit audio when possible. Not only does it reduce file sizes, but it also improves performance when the Mac is processing other tasks—such as animations—at the same time.

HOT TIP

Sound Hardware

If you want to record sound, you'll need either a microphone or a sound digitizer, depending on your Mac model (for the specifics, see "The Mac's Built-In Sound Capabilities" on page 682). A good pair of external speakers can vastly improve the quality and volume of your audible output—particularly useful if you're playing to a crowd. And if you want superior, CD-quality sound, you'll need the 16-bit capabilities of an AV Mac or a digital audio board.

Microphones. The Mac microphone situation is a bit confused. In the beginning, there was no audio input jack and therefore no microphone. When Apple released Macs with audio input jacks, it included the **Apple Microphone**, a jumbo-lozenge-shaped mic. Later, Apple quit bundling the microphone but still offers it separately for $20. Some models have a built-in microphone, which is hidden beneath a couple of perforations in the case and picks up the computer's noise as well as your dulcet tones. Now Apple is equipping Macs with an audio input jack that supports a less noisy *line level* (the same kind of signal that goes into and out of an audio CD player, tape deck, or VCR) and no microphone—but for $30 you can get its **PlainTalk microphone.**

Sound File Formats

(CB)

Just as there are various graphics file formats, sound files also come in a variety of (oft-incompatible) flavors. Here are the most common file types.

Icon	Kind	File Type	Notes
	System 7 sound file	sfil	Stored in the System file and appears in the Sound control panel. To hear it double-click the icon. Put one in the Startup Items folder and it will play each time you start the Mac.
	SoundEdit Pro AIFF file	AIFF	Audio Interchange File Format is the industry standard for audio files. QuickTime, Audioshop, and Premiere save in AIFF format.
	SoundEdit file	FSSD	Older file format produced by the original version of macromedia's SoundEdit.
	SoundEdit Pro file	jB1	Native file format of SoundEdit Pro.
	Audioshop file	snd	System resource found inside applications and HyperCard stacks. You can suck them out of programs with a conversion utility.
	Kaboom .WAV file	BINA	A format generated by Microsoft Windows applications. Nova Development's Kaboom! Factory can convert these files to Mac formats.

Apple's motive for changing the audio-input configuration isn't as capricious as it may seem. It's indicated by the name *PlainTalk:* The cleaner line-level input should help the speech-recognition capabilities being implemented in the AVs and future Macs. This design switch does mean, however, that you can't use an Apple Microphone with the newer, PlainTalk-ready Macs. Likewise, the PlainTalk microphone isn't backward-compatible.

If you want a non-Apple mic, there are numerous and better-sounding alternatives to the Apple Microphone. Sound maven Craig O'Donnell recommends

Radio Shack's $25 **Tie-Clip Omni.** However, you have only two alternatives to the PlainTalk mic:

- Get Jabra's $170 **Ear Phone,** which combines a microphone and speaker and supports speech recognition.
- Connect your Mac to an audio mixing board—all the cool cats dig the **Mackie 1202** mixer ($400)—and use the microphone of your choice.

MacRecorder. If you have an older Mac that lacks an audio input jack, you'll need a serial port recording device—a *digitizer*—to capture sound. The most

Sound Conversion Utilities (CB)

Every sound format isn't recognized by every program (surprise, surprise). To import your favorite sound bite into your favorite program, you may have to convert it to a different format using one of the utilities below.

Program	Import Formats	Export Formats
SoundExtractor shareware $5	FSSD, snd, System 6 suitcase sounds, SoundEdit Pro	sfil
SoundConverter Pro shareware $20	sfil, snd, FSSD, Sound Mover suitcase	sfil, FSSD, System 7 suitcase, Sound Mover suitcase
Sound Mover shareware $25 for Sound Manager package	sfil, snd, FSSD, System 6 sounds, SoundEdit Pro	snd, Sound Mover suitcase
Balthazar freeware	Windows .WAV files	sfil
Movie2Snd freeware	MooV (QuickTime)	sfil
Soundtrack freeware	MooV	AIFF
Audioshop 2 Opcode Systems $150	sfil, snd, FSSD, AIFF, MooV, Macromedia Director	sfil, snd, FSSD, AIFF, MooV, Macromedia Director
Kaboom! Nova Development $50	sfil, snd, FSSD, AIFF, MooV, .WAV	sfil, snd, FSSD, AIFF, MooV, .WAV
SoundEdit 16 Macromedia $380	sfil, snd, FSSD, AIFF, MooV, .WAV, SoundEdit Pro, Sound Designer II, Studio Session Instrument	sfil, snd, FSSD, AIFF, MooV, .WAV, SoundEdit Pro, Sound Designer II, Studio Session Instrument

popular digitizer is Macromedia's **MacRecorder** ($100 alone, or $350 as part of the **MacRecorder Sound System,** which includes SoundEdit Pro, an 8-bit sound editor). MacRecorder includes a volume control and two input jacks—microphone and line level—for recording with the microphone of your choice or from other electronic sources such as tape or CD players.

Affordable 16-bit sound cards. Mac-Recorder's 8-bit capabilities aren't going to thrust you to the top of the charts. If you want CD-quality sound, you need an AV Mac or a 16-bit digital audio board.

Musicians seeking the cleanest sound will appreciate the superior signal-to-noise specs and powerful sound-editing software in the **Audiomedia II** package ($1,300, Digidesign). The stereo, 16-bit sound card features analog as well as digital input and output jacks and 44.1 and 48 kHz sampling rates. Bundled with it is **Sound Designer II,** a top-of-the-line sound editor. The $1,000 **Audiomedia LC** brings the same power—minus the digital jacks—to LC, Performa 400, and Color Classic owners.

Multimedia types looking for AV compatibility, a shorter NuBus board that will fit in the Quadra 610, or the chance to save a few bucks should check out the **NuMedia** board ($700, Spectral Innovations). It uses the same DSP processor found in the AV Macs to record and play 16-bit sound and is bundled with Passport Producer 1.2. For $500 you can get **NuMedia 2,** which lacks the digital jacks and includes Opcode's Audioshop 2.

Speakers. The Mac's internal speaker is fine for delivering system beeps, but its output quality is too wimpy for a multimedia project. The speakers built into Mac AV monitors are a vast improvement, but they can't be repositioned for use with an audience. If you want to really *hear* the sounds emanating from your Mac, plug a pair of speakers into the Mac's external speaker jack. Computer speakers come in various prices and sizes, but they share two characteristics not common to stereo speakers: They're *shielded* (if you stick one next to your monitor, it won't look like your Mac has suddenly ingested peyote), and they're *powered* (they have a power cord).

The Mac's Built-In Sound Capabilities (CB)

Mac model	Internal speaker	Speaker jack	Audio input
128, 512, 512Ke, Plus, SE, Classic	left channel	left channel	serial port
SE/30	stereo mixed to mono	stereo	serial port
Classic II, Performa 200	left channel	left channel	Apple Microphone
Color Classic	left channel	left channel	PlainTalk microphone, built-in microphone
II, IIx, IIci, IIcx, IIfx	left channel	stereo	serial port
IIsi	stereo mixed to mono	stereo	Apple Microphone
IIvi, IIvx	left channel	left channel	Apple Microphone
LC, LC II, LC III	left channel	left channel	Apple Microphone
LC 475	stereo mixed to mono	stereo	PlainTalk microphone
LC 520, Performa 550	left channel	stereo	PlainTalk microphone, built-in microphone
Performa 400, 405, 410, 430, 450, 460, 466, 467, 600	left channel	left channel	Apple Microphone
Centris 610, 650	stereo mixed to mono	stereo	Apple Microphone
Quadra 605; Performa 475, 476	stereo mixed to mono	stereo	PlainTalk microphone
Quadra 610, 650, 700, 800, 900, 950	stereo mixed to mono	stereo	Apple Microphone
Quadra 660AV, 840AV	stereo mixed to mono	stereo	PlainTalk microphone (16-bit)
Workgroup Server 60, 80, 95	stereo mixed to mono	stereo	Apple Microphone
Power Mac 6100, 7100, 8100	stereo mixed to mono	stereo	PlainTalk microphone (16-bit)
Portable	left channel	stereo	serial port
PowerBook 100	left channel	left channel	serial port
PowerBook 140, 145, 145B,	stereo mixed to mono	stereo	Apple Microphone (optional on 145B)
PowerBook 160, 165, 165c, 180 180c	stereo mixed to mono	stereo	Apple Microphone, built-in microphone
PowerBook 520, 520c, 540, 540c	stereo	stereo	built-in microphone, PlainTalk mic (16-bit)
PowerBook Duo 210, 230, 250, 270c	left channel	left channel (with dock)	built-in microphone
PowerBook Duo 280, 280c	stereo mixed to mono	left channel (with dock)	built-in microphone
PowerBook Duo MiniDock, DuoDock, DuoDock II	—	left channel	Apple Microphone

For personal use and small-scale presentations, give a listen to Altec Lansing's $130 **ACS 100s,** Labtec's $150 **CS-1400s,** Yamaha's $150 **YST-M10s,** or Apple's $180 **AppleDesign Powered Speakers.** If you require the really *big* sound and could use extra inputs for audio CDs and MIDI (discussed in the "Music" section, below), take a gander at the $400 **Pattern 100s** from Atlantic Technology.

Recording and Editing Sound

There are numerous ways to get sound into the Mac, which you can use to add voice annotation to programs that support it (including Microsoft Word and Excel and CE Software's QuickMail) or to create special effects for a multimedia show. Here are our favorite techniques for capturing and playing with sounds.

Using the Sound control panel. System 7's Sound control panel provides a mini recording studio for sound effects up to 10 seconds long. The only equipment you need is a microphone. Here's how you do it:

- Open the Sound control panel.
- Click the Add button, which brings up a recording dialog box.
- Say something and watch the lines coming from the speaker icon. If you see a straight vertical line, the input is too loud. Either move the microphone further away or restrain those strident tendencies.

- Click the Record button and have at it for up to 10 seconds.
- Click the Stop button (or press Return).

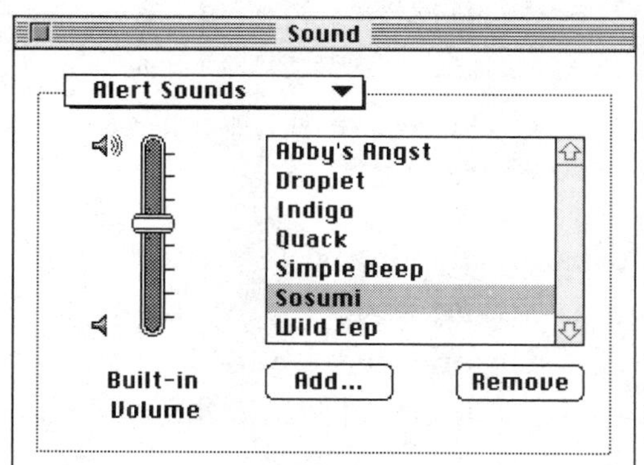

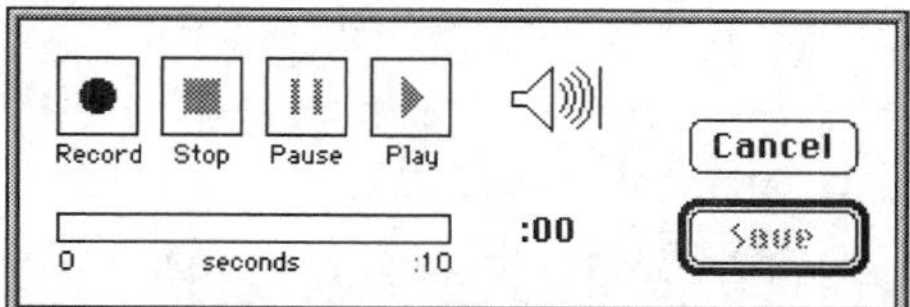

If your Mac has a microphone or digitizer, you can record sounds with System 7's Sound control panel (left). Just click the Add button, which brings up a dialog box with VCR-like controls (above). If a vertical line appears after the speaker icon, as shown here, you're talking too loud.

- Give a listen by clicking the Play button.
- If you're satisfied, name and save your new sound. Otherwise, re-record it.

Your new sound is automatically stored (in sfil format) inside the System file. To use it elsewhere, open the System file (by double-clicking it) and drag it out.

HyperCard's Audio Palette. You can't edit sounds with the Sound control panel. You're also stuck with a 22-kHz sampling rate, no compression, and a 10-second recording time. However, if you have HyperCard 2 (sorry, not the HyperCard Player shipped with the Mac), you've got a nifty sound utility at your fingertips. The built-in Audio Palette lets you record at either 11 or 22 kHz with 3:1, 6:1, or no compression; provides some basic sound-editing tools; and expands recording time to available memory.

Before beginning your audio explorations, make sure the Audio Help stack is cohabiting with HyperCard. To record, open a stack and select Audio from the Edit menu. Up pops a recording console that works much like the Sound control panel. To muck with a particular audible tidbit, click the Edit button. Click and drag across the graphic representation of the sound wave to select a section; you can use standard commands such as Cut, Copy, Paste, and Clear. When the sound is saved, HyperCard places a button titled Play [*your sound's name*] in the stack from which you chose Audio. To export the sound (which is a snd resource) for use elsewhere, you'll need a conversion utility (see the table "Sound Conversion Utilities" on page 680).

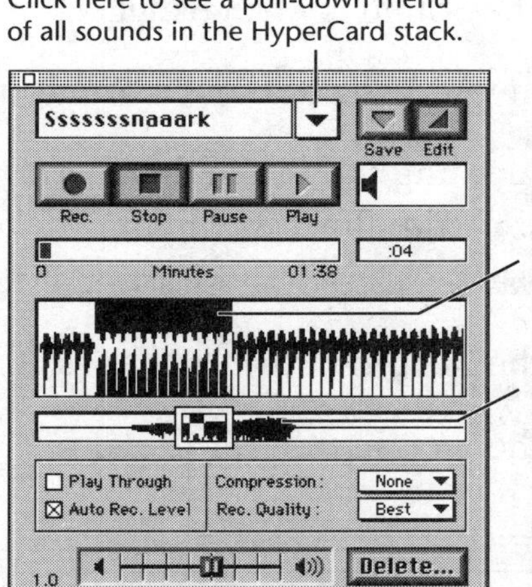

HyperCard's Audio Palette is a handy utility for both recording and editing sounds.

Sound editors. HyperCard isn't the only tool available for basic sound editing. There are several shareware utilities, such as **Sound Mover** (part of the $25 Sound Manager package), as well as commercial utilities like **Kaboom! Factory** (part of Nova Development's $50 Kaboom!; see Chapter 13) and **SoundMate**

(part of Motion Works' $250 Multimedia Utilities, see "Editing Movies" in the "Video" section, below). For full-bore sound editing, however, you'll need to look a bit further.

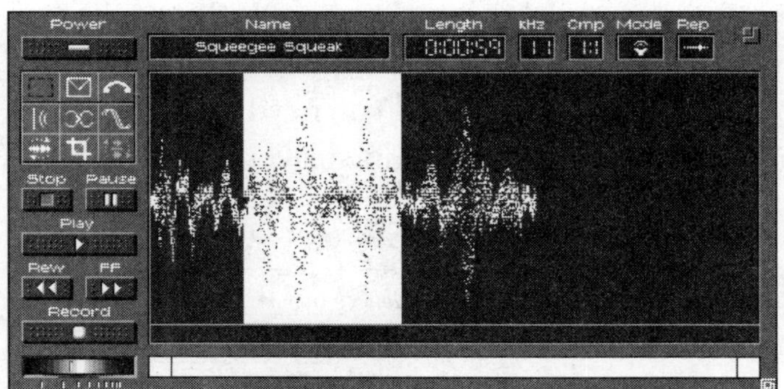

Audioshop has an attractive interface, and its editing controls let you add reverb, echo, and flanging (among other things) to your sounds. For that authentic Beatles sound, you also can play sounds backward.

Audioshop 2 ($150, Opcode Systems) is a moderately featured sound editor that lets you record and edit 8- and 16-bit sound and add effects such as reverb and echo. You can play audio CDs from a CD-ROM drive from within the program and capture and edit their music tracks. Audioshop can record 16-bit audio from AV and Power Macs and machines outfitted with Spectral Innovations' NuMedia sound card (see "Affordable 16-bit Sound Cards," above). Audioshop also can create a playlist of—and then play—every sound, from every application, on your hard drive.

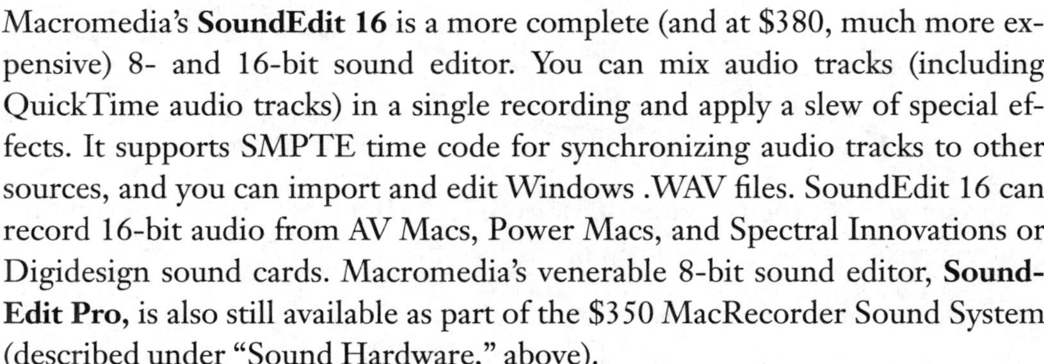

Macromedia's **SoundEdit 16** is a more complete (and at $380, much more expensive) 8- and 16-bit sound editor. You can mix audio tracks (including QuickTime audio tracks) in a single recording and apply a slew of special effects. It supports SMPTE time code for synchronizing audio tracks to other sources, and you can import and edit Windows .WAV files. SoundEdit 16 can record 16-bit audio from AV Macs, Power Macs, and Spectral Innovations or Digidesign sound cards. Macromedia's venerable 8-bit sound editor, **SoundEdit Pro,** is also still available as part of the $350 MacRecorder Sound System (described under "Sound Hardware," above).

A standout application for serious 16-bit multitrack digital audio recording is OSC's $400 **Deck II.** You can record and edit four audio tracks with a Digidesign sound card, six tracks with a NuMedia card or Quadra 660AV, and eight tracks with a Quadra 840AV. Deck II sports many professional features, including nondestructive editing, automated mixdown, and support for both SMPTE and MIDI time code (which lets you synchronize it with a MIDI sequencer, giving you a virtual recording studio).

Capturing sound from audio CDs. If you don't have one of the programs mentioned above, you can still pluck your favorite Lyle Lovett tune off of an audio CD and save it as an audio-only QuickTime file. All you need are System 7, Sound Manager 3, Quick-Time 1.5 or later, a Quick-Time player utility, and an AppleCD 300 or 300i CD-ROM drive. Here's how:

- Load an audio CD into the AppleCD 300.
- Fire up a QuickTime utility such as MoviePlayer or Popcorn (see "Simple Editing" in the "Video" section, below).
- Open the CD from the utility and double-click on an audio track.
- A Save dialog box will appear. Click the Options button.
- In the Import Options dialog box, choose the parameters for capturing the audio track. You can capture just a piece of the track by setting start and stop times. To hear your selection, click the Play button.

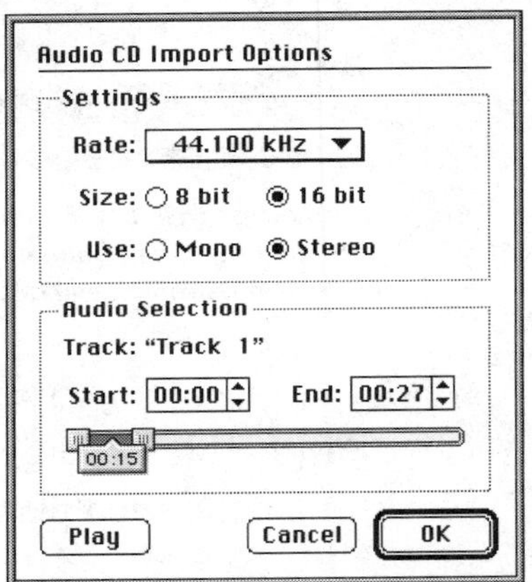

QuickTime utilities such as MoviePlayer have a special dialog box that lets you capture music from an audio CD and turn it into an audio-only QuickTime file. (You also need an AppleCD 300 CD-ROM drive.)

- Remember that digital audio files are huge. Higher sampling rates, more bits, and stereo tracks gobble up more disk space.
- Press OK, name your track, and save it. Since it's an audio-only QuickTime file, you'll only see the Standard Controller bar during playback, without an accompanying movie frame.

Music (CB)

To create and manipulate synthetic music on the Mac, you need *MIDI* (Musical Instrument Digital Interface), a technology that enables the computer, in concert with electronic instruments, to record and play musical performances. Using MIDI-compatible hardware and software, you can compose, reproduce, and score music for a single instrument or an entire orchestra. And MIDI music is now more accessible to nonmusicians, thanks to the plug-and-play ease of General MIDI instruments and the incorporation of a music track in QuickTime 2 (see the "Video" section, below).

Throwing together a MIDI system is remarkably easy to do. To make the Mac warble, you need just three things:

- **A MIDI-compatible instrument.** Options include synthesizers, samplers, controllers, and sound modules.
- **A MIDI interface.** This external box connects to the serial port and translates between your MIDI instrument(s) and the Mac.
- **MIDI software,** usually a *sequencer,* which lets you build multitrack recordings. You can also create sheet music from MIDI input using *notation software*.

All of these items, including the software, can be found at a good musical instrument store.

Sharing the Serial Port (CB)

The Mac communicates with MIDI devices via the serial port. If you'd rather not dedicate your precious modem or printer port to MIDI, you have three options:

- Buy a General MIDI instrument, such as E-mu's SoundEngine Music Module, which has an additional serial port for connecting to a modem or printer.
- Buy a switchable MIDI interface that, with a push of a button, directs serial information either to MIDI or to your modem or printer. Prices start at $60 for Opcode's *MIDI Translator II.*
- Buy a $20 serial switch box at your local electronics shop.

Synthesizers and Samplers

A *synthesizer* is a device that can recreate a variety of sounds electronically, while a *sampler* doesn't create sounds but instead plays back digital recordings (samples) of natural

MIDI Defined (CB)

The MIDI standard, adopted by musical instrument makers in the early 1980s, provides a common language and interface (a five-pin plug), so that hardware from different companies can reliably connect and communicate with one another. MIDI's language is sort of a musical PostScript. Instead of sending instructions to a printer, however, MIDI transmits musical instructions—such as "play middle C" or "sustain that note" (digitally, of course)—between the Mac and MIDI hardware.

A MIDI file thus contains the instructions needed to play a piece of music, rather than the actual sounds produced by a performance. It records when each note was played, what the note was, how hard it was played, and for how long. Basically, it's like the roll of paper that tells a player piano what to play, as opposed to an audio tape you play back on a stereo. And because MIDI files contain only musical instructions, they are teensy in comparison to digital audio files.

More recently, companies adopted *General MIDI,* a subset of the MIDI standard that (among other things) standardizes the order of sounds within MIDI instruments. For example, selecting program 1 always produces an acoustic piano sound on any MIDI device that incorporates the General MIDI specs (not all of them do). Likewise, the violin sound never strays from program 41, and applause is always program 127.

sounds. Both devices are often incorporated into keyboards, but they can take other forms—for example, Digidesign's $2,000 **SampleCell II** is a NuBus card.

Controllers

If you want to play music into your Mac for recording or *notating* (turning into sheet music), one of your MIDI instruments should be a *controller.* These devices—which include keyboards, guitars, basses, violins, wind instruments, and drum pads—make absolutely no sound on their own. Instead, they control the sound generated by an external synthesizer or other MIDI device. You'll want your instrument to play more than one kind of sound—say, a piano, bass, and trumpet—simultaneously for that full orchestral effect. So be sure your synthesizer or sound module is *multitimbral,* allowing you to play 16 different sounds at once.

The MIDI Interface

MIDI instruments communicate with the Mac through the *MIDI interface*, a small box with MIDI input and output ports. You can pay up to $1,000 for a professional interface, but Opcode Systems' $60 **MIDI Translator II,** with hookups for three instruments, is fine for the casual MIDI musician.

Sound Modules

Not everyone can sit down at a synthesizer keyboard and plunk out a dynamic, ten-minute soundtrack for a multimedia presentation. That's why there are *sound modules* (plug-and-play MIDI synthesizers), which play prerecorded sequences sent to them from sequencing programs, games, or multimedia applications. In fact, a sound module doesn't *have* a keyboard or any other means of inputting sounds. Just hook it up to the Mac's serial port (you normally don't need a MIDI interface) and use a program such as Passport Producer Pro (described in the "Presentations" section of this chapter, below) to synchronize a sequence with your presentation.

When selecting a sound module, let your ears be the judge. You can always buy new software, but you can never make that piano sound less cheesy. Also look for units that incorporate the General MIDI specs, so you'll be assured of always hearing the same sounds, no matter what software or hardware you use them with.

Prerecorded Sequences (CB)

You can add new sequences to your sound module's repertoire by purchasing them at music stores or via mail order. Look for ads in magazines such as *Keyboard* and *Electronic Musician*. Expect to pay between $7 and $10 per sequence, $20 or more for collections. Prerecorded sequences are also included with each issue of *Nautilus*, the CD-ROM magazine. (For more on *Nautilus*, see Appendix B, "Where to Find More Information").

The choices include the **SoundEngine Music Module** ($600, E-mu Systems), **Audio Gallery** ($500, Korg), **Hello! Music!** ($500, Yamaha), and **SC-7 Sound Module** ($400, Roland). Each package contains a General MIDI sound module, which uses digital samples as the basis for its sound, and software. SoundEngine contains the finest software of the bunch: Opcode's EZ Vision (see "Sequencers," below) and

Edit One, an editing application. The SoundEngine and Audio Gallery modules sound the best to my ears. Roland's SC-7 module is a good choice for musicians on a budget, but the sound module that comes with Hello! Music! sounds tinny, and the included software, Passport Designs' Trax, is nothing to write home about.

Sequencers

MIDI is popular among composers and musicians because it lets them do *sequencing*, that is, record music instrument by instrument (track by track), then play back the entire composition with perfect synchronization. They compose and edit their performances in programs called *sequencers*. The resulting MIDI files are naturally called *sequences*. When saved as *Standard MIDI Files*—a format that allows sequences created by one program to be read by another—they can be imported into notation programs or another sequencer.

Sequencing programs let you manipulate MIDI data in ways that are impossible with tape. After you record a piece of music, you can use the sequencer to change the pitch, stress, or duration of any note; align notes to beats automatically; copy and paste sections; increase or decrease the tempo of the piece; or transpose the piece to another key. Unlike a digital sound editor, in which you work with a picture of a sound wave, a sequencer displays individual MIDI events such as notes, velocity (how hard you hit the key), and duration (how long you play the note), so you can work with the events directly.

Entry-level sequencers. There are a half-dozen entry-level sequencers that don't include such arcane capabilities as time-code synchronization or extensive MIDI data editing. Of them, **EZ Vision** ($100, Opcode Systems) packs the most bang for the buck. Along with the usual features, such as graphic and event-list editing of note data, you'll find graphic editing of MIDI controller data, color support, and publish-and-subscribe integration with **Galaxy,** Opcode's $150 librarian program, and **Galaxy Plus Editors.** The latter is a $400 program that lets you edit as well as archive synthesizer *patches* (sounds) and then have their names appear in EZ Vision or Vision sequences for easy reference. If you want to edit your tunes using standard music notation, you have two worthy $150 choices: Opcode's **Musicshop**—EZ Vision with notation—and Steinberg's **Cubase Lite.**

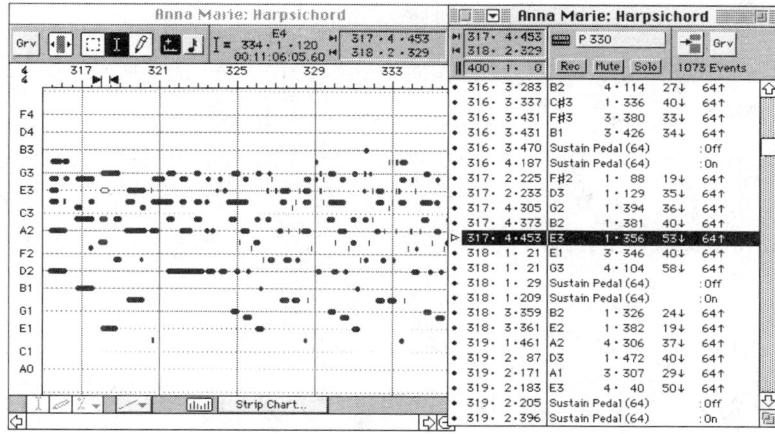

Like most professional sequencers, Vision displays music data in two ways. The graphic editing window (left) displays notes as dots; the longer the dot, the longer the note will play. The event-list window (right) displays notes as MIDI data. The selected line indicates that an E was played on the 4th beat (453rd tick) of measure 317 and that the key was struck with medium force (53 out of a possible 128).

Pro sequencers. For years the two big guns in professional sequencers, Mark of the Unicorn and Opcode ahve battled for supremacy. At press time, Opcode's **Vision 2** ($500) had the upper hand over **Performer 4.2** (also $500). Prior to the release of version 2, many musicians liked Vision's proprietary publish-and-subscribe relationship to Galaxy and its superior graphic-editing capabilities, but Performer users admired its more intuitive interface and the ability to edit sequences via music notation. Version 2 has silenced the critics, however, with its notation editing, colorful redesigned interface, and free copy of Galaxy. That is, until the release of Performer 5....

Of course, there *are* other pro sequencers. OSC's **Metro,** for example, doesn't have the expansive features of Vision and Performer, but for $225 it packs enough power to make it a serious contender. In addition, two European heavyweights have sloshed to our shores: **Notator Logic** ($400, Emagic) and **Cubase** ($500, Steinberg). Both are powerful and complex MIDI packages that not only offer sequencing but also notation, patch-editing, and MIDI-programming modules. While they don't rival dedicated notation and editing programs, these modules do make Performer's and Vision's efforts look weak.

Unfortunately, every professional sequencer except Metro and **Master Tracks Pro** ($400, Passport Designs) is copy-protected. We hate it, you hate it, and the companies claim to hate it, too. These programs have become so complex that the casual scumbucket with a pirated copy, no manual, and no access to tech support is unlikely to glean much benefit. So, developers, cut the paranoia—and the copy protection.

Notation Programs

Turning musical ideas into legible sheet music used to be a time-consuming and expensive task. Today anyone can turn out good-looking musical scores, thanks to the meshing of computers, laser printers, MIDI, and notation software (also called *scoring programs*). These programs let you create and edit a musical score, using standard music notation. You can compose a score in one of four ways:

- Point and click to compose directly onto a standard music staff.
- Enter notes via the Mac's keyboard. (Typing G5, for example, gives you a quarter note in Finale.)
- Enter notes by playing them on a MIDI keyboard or other controller.
- Import MIDI files created with a sequencer. The notation software automatically transcribes the data onto the score.

The first serious notation software to appear, Coda's **Finale,** used to be the program everyone loved to hate, thanks to its four-figure price and hundreds of

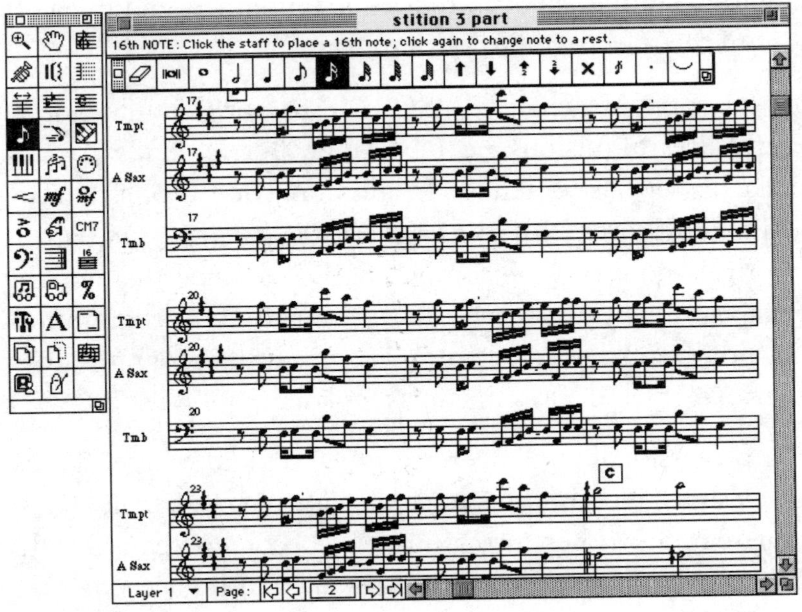

A notation program such as Finale lets you create professional-looking sheet music. The easiest (and most tedious) way to enter music is to click rhythmic values in the note palette (top) and place them directly on the staff. Most notation programs also offer Mac keyboard and MIDI input.

nested dialog boxes. Version 3 has changed all that: The nested boxes are gone; the price is now $750 ($275, academic price); and the documentation has been rewritten. In short, the program has become almost a pleasure to use (after you devote a bit of study to it). Just about anything you can think to do with music notation can be done with Finale. But if you're on a budget or looking for an entry-level program, plunk down $350 for **Finale Allegro** (formerly Music Prose) instead. It contains many of Finale's features but limits you to 32 staves (lines of music) and doesn't provide Finale's specialized—some may say arcane—editing tools.

Despite its refinements, Finale is still neither the most accessible nor the fastest notation program. Temporal Acuity's **Nightingale** ($500; academic pricing available) doesn't pack all of Finale's power, but it's easier to use and speeds right along. Coolest feature: You can scan in a preprinted score and then edit it.

GOOD FEATURE

You might also check out **Songworks** ($130, Ars Nova), a composition/notation package that lets you enter a melody line on a single musical staff (called a *lead sheet*), then generates harmonies for your tune. Or you can build your song the other way 'round by entering a chord progression and asking for melodic suggestions. Because Songworks doesn't require a MIDI device in order to make sounds—it contains internal sounds that can be played from the Mac's keyboard—it's a terrific aid for PowerBook-toting composers.

Music Training

If you're not quite ready to score a digital orchestra or go onstage with a MIDI rock band, you can still take advantage of the Mac's musical talents by training yourself with one of the programs below.

Practica Musica. This MIDI-compatible $130 program from Ars Nova is the best thing going on a floppy disk for ear training and the study of traditional music theory and harmony. You work through exercises that test your powers to sight-read notes, to play intervals and chords, and to notate pitches that the program plays. Version 3 adds rhythm-tapping exercises, exercise customization—you can, for example, focus ear-training exercises on the harmonic minor scale in D—and, as programmer Jeffrey Evans puts it, "more richness of stuff."

Auto-Accompaniment Software (CB)

In years past, musicians without a 24-hour backup band had to settle for lonely hours of solitary practice. Now you can have a virtual band at your beck and call with **MiBAC Jazz Improvisation Software** ($125, MiBAC Music Software) or PG Music's **Band-in-a-Box** ($60, standard edition with 24 accompaniment styles; $90, professional edition with 75 styles).

Both products give you a small backup band—drums, bass, and piano (Band-in-a-Box also throws horns and strings into some arrangements)—that can play in any key, at any tempo, and is generous enough to let you have *all* the solos. You simply type in the chord changes you want it to play. MiBAC focuses entirely on jazz and is a fine choice for musicians interested in this hep genre. Band-in-a-Box contains a more versatile band that, in addition to jazz and rock, can handle everything from reggae to a polka.

Claire. This $130 Opcode program is a real boon for microphone-equipped Mac users interested in honing their intonation skills. **Claire** leads you through a customizable series of singing exercises based on the European *solfège* (do, re, mi) system, listens to what you sing, and offers friendly feedback regarding your ability to sing on key. It also provides an excellent introduction to sight-singing.

The Miracle Piano Teaching System. One benefit not listed on the cover of this book is that the three secrets to mastering the piano are hidden within its pages. Here they are:

- Play the right notes.
- Play them at the right time.
- Play them the right way.

The Software Toolworks' highly hyped **Miracle Piano Teaching System** might help you with the first two tasks, with its cute games and precious exercises, but no one except a living, breathing teacher can help you with the third. My advice as a piano teacher: Use the $500 to enroll in a junior college course.

Video

Movies on the Mac? Once upon a time, it didn't seem possible, considering that a *single second* of TV-quality video requires *30MB* of data. (Whew.) Then along came QuickTime, Apple's remarkable technology that lets you manipulate digital movies almost as easily as text and graphics.

With QuickTime, you can make, play, and edit movies and combine them with other elements to create anything from a business report to a multimedia extravaganza. Stick a home movie of your kids into a letter written in Microsoft Word and e-mail it to your friends. Prepare a sales presentation in Persuasion with a video that shows your hot new product in action. Combine movies, audio, and animation to create the next hot-selling CD-ROM game. It's all doable, using off-the-shelf software, thanks to QuickTime.

Two quick notes on terminology: As used here, *video* means the electronic signal normally produced by television, not by the Mac's video display (the monitor and board). And *full frame, full motion* means 640 by 480 pixels at 30 frames per second (fps)—equivalent to the NTSC television broadcast standard. In most cases, you won't attain this size or speed on your Mac.

1. Movie frame
2. To adjust a movie's volume, click and hold the Volume Control button to bring up the Volume Slider.
3. Play/Pause button
4. The Slider indicates where you are in a movie. Drag its thumb to move around in the movie, or click a spot on the Slider to jump to that point in the movie.
5. Step Backward and Step Forward buttons. Control-click either button and a shuttle control will appear that lets you play a movie backward or forward at just about any speed. Dragging the shuttle's thumb adjusts the speed of playback as well as the direction.
6. The Resize Window button lets you click and drag to resize the movie frame. For optimum playback, use a multiple of the original frame size—twice as big, for example, or half the size. The frame automatically resizes in the appropriate increments if you hold down Option while dragging the button.
7. To restore a movie's original frame dimensions, click the Zoom box.

The Standard Controller provides a VCR-like interface for playing QuickTime movies.

QuickTime (MM)

QuickTime isn't a piece of software; rather, it's a broad-based technology for storing and displaying time-based data. There are four key components: system software, a special file format, a standard user interface, and compression.

QuickTime Controller Shortcuts (MM)

The Standard Controller has several shortcuts for movie playback:

Play	Press Spacebar or Return, or double-click in the frame
Pause	Press Spacebar or Return, or click once in the frame
Mute the sound	Option-click the Volume Control button
Step forward	→
Step backward	←
Jump to end	Option-click the Step Forward button
Jump to beginning	Option-click the Step Backward button
Play in reverse	Cmd-click the Step Backward button, or Shift-double-click in the frame
Play every frame	Hold down Option and begin playback

The system software. To use QuickTime, you must have System 6.0.7 or better, a color-capable Mac (an '020 or better), and at least 2MB of RAM. Physically, QuickTime is an extension that goes in the Extensions folder inside the System Folder. (System 6 users should put it directly in the System Folder.) It comes with the system software and with most applications that require it. It's also freely available from user groups and online services.

With QuickTime installed, you can copy and paste movies as easily as you can text and graphics. You can open (or place) and play movies in any application that supports QuickTime, an ever-growing list that includes word processors, spreadsheets, graphics programs, and presentation packages. Some applications also let you create and save QuickTime movies.

The file format. QuickTime adds a new file format, MooV, to the system's repertoire. MooV stores the synchronized tracks of a QuickTime movie, including a control track and one or more tracks each for video, audio, and text. Any application that recognizes the MooV format can open and play QuickTime movies, and movies you make are saved as MooV files.

The user interface. QuickTime supplies a VCR-like interface for playing movies, which appear in a small window, or *movie frame*. Most applications that support QuickTime movies display the Standard Controller during playback. (Audio-only QuickTime files display the controller only, without a movie frame.) When a movie isn't playing, the controller is often replaced by a *badge* (a small filmstrip icon) in the lower-left corner of the frame. Click the badge to produce the controller and play the movie.

QuickTime compression. There are no two ways about it: Movies are multi-megabyte affairs. A single 24-bit full-screen image (640 by 480 pixels) is about 1MB in size, and as mentioned, the Mac would have to display 30 of these images each second to emulate TV-quality video.

Shoving around this much data is beyond the scope of existing Macs, so QuickTime uses several ploys to make computer-based movies feasible. One concession is to reduce the movie's screen size—a typical frame in QuickTime 1.6 is 240 by 180 pixels. Another workaround is to reduce the frame rate during playback (see "Playback Speed," below).

Compression Settings
Compressor
Video
Color
Quality
Least Low Normal High Most
Motion
Frames per second:
☒ Key frame every 24 frames
More... Cancel OK

In most programs that save QuickTime movies, you choose a compressor and adjust its parameters in the Compression Settings dialog box.

The key strategy, however, is compression. QuickTime has built-in compressors that can make file sizes 10 to 20 times smaller, usually with little effect on image quality. (Your mileage may vary!) During playback, QuickTime (via the compressor) automatically decompresses the image before displaying it. See "QuickTime Compressors," above, for a list of the common compressors.

Playback speed. One of QuickTime's major achievements is its ability to play movies at the correct speed on any QuickTime-compatible Mac. Run a 240-by-180-pixel movie on a Quadra 840AV and it smoothly plays at 30 fps.

QuickTime Compressors (MM)

Most programs let you choose a compressor and specify its parameters when you save a movie. Each compressor is optimized for a particular image type and produces a different trade-off between image quality and file size. If you don't specify a compressor and compression ratio, the default is usually Video at Normal quality. QuickTime has several built-in compressors:

- **Video.** Good general compressor for 16-bit video sequences. Fast enough to compress video as it's captured, but compression is relatively low, resulting in large file sizes.
- **Cinepak.** Most efficient compressor—makes the smallest movies with the smoothest playback. However, compression takes an extremely long time (often overnight). So movies should first be saved with the Video or None compressor, then recompressed at the end of the editing process with Cinepak.
- **None.** Usually best for capturing live video because data is saved directly to disk without compression. (Be sure you have lots of storage available.) Because capture rates are limited mainly by hard disk speed, None often produces higher frame rates than Video does. Files are huge, however, and should be recompressed with the Video or Cinepak compressor to reduce the file size.
- **Animation.** Best for computer-generated animation.
- **Graphics.** Good choice for 8-bit still images. Not an efficient compressor for animations and movies or for 24-bit images.
- **Photo-JPEG.** Ideal for compressing photographic images; can achieve high levels of compression. Compression/decompression is slow, however, making it unsuitable for video sequences without additional hardware (see "High-End Video" in this section).
- **MPEG.** Available with QuickTime 2, this video-compression standard was developed by the Moving Picture Experts Group. It should offer good performance (perhaps better than Cinepak), but compressing a movie with MPEG may require a lot of processor power.

Finally, although it doesn't appear in the compressor list, QuickTime has a Photo CD decompressor that converts images from Kodak's Photo CD discs into PICT files. (For more on Photo CD, see Chapter 15).

Run the same movie on an LC 475 and you'll see a jumpier 15 fps, but it plays in the same amount of time and all elements, including audio, remain synchronized: That's because QuickTime skips frames as necessary to keep the video synchronized with the audio. (Faster playback is on the way; see the box "QuickTime 2" on page 700.)

In general, a movie begins looking smooth at 15 fps. Movies can be captured at varying frame rates, but if your movie came from NTSC video, it will play better if the frame rate is evenly divisible into the 30 fps NTSC standard—15 fps will produce better results than frame rates such as 13 or 16 fps.

When making movies, you must balance frame rate against other factors, including compression scheme, color depth, video-capture frame rate, and content. (Pans, zooms, and frequent cuts don't compress as efficiently, for example, because QuickTime can't use temporal compression. For more on this, see "More QuickTime Tips," below.) One limitation you can't overcome, however, is the data-transfer rate of storage devices. The relatively slow transfer rates of CD-ROM drives, for example, reduce frame rates, although this problem is diminishing as newer, faster drives appear.

Making Movies

To play a movie, all you need are a QuickTime-compatible Macintosh and a QuickTime-savvy application. To create a movie, however, you need special software and/or hardware. (If you don't have the time or inclination to make your own movies, see the box "Clip Media" on page 675.) There are three ways to make QuickTime movies:

- Generate movies using presentation programs, animation and 3-D packages, spreadsheets, or screen-capture utilities.
- Capture audio and video using digitizing hardware.
- Edit existing movies using a video-editing application.

Creating animations (MM/AA). A wide variety of applications can generate and save animations as QuickTime movies. For example, Excel 4 can animate its charts, allowing you to fly around a 3-D bar chart or show a chart series growing over time. (To play the animation, you'll need a QuickTime utility such as MoviePlayer.) With Canvas 3 and Kid Pix, you can create QuickTime animations that play back a series of drawings as a slide show. You can also capture your on-screen activities as a QuickTime movie—for a tutorial, say, or a product demo—using CameraMan or Spectator; see "Screen-Capture" in Chapter 13 for more details.

QuickTime 2 (MM/CB)

By the time you read this, QuickTime 2 should be available, offering bigger, faster movies—perhaps double the performance available with QuickTime 1.6—and more support for professional multimedia endeavors. Apple claims that QuickTime 2 will allow an LC 475 to play a 320-by-240-pixel movie at 30 fps (that's up from 240 by 180 at 15 fps), and that full-frame (640 by 480) movies will run at 15 fps. The new MPEG (Moving Picture Experts Group) compressor will provide the video-compression standard that's touted as a necessary step for interactive television, and QuickTime 2's built-in support for SMPTE time code will benefit those producing broadcast-quality video.

QuickTime 2 will also have a music track, complete with a built-in subset of General MIDI instrument sounds. It will let you create and play music through the Mac's internal speaker or send MIDI data out the serial port to external MIDI devices. Although the music track has a nonstandard file format, it will be General MIDI–compatible, allow you to import a Standard MIDI File into a movie, and let you record directly into a QuickTime file with a MIDI instrument.

Presentation, animation, and 3-D programs are especially QuickTime-adept: Cinemation, Typestry, and Macromedia Director are good examples. (Typestry is described in Chapter 14; the other programs are described later in this chapter.) Infini-D and Virtus WalkThrough Professional (described in Chapter 15) can use a QuickTime movie as a modeling surface on an object—for example, as a moving picture on a wall.

Apple's QuickTime CD-ROMs (MM). To get a feel for what QuickTime can do, buy Apple's **QuickTime Starter Kit.** For $100, you get a CD-ROM of sample movies and images plus floppy disks containing five QuickTime utilities. One of them, MoviePlayer, is a good player utility, but you can get it free elsewhere (see "Editing Movies," below). Another, Movie Recorder, is a basic video-capture program, although most digitizing boards come with such a utility. There's also PixelPlay, a screensaver utility that plays QuickTime movies.

But it's the other two utilities that make the package worth the price. Movie Converter can turn a series of PICT images into a QuickTime movie, recompress or resize an existing movie, or convert it into a PC-compatible file. Picture Compressor compresses still images and, although slow, it's handy if you want to use the Photo-JPEG compressor on photographic images.

Some QuickTime programs, such as ComboWalker, can create a custom file icon (left), which is more informative than a generic movie icon (right).

Serious movie-makers should get the **QuickTime Developer's Kit** ($200, APDA). This CD-ROM includes the utilities found in the Starter Kit, plus sample code, *XCMDs* (for adding QuickTime capabilities to HyperCard), MovieShop, and ComboWalker. You should use MovieShop to recompress any movie destined for a CD-ROM, because it will optimize the movie for best playback. ComboWalker can flatten a movie (reduce it to just a data fork, making it playable using QuickTime for Windows) and turn a movie's poster frame into a custom file icon. (Baseline Publishing's $25 **I Like Icon** can go a step further: Double-click a movie's file icon and it plays a teeny-tiny version of the movie.)

Digitizing video (MM). To capture video from a camcorder, television, VCR, or videodisc player, you'll need a video-digitizing board (unless you have an AV Mac, which has a built-in digitizer). Plug your camcorder into the board and turn it on, click Record in the on-screen software, and the board converts the incoming video signal into a QuickTime movie and saves it to your hard disk.

There is a wide array of digitizing boards to choose from, but if you're just starting out, **VideoSpigot** ($430, SuperMac) and **Movie Movie** ($350, Sigma Designs) provide good quality at a low price. Both boards achieve reasonable frame rates (depending on your Mac), although they're limited to maximum frame sizes of about 320 by 240 pixels. Movie Movie is slightly faster and also captures audio. If you use VideoSpigot, capture your video with the bundled ScreenPlay application; its proprietary compression software boosts frame rates by about 30 percent over programs such as Premiere.

If you're more ambitious, both SuperMac's **Spigot II Tape** ($1,000) and Radius' **VideoVision** ($2,000) can capture full-frame still images and output movies to videotape. VideoVision also captures 8-bit stereo sound and doubles as a 24-bit display board (saving an extra purchase and a CPU slot), but surprisingly, its capture rates are slower than the low-cost boards unless you add pricey compression hardware (see the box "High-End Video" on page 705).

Editing Movies

Once you've made a few movies, you'll probably want to edit them. Video-editing software lets you cut and paste movies, add transitions and special effects, optimize image quality for playback on different machines, and, in some cases, record video (if you have a digitizing board).

BARGAIN

Simple editing (MM/AA/Greg Wasson). For basic cut-and-paste movie editing, all you need is **MoviePlayer** (also called Simple Player), Apple's freebie QuickTime utility. Besides letting you shorten movies or add clips to an existing movie, MoviePlayer can loop movies during playback, instantly double or halve the frame size, and change the *poster frame* (the still image that represents the movie when it's not playing).

EasyPlay, a $20 shareware utility, lets you view, edit, and catalog movies. Each catalog can contain 4,000 entries. You might also enjoy **Theater Maker** ($10), which creates stand-alone QuickTime applications that display a movie within a larger background (for example, an image of a TV set). You can get all of these utilities, plus others such as Aladdin's **Popcorn,** from user groups and on-line services.

HOT TIP

There are two ways to copy or cut a piece of a movie. You can position the Slider thumb at the beginning of the desired section, then hold down Shift and begin playing the movie. When you release Shift, the movie stops and the played portion is selected. Alternatively, you can press Shift while dragging the thumb in the Slider. You can then copy or cut the selected portion. To insert it into another location in the same movie (or another movie), move the thumb to the desired point and paste.

BARGAIN

Producing movies on a budget (AA/MM). If you want a more robust movie-editing solution but are short of cash, consider these wallet-conscious packages. **QuickFLIX!** ($150, VideoFusion) has an intuitive interface that walks you through every step of the movie-making process, from video recording to editing, titling, and special effects. Aimed at novice users with LC-class machines, it eschews the advanced video-editing features of Premiere and VideoShop, while offering many of the special effects in big brother VideoFusion (described under "Special Effects," below).

Motion Works' $250 **Multimedia Utilities** covers the movie-making gamut. MovieEdit lets you add sound, titles, graphics, and additional video to QuickTime movies; SoundMate records and edits sounds; TransMorph does simple warping and morphing of images; MotionPaint creates animated cel sequences; MovieClick adds "hot spots" (programmable buttons) to movies; and CameraMan records your on-screen activity as a QuickTime movie.

Premiere (MF/AA). Adobe's **Premiere** is the leading video-editing package, with good reason: It has the most flexible interface for editing movie clips, the heart of most multimedia projects. Premiere 4 handles up to 99 video and 99 audio tracks, letting you adjust motion, filters, and transparency separately for each track. The Trimming window makes it easy to edit the heads and tails of video clips, and previewing your creative progress, especially repeated previews of the same segment, is relatively fast. Premiere has robust title-making tools, and it provides a good selection of filters and transition effects, although not as extensive as those in dedicated special-effects programs (described under "Special Effects," below). Many filters, including some for Photoshop, incorporate a time factor—the Photoshop Twirl filter actually twirls, for example. You can digitize video from within Premiere, and high-end users can generate SMPTE time code and edit decision lists (EDLs) for broadcast-quality work.

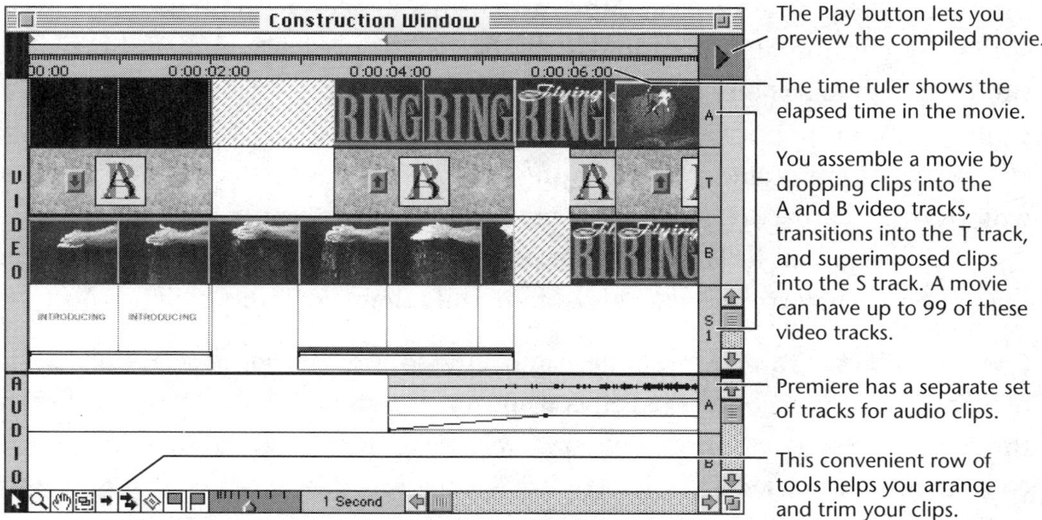

In Premiere, Adobe's popular video editor, you perform most editing tasks in the Construction window, a timeline with multiple tracks for video and audio.

Most of Premiere's tools are usable by beginning movie-makers as well as video pros. If you don't receive Premiere bundled with a digitizing board, however, its $800 price (which includes a CD-ROM of movies and tutorials) is steep for novice use. In that case, consider the Limited Edition of Premiere that's bundled with Photoshop LE in Adobe's **Audition** package ($250), which also includes a CD-ROM of stock photos and movies. Premiere LE has most of the full version's essence (minus higher-end features such as EDLs and titling), and you can upgrade later if you want.

BARGAIN

Like Photoshop, Premiere lets you add new capabilities via plug-in modules. It supports many popular Photoshop plug-in packages, such as Kai's Power Tools and Aldus's Gallery Effects series (see "Plug-In Power" in Chapter 15). Or check out **Dynamic Effects** ($120, Gryphon Software), a set of 20 Premiere-specific filters that includes time-distortion, ghosting, and vintage-movie effects. If you're working with videotape, Abbate Video's **VTK Plug-In Pack** ($100) lets you control virtually any VCR or camcorder from within Premiere.

VideoShop (MM). If you don't need the bells and whistles of Premiere, **VideoShop 2** ($500, Avid Technology) offers a simpler approach to editing a movie. In Premiere, you drag video clips into separate A and B tracks, align them, and then drag a transition filter into a third channel. VideoShop lets you simply drag clips one after the other into its Sequencer window and apply transitions by clicking and dragging at the border of two clips. VideoShop offers similar (albeit less robust) features to those in Premiere—from special effects to titling to audio support—and its tools for combining and layering movies make VideoShop a good choice for creating composite-video effects. The program won't satisfy hard-core video mavens, however. For example, it can't convert digital edits into an EDL for videotape editing, although by the time you read this Avid may have released an add-on module that adds time-code support.

Special effects (MM/AA). Premiere and VideoShop have good selections of filters and transitions, but for advanced special effects you'll also need a program that specializes in *compositing*, *filtering*, *morphing*, *warping*, motion control, and color manipulations.

GOOD FEATURE

VideoFusion ($650, VideoFusion) is speedy and easy to use, with excellent tools for the mid-range user, including dynamic morphing, image warping, and a

VideoFusion lets you choose between a timeline window (bottom) and a storyboard format (top left) for adding special effects to movies. You can preview the results in a player window (upper right). QuickFLIX!, the budget-priced video editor, offers this same interface.

nifty Pan Zoom Rotate effect. If you have a wad of cash and the desire for broadcast-quality special effects, CoSA's **After Effects** ($2,000) is the way to go. It can animate movies or still images over time, altering their position and layering them with other movies. None of the effects are final until the movie is output, so you can build effect upon effect, yet still go back and edit the first one.

You'll need an '040-class machine to use **Video Graffiti** ($400, Neil Media), but it's the first program to offer *rotoscoping*—the ability to paint on frames of a QuickTime movie, individually or while it plays—within a single

High-End Video (MM)

If you're serious about capturing and outputting NTSC-quality video, you'll need more—a lot more—than QuickTime. Even with its built-in compressors, QuickTime can't display full-frame, full-motion video without a very fast processor (at least a 33-MHz, '040-class machine), a compression board, and a large, fast hard disk (with at least a 10MB-per-second transfer rate).

A *compression board,* which has a special chip that runs the compression algorithm (usually Photo-JPEG), will dramatically increase video-capture rates, giving you full-frame, full-motion video. The boards to consider come with **DigitalFilm 1.5** ($4,000, SuperMac), **MoviePak2 Pro Suite** ($4,200, RasterOps), and **VideoVision Studio** ($4,500, Radius). All can double as video display boards, capture both video and audio, and perform RGB-to-NTSC conversions for video output. RasterOps also has a mid-range package, **MoviePak Presenter** ($1,500), and it offers daughterboards that add compression capabilities to some of its video cards.

If you want to edit and/or catalog material on videotape, a couple of budget-minded products let you do it directly from the Mac. **VideoDirector** ($200, Gold Disk) and **Video-Toolkit** ($280, Abbate Video) give you on-screen controls for operating most VCRs and camcorders. Once you've finished making your edits, the programs use the edit decision list (EDL) to automatically assemble the final tape (you'll need two VCRs).

application (finally, an easy way to add light-saber effects to your sci-fi movies!). Previously, you had to export movies from Premiere or VideoShop and paint them frame by frame in Photoshop or Painter.

Morphing (MM, Ben Long). From *Terminator 2* to Michael Jackson videos to razor-blade commercials, morphing is hot stuff. This unusual transition uses stretching and blending techniques to create the illusion that one image has melted into another. For example, a woman's face could turn seamlessly into a lion's head. VideoShop, VideoFusion, and Motion Works' Multimedia Utilities offer some morphing capabilities, but for the best results consider a dedicated program. Morphing is a limited effect, however, so be sure you'll use it before whipping out your credit card.

GOOD FEATURE

Morph ($240, Gryphon Software) lets you morph either two still images or two videos, creating a QuickTime movie as output. You define the morph by applying reference points to each image and arranging them so Morph knows what part of the first image maps to which part of the second image. Some people think **Elastic Reality** ($350, Elastic Reality) produces better results, because it uses Bézier curves to let you more precisely define the morphing areas, and you can morph different image areas at different rates.

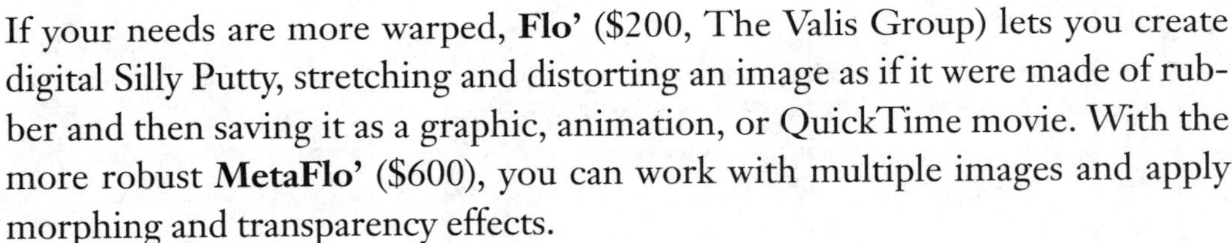

If your needs are more warped, **Flo'** ($200, The Valis Group) lets you create digital Silly Putty, stretching and distorting an image as if it were made of rubber and then saving it as a graphic, animation, or QuickTime movie. With the more robust **MetaFlo'** ($600), you can work with multiple images and apply morphing and transparency effects.

More QuickTime Tips

HOT TIP

Startup and screensaver movies (AA). Want your Mac to play a favorite movie during startup? Rename any MooV file Startup Movie and put it in the Startup Items folder (inside the System Folder). How about when your Mac goes to sleep? Two free utilities, **Movies 'Til Dawn** and **Movies After Dark,** can automatically play movies as screensavers if you also have After Dark (see "Screensavers" in Chapter 13).

Trading color for speed (MM). For the best trade-off of color vs. speed, record and save movies in 16-bit color. (In the Monitors control panel, that's Thousands or 65,536 Colors.) A 16-bit movie looks almost identical to a 24-bit movie and it plays *much* faster, because the Mac is only processing two-thirds as much data. In recognition of this, QuickTime's Video compressor only stores 16 bits of data, even if the movie was captured in 24 bits.

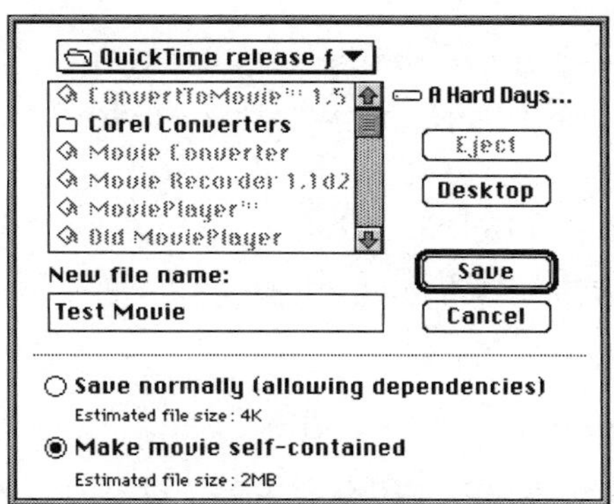

You can make a movie self-contained—without links to other movie files—by choosing Save As in MoviePlayer and then clicking the appropriate radio button. Note the enormous size difference between the two options.

Self-contained movies (MM). Because of the large amounts of data involved, the Mac doesn't usually copy the actual movie when you paste or place one into a presentation, text file, or composite movie. All that's stored in the document is a *reference* (a pointer to the original movie's location). This strategy is faster and greatly reduces file sizes, but it means the original movie (with its original name) must remain accessible to the document. Otherwise, when you open the file the movie won't play—a potentially embarrassing situation.

If you're using a video-editing program (MoviePlayer, Premiere, et al.), you can minimize problems by saving movies without references (also called *dependencies*). When you choose this option, the program incorporates all movie data into the main file and severs the links. The result is a completely self-contained—albeit larger—file.

Playing movies backward (MM). If you've tried this trick (see the box "QuickTime Controller Shortcuts" on page 696), or jumped to an arbitrary point in a movie, you've probably experienced delays and poor playback. The culprit is *temporal compression*, a technique QuickTime uses to further reduce movie size. Instead of saving every frame, QuickTime saves the difference between consecutive frames. This means that to display frame 4, QuickTime must first read frames 1, 2, and 3. An entire movie frame, or *key frame*, is saved only at specific intervals (say, every 15 frames).

If you want to play a movie smoothly in reverse or quickly jump to any frame, recompress the movie with different settings. Open the Compression Settings dialog box and reduce the key-frame number or set the Temporal slider (accessed with the More button) to Low or Least. Remember that these strategies will increase file size.

Premiere Tips

(MF)

Managing Premiere's transitions. Premiere 3 has more than 60 snazzy transitions—a bounty of digital riches. But what if you're unsure which one you want and need to compare a few alternatives, such as several kinds of dissolves? Or what if you can't remember the name of a desired effect? Scrolling down the long Transitions window to recall (or find) an effect is tedious, but there's a solution: Rename the transitions.

Each one is a separate file in Premiere's Plug-Ins folder. Open the folder and rename the transitions to change their alphabetical order. This little secret lets you:

- **Put favorite transitions first.** Add a space or two in front of the names of transitions you rely on most frequently. They'll appear at the top of the Transitions window.
- **Group transitions by category.** Insert a category name before each plug-in's name. For example, transitions that "peel" an image to reveal the next image (such as Center Peel) can be renamed Peel; [*Name*] (e.g., Peel; Center). All peel effects will then cluster together in the Transitions window.

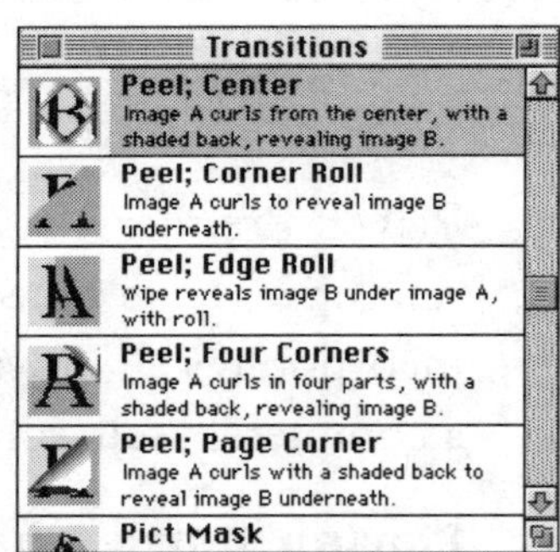

Locating a transition in Premiere's Transitions window is much easier if you change the names so that related effects, such as peels, appear together.

To make your editing even more efficient, use the same renaming technique to sort the contents of the Filters dialog box.

Filter-size sensitivities. Several Premiere filters have an annoying quirk: When you preview the filter in a smaller window than your movie's final frame size, the effect appears at an inaccurately large scale. This can mislead you into

Original  **Preview effect** 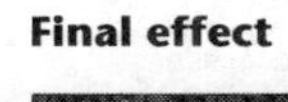 **Final effect**

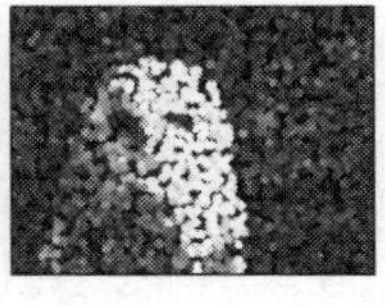

Certain Premiere filters don't always preview correctly, which can mislead you into choosing the wrong filter settings. In a half-size Preview window, for example, the Pointillize filter produces results that are twice as large (middle) as the actual effect that appears in the finished movie (right).

choosing the wrong filter settings. The built-in previews within Premiere's filter dialog boxes unavoidably suffer from this quick. When preview accuracy counts, here's an alternative.

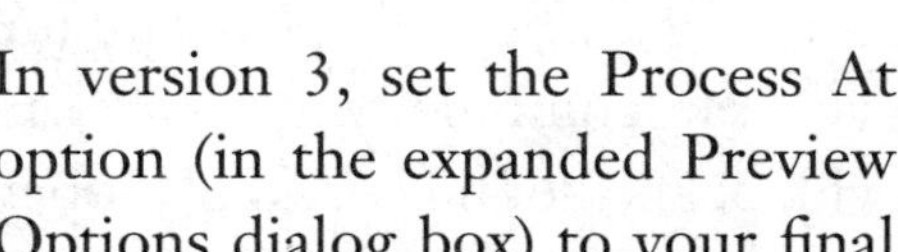

In version 3, set the Process At option (in the expanded Preview Options dialog box) to your final output size. Then use another preview command, such as Snapshot, for WYSIWYG results. An extra benefit: The correctly sized temporary preview files that Premiere creates may reduce the compiling time for your final movie.

Earlier versions of Premiere don't have the Process At option. In that case, set the Preview window to your final frame size (at least temporarily) before triggering a preview. (To quickly snap to standard frame sizes, hold down Option as you drag the lower-right corner of the Preview window.)

Unfortunately, all of these methods require extra compiling time. So if you have a slow Mac, stay aware of the filter-size problem when you preview. For future reference, here are the filter culprits: all Blur filters, all Sharpen filters, Convolution Kernel, Crystallize, Mosaic, Pointillize, Stylize, Tiles, and ZigZag.

Freezing a frame. Inevitably, one of your video clips will be slightly too brief for your needs. Premiere has a Speed command that can stretch a clip's duration, but it also slows the pace of action and any attached sound.

If the clip is followed by a transition, here's another approach: Create a PICT image of the clip's last frame, using the Clip Window and the Frame as PICT command. Then place the PICT immediately after the too-short clip so that it overlaps the last second or two of your transition. (Drag the PICT clip's edge, if necessary, to adjust its duration.) Few viewers will notice a frozen image in the final frames of most transitions because it's sufficiently obscured by the transition's effect.

Presentations

If multimedia is defined as the blending of different types of media, then presentation software is its very essence. That's right: Those slide-making programs that marketing and business folks use every day for sales, education, and training are actually powerful multimedia tools. With a presentation program, you can combine text, charts, and illustrations—and, if you wish, animation, video, and sound—into eye-opening visuals that keep the audience awake and get your points across in style. You can choose from a variety of output options, including on-screen presentations, 35mm slides, overhead transparencies, audience handouts, and videotape.

What to Look For (SC)

Presentation software comes in two basic flavors. *Traditional presentation programs*, such as PowerPoint and Persuasion, are essentially slide-making tools for business presentations chock full of charts and bullet points. If you're doing an on-screen slide show, you can add QuickTime movies and sounds.

Multimedia presentation programs output only to the screen (or videotape), but they offer more pizzazz. Not only can you combine elements from a variety of sources—including sounds and movies—but you also can define precisely when and how they will come and go over time. For example, you could have a pie chart roll onto the screen and break apart. Then each slice tumbles off the screen in a different direction while theme music pounds in the background. Two seconds later, the company logo fades in while a narrator adds a pithy comment. Most multimedia programs also offer rudimentary interactivity, allowing you (or a client) to jump to different points in the presentation at will.

Whether you opt for an old-fashioned or new-fangled presentation program, here are some key features to look for.

Import capabilities. You'll probably create most of your media elements elsewhere, so be sure the program imports the file formats you need for text, graphics, animation, video, and sound. Typically, traditional programs offer better support for spreadsheet data, while multimedia programs can handle

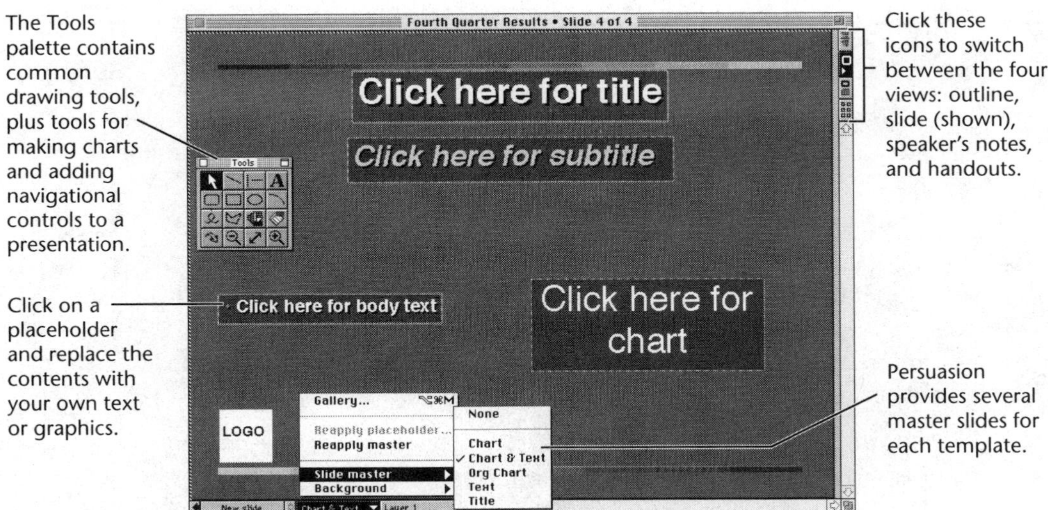

Presentation programs such as Persuasion provide a variety of templates—predesigned slides with color-coordinated backgrounds and formatted text.

more sound and animation formats. For a peek at some prepackaged art, movies, and sound, see the box "Clip Media" on page 675 and "Clip Art" in Chapter 15.

Media creation and editing. You don't want to import everything, so look for text-formatting features (including a spelling checker!) and basic drawing tools. Traditional programs can create graphs from scratch, while some multimedia presenters have sound editors. But if, for example, you require a truly sophisticated chart, you'll have to produce it in a dedicated program such as DeltaGraph Pro (see "Graph-ically Speaking" in Chapter 15).

Run-time player. This is critical if you want to hand out copies of presentations. A run-time player is a limited version of the program that plays back presentations but can't create them. You can freely distribute it with your presentations, so that clients can view them without the full program installed on their computer.

Don't forget to include external source files (such as QuickTime movies) when you distribute the presentation. And stick to core fonts such as Helvetica and Times so the text will look good on everyone's Mac.

Presentation Polishers (SC/AA)

The text is in place, the charts are drawn—now it's time for the finishing touches. Here are some clever utilities that can help you pick a pleasing color scheme and smooth the rough edges on your graphics.

If you aren't using a template, Pantone's $100 **ColorUP** can take the guesswork out of selecting colors that work well together for slide backgrounds, text, graphs, and so forth. Tell ColorUP your target output medium—screen, slides, and so forth—and it helps you choose coordinating colors that won't make people flinch or squint. When you import ColorUP's palette to Persuasion or PowerPoint, the palette colors are automatically assigned to specific presentation elements, such as titles or pie chart slices.

Let the ugly truth be known: Digital graphics often have jaggy edges, a problem that's magnified when they're projected on a large screen. **Smoothie** ($150, Peirce Software) anti-aliases the edges of PICT images, vastly improving the image quality of graphics created in drawing and presentation programs. **JAG II** ($130, Ray Dream) works the same magic on 3-D images, animations, QuickTime movies, and bit-mapped (TIFF, PICT) graphics.

If you don't have Smoothie or JAG, here's an alternative that works pretty well: Make the original image as large as possible, then scale it down to the proper size when you place it in the presentation program.

Templates. A healthy selection of predesigned slides or scenes makes creating consistent, professional-looking presentations faster and easier. The backgrounds, color schemes, text placement and formatting, charts and graphics, and (in some cases) animation are already in place. Just substitute your material for the placeholders, and away you go.

Transition effects. For on-screen presentations, you can vary the way one slide or scene is replaced by another. Wipes, fades, and dissolves can add subtle interest. Some programs offer funkier effects such as checkerboards and vertical blinds.

Tip: Use a program's build feature to reveal bullet points or chart elements one slide at a time. It adds drama and helps ensure that the audience will be listening to you instead of studying the slide.

Cross-platform compatibility. If you work in a mixed-platform environment, look for programs with Windows versions that allow users to open and edit presentations created on the Macintosh, and vice versa. Most slide-based presentations should convert with only minor changes, such as text reformatting (due to font differences).

Traditional tools. Slide-making programs have a few more key features:

- The *outliner*—a defining feature of these programs—lets you quickly enter or import text. Outline entries should be linked directly to slides, so that any text changes you make show up in the slide, and vice versa. It also should be easy to change the order and hierarchy of items in the outline.
- A *master slide* acts as a guide for individual presentation slides. Backgrounds, text placeholders, and graphics (such as a company logo) that you put on a master appear on any slide tied to that master. This lets you quickly format a large number of slides and ensure a consistent look for the presentation.
- A *slide sorter* lets you quickly rearrange a presentation by clicking and dragging thumbnails.
- *Audience handouts* and speaker's notes often contain thumbnails of the slides along with explanatory text.

Multimedia tools. Multimedia programs have specialties of their own:

- A *timeline* lets you control the comings and goings of each element—logos, movies, sounds, and so on—in the presentation by specifying start and end times.
- *Slide-import capabilities* help convert a traditional slide presentation into a multimedia extravaganza.

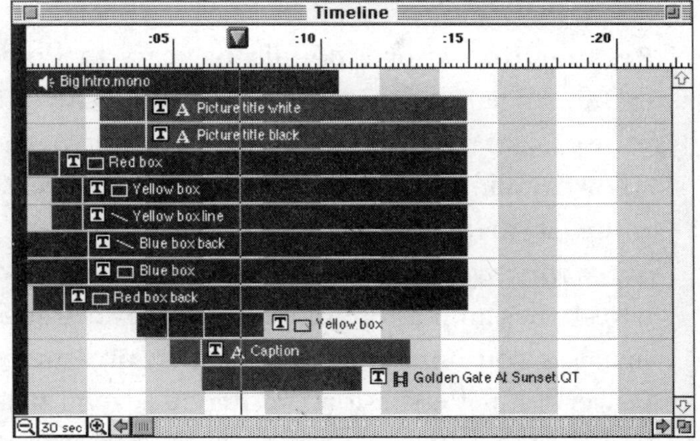

Multimedia presentation programs use timelines to let you control the comings and goings of movies, graphics, titles, and sounds. In Action! (shown here), each element is represented by a bar. Drag the bar to change when an object appears on screen and stretch the bar to lengthen the time it stays there.

- Basic *animation tools* let you add motion to text and graphics. For example, you could direct a circular corporate logo to bounce around a scene, then come to rest on top of an *i*.
- *Interactivity* means you can add buttons that let you (or another viewer) decide where to go in a presentation or when to play a QuickTime movie. This makes multimedia presentation programs good choices for producing training materials and kiosk displays.

Traditional Presentation Programs (SC)

Slide-making applications are the workhorses of business presentations, meeting the needs of most of the people most of the time. You can't go wrong with either Persuasion or PowerPoint (described below). Both offer good outliners and text handling, drawing tools, robust charting capabilities, numerous templates and transitions, a run-time viewer, and hot links to other programs—which means you could, for example, double-click on a table imported from Excel to open it directly into Excel for editing. If you're presenting mostly charts and graphs, also consider DeltaGraph Pro, a super graphing program with decent presentation features to boot (see "Graph-ically Speaking" in Chapter 15).

Persuasion. After a couple of years in PowerPoint's shadow, **Persuasion** ($500, Aldus) is again king of the hill, at least temporarily. Version 3 is easier to use, with floating palettes and better navigation icons, and its improved color handling ensures that color slides convert nicely to grayscale or black and white, so that audience handouts are now legible. *[I like the nudge controls and automatic kerning.—AA]* Beefed-up options for on-screen presentations include bare-bones animation; more control over transitions; and an autojump feature that lets you branch to other slides, presentations, or programs. And, unlike PowerPoint, Persuasion can juggle several master slides in a single presentation. For example, you could use one master for bullet-point slides, another for charts, and a third for titles. Persuasion's biggest drawback is its clumsiness in exchanging presentations with the Windows version.

GOOD FEATURE

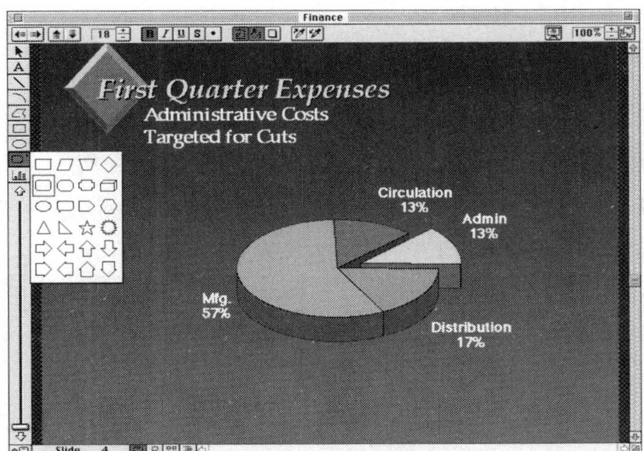

PowerPoint is a full-featured traditional slide-making program with a variety of tools neatly arranged around the window. It offers excellent graphing capabilities, and a handy shape tool (left) helps you draw perfect polygons.

PowerPoint. The original presentation program has that familiar Microsoft look and feel: a handy toolbar up top and hot links to other programs. **PowerPoint 3** ($500) has only a single master slide, but the ability to format slide text in outline view is a real time-saver. A versatile shape tool lets you quickly draw perfect stars, arrows, and triangles, and the artistically challenged will appreciate the color coach, which helps you select coordinated colors for your presentations. PowerPoint's near-flawless ability to transfer presentations to and from its Windows version is a definite advantage over Persuasion. Watch for version 4, which will sport more production aids and design features, such as improved toolbars, easier creation of organizational charts, and limited interactivity.

GOOD FEATURE

CA-Cricket Presents III. At $130, Computer Associates' presentation program costs hundreds less than its competitors, and it shows. It's hobbled by an outliner that isn't part of the main program—you must generate outlines in a separate (bundled) utility and import them, a cumbersome process. Menu arrangement is clumsy and charting options are limited, but it does have one nifty feature: You can edit QuickTime movies, adding titles, sounds, animation, and objects to individual frames. You can also export an entire presentation in QuickTime format, which lets you place (and run) it in other applications.

BAD FEATURE

Multimedia Presentation Programs

Multimedia programs have a steeper learning curve than their traditional cousins, but take heart: They're aimed at business folks, not multimedia gurus, and they're *much* less complex than full-fledged authoring programs such as Macromedia Director (described in the "Authoring Tools" section, below).

Some programs are based on the familiar slide metaphor, while others treat presentations as movies.

Action! (SC). The prototypical multimedia presenter, Macromedia's **Action!** uses a slide-based interface and represents time-based events with horizontal bars in a Timeline window. Drag a bar to change when an object appears on screen and stretch the bar to lengthen the time it stays there. This leaner, cheaper ($500) sibling of Macromedia Director provides all the basic multimedia-presentation tools, but it doesn't have any standout features to push it above the competition. Converting slide presentations is also a pain, because each slide must be imported separately as a PICT file.

BAD FEATURE

Astound (SC). You don't have to choose between a traditional and multimedia presentation program: Get **Astound** ($400, Gold Disk), the only program that offers the best of both worlds. Like traditional programs, it uses a slide-based approach and supports outlines, 35mm slides, overheads, and speaker's notes. You can even create charts and edit text (including spelling checks). Yet Astound also provides a full range of multimedia tools, including a timeline, rudimentary animation tools, interactive buttons, and a sound editor. To top it off, Astound has a well-designed interface that's relatively easy to use, and its transition effects are positively stunning.

GOOD FEATURE

Cinemation (SC). If you want a program that's easy to learn—particularly if you only create a few presentations a year—choose **Cinemation** ($500, Vividus). It treats presentations as movies: The Filmstrips window displays thumbnails of each frame in your movie, and the currently selected frame is displayed in the main window, where you add graphics, movies,

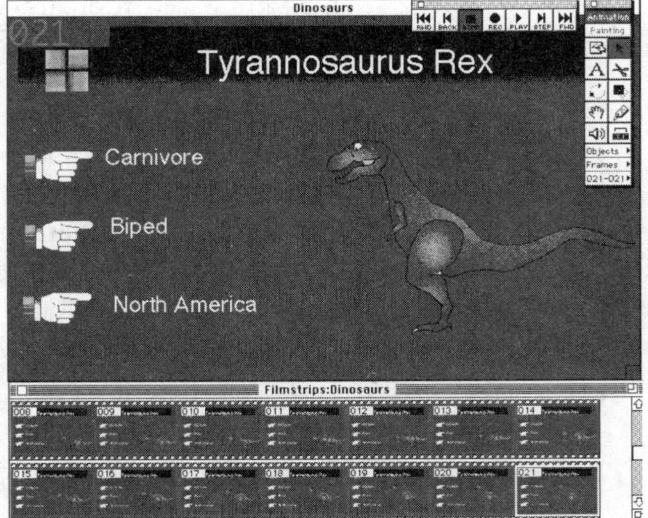

Instead of using a timeline or slide-based approach, Cinemation treats presentations like movies. You select a frame to edit in the Filmstrips window (bottom). The frame then appears in the large drawing window, ready for you to add text, graphics, animations, and sounds.

and sound and set up animations. This approach makes it difficult to time events precisely, but sequencing events relative to each other is a snap. You can export finished presentations as QuickTime movies. Best feature: Cinemation can quickly convert and animate an entire slide-based presentation (from, say, PowerPoint) by importing it as a Scrapbook file (see the box "Instant Presentations" on page 718).

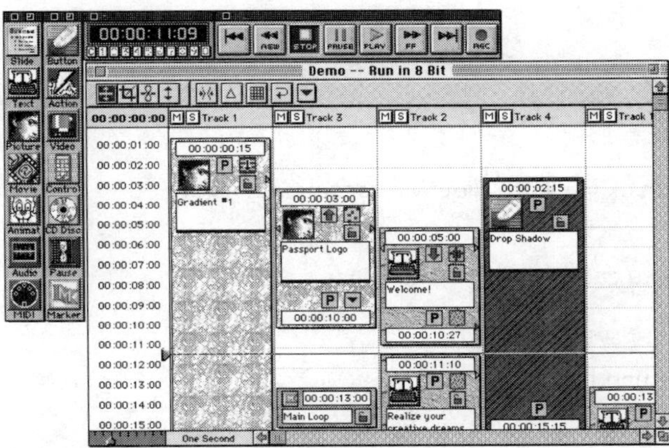

To create a presentation in Passport Producer Pro, you drag media types—such as text, sound, movies, and interactive buttons—from the toolbox (left) into tracks in the Time Sheet window. You can preview the presentation with the VCR-like controls at the top.

Passport Producer Pro (MM). A precise timeline, intuitive interface, excellent MIDI features, cross-platform capabilities, and AppleScript support are what set **Passport Producer Pro** apart from the competition. You build presentations by dragging and dropping media elements into tracks along a timeline. You can add path-based animations and interactive buttons for branching to other sections or executing an AppleScript script. Passport Designs also makes music software, and accordingly, Producer Pro has the best features for playing and editing MIDI files. Video professionals will appreciate the support for SMPTE time code and the ability to control external hardware such as VCRs and videodisc players. Producer Pro's biggest drawback: its $1,000 price tag.

Presentation Tips

Keep it simple (AA). Transitions, animations, movies, and sounds liven things up, no doubt about it, but too many will distract, instead of impress, your audience. Too much activity may also overstress your Mac, causing the presentation to become slow and jerky. Try using just one or two eye-catching effects to guide viewers to specific points.

Color concerns (AA). Use 8-bit color whenever possible, because the Mac can process it much faster than 24-bit color. For instance, create 8-bit animations

Instant Presentations (SC)

In a hurry? A real hurry? The fastest way to create an animated presentation is to combine two products: a traditional program (such as PowerPoint or Persuasion) and Cinemation. Excluding typing time, you can complete a text-oriented, 20-scene presentation in a half-hour. Here's how:

- Create an outline in PowerPoint's Outline view.
- Apply a template.
- Add any master slide items, such as a logo or date.
- Save the presentation in Scrapbook format.
- Launch Cinemation and import the Scrapbook file. Each slide will become a separate frame in Cinemation.
- Apply a Cinemation AutoMotion template to each frame.
- Play it back, then tweak as needed.
- Save it, hand the disk to your boss, and demand a raise.

Even if you have more time, it can still pay to base a multimedia presentation on a traditional one. Unlike their flashier siblings, traditional programs offer better backgrounds, streamlined text entry, find-and-replace features, spelling checks, and bodacious charting options. You can create a traditional presentation, then import it into a multimedia program and jazz it up.

and save them with the QuickTime Animation compressor set at highest quality (this also reduces file sizes). (For more on QuickTime compressors, see the box on page 698.)

File management (AA). Keep all the source files in the same folder with the presentation so they'll be available when you run it. This is important because many programs create a link to movies, sounds, and graphics instead of importing them. If you're distributing the presentation, keep in mind the space limitations of floppy disks and don't forget the run-time player!

Presentations to go (SC). If you plan to take your show on the road with a PowerBook, here are a few tips:

- Several programs provide templates specially designed to look good on a PowerBook screen.

- Keep it simple. QuickTime movies, jazzy sounds, and intricate drawings won't cut it on most PowerBooks.
- If you don't have a color PowerBook, test-drive the presentation in black and white or grayscale to be sure contrasting colors and text show up well. (Persuasion 3 has a built-in grayscale preview.)
- Stick to core fonts (see "Fonts Everyone Has" in Chapter 14). You'll save hard disk space and, in an emergency, won't have problems running the presentation on someone else's Mac.
- Bring backup—PowerBook batteries and some floppies with an extra copy of your presentation and the run-time player.
- A PowerBook screen works only for a handful of viewers. For larger groups, hook up an external monitor, video projector, or LCD projection panel.

Authoring Tools

Traditional presentation programs are great for producing on-screen slide shows, and their multimedia cousins even provide limited interactivity. But what if you want users to type in information and, based on what they enter, have the program respond in different ways? If your multimedia needs are this complex, you need an *authoring program* such as HyperCard, Macromedia Director, or the Apple Media Tool. Authoring packages are more difficult to learn and use than presentation programs, but they also give you more flexibility and control over the finished product, which could be an interactive sales kiosk, on-line training system, simulation, educational program, or a CD-ROM-based game (to list just a few possibilities).

```
on mouseUp
        go to next card
        put the date into card field "The Current Date"
end mouseUp
```

This simple HyperTalk script could be attached to a button that, when clicked, goes to the next card (screen) and displays the current date in the appropriate field.

What to Look For (MM/AA)

Authoring programs range from simple point-and-click software to full-blown programming environments. Here are some key features to consider when picking a package.

Scripting. In addition to the usual features found in multimedia presentation programs, most authoring programs offer some kind of *scripting language,* which lets you write simple programs, called *scripts,* to perform specific activities. HyperCard, for example, has a scripting language called HyperTalk.

With scripting, you can add a level of interactivity beyond mere button-pressing, greatly expanding the kinds of projects you can create. For example, you could produce a real estate advisory program that asks home buyers to enter information on their price range and desired location. Based on this data, the program would display digitized photos with details about houses that match their criteria. Depending on the scripting language, you could also write scripts that play QuickTime movies, call on other programs to perform certain tasks, or operate a device, such as a videodisc player, from within the presentation.

GOOD FEATURE

Scripting has two advantages over a programming language such as C or Pascal. First, a scripting language such as HyperTalk is easier to learn because its syntax is more like standard English. Second, HyperCard and other authoring programs simplify scripting by including prewritten script segments that you can use to quickly add graphics, text fields, and buttons to your multimedia project.

Expandability. On the down side, most scripting languages don't do everything a full-fledged programming environment can. Happily, in most cases you can use plug-in modules to add capabilities not intrinsic to the program.

GOOD FEATURE

HyperCard, for example, doesn't provide native support for color and can't access a device via the serial port. You can add these features, however, by using a HyperTalk script to access the appropriate external command (XCMD). In fact, XCMDs have become a standard approach for adding functionality and most authoring programs support them—particularly useful since XCMDs are a key way of adding control for external devices such as VCRs and videodisc players. There are a wide variety of XCMDs available from user groups and on-line services, and Heizer Software is a good source for commercial packages.

Multiplatform Multimedia (MM)

One day soon you'll be able to create presentations that run—without further modification—on multiple platforms. The key is Script X, a cross-platform multimedia scripting language, due for release any day from Kaleida Labs, a joint venture of Apple and IBM.

While you could write your production in Script X from scratch, most folks will probably wait for companies to update their products to save in Script X format. (Several companies, including Macromedia and Apple, have announced plans to do so.) This means you'll still create multimedia productions as usual, using existing programs such as Macromedia Director or the Apple Media Tool. But you'll save the presentation in Script X format, and the resulting file will play on any computer that has a Script X player (expect Mac and Windows versions first).

Many programs are also adding support for AppleScript, Apple's systemwide scripting language (see Chapter 3). AppleScript enables applications to talk to each other, adding a great deal of programming power. You could, for example, create a kiosk presentation in HyperCard that uses AppleScript to save entered data to a FileMaker database.

Run-time player. If you want to give your multimedia projects to others to run on their machines, be sure to evaluate the *run-time player*, a limited version of the program that lets people view presentations but not edit them. Some companies let you freely distribute the run-time players with projects. Macromedia, however, requires a 1 to 2 percent royalty for commercial distribution of Authorware-based productions, and Apple charges $500 per title for commercial distribution of projects produced with the Apple Media Kit. (Educational and nonprofit organizations can distribute Media Kit projects for free.)

Cross-platform compatibility. If you're a serious multimedia developer, you'll soon start thinking about developing for that *other* operating system, Windows. Both of Macromedia's products, Macromedia Director and Authorware, have Windows versions that are compatible with their Mac counterparts, allowing you to open, edit, and run Mac-originated projects. Developing cross-platform projects may soon be easier, however; see the box "Multiplatform Multimedia," above.

Authoring Programs

Mac-based multimedia has been around (and over-hyped) since 1987, so it's surprising how few products for multimedia authoring are available.

HyperCard (MM/AA). Apple originally developed HyperCard as a do-it-yourself construction kit to let Mac users easily create custom applications. It soon became the darling of multimedia developers, however, because it was easy to use, had a scripting language, was easily extensible via XCMDs, and came free with every Mac.

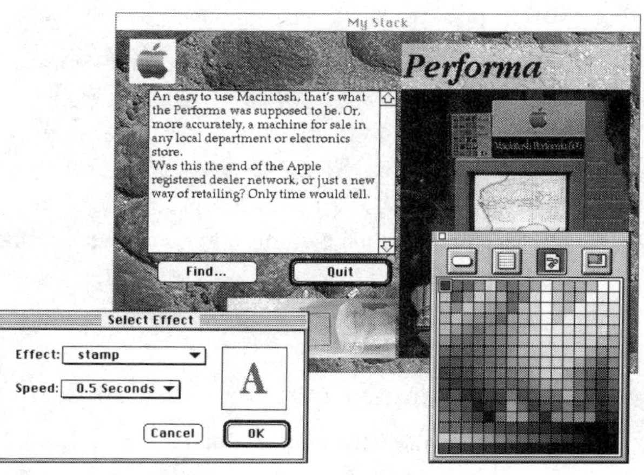

HyperCard, the Mac's first authoring tool, is a good choice for beginners, but it also can produce more sophisticated presentations. Version 2.2 finally lets you assign colors to buttons, fields, and backgrounds and apply transition effects between cards.

HyperCard presentations, called *stacks*, are made up of individual screens called *cards*. These cards can contain text, pictures, sounds, buttons, and—with appropriate XCMDs—animations and QuickTime movies. Scripts can be attached to cards, buttons, or text fields and triggered in a number of ways: when a card is displayed, when the cursor is over a button, or when you click in a field or on a button. To make new stacks, you can copy selected cards and buttons from existing stacks, or you can design new cards with HyperCard's text and paint tools and then use HyperTalk to create and attach scripts that make the stack do exactly what you want.

A run-time version of HyperCard, called the **HyperCard Player**, comes with every Mac, allowing you to play existing stacks. To create stacks, you need **HyperCard 2.2** ($250, Apple). The package contains the HyperCard programming environment plus sample stacks, stack templates, XCMDs, ready-made buttons, and the QuickTime Tools stack, which lets you insert and play movies in stacks. Version 2.2 corrects a long-standing HyperCard deficiency—no color support—with Color Tools, an XCMD that lets you add 256-color images to cards and colorize buttons, fields, and backgrounds. Opening Color Tools takes several seconds, however, and there are no color paint tools. And, when you first open a colorized stack, no color appears for a few seconds as HyperCard loads the XCMD. (You can remedy this by having a black first card and then moving to a colored one once HyperCard opens the XCMD.)

HyperCard 2.2 is also more extensible, adding support for AppleScript and WorldScript (which lets you create multilingual stacks) to its repertoire. Third parties offer their own enhancements, too. **ADDmotion II** ($95, Motion Works) is an XCMD that lets you create and animate characters on a card; at press time it was included in the HyperCard 2.2 package. **Fast Pitch Pro** ($80, OBjectic Systems) can convert HyperCard stacks into slide shows—complete with color graphics, movies, and sounds—without using HyperTalk scripting.

When to use it: HyperCard is a good choice for beginning multimedia authors, because it's cheap and you can quickly produce simple projects. It's particularly good for presentations involving lots of text. Because support for color, animation, and QuickTime movies isn't part of the core software, however, it doesn't handle these features as well as, say, Macromedia Director. But don't be fooled into thinking HyperCard can't handle complex projects—it was used to create Myst, the best CD-ROM game yet invented (see Chapter 20).

If you're a budding HyperTalk user, you can learn a lot by looking at other people's scripts. To see (or edit) the scripts behind a stack, first set the user level to 5 (Scripting) by choosing it on the Preferences card (Home menu). Then select the Button or Field tool, double-click on the desired object, and click Script in the resulting Info dialog box.

Two more quick tips: To keep two (or more) stacks open at the same time, hold down Shift each time you open a new stack. And if the menu bar isn't visible in a stack, ⌘ Spacebar will make it appear, allowing you to access menu commands.

SuperCard (MM/AA). **SuperCard** ($500, Allegiant Technologies) is basically an upscale version of HyperCard. Its scripting language, SuperTalk, is a superset of HyperTalk and it can convert HyperCard stacks and use XCMDs. Traditionally, SuperCard has had two key advantages over HyperCard: built-in color support and multiple on-screen windows. (As noted, HyperCard lets you open several stacks simultaneously, but switching between them is slow and cumbersome.) It also offers color drawing tools and can create cards of any size.

Unfortunately, SuperCard spent several years in limbo and lost its momentum. In early 1994, however, Aldus sold SuperCard to Allegiant Technologies, a startup company that includes members of the original development team. A long-overdue upgrade, version 1.7, provides integrated QuickTime support, enhanced sound capabilities, new scripting features, hypertext links, and greater support for HyperCard XCMDs. Allegiant also plans to release a Windows run-time player for SuperCard.

When to use it: SuperCard has most of HyperCard's strengths, and then some. It's an excellent general authoring tool, particularly in the educational arena.

Macromedia Director (MM/AA). **Macromedia Director 4** ($1,200) began life as an animation program, then Macromedia added scripting, making it possible to create interactive presentations. Today Director is the most popular multimedia authoring program, used to create everything from sales presentations to on-line help systems. Several popular CD-ROM games, such as Iron Helix, were developed in Director.

GOOD FEATURE

Director creates frame-based animations and provides rich tools for generating artwork, animations, and QuickTime movies. Using a timeline, you can combine and synchronize up to 32,000 elements to create sophisticated multimedia projects. Scripts can be attached to any frame or onscreen object; the scripts are executed when the frame is displayed or when the user clicks the object.

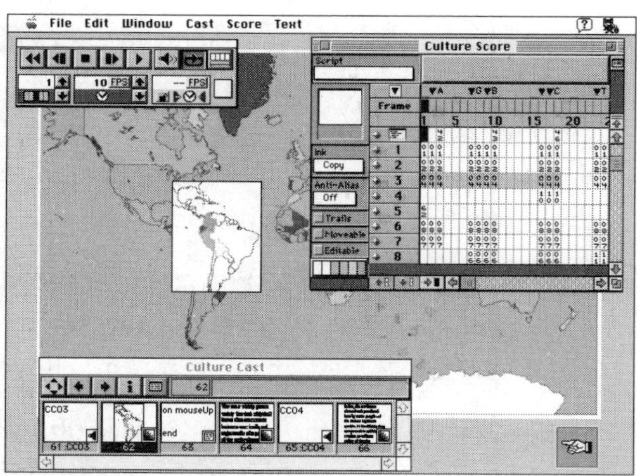

Macromedia Director is the most popular authoring program, in part because of its animation capabilities. Individual elements, such as graphics and Lingo scripts, are stored in the Cast window (lower left). You arrange these cast members on the Stage (main screen) and record their position in each frame in the Score window (upper right).

Lingo, Director's scripting language, is similar to HyperTalk, yet it's different (and complex) enough to cause confusion if you use both languages. Director can use XCMDs and also has its own plug-in modules, called *XObjects*, for controlling external audio and video devices. On the down side, Director is a complicated and expensive program and can be intimidating for new users. It's also memory-intensive—it prefers to load an animation into memory before playing it—and it doesn't handle text-based data very well.

When to use it: If you want lots of animation and graphics, choose Director.

Authorware Professional (MM). Macromedia's other authoring tool, **Authorware Professional 2,** is *much* more expensive ($5,000). It's designed primarily for computer-based training and educational courseware and includes functions for asking questions and recording the answers.

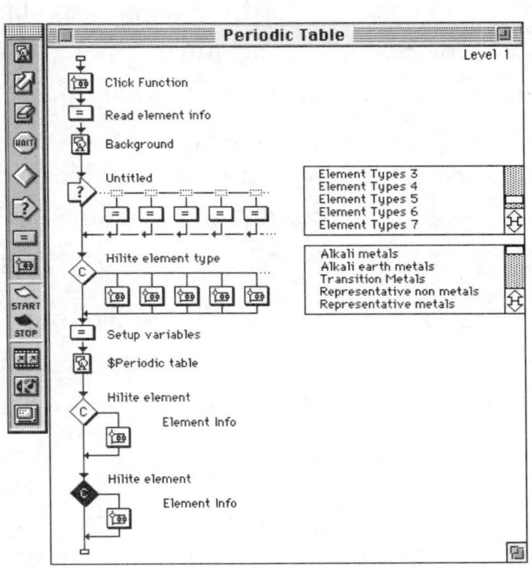

Instead of supplying a scripting language, Authorware lets you create a multimedia project by arranging icons in a flowchart. The icons represent different presentation elements, such as animation or user input.

Authorware doesn't have a scripting language. Instead, you organize icons—which represent elements and actions, such as a graphic or test of user input—into a flowchart that shows how the components will work together. This approach is faster and easier to use than scripting. You can create simple animations in Authorware and import Director presentations and scripts. It includes built-in support for videodisc players, and you can run the same presentation on both Mac and Windows machines from a single network server.

When to use it: Consider Authorware if you're doing training or educational projects.

Apple's multimedia tools (MM). Finally, if you can't face scripting and or the cost of Authorware, consider the **Apple Media Tool.** This $800 authoring program eschews scripting, offering instead an object-oriented approach that

resembles that of presentation tools such as Action! and Passport Producer Pro. You import media elements and arrange them into screens, applying transitions and defining how users will interact with buttons. The Media Tool has three key advantages: It's easy to use, it can save your production in formats playable on Windows or Power Mac machines, and a future version will support Script X. It won't replace Macromedia Director, however, because it doesn't animate, paint, edit video, or record sound.

If you need more control (such as tracking user responses) and you're ready to try some real programming, Apple also sells the **Apple Media Tool Programming Environment** ($1,000), a high-level language that lets you customize your production to the *n*th degree. And, last but not least, you can get both products bundled together—along with VideoFusion's FusionRecorder and a CD-ROM of sample projects with source code—as the **Apple Media Kit** ($1,500, Apple). All three products are available from APDA, Apple's developer group.

CD-ROM

When to use it: The Apple Media Tool is a good choice for kiosks or simple interactive presentations. Choose the Programming Environment for complex customized presentations.

18 Education & Reference

ONE OF THE EARLIEST PROMISES OF COMPUTERS was that they would put a vast amount of information at your fingertips. With the advent of CD-ROM technology, that promise has come true on the Macintosh.

Millions of megabytes of information—covering a vast array of subjects—have been collected, compiled, sorted, indexed, annotated, and condensed for your reference. Digital reference materials offer one great advantage over their paper counterparts: You can quickly search for and retrieve the information you need.

But what's more exciting is that developers have taken advantage of multimedia technology to enrich and enliven their material with graphics (including illustrations, drawings, and photographs), sounds (including voice-overs and music), and moving pictures (including videoclips and animations). This multimedia data is not merely adornment; it's designed to provide added understanding and insight to the information you're reviewing.

You'll find an abundance of titles and topics to choose from in the market; this chapter, which introduces you to more than 160 titles within six broad categories, only scratches the surface.

Contributors

Connie Guglielmo (CG) is the chapter editor.

Carolyn Said (CS), a senior editor at *MacWEEK,* wanted to research dictionaries and encyclopedias for this chapter so that she could decide which ones to use at home helping her son, B.B., with homework and research projects.

Lee Sherman (LS) is a San Francisco–based freelance writer whose work has appeared in *MacWEEK, NewMedia,* and *NeXTWORLD.* Now, he is also an amateur astronomer.

Contents

Compendiums vs. Interactive Experiences (CG)

You'll find a mixture of products here, and not only in terms of subject matter. To me, reference and education titles can be broadly defined in two categories: compendiums and interactive experiences. Information compendiums are products that provide a compilation of facts, or the complete text of some book or reference tome in digital format. Although there may be some multimedia data included (sound, animations, or the like), these products are mostly text-based and designed to provide quick, easy, and random access to information. Interactive experiences, on the other hand, are those products that use multimedia technology to bring a subject or topic to life by allowing you to look at the information in a way not possible in a static book format. These titles use sound, animations, video, graphics, and even text to maximum effect.

Take digital books as an example. You'll find the complete works of William Shakespeare (and other authors) in digital format. Compendiums are those products that contain the complete text of his plays, poems, and sonnets, with annotations, indexes, and a good searching engine. For a graduate student writing a thesis on how the word *nature* is used by Shakespeare, such a product is a dream; just type in the word and all references are found for you.

But you'll also find digital books that provide the complete text of one or a few of Shakespeare's works, and then delve more deeply into those works by including a biography of Shakespeare, a historical summary of the times he lived in, illustrations and artist renderings of how the plays were originally staged at the Globe Theater, and maybe videoclips from a movie of that work. For a student just discovering Shakespeare, this presentation provides insight into the author and his work.

So when you're looking into these titles, remember to ask yourself what you're after: a compendium or an experience.

CD-ROM Love Fest

(CG)

Although you'll find lots of products on floppy disk, the majority of reference works are being published on CD-ROM discs. Why overwhelmingly CD-ROM? The bottom line is that CD-ROM discs are currently the most cost-effective way to store massive quantities of data (upwards of 650MB on a single disc, compared to 1.4MB per floppy). If you're serious about using multimedia-enriched reference materials on a frequent basis, you'll need to consider getting a CD-ROM drive, if you haven't already.

Some educational titles that use video at the center of their presentation are distributed on *laserdisc,* the same format used to distribute high-quality movies for home use. (Beware, though: Not all laserdisc players are created equal. Only certain players have the computer hook-up necessary to work with your Mac, so don't assume that the laserdisc player you've got hooked up to your TV set will work with your Mac.) These products usually come with HyperCard stacks that you install on your Mac and that control the laserdisc. You click on icons or buttons (which usually resemble a video camera) when you want to play a video segment, and the stack automatically queues the laserdisc player, searches the laserdisc, and then displays the videoclip either on a TV screen or (if you have the appropriate video cards installed) on your Mac monitor.

Literature

(CG)

Most of these titles bring another dimension to the reading experience by adding supplemental material in the form of sound, graphics, and animations. Sometimes, though, the additional material you'll find will just be expanded pop-up footnotes.

Voyager's Expanded Books

In the same way paperbacks revolutionized the publishing market by making books available in small, lightweight editions, Voyager's Expanded Book series of fiction and nonfiction books on disk (originally designed with PowerBook and Duo users in mind) have redefined portability for the digital age. Click on the arrow to turn the page, or use the search tools to trace a character through a novel: The thoughtful layout and design make these books highly readable, and after a while, you forget that you're reading a book on disk rather than one on paper. The more than 60 titles in the series sell for under $30, with the majority carrying a $20 list price. The range of titles (including many current best-sellers) is impressive: **Jurassic Park, The Autobiography of Malcolm X, The Pelican Brief, Conduct Unbecoming, Of Mice and Men,** the complete works of Jane Austen, lots of science fiction (including everything ever written by Isaac Asimov), and even children's favorites such as **A Wrinkle in Time.**

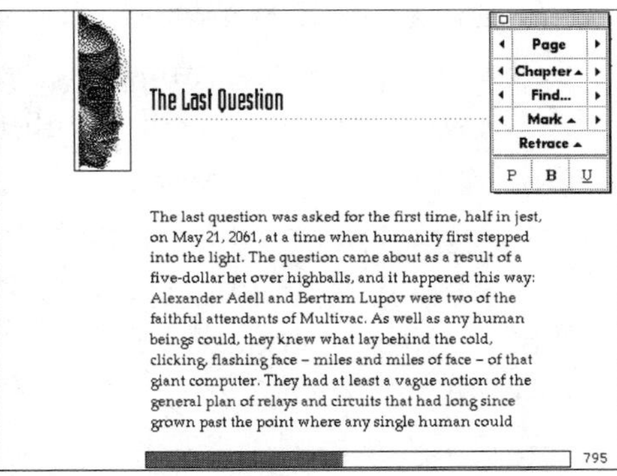

Voyager's Expanded Book series puts best-sellers and classics in digital form. But they're more than just disk-based versions of the books: You'll find an elegant interface and pop-up annotations that enrich the text. If you want to look up a previous passage or go to your favorite scene in the book, the fast search tool will find it for you.

Classic Literature

We'll never know whether William Shakespeare would have been even more prolific with a Mac, but developers have lined up to make sure that his words live on. Many of these works are compendiums, including Creative Multimedia's **Shakespeare on Disc** ($30), a CD-ROM containing 37 plays and 159 sonnets and poems; and **Shakespeare's Works** ($50) from Books-on-Disk, which gives you quick text access (on floppy disk) to the plays and sonnets.

For an interactive look at the plays, check out Shakespeare on Disc's (that's the developer's name) **Shakespeare and the Globe Theater** ($130), a HyperCard-based presentation that provides a comprehensive introduction to the playwright (his life and times) and the historical setting in which his plays were staged. Intellimation has also developed a HyperCard-based look at old Will with **Shakespeare's Life and Times** ($80), designed for 11th and 12th graders. Thanks to HyperCard, you'll be able to jump from one topic to related topics by clicking on the buttons (or links) plotted out by each developer.

To study a single play in depth, look for titles such as The Voyager Co.'s CD-ROM-based version of **Macbeth** ($100), an interactive experience that offers annotations, commentary, and the complete performance of the tragedy by the Royal Shakespeare Company. Learning Tomorrow has also spent lots of development time creating HyperCard-based interactive multimedia presentations of **Macbeth** ($70) and **Romeo and Juliet** ($70), each providing historical information about the plays and times they depict as well as full text. MacBeth, for example, is built around the script of the play, allowing you to read the text, look up selected words in the glossary, or play through an animated version of the action. There's also a section that has a "director" leading you through an analysis of the four main characters from an actor's point of view.

An interactive version of Shakespeare's Macbeth from Learning Tomorrow is built around a script of the play, allowing you to, among other things, play through an animated version of the action. The synopsis view is shown here.

For other classics compendiums, look into Shakespeare on Disc's floppy-disk-based version of Oscar Wilde's **The Importance of Being Earnest** ($60) or **Milton on Disk,** a floppy-disk-based package containing the complete works of the 17th-century poet. ($130).

If you are interested in classic literature but don't have the time to read, Bureau of Electronic Publishing publishes the ultimate compendium: **Monarch Notes on CD-ROM** ($70), containing more than 200 summaries and notes on authors ranging from Shakespeare to Kafka to Woolf.

And for literary commentary in a somewhat more interesting and interactive form, check out The Voyager Co.'s **Poetry in Motion** ($30), a CD-ROM with audio, graphics, and over 90 minutes of QuickTime video that gives 18 modern poets (including Allen Ginsberg, William S. Burroughs, and Tom Waits) a chance to recite/perform their work and comment on it (interviews with some of the authors are also included).

Mysteries and Horror

If you're into mystery, Creative Multimedia publishes a CD-ROM offering Sir Arthur Conan Doyle's complete text with **Sherlock Holmes on Disc** ($30).

Discis Knowledge Research will get your heart thumping with an interactive CD-ROM version of Edgar Allan Poe's classic short story, **The Tell-Tale Heart** ($60), or turn to Queue's compendium of classic horror: a color CD-ROM ($50) containing the text, with graphics, narration, and questions, called **The Frankenstein, Dracula, and Dr. Jekyll & Mr. Hyde CD.**

Religion

Even the oldest texts have found new life on CD-ROM. Davka publishes the **Judaic Classics Library** ($500), which is interactive CD-ROM storytelling, as well as floppy-disk-based compendiums such as **Talmud Tutor** ($60) and **HyperHanukkah** ($40).

The Time Warner Interactive Group offers the CD-ROM-based **New Family Bible** ($50), with color painting and audio dramatizations of 40 stories from the Bible covering Biblical events from the Garden of Eden to Moses' journey to the Promised Land. There are also maps of Biblical lands, family trees of the characters, and audio pronunciation of names and places in both English and Hebrew.

Time Warner's New Family Bible contains 40 stories from the Bible, covering events starting with Adam and Eve's misadventures in the Garden of Eden.

For the complete text of the Bible, there's the **Holy Bible** ($60) from Linguist's Software and **The King James Bible** ($50) from Books-on-Disk. Medina Software offers several text-based compendiums related to the Bible, including **MacGospel** ($13), which presents the gospels of Matthew, Mark, Luke, and John.

Classic References (CS)

Electronic media's ability to quickly find a particular word is perhaps nowhere more useful than in the books created just for that purpose: dictionaries and encyclopedias. Most of the big names in reference books—*Webster's*, *Random House*, *Compton's*, and even the venerable *Oxford English Dictionary*—have seen that advantage and have jumped on the electronic bandwagon. Some of them have depended on the benefits of the search feature alone to get you to spend your money, but others—especially the encyclopedias—take more advantage of the medium, bringing words and concepts to life with colorful and detailed graphics such as illustrations, maps, animations, and even QuickTime video. And many companies take advantage of the massive storage power of CD-ROM to bundle several reference works in a single package.

Dictionaries

In the beginning was the word, and it was written down by Noah Webster (and a few others). You'll find several versions of Webster's dictionary in electronic form. What's the difference among them? A matter of deciding which words make the final cut as the core set of terms considered fundamental to our language today. In addition to the text, you'll find these works enlivened by graphics and illustrations.

WordPerfect publishes the **Random House Webster's Dictionary & Thesaurus, College Edition** ($100). It gives definitions for more than 180,000 words and offers the added benefit of linking those words to more than 275,000 synonyms. WordPerfect also offers the **Random House Webster's School and Office Dictionary** ($30), which contains 60,000 definitions. Highlighted Data, meanwhile, sells **Webster's Ninth Collegiate Dictionary** ($200), which includes 200,000 definitions.

If *Webster's* way of defining the language doesn't appeal to you, electronic versions of other popular dictionaries are also on the market, including Random House's **Unabridged Dictionary, Second Edition,** offering 315,000 entries on CD-ROM for $80; packaged with the hardbound book, it's $160.

SoftKey International has brought the **American Heritage Electronic Dictionary** to market in two editions: the **Deluxe Edition** ($130) includes 310,000 definitions; the **Standard Edition** ($60) has 116,000 definitions.

But real word mavens will want **The Oxford English Dictionary, Second Edition** from Oxford University Press ($900). The CD-ROM contains more than 500,000 definitions (including word origins) and 2.4 million illustrative quotations.

More Help for Writers

Having conquered the application-software market, Microsoft is ready to tackle the reference market with a heavyweight reference CD. Its **Microsoft Bookshelf** packs seven books onto one disc, including an encyclopedia, a dictionary, a thesaurus, a book of quotations, an atlas, and a world almanac, all for the low price of $100.

Microlytics offers both **Word Finder Plus** ($40), which has 1 million synonyms and 50,000 definitions, and an electronic version of **The Elements of Style** ($30), with all the text from Strunk and White's classic book.

For poets and others who care, **A Zillion Kajillion Rhymes** ($50) from Eccentric Software that can generate rhymes for almost any word.

Encyclopedias

Encyclopedias seem like a natural for the Mac, which can add multimedia extras such as videoclips of historic events, animations to illustrate concepts, soundbites of famous speeches, and, of course, fast searches and hypertext buttons that can take you to related material with a click of the mouse. The differentiating factors seem to be the number of ways you can search the encyclopedias (Compton's for instance will narrow the search to only entries with graphics, if that's what you're interested in), and the way they slice and dice the data for you with timelines and topic and thematic outlines. Of course, for most people, price may be the overriding sell, and the good news is that street prices put these

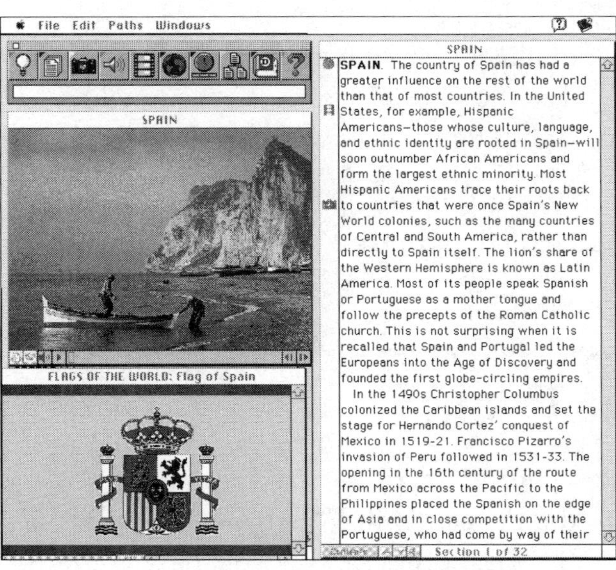

For the price ($150), Compton's Interactive Encyclopedia puts a lot of information at your fingertips. In addition to the text articles (about 34,000 of them), this CD-ROM-based multimedia encyclopedia has lots of graphics, sounds, videoclips, and an impressive search engine that the company unsuccessfully tried to patent.

tomes of wisdom at a price point well below what you would have to pay for their paper-bound counterparts.

CD-ROM

Compton's New Media offers **Compton's Interactive Encyclopedia** ($150), a CD-ROM based on *Compton's Encyclopedia* that boasts an elegant interface, 34,000 articles, 7,000 pictures, more than 50 minutes of sound, 89 videos, a timeline, a topic outline, and a browser path to related subjects. A few years ago, this CD-ROM would have cost you about $300, but the company decided to drop its price after Microsoft announced it was getting into the reference market with Encarta.

Microsoft's **Encarta** ($140) features 26,000 articles organized both alphabetically and thematically (based on *Funk & Wagnall's Encyclopedia*, but significantly expanded by Microsoft), as well as more than 100 animations and videoclips, thousands of photos, interactive charts and simulations, more than eight hours of audio, a timeline, an interactive atlas, and a game called MindMaze.

CD-ROM

The New Grolier Multimedia Encyclopedia ($400) from Grolier Electronic Publishing provides the complete text of the 21-volume *Academic American Encyclopedia* (33,000 articles), thousands of illustrations, pictures, and maps, plus four hours of videoclips, animations, and sound. The disc also offers a timeline and an outline arranged by branches of knowledge.

Last but not least, Microlytics publishes the **Random House Encyclopedia** ($70): 20,000 text-only articles distributed on floppy disks.

History and Current Events (CG)

The past and not-too-distant past keeps getting rewritten—and repackaged—in digital form. From the Civil War to the Persian Gulf War, from Columbus to Martin Luther King, Jr., important historical events and people have come under the scrutiny of developers eager to package history for you in multimedia presentations.

Military Confrontations

War is a popular topic for multimedia reference works, designed to appeal to history buffs or teachers who need supplemental material for their classes.

The battles, people, and events of the Civil War have been packaged in **Point of View: The Civil War and Reconstruction** ($250), a laserdisc presentation with graphics, audio, and video designed for 8th to 12th graders and distributed by Scholastic Software.

Using its relationship with Time *magazine as a source of stories and photographs, the Time Warner Interactive Group put together a CD-ROM entitled Desert Storm: The War in the Persian Gulf.*

CD-ROM

Using photos and text that appeared in *Time* magazine, the Time Warner Interactive Group has put together two CD-ROMs about relatively recent events: **Desert Storm: The War in the Persian Gulf** ($40) and **Seven Days in August** ($60), which traces the creation of the Berlin Wall and the escalation of the Cold War. The photos are compelling, the writing straightforward, and the interface thought-fully designed; the fact that both titles came out relatively soon after the events is a sure indication that Time Warner will continue to repackage news and photos in an interactive medium.

CD-ROM publisher Quanta Press wins the war of titles with its USA Wars series, which includes text and graphic-based compendiums of the **Civil War, Desert Storm, Korea,** and **Vietnam** ($70 each), and **World War II** ($80).

World History

More sweeping views of history are offered by a variety of publishers who recognize that reading about the past can be, well, boring. That's why these CD-based titles strive to create interactive experiences.

Bureau of Electronic Publishing has picked no less than the **History of the World** as the subject matter for its CD-ROM ($125, with annual updates). The company also offers **The Multimedia World Factbook** ($30), a CD-ROM that profiles 248 countries using text, statistical data, and lots of imagery.

The **Time Traveler CD** also takes on a large chunk of history: This interactive CD-ROM ($160) from Orange Cherry/New Media Schoolhouse covers human history from 4000 B.C. to the present through words and pictures and is designed to bring history to life for students.

For information on the Middle East, Quanta Press offers its **Middle East Diary** ($100), a CD-ROM containing reports on both events and people that shaped the region, as well as **European Monarchs** ($80), a CD-ROM with stories, images, and the family trees of Europe's kings and queens.

Special Interests

Among special-interest historical works, Quanta Press publishes a CD-ROM ($70) containing a text and image database about **North American Indians,** while AfroLink Software's HyperCard-based **Who We Are** ($122 black and white; $144 color) tackles the subject of black world history.

U.S. History

Great Wave Software offers **American Discovery** ($50), an interactive look at U.S. geography and history with maps, photos, illustrations, and a basic overview of American history that might appeal to students reluctant to spend time with their textbooks but who might be willing to explore with their computer.

For an unusual look at the United States, you might look into (or convince your local school to look into) **GTV: A Geographic Perspective on America History** ($800, Optical Data), a beautifully designed laserdisc-based presentation put together by the National Geographic Society. Filled with two hours of video, 1,600 still images, and 200 maps, it does a great job of enlivening learning about history and geography by showing you rather than telling you about the land, and the reason settlers settled where they did on their westward move from the Atlantic to the Pacific.

In addition, The Voyager Co. offers **Who Built America?,** a thoughtfully designed CD-ROM put together by the American Social History Project that explores through words and pictures the people and events that shaped U.S. history from 1876 to 1914 ($100; $350 for the education edition with teaching guide). With its background audio and stylized photographs, this presentation has the look and feel of a PBS documentary—a good one.

CD-ROM

U.S. Presidents

Forget what the polls say; presidents are popular people. The approaches to them range from the respectful (deep-voiced narrators explain their lives and achievements) to the playful (a learning game for kids). Applied Optical Media's **Atlas of U.S. Presidents** is a CD-ROM ($40) containing biographies, portraits, and information about 41 presidents, with audioclips from public speeches made this century.

CD-ROM

Facts & Faces of U.S. Presidents ($50) is a HyperCard-based floppy disk presentation from Visatex for schools (ages eight and up). Tanager Software offers **The Secret Codes of C.Y.P.H.E.R.: Operation U.S. Presidents** ($60, with school lab versions available), which takes a game approach to presidential history.

And if you're interested in learning more about FDR, Multi-Educator offers a CD-ROM called **Franklin Roosevelt: History Maker** ($55) that delves into his life (and famous wife), and the particular challenges he had to tackle during an unprecedented four-term reign at a time when the country was facing crises such as the Depression and World War II.

CD-ROM

Other Lands and Languages (CG)

Visit exotic locations and learn the customs and languages of people from around the world with these guides, which rely heavily on your interaction to get their message across, whether you're learning a new language or honing your geography skills with an electronic atlas.

Learning New Languages

If you've given up on books and tapes but are still interested in perfecting your Spanish or learning French, interactive language learning tools might inspire you on your quest to master a foreign language. And you'll find that when it comes to foreign languages, Mac developers are verbose.

Language basics. HyperGlot Software covers the globe with a sweeping line of software for a variety of languages using several approaches. There's the immersion techniques of Berlitz in the **Berlitz Think & Talk** series ($200 each). **French**, **German**, **Italian**, **Russian**, **Japanese**, and **Spanish Word Torture** ($50 each) are HyperCard-based stacks that present you with vocabulary quizzes. You'll also find products that emphasize one aspect of language learning, such as reading skills or grammar, including **French Reading Lab 1** ($30) for improving your French reading skills, and **German Passive Voice** ($60) for learning German tenses.

Gessler Educational Software has its own approach to teaching French, German, Latin, and Spanish, which has developed into a line of products called the **Transparent Language** series ($140 each), while Fairfield Language Technologies offers a series of multimedia CD-ROMs ($400) as part of its **Rosetta Stone Language** series designed to immerse you in Spanish, English, French, or German. Lingo Fun, on the other hand, has developed the **Computerized Grammar** series, including introductions to French, German, Italian, Latin, and Spanish grammar ($60).

At least two developers have become known for specializing in Japanese-language learning aids: Anonae Software, which offers **Japanese Language Instruction: Kanji Exercises No. 1** ($65) and **Hiragana/Katakana Exercises** ($45); and Qualitas Trading Co., which developed **KanjiCard** ($200) and **JapanEase, Volumes 1 and 2** ($100 each).

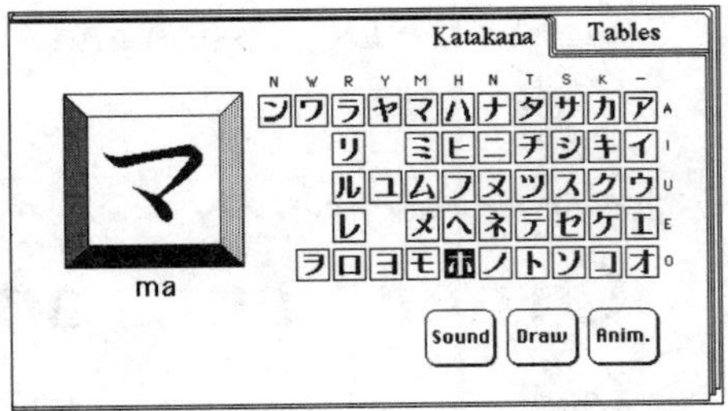

Learning a new language can be easy with one of the many interactive learning programs available on the Mac, including JapanEase, a Japanese-language program from Qualitas Trading Co.

Learning languages with pictures. **Language Discovery** ($50) from Applied Optical

Media offers you a visual guide to learning 1,000 words in English, French, German, and Spanish. Each word is accompanied by a picture of the object, put in the context of everyday scenes from life (picture the rooms in your home with everything labeled in a foreign language).

If you like learning through association with pictures, there's also **PictureIt!** ($70), a foreign-language picture dictionary from Penton Overseas.

Maps and More

Applied Optical Media offers two CD-ROM-based atlases: **The American Vista Atlas** ($80) charts out the United States using maps from Hammond and incorporates data from the 1990 U.S. Census, **The World Vista Atlas** ($80), an international atlas based on maps from Rand McNally, contains standard phrases in the major languages of each of the more than 200 countries included.

Educorp Software also offers a series of CD-ROM-based maps (each $60), including the **USA Relief Map,** which gives you an atlas of the United States and aerial photographs of major metropolitan areas; and the **World Relief Map,** created from satellite data and showing topographic detail. Both use color to maximum effect.

For an unusual perception of the world, there's the **CIA World Factbook** and the **KGB World Factbook** ($50 each), CD-ROMs from Quanta Press.

And The Software Toolworks offers its popular **World Atlas** ($80 for disks; $70 for the CD-ROM version), an atlas, almanac, and fact book with more than 250 detailed maps that has become a de facto standard for Mac-based atlases because it's so easy to use and understand.

Travel Guides

Always dreamed of seeing the Great Barrier Reef or visiting the Amazon Rainforest? You can with **7 Natural Wonders of the World** ($70), from InterOptica Publishing, a color CD-ROM that lets you explore the Seven Wonders through QuickTime movies, digital video, animations, graphics, maps, photographs, and interactive text. InterOptica also offers other CD-ROM explorations, including tours of the **Great Cities of the World** ($50), **Great Wonders of the World** ($70), and **The Orient—Multimedia Guide to the Far East** ($50).

The Voyager Co. offers an introduction to Japanese customs and language with the CD-ROM-based **Exotic Japan** ($60), which provides enough lessons and quizzes (and the chance for you to record and replay your voice as you go through the pronunciation guide) for you to feel like you're ready to visit the country.

If you're interested in underwater adventures, you can journey through the Atlantic with a humpback whale and learn about more than 100 other species in **A World Alive** ($50, Voyager), an interactive documentary on CD-ROM that also includes a game to test what you've learned. The disc is built around a 30-minute documentary (that you can play from beginning to end if you're not into interacting) that was compiled in collaboration with the St. Louis Zoo and narrated by that man with the great voice, James Earl Jones.

And Amazing Media has put together diving tours of undersea locations including the Galapagos, the Red Sea, the Sea of Cortez, and the Caribbean in its **Oceans Below** ($50) CD-ROM (which is distributed by The Software Toolworks). The disc contains more than 200 videoclips and 125 photographs of animal and plant life, and plane- and shipwrecks. The images, especially the close-ups of underwater reefs, will make you long for a vacation, but you may find the two scuba diving guides slightly annoying as they prattle on and suit up at each new locale while the QuickTime videos and images load.

Oceans Below takes you on diving tours of undersea locations in the Caribbean, among other exotic places. Discover shipwrecks, meet the animal and plant life, and just get away from it all—without leaving your desk.

Art and Music

(CG)

Since the early days of desktop publishing on the Mac, creative professionals have been using scanners and page layout and photo manipulation software to create digital versions of coffee-table and illustrative art books. You'll find these titles filled with beautifully rendered digital versions of photographs and other works of art and vitalized by sound, animations, video, and other media.

Finding Out About Art

For a wealth of art-related titles, a good starting point is The Voyager Co. It offers more than 200 high-quality, interactive laserdisc presentations (starting at $60), including interactive tours of the art holdings of **The Louvre, The National Gallery of Art,** and **The Art Institute of Chicago,** and looks at the works of artists such as **Michelangelo** and **Vincent van Gogh.** The HyperCard-based presentations contain historical, biographical, and art commentary, as well as broadcast-quality video tours of the museums and full-color photographs of the works being discussed.

For a detailed look at Impressionism, Quanta Press publishes **Coate's Art Review—Impressionism** ($80), a CD-ROM containing images created by Impressionist artists as well as a database containing background information on this period in art history and lists of museums and their collections.

Coffee-Table Books

Photography and coffee-table books have also gone digital. Instead of a minimalist caption describing the photo, photographers are now using the medium to bring more context to the work and to create mood, turning what would have been just static presentations of their photos into true interactive experiences.

From Alice to Ocean ($140, Claris) is a book and CD-ROM package created by Rick Smolan, well-known photojournalist and cocreator of the A Day in the Life series of photography books. The disc contains photographs and an interactive presentation that documents the one-year trek of Robyn Davidson through the Australian Outback, where she was accompanied by three camels, her dog, and (intermittently) photographer Smolan, who was on assignment for *National Geographic.* For a while, Apple was bundling a QuickTime-based CD-ROM version of this title with all its CD-ROM-equipped Macs, so you might already it in your CD-ROM library.

From Alice to Ocean is a book/disc bundle that takes you along on a trek across the Australian Outback with Robyn Davidson, her dog, and three camels.

There's also **I Photograph to Remember** ($40, Voyager), a CD-ROM presentation of Latin American photographer Pedro Meyer's family memoir and intimate recollections of the last years of his parents lives. The disc is narrated in English and Spanish by Meyer.

Studying Music

If you're interested in learning to play an instrument, turn to the reviews of some of the music instruction programs listed in the "Music" section of Chapter 17. What you'll find here are programs designed to increase your understanding and appreciation of composers and their music. Although there are several small publishers offering products in this subject category, two publishers rule this market: The Voyager Co. and the Time Warner Interactive Group.

One piece, between the notes. Voyager's CD Companions (built using Apple's HyperCard) lets you listen to an entire composition as the text commentary scrolls by, or click to bring up a glossary of music terms and theory, or click again to read about the life of the composer. Four of the titles in the series are annotated and researched by Robert Winter, a pianist and instructor at UCLA; these include **Ludwig van Beethoven: Symphony No. 9, Igor Stravinsky: The Rite of Spring, Antonin Dvorák: Symphony No: 9 "From the New World"** (each list for $80), and **Wolfgang Amadeus Mozart: The Dissonant Quartet** ($60). Other CD Companion titles include **Franz Schubert: The Trout Quintet** ($60) and **Richard Strauss: Three Tone Poems** ($60).

Time Warner offers a series of HyperCard-based CD-ROMs that also let you explore a specific piece in depth. This series includes Brahms's **A German Requiem,** a two-disc set filled with musical and historical background; and **The String Quartet,** ($66 each) which features a recording of Beethoven's String Quartet No. 14, with lots of additional information about string quartets in general. As with the Voyager series, you can just play through the music, but the real fun begins when you sit down and get involved in the intricacies and subtleties of the composition and explore the life and times of the composers.

GOOD FEATURE

Musical samplers. Orchestra: The Instruments Revealed ($80, Time Warner) shows you what instruments look and sound like and how they are played, using graphics and audio examples. The disc features the London Symphony Orchestra's performance of "The Young Person's Guide to the Orchestra."

CD-ROM

The titles in Voyager's So I've Heard series ($25 each) are designed to be music samplers, offering you commentary and soundclips from an array of composers. Three volumes are currently available (and several more were in the works as of this writing): **Volume 1: Bach and Before** takes you from the music of ancient Greek rituals to Bach; **Volume 2: The Classical Ideal** is an earful of the work of 18th century composers such as Mozart and Haydn; and **Volume 3: Beethoven and Beyond** explores Beethoven's impact on the classical music scene.

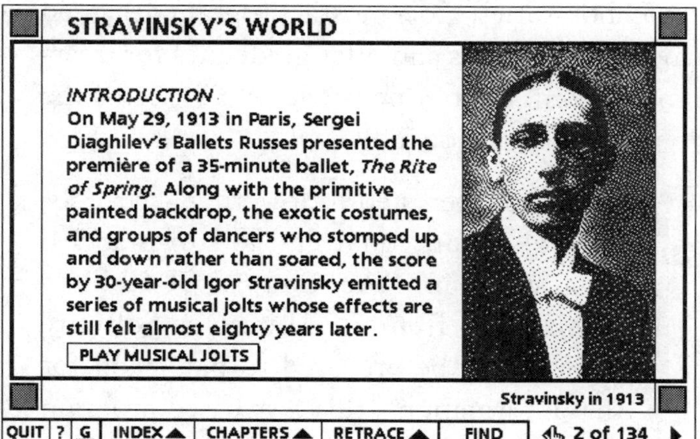

Voyager's CD Companion series does more than introduce you to some music by great composers. It allows you to listen to the music as text-based commentary scrolls by, click on a particular phrase to learn more about the composers' technique and music composition in general, or learn more about the composers' lives and times.

The great thing about all of Voyager's offerings is the time and thoughtfulness the company puts into designing the interface to its products: You'll find the screens easy to read, punctuated with elegant illustrations, and designed with search tools and icons that make it a pleasure to explore the topic at hand.

GOOD FEATURE

Science, Health, and Nature

Whether you need to know more about animals, vegetables, minerals, Earth, or beyond, you'll find that many topics have been well researched by enterprising Mac developers.

Health

(CG)

You won't find a cure-all in these works, but you will find well-researched and well-intentioned products designed to educate you about specific health issues.

CD-ROM

The **Mayo Clinic Heart Disc** ($60), a CD-ROM distributed by Interactive Ventures, tells you everything you could possibly want to know about heart health and heart disease, including videos of medical procedures that have been performed at the renowned Mayo Clinic. For a broader view of health matters, the company also distributes the **Mayo Clinic Family Health Disc** ($100), a home medical reference also on CD-ROM that describes symptoms and treatments for a variety of health problems ranging from the flu to tuberculosis.

Parents: If you've still got questions after consulting *Dr. Spock*, there's **Personal Pediatrician** ($60) from Lundin Laboratories, a diagnostic program designed to help you identify children's medical problems and offer guidelines for treatment. Still, as a parent I have to say a call to your pediatrician still seems the best diagnostic tool of all.

FAST FOODS

FAST FOODS	PORTION	total CALS	SA-FA CALS
✓ Kentucky Fried Chicken, wing + thigh	1 dinner	902	107
Kentucky Fried Chicken, drumstick + thigh	1 dinner	765	95
Kentucky Fried Chicken thigh	1 piece	257	39
Kentucky Fried Chicken drumstick	1 piece	117	15
✓ Kentucky Fried Chicken breast	1 piece	199	29
✓ Kentucky Fried Chicken Extra Crispy drumstick	1 piece	155	21
Kentucky Fried Chicken Extra Crispy breast	1 piece	286	44
Kentucky Fried Chicken wing	1 piece	136	21
Long John Silver's fish	1 serving	483	70
McDonald's apple pie	1	253	33
McDonald's regular fries	1 serving	220	33
✓ McDonald's chocolate or vanilla shake	1	383	47
McDonald's hot cakes w/butter and syrup	1 serving	500	43
McDonald's Egg McMuffin	1	327	59
✓ McDonald's Filet-o-Fish sandwich	1	432	71
McDonald's cheeseburger	1	307	58

Clear all marks | Ledger | Done | <<Mark foods by clicking>>

Still don't know what all the worry and talk about cholesterol is about? Take Control of Cholesterol from the Lifestyle Software Group is an inexpensive program loaded with lots of practical information, but unfortunately the questionnaire format leaves a lot to be desired.

If you're interested in lowering your cholesterol count, you'll find lots of practical suggestions in **Take Control of Cholesterol** ($20) from the Lifestyle Software Group. But be prepared to pay a toll for that information—this text-based program is a series of not-very-well-laid-out questionnaires and checklists on screen, making it a rather sterile (maybe that's the point?) and uninviting way to explore the topic.

For straight talk on AIDS, there's ABC News InterActive's **Understanding Ourselves: AIDS** HyperCard-driven laserdisc presentation ($400, distributed by Scholastic Software), a well-designed and compelling study of AIDS and its causes, treatments, and ramifications on the lives of people touched by the it. Your narrator is C. Everett Koop, the former U.S. Surgeon General.

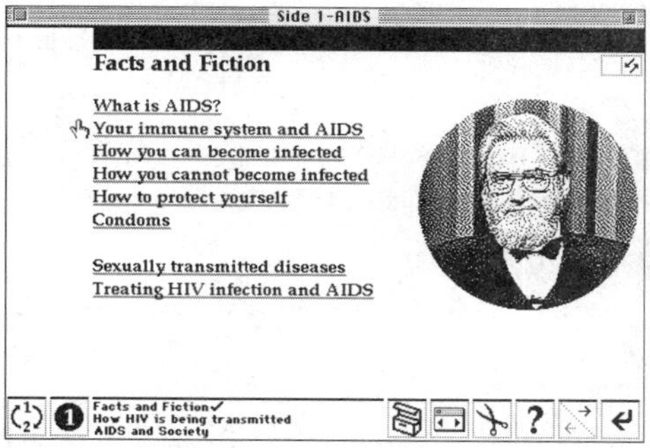

ABC News InterActive offers a HyperCard-driven laserdisc presentation that explores the AIDS epidemic, including causes, prevention, and the impact the disease has had on real people infected with it.

Flora and Fauna (CG)

You never know when you'll need to be conversant in cow talk; that's when you'll be glad that Quanta Press offers **About Cows** ($30), a full-text database, with good searching tools, on CD-ROM.

CD-ROM

Audubon's Mammals ($100) from Creative Multimedia offers the illustrations that John James Audubon (known for his bird prints) produced in 1840 under the title *Quadrupeds of North America.* Creative Multimedia has added text describing the habitat of each mammal, as well as sounds. For bird watchers, the publisher also offers a CD-ROM called **Birds of America** ($100) that contains the complete text (and 500 color bird lithographs) from the 1840 edition of Audubon's book of that name.

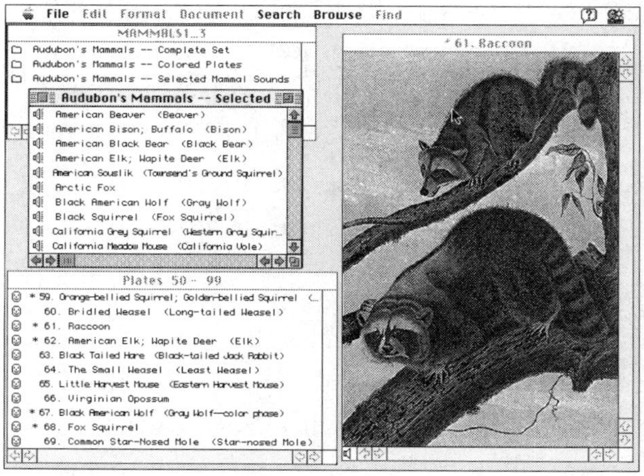

Creative Multimedia introduces you to the mammals of America using the 1840 edition of John James Audubon's **Quadrapeds of North America** *as its reference point. Added text and sounds enliven digital versions of Audubon's drawings.*

For an authoritative overview of animal (and plant) life, Educorp (one of the largest distributors of CD-ROM titles) offers **The Encyclopedia of Life** ($130). The easy-to-use interface lets you delve into 3,700 text entries, launch 130 QuickTime videoclips, choose from among 600 color images, and search through the glossary covering the millions of plants and animals that inhabit the planet.

GOOD FEATURE

The Expert-Center for Taxonomic Identification (ETI), based at the University of Amsterdam, has put together a series of well-researched and well-crafted multimedia CD-ROMs dealing with some unusual animal life. **Birds of Europe** ($150) is very well designed and beautifully illustrated: The colorful drawings and illustrations were clearly chosen by someone who really loves and appreciates birds. ETI's enthusiasm for its subjects also extends to the design of its other programs, including **North Eastern Atlantic & Mediterranean Fish** ($200); **Linnaeus Protist** ($32), which describes microscopic plants and animals living in the North Sea; **Pelagic Molluscs of the World** ($500), a study of clams and other related ocean life; and **Turbellaria of the World: A Guide to Families and Genera** ($100), a look at aquatic flatworms.

Operation: Frog ($100), from Scholastic Software, dissects a frog for you. Pick a body part, and you get to cut through the various layers and organs in exquisite (and annotated) detail. At least you don't have to smell the formaldehyde.

CD-ROM

Meanwhile, endangered species are the topic of a CD-ROM version of Douglas Adams's (better known for his *Hitchhiker's Guide to the Galaxy*) and photographer Mark Carwardine's book, **Last Chance to See** ($60, distributed by Voyager). Adams reads the entire text on the disc, which includes more than 700 color photos and information about the status of each species.

And although they are no longer around us except in museums and at the movies, dinosaurs are a popular topic for multimedia presentations. The three described here seem designed with kids (say eight and up) in mind: The interfaces are very simple, the text is big, and the carefully drawn color illustrations show how fearsome some of the dinosaurs might have looked. Choosing among them may come down to preferences on how the screens are designed, since they're all comparably priced.

CD-ROM

Disc-O-Saurus ($70) from timebox inc. has nicely rendered illustrations and well-written descriptions. **Dinosaurs! The Multimedia Encyclopedia** ($80) from Media Design Interactive includes maps, interviews with the world's leading paleontologists, and shots of dinosaur skeletons filmed at museums around the world. The **Encyclopedia of Dinosaurs** ($65, distributed by Educorp), has information on 400 dinosaurs, with pop-up maps that show where each species has been found. There's also a video tour of important excavation sites.

Ecology

(CG)

For anyone interested in learning about ecology, the **ECODISC** ($300, Educorp) is an amazing experience (it works in nine languages). You explore and learn by wandering through this beautifully designed simulation of a real nature reserve (in summer or winter).

Earthquest offers colorful and animated explorations of the world and ecology in **Earthquest** and **Earthquest Explores Ecology** ($60 each), both of which contain lots of easy-to-follow information and compelling images. Educorp distributes **The Big Green Disc** ($45), a fully narrated documentary filled with color video, animated diagrams, and photo essays about issues affecting our planet. The program lays out the problems—global warming, acid rain, ozone depletion, and then lets you decide whether you want to explore their causes and effects.

Outer Space

(LS)

Astronomy programs—from desktop planetarium software that can display depictions of the night sky as accurate as anything you can see in a science museum, to interactive multimedia explorations of space—let you travel to the stars without ever having to leave your desk.

Studying astronomy. Carina Software's **Voyager II** ($160) displays celestial phenomena, including stars, planets, galaxies, and constellations, on any given date in history, as viewed from any point throughout our solar system. It is among the fastest astronomy programs available, displaying accurate renderings in seconds. Star trippers will enjoy exploring the universe while serious students of astronomy can call on the program's extensive database to locate a particular star or planetary object on a star chart. The database seems complete, and yet the program takes up just three megabytes on a hard disk.

Redshift ($100), from London-based Maris Multimedia, is the ultimate in astronomy software. Instead of the line drawings used in other programs, it displays awe-inspiring 3-D planetary models; detailed surface maps of the Earth, Moon, and Mars; and more than 700 colorful photographs of a high enough quality to be used for scientific analysis. Hypertext links in the photo gallery

CD-ROM

take you directly to entries from the *Penguin Dictionary of Astronomy*. The program also lets you record your travels through space and save them as a movie that can be played back within any program that supports QuickTime. Orbital data provided by the Jet Propulsion Laboratory ensures scientific accuracy.

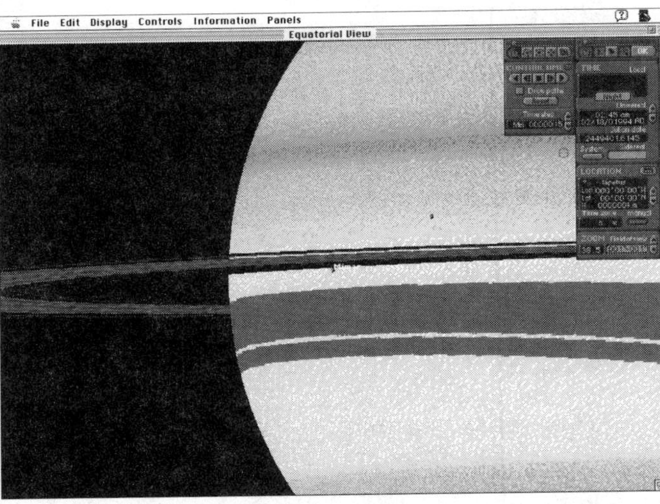

Redshift, the ultimate in astronomy programs, displays 3-D planet models and makes use of scientifically accurate orbital data provided by the Jet Propulsion Laboratory.

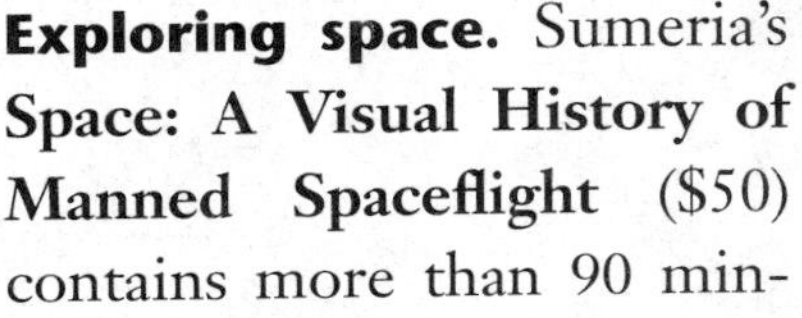

Exploring space. Sumeria's **Space: A Visual History of Manned Spaceflight** ($50) contains more than 90 minutes of footage taken from the NASA video and film library, provided in QuickTime format. Also included are mission histories for the Mercury, Gemini, Apollo, and Space Shuttle projects, and descriptions of space-based science experiments, life in zero gravity, satellite deployment, and space stations.

In Multicom's **Americans in Space** ($60), 500 photographic images and one hour's worth of full-motion video in QuickTime format tell the story of America's efforts in space, beginning with early experimental rockets and the X-15 program and ending with plans for space stations still on the drawing board. An interface modeled on a Mission Control room serves as command center for accessing the disc.

How about an interactive tour of our solar system based on the Time-Life Books series Voyage Through The Universe? **The View From Earth** ($56), from the Time Warner Interactive Group, presents an easy-to-use interface that takes you immediately to the planet of your choice. Unique to the disc is the extensive information it provides on the solar eclipse. Astronomers interested in tracking a solar eclipse can use the program to determine the best possible location for viewing any single eclipse. The program's Eclipse Tracker consists of a world map and a schedule of past, present, and future eclipse occurrences.

19

Kids' Stuff

SET KIDS, NO MATTER WHAT AGE, in front of your Macintosh and see if you can pry them away. The conventional wisdom was that titles and games for kids had to be packaged under an "educational" label; well, we say phooey to that. Any parent or teacher will tell you that kids are born learning machines. If they're having fun and engaged, they're learning something, whether it's hand-eye coordination as they maneuver the mouse and cursor, a few new vocabulary words after reading through an interactive story, or even just getting comfortable using a computer.

In the pages ahead, you'll find a sampling of some of the hundreds of titles available for kids. Deciding what to include was difficult because there's so much great software for kids, and new titles are arriving every day. According to one industry research group, kids' software is the fastest growing market segment, so we've included information on how to get to the source of these new titles.

How did we settle on the titles described in this chapter? We talked to parents, educators, and, of course, kids to come up with a list of popular titles. You'll find six main categories of products, including interactive stories and adventures and painting, drawing, and math programs. Have fun!

Contributors

Connie Guglielmo (CG) is the chapter editor.

Anita Malnig (AM), an executive editor of *MacWEEK,* is author of several children's nonfiction books and a former children's book editor. On this chapter, she received expert advice from her three-and-a-half-year-old son, Tomás.

Dan Ruby (DR) is the former editor and publisher of *NeXTWORLD* magazine. **Twyla Ruby (TR),** age eight, writes a column on children's software, called "Twyla's World," which appears in *Electronic Entertainment* magazine.

Carolyn Said (CS), senior news editor for *MacWEEK* magazine, collaborated on her reviews with her son, B.B., age ten, and two friends, Honey Bee Evans, ten, and Walker Shapiro, eight.

Sharon Zardetto Aker (SA), Nancy E. Dunn (ND), and **Susan McCallister (SM)** contributed to previous editions of *The Macintosh Bible*, from which parts of this chapter were taken.

Contents

Interactive Stories

Interactive stories are more than just books in digital form; with sound, animation, and the ability to let kids interact with the characters, interactive titles let you and your child become part of the adventure. You'll find stories for kids of all ages, with both familiar titles re-created in the new medium and new titles designed specifically to be "read" on a computer.

The Living Books Series (AM)

If you have a CD-ROM player and young children, Living Books from Brøderbund Software should be part of your CD collection. The current four titles are all well produced, with good use of color, animation, and sound, and they're faithful to the original titles (a paperback version of each book is bundled with the CD discs). They're also funny and engaging, and they get to the opening page of each story quickly and easily—important considerations when dealing with the attention span of five-year-olds.

CD-ROM Is for Kids (CG)

Because of their large storage capacity and the relatively low cost of the discs, CD-ROM is becoming the medium of choice for kids' software. If you're interested in having your kids play with titles on the Mac, then you should think seriously about buying a CD-ROM drive. If your Mac didn't come bundled with a CD-ROM drive, not to worry: Drive prices are coming down fast, and you should be able to easily find drives that cost less than $200 (compared with $400 to $500 just one year ago).

Each interactive book is set up the same way: You can choose to have the story "read" or you can choose to "play." In play mode, each page is read aloud as the words read are highlighted; then the child (or you) clicks on just about any character or object on the page and something delightful and silly happens. Only The New Kid on the Block has a slightly different scenario (see below). Each CD can be read in English or Spanish; Just Grandma and Me offers Japanese as well.

Just Grandma and Me. The original title that broke ground in this genre, **Just Grandma and Me** ($40) holds its own as one of the best. It's based on the same title by well-known children's author and illustrator Mercer Mayer and captures the playful, appealing nature of his books. The large, boldly drawn illustrations,

Just Grandma and Me, the premier interactive book in Brøderbund's Living Books series, takes you along as Little Critter spends a day at the beach with his grandmother.

with each page relatively uncluttered, are just right for three- to six-year-olds. The text is spare with a nice, large, readable font. The story is simple—Little Critter spends the day at the beach with his grandmother—and the added adventures don't stop. Click and a cow moos; click again, and the Little Critter gets caught in the beach umbrella; click once more and the starfish dance. My three-year-old son, Tomás, chortled at the antics and pretty much learned the story by heart.

CD-ROM

The Tortoise and the Hare. Also designed for three- to five-year-olds, **The Tortoise and the Hare** ($40) is simply told and the brightly colored illustrations are childlike, although the graphics lack the finesse and artistry of Mercer Mayer's work. The same goes for the retelling of the story—it's good, but it's just not simple in the artful way of Just Grandma and Me. The antics will please kids for sure, but I (the critical adult) thought they lacked some of the spontaneous silliness of Just Grandma and Me. But the Tortoise definitely has his plodding charm, and the old Hare outwits himself and a lesson is indeed learned. The production of the paperback book wasn't up to par with the others in the series, and the illustrations looked like they were printed on a laser printer.

CD-ROM

Arthur's Teacher Troubles. While younger kids (under five) can—and do—enjoy this, the longer, wordier text of **Arthur's Teacher Troubles** ($50) will work best with slightly older

Educational Discounts (CG)

You'll find the suggested retail price of products listed throughout the chapter (of course, street prices are much lower). But educators should know that most companies offer educational pricing on those products, with even greater discounts when products are purchased in quantity. Some developers also offer additional educational material, such as classroom editions or curriculum support. Be sure to call the publishers and ask about these specials if you're interested in using these products in a classroom setting.

Arthur has lots of problems on his hands: a troublesome teacher, an annoying kid sister, and a 100-word list to memorize for the school spelling bee. Marc Brown's Arthur's Teacher Troubles has been made into an interactive book by Brøderbund.

kids. Based on the misadventures of Arthur, the hero of a series of stories by author Marc Brown, this story sees poor Arthur stuck with a demanding teacher named Mr. Ratburn, a list of 100 words to memorize for a spelling contest, and an irrepressible little sister who won't let him forget how much he has to study. But silliness abounds here, too: Click and a dragon toy spits fire, the fire extinguisher goes berserk, and the little sister falls off the bed in the midst of taunting Arthur. The story is well written and well illustrated (Arthur's woebegone face is sympathetic and funny at the same time). The goofy antics simply add to the fun already there.

The New Kid on the Block. Jack Prelutsky is an oxymoron—a successful poet. School kids love his rhymes about the trials of home and school life, and Living Books has brought them to life in **The New Kid on the Block** ($10). James Stevenson's illustrations differ greatly from the pictures in the previous titles—the more sophisticated black-and-white cartoons will appeal to older kids, but probably not as much to the littler ones. The poems are fabulous and the narration is excellent, as are the little animations that happen in the "read" part of the package. The letdown for me was that the animations in the "play" part don't offer that much more than what's in the read section. In the title poem, when the narrator gets tweaked in the read part, he gets a little pull on his sleeve; in play, he gets a big pull. You can read the lines over and over again in play, however, and that's probably a big plus for the kids who are real Prelutsky fans. I suspect this title may work very well in a classroom.

Zoom Books Series

(AM)

CD-ROM

T/Maker Comapny has gotten into kids software with a planned series of interactive stories, the first title of which is **Four Footed Friends.** By the time this book is published, expect more titles in the series to be out on the market.

Four Footed Friends ($30), based on a 1914 children's book, captures the artistry of interactive stories while letting go of some of the comic qualities of the Living Books titles. This adventure can be read in English, Spanish, French, and Japanese. Both a CD-ROM and a floppy disk version are available.

GOOD FEATURE

The book has an exceptionally long introduction; I was greatly relieved to discover I could bypass it. But once I got into the book, I was immediately impressed by the artistry and crafting of the package. The original drawings of carefully drawn animals in costume, the accompanying background drawings, and the QuickTime animations are simply top-notch.

Each animal has a charming four-line poem describing it. Then the added fun begins: Click on a bookworm to get a scanned photo of the real animal with some information about it and maybe a little game; click on another animal for the spelling and definition of a related word—like *hay* in the cow section. The next worm gives you a watercolor set and a black-and-white drawing to color in. Another button lets you navigate through the package, allowing you to go to whatever animal you want.

In T/Maker's Four Footed Friends, each animal you meet is in full costume and accompanied by a four-line poem describing it. But there's more than meets the eye in this interactive retelling of a 1914 children's book.

Although some kids might want to go for the quick laughs to be found in the Living Books series, Four Footed Friends is the kind of title I have been dreaming about—a superior, complex crafting of a multimedia title. Many of us have been wondering when some original art would find its way into this medium. I just found it.

Discis Book Series (DR/TR)

Discis Knowledge Research has put together electronic story books ($40 per title; 12 titles available) designed for kids over six. By combining the text of the original work with dramatic narration, color illustrations, music, and sound effects, Discis has provided a rich learning experience for beginning readers. Besides listening to the narration, you can click on items in the accompanying illustrations to learn the correct spelling and pronunciation. Unlike electronic book titles from other companies, the Discis books do not include animation, so while the titles are useful for teaching vocabulary and spelling, they have limited appeal for kids who can already read. The series includes classics such as **Aesop's Fables, Cinderella,** and **The Tale of Peter Rabbit,** as well as contemporary titles such as **Heather Hits a Home Run, A Long Hard Day on the Ranch**, and **Scary Poems for Rotten Kids.**

AmandaStories (SM/CG)

Charming and fun. That's the best way to describe these wonderful creations by Amanda Goodenough (published by The Voyager Company), a must-have for any parent of a toddler. The disc ($60) contains ten stories, featuring the exploits of Your Faithful Camel and a mischievous black cat named Inigo (who is named after the sword fighter Inigo Montoya, a character in the book *The Princess Bride*). Inigo gets into all sorts of trouble, but always manages to find his way out of it—and a few friends along the way—and live happily ever after.

The stories are colorful picture books made into HyperCard stacks, with several hidden buttons behind each picture so a story can be "read" several different ways. Each adventure includes very basic sound and animation, and the drawings are simple, uncluttered, and delightful, making them perfect for toddlers. But even older kids (and adults) can be easily drawn into the stories. The **AmandaStories** are also a great example of what you can do with HyperCard, Apple's interactive authoring environment (a reader version is bundled with every Mac).

Interactive Adventures

If you've always been envious of Alice journeying through Wonderland, then make sure your kids have Wonderlands of their own to explore. Some of the worlds re-created in these adventures are imaginary places, but you'll also find familiar settings such as backyards and houses where, of course, unexpected things happen.

The Treehouse, The Playhouse, and The Backyard (CS)

Chock-full of things to do, Brøderbund's **The Treehouse** ($40) is the ideal clubhouse, the one you wish you'd had as a kid. Players pick an opossum playmate with whom to explore a bevy of activities: a musical maze, a theater where you make up silly sentences, and a counting game, to name a few. Clicking around The Treehouse turns up plenty of interesting reactions: clouds change shape and the opossums and birds can be fed. At my house, even children older than the targeted ages of five through eight were occupied for hours. From an educational standpoint, the musical activities are particularly strong: Children can learn facts about the different instruments and hear their sounds, compose and play short songs, and learn music-reading skills.

With The Treehouse, you get a clubhouse unlike anything you could build in your backyard.

Bear in mind that some of the activities require reading; if your child is preliterate, Brøderbund's **The Playhouse** ($35) or **The Backyard** ($35) offer similar environments full of fun activities for children ages three to six. The Playhouse features a clock that teaches how to tell time, an ABC book, and a counting board game. The Backyard offers activities that teach animal habitats, mapping and directional skills, strategy, and logic. As in The Treehouse, clicking on scattered objects produces interesting results—a radio plays music,a balloon pops. Either game would make an excellent first introduction to the Mac.

A Silly Noisy House and Rodney's Wonder Window (SM/CG)

These colorful CDs from The Voyager Co. will lead your kids on adventures through worlds beautifully conceived by their creators. **A Silly Noisy House** ($60), created by Peggy Weil, is an imaginative adventure designed for three-year-olds and up. As in The Playroom, when you click areas of the screen or objects in a room, things happen. The game begins with a cross-section of a large house: Just click on a room to zoom in. Each room has several different views and is loaded with objects that—as promised—do silly, noisy things. A pitcher fills glasses with water, a rocking horse makes galloping sounds, a pie erupts with blackbirds as you hear *Sing a Song of Sixpence.* Some objects are unpredictable, responding to clicks in different ways at different times. The animation is great, and the sound is impressive.

You really don't have to be a kid to enjoy the colorful, fun, and unusual scenarios you'll find behind **Rodney's Wonder Window** ($40), created by artist Rodney Alan Greenblatt. There are 24 interactive episodes filled with animations and sounds. If your children like to pick out their own clothes, have them order "Data Shorts" in their favorite fabric (plaid, knotty pine, or X-ray, among others). Or take a trip to the "Probe and Poke Pet Shop," then maybe watch a movie of Chip and Peg's adventures in ShapeLand. It's wacky, weird, wild, and fun.

Scooter's Magic Castle (DR/TR)

Kids explore a castle full of games and activities in this entertaining collection from Electronic Arts ($50) designed for five- to eight-year-olds. Upon entering each room of the castle, kids discover a new challenge that teaches such skills as memorization, pattern recognition, logical thinking, and creativity. Since each learning activity is packaged with colorful graphics and amusing animations, the kids think they're just having fun. Each activity is available in three levels of difficulty, so **Scooter's Magic Castle** remains interesting for more than a short time. But since the program doesn't provide an overall goal for winning, the video-game generation may lose interest with the wander-around-and-look-for-something-new approach.

Paint, Draw, and More

Creating art on the Mac can be quite an experience for someone who has never played with a paint and draw program. In these kids' programs, you'll not only find many of the familiar tools you'd see in the grown-up programs—brushes, erasers, shapes—but also so much more: brushes that make sound effects, rubber stamps, animated tools, and the like. The only problem you may have with these programs is that you can't leave them alone long enough for your kids to have a turn. Be nice and share!

Kid Pix (CS)

Kid Pix ($40) is a joy. A paint program designed especially for children (former Apple CEO John Sculley once demo'ed it at a trade show, proving that anyone can use it!), it brims with magical and sometimes mysterious features. A Wacky Brush tool offers dozens of delightful ways to paint, ranging from splattering paint to flinging galaxies of stars to spawning crawling caterpillars. Rubber Stamps let children festoon their creations with more than 100 items, including dinosaurs, ice-cream cones, light bulbs, bugs, bikes, and traffic lights. The Electric Mixer tool lets artists transform their drawings in crazy, mixed-up ways, swapping colors, highlighting, splashing paint or burying the drawing in snowflakes. Goofy sound effects, such as paint that gurgles when it's poured and exploding firecrackers, add to the feeling that you have entered an enchanted parallel universe.

The Eraser tool offers dramatic dooms such as a Firecracker that clears the screen in one big, satisfying blast; a Black Hole that swallows up everything; or Hidden Pictures that appear as you erase.

But wait, there's more: Brøderbund also offers **Kid Pix Companion,** a $30 add-on to Kid Pix that spins the paint program into motion with multimedia features such as Wacky TV, which is a QuickTime movie player complete with silly special effects and a selection of daffy small movies. Companion includes a separate program called SlideShow, which provides a nice, simple interface for creating slide shows, complete with graphics, sound, and transition effects. Companion adds gobs more rubber stamps to Kid Pix, several new Hidden Pictures, and new features that let kids color in line drawings or get inspired by funny voices suggesting weird and wild ideas for drawings ("I am Commander Salamander with a set of sharp, crooked toenails, and I float in the ocean.")

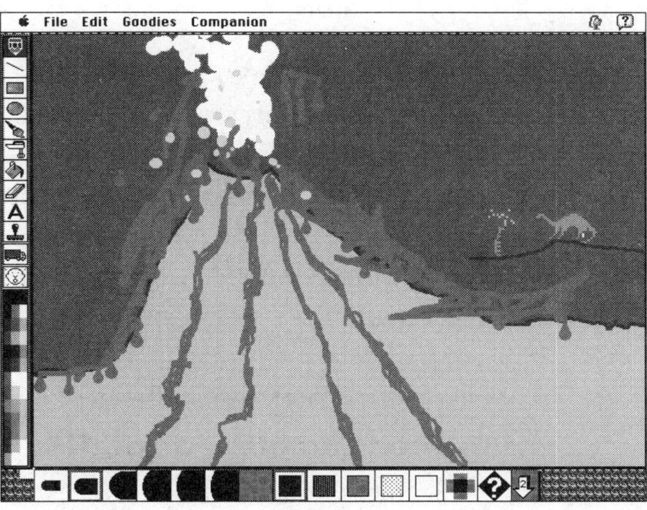

The premier drawing program for kids, Kid Pix lets you create pictures using an assortment of unusual tools, including rubber stamps and animated brushes. There are sound effects, too, and several really fun ways to "erase" your pictures.

Art Center

(DR/TR)

If Brøderbund's Kid Pix set the standard for children's paint programs, Electronic Arts (with its new EA*Kids line) extends the concept by providing five modules for creating images in a single package. The **Art Center** ($50), for three-year-olds and up, contains a sticker book, a costume designer, a paint box, a coloring book, and a geometric shape assembler. Each module offers delightful sounds and a library of premade images. The interface of tools panel, color picker, and brush effects is intuitive.

Younger kids will catch on quickly with the beginner level and should be entertained for hours. But older children may find themselves confined by the limited sizing and rotation options. They may also be frustrated by the inability to move their work between modules. There is no way to place a sticker on a costume or use a paint-box tool in the coloring book. Also missing is any kind of move-to-front or move-to-back function, which often makes it difficult to achieve the desired effect.

Fine Artist (CS)

Microsoft's **Fine Artist** ($65) wasn't out in time for us to play with, but it promised a bevy of features to help kids create everything from animated pictures and multimedia slide shows to posters, comic strips, buttons, and stickers. A Drawing Tricks Floor offers basic tutorials on art techniques such as drawing with a grid. Other features include more than 125 clip art stickers, 76 custom colors and patterns, 72 paintbrush styles, dozens of wacky sounds, and lots of special effects.

Sharing Your Computer With Kids (CG)

You'd really love to give your child access to all the kids' games and titles you've loaded on the Mac, but you're concerned they might inadvertently get access to your files, and, in the worst-case scenario, trash something important. Mac software developers are a step ahead of you, offering programs that let you configure your system so that kids can access only the files and folders *you* want them to access.

Apple, for instance, offers **At Ease,** a simplified version of the Finder that comes with Performas but can also be bought separately for other Macs. Among other features, At Ease lets you determine which folders and applications your child can gain access to and automatically saves all files into personalized document folders. (At Ease is described more fully in Chapter 4.)

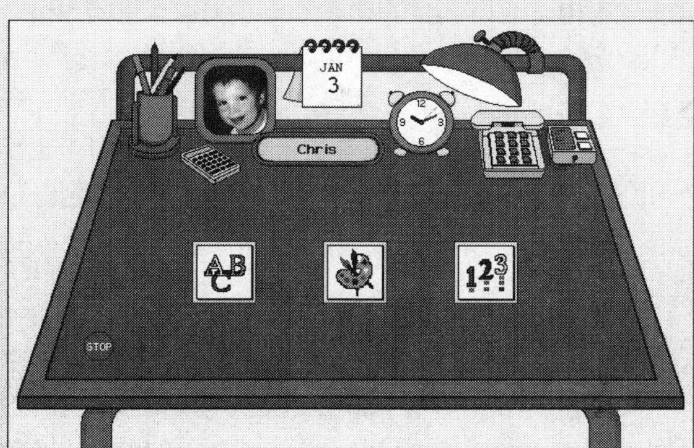

KidDesk, from Edmark, may become one of your favorite programs: It allows you to set up a special desktop that gives kids access to only certain files and folders. And that means no more worries about what files your children might accidentally trash.

Edmark developed **KidDesk** ($40, or $54 for a school edition). It lets you set up a special desktop showing only the icons you've selected, as well as utilities that kids can play with, such as a talking clock, a working calculator, a calendar, and even a screen saver. A parents-only password must be entered in order to gain access to the "grown-up" desktop.

Making Up Stories (CS)

All these programs are based on the same solid premise: Children love to make up stories and illustrate them. Each provides a rudimentary word processor, paint tools or prefabricated graphics, and some sound effects.

Storybook Weaver and My Own Stories

MECC's **Storybook Weaver** and **My Own Stories** ($50 each) rely on clip art graphics. They offer hundreds of images and dozens of sounds and background scenes. Storybook Weaver draws its images (knights, trolls, treasure chests) from folklore; My Own Stories offers contemporary symbols (shopping malls, Frisbees, fire trucks).

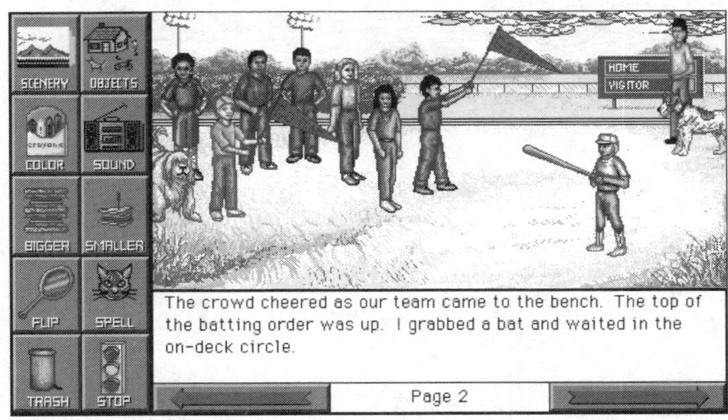

Making up your own stories is easy to do with My Own Stories from MECC. Choose from hundreds of clip art images of modern-day images to illustrate the stories you and your kids think up.

Kid Works 2

Davidson & Associates' **Kid Works 2** ($60) comes with ready-made picture elements too, but it also includes a paint program, giving children more room to express themselves in their illustrations. Children can substitute any of numerous pictures for some words in their story. A text-to-speech feature lets children hear their stories read aloud.

Creative Writer

Microsoft's **Creative Writer** ($65), new this year, packs more features than the three other programs I looked at. In fact, I was exhausted after playing with it. It places users in the fantasy world of Imaginopolis, where they can create projects like banners, newsletters, or greeting cards, as well as stories. The word

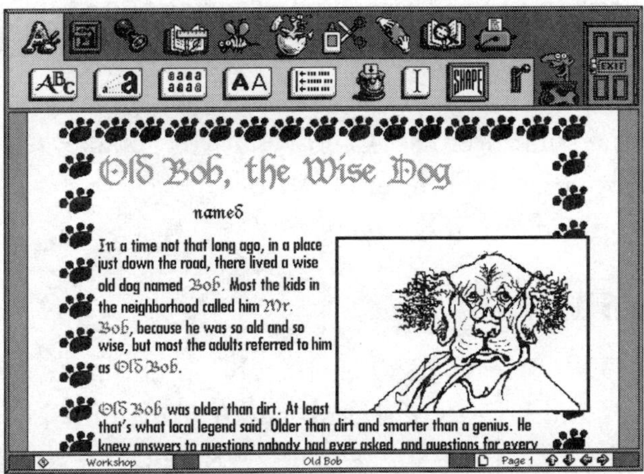

In Imaginopolis, brought to you by Creative Writer from Microsoft, kids can create amazing stories using special fonts, special effects, and lots of images, borders, and backgrounds.

processor has tons of fonts, type styles, and such special effects as "shape" words; zany sounds and other special effects liven up both writing and drawing; and a "Splot Machine" brims over with 8,000 kooky story ideas. It includes about 100 clip art images and dozens of borders and backgrounds. One handy feature more kids' programs could use is an Undo that goes as far back as 20 steps. The program has exhaustive context-sensitive help.

Geography, History, and Beyond

If you're looking for interesting and innovative ways to get your children interested in history and geography, you'll find lots of titles. But like everything else in this chapter, these programs offer a lot more than just history lessons on disk: They're games, stories, and interactive adventures designed to engage your kids while they explore the world and its history.

Carmen Sandiego Series (Mary Toth)

CD-ROM

Brøderbund's wildly successful Carmen Sandiego series started with **Where In the World Is Carmen Sandiego?** ($30) and now includes titles that take Carmen (and your kids) to Europe, the U.S.A., and space, with both regular and "deluxe" (CD-ROM) editions packed with sound effects, music, graphics, and animations. Titles range in price from $30 to $60, and, depending on the title, you'll also get a paperback edition of the *World Almanac and Book of Facts*, *Fodor's U.S.A.* travel guide, the *New American Desk Encyclopedia*, or *What Happened When*, a 1,300-page encyclopedia of American history and culture.

In case you've somehow missed out playing Carmen Sandiego (or watching the TV game show for kids that airs on public television), I'll explain: You learn about history and geography by trying to track down Carmen and her band of thieves as they journey through the world (and through time). You're assigned a mystery case, and you have to collect enough clues to get an arrest warrant and find the suspect before time runs out.

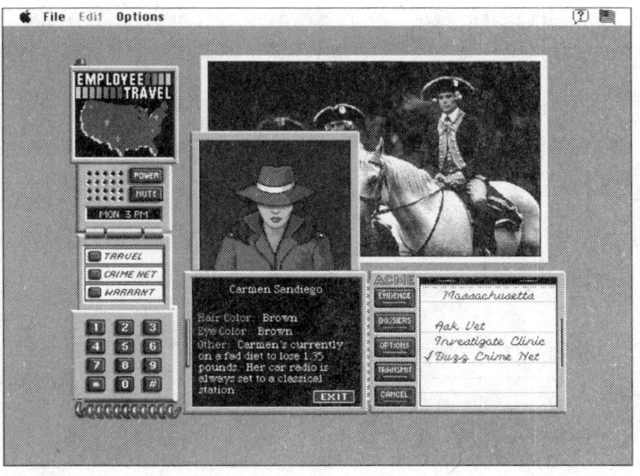

You're on the lookout for the brilliant and elusive Carmen Sandiego and her band of thieves in this series of geography adventures created by Brøderbund. Follow the clues as you follow the thieves around the globe and through time.

You call on informants and witnesses who offer clues about who the crook is and hints about the best time and place to track the suspect. For example, if a clue says the suspect stole something from Francisco Pizarro, you'd know to travel to 16th-century Peru. And just on the off-chance you wouldn't know, you'd turn to the encyclopedia that's included.

GOOD FEATURE

The whole series is a great way to teach reading skills and improve knowledge of history and geography, but it's also great for teaching kids (and their parents) how to use reference materials.

Eagle Eye Mysteries (CS)

If your child is hooked on Encyclopedia Brown, Nancy Drew, or the Hardy Boys, he or she might enjoy exploring **Eagle Eye Mysteries** ($60) from Electronic Arts (part of their new EA*Kids label). The player joins with a couple of young detectives to solve mysteries in the small town of Richview. The sleuths visit various locations around town to gather clues and interview people. When they're done investigating, they review the information collected, select pertinent clues, and accuse a suspect. Cases are organized into three levels, each progressively more difficult.

The concept is great; the actualization is adequate but not enthralling. In fact, the interface looks like a straight port from the IBM PC. The program helps children sharpen their wits by learning about deductive reasoning, but its attempts to teach facts about science, history, and other topics are somewhat heavy-handed. Eagle Eye Mysteries kept my kids interested, but after running through the 50 included mysteries (each takes about 10 to 20 minutes), there was nothing new left to do.

BAD FEATURE

MECC's Trail Books (CS)

MECC has taken to heart the saying, "The journey is its own reward." The company offers educational games in which players "travel" a route packed with adventures, information, and colorful characters.

The Oregon Trail. The Oregon Trail ($50 for the disk-based version; $70 for the CD-ROM edition) replicates the covered wagon route followed by westward-bound pioneers in 1848. Players select a name, a profession (such as a schoolteacher or blacksmith), and traveling companions. They are assigned a certain amount of money and offered a chance to stock up on supplies before embarking on the 2,000-mile trek from Independence, Missouri, to Oregon's Willamette Valley. Following an animated route, the pioneers must contend with hazards such as river crossings, disasters such as illness or wagon breakdowns, and day-to-day decisions such as how much food to consume. The travelers encounter other emigrants and local residents along the way, and they can stop to trade or buy supplies, as well as to hunt.

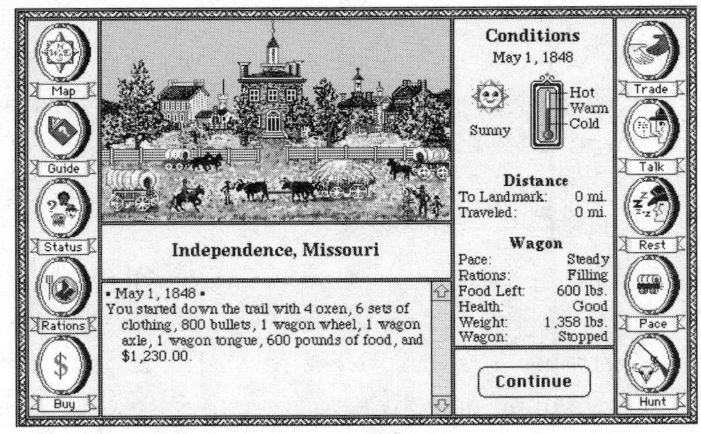

You'll feel like you're part of the wagon trail as you journey along The Oregon Trail as a member of a covered wagon expedition in this interactive geography/history adventure from MECC.

GOOD FEATURE

This is a top-notch educational title. The simulations are realistic (especially in the CD-ROM version), the scenario is gripping, and there is a substantial amount of historical information skillfully interwoven throughout. Children playing the game seem to gain a real understanding of the pioneers' experience and get caught up in the excitement of the journey. When my son plays it, a friend or two or three usually crowds around the Mac and calls out advice and opinions on what to do next—or jostles for control of the mouse!

The Amazon Trail. With **The Amazon Trail** ($60), MECC switches the journey to a canoe trek up the Amazon River. Its scenario is that a mysterious disease has afflicted a hidden Inca village; a secret medicinal plant hidden in the rainforest is the villagers' only hope for salvation. The player must find the plant and then the people, along the way stocking up on other items the Inca king might desire. The trip weaves in and out of time, allowing the traveler to meet up with explorers, naturalists, scientists, and others who shaped the development of the Amazon. Players can stop to explore the rainforest, clicking on plants or animals to identify them. They have to spear fish out of the river for food (my children thought this was the best part). A guidebook gives detailed information about the flora and fauna, and pronounces names aloud. Players visit landmarks along the way, where they can talk to people (many of them actual historical figures) and trade for supplies.

The Amazon Trail contains a wealth of beautifully presented information, touching upon history, ecology, geography, and cultures of the rainforest. The color animations are absolutely stunning. Digitized photographs and speech and authentic South American music provide nice touches of realism.

Headline Harry and the Great Paper Race (CS)

Headline Harry ($60), from Davidson, pairs the player with ace reporter Harry, who's racing to scoop the competition on important news stories circa 1950 to 1990. In addition to learning U.S. geography, players get the lowdown on important historical events and pick up some news-gathering skills.

Swamp Gas (Cameron Dunn)

Swamp Gas ($50), from Inline Software, helps kids eight years old and up (reading is required) learn U.S. geography as they guide a little alien and its UFO through missions around a map of the United States. After you complete each trip, you get to play one of three silly arcade games (they're all fun) that use slapstick maneuvers (banana peels, pies in the face) rather than fighting.

I like to play at the beginner level—finding states by shape—because there the game gives hints if you ask. Kids (or grown-ups) who know more can try to find cities. To make it tougher, you can set the game to ask multiple-choice questions about the state, or you can choose more stops per mission—up to 50! Play by yourself or with up to three people.

Math and Reading

A great many kids' programs set out to teach math and reading—perhaps more than any other subjects. You'll find that some developers offer a series of math and reading programs (all built around the same character) designed for different age groups. But even the best programs can't do it alone. Be prepared to spend time with earlier learners and they'll eventually get so good at using the programs that they'll ask you to go away so they can work through the problems and learning games on their own.

KidsTime (SA/ND/SM)

KidsTime ($50), from Great Wave, was one of the first Mac programs for young kids, and it has stood the test of time. It includes five activities, the first three of which teach skills to kids who can't read yet: ABKey builds character recognition, Match-It teaches recognition of identical and similar objects, and Dot-to-Dot teaches number recognition and sequencing.

Although recommended for ages three to eight, KidsTime's two other activities can keep a ten-year-old involved. StoryWriter lets you type a story, interspersing pictures from a special font. The program then reads the story back to you in a robotic computer voice, saying the word for the picture. KidsNotes is a terrific music program—no surprise since the same company publishes a professional-level music program called ConcertWare+.

Reader Rabbit (SA)

Reader Rabbit 1 ($60), from The Learning Company, is a program for early readers (ages three to six) that uses three-letter words exclusively. The program has four activities, two of which I like. In one, a letter appears on one of three blank spaces, and you have to choose words that have that same letter in the same position. Words that don't match get dumped into the garbage. And once you've come up with enough correct words, a rabbit does a dance—with good sound and animation. In the other activity I like, you have to fill the cars of a train with words that share two out of three letters with the words in the preceding car. When the cars are filled, the train drives off the screen. If you like the program, you might check into the many other (age-appropriate) Rabbit-based adventures for learning reading and math skills.

Super Solvers OutNumbered!, NumberMaze, and New Math Blaster Plus (ND)

I looked at three math games from different developers; each program is designed to teach math fundamentals and is geared toward similar age groups.

Super Solvers OutNumbered! Anytime a new user signs on to **Super Solvers OutNumbered!** ($60) from The Learning Company, the game goes into beginner mode, explaining the rules on-screen as you play. My eight-year-old installed it himself and started playing without one look at the instruction booklet. It's a great game that combines arcade-style action and logical problem-solving, and unlike many educational games, it induces you to drill by making that a prerequisite for more play. When you solve arithmetic problems (you can control how hard they are), you win clues that help you find out where the bad guy is hiding. The problems are interesting—more like puzzles than drills—and there's even an on-screen calculator to help make sure the focus isn't on arithmetic. I enthusiastically recommend this titles for kids seven to ten who can read pretty well.

GOOD FEATURE

NumberMaze. In **NumberMaze** ($50, or $70 for the color version) from Great Wave Software, you guide a playing piece—a galloping horse, a roadster, and a mouse—through a maze. You have to solve problems to get around obsta-

More Fun!

(CG)

Where do you go to find out about and buy titles for kids? Fortunately, there are lots of sources and developers.

According to the Software Publisher's Association, an industry group that puts out all sorts of statistics and figures, the three largest developers of educational (a.k.a. kids) software are The Learning Company, Davidson and Associates, and Brøderbund Software. Each of the companies publishes catalogs (yours for the asking) describing the titles they offer in various subject categories and for different age groups.

But the Mac market is also populated by hundreds of other companies offering dozens of titles. Among those companies you'll find Edmark Corp., which offers creative learning programs such as Thinkin' Things and Millie's Math House for teaching kids numbers, shapes, and patterns; Optimum Resource, which offers the award-winning Stickybear series of programs teaching math and reading; Ventura Educational Systems, which offers more than 35 titles for kids and teachers covering math, science, geography, and history; and the Chariot Software Group, which also offers software programs and tools for both kids and teachers.

But there are many more developers, some offering just one or two titles, and many subject categories we didn't get a chance to cover in this chapter (such as astronomy programs for kids). Chances are, their products will be available from one of the distributors specializing in kids' and educational titles, such as Educorp, Educational Resources, and Learning Services (you'll find them listed in the resources section at the end of this book).

cles. Beginners count objects like turtles or toy sailboats. The problems gradually get harder, through 48 levels of difficulty, which include all types of computation and word problems. You can get hints if you're having difficulty (the program concentrates on trouble areas automatically). My son started using it as toddler just learning to count, and he still likes it in third grade.

New Math Blaster Plus. I found this program ($60), from Davidson, the weakest of the three math games I looked at. Three of its four modules are arithmetic drills, in six levels, from single-digit problems to fractions (no word problems), mixed with some arcade play. Only the fourth requires reasoning, rather than instant recall of math facts. **Math Blaster**'s strength is its variety of games, but the math is monotonously dull. My 8-year-old couldn't start this one up on his own, and the manual didn't help because it's directed to teachers rather than players. Davidson says it's appropriate for ages 6 to 12, but I think kids older than 10 would get bored with it pretty fast.

BAD FEATURE

20

Games & Hobbies

OK, ’FESS UP. We know you don’t spend *all* those hours in front of the Mac crunching spreadsheets. The rapidly growing market for personal software proves that a lot of you also use your computers for recreation and relaxation. In fact, Mac users spent more than $40 million on games in 1993, a number that’s growing rapidly as more sophisticated software—replete with color, interactive play, and stereo sound—captures the imagination (and pocketbooks) of digital gamesters.

In this chapter you’ll find our takes on some of the best Mac games, from arcade hits to epic adventures, plus some game-winning strategies. But games aren’t the only desktop diversions. You’ll probably be surprised by the variety of hobby software that’s available in categories such as gardening, sports, cooking, crafts, collectibles, and genealogy.

So take a break, kick back, and turn the page. This chapter’s for your off-duty hours.

Contributors

Aileen Abernathy (AA) is the chapter editor.

Christopher Breen (CB) is a writer and musician based near San Francisco. A contributing editor to *MacUser,* he also writes for several gaming magazines and is trying to convince his mother that he really *can* make a living playing computer games.

Shelley Cryan (SC) runs a consulting business in New York and writes frequently for computer magazines. She wishes her real garden looked as good as those she creates on screen.

Victoria von Biel (VvB) is the features editor at *Computer Life,* located in San Francisco. She has used her five years in the computer industry as an excuse to find the perfect cooking program.

Contents

Games

Mac gaming ain't what it used to be—and that's great news for the recreationally challenged. Faster, cheaper color Macs and CD-ROM technology have combined to bring us stunning new arcade hits, science fiction and fantasy adventures, strategic conquests, brain games, flight simulators, and head-to-head network challenges. There's also *edutainment*, a term coined for children's titles that blur the line between games and education (for more on educational games, see Chapter 19).

Games are at the forefront of multimedia technology. Titles such as Myst and The Journeyman Project blend photorealistic 3-D imagery, animation, video, and CD-quality sound. Plus, they're *interactive*—you have control over the characters' movements and the order in which goals are accomplished.

So, what's your addiction?

Rules of the Games

Before we look at our favorite playthings, here are a few things to keep in mind.

Free (and cheap) games (AA/CB). Some of the coolest games are *really cheap*—even free. A wealth of shareware and freeware is available from on-line services and user groups. Many commercial games covered here also have older shareware versions and/or demos that you can try before you buy. One good foraging area is the Macintosh Entertainment Forum on CompuServe, and Educorp offers the $50 **Game Room** CD-ROM, which contains more than 800 such games. We supply our own selection of recommended shareware titles (sorry, there are just a couple of small games) on the *Mac Bible* disks, available by sending in the card at the back of this book, or on the CD-ROM that came with this book, if you bought that edition. And please, pay the (negligible) shareware fees to the authors so they will continue to develop and support this stuff.

System requirements (AA). As their complexity increases, more and more games require color, multimegabytes of memory and hard-disk space, and CD-ROM drives (see "Everything's Coming Up CD-ROM" in this chapter). But that's not true of all games, including some of the best ones, so if you're a Mac

Classic or PowerBook owner, don't despair (see "PowerBook Gaming" in this chapter). To avoid disappointment, though, find out the minimum system requirements—including Mac model, system version, RAM, and disk space—for a game before you buy it.

Some games use fancy programming tricks that may cause memory conflicts with your extensions or applications. If you have trouble, turn off unnecessary extensions and quit any open programs. Still having problems? Call tech support; a newer version of the game (or application) might help.

Copy protection (AA). Some companies try to minimize pirating by copy-protecting their games. One approach—favored by titles such as Prince of Persia, Wordtris, and Lemmings—requires you to supply arcane information from the instruction booklet each time you start the game. Other games, such as Spectre, use a serial-number-based system that prevents you from launching duplicate copies over a network. We hate copy protection of any sort—you lose the booklets, network checks sometimes cause system hang-ups—which is why we applaud companies such as Delta Tao, which refuses to copy-protect its games. What it loses in stolen copies of Spaceward Ho!, Strategic Conquest, and Eric's Ultimate Solitaire it more than makes up in customer goodwill.

The Ultimate Joysticks (CB)

Let's face it, mice are lousy tools for piloting planes or maneuvering past slobbering bogeymen. For more agility (and less wrist strain), Advanced Gravis offers two excellent alternatives that plug into the ADB port: the **MouseStick II** ($100), a five-button flight joystick, and the **GamePad** ($50), a Nintendo-style game controller. Both products ship with preconfigured settings for many popular games, but you can change them or create your own sets from scratch. You can also make game sets "application-aware," so they will automatically load whenever you launch the corresponding game.

For arcade games, the best thing about the GamePad is that you can have one button fire repeatedly without lifting your finger. Not only does this make you a more deadly adversary, but it also relieves the potentially damaging finger fatigue.

If you're a flight-sim fanatic, check out ThrustMaster's line of mouse alternatives, all of which plug into the ADB port. The **Flight Control System** ($150) and **Weapons Control System** ($100) aren't cheap, but they are studded with buttons that provide you with maximum control over your aircraft. For another $150, you can get your feet into the action with the **Rudder Control System**.

Arcade Action

Limber up those fingers, because this category has something for everyone: traditional shoot-'em-ups, games of skill, hyperkinetic run-'n-jumps, and the latest in digital pinball.

Warning: Arcade games are addictive, and constant play can strain your trigger/ducking/flipper fingers (and the attached wrist). If you spend hours rat-a-tatting on the keyboard, we recommend you purchase a GamePad (see "The Ultimate Joysticks" on the previous page).

Prince of Persia (CB). Ever since the days of Dark Castle, Mac gamers have shown a proclivity for catapulting their digital alter egos off high perches and across deep chasms. **Prince of Persia** ($35) from Brøderbund is a superior example of the run-'n-jump genre. You (the Prince) have been locked in the dungeon by the evil Grand Vizier Jaffar. To win the big smooch from the Sultan's daughter, you must scale walls, leap deep chasms (in a single bound), battle scimitar-swinging thugs, and tiptoe through the steel jaws of death.

To win the fair princess in Prince of Persia, you must escape from a dungeon filled with deadly spikes and gnashing steel blades, not to mention bottomless pits, poisonous potions, and enemy swordsmen. Could a kiss really be worth all this?

The graphics are excellent and character movement is quite lifelike. You'll find yourself gasping as you propel the Prince across a seemingly impassable void. You might also find yourself groaning as you are run through for the 57th time by the fat guard on Level 6, which makes the game an excellent candidate for Axis the Gamecheater (see "Cheaters Anonymous" on page 778). This is one color game that also looks and runs great on a PowerBook or Mac SE, and there are patches posted on-line to circumvent the annoying copy-protection scheme (look for PoP Patcher). Watch for **Prince of Persia 2: The Shadow and the Flame,** which has an expanded story line and even more challenges.

Crystal Crazy (CB). This is the long-awaited sequel to that hugely popular grab-the-goodies diversion, Crystal Quest. This time around you're a space cow, piloting a flying bedpan among the stars. Along the way you gather crystals, shoot annoying critters, and, once the crystals are in hand, get out while the getting's good. But **Crystal Crazy** ($50, Casady & Greene) also has you smashing breakable objects, piecing together puzzles, and sinking pool balls—all while facing down new adversaries, such as the predatory space bunny and the Zinkleflashoxicationizer. The game runs nicely in black and white and is a good choice for PowerBookers, but use your headphones on the plane—the sounds are super but could provoke a humorless seat mate.

POWERBOOK

Firefall Arcade (CB/AA). Remember Centipede, the arcade game where you shot at a multisegmented insect that, with each hit, broke apart in infuriating ways? It's back, in the guise of **Firefall Arcade,** a $50 bug killer from Inline Software. Firefall not only includes most of the charms of our old friend (although we miss the cans of DDT), but it also offers glorious improvements. Your targets are fireworms that weave down the screen and, when shot, form colored barriers. New hazards lurk, such as slideworms and a relentlessly pursuing cube. Fortunately, bonus pieces containing temporary shields, invincibility, and double shots occasionally rain down from destroyed barriers. Our fun came to an abrupt halt, however, when the game suddenly ended after nine levels. Arcade games aren't supposed to *end;* the whole point is to eternally chase after higher scores and progress just one more level. Most games of this genre have 100 levels, not *9*. Argh.

BAD FEATURE

Maelstrom (CB). For a mere $15, you can enjoy this '90s update to that '80s hit, Asteroids. The current Grand Poobah of space-arcade shareware games, **Maelstrom** has a simple setup: You pilot a spaceship amidst a field of asteroids, blasting them into nothingness while fighting off alien spaceships and gathering goodies. Author Andrew Welch has produced a stellar (pardon the pun) product, with professional-quality graphics. If you tire of the built-in sounds, you can download alternate sound files from an on-line service. Unfortunately, Maelstrom won't run in black-and-white mode, but color users can set their Mac's clock to December 25 for a holiday treat.

HOT TIP

Two other shareware titles worth mentioning are **Space Junkie,** a $15 space-invaders game reminiscent of Galaxian, and **Cyclone,** a $10 diversion that hearkens back to Atari's Star Castle. Like Maelstrom, both are color-only games. Also, if you have More After Dark, one of your screen-saver options is **Lunatic Fringe,** a mildly entertaining space shoot-'em-up.

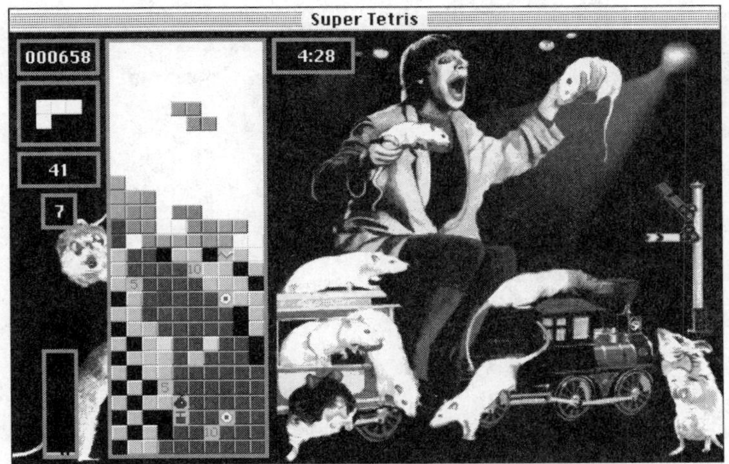

Super Tetris has a simple premise: Maneuver the falling blocks to plug holes and form complete lines. See how many lines you can form in five minutes—but don't get distracted by the antics of the Moscow Circus.

Tetris (AA). The rules are simple, the game is addictive. Blocks composed of four squares in various configurations fall randomly from the top of the screen, and you manipulate them to form complete lines at the bottom. From this basic premise, Spectrum HoloByte (and Russian developer Alexey Pajitnov) built a dynasty. The original Tetris became an instant classic when it was released in 1988; the current iteration, **Super Tetris** ($45), features scrolling pits, falling bombs, and hidden treasures, plus you can play games against the clock or a live opponent.

Another favorite, **Wordtris** ($40), rains letters that you must arrange into words. The lower levels are too easy (but great for kids); the advanced levels demand that you pluck words from your brain at lightning speed. If you have a CD-ROM drive, however, the best deal is **Tetris Gold,** a $50 CD-ROM that contains the entire Tris clan, including the lesser-known **Welltris** and **Faces.**

Tetris is an excellent game for PowerBooks and low-end Macs. If you're more miserly, Steve Chamberlain's freeware version, **Tetris Max 2,** has larger pieces and (unlike the commercial version) music that doesn't immediately get on your nerves.

Cheaters Anonymous (CB/AA)

My name is Chris, and I'm a cheater. I admit it, there's nothing I like better than seeing my SimCity 2000 funds skyrocket. (Type *porntipsguzzardo* in version 1. Version 1.1 users must bring the Map window to the front, type *pirn*, click on the floating Status window, and then type *topsguzzardo.*) And I hate running out of ammo in **Lunicus** ($70, Paramount Interactive). (Stay on the top floor, use all the ammo in the lockers, then enter the elevator and push the Up button. When you emerge, all the lockers are restocked!) I'd feel ashamed—if there weren't millions of other people just like me. How else do you explain the success of **Axis the Gamecheater** and the **Universal Hint System**?

Axis ($40, Baseline Publishing) is a control panel that lets you add lives, money, shields, time, and more in dozens of shareware and commercial games. You can repair a damaged Hellcat, improve the Prince of Persia's health, or add extra Gliders. To add new cheats, just download a fresh collection of GEMs (Game Enhancement Modules) from an on-line service or order a disk from Baseline.

The Universal Hint System ($10, shareware) is particularly helpful for adventure games such as Might and Magic or Wizardry, in which a simple hint or glance at a map can speed you on your way. Need more explicit instructions? Prima Publishing has excellent, fun-to-read walkthroughs for Myst, Prince of Persia, and SimCity 2000 ($20 each), while Osborne/McGraw-Hill offers strategy guides for SimCity Classic, SimCity 2000, and King's Quest ($20 each) and for Wizardry ($28).

For more game goodies, check out the monthly electronic magazine *Inside Mac Games* (IMG Publishing). You'll find an abbreviated version on major on-line services, or you can get the full version on disk ($28/year) or as a 1.3MB file over Internet ($18/year).

Diamonds (CB). For a fresh spin on the break-out genre, try **Diamonds 2** ($50) from Varcon Systems. You remove wall after wall of different-colored bricks by banging a ball against them. The catch is that you can only remove bricks that are the same color as your ball. That means bouncing the ball against special Paintbrush bricks while contending with Lock, Reverser, and Trap bricks. It's *not* as easy as it sounds—if you get complacent, try **More Diamonds** ($20). In black-and-white mode, it's tough to distinguish among the different patterns that mark the ball and bricks, so if you have a monochrome Mac, try the $20 shareware version, **Diamonds 1.6,** first.

Glider (AA/CB). Your mission: to pilot a paper airplane through a very large and wacky house while avoiding obstacles such as balloons, faulty electrical sockets, 'copters, and paper shredders. Maintaining airspeed means guiding the hapless plane over poorly placed (player's perspective) air vents. **Glider 4** ($50, Casady & Greene) is a lot of fun, and if 60 rooms aren't enough, the Room Editor lets you devise your own tortures. **More Glider** ($20) contains six additional houses and a level of challenge that may tempt more unscrupulous readers to cheat (again, see "Cheaters Anonymous" on the opposite page). Glider is another good PowerBook game, and if you're budget-minded, a black-and-white shareware version, **Glider+,** offers 15 rooms of fun for $8.

Pinball simulations (CB). First there was Tristan. Then came Eight Ball Deluxe. Now pinball developer Little Wing has given us the ultimate challenge: **Crystal Caliburn** ($60, StarPlay). The game has a Holy Grail theme and sports two ramps, multiball play, and a bewildering array of bonus targets. A wonderful simulation, but the table is slower than that of **Eight Ball Deluxe** ($50, Amtex), a re-creation of the classic Bally machine. Both games capture the feel of a real pinball machine, with realistic bumpers, sounds, gravity (although the ball "floats" too much in Crystal Caliburn), and the ability to give the machine a strategic nudge (via the Spacebar).

To rack up big bumper points, nudge the table (with the Spacebar) when the ball is in this area.

Practice using the left flipper to shoot the moving ball up the Camelot Castle ramp (right). To bring home the Grail—and a huge score—you must hit this ramp on the fly.

To make the Glass Island ramp (left), trap the ball with the right flipper, release it, and then flip when the ball reaches the center of the orange line.

Crystal Caliburn is the next best thing to a real pinball machine, with realistic ball movement, three-dimensional ramps, and a plethora of bonus targets. Your goal is to fill the Round Table with deserving knights and then retrieve the Holy Grail. Warning: This is one tough table!

Strategy and Brain Games

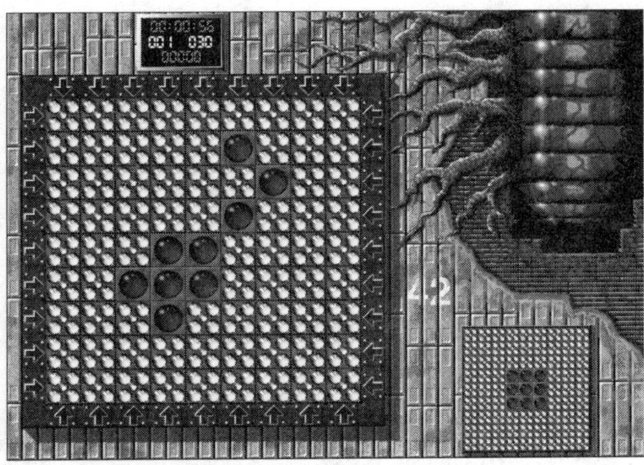

Cogito makes Rubik's Cube seem easy. The idea is to restore the marbles to their original design (shown at the lower right), using the arrows around the edge of the board to move rows and columns. Level 1 is easy, but only a master strategist will make it through the remaining 119 levels.

Do you prefer mental gymnastics to physical ones? These puzzlers will give your brain a good workout.

Cogito and company (CB/AA). Imagine a particularly diabolical version of Rubik's Cube, with cool graphics and a soundtrack reminiscent of bad German synthesizer music from the mid-'70s (yes, you can turn it off). That's the basic idea behind Inline Software's **Cogito,** where you must return a scrambled set of marbles to their original configuration. Unlike the Cube, though, the designs and moves become more complex with each of the 120 levels.

BARGAIN

Cogito costs $50, but don't waste your money—get **Three Great Plays** instead. For the same price, you get Cogito plus two more of Inline's brain-teasers, **Tesserae** and **3 in Three**. Tesserae is a mosaic scrambler similar to Cogito, while 3 in Three follows the amusing adventures of a number 3 who's lost in the Mac's innards. To return her to her spreadsheet, you must solve dozens of puzzles. Big fun. Plus, all of these award-winning perplexers look and run great on memory-constrained monochrome Macs.

HOT TIP

Lemmings (CB/AA). The original **Lemmings** ($50, Psygnosis) and its sequel, **Oh No! More Lemmings** (also $50), are two of the cutest action/puzzle games around. You're responsible for safely guiding a load of little green-haired mammals through more than 100 levels of hostile territory. To succeed, you must put the brainless creatures to work. If, for example, you are confronted by a steep pinnacle followed by a pit of fire, you would select one lemming to claw through the pinnacle and, once through, convert him into a bridge builder for crossing the pit. Meanwhile, don't forget to transform the critter directly behind him into a blocker, lest the idiot hordes merrily march into the flaming pits of hell. Once the bridge is built, you can nuke the blocker (our favorite part!) and proceed to the next baffling level.

Kids will find the creatures irresistible but the higher levels too taxing. Adults will quickly tire of looking up access codes in the manual each time they play. Fortunately, you can send the master disk to Psygnosis along with $5 and receive a version without the annoying copy-protection scheme.

Editors Poll: What Game Do You Play Most Often?

AA: I'm addicted to Super Tetris and Shanghai, which I use as free-association tools when I need to give my brain a break. When I want something even less mentally taxing, I play Maelstrom, Crystal Caliburn, or Spectre VR. And I can spend hours (and hours) on tantalizing puzzles such as Myst.

DB: I think there's something wrong with me. I'm the only computer tweak I know who doesn't like computer games. I look at a computer screen enough already. There's got to be people like me out there, right? Right?

Excuse me, I have to go play another game of ping pong in our rec room.

EC: I generally play the same game maybe two or three hours a day for weeks on end, only to abruptly give it up and never play it again. Tetris is a special case: I played it so long and hard that eventually everything I saw (including the bricklike sidewalks of Barcelona, where I lived) seemed to be falling into Tetris formations.

DD: I'm completely addicted to Shanghai. It switches me to right-brain mode (you have to think visually, not logically, to make the matches), and since I can (after lots of practice) finish a game in about four minutes, I can always kid myself that I'll play just one game and then get back to work.

CG: Tetris (personal best: 114 lines) and Klondike, a simple little game of solitaire that you can play into the night!

JK: Scott Macneil's Minesweep. When I'm starting to get fuzzy-brained, it wakes me up to solve a straightforward logical problem (or to have a bomb explode if I'm not being so logical). Each game only takes a few minutes, and it ends with a sense of accomplishment, not frustration (which is what I get from playing games like Tetris).

BW: My favorite, believe it or not, is the Microsoft Word speller and thesaurus, which I play for about an hour a week. The spell checker is only really so-so when it comes to figuring out the suggested spellings of misspelled words, so it's really a riot to give it a few choice misspellings, on purpose, and see what it comes up with.

Oxyd (CB). **Oxyd** is a brain-teaser—and partially a game of skill—that forces you to devise ingenious solutions to seemingly insurmountable obstacles. The idea is to navigate a black marble through 100 levels of perplexing landscape. Along the way, you encounter such difficulties as marble-swallowing quicksand, laser traps, and crumbling floors. The original Oxyd is freely available on-line. To play beyond the first 10 levels, however, you must send $40 to Dongleware to obtain a code book that unlocks the remaining 90 levels. An additional 100 levels are available for cooperative play over a network. If you're not all puzzled out, there's a commercial sequel, **Oxyd Magnum** ($60).

Pax Imperia (CB). You're out to conquer the galaxy, and all you have to do is build a fleet of spaceships, impose colonies on other worlds, provide a strong defense, and maintain a stable economy. And those are the easy tasks. In addition, you must design your ships, spy on the neighbors, and assassinate troublesome dignitaries. **Pax Imperia** ($70, Changeling Software) is a very complex—but ultimately satisfying—space odyssey. On a network, you can vie with up to 16 opponents for ultimate control of the universe.

Two other conquer-the-galaxy games that aren't quite so feature-laden are **Spaceward Ho!** ($60, Delta Tao) and **Galactic Empire** ($15, shareware).

Space Operas (CB/AA)

The first successful Mac CD-ROM game, Reactor's **Spaceship Warlock** ($95), eschewed arcade action for pure exploration and won raves for its state-of-the-art 3-D graphics. Following in its footsteps, several companies have thrown their best minds (if not their best storytellers) at space operas. You know what I mean: Hostile superior intellect from far-off galaxy threatens frolicking, peaceful Terrans, and it's up to you to save the world. If you like this genre, and have an 8-bit monitor and 5MB of memory, here are two games you'll enjoy.

Iron Helix. This is the best of the sci-fi sagas. Your $75 mission is to disable a biological weapon (code-named Iron Helix) in the belly of a renegade spaceship bent on the destruction of a planet of frolicking, peaceful Terrans. To accomplish this, you remotely control a robotic probe through the dark and eerie passages of the ship, collecting genetic codes and studying the crew's video

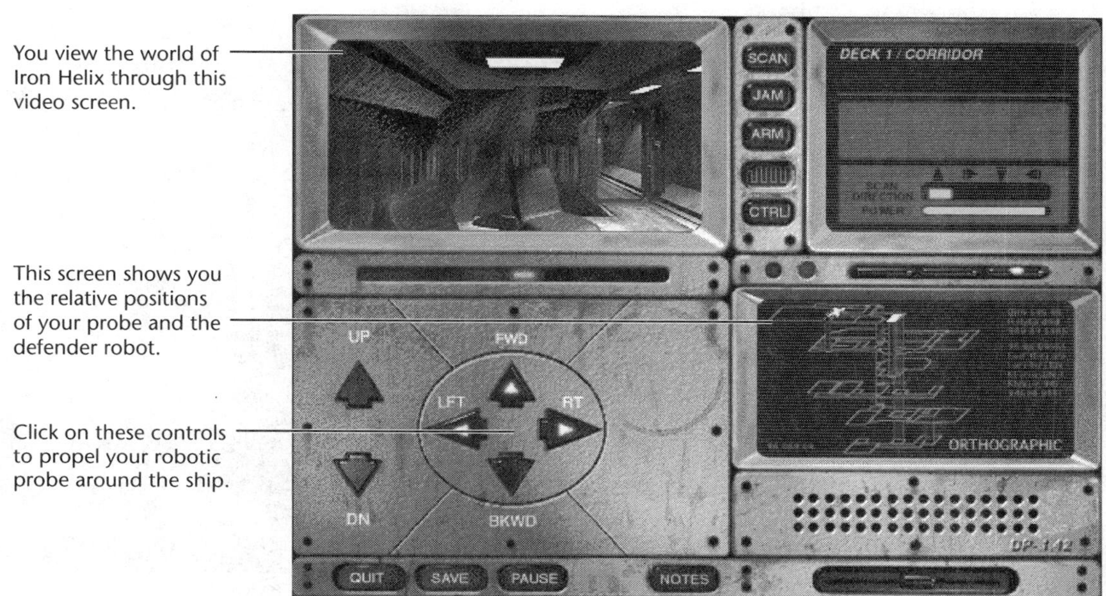

Iron Helix is a classic space opera: To protect a planet of frolicking, peaceful terrans, you must disable a biological weapon on a renegade spaceship while being relentlessly pursued by a hostile robot.

messages. Hot on your heels is the ship's defender robot and you, darn the luck, haven't a single weapon at your disposal. (If your pursuer gets too close for comfort, duck into an elevator—the robot can't use it—or hide in the secret shaft in engineering.) Rendered entirely in 3-D animation, Spectrum HoloByte's **Iron Helix** is a good, high-tech cat-and-mouse game that, for CD-ROM, runs at a fairly brisk clip.

The Journeyman Project. You belong to a culture of frolicking, peaceful Terrans threatened by a hostile superior intellect—in this case, a time-traveling saboteur. As a member of the Temporal Protectorate, you must prevent said HSI from revising history by traveling back in time yourself and repairing his temporal rips. To achieve your goal, you must solve several puzzles (some a bit far-fetched for my taste). More than one solution exists for each, and you get extra points for nonviolent responses. Unlike Iron Helix, which forces you to complete tasks in a particular order, **Journeyman** is unstructured, allowing you to proceed as you see fit.

Journeyman ($80, Quadra Interactive) exhibits the kind of slick graphics—including 30 minutes of video shot with professional actors—and sound quality we've come to expect from CD-ROM titles, but drive-access times can be glacially slow.

Adventuring We Go

(CB)

Fantasy and role-playing games are long-time gaming favorites (see "Oldies But Goodies" in this chapter), and they're improving with age.

Myst is a must-have adventure for any owner of a CD-ROM drive. You'll be spellbound for hours (days, weeks...) as you explore surrealistic worlds and try to solve Myst's intriguing mystery.

Myst. If you still need a reason to buy a CD-ROM drive, here it is. **Myst** ($60, Brøderbund) is a breathtakingly gorgeous adventure with a compelling plot from brothers Rand and Robyn Miller, the creators of three award-winning children's titles (**The Manhole, Cosmic Osmo,** and **Spelunx and the Caves of Mr. Seudo,** $35 each from Brøderbund).

You begin the game on deserted Myst Island. As you wander around, you uncover an intriguing but disturbing mystery involving the absent landlord, Atrus. To unravel the mystery and find Atrus, you must solve a variety of original, clever puzzles that require close attention to detail. This may sound like standard adventure fare, but Myst is a seminal work, forever changing our expectations of what a CD-ROM game should be. Every scene has a surreal, photograph-like quality; the QuickTime movies are seamlessly integrated into the 3-D graphics; the soundtrack and environmental sounds add just the right touch of atmosphere; the plot is believable; and the puzzles are tough but fair. And, unlike many adventure games, Myst is nonlinear and nonlethal. You are welcome to try any boneheaded stunt at any time without fear of an untimely end.

Tip: Keep your ears as well as your eyes open, because many of Myst's clues are aural in nature. You could easily spend hours banging your head against the screen until you realize that when you made that last turn, the Mac went *bawang* instead of *poing*. It's worth your while to figure out why.

Might and Magic III, Isles of Terra. Most role-playing games for the Mac are converted DOS products that appear to have been ported during someone's lunch break—and I *do* mean you, Strategic Simulations, and your officially licensed Advanced Dungeons & Dragons series. Fortunately, New World Computing took more care with the Might and Magic series. If you like assembling a group of magical creatures and leading them through dark and scary places in an epic quest for gold and glory, **Isles of Terra** ($60) is for you.

Pathways Into Darkness. Warning: This is a terrific game, but it's not for the squeamish. Bungie Software's $70 adventure asks you to march into the bowels of an ancient, maze-filled Yucatán pyramid and prevent an alien presence from destroying the world. And wouldn't you know it, the place is crawling with icky creatures that want to cut your mission short. (Tip: The key to survival is ducking—a lot.) Despite the overhead of 3-D texture-mapped graphics (which reveal every gruesome detail), game play is remarkably smooth. Blood-curdling stereo sound clues you in to the location of the next beastie, and the graphics are just that: graphic.

CD-ROM

Modern mysteries. If you prefer more traditional software sleuthing, the three volumes of **Sherlock Holmes, Consulting Detective** ($70 each, Viacom New Media) let you tag along with Holmes and Watson through the streets of Arthur Conan Doyle's London. To solve the murders, you interview suspicious characters, track down leads provided by Scotland Yard and the Baker Street Irregulars, and scan the *London Times* for clues. Each CD-ROM volume contains three original mysteries that feature 90 minutes of live-action video, with fine performances by the actors. Creative Multimedia's Virtual Murder CD-ROM series employs more modern investigative techniques. In **Who Killed Sam Rupert?** ($40) and **The Magic Death** ($50, or $70 for both games), you run forensic tests on the evidence, review QuickTime testimony from prime suspects, comb through the victim's personal effects, check your suspects' alibis, and suffer through press conferences.

Simulated Reality

Ever wondered what it would be like to play God? How about something less nervy (relatively speaking), like flying an F/A-18 Hornet into battle? Here's your chance to find out.

In SimCity 2000, you're the mayor of a futuristic city populated by demanding citi-sims who want it all: industry and *clean air, convenient housing* and *open space, low taxes* and *low crime rates. Can you strike a balance and turn your city into a thriving metropolis?*

Maxis's Sim Series (CB/AA). Each of Maxis's award-winning Sim products elevates you to Most Exalted Person on High and lets you throw your weight around in matters ranging from urban planning, to the development of life, to the successful running of an ant colony. In **SimCity 2000** ($70), you don the hat of an ambitious mayor responsible for controlling the myriad factors—from taxes to crime to the environment—that make a city grow and prosper. New features include 3-D landscapes, subways, an underground water system, humongous arcologies (cities within cities), prisons, marauding aliens, and the ability to create your own terrain. For another $20, you can get **SimCity 2000 Scenarios, Vol. 1: Great Disasters,** which tests your mettle against real and not-so-real natural disasters, including Midwest flooding, California earthquakes, and rioting lawyers in Washington, D.C.

The Sim series also includes **SimEarth** ($50), **SimLife** ($70), **SimAnt** ($50), and the one that started it all, **SimCity Classic** ($40). (Someone missed the, uh, boat when naming the $70 **A-Train.**) SimEarth and SimLife, in particular, are entertaining exercises in evolution, where you tinker with the environment and gene pool, respectively, to tailor life to your liking. Intelligent, lion-headed salamanders, perhaps?

While there aren't any points to rack up, the Sim series has a fair dollop of humor—watch for Santa on Christmas Eve in A-Train, listen to the delighted *oo-la-LA* when animals mate in SimLife, or type the word *joke* in just about any game. Maxis also offers tips on CompuServe's Game Publishers Forum B. Plus, these products have the finest, funniest, and most enlightening manuals around (essential, considering the complexity of these games).

HOT TIP

Civilization (CB). From small things, big things one day come. Never was this statement more true than in MicroProse's $50 epic god-game, **Civilization.** As the name implies, your job is to take a small tribe wandering about in 4000 B.C. and nurture it into a booming, global civilization of the future. You achieve this goal by acting as a god-in-training who, with each success, gets more complex assignments. Initial responsibilities entail setting up a functional village and providing a small defense force to protect the citizens. As your tribe prospers, you must establish trade routes, barter or war with neighbors, deal with global warming, and fling groups of your citizens into the cosmos to establish space-based colonies.

Flight simulators (CB). It's no contest: Graphic Simulations makes the best flight sims on the Mac market. **Hellcats Over the Pacific** ($70) is a World War II prop-fighter operating in the Pacific Theater, and **F/A-18 Hornet** ($80) is a modern-day jet-fighter complete with electro-optical weapons, Sidewinder missiles, and advanced radar. Chair-jockeys are routinely amazed when they strap in and find how smoothly the scenery scrolls by and how quickly their aircraft responds. Both simulations let you plug in additional theaters of war, such as **Hellcats: Missions at Leyte Gulf** ($35).

GOOD FEATURE

Chuck Yeager's Air Combat ($60, Electronic Arts) features aircraft from WWII, Korea, and Vietnam and, as the name implies, this sim focuses on dogfighting. The frame rate isn't as smooth as that in Graphic Simulations' products, but the wealth of missions and aircraft make CYAC a worthy contender. At press time, Parsoft Publishing's **A-10 Attack!** was still in development (and unpriced), but it looks to be the most happening game on two wings. It was created by Eric "Hellcats" Parker, so check it out if you have the slightest interest in lounge-chair aviation. (And yes, I *did* intentionally exclude Microsoft's long-in-the-tooth Flight Simulator 4.)

THINGS TO COME

Electronic Board Games

Not so long ago, we had to amuse ourselves with cards, board games, and crossword puzzles. Then came computers. Then came digital versions of our favorite B.C. (Before Computers) pursuits.

Chessmaster 3000 (CB). For players who yearn to strengthen their chess game or learn a lesson in humility, **Chessmaster 3000,** from Software Toolworks, is more than happy to oblige. The attractive $50 game has a powerful artificial-intelligence engine and offers a host of features, including a library of 150,000 opening moves, an interactive tutorial, and tournament play for as many as ten players. By following the guidelines provided in the on-line help file—a necessary inclusion, since the printed docs are on the skimpy side—you can even create customized chess pieces.

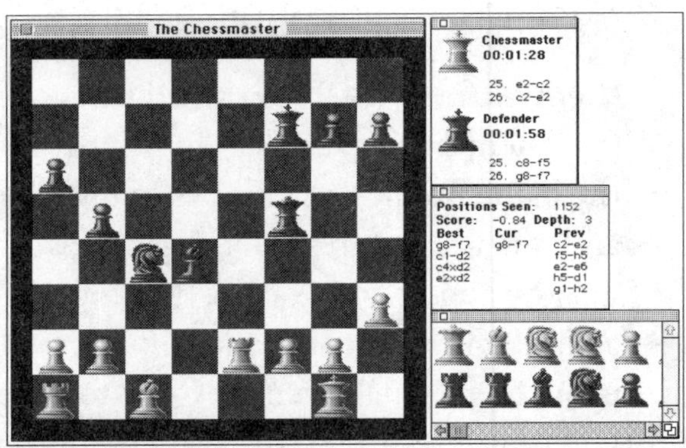

Besides providing a tough and tireless opponent, Chessmaster 3000 can recreate classic chess matches, such as this 1876 game from Henry Edward Bird.

Monopoly and Risk (CB). For years Parker Brothers fended off shareware authors attempting to clone its intellectual property. Then Virgin Games finally secured the digital rights for **Monopoly** ($40) and **Risk** ($50). These are faithful renderings of the originals, which you can play with friends or against the computer (or both). You may get eyestrain from squinting at the 9-inch game boards, however; Virgin didn't program the games to resize for larger monitors.

GOOD FEATURE

Scrabble (CB). Virgin also offers the official **Scrabble** release ($40), but the Sheppard Company's **Maven** beats the pants off it. Not only does Maven feature a larger board and play at a more advanced level (my cat could beat Scrabble's Level 1), but you also can put premium squares anywhere you like—scatter Triple Word Scores to your heart's content—and the Simulation feature reveals how a game will play out over several moves. The $75 price is a bit steep, but true Scrabble aficionados will feel richly rewarded.

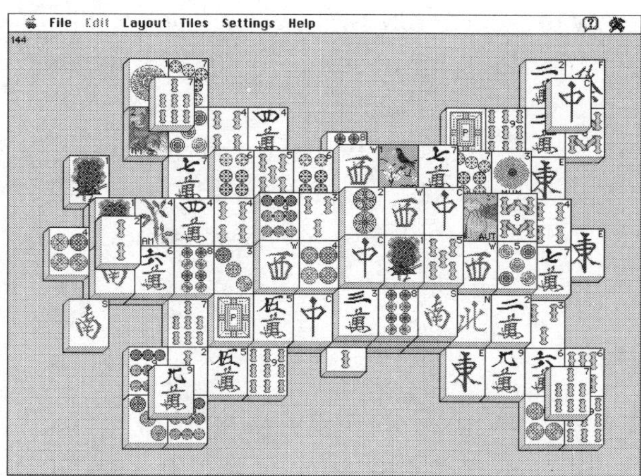

It sounds simple: Just remove accessible tiles from the pile in matched pairs. But the Ox is one of the toughest layouts to win in Shanghai, an addictive game favored by Mac Bible *editors. If you don't like the Mah-Jongg tiles shown here, you can choose from seven other tile sets.*

Shanghai II: Dragon's Eye (AA). **Shanghai II** ($30, Activision) is deceptively simple and completely addictive. The idea is to remove tiles from a decoratively arranged pile by snapping off accessible matched pairs until you run out of moves, tiles, or time. Shanghai II offers eight different tile sets (from Mah-Jongg to Sports), a variety of game layouts based on the Chinese zodiac (from the simple Snake to the practically impossible Tiger), and a Layout Construction Set for creating your own formations. Play solitaire (as I do) or against an opponent in the special Dragon's Eye challenge. A freeware offering, **Gunshy,** offers a much simplified version of the game.

Card games (CB/VvB). Digital versions of solitaire are favorite time-wasters for computer jockeys everywhere. **Eric's Ultimate Solitaire** ($60, Delta Tao) contains 17 playing-card hits, including Klondike, Canfield, and Forty Thieves. Sure, you could get most of them as shareware, but you'd miss the on-line help, clever graphics, cheatability, and digital sound. For shareware groupies, **Klondike** ($10) is the long-time champ of addictive solitaire. A shareware newcomer, **Hearts** ($15), can liven up a slow Saturday night for you or a network of lonely hearts. You can ensure a win by choosing from three skill levels (Smart, Average, or Dumb as a Stump), giving yourself a hefty handicap, or using the tutorial mode.

Crossword puzzles (AA). Do you do crosswords in ink, only to regret your bravado when you reach 41 Down? Welcome to the world of digital puzzling, where you can delete rash wordplay with a keystroke. The Premium Edition of **Lyriq Crosswords** ($30) is all a serious word lover could want, with more than 250 puzzles from *The Washington Post*, *Penny Press*, and *Crossword Magazine*, and four levels of play (from Kids to Expert). Lyriq provides optional hints, timed

tournament play, and puzzle printing for die-hard inkers. The interface is elegant, with nifty touches such as automatic skipping of filled-in squares when you enter a word. Additional puzzle packs are $10 to $25. For more casual puzzlers, **Take a Break! Crosswords** ($50, Dynamix) supplies 750 puzzles developed with Dell Magazines, while **CrossPro** ($40, Aspen Gold) has 250 crosswords from Stavrolex. Both Lyriq and CrossPro have low system requirements, making them great PowerBook companions.

Network Gaming (CB)

Ever daydreamed about getting even with that joker in Accounting who keeps losing your expense reports? If you're on a network, challenge him to one of these friendly games. (Oh sure, you could play cooperatively, but where's the fun in that?) You can also set up network showdowns with Pax Imperia and the flight simulators F/A-18 Hornet and Chuck Yeager's Air Combat.

Spectre VR. Velocity Development was a pioneer in network shoot-'em-ups with its futuristic 3-D tank game, Spectre. Three years and two sequels later we have the $60 **Spectre VR** (virtual reality, get it?), boasting a dozen network scenarios (for up to eight players) plus a terrain editor, VRchitect. As you race (or fly!) the tank around the playing field, you must not only avoid the deadly love taps of your friends, but also keep an eye peeled for intelligent acid pools and cybermud. Fortunately, you have several new weapons at your disposal;

PowerBook Gaming (CB/AA)

The point of owning a PowerBook is to travel light and travel smart. Therefore, the perfect PowerBook game will not require the following:

- a refer-to-the-manual copy-protection scheme
- more than 2MB of hard disk space or memory
- color
- a keypad
- a CD-ROM drive

Most of these guidelines also apply to games that will fit (and run) comfortably on the Mac Classic, Performa 200, and old warhorses such as the Plus and SE. This needn't limit your playtime (much)—check out Tetris, Oxyd, Cogito, 3 in Three, Shanghai, Prince of Persia (once you remove the annoying copy protection), card games, crossword-puzzle software, and reissued classics such as Zork and Shadowgate.

unfortunately, the controls are confusing and you may be annihilated while fumbling for the right one. Warning: Some users have reported sluggish game speed on less-than-sprightly machines. *[Spectre is also an excellent single-player game.—AA]*

Super Maze Wars. What the concept lacks in originality—racing around a maze, grabbing goodies, and blasting your buddies—**Super Maze Wars** ($65, Callisto) makes up for in execution. Its 3-D graphics aren't as detailed as those in Spectre VR, because it uses the computer's processing power for raw speed instead. Throw in well-designed controls, radar, and some ButtKicker missiles, and you have the makings of a fine search-and-destroy network game.

Bolo. As many as 16 people working in teams can play this $25 shareware tank game, which stresses strategy over brute firepower. That's correct: The point is not to mindlessly careen about, blowing up whatever passes before your gunsight, but rather to work in tandem with your buddies in order to achieve a common goal (such as ambushing the opposing team).

Oldies But Goodies

(CB/AA)

Once upon a time, the Mac had a whopping 512K of memory and adventure games were text-based. Because they couldn't distract you with glitzy animation, graphics, and sound, the games had to have compelling plots. You know the routine:

- Character finds him/herself standing about empty-handed.
- Character wanders around collecting odd items.
- Character employs items to solve puzzles ("Use the lucky charm to frighten the rabbit").
- Character enters maze and gets lost.
- Character meets sad end.
- Player buys graph paper and starts over.

Some of the best titles from this era have been updated and make perfect playtoys on low-memory monochrome Macs. Remember the Zork series? Infocom sold 3 *million* copies of these fantasy games in the 1980s. Well, they're baaack. Activision has released **The Lost Treasures of Infocom I,** which has all 5 games, along with 15 other favorites such as Planetfall, Deadline, and The Hitchhiker's Guide to the Galaxy. All in all, weeks (or maybe years) of frustrating fun for just $50 ($60 on CD-ROM). Another $30 gets you volume II, which has 11 lesser-known games (the $40 CD-ROM has 14). Sadly, neither volume contains my favorite Infocom title, Leather Goddesses of Phobos.

Not to be outdone, Viacom New Media has reissued three classic Mindscape titles—**Shadowgate, Uninvited,** and **Deja Vu I & II**—for $40 apiece. These were the first adventure games to have a graphical interface, eclipsing the days when you typed seemingly reasonable commands only to be confounded by the computer's stubborn "Huh?"

Hobbies

Hobby software is a relatively unknown software niche. Its products are (usually) inexpensive and aimed at nonprofessionals, do-it-yourselfers, collectors, and enthusiasts of all stripes. On the following pages we've gathered a plethora of programs (and a few tips) for personal pursuits such as genealogy, gardening, home remodeling, sports, movie watching, cooking, baseball-card collecting, sewing, and model railroading.

Much of this software comes from small companies, often written by the hobbyists themselves to meet their own needs. As a result, some programs are superb, while others leave a lot to be desired. In some categories, the shareware offerings are better (or at least cheaper) than the commercial products. But take heart: The booming home-software market has developers working overtime, and we expect higher-quality hobby programs to appear in the near future.

Home Sweet Home (SC)

Need to remodel the kitchen? Hate the backyard? You can sketch a better home or garden with a few clicks of the mouse, thanks to a spate of home-design programs aimed at amateur architects and landscapers.

Architecture. The programs for would-be architects aren't as sophisticated as computer-aided design (CAD) programs (see Chapter 15), but they cost *much* less, are easier to learn, and meet the needs of most nonprofessionals. **Design Your Own Home: Architecture** ($100, Abracadata) lets you create both floor plans and elevations, complete with wiring, plumbing, and insulation. It offers several predrawn windows, doors, bathroom fixtures, and other design elements. It needs just 512K of application RAM and can run off a floppy, so it's a good choice if you're hardware-constrained.

If you've got 1MB of RAM and a hard drive, however, opt for **Expert Home Design** ($50, Expert Software) instead. Expert covers the basics as well as DYOH: Architecture does, plus it's cheaper and offers more features. For example, you can draw different parts of a design (such as wiring and carpeting) on different layers, and it includes a furniture library for basic interior design (but see below). It also lets you rotate walls and furnishings to any angle, which could be handy if you're designing bathrooms for the Pentagon.

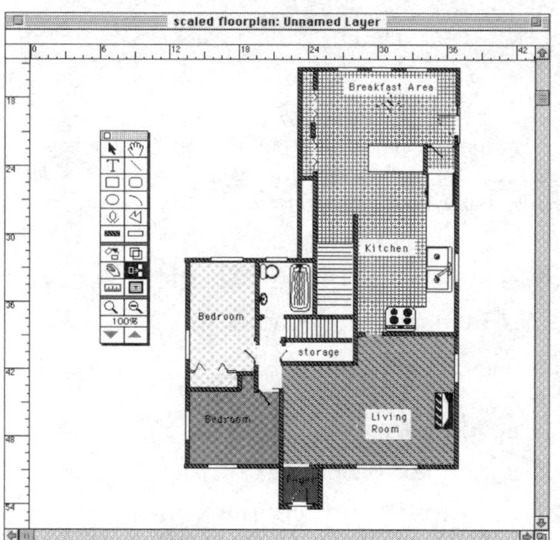

Expert Home Design makes it easy to sketch your dream house, complete with wiring, plumbing, carpeting, fixtures, and even furnishings.

Interior design. If you're interested in furnishing a home rather than building one, pass up **DYOH: Interiors** ($100, Abracadata), which is basically DYOH: Architecture with different clip art. Its simplistic features are good only for a quick-and-dirty evaluation of whether the bed, dresser, and bookcase fit against the wall, a scenario for which a tape measure or muscular cousin Leo could do just as well.

Instead, get **MacInteriors** ($130, Microspot), which offers a full-color, 3-D approach to space planning. It has basic tools for sketching walls, windows, and doors, but the real fun begins when you start fussing with the furniture. The extensive library contains fairly realistic looking objects, from sofas and tables to potted plants (tall or short), computers, and bunk beds. You also can draw your own furniture and attach descriptions and prices. A standout feature is MacInteriors' perspective view, which lets you do a walkthrough of your redesigned habitat, giving you a real feel for what the rooms will look like.

Landscaping. Both Abracadata and Expert Software offer landscaping programs to round out their home-design suites, but give them a pass. For landscaping an entire yard, **Mum's the Word Plus** ($120, Terrace Software) combines a detailed, 600-plant database (which you can add to) with a well-designed planting scheme. Mum's helps you select flowers, shrubs, trees, grasses, and ground covers according to specific criteria—such as shade or drought tolerance—then places colored symbols where you've planted them. Once you've decided on the plants, Mum's creates a shopping list for your nursery visit.

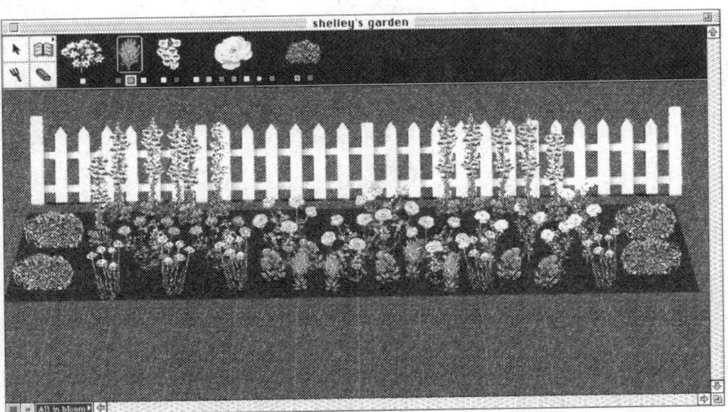

To design a garden with FLOWERscape, just select a blossom from the plant strip (top) and click it into your plot. Once you're done planting, you can see what the realistic-looking flora will look like in any given month using a pop-up menu.

If you're a vegetable gardener, another Abracadata product, **Sprout!** ($80), offers carrots as well as kohlrabi in its well-stocked database. Sprout! has a planting and harvesting calendar, plus it can tell you how many people your garden will feed if everything grows as planned. Tips about planting are geared to novices, making it easy to mind your queues of peas.

Do you value beauty over sustenance? **FLOWERscape** ($75, Voudette) helps you design flower gardens. FLOWERscape is incredibly easy to use and—unlike other programs discussed here—it uses scanned photographs to provide realistic images for the 150-plus flowers in its database. FLOWERscape suggests flowers based on your criteria—height, color, climate, and so forth. You pick the flowers you want, then plant them with a mouse click. FLOWERscape can even show you what your garden will look like, barren or blooming, in any given month.

Growing a Family Tree (VvB)

If you're more interested in cultivating your family tree than the one in the backyard, you know that genealogy is a serious business, requiring long hours of research, meticulous record keeping, and the sleuthing skills of Sherlock Holmes. While the quality of much genealogy software is poor, two programs stand out, and both are firmly endorsed by Mac-based genealogists.

Tip: Whichever genealogy program you buy, make sure it imports and exports files in GEDCOM format (both programs mentioned below can do this). This will let you trade files with other genealogists or use the files in other genealogy programs.

Personal Ancestral File. PAF is distributed by the Church of Jesus Christ of Latter-day Saints (better known as the Mormon Church), which oversees the world's largest genealogical data collection at its Family History Library in Salt Lake City, Utah. This easy-to-use, HyperCard-like database can store your research notes and lets you create printable pedigree charts (family trees) and other custom-designed reports. PAF is a steal at $35, and although it's an ideal entry-level program, it's powerful enough to do almost anything a genealogy buff could want. And don't worry about being swamped in religious arcana: PAF was developed to help Mormons apply for LDS ordinances, but you can omit all references to the church.

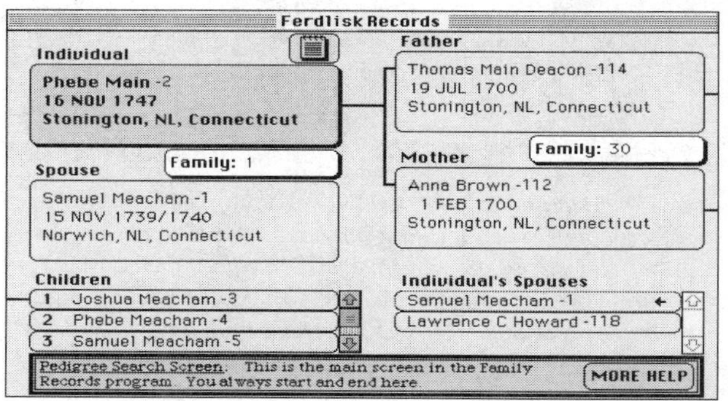

Originally developed by the Mormon Church, Personal Ancestral File is easy to use, inexpensive, and powerful—an ideal choice for genealogists of all stripes.

Reunion. At $170, **Reunion 3** is considerably more expensive than PAF, but users rave about the program and Leister Productions' technical support. My version was HyperCard-based, but an upgrade

due in mid-'94 will be a faster stand-alone application. Reunion includes a drawing program for creating pedigree charts and descendant's charts, and you can add digitized photos to charts, as well as explanatory text under each individual's name.

A Couch Potato's Guide to the Movies (VvB)

If you've ever wandered around a video store undecided between *8½* and *Don't Tell Mom the Babysitter's Dead*, help is here. CD-ROM guides to the movies—complete with QuickTime film clips—are a hot commodity. But don't despair if you don't have a CD-ROM drive: There's even a program on old-fashioned floppy disks.

Cinemania '94. Despite its price tag, Microsoft's $80 CD-ROM is likely to be the front-runner in this increasingly crowded field. *[When has Microsoft ever come in second?—AA]* Not yet released at our deadline but *extremely* popular in its Windows incarnation, Cinemania boasts 20 film clips, 160 snatches of dialog, and thousands of stills from 19,000 films. Film reviewers Pauline Kael, Roger Ebert, and Leonard Maltin offer their opinions, plus there are articles on film genres and history, as well as the contents of Ehraim Katz's *Encyclopedia of Film*. Even the interface looks good.

Movie guides are a popular CD-ROM offering, but only MovieSelect can make recommendations based on personal taste. Just select a movie category (such as Comedies), then choose three favorites from the scrolling list. When you're done, MovieSelect will display a printable list of suggestions from its database.

Criterion Goes to the Movies. Voyager's $25 entry in the movie derby is an exquisite compilation of highlights from its Criterion Collection of laser discs, ranging from *Citizen Kane* and *Lawrence of Arabia* to *2001: A Space Odyssey* and *Boyz N the Hood*. The CD-ROM has essays on each of the 150 movies, cast and credit lists, stills, plot synopses, and—best of all—QuickTime movies of memorable scenes. This disc doesn't have information on thousands

Everything's Coming Up CD-ROM (AA/VvB)

Because of their size and complexity, many hobby and game applications now ship only on CD-ROM. Hundreds of titles are now available, ranging from hobby discs such as Virtual Tarot, Cinemania, and Baseball's Greatest Hits to hot games like Iron Helix and Myst. In fact, CD-ROM may be the dominant way of distributing games by the time you read this.

CD-ROM drives are cheaper and faster than ever, so if you don't already own one, consider the investment. Those silver discs are going to multiply exponentially as users' appetite for high-quality graphics, animation, movies, and sound continues to grow. (For more on CD-ROM drives, see "CD-ROMs" in Chapter 5.)

Tip: CD-ROM-based software needs *lots* of RAM to run effectively. Even if you copy an application to your hard disk drive from a CD-ROM, chances are it will still need to access files on the disc. So allocate as much RAM as possible to the program by selecting its icon, choosing Get Info (Cmd I), and bumping up the Preferred Size in the Memory Requirements box.

of films, but it's a must for true movie buffs. *[It's also an extended commercial for Criterion laserdiscs.—AA]*

MovieSelect. This $60 CD-ROM from Paramount Interactive has one really cool feature: It can suggest movies you might like based on which movies you've enjoyed in the past. Just pick three favorites from a list of representative titles and **MovieSelect** displays a list of recommended videos culled from its database of 44,000 movies. You can even print the list and take it to the video store.

Movies, Movies, Movies. Finally, for Mac users without a CD-ROM drive, there's **Movies, Movies, Movies** ($35, MacKay Associates). This no-frills set of text files gives you the cast, director, year released, quality rating, and plot for around 2,800 movies. You can view the files with a word processor or import them into HyperCard or a database manager. Updates are (usually) available each spring for $15 (MacKey is a one-man operation).

Sports (AA)

The Mac might seem an odd piece of athletic equipment, but if you're serious about staying (or getting) in shape, it could prove more useful than a fancy sports watch. Sports-related programs can help you monitor your training progress or teach you some new moves. And if you're a fan instead of a player, there are CD-ROMs chock-full of sports trivia.

The Athlete's Diary. Developed by a triathlete, this versatile sports log ($50, Stevens Creek Software) helps you plan, track, and evaluate a fitness regimen for up to eight sports of your choosing, from cycling and swimming to aerobics and weights. You can record and analyze virtually anything: average pace, total time/distance, personal records, optimum heart rates—even whether those new running shoes have improved your performance. A charting feature gives you visual feedback on your progress. Entering post-exercise data takes seconds and the program requires just 1MB of RAM. Put it on your PowerBook and you'll have no excuse for not exercising during road trips.

GOOD FEATURE

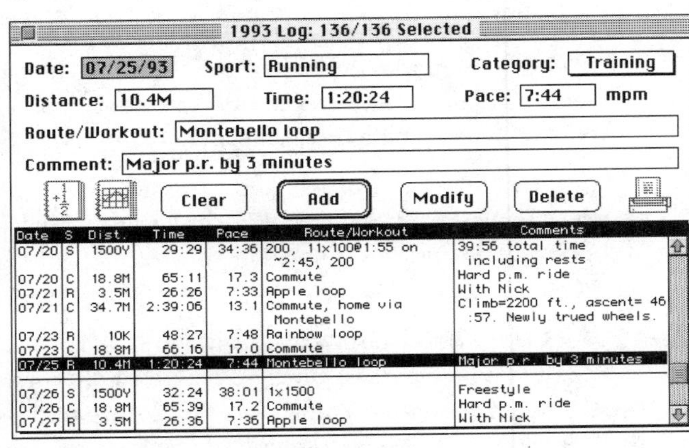

The Athlete's Diary helps you plan and track a physical fitness regimen for up to eight sports. Entering workout data is a snap, and you can monitor your progress in a variety of ways.

The Outdoor Athlete. For the price of a month at Nautilus, you can get **The Outdoor Athlete** ($40, Johnson Books), an excellent cross-training guide for backpackers, climbers, skiers, mountain bikers, and water-sports enthusiasts. Based on personal trainer Steve Ilg's book of the same name, the CD-ROM contains step-by-step techniques for achieving peak physical form, advice on nutrition and cardiovascular health, and a healthy dollop of "holistic" wisdom. How do you actually *do* an abdominal crunch or a back squat? A QuickTime movie provides an enlightening show-and-tell. The only weak link is the journal-keeping feature.

Sports trivia. If you prefer the sidelines to the playing field, these CD-ROM-based collections of sports trivia will make you the envy of the bleacher section. The **Sports Illustrated 1994 Multimedia Sports Almanac** ($60, StarPress Multimedia) supplies video and audio highlights from major 1993 sporting events (such as the Super Bowl, the World Series, and the NCAA Final Four), an entire year of *Sports Illustrated* on disc, and loads of statistics for collegiate and pro sports. **Baseball's Greatest Hits** ($80, Voyager) captures 65 of the most memorable moments in America's Pastime in QuickTime movies, photographs, interviews, statistics, period writings, and six hours of play-by-play audio clips. You can hear Ty Cobb give base-stealing advice, watch Hank Aaron hit No. 715, or play the most arcane trivia game yet devised.

But the most entertaining compendium of sports trivia, hands down, is **The Great Golf CD** ($80). The full-color interface uses pictures, movies, anecdotes—even songs about golf!—to take you on an oft-humorous tour of the sport from A.D. 1400 to the present. By clicking the animated icons (Lee Trevino's wagging head is my favorite), you can learn about golf's history, courses, events, people, and equipment. This is the second superb multimedia title from Eden Interactive, which previously released **Greg LeMond's Bicycle Adventure** ($60, also available on floppy disks), an award-winning look at the cycling world from Leonardo da Vinci's crude sketches to today's road racers.

The Great Golf CD provides a humorous and informative look at life on the links. Click on one of the animated icons, and you'll uncover anything from golf's debut in the Olympics, to footage of great shots, to jokes you can share with your favorite foursome.

Mac Can Cook

(VvB)

It's not cool to admit you use the Mac to file recipes, but I don't care—I've been doing it for years, and until recently it wasn't easy. Unlike PC-based foodies, Mac gourmets haven't had access to decent recipe programs that let you scale recipes, create shopping lists, and search for recipes by different criteria.

If you're tempted to buy a cookbook on CD-ROM—lured by such high-profile names as the **Better Homes and Gardens Healthy Cooking CD Cookbook** ($60, Multicom)—put away your credit card. These CD-ROMs are slow and the quality of the software is (so far) poor. But keep your eyes on this category, because higher-quality cooking CD-ROMs should appear in the near future.

Mangia! In 1993 Upstill Software released **Mangia!** ($50), the first truly powerful cooking program. You can enter recipes and keep tabs on what's in your pantry, so that a quick search through the recipes will locate one you can make for dinner without having to go shopping. It lets you categorize recipes by course, season, main ingredient, or nationality. You can design a series of menus (for the week or a special occasion, for example), and then print a shopping list based on what you don't have in the pantry. Plus, you can rate recipes based on criteria such as low fat, good for crowds, or family favorite.

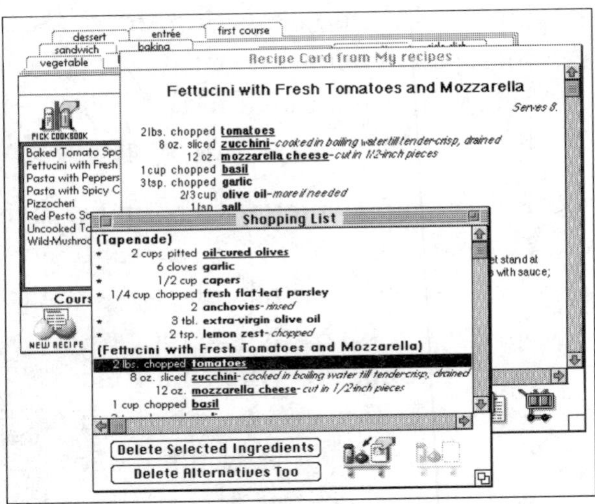

Forget the Cuisinart; Mangia! is the best kitchen aid of the '90s. This powerful cooking program lets you store, search, and view recipes in a variety of ways (by course or cooking method, for example). It places asterisks next to ingredients you already have, and you can print a shopping list with items sorted by their location in the supermarket.

Mangia! can't import or export recipes, however, which means painstakingly typing every single ingredient in every single recipe (you *can* cut and paste notes or directions from a text document, which is some help). Its idiosyncratic entry mode requires you to enter the ingredient, amount, and any notes (chopped or grated, for example) in separate fields. Annoying, yes, but doing it this way does make the program's search function more powerful. Version 1.1, which should be out by now, will solve the import/export problem, and version 2 is due in early '95.

Tip: Create a new category in the Ingredients dictionary called Nonfood Items and in it put such things as dish-washing liquid, toothpaste, toilet cleaner, and paper towels. Now when you compile a shopping list, you can add these items as Miscellaneous Ingredients so you don't forget them.

MasterCook Mac. While it isn't as pretty as Mangia!, **MasterCook Mac** ($40, Arion Software) has some excellent features. First, it calculates the nutritional value of your recipes. Second, you can swap files with the Windows version,

MasterCook, and version 2 (due out in late 1994) will import Windows formats such as MealMaster. Third, the shopping list tallies quantities for the same ingredient used in several recipes (so you don't get five entries for onions), and the program adjusts measurements for scaled recipes (if you double a recipe that calls for 4 ½ teaspoons of yeast, it will appear as 3 *tablespoons* of yeast in the doubled version). Finally, MasterCook includes a wine-list manager and bartender's guide.

Tip: If the 1,002 recipes included with MasterCook Mac aren't sufficient, you can call Arion's free BBS (512/327-9814) and download any of its 10,000 or so recipes.

The Nutritionally Correct Mac (VvB)

The flip side of eating and drinking is dieting. Most nutrition software has a database of foods and records what you eat, supplying a running tally of calories consumed as well as nutritional information and statistics. Unfortunately, many programs are badly executed and surprisingly expensive.

The Diet Balancer ($80, Nutridata Software) asks you basic questions—age, sex, height, weight, special medical conditions (including pregnancy and lactation), and exercise regimen—then guides you in recording food choices and helps you plan meals. Optional disks contain brand-name foods and sample week-long meal plans for low-calorie, high-fiber, low-sodium, diabetic, and other diets. You also can plot your weight loss on a chart. The Diet Balancer has an edge in interface and ease of use over a similar program, **Nutri-Calc Plus** ($160, Camde), but the latter has one sensible feature: You can use a Recipe option to add the grouped ingredients of a dish (such as a soup) to the database, so that inputting foods is a bit easier. You also can customize the food lists in both programs, so if, for example, you're following a Weight Watchers diet, you can record the required exchanges.

One drawback to nutrition programs is that they are time-consuming to use properly, because you must scroll through long food lists to locate every item eaten, then record the amount and when you ate it. As a result, you might think twice before gobbling that Pop-tart (210 calories) or swilling a Brandy Alexander (196 calories). On the other hand, you might just not record them.

Collectors' Additions

(AA)

A computer is the ideal tool for organizing and tracking the data associated with hobbies, such as stamps, coins, sports cards, and comic books—both for personal pleasure and for insurance, tax, and investment purposes. One approach is to create your own database from scratch, using a program such as FileMaker Pro (see Chapter 11). You can save time and effort, however, by getting a specialized database that already contains information on thousands of issues. You enter a few identifying details about each item in your collection, and the program automatically inserts prices and other data into the record. You can view, search, sort, and print your collections according to a variety of criteria.

Unfortunately, even though each of these hobbies has tens of millions of participants, there's little decent software available—with the following exceptions.

GOOD FEATURE

Baseball cards. Ever wonder if the baseball cards you collected as a kid are worth anything? To find out, dust off those shoe boxes and boot up **The Card Collector** ($50, AbleSoft), which contains data for 70,000 baseball cards from a dozen companies, including Donruss, Fleer, and Topps. The database covers 1948 through 1993 and includes names, card numbers, prices for varying card conditions, and preset rookie flags. The Card Collector, which has sold more than 60,000 copies in its DOS incarnation, has an attractive interface and nice touches, such as checkboxes for flagging special subsets of your collection and report forms for inventories and user-defined want lists. The database doesn't include team information, though, so you're out of luck if you want to find every card for the 1969 New York Mets. AbleSoft offers price and data updates via disk or its 24-hour bulletin board, and card junkies take note: Databases are also available for football, basketball, and hockey cards.

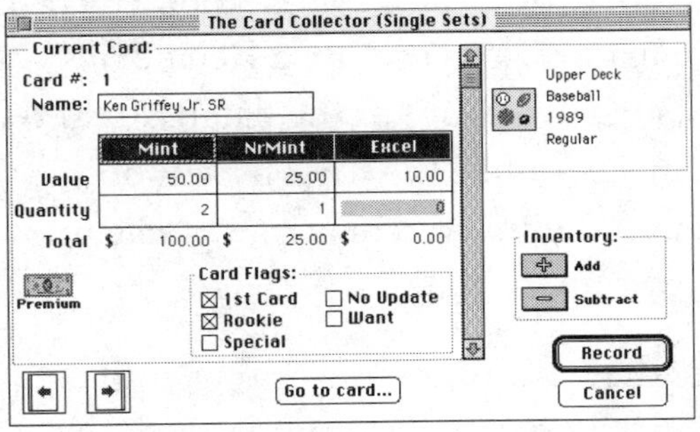

The Card Collector is an elegant solution to the problem of baseball management—cards, not teams. Just enter the quantity for each card you own and the program fills in the value, special flags, and premium status.

Bird watching. If you're an avid bird watcher—the type who maintains a life list of every bird ever seen—get **Bird Brain,** a $125 labor of love from Ideaform. Espied the elusive marbled murrelet? Enter the

Getting It On-Line (VvB/AA)

No matter what your hobby or gaming preferences are, you really should hook up with an on-line service such as CompuServe or America Online. These services have sections devoted to every genre covered here, where you'll find the latest shareware goodies as well as thousands of people who are dying to share their knowledge with you.

On CompuServe, for example, forum names include Cooks Online (*the* place for Mac foodies to hang), Genealogy, ShowBiz, Health & Fitness, Crafts, Collectibles, Gardening, and the Gamers Forum. (Heck, there's a separate forum just for flight-simulator freaks.) For more on on-line services and bulletin boards, see Chapter 22.

details in Bird Brain's well-designed database and it automatically adds the bird to your ABA, AOU, and World Life lists. The program contains common and scientific names for more than 1,900 birds of North and Central America and Hawaii, and provides many shortcuts for data entry and searches. You could, for example, retrieve all sightings of great blue herons at Pescadero Marsh or the birds you saw in Tennessee in May 1994. You can also create custom list types and formats for printed reports. For ornithologists with a larger flight range, **World Bird Brain** ($175) has a database of 10,000 birds.

Stamps, coins, and comics. Ninga Software offers a trio of $50 products for philatelists, numismatists, and comic-book lovers. A lifelong stamp collector, I installed the U.S. version of **HobbySoft Stamp Keeper** with high hopes of converting my Microsoft Word–based records into something more practical. Alas, the program is an ugly DOS port, difficult to navigate and missing key features. Stamp Keeper automatically supplies pricing and descriptive data, but the 3,000 stamp issues in its database don't include envelopes, postal cards, or revenues. There are no prices for first-day covers, and the Comment field is limited to 13 characters. And you can't flag individual issues, so there's no way to create custom want lists.

Ninga's HobbySoft programs for coins and comics share the same awkward interface and limited feature set; the only difference is the accompanying database. **Comic Keeper's** database, for example, includes cover date, strip title, and artist names. The HobbySoft products may be more useful than researching and entering all the data yourself, however, especially if you're computerizing a large collection. (Besides, you can always export the finished catalog as a tab-delimited text file and then work with it in the more friendly environs of Word, Excel, or FileMaker Pro.) Annual updates are $30 and other versions (such as Canadian) are available for the stamp and coin programs.

A Stitch in Time (VvB)

Until recently, I didn't think a Mac could be much help when it came to hands-on activities such as sewing, knitting, crocheting, and embroidering. *Au contraire*. The programs below can actually enhance the creative experience by letting you design your own patterns or adapt existing designs.

Sewing. Anyone who sews (I'm reluctant to call them sewers) will find **Fittingly Sew** or **Dress Shop** a godsend. Both programs let you design and fit clothes on screen and then print the altered pattern so that (theoretically) everything you sew fits perfectly. As a ham-fisted, albeit enthusiastic, person-who-sews, I was a little intimidated by these programs, but if you know your sewing basics, both are easy to use and have good documentation.

LivingSoft's Dress Shop ($130 complete, or $30 per component) is aimed at Mac users who have little sewing experience. The program includes 40 basic patterns—including dresses, blouses, pants, a cape, and leggings—and guides you through the task of fitting and adapting designs. Fittingly Sew ($170, Bartley Software) is aimed at the more experienced tailor who wants as much flexibility as possible. Fewer boilerplate garments are included, but you have more leeway in adapting them. You can get demo versions of both programs from the developers or from CompuServe's Crafts Forum.

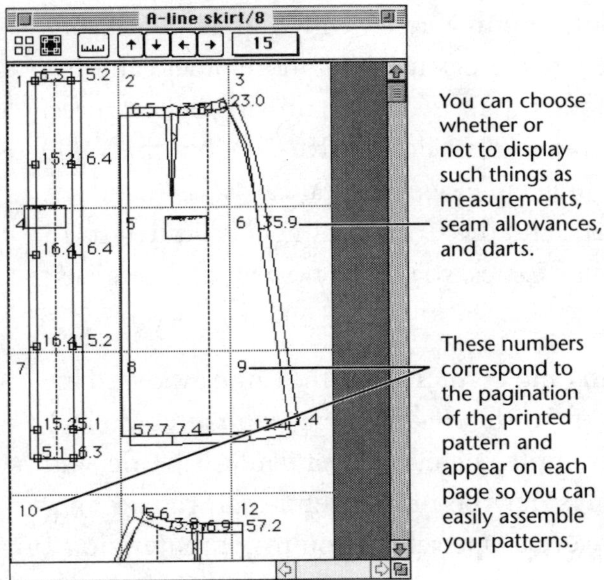

Fittingly Sew lets you tweak paper patterns on screen, ensuring the best possible fit for your clothes.

Knitting. ColorKnit is a $15 gem that lets you design grid-based patterns—including amazingly complex Fair Isle–type designs—that can be printed or exported as PICT files. A well-designed shareware program, ColorKnit uses standard Mac painting tools, and the on-screen documentation is clear and to the point. If you don't have a color monitor, don't be put off by the name—you can use ColorKnit with a monochrome Mac, too.

Stitch Painter ($85, Cochenille Design Studio) is similar to ColorKnit, only more sophisticated and more expensive. This program also can be used by embroiderers, crocheters, weavers—anyone who designs patterns using a grid. It's essentially a specialized paint program that lets you create a repeated motif, which can be flipped, rotated, recolored, and resized. An enhanced version (**Stitch Painter Gold,** $165) adds an editable texture palette and other features. Cochenille sells two other handy products: **Bit Knitter,** a $250 hardware and software package that lets you hook up your Mac to a Studio, Brother, or Passap knitting machine, and **Stitch Editor** ($110), which lets you turn scanned or computer-generated images into patterns.

Finally, serious knitters will enjoy **Knit One** ($80, Penelope Craft Programs), which lets you alter knitting and crochet patterns so they can be used with different thicknesses of yarns and wools and varying needle sizes.

GOOD FEATURE

Special Interests

But wait, there's more: programs that didn't fit in the other categories but are too neat to ignore.

Design Your Own Railroad (AA). An indispensable tool for model railroaders, **Design Your Own Railroad** ($80, Abracadata) lets you forgo the trial-and-error approach to creating a railroad that fits in the den. With this simplified CAD (computer-aided design) program, you can plan an entire to-scale layout—including stations, depots, overpasses, and scenery—before laying a single piece of track. DYORR also has a full-blown simulator, allowing you to assemble and run trains on the completed design. You can test a layout before buying materials or—if you don't have the space or budget for a real model railroad—just

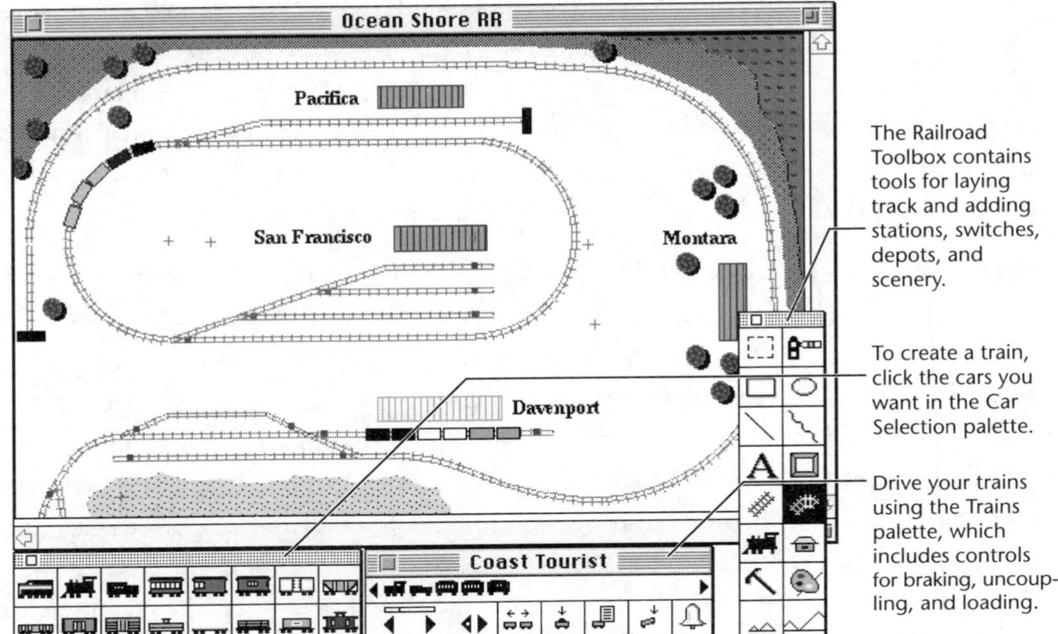

Design Your Own Railroad is the ideal Mac toy for model railroaders. You can design and build precision, to-scale layouts, then barrel down the tracks in a custom-built train.

enjoy being an armchair modeler. And if you want to challenge your operating skills, DYORR will let you race against the clock to complete switching maneuvers or freight moves. Toot, toot!

Handwriting Analyst (AA). According to graphologists, your handwriting reveals your personality, warts and all. So if you'd like to check your compatibility with a potential mate or choose the right boss (or employee), get their John Hancock and a copy of **Handwriting Analyst** ($80, Wintergreen Software). Answer a series of multiple-choice questions about the signature or writing sample, and the program produces a detailed profile of the writer's personality. My signature generated some mixed reviews: "She tends to be both creative and methodical in her approach to problem-solving." Other remarks, however, were quite specific: "She is inclined to talk out loud when alone" (oops). The manual has a fascinating section that explains the personality traits associated with each letter formation—fat *y* loops, for example, mean you strive to accumulate money and possessions. (Nope, not me.)

Wine and spirits (VvB). Oenophiles will appreciate **Wines of the World** ($60, Multicom), a delightful CD-ROM that supplies information on wine quality, wine appreciation (storing wine, reading a label, judging quality, and so on), and wine-making regions of the world. It has color photographs and QuickTime movies, but its best feature is the 20,000-wine database. You can search for a wine by type, producer, vintage rating, and/or price; catalog your own wines; and enter tasting notes—not a bad idea, as some of the ratings are rather idiosyncratic. If you just want to catalog wines without a lot of fuss, two popular shareware offerings are **CellarKeeper** (free) and **Le Sommelier** ($15).

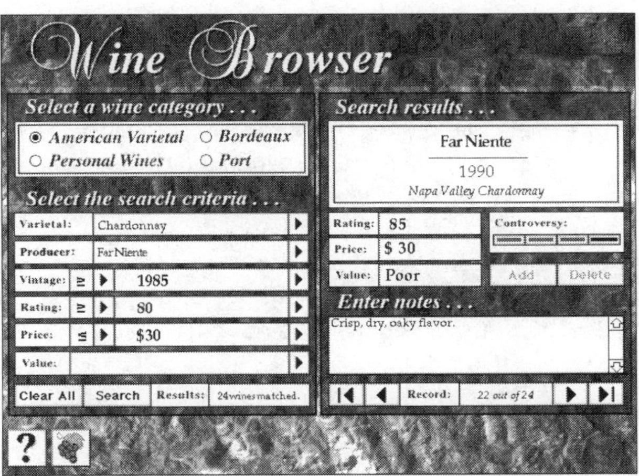

Oenophiles will appreciate Wines of the World, a CD-ROM that lets you search a 20,000-wine database for just the right vintage. You can also enter your own wines and tasting notes—not a bad idea, actually, as some of the ratings are rather idiosyncratic.

If you prefer hard liquor, **MacCocktail** ($80, Blackfire) contains more than 200 drink recipes, each with a full-color photo, as well as QuickTime videos illustrating the basics of mixology, such as how to prepare a layered drink. You can add new recipes and comments to the database or figure out what drinks can be made with the liquor that you've got on hand. Blackfire is also developing CD-ROMs covering specialty coffees and microbreweries.

Editors' Poll: What's Your Favorite Shareware?

AA: Disinfectant, an indispensable utility for safeguarding your disk against viruses. It's freeware and regularly upgraded by the author! I also use Compact Pro and MoviePlayer fairly often and indulge in an occasional game of Maelstrom.

DB: I can't say I have one favorite shareware program any easier than I can say I have one favorite movie or music group. I figure I need them all! Compact Pro is indispensible. Zterm is quite good. I also commonly use Add/Strip for processing text that I get off on-line systems and Disinfectant to protect myself from viruses. I can't do without SCSIProbe (you know you're a computer geek when you start complaining that the Mac allows only seven SCSI devices).

EC: David Rakowski's fonts. They are beautiful and well-crafted, and I've never seen commercial versions available. And his readme's are worth the shareware fees all by themselves.

DD: There are a few I really depend on. The one that saved me the most troulbe is probably ZipIt, a Mac utility that compacts files in the PC-standard PKZIP format. That finally let me send Mac files to PC users by e-mail without a problem. Compact Pro is great, too. I also really like MenuChoice, which lets you get to your control panels from the Apple menu (by making the menu hierarchical) and SmartKeys, which automatically fixes one of my main typos: typing two capital letters in a row. And SpeedyFinder, for one essential feature: a keyboard command for emptying the Trash. (I know it's just me, but I can't stand to have a bulging Trash can.)

CG: Klondike, my favorite Solitaire game.

JK: Compact Pro is the most essential. Runners up: MenuChoice, which makes your menu hierarchic; WindowShade and WindowRanger (which are only available on ZiffNet/Mac). System 7.5 will actually make all these, except Compact Pro, obsolete.

HN: SCSIProbe. It's freeware, not shareware, but I can't imagine how I'd live without it.

BW: I like GraphicConverter by Thorsten Lemke, which is very good at converting image and drawing files between formats.

PART

Extending Your Reach

Editors' Poll: What On-Line Services Do You Subscribe to? Favorite Forums?

AA: CompuServe (90 percent) and AppleLink. On CompuServe, I frequent the MacUser and Desktop Publishing forums (although not frequently these days; it's too addictive!). In researching our *Mac Bible* chapters, my contributors and I found several other CIS forums to be invaluable resources due to their knowledgeable, friendly participants and wealth of shareware.

DB: I'm on CompuServe almost every day, America Online every other day, and AppleLink a couple of times a week. I tried Prodigy and decided it was a cruel joke. I canceled my subscription after two days.

EC: I'm on CompuServe (72102,242) and AOL (LCastro). I fell in love with CompuServe's Crafts forum right from the beginning, though it's been a while since I've been around. I thought it was so cool that nobody talked much about computers. And the people are so nice! The Internet forum on AOL is pretty hip, as is the Sports forum, which is the only place I've found since I've been back in the States that has up-to-date scores of the Barcelona football team (that's soccer to you).

DD: I got CompuServe just because I needed an e-mail address, and most people I knew seemed to have CompuServe. Now that I'm working on the *Bible,* I use AOL and AppleLink to receive mail, too. I'm also beta-testing Apple's eWorld program, which seems like it could be fun. Mostly, I want to be where most people can reach me most easily. I was thinking of switching to AOL as my primary address just because I could be DarcyD@aol.com instead of 71332,3264, and everyone seems to be on AOL, too. CompuServe is where the forums are, but I don't use them much, except ZiffNet Mac, where I go to download shareware.

CG: I'm on line with AppleLink, MCI Mail, and CompuServe (ZiffNet). I really don't have a lot of time to spend logging on to any forums. I use the services primarily to send and receive (lots) of e-mail.

JK: America Online and CompuServe. I don't spend much time on the forums.

HN: CIS, AppleLink, AOL, MCI, and eWorld. Favorite forum: MacWEEK Forum on ZiffNet via CIS.

BW: I originally started with MCI Mail, and after a few years moved to harder stuff, like CompuServe and AOL. I live in a small town, so CompuServe has been my professional window on the world. Many of the contributors to the Networking chapter, for example, are people I met on CompuServe. I'd like to find the time to hang out on a given forum and sustain a relationship, but I'm spread too thin these days.

21 Printing

For better or worse, paper remains the Main Street of information exchange. Far from creating a paperless office, personal computers have made it cheaper and easier to print things on paper.

The Mac and PostScript brought graphically cool printing to the desktop, and time has only made it better. Inkjet printers costing less than $300 have practically relegated the ear assault and coarse printing of dot-matrix printers, like the old $600 Apple ImageWriter II, to the humble task of printing multiple forms and labels. Inkjets are now the happenin' thing at the low end.

As for laser printers, 600 dots per inch is the new standard for resolution, finally putting some teeth in the concept of laser-based "typeset quality." Bargain basements are now stuffed with 300-dpi PostScript printers costing less than $1,000.

In fact, prices have come down on all classes of printers, creating more choices than you've ever had before. Do you need to print photographic quality in color? Are inkjets the best for printing presentations? Or do you need a color printer at all? We'll answer those questions for you and show you how to take advantage of the various types of industrial-strength printing equipment found in service bureaus.

Contributors

Bob Weibel (BW) is the chapter editor.

Jim Felici (JF), ex-managing editor of *Publish* magazine, is now a free-lance writer and *bon vivant* residing in Fontès, France.

Randy B. Singer (RS) is a practicing attorney and Apple Legal Fellow who leads user groups for attorneys using the Mac.

Sharon Zardetto Aker (SA), Nancy E. Dunn (ND), and **Arthur Naiman (AN),** edited previous editions of the *Mac Bible,* from which parts of this chapter were taken.

Contents

How Printing Works

You've seen it on screen, now you need it on paper. The Mac makes printing easy, hiding the otherwise complex task of integrating your software with the printer hardware to produce the results you want. When you select a printer from the Chooser and print, the Mac has to convert its method of storing and representing text and graphics into a form the chosen printer expects. Printers differ in their graphical capabilities, and each generation of Mac system software offers new ways of printing. Here are the basics.

Print Drivers

(JK/SA/AN/ND/RS/BW/Susan McCallister)

Printer drivers are programs that tell the Mac how to prepare print data for your printer. Without them, each application would need additional programming to handle all the types of printers you might use.

So, in addition to physically connecting your printer to the Mac, you also need a printer driver to connect your software to the printer. Apple supplies drivers for the ImageWriter, the StyleWriter, and the LaserWriter. Some third-party printers have their own drivers, although many are designed to use Apple's drivers.

You may not need a separate driver for each type of printer you use; sometimes a single driver works for several related printers. For example, Apple's LaserWriter driver works for any PostScript laser printer.

Printer drivers go into the Extensions folder in your System Folder; if you drag them onto the System Folder icon (not the window), the Finder will put them in the Extensions folder automatically. (In System 6, printer drivers go in the System Folder, but not into any folder within it.)

Once your printer drivers are installed in the Extensions folder, you still have to tell your Mac which one to use. The standard way to do that is to select Chooser from the menu and click on the printer you want to use (Apple's QuickDraw GX, which we discuss later, offers alternate scenarios). The printer driver you select in the Chooser generates Page Setup and Print dialog boxes relevant to the capabilities of the printer. Many applications substitute their own dialog boxes for these basic ones to give you even more printing options.

When you use the Chooser to switch from one type of printer to another—from a StyleWriter to a LaserWriter, say—you need to let any open applications know that. That's because different kinds of printers use different print areas on the page, even different character spacing. To hip an application to the change, open its Page Setup dialog box and then close it again (you don't have to change any settings). You should also do the same thing to activate a newly installed printer driver. (A dialog box will warn you when you need to do this.)

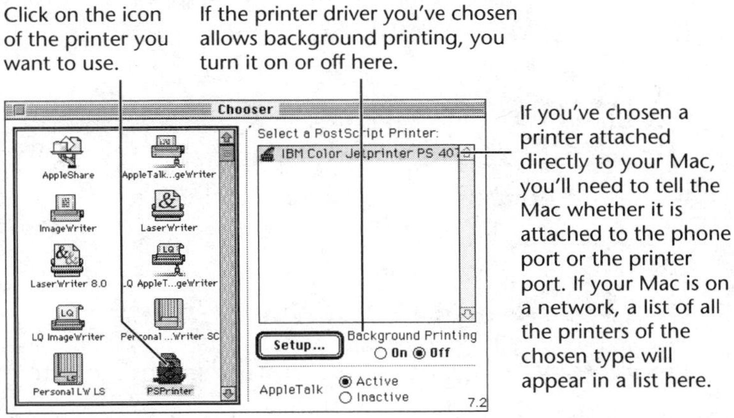

Click on the icon of the printer you want to use.

If the printer driver you've chosen allows background printing, you turn it on or off here.

If you've chosen a printer attached directly to your Mac, you'll need to tell the Mac whether it is attached to the phone port or the printer port. If your Mac is on a network, a list of all the printers of the chosen type will appear in a list here.

You use the Chooser to tell your Mac what printer you want to use.

Background Printing (RS/BW/SA/AN/JK)

Macs can send out print jobs faster than printers can process them, which often leaves the computer waiting for the printer. A print spooler is a program that temporarily stores print jobs on disk and takes over feeding the printer in the background. Since the Mac creates this print file quite quickly, you can get back to work and leave the computer and the printer to talk to each other in the background. (*Spool* is an acronym for simultaneous print operations on-line.)

Most Mac printer drivers let you simply click an On or Off radio button to turn background printing on or off. Two system files are at work behind the scenes during background printing: PrintMonitor, for System 7 (which installs as both a Control Panel and a System Extension), and Backgrounder, which is required for background printing under System 6. (The Apple installer for the LaserWriter driver should do this automatically, although the System 7 installer will also work.)

PrintMonitor keeps track of which document is printing, how many pages are left to go, which other documents are waiting to be printed, and so on. It is launched automatically when a print job is started, and you can check the status of a print job by choosing PrintMonitor from the Application menu. When the printer needs attention (because it's out of paper, for example), PrintMonitor flashes its icon in the upper-right corner of the screen, alternating it with the Application menu icon. (In System 6, it does the same with the menu icon.)

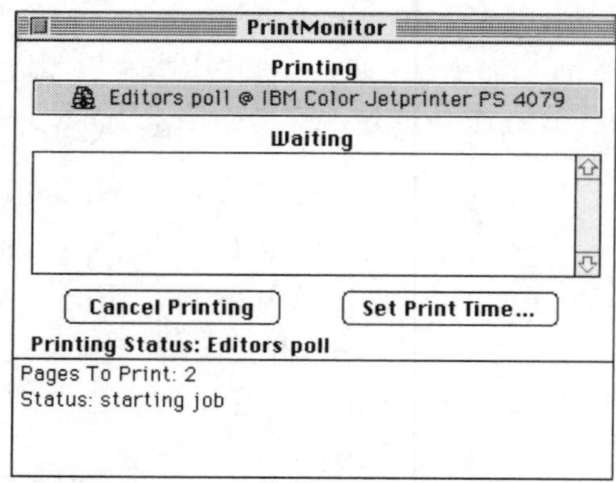

You can view PrintMonitor by selecting it from the Application menu. Here you can check on the status of a print job, cancel it, or set a time for it to be printed later (handy for printing long documents after hours, among other things).

QuickDraw and PostScript Printing (BW)

QuickDraw is a graphics description language, the part of the Macintosh operating system that handles the screen display—drawing lines, managing color, controlling windows, basically handling all the graphics. The PostScript page description language is also a graphical programming language, used mostly for imaging on printers (it was introduced with the first LaserWriter printer). PostScript handles a greater variety of graphical functions, and with greater precision, than QuickDraw.

Macintosh printers can be divided into two types: those that rely on QuickDraw's description of the image to be printed and those that use PostScript information, translated from QuickDraw by a PostScript printer driver.

In either case, the QuickDraw or PostScript information must go through one more translation before it is printed: It must be converted to a raster—a pattern of dots that can be printed. For QuickDraw printers, this translation is done by the Macintosh's own processor. For most PostScript jobs, it's done by a computer, called a raster image processor or PostScript interpreter, within the printer itself.

You can print QuickDraw graphics to a PostScript printer, but you can't print PostScript graphics to a QuickDraw printer (the special interpreter is missing).

A special exception is made for fonts. By using ATM (available from Apple or Adobe, or installed automatically with System 7.5), you can turn the Mac's processor into a PostScript font interpreter, as described in Chapter 14.

Printing Under QuickDraw GX (BW)

QuickDraw came up the river, had a child, and Apple called it QuickDraw GX. It grew strong and came of age in 1994 with graphical imaging and typographic features that put it more in league with PostScript. Apple provides it as a System extension with System 7.5, and it can be used with any System version after 7.1. We discuss the basics of QuickDraw GX in Chapter 3, "System Software," and how it affects typograpy in Chapter 14, "Fonts." It also has lots of repercussions for printing, introducing, among other things, a new Chooser, new drivers for Apple printers, and PrinterShare GX, which replaces PrintMonitor. Here are some of the new features you'll see:

- A desktop icon will appear for each printer you select using the new GX Chooser. After that you can print a file by dragging it onto a printer icon.
- Any printer connected to your Mac, even via the serial port, can be shared over a network.
- Under the new drivers, the GX Print dialog box lets you select, at print time, any printer for which you've created a desktop icon, as above—no last-minute trips to the Chooser.
- The GX Print One command (⌘P) prints a single copy of your document using your latest Print dialog box settings.
- Printing software extensions will add custom print tools, such as the ability to print the word *Copy* screened across each page. Third-party vendors can also develop printer extensions.
- Each desktop printer has its own print queue, which you can move to a different printer if you want. Double-clicking on a job name will let you see a print preview.
- The myriad new graphics functions of QuickDraw GX will translate into greater graphical potential for QuickDraw printers.

Types of Printers

You need the right printer for the job. Picking the wrong type of printer is a waste of money, no matter how good a deal you got. Here's what's out there.

Black and White

(BW/RS)

Elegant, basic black: still the cheapest, most common form of printed matter. Even people who own a color printer use black-and-white printers to cheaply print copy for proofing and informal communications.

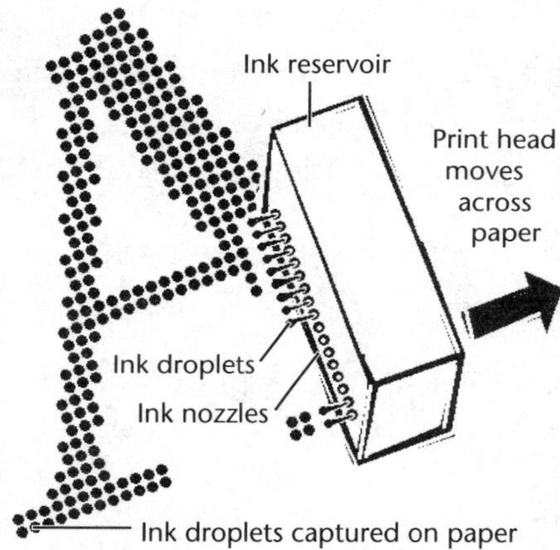

Inkjet printers squirt tiny drops of ink from an array of tiny nozzles that pass back and forth across the paper.

Inkjet printers (RS/BW). Inkjet printers form characters out of little dots created by tiny jets of ink. Inkjet technology has largely taken over the market once occupied by dot-matrix impact printers: They're inexpensive, quieter, often faster, and produce better-looking text and graphics than dot-matrix impact printers. Apple's StyleWriter II and Hewlett-Packard's DeskWriter are two inkjet printers that are compatible with the Mac.

Laser printers (RS/BW). Printers like Apple's LaserWriters print images by beaming flashes of laser light onto a photo-electric drum. A dry ink powder (called toner) sticks electrostatically to the imaged portion of the drum, as in a photocopying machine. A hot fuser roller presses and bonds the toner to the paper. Laser printers are bigger, heavier, and more expensive than inkjet printers, but print quality is usually better.

Thermal fusion (RS). Thermal fusion printers employ tiny heated elements in the print head that push a ribbon against the page, bonding a waxy ink to the paper. Desktop and portable varieties of thermal fusion printers compete with black-and-white inkjet printers. Cost per printed page is generally higher than for inkjet printing, but there's no liquid ink to run or smear.

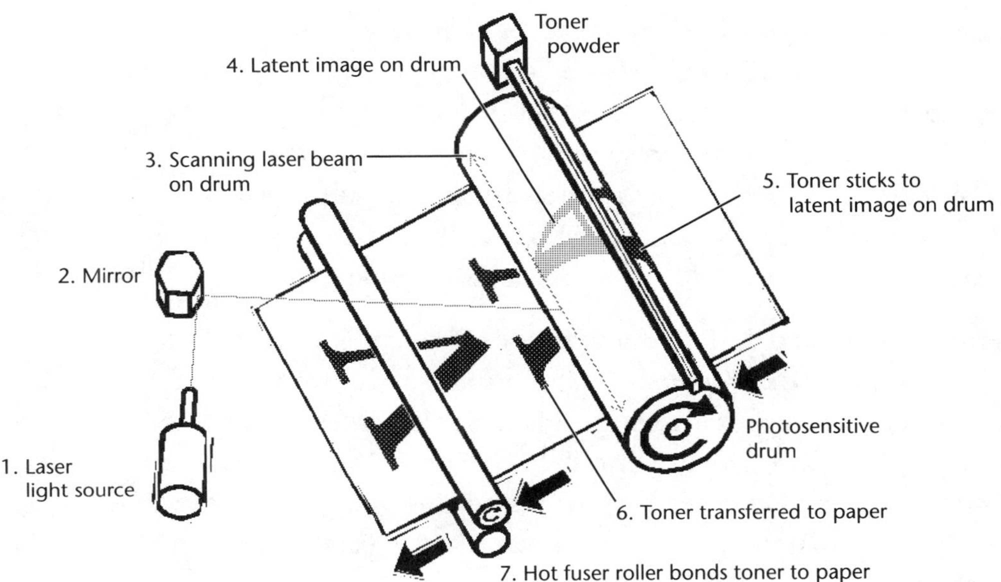

Laser printers print indirectly. They first create an image on a photo-sensitive cylinder (drum). Electrostatic toner powder sticks to the image on the drum and is then bonded to the paper.

Dot-Matrix Impact Printers (AN/JK/BW/RS)

Dot-matrix impact printers form characters out of a pattern of dots created by a row of pins hammering on an inked ribbon lying against the paper. The number of pins can vary, with 9-pin and 24-pin being two common configurations; the more pins, the better the print quality. If you're printing multiple forms that use carbon or NCR paper, neither laser nor inkjet printers will do the job. You need an impact dot-matrix printer, like Apple's ImageWriter II.

Color Printers (BW/RS)

In the past you were lucky if an affordable color printer could handle up to a dozen colors. Fortunately, that's changed, thanks to improved technology and the economics of mass marketing.

Color inkjet (BW). It didn't take long for engineers to design inkjet printers sporting three or four separate print heads, each spraying a different color of ink. Typically, these are the three primary colors, cyan, magenta, and yellow, with black often included for improved text and image printing. Cheaper models print only a handful of colors, good for simple charts, diagrams, and graphs. More expensive models include PostScript interpreters for printing elaborate color text and graphics for presentations and design comps. To approximate different colors and shades, the printer driver must dither (that is, create patterns of dots, or halftones for each color. At 300-dpi resolution, these patterns can have a rather coarse appearance, like cheap comic books.

Thermal-wax transfer (RS). Using rolls of plastic film coated with four different colors of wax-based pigments, these printers lay down each of three or four primary colors when printing a page. Heating elements melt the wax and transfer it to the paper. (There are also "phase-change" thermal-wax printers that melt sticks of wax pigment and apply it much as inkjets do.) Both types apply each color in a separate pass, which means that the page being printed must go through the printer several times. Like color inkjet printers, thermal-wax printers must also use halftone or dithering techniques to simulate a wide range of colors and shades.

Thermal-wax printers create attractive, glossy prints that are slightly raised from the page. The wax-transfer variety usually requires special paper, though some companies, like Tektronix, have options that allow you to use plain paper, which the printer primes during printing.

Thermal-wax printers are popular for printing hard-copy and overhead-transparency presentations and color design comps.

Dye sublimation (RS/BW). Dye-sublimation printers work in much the same way as thermal-wax printers, but instead of melting wax-based pigments, dye-sublimation pigments become gaseous (sublime) when heated by the print head. The sublimed dye then penetrates the paper's special coating. Dye-sublimation printers don't have to use dithering or halftones to create different colors or shades of colors. They can blend the correct amount of each primary color (cyan, magenta, yellow, or black) to create just the right color at each printed dot. That's why they're called continuous-tone printers. A good dye-sublimation print looks like a color photograph. Not too long ago $40,000 was cheap for a dye-sublimation printer. Now many cost less than $10,000, and some are below $5,000.

Color laser (BW).The least expensive color laser printers, like the QMS ColorScript Laser 1000, are still over $10,000. QMS markets it as a "business" machine, although most studies show that general business users aren't willing to spend much more for color than they are for black and white. You can hook your Mac to a $40,000-plus Canon CLC copier, as some big-budget firms do. With sufficient memory, the Canon CLC can print continuous tone images, a benefit of the transparent toner the machines employ. Lower-priced color lasers, like the ColorScript Laser 1000, use opaque toner, so continuous-tone images and tints are printed as halftones. At 300 dpi, they look rather rough, anything but photographic.

GOOD FEATURE

What Type of Printer Do You Need?

There's what you want, and there's what you need. Your transaction printouts might look nice in color, but can you afford the expensive inks, and possibly slower printing? Can your software easily format the reports in color? If you need only four colors, then there's little point in paying for a printer that prints millions. This section should put your basic options in perspective.

Color or B&W? (BW)

This used to be a simple question to answer: "You wanna print color pictures, charts, graphs? Get a color printer." There's no question that good color design makes information graphics easier to comprehend while putting a slick spin on your image.

But the interest in color is spilling over into a hybrid area now dominated by black-and-white desktop printing. In the glut of sales and promotional documents competing for attention these days, a document sporting colored headlines, callouts, illustrations, and charts is more likely to catch someone's attention. That requires a printer that's good at both black text *and* color, but that isn't too pricey.

While most of us choke at the sticker price on color laser printers, inkjet technology is coming to the rescue. (See our picks for color inkjet printers below.)

Print Quality

(BW)

Although it's ultimately a subjective judgment, print quality is usually rated in terms of *resolution*. All the printers we discuss in this chapter use tightly packed arrays of dots to create the shapes we see on paper. The tighter the array of dots, that is, the more dots per inch (dpi), the higher the resolution, and the finer the images appear.

Inkjet printers produce 300 or 360 dpi, a respectable resolution that comes close to laser printing in quality. (The different types of inks used make some difference in quality, too, as described later in this chapter.)

Most laser printers print 300 by 300 dots per inch, but some give you 400 by 400, 600 by 600, 800 by 300, 1,000 by 400, 1,200 by 600, and even higher. The dots per square inch range from 90,000 to 720,000—which means that at the high end, they provide more than five times the resolution of the best inkjets. Some laser printers also offer various forms of *enhanced resolution*, which smooths jagged edges and/or sharpens grayscales to give the appearance of higher-dpi output.

Even 720,000 dpsi is nothing compared to the 1,270 dpi of a Linotronic 300 imagesetter—1.6 million dpsi, nearly 18 times the resolution of a LaserWriter and almost 70 times that of an ImageWriter. The 3,386-dpi Linotronic 330 produces about 11.5 million dpsi—more than 125 times the LaserWriter's resolution and almost 500 times the ImageWriter's.

Portability

(BW/RS)

The PowerBook has liberated Mac users from their desktops, and fortunately battery-powered portable printers are affordable companions. The best of these are inkjet printers, like Apple's $440 **Portable StyleWriter** or Hewlett-Packard's

$380 **DeskWriter 310,** and their print quality is practically indistinguishable from that of laser printers. But road warriors pay a penalty for portability since these printers tend to be quite a bit slower than equivalent desktop options.

PostScript (RS/AN/JK/BW)

As previously mentioned, there are two basic kinds of printers—those with PostScript (Adobe's page description language) built into their processors, and those without. PostScript used to be a very pricey luxury, but now the difference between the PostScript and non-PostScript versions of a printer can be as little as $500. You'll find many color inkjet, thermal-wax, dye-sublimation, and laser printers that use PostScript.

If you're creating pages ultimately destined for a high-resolution imagesetter, you'll need a PostScript printer for proofing your pages. The same holds true if you intend to use EPS (Encapsulated PostScript) format clip art or other PostScript-based graphics.

You can also print PostScript graphics on a non-PostScript printer by using an interpreter program like TeleTypesetting's **T-Script Basic** ($85) but it tends to really slow printing. For professional desktop publishing and graphics work, there's no substitute for a PostScript laser printer. But if you mainly print text and non-PostScript graphics, a less expensive QuickDraw printer will probably give you everything you need.

One more issue to consider when deciding between PostScript and QuickDraw printers is speed. The fact that QuickDraw printers rely on the Mac's own processor to rasterize the image means that you and your printer are both sharing the Mac's processor, slowing down both of you. The on-board computer of a PostScript printer relieves the Mac of that task.

Cost (BW)

You get what you pay for: a fast, high-resolution, PostScript, color printer can cost upwards of $5,000. But trade off one or more of those qualities, and you can do quite respectably for under $1,000. The best buys are inkjets, with 300-dpi resolution for under $300. The tradeoff there is speed. The graph on page 825 shows the basic price points for different kinds of printers.

Level 1 vs. Level 2 PostScript (RS/BW)

Software support for PostScript Level 2 has been slow in coming, but the new Mac PostScript drivers finally take advantage of it. That means having to install Apple's LaserWriter driver version 8 or Adobe's functionally equivalent PS Printer version. (Both companies worked together to develop the drivers, which though cosmetically different to a slight degree, function identically.) Postscript Level 2 has many advantages over Level 1; here are a few:

- generally faster operation
- caching of forms that will be printed repeatedly
- better control of the unique capabilities of individual brands and models of printers
- easier print-job setup for paper sizing, multiple trays, and scaling
- color support with color matching between screen and printer
- data compression/decompression to speed jobs to the printer
- improved memory allocation

These features aren't critical for many printing tasks, so don't necessarily ignore a great deal on a Level 1 PostScript laser printer.

GOOD FEATURE

Aside from exploiting Level 2 features, the Apple and Adobe versions of the Level 2 driver take better advantage of your printer's features—everything from installed RAM, to page-image size, even the number of paper trays. These details are stored in PostScript Printer Descriptions (PPDs). The Apple driver package includes PPDs only for Apple printers, while the Adobe version includes all currently available PDFs, almost 5MB worth—certainly the way to go if you use a non-Apple PostScript printer.

In almost every category, you'll find bargains if you look in the PC section of the store. It's actually fairly easy to adapt a PC printer for a Macintosh, as described in the box on page 826.

Speed (BW)

Most printers have some sort of rated speed, but those textbook figures rarely factor in the time the printer spends processing the print data prior to actually spitting out paper. This is especially true for PostScript printers, which bear the awesome task of crunching complex PostScript programs. A four-page-per-

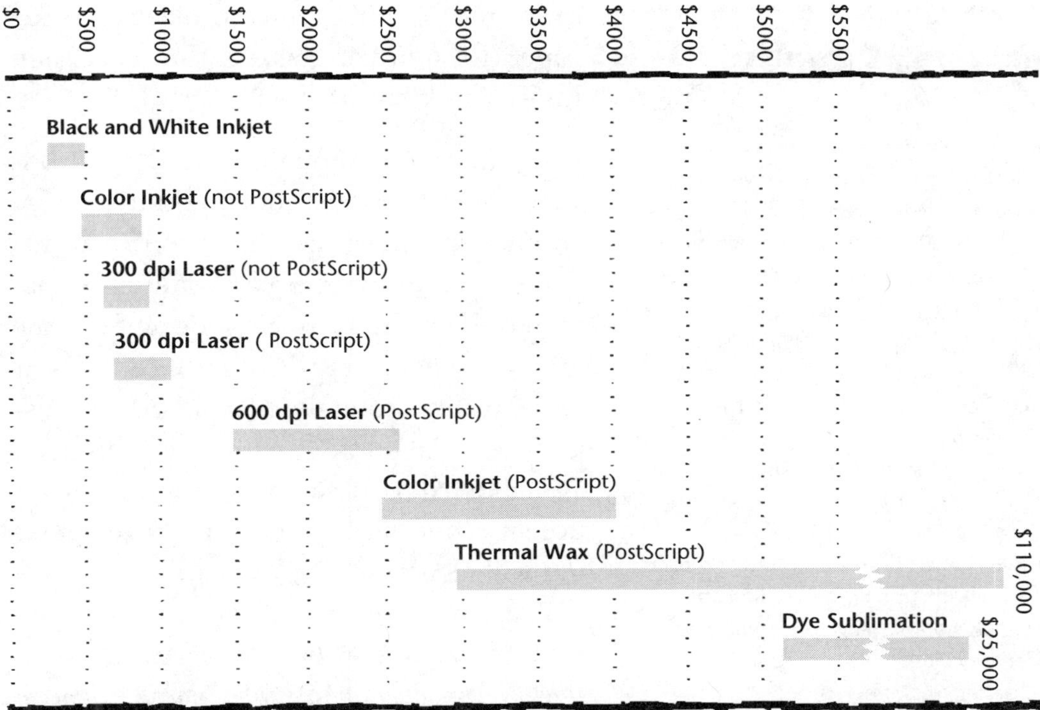

This chart gives some idea of the relative prices of different kinds of printers.

minute laser print engine, for example, with a high-speed PostScript processor, may well outpace an eight-page-per-minute model with a slow processor.

Inkjet Printers

Inkjet printers have become the personal business printer of choice, given their low price, small size, crisp print quality, and the other traits we discussed in the "Types of Printers" section above. Inkjet speed is typically rated in characters per second, like dot-matrix printers, though Hewlett-Packard has started rating its high-end color printers, like the DeskJet 1200C/PS, in pages per minute. But if you can afford a dot-matrix printer, you can definitely afford an inkjet, as you'll see below. Some people prefer the inkjets' output to that of laser printers because the blacks are blacker—although the output is also less

Adapting PC Printers for the Mac (RS)

You *can* use a PC printer with a Mac; you just need a Macintosh driver and a serial-to-parallel converter cable. The best kit is GDT Softworks' **PowerPrint** ($149 list, $100 mail order). It includes a serial-to-parallel converter, intended for printers that only have a PC standard Centronix parallel port. The converter draws power from both the printer and from your Mac ADP port, no wall plug needed. The PowerPrint software has print drivers for just about every dot-matrix, inkjet, and laser printer. The latest version of PowerPrint has a built-in spooler, grayscale capability, color printer support, multiple feeder trays, text rotation, scaling, multiple paper sizes, and so on.

crisp since the ink tends to bleed into the paper (for more on this, see the "Laser and Inkjet Paper" box below).

Keep in mind, though, that despite advances in ink formulation, no printout from an inkjet printer is as smearproof as prints from a laser printer. If you print envelopes with these printers, don't get caught in the rain on your way to the post office! (If your inkjet print absolutely must be smear resistant, you can spray it with artists' fixative, available from art supply stores, but this is not an economical practice and overspraying will also cause it to smear.) *If you use a fixative, make sure you use it in a well-ventilated area. Last time I tried one, the room smelled like overripe bananas for a couple of weeks. It probably causes cancer, too.—DD]*

DeskWriter vs. StyleWriter II (JK/Larry Pina/RS)

Hewlett-Packard's $400 **DeskWriter** and Apple's $360 **StyleWriter II** are now the most popular printers for personal and light business use. They're fairly quiet and inexpensive, with print quality that rivals a laser printer's (at 300 dpi for the DeskWriter and 360 dpi for the StyleWriter).

Since these aren't PostScript printers, neither can print PostScript text or graphics without some help. For ways around this drawback, see the "QuickDraw and PostScript Printing" section above. The DeskWriter comes with 35 TrueType outline fonts. The StyleWriter comes with a total of 39 TrueType fonts, although if you use System 7, you already have most of them, which you can use with either printer.

Both printers have spoolers to let you keep working while your files print in the background. (If you have an older, nonspooling version of either printer's driver, see your dealer about getting a free update.) But using these spoolers involves a tradeoff: You get your desktop back sooner, but your pages will print more slowly and might display more banding (thin white lines through an entire line of print).

Choosing between these two printers is tough, since both manufacturers have continually released updated drivers that add features and increase speed. The DeskWriter is easier to use on a network, since it's a true AppleTalk/LocalTalk device that can be networked directly in the normal Mac way.

GOOD FEATURE

The StyleWriter, on the other hand, is simply a serial device that uses Apple's Grayshare software to network in a backassward way. Grayshare allows the Mac to which the printer is attached to act as a server for the printer. Other Macs networked with that Mac can access the printer attached to it. But the printer itself is not part of the network; instead, it is dependent on its host Mac for access to the network. If that Mac is turned off, the upshot is no printing for the rest of the network. This setup will also create a performance hit on the local/host Mac because of the processing it must do to direct print jobs to the printer.

Inkjet Printer Ink Supplies (BW/RS)

Printing with inkjet ink costs more per page than with laser printer toner. An ink cartridge for Apple's StyleWriter II, for example, costs around $25 and prints about 466 pages of text. That's more than five cents a page, compared to about two cents a page from a $90 LaserWriter printer cartridge. Printing high volume or lots of high-ink-coverage graphics could empty a cartridge every two or three days.

Mail-order ink-cartridge pricing is typically about 20 percent less than list, not nearly as dramatic as discounts on many toner cartridges. There are ways to cut ink costs further, though, as we explain below.

Refilling inkjet cartridges (RS). You can save a lot of money by refilling your printer's ink cartridges instead of buying new ones. Most cartridges are good for ten or more refills. JetFill and American Ink Jet Corp. sell syringelike devices (the eponymic **JetFill** and the **CompuJet**, respectively) that come with smear-resistant black ink ($10) or colored ink ($11), about $10 less than buying a new DeskWriter or StyleWriter cartridge.

BARGAIN

If you want to save even more money, you can make your own refill kit. The method described below is for the DeskWriter, but you can probably also use it with the StyleWriter, even though it has a different type of ink reservoir.

All you need is a syringe and some ink. A medical syringe with a needle works best; otherwise a hobby syringe (meant for model airplane glue) will do. Hobby stores sell them for around $1.50.

For ink, I recommend Sheaffer Skrip (about $2 for two ounces; if you want black ink, get the jet black). It's water soluble and smears more easily than HP's ink, but it's a lot cheaper and shouldn't clog the print head as much. One bottle will fill the cartridge about five times. (DeskWriter cartridges have a sponge in them that holds some black ink even after they're empty, so don't try to refill them with colored ink.) You might also want to try the ink that's available from MacFriends. It's more expensive, but it's made expressly for inkjet printers.

To refill the cartridge, take it out of the printer (if the print head is clogged, soak it in alcohol to clear it). Remove the plug that covers the filler hole on the side of the cartridge, and put 12 cc's of ink in the syringe. If your syringe isn't graduated, measure the ink separately, or gradually fill the cartridge with small amounts of ink.

Put the tip of the syringe over the hole in the top of the cartridge. Seat it as well as you can, and then inject the ink. You can expect some overflow from both ends of the cartridge, so do this over a sink.

The manufacturers of inkjet printers haven't stood still for this, though. The latest cartridges for the DeskWriter and the StyleWriter now have unremovable plugs. (I know; I've mangled several of them beyond recognition, but they still refused to come out!) Fortunately, the inkjet refill kits include needles for piercing these seals. Just keep the filler from one of these kits and use it to refill your cartridges with ink in the future.

Remanufactured inkjet cartridges (BW). If refilling sounds too scary, Cybersight sells fully guaranteed remanufactured inkjet cartridges. (They even guarantee your printer!) A **Cybersight Renew** cartridge for the Apple StyleWriter II, for example, costs only $14 ($13 if you buy a six-pack), or about 48 percent less than new. Cybersight also offers bulk rates for 20 or more cartridges of the same or different types, which can shave 50 percent off Cybersight's own pricing.

Inkjet Printer Tips

Don't let cartridges dry out (ND). Try to avoid opening a new ink cartridge if you know you're not going to be using your printer for awhile—the ink may dry up before you get a chance to use it. Standard DeskWriter cartridges normally print about 300 pages, but my friend Tom's newly opened cartridge languished for six months and then ran out of ink after only 50 pages. Take his advice and change the cartridge *after* your vacation.

Unclogging ink cartridges (ND). Sometimes ink clogs some of the fine holes in inkjet print heads, so you see blank stripes in whatever you're printing. To clear the holes, you can try using the Prime feature on the DeskWriter or StyleWriter, but that doesn't always work—and it shortens the life of the cartridge.

Instead, try printing a heavily inked page one or more times. You can make a suitable page to print by going into a graphics program, drawing a box that fills a whole page, and filling it with black (or a dark pattern). It this fails, you can try soaking just the print head (not the whole cartridge) in some alcohol.

Prime mechanism upgrade (ND). Early DeskWriters have prime pumps that can malfunction and create a messy ink spill inside the printer near the ink cartridge. These defective pumps sometimes make clogged print heads worse, rather than fixing them. HP offers a free upgrade kit to owners of DeskWriters with serial numbers whose first four digits are lower than 2937.

Updating the driver of the StyleWriter I (RS). When Apple discontinued the StyleWriter I and introduced the StyleWriter II, it unfortunately stopped updating the driver for the StyleWriter I. The StyleWriter II, which is virtually

the same printer only with a slightly revised and faster print engine in a sleeker case, kept getting faster and better at grayscale printing with each driver revision. A few inquisitive souls tried out the driver for the StyleWriter II on the StyleWriter I and found that it worked, but that certain features of the StyleWriter II driver, such as the print head clearing command, would seriously damage their StyleWriter I's.

Igor Livshits cured cross-driver problem with his freeware **StyleWriter I+ Hack** (available from on-line services and user groups), which helps you remove dangerous features of the StyleWriter II driver. The StyleWriter II driver isn't free, though, so you must buy a set of Apple's latest system software to get it legally.

A better solution is to get **WonderPrint** ($60) from Delta Tao Software. This little extension gives you even faster printing and better grayscales than using the StyleWriter II driver on a StyleWriter I.

DeskWriter drivers (LP/RS/ND). Early versions of the DeskWriter driver didn't work well with System 7's memory features. If you tried to print with virtual memory on, you'd get an alert that said, "Datacomm buffer overrun—no DTR handshaking." If you had 32-bit addressing on, you'd get a system error when you issued the Page Setup or Print commands. HP fixed these problems in version 2.2 of the driver. Version 2.2 also made it possible to use fonts like Sonata (for music notation) that use negative kerning to make characters overlap.

Recent versions of the DeskWriter driver increase printing speed, use better dither patterns for printing grayscales, and include a spooler for background printing. You can get the latest driver from user groups, on-line services, and bulletin boards.

Networkable DeskWriters (Larry Pina). If you're buying a used DeskWriter to be shared by Macs on a network, make sure it's the newer model, HP2279A, which has a blue DeskWriter label. The original model, HP2278A (its DeskWriter label is red), isn't networkable.

Proofing on a StyleWriter (RS). If you want to proofread on a StyleWriter before printing on a laser printer, get the BetterWriters print driver from GDT Softworks. This driver lets you scale the printout in 1 percent increments. Setting the printout to 97 percent approximates a laser printout, and it also lets you use a StyleWriter with some applications that expect you to have a laser printer. (This tip may work on any inkjet, but you may have to experiment.)

Laser Printers

Steve Jobs decided that Apple's first laser printer should also launch Adobe System's PostScript page description language into the consumer sphere. The first LaserWriter listed for over $6,000 in 1985, but people paid it. For graphic artists and publishers, PostScript was probably *the* best reason for buying a Mac (and, of course, PageMaker).

Choosing a Laser Printer (BW/RS)

The Macintosh laser printer market has exploded, with more models on the market than we could possibly describe here. Prices continue to free-fall, while printing speed, resolution, and convenience have soared. Before we talk about a few specific printers, we'll take an overview of laser printer features and the issues surrounding today's laser printer market.

PostScript clones (BW). Some printer manufacturers felt shut out of the PostScript printer market because of Adobe's initially stringent licensing policies. That, or they wished to add features (like resolution enhancement) that Adobe's PostScript hardware/software designs had failed to address. As a result they developed or licensed PostScript-compatible interpreters that performed like Adobe's patented PostScript. Over the years they've gotten pretty reliable, certainly for Level 1 PostScript.

When a printer has the price and features you want, and it's a clone, don't hesitate to buy it unless there's a genuine Adobe-licensed equivalent. Most of the inexpensive, B-size (11- by 17-inch tabloid) laser printers on the market are clones, for example, and we know many satisfied customers. The same holds

The Engine

(BW)

There are hundreds of laser printers on the market, but the print engines driving them are made by only a few companies. Canon is the main supplier by far, with IBM/Lexmark, Fuji/Xerox, Sharp, Ricoh, Minolta, and Kyocera playing catch-up. This situation maintains healthy competition and avoids dealers having to stock hundreds of different brands of supplies and components.

For most printers, the toner reservoir, drum, and developer are incorporated into a single cartridge that you can throw away or recycle when the toner's gone. Other engines, notably from Sharp, Kyocera, and Ricoh, have separately installed toner, developer, and drum units, which you replace individually as they wear out. Going by the manufacturer's replacement ratings for these expendable parts, neither approach seems dramatically more economical.

Since printers that use the same engine are more alike than different, laser printers are often classified by the type of engine they use. Here's a guide to those currently in common use.

Common Cartridges or Component Systems

Engine	Cartridge/ component name	Printers	Duty cycle in pages at 5 percent coverage
Canon CX	EP cartridge	LaserWriter, LaserWriter Plus	3,000
Canon SX	EP-S cartridge	LaserWriter II, IINT, IIf, IIg	4,500
Canon NX	IIIsi cartridge	HP LaserJet IIIsi	6,000
Canon LX	EP-L cartridge	Apple Personal LaserWriter NT, QMS 410	3,000
Canon EX	EP-E cartridge	HP LaserJet 4, LaserWriter Pro 600, 630	6,000
Canon BX	EP-B cartridge	Xante 8100, NewGen TurboPS 660B, QMS 860	6,000
Minolta	Imaging Cartridge 2	NEC SilentWriter II 90	8,000
IBM 4019	4019 cartridge	IBM 4019 printers	5,600
Fuji/Xerox	EP cartridge	Dataproducts LZR 1560	12,000
Sharp 9500	three-component	Sharp JX 9500, TI Microline	Separate ratings for developer, toner, and drum
Ricoh 4080	R4080 three-component	Ricoh 4080, QMS 1500, DEC Scriptprinter	Separate ratings for developer, toner, and drum
Ricoh	R6000 three-component	Ricoh 6000, IBM PagePrinter	Separate ratings for developer, toner, and drum

true for high-resolution (over-600-dpi) lasers. Companies like LaserMaster, NewGen, and Xante make it easy to upgrade the PostScript-compatible interpreter, and they generally stay on top of compatibility problems. Adobe-licensed PostScript printers have had bugs, too!

Resolution and resolution enhancement (RS/BW). The new standard in quality is the 600-dpi resolution provided by relatively inexpensive laser engines like the Canon EX found in printers like the Apple LaserWriter Pro 630 and the Hewlett-Packard LaserJet 4M. Once costing over $10,000, some 600-dpi printers are now less than $2,000, not much more than 300-dpi printers. Some even threaten to break the $1,000 price point. You'll definitely notice the difference between 300-dpi and 600-dpi printing. The jaggies almost disappear from text, and it's even more dramatic when printing graphics and scanned-in photos.

Vendors such as Apple, LaserMaster, NewGen, Xante, and others sell printers with controller circuitry that manipulates the laser beam to create a higher apparent resolution, beyond the 400 dpi or 600 dpi of a standard laser engine. For comparative purposes, "enhanced" resolutions are hard to quantify because different vendors use different electronic techniques. One vendor's "800 by 800" enhanced resolution may look as good as another's "1,000 by 1,000." If you're looking for better text quality, start looking at HP's LaserJet 4 printers based on the Canon EX engine, which combine true 600-by-600-dpi resolution with HP's resolution enhancement technology, and compare it with higher-resolution models from Xante, LaserMaster, NewGen, and so on.

Resolution enhancement that improves text and graphics doesn't always improve grayscale images, so vendors now provide additional grayscale enhancement. Apple's PhotoGrade grayscale enhancement, introduced with LaserWriter IIg, is quite good; in fact, it's better at 300 dpi than most grayscale printing at 600 by 600. Other vendors have been upgrading their grayscale enhancements quicker than we can test them, so if grayscale's your game, check out the current models.

Just remember that 1,200 dpi on a toner-based printer doesn't compare with the sharpness of a 1,200-dpi photoimagesetter. The laser-drum-toner process produces a rather sloppy, nonuniform dot in comparison to the photo-chemical process of imagesetters. Also, it's very important to test different toner density settings on "enhanced-resolution" printers, since density, which tends to wander, can make a huge difference in print quality.

Speed (RS/BW). Laser printers' rated speeds range from about 4 pages per minute to 40 and beyond. That speed indicates how fast the printer can push through blank pages. But it doesn't account for the time it takes to process the page prior to printing—and for PostScript printers, that can be considerable. Vendors are now incorporating fast *RISC* (Reduced Instruction Set Computer) processing chips, which are optimized to execute one or more instructions per computer clock cycle. Compare that to general-purpose processors like the 68000 series, which use several cycles to execute more complex instructions that aren't easily optimized for printing. The faster RISC chips help printers process pages for printing at a rate closer to the actual page-per-minute speed of the printer engine—especially important for complex graphics and large scanned images.

RAM (JF/BW). PostScript printers need a lot of memory. They use almost a megabyte to hold the image of a page before it's printed and nearly another half-megabyte to do the calculations creating those page images. Any leftover memory is used for storing fonts and for caching images of letters it has already drawn, so it doesn't have to draw them from scratch again next time they're needed. In a PostScript printer with 2MB of memory, less than 400K is available for font storage—enough for perhaps ten typical PostScript fonts (less for the porkier TrueType variety). If you use many fonts, your best bet is a printer that has more than 2MB of RAM (for a letter-size printer). Adding a hard disk to your printer is an expensive option, but it's popular mainly among graphic arts and publishing pros.

With enough RAM to hold all the fonts and forms for a print job, your printer won't waste time automatically downloading them during printing (see "Automatic PostScript Font Downloading" in Chapter 14). Some printers will also use additional RAM for *double-buffering*, wherein one page gets ready while a previously processed page is fed to the print engine.

You can now add RAM to most printers, usually by installing RAM SIMMs (Single In-line Memory Modules). There are several types of SIMMs on the market, so check out which one your printer accepts before buying any.

Network connections (BW). Although LocalTalk has been the standard connection for Mac printers, Ethernet cabling typically moves print data at least four times faster than LocalTalk, a big advantage when printing bitmapped image files and other large job files. That's why your new laser printer purchases should have an Ethernet interface built in or provided as an option. Make sure the printer's Ethernet interface handles AppleTalk protocols. Some can also handle TCP/IP, DECnet, or Novell Netware, if you also want to let networked Unix workstations, DEC Vaxes, or PCs, respectively, print directly to the printer. Some printers can handle several protocols at once. You can use LocalTalk-to-Ethernet bridges or routers to connect LocalTalk-based printers to Ethernet networks, but if you do, you lose the speed advantage of Ethernet. (For more on all these networking terms, see Chapter 23.)

Emulation and Context Switching (BW)

Many printer controllers can determine the appropriate language interpreter, PostScript or PCL, for example, for a given job coming over a printer port. Simple context switchers search the first part of a job for some known PostScript codes, particularly the %! character pair that's part of the PostScript header commonly placed on PostScript print jobs. If it doesn't spot %! or other clues, it assumes the job is PCL and switches to PCL emulation.

Trouble is, your printer may run out of paper in the middle of a PostScript job, for example, causing the job to "time out" while you reload. When you resume, the printer doesn't recognize the PostScript codes from the middle of the job and mistakenly switches to PCL. For that reason, LaserMaster's Unity line of printers maintains a special print buffer designed solely to accept one byte of a job every few minutes so that the printer doesn't time out and switch context inappropriately.

QMS, which pioneered context switching, takes an even more sophisticated approach. Its ESP (Emulation Sensing Processor) goes beyond checking for a few common PostScript codes and instead uses statistical analysis to determine the probability that the job is PostScript. QMS maintains a database of PostScript jobs, especially those known to confound ESP. QMS periodically processes this database into refined upgrades of ESP, which have consequently "learned" to recognize PostScript more reliably.

PCL support and automatic port switching (BW). Most laser printers now sport LocalTalk, Centronix parallel (common on PCs), and RS-232 serial ports, and a few include Ethernet. In the old days you had to throw a switch or fiddle with some buttons and sometimes even restart the printer in order to switch between ports. These days, that's retro; many printers now automatically switch to whichever port has a job coming in. Some can even automatically switch from a PostScript processing mode to a LaserJet PCL (Printer Control Language) mode (common on PCs). Some, like QMS printers sporting their Crown architecture, can even switch between PCL and PostScript without erasing downloaded PCL or PostScript fonts.

Resident fonts (BW). Most PostScript laser printers come with at least 13 built-in fonts, typically Times, Helvetica, and Courier (each in regular, bold, italic, and bold italic weights), plus Symbol. Many come with 35 fonts, adding Bookman, Avant Garde, Palatino, New Century Schoolbook, and Zapf Dingbats to the basic 13. A few come with more. These fonts are coded into ROM (Read-Only Memory) chips inside the printer.

GOOD FEATURE

Some printers, like the LaserMaster Unity models, may include more than a hundred fonts stored on a hard drive mounted inside the printer, which you can add to or delete. Most Accel-a-Writer printers from Xante have 512K of *flashROM* (expandable to 1MB) to which you can download your own set of fonts that are then stored as though they were built in.

Paper handling (BW). A heavily used shared printer should have at least one paper tray holding at least 240 sheets (see the following box about paper-tray options). Most of the faster (12-ppm to 20-ppm) printers on the market have ample paper-handling options.

And consider paper size. Laser printers capable of printing tabloid-size (B-size) pages were once *beaucoup* pricey: $15,000 and up. Now they start at around $5,000, thanks to Canon's 600-dpi BX laser engine. Even if your final production is letter-size, you'll want a B-size printer if you need to show crop marks and bleeds that extend off the page.

The Best Buys (RS)

There are so many brands of laser printers on the market now that it's hard to know which is best for your needs. One surprising thing, though, is that the same companies keep producing the best values over time. Apple, with its recent tactic of coming out with new models about every three months, often has

Paper-Handling Enhancements (BW)

If you're constantly racing to add paper or feed an envelope to your shared laser printer, it's time to consider some paper-handling options and upgrades.

First, see what your printer vendor offers. Apple's Personal LaserWriter LS and NTR, for example, came with only a 50-sheet multipurpose paper-input tray. But Apple still sells the $100 Personal LaserWriter 250-sheet cassette base, which adds another 250-sheet cassette feed to the bottom of the printer. That feeder also accepts Apple's $75 Personal LaserWriter envelope cassette or legal cassette, in addition to providing a second 250-sheet feed for Personal LaserWriter NTs.

GOOD FEATURE

The LaserWriter Select accepts a $150 optional 250-sheet feeder, and a $300, 500-sheet feeder. You can also get a 500-sheet feeder for the LaserWriter Pro models and an envelope feeder holding 75 envelopes, both priced at $400.

Third-party vendors also sell humongous paper feeders for many Mac-compatible laser printers. **Jet Tray 1500,** from Genesis Technology, is a single-bin, 1,500-sheet feeder costing only $495. Its Model LCS 15-SX, for example, works with LaserWriter II's, QMS PS810/815's, and other SX-engine printers. The $495 Genesis **Jet Tray 250E** fits 250 Commercial 10 envelopes.

If you commonly print using a mix of papers and envelopes, consider a multibin sheet feeder like one from BDT Products. With BDT's $3,300, six-bin feeder, for example, you can load letterhead, second-page, plain bond, and legal papers, plus envelopes. Each paper bin holds 220 sheets, and the envelope bin holds 50 envelopes. BDT also sells three-, four-, and five-bin feeders. Macs connect to the printer as normal, while the sheet feed connects to the printer via its RS-232 serial port. BDT's LaserStation software initializes the printer's serial port and lets people choose different bins from their Macs.

some of the most attractive printers available, at least until the third parties catch up. But you often can't go wrong with models from Hewlett-Packard, NEC, or Texas Instruments.

We can't cover them all, but here are some recommendations.

BARGAIN

A dirt-cheap PostScript-compatible printer (RS). The Star Micronics **LaserPrinter 4 StarScript** isn't the best 300-dpi laser printer on the Mac market, nor the most compact (though it does have quite a small footprint). It's even hard to find. But it is the cheapest PostScript-compatible laser printer currently available for the Mac. The brochures don't give a list price, but at press time it was going for as little as $560 at local computer stores. For that you get a

10-MHz RISC processor, Star's own PostScript emulator, 2MB of RAM, 35 resident fonts, and a four-page-per-minute print engine, in addition to Hewlett-Packard LaserJet IIp compatibility. Being a PostScript clone, it might not suit a graphic arts professional (give it a try in the store), but I couldn't trip it up.

A good, cheap PostScript printer (RS).The 300-dpi Texas Instrument **microWriter PS23** is the heir apparent to Texas Instruments' long-standing popular bargain, the microLaser PS17. It has a list price of $800 and is often sold for well below $700. It has a lot of nice features, including true Adobe PostScript Level 2 (not a clone), HP LaserJet compatibility, and a 250-page feeder tray. Its 13.8- by 14.8-inch footprint leaves plenty of work space on your desk.

The microWriter PS23 actually uses light-emitting diodes (LEDs) instead of a laser. TI claims they are more reliable and slaps a five-year warranty on the print head to back it up. The printer's software even lets you switch between paper trays or the envelope feeder within a single document, all from the Print dialog box. The PS23 comes with 2MB of RAM, which you can upgrade to 4MB. Make sure you order the PS23; the plain microWriter from Texas Instruments isn't Mac-compatible.

A 600-dpi bargain (RS).It's no secret that the popular Texas Instruments laser printers are based on Sharp engines. Sharp now has its own line of Mac-compatible laser printers—hot values all. The 600-dpi Sharp **JS-9460PS** laser printer's 16-MHz RISC processor pumps a six-page-per-minute print engine, with enhanced grayscale technology and the reliable PhoenixPage PostScript emulator. It's got the same small footprint as the Texas Instruments microWriter. Sharp's SoftBand technology stretches its 2MB of RAM. The Sharp JS-9460PS lists for $1,200, though it is heavily discounted by mail-order vendors such as MacMall to as low as $800, making it limbo-lowest among the 600-dpi PostScript crowd.

The best personal 600-dpi laser printer (RS). In the hotly contested 600-dpi, light-duty laser printer class, Apple, Texas Instruments, and NEC have worthy entries. One high-value standout is the $1,730 Hewlett-Packard **LaserJet 4MP.** A four-page-per-minute engine and true Adobe PostScript Level 2 interpreter are driven by a 20-Mhz RISC processor, using a caching scheme to speed printing. The printer comes with a whopping 6MB of RAM, upgradable to 22MB, 35 PostScript internal fonts, and a 250-sheet paper tray. It has several energy-saving features, which can save you quite a bit on your electrical bill (most laser printers consume enough wattage to light a small home). The 4MP consumes only about 5 watts per hour when in dormant mode and 15 watts per hour in powersave mode.

GOOD FEATURE

And let's not forget HP's resolution-enhancement technology (REt). As with the other 600-dpi LaserJet 4 models, the combination of 600-dpi resolution and HP's REt produces breathtaking print quality you must see to believe.

Toner

If you've been paying close to list price for brand-new toner cartridges down at the corner store, you can probably guess why we're offering a few smart buying and conservation techniques. Use 'em and cut your toner costs in half.

Adjusting toner density (JF/RS/BW). If you print mainly text, you can crank the print density way down on your laser printer. Only at the very lowest setting does type start to look pale, although large, solid areas of black will begin to suffer below a mid-range setting. This can extend the life of your toner cartridges considerably.

Working Software makes a neat product called **Toner Tuner** ($25 list) that lets you adjust the darkness of a print from the Print dialog box prior to printing. It's not only more convenient than most utilities, but it's also a good option for printers lacking toner-density adjustment. Toner Tuner works with any type of printer, even inkjets.

If you're shopping for new printers, be aware that special hardware in Hewlett-Packard's LaserJet 4ML and 4MP lets you select an "EconoMode" that saves toner by printing 50 percent fewer printer dots. Somewhat more refined than Toner Tuner, EconoMode prints solidly along the leading edge of text and graphics, more lightly for the remainder. *I tried this but found it unacceptably light, even for drafts. However, the HP LaserJet Utility offers a Print Density setting that lets you choose between five density levels, and I've found the lightest one to be just right.—DD]*

Getting the last drop (JF). As your toner cartridge approaches the end of its useful days, there are a couple of ways to extend its life.

- When the "low toner" light comes on, open the printer, remove the cartridge, and give it a few brisk shakes from end to end to jog the remaining toner around. Don't turn the cartridge upside down; just make motions like you're sifting flour. You should be able to this a dozen times or more before the "low toner" light refuses to turn itself off and the cartridge is really getting empty.
- If you're running out of toner when stores are closed, you can use a can of aerosol acrylic fixative from an art supply store (it's used for fixing pastel and charcoal drawings) and spray any pages on which the image is becoming faint. The spray dissolves and darkens the toner, resulting in richer blacks. It'll do until you can buy more toner.

Discount toner cartridges (BW). The Canon SX toner cartridge in your old LaserWriter IINT prints about 4,000 text-based pages and lists for $130. At 100 pages per business day, that amounts to around $750 a year in toner. Fortunately, without much effort you can get that figure down to around $300.

First off, don't end up buying cartridges one at a time from corner retailers; buy at discount stores, if you insist on new cartridges. My local Connecting Point computer store, for example, charges $100 for a brand-new SX cartridge, whereas OfficeMax office supply superstores sell it for $74. Mail-order SX cartridges cost around $85 each, down to about $80 if you buy a dozen, including shipping.

Apple-brand cartridges are often more expensive than identical ones from Hewlett-Packard or Canon, so buy the equivalent HP or Canon brands indicated in the chart below.

Hewlett-Packard Equivalents for LaserWriter Toner Cartridges

Printer	Cartridge Name	Printer Engine	HP Equivalent
LaserWriter, LaserWriter Plus	EP	Canon CX	LaserJet, LaserJet Plus
LaserWriter II, IINT, IIf, IIg	EP-S	Canon SX	LaserJet II, LaserJet III
Personal LaserWriters	EP-L	Canon LX	LaserJet IIP, IIIP
LaserWriter Pro 600, Pro 630	EP-E	Canon EX	LaserJet 4

Recycled toner cartridges (BW). If you really want to save on toner, you should consider recharged (refilled) or remanufactured cartridges. Recycled SX cartridges, for example, price out at $40 to $70, instead of from $70 to $100—way less than new, and better for the environment.

Not all reused cartridges are the same quality, however. Here's the rundown:

- **Recharging.** Recharging a cartridge means simply refilling an empty cartridge with fresh toner. Nothing is done about worn or damaged parts and, as a consequence, print quality and reliability after recharging aren't usually guaranteed. That's a bit dicey in our view. Before third-party manufactures began providing replacement cartridge parts, drill 'n' fill was the only game in town, and a bit risky.
- **Remanufacturing.** Remanufacturing entails much more than refilling. The cartridge is disassembled, cleaned, and inspected. Worn parts, including the imaging drum, are replaced as necessary. As a result, remanufactured engines commonly come with guarantees. Even Hewlett-Packard is remanufacturing SX-engine cartridges, offering a $95 mail-in replacement kit for its high-quality **Optiva 95R.**

But how do you know exactly what you're getting from a remanufacturer? Call and ask. Do they have a clean, modern facility, or are they operating out of a garage? Do they replace worn drums with new ones, or do they simply polish or recondition them by spraying on a photo-sensitive coating? What's the guarantee lifetime, six months, or just 60 days?

Super Cartridges (BW)

Some remanufacturers, such as Codo and Black Diamond produce rebuilt cartridges with superior long-life drums and magnum loads of toner. Codo's **PERMAJET Plus** double-capacity cartridge has a long-life drum and double the toner of original cartridges, with a rated page yield (5 percent coverage) of 8,000 as compared to the 4,000-page yield of original SX cartridges. It sells for about $89 through mail-order firms like Richard Young Products and others. Codo rates another of its super SX cartridges, the **Toner Tank,** at 20,000 pages. It comes with a standard 4,000-page toner load, plus four additional refills, selling for about $250. Either option works out to about a penny per page.

Black Diamond conservatively rates its Supercartridge at 12,000 pages. ISSI Data Products, a corporate office supplier in Seattle, sells the Black Diamond for $150 for a single unit (about a penny a page), $130 each in volume.

Quality varies on remanufactured cartridges, so test a brand out before ordering it in bulk.

GOOD FEATURE

Disposing of toner cartridges (RS/BW). Our best advice is: Don't throw out toner cartridges, even if you buy only new cartridges. Many cartridge recyclers will buy CX, SX, LX, NX, EX, and other cartridges. Apple not only has a cartridge recycling program, it'll donate one dollar to a conservation charity for each empty cartridge you return.*HP has my loyalty. New HP cartridges come with a prepaid UPS shipment label in the box. You just pack your old cartridge in the new wrapper and box, slap on the sticker, and hand it to a UPS driver.—DD]*

Since not all used cartridges are in demand, you may have to throw one away. Place the cartridge back in its shipping bag or another plastic bag (ZipLocks are handy) and tie or tape it completely shut to prevent residual toner from escaping.

WARNING

Some cartridges may be hot when they come out of the machine, so let them cool down in the printer before removing.

Laser Printer Tips

HOT TIP

Manual PostScript font downloading (JF). Manual downloading copies fonts into the printer's memory so they stay there until the printer is turned off. You manually download fonts with a special program, such as Apple's LaserWriter Font Utility (included with the System) or Adobe's Downloader (free with Adobe fonts). If your printer has a hard disk, these programs can copy your fonts permanently onto it, where they'll stay until you erase them.

The benefit of manual downloading is that your pages print faster, because you download the fonts just once (in the morning, say, when you start your printer), not every time you print.

If you're going to print several times using the same fonts, you'll save time by manually downloading them, even if you'll be using other fonts later in the day. When you've finished using one set of fonts, restart your printer to clear its memory; then download the next batch. The time it takes to manually download the fonts is paid back each time you print using those fonts by saving about 15 seconds per font used in each document.

If you're stuck with a 2MB-or-less printer, your best strategy is to manually download each day the handful of fonts you most commonly use (four to six fonts for a 2MB printer, one to two for a 1.5MB model). This will leave enough memory for printing most typical jobs (using three fonts or fewer) using automatic downloading. If you're starved for printer memory, avoid TrueType fonts, which munch more RAM than PostScript fonts do.

Only in the most desperate circumstances should you select "Unlimited Downloadable Fonts in a Document" in the Page Setup dialog box. This causes the Mac to download only a single font to the printer, deleting it when another font is called for. This means a 30-second delay for every typeface change, even if it's only for italicizing a single word.

PostScript printer memory madness (JF). Managing limited memory in a PostScript printer can make you nuts. It's hard to know exactly how much memory is available, because Apple's LaserWriter Font Utility cleverly won't tell you this vital information. For that, you need Adobe's Downloader.

Avoid ghosting (JF). If you're using your laser printer to make many copies of a page, you may notice that you get a ghost image of one part of the page invading another part of the page, especially in large areas of solid black. You can avoid this ghosting by cranking up the print density setting to near its maximum.

Cleaning out paper dust (JF). A photographer's can of compressed air is useful for blowing away all the paper "dandruff" that accumulates inside your laser printer.

Printing envelopes (JF). To minimize paper jams when printing envelopes, use your fingernail as a brayer to flatten out all the seams of the envelope before printing, particularly the edge of the envelope that first meets the rollers.

Feeding single sheets on the LaserWriter II (AN/JK). The LaserWriter II and many other Canon-engine printers will pull a single sheet of paper from the slot on the top of the paper tray, whether you tell it to or not. So if you're working on a nonnetworked LaserWriter II, all you have to do is put a sheet of paper in the slot; you don't gain anything by clicking the Manual Feed button in the Print dialog box.

Try this on a shared network printer, though, and someone else's print job may use the single sheet first. So click the Manual Feed button, and your Mac will tell you to insert the sheet when the printer is ready for your job.

Protect cartridges from light (BW). Even though toner cartridges look light-tight, they're not. Stuffing them back into their light-proof shipping bags will prevent damage to the photo-electric drum inside. Once overexposed to light, the cartridge may start showing one or more bands of overly light printing across the page, caused by exposure lines on the drum. All you can do then is send it in for remanufacturing.

Laser printer hang-ups (AN/RS). Laser printers sometimes get confused and hung up (just like the rest of us). When this happens, restart the printer with the LaserWriter Utility (or some similar program). If that doesn't help, restart your Mac (with the Restart command on the Special menu).

If there's still a problem, turn both the Mac and the printer off and wait five minutes before turning them back on (check all the cable connections while they're both off). If *that* doesn't help, replace your printer drivers. If *that* doesn't help, reinstall your system software as described in Chapter 3.

If it's still no-go, you may actually have a hardware problem.

Faster bitmap printing (AN/SA/JK). The LaserWriter driver gives you a number of useful options in the Page Setup dialog box. One of these is Faster Bitmap Printing, which preprocesses bit-mapped images before they're sent to the LaserWriter. Apple states that "in rare cases, some documents may not print with this option turned on," but we've never experienced that. If it happens to you, just turn the option off and try again.

Graphics smoothing (AN/SA/JK). The Graphics Smoothing or Smoothing Bitmap option in the LaserWriter Print dialog box reduces the jaggies on bit-mapped graphics—for example, the stair-step effect around curves turns into a slightly squiggly line. This option only works for Apple's LaserWriters, not for other brands of PostScript printers. Some programs (like PageMaker) have smoothing routines of their own that work on all PostScript printers.

Better bitmaps (AN/SA/JK). Do the MacPaint images you placed in your document show distracting crosshatch patterns when printed on your laser printer? The Precision Bitmap Alignment option in the LaserWriter Page Setup dialog box improves bit-mapped graphics by reducing the entire image on the page to 96 percent of its normal size. This gets around the incompatibility between the 72 dots per inch of the Mac's screen and the 300 dots per inch of a laser printer's output (300 divided by 72 is 4.1666, but 96 percent of 300 is 288, into which 72 goes exactly 4 times).

There's a neat trick that avoids having to reduce the whole document—just enlarge the graphic to 104 percent of its original size (of course, this only works in programs that give you that precision). But be aware that neither this approach nor Precision Bitmap Alignment will work if the graphic has already been reduced or enlarged from its original size. PageMaker's "magic stretch" feature ensures that you scale bit maps to the percentages compatible with your printer's resolution.

Labels and envelopes for laser printers (AN/SA/DD). Unless it's made especially for laser printers or copiers, don't print on any material that contains glue. The heat in the printer can cause labels to peel off inside the printer and can seal envelopes. If you've *got* to print envelopes in your printer (of course you do), just make sure to be waiting at the output end, to peel them open before they seal permanently.

Avery makes labels specifically designed for laser printers. Because a special adhesive is used, the labels don't peel off when subjected to the high heat inside the printer. We've used them at the office and haven't had any problems with jamming. They come in three sizes: 1 inch by 2⅝ inch (product codes 5160 and 5260), 1 inch by 4 inch (product codes 5161 and 5261) and 1½ inch by 4 inch (product codes 5162 and 5262) and are available at most office supply stores.

Dot-Matrix Impact Printers

No, we're not talking visual impact here, but the impact of steel on paper used by dot-matrix impact printers. As we mentioned previously, the print quality, low price, and relative speed and silence of inkjet printers leave only one reason for buying an impact printer: printing multiple forms.

Choosing an Impact Printer (BW/RS)

In printing multiple form, checks, and so on, most people aren't splitting hairs about print quality (resolution). Speed, price, and Macintosh compatibility are the relevant issues.

Resolution. Dot-matrix print resolution is determined by the number of pins in the print head. Apple's 9-pin ImageWriter II dot-matrix printer prints text at 72 dpi, although at Best quality the pins overstrike to generate 160 dpi across and 144 down. This mode of printing is known generically as "near-letter-quality," or NLQ, a feature of most dot-matrix impact printers. Dot-matrix printers sporting 24-pin print heads achieve over 300 dpi, but since the dots are larger than inkjet or laser dots, print quality isn't as fine. Apple also used to make a 27-pin version of the ImageWriter, the ImageWriter LQ, for "letter-quality." The LQ had a lot of problems and has been discontinued.

Speed. Dot-matrix printers are rated in "characters per second," or cps. The ImageWriter II is rated at 250 cps, although that's only in draft mode. At Best mode it prints less than half that fast. This holds true for most models sporting a "near-letter-quality" mode.

Compatibility. Most dot-matrix printers on the market aren't compatible with the Macintosh. Mac-compatible dot-matrix printers imitate the 9-pin Image-Writer II and use Apple's ImageWriter driver. At this writing we don't know of any Mac-compatible 24-pin dot-matrix currently being sold.

Price. There are lots of nine-pin dot-matrix printers on the market selling for less than $200. Trouble is, they're not Mac-compatible. Factor in the cost and hassle of a conversion kit like GDT's PowerPrint described in "Adapting PC

Printers for the Mac" on page 826, and you may feel like spending a little more for a compatible model.

Your Choices

(BW/RS)

Stores still sell ImageWriter II's for about $450, but some nice ImageWriter-compatible printers are also around. Seikosha's nine-pin, 150-cps **SP-2400AP** lists for $400 (only $250 from MacWarehouse). The wide-carriage **SP-2415AP** lists for $570. GCC's **WriteImpact** nine-pin, 192-cps dot-matrix is a bit pricey, though somewhat faster, listing at $600.

Color Printers

In the "Types of Printers" section above we covered the basic technologies employed in color printers. Now we're going to name some names as we offer up some good deals and further buying considerations.

Color Inkjet

For low-cost color printing, color inkjet is the way to go. It provides 300-dpi resolution on plain paper, for street prices as low as about $500.

Hewlett-Packard DeskWriter C (RS/BW). Hewlett-Packard pretty much has the low-cost (read: under $1,000) color printer market to itself. The $500 **DeskWriter C** is basically a black-and-white printer, but you can swap out the black ink cartridge for a three-color cartridge. However, because there's no black ink in the color cartridge, black areas are printed using a composite black made by overprinting all the colors. Trouble is, the resulting black is really more of a greenish dark gray. This is especially rough on text, although you can set the printer to pause between text and graphics so you can pop in the black or color cartridge. If this sounds unacceptable, you'll need to pay more for a color inkjet that includes true black ink in its color array. See the description of the HP550C, below.

Hewlett Packard DeskWriter 550C (RS). The **HP DeskWriter 550C** is much improved over the DeskWriter C. In fact, it may be HP's best value in a color printer. It doesn't require any cartridge-swapping in order to print color, and it will print true blacks, for text, since it accommodates two ink cartridges—one for black ink and a second that contains cyan, magenta, and yellow inks.

There's one drawback, though: The 550C uses the color cartridge exclusively to produce all the colors in a graphic, including black (with mediocre results, as with the DeskWriter C). Fortunately, if a page contains text and graphics, the 550C automatically switches to the true-black ink to print the text.

Notwithstanding the above, the HP 550C is one hell of a buy, with a list price of only $600. This printer is especially nice for doing business graphics like charts and graphs and the odd flyer that has colorized fonts. It's even good for proofing color output before taking the final product to a service bureau. Of course, it isn't fast, being both a QuickDraw printer and an inkjet, with the complex computation necessary to interpolate color, but at this price you can afford to wait.

At press time, HP had just introduced the $720 DeskWriter 560C, sporting 600- by 300-dpi black printing, using a superior formulation of black ink in addition to a three-color cartridge like that of the 550C. Color control has been further automated with ColorSmart drivers (compatible with Apple's ColorSync) that adjust color on the fly to get the best color out of the different text, graphics, and image portions of a single page. ColorSmart drivers are also available at no charge for the DeskWriter 500C and 550C.

Canon BJC-600 and 820 (RS). The **Canon BJC-600** is a four-color, 360-dpi inkjet printer that lists for $720 and has a street price of well under $500. Its color and resolution are excellent.

What's the catch? The BJC-600 is *not* a Macintosh-compatible printer. But with the addition of a GDT PowerPrint package (see the box on page 826), it will work perfectly with your Mac. In fact, this is more or less what Apple did to come up with the stillborn Apple Color Printer, based on the wide-carriage **Canon BJC-820**. You can have the equivalent package (minus the option to use extra-wide paper) for around $1,000 less with the BJC-600/PowerPrint combination.

Actually, for some reason, the BJC-600 has much superior output quality compared to the BJC-820 or the Apple Color Printer. This wouldn't seem to make sense, since they are basically the same technology from the same company, but there it is.

Apple Color StyleWriter Pro (BW). Perhaps for that reason, as we went to press Apple announced a $630 Color StyleWriter Pro based on the Canon BJC-600 engine. Like the StyleWriter, the Color StyleWriter Pro uses Grayshare to share the printer over an AppleTalk network. Unlike the Hewlett-Packard 550C, the Canon engine doesn't have problems with the black ink reacting with the color ink since it uses individual cartridges (which you can replace separately).

Good, but more-expensive, inkjets (RS). HP's hot new $2,400 PostScript **DeskWriter 1200C/PS** has an advanced 104-nozzle print head that puts it at the head of the color inkjet pack for both color graphics and text, with a speed and low cost per page that are clearly tempting.

If you need to print tabloid, 11- by 17-inch pages, there are a couple of other PostScript color inkjets we like: the **HP PaintJet XL300** ($4,000 list) and the **Lexmark/IBM Color Jetprinter PS 4079** ($3,200). The XL300 may nudge the Jetprinter slightly in terms of color quality, and it's got Adobe PostScript Level 2 compared to the Phoenix Level 1 clone used in the Jetprinter. But it's also rather large, heavy, and noisy in comparison to the cheaper, sleeker, lighter Jetprinter. The Jetprinter controller actually stores its interpreter code in a removable ROM SIMM, making for easy controller upgrades. In fact, a recent upgrade seemed to boost both speed and color balance.

Thermal Wax

Until recently, the cheapest thermal-wax printers were priced in the $3,000 to $4,000 range—too high for many small businesses and certainly out of the question for home use. This has changed in a big way, as you'll see below.

GOOD FEATURE

A great thermal-wax printer (RS). Tektronix's **Phaser 200e** (list price $2,000) is top quality, the first thermal-wax printer (along with the Phaser 220i) to achieve 600- by-300-dpi resolution. It has a 16-MHz RISC processor, PostScript Level 2, 4MB of RAM, and 17 resident fonts. And it's fast compared to

Laser and Inkjet Paper

(BW/AN/RS)

Printer vendors naturally recommend paper and other media that show off print quality to best effect. Trouble is, top-quality paper doesn't come at everyday prices. We'll explain a few things about laser and inkjet paper and show you how to find good paper that won't break your budget.

Laser printer paper

Since laser printers work similarly to photocopiers, it's no surprise that they use the same kind of paper—often labeled as "xerographic."

Laser printer vendors recommend the more expensive brands of 24-pound laser/copier papers that are smoother, whiter, and more opaque than cheaper brands. QMS, for example, recommends premium laser bonds like **Hammermill Laser Plus,** or **Weyerhaeuser First Choice** ($13.50 and $8 per ream, respectively, from Paper Direct mail order). But frankly, we can rarely bring ourselves to pay that much. You'll usually find us lined up at office supply discount stores buying 20-pound bond for $19 a case (10 reams). It's amazing what you'll find, so buy a lot when you find it.

Recycled laser paper

Recycled 20-pound laser/copier paper has also gotten pretty cheap. Local stationers typically sell **Weyerhaeuser's Recycled Laser Copy** for $4 a ream. You can get it for as low as $27 a case at paper-supply retailers. Weyerhaeuser Recycled is 50 percent waste paper, including 25 percent postconsumer waste. "Postconsumer" is key here, referring to the paper we drag to the curbside instead of throwing away. By EPA standards a paper stock can be labeled "Recycled" if it contains 50 percent recycled paper with 10 percent postconsumer waste.

But the most environmentally correct recycled papers are those like **Unity DP,** a European paper that's 100 percent recycled with at least 50 percent postconsumer magazine and newspaper waste. Another big point: It's made without use of chemical bleaches. This reduces cost and water pollution levels but produces a grayer-looking paper—an attractive, natural appearance, we think. It's priced around $3.50 a ream. Hammermill also produces a Unity DP entirely from de-inked newspapers and magazines.

Color inkjet paper

If you look closely at any inkjet printer's output, you'll notice that the ink spreads a bit into the fibers of the paper, creating a fuzzy edge around everything. Absorbency is the key factor in choosing paper: the less, the better.

In general, color inkjets tend to look better on special coated papers because the ink stays at the surface. On uncoated papers the color inks sink into the paper, leaving the surface slightly uncovered and producing a low-saturated, washed-out look. Also, different colors sink in differently, causing color shifts.

HP color DeskJets, for example, look terrific on HP's **LX JetSeries Glossy** stock—colors are vibrant and accurate (it's more of a plastic than a paper). We can't quite swallow the buck-a-page price, though: $60 for 50 sheets! (We've seen it mail order for $48.) Randy's found something cheaper and equally good if not better: **Super Color Ink Jet Pape**r from Micro Format, at $19 for 150 pages. Randy turns his printer's ink output way down, since this paper really keeps the ink from sinking in *and* from spreading.

Cheaper alternatives compromise quality. Bob hasn't found a good alternative to IBM's coated stock for his Lexmark Jetprinter, although Hammermill's Laser Plus and Strathmore's Legacy aren't bad for preliminary prints.

B&W inkjet paper

For black-and-white inkjet, on the other hand, Canon and others recommend an uncoated ultra-white, 25 percent cotton paper like Crane's **Crest** fluorescent white (typically $12 for 100 sheets). The ink contrast against the white looks good and the fiber structure minimizes ink spread. (It's OK for the ink to sink in rather than spread out.)

With some experimentation you can find good, two-sheets-for-a-penny alternatives for B&W inkjets, since many bargain bonds work well. It's hard to guess which, though, since many national brands are manufactured at different mills using different formulations.

Black-and-white text may actually look worse on coated paper since the ink spreads more than it does on uncoated paper. For example, on Bob's Lexmark Jetprinter, colors look best using the IBM coated stock, but black text looks sharper on 25 percent cotton bonds and even cheapo laser bond.

other color printers, about two pages per minute. Plus, it prints on plain paper, using Tektronix's ColorCoat option, and it handles transparencies with ease.

GOOD FEATURE

Prints from the Phaser 200e are sharp; the blacks are deep black and small lines are rendered crisply. Like other thermal-wax printers, shading and various color tones are dithered or halftoned, not photo-realistic. It's good for technical illustration, design comps, and advertisements, though disappointing when printing scanned-in photographs. Tektronix backs its printers with on-site service and toll-free technical support.

The cheapest thermal-wax printer for the Mac (RS). Fargo Electronics manufactures a small thermal-wax color printer that's sold under several different brand names. Fargo sells it as the **Primera Color Printer** for only $1,000 list. It's also sold as the **NU Design Color Printer** by DTP Direct for the same price. Both also require a $250 Macintosh interface kit. Though the resolution on these printers is only 203 dpi, the output is distinguishable from that of 300-dpi thermal-wax printers only when compared side by side.

Dye Sublimation

There are two classes of dye-sublimation printers on the market: those designed primarily for rendering retouched photos and computer-generated art, and those designed primarily for proofing pages containing continuous-tone images, type, and graphics.

Photo only (BW). The venerable **Kodak XL7700** and newer **XLT7720** ($25,000) and the **Sony UP-D7000** ($9,000) are three examples of dye subs favored by photographers and computer artists. Resolution is typically 150 to 200 dpi (203 dpi for the Kodaks, 163 dpi for the UP-D7000). They lack built-in PostScript interpreters and LocalTalk interfaces, using SCSI or GPIB connections instead. The accent is on high-quality media and color balance, so they're typically used to get a photo-quality proof of an edited color photo or computer-rendered scene, or a hard-copy version of a computer video presentation or multimedia display, rather than for full-PostScript publications.

Proofing (BW). For the document-proofing market, dye-sublimation printers like the Tektronix **Phaser IISD, GCC ColorTone,** or **RasterOps CorrectPrint 300** sport built-in PostScript processing, 300-dpi resolution, and typical Mac interfaces like LocalTalk, in addition to SCSI. The higher dpi rating makes for better text and possibly a crisper image in a few cases.

PostScript is important if you're going with imagesetter color separations as your final production process.With type and graphics as well as scanned photos supported by PostScript, this type of printer is also very good for comping package design and color point-of-sale displays that employ all three elements.

A dye-sublimation bargain (RS). Would you believe dye-sublimation printing for less than $1,300? For $250 you can upgrade the Fargo **Primera Color Printer** (discussed under "Thermal Wax," above) to be a true dye-sublimation printer. DTP Direct sells the NU Design with upgrade for only $1,200, and the dye-sublimation output of these printers is beautiful.

The only drawback (and there has to be *one* at this price) is that prints lack the brightness you'll see in more expensive dye-sublimation printers like the Kodak XLT7720. This is probably because these Fargo printers use a composite black in dye-sublimation mode. But at this price it's forgivable. If you are considering a color printer, it is highly recommended that you call one of the two companies mentioned above that sell this printer and ask them to send you a sample of both the thermal-wax output and the dye-sublimation output.

Color Printing Tips

Glossy blacks from thermal wax (BW). Sometimes the straight black from a thermal-wax transfer printer may have a matte texture or tiny gaps in coverage. You can get a glossier, more solid looking black by specifying 100 percent of cyan, magenta, and yellow, in addition to black (provided your software lets you specify colors that way).

Single-ink text (BW). When you're printing color text in small point sizes, you're better off using a single color ink: cyan, magenta, or yellow. Most other colors use a halftone or dither pattern made of different-color ink dots, which makes small type look unacceptably coarse.

Monochrome proofs (BW). This may sound obvious, but use a monochrome printer to proof the basic text and graphic layout of your color documents. The cost per page is invariably cheaper than that of a color printout, and you'll spot a lot of errors that don't relate to color.

Keep track of good colors (BW). Because of peculiarities in ink formulations or color dithering and halftone techniques, some colors and shades simply look better than others on a given printer. If a specified color just doesn't come off well, experiment with slightly different values. When you find one that works, record its color specs so that you can re-create it, or save a sample of the color in a document to retrieve later.

Special-Purpose Printers

Beyond the mainstream you'll find some interesting breeds of printer, designed for special tasks and circumstances. Check 'em out.

Label and Address Printing

(Karen Faria/JK/BW)

CoStar's **AddressWriter** sells for around $300 mail order, and for that you get an eight-pin printer designed specifically for printing addresses directly onto envelopes or postcards (or, with an optional $75 attachment, labels). It's compatible with Macs and PCs, and a $200 LocalTalk upgrade lets you share it on a Mac network.

Its bundled software stores up to 1,600 addresses, and the addresses can even include PICT graphics. It also generates and prints a postal bar code for each address. The bar code not only speeds up delivery of your mail, but it can also save you up to 20 percent on bulk mailings.

For quick, quiet label printing, CoStar makes the **LabelWriter II** and **LabelWriter II Plus** thermal-fusion printers, available mail order for around $185 and $240, respectively. The II prints standard 1⅛-inch-wide shipping labels, while the II Plus prints wider, 2¼-inch labels for shipping, floppy disks, video cassettes, and so on.

Bob, you'd spend money on these? Word and WordPerfect have good templates for standard labels. Plus there are great utilities like DynoPage and DynoDex for easy label printing on any printer. TouchBase also includes excellent templates for labels. I personally recommend the shareware package ***Easy Envelopes*** *by Andrew Welch for doing envelopes with bar codes. It's dead easy to use, and cheap.—RS] Randy, anyone who does a variety of correspondence or fulfillment during the day wants push-button labeling. I use templates and addressing utilities myself, and I still end up fiddling with the damn things instead of getting work done. I only send two or three letters a day, otherwise I'd blow my next royalty check on an AddressWriter.—BW]*

Portable Printers (RS/JK)

If you'd like to print a report from your PowerBook while airborne over the Rockies, you'll want a lightweight, compact, battery-powered printer. Even if you don't need battery power, these small printers are perfect for those accidental tourists traveling light. There are two types: inkjet and thermal fusion, both equally quiet.

Two portable inkjets (RS/JK). Apple's **Portable StyleWriter,** at $440, is quite slick, although it's simply a Canon Bubble Jet portable printer using a GDT driver and a serial-to-parallel converter. You can get the same printer, without the little Apple logo, for much less money, as you'll see.

The Canon **BubbleJet BJ10ex,** the **Canon BJ-5,** the Star Micronics **StarJet SJ-48,** and the **Brother HJ-100i** are essentially the same inkjet printer sold under different names and model numbers. They're also the same printer as the 360-dpi Apple Portable StyleWriter, except they're PC-only. Add a GDT PowerPrint package, and they become well-priced Mac-compatibles. At less than five pounds, they fold up into notebook size (about 12 inches by 8½ inches by 2 inches), use plain paper, and are unusually quiet (about 45 dB). All of these Canon-based portable printers list for $500 and commonly sell for a lot less (often for less than $200). Add about $50 if you want the optional rechargeable battery.

Another popular inkjet portable printer is the Hewlett-Packard **DeskWriter 310**. Unfortunately it is more expensive than the above portable inkjets (list $380, battery not included), though smaller (12 inches by 5¾ inches by 2½ inches). You can upgrade it to print in color, however. (Unfortunately, like the DeskWriter C it will only print composite blacks in color mode.)

Thermal-fusion portables (RS). The $400 **Citizen Notebook Printer II** uses *thermal fusion*, bonding a waxy ink to the paper. The waxy ink doesn't spread on the page like that of inkjets, giving its 360 dpi an impressive laserlike crispness (if you use the higher-quality ribbon).

The $1,000 Mannesmann Tally **MobileWriterPS** is decidedly more expensive and less portable than the rest, but it provides Adobe PostScript, six-page-per-minute printing, and print quality indistinguishable from a desktop laser printer. At eight pounds it's about the same size and shape as a PowerBook, has a built-in 80-sheet paper feeder, and its battery and one ribbon are good for about 150 pages. This printer can double as both your desktop business printer and a portable. At $15 per ribbon, though, you're paying about ten cents per page, compared to two cents per page or less for toner-based laser printers. Nor does it print as well as laser printers on cheaper bond paper.

Using Service Bureaus

When you need better-quality printing than you're equipped to handle, you can often get the job done at a service bureau. Most service bureaus offer laser printing, dye-sub, and large-format color printing as well as high-resolution (1,200 to 3,600 dpi) imagesetter output to film or paper. Some offer do-it-yourself access to their equipment, while others ask you to drop off your files for processing.

Before You Deliver Your Files (BW)

Getting files printed at a service bureau isn't quite as casual as dropping off your laundry. You've got to make sure that the service bureau has the files it needs, that it has the fonts and software you need, and that everyone is clear on what to expect. Here are some guidelines and tips.

Setting up your files. When you deliver your files to a service bureau, make sure to include not only the document files, but also any graphics files included in the documents.

Fonts and software. Services bureaus usually have the major applications installed—PageMaker, QuarkXPress, Photoshop, and so on—with which to load and print your documents. The service bureau also needs to have the fonts you used in your document. The assumption is, of course, that they, too, own those fonts. If they don't, you're faced with a moral dilemma. You'd be violating your license agreement to copy a font for your service bureau to use, but circumstances often force people to do it.

Always let the service know the exact font name, version number, and vendor of the fonts you've used. It's a good idea to include a suitcase of the screen fonts—critical if you're using any custom kerning-pair adjustments.

If a service bureau you want to use doesn't have the fonts and software you need, there is a way around it: Print your file to disk as described below.

Filling out the form. Unless you're renting the equipment by the hour and doing the output yourself, most service bureaus require you to fill out a form that describes the files you are supplying and the type of output you want.

If you're asking for film, confirm how your print shop wants it—film positive or negative, right-reading emulsion up or down—and make sure the service bureau knows what that means.

And one more thing: If a service bureau has more than one type of laser printer and/or imagesetter, make sure you know the rate for the one you want to use. Rates may be higher for higher-resolution imagesetting, film, complex (long-running) jobs, and faster turnaround, among other things. So ask, don't presume.

Printing to PostScript Files (SA/JK/Larry Pina/AN/BW)

You can turn any Mac document into a PostScript text file that can then be printed on any PostScript device without using the application that originally created the document. Since the PostScript file can include font, graphic, and image file data, this process saves you from having to provide all those files separately—a nice tidy package, though possibly a huge one.

Generating a PostScript file in version 7.0 or later of the LaserWriter driver is easy. Just open the document and choose Print from the File menu. In the Print dialog box, click the PostScript File button (the File button in the Destination options for version 8.0 of the Apple and Adobe drivers). The Print button becomes a Save button. Click on it and you'll get a dialog box that asks you where you want to put the file and what you want to call it.

Version 8 of the Apple and Adobe drivers give you additional options:

- You can choose to capture the job as a PostScript print job or as an EPS file with standard bit-mapped, scalable PICT, or no preview image.
- You can select between PostScript Level 1 or Level 2 compatibility.
- You can elect to include or not include fonts, or to simply exclude the basic 13 fonts built into most PostScript printers.
- You can choose between ASCII and the more compact binary-encoded PostScript formats.

With earlier versions of the LaserWriter driver, there was no PostScript File button to click; instead, you had to click the OK button and press ⌘P within about a second. (If you didn't press ⌘P fast enough, the document would print rather than be saved as a PostScript file.)

The PostScript file created by either of these methods can be opened (and altered, if you're a PostScript programmer) in any word processor. To print it, you don't open it and then choose Print; that will just give you a printout of all the PostScript commands in the file. Instead, you *download* the PostScript file to the printer the same way you do fonts, with the LaserWriter Font Utility or a similar program.

Service Bureau Tips

HOT TIP

Proof your pages on a laser printer before getting high-resolution output (BW). Remember, you're spending $7 to $15 or more for each page of image-set paper or film. It's always worth it to get a laser proof, and check it carefully, before you send your files for final output.

Set up the page for PostScript output (BW). On your own machine, open the Chooser and select the LaserWriter icon (or whatever printer driver icon corresponds to the laser printer you'll use). Select Page Setup from the File menu, make any changes you want (or no changes), and click OK. Now go through your document to make sure it still looks right. Remember that different printers use different margins from the LaserWriter, and there are other incompatibilities, so you may need to make some changes.

Lock your floppies (BW). Service bureaus are notorious sources of viruses. Make sure your disks are locked when you deliver them to avoid any accidental contamination.

Optimize the document (David Van Ness/JK/AN/Dale Coleman). To keep the file size down, delete any extraneous art from the pasteboard margins. Similarly, check illustrations for undefined colors or unnecessary placed art by choosing the Select All command, Shift-clicking to deselect everything you recognize and then investigating any remaining objects.

Ask for help with trapping (David Van Ness/JK/AN/Dale Coleman/DD). If your job has color separations, find out from the company that's going to print the job how much color *trapping* it needs (that's making darker colors overprint lighter colors by a certain distance, to avoid unsightly gaps where they meet). It sounds easy, but it's really complicated; if you don't know what you're doing, ask for help.

Avoid the Imagesetter RIP killers (BW). PostScript imagesetters have a far tougher job than laser printers given their higher resolution, and consequently they work differently inside. What's hard for a PostScript printer to swallow will likely choke an imagesetter's raster image processor. Be kind, in the following ways:

- Don't embed one EPS file within another if you can avoid it, especially when there's a font specified within. The font spec can get lost or the resulting PostScript code may get too convoluted to process.
- Don't drastically scale down a large scanned image to obtain a thumbnail size. Resample the image to the proper pixel resolution.
- Beware of complex PICT graphics. PICT is a notoriously ambiguous file format and its PostScript processing has caused many tears.
- Avoid long paths and excessively large, complex masks. The calculations involved may simply overwhelm the processor. Break complex curves into simpler ones and/or remove unnecessary control points. Use several simpler masks instead of one complex one.

- Avoid scaling and rotating complex EPS graphics in your page layout program. Doing so can lengthen print time or choke the imagesetter processor. Do the required scaling or rotating in your graphics program, and then reimport it into your layout.

Getting negative, right-reading film (AN/SA/JK). If you need to adjust a PostScript printout to conform to a print shop's requirement of right-reading film with emulsion up, or down, and so on, clicking on the Options button in the Print dialog box gives you several relevant choices. (A dog of indeterminate breed—with a very thick tail—demonstrates the effect of each option as you select it, though a lowercase *a* does it on Adobe's PSPrinter driver.) For example, you can flip the entire image on the page vertically or horizontally, and also "invert" a printout, changing whites to blacks and blacks to whites to create a negative image.

Telecommunications

TELECOMMUNICATIONS—the transfer of information between computers over telephone lines—take you and your Mac beyond the confines of your desktop and your office. Just plug in a modem, fire up some communications software, and you're headed onto the information superhighway.

The traffic regulations and road signs may be confusing at first, but with a little patience you'll be on your way. Whatever your destination—be it a colleague's computer or the global Internet, a local bulletin board or a national on-line service, or maybe just the office network—odds are you'll soon find your Mac and modem an indispensable way to keep in touch. Before long you could be chatting familiarly with electronic friends you've never seen, trading messages and files with associates around the world, getting answers to your computer questions (and maybe even offering a few tips to others), and decking out your Mac with the latest free and shareware software.

Contributors

Henry Norr (HN) is the chapter editor.

Randy B. Singer (RS) is an ardent telecommunicator. You can find him on America Online as RBS, on AppleLink as Law.Singer, on Planet-BMUG as Randy Singer, on eWorld as RandySing and on the Internet as RBS@AOL.com. He often answers technical questions in the MacBible/Peachpit Press forum on America Online.

Arthur Naiman (AN) and **Sharon Zardetto Aker (SA)** edited earlier versions of the *Mac Bible,* from which parts of this chapter were taken.

Contents

All About Modems

To telecommunicate, you need a *modem* ("MOE-dem"), a small piece of hardware that lets you hook up your computer to a phone line and transmit and receive data. The name is short for *mo*dulator-*dem*odulator. On the sending end, a modem translates (modulates) digital information from your computer into sounds, which then travel over telephone wires; the modem on the receiving end translates (demodulates) the sounds back into digital data.

Modems can be either external or internal (installed in expansion slots inside your Mac). Internal modems are the norm among PowerBook users because that way you don't have to carry around another device when you're on the road. They are common on PCs too, but on desktop Macs they are extremely rare. Unless you have some special space constraints, go with the crowd. (There's more on buying modems below.)

A modem won't do anything until it receives instructions from software running on your Mac. Virtually all modern modems are *Hayes-compatible*. That means they are built to obey the *Hayes command set*, a modem-control language originally developed by Hayes Microcomputer Products, one of the pioneering manufacturers of modems for microcomputers. (It's also called the *AT command set*, since Hayes used AT at the beginning of each command as a signal to the modem to pay ATtention.)

The Killer Vs (HN)

The Hayes commands are the standard for how computers talk to modems, but we also need standards for how modems talk to each other. For that reason the manufacturers of modems and the chip sets they use spend vast amounts of time hashing out standards, both among themselves and through an international organization now called the *ITU-T* or *ITU-TSS*, for International Telecommunications Union-Telecommunications Standards Sector. (You may still see this body referred to as *CCITT*, after its old French name, which was translated as the Consultative Committee International Telegraph and Telephone.

This group has addressed three main aspects of telecommunications: transmission speed (measured in bits per second), error checking, and data compression. Its standards are identified by a *V.* followed by a number (and sometimes the word *bis* or *ter*, which are French for "second" and "third"). Here's what they mean, and why you do (or don't) need to pay attention to them.

Speed. The speed at which modems transfer data is measured in *bits per second* or *bps*, as in "Don't buy a modem that doesn't do at least 9,600 bps." You'll often hear the word *baud* used instead of bps, as in "2,400-baud modems are just too slow," even though that usage is technically incorrect—*baud* properly refers to a related, but different, aspect of modem performance.

The major standards regulating data and fax modem communications at different speeds are listed in the table at right.

Telecommunications Standards (JK/RS/HN)

Standard	Speed in bps
V.22bis	2,400
V.32	9,600
V.32bis	14,400
V.32terbo*	19,200
V.34, V.Fast*, or V.FC*	28,800
V.17	14,400 fax
V.29	9,600 fax

*Unofficial interim standards.

THINGS TO COME

By the time you read this, V.34 (also known by its nickname, *V.Fast*) should be an official, approved standard, but at this writing it is not; the companies involved have been haggling for more than two years about the final details. Since customers always want better performance, two groups of modem makers have settled on unofficial interim standards for higher speeds while they wait for the final ITU-T documents.

One of these semistandards, *V.32terbo*, allows communications at up to 19,200 bps—provided that both sender and receiver are V.32terbo devices, because, like other modems, they can't communicate faster than the highest common denominator. Companies supporting V.32terbo include AT&T, Global Village Communications, and Apple (in its Express Modem II for the PowerBook 500 series).

A rival industry faction, including Hayes and several other leading modem makers, has rallied around a different quasi-standard. This one, known as *V.FastClass* or *V.FC* because it's based on the working draft of the V.34 or V.Fast

Figuring Actual Transfer Rates (HN)

When you are shopping for a modem, it's important to pay attention to the speeds and standards supported by the various models—a 14,400-bps modem really is a lot faster than a 9,600-bps model. But many other factors influence the transfer rates, or throughput, you'll experience in real-life telecommunications.

A 2,400-bps modem, for example, can transfer 300 bytes per second—in theory. But there is always extra overhead involved in telecommunications—setup negotiations between the two modems, special *stop bits* that sometimes mark the beginning and end of bytes of data, and occasional retries when some data is not received properly. All of this reduces real data-transfer rates. As a very rough rule of thumb, assuming no data compression and normal amounts of line noise, divide the bps rate by 10 to approximate the actual transfer rate in bytes or characters per second. (Remember that in the binary system computers use, it takes eight bits, or one byte, to represent a character.)

In other words, two 2,400-bps modems will typically transfer about 240 bytes per second, or around 14K per minute; with 14,400-bps modems, you can expect to average 1,400–1,500 bytes or characters per second (84K–90K per minute).

Remember, though, your mileage may vary. A noisy line or bad connection can drastically reduce your throughput. And if you download a file from a BBS or on-line service at a time of day when the system is crowded, expect lower-than-optimal transfer rates even if the connection is clean, because the computer at the other end of the line may sometimes leave your modem sitting idle while it services other users.

On the other hand, you can boost effective throughput to significantly higher levels by using data compression: If you can compress a 1-meg file down to, say, 500K, you can send it over the phone in half the time. (see "Data Compression," on the next page).

specification, supports speeds up to 28,800 bps. Most makers of these modems have promised buyers that if a hardware or software upgrade is necessary to ensure compatibility with the final V.34 specification, they'll offer it free or at nominal cost.

V.32terbo modems will generally *not* be upgradable to V.34.

Error correction. Today's modems are amazingly accurate, but they do make mistakes. (How would you like to try to interpret 14,400 sounds a second that have been transmitted over a noisy copper wire?) That's why they need *error detection* and *error correction*—ways to verify that the receiver received what the sender sent and to request a retry if that didn't happen. File-transfer protocols (described below) incorporate their own software-based error checking, but with high-speed devices it makes sense to have hardware help carry the burden.

The current error-correction standard, called *V.42*, incorporates several technologies, including several parts of the *Microcom Network Protocol (MNP) Levels 2, 3, and 4*, a scheme originally developed by modem-maker Microcom. Most modems that don't support V.42 *do* support MNP 2, 3, and 4, since Microcom has put them into the public domain.

An additional error-correction technique not included in V.42 is Microcom's MNP Level 10. It's especially designed for adverse conditions, such as exceptionally noisy lines and cellular connections. In normal home or office use, it shouldn't be necessary, but look for it if you are shopping for a cellular modem to connect to your PowerBook.

Data compression. To the extent that data can be compressed before transmission, you can get more effective *throughput*—in other words, send and receive your files faster—with any modem, whatever its transmission speed. That's why most Mac files in on-line libraries are compressed with software like Aladdin's StuffIt or the shareware Compact Pro (see Chapter 13). The idea behind hardware compression is similar, but it's simpler because it requires no effort on the part of either sender or receiver—the modems should compress and decompress the data automatically.

But hardware compression only works if both devices are using the same technology, so modem vendors have agreed on a standard—although, in an apparent effort to maximize confusion as well as throughput, the CCITT named the standard *V.42bis* even though it's quite distinct from the V.42 error-correction protocol. Exactly how effective it is depends on many factors, including the nature of your data, but V.42bis generally seems to increase throughput by 50 to 100 percent. (And most V.42bis modems are smart enough not to waste time trying to compress data you've already compressed with a utility.) Microcom's alternative compression scheme, *MNP Level 5*, is less efficient, and it apparently wastes time trying to squeeze a few extra bytes out of data that is already compressed.

Vendors regularly imply that compression is much more efficient than it really is. For V.42bis, for example, they generally assume a 4:1 compression ratio. In ads for 2,400-bps (V.22bis) modems with V.42bis support, for example, you'll often see claims of "throughput up to 9,600 bps" (or some such), while 14,400-bps modems with compression are supposed to transfer up to 57,600 bps.

Buyer beware: These claims may not be literally false, but they are bogus because they are based on ideal conditions—you'll probably never achieve those levels of throughput, and certainly not on a regular basis. In particular, don't mistake a V.22bis modem with compression for a real V.32 modem, no matter how often the number 9,600 appears in the ad.

How Much Speed Do You Need? (HN/RS)

Simply put, telecommunicating is slow. In fact, it requires more waiting than most anything else most of us do with our Macs. Worst of all, when you log onto a commercial on-line service or dial a long-distance number, you have to pay to wait!

That's why there's no such thing as a modem that's too fast—provided that you can use and afford the speed. For most users, it doesn't make sense to be too far out on the cutting edge in performance, because the very fastest modems command a premium price, and odds are that most of the colleagues and services you connect to don't have modems that match. (And some on-line services charge extra for their highest speeds, so even if they can keep up with your modem you might not be getting as big a bargain as you thought.)

But once a new modem technology has been available for a year or two, prices for it typically plummet. At the same time, on-line services add reasonably priced support for the higher speed, and the faster modems are likely to start showing up at other organizations you do business with. At that point it's foolish not to make the leap to the new performance plateau.

That's the stage we have reached with V.32bis—14,400 bps—fax modems in 1994. It simply doesn't pay to buy anything less; slower modems may still be a bit cheaper, but the savings are small. If you can't afford a V.32bis modem now, wait until you can, or borrow against the money you'll save in on-line time. On the other hand, at this writing, V.32terbo and V.FastClass modems still command a premium and aren't yet widely supported; they probably don't make sense unless you regularly send large files to someone else who's prepared to buy a similar modem.

But keep an eye on V.34 modem prices—modems based on the draft versions of the standard are already sliding down the same price curve V.32bis devices followed.

Fax Modems

(Steven Schwartz/JK/HN)

More and more modems at lower and lower prices come with *fax* capability. They enable you to send memos, press releases, or anything else you create with any application on the Mac, to any fax machine without first printing it on paper. Instead of printing to a printer, you "print" to the fax modem and enter the phone number of the fax machine you are sending to; the fax modem software converts your document to an image in fax format and sends it over the phone line.

Some low-end fax modems are "send-only" when it comes to faxing—though they can send and receive computer data, they can't handle incoming faxes. But most fax modems nowadays can receive as well as send. As long as your Mac and modem are on (and the fax-modem software is installed and set to auto-answer), receiving a fax is automatic; incoming faxes are stored on disk, and software lets you know when they arrive.

Fax software usually comes in at least three parts: a Chooser driver for sending faxes; an extension or control panel for receiving them; and an application for viewing faxes you receive, maintaining a phone directory, setting your preferences, and so on.

Fax modems vary in the speed at which they send and receive faxes, and these speeds don't necessarily match the same modem's data-transfer speed. Don't buy a fax modem that doesn't support fax speeds of at least 9,600 bps, the rate supported by most stand-alone fax machines. Many of the latest fax modems support the *V.17* protocol, which allows fax speeds of 14,400 bps. This won't do you any good if you are communicating with a standard fax machine, but it will if you are communicating with another V.17 fax modem.

Fax Modem vs. Fax Machine (RS/HN)

In terms of sending faxes, fax modems can be fabulously convenient, at least if you create most of what you want to send on the Mac. They're cheaper to buy than regular fax machines (especially if you are buying a high-speed modem anyway—nowadays there's almost no premium for faxing capabilities). They save paper, since you don't have to print a copy just to put in the fax machine. And if you're running Adobe Type Manager or TrueType on your Mac, your documents will look much crisper and cleaner than standard faxes (causing the receiver to wonder how you did it!). The only downside, with respect to sending, is that you can't easily send material you didn't create on the Mac. (You need a scanner to get other info into your Mac first.)

For receiving faxes, however, the picture is much more complicated. On the plus side, there is still the cost savings. You can save paper by reading some faxes on screen, and when you do print, if you have a laser or inkjet printer, you get much better quality than from most fax machines. And if the fax was sent to you in high-resolution mode and you have optical-character-recognition (OCR) software (see Chapter 8), you can convert the contents into text that you can edit in your word processor.

The disadvantages of fax modems for receiving, though, are significant. Your computer has to be on to receive faxes. Processing a fax in the background strains the capabilities of all but the fastest Macs—you might notice your machine getting painfully sluggish while receiving. Received faxes take up a lot of room on your hard disk, and they are much harder to read on the Mac's screen than as hard copy from a fax machine; fax machines, after all, print at 200 dpi, compared with the Mac screen's 72 dpi. Besides, scrolling through a document is slower and more cumbersome than flipping through actual pages. Sure, you can print it out, but that ends up taking much more time and effort than just grabbing the incoming copy off a regular fax machine. (Though the new 3.0 version of FAXstf, with it's optional AutoPak, can be set to automatically print out all incoming faxes, just like a regular fax machine.)

The ideal arrangement, of course, is to have a fax modem for outgoing messages created on your Mac and a regular fax machine for incoming messages or other outgoing items. And then, of course, you'll want a scanner and OCR software in case you want to convert anything incoming to digital text....

Reliability, Compatibility, and Support (HN)

Specs and standards don't tell you everything about a modem—between two units with seemingly identical features, subtle differences, especially in their ROMs, can make the difference between smooth sailing and constant hassles. Some modems work fine with others of the same brand and with many other brands but have major problems with certain other manufacturers' units.

Unfortunately, it's not easy to get a handle on such issues; magazine reviews usually aren't much help. Your best bet is talk to others who are already using the model in question. Ask around among friends or at a user group, or go on-line: Most major modem makers have their own BBS (bulletin board service) and/or a customer-support forum on CompuServe, America Online, or other service. *[Of course, if you don't have a modem yet, it's hard to get on-line to find out which one to buy.—RS]* Scanning such forums provides invaluable insight—both in terms of the problems users may be reporting and the attitude the company's representatives display. Tech support is important—odds are you'll need it sooner or later. An on-line forum with knowledgeable reps providing prompt and friendly

A Fax Modem That's Also an Answering Machine?! (RS)

Yep, it's true. Many modems can now answer your phone like an answering machine and store your messages on your hard disk; some even provide comprehensive voice-mail capabilities comparable to an expensive business voice-mail system. Modems that feature various levels of this capability are the **LineLink 14.4** from MacWarehouse ($100 for the modem, plus $40 for the voice upgrade), the **Prometheus Ultima Home Office** ($310), the **SupraFAXModem V.32bis** ($250, plus $100 for ROM and software upgrade), various models from ZyXEL, and my favorite, **WaterMark Message Central** from High Tide Software, a $500 package that includes a modem, cables, and software.

The least expensive of these products act just like a simple answering machine. Some provide individual mailboxes (a personal message area for each member of your household or business.) The High Tide product is at the high end and has voice-mail capabilities similar to those of other commercial products costing three times as much. WaterMark Message Central is truly Mac-like in its operation and spectacular! Along with impressive voice-recording-quality and security features, it allows an unlimited number of mailboxes and an unlimited number of choices in the outgoing message tree (i.e., you can give a caller the choice to push, for example, 1 for sales, 2 for tech support, etc., and then can give an unlimited number of choices for numbers to push on the next level, and the next, that they get to). This nesting capability is what makes the High Tide product so special. It allows the user to set up this system to route any call correctly. It can allow a business of almost any size to free its receptionists from phone-answering duties.

[Sounds like voice-mail hell to me. Don't get carried away, or you'll free up your staff but lose your customers!—HN] [Actually, the product is so sophisticated that it can eliminate voice-mail hell. Each caller can create his or her own password-protected outgoing mailbox from which to pick up messages.—RS]

support is both a valuable resource in its own right and a telling sign about the company's culture; if it doesn't offer on-line support, or messages go unanswered for days, I'd stay away.

And don't forget to find out in advance about the vendor's return and warranty policy.

Tester's Choice (RS)

Listed below are what I consider the best three modems currently available for use with the Macintosh, rated 1-2-3, along with some pros and cons for each. Price, as well as performance, was definitely a consideration in choosing these modems. They are all external fax modems and come with a hardware handshaking cable. (For more on handshaking cables, see "Flow Control" under "Setting Up the Connection," below.)

Keep in mind that prices—both for these modems and their competition—are likely to have declined since this was written, and new models supporting the final V.34 standard should be appearing. These recommendations are not cast in stone.

#1. AT&T Paradyne DataPort 14.4. This modem (the Macintosh version is model #3710-A1-202) can be purchased directly from AT&T for $240, but you may be able to find it for less. It comes with Smith Micro Software's QuickLink II software for data and fax. The software is junk, in my opinion, but the modem is quickly approaching legendary status among BBS operators. It will happily connect with any other brand of modem, and it seems to be impervious to line noise (a big problem with many high-speed modems). Other features include a proprietary technology for handling problems associated with connections over cellular phones, a toll-free number for technical assistance, and a lifetime warranty!

GOOD FEATURE

#2. U.S. Robotics Sportster 14.4/Mac & Fax. The **Sportster** comes with a stripped-down version of Software Ventures' MicroPhone and STF Technologies' FAXstf software for fax transmissions. USR recently dropped the suggested retail price of this modem to $330, and I've seen it selling for as little as $150—an incredible deal. The construction looks cheap, but I have yet to hear

BARGAIN

of an owner having a reliability problem—and it performs better than many modems costing twice as much.

#3. Global Village Communications' TelePort Gold. Global Village's modems come with ZTerm (with the usual shareware fee waived) and Global Village's own fax software, which includes optical character recognition. Suggested retail price at this writing is $400, but I've seen it selling for $260. This modem is the closest thing there is to a plug-and-play high-speed modem for the Macintosh. The fax software may be the best in the industry, and ZTerm, though not flashy, is solid. If you plan on heavy faxing, the quality of Global Village's software may make this modem almost as good as AT&T's.

GOOD FEATURE

Penny Wise?

Here are some other modems that illustrate both the benefits and the risks in choosing economy modems.

SupraFAXModem V.32bis (Steven Schwartz/RS). When the **SupraFAXModem V.32bis** hit the market a couple of years ago, it was one of the first of a new generation of high-speed modems available at a reasonable price (now $250, including cable and software). It offered 14,400-bps performance for fax as well as data; support for the V.42, V.42bis, and MNP 5 protocols; a unique alphanumeric LED status panel; a stripped-down version of MicroPhone and FAXstf; and an answering-machine option via a $100 ROM and software upgrade.

This modem sold in huge numbers, and many buyers loved it. But a significant number of users found that line noise often made it hang up suddenly when trying to connect, or caused it to connect at less than full speed. It also didn't like to connect to certain brands of fax machines or with other Supra modems. Supra came out with several ROM upgrades to try to cure the problems; they're available from the company for $20, and upgrading is definitely a good idea if you've got an older unit. (To find out what version of the ROMs you have, open your telecommunications program and, when not connected to a service, type *ATI* and hit [Return].)

Supra has since come out with a less-expensive version of its V.32bis modem, called the **SupraFaxModem 144LC.** At a list price of $190 it is currently one of the better buys in the high-speed modem market. Unlike its more expensive sibling, the LC has just the usual indicator lights on the front panel instead of an alphanumeric readout.

Technology Concepts LineLink 14.4 (RS). The **LineLink 14.4** is a V.32bis 14,400-bps fax modem priced at only $100 from the mail-order house MacWarehouse. Fax software is an additional $30, but it's the excellent MaxFax from Prometheus; for $40 you can get both MaxFax and voice capabilities! A poorly kept secret is that this modem is made for MacWarehouse by Prometheus, a well-known and respected company.

The modem works well when set up properly, but the case, speaker, and on/off switch are of cheap construction. In addition, the manual is even poorer than most. Though the optional MaxFax software is excellent for faxing, the bundled data software, MacKnowledge, is too complicated for most users.

This is not a modem that I would trust for use in a business environment, but at $100 it might be a reasonable gamble for home use. Personally, I would spend the extra money for a USR Sportster. I advise that you buy only with a gold credit card, which will double the length of the warranty.

Communications Software (HN)

As with everything else you do on the Mac, good telecommunications hardware won't get you far without matching software. The modem determines your maximum throughput, but even that depends on the software to configure it. And in 101 other ways, software determines how easy and convenient it is to telecommunicate. A program with clear configuration screens, a comprehensible menu structure and graphical interface, support for the leading file-transfer protocols, a built-in address book, and an easy way to automate frequently repeated operations can make the whole process fast and fun; conversely, cumbersome software can make all communications a drag.

General-Purpose Packages

Most communications programs are general-purpose, which means that they can communicate with most other software and on-line services; in contrast, some services, such as America Online and eWorld (both described below), require and provide their own service-specific software. General-purpose programs are also called *terminal emulators* because the first such programs were developed to dial in to mainframes or minicomputers, and they worked by fooling these hosts in to thinking the computer calling in was just another terminal of the sort normally attached to such systems.

Mac telecommunicators can now choose among a number of powerful and polished general-purpose communications packages. For most purposes any of them will do the job, but here are some considerations to bear in mind:

- If you use the same services at all regularly, scripting can save you a lot of time and hassle, because a script can automatically choose the proper settings, dial the call, go through the log-in procedure, and take you to your favorite areas.
- If you plan to download files, look for a software package that supports the fastest protocol in use on the systems you call: For most local BBSes, you'll want to be able to use ZTerm, but if you call CompuServe the most, don't worry about ZTerm—CompuServe doesn't use it. Look instead for support of CompuServe's own B+ protocol.
- If you'll need to log into a host computer at work or school, check to make sure the software you buy provides the terminal emulations you need. (That's ordinarily not a problem, but some systems do require unusual emulations.)
- If you plan to get into the Internet, you'll want to smooth your way on the information superhighway with a package that includes special networking software and graphical tools specifically for Internet. (Right now MicroPhone Pro is the only one of the programs listed below that includes Internet software, but others are likely to follow suit.) Of course, if you expect to spend a lot of time surfing the Internet, you should consider a package designed specifically for that purpose—see the section on "Internet Applications" and the box "Easier Ways In" later in this chapter.

The Communications Toolbox (HN)

If you look into a lot of recent Mac communications programs, you may notice that the configuration dialog boxes in many of them look suspiciously similar. Is this evidence that developers are simply copying each other's look and feel?

Not exactly. What you are seeing are dialogs created with the help of the *Macintosh Communications Toolbox* (a.k.a. the *Comm Toolbox,* or *CTB*), a piece of Apple system software that was introduced as an add-on to System 6 and then rolled into System 7. It provides a uniform framework for communications (including nicely designed dialog boxes) and a set of basic communications tools, all of which are available to any application that supports the toolbox. The goal was to make it easier for developers to add communications capabilities to their software, enable multiple applications to share the same tools, and spare users from having to confront a new interface in each program. *[The unfortunate reality is that if a program utilizes the CTB, it often has inferior performance to one that does not.—RS] [Actually, every one of the programs listed below, except ZTerm and White Knight, make some use of the CTB, and White Knight will soon join the crowd. It's true that the CTB by itself provides only basic capabilities, so developers still have to do their own work to deliver more sophisticated features. It's also true that Apple is planning a major overhaul of the whole way the Mac operating system handles communications and networking; eventually that will make the CTB obsolete.—HN]*

In addition to standard dialog boxes, the Comm Toolbox defines three standard types of tools:

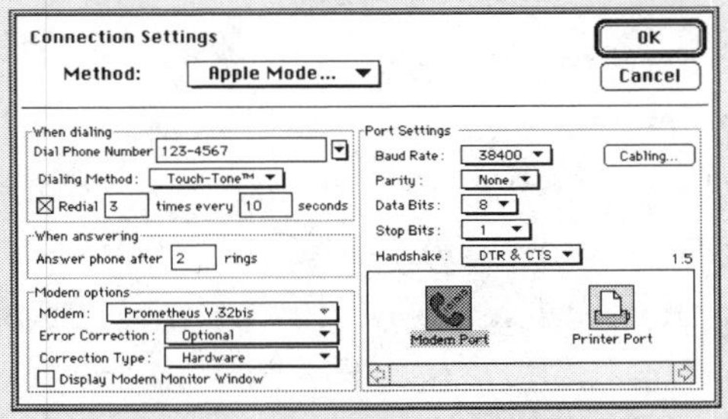

- *Connection tools,* which define how the Mac is to be connected to another computer. In addition to the Apple Modem Tool, there's a Serial Tool for direct connections, a Telnet tool for TCP/IP connections, and several other tools for different kinds of network connections.
- *Terminal tools,* which define the types of terminals that communications programs can emulate—TTY, VT102, or VT320, for example.
- *Transfer tools,* which implement file-transfer protocols such as Xmodem or Zmodem.

Most Macintosh communications programs now incorporate Apple's Communications Toolbox (CTB). Although different programs implement the CTB interface differently, most have settings screens that look more or less like this one, taken from ClarisWorks' communications module.

Under System 7 these tools get installed in the Extensions folder, and you have access to them from any Communications Toolbox–based application. If, for example, you install Aladdin's SITcomm program, you'll have a Zmodem tool that's also available for use in, say, ClarisWorks' communications module, even though that program did not come with Zmodem support.

Here are capsule descriptions of several of the most notable programs:

MicroPhone Pro (HN). Software Ventures now offers several versions of its **MicroPhone** package, with varying feature sets and prices to match. The top-of-the-line **Pro** package, priced at $300, is the most versatile and feature-filled of all the Mac communications programs; some have begun to deride it as a bloated hodgepodge. In addition to the feature that made it famous—a powerful but easy-to-use script editor—it now offers support for a half-dozen terminal types and all major file-transfer protocols (including Zmodem, CompuServeB+, and Kermit, described in the box on page 881). It also includes software for setting up your own dial-in BBS, as well as custom graphical front ends to CompuServe, GEnie, and MCI Mail. For Internet users, the box includes Apple's essential MacTCP and MacSLIP, a driver that makes it possible to establish a full TCP/IP connection over a phone line, plus Internet news and mail readers, a Telnet tool, and the Fetch file-transfer application. (For more on BBSes, on-line services, and the Internet, read on.) Software Ventures once promised to add fax software; for now it continues to bundle FAXstf.

White Knight (HN). The FreeSoft Co.'s $140 **White Knight** (previously Red Ryder) once reigned supreme as the most powerful of Mac telecommunications packages, with an extensive scripting system—really a programming language—built-in. But the program has stagnated in recent years: It's one of the few that (at least as of this writing) provides no support for the Mac Communications Toolbox (see the box on the previous page), and its manuals and menus remain cluttered and confusing. It supports Zmodem transfers but offers no Internet tools. Many veteran experts continue to rely on it, but it's hard to see what would attract new customers.

BAD FEATURE

Smartcom II (HN). Another favorite with many Mac old-timers is Hayes's **Smartcom II** ($150). It's lean and fast but provides a wide range of scripting and protocol options and a customizable, button-based graphical interface. The latest release integrates Apple's PowerTalk electronic-mail system, so you can mail material clipped from an on-line session straight to colleagues on your local network or anywhere else PowerTalk can reach. The new version also provides full support for Hayes's blazingly fast V.FastClass modems.

GOOD FEATURE

SITcomm (HN/RS). The $120 **SITcomm** comes from Aladdin Systems, developer of the StuffIt series of data-compression utilities, and the connection is easy to see: Not only does the first part of the program's name come from the file-name extension commonly used to indicate a StuffIt archive, but automatic file compression and decompression is built-in. The program makes it easy to log on to a variety of services, and it comes with its own Zmodem tool, but the only other scripting capability it offers is by way of AppleScript—a system that's too complicated for most nonprogrammers. (Besides, neither AppleScript nor documentation for scripting is included in the package.)

CrossTalk (HN). Long among the best-selling communications packages in the IBM PC world, **CrossTalk** ($195) from Digital Communications Associates (DCA) finally reached the Mac in 1993. Its ancestry might make some suspect a PC port lacking the graphical character and elegance Mac users expect, but that's not the case. The Mac version makes extensive use of Apple's Communications Toolbox (DCA developed its own Zmodem tool, as well as terminal tools for several unusual terminal types). Scripts developed with the program's sophisticated scripting language can be launched by clicking on icons, buttons, or other objects placed in custom QuickPads (floating palettes); predefined QuickPads for a dozen on-line services, including the Dialog information service and the Official Airline Guide, are included. Best of all, users in organizations that have both Macs and Windows PCs can use the very same scripts and QuickPads on both platforms.

MAC BIBLE DISK

ZTerm (RS). The shareware program **ZTerm** has become a de facto standard, appealing not only to cash-strapped Mac telecommunicators but also to everyone who appreciates lean, focused, and inexpensive software. It uses Zmodem, supports all baud rates, includes a basic scripting facility, and measures only about 250K—compared with over 1 meg for a basic MicroPhone II setup! You won't find many bells and whistles you don't need, but it does some things better than even the most expensive communications programs—for example, it's excellent at handling color ANSI graphics and PC-based bulletin boards, which competitors have only recently begun to figure out. With a registration fee of $30, ZTerm is a bargain, and it may be all you ever need, or want, in a communications program.

Fax Alternatives (RS/HN)

The best fax software available today comes only with certain vendors' modems. The very best is Global Village's, which is included with the company's TelePort and PowerPort modems. MaxFax, which comes with Prometheus fax modems, is also excellent, though it lacks an OCR option.

If you have a different modem, neither of these packages will work with it, but that doesn't mean you're stuck with the software that came with your own modem: At least two vendors market fax software that works with most fax modems on the market today.

The best, and most popular, of these is **FAXstf 3,** which STF Technologies sells for $60. (An older and less elegant version of FAXstf comes bundled with many modems). FAXstf includes many components, and sometimes it's hard to remember which does what, but perhaps that's the price of having so many features. In addition to the normal fax features, FAXstf lets you add new phone-book entries on the fly and comes with a DA you can use to quickly compose short faxes. A $90 add-on package, previously called FaxManager Plus but now rechristened **STF AutoPak,** provides optical character recognition, automatic printing, and other advanced features that the basic version lacks.

The other contender is **Delrina Fax Pro**, a new Mac package from the leader in the Windows fax-software market. Fax Pro costs $130, but it includes OCR. Like FAXstf, Fax Pro provides an wide variety of features, including a DA for faxing quick notes, automatic retransmission of pages that did not get through, and extensive logging and fax-management options. On the other hand, it's slower than FAXstf, the graphics it generates are not as good, and as a relatively new Mac program it's still a little rough around the edges.

Users of both products have reported a number of bugs and glitches. But Delrina provides excellent support. (The day after I requested an update to Version 1.5 on CompuServe, it arrived free of charge on my doorstep.) The same can't be said of STF's customer support—many users report receiving no response to repeated toll calls seeking assistance.

Setting Up the Connection (HN/RS)

Because there are multiple standards in telecommunications, any versatile communications program has to offer an array of configuration choices—most telecommunications programs need at least minimal fiddling with their settings to get everything working correctly. (That's what makes telecommunications one of the most difficult tasks on a computer to master.) To make matters worse, most manuals that come with modems and telecom software are poor.

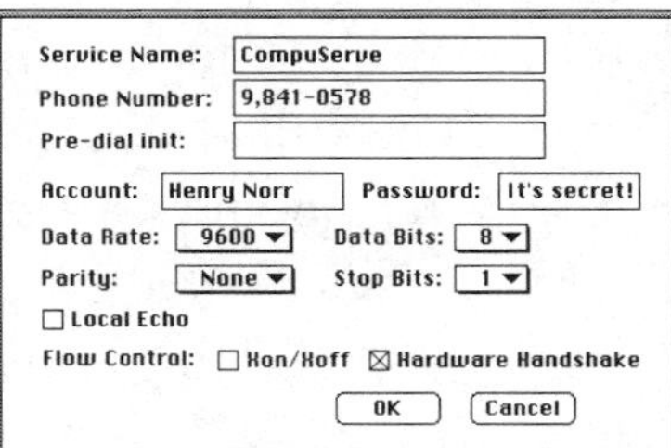

Telecommunications programs typically have complex screens for setting parameters. Even with a relatively simple program such as ZTerm, the popular shareware package, you have to go through several dialog boxes to get everything configured.

The good news is that once you have your software set up and running properly, you can normally forget about most of these settings and put the manual on the shelf—at least until you get a new modem, switch to another program, or try a new on-line service.

Bits per Second

Most modems are capable of handling not only their rated top speed but also several slower speeds; a 14,400-bps modem, say, can transmit at 9,600, 2,400, and 1,200 bps. When two modems connect, they negotiate to determine the highest transfer rate they share; if line noise or other problems make it impossible to carry on at the rate originally determined, they should drop down automatically to a lower rate. Some (but not all) modems are even smart enough to move back up to a higher rate if line conditions improve.

But no modem will use a higher speed than your software is set for, so be sure your software is set to the speed you want.

Flow Control

Modems generally can't transmit data over the phone line as fast as your Mac can send it to the modem over a serial cable, and sometimes the computer can't keep up with the data the modem is trying to deliver. If either device feels it's in danger of gagging on excess data, it can signal to the other to stop sending data until the backlog has been processed. This coordination process is called *flow control* or *handshaking*. (The latter term is also used for what the negotiating modems do when they're first connected to determine the speeds and protocols they have in common. If your modem's speaker is on, you can hear them screeching at each other.)

Lower-speed modems (2,400 bps and slower) usually rely on a flow-control technique called *Xon/Xoff* (pronounced "ex-on ex-off"): They can send the computer on and off signals between chunks of data. If you are dealing with such a modem, make sure to turn on the Xon/Xoff switch that you're sure to find in some settings dialog box or menu in your communications program.

Modems that work at 9,600 bps and faster, however, support *hardware handshaking*—a scheme that uses special circuitry in the modem and computer, plus dedicated lines inside the cable, for signaling. (In some programs the control for hardware handshaking is labeled *RTS/CTS*, or Request to Send/Clear to Send, after the names of the special flow-control signals.) Hardware handshaking is faster and more reliable than Xon/Xoff, so be sure to turn it on if you have a high-speed modem—assuming, of course, that you have the required *hardware handshaking cable*.

Cables that come bundled with high-speed modems are generally the hardware-handshaking type; if you have to purchase a cable, specify that you need hardware handshaking. If you upgrade from an older (2,400-bps) modem, you probably don't already have a hardware handshaking cable, so be sure to get one.

Other Terminal Settings

Depending on the program or service you are communicating with, you may need to send and receive data in chunks of either seven or eight bits; your software should offer a choice under the heading *data bits*. *Stop bits* mark the end of one byte and the beginning of another. *Parity* is an old-fashioned way of checking that the other computer received exactly what you sent. Far and away the most common setting is eight data bits, one stop bit, and no parity. Those are the default settings in most Mac telecommunications programs; don't change them unless you know what you're doing.

File-Transfer Protocols

You can send plain-text (ASCII) files via modem with no special protocol or error checking: Any communications program can send an unformatted text file character by character, as if you were typing it out. That's sometimes necessary if you are sending data to an old device, such as a Tandy Model 100 laptop, that doesn't use protocols. But there are lots of problems with text transfers: Characters may get dropped or garbled, and unless you go through some special tricks, you can't send a formatted document or a graphic image that way.

To send anything but plain text, or even if you just want to make sure a text file arrives intact, you need to use a *file-transfer protocol*—a set of conventions for

Xmodem, Ymodem, Zmodem (HN/RS)

Here's a guide to some commonly used transfer protocols, ranked roughly in order of preference:

- *Zmodem* should be your choice whenever possible. It's the fastest, can send multiple files in a batch, includes the files' names and other information about them, and can resume interrupted transfers right where it left off, so you won't have to cover the same ground twice.
- *Ymodem* (and an even faster variant called *Ymodem-G)* also supports batch transfers and file names. Ymodem-G contains no error-checking protocol. It's a very fast way to transfer files, but use it only with modems that do error correction in hardware or when two computers are hard-wired together directly.
- *CompuServe B+* is the latest in a series of proprietary "B" protocols the CompuServe Information Service developed for its use on its own network. It's useless anywhere else, but it's your best choice if you are downloading from CompuServe. (It's not quite as fast as Zmodem, but CompuServe doesn't support Zmodem.)
- *Xmodem* is an older protocol that is still widely used, in part because it's supported by virtually all communications programs, while its Y and Z cousins are not. But because it sends data in smaller packets it's relatively slow, and, unlike Zmodem and Ymodem-G, it waits for acknowledgment of a packet before starting to send another. It uses an error-detection technique called *checksumming,* but some implementations give you another option called *CRC,* for cyclical redundancy checking. Choose the latter if available.
- *Kermit* works with a wide range of computers and telecommunications equipment, including mainframes that don't support newer protocols. Because of its versatility and easy configuration, it's still a favorite among many government and university users. But it's generally slower than the alternatives, and it's not supported on most services.

Zmodem for the Comm Toolbox (RS)

Zmodem has long been a sore spot for users of applications that rely on the Mac Comm Toolbox. That's because Apple in its wisdom chose to deliver an Xmodem tool rather than one implementing the superior Zmodem alternative, as standard equipment in the CTB. A few developers, such as Aladdin and DCA (developer of Crosstalk, a PC favorite recently released for the Mac), have created their own Zmodem tools but don't sell them separately; that means users of CTB-based integrated packages, such as ClarisWorks, Microsoft Works, and Symantec's GreatWorks, haven't been able to use Zmodem unless they shell out for a specialized communications application they may not otherwise need.

Fortunately, a better solution has recently materialized: A small company called Mark/Space Softworks now markets a Zmodem tool that works with any CTB-based application. Just drag it to your System Folder, and it will be put in the Extensions folder. It's called—surprise!—the **Mark/Space Zmodem Tool,** and it costs just $30. In addition, the company distributes a demo version free of charge through user groups and on-line services. The demo version doesn't support uploading but works fine for downloading. You might also want to check out Mark/Space's own simple CTB-based application, **Communicate Lite** ($50).

how much data will be packaged, sent, and verified. These protocols are independent of the computer, the modem, and even the communications software you are using: When a Mac user sends a file using the shareware program ZTerm, the Zmodem protocol, and a Zoom or ZyXEL modem (for instance), any modem connected to any computer running any program that can handle Zmodem transfers should be able to receive the file correctly. Not all communications programs and services support all protocols, though, so you may not be able to stick with only one.

The MacBinary Imperative (HN)

Virtually every Mac telecommunications program has a setting for enabling something called *MacBinary*. It should be on by default, and you should leave it on unless you have some very special reason to turn it off.

MacBinary is not a protocol but a file format. It was devised by Mac telecommunications pioneers to deal with some unique Mac features, including the fact that the Mac divides files into two segments (called the *data fork* and the *resource fork*) and stores some information about files, such as type and creator codes, creation and modification dates, and icons, in the Finder rather than the file itself. MacBinary solves these problems by combining both forks in a single block and adding a 128-byte header with the Finder information; when receiving a file, MacBinary-aware applications recognize the header, decode the file, and restore it to standard format.

When MacBinary is turned on and you initiate a file transfer, your software will convert the file into the MacBinary format. If it's sent to a PC or a mainframe, it will stay in MacBinary format, but if it reaches a Mac via a Mac communications program, it will automatically be converted back to its original format. If you download a Mac file to a PC and take it to a Mac on a floppy or over a network, you'll have to convert it yourself before it's usable. (To find out how to do that, see Chapter 25).

On-Line Services (HN)

An *on-line service* is like a combination electronic post office, user group, debating society, newsstand, library, and shopping mall. Members of a service—computer users who have obtained accounts on the service by agreeing to pay the required fees—can get access to these features by using a modem to connect their computer to the service's mainframes over phone lines. Odds are that the service's central computers are far from you, but major services have *local nodes* or *access numbers* in every metropolitan area, so unless you live in the boonies, you shouldn't have to pay long-distance charges.

What They Offer (HN)

Each of the major services—CompuServe; America Online; AppleLink and its new heir apparent, eWorld; GEnie; Prodigy; and the others—has some unique features, but they are similar in many ways. You'll find most of the following features on all of them.

E-mail. Once you've dialed in and *logged on* (entered your name and password or account number), you can exchange files and private messages—electronic mail, or *e-mail* for short—with others who subscribe to the same service. More and more, you can also communicate with subscribers of other services. For an extra charge, some services will even convert messages to fax format or hard copy, and then forward them (in the latter case by overnight mail) to clients and associates who don't regularly sign on to any service.

Forums. Besides private, person-to-person communications, most services provide *forums* on which subscribers can give and get advice, share tips and rumors, and debate issues large and small. Messages are posted for all to see, so anyone can join in or read the message traffic without participating (that's called *lurking*). Forums usually have moderators—called *sysops* (pronounced *SIS-ops*, for system operators)—to answer questions, direct traffic, and maintain a bit of order.

Forums are also known as round tables or *SIGs* (for special interest groups). Sometimes they're called bulletin boards, but that usage is confusing when you're talking about a commercial on-line service: Most people use the term *bulletin board service*, or *BBS*, to refer to smaller-scale, typically noncommercial dial-up services. (See "The BBS Alternative," below).

Tech support. Many computer hardware and software companies provide support to their customers through on-line services. In addition to enabling you to ask questions, report problems, and get authoritative advice at any time of the day or night without spending hours on hold, on-line support forums are great places to compare notes with fellow users and download software updates, sample files, scripts, and other goodies.

Software libraries. All of the services maintain electronic libraries from which you can download software—mainly freeware and shareware, but now also some commercial products. The major services have tens of thousands of downloadable files—utilities, pictures, sounds, movies, HyperCard stacks, even full-blown applications.

News and information. On-line services also let subscribers browse up-to-the-minute news, weather, sports reports, stock prices, and other information. Specialized databases posted on or connected to the services offer access to statistics, bibliographies, legal cases, and articles originally published in hard copy.

Chat. On some services you can *chat*—type messages back and forth in real time—with others who happen to be on-line when you are, either in private conversations or in open *conferences*.

Shopping. Nowadays you can even shop in electronic malls—not only for computer hardware and software, but also for airline tickets, books, gifts, and even groceries.

How Much Does It Cost? (HN)

Depending on what you do, where you do it, and how long it takes, getting on-line costs something between a pittance and a fortune, and figuring out where on that spectrum you'll fall isn't always easy.

Broadly speaking, the services generally charge by the hour—or more precisely by the minute. But some have a monthly base charge, which may or may not include a certain number of hours on-line or unlimited access to selected services. Some services charge more during business hours than for access at night and on weekends and holidays. High-speed connections often cost more than slower ones. AppleLink, in addition to billing for time spent on-line, charges extra for material you download. On some services a few areas are free, while other sections, notably some of the research databases, carry steep surcharges.

Fortunately for users, prices overall have declined steadily, thanks mainly to increasing competition. If you're careful (and you don't get too much mail), you should be able to maintain an account and use it actively—checking your mail regularly, browsing a few forums and even downloading occasional files—for $10 a month. At the other end of the spectrum, the sky's the limit. And be careful—getting on-line can be as addictive and expensive as a drug habit.

On-Line Options (HN/RS)

No one service is right for everyone—each has longtime users and enthusiastic champions as well as harsh critics in the Mac community. Since most of them offer free introductory subscriptions, your best bet may be to try them all until you find one that feels comfortable.

GOOD FEATURE

America Online. If you haven't used an on-line service before, America Online (AOL) is a good place to start. It's got a nice graphical interface for both Mac and Windows, large libraries of downloadable software, electronic versions of many leading newspapers and magazines, support forums for many Mac vendors, and a pioneering Internet Center, which offers access to selected features of the worldwide Internet. AOL is also relatively cheap. Currently the monthly charge is $10 for five hours of access, any time day or night; additional time is $3.50 per hour, and there's no extra charge for "premium" services.

BAD FEATURE

On the other hand, the service has some serious deficiencies. Its interface, though pretty, requires so much mouse clicking that it can get tiresome. Its message boards don't support real *threading* of messages (displaying messages and any replies to them together to make it easier to follow a discussion).

Mac Bible On-Line (AN/RS)

The *Macintosh Bible*/Peachpit Press has its own forum on America Online. Just choose Departments from the Go To menu, then click the Computing & Software button, then on the Books & Magazines icon, then on the Macintosh Bible/ Peachpit Press item. A faster way to get there is to simply choose Keyword in the Go To menu, type in *macbible* and then hit Return. Once there, you can (among other things) leave messages for your favorite Peachpit authors and ask questions in the Message Center.

CompuServe. CompuServe, a larger and older service than AOL, offers access to more information on more subjects than any other service. It serves users with all kinds of computers, and it's got plenty of Mac software and discussions, both in a group of forums known as MAUG and in *MacUser* and *MacWEEK* forums on ZiffNet (a separate service accessible through CompuServe). Many Mac hardware and software vendors also maintain support forums or an informal presence on CompuServe.

Until recently, CompuServe was expensive compared with AOL, but recent rate cuts have made it much more reasonable. Under the standard plan, a monthly fee of $9 provides unlimited access to dozens of news, sports, reference, shopping, travel, and entertainment services, plus the right to send the equivalent of 60 three-page e-mail messages. For other areas, such as the Mac forums, hourly rates are $4.80 per hour for 2,400-bps and slower speeds or $9.60 per hour for 9,600- or 14,400-bps access. ZiffNet membership costs $3 per month plus standard hourly connect charges, but a few services, such as downloading *MacUser*'s utility of the month, are free of all charges.

Perhaps because it's been more expensive, the clientele on CompuServe and ZiffNet Mac forums is more heavily weighted toward computer professionals, journalists, and business users than on AOL (though many such people turn up there, too!). You can usually get an authoritative answer to any Mac question in a matter of hours.

CompuServe runs on ancient character-based software, which you can (if you wish) navigate DOS-style by typing in cryptic commands. But the service now offers two applications that create graphical shells enabling you to point and click your way around.

CompuServe Information Manager for Macintosh, a.k.a. **MacCIM** ($25), takes an interactive approach similar to AOL's. It lets you read mail and prepare replies off-line, but it's really designed to make it easier to navigate the service while you are on-line.

CompuServe Navigator ($70, with a $25 credit for on-line time) lets you create completely scripted (automated) sessions that reduce your on-line time: Once you tell it which forums to visit, message threads to read, libraries to search, or files to download, and so on, the program will dart on-line, carry out your instructions at full speed, and then log off—all without intervention on your part. You can read them and prepare replies to mail and forum messages off-line, at your leisure and without hourly fees.

Navigator's interface can be confusing, and some functions aren't as reliable as they should be in a product that's been on the market for more than seven years. But on the whole it's a terrific boon for heavy users.

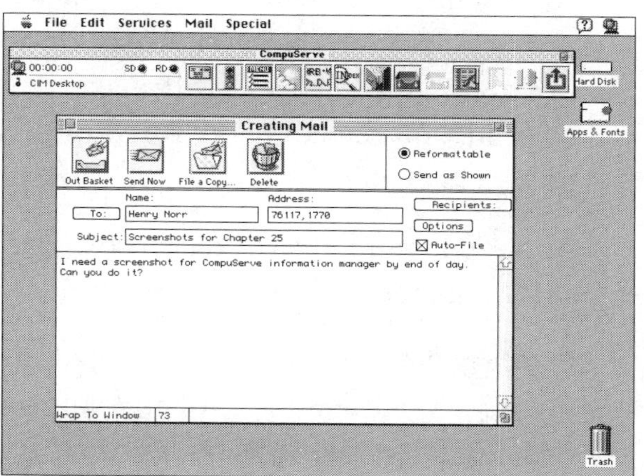

CompuServe Information Manager gives a graphic user interface to the CompuServe Information Service. You can also log on and use text commands with any communications software. The icon bar gives one-click access to common services such as mail and stock quotes. Mail message windows, like the one shown here, can draw on personal address books.

CIM's a better choice for new or occasional users of CompuServe, and for anyone who likes to explore the service on a whim. Nav's a better choice if you regularly visit the same areas and simply want the process automated.

AppleLink and eWorld. AppleLink, Apple's own original on-line electronic-mail and information service, was once just for Apple employees, dealers, developers, user groups, and universities, but in recent years the company has made accounts available to anyone who can afford them. eWorld is a new Apple-run service that just got off the ground in mid-1994.

The main value of AppleLink is access to Apple information, such as product spec sheets, press releases, tech notes, and system-software updates. The system's structure, however, is chaotic, and many sections are not maintained with any regularity. Worst of all, it's fabulously expensive: up to $37 per hour for 9,600-bps access.

There's probably no reason for anyone to join AppleLink at this point because Apple plans to phase it out in favor of eWorld. The latter is a vast improvement. Its interface is attractive and easy to use, though like the AOL interface it's based on, it involves constant mouse-clicking and a clutter of windows. *[Which I personally prefer to a bunch of key-tapping and a plethora of cryptic commands.—RS]* At $9 a month (including two off-peak hours) and $5 or $8 (off peak or prime time, respectively) per hour, eWorld will at least be in the ballpark as far as pricing goes. Apple says it will make the data now on AppleLink available on eWorld, and the company is recruiting lots of other vendors and information providers, including ZiffNet Mac, to set up their own sections on the service.

Apple will bundle eWorld user software with all of its products, so the service is almost guaranteed a huge user base.

Prodigy (SA/JK/RS). Prodigy is an on-line service sponsored by Sears and IBM; there's a special version of the software for Mac owners. Despite its name, Prodigy is no *wunderkind.* It won't run in the background, the menu isn't available when you're in it, and it's hard to get 9600-bps service outside of major cities. Even worse, the bottom of every screen is reserved for ads—for things like mouthwash.

BAD FEATURE

Prodigy does have at least one valuable feature: You can look up politicians' biographies and voting records, and the campaign contributions congressional and presidential candidates have received. But access to this information alone doesn't make Prodigy worth signing up for, even at $13 per month (extra for special services).

Anyone even thinking about signing up should know one more thing about Prodigy: They read and censor user's posts! (Their explanation is that this is a family-oriented board.) Another stroke against them: They started charging for excess e-mail messages (after advertising that all such services would be free), and then deleted all public messages discussing and/or complaining about this action! This type of behavior did wonders for America Online's growth. And the difference between the look of Prodigy and that of America Online is the difference between artwork created in an early version of MacPaint compared to the same artwork created in Adobe Illustrator.

The BBS Alternative (HN)

An electronic BBS is sort of a home-grown, low-rent on-line service. Your local BBS won't have all the latest news, and you probably can't order your airline tickets on it. But what you get, you get for free (more or less): BBSes generally don't charge for on-line time, though some require a modest annual membership fee. *[Some "charge" in the form of requiring you to participate in discussions by posting at least once every certain number of calls.—RS]*

Like their commercial cousins, BBSes typically have libraries of downloadable software and forums for discussion of computer matters and other subjects. Most boards also let members exchange private e-mail; since many BBSes are now linked to each other and/or the Internet (see below), you may be able to send messages anywhere, even to correspondents on commercial services.

Some BBSes are focused on the Mac or on computers more generally; others are defined by their members' interest in a particular hobby. Some are open to anyone; others are sponsored by a particular organization and limited to its members or set up by a company for its customers.

One disadvantage of most BBSes, compared with commercial services, is that they can't handle as many callers at once. If you're calling a popular board, particularly in the evening, you are likely to get a busy signal—a rarity with commercial services. Most BBSes also limit the length of each call or the amount of time you can spend on-line per day. Commercial services, for better or worse, are happy to have you ringing up a bill 24 hours a day.

Another traditional disadvantage of BBSes is that they've usually had text-based, rather than graphical, user interfaces. That's begun to change, though, as many BBSes have switched to graphical software systems such as **TeleFinder** ($425) from Spider Island Software, **NovaLink Pro** (starting at $100) from ResNova Software, and especially **FirstClass** from SoftArc ($95 per server with a variety of multiclient software packages starting at $395). One of the great things about FirstClass systems is that even if you don't have the graphical client software, you can still log on. If you then download the free client software, you'll have a much nicer experience the next time.

Thousands of individual BBSes around the world have linked together to form a loose metanetwork called FidoNet. *The BMUG Guide to Bulletin Boards and Beyond* ($20, or $15 for members) explains how to access the BBSes that are part of FidoNet and even can help you start your own BBS.

The Internet (HN)

Unless you've had your head in the sand for the last couple of years, you've undoubtedly heard about the Internet—or just "the Net," to those in the know—the amorphous digital network that already connects millions of computer users around the world and is widely heralded as a prototype for the emerging information superhighway.

Until recently, it wasn't easy to get access to the Internet unless you were connected to a large government, educational, or corporate institution that was wired into the Net. You had to go through a system administrator to set up your account and configure your machine And once you got an account, you had to master a bunch of cryptic Unix commands before you could even begin to find your way around.

All that has changed in the last few years. A suite of excellent shareware and free Mac software has made the Net manageable (if still not exactly friendly), and commercial Mac developers have followed with several packages of high-quality access tools. Most commercial on-line services have set up gateways to the Internet, so you can easily exchange mail with Internet users even if you don't have your own account. America Online has begun to offer a wide array of Internet services, and other services are likely to follow with similar arrangements. And for those who want a direct Internet account and don't have access through work or school, local-access providers all over the country now offer relatively inexpensive individual accounts.

What Is It?

The Internet is not a specific service, with its own organization, central computers, and fee structure. Rather, it's a loosely structured network of networks, a worldwide digital web. It began as a way to connect Unix networks at research labs, universities, and defense contractors to each other and to the Pentagon and other government agencies, but it's grown to encompass thousands of corporate networks, nonprofit groups, and dial-up service providers who sell accounts to individuals. And in recent years the major commercial on-line services have tied their systems into the Internet so their users can communicate with anyone on the net, and vice versa.

More Info About the Internet (HN)

The Internet is much too big and diverse to be covered in depth here. If you want more details, bookstores are now bulging with Internet titles. Two excellent Mac-oriented titles, both of which provide Internet-access software, are Adam Engst's *The Internet Starter Kit for Macintosh* (Hayden) and Michael Fraase's *The Mac Internet Tour Guide* (Ventana).

There are also dozens of electronic guides to the Internet. My favorite (I'm giving myself away here) is one called *The Big Dummy's Guide to the Internet,* which is available in both plain text and HyperCard formats; you can find it on any of the major on-line services.

All of this has meant exponential growth. No one knows for sure how many people are connected to the Internet, but at this writing the total is generally estimated at some 20 to 30 million people. That figure is clearly somewhat inflated because it includes many people who work at organizations tied into the net but don't actually use it. But there's no doubt that the number is huge and growing fast.

What It Offers

GOOD FEATURE

As the Internet grows, new services keep emerging: Among other things, you can now explore hypertext databases that link documents in libraries around the world, send faxes without paying long-distance charges, download digitized-music recordings, and tune in to radio-like audio programming. Most Internet users, however, do the same things that others do on commercial networks and local bulletin boards—exchange e-mail, download files, and share news and ideas with others interested in the same topics. But the very size of the Internet means there's more of all that—more potential correspondents, more data libraries, and more topical forums (known on the Internet as *newsgroups*).

GOOD FEATURE

E-mail. The most obvious allure of the Internet is that it allows you to exchange messages with people all over the world, regardless of the kind of computer they use, the software they run, or the particular network they connect to. As long as they are part of an organization that's got an Internet connection, or a member of almost any on-line service, you should be able to put a message in their mailbox in a matter of minutes.

Newsgroups. One of the most compelling features of the Internet is access to *Usenet newsgroups*— something on the order of 5,000 forums focusing on topics ranging from floating-point math to football to philosophy. (There are at least four newsgroups devoted to various aspects of *StarTrek*, and about 20 dealing with the Mac.) Though the term "newsgroup" may make them sound authoritative, in most cases they are just discussion groups—like forums on CompuServe or AOL—in which participants with varying levels of knowledge share their insights and their ignorance. Some groups have moderators, which usually ensures a certain level of focus, while others are completely freewheeling. Usenet is actually a separate Unix-oriented network, but it's linked to the Internet, so once you're on the latter, you can get access to the newsgroups.

Internet Addresses (HN)

Several different addressing schemes are used in different parts of the Internet, but the standard format is *username@domain.top domain.* The @ (or Shift 2) is pronounced "at," and the periods are pronounced *dot.* Spaces and commas are not allowed, but you can use extra periods, dashes, or underscore characters instead. The entire address is normally written in lowercase because that's the fashion on the Net; aside from the password schemes on some Internet systems, most of the Net is actually not sensitive to case.

Most users choose their last name, with or without their first name or initial, as their username, but some people use abbreviations, nicknames, numerical IDs, or titles. (Bill Clinton's username is *president.*) If you get an account through your company or university, you may have to follow its naming conventions.

A domain is basically the name of a particular organization or network. Some domain names have of several words, separated by periods; at some large organizations there are mid-level domain names identifying different parts of the organization or even different machines.

In the U.S., a top domain is a three-letter code that identifies the type of organization: *.com,* meaning commercial, signifies a private business; *.edu* means an educational institution; *.gov* means—guess what? And so on. Non-U.S. accounts, as well as a few in this country, use a two-letter country code as the top domain.

By this writing, all the major on-line services have Internet *gateways,* so you can exchange mail via your favorite service with anyone anywhere on the Internet (including subscribers to other commercial services that also have gateways). The format and procedures for sending messages to Internet addresses vary depending on which service you are starting from. In some cases there are length limits on messages sent through a gateway, and often you can't enclose files with messages. Check with your on-line service for details.

If you are on the Internet already and want to send a message to someone on a commercial on-line service, you must use his or her account name or identifying number on that service before the @ sign, with the service's domain and top domain following—for example, *HenryNorr@aol.com* or *76117.1770@compuserve.com.* (The comma in CompuServe addresses has to be changed to a period.)

Fetching files. Hundreds of thousands of files—shareware and freeware for every platform, updates for Apple system software, satellite images, digitized sounds, government reports, great literature in text format, and almost anything else you can think of—are available for downloading over the Internet. The phrase to know is *ftp*. It stands for *file-transfer protocol*, but the acronym has become an adjective (*ftp sites* are computers on the Net from which you can download files using the protocol) and even a verb (you ftp the files you want).

Many sites, or *archives*, allow *anonymous ftp*—that is, anyone can log on to the archive just by entering the username *anonymous* and any text as a password (though it's considered good form to use your e-mail address as the password).

Browsing information. The mail systems, libraries, and forums of the commercial on-line services are roughly analogous to the Internet services mentioned so far, but there's no real equivalent to the information-browsing options the Internet offers. Thousands of universities, libraries, government agencies, private organizations, and individuals have put millions of pages of information—databases, directories, statistics, images, even the full text of research reports and books without copyrights—on hard disks accessible through the Net.

Finding your way through this vast mass of data is a major challenge. Several different, overlapping schemes for indexing, linking, searching, and retrieving information are in use on the Internet. These are the best-known systems:

- *Gopher*, a system of interconnected databases (known as Gopherspace) listing files, directories, images, sounds, and just about anything else the people who maintain Gopher servers want to incorporate.
- *WAIS* (Wide Area Information Servers), a system for indexing and searching text data. WAIS and Apple's AppleSearch product evolved out of the same research, and AppleSearch will soon be able to search WAIS libraries.
- *World-Wide Web*, an ambitious scheme for creating hypertext links among a variety of kinds of information located all over the world; clicking on a word in the file you are reading can take you automatically and almost instantly to a file halfway around the world with more information on the subject.

Fortunately, there are now first-rate Mac programs offering point-and-click access to each of these information-retrieval schemes (see "Internet Applications," below).

Getting on the Net

Before you can start to use the Internet, you need to get an account established, and depending on how you're connecting and what kinds of services you require, you may need to install some special networking software.

For mail-only dial-up access. The simplest kind of Internet connection is a dial-up link. If you don't have one through your business or school, you can get a basic dial-up account relatively cheaply (many providers offer them for $20 a month or less, with unlimited access), and they require no special hardware or software—just a modem (the faster the better) and any Mac telecommunications program.

In most cases, these accounts work only for sending and receiving mail; you probably won't be able to join newsgroups, download files, or browse remote databases.

For full dial-up access. To get access to all Internet services via modem, you need software that lets your Mac speak *TCP/IP* (the networking protocol used on the Internet) and extra software for creating a TCP/IP connection over a phone line. And you need an account configured to support this kind of connection.

MacTCP (an Apple system extension that Macs need in order to join TCP/IP networks) currently comes bundled with many Internet-oriented software packages (including the free version of Eudora, described below). Starting with System 7.5, MacTCP will become a standard part of the Mac operating system.

SYSTEM 7.5

To establish a TCP/IP connection by phone you need a driver that implements either *SLIP* (Serial Line Internet Protocol) or *PPP* (Point-to-Point Protocol). The latter is newer and apparently somewhat faster and more flexible, but for most people the deciding issue is which one is supported by the system you intend to dial in to. (Not all organizations and service providers offer these options, but the number that support one or both is increasing rapidly.) The main commercial Internet communications packages (described below) include SLIP drivers, and Intercon System allows its **InterSLIP** software to be distributed freely. PPP drivers are harder to come by, but Intercon now offers **InterPPP** for $100, and there's a free package called **MacPPP**.

Configuring MacTCP and SLIP or PPP is definitely a pain. Your best bet is to get help from an expert—your service provider, your network administrator, or a friend with lots of TCP/IP experience.

Choosing a Service Provider (HN)

Scores of companies—some with local nodes all over the country, some limited to particular regions—now offer dial-up Internet access. One way to get a list of providers in your area is to check your bookstore or library—most Internet books include such lists. But more providers spring up every month, and options and rates change, so the lists in books soon get out of date.

Two regularly updated lists of providers—called PDIAL and nixpub—are widely distributed on the Internet. Of course, that won't do you much good if you need the list precisely because you don't already have access, but you may be able to get a copy through a user group or commercial on-line service.

The best bet is probably to inquire through a local BBS or user group. That way, you'll get not only names and numbers but also warnings about such problems as local nodes that are always busy or tech-support staffers who snort contemptuously because you don't know Unix inside and out. (I have an account with one of the larger providers, Netcom. When I sent a note to tech support because the system was refusing to let me log in about one call out of every three, I got a curt message back saying "any timeout or delay problems need to be resolved by software on your end.")

Remember that not all providers support SLIP or PPP. Choose one that does, if you want the option of full access to all Internet services.

The rate structures for these services can be complicated. Be sure to factor in not only monthly fees, but also setup charges, access limitations, and hourly rates, if any. Rates for SLIP and PPP accounts are usually higher than for simple dial-up access, and it's more likely that there will be an hourly charge.

POWERBOOK

Look for a provider with a local number near you to avoid phone-line charges. If you travel a lot and take a PowerBook, try to find a provider that also has local nodes in the places you are apt to visit.

Internet Applications

Once you've got the plumbing taken care of—your account's established and the necessary networking software is installed and configured—you'll need to choose one or more applications as your front end to actual Internet services. If you're comfortable with the Unix command line, any terminal program will do. But if you'd prefer a graphical interface, you have lots of excellent options—some free, some shareware, and some commercial.

Free and shareware programs. The last few years have brought an array of nifty free or low-cost products that put a Mac interface on Internet services. For mail, the standard is **Eudora,** by Steve Dorner. There's a freeware version, but now there's also a $65 commercial version published by Qualcomm. For now,

Easier Ways In

(HN)

There are now a couple of neat ways to bypass most of the hassles of getting on the Internet while getting access to many of its services.

America Online

America Online, like other commercial on-line services, now offers a variety of Internet services, including mail, newsgroups, and Gopher and WAIS searching, as part of its regular selection of features. That means anyone with an AOL account can now cruise the Net just like the heaviest Internet jocks (they're sometimes called *net heads*). You don't pay anything extra—just AOL's standard monthly and hourly rates—and you work through the service's standard graphical interface. It's hardly speedy, and there's an annoying lot of clicking though folders and dialogs, but it sure beats the Unix command line. If you're a net novice, AOL is great place to get your feet wet. Just go to the icon called Internet Center and you're on your way.

GOOD FEATURE

Delphi

Delphi, another national on-line service, offers access to the Internet through its regular dial-in service, which you can log into with any standard communications program. The list of Internet features supported is much more extensive than AOL's, and rates are at least competitive. It costs $10 a month with four hours' access and $4 for each extra hour, or $20 a month for 20 hours' access and $1.80 for each extra hour. With either plan, there's also a $3 monthly surcharge for Internet access. The problem is that you have to use Delphi's sometimes-cumbersome menu-based system; there's no point-and-click GUI, as on AOL, and you can't use the cool, graphical Mac applications you could if you had your own connection.

WorldLink

Another easy option is Intercon Systems' WorldLink. The $30 package includes an account with a major Internet service provider (Performance Systems International, or PSI), which has local numbers in 70 cities and 17 countries. WorldLink doesn't require MacTCP, SLIP, or PPP, yet, starting with version 2.0, it lets you participate in newsgroups and download files via anonymous ftp. The service charge is only $9 per month, regardless of how much time you spend on-line, if you can tolerate a 2,400-bps connection; for 9,600-bps access, the fee is $19 per month—no more than most service providers charge for a mail-only dial-up account. Remember, though, that WorldLink *won't* give you access to all Internet services. If, for instance, you want to use Mosaic, the much-ballyhooed graphical interface for the World-Wide Web, over the phone, you'll need a SLIP or PPP account.

the core capabilities are the same in both versions, though the commercial release includes some useful extra features, such as a filtering scheme that can set priorities and automatically rename or file your mail on the basis of the subject, sender, or other variables.

For reading and replying to newsgroups, there are at least three good options: **Newswatcher**, **Nuntius**, and **InterNews.** For downloading files, use a program called **Fetch** if you already know what you want and where it is; if you are browsing, the best bet is **TurboGopher.** All of these are freely distributed, but Dartmouth College, where InterNews and Fetch were developed, requires a $25 fee for each copy in use at for-profit enterprises.

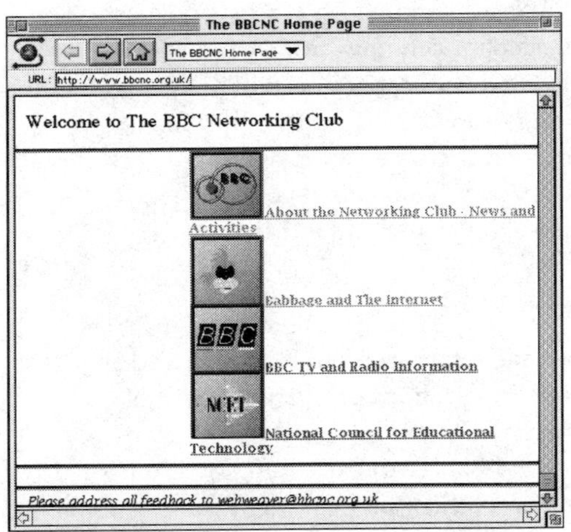

Mosaic provides a colorful and easy-to-use interface to the World-Wide Web, a hypertext system linking text, images, and other data around the world via the Internet. Any organization setting up a Web server can create its own custom "home page." This one is at the British Broadcasting Company.

A free program called **Mosaic,** developed by the National Center for Supercomputing Applications, has recently caused a sensation in Internet circles. It provides a slick graphical interface to the World-Wide Web hypertext system linking resources at Internet sites all over the world. Just click on something you are interested in and you are automatically connected to the source. It's hard to explain just what it is, but it's definitely slick. (So is John Hardin's **MacWeb**, another free World-Wide Web browser that appeared just as this book was going into production.)

Commercial programs. Overall, the quality, stability, and range of the freeware and shareware tools listed above (and many others not mentioned here) is excellent, but some users may prefer a commercial package with a single interface, printed documentation, and professional tech support. The granddaddy in this category is Intercon System's **TCP/Connect II,** which is available in several versions starting at $200; the full version, which includes MacTCP, SLIP software, and facilities for mail, file transfers, and news, is $500.

A less expensive option (and one I've found much easier to set up and use) is Synergy Software's **VersaTerm-Link**, which is now included with three other Synergy packages: **VersaTilities**, a $145 collection of networking utilities; **VersaTerm**, a $200 terminal-emulation package; and **VersaTerm-PRO**, a $300 version that includes some terminal emulations for high-end graphics. VersaTerm-Link lets you run any TCP/IP application, but it also has its own array of built-in features for mail, file transfer, and news, including one unique news feature of special value to users paying by the hour for SLIP access: It can download newsgroup messages direct to your disk without making you open each one. You can read them later at your leisure, without worrying about on-line charges.

The latest developer to add Internet access tools is Software Ventures, which now bundles separate Internet news and mail readers, plus Fetch for file transfers, with its MicroPhone Pro (described along with other general-purpose telecommunications programs, above). The news and mail programs lack some of VersaTerm-Link's features (including news downloading), but they work fine.

TCP/Connect II, VersaTilities, and MicroPhone Pro all now come with MacTCP and SLIP software.

Several other comprehensive Internet software packages are currently under development and should be available by the time you read this.

Telecom Tips

Pay attention to that garbage (SA/RS). Intermittent garbage (bizarre characters that have no apparent meaning) on the screen when you're communicating with another computer usually means you've got a noisy phone connection or line noise. If you're just typing messages back and forth with someone, don't worry about garbage as long as you can read through it. But if you're transferring files, hang up and try again for a cleaner connection. Dropping the bps rate (from 14,400 to 9,600 or from 2,400 to 1,200) sometimes helps, too.

If you're getting nothing but garbage on the screen, it may be because you and the computer you're connected to are trying to communicate at different bps rates. Most programs let you change the rate right in the middle of a session, so try that and see if it eliminates the garbage.

Closing the serial port (RS/HN). Sometimes, when you switch from one communications program to another, or even if you try to start the same program after a crash while it was on-line, you get an error message that the modem port is in use and that the program you are launching cannot use it; under some circumstances the program may even crash. That's because the first program told the Mac operating system it was using the port, and the system, for obvious reasons, won't let two programs try to send data out the same port at the same time.

Restarting your Mac will solve the problem, but an easier solution is to run **CommCloser** (or the similar **Gremlins**), a tiny utility available from most user groups and on-line services. Click the Modem button and the program will quickly close the serial port; you can then start up your telecom program. Russ Nelson, author of CommCloser, asks only for a donation of any form or kind; even a postcard will do.

Russ Nelson's CommCloser makes it easy to close a serial port that's been left open by another application.

Disabling Call Waiting (Dale Coleman/JK/AN). Call Waiting—the phone service that interrupts calls with signals when someone else is calling and lets you switch between the two calls—disrupts data transmissions. Most phone companies let you temporarily disable Call Waiting for the duration of any outgoing call. Just precede the number you're dialing with **70* (on a tone line) or *1170* (on a pulse line). When the call is over, Call Waiting returns automatically.

If you're using a Hayes-compatible modem, type **70,* (include the comma) in front of whatever number the modem's set up to dial in your communications software. When you tell the modem to dial, it will disable Call Waiting, pause for a second or two to allow the dial tone to return, and then dial the phone number (the comma after **70* generates the pause).

Saving time and money on-line (SA/JK/HN). Here are five things you can do to make your on-line sessions more efficient:

- Although many services have higher hourly fees for higher bps rates, you should still use the highest rate your modem can handle when sending or downloading files. Few services charge twice as much for a 9,600-bps connection as for a 2,400-bps one, even though transmissions take less than half the time.
- If you are sending files to a friend or colleague, be sure to compress them first.
- If your communications software lets you create scripts or otherwise automate on-line procedures like posting and retrieving messages, use that capability. Scripts run faster than you can work in real time.
- Prepare your messages and files off-line. Why pay for on-line time when all you're doing is writing?
- If you have to interrupt your work while on-line, try going into a customer-service or help area; the hourly charge is usually waived there. You'll save yourself the time and trouble of logging on again and won't have to pay for the connect time (but if you're away *too* long, the service may hang up on you).

Traveling prepared (HN). A few tips for staying connected while you're on the road with your PowerBook:

- If you think you might need access to your home machine or office network while you're gone, install **Apple Remote Access** (ARA) before you leave ($70 for the Client software, $250 for the Personal Server). It puts all the services you're used to—printers, file servers, e-mail, and so on— right on your desktop, no matter where you are. A useful adjunct is Trilobyte Software's **ARA-Commander** ($30), which adds a slew of useful conveniences missing from Apple's package. It enables you, for example, to create "connectors"—simple, memory-saving mini-applications that can create an ARA connection, then automatically open files you've preselected on the remote computer.

- If you intend to log on to on-line services during your travels, you can save yourself a lot of hassle by looking up the local access numbers for the places you'll visit before you leave, instead of trying to do it after you reach your destination.

- Need a printer when you're stuck in a hotel room with only a PowerBook? Easy—if you have a fax modem. Just fax the document to the hotel fax, run down and pick it up, and you're all set.

- A company called Konexx makes some telecommunications accessories that can help you make your connection when nothing else will, including an adapter that lets you communicate through digital PBX systems, adapters that you plug into European and Asian phone systems, and even an acoustical coupler that lets you transmit at rates up to 9,600 bps even if the only phone around is a pay phone. It's not always easy to find the Konexx products, but APS Technologies, the mail-order storage vendor, carries them, as does modem-maker Global Village Communications (under its own name).

23 Networking

Back when a PC network interface card cost a luxurious $700 to $1,000, the Mac Plus had networking built-in. That built-in Mac network, known as AppleTalk, couldn't do much more than connect a LaserWriter printer, but it's grown by staggering proportions.

Whether you only need to connect to a printer, share a few files among a small workgroup, or connect a global corporation, the pieces are all here now. In this brief chapter we'll show you what's possible and provide a framework for understanding Mac networking.

If you're tired of scampering from Mac to Mac, sharing files via disks, you should know that, with System 7 file sharing, there's little reason to, as this chapter explains. You say your Mac workgroup has tripled in size and now your LocalTalk network creeps along? We'll show you what's involved in speeding up and enlarging your network. Is your staff on the road a lot, or just tired of commuting? In this chapter you'll find out how to set up your network for remote network access by roving PowerBooks or home-office Macs.

Contributors

Bob Weibel (BW) is the chapter editor.

James Anders (JA) is senior consulting engineer with Computer Methods Corporation. His most recent book is *LiveWired: A Guide to Networking Macs* (Hayden).

Ron Colvin (RC) designs and maintains big, BIG networks, for the U.S. Army, NASA, the U.S. Veterans Administration, and commercial clients.

Dorian Couglas (DC) is a consultant and trainer for Network Frontiers.

Paul Hurley (PH) is director of computer services for a large law firm in Sacramento, California.

Randy Titchner (RT) handles the networks at Boston College in Chestnut Hill, Massachusetts. You name it—VAX, PC, Mac—the college has it somewhere.

Sharon Zardetto Aker (SA), Nancy E. Dunn (ND), Stephen Howard (SH), Arthur Naiman (AN), and **Charles Rubin (CR)** contrib-uted to earlier editions of *The Macintosh Bible,* from which parts of this chapter were taken.

Contents

Who Needs a Network? (BW)

Sure enough, you're getting a lot more work done with your new Mac, and now, you're working with new partners or handing out Macs to the rest of your staff. Suddenly your old, informal system of sharing documents and ideas isn't up to the new pace. Plus you've got new printers, modems, and other relatively expensive pieces of equipment to share. It's time to get networked—time to connect those Macs so that someone can send a document or just a brief reminder to someone else, get easy access to companywide documents, or maybe just print something without leaving their seat. If any of the features described below seem attractive to you, it's time to set up a *local area network (LAN)* for your Macs.

File Sharing

If the interoffice mail tray next to your Mac still bears interoffice memos with attached routing slips, you need to ask why. Everything you need in order to share files is built right into System 7. When you've finished your part of a project you can quickly invoke file sharing so that others on the production line can use their Macs to read or copy the file from your hard disk. No more sailing disks between cubicles.

E-Mail

If file sharing is the network circulatory system for documents, e-mail is the nervous system, serving to trigger activity, to stimulate, to light fires or put them out. When, for example, your contribution to a group project is complete and the file is ready for sharing, you still need to notify your next-in-line salary slave before you can put your feet up. A simple electronic mail system might only flash a message on someone's screen. More sophisticated systems store messages in electronic mailboxes and notify people to check and retrieve their mail. Many even allow you to attach document files to messages, and thus serve as a means of file sharing as well.

Memos and reminders are perfect fodder for e-mail: no more slips of important paper blowing in the wind or getting buried in the heap on your desk. You can quickly nudge a single individual or a whole department, checking electronically to see if everyone has received the message. Most mail systems make replying to a message quick and easy—a great catalyst for decision making.

Sharing Resources

There's more to computer networks than sharing files and e-mail; you can also share equipment such as printers and modems. AppleTalk's primary function on early Macs was to connect expensive LaserWriter printers, and most Macintosh-compatible printers come with the same built-in LocalTalk ports as do Macs. Connect the printer to your Mac with LocalTalk, and it should appear in your Chooser, ready to use, even if it's down the hall.

High-speed modems are also commonly installed as shared resources. Most people on a network don't use a high-speed modem often enough to justify buying one for each, but with a little specialized hardware and software, you can access the modem as if it were connected directly to your Mac.

And shared resources don't have to be hardware. Centralized information directories and databases are other examples of valuable resources that can be shared over a net.

Growing a Network (JA/BW)

Once you decide you need a network, you've got to decide on what kind of network to install, and that depends on many factors. Let's look at an example of how Mac networks form and grow. Let's say you're starting out in your grandmother's basement. You have a credit card and no capital except a few ideas that you think could take you and your equally broke partner into the Fortune 500. You start off with a pair of Mac IIcx's, using the venerable "sneaker net" to share files. But when you buy a LaserWriter Pro networkable printer, it's time to network.

LocalTalk Daisy-Chain Network

Your cheapest network option is LocalTalk, which has been built into every Mac since the Plus. All you need is a LocalTalk connector for each device (including the PostScript laser printers) and some cabling. You plug them in, go into System 7's control panels to set up file sharing, buy an inexpensive e-mail package, and voilà. You're sharing files, the printer, and e-mail.

Ethernet Daisy-Chain Network

As soon as you start telephone marketing with your new multiuser order-entry database, your network bogs down. You need more speed, and Ethernet is the ticket. The price of Ethernet connections have plummeted, and Ethernet is even built into many new Macs, making LocalTalk networks obsolete for all but the smallest installations, where performance isn't a concern. This means you'll need some kind of Ethernet adapter for each device, as we discuss below.

If you have a LaserWriter II, you can invest in a LaserWriter IIG upgrade card, which provides the Ethernet connection. (A few other brands have optional Ethernet interfaces, so check.) You can purchase one of the many LocalTalk-to-Ethernet adapters for the printer, but although these devices make it easy to connect a LocalTalk device to the Ethernet, they still limit communications to LocalTalk speeds. From now on, all future devices should be Ethernet-equipped.

Your next decision is which kind of Ethernet cable will best serve your needs. Thick-wire, or 10Base-5 Ethernet, is primarily used for large campus and corporate backbone networks. You're not that big yet. Instead, you could get Ethernet adapters for all the Macs, and daisy chain thin-wire Ethernet, (10Base2) where the LocalTalk/PhoneNET cabling used to be.

Structured Ethernet Wiring

When your burgeoning empire moves to a new three-story building, with more growth on the way, it's time to rethink your network and go with a "structured wiring" approach. At this point, unless you got a Masters in computer science along with your MBA, you'll want to hire a consultant to help you properly plan and install this phase of growth. The stakes here are high—we're talking tens of thousands of dollars in equipment.

A structured wiring plan should be modular and logically organized to make expansion easy. In a typical setup, each floor of the building would have a wiring closet containing an intelligent hub (described in our "Network Hardware" section, below). The hub's chassis would let you add network adapter cards of varying types.

Each hub is in turn connected with fiber-optic cables to a multiport AppleTalk router in a master wiring closet. Like the hubs, the router also offers several slots for adding various network adapters, providing the flexibility and room for expansion that's key to this setup. By using fiber to connect the three hubs, you'll leave the door open for FDDI (Fiber Distributed Data Interface) or some other high-speed networking method.

You'll want to create AppleTalk zones to organize the network services. Typically, you'd create three zones: First Floor, Second Floor, and Third Floor. Each router port should be configured with its own unique AppleTalk network range and zone name.

As your traffic increases, you can install FDDI cards in your backbone routers and each of their network hubs. That way, instead of a 10MB Ethernet, you'll have a 100MB-per-second transmission speed to accommodate the additional traffic loads you'll encounter.

Starting Simple

As you can see, networking Macs can be both very simple or very complicated, depending on the size and range of your network. In the next section, we'll describe the factors that would influence the decisions outlined here and define some of the terms we just threw at you.

Putting Together a Network

In some ways, networking Macs is easier done than said: It's easier to plug your Macs together in a simple AppleTalk network and start sharing files and printers than it is to even begin explaining what's actually going on. That's because the AppleTalk network technology is designed to handle many network issues automatically, behind the scenes. That plug-'n'-play beauty of the Macintosh is the honeymoon glow of young, uncomplicated Mac networks, however. As your organization grows, you'll need more speed and range than the built-in LocalTalk/AppleTalk Mac network provides. That's when you'll have to actually know something about AppleTalk and other forms of networks. We hope this section will at least help you ask the right questions.

Network Protocols (RC/BW)

In local area networks, all the computers are strung along a single wire, a sort of "party line" over which all the digital communication takes place. That saves on cabling, but it creates the potential for incredible chaos. Just picture things if all the phones on your block were connected in a single, huge party line. Picture the interruptions, the eavesdropping, the total jam you'd be in. Sooner or later you and your neighbors would start developing rules and procedures (let's call them *protocols*)—hang up if the line is busy and try again later, keep calls short, hang up if an incoming call is not intended for you, and so on—to guarantee at least a semblance of orderly communication.

Solving this "party line" problem is the crux of networking. Although you can see and touch network cabling, it's the invisible sets of complex rules and digital procedures—the protocols—that really make a network run. In fact, for any network there may be dozens of separate protocols at work, many operating in different ways at the same time.

Protocol layers and functions. I once overheard this snippet of conversation at a truck stop on I-5: "What kind of network they *got*, anyway?" "I think it was Ethernet," came the frank reply. I later asked a magazine art director what kind of network *she* had. The answer: "AppleTalk." Soon after, someone on the elevator was talking about a specific kind of network in *his* office, called 10BaseT.

Protocol Hierarchy (BW)

If you've followed this discussion so far, you'll gather that different kinds of protocols function in layers, with each layer serving the one above it. Picture the shipping department of an office building. The *cabling scheme,* such as 10BaseT, would serve as the streets and roads. Ethernet, or some other *access scheme,* might then be the truck or other vehicle hauling the load. Various layers of AppleTalk protocols on the management floors might then define how the truck is loaded, how the messages are addressed, how they're packaged, how they're tracked and insured, and how they're created in the first place. Apple's *EtherTalk,* for example, is simply a scheme that runs AppleTalk protocols over Ethernet.

Now suppose we replace the 10BaseT cabling with another kind, such as 10Base2 coaxial cable. We can still run our Ethernet trucks down the newly specified streets (maybe with just a change of tires). Nothing else changes; the AppleTalk folks upstairs still handle things as they did before.

Suppose again that our shipping department also serves another organization in the building known as TCP/IP. The TCP/IP people have their own way of creating network messages, packaging, and addressing. Fortunately, their stuff still fits into our standard Ethernet trucks. With a little dovetailing, we can, in many instances, mix and match protocols, as long as we pay attention to the different layers they occupy.

One of the best ways to understand this hierarchy is to look at a standard conceptual framework known as the *OSI (Open Systems Interconnection) reference model,* which describes an overall network architecture in terms of seven hierarchical layers (illustrated below). Apple designed AppleTalk with this OSI model in mind, and much of Apple's network documentation refers to it.

The OSI Reference Model

Layer	Name	Example
7	Application	PageMaker, Chooser
6	Presentation	PostScript format (from LaserWriter driver)
5	Session	Establish printer connection
4	Transport	Get printer name for Chooser, ensure reliable data transmission
3	Network	Package and address the print messages
2	Data link	Network adapter (EtherTalk, Token Ring), cable access
1	Physical	Network cable (LocalTalk, 10BaseT, Thin Ethernet)

But here's the point: All these people could have been talking about the same network. These three terms, Ethernet, AppleTalk, and 10BaseT, could actually describe different parts of a single network. How? The functions they name are all separate, each only describing a part of the whole network. Network folks tend to think of these different parts as occupying separate "layers," based on their function (see the box "Protocol Hierarchy" on the opposite page).

10BaseT, for example, is a wiring scheme, using twisted-pair cabling similar to phone wire. *Ethernet,* on the other hand, is a somewhat broader term, defining how computers and other devices should access the wiring. Ethernet can and does run on other types of wiring, not just 10BaseT. And *AppleTalk* refers to an entire group of protocols created by Apple that governs almost every other aspect of networking, that is, how computer messages are organized and sent so that they arrive where they're supposed to without error.

If you've got a Mac-only network, you can pretty much safely stick to AppleTalk (lucky you). If you've got to connect with other kinds of computers, however, you'll need to know about—and coexist with—other protocol suites.

AppleTalk. As mentioned above, when we say "AppleTalk protocol" we're really talking about a large group of protocols that govern AppleTalk networks. (The term "AppleTalk" once also referred to cabling, but the cabling is now called *LocalTalk.*) AppleTalk achieves its plug-'n'-play nature by automatically handling a lot of techie things like assigning workstation and network addresses, routing messages between networks, and so on. Instead of dealing with cryptic numbers, you can assign names to workstations, or to sections of your network called *zones.* These things are unique to AppleTalk and are part of why it's so easy to use. In fact, you won't know how good you have it until you have to deal with systems using other protocols that aren't as friendly.

GOOD FEATURE

TCP/IP. If you're using a Macintosh in a multivendor environment including Unix workstations—DEC VAX, Sun SPARCstations, and so on—99 percent of the time *TCP/IP* will be the commonly supported protocol. TCP/IP stands for Transmission Control Protocol/Internet Protocol and was designed over many years to support the Internet, the largest computer network in the world (described more fully in Chapter 22). Although other protocol standards have been put forward, TCP/IP has become the de facto internetworking standard. We'll get into it in more detail later.

If your Mac is connected to an Ethernet network, you can make it talk TCP/IP by installing Apple's **TCP/IP Connection for Macintosh** software (about $100 on the street). If you've got System 7.5, you've already got the main component of this product, MacTCP. Once one of these products is installed, and you select TCP/IP from the Networks control panel, your Mac starts talking TCP/IP as well as AppleTalk. The problem with TCP/IP in a Mac environment is that you have to explicitly specify a lot of network settings, such as device addresses, that simpler Mac systems handle automatically.

IPX (Netware). IBM and Microsoft were so slow in coming out with a decent network operating system for PCs that a third company, Novell, came up with Netware. Created from the ground up without using DOS, Netware's speed and relative reliability made it the most widely installed network operating system in businesses. The main networking protocol used by Netware is *IPX*, which stands for Internetwork Packet Exchange.

DECnet. The modular, high-performance design of Digital Equipment Corporation's VAX minicomputers has made them popular in business, research, and academic environments. While many VAX computers also run the Unix operating system with TCP/IP network protocols, others run proprietary VAX operating systems with network protocols called *DECnet*. Apple and DEC formed a technical alliance that eventually produced a product from DEC called **Pathworks for Macintosh** ($305), which includes DECnet for Macs. This allows Macs to act as VAX terminals and take advantage of VAX printing, file transfer, printing, e-mail, and other services.

Topologies (JA/BW)

The network protocol you use has an effect on the layout, or *topology*, you choose for your LAN. Certain types of networks require certain layouts, though some can run on a variety of schemes.

Daisy chain. A *daisy-chain* setup—the topology used for LocalTalk networks—simply strings computers and other devices along using a series of separate cable links, forming a chain. The chain can be straight or twisted into a pretzel, as long as you don't connect the two ends together—no circles or loops. The network connector at each computer provides two connector jacks, one for the computer or device on one side and one for the computer or device on the other. For the computers at each end of the wire, there's only one cable connection; a *terminating plug* is sometimes fitted into the remaining empty connector.

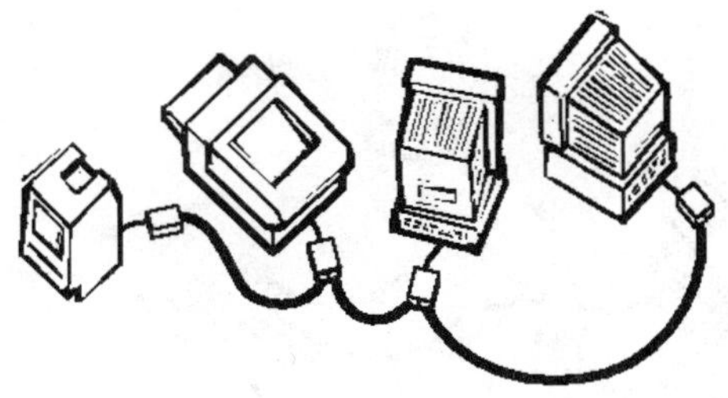

In a daisy-chain connection such as that used by LocalTalk networks, a separate piece of cable runs between each node. In LocalTalk networks, the wires plug into LocalTalk connector boxes, which plug into each Mac's printer port.

Bus. In a *bus* topology, network devices are strung linearly along a single cable, not chained together with separate lengths of cable. Each device requires a *tap*, which actually penetrates the cable insulation to contact the live wire. A bus often forms a *backbone* connecting separate networks.

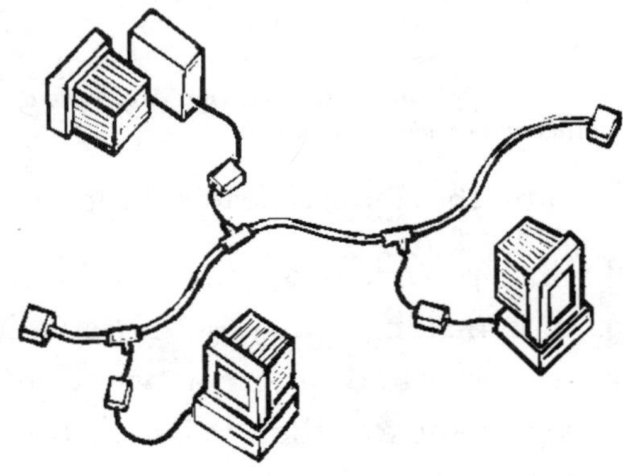

A bus topology uses a continuous length of cable. Connecting computers use a transceiver and some form of tap to hook into the bus. Terminators at each end of the bus minimize signal reflections.

Ring. Networks based on *Token Ring* and FDDI protocols, which we discuss below, use a ring-shaped topology. In this setup the cable makes a complete loop back to where it started, forming a circle, or ring.

Star. In the *star*, or radial, topology, several separate runs of cable converge at a central *hub* or *concentrator*, usually with only a single device connected at the end of each cable run. (Hubs are described under "Network Hardware," below.)

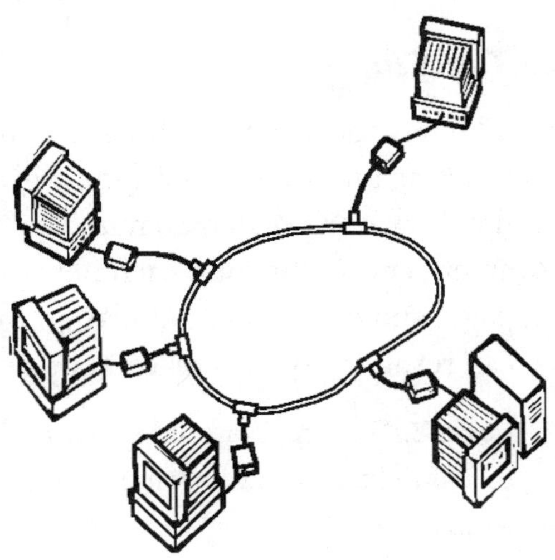

A ring topology (used with Token Ring networks) uses a continuous loop of coaxial cable. Each node requires a plug-in board, which connects to the cable via a transceiver and a tap.

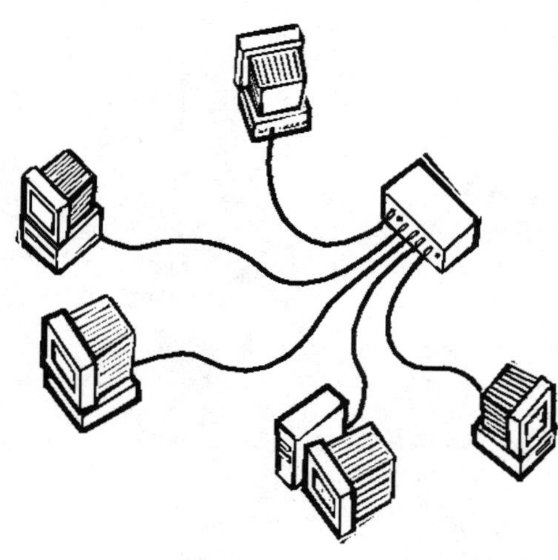

A star topology connects separate runs of cable to a central hub or multiport repeater.

There are two types of networks using star topology: *passive stars* and *active stars.* A passive star connects cable runs at a central hub, but it doesn't do anything to boost or direct signals from one cable to another. Consequently, the passive star starts running out of steam after you've connected half-a-dozen or so devices. Active stars, however, use concentrators or *multiport repeaters* (also described below) to amplify (repeat) the signal coming from any segment to keep it from getting too weak (attenuating). Consequently, these active hubs can be designed to handle a large number of cable runs; the signal repeaters keep the whole thing struttin'.

GOOD FEATURE

Stars provide two main benefits over other topologies. First, they're more modular, making for easier, more logically organized network expansion. Second, it's easier to diagnose network problems at the star hub, where all the separate legs come together. When a problem occurs on one leg, it's easy to isolate that leg and fix the problem without bringing down the whole network. The downside, of course, is that when the hub itself goes down, so does the entire network that's dependent on it. Bus and daisy-chain networks are less centralized, hence less prone to total failure.

The Cable (JA)

The next decision you'll have to make concerns the type of wiring you'll use. Once again, if you're sticking with LocalTalk, your job is simple. With Ethernet, however, you have a number of options. The type of wiring you choose has an effect on how long each network segment can be (see the table on the next page) and can lay the foundation for future network growth. The wrong choice can result in costly replacement when you're ready to extend your network.

LocalTalk. The original version of Apple's LocalTalk cable supported only up to 1,000 feet of total wiring with a maximum of 30 nodes. LocalTalk always uses a daisy chain topology.

Speed, Length, and Node Limits for Different Types of Cable

Cable Type	Maximum number of nodes per segment	Maximum cable run	Maximum transmission speed
Apple LocalTalk	30	1,000 feet	230.4K/second
PhoneNET LocalTalk	30	3,000 feet	230.4K/second
10BaseT Ethernet (twisted-pair)	1	100 meters	10MB/second
10Base2 Ethernet (thin-wire)	30	189 meters	10MB/second
10Base5 Ethernet (thick-wire)	100	500 meters	10MB/second
FDDI multimode optical fiber	500	100 kilometers	100MB/second

Phone-type LocalTalk (PhoneNET) was originally developed by Farallon to use standard telephone cabling (and telephone RJ-11 connectors) instead of the more expensive LocalTalk cabling. PhoneNET extended AppleTalk's total wiring limit to 3,000 feet, and through the use of star repeaters and quality wiring, it is possible to put 50 or 60 nodes on a PhoneNET network without too much distortion.

If you have a network of any size, PhoneNET-type hardware can save you lots of money, and imitations of it can save you even more. At the college where Rich teaches, they use an inexpensive and reliable PhoneNET clone, Trimar's **CompuNet,** which costs just $15 per connector, or $10 each if you buy ten or more. Focus Enhancement sells its **LocalTalk TurboNet Connectors** for about the same price as the Trimar product. (If you already have LocalTalk cabling, just switch over to PhoneNET-type hardware for any additional needs. Farallon makes an adapter for connecting LocalTalk to PhoneNET systems, so you won't lose whatever you have invested.)

Ethernet. Ethernet—a set of protocols that describes how digital signals are transmitted and how computers access the cable—is not specific to any one kind of cabling, and several kinds of cable are currently used, as we describe below. Ethernet isn't specific to any particular set of protocols either. It's purposely designed to handle multiple protocols, including AppleTalk, TCP/IP, Netware, and others.

There are three main types of Ethernet cabling currently in use:

- **10BaseT (twisted-pair) Ethernet.** 10BaseT, the newest type of Ethernet wiring, has gained rapidly in popularity because it uses unshielded twisted-pair wiring (a kind of telephone wire), which is cheaper and easier to install than the earlier types we discuss below. (The *T* in 10BaseT stands for telephone.) Unless you're using the new daisy-chainable Farallon EtherWave units (discussed below), you're talking an active star topology (see "Topologies," above) that uses a 10BaseT hub to connect many separate runs of cable. On a 10BaseT star network, each run of wire is limited to a maximum of 100 meters, or just over 300 feet. The number of devices depends on the make of the hub; high-end hubs can support more than 100. Daisy-chained EtherWave networks are limited to a maximum of 100 meters, and each EtherWave daisy-chain can support up to 7 devices.

  When shopping for 10BaseT wiring, look for Level 5, the highest grade. Call Black Box Corporation for its nifty networking catalog and order a spool of it. It's not much more expensive than lower-rated cabling and could be used for future higher-speed wiring such as the twisted-pair copper variant of FDDI known as CDDI (discussed below).

- **10Base2 (thin-wire) Ethernet.** 10Base2 Ethernet allows up to 30 daisy-chained devices per each 189-meter segment of coaxial cable (a type that uses a single-wire conductor surrounded by layers of electrical shielding). (The *2* in 10Base2 stands for the 200-meter maximum cable length; they rounded up.) Thin-wire Ethernet can use a daisy-chain topology or with a *multiport repeater*, an active star layout. The use of thin-wire star topologies is rapidly declining due to the arrival of the newer, more flexible twisted-pair Ethernet.

- **10Base5 (thick-wire) Ethernet.** 10Base5, or thick-wire, Ethernet is a stiff twin-axial (one wire inside another wire) cable about ⅜ inch in diameter, with a 15-pin D-style connector. (The *5* in 10Base5 stands for the 500-meter maximum cable length.) The cable is terminated at both ends with special fittings that minimize signal reflections that would otherwise degrade communications, so it permits a maximum of 200 devices on a 1,640-foot segment.

Thick-wire Ethernet is often used as a central backbone connecting secondary networks throughout a building, although fiber-optic Ethernet and FDDI (see below) are rapidly replacing thick-wire as a backbone media.

Token Ring. Ethernet devices listen to the cable before transmitting. Token Ring devices, on the other hand, wait their turn until an electronic token—something like a baton in a relay race—comes their way. Because of this fundamental difference, Token Ring networks can be faster than Ethernet networks when there's lots of network traffic. Most decisions to use Token Ring technology, though, are made because of IBM's adoption of Token Ring as its preferred LAN cabling. There are currently two implementations of Token Ring, one rated at 4 megabits per second and the other at 16.

FDDI and CDDI. Likely to succeed Ethernet, FDDI is an ANSI and ISO standard network based on dual-fiber-optic rings. FDDI has a bandwidth (or data throughput rate) of 100 megabits per second, 10 times that of Ethernet. FDDI networks can contain 1,000 nodes, no more than 2 kilometers apart, for a total aggregate distance of 100 kilometers. Apple offers FDDITalk drivers, though FDDI cards are still a bit on the expensive side at over a $1,000 per card; but just as the cost of Ethernet cards dropped several years ago, expect the same to happen to FDDI cards as well. FDDI cards are currently offered by several companies, Cabletron, Codenoll, and Spectra Systems among them. While FDDI is still rare on the desktop, it's becoming more prevalent as a backbone cabling system.

THINGS TO COME

Although FDDI is gaining in popularity, there are other upcoming standards vying for acceptance. A proposed CDDI (Copper Distributed Data Interface) standard would offer the performance of FDDI using less-costly copper cabling. HP and AT&T are proposing an upgrade to the Ethernet standard to achieve FDDI performance levels (100 Mbps) using 10BaseT twisted-pair wiring. Instead of two twisted pairs, this approach requires four twisted pairs.

Network Hardware

As long as you stay within the limits of a 30-node, 3,000-foot AppleTalk network, LocalTalk cabling is all you need to create a net. Once you outgrow that, however, there are a few other devices you'll need so you can adapt your

Dial-Up Connections (PH/BW)

One thing about a good network—it's awfully hard to leave behind. Whether you're roving with your PowerBook or handling some office business from home, you can still reach your file servers and e-mail over the phone lines. AppleTalk dial-in access has been around for years. The Hayes InterBridge, Shiva NetBridge, and Solana S-Server were early products using proprietary drivers to send AppleTalk protocols over the wires via modem. Now Apple has set the standard with the Apple Remote Access protocol, which finally integrates dial-in access at the Mac System level.

The first product, AppleTalk Remote Access 1, originally shipped with early PowerBooks. It then became a separate product, and has now been superseded by Apple Remote Access 2.0. Whereas version 1 was a server-client combination under one price, ARA 2.0 sensibly breaks those functions into two separate products. Now you buy the **ARA Personal Server** for $225. It comes with client software for one user. Additional client copies are $30 each.

Still, it could get a little expensive using a dedicated Mac for each AppleTalk network dial-in line, and ARA needs too much computing power to reside on somebody's workstation. Fortunately, you've got some options. We're sold on Shiva's **LANRover/E** (for Ethernet), an ARA-compatible box that serves four ($2,300) or eight ($3,300) separate modem lines. It's got great software for managing the LANRover from a remote computer, and it goes beyond remote access, also letting your local Macs dial out through the modem lines. Plus, it supports Internet Protocol addressing, so if you're connected via a LANRover/E and have an IP address, you can access the Internet without using an AppleTalk-to-TCP/IP gateway. (See Chapter 22 for more on getting on the Internet.)

Another option is Apple's **ARA MultiPort Server,** a $1,800 combination of a NuBus four-port serial card supporting four modems and some fairly comprehensive management software. You can add up to three additional $1,500 four-port expansion cards to control a maximum of 16 dial-in modems (there's no dial-out as of this writing).

Each of these server solutions requires a separate modem for each line. To simplify configuration and troubleshooting, we recommend settling on one manufacturer for your modems and selecting the fastest modem possible. At this writing that means modems that follow the V.32bis and V.42bis standards (described in Chapter 22). When the new V.34 standard (also known as V.Fast) becomes more widely available, it should make a great ARA modem. Remember, in order to take advantage of the server modem's speed and error correction, your client modem should also follow the same standards.

HOT TIP

Whichever way you go, ARA is easy to use. Where Paul works he shows the staff how to log on and mount a file server, or even their own Mac, from their laptops. Then they simply make an alias of the remote volume. From that point on, all they have to do is double-click the alias, which has stored the dial-in phone number, their user name (but not their password), and the network path to the volume they've mounted.

Ethernet connection to the type of cable you've chosen, strengthen the digital signal over longer stretches of cable, create a hub for a star topology, and connect separate LANs into a larger network.

Adapters (RT/RC/BW). Once you go beyond the LocalTalk circuitry built into your Mac, you'll need some kind of adapter in order to take advantage of Ethernet, Token Ring, or some other type of cabling.

Even Macs with built-in Ethernet require an external adapter, which fits them for the specific type of Ethernet cabling you're using. Here's a rundown of your options:

- If you have built-in Ethernet circuitry on your Mac, you can use FriendlyNet adapters from Apple, Asanté, Dayna, and others to adapt the built-in Ethernet to a particular form of Ethernet cabling. (Such devices are called *transceivers.*) The $175 Apple **Ethernet AUI Adapter** comes in thick, thin, and twisted-pair varieties.

- NuBus and LC Ethernet adapters provide Ethernet for Mac models lacking built-in Ethernet. There are scads of them on the market, some priced below $100. Apple lists a 10BaseT NuBus adapter for $180. Some boards, like Apple's **Ethernet LC Card** and **Ethernet NB Card,** require an additional transceiver adapter (the Apple Ethernet AUI, cited above, for example), but Apple now sells them bundled for $180 and $280, respectively. You'll only need a new transceiver if you change to a different kind of cabling.

- If you want to daisy-chain 10BaseT Ethernet, try Farallon's **EtherWave** products. If you've already got Ethernet on your Macs, a $130 **EtherWave Transceiver** (AUI or FriendlyNet [AAUI]) will let you daisy-chain them over 10BaseT wiring. **EtherWave NuBus** and **LC** cards list for $230. Newton and SCSI adapters run $380, and there's even a $420 EtherWave adapter box for LocalTalk printers.

  Tut Systems' **Silver Streak** Ethernet transceivers and adapters let you daisy chain up to 30 devices, using ordinary, flat telephone cable. Silver Streak isn't 10BaseT-compatible, although Tut offers a $200 10BaseT converter. AUI and FriendlyNet transceivers list for only $100. NuBus and LC adapters list for $250.

- SCSI Ethernet adapters give your slotless Mac Plus, Classic, or PowerBook, for example, a chance to get out on the Ethernet. One of the cheapest is Focus Enhancements' **EtherLAN SC** ($200, for twisted pair). Asànte's $460 **Mini EN/SC** works with both thin Ethernet and 10BaseT.

Repeaters (JA/BW). *Repeaters* take the electrical signals that represent the 1s and 0s of the digital transmission and retransmit them to another network segment, allowing the signal to carry over longer distances. They don't filter or direct network traffic in any way.

In the Macintosh networking realm, there are many LocalTalk repeaters. An example is Farallon's **StarController** ($1,400), which is a multiport repeater that supports multiple cable segments. Many vendors also offer Ethernet repeaters, the most common being 10BaseT hubs, which are multiport repeaters using twisted-pair Ethernet connections.

Bridges (JA/BW). *Bridges* are one step higher than repeaters on the network evolutionary scale. Bridges examine the source and destination of network frames and can minimize traffic by passing only those frames that are destined for nodes on the other side. This way, you can increase the size of the network without bogging the whole thing down with additional traffic. Unlike *routers* (discussed below), however, they don't know or care about network addresses and zones. Ethernet bridges have long been used to interconnect LANs over long distances. With Ethernet bridges, organizations can connect two geographically remote Ethernet LANs and make them appear as a single connected entity.

Currently there's only one company offering LocalTalk-specific bridges: Tribe. Its **LocalSwitch** ($2,500) and **TribeStar** ($1,800) use the LocalTalk-specific node number to keep track of node locations. They then use those numbers to limit traffic to only those segments containing the valid nodes.

Routers (JA/BW). *Routers* make decisions on how best to route traffic between networks. Since they actually look at the network source and destination addresses of a specific protocol's message structure, they are fundamentally different from bridges, which generally process network frames without concern for the networking protocol used within.

Routers are the fundamental building blocks of large AppleTalk networks. Without routers, you'd be restricted to 30 to 50 devices on a LocalTalk network and several hundred devices on an Ethernet or Token Ring network. Also, AppleTalk routers create and maintain AppleTalk zones and multiple networks. You can't have zones or linked networks without an AppleTalk router. (See the box "AppleTalk Network Numbering and Zones," on the next two pages for more on those.)

Network Hardware: Not Always What It Seems (JA)

Early AppleTalk "bridges," like the Hayes Inter-Bridge, were technically routers. Vendors also use the term "bridge" for certain low-cost LocalTalk-to-Ethernet devices, like Compatible Systems' Ether•Write, Dayna's EtherPrint, and AsàntePrint, used to cheaply connect LocalTalk printers, shared modems, or PowerBooks to EtherTalk-based LANs. (Unlike routers, these cheaper devices don't create or maintain AppleTalk networks and zones, and they handle only a limited number of LocalTalk devices.) When shopping for network connections, pay attention to what the device does, not what it's called; the terms can get confusing.

There are AppleTalk routers, DECnet routers, TCP/IP routers, and Netware routers. There are even routers that can route multiple protocols concurrently. Many AppleTalk routers have a LocalTalk port and an Ethernet port. A good example of a *multiprotocol router* is the **Shiva FastPath** ($2,000), which handles LocalTalk-to-Ethernet AppleTalk routing but can also route DECnet and TCP/IP protocols. A multiprotocol router does not convert one protocol into another; it simply routes each protocol according to its protocol type. It's as if three separate routers, for AppleTalk, DECnet, and TCP/IP, were merged together as a single unit.

Gateways (JA/BW). *Gateways* provide protocol translation services on the network and can be used to connect different kinds of networks. Most gateways also function as multiprotocol routers.

Gateways provide a centralized alternative to placing a "foreign" protocol, such as TCP/IP, on your Macs. Cayman's **GaterShare** software, for example ($995 for the software, $2,800 for the GaterBox router/gateway it runs on) converts Network Filing System (NFS) protocols, common on Unix workstations, to AppleTalk Filing Protocol (AFP), letting a Mac access workstation files as if they were on an AppleShare server. (NFS was developed by Sun Microsystems

AppleTalk Network Numbering and Zones (JA)

If you've got more than 30 nodes on your AppleTalk network, chances are you're using an AppleTalk router to divide it into a couple of subnetworks. This keeps network traffic more localized to each part of the network, and it makes it easier to organize a far-flung network. Each subnet of your internetwork has a unique number. AppleTalk is alone in also letting you apply a name to a subnet or group of subnets. These names reflect "zones," a logical organization designed to make the net easier for users to navigate. The network numbers are used by AppleTalk; the zones are there for you.

AppleTalk networking actually comes in a couple of "flavors," the original, known now as Phase 1, and a newer, Phase 2 AppleTalk. This is important to know because network numbering and zone naming work differently depending which version you're using.

AppleTalk Phase 1

Phase 1 networks can have only a single network number per cable segment. Since AppleTalk supports only 256 potential nodes per network number, each cable segment is limited to 256 devices. Actually, the limit is 254 devices, since 0 is unused and 255 is reserved for broadcasts heard by all devices.

The 254-device limit isn't a problem on LocalTalk and PhoneNET since LocalTalk has a recommended limit of 32 devices. But EtherTalk clearly hit the wall at 254 nodes per cable (including cable segments added via bridges or repeaters)—bad news for large organizations that want to start plonking Macs onto their Ethernets.

Phase 2 vs. Phase 1 Network Number Assignment

Phase 2 breaks the 254-node address limit by letting you have more than one network number per cable. You can, in fact, assign a whole range of network numbers to an Ethernet or Token Ring cable segment, dramatically increasing the number of potential addresses. In a Phase 2 network, the network numbers can range from 1 to 65,534. A special range, called the *startup range,* runs from 65,280 through 65,534. This leaves the numbers 1 through 65,279 for general assignment.

Here's how the node and network numbering work under Phase 1 and Phase 2, depending on whether a router's installed:

- **Phase 1 with no routers.** (Applies to LocalTalk and the now extinct first version of EtherTalk.) The network number is always zero.
- **Phase 1 with routers.** The network number is a number between 1 and 65,536. Each network segment, either LocalTalk or the old EtherTalk, must have a single number assigned. No duplicates are permitted.
- **Phase 2 without routers.** (Applies to the current version of EtherTalk and TokenTalk [AppleTalk over Token Ring wiring].) The network numbers fall in a range between 65,280 and 65,534. This is known as the startup range. There are 254 numbers in this

range that are used by AppleTalk nodes as they come onto the network. This means that for a single, logical segment of Ethernet, there can be 254 networks, each having 253 nodes. This multiplies for a total of 64,262 AppleTalk devices per segment. If you need more than that, an AppleTalk router will be required. Network numbers, like the node number, are chosen at random. One Macintosh could be node 23 in network 65,288 and an adjacent Mac could be node 23 in network 65,500.

- **Phase 2 with routers.** In this case network numbers range between 1 and 65,279. Zero isn't used and 65,280 through 65,534 are reserved for the startup range. Still, with 253 nodes per network number, you could have 16 million nodes per network segment. Although you could use the entire range of numbers for a single segment, it would be wasteful. You're better off assigning a modest range of numbers to a cable, leaving room for growth and expansion.

Assigning Network Ranges

It makes sense to assign fixed network number ranges to the various divisional locations. One location could use 1 to 100 and another could have 101 to 200. That way, local network managers could add routers by using network numbers in their preassigned range. For example, the network numbers could be allocated so that the network on the first floor would be networks 1 to 20, the second floor would be 21 to 40, and the third floor would be 41 to 60. The numbers 61 to 100 would be reserved for future growth.

to provide enhanced file-transfer services and to support network-savvy applications. AFP is Apple's file-sharing system for Macs.) The Mac doesn't have to run NFS. This approach may not be as fast as running the same native protocols on each machine, but it can be a simple and cost-effective way to share dissimilar network services.

Hubs (JA/BW). A network *hub* is the central device on any active star network (which we discuss in the "Topologies" section, above). We mentioned that hubs are often called *concentrators* or *multiport repeaters.* They may have 8, 12, 16, 24, or more ports. Each run of cable composing the star topology connects to one of these ports. The hub amplifies the signal coming into a port before sending it out onto the rest of the network.

Since hubs amplify a network signal, they extend the distance the signal can travel. Also, hubs break networks into shorter lengths of wire, and the shorter the wire, the less chance of signal error. Some hubs also process the signal to resynchronize its timing, while others add sufficient intelligence to recognize disruptive signals and automatically close down the offending port. The term "intelligent hub" applies to hubs that perform extra diagnostic and maintenance functions, or also provide bridging and routing.

Are You Being Served? (Martin Labelle/James Reynaldo/BW)

There are two ways to set up network services. In a *peer-to-peer* arrangement, say for file sharing, each networked Mac is capable of sharing files. In a server-based setup, all shared files must be kept on a central file-sharing computer. Before your co-workers can access your file, you must copy it from your computer to the file server, which then shares the file. System 7's file-sharing feature is peer to peer. Apple's AppleShare file-sharing software represents the server-based approach. (Both approaches are described under "File Sharing," below.)

Since "service" is the raison d'être of computer networking, whether it's print spooling, file sharing of centralized data bases or documents, e-mail, or shared modems, your network is likely to require at least one type of server. Although you can run several services from a single Mac if you have to, matching the right Mac with the right server software is a tricky business. You need to consider the number of people accessing the server at any one time, how many and what kind of services you've installed, the kinds of files you're sharing, and the speed of your cabling (LocalTalk vs. Ethernet, for example). Given the number of interrelated factors, we'll throw out a nonlinear potpourri of considerations to help you weigh the alternatives:

HOT TIP

- If you store thousands of 100K or smaller files on a file server, then the server should be able to complete file requests quickly. If, on the other hand, you're storing multimegabyte image files, you'll want a dedicated Mac with a fast CPU and faster network cabling than LocalTalk. Still, if people don't use the server a lot, then you won't need the fastest CPU.
- In our experience, AppleShare version 3 running on a 68030 (LC III, IIci, IIsi) with at least 8MB of RAM is the minimal setup for a workgroup of 25 users. If you have a 68040-based Mac as a server, there's no reason not to go with

AppleShare 4 (it's faster). And get the biggest, fastest hard drive you can afford—you'll never regret it.

> ### *The Apple Workgroup Servers* (BW)
>
> Apple now offers some Mac server package "deals," consisting of network-ready Macs bundled with the latest AppleShare versions. Dubbed the Apple Workgroup Servers, they're at least an object lesson in the kind of server hardware Apple thinks you might need. Turn to Chapter 2 for a description of the different models.

- You usually know your server setup is too slow when users start consistently complaining about it. If only a couple of people tend to complain, find out whether they're inadvertently doing hog-city stuff. Launching applications from a server will definitely slow you down over LocalTalk, as will double-clicking a Word document from a mounted server drive or sharing font suitcases. LocalTalk just can't take it. It's good practice to always copy files to your desktop before opening them.

HOT TIP

- Different types of server software can often work together on the same Mac. Martin runs Apple's Apple Remote Access on the same machine as his AppleShare file server, no problem. (And that way, ARA can just tap into the AppleShare user list, so he doesn't need another utility to create a user's account for the ARA server.)
- It's not a good idea to allow the file server, such as AppleShare, to also act as a print server on a LocalTalk LAN. The aggravation of having to restart the server every time the spooler hangs up isn't worth it.
- In James's experience, you're better off upgrading (for example, purchasing faster drivers or CPU accelerators) for the server hardware you already own and handing the cream of newly purchased Macs over to individual users. Any network—whether it's 5 users or 5,000—is only as good as the people on it. The real work is done by the workers, and it is done better with better tools.

File Sharing

We introduced the concept of file sharing back in the "Who Needs a Network?" section. It's worth pointing out that Apple didn't provide any means of file sharing when it introduced AppleTalk with the Mac Plus. Sneaker-net ran rampant until a company named Centram Systems West introduced TOPS (Transcendental Operating System), peer-to-peer file-sharing software for Macs and PCs. TOPS is now history, and Apple itself provides for both peer-to-peer and server-based file sharing, through System 7 and AppleShare, respectively.

System 7 Peer-to-Peer File Sharing (JK/CR/SH)

Making use of System 7 file sharing starts with a trip to the Sharing Setup control panel. Click the Start button to activate file sharing on your Mac. The names you enter under Network Identity will appear on everyone's Chooser.

System 7's file sharing lets Macs on a network access each others' files. It's a great way to copy files from one Mac to another—much easier and faster than carrying floppies back and forth. You can also work on a file located on another Mac without copying it to your own, but that generally slows down both Macs.

Your files are private until you turn on file sharing by clicking the Start button in the Sharing Setup control panel. Then you select a disk, folder, or file to share and choose the Sharing command from the File menu. In the dialog box that appears you can set up access privileges for other users on your network, restricting them to merely looking at your files, or allowing them to make changes, rename, move, or delete them.

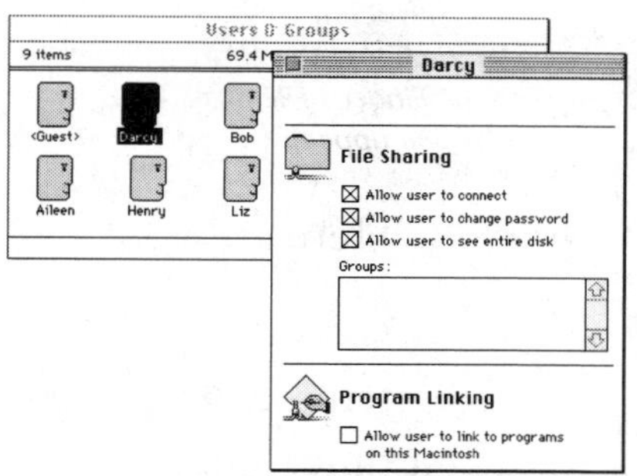

The Users & Groups control panel lets you grant sharing privileges to different users or groups of users.

If you want to assign different degrees of access to different users, you'll have to register each user's name (and give them passwords if you want) in the Users & Groups control panel. You can also organize users into Groups, so you can set access privileges for several of them at once. The File Sharing Monitor control panel lets you keep track of who's using which of your shared items.

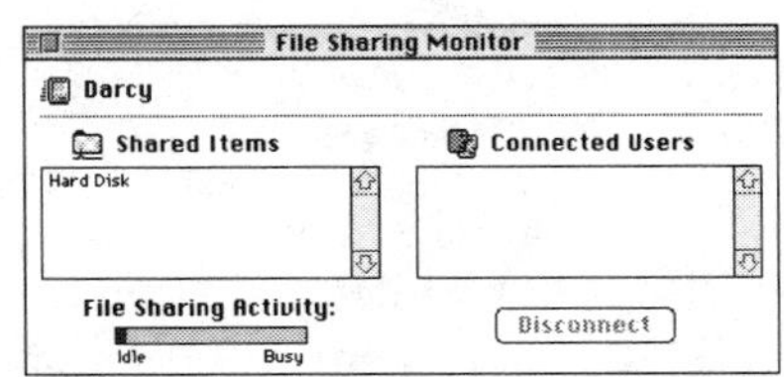

Once you've set up file sharing on your Mac, you can use the File Sharing Monitor control panel to see which files, folders, or disks you've shared, and who's currently using them.

To access shared files on someone else's Mac, you open the Chooser, click on the AppleShare icon, select the Mac's name in the box on the right, and click OK. In the next couple of dialog boxes, you'll be asked to enter the name under which you were registered and your password (if any), and to select the shared item you want to use. When you've clicked OK in the last dialog box, the shared item's icon shows up on your desktop, just like another disk.

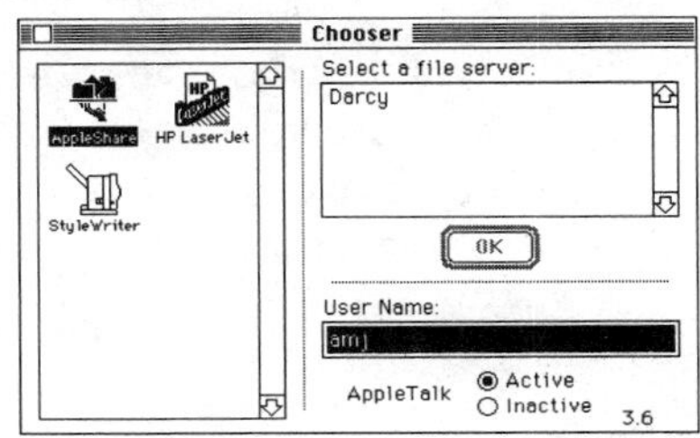

To gain access to files on a server or another user's Mac, select the shared volume in the Chooser.

In the same way, you can access all the contents of your own Mac's hard disk from another networked Mac; just enter your owner's name and password (you entered them in the Sharing Setup control panel when you turned file sharing on).

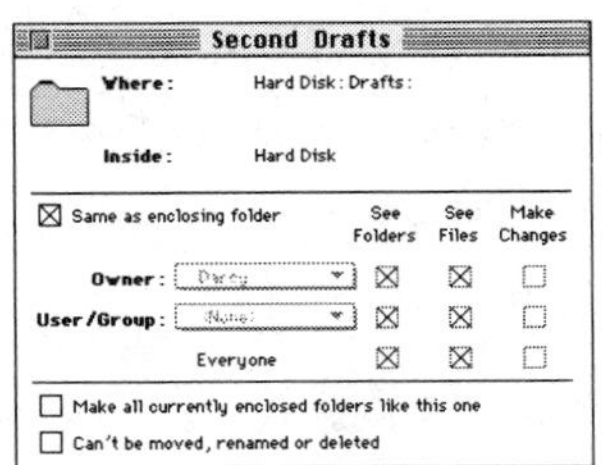

To set up access privileges for a file folder, or disk volume, select it on the desktop and choose the Sharing command in the Finder's File menu. This dialog box will appear.

Although only System 7 Macs can share their files, Macs running System 6 can access files on other Macs—all they need is the AppleShare workstation software, which comes on System 6 installation disks since version 6.0.4. To share files from a System 6 Mac, you need Public Folder (described in the box by that name on the next page).

File sharing's main costs are that it uses up memory in the host Mac (the one that's sharing files) and slows it down. Here are a few tips on how to minimize that tendency:

HOT TIP

- You can bypass most of the procedure for getting a shared item onto your desktop by making an alias of it once you get it there the first time. The next time, just double-click the alias and click OK in the dialog box that appears. (See "System Software Tips" in Chapter 3 for more on setting up aliases.)

Public Folder

(BW/JK/Rich Wolfson)

Public Folder provides basic file-sharing capabilities to System 6 Macs. Available free from Claris if you've got one of their other products, and downloadable from most bulletin boards and on-line services, it allows anything that's placed in a root-level folder named Public to be seen and copied by any other Mac on the network (provided it has the Public Folder init running).

Transferring files is much faster with Public Folder than using a file server as an intermediary. But Rich's favorite use for Public Folder is to accomplish something that would otherwise be impossible with System 6 Macs—copying the contents of one hard drive to another.

Normally, you'd need a spare hard drive or file server for an intermediary transfer. With Public Folder, you just hook an ImageWriter cable into the printer port of both Macs and run Public Folder on both machines. With AppleTalk turned on in the Chooser, the machines can communicate with each other and can copy files from each other's Public Folder.

- You can share up to ten separate items (files, folders, or disk volumes), but unless you're setting up different access privileges for each of them, it's much easier to gather everything you're sharing into one folder and share *it.*
- The fewer people with whom you share files, the less time your Mac will spend responding to their requests. Ask the people with whom you share files to free up your Mac by disconnecting as soon as they've copied what they need.
- Share as few files as possible. The fewer files you share, the fewer opportunities there will be for someone else to accidentally delete or rename your files or see something they shouldn't.
- Use as little security as possible. You should be able to control access to your sensitive files by being careful which folders you share. As soon as you start creating users and groups and setting privileges for them, you'll find yourself tangled in a web of security that you'll constantly be asked to change. A lot of people will forget their passwords, and there's no place to look them up—you can only create new ones.
- If you do register users, make sure all owners of file-sharing Macs on the network register users with the same names. If someone named Margaret were

registered as Meg on one Mac, Peggy on another, and Maggie on a third, she'd have to remember which Mac had her set up under which name.

AppleShare File Sharing (BW/SA/SH/JK)

AppleShare, Apple's file-server software, can turn any Mac on a network into a dedicated file server. With AppleShare running, the file server's hard disk appears to everyone on the network as another icon on the desktop, with its own window, folders, and files. AppleShare predates System 7 file sharing (described above) and has some similar security features; each file or folder can have an "owner" and only someone with appropriate access privileges can get at it. A network administrator can set up work groups with various levels of access privileges. AppleShare also includes the AppleShare Print Server, which spools print jobs (see "Background Printing" in Chapter 21).

AppleShare 3 now shares the lineup with two beefier products: **AppleShare 4,** a speed-optimized version that only runs on 68040 and higher Macs using System 7.1 or later; and **AppleShare Pro,** which runs only on A/UX (Apple's Unix-based operating system, discussed in Chapter 3. The table below gives you an overview of their comparative price and performance.

Comparison of AppleShare Versions

	Concurrent log-ins	Recommended number of concurrent users	List price
AppleShare 3.0	120	15	$1,200
AppleShare 4.0	150	30	$1,900
AppleShare Pro	200	50	$2,400

Electronic Mail

Nothing glues a workgroup together better than electronic mail, as we discussed in the opening section of this chapter. E-mail, in its classic "store-and-forward" form, consists of e-mail server software running on a server computer, and a client (or front-end) portion running on each individual's Mac. The mail server acts as a sort of electronic post office where messages come in, are sorted, and are then stored in each individual user's personal mailbox. Using the front-end client software, you can open your mailbox at your convenience and retrieve your mail. An alternate, "broadcast" form of e-mail shoots messages straight to individual desktops, often a good option for small (five- to-ten-person) networks or for network conferencing.

E-Mail Features

(PH)

Given the number of features competing vendors have added to the basic mail packages of yesteryear, there's more to e-mail than you might realize. Here are some of the things you can expect to find:

- **Mail messaging.** This is the typical posting of messages to one or more electronic mailboxes.
- **Transport medium for files.** You can attach one or several document files to a single message, which means your mail system can also serve for file exchange.
- **Conferencing.** Some e-mail packages provide a message-passing system with a conference screen. Several people can get an interactive conference session going, not unlike what you'd find on CompuServe or America Online (described in Chapter 22).
- **Remote mail access.** Some e-mail packages let you hang a modem off the mail server, letting remotely located Macs dial in to send and receive mail messages.
- **Gateways.** The boundaries of your e-mail activity may extend beyond your local network into the realms of public e-mail services such as AppleLink, CompuServe, MCI Mail, and America Online. Some e-mail packages provide gateway software that lets you automatically exchange mail with these services. With a gateway, you don't have to quit your local e-mail to log on to the outside service.

AOCE and PowerTalk (BW)

It's e-mail! It's groupware. No, wait, it's an application development system. No, it's a state of mind! Well, whatever it is, the Apple Open Collaboration Environment (AOCE), which first showed its face at the debut of System 7 Pro and now ships with System 7.5, will change the way you communicate via your Mac.

PowerTalk is the client portion of AOCE, bringing e-mail and other forms of messaging down to the Finder level. If you find yourself having to check QuickMail, CompuServe, Internet, and AppleLink throughout the day, for example, PowerTalk, with the help of third-party software, will let you combine these and other types of communications into a single desktop mailbox called the In Tray.

PowerTalk initially provided only a bare-bones e-mail program called AppleMail, for AppleTalk networks. But you can purchase "personal gateways"—Apple may eventually bundle some—that link PowerTalk to other e-mail packages or public and private mail carriers. Mail-gateway vendor StarNine Technologies offers **Mail*Link Internet** for PowerTalk, for example, starting at $100 per user, enabling e-mail exchange with Unix mail systems and the Internet. StarNine also sells PowerTalk gateways to Microsoft Mail, QuickMail, and others. CE Software sells QuickMail-AOCE, $100 per single user, $600 for the ten pack. The **FAXstf 3.0 AutoPak** gateway from STF Technologies ($50 for the AutoPak, $40 for the basic FAXstf software) lets your PowerTalk mailbox send and receive faxes.

Some vendors are building PowerTalk compatibility into their applications so you can e-mail documents from within your application as easily as you can print them. Claris's MacWrite Pro 1.5 and WordPerfect were a couple of early adherents. Another example is Caravelle Networks' **NetWorks 3.0.2** network monitoring software ($300), which will send you PowerTalk mail at the first sign of network trouble.

A key aspect of PowerTalk is the Information Card. You create an Information Card for each person with whom you communicate. It lists the e-mail address they'd like you to use, the street address, and other particulars. Drag a document onto an information card, and PowerTalk knows where to send it. A group of Information Cards is called a *catalog,* although other kinds of network resources can be developed as catalogs as well. Catalogs can be used to develop groupware applications.

What about passwords for all your e-mail and file-server connections? PowerTalk's "key chain" lets you type in just a single password, which in turn will automatically handle password negotiation for your server and e-mail access.

PowerTalk will handle these store-and-forward mail functions without a server, but Apple is shipping software called **PowerShare Collaboration Server** ($1,000), which adds centralized mail management and store-and-forward messaging and shared catalogs, plus encryption and public-key-based message authentication.

The Shrinking World of E-Mail (PH/BW)

The Apple Open Collaboration Environment (AOCE) has sparked some changes in the e-mail scene (see the box "AOCE and PowerTalk" on the previous page). Microsoft announced that it would no longer develop the Mac-based mail-server portion of its popular MS Mail product. Instead, Microsoft is recommending that users move to a new MS Mail server that will run on PCs using the Windows NT multitasking operating system. Microsoft will, however, develop Mac e-mail service as an AOCE PowerTalk module. That'll all take awhile to get rolling, so for now MS Mail is in a state flux.

Many of the popular mail products for the IBM PC, including Lotus's cc:Mail and Da Vinci eMAIL, now are including a Macintosh desktop front-end client, as well as front-end clients for DOS, Windows, and OS/2. Note, however, that these products require a PC to run the mail server.

That leaves QuickMail, which we describe at length below, as the main Mac-based e-mail server, though some economy-class e-mail packages such as WordPerfect Office (described in Chapter 12) and Casady & Greene's Snap MAIL may fill some needs.

In fact, **Snap MAIL** ($200 for five users) may be poised to move into the vacuum created by Microsoft's repositioning of MS Mail. It has many of the features of full-blown packages, including message encryption for information privacy, but it currently lacks external mail gateways and compatibility with non-Mac systems. C&G plans to add those, however. The package is easy to administer, and it doesn't necessarily require you to dedicate a Mac as a mail server. At $200 for a five-user package, it also costs only about half as much as programs like QuickMail.

QuickMail (PH)

In CE Software's **QuickMail** ($450 for five users), you'll always have a Mac as the mail server, even if you have PCs connecting via QuickMail's PC client software. It's a natural choice for Macintosh nets that have a few PCs attached. And thanks to the Macintosh interface, QuickMail is very easy to administer and so is a good overall mail package even if half the connected machines are PCs.

QuickMail is a full-featured mail system, which means that it includes all the bells and whistles outlined under "E-Mail Features," above. On the network I manage, QuickMail does more than handle mail messages. For example, we can attach up to 16 files to a single QuickMail message, allowing us to send the file(s) along with a message that explains what to do with them, and when.

We're also using the QuickMail message-passing system, which lets us call up a QuickConference screen, select the person or persons we want to beam a message to, type in a message, and shoot it directly to their Mac, where it pops up on screen.

Several people can also get an interactive conference session going in QuickMail. We find it useful in conferencing between offices located in different cities, since they're connected via a high-speed backbone network. Everyone can follow the conference, selecting and saving relevant text from the screen. (QuickMail won't log the entire conference.)

Remote dial-in mail. When someone doesn't have his or her own e-mail account but wants to get onto our network, the QuickMail dial-in feature lets us set them up with a QuickMail mailbox that they can access via a modem. They dial in, enter a password, and with standard terminal emulation (and Xmodem or Zmodem file-transfer protocols), they can send and receive messages and attached documents using standard telecommunications software. If they're using an IBM PC, Unix workstation, or any system sporting the required terminal emulation and file-transfer protocols, all they see are simple ASCII screen prompts. If the person remotely connecting to QuickMail has a Mac, the standard QuickMail package includes an excellent program called QM Remote, which provides the same interface as the standard QuickMail client software. As an added advantage, QM Remote lets you create your QuickMail messages off-line and then send and receive all your waiting mail messages at once, in the evening, for example, when phone rates are cheaper.

E-mail gateways. With QuickMail's built-in e-mail gateways you can send or receive electronic mail from MCI Mail, AppleLink, and CompuServe without leaving QuickMail to log on to these services directly. Third-party gateways from StarNine Technologies are also available for linking e-mail systems for

Novell MHS, IBM AS/400 systems and mainframes, and even the Internet. The gateway software automatically connects to the outside mail system, appropriately reformats the message, and handles enclosed files. You can set it to automatically connect and exchange mail once a day or every few minutes, as you wish. My firm uses QuickMail's AppleLink gateway quite frequently, so instead of signing onto AppleLink we just create a normal QuickMail message, enclose a document if necessary, and then sent it to our AppleLink account.

It is also very easy to exchange QuickMail messages between remote QuickMail sites. We use a QuickMail-to-QuickMail gateway to exchange messages with several of our clients who use QuickMail. To address a message to a remote QuickMail site, you simply include the person's name and his or her QuickMail phone number.

You'll need to set up a gateway mail center on your QuickMail server. That setup does require you to run the QuickMail administration software all of the time, because it's that software that actually controls the modem. It runs as a separate task under System 7, so you'll need to have sufficient RAM for it.

HOT TIP

If you have several QuickMail servers (we have 12, in order to handle our 200 local users, since each QuickMail server can handle up to 32 active users at one time), pick one to handle the gateways. In my office, the one that's least busy has the modem attached, and that's the one that communicates with the outside world.

Network Management Tools (DC/BW)

Your network is now spread over three floors, and lately, just before lunch time, people complain that they can't print or reach their e-mail. To find out what's going on you'll need a network management and troubleshooting utility. There are several management issues to consider, and there are good products to handle all of them. The problems and solutions are described in this section.

Performance

Is the problem that everyone is simply hopping on the network before lunch, grinding performance to a halt? A program like Neon Software's $495 **TrafficWatch II** (originally from Farallon) checks the LocalTalk or Ethernet traffic on your network, giving you a graphical analysis of overall traffic patterns and error levels, right down to the node. Thus informed, you can decide how to reconfigure your network to remove the bottleneck.

Fault Finding

When your users complain that their laser printer has vanished from the Chooser, you have a fault. The question is, where? You can start looking with Apple's venerable $130 **Inter•Poll** utility. Inter•Poll shows you who and what's on the network: what System, Finder, and printer drivers they're using; the name and ID number of each device; and what type of computer it is and its zone name. You'll soon notice if it's just the printer or the whole network zone that's gone down.

You can also find out who's resetting the LaserWriter as a result of using an old printer driver or who needs a System update. Inter•Poll's interface is functional, if not elegant. The program is simple to learn and use, and it works across network bridges. You install an init, called the Responder, on each user's Mac. When polled by Inter•Poll, the Responder sends along information about the Mac's system.

More expensive troubleshooters such as AG Group's **NetWatchMan** or Caravelle's **NetWorks,** both $300, keep an eye on network services and let you know when something goes down—before irritated users start calling you. Some, such as NetWorks, can even call your beeper.

Neon's **LANsurveyor** ($400 for five zones, $700 unlimited) compiles a map of your network and checks whether any devices suddenly go down. In addition to Responder data, LANsurveyor can gather SNMP (Simple Network Management Protocol) information from routers and from any other device supporting SNMP, as well as Macs running the AppleTalk Connection SNMP agent.

(SNMP, which is related to TCP/IP, has become a de facto network management standard.) It even gives you router packet counts. Farallon's NetAtlas also maps your network, but we think LANsurveyor's method does a better job of showing how your network actually functions, giving you a better organizational view.

GOOD FEATURE

AG Group's **LocalPeek** and **EtherPeek** ($500 and $800, respectively) and Neon's **Netminder** ($600 for Ethernet, $400 for LocalTalk) are *protocol analyzers:* They don't just count packets, they pry into them, often revealing very obscure network problems. You can, for example, set filters to simply capture the traffic between two nodes and then analyze the packet information to see precisely what's going wrong. Netminder even applies artificial intelligence routines to sniff out potential trouble and trace the problem packets back to their source. Aside from fault isolation, you can do some very refined traffic analysis with these protocol analyzers, although they're not for beginners.

Configuration

When it comes to configuring networks and zones on an AppleTalk router, for example, you'll probably use whichever utility the vendor supplies. One great thing about Shiva's line of routers and Apple Remote Access servers is Shiva's Net Manager software, which works across its entire product line.

Accounting

Part of a net manager's job is asset control: keeping stock of the software and hardware options currently installed on the network Macs. MacVONK's **NetOctopus** ($645 for a server and ten users) and Technology Works' **GraceLAN Network Manager** excel at gathering details—System, Finder, and AppleTalk versions; printer drivers; names and versions of applications and system extensions; installed RAM, video boards, SCSI devices; and more—about your Macs.

NetOctopus can also use Installer scripts to update or install applications over the network. Other asset control programs, like the $750 **Status*Mac** from On Technology, have simpler updaters, good for updating files, folders, system extensions, and control panel devices.

Security

If you deal with government-classified information or trade secrets, or you simply don't want your staff pirating licensed software off your network, you'll need security software that controls access to your Macs. One of the desktop security utilities covered in Chapter 13 will let you batten down the hatches with a combination of encryption and password protection for workstation Macs and servers.

If the people on your network are sharing files via System 7 file sharing, you may want them to monitor who's actually using the files. While Apple's File Sharing Monitor control panel will show you which registered users are logged on to your Mac, logged-in guest users are just listed as "<Guest>." The $50 **Nok Nok** utility from the AG Group reports the user name, machine ID, and network zone of any Mac using System 7 file sharing to access a host Mac. Nok Nok alerts users when someone connects, and it also keeps a log of such connections. **Nok Nok A/S** ($175) offers similar monitoring for AppleShare servers.

Timbuktu and Timbuktu Pro (RT/BW)

When you use Farallon's **Timbuktu** ($150 a copy, $2,000 for a 30-pack), your screen reflects what's happening on another machine in the network. You can simply observe the other machine or actually control it with your own mouse and keyboard, as if they were attached to the remote computer. This is invaluable when someone on another floor, or in the next building, needs help. Network administrators with out-of-the-way file servers will also love Timbuktu. AppleShare lets you perform administration functions only at the server, so Randy's admin group at Boston College uses Timbuktu to add users or change privileges from another networked Mac.

Randy has also installed Timbuktu at BC's public Mac facility so that attendants can help students with software questions without having to leave their posts. Administrators were careful to remove the Timbuktu control panel after installation so that students can't change settings and connect to administration Macs. But **Timbuktu Pro** ($200) is less of a kludge. Timbuktu Pro supports TCP/IP and ARA and has enhanced password protection. And you can even do remote control over the Internet with it! An optional $700 Administrator's Toolkit (free with a $5,500, 100-copy pack of Pro) sets passwords and access privileges.

Networking Tips

Network Design

Using routers for efficiency (RC). AppleTalk is very chatty, sending a lot of traffic just to keep track of itself for you. You might want to put a router on your LAN just to isolate some of that "chat" traffic.

For example, if you have 50 Macs on a single piece of cable, every time someone opens their Chooser, every other connected Mac must respond, answering "I'm here, this is my address, here are my services." If you stick a two-port router, such as a Compatible Systems Risc•Router in the middle, the router keeps track of who and what is connected to each side. From then on when somebody on side A opens the Chooser, only the nodes on side A, the router port A, and router port B respond, not all the other Macs on side B.

AppleTalk routers, however, are also chatty, updating each other every 10 seconds or so. Routers that use the new AppleTalk Update Routing Protocol (AURP) will handle this more efficiently. Without AURP, a router rambles off everything it knows during the update. With AURP, it only sends the information that's changed since the last update, which cuts down significantly on the traffic problem. AURP first appeared on the Apple Internet Router, but Shiva, Cisco, and other vendors will support it, too.

Separate zones for remote LANs (JA). In line with the above tip, traffic generated by Mac Chooser requests can really bog down the relatively slow speed of wide-area network (networks that span geographically separate sites) or ARA links, especially if you've included geographically separate LANs under the same zone name. Therefore, while you could theoretically name networks in San Jose and Las Vegas with the same zone name, such as "Production," it would cause additional and unwanted WAN traffic. This is true no matter what kind of WAN link you decide to use and should be avoided.

Don't skimp on wiring (RC). Always insist on putting in more wiring than you need up front. Installation labor costs account for over 65 percent of the total job. Skimping on cabling now will cost you double later because you'll end up installing what you should have in the first place and paying labor costs twice. Your in-house work force will also lose job time because the network will be down while workers are climbing on desks to get into the ceiling area.

Network Management

Monitor lightly (DC). Network monitoring and profiling software like LANsurveyor, NetWorks, and GraceLAN are great for troubleshooting and gathering performance or inventory data about your network. But used recklessly, they can bring your network down. That's because they generate a lot queries over the network, and that (and the responses to those queries) creates a lot of traffic. If you instruct GraceLAN, for example, to identify the installed applications on each Mac, especially at a peak traffic hour like right before lunch or while everyone is logging on in the morning, you can grind your network to a halt. The same holds true with LANsurveyor: If you're checking each network device every 30 seconds, there won't be much room for other traffic. Moral: Set up these products to do their jobs as unobtrusively as possible.

The right tools (RC). As network administrator, insist on having the right tools, even if they seem extravagant at first. For example, you may need network monitoring software, a cable tool kit (with cable scanner), spare parts (network cards, cables, connectors), and even a laptop with a network adapter. These items are invaluable to someone trained in their use, as any network manager ought to be. They not only provide you with instant access to troubleshooting capabilities, but in the long run they will save the company money when it doesn't have to contract out that work at high labor rates.

Know thy vendor (RC). Stay on good terms with a local vendor. Mail order is nice, but nothing can replace a good relationship with a local vendor in times of trouble.

Watch those wiring closets and computer rooms (RC). Keep access restricted to authorized personnel and keep tabs on the condition of the rooms. Do not allow them to be used as storage rooms for office supplies or old boxes or records. This presents safety hazards and extra trouble if you need to work in those rooms, and it restricts ventilation of your expensive communications equipment.

Editors' Poll: Ever Used the Internet (Other Than Through an E-mail Gateway)?

AA: Nope. I would like to, though.

DB: I use the Internet just a little, but I plan on learning more. I think the "information superhighway" is mostly hype, but there are certainly benefits from being connected to such a large group of people.

EC: I'm searching for an independent service provider, or whatever you call them, for Northampton, Massachusetts. I can't believe there aren't any. For some reason Delphi and the rest of them make me suspicious, I wish I was a student and could get a local, use-it-as-much-as-you-want account. There's so much out there, and so many people to talk to, and so much information. AOL's Internet services (not just a gateway) are pretty good.

DD: When I was at *NeXTWORLD* magazine we had a connection, and our technical editor set us up with a bunch of newsgroup feeds. I loved being able to e-mail just anybody (I found out during that time that my brother and sister both had Internet connections through their work!), but I found the newsgroups a frustrating waste of time—so much flaming! I was so busy at that job, though, that I gave it about two days and never explored further.

CG: I've logged on to the Library of Congress and several other government information sources, but I haven't really put in a lot of mileage on the Internet information highway—yet.

JK: Not really.

HN: Yep. I have a SLIP account at Netcom and use it to read USENET newsgroups.

BW: No. Again, it's something I intend to do when I find the time.

24 Sharing Files

LET'S SAY YOU'VE BEEN WORKING for days with Microsoft Word, pulling together an important report. It's midnight, and before you hand your work to your boss tomorrow morning, you want your colleague in Edinburgh to read it over. It's 9 a.m. there; she's just reported to work, and if you e-mail the file to her office, she should be able to make her changes in the file and get it back to you by the time you wake up in the morning.

But wait: You've got a problem. Your colleague has a Mac, all right, but she doesn't use Microsoft Word. The document is full of special formatting—bold and italic type and some complex tables. You don't want to have to get 50 pages back by fax and manually input her changes in the morning.

This chapter covers some of the ways to work around the problems of sharing information between different programs.

Contributors

Darcy DiNucci (DD) is the chapter editor.

Jamie Brown (JB) is a systems administrator at Forensic Technologies in San Francisco. He spends his free time with his lovebird, Loki.

Henry Norr (HN) is editor emeritus of *MacWEEK* magazine and an editor of this edition of the *Mac Bible.*

Ross Scott Rubin (RSR) is the author of *Yakety Mac: The Telecom Tome* (Hayden) and the original edition of Hayden's *PowerBook Power Book.* A forum consultant to America Online's Mac Hardware Forum, he is a staff columnist for *CONNECT* magazine and contributes regularly to *MacWEEK, MacUser,* and *Mac Home Journal.*

Contents

File Formats and How They Work (DD/JB)

Text is text, right? Why wouldn't your friend in Scotland be able to open a simple word processing document in whatever word processor she happens to use?

Well, if it *were* just text, she could. Most English-language programs use a standard code called ASCII (see the box by that name on this page) to spell out the letters of the alphabet and basic punctuation. Where you've got a problem is with all the other information that's saved in a file: the placement of items on the page, the typefaces they use—all the information that tells the program how to display and print the information just as you've specified.

This extra information is generally in a language known only to the program that created it (another way of saying that each program has its own *file format*), and trying to open a file in a program other than the one it was saved in can cause trouble. In some cases, you can't open the file at all; the new program simply won't recognize it as a file. In other cases, you can open the file, but it will be full of all sorts of extra characters—symbol characters, missing-character boxes, and rabbits (yes, we've seen rabbits).

ASCII (JB/HN)

ASCII (pronounced "as-key") is an acronym for the American Standard Code for Information Interchange, which is a universal system of numbering characters. Every text character, tab mark, paragraph mark, punctuation mark, and other common text symbol has its own ASCII number, which all Macintosh programs understand. When you press a key, the code is stored in your document, so any other program can match it to the corresponding symbol in any font.

The Mac uses an extended (256-character) version of the ASCII standard. Many other platforms support only the original 128-character version. That's why some characters you can create in a Mac text editor, like *é*, may not be displayed if you paste the text into an on-line service.

Most applications use ASCII to code the text you type in, then add their proprietary formatting and layout codes around it. If you want to share files between programs, ASCII is always a safe way to get the raw text (and nothing else) across.

Opening Files You Don't Have the Application For

Almost anyone who has worked on the Mac for even a short time has seen the annoying dialog box that tells you your document could not be opened because "the application that created it could not be found."

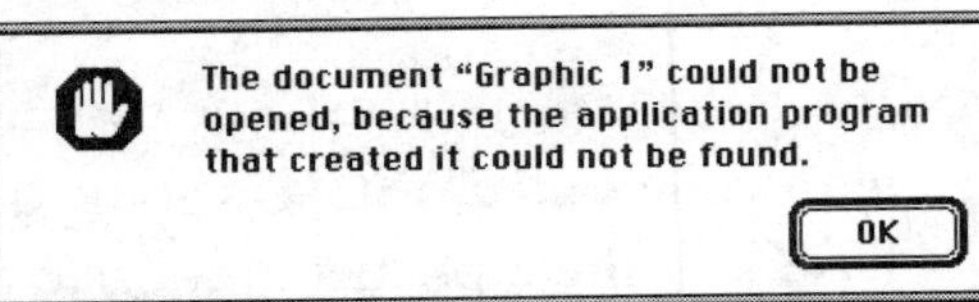

This dialog box warns you that opening a document won't be as easy as you thought.

If you're using a system before 7.5, and the document is a text file or a PICT file, the Mac will ask you whether you'd like to open the document with TeachText, the basic text editor that Apple included with earlier system versions. (SimpleText replaces TeachText in 7.5.) If you are just trying to get a look at the contents of a file (and the Mac gives you the option), TeachText might be worth trying. If what you want to do is get in there and use the information, you'll want to look for a better alternative. Some of those options are outlined in this section.

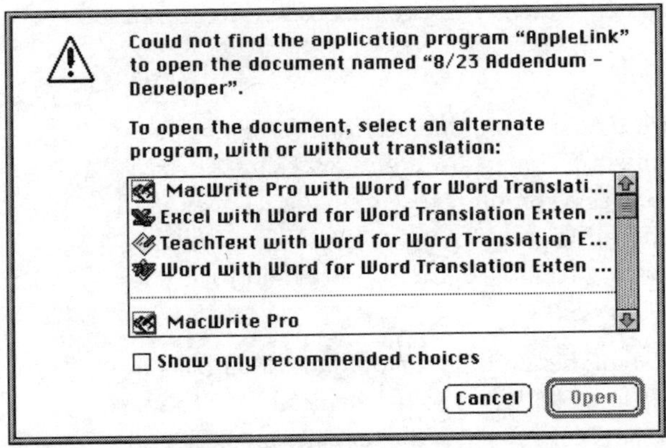

Easy Open adds new options to the standard "Application not found" dialog box, listing all the programs on your system that can open the file.

Luckily, Apple is taking steps to make sure that scenario happens less and less. Starting with System 7.5, Apple bundles Easy Open and a set of document translators that make opening strange files easier.

If you don't have System 7.5 and don't plan to upgrade, don't worry: You can still get many of the same benefits with earlier systems using third-party programs.

File Types and Creators (JB/HN)

When you double-click on a file icon in the Finder, how does the Mac know what program to open?

The Finder keeps track of which programs created which files through a system of four-character codes called Types and Creators. A four-letter *Type code* identifies the nature of the file, regardless of the application that created it. All applications have the same type code, APPL, regardless of the kinds of files they create; all ASCII text documents have the code TEXT, and dozens of different programs can create graphics files of the Type PICT, for example. Some applications, however, use proprietary type codes for their files.

Another four-letter code, the *Creator code*, tells the Finder which program "owns" the document: It distinguishes a text file created with Microsoft Word (MSWD), for instance, from one created with MacWrite Pro (MWPR). This determines which program's icon is attached to the document and which is launched when you double-click the file, among other things.

When none of your programs can open a file, you can assign a new Creator to the file using one of several shareware and commercial utilities designed for that purpose. This will allow you to at least open the file, although the results may not be very satisfactory: You may still end up with those rabbits and missing character boxes. Changing codes can be useful if you have to get the actual ASCII text from a file and when you have no other way to open or translate the file. *[When I don't have the application that created a file but I really only need the text or pictures from it, I use* ***CanOpener****, a $125 utility from Abbott Systems that can display and extract text and PICT images from any file. (It can also search for a particular word or phrase inside any file on your disk.)—HN]*

If you want to try changing the creator code, your options for doing it include the shareware **System 7 Pack** and **SpeedyFinder 7** (also mentioned under "Easy Open" in this chapter). Connectix's **Hand-Off II** ($100) has one of the most flexible approaches to the problem, but several popular collections of System 7 utilities, including Now Software's **Now Utilities** ($130), and Management Science Associates' **ALLright Essentials** ($130) allow this kind of application substitution, too. If you're a power user, you can also take on the task in ResEdit (described in Chapter 13).

Easy Open (JB/HN)

Easy Open is a system extension provided with System 7.5 and with some translation programs (described under "Translation Programs," below). Among other things, it replaces the standard "Application not found" alert with a dialog box that offers some options.

The Claris XTND and Microsoft EC Systems (JB/HN)

In addition to their built-in translation capabilities, many applications let you add extra "plug-in" translators. Many such programs use XTND, a scheme developed by Claris and available for licensing from Apple; Microsoft products use their own translation scheme.

XTND

XTND (pronounced "*extend*") is shipped with all Claris applications and a variety of programs from other developers, including Nisus, WordPerfect, In Control, and On Location. Claris and other developers provide a number of conversion filters that work with the system, and DataViz, the leading commercial developer of translators (described under "Translation Programs," later in this chapter), has adapted its translators to work with programs that support XTND.

When the XTND engine is installed, XTND translators appear in pop-up menus in the Open and Save As dialog boxes of programs that support the technology, allowing you to open and save files in any of the supported formats.

Microsoft's External Converters (ECs)

The Word and Works EC (external converter) systems were developed by Microsoft and aren't as widespread as XTND filters. Microsoft Word ships with many translators, and you can add converters from other vendors at your discretion. A number of EC translators also come in DataViz's MacLink package.

When Easy Open is installed, you are given a list of all the programs on your hard drive that can open that document. You choose from the list, and the document is opened with that program. (You can also tell Easy Open to automatically use the last application you selected for a particular file format.)

Easy Open also handles translations for files that you drag and drop onto an application icon. If a translator exists that will translate the file for that application, it will be automatically executed, and the application will open the translated file.

When Easy Open is installed by itself, there is no difference between using the dialog box or opening the document from within one of the programs on the given list directly—you get the best results the program alone can muster. But System 7.5 also ships with a set of translators from DataViz. When these translators are installed, Easy Open adds them to the list of options. (Keep reading for more on translation programs from DataViz and others.)

Easy Open adds a couple other nice features, as well. First, instead of the default Macintosh file icon for files you don't have the applications for, you get the correct program icon. Also, Easy Open lets you create your own "Document Converters," tiny 4K drag-and-drop applications that convert documents into a format you've specified.

If you don't have Easy Open, there are some shareware utilities that do some of the same things. Adam Stein's **System 7 Pack** ($30) and Victor Tan's **Speedy-Finder 7** ($20 Australian) both include features that let you associate new programs with file types and pick a new program when the original creator isn't available—as well as a host of other handy tools.

You Also Need the Fonts (DD)

Even if you've got the right application to open a shared file, it may still look funny when it opens on your screen. If you don't have those fonts installed, the text will show up in Geneva (or whatever "default" font you've chosen in your application). Your first hint that something is wrong (I mean, someone *could* have meant to format their entire newsletter in Geneva) might be a table whose columns jump all over the place or a headline that doesn't fit its measure.

There are a few ways to make sure this doesn't happen. One is to format any documents you intend to share with fonts you know the other person has. Using the basic fonts that come with the system (described in the box "Fonts Everyone Has" in Chapter 14) is always a safe bet. Most people have these fonts installed in their system, and if they don't, they've usually got them around somewhere.

Adobe sells a product called **SuperATM** ($100) that solves the problem by creating fonts on the fly that match the metrics of the original document fonts. The product is based on Adobe's everyday ATM (Adobe Type Manager) product, which interprets PostScript fonts for screen display. The "super" version adds a database of Adobe PostScript font metrics and installs two Multiple Master fonts (a serif and a sans-serif). With this information, SuperATM synthesizes fonts that match the character widths and essential style of the original fonts. They don't look perfect, but at least when you open the document, your line breaks are right and you get a sense of what the original creator intended.

Another method is to use a document format specifically designed for the electronic distribution of files, such as those described under "Electronic Publishing Tools" later in this chapter. Most of those programs have ways of making sure that readers who don't have the right fonts will still see something approaching your original design on screen.

Instant Translations

(JB)

Almost any software can open plain ASCII text files. Most leading software can also open a range of other formats. Here's a guide to which programs can open which other programs' formats and interchange formats. Remember, though, that in any translation, some information that depends on advanced features (special formatting, formulas, or calculations) in the source software may be lost.

Word Processor Formats	MS Word		MacWrite	Write-Now	Nisus	WordPerfect		MS Works		ClarisWorks	Text	RTF	TIFF	EPS	PICT
	Mac	PC				Mac	PC	Mac	PC						
Microsoft Word 5	●	●	●		●		●	●	●		●	●	●	●	●
MacWrite Pro	●	●	●	●		●	●	●		●	●	●	●	●	●
WriteNow 3	●		●	●			●				●		●	●	●
Nisus 3.4					●					●	●		●	●	●
WordPerfect 2	●	●	●	●		●	●				●	●	●	●	●
Microsoft Works 3	●	●	●		●		●				●	●	●	●	●
ClarisWorks 2	●	●	●	●		●	●	●		●	●	●	●	●	●

Spreadsheet Formats	Excel	1-2-3	MS Works	ClarisWorks	Text	Tab-delimited	Comma-delimited	DBF	SYLK	RTF	DIF	TIFF	EPS	PICT
Microsoft Excel	●	●			●	●	●	●	●		●			●
Lotus 1-2-3	●	●			●	●	●		●					●
Microsoft Works	●	●	●		●	●	●		●	●		●	●	●
ClarisWorks	●		●	●	●	●	●	●	●	●		●	●	●

Graphics Formats	Photoshop	Illustrator	FreeHand	Canvas	Painter	EPS	PICT	TIFF
Photoshop 2.5	●					●*	●	●
Illustrator 5		●						
FreeHand 4			●			○		
Canvas 3				●		●	●	●
Painter 2					●	●*	●	●

* Photoshop and Painter turn EPS into bit maps as they open them.

● Files can be opened and modified.
○ Files can be opened for viewing only; they cannot be modified.
● Files can be placed in a document but not opened directly.

Built-In Translation (DD)

If you don't have Easy Open or another system extension that automatically offers alternative applications for opening files, you can try different options yourself. Get out of the "Application not found" box and open an application that uses the same kind of file. Then try to open the file using that application's Open command. Many programs have built-in translators for foreign files, and you will be able to open the file with all the information and formatting intact (see the box "Instant Translations" these two pages). Others won't do such a clean job, but if you need to get the file open, this method is always worth a try. Once you've got the file open, you can use Save As to save it in your own program's format, and the next time you double-click it, it will open automatically.

Translation Programs

Programs that are dedicated to transferring files from one format to another are multiplying almost as fast as the formats they are designed to convert. And many of the filters provided for these programs plug directly into Easy Open and into other applications.

MacLinkPlus (HN). DataViz, the pioneer developer of format-translation tools for the Mac, has developed filters for more than 1,000 format combinations, including graphics, database, and spreadsheet formats as well as numerous word processing options. The DataViz translators work with Easy Open, XTND, Microsoft's applications, and DataViz's own translation utility.

If you have System 7.5, you already have a set of DataViz translators, but the company also sells them in several retail packages. The basic version, **MacLinkPlus/Easy Open** ($110), includes the full set of filters plus Apple's Easy Open extension. **MacLinkPlus/Translators Pro** ($150) adds Macintosh PC Exchange, the Apple extension for mounting DOS floppies on the Mac desktop. The top-of-the-line **MacLinkPlus/PC Connect** ($200) combines all that with a serial cable and software for linking a Mac and PC directly. (See the next chapter for more on that.)

Word for Word (JB). **Word for Word** from Mastersoft ($150) converts over 100 different formats created by Macintosh and PC word processing applications. You simply tell the application what documents you want to convert, what format you want to convert them to, and where you want to save the new files. The program scans each of the documents to be converted, determines what format they were in originally, and translates them into its own format and then into the type of document you have specified. It converts as many attributes of the original application (text, formatting commands, page layout specs) as it can to matching features in the new application; commands it can't translate are marked in the new document so they can be easily spotted and manually translated.

Word for Word is my favorite translation package. Although its use of its own translation format (and not XTND) does make it less convenient to use than the DataViz translators (unlike XTND filters, Word for Word's aren't available from the Open dialog boxes of most programs), I think it gives far superior results. It even translates graphics embedded in word processing files. Another benefit is the sheer number of its translators: Chances are, if a word processing document has been created on a Macintosh or PC, Word for Word can convert it to something you can use. Mastersoft's manual explains in detail all of the special features it has trouble converting, and what you can do to minimize the pain and suffering of translation. And, if worse comes to worst, call them with questions—their technical support is one of the best I have ever dealt with. The Word for Word package includes Apple's Easy Open extension.

Graphics Converters (RSR/HN/Ben Long/Greg Wasson). Service-bureau operators and others who have to deal with a wide variety of graphics files often rely on Adobe Photoshop for translation, since it can read and write so many formats. Dedicated graphics-conversion packages, including Equilibrium Technologies' appropriately named **DeBabelizer** ($300), a streamlined sibling called **DeBabelizer Lite** ($130), and TechPool's **Transverter Pro** ($400), offer a broad range of PC and Mac graphics format translations. DeBabelizer also supplies tools for batch processing and editing, which you can use, for example, to automatically open a series of scanned images, remove moiré patterns, sharpen each image, and save them all as TIFF files. The DeBabelizer products are designed mainly for bit-mapped graphics such as scanned images, while Transverter Pro is oriented toward PostScript art, though it can convert files to other formats.

GraphicConverter, a $35 shareware tool from Germany, is a sort of shareware version of the commercial products described above. It also boasts some powerful features, including batch processing and paint tools for manipulating graphics. (It requires System 7, a color monitor, and at least 2MB of free RAM.) **Imagery,** a free program, has fewer features, but it can also handle lots of translations.

MAC BIBLE DISK

Sharing Files With Others

While solutions such as the XTND translators and Easy Open are making files easier and easier to share, you can never *count* on colleagues having the applications—and especially the fonts—they need to be able to receive all your information intact. The guidelines and software described in this section will help you make sure your message gets across.

Interchange Formats

Some file formats can be read by almost any application. ASCII (described in the box by that name on page 943) is one. The native formats of the industry's top programs—Microsoft Word and Excel, FileMaker, MacWrite, and WordPerfect, for example—are usually supported by translators in their competitors' programs. There are also a few other formats (called *intermediate* or *interchange* formats) that have been agreed on as standard paths between programs. In some cases, you'll lose some formatting in the translation, but they're your next stop when native formats don't work.

Text formats (DD/HN). For text, ASCII is a sure bet. It can be read by any text-processing program. And if all you need to get across is the text, but no formatting (not even boldface and italic), ASCII is as good as any other format, and the small file size is a bonus.

Many programs will give you a few other choices in their Save As dialog boxes that can help you retain italic, bold, and other formatting you don't want to lose. Microsoft Word, for example, offers two methods for turning a formatted word processing file into ASCII text without losing its formatting forever. *Text With Layout* is the more primitive of the two. If that is selected, spatial formatting—indents, tabs, tables, and line and paragraph spacing—is re-created by inserting spaces in the file. With *RTF*, or *Rich Text Format* (now also called *Interchange Format*), formatting instructions are preserved, along with the document's contents, as text; Microsoft applications and a handful of others that support the format can interpret these instructions and re-create the formatting.

Unless you know that the destination application properly supports these formats, however, you are better off saving your data for transfer as simple plain text. Programs that don't support Text With Layout or RTF will just be confused by the extra information.

Spreadsheet and database formats (RSR/HN/JB). ASCII is a standard format for transferring information from spreadsheets and databases as well as word processors, but such programs need more information than just the text. They need to be told what text goes in each field and how to separate groups of fields into records. The standard way to do this is to place either tabs or commas between the fields (or columns), and returns between the records (or rows), in a format called *tab-delimited text* or *comma-delimited text*. Nearly all spreadsheet and database applications, including personal information managers, let you import and export data in these formats. It doesn't matter whether you choose tabs or commas, as long as the program into which you plan to import the file can handle those delimiters.

There are several other standard tabular formats that hang onto more information than the ASCII formats. *SYLK*, *DIF*, and *DBF* are among the most frequently used. SYLK, the SYmbolic LinK format, is designed to store numbers and is used primarily by spreadsheet programs; it preserves text, numbers, formulas, and text formatting. DIF (Data Interchange Format) and DBF (the format for dBase) are used mostly for databases; they preserve the field names but no text formatting. Most applications support one or more of these formats, but keep in mind that they do not include the formatting and layout information you will get by saving in an application's native format. They are used primarily to get data from one program to another and keep it in the right place. And in every case, moving data between databases is a tricky proposition, requiring the recipient to create a layout for the data in the destination program before importing it.

Graphics formats (AA). As described in Chapter 15, graphics programs are generally split into two camps. Paint programs use *bit-mapped* graphics, that is, they record images as a grid of colored pixels ("bits" in computerese). Draw programs use *object-oriented* graphics—they store each element of an image as a discrete object that can be manipulated separately. Also as explained in Chapter 15, most graphics programs can save both in their own native formats and in a number of other formats that can be used to transfer images among programs.

The most common graphics interchange formats on the Mac are *TIFF* (tag image file format), *EPS* (encapsulated PostScript), and *PICT* (not an acronym). Each has its own uses and limitations.

- TIFF, the most common interchange format for bit-mapped graphics, can contain images of any resolution and color depth. It's supported by every graphics program that works with bit maps, but because the format has several variations, occasionally an application may have trouble opening a TIFF file created by another program.

- EPS is the standard format for storing high-resolution PostScript illustrations. Unlike pure PostScript files, EPS files usually have two parts: the PostScript language description of the graphic, readable by the raster image processor (RIP) on PostScript output devices, and a bit-mapped PICT image used for on-screen display. A drawing saved in EPS format can be imported into other documents and scaled and cropped, but its contents are often no longer editable, even by the program that created it. (Illustrator and FreeHand can open EPS files for editing; Photoshop can, too, although it translates EPS into it's own, bit-mapped format along the way.)
- PICT files are encoded in QuickDraw, the Mac's native graphics language, and can contain both bit-mapped and object-oriented graphics. PICT is the standard format for graphics that are cut or copied to the Clipboard and for drawings that won't be output on PostScript printers.

Electronic Publishing Tools

Say instead of asking for preliminary feedback and editing from your friend in Edinburgh, she was just one of the people on the distribution list for your report. She and several other colleagues need to read your findings before an important client meeting the next day. You've carefully formatted it, inserted lots of graphics and tables, and used lots of different fonts. You want to be able to send it to a lot of different readers, who use lots of different word processors, and you want them to see it in just the form it's in.

A passel of programs aimed at answering this problem have sprung up recently, including Adobe's Acrobat, No Hands Software's Common Ground, Farallon's Replica, and WordPerfect's Envoy. And if you have QuickDraw GX, you've got a built-in solution, QuickDraw's portable digital document (PDD) format.

All of these programs let you exchange fully formatted documents between computers without worrying whether the recipient has the application that created them or (in most cases) the fonts they include. And with the exception of

QuickDraw GX, these programs can create electronic files that can be read on both Macs and PCs running Windows. They also have uses far beyond the one we'll talk about here: delivering documents to readers who don't have the right apps and fonts. All these vendors have big plans for features—full-text search and indexing capabilities, for example—that will make them suitable for building the electronic document archives that could make possible the paperless office we've been hearing about since computers were invented.

THINGS TO COME

Most of these programs work in a similar way. To create a document, you choose the program's driver in the Chooser (or just hold down a special modifier key) and "print" it to disk using the standard Print command. (All these programs supply a quickie drag-and-drop creator application.) All of them also supply ways to compress the files they create for faster communication across e-mail systems. At the other end, a recipient uses a "viewer" application to read the files. In most cases, the recipient can't edit the electronic documents directly, but in most of the programs they can add annotations in the form of posted notes.

Despite these similarities, these electronic publishing packages differ from one another in several important ways:

- how they handle fonts
- how compact their files are
- the features they supply for navigating and annotating the electronic documents they create

All the programs in this new category have hit the ground running and are in heated competition to add new features fast, so check the latest versions when you're in the market to see who's got what. The descriptions here attempt to outline the differences in approach between the different products, as well as their features at press time.

QuickDraw GX's PDDs (DD). The biggest benefit of QuickDraw's PDD format is that you don't need any special program to create documents with it. It's built right into System 7.5 or any system that uses Apple's QuickDraw GX extension. (The GX extension and how to get it are described in Chapter 3.)

PDD files can be read by anyone who also has QuickDraw GX installed (via the SimpleText application that comes with every Mac that has System 7.5), but it doesn't allow the recipient to search for text or add annotations. The resulting file sizes are also fairly large (see the table of file sizes on page 959).

QuickDraw GX offers three options for embedding fonts: no fonts (if you know the people at the receiving end will have the fonts on their system), nonstandard fonts (if you can count on them having the basic system fonts installed), and all fonts (if you want to make sure they see the file correctly no matter what fonts they have installed).

The greatest limitation for some users will be that the PDD format can't reach across platforms: The fact that it depends on GX's graphics engine limits its distribution to a fraction of Mac users and locks out Windows users and other audiences. For Mac users who have GX, however, it's unbeatably convenient.

Adobe Acrobat (RSR/HN/DD). Acrobat is the most heavily hyped, the most expensive, the most feature-rich, and the most demanding in terms of hardware requirements of all the products described here. The basic package, **Acrobat Exchange** ($195) includes the PDF Writer (a driver for creating the portable files, called PDF, or Portable Document Format, documents); the Exchange app serves as the viewer. Another application, the **Acrobat Distiller,** can create

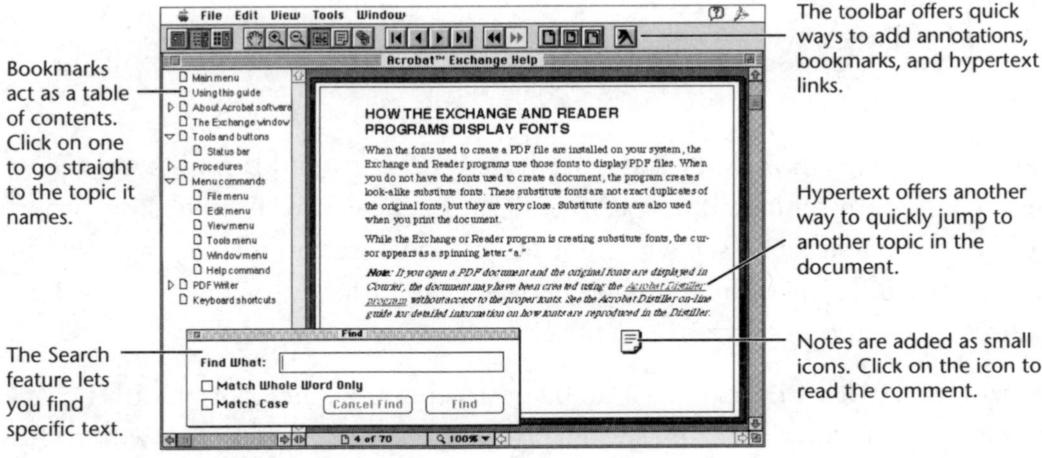

Adobe Acrobat offers a complete set of annotation and navigation tools with an elegant interface. Unlike the other electronic publishing programs, though, it requires that each document recipient buy his or her own copy of the viewer.

PDF files from PostScript files. It also adds compression features and some advantages for high-resolution graphics, but it will set you back an extra $700 for the basic version and $2,500 for the network version (which includes batch processing). Each recipient of a PDF file must have his or her own copy of Exchange or of the **Acrobat Reader,** which costs $50 when purchased separately. Although Acrobat will run on a Mac Plus with 2MB of free RAM, performance is unacceptably slow on older machines, and Acrobat Exchange alone requires 7.5MB of disk space.

Acrobat has a rich set of annotation features, at press time rivaled only by WordPerfect's Envoy. It offers not only basic text-search features but also posted notes for annotating the document; thumbnails, which present the pages in the document in reduced form, letting you quickly find and jump to the page you want to see; multilevel "bookmarks," for allowing quick access to marked locations in the document; and *hypertext* links, which jump you to related parts of a document when you click on them. And the interface is the most elegant of all the products reviewed here.

PDF files show the fonts in the original document only if the machine at which the document is being read has the fonts installed; otherwise, Acrobat uses Adobe Type Manager and the company's Multiple Master technology (the same technique used for Super ATM) to create fonts approximating the originals. If the file is created with Acrobat, the graphics are stored as screen-resolution bit maps. Distiller, however, rasterizes EPS files, retaining all their original resolution at any magnification.

Adobe has published the PDF format as a standard that other developers can take advantage of. At press time, Adobe had announced that Illustrator 5.5 would be able to write and edit PDF files (and now that Adobe will acquire PageMaker in its merger with Aldus, PageMaker probably won't be far behind), so graphic artists who use those programs might have a preference for Acrobat's format. Acrobat's features also make it a strong candidate for document archiving and electronic publishing, but they're probably overkill for the simple exchange of electronic documents. And Acrobat's requirement that each recipient must be equipped with an Acrobat reader makes the product most practical for businesses that mean to adopt the product companywide.

Common Ground (DD). No Hands Software calls its **Common Ground** format "DigitalPaper" (DP), a moniker borne out by its approach of creating bit-mapped images of your documents that can be distributed almost as freely as paper. It's an easy, one-step process, and unlike Acrobat users, creators of Common Ground documents can embed a mini-viewer into their files so that they needn't worry whether readers at the other end have their own copies of the Common Ground Viewer. (Embedding a viewer adds about 90K to the file.) Common Ground also uses proprietary technologies to embed font data so that the recipient needn't have the fonts installed at his or her end. The Common Ground package lists for $190. Common Ground also has lower system requirements than Acrobat has; creating and viewing documents is relatively quick on low-end Macs, and the program requires only 700K of hard disk space.

Recipients who use the embedded mini-viewer can page through the DP document and zoom in and out, but not much else. Even the full-featured reader included with the Common Ground program limits navigation options to paging through or searching for text strings; in version 1.1 (the current version at press time) there were no hyptertext or bookmark features. Recipients can copy text or graphics from DP documents, but they can't annotate them. Common Ground saves different versions of the file, at resolutions ranging from 72 to 300 dpi, so that graphics remain sharp when viewed on screen, even at high magnifications, though high-resolution printing will test their limits.

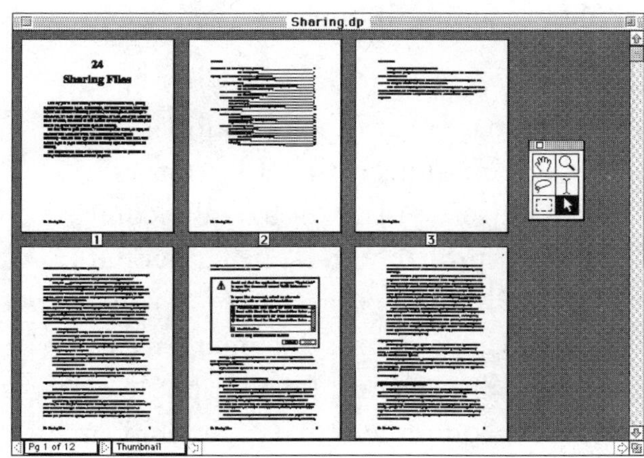

Common Ground's thumbnail view, shown here, is one way to view a digital paper document. You can magnify and search through the electronic documents and cut and paste graphics and text, but you can't add annotations.

Common Ground does have a few of its own bells and whistles, however, including the ability to password-protect documents or assign a "read-only" status to them (so they can't be printed or copied). In its latest version, it offers JPEG compression (through QuickTime), greatly reducing file sizes for files that include high-resolution graphics (although the raw file size was larger than any other program except QuickDraw

Electronic Publisher Files (DD)

These tests were done on a 69K, four-page QuarkXPress document that included four fonts and three TIFF files (an additional 518K).

Product	File Size without viewer	with viewer
QuickDraw GX[1]	243K	n/a
Acrobat	72K	n/a
Common Ground	173K	260K
Envoy[2]	20K	356K
Replica	56K[1]	453K[1]

Notes

1 Using the "Include all fonts" option.

2 The version tested was a prerelease version; WordPerfect says file sizes for the release version should be about the same.

GX, as noted in the table above). It also boasts support for Apple's AOCE technology (described in Chapter 23), allowing users to e-mail DP files from within the Common Ground viewer, and includes a filter that plugs into Easy Open, letting users open editable DP docs in text-editing apps.

Replica (RSR/HN/DD). Farallon's **Replica** ($190) has a lot in common with Common Ground. It's digital documents can include a viewer so that they can be e-mailed to anyone, regardless of whether they have Replica installed. (Farallon takes the free-viewer approach a step further by installing the Replica viewer on the recipient's computer permanently so that it need be sent along only once.) It offers password protection and read-only encoding by the sender, and a limited set of navigation options, including paging and text search, but currently no hypertext, bookmark, or annotation features.

In Replica, graphics and font depiction is based on the TrueType capabilities common to both the Mac and Windows. When saving a document, Replica gives you four font-embedding options: no fonts; screen fonts only; screen and printer fonts for all non-System fonts; and screen, printer, and TrueType fonts. Only with the last option can you be sure that your reader will see the document as you intended it. (It also results in the largest file size.) In our tests,

Replica and Envoy tied for the least-satisfactory treatment of graphics: embedded TIFFs become unreadable at higher magnifications.

Envoy (DD). WordPerfect's entry, called **Envoy,** hadn't been released when we wrote this, but advance reports and tests showed impressive capabilities that rivaled or surpassed Acrobat's, with the low hardware requirements and free-viewer distribution of the other products. It will sell for—you guessed it—$190.

As with the other products, the recipient can use the viewer (freely embeddable in the Envoy document) to zoom in and do text searches on the file, and the file's content can be cut and pasted as ASCII text or PICT graphics into other applications. Like Acrobat, though, it goes beyond that basic set to offer thumbnails, bookmarks, hypertext links, and annotation capabilities—plus a highlighter tool. And its annotation features surpass even Acrobat's: The notes can be color-coded, identified by author, given different icons, and identified by

MarkUp: For Detailed Collaboration (DD)

Mainstay offers an electronic publishing solution for editors and others who want to comment on electronic documents with precision and old-fashioned proofreading marks instead of posted notes. **MarkUp** ($195) uses the same print-to-disk method as the other electronic publishing apps, and it lets you embed a viewer for recipients who don't own the program. (As with the others, embedding a viewer adds significant bulk to the file.)

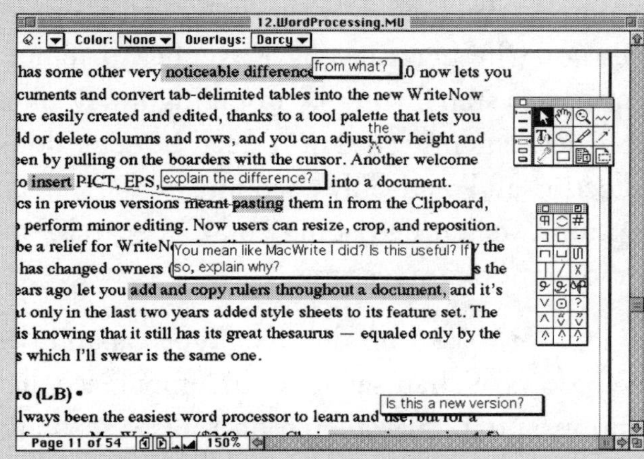

MarkUp offers copyediting marks, a highlighter tool, and text boxes for editing and annotating electronic documents.

What Mainstay offers that the others don't are carets, transposition marks, and other symbols dear to copyeditors, along with the ability to add boxes for lengthier comments. Each reviewer's comments are added in a separate overlay, which can be viewed all together or separately, and marks can be coded with any of eight colors. MarkUp users can also create a change log showing the time of each editing session.

type. Recipients can search on any of these attributes, finding only the notes added by their boss, for example. As with Common Ground and Replica, creators of Envoy files can add password protection or read-only status to the files.

Envoy saves a description of each font with the file. If the recipient has the right fonts installed, no problem: The document is shown in its original state. If not, Envoy selects the closest match possible from the fonts that are installed and adjusts the character spacing to fit the metrics of the original font. Line breaks remain intact, but this method is less apt to preserve the original look of the document than that used by the other programs.

In my test file, Envoy's other weakness was its lack of graphics resolution: The resolution of the bit-mapped graphics broke down quickly at higher magnifications. Envoy also had my least-favorite viewer, offering a whole band of navigation tools, with almost nothing working just as I'd like. For example, the Find feature has no "Whole Word" option, and bookmarks are accessed from a pop-up menu at the bottom of the screen instead of being implemented in the elegant table-of-contents view used in Acrobat.

Editors' Poll: Can You Think of Anyone Who Should Buy a PC Rather Than a Mac?

DB: I know of a guy who should buy a PC rather than a Mac. I hate him. I don't hate many people, but this guy really gets my goat. He should use a PC. It would serve him right.

EC: No.

DD: Well, the many times I've been asked to recommend one or the other, it's always been the Mac. Even in the old days, when there was a great cost differential, I just felt the ease of working with the Mac was worth the premium. OK, I guess if you wanted a laptop, for word processing only, you might still get a DOS-based one (they're still cheaper than PowerBooks).

CG: Although I personally like the Mac, I see a lot of reasons that someone might want a PC. If everyone in your office uses Windows and you want to do work at home, then it makes sense to buy a comparable system. With all the low-cost Macs these days, though, price is no longer a reason.

JK: Someone who has a lot of PC software (or has to work with PC software) and isn't ready to spring for a Power Mac with 16 megs of RAM and SoftWindows.

HN: Sure—anyone who needs to use a DOS-only vertical application or a dBASE database or such.

BW: This is a rather, uh, personal topic, and frankly I don't think this is the time or place for it. OK?

25

Coexisting With PCs

SAD TO SAY, most personal computers aren't Macs. In fact, there are something like ten or twelve IBM-style PCs for every Mac in existence. So odds are a time will come, if it hasn't already, when you'll want to read some files created on a PC, or send some data to a friend, client, or colleague who uses one. Perhaps you'll want to put both kinds of machines on the same office network. Or maybe you'll even need a program written for DOS or Windows and want a way to run it on your Mac.

Not long ago, most of those things were out of the question. While the insides of Macs and PCs may look similar, from a technical point of view they are very different, and teaching them to cooperate has been a long and painful process. The schooling is not complete yet, but we have progressed to the point where exchanging data between the computer families ("across platforms," as the computer industry calls it) is commonplace and simple. And Macs and PCs can now share more than data files. Look-alike versions of most major applications are available for both systems; you can plug them both into the same networks and electronic-mail systems; and they can share peripherals. If necessary, you can even run DOS or Windows on your Mac.

Contributors

Henry Norr (HN) is the chapter editor.

Ross Scott Rubin (RSR), is the author of *Yakety Mac: The Telecom Tome* and the original edition of *Hayden's PowerBook Power Book* (both from Hayden). A forum consultant to America Online's Mac Hardware Forum, he is a staff columnist for *CONNECT* magazine and contributes regularly to *MacWEEK* and *MacUser,* and *Mac Home Journal.*

Contents

Getting It There

There are many ways to move data between a Mac and a PC—probably more than you think. Which approach you should choose depends on the distance between the machines, the size and nature of the files you have to transfer, how often you expect to be doing such transfers, and, of course, your budget.

PC Floppy Disks in Mac Drives (RSR/HN)

Probably the most common method of transferring information between Mac and PC is "sneakernet"—walking a floppy disk from one machine to the other. A decade ago, when PCs used 5.25-inch floppies—the black ones that really were floppy—this wasn't easy, since the disks didn't fit into the Mac's 3.5-inch floppy drives, and vice versa. In the late 1980s the PC world caught on to the advantages of the smaller, sturdier and more capacious 3.5-inch format, and now most new PCs have at least one 3.5-inch drive. But the road was still not clear, because the 400K or 800K floppy drives used in early Macs were based on a proprietary design—the brainchild of Apple cofounder Steve Wozniak himself—that made them incapable of reading or writing even 3.5-inch PC-format floppies.

The *SuperDrive*—the 1.4MB floppy mechanism Apple introduced in 1988 and now uses in all Mac models—took care of the mechanical incompatibility. For the first time, Macs and PCs could share the same floppy disks. But you still couldn't just insert a disk from a PC and see its icon, folders, and files on the Mac desktop, because the Mac didn't know how to read PC directories; unless you bought special software or opened a utility called Apple File Exchange, the Mac would tell you the PC disk was unreadable. Only recently, in certain Performas and the Power Macs, and then under System 7.5, has Apple finally made software that mounts DOS disks on the standard desktop equipment.

Apple File Exchange (RSR/HN). Apple's original solution to the problem of reading DOS directories was Apple File Exchange (AFE), which comes free with the Mac system software (look on the disk called Tidbits). Only after starting up AFE could you insert a DOS disk, have it recognized as such, and see or copy what was on it. (It also works with ProDOS disks from the Apple II.)

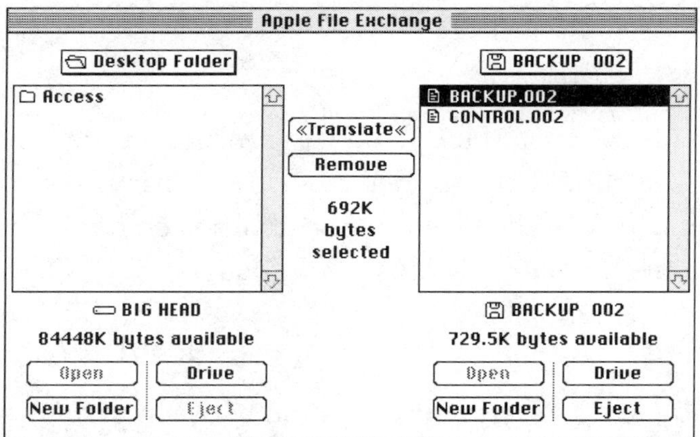

Apple File Exchange's main window displays two lists. The contents of your hard disk are on one side (generally the left), while the contents of the DOS floppy are on the other. Selecting files and clicking buttons lets you copy files to or from the DOS disk. A menu command lets you format a floppy as a DOS disk.

Apple File Exchange is not especially user friendly, and it's now possible to do everything it does more easily with more modern utilities. But it can still be useful, and you can't beat the price.

Just moving a file from PC disk to Mac disk doesn't guarantee that Mac programs can read the file, because the information inside it might be stored in a way Mac programs can't understand. Ditto in the other direction, with Mac documents copied to a PC disk. That's why AFE and similar programs were designed not just to copy files, but also to translate them. (Unfortunately, this kind of translation only works with data documents; making actual programs written for one machine work on the other is a bigger task, one that a simple utility can't handle.)

Aside from a simple converter for text files, AFE has always shipped with one translator, which converts between the old MacWrite format and a PC word processing format called DCA-RFT. But other companies developed additional translators that show up as menu options in AFE. The most notable products of this sort are DataViz's **MacLinkPlus/PC** and **MacLinkPlus/Translators,** which include translators, or *filters*, for hundreds of combinations of Mac and PC word processors, spreadsheets, databases, and graphics programs. (Note that DataViz's filters now also work with the XTND, Easy Open, and Microsoft translation schemes described in Chapter 24.)

DOS Disk Mounters. The easy and elegant way—the real Mac way—to deal with DOS disks is to make it possible to insert them any time, like any other disk, and to see their contents in standard Finder windows and Open dialogs. Apple promised to build such capabilities into the Mac operating system back in 1988, when it introduced the SuperDrive, and by the time you read this, the promise should have come true. At this writing, though, you can make your Mac work this way only if you purchase and install a special system extension.

Three such programs are widely available: Dayna's **DOS Mounter Plus** ($80), Insignia Solutions' **AccessPC** ($130), and Apple's own **Macintosh PC Exchange** ($80), which uses technology developed by Insignia. The Apple product, which is now included with many new Macs and Performas and will be distributed as an extension with System 7.5, has the most inviting interface, but it also consumes the most memory, and unlike the other two, it won't work with System 6. DOS Mounter Plus and AccessPC have more features: Both let Mac users connect to the most common kind of PC networking software (Novell Netware), and both work with other DOS-formatted removable media such as SyQuest, Bernoulli, and magneto-optical cartridges. AccessPC also includes Mastersoft's Word for Word translation filters for a variety of word processing formats. (For more on Word for Word, see Chapter 24.)

GOOD FEATURE

Dealing With 5.25-Inch Floppies (RSR/HN)

Even when Macs and PCs used completely different types of floppies, the need to exchange files led developers to try to bridge the gap. As far back as 1985, Dayna Communications developed an expensive contraption called MacCharlie—a PC that wrapped around the Mac and used its screen, enabling users to run DOS programs and transfer files between Mac disks and PC floppies.

A few years later Apple brought out the Drive 5.25, an external drive for the Mac that could read and write 5.25-inch PC floppies. But it too was expensive, and it required you to install a special card in a Mac SE or Mac II. Then Dayna struck back with a much better solution: the DaynaFile, an external SCSI device that could hold two standard PC floppy drives, in either 5.25- or 3.5-inch format.

The DaynaFile is still around (now in a smaller casing called the **DaynaFile II**). It costs $600 for one drive, $900 for two, and it's still the best option if you frequently need to read 5.25-inch PC disks from your Mac. Fortunately, that's rarely necessary nowadays, since most PCs use 3.5-inch floppies and most Macs have SuperDrives that can read them.

If you occasionally run across some old 5.25-inch PC floppies but you don't need regular access to them, your best bet is to take the floppies to a PC with both 5.25- and 3.5-inch floppy drives. Copy the files from the big disk to the little one, take the latter back to your SuperDrive-equipped Mac, and you're off. (PCs with both sizes of floppies aren't hard to find. In a pinch, you can even add a 3.5-inch drive to most PCs, if you know what you are doing or can find someone who does. It shouldn't cost more than about $50.)

It's Not Just Floppies Anymore (HN)

If the files you are trying to move between platforms are too big to fit on a floppy, you've got a problem. One solution is to use matching high-capacity removable-media drives—SyQuests, Bernoullis, or magneto-opticals (all described in Chapter 5)—on both the Mac and PC sides.

Recent versions of both Dayna's DOS Mounter Plus and Insignia Solutions' AccessPC can mount PC-formatted removable cartridges on the Mac desktop, and both now include software that lets you format DOS cartridges from the Mac; they even let you divide cartridges into separate Mac and DOS partitions. The most versatile cross-platform formatter, however, is Software Architects' **FormatterFive** ($200), which can apply PC formatting to hard drives as well as to removable media from the Mac.

Don't forget, though, that you won't be able to connect Mac drives to your PC unless it's got a SCSI adapter. That's not a standard item in your average PC clone, but these days adapters are not uncommon and not expensive. (See Chapter 5 for more on SCSI.)

All these extensions let you read, write, and format PC disks. Using any of them is pretty straightforward. When they are loaded, any inserted PC disks appear in the Finder and in Open and Save As dialogs, just like Mac floppies. When you double-click the disk's icon (which may include a "D" for DOS or "PC" to identify its origin), you get a window showing its contents; DOS directories and subdirectories are shown as folders. You can copy files and folders to and from the disk just by dragging.

Mac Disks in PC Drives (HN)

Just as Mac developers have figured out how to read PC disk formats on the Mac, PC developers have come up with utilities that let you read, write, and format Mac floppy disks (high-density only) on a PC. There are several such programs. Some, such as PLI's **Mac to DOS** ($100) and REEVEsoft's **MacSee** ($35 shareware, $80 commercial), are separate applications—you need to launch them and use their commands to move files. A couple of recent competitors, such as **MacDisk** ($100) from Insignia Solutions and **MacAccess** ($70) from Hypro Technologies, are not applications, but *TSRs*, or *terminate-and-stay resident* programs—the DOS equivalent, roughly speaking, of a Mac system extension.

The virtue of the TSRs is that they enable you to see and open files from your Mac disk from anyplace where you see your DOS and Windows files, including DOS, the Windows File Manager, and the Open dialogs of Windows applications. (You see only truncated versions of the Mac file names in these places, but blame DOS, not the utilities, for that; you can always see the full Mac names by launching MacDisk or a Hypro utility called **MacShow.**)

Between the two TSRs, Insignia's MacDisk is the more powerful, at least as of this writing. But MacAccess is included in **ConversionsPlus,** DataViz's $150 PC-Mac format-translation package for DOS and Windows. (It works like the company's MacLinkPlus products, described in Chapter 24, except that it runs on the PC side of the fence.) If you plan to do a lot of format translation and for some reason prefer doing it on the PC, that's an economical bundle.

Mapping DOS Extensions (RSR/HN)

One of the several factors that complicate file transfers between Macs and PCs is that they use different schemes to associate data documents with applications. DOS doesn't know Mac file types (see "File Types and Creators" in Chapter 24) from blood types; it just ignores the four-letter type and creator codes on documents you transfer. For its part, the Mac, left to its own devices, has no way of interpreting the three-character filename extensions that identify the creating application in the PC world (.XLS for Excel worksheets, .WP for WordPerfect documents, and so on). When you transfer a DOS or Windows file to the Mac, the Mac ordinarily assigns it a generic Type and Creator.

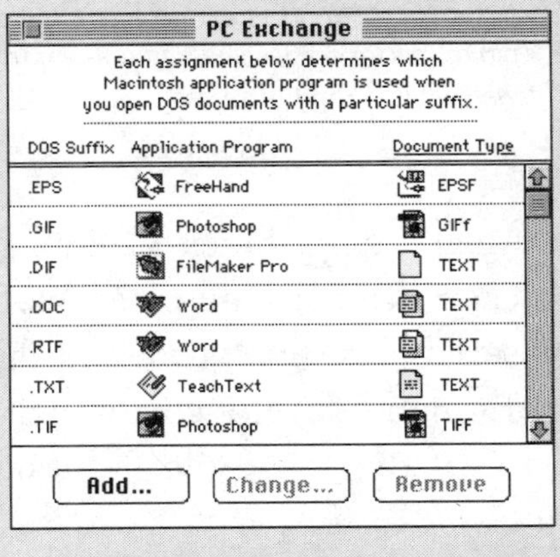

PC Exchange

Each assignment below determines which Macintosh application program is used when you open DOS documents with a particular suffix.

DOS Suffix	Application Program	Document Type
.EPS	FreeHand	EPSF
.GIF	Photoshop	GIFf
.DIF	FileMaker Pro	TEXT
.DOC	Word	TEXT
.RTF	Word	TEXT
.TXT	TeachText	TEXT
.TIF	Photoshop	TIFF

Add... Change... Remove

Apple's Macintosh PC Exchange, available from Apple or included as an extension with System 7.5, lets you map DOS extensions to Macintosh file types. The program automatically makes the translations.

All three commercial DOS-disk-mounting utilities—Dayna's DOS Mounter Plus, Insignia Solutions' AccessPC, and Apple's Macintosh PC Exchange—offer a handy feature called *extension mapping.* Using the utilities' control panels, you can associate a particular Type and Creator code with any DOS extension. You can, for example, assign the Creator "MSWD," which designates Microsoft Word on the Mac, to all PC files ending in .DOC, the extension Word uses in its PC and Windows versions; the Type can be set to "TEXT."

What you get in exchange for the time you spend setting up these mappings is the ability to open a PC file into the Mac application you want just by double-clicking; otherwise, you'd have to open the application some other way and get to the file you want via the Open dialog box.

Note that Types and Creators are among the few aspects of the Mac system that are case-sensitive. That means that a file with the Creator "FOOB" and one with the creator "foob" could launch two different applications.

Direct Serial-Cable Connections (RSR/HN)

Sneakernet is a simple solution if you don't have too much data to share and you have 3.5-inch floppy drives on both platforms. But it can be a pain if you have multiple megabytes to move, or if you're using a PowerBook 100 or a Duo and you don't feel like schlepping an external floppy drive along.

The cable. One solution under those circumstances is to connect the Mac and PC directly by cable. A common type of cable known as a *null modem cable*, with a round 8-pin end and a trapezoid-shaped 9-pin end, can connect a serial port of the Mac to the serial (COM1) port of a PC.

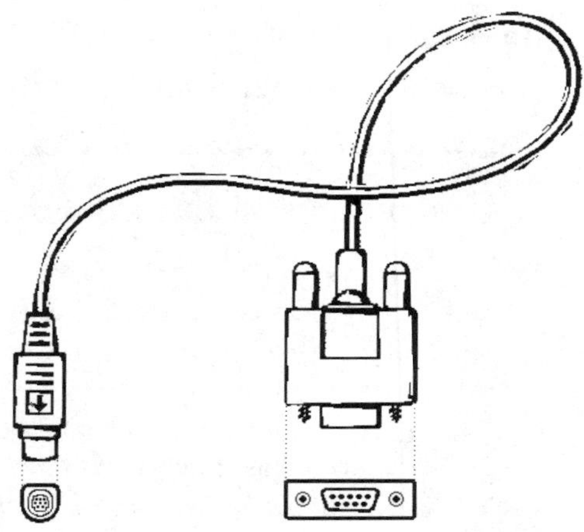

A null modem cable, which you can use to attach a Mac and a PC for direct data transfer, has a round 8-pin connector on one end and a 9-pin, trapezoid-shaped connector on the other.

POWERBOOK

Both the modem and printer ports of a Macintosh are serial ports, but the printer port won't work with a null modem cable (or modem) if you have AppleTalk active. If you are a PowerBook user with a printer port but no modem port, make sure to make AppleTalk inactive by disabling it in the Chooser.

The software. Establishing a physical link between the machines is only part of the problem; before they can start to talk, each machine must have software capable of moving text or files across the serial port. Such programs are called *terminal emulators* because they were originally developed to enable personal computers to talk to mainframes just as if they were old-fashioned data terminals.

If the machine you need to communicate with is running Windows, you're probably in luck. Microsoft includes a terminal emulator called—hold onto your socks—**Terminal** with every copy of Windows. It's simple and low powered, but the price is on target. If the machine runs only DOS, you'll need to use some other program such as **ProComm** or **CrossTalk.**

On the Macintosh side, any standard communications program will do; if you don't already have one, the shareware package **ZTerm** is a great bargain.

The connection. With your software and cable in place, it's time to set up the connection.

1 Match the settings.
The key to making Macs and PCs talk via cable is to make sure you are using the same settings. By convention, that means 8 bits, 1 stop bit, and no parity (sometimes abbreviated 8N1). The meanings of these settings are rooted in telecommunications trivia; the important part is that they're set identically on both the Mac and PC.

Then set the port speed to the highest speed both programs support—38,400 bps should do. Once both programs are running, you should be able to type back and forth such witticisms as "Watson, come here, I need you."

2 Initiate the transfer.
To send files from the Mac, hunt around your terminal emulator's menus for a command called "Send File" or something similar. This should reveal a dialog box similar to the standard Open dialog in other Mac programs; just double-click the file you wish to send.

3 Pick a protocol.
Most popular terminal emulators give a choice of *file transfer protocols*—a kind of language both sides agree to speak when setting up and executing the transfer; the most common of these are XModem, YModem, and ZModem. Generally, sending files via ZModem is fastest and easiest, and popular telecom products on the PC support it. If you're receiving the file via Zmodem, you may not need to

Mac Emulation Under DOS? (HN)

The most unusual of the several PC programs that make it possible to read and write Mac disks on a PC comes from ARDI, a small company in Albuquerque, New Mexico. Called **Executor/DOS,** the $100 program doesn't have all the features of competitors such as MacDisk, and it works only under DOS, not Windows. What makes it intriguing is that it also enables you to run some Mac applications in emulation on PCs with a 386 or later chip—a capability no other developer has offered.

The SCSI Alternative for PowerBook Users (HN)

POWERBOOK

If you have a Mac PowerBook and a PC with a SCSI card installed, you have an option that's faster and easier (once set up) than any serial connection: linking up the two machines in what's known as *SCSI disk mode,* a scheme that lets the notebook's hard disk function as an external drive for the desktop machine.

Most PowerBook models allow such connections to desktop Macs with no added equipment except a special "SCSI disk adapter" cable (about $40), but to make the link to SCSI PCs you need another product—Software Architects' **Laptop Liberator.** The $195 package includes a small hardware adapter (called the PowerBridge) that's attached to SCSI cables from both machines, plus software that lets you create a DOS partition on the PowerBook hard drive.

Once you've got everything connected, you can mount the Mac disk's DOS partition on the PC and move files back and forth with standard DOS commands. Since it's easy to connect other Macs to a PowerBook, and you can simply drag Mac files to the DOS partition, the PowerBook becomes an effective high-speed bridge to the PC.

do anything further—the transfer begins automatically. (For more on file transfer protocols, see Chapter 22.)

Receiving files. Receiving files from a PC is, as you might expect, very similar. The PC initiates the transfer. On the Mac side, if you're not using ZModem, you may need to choose "Receive XModem" or a similar command depending on the protocol used. Software Ventures' **MicroPhone Pro,** for one, has a dandy feature that can start receiving files automatically regardless of the protocol used.

This whole procedure sounds more complicated than it really is—once you get used to it, it takes only a minute to set up, and it works pretty well, especially if the files you have to transfer are simple text documents. Remember, though, that if you find yourself using a cable connection often, it's time to consider getting a permanent one—a network link, as described on the next page.

Modem Connections (RSR/HN)

By sending computer data across telephone lines, modems let users share files over long distances and across geographic boundaries. They can also help you overcome the barriers that divide computer platforms, even if they're in the same office. If you've got a modem on your Mac, for example, you can call a modem-equipped PC directly and share files using communications programs on each end. If you both subscribe to an on-line service such as CompuServe or America Online, or to a local BBS, you can also send files through the e-mail services supplied there. (Remember that you are paying by the hour for these services, so uploading and downloading big files can get expensive.)

Connecting a single Mac and PC via modem is similar to linking them via direct cable, with a few extra considerations. Of course, before you start communicating, one person will need to dial the other. You can set up your modem to wait for a call by typing *ATS0=0* once you open your terminal emulator. Furthermore, instead of using the maximum speed listed in your terminal emulator, as you can with a direct cable connection, you'll be limited to the maximum speed of your modem—normally, 2,400 bps, 9,600 bps, or 14,400 bps. (If your modem will do 14,400 bps but that speed isn't listed in your software, choose the 19,200 bps setting.) The communications software on the Mac side should have MacBinary enabled unless you are sending just text files (for the reasons explained in the box "Fork It Over," on page 974).

Network Connections (RSR/HN)

If you frequently need to pass files between Macs and PCs in the same office (or even at home), and the files are large (or you're tired of sneakernet), and you can afford to spend a few hundred dollars on the problem, tying your Macs and PCs together on a *local area network (LAN)* is worth considering. There's no denying that networking Macs and PCs is considerably more complicated than just connecting Macs. Some of the considerations entailed in setting up Mac-only and multiplatform networks are covered in Chapter 23. Here we'll talk about the special considerations brought up when PCs are added to the picture.

The hardware. There are several ways to add LocalTalk (the networking scheme built into every Mac) to your PCs. At least two companies—Farallon Computing and CoOperative Printing Solutions (COPS)—market add-on cards that give PCs a Mac-style LocalTalk connector; you can then wire them to Macs and LaserWriters with Farallon PhoneNET connectors (or equivalents from other companies) and inexpensive twisted-pair wire. There are also a couple of solutions that let you use the PC's parallel port for LocalTalk connections (see the box "Connections Without Cards" on page 976).

Fork It Over (HN)

All Mac applications are divided internally into two parts known as the *resource fork* and the *data fork;* most Mac documents have only a data fork, but some have a resource fork as well. That's a piece of techie trivia you should never need to know if you're using just a Mac, but it may be important if you store Mac files on a PC. Pay close attention if you ever plan to download Mac files from a BBS or on-line service to a PC and then move them to the Mac. Too many users have wasted too many hours because they didn't understand the issues involved and how to solve them.

The problem is that PCs, as well as Unix machines, mainframes, and other kinds of computers, don't know a thing about forks (they eat with their hands). They also don't understand the information the Mac Finder keeps for every file, such as its full name, icon, Type and Creator, and creation and modification dates.

If you are just trying to send a drawing, say, or a spreadsheet or word processing file from your Mac to a PC user, then you don't have to worry about all the extra information; PC programs just ignore it anyway. But if you're dealing with a file that's going to be used someday on a Mac, then it's either convenient (in the case of a data document) or absolutely critical (in the case of an application) that all elements of the file be preserved, and in a way that allows the file to be reconstructed properly once it's back on a Mac.

The basic solution to this problem lies in a file format called *MacBinary,* which was worked out a decade ago by communications developers eager for a standard way to keep Mac files intact when sending them through on-line services. When you *send* a file through a terminal emulation program with MacBinary enabled (turned on), the data and resource forks are combined, along with the Finder attributes, into a single whole. If such a program *receives* a MacBinary file, it recognizes the format and decodes it, returning the file to standard Mac form.

Most Mac communications programs have MacBinary on by default, and for most people there's no reason ever to turn it off. But it's a good idea to double-check that it's on before using a Mac terminal emulation program to send files to a PC—either over a local cable connection or via modem. (Depending on the program you are using, there might be a menu command, a dialog box checkbox, or a Preference setting for MacBinary.)

Mac files posted in on-line libraries, whether or not they've been compressed, are usually in MacBinary format. That's no problem if you download such files to a Mac (as long as you have MacBinary enabled) because, as noted above, your communications software processes them as they arrive. But DOS and Windows telecom programs don't know anything about MacBinary, so after you've downloaded to a PC, it's up to you to make sure the reprocessing gets done.

One way to do that is to transmit the file from the PC to the Mac using a communications program on the Mac side that has its MacBinary option turned on; the effect is the same as if you'd downloaded it from the BBS to the Mac in the first place.

Another option is REEVEsoft's **MacSee,** a nifty PC utility available on-line in a shareware version (there's also a commercial version). Either version lets you read and write high-density Mac floppies and SyQuest disks (see "Mac Disks in PC Drives," earlier in this chapter). What makes MacSee unique is that it has a MacBinary translation option built in: As you move a file from the PC to the Mac disk, you can tell MacSee to process a MacBinary file back into its original Mac form.

Alternatively, you can bring the file back to the Mac in MacBinary format and do the reprocessing there. Many Mac utilities will do the job, among them a classic freeware application called **Binhex,** an Apple File Exchange translator called **MacBinary to Mac** ($5 shareware), a System 7 drag-and-drop utility called **MacBinary II+** (free), Bill Goodman's **Compact Pro** shareware compressor, and shareware and commercial versions of Aladdin Systems' popular **StuffIt** compression utility. (Compression utilities are described in Chapter 13.)

Both Macs and PCs can also use Ethernet, a faster networking scheme, and that option makes sense if you plan on transferring large files frequently, especially if you have a new Mac with Ethernet support built in. Farallon's new **EtherWave** line and Tut Systems' **Silver Streak Connectors** make setting up and configuring Ethernet networks *almost* as much a plug-and-play proposition as LocalTalk.

The software. Just connecting the Mac and PC, whether with Ethernet or with LocalTalk, won't do you much good unless you've also got software capable of sending and receiving useful information over the physical connection. Again the leaders in this area are COPS and Farallon. **COPSTalk for Windows** ($180) lets Windows users share printers, directories, and drives with Mac users, in almost exactly the same way Mac users can with System 7 file sharing. Farallon's **PhoneNET PC** software ($200) does most of the same things under both DOS and Windows, although it does not enable Mac or other PC users to mount another PC user's disk on their own desktop. You can fill that void with Miramar Systems' **Personal MacLAN Connect** ($200).

Or you can use PhoneNET PC in conjunction with Farallon's Timbuktu for Windows and Mac—amazing programs that let the user on either machine see the screen of the other in a window on the desktop. In effect, you can put a

Connections Without Cards (HN)

If you want to avoid the hassle of adding a LocalTalk or Ethernet card to your PC, you now have another option: an external AppleTalk connector that plugs into its parallel port, the one usually used for PC printers.

The first such product, the **Coactive Connector** from Coactive Computing ($200), also requires similar connectors ($50) to be attached to the printer port of all Macs linked to the PC and to the LocalTalk port of any printers to be shared; the machines could then be connected with phone wire. Coactive's software lets PC users and Mac users share files on any connected computer. It also gives PC users access to any attached AppleTalk printer.

A new challenger, **PCTalk** from Apexx Technology ($200), likewise plugs into the PC's parallel port, but it creates a standard AppleTalk port instead of a special proprietary connector; you need only attach a standard PhoneNET or compatible connector, then run telephone wire to a regular PhoneNET box on the Mac. Apexx doesn't provide any software, but it offers more expensive bundles that combine the adapter with Farallon's PhoneNET PC and Timbuktu for Windows software.

Windows screen on the Mac, and vice versa. You can even control the other machine remotely, just by using your mouse to pull down menus and select commands within the window that represents the other desktop.

All of this makes for a very convenient setup, but it doesn't come cheap: Farallon's **Timbuktu for Windows PhoneNET Kit** (a bundle that combines the LocalTalk card, a PhoneNET connector, and Timbuktu for Windows and PhoneNET PC software) lists for $380; a comparable kit with EtherWave instead of the LocalTalk card is exactly the same price. A copy of **Timbuktu Pro** for the Mac is $200. (At least Farallon offers sharp discounts for volume purchases.)

Server-Based Networks (RSR/HN)

When a network is large and the traffic heavy, it's more efficient to set up a *server*, a machine that functions as a central repository for everyone else on the network. (You can find more on the whys and wherefores of servers in Chapter 23.)

If the network will be mainly Mac with some PCs, Apple's own AppleShare (see Chapter 23) can handle the job: PhoneNET PC and COPSTalk both include client software that lets PC users log on to an AppleShare server, and Apple has announced plans to offer its own AppleShare client software for Windows.

In predominantly PC settings, however, it's the Mac that has to fit in with PC standards—specifically, with Novell Netware, the DOS/Windows world's most popular networking software. (PC people call it a *network operating system.*) Novell offers a special add-on for Netware that teaches it how to speak Apple-Talk so it can communicate with Macs; the product is appropriately named **Netware for Macintosh.** Once it's installed on a Netware server, Mac users can access the server through the Chooser, along with AppleShare servers or shared Mac volumes, and Netware directories look just like Mac folders. You can also take advantage of Novell print queues so that printing can be centrally managed.

While Netware for Mac gives you the closest interaction with a Novell server, it is an expensive investment if you're the odd Mac in a sea of PCs (it's $500 for 5 users or $3,000 for 200 users). There are two alternatives that give you access to Netware at a lower cost, by making your Mac look to the server like a PC: Dayna's **DOS Mounter Plus** and Insignia Solutions' **SoftNode, SoftPC Professional,** and **SoftWindows.** At $100, DOS Mounter is much cheaper than the others, which can cost up to $500 depending on the version, but only the Insignia products allow you to run PC applications on your Mac.

Reading Files

So far, this chapter has covered only ways to get files from the Mac to the PC and back. But suppose that somehow—by hook, crook, or floppy disk—you've gotten your PC files to the Mac. Congratulations are in order, but the battle is not over yet: Next you have to find a way to read those files.

The techniques for solving this complex set of problems are similar to those discussed in Chapter 24 for interchanging files among Macs with different software; in fact, many of the products and interchange formats you might use to solve file-exchange problems among Macs also help when you are moving files between Macs and PCs.

There are four primary strategies:

- relying on applications that have versions on both platforms
- using special utilities and filters to translate between Mac and PC formats
- saving files in intermediate interchange formats understood on both sides
- generating platform-independent versions of your documents with one of the new generation of electronic publishing tools

Cross-Platform Applications (RSR/HN)

Today almost every successful Macintosh application is also available in a Windows version; likewise, many programs that started on Windows have since moved to the Mac. In most cases these programs use identical or similar file formats on both platforms, and they generally offer about the same features, so the Mac version can read files created on the PC, and vice versa.

Other things being equal, choosing the same application on both the Mac and the PC makes sense if you plan to share files across platforms—it eliminates, or at least drastically reduces, the translation hassle, and it ensures that the users on both sides will be dealing with the same terminology (more or less) and features when discussing changes to a file.

There are some caveats, however. First, sharing features and file formats is *not* an absolute guarantee that documents will look precisely the same on both platforms. Differences in fonts are notorious for mucking up line endings and document lengths in word processing and desktop publishing files, for example. Other small differences show up in all too many programs. And cross-platform sharing isn't always as easy as just opening the other file. In some cross-platform applications, such as Quicken, you have to use a special intermediate file format, which makes going back and forth from Mac to PC much less convenient.

Still another complication is that software publishers often allow long lags between Mac and Windows releases of new versions of the same product. For many months, for example, Illustrator 4 was available only for Windows, and

Major Applications Available for Both the Mac and Windows

Category	Applications
Word processing	Microsoft Word, WordPerfect
Spreadsheets	Lotus 1-2-3, Microsoft Excel
Graphics	Adobe Illustrator, Adobe Photoshop, Aldus FreeHand, Aldus IntelliDraw, AutoCAD, Canvas, ClarisDraw, ClarisImpact, Deltagraph Pro
Databases	FileMaker Pro, Microsoft FoxPro, Omnis, Oracle
DTP	Aldus PageMaker, FrameMaker, QuarkXPress, Ventura Publisher
Presentation	Action!, Aldus Persuasion, Astound, PowerPoint
Other	ACT!, ClarisWorks, CrossTalk, Managing Your Money, Master Tracks Pro, MicroPhone Pro, Microsoft Project, Microsoft Works, Passport, Quicken

then Illustrator 5 was available only for the Macintosh. That can cause problems if you are exchanging files between machines. The user with the newer version may have to save in the older format—and therefore may not be able to take advantage of the newest features—if the document has to be portable. If you are running a cross-platform operation, it might even be worth holding off on upgrading one side until the other side catches up.

Finally, remember that cross-platform compatibility isn't everything, and the whole strategy of picking such applications doesn't always make sense. If you and the Windows user in your life already own different programs, have each mastered the software you've got, and can manage to share the data you need to, then it may not be worth investing time and money in new software, even if sharing files involves a few extra hassles and glitches. Likewise, one or both of you may find that a different application, one that's not available on both platforms, is easier to use or offers special features that are important to you.

Translation (RSR/HN)

In cases where a cross-platform app isn't available, or you simply decide to use a Mac-only application for other reasons, you may need to turn to a *translation utility*—a software package that reads in files in one format and generates an equivalent—ideally, an exact replica—in a different format. Translators for many common DOS and Windows formats come with some major Mac applications in every category (see the box "Instant Translations" in Chapter 24). If those translators don't meet your needs, dedicated translation utilities such as

DataViz's **MacLinkPlus** packages, Mastersoft's **Word for Word,** Equilibrium Technologies' **DeBabelizer** and **DeBabelizer Lite,** and TechPool's **Transverter Pro** (all described in Chapter 24) offer many additional filters.

Intermediate File Formats (RSR/HN)

If you are dealing with a PC program for which there is no Mac equivalent or even translator, you may not be able to use the file on the Mac in its native file format; same with a Mac file you are sending to a PC.

In those cases you'll need to save the file in an *intermediate* or *interchange* format—ASCII and RTF for textual data and word processing files; GIF, TIFF, EPS, and others for graphics; and so on. (The major interchange formats are described in Chapter 24.) These formats give you considerable flexibility in moving a document among applications and across platforms, but they often require sacrificing some of the original formatting and detail.

Text and word processing. Alas, even pure text files do not translate perfectly from PC to Mac or vice versa. First, there's the difference in the basic character sets used; the Macs use an extended ASCII character set of 256 characters, including symbols and accents not normally available on PCs.

An even more common problem is that the Mac and the PC use different ways to indicate the end of a line. Specifically, PCs use a symbol called a *line feed;* Macs use carriage returns, the same symbol used for paragraph breaks. If a Mac text editor such as TeachText or word processor such as Microsoft Word reads a DOS text file, you'll notice little rectangular boxes at the beginning of each line; these represent the line-feed characters.

Surprisingly, Word and most other Mac word processors don't provide a simple way to get rid of these line feeds, but text-processing utilities and text editors such as Baseline Publishing's Vantage typically do. (See Chapter 8 for more about Vantage and other text editors.) One the most elegant solutions is a $5 shareware application called **DOSWasher,** by N. Jonas Englund. Simply drop the DOS text file on DOSWasher and it becomes a Mac text file. Drop a Mac text file on and it becomes a DOS file.

BARGAIN

If you're dealing with formatted word processing documents, major Mac word processors such as Microsoft Word and WordPerfect usually do a good job of translating files created with their PC counterparts. Since most other PC word processors support at least some versions of the Word or WordPerfect file formats, you can use them as a kind of bridge across platforms. The Word for Word and MacLinkPlus programs also translate among hundreds of PC formats; they are particularly useful if you need to convert files from older programs.

Spreadsheet and database information. Tab-delimited or comma-delimited text is a standard format for transferring information from spreadsheets and databases across platforms as well as from program to program on the same platform: Nearly all such applications, including personal information managers, let you import and export data in one or both of those formats. The data is stored as ASCII text, the delimiter character separates fields or columns, and carriage returns normally mark the ends of records or rows.

There are several other interchange formats recognized by many spreadsheets and databases on both Mac and PC. DIF (data interchange format) preserves values but loses formulas; .WKS, the original Lotus 1-2-3 format, preserves the formulas, as does the SYLK (symbolic link) format. Use SYLK if you want to preserve the text formatting in your spreadsheets.

Graphics formats. Graphic images are frequently moved across platforms, and although there are some quirks in the process, several relatively painless solutions are available. A common one is to rely for translation on applications that read and write multiple formats, particularly Adobe Photoshop and Deneba Software's Canvas. Another approach is to turn to a utility such as DeBabelizer or Transverter Pro or their shareware competitors.

Remember that PICT, while ubiquitous in the Mac world, is not widely supported in the PC market, although a few PC programs can read it directly and most conversion utilities can translate it into something more universal.

Tag Image File Format (TIFF), the de facto standard among graphics professionals and serious desktop publishers for scanned images and bit maps, is platform-independent, but subtle differences exist between the Mac and PC

versions. Photoshop, MacLinkPlus, and the freeware program FlipTIFF can help when you are translating TIFF files between Mac and PC formats.

The TIFF specification provides an option for compressing image data, but not all programs that read standard TIFFs can handle compressed files.

If your conversion utility doesn't do it for you (most do), make sure the Mac file type is TIFF after you've converted a PC TIFF file.

The EPS format allows both Mac and Windows users to save bit-mapped screen representations of screen images along with PostScript. Those previews, however, don't travel well across platforms, so don't include them if you'll be trading them with a Windows user. When bringing EPS files to the Mac, be sure to change their Type code to EPSF.

CGM, or Computer Graphics Metafile, is a platform-independent graphics format endorsed by the U.S. Department of Defense as part of an effort to standardize government and defense industry documentation. It's increasingly common on the PC, but its acceptance has been slow on the Mac. Deneba Software's Canvas, for one, can read and write CGM files.

Compression standards. As with other products, the Mac and the PC have different standards when it comes to compression. **PKZip** ($47 from PKWare) is the most popular PC equivalent to Aladdin Systems' StuffIt family and Bill Goodman's shareware Compact Pro on the Mac.

If you receive a file with the suffix *.zip*, it has almost certainly been compressed with PKZip (or else someone is playing a cruel hoax on you). If it's a PC application and you are using a Mac, you might as well leave it compressed, since it won't run on the Mac anyway. But if it's a data file you plan to translate or open with a compatible Mac application, you will need to decompress it before you can use it.

Fortunately, several Mac programs can help with the task. **StuffIt Deluxe** ($120) has an Unzip command in its Translate menu; follow the dialog boxes from there. (The program can also decompress a wide variety of other compression formats used on Unix as well as DOS systems.) Several freeware

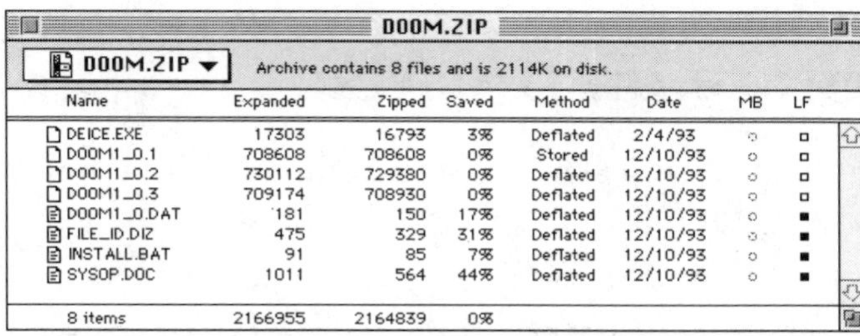

DOOM.ZIP

DOOM.ZIP ▾ Archive contains 8 files and is 2114K on disk.

Name	Expanded	Zipped	Saved	Method	Date	MB	LF
DEICE.EXE	17303	16793	3%	Deflated	2/4/93	○	□
DOOM1_0.1	708608	708608	0%	Stored	12/10/93	○	□
DOOM1_0.2	730112	729380	0%	Deflated	12/10/93	○	□
DOOM1_0.3	709174	708930	0%	Deflated	12/10/93	○	□
DOOM1_0.DAT	181	150	17%	Deflated	12/10/93	○	■
FILE_ID.DIZ	475	329	31%	Deflated	12/10/93	○	■
INSTALL.BAT	91	85	7%	Deflated	12/10/93	○	■
SYSOP.DOC	1011	564	44%	Deflated	12/10/93	○	■
8 items	2166955	2164839	0%				

**Tommy Brown's ZipIt lets you easily compress Mac files in PKZip format for Mac-to-PC telecommunications. The program also unzips PKZip archives.*

utilities also decode Zip files. **ZipIt,** a $10 shareware item that looks professional in quality, is unique in enabling you to create as well as decompress Zip archives. (Best of all, author Tommy Brown regularly updates the program to match the frequent updates to PKZip.)

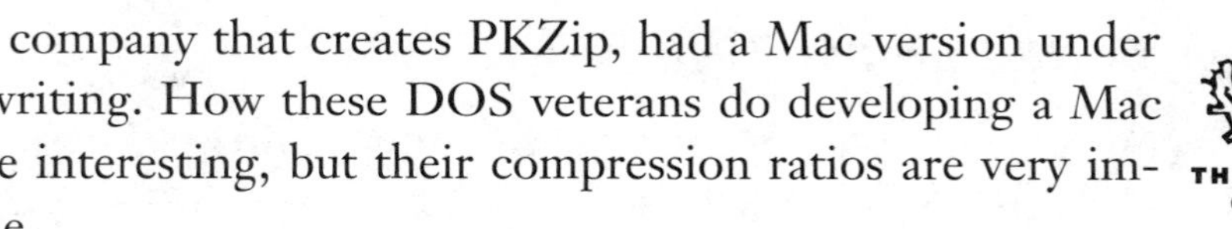

Finally, PKWare, the company that creates PKZip, had a Mac version under development at this writing. How these DOS veterans do developing a Mac program should prove interesting, but their compression ratios are very impressive on the PC side.

If you don't have ZipIt and want to compress a file before sending it to a PC user (to save time on long-distance charges, for instance), the developers of StuffIt and Compact Pro have created decompression-only DOS utilities for expanding their archives on PCs. The programs UNSITI.EXE (for StuffIt) and EXTRAC.EXE can be found on on-line services. When run on a PC, they provide a means of decompressing Mac archives sent via modem, network, or disk.

Electronic Publishing Tools (HN)

Electronic publishing products such as **Adobe Acrobat,** No Hands' **Common Ground,** Farallon's **Replica,** and WordPerfect's **Envoy** all have one reason for being: to solve the problem of cross-platform document distribution. These utilities offer a variety of features for searching and annotating files, but remember that once a file has been converted to one of these formats, it may no longer be editable even by the program that created it. (You'll find more on these programs in Chapter 24).

Running PC Software on the Mac

The availability of cross-platform applications and the increasing ease of data exchange has greatly diminished the need for Macs and PCs to run each other's applications, but there may still be times when you'd like to run some DOS or Windows software on the Mac—a company-standard database developed in dBase or Paradox, or perhaps a specialized application that's available only on the PC, or a even just a hot game that isn't offered on the Mac. Today, three products allow you to run such software right on your Macintosh.

SoftPC and SoftWindows (RSR/HN)

As its name implies, Insignia Solutions' **SoftPC** ($165 to $500, depending on the version) emulates a PC in software. It runs on Macs with 68K processors (that is, those that don't have PowerPC chips). **SoftWindows** is a new version for Power Macs; it's $500 if purchased separately, but Apple bundles it with some Power Mac configurations. Both SoftPC and SoftWindows in effect fool DOS and DOS applications into thinking they are running on a system with PC-standard hardware, including an Intel processor. Behind the scenes, they translate the instructions issued by the PC software into terms understood by the Mac. The result is that MS-DOS (which is included), most DOS programs, and (with SoftWindows) most Windows software can run in a window on your Macintosh. You can even cut and paste text between Mac and DOS/Windows windows.

GOOD FEATURE

The programs use a portion of the Macintosh's hard disk and RAM to serve as their PC counterparts. The PC "hard disk"—actually a large file on the Macintosh disk—can be mounted on the Mac desktop with Insignia's AccessPC program. You can also designate a folder on the hard disk to be shared between the Mac and the PC.

BAD FEATURE

The Insignia software maintains a surprising degree of compatibility with most PC software. At this writing, though, it still emulates an Intel 286, so some recent programs that need the "enhanced mode" of the 386 or a later Intel chip simply won't run. That includes the latest versions of WordPerfect, Quattro

Pro, FoxPro, Paradox, and Lotus Improv, and the list is growing fast. Insignia says it expects to deliver a 486 emulator by the end of 1994.

Because Insignia includes Microsoft's CD-ROM drivers, SoftPC and SoftWindows can run most PC CD-ROMs. But the emulation doesn't yet include a PC sound card, such as the de facto standard Sound Blaster, so Windows multimedia titles run in silence.

The biggest problem with SoftPC is its speed. Ordinarily, a 68030-based Mac is roughly comparable in speed to a 386-based PC, whereas a 68040-based Mac is comparable to a 486-based PC. With SoftPC, the rule of thumb is that you go back about a generation of Intel processors in speed. On an '040-based Macintosh (a Centris or Quadra), DOS programs under SoftPC run as they would on a 386. On an '030 Macintosh (like a IIci or LC III or Performa 600), programs will run as they would on a 286 (roughly as fast—or, more accurately, as slowly—as a Mac Plus). Needless to say, SoftPC on a 68000-based Mac (such as a Mac SE) is excruciatingly slow.

SoftWindows does much better on Power Macs: Performance is in the 386 to low-end (25-MHz) 486 range.

Generally speaking, SoftPC and SoftWindows are convenient solutions if you need only occasional access to older DOS or Windows software and if a leisurely pace doesn't bother you. If you are using PC programs regularly, if you require the latest versions, or if you are the type that demands quick response from your computer, they're probably not for you.

OrangePC (RSR/HN)

If your Mac has a NuBus slot (i.e., if it's a member of the Mac II, Centris, or Quadra families, except the Quadra 605, or if it's a first-generation Power Mac) and you have some money to spare, you can get higher performance and more compatibility by installing **OrangePC,** a PC on a card from Orange Micro. Since it includes a real 486 processor, the OrangePC doesn't have a problem running programs that require a 386 or 486, and it can run them fast.

The cards contain their own RAM so you don't have to sacrifice any of your Mac's memory to run PC software. They even have slots for PC expansion boards so you can add networking cards or sound cards. Like SoftPC and SoftWindows, the Orange cards let you run DOS software in a window, but you must purchase Windows yourself.

For the Macs that support it, the Orange Micro cards come close to the best of both worlds, but nobody ever said that living in utopia was cheap: Prices currently range from around $900 to $2,750, depending on the processor you choose and the amount of memory on the card.

Quadra 610 DOS Compatible (HN)

In the spring of 1994 Apple began shipping a Mac that could also function as a PC—the Quadra 610 DOS Compatible—and an expansion card that added the same capabilities to existing Quadra and Centris 610 machines. It was a neat and inexpensive solution to the cross-platform compatibility problem—so neat and inexpensive, in fact, that the machine and the add-on card sold much faster than Apple had expected. Within a couple of months both products were out of stock, and Apple decided not to make any more of them.

At this writing Apple hasn't said for sure whether it will eventually offer a successor to these products or concentrate on the SoftWindows solution.

Peripherals That Go Both Ways (RSR/HN)

In the past, peripherals that could be used with both Macs and PCs were few and far between. Many PC peripherals attach via a parallel port that is absent on Macs. Mac keyboards and mice, on the other hand, attach via the Apple Desktop Bus, which is absent on PCs. But now, more and more peripherals are learning to work on both sides of the fence. If you have both Macs and PCs, you may want to look for peripherals that can be used with either one.

Modems. Modems have long been one of the least choosy devices when it comes to platform; generally, you just need to specify a Mac or PC cable.

Printers. Printers, on the other hand, have been a bigger problem. Most PC printers require a parallel port; if you found a serial PC printer, the printer drivers that come with the Mac wouldn't work; and even if you had a network printer that could support both Macs and PCs, you'd often have to reconfigure DIP switches and the like depending on the source of the job.

Now all that is changing. GDT Softworks offers a $150 package called **PowerPrint** that provides a serial-to-parallel converter cable, print-spooling software (allowing you to use your Mac while it's printing), and drivers for most common PC printers. (Apple sells a version of the GDT product under the name **Apple Print Pack.** It costs less—$100—but it doesn't support nearly as many printers as the original, and it's missing the spooler and other useful PowerPrint features.) Most new office printers have multiple ports and automatic switching technologies, so you can connect them to Macs and PCs simultaneously and they'll sense whether to use PostScript or older PC formats to produce the document image. (See Chapter 21 for more on some ambidextrous printers.)

GOOD FEATURE

Monitors. In the display domain, Macs no longer require special monitors. Most of Apple's recent models can drive many standard PC monitors (VGA or SuperVGA); all you need is a cable adapter such as James Engineering's $20 MacVGA. And most major monitor manufacturers—now including Apple—offer "multisync" monitors that can accommodate video signals from Macs as well as many different PC video cards. High-end NEC models even allow dual inputs so you can switch between Mac and PC video signals instantaneously.

SCSI devices. Since the Mac Plus, SCSI has been a standard way to connect hard disks, CD-ROM drives, and scanners to the Mac. Although available in the PC world, SCSI hasn't been a standard there—it's not built into most PCs, and SCSI adapters from different third parties are often incompatible. But SCSI is becoming steadily more common on PCs, and standardization is starting to take hold. If your PC has a SCSI card from a well-known manufacturer such as Adaptec, there's a good chance that it will work with SCSI hard drives, CD-ROM players, and scanners marketed for the Mac. (You will, however, need to get PC drivers, either from the hardware manufacturer or a third party.)

Editors' Poll: What Dream Feature Would You Like to See Added to the Mac?

AA: Artificial intelligence, so it will write my stories for me. No, wait…voice-controlled typing, like that old *Star Trek* episode with the voice-activated typewriter.

DB: My favorite future vision is the meta-computer model, where you don't know what machine you're using or where it is or anything. You just plug in, and you're part of the worldwide network, running a program on a computer in Sweden and editing a file on a computer in Tokyo. I'm not holding my breath, but the concept makes sense to me.

EC: This is just a little thing, but I wish desktop Macs could sleep like PowerBooks. I hate restarting (and watching the init procession), and lately I've been having to leave my Mac on all night to catch faxes sent from far-away time zones. A sleepable call-activated Mac would solve both problems, without wasting energy and time.

DD: Well, if Apple can make OpenDoc work the way it should, that would be great for me. I love the idea of transparently going from task to task without changing applications.

JK: The ability to cook a tasty dinner, clean my apartment, and give me back rubs. (No matter how nicely I ask for these things, it always just sits there.)

HN: I think a dictation system that really worked accurately and without imposing any limitations on vocabulary and phrasing would be way cool.

BW: Macs of the future should have bio-feedback sensors to alert you to your endocrinological state, should it exceed a healthy balance.

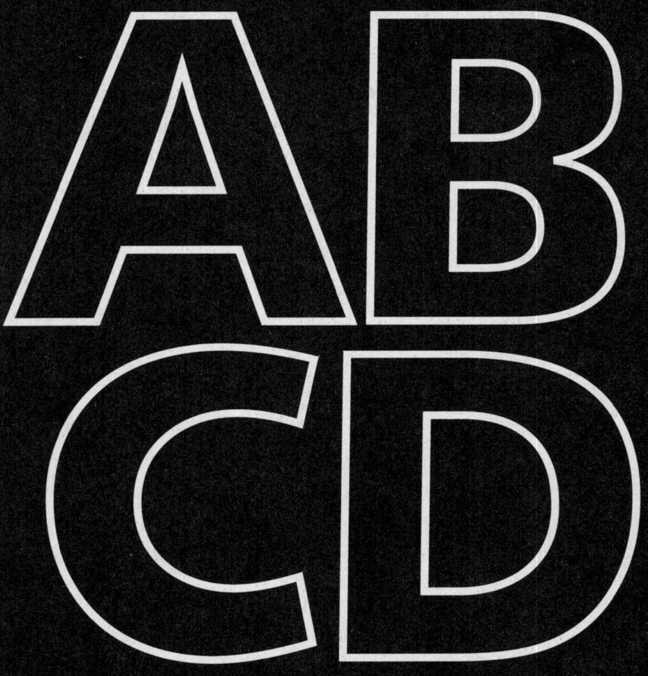

Appendixes

Editors' Poll: Have You Ever Suffered From a Repetitive Stress Injury?

AA: Not really.

DB: We got a ping-pong table in our office recently, and we've decided it may have been the best ergonomic decision we ever made. Don Sellers, author of *Zap!,* told us that the two best things you can do to avoid computer injuries are to reduce stress in the office and to get up and move! Excuse me, I've got to go play a game of ping-pong now.

EC: No, I know a lot of people who say they have, but I never have.

DD: Never a full-blown case. But once when I was working on a writing project, I started getting some pains. Right away, I bought a wristrest for my keyboard and mouse pad. It only seems to start up when I've been writing (and not breaking it up with other stuff) for about three weeks straight.

CG: Yes. Working on my computer eight to ten hours a day gave me massive pains in the wrist. At the time, I don't think there was a lot of talk about carpal tunnel syndrome. I now use one of those wristrest pads (it's blue, like my mouse pad) and I try to take breaks while typing. I'm still in search of the perfect keyboard, and I'm optimistic that there will be ones that are better from an ergonomic point of view in the near future. Otherwise, I imagine that in then next ten years, we'll have a generation of teenagers with carpal tunnel.

JK: No, but I'm continually trying to improve the ergonomics of my work situation. First I bought an ergonomic chair, then a desk with a keyboard shelf, then casters for the desk to get the keyboard shelf off my thighs and up to the level of my hands, and I'm waiting for my Apple adjustable keyboard to arrive.

HN: Yes, I've had several bouts of what was diagnosed as incipient carpal tunnel syndrome. Definitely a drag, but wearing a brace got it under control.

BW: After years of using computers, I'm discovering that the endurance of the tendons in my hands is dropping rapidly. I simply quit for a short while when I start noticing pain, basically to avoid injury. Sometimes I think that clicking and dragging with the mouse is harder on the hands than using the keyboard.

Staying Healthy at the Mac

THE MAC IS AN EXCITING COMPUTER, and people tend to get so involved with using it that they're often unaware—until it's too late—of the subtle but sometimes serious effects that using a computer can have on the body, some of which can cause permanent disabilities. This appendix discusses computer-related health threats and what you can do about them.

Contributors

John Kadyk (JK) is the editor of this appendix.

David Hauer (DH), like most musicians, is inordinately preoccupied with hands. He prefers not to unduly stress his own when working at the Mac.

Arthur Naiman (AN), creator of the *Mac Bible,* wrote much of the health-related material in the previous edition.

Don Sellers (DS) is a Seattle-based computer writer, editor, educator, documentary film-maker, and author of the book *Zap! How Your Computer Can Hurt You—And What You Can Do About It* (Peachpit Press).

Contents

Eye Problems and Headaches

Eyestrain, or eye fatigue, is the most common computer-related health complaint. People who use computers for extended periods usually experience some degree of eyestrain, although they may not notice it until a headache develops.

The Problems (DS/AN)

After long work at a computer, the eye muscles get tired and refuse to focus, to which people typically respond by trying harder to focus. That, in turn, often leads to tension in the neck muscles, and then to headaches.

You can get eye fatigue from just looking at the screen too long; from using a screen that's dirty, out-of-focus, or obscured by reflections; or from constantly shifting your focus back and forth from the screen to a printed page. Many of us can't avoid these activities in our work, but we *can* eliminate other conditions that strain our eyes and take steps to relieve the strain we can't avoid.

The American Association of Ophthalmologists says monitors present no hazard of permanent damage to the eye, but some eye researchers say that computer work, like any extended close work, can lead to *myopia* (near-sightedness). According to James Sheedy of the University of California at Berkeley optometry school, working regularly at a computer screen can also accelerate *presbyopia*, the inability to focus at varying distances that usually hits people in their forties.

What to Do About Them

Now that you know what eyestrain is, here are some of the ways you can reduce the factors that contribute to it.

Get a good monitor (JK/DS). Choose a monitor that's bright, sharp, has good contrast, and is free of flicker. Don't underestimate the importance of brightness, especially if you work in a well-lit environment. A monitor that looks bright enough in a dim room may be completely inadequate for a brighter situation. Most people won't notice any flicker if the monitor has a refresh rate of 70 Hz or above, but some people are particularly sensitive to it, so make sure the screen image looks perfectly steady on any display you're thinking of buying. (67 Hz is usually OK for 14-inch monitors, but bigger monitors need faster refresh rates to look stable—see Chapter 6 for more info). Curved screens make glare worse, so look for a flat screen.

Avoid reflections on the screen (DS/JK). It's much harder for your eyes to focus on a screen that's covered with reflections (also called *glare*). Reflections usually come from a light source in front of your monitor: a desk lamp, an overhead light, or a window in the wall behind you. But putting your monitor in *front* of a window can cause problems too: sunlight shining on an object in front of the monitor can create as bad a reflection as a light bulb. *[There's a window behind my computer, and when the sun shines through it, if I'm wearing a light-colored shirt it can cause a reflection on the screen. So I change to a dark-colored shirt on bright afternoons.—JK]*

HOT TIP

Try to set your monitor up to avoid these problems. You can even build a light-shade around your screen—using cardboard and tape—to help shield it from light coming from the side or overhead (black cardboard with a matte finish works best). Glare reduction treatments and coatings for your screen can help too, but they can also lead to other problems, like making the image fuzzier or making the reflective effect of dirt and finger oil much worse than it would otherwise be. You can also buy filters that fit around your screen. They, too, can make the image either better or worse, depending on the filter's type, its quality, and your lighting and monitor conditions; so if you decide to buy one, try to get a money-back guarantee in case it's not right for your situation.

Keep the screen clean (DS). The static electricity on computer screens attracts dust and grime, which reduces brightness and contrast, causing a fuzzier, dimmer image. Clean your screen regularly, using the procedure recommended in its manual (some screens have coatings that some cleaning products can damage).

Work in an evenly bright environment (JK). If your work environment is much brighter than your monitor, or vice versa, your eyes will be constantly readjusting whenever you shift your gaze. Try to balance the brightness of your screen with that of the wall behind your monitor, the task lighting at your desk, and the overall brightness in the room. (Because of the window behind my monitor, I'm constantly readjusting my monitor's brightness on partly cloudy days; on really bright days, I cover the window with a thick, dark blanket and keep my monitor's brightness low.)

Use a readable type size (DS/JK). For the purpose of avoiding eyestrain, it's recommended that you sit 18 to 24 inches from the monitor, but if you've got an older monitor and want to avoid the possible harm of electromagnetic radiation (see "Radiation," below), you should sit 28 to 30 inches away. Whatever distance you work at, set the type size in the documents you work on so that you can read the screen without undue strain at that viewing distance.

Get your eyes checked (DS). Computer work is particularly demanding on the eyes, so it may lead you to discover eye problems that wouldn't otherwise bother you. If you already wear glasses or contacts, consider getting your eyes rechecked—many forms of eyesight correction can cause rather than correct problems at the computer. You may need custom eyesight correction for the times you're at work.

Take breaks and exercise (DS). The National Institute of Occupational Safety and Health recommends getting away from the screen for 15 minutes every one or two hours of intense work at the computer. If that's not realistic for you, take breaks as often as you can. Spend the interval doing noncomputer work, or—as one doctor recommends—put your feet up, your head back, and close your eyes and relax (general stress increases the strain on your eyes, too). *[Before you take up this regimen, maybe you should alert your boss that it's doctor's orders.—DD]* Exercise your eyes every ten minutes or so by focusing on as distant an object as possible for five or ten seconds.

Neck and Back Pain

Neck and back pain are related, and they are often symptoms of posture problems that can affect the entire body. Good furniture is one way to help solve the problem, but you don't necessarily have to spend a lot of money, if you just pay some attention to how you work.

The Problems (DS/JK)

As you've probably noticed, hours of sitting in one position, with your arms extended over the keyboard and your neck craned to see the screen, gives you a stiff, aching back and neck. You may not realize that it also compresses the spine, as well as putting a load on your tendons, muscles, and nerves.

When nerves at the spine become pinched, irritated, or compressed, the entire nerve pathway can be affected, which can cause a myriad of symptoms throughout the body. Pain or tingling in the foot, for example, may mean nerve damage in the spine.

You can try to avoid these problems by paying close attention to the way you sit at the computer.

What to Do About Them

Sitting in the right position and getting up regularly to take breaks can be the best way to avoid neck and back pain.

Good sitting posture (DS/JK). What's the right posture? Slouching (leaning forward from the waist, with no support for the lumbar vertebrae) can lead to all sorts of problems, but "sitting up straight" isn't necessarily ideal either. It's more important that you sit comfortably, with your chair supporting your back and maintaining a healthy inward curve at your lower back.

Generally, the best way to get that kind of support is to lean back slightly into the backrest of a chair that's well designed and well adjusted. Making an angle greater than 90 degrees between your legs and your trunk also helps to avoid lower-back problems. You also want to avoid craning your neck forward and rounding your shoulders inward.

If you're going to be sitting throughout a workday, you'll want to be able to shift your position periodically, so you need a chair that can accommodate a range of postures.

Positioning your monitor (JK). If you're always looking up, down, or sideways to see your monitor, your neck will start to feel stiff and sore and can develop chronic problems.

Selecting a Chair (DS/JK)

The point of an adjustable chair isn't to let you find the one perfect position you can sit in all day without budging: A good chair should make you comfortable in a number of different postures. Get one with a backrest that adjusts up or down and whose tilt you can change (it should also be tall enough to support your upper back when you lean against it). The seat should also be adjustable to tilt forward or backward. Since the positions of the seat and backrest are related, you should be able to adjust both at once *while you're sitting,* by just moving around until you find a comfortable position and then setting it with a lever.

You should also be able to adjust the seat height so that when you sit with your hands on the keyboard, your feet are flat on either the floor or a footrest, and your elbows are level with your wrists and hands. Armrests are often recommended, but it's unclear whether it helps to use them while typing.

Not all chairs—even those that appear to be on the forefront of design—are based on modern ergonomic principles, and there's no perfect chair for everyone; you need to try some out to find one that's right for you.

Kneeling chairs have forward-tilting seats and a support for the knees, which bear a lot of body weight. These chairs have their advantages, but they put a lot of stress on the knees, tire the back, and are difficult to get in and out of. Many experts in ergonomics feel these flaws far outweigh the advantages of kneeling chairs.

Set up your monitor so that the top of the screen is at or slightly below eye level. That may mean putting it next to your Mac rather than on top of it, or putting a stack of magazines under it. If you've got a tall monitor, like a one- or two-page display, try to keep your work near the top of the screen (I'm always moving and scrolling windows to avoid having to look down).

If putting your monitor right in front of you on the desk doesn't allow you to sit far enough back from it, get a slide-out shelf for your keyboard or get a bigger desk. Putting your monitor off to the side is not a good idea if you use your computer a lot. (I used to work with the monitor at the end of the desk—so I had to turn sideways to see it—and ended up with a painful neck problem that took months of physical therapy to correct.)

If you're willing to invest some money, you can get a heavy-duty swing arm that will hold your monitor just where you want it, and swing it out of the way when you're not using it. Check office furniture stores or catalogs.

Wrist and Arm Problems

Although pain in the wrists and arms is very common, don't ignore it—it can lead to permanent disabilities.

The Problems (JK)

The repetitive movements and unnatural positions involved in using a keyboard and mouse all day can lead to a group of problems known as *cumulative trauma disorders (CTDs)* or *repetitive stress injuries (RSIs)*. For computer users, these usually take the form of inflamed tendons (tendonitis) or inflamed tendon sheaths (tenosynovitis), or *carpal tunnel syndrome (CTS)*, a nerve problem that's often the result of tendon problems. (The mechanics of operating a typewriter—hitting the carriage return, changing sheets of paper, and so on—apparently spared keyboard users from these problems in the days before personal computers. The incidence of CTDs has skyrocketed since computers replaced typewriters.)

Carpal Tunnel Syndrome (JK/DS). The median nerve, which carries feeling from the hand and controls some of the finger muscles, passes through a narrow tunnel of bone and ligaments on its way through the wrist. If the tendons that also pass through this tunnel become inflamed and swollen, they can compress the median nerve and the blood vessels supplying it, causing CTS.

CTS symptoms include pain, numbness or tingling in the hands, especially in the first three fingers and thumb, but often in the forearms as well. CTS also causes burning pain in the wrist during time away from the computer, particularly in the middle of the night. Night burning and numbness are among the best diagnostic indicators of CTS.

But CTS means more than just pain—advanced cases can leave permanent nerve damage, severely limiting hand movement and coordination. Some CTS sufferers lose their ability to use a keyboard and have to change careers.

Mouse dangers (DH). Keyboards are most often blamed for CTDs, but using the mouse can also help bring them on. In fact, certain mouse activities can be very stressful, since it's normally only a single finger that does all the repeated moving, and this motion occurs while the rest of the hand is partially flexed.

What to Do About Them

A number of factors contribute to CTDs, including bent wrists, the speed and force of hand movements, and one's overall level of stress (one study found that reporters on deadline were more likely to get CTS than others who used the keyboard just as much).

Keep the wrists flat and straight (JK). This means your keyboard has to be at the right height, so that your arms aren't reaching up or down for it but are parallel to the floor. If your desk is too high, you may want to get a keyboard shelf that attaches under your main desk surface and slides out like a drawer. (The desk I used to work on placed the keyboard too high, so I bought one with a keyboard shelf, and that was too low; finally, I raised the new desk a little by installing casters under its legs, which put the keyboard at just the right height—and I can now move the desk around.)

Avoid resting your wrists on the desk in front of the keyboard, since that creates an upward angle that's considered a major contributor to CTS. If this posture is already habitual for you, you can get a wristrest to put in front of your keyboard (computer stores and business supply stores have 'em), or consider getting a keyboard that has wristrests built-in, such as the Apple Adjustable Keyboard or the Kinesis Ergonomic Keyboard (see Chapter 6 for more on them). But be careful

A Really Adjustable Workstation (AN)

A small company in Boston called Soho has come up with a computer workstation that's more fully adjustable than any I've ever seen. Any or all of its three 16-inch by 32-inch shelves can attach to either the front or the back of the desk (the normal configuration is one shelf low in the front for the keyboard and two higher shelves in the back for the computer, monitor, and peripherals).

Shelves can be set at any height between 22 inches (20 inches if you remove the casters) and 52 inches, and the keyboard shelf tilts up to 45 degrees. Adjusting the height (or angle) of a shelf involves nothing more than turning two knobs, yet when the shelves are in place, they can bear up to 100 pounds each, enough for even the largest monitor (the entire workstation can handle 150 pounds total).

The shelves are made of particle board, but they are completely sealed with laminate and banded around the edges. The Soho table lists for $450 but the average street price is around $300. It comes with a one-year warranty.

how you use wristrests—the wrong kind of pressure on nerves in your arm can get you into trouble.

A wristrest—or a rolled up towel—can help keep your wrists straight as you're typing.

It's also bad to bend your hands outward at the wrist, which is unavoidable with an ordinary keyboard. The Apple and Kinesis keyboards address this problem, too.

Work defensively (DS/DH). Once you've set up your desk and keyboard so that your wrists don't bend, here are some guidelines to work by:

- Cultivate a light touch on the keyboard and mouse. Don't use too much force when typing, clicking, or dragging.
- Keep your wrist straight when you move the mouse. If necessary, adjust the tracking speed in your Mouse control panel to make it easier to get the pointer where you want it.
- If your mouse feels awkward or uncomfortable, consider one of the ergonomic models on the market.
- Don't rest your wrists or forearms against hard edges, since that can compress nerves.
- Stay warm. Working at cold temperatures may increase the chance of developing CTDs.
- Vary your work to include tasks away from the computer, and spread those duties out over the day so you get up from the desk regularly.
- Sit in a good posture, and vary your position during the day (see the box "How to Sit at Your Mac" on the next page).
- It's worthwhile to experiment by alternating the hand you move the mouse with. The dexterity required is usually less than that necessary for normal writing, so even those of us who aren't ambidextrous can manage it.

Treating CTDs (DS). Occasional or mild CTD symptoms may disappear with rest and the help of over-the-counter anti-inflammatory pain relievers like aspirin or ibuprofen. But when the symptoms get more severe, self-treatment isn't advisable; arm or wrist splints and slings, arm rests, wristrests and other products advertised as preventing or treating CTDs can actually worsen an existing problem if they aren't used properly. Let a medical professional—preferably with a background in CTDs—guide you. Treatments range from

How to Sit at Your Mac

(JK)

The way you set up your Mac and how you sit while you're using it have effects on all of the health problems discussed so far, and others as well. A picture's worth a thousand words (and is much easier to refer to) so here's one showing the major things you should consider. *[Use it as a starting point, but don't forget to change your position around often. If you sit in the position shown for eight hours straight under stress, you're going to get injured.—DS]*

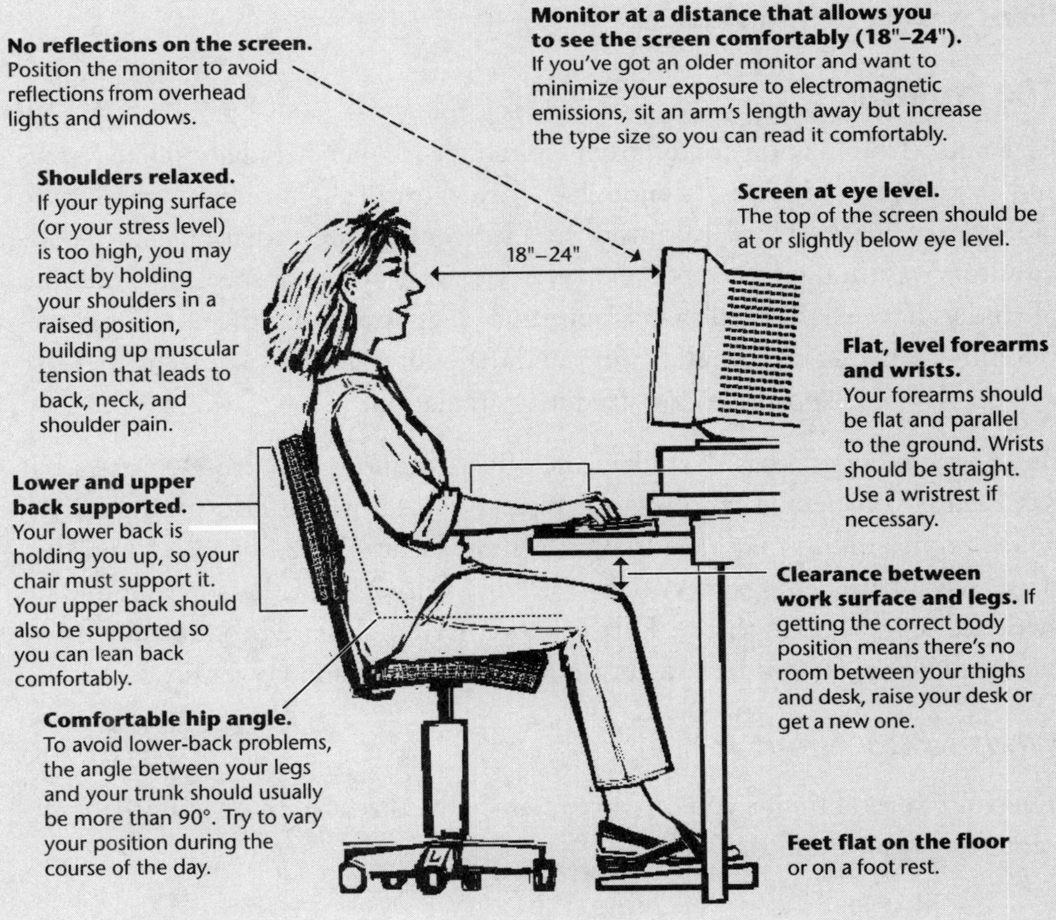

No reflections on the screen. Position the monitor to avoid reflections from overhead lights and windows.

Monitor at a distance that allows you to see the screen comfortably (18"–24"). If you've got an older monitor and want to minimize your exposure to electromagnetic emissions, sit an arm's length away but increase the type size so you can read it comfortably.

Shoulders relaxed. If your typing surface (or your stress level) is too high, you may react by holding your shoulders in a raised position, building up muscular tension that leads to back, neck, and shoulder pain.

Screen at eye level. The top of the screen should be at or slightly below eye level.

18"–24"

Flat, level forearms and wrists. Your forearms should be flat and parallel to the ground. Wrists should be straight. Use a wristrest if necessary.

Lower and upper back supported. Your lower back is holding you up, so your chair must support it. Your upper back should also be supported so you can lean back comfortably.

Clearance between work surface and legs. If getting the correct body position means there's no room between your thighs and desk, raise your desk or get a new one.

Comfortable hip angle. To avoid lower-back problems, the angle between your legs and your trunk should usually be more than 90°. Try to vary your position during the course of the day.

Feet flat on the floor or on a foot rest.

simple rest to anti-inflammatory medications or injections to surgery. The important thing is to do something about your pain sooner rather than later. People who decide it will go away by itself, or that help can wait, are the ones who end up permanently injured.

Radiation

Desktop computer monitors produce electromagnetic radiation in low-frequency ranges known as *ELF (extremely low frequency)* and *VLF (very low frequency)*. The word *radiation* itself sounds threatening, and because it's invisible and the experts are undecided as to whether or not it's harmful, the possible threat is all the more mysterious.

The Problem (DS/JK)

ELF and VLF radiation are different from high-frequency radiation like X-rays and gamma rays, which carry enough energy to break chemical bonds and cause biological change. Until recently, the electromagnetic radiation emitted by monitors was thought to be benign. Over the last 15 years or so, a small number of studies have challenged that assumption, suggesting that the chances of developing leukemia and other cancers, and the odds of miscarriage, may increase with prolonged exposure to low-frequency radiation.

But a lot of research hasn't studied the effects of monitors directly; instead, it has focused on people who live near power lines, which also produce ELF fields. Some studies that have looked at monitor use have linked it to miscarriage (see "Other Things to Watch Out For," below), but others have found no evidence of any health threat. Furthermore, ELF fields are produced by many electrical devices in modern society, not just monitors and power lines.

What to Do About It (DS/JK)

There are several things you can do to reduce the threat (if there is any) of radiation from your monitor.

Get a low-emissions monitor. As mentioned in Chapter 6, Sweden has created low-ELF and -VLF standards for monitors sold in that country, and most current monitors meet their low MPR II emissions standards.

Turn your monitor off. Don't leave your monitor on when it's not being used. Many current monitors will power down automatically in order to comply with the U.S. government's Energy Star requirements; look for them if you're in the market for a new monitor.

Keep your distance. Sit at a distance from your monitor, particularly if it's an old one. Emission levels drop off rapidly as you move back from the screen. For MPR II–compliant monitors, just sitting at a normal viewing distance of 18 to 24 inches should bring ELF and VLF radiation down to or below normal background levels. With most older monitors, sit an arm's length away (about 30 inches) to bring them down that low. The radiation coming from a monitor's back and sides is stronger, so you should sit at least four feet away from monitors in your vicinity. (Be aware that walls and partitions don't block electromagnetic fields.)

WARNING

Install an emissions filter. If you've got an old monitor (which is likely to produce higher emission levels than current models) and want to reduce its emissions, NoRad makes flexible bands you can install around the outside of the monitor to absorb magnetic fields ($65 to $131, depending on your monitor's size). Grounded screen filters can block the electrical component of ELF, but not the magnetic component, and some evidence suggests that the magnetic component is more likely to be harmful.

General Advice

As you may have noticed, many of the problems described above stem from some of the same contributing factors. That means that a few basic precautions can help avoid problems in several areas.

A Good Book on All This (JK)

The material in this appendix under Don Sellers's name is adapted from his book, *Zap! How Your Computer Can Hurt You—And What You Can Do About It* ($13, from Peachpit Press), which gives much more thorough coverage of computer-related health threats than we have space for here. It also provides a huge list of related resources, including other books, periodicals, and organizations, plus sources of ergonomic hardware, software, and furniture.

Make Sure to Take Breaks (JK)

There are programs designed to interrupt your work periodically and guide you through a series of exercises designed to alleviate the problems associated with sitting at work all day, but to me, they're self-defeating; what you really need is to get away from the computer and move around, and no software is going to help you do that. Instead, get a book on stretching, join a yoga class, or begin an exercise routine.

Lower Your Stress (DS/JK)

With too much stress, the body stays on constant alert, resulting in tensed muscles, shallow breathing, and surging hormones. Stress overload exacerbates virtually any health problem you can think of, including most of those discussed in this chapter. So do what's necessary to keep your stress under control, including exercising regularly and eating a balanced diet.

Don't Wait Until You're Suffering (DS)

People constantly adjust to awkward or constrained positions, chairs of the wrong height, or bosses who put them in lousy moods. The body and mind compensate for these problems, minimizing the immediate results. But the worse computer-related injuries get, the harder they are to fix. So listen to your body, and when something hurts, do something about it. If you don't take the time to be healthy now, you may have to use it to be sick later.

Make Sure Products Are Really Ergonomic (DS/JK)

Just because a product is labeled ergonomic doesn't mean that it is. The American National Standards Institute (ANSI) and the U.S. Occupational Safety and Health Administration (OSHA) issue some recommendations, but neither organization has a certification process to determine whether a product actually conforms to those recommendations. Beware of unsupported claims.

Even good products aren't necessarily right for every user. For example, many people rave about ScanCo's **MacTable,** which Apple has sold through its catalog. But a computer author we know who's five feet, seven inches tall found to his dismay that its keyboard shelf wouldn't go any lower than 28 inches (although the front edge could be tilted down to 26 inches). That's around the top of the height range recommended by the American National Standards Institute and certainly too high for many Mac users.

Other Things to Watch Out For

Most of the material in this appendix applies to everyone, but here are a couple of special-case situations to be aware of.

Using Computers During Pregnancy (DS)

Should you stop using your Mac during pregnancy? Probably not, but here are some reasons to limit the amount of time you spend at the computer.

Miscarriage. There's conflicting evidence about miscarriage and computer use. A large-scale study done in 1988 found a doubled rate of miscarriage among women who worked more than 20 hours a week at a computer. A 1992 study of women who had been exposed to high levels of ELF from computer monitors found a miscarriage rate that was nearly three times that of women exposed to low levels or none at all. A third study found no link between miscarriage and VLF radiation, and a fourth found no increased risk of miscarriage from computer use at all. Whichever studies you decide to believe, you can at least minimize your exposure to radiation by following the recommendations listed under "Radiation," above.

CTDs. Up to 35 percent of pregnant women—whether or not they work on a computer—experience carpal tunnel syndrome or tendon inflammation during or immediately after pregnancy. The cause may be hormonal changes that occur and can lead to an increase in fluid retention and swelling. Using a keyboard and mouse can contribute to these conditions too, so be on the lookout for them and prepare to take remedial steps if they do appear.

Sitting. Because of the fluid retention mentioned above, pregnant women who sit at work often experience a fluid buildup in their legs and feet. You can minimize the resulting discomfort by just getting up, stretching, and moving around. You might also consider a 20-minute rest in the afternoon, lying on your left side, to promote circulation and reduce the buildup of fluid. Swimming, walking, or other moderate exercise will also promote good circulation.

On the positive side, sitting on the job seems to result in fewer premature births than standing (but women who have active jobs like waitressing apparently do the best of all).

Epileptic Seizures in Children (DS)

Small numbers of children have reportedly experienced epileptic seizures while playing video games. Little scientific research has been conducted on video games and epilepsy, and there's no evidence that video games can cause it. But it is known that flashing lights or flickering images can cause seizures in children who are photosensitive. Parents of children who have epilepsy are encouraged to check with their doctors about photosensitivity.

B

Where to Find More Information

WHEN YOU'RE TRYING TO FIND THE RIGHT PROGRAM or figure out which Mac is best for you, there are two routes you can try: magazines or other users. Magazines tend to have more complete reviews, but users are almost always more frank, since they needn't worry about offending potential advertisers.

In this appendix we'll tell you how to find magazines and books you'll probably find helpful and how to find the best source of all—Mac user groups.

Contributors

Elizabeth Castro (EC) edited this appendix.

Arthur Naiman (AN) and **Nancy E. Dunn (ND)** contributed to earlier editions of the *Mac Bible,* from which parts of this appendix were taken.

Contents

Magazines and Newsletters

Devoted to the Mac

Shortly after the dawn of creation, that is, January of 1984, journalists and publishers jumped on the trail of the Mac. Here's a rundown of what they've come up with.

Macworld (EC). *Macworld* magazine ($4 an issue, $30 a year), born the same day as the Mac itself, devotes a considerable amount of space to product reviews and lab tests (and to advertisements), but it also seems more willing to tackle original and nonconventional stories—one landmark issue addressed the subject of computers in America's schools.

MacUser (DD). *MacUser* ($3 an issue, $27 a year), a hefty magazine like *Macworld*, puts most of its energy (and the considerable resources of the Ziff-Davis labs) into thorough product testing and comparison.

MacWEEK (EC). Since *MacWEEK* comes out more often—can you guess how often?—it is the best source for the latest news and gossip: what products are coming out and when and what's happening to the business end of the market. Unfortunately, it's pretty hard to get your hands on one. You can't really find it on newsstands, and subscriptions are a steep $100 a year—though you can get a free subscription if you manage or purchase (or claim to manage or purchase) lots of Macs or Mac products.

Lots of Advertising (EC)

Just the thought of a huge Macintosh magazine is enough to make you wonder how you'll get around to all those other important leisure activities you have planned. But don't despair. You can safely ignore more than half of the pages and still not miss a single article. It's all in the advertising. *MacUser* and *Macworld*, the largest magazines at some 250 pages each, are also the most heavily weighted down with ads—about 60 percent. *Mac Home Journal*, with only 130 pages, has just under 50 percent of its pages covered with ads, while *Wired*, with almost 150 pages total, devotes only 35 percent to advertisements. *Flash* is the least encumbered by ads—under 25 percent of its 100 pages. *[On the other hand, a lot of people find the ads in the fat magazines almost as useful as the editorial pages—they are a good way to find out what products are out there.—DD]*

Mac Home Journal (EC). Like cities, it seems that magazines should either be huge or tiny; with few exceptions, the middle ground lacks symphonies and specialty bookstores while not quite escaping from crime and dirt. *The Mac Home Journal* ($20 a year) seems too small to serve the home-office crowd adequately—there are no "Mac Home Journal labs" to provide the detailed, technical reviews like the ones that appear in *Macworld* or *MacUser*. On the other hand, the magazine seems unwilling to devote too much energy to home use or game playing. Which leaves the reader with a little of this and a little of that, but nothing very focused or in depth.

Cobb Group newsletters (ND). The Cobb Group publishes several excellent monthly newsletters for Mac users. *The Mac Authority* ($50 a year) contains general Mac techniques and tips. Four others focus on popular Microsoft products: *Inside Word* ($50 a year), *Excellence* ($50 a year), *Inside Microsoft Works* ($40 a year), and *Inside FileMaker Pro* ($60 a year). *Inside HyperCard* ($60 a year) is aimed at stack developers.

BMUG Newsletter (EC). This 500-page "newsletter," published twice a year by the folks at BMUG (see the entry on BMUG under "User Groups," below), is jam-packed with reviews, commentary, and tips written by honest-to-goodness users. There's not a single ad, and that frees up BMUG's staff to say exactly what they think about the products they review and talk about. The newsletter is included free with membership in the user group, but I'd buy it even if it wasn't. (Nonmembers as well as members can buy back issues of the *BMUG Newsletter* for $7 each, directly from BMUG.)

The 1993 BMUG Shareware Disk Catalog (ND). This $23, 700-page directory (published by Addison-Wesley) catalogs the 340 disks'-worth of freeware and shareware in BMUG's library. Even if you're not planning to buy any of these

Mac History Books (EC)

If you're interested in how two guys in a garage started a billion-dollar company, and how one of them got kicked out half way through, check out a couple of the following:

Steve Jobs: The Journey Is the Reward by Jeffrey Young (pro-Jobs, pro-Wozniak)

Accidental Millionaire by Lee Butcher (anti Jobs, pro–everyone else)

West of Eden by Frank Rose (pretty even)

Odyssey by John Sculley (pro-Sculley, doesn't talk much about anyone else)

Hackers by Steven Levy (an amazing book that explains where Woz came from)

Other Books (EC)

There are probably a hundred books that offer information on how to use the Mac. Unfortunately, *this* book isn't the place to talk about them (it's hard to sound sincere when you're blasting the competition...). Just the same, my recommendation is to avoid books in a series—they tend to put more emphasis on looking alike than on getting down to the business at hand. And although bookstores hardly ever have a decent Mac selection, that doesn't mean the book you want doesn't exist. The best way to find out what's out there is to call the publisher and ask for a catalog—my favorites are Peachpit (OK, I couldn't help it), Ventana Press, and IDG Books; check Appendix D for telephone numbers. When you've found what you want, you can order the book from your local bookstore.

programs from BMUG, the brief descriptions (and compatibility details) can help you find useful software on-line or at your local user group.

Macintosh Product Registry (EC). If you want to know what software is available for the Mac, the *Macintosh Product Registry*, published by Redgate Communications ($15 for one issue, $40 for a year) is the most complete listing around. Updated quarterly, the listing offers a paragraph or two about almost every program written for the Mac, including major features and company contact info.

The CD version ($40) delivers the book in a HyperCard stack, letting you search for programs by company and product name. The stack is a great idea and includes the same information as the book, but its bare-bones construction makes you think they put it together at the last minute.

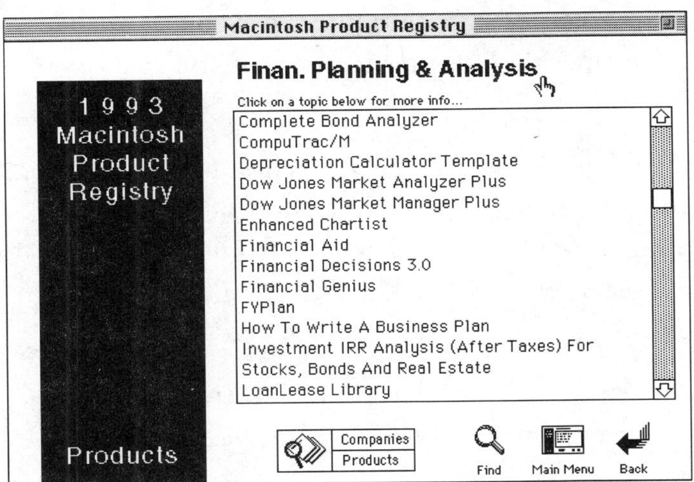

The Macintosh Product Registry *lists almost every product available for the Mac.*

Nautilus (ND/EC). Nautilus is a $135-a-year "magazine" that appears monthly on CD-ROM disk. It's a good way to get big clip art and sound files that would cost a fortune to download from an on-line service, demo versions of software, upgrades for popular programs (including system software—one subscriber was delighted to receive System 7.1 even before his local user group did), and shareware from international bulletin boards. Nautilus also includes articles of general interest: A recent issue included info and a QuickTime video on cougars and bobcats and an explanation of the déjà vu phenomenon (complete with a mini-program designed to provoke a déjà vu experience in the viewer). Nautilus's interface has improved—it's easy to get around, and the programs, videoclips, and sounds you can copy from the CD are placed at your fingertips. Be sure and use the Installer to install the Nautilus startup files and index on your hard disk. This will make the program go a lot faster.

Nautilus offers both general-interest articles and Macintosh-related information. Almost everything is bolstered with a QuickTime video, sound, or a mini-program.

Computers in General

If your interests extend beyond the Mac and into computers in general, there are a number of multiplatform magazines that may have just what you're looking for.

Computer Select (EC). If you can't decide which magazine is best for you, buy them all! Computer Select from Computer Library (a division of Ziff-Davis Publishing), offers a year's worth of computer-related articles from 150 different sources (including *MacUser*, *Macworld*, and *MacWEEK*, but also the *New York Times*, *PC Magazine*, and *Aldus Magazine*) on each monthly CD.

Although not all of the articles appear in full-length form (an abstract appears in the place of some), it's hard to exaggerate about the enormous amount of

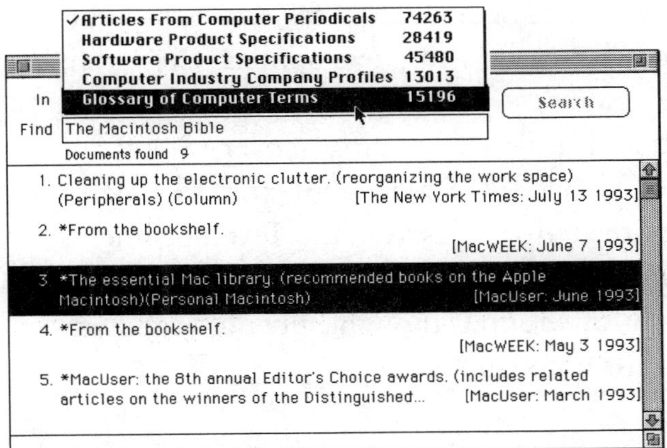

Computer Select's electronic catalog of computer-related articles is an enormously useful resource.

GOOD FEATURE

information suddenly available with Computer Select. With some 75,000 articles, 13,000 company profiles (complete with names, addresses, and phone numbers), and 15,000 definitions of computer terminology, you'll be happy to hear that Ziff uses its proprietary "Answerware" database format, which lets you search any topic (with logical operators like AND and OR) in a matter of seconds.

It's biggest drawback? The $1,000 yearly subscription rate.

Flash (EC). If you have a laser printer, you need *Flash* ($15 a year for six issues), the "Premier Journal for Desktop Printing." It's chock-full of articles on laser printer repair, using transfer toner to print on T-shirts and mugs, and writing PostScript code, as well as desktop publishing tips, book and product reviews, commentary, and some very funny comics.

NewMedia (EC). If you want to be on top of the latest and greatest in the burgeoning world of multimedia, pick up a copy of *NewMedia* ($50 a year). It reviews the most important video, graphics, and sound software and hardware and gives you an idea of where it's all headed.

GOOD FEATURE

Wired (EC). It's not easy to describe *Wired*, an attractive, compelling new magazine whose mission seems to be to put technology in a social context. Rejecting what publisher Louis Rossetto calls the "ad sales formula cum parts catalog" mentality of national computer magazines, *Wired* goes beyond features and upgrades, even the Mac itself, and seeks to capture the significance of the digital revolution as it evolves and, somehow, put it down on paper. It's incredible. You can get *Wired* for $40 a year.

Co-Net CD (EC). The Co-Net CD ($27 for one issue, $50 for two-issue year subscription), available from the Trace Research and Development Center at the University of Wisconsin-Madison, includes a wealth of resources for people who have disabilities. Abledata is a HyperCard-based catalog of over 18,000 rehabilitation and assistive devices. The Cooperative Service Directories list people and agencies that provide disability-related services. And the Text Document Library includes a collection of key disability-related documents regarding law, ADA, accessibility, and funding. The information is thoughtfully put together; Abledata, for example, is accessible to the vision-impaired.

User Groups

User groups are clubs made up of people who are interested in computers in general, a particular kind of computer, a particular kind of software, or even an individual program. They're typically nonprofit and independent of any manufacturer or publisher.

User groups are an excellent source of good information—which isn't surprising, since sharing information is their main purpose. Nowhere else are you likely to find so many dedicated people eager to help you solve your problems, none of whom would dream of charging you a nickel for it. (On the other hand, a lot of their opinions and recommendations have to be taken with a grain of salt.)

User group meetings are usually free and open to the public. Joining the group normally costs somewhere between $20 and $60 a year and gives you access to the group's library of public domain software and shareware and usually some sort of discount on commercial software and hardware. Many user groups also offer tech support, either by telephone or in person.

Large groups often feature guest speakers from the computer industry who describe new products at their meetings. They also have subgroups called *SIGs* (special interest groups) for members who have particular interests or needs: beginners, developers, musicians, graphic artists, desktop publishers, and so on.

Finding a Local User Group (EC)

Unless you live in a very remote area, finding a local user group shouldn't be hard—especially if there's a college or university nearby. Either check with an Apple dealer (any good one will know all the local user groups) or call 800/538-9696, which is Apple's user group hot line (you give them your ZIP code and they give you the names and numbers of up to three user groups in your area). If you can't find a group in your community, get together with some other Mac users and start one of your own.

The Biggies

There are a few user groups that are so big, or so old, that they serve as an example for all the rest. And even if you don't happen to live near them, their enormous software libraries (which you can generally order by mail on floppies or CD), incredible newsletters brimming with news and tips, member discounts, and fantastic free tech support make long-distance membership very tempting. Of course, it'll be hard to get to the meetings, but that's even hard for people who live close by.

Below we describe the largest and oldest Macintosh user groups.

Boston Computer Society (AN/EC). There are more than 45 SIGs in the country's largest user group, the Boston Computer Society, and each of them publishes a newsletter (in addition to BCS's own slick magazine). When you join BCS (for $40 a year), you get to choose two SIGs to belong to (more than that costs extra). BCS's Mac SIG has more than 10,000 members and its newsletter, *The Active Window*, is excellent. In addition, it offers great tech support, advice on buying software and hardware, and discounts to members for third-party items (one month was printers, for example).

BMUG (EC). BMUG's motto is "We give away information." With more than 12,000 members all over the world and offices in Berkeley and Boston, BMUG is truly a Mac institution. BMUG sends out a 450-page, advertisement-free newsletter twice a year to its members (see page 1010) and offers tech support, hard disk salvaging, and a great BBS (actually two, one on each coast). BMUG also publishes excellent books: *The Zen of ResEdit* and *The Tao of AppleScript* are just two I'd recommend. One of the members' discounts is free shipping from MacWarehouse. BMUG also maintains an extensive public domain and shareware library and publishes, on CD-ROM, a comprehensive collection of noncommercial software.

NYMUG (EC). With almost 5,000 members and 40 different Mac-related SIGs, NYMUG, the New York Macintosh User Group (memberships $40 a year) is one of the largest Macintosh user groups. It publishes a monthly bulletin, called *Mac Street Journal*, and holds meetings for SIGs as varied as "Mac Kids Club," "Electronic Imaging," "Medical/Dental," and "C & Pascal." (I want to know if they call themselves NYMUGgers…)

APDA (ND). APDA started out as a sort of user group—the Apple Programmers and Developers Association. Now it's an Apple service that provides tools for programming, including languages, utilities, books, and training. Call for the free catalog (the contact information is in Appendix D).

Buying Macs and Mac Products

THERE'S NOTHING WORSE than buying computer equipment. You're never sure who's telling the truth, or if your purchase will be worth next to nothing the day after tomorrow when the SuperDuper models come out. There's no getting around it: Buying computer equipment and the software to run on it can be very stressful. And to make matters worse, those things are expensive! Make a mistake and you'll really regret it.

This chapter is designed to give you all the information you need before you make a purchase so that you don't bang your head against the wall later. There's not much you can do about plummeting computer values, but at least you'll know that you've done the best you can.

Contributors

Elizabeth Castro (EC) is the appendix editor.

David Hauer (DH) put on his SIGGraph '82 T-shirt again last year (having spent the intervening time playing music) and hasn't taken it off since. He's a Mac consultant and animator.

Larry Pina (LP) is a software developer and technical writer based in Westport, Massachusetts. He is the author of *Mac Classic and SE Repair and Upgrade Secrets* (Peachpit Press).

Arthur Naiman (AN) was the original author and editor of *The Macintosh Bible.*

Contents

Buying a Mac

In 1984, buying a Mac was easy because there was only one to choose from. Today, Apple sells over 20 different models, and you can find another 20 or so that have been discontinued. Check out Chapter 2 for information on the kinds of Macs you'll be choosing from (at least when this was written). Then, before you buy, do some research to see where they offer the Mac you want at the best price.

Buying a New Mac (EC)

Shopping for a new computer is a lot like shopping for any big-ticket item: You'll find a wide variety of prices for the same item from different dealers, and you'll be better off all around if you can find a dealer you can trust. That said, though, there are a few special considerations to keep in mind when shopping for a Mac. Here's a rundown of them.

Apple's falling prices. There's one thing about buying a Mac that you've got to have crystal clear: If you wait three months, it's price will probably go down. And if you wait three more months, it'll go down further. Macs do not make good financial investments. On the other hand, they are a great tool, and if you never buy one, you'll never have one.

You should probably also know that Apple tends to introduce new models (and discount or discontinue older ones) every three or four months. Check on-line services (like America Online) or *MacWEEK* magazine to see if there are any hints about the imminent demise of a computer you're interested in. The electronic newsletter TidBITS, published by Tonya and Adam Engst and available by subscription right to your e-mailbox, is also a great source of information about new products and falling prices.

If you can bear to forgo the "very latest" in Mac technology, you can often get a great deal by buying those discounted and discontinued models. Keep in mind, though, that there are two common reasons Apple discontinues its models of computers. One is that the old model is too close in features to a new model (the Centris line, Quadra 800, and SE/30 are good examples), and buying one

Apple's Falling Prices: A Case in Point (EC)

Just four months after Apple announced the Mac IIvx, it shaved $1,000 off the price and offered a faster Centris for even less than the original IIvx. Since both *MacUser* and *Macworld* had heavily promoted the IIvx, readers were just a mite ticked off, but they shouldn't have been so surprised. The original Mac was introduced in January of 1984 and by September, when Apple announced the Mac 512, the original Mac (with 128K) had dropped $300 in price. If you buy a 128K Mac today, it'll cost you less than $50.

The moral of the story: Check around before you buy. If you already have a Mac, go on-line and ask if there are any rumors about the Mac you're interested in. And ask if there are any upgrade paths from your Mac to another one.

of those may be a very good buy. Another, though, is that Apple knows something you may not about future technology plans, like the fact that 68030 processors are on the way out since they are not upgradable to PowerPC. In that case, the purchase may not be such a great idea, unless you don't care much about future upgradability.

Finding a good deal. When looking for the best price on a Mac, call several dealers, and then do some bargaining. I asked five different dealers for quotes and there was more than a $300 difference between the highest and the lowest. (Surprisingly, all of them were lower than the mail-order prices quoted in *MacUser* that month.) And don't forget: If you order your Mac shipped from another state, you won't have to pay sales tax—and you can still bring it into your local dealer for service (see the next entry).

BARGAIN

Some vendors offer a special price if you buy a specific configuration or a particular model Mac together with a particular keyboard and monitor. Think of it as an Apple Value Meal.

ApplePrice (EC)

This may sound crazy, but there is no official price for any Apple product. If you call Apple and ask for a one, they'll just refer you to your local dealer. The amounts quoted in magazines and in Apple's ads (and in this book) are called "ApplePrice," which is an estimate of the street price, according to Apple.

When you're comparing prices between Apple equipment and the same item from another manufacturer (not on Macs, of course, but on things like hard drives or monitors), remember that the ApplePrice is a lot closer to what you'll finally pay than the other manufacturer's list price, which may be much higher than the price you'll actually pay at a dealer.

Warranties and guarantees for new Macs. Apple offers a one-year warranty on every hardware product it sells. That means that Apple or an Apple Authorized Service Provider will fix any hardware problem you have free of charge. Whether they will fix it on-site or when you bring it in for service depends on the problem you have. Sometimes Apple will even send replacement parts by courier service—before you even send in your old one.

This is an Apple guarantee, and it's valid even if you buy your Mac from a mail-order company or even another person—as long as nobody but an Authorized Apple Service Provider has touched your Mac's innards and you have a dated sales receipt with your equipment's serial numbers on it.

One of the nice things about the Apple guarantee is that it is good throughout the world. So if you are in Barcelona on a business trip and your PowerBook dies, you'll be happy to know you can bring it to any Authorized Apple Service Provider for service. (You may have to pay for it, but Apple will reimburse you once you get back to the U.S.)

Service. You'd think that if you're about to plunk down a couple of thousand dollars, the salesperson would automatically treat you nicely, but it just ain't true. This is one of those things that I've never understood about Apple: It's hard to find a dealer who knows what he's talking about, and even if you do, it's even harder to find one who's willing to spend a few minutes sharing that knowledge with you. Maybe it's because Macs are so easy to sell, who knows? At any rate, they may be in the minority, but knowledgeable dealers do exist: Don't settle for less.

800/SOS-APPL (EC)

Apple has a free technical support line (800/SOS-APPL) but unfortunately it is so popular that you sometimes have to wait up to 45 minutes listening to minimalist music while you're on hold. I can almost stand waiting, but the music makes me go berserk. They should let you leave a message (and then get back to you later) or, heaven forbid, hire more people to answer the phones. At the very least, they should let you shut off that music. Here's a tip that will be worthless once published: They say the best time to call is between 9 and 10 a.m. and 3 and 5 p.m., central time, Tuesdays, Wednesdays, and Thursdays.

Plugs and Volts

(EC)

If you're planning to take your new purchase along with you on a trip, you should know that those little American flat pronged plugs are not very common outside of this country. So even though PowerBooks (and most laptops) can use the 220 volts that are common in Europe or the 100 volts that they use in Japan, it won't do you much good unless you have an adapter that lets you plug it in.

If you're bringing a desktop computer, a hard disk, or a printer along, be sure to check what voltage it will accept (either by consulting the technical information booklet that comes with it or by looking on the plug itself next to the word *Input*). If your hardware won't work with the voltage at your destination, you'll have to buy a transformer.

The tough stuff comes when you try to plug your modem into the local telephone lines. There are almost 40 kinds of telephone plugs in the world, with four different ones in Germany alone. And you'll need local access numbers if you want to plug into CompuServe or other on-line services. Although some countries do use RJ-11 plugs (as we do in this country), it's a good idea to check first; then you'll know whether you need an adapter.

For adapters, transformers, and friendly advice, try Bon Voyage (800/995-9716), a travel bookstore and travel-necessity mail-order warehouse in Fresno, California.

Buying a Used Mac

(EC)

Though hardware prices continue to fall, Macs still cost more than yo-yos, and many people wonder whether it isn't smarter to buy one used. Although there are obvious risks associated with doing that, Macs are pretty reliable. Far fewer than 1 percent of all Macs are shipped with faulty hardware (not counting disk drives), and most problems turn up within the first 90 days or so of use.

Why not? One question to ask about a used Mac is whether Apple provides an upgrade path from it to a current model. If not, you're likely to have increasing difficulty finding compatible hardware and software as the years go by; in addition to the obvious problem of keeping up with the pack in terms of processing speed and power.

If you are considering buying an older Mac and then adding an accelerator and extra memory, be sure to check prices on the new Macs first. Prices have been dropping so drastically that you might be able to buy a new, faster Mac for less than a used, souped-up model.

Where to look. One of the best places to find a used Mac is through the classified advertisements in a user group newsletter (see Appendix B for more on user groups). Some dealers also have second-hand Macs and may offer some limited guarantee. No matter who you buy the computer from, if it is less than a year old, the original Apple guarantee will still be valid as long as you have the original dated invoice that includes the computer's serial number.

How Much Is It Worth Now? (EC)

Many Mac magazines, including *Macworld* and *MacWEEK,* publish a monthly listing of used Mac prices. Your local user group is another good source of information for the going rate on a used Mac.

You can also call the American Computer Exchange, a service that connects buyers and sellers of all kinds of computer equipment (for a commission); see Appendix D for contact information.

Checking Out a Used Mac (LP/DH/AN)

To reduce the chances of getting slimed, it's a good idea to check out a used Mac pretty thoroughly before you buy it. The few easy checks described here could save you a lot of teeth-gnashing later. (If you need help with some of the terms used in this section, consult Chapter 2.)

Check the memory. Choose About This Macintosh on the menu to make sure you're getting all the RAM claimed. And use a utility like RAM Check to verify that all the RAM is in working order.

Check the hard drive. If the system includes a hard drive, reformat it and then run a utility like SCSI Evaluator or FWB's Hard Disk ToolKit to check for speed and bad sectors; if it finds bad sectors, the disk may not be reliable. This may take some time, but it's as good a way as any to put a machine through its paces.

Check the keyboard. Sometimes an otherwise perfect Mac will have a keyboard with one or more broken keys. Be sure to test them all. Stiff, sticky keys aren't much better than broken ones; they'll drive you crazy, and you'll have to fix them or get a new keyboard.

Check the mouse. The mouse can sometimes be bad too. To test it, wiggle both ends of the cable as you move the pointer around the screen and click. If the pointer does not move smoothly, there may be a problem with the connection (then again, it may just be dirty; see Chapter 6 for more information on how to clean a mouse).

Check floppy drives. There are two parts of a floppy drive that you should check out. If you want to make sure the Mac has a SuperDrive—the up-to-date Macintosh floppy drive that uses high-density, 1.4MB disks—insert a high-density disk in the drive. If you get a message saying "This disk is unreadable. Do you want to initialize it?" it's probably not a SuperDrive. (It could also be that the drive needs service or cleaning, as described in Chapter 5.)

If a floppy disk is hard to insert—or worse, hard to get out—and the drive seems sticky or gummy, it may be time for a cleaning or for a new drive.

The 800K floppy drives in Pluses, early SEs, and early Mac II's were built by Sony, but they're not all the same. The original ones have black labels and tend to have problems ejecting disks. More recent drives are more reliable; they have red labels. (You have to take the case off to see the labels.)

Check the screen. To assess wear-and-tear on a screen, turn off the power. If you see a ghost of the menu bar on the black screen, it's near the end of its life.

If you suffer from astigmatism, then wear a white shirt or shine a flashlight at the screen. If you can clearly see your reflection, then using that monitor day after day may cause headaches and even backaches (because you'll be unconsciously twisting every which way in an attempt to minimize the glare).

Check the video card. To find out which kind of video card—if any—is in a used Mac, go to the Monitors control panel. You may only be able to select black and white, which means it's got a 1-bit card. If you can select 16 colors (or shades of gray), it's got a 4-bit card. If you can select 256 colors, it's got an 8-bit card. If you can select millions of colors, it's got a 24-bit card. The more bits—and colors—the better.

Click the Options button. If it says Macintosh II Video Card, the card is low-resolution. If it says Mac II High Resolution Video Card or Macintosh Display

Looking at an Older Mac (LP)

All Macs aren't alike—even Macs with the same model names. Some older Mac models went through midlife revisions that had a big impact on their reliability or performance. To make sure you're getting the best of the breed, try these tests.

Pluses

A Mac Plus may have one of three ROM versions. Versions 1 and 2 don't work very well with SCSI drives. To tell which version a given Plus has, boot from a floppy and press the interrupt button. (On most Macs, that's on the side, in a two-button set. The interrupt button has a downward-pointing arrow on it.)

You'll see a >. Type *DM4000000* after it and hit Return. The ROM version will be shown in the second and third columns of the top row. 4D1E EEnn indicates version 1, 4D1E EAnn indicates version 2, and 4D1F 81nn indicates version 3 (the one you want). To exit the debugger and return to Finder, type *G* and then Return.

SEs

Early SEs have a squirrel-cage fan that tends to be annoyingly loud and may cause video interference. Later models have a quieter, noninterfering propeller fan.

There are two versions of the SE logic board. The early model (part number 820-0176) doesn't work as well with expansion cards and SIMMs as the later one (part number 820-0250). Unfortunately, to tell which model you've got, you have to remove the logic board and read the label printed to the right of the 68000 chip.

Mac II's

Lift the lid and read the part number stenciled on the left-rear corner of the logic board. Later models (part number 820-0288) are almost 25 percent faster than earlier models (part number 820-0163).

Mac IIcx's and IIci's

The ci has limited 8-bit video built into the logic board, so it may not come with a video card. The ci's built-in video works fine with Apple monitors, but it doesn't support NTSC and PAL video equipment.

The ci has space for a cache card, which increases the processing speed. All models sold in 1991 and later included one free.

Card (the most advanced), it's high resolution and will work better with NTSC and PAL video equipment like camcorders, VCRs, and TVs. (Of course, it may not be an Apple board at all, in which case you'll have to call the dealer or manufacturer to find out what that specific board can do.)

Buying Other Stuff

(AN/EC)

This book is filled with specific evaluations and comparisons of Mac programs. What follows here are some general guidelines on what to keep in mind while you're shopping and how to decide where to buy.

Before You Buy Anything

Here are some rules of thumb that apply to both hardware and software.

Start with the best. If you can figure out which is the best program, buy it. Don't tell yourself "Well, I really can't afford that," or "I can get by with less." This is almost always a false economy: You end up having to pay to replace the defective product (or program), and you also lose the time you've invested learning to use the first one.

Trust good publishers. Since movie reviewers spend most of their time telling you the plot (and usually can't even do that with any accuracy), one of the best ways to decide if a movie is worth seeing is to find out who directed it. Similarly, one of the best ways to tell if a program is worth buying is to judge by the company that publishes it. If you like one piece of software by a publisher, chances are you'll like another.

Get the support you need. There's a saying in real estate that the three most important things to consider when buying property are location, location, and location. Likewise, the three most important things to consider when buying a computer product are support, support, and support. (Support is the availability of someone to answer your questions, usually on the phone, and to fix things if they go wrong.)

Support is the reason it often makes sense to pay a little more to buy from a vendor whose staff knows something (whether it's a local store or a mail-order distributor). Don't imagine you can depend on the publisher's telephone support line. Most of them are so understaffed that you might as well just play a tape recording of a busy signal and not tie up your phone. (Get this: WordPerfect has a disk jockey who gives "traffic reports" to let you know how long you'll have to wait on hold for each department. You've got to hear it to believe it.)

Take reviews (including ours) with a grain of salt. One problem with reviews is that most reviewers aren't like most users. They tend to have much more experience with Mac programs and to be much more interested in exploring the Mac as an activity in itself. (We call this tendency "expertosis"; it also causes a problem with manuals.)

Another problem is that reviewers are seldom given enough time to really get to know the ins and outs of the software they're evaluating. Lots of programs are complicated enough that you don't really get a feeling for their strengths and weaknesses until you've used them fairly heavily for a couple of months.

A third problem is that magazines are supported by advertising revenues, and though we're always surprised by how tough they're willing to be in spite of that fact, no magazine's reviews are going to be, on the average, 75 percent or even 50 percent negative.

Still, reviews are a great place to learn about products. Just don't treat them as gospel—even when they appear in the *Bible*. (In fact, especially when they appear in the *Bible*. Magazines can afford to do a much more comprehensive and thorough job of evaluating whole classes of products. All we can do is give you the opinions of an expert or two, or—at best—the general consensus among the Mac experts we know.)

Compatibility. Make sure that the product you want to buy is compatible with the ones you already own. Make sure you know what you have, and then explain it to the vendor and ask if the new product will be compatible.

Get a money-back guarantee. Many vendors offer a money-back guarantee in case you're not satisfied with what you've bought. However, many don't. Make sure, before you buy, that you'll be able to send it back if it's not what the doctor ordered.

Don't pay retail. Whether you're buying a printer or a word processor, you would do well to check around before you buy. Prices vary from region to region, and from dealer to dealer—sometimes a lot. Generally, the best prices for software are found in mail-order catalogs. The best deals in hardware, on the other hand, are often found in large cities (like New York).

The prices quoted in this book are generally retail prices—we had to be consistent so that you could compare from one program to the next. Street prices are often 30 to 50 percent less.

Before You Buy Software

Here are the *Mac Bible* rules of looking for software.

Ease of use—insist on it. One of the major reasons people buy the Mac is to avoid a lot of intimidating, user-hostile gobbledygook. For software to be easy to use, it should be hierarchically organized. This means that most basic operations are simple and central to how the program works and the more advanced operations are off to the side, so you don't even know about them until you need them.

Since all Mac programs are designed with a similar interface, a good program should look familiar, even if you've never seen it before. That means you should immediately be able to see how to create, open, close and save documents, copy and paste, and quit.

You want a great manual you don't need, with an index. No matter how great a program is, it doesn't do you any good unless you can figure out how to use it. Mac software should be so clear, its menu commands so understandable, that you only need a manual to fill you in on the details. The manual should be illustrated, well written, and have a good index.

Even the worst manuals are a great place to look for tips, which are usually marked with a special icon or set off in boldface or italics. Quark's manuals are a good example: They're almost impossible to understand when you're trying to learn the program, but if you skim them, you will glean more than a couple of good tricks.

You won't get consistency, so settle for customizability. Although the commands in Mac software are much more standardized between programs than those on the PC, they're still not nearly as standardized as they should be. One thing that really irks me is the lack of consistency around the commands for boldface, italics, and plain text.

Does this lead to frustrating typing mistakes? Is the Pope Catholic? Do politicians lie?

You can use QuicKeys or Tempo to customize most programs, but some are structured so you can't change all their commands. For example, in PageMaker, you can't change the command for plain text because there's another command with the same name (Normal) on an earlier menu.

Since there are lots of people who are now very used to lots of different commands, true Macintosh consistency is a lost cause. What you can get instead (and which is almost as good) is the ability to change a program's commands to what you want them to be.

No program is an Iland, intire of it selfe. Unless you plan on buying one sole program to satisfy all your Macintosh needs, make sure the programs you buy let you save your documents in several formats and export and import documents to other programs.

Speed counts. As many people have learned to their sorrow, ease of use isn't everything. How fast a program runs can be even more important. Unfortunately, that's seldom mentioned in ads or by salesclerks and it's one of the hardest things to evaluate in an in-store tryout. But delays of even a few seconds can be very annoying if you keep running into them. Because of that, speed is one of the prime things to look for in a program.

Don't use a bazooka to kill a fly. If you're using PageMaker 5 to compose your e-mail, don't be surprised if you're gray before your time. Huge programs take up a lot of memory and disk space and do a lot of things well, once they get around to doing them. But if you need to do something simple, a snappy little program dedicated to the task will run circles around the big guys.

Shareware, freeware, and public domain software are worth trying. Shareware is a concept that got started with computers and it's a great idea that should be supported. The idea is that programmers who come up with a neat application or utility distribute it through user groups and on-line services to other computer users. And if you like the program and use it in your work (or play), you pay for it. This gets a lot of really useful, really inexpensive programs out into the world, bypassing corporate expenses like advertising and distribution.

GOOD FEATURE

If you do end up using a shareware program, make sure you pay for it. If you don't, you may save money in the short run, but if the people who write shareware have to find some other way to make a living, they won't be able to upgrade the program you're using or create anything new.

Lots of programs are available absolutely free, thanks to the generosity of their authors. *Freeware* means the author stills owns the copyright (which means you can't change the software), while *public domain software* is said to belong to everyone (and thus is open to a good hack).

You can get shareware, freeware, and software in the public domain (all of which are sometimes collectively known as "publicly distributable software") from good computer stores (if you've done business with them), user groups, or bulletin boards (see Appendix B for more on user groups and Chapter 22 for more on bulletin board services). You often have to put up with skimpy documentation, or none at all, and early versions of most programs have bugs. But there's a lot of terrific stuff, some of it better than commercial programs.

Beware of vaporware. So much software has been promised that never saw the light of day (or saw it on a day many months after it was supposed to) that there's even a name for it—*vaporware*.

So when some salesclerk (or ad, or friend) tells you that a new product will be along "real soon now," don't depend on it. Few computer products come out on time, and some end up being nothing more than vaporware.

MAC BIBLE DISK

The Mac Bible Software Disks (DD)

The Mac Bible Software Disks (Peachpit Press, $10) include several of the shareware and freeware programs recommended in this book. For $25 more (if you didn't get the package deal: the book and disk combo for $42), you can get the Macintosh Bible CD-ROM, which includes more software as well as lots of program demos, clip art, and shareware fonts.

If possible, try before you buy. Any decent computer store will let you sit and play with software for hours at a time, as long as no one else wants to use the machine (unfortunately, someone almost always does). Trying a program in a store will often (but not always) give you enough of a feeling for it to decide if you want to buy it.

Some software manufacturers offer free (or low-cost) demo versions so you can try out the program at home before deciding on your purchase. Another good place to find demo software is on CD-ROMs (see the boxes "The Macintosh Bible Disks" on page 1030 and "Unlocking Your Software From a CD" on page 1032). Typically a demo version works exactly like the original but won't let you save, print, or export.

Thou shalt not steal. Pirating software is a short-sighted solution to your economic woes. Even if you save a couple bucks by copying your friend's program, you won't get the upgrades, the manuals, or the support that comes from having the real McCoy. (Sorry.)

And if people can't make money developing software because everyone is stealing their software instead of buying it, soon there won't be any good programs at all. Then what'll you do?

Before You Buy Hardware (AN/EC)

Here are some things to remember when you're looking for hardware of all sorts.

Get what you need. If you want something—a big screen instead of a 14-incher—you'll usually be happier if you figure out some way to justify having it. I've seldom if ever heard anyone say, "I really shouldn't have bought this [expensive piece of computer equipment]. I really could have gotten by with [something simpler and less expensive]." But I can't count the number of times I've heard people who've gotten some powerful new piece of hardware say, "How did I live without this?"

You can never have too much. How do you know how much is enough? Actually, there are some things that you can never get too much of, among which are hard disks, RAM, and Ben and Jerry's Heathbar Crunch ice cream. If you're buying a hard disk, buy twice as much as you think you'll need. If you're buying RAM, buy as much as you can afford. If you're buying Heathbar Crunch, fill up your freezer.

Check out the OEM. When buying hardware, remember that what really counts is often not the name on the box, it's the OEM ("oh-ee-em," or original equipment manufacturer). Overall quality is determined by the OEM; service and technical support depend on who you buy the equipment from. (The chapters covering hardware in this book point out some good names to look for.)

Get a long warranty. Look for a good long warranty—at least a year. Lots of companies offer two-year, three-year, or even five-year warranties. (Of course, those companies may not be around in five years, or even two, and that's definitely something else to consider.)

Where to Buy (EC)

You can buy Macs, hardware peripherals, and software in three basic places: at an Apple Authorized Reseller, at warehouse and department stores, or by mail order.

Apple Authorized Resellers

Apple dealers (called "resellers" by Apple) tend to have competitive prices on Macs and hardware, but they overprice their software. They generally provide average to good service and are fairly reliable. They are not known for having

Unlocking Your Software From a CD (EC)

If mail order isn't fast enough for you, try a locked CD. A locked CD is generally filled to the gills with software, which you can unlock once you've given your charge-card number to a sales representative, by phone.

Locked CDs have several good features: the disks often include information and demo versions that give you a good idea of how the program works before you buy it, and once you decide, you can have the program installed on your hard disk right away. Unfortunately, the manuals, which are generally sent later (if at all), will still take a few days to get to you. And the software used to run the CD and take you on a tour of its contents can be really slow.

Apart from specialized CDs like **Adobe's Type On Call** ($65), which includes Adobe's entire font collection, and **Club Kidsoft** ($3), which specializes in educational software and games for kids, many mail-order companies offer CD mixes with a variety of software. Apple distributes a CD of its own, **Software Dispatch,** that is free of charge.

the most helpful or knowledgeable staff, although there are exceptions. They can, and generally will, order you any Apple product and often can provide authorized service and repairs if anything goes wrong.

Why do some resellers (generally mail-order companies) opt *not* to be Apple Authorized Resellers? Apple requires it's Authorized Resellers to buy $1 million in equipment per year (in most areas), have a certain amount of working capital (anywhere from $150,000 to $300,000, depending on the region), invest in promotional activities (to the tune of $20,000 if the dealer is located in the Northeast, for example), and have an Apple Product Manager on staff, on site. In addition, Apple checks out the store's floor space, appearance, and frontage, in an effort to protect its image.

Warehouse and Department Stores

The Performa line is available at Sears and warehouse stores like Price Costco. You are likely to find a good price at such stores, and get some free, bundled software, but you probably won't get a lot of support or advice from them. You also won't find much selection, and they're not likely to carry many peripherals (apart from printers).

Mail Order

Buying computer equipment by mail is blindingly fast. You can order a program one day and have it the next, as long as it's in stock. In addition, mail-order companies tend to offer the lowest prices, and they don't skimp on support or information. You should make sure that the company you are dealing with has a good reputation and that they've been in the business for awhile. And you should pay by credit card whenever possible; if there is any problem, you can instruct your bank not to pay the charge. Returns and repairs vary from vendor to vendor; ask before you buy, as some companies will bill you for a "restocking charge" on returns.

HOT TIP

Although Apple had its own catalog for a time (it was discontinued in early 1994), its prices were not really very competitive. It's recently decided to authorize other mail-order companies, like CompUSA, Elek-tek, and *Crutchfield Magazine* as official Apple Authorized Resellers.

If you're looking for software, call MacWarehouse, Rocky Mountain Computer Outfitters, MacConnection, or The Mac Zone. All of these companies will send you a free catalog (which is a great way to find out what software is available), and the latter two both offer demo-filled CDs that can make the full version appear on your desktop when you say the magic word (see the box "Unlocking Your Software From a CD" on the previous page).

Invisible Ads in Software Catalogs (EC)

If you've ever wondered why some programs seem to get preferential treatment in a software catalog, perhaps you won't be surprised to hear that software manufacturers have to pay to have their products appear. A bare-bones mention in a national mail-order catalog starts at around $5,000—and you wondered how they could make a living selling software so cheap!

Although the prices at all these dealers are about the same, call around to compare, and ask if the software you're interested in is bundled with anything else.

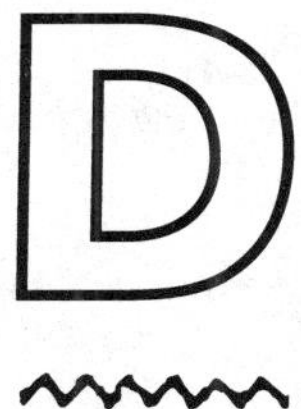

Contact Information

This appendix provides the information you need to get hold of the software publishers and hardware manufacturers of the products mentioned in this edition of the *Mac Bible*. By calling the numbers listed here, you can find out about the current availability of products you're wondering about, their current list price, and local sources. You could probably also order the product, but, as explained in Appendix C, that may not be a great idea, since you can usually find the product from outside sources at prices much lower than the manufacturer's list price.

The information was up to date at press time, but, as proven by the trouble we had tracking down some of these companies, these things can change fast. We've included e-mail addresses for companies that advertise them as part of their customer marketing materials. In those cases, we've used these abbreviations: AOL = America Online, AL = AppleLink, CIS = CompuServe Information Service, and MCI = MCI Mail. We've also included phone numbers for private bulletin board services (BBSs) for the companies that supply them.

Abacus Research and Development (ARDI)
1650 University Blvd. NE,
Suite 101,
Albuquerque, NM 87102
505/766-9115, fax 505/247-1899

Abbate Video
14 Ross Ave., 3rd Floor,
Millis, MA 02054-1545
800/283-5553, 508/376-3712,
fax 508/376-3714
AOL: abbate vid

Abbott Systems
62 Mountain Rd.,
Pleasantville, NY 10570
800/552-9157, 914/747-4171,
fax 914/747-9115

AbleSoft
4102 George Washington Hwy.,
Yorktown, VA 23692
800/545-9009, 804/898-8484,
fax 804/898-8282,
BBS 804/898-8686

Abracadata
P.O. Box 2440, Eugene, OR 97402
800/451-4871, 503/342-3030,
fax 503/683-1925
CIS: 70751,620

ACI US
20883 Stevens Creek Blvd.,
Cupertino, CA 95014
800/384-0010, 408/252-4444,
fax 408/252-4829
AL: D4444; CIS: go acius

Activision
11601 Wilshire Blvd., Suite 1000,
Los Angeles, CA 90025
800/477-3650, 310/473-9200,
fax 310/479-4005
CIS: go gambpub

Addison-Wesley Publishing
One Jacob Way,
Reading, MA 01867
800/447-2226, 617/944-3700,
fax 617/944-9338

Adobe Systems
1585 Charleston Rd.,
P.O. Box 7900,
Mountain View, CA 94039-7900
800/833-6687, 415/961-4400,
fax 408/562-6775,
BBS 408/562-6839
CIS: go adobe

Advanced Gravis Computer Technology
1790 Midway Ln.,
Bellingham, WA 98226
604/431-5020, fax 604/431-5155,
BBS 604/431-5927
CIS: go macdven

Advanced Laser Graphics
1835 K St. NW, Suite 745,
Washington, DC 20006
202/298-1750, fax 202/331-1115
CIS: 72510,474

Advanced Software
P.O. Box 65670,
West Des Moines, IA 50265
800/346-5392, 515/225-9620,
fax 515/225-2422

AEC Software
22611 Markey Ct., Bldg. 113,
Sterling, VA 20166
800/346-9413, 703/450-1980,
fax 703/450-9786

Affinity Microsystems
1900 Folsom St., Suite 205,
Boulder, CO 80302
800/367-6771, 303/442-4840,
fax 303/442-4999

AfroLink Software
1815 Wellington Rd.,
Los Angeles, CA 90019
213/731-5465, fax 213/730-0653

Agfa Division of Miles
90 Industrial Way,
Wilmington, MA 01877
800/424-8973, 508/658-5600,
fax 508/687-5328

The AG Group
2540 Camino Diablo, Suite 200,
Walnut Creek, CA 94596
800/466-2447, 510/937-7900,
fax 510/937-2479

Aladdin Systems
165 Westridge Dr.,
Watsonville, CA 95076-4159
800/732-8881, 408/761-6200,
fax 408/761-6206

Aldus
411 First Ave. S.,
Seattle, WA 98104-2871
800/685-3652, 206/628-2320,
fax 206/343-3360,
BBS 206/623-6984
CIS: go aldus

Aldus Consumer Division
5120 Shoreham Pl.,
San Diego, CA 92122-5926
800/888-6293, 619/558-6000,
fax 619/558-8723

Alias Research
110 Richmond St. E.,
Toronto, ON, M5C 1P1, Canada
800/447-2542, 416/362-8558,
fax 416/362-4696

Alki Software
300 Queen Anne Ave. N.,
Suite 410, Seattle, WA 98109
800/669-9673, 206/286-2600,
fax 206-286-2785

Allegiant Technologies
6496 Weathers Pl., Suite 100,
San Diego, CA 92121
619/587-0500, fax 619/587-1314

Alphatronix
4022 Stirrup Creek Dr.,
P.O. Box 13978,
Research Triangle Park, NC 27709
919/544-0001, fax 919/544-4079

Alsoft
P.O. Box 927,
Spring, TX 77383-0927
800/257-6381, 713/353-4090,
fax 713/353-9868

Altec Lansing Multimedia
P.O. Box 277, Milford, PA 18337
800/548-0620, 717/296-4434,
fax 717/296-2213

Altsys
269 W. Renner Rd.,
Richardson, TX 75080
214/680-2060, fax 214/680-0537
AL: d0590; CIS: 76004,2071;
MCI: 271-8914

Alysis Software
1231 31st Ave.,
San Francisco, CA 94122
800/825-9747, 415/566-2263,
fax 415/566-9692

American Computer Exchange
6065 Roswell Rd., Suite 535,
Atlanta, GA 30328
800/786-0717, 404/250-0054,
fax 404/250-1848

American Ink Jet
13 Alexander Rd.,
Billerica, MA 01821
800/332-6538, 508/667-0600,
fax 508/670-5637

American Power Conversion
132 Fairgrounds Rd., West
Kingston, RI 02892
800/800-4272, 401/789-5735,
fax 401/789-3710

America Online
8619 Westwood Ctr. Dr.,
Vienna, VA 22182-2285
800/827-6364, 703/448-8700,
fax 703/448-0760

Amtex Software
P.O. 572,
Belleville, ON,
K8N 5B2, Canada
613/967-7900, fax 613/967-7902

Anonae Software
P.O. Box 7629, Berkeley, CA 94707
510/527-8006

APDA (Apple Programmers and Developers Association)
P.O. Box 319,
Buffalo, NY 14207-0319
800/282-2732, 716/871-6555,
fax 716/871-6511
AOL and AL: apda;
CIS: 76666,2405

Apexx Technology
506 S. 11th St., Boise, ID 83702
800/767-4858, 208/336-9400,
fax 208/336-9445

Apple Computer
1 Infinite Loop,
Cupertino, CA 95014
800/776-2333, 408/996-1010,
tech support 800/767-2775,
fax 408/974-6726,
fax on demand 800/505-0171,
CIS: go aplsup

AppleLink
Apple Online Services,
1 Infinite Loop, MS: 41-D,
Cupertino, CA 95014
408/974-3309

Applied Optical Media
1450 Boot Rd., Bldg. 400,
West Chester, PA 19380
800/321-7259, 215/429-3701,
fax 215/429-3810

Appoint
6377 Clark Ave., Suite 111,
Dublin, CA 94568
800/448-1184, 510/803-8850,
fax 510/803-1995

APS Technologies
P.O. Box 4987, 6131 Deramus,
Kansas City, MO 64120-0087
800/233-7550, 816/483-1600,
fax 816/483-3077

Ares Software
565 Pilgrim Dr., Suite A,
Foster City, CA 94404
800/783-2737, 415/578-9090,
fax 415/378-8999
AOL: aressw; AL: ares;
CIS: 70253,3164

Arion Software
3355 Bee Cave Rd., Suite 503,
Austin, TX 78746
512/327-9573, fax 512/327-3786,
BBS 512/327-9814
AOL: arion2; CIS: 73740,2207

ARRO International
P.O. Box 167, Montclair, NJ 07042
800/243-1515 ext. 485 (orders only), 201/746-9620,
fax 201/509-0728

Ars Nova
P.O. Box 637, Kirkland, WA 98083
800/445-4866, 206/889-0927,
fax 206/889-0359
AL: arsnova

Artbeats
P.O. Box 1287,
Myrtle Creek, OR 97457
800/444-9392, 503/863-4429,
fax 503/863-4547
AL: artbeats, CIS: 74221,125

Asanté Technologies
821 Fox Ln., San Jose, CA 95131
800/662-9686, 408/435-8388,
fax 408/432-1117
Internet: sales@asante.com

ASD Software
4650 Arrow Hwy., Suite E-6,
Montclair, CA 91763
909/624-2594, fax 909/624-9574

Ashlar
1290 Oakmead Pkwy., Suite 218,
Sunnyvale, CA 94086
800/877-2745, 408/746-1800,
fax 408/746-0749

Aspen Gold Software
P.O. Box 370486,
Denver, CO 80237-0486
303/745-5448
AOL and AL: aspengold;
CIS: 73543,107

AT&T Paradyne
P.O. Box 6457, Salinas, CA 93912
800/554-4996, 813/530-2000,
fax 813/530-2398

Atlantic Technology
343 Vanderbilt Ave.,
Norwood, MA 02062
617/762-6300, fax 617/762-6868

Attain
48 Grove St.,
Somerville, MA 02144-2500
800/925-5615, 617/776-1110,
fax 617/776-1626

Atticus Software
456 Glenbrook Rd.,
Stamford, CT 06906
203/348-6100, fax 203/964-8271
AOL: atticus sc; CIS: 75300,3173

Autodesk
2320 Marinship Way,
Sausalito, CA 94965
800/964-6432, 415/332-2344,
fax 415/331-8093

auto•des•sys
2011 Riverside Dr.,
Columbus, OH 43221
614/488-9777, fax 614/488-0848

Automated Graphics
1911 W. Wabansia Ave.,
Chicago, IL 60622
312/384-3833, fax 312/384-4539

AviComp Macintosh Solutions
229 Fort Mitchell Ave.,
Fort Mitchell, KY 41011
606/341-0055
CIS: 72137,2317

Avid Technology
Metropolitan Technology Park,
One Park West,
Tewksbury, MA 01876
800/949-2843, 508/640-6789,
fax 508/640-1366

B

Bartley Software
72 Robertson Rd., Box 26122,
Nepean, ON K2H 9R0, Canada
800/661-5209, 613/829-6488
CIS: 72133,3102

Baseline Publishing
1760 Moriah Woods Blvd., Suite 5,
Memphis, TN 38117-7118
800/926-9677, 901/682-9676,
fax 901/682-9691
AL: baseline.pub; CIS: 75300,1576

BDT Products
17152 Armstrong Ave.,
Irvine, CA 92714
800/346-3238, 714/660-1386,
fax 714/474-0480

BeachWare
9419 Mt. Israel Rd.,
Escondido, CA 92029
619/735-8945 (also fax)
AL: beachware

Bear Rock Technologies
6069 Enterprise Dr.,
Diamond Springs, CA 95619
800/232-7625, 916/622-4640,
fax 916/622-4775

Berkeley Data Access
2560 Bancroft Way, Suite 3,
Berkeley, CA 94704
510/644-2396 or -9999,
fax 510/649-9542

Berkeley Systems
2095 Rose St., Berkeley, CA 94709
800/877-5535, 510/540-5535,
fax 510/540-5115

Best Power Technology
P.O. Box 280, Necedah, WI 54646
800/356-5794, 608/565-7200,
fax 608/565-2221

Best!Ware
300 Roundhilll Dr.,
Rockaway, NJ 07866
800/322-6962, 201/586-2200,
fax 201/586-8885

Binary Software
2218 Wilshire Blvd., Suite 900,
Santa Monica, CA 90403
800/824-6279, 310/449-1481,
fax 310/449-1473

Bit Jugglers
785 Castro St., Suite C,
Mountain View, CA 94041
415/968-3908, fax 415/968-5358

Bitstream
Athenaeum House, 215 First St.,
Cambridge, MA 02142-1270
800/237-3335, 617/497-6222,
fax 617/868-4732

Black Box
P.O. Box 12800,
Pittsburgh, PA 15241
800/552-6816, 412/746-5500,
fax 800/321-0746 or
412/746-0746

Black Diamond
1853 Del Rio Dr.,
Lafayette, CA 94549
800/431-4969, 510/933-9073,
fax 510/926-0338

Blackfire
1319 Amethyst St., Suite A,
Redondo Beach, CA 90277
800/556-7207, 310/798-0202,
fax 310/379-1182
AOL: the fenix

Blyth Software
989 E. Hillsdale Blvd., Suite 400,
Foster City, CA 94404-1613
800/346-6647, 415/571-0222,
fax 415/571-1132

BMUG (Berkeley Macintosh Users Group)
1442A Walnut St., Suite 62,
Berkeley, CA 94709-1496
800/776-2684 (sales only),
510/549-2684, fax 510/849-9026,
BBS 510/849-2684
AOL and AL: bmug;
CIS: 73237,501

Bon Voyage
2069 W. Bullard,
Fresno, CA 93711
800/995-9716, 209/447-8441
(also fax)
CIS: 70754,3511

Books-On-Disk
311 Harvard St.,
Brookline, MA 02146
617/734-9700, fax 617/734-3974
AL: d2158; CIS: 72662,13

Boston Computer Society (BCS)
1972 Massachusetts Ave.,
Cambridge, MA 02140
617/864-1700, fax 617/864-3501,
BBS 617/864-3375

Bravo Technologies
P.O. Box 10078,
Berkeley, CA 94709-0078
510/841-8552, fax 510/841-8559

Brøderbund Software
500 Redwood Blvd., P.O. Box 6121,
Novato, CA 94948-6121
800/521-6263, 415/382-4400,
fax 415/382-4419

Bungie Software Products
5455 S. Hyde Park Blvd.,
Chicago, IL 60615-5805
312/493-2849, fax 312/493-4557
AOL: bungie1; AL: bungie

Bureau of Electronic Publishing
141 New Rd.,
Parsippany, NJ 07054
800/828-4766, 201/808-2700,
fax 201/808-2676

C

Cabletron Systems
35 Industrial Way,
Rochester, NH 03867
603/332-9400, fax 603/332-7386

Caere
100 Cooper Ct.,
Los Gatos, CA 95030
800/535-7226, 408/395-7000,
fax 408/354-2743

CalComp Digitizer Division
14555 N. 82nd St.,
Scottsdale, AZ 85260
800/458-5888, 602/948-6540,
fax 602/948-5508

Calera Recognition Systems
475 Potrero Ave.,
Sunnyvale, CA 94086
800/422-5372, 408/720-8300,
fax 408/720-1330

Callisto
182 W. Central St.,
Natick, MA 01760-9582
800/544-4511, 508/655-0707,
fax 508/650-4626
AOL: callisto1; AL: callisto;
CIS: 71302,3374

Camde
449 E. Saratoga St.,
Gilbert, AZ 85234-7772
602/926-2632, fax 602/437-1055

Canon Computer Systems
2995 Redhill Ave.,
Costa Mesa, CA 92628
800/848-4123, 714/438-3000,
fax 714/438-3099

Canto Software
800 Duboce Ave., Suite 101,
San Francisco, CA 94117
800/332-2686, 415/431-6871,
fax 415/861-6827
AL: canto

C.A.R.
4661 Maryland Ave., Suite 200,
St. Louis, MO 63108
800/288-7585, 314/454-3535,
fax 314/454-0105

Caravelle Networks
301 Moodie Dr., Suite 306,
Nepean, ON, K2H 9C4, Canada
800/363-5292, 613/596-2802,
fax 613/596-9659
AL: cda0362; CIS: 72410,2406

Carina Software
830 Williams St.,
San Leandro, CA 94577
510/352-7328, fax 510/352-2343

Cartesia Software
5 S. Main St., P.O. Box 757,
Lambertville, NJ 08530-9977
800/334-4291, 609/397-1611,
fax 609/397-5724

Casa Blanca Works
148 Bon Air Ctr.,
Greenbrae, CA 94904
415/461-2227, fax 415/461-2249

Casady & Greene
22734 Portola Dr.,
Salinas, CA 93908-1119
800/359-4920, 408/484-9228,
fax 408/484-9218
AL: d0063

Castle Systems
1306 Lincoln Ave.,
San Rafael, CA 94901
415/459-6495 (also fax)

Cayman Systems
400 Unicorn Park Dr.,
Woburn, MA 01801
800/473-4776, 617/932-1100,
fax 617/932-0853

Central Point Software
15220 NW Greenbrier Pkwy.,
Suite 150, Beaverton, OR 97006
800/964-6896, 503/690-8088,
fax 503/690-8083,
BBS 503/984-5366
CIS: go central

CE Software
P.O. Box 65580,
1801 Industrial Circle,
West Des Moines, IA 50265
800/523-7638, 515/221-1801,
fax 515/221-1806
AL: ce.sales; AOL: cesoftware;
CIS: 76136,2137

Changeling Software
596 Elm St.,
Windsor Locks, CT 06096-1603
800/769-2768, 203/292-5087,
fax 203/292-5089
AOL: changelins;
AL: changeling; CIS: go gamcpub

Chariot Software Group
3659 India St., Suite 100,
San Diego, CA 92103
800/242-7468, 619/298-0202,
fax 619/491-0021

CharisMac Engineering
66 P&S Ln., Suite D,
Newcastle, CA 95658
800/487-4420, 916/885-4420,
fax 916/885-1410

CheckMark Software
724 Whalers Way, Bldg. H,
Fort Collins, CO 80525
800/444-9922, 303/225-0522,
fax 303/225-0611

Chena Software
905 Harrison St.,
Allentown, PA 18103
800/245-4577, 215/770-1210,
fax 215/770-1043

The Chip Merchant
4870 Viewridge Ave.,
San Diego, CA 92123
800/426-6375, 619/268-4774,
fax 619/268-0874

Church of Jesus Christ of Latter-day Saints
1999 W. 1700 S.,
Salt Lake City, UT 84104-4233
800/537-5950, 801/240-1174

Citizen America
2450 Broadway, Suite 600,
Santa Monica, CA 90404
800/477-4683, 310/453-0614,
fax 310/453-2814,
BBS 310/453-7564

Claris
5201 Patrick Henry Dr.,
Santa Clara, CA 95052-8168
800/325-2747, 408/727-8227,
fax 408/987-3932
AOL: Claris

Club KidSoft
718 University Ave., Suite 112,
Los Gatos, CA 95030-9958
800/354-6150, 408/354-6100,
fax 408/354-1033

CoActive Computing
1301 Shoreway Rd., Suite 221,
Belmont, CA 94002
800/825-2638, 415/802-1080,
fax 415/593-9304

The Cobb Group
9420 Bunsen Pkwy., Suite 300,
Louisville, KY 40220
800/223-8720, 502/491-1900,
fax 502/491-8050

Cochenille Design Studio
P.O. Box 4276, Encinitas, CA 92023
619/259-1698, fax 619/259-3746

Coda Music Technology
6210 Bury Dr.,
Eden Prairie, MN 55346
800/843-2066, 612/937-9611,
fax 612/937-9760
CIS: go coda

Codenoll Technology
1086 N. Broadway,
Yonkers, NY 10701
914/965-6300, fax 914/965-9811

Codo Manufacturing
Avenue B, Leetsdale, PA 15056
800/245-1294, 412/741-2010,
fax 412/741-2785

ColorAge
900 Technology Park Dr.,
Billerica, MA 01821
800/437-3336, 508/667-8585,
fax 508/667-8821

Common Knowledge
124 University Ave.,
Palo Alto, CA 94301-1637
800/954-3800, 415/325-9900,
fax 415/325-9600

Communication Intelligence
275 Shoreline Dr.,
Redwood Shores, CA 94065
800/888-9242, 415/802-7888,
fax 415/802-7777
CIS: go cic

Compatible Systems
P.O. Box 17220,
Boulder, CO 80308
800/356-0283, 303/444-9532,
fax 303/444-9595

Component Software Industries
P.O. Box 201, Rocky Hill, NJ 08553
800/633-4252, 609/497-4501,
fax 609/497-4008

Compton's NewMedia
2320 Camino Vida Roble,
Carlsbad, CA 92009
800/862-2206, 619/929-2500,
fax 619/929-2511

CompUSA
15167 Business Ave., Suite 194,
Dallas, TX 75244-9659
800/266-7872, 214/888-5770,
fax 800/329-2212 or
214/888-5706

CompuServe
P.O. Box 20212,
Columbus, OH 43220
800/848-8199, 614/457-8600,
fax 614/457-0348

Computer Associates International
One Computer Associates Plaza,
Islandia, NY 11788-7000
800/225-5224, 516/342-5224,
fax 516/342-5734
AL: ca.cricket; CIS: go ca

Computer Library (Ziff-Davis Publishing)
One Park Ave., 5th Floor,
New York, NY 10016
800/827-7889, 212/503-4400,
fax 212/503-4414

Connectix
2655 Campus Dr.,
San Mateo, CA 94403-2520
800/950-5880, 415/571-5100,
fax 415/571-5195

Contour Designs
P.O. Box 1763, Los Altos, CA 94023
415/941-1000, fax 415/941-1474

CoOperative Printing Solutions (COPS)
5950 Live Oak Pkwy., Suite 175,
Norcross, GA 30093
404/840-0810, fax 404/448-7821
AL: cops; CIS: 70671,3371

CoSA
411 First Ave. S.,
Seattle, WA 98104-2871
206/628-4526, fax 206/343-4240

CoStar
100 Field Point Rd.,
Greenwich, CT 06830
800/426-7827, 203/661-9700,
fax 203/661-1540

CRA Z Software
P.O. Box 6379,
Haverhill, MA 01831
508/521-5262

Creative Media Services
2936 Domingo Ave., Suite 5,
Berkeley, CA 94705
800/358-2278, 510/843-3408,
fax 510/549-2490

Creative Multimedia
513 NW 13th Ave., Suite 400,
Portland, OR 97209
800/262-7668, 503/241-4351,
fax 503/241-4370,
BBS 503/241-1573

Creative Software Solutions
41 Timberlake Dr.,
Fayetteville, TN 37334
615/438-0727

Creative Solutions
4701 Randolph Rd., Suite 12,
Rockville, MD 20852
800/367-8465, 301/984-0262,
fax 301/770-1675

Creative Think
P.O. Box 7354,
Menlo Park, CA 94026
415/321-6775, fax 415/321-0609
CIS: 72234,2450

Crutchfield
1 Crutchfield Pk.,
Charlottesville, VA 22906
sales 800/388-7700, catalogs
800/955-9009, 804/973-1811,
fax 800/388-9756

CTA
25 Science Park, Suite 310,
New Haven, CT 06511
800/252-1442, 203/786-5828,
fax 203/786-5833

Curtis Manufacturing
30 Fitzgerald Dr., Jaffrey, NH 03452
800/955-5544, 603/532-4123,
fax 603/532-4116

D

Dantz Development
4 Orinda Way, Bldg. C,
Orinda, CA 94563-9919
510/253-3000, fax 510/253-9099

DataDesk International
9524 SW Tualatin-Sherwood Rd.,
Tualatin, OR 97062
800/477-3473, 503/692-9600,
fax 503/691-1101

DataViz
55 Corporate Dr.,
Trumbull, CT 06611
800/733-0030, 203/268-0030,
fax 203/268-4345

DataWatch
P.O. Box 13984,
Research Triangle Park,
NC 27709-3984
919/549-0711, fax 919/549-0065

Davidson & Associates
19840 Pioneer Ave.,
Torrance, CA 90503
800/545-7677, 310/793-0600,
fax 310/793-0601

Davka
7074 N. Western Ave.,
Chicago, IL 60645
800/621-8227, 312/465-4070,
fax 312/262-9298

Dayna Communications
849 W. Levoy Dr., Salt Lake City, UT
84123-2544
800/531-0600, 801/269-7200,
fax 801/269-7363

DayStar Digital
5556 Atlanta Hwy.,
Flowery Branch, GA 30542
800/962-2077, 404/967-2077,
fax 404/967-3018
AOL: daystar ol; AL: daystar.info;
CIS: 75300,1544

Decision Maker's Software
1910 Joslyn Pl., Boulder, CO 80304
fax 303/449-6207
AOL: jgcman; AL: d0391;
CIS: 70337,2143

Delphi
1030 Massachusetts Ave.,
Cambridge, MA 02138
800/695-4005, 617/491-3393,
fax 617/491-6642

Delrina
6830 Via Del Oro, Suite 240,
San Jose, CA 95119-1353
800/268-6082, 408/363-2345,
fax 408/363-2340

DeltaPoint
2 Harris Ct., Suite B-1,
Monterey, CA 93940
800/446-6955, 408/648-4000,
fax 408/648-4020
AOL and AL: deltapoint;
CIS: 76004,1522

Delta Tao Software
760 Harvard Ave.,
Sunnyvale, CA 94087
800/827-9316, 408/730-9336,
fax 408/730-9337
AOL: deltavee

Deneba Software
7400 SW 87th Ave.,
Miami, FL 33173
305/596-5644, fax 305/273-9069
AOL and AL: deneba;
CIS: 76004,2154

Desert Sky Software
5201 N. 7th St., Suite 202,
Phoenix, AZ 85014
602/279-4600, fax 602/279-4768

DGR Technologies
Bottom Line Distribution,
1219 W. 6th St., Suite 205,
Austin, TX 78703
800/235-9748, 512/476-9855,
fax 512/476-6399

DiagSoft
5615 Scotts Valley Dr., Suite 140,
Scotts Valley, CA 95066
408/438-8247, fax 408/438-7113

Diehl Graphsoft
10270 Old Columbia Rd.,
Suite 100, Columbia, MD 21046
410/290-5114, fax 410/290-8050
CIS: 72662,1320

Digidesign
1360 Willow Rd.,
Menlo Park, CA 94025
800/333-2137, 415/688-0600,
fax 415/327-0777

Digital Communications Associates (DCA)
1000 Alderman Dr.,
Alpharetta, GA 30202
800/348-3221, 404/442-4000,
fax 404/442-4361

Digital Eclipse Software
5515 Doyle St., Suite 1,
Emeryville, CA 94608
800/289-3374, 510/547-6101,
fax 510/547-6104

Digital Equipment Corp. (DEC)
146 Main St., Maynard, MA 01754
800/344-4825, 508/493-5111,
fax 800/234-2298 or
508/493-8780

Discis Knowledge Research
45 Sheppard Ave. E., Suite 410,
Toronto, ON, M2N 5W9, Canada
800/567-4321, 416/250-6537,
fax 416/250-6540

Dongleware Publishing
35 Howard St.,
Cambridge, MA 02139-2909
800/228-6993, 617/497-1130

Dream Maker Software
925 W. Kenyon Ave., Suite 16,
Englewood, CO 80110
800/876-5665, 303/762-1001,
fax 303/762-0762

DS Design
2440 SW Cary Pkwy., Suite 210,
Cary, NC 27513
800/745-4037, 919/319-1770,
fax 919/460-5983

DTP Direct
5198 W. 76th St.,
Edina, MN 55439
800/448-8231, 612/832-5406,
fax 612/832-0052

Dubl-Click Software
22521 Styles St., Woodland Hills,
CA 91367-1730
800/266-9525, 818/888-2068,
fax 818/888-5405

Dynamic Engineering
435 Park Dr.,
Ben Lomond, CA 95005
408/336-8891, fax 408/336-3840

Dynamix
1600 Millrace Dr.,
Eugene, OR 97403
800/757-7707, 503/343-0772,
fax 503/344-1754

E

Earthquest
125 University Ave.,
Palo Alto, CA 94301
415/321-5838, fax 415/322-3817

Eastgate Systems
P.O. Box 1307,
Cambridge, MA 02238
800/562-1638, 617/924-9044,
fax 617/923-4575

Eastman Kodak
343 State St., Rochester, NY 14650
800/235-6325, 716/724-4000
CIS: go kodak

Eccentric Software
P.O. Box 2777,
Seattle, WA 98111-2777
206/628-2687, fax 206/628-2681

Ecological Linguistics
P.O. Box 15156,
Washington, DC 20003
202/546-5862

Eden Interactive
1022 Natoma St., Suite 2,
San Francisco, CA 94103
800/743-3360, 415/241-1450,
fax 415/241-1459

Edmark
P.O. Box 3218,
Redmond, WA 98073-3218
800/426-0856, 206/556-8400,
fax 206/556-8998

Educational Resources
1550 Executive Dr., Elgin, IL 60123
800/860-9003, 708/888-8300,
fax 708/888-8689

Educorp
7434 Trade St.,
San Diego, CA 92121-2410
800/843-9497, 619/536-9999,
fax 619/536-2345

Elastic Reality
925 Stewart St.,
Madison, WI 53713
608/273-6585, fax 608/271-1988

The Electric Typographer
2216 Cliff Dr.,
Santa Barbara, CA 93109
805/966-7563

Electronic Arts
1450 Fashion Island Blvd.,
San Mateo, CA 94404-2064
games 800/245-4525,
children's titles 800/543-9778,
415/571-7171, fax 415/571-7993
CIS: go gamapub

Electronics For Imaging
2855 Campus Dr.,
San Mateo, CA 94403
800/285-4565, 415/286-8600,
fax 408/848-5784

Elek-tek
7350 N. Linder Ave., Dept. C1133,
Skokie, IL 60077
800/395-1000, ext. 7708,
708/677-7660, fax 708/677-1081

Emagic
P.O. Box 771,
Nevada City, CA 95959
916/477-1051, fax 916/477-1052

E-mu Systems
1600 Green Hills Rd.,
P.O. Box 660015,
Scotts Valley, CA 95067-0015
408/438-1921, fax 408/438-8612

Engineered Software
615 Guilford-Jamestown Rd.,
P.O. Box 18344,
Greensboro, NC 27419
910/299-4843, fax 910/852-2067

Equilibrium Technologies
475 Gate Five Rd., Suite 225,
Sausalito, CA 94965
800/524-8651, 415/332-4343,
fax 415/332-4433

EveryWare Development
6543 Mississauga Rd.,
Mississauga, ON, L5N 1A6, Canada
905/819-1173, fax 905/819-1172

eWorld
Apple Online Services,
1 Infinite Loop, MS: 41-D,
Cupertino, CA 95014
800/775-4556, 408/974-1236

Expert-Center for Taxonomic Identification (ETI)
University of Amsterdam,
P.O. Box 4766, 1009 AT
Amsterdam, The Netherlands
31/20/525-7239,
fax 31/20/525-7238

Expert Software
800 Douglas Rd., Suite 750,
Coral Gables, FL 33134-3160
800/759-2562, 305/567-9990,
fax 305/443-0786
AL: expert

ExperVision
3590 N. First St.,
San Jose, CA 95134
800/732-3897, 408/428-9988,
fax 408/456-0823

F

Fairfield Language Technologies
122 S. Main St., Suite 400,
Harrisonburg, VA 22801
800/788-0822, 703/432-6166,
fax 703/432-0953

Farallon Computing
2470 Mariner Square Loop,
Alameda, CA 94501-1010
800/998-7761, 510/814-5000,
fax 510/814-5020

Fargo Electronics
7901 Flying Cloud Dr.,
Eden Prairie, MN 55344
800/258-2974, 612/941-9470,
fax 612/941-7836

Flash
Riddle Pond Rd.,
West Topsham, VT 05086
800/252-2599, 802/476-3309,
fax 802/439-6463
CIS: 73130,1734

Focus Enhancements
800 W. Cummings Park,
Suite 4500, Woburn, MA 01801
800/538-8866, 617/938-8088,
fax 617/938-7741
AOL: focus tech; CIS: 71075,1262

FontHaus
15 Perry Ave., Suite A7,
Norwalk, CT 06850
800/942-9110, 203/846-3087,
fax 203/849-8527

Font World
2021 Scottsville Rd.,
Rochester, NY 14623-2021
716/235-6861, fax 716/235-6950

Footprints
2469 E. 7000 South, Suite 207,
Salt Lake City, UT 84121
801/942-1580, fax 801/942-1582
CIS: 76377,1260

Form and Function
1595 17th Ave.,
San Francisco, CA 94122
415/664-4010, fax 415/664-4030
AL: x1968

Fractal Design
335 Spreckels Dr., Aptos, CA 95003
800/297-2665, 408/688-8800,
fax 408/688-8836
AOL: fractal; CIS: go fractal

Frame Technology
1010 Rincon Circle,
San Jose, CA 95131
800/843-7263, 408/433-3311,
fax 408/433-1928

Freemyers Design
575 Nelson Ave.,
Oroville, CA 95965
916/533-9365

The FreeSoft Company
105 McKinley Rd.,
Beaver Falls, PA 15010
412/846-2700, fax 412/847-4436

FWB
2040 Polk St., Suite 215,
San Francisco, CA 94109
415/474-8055, fax 415/775-2125

GCC Technologies
209 Burlington Rd.,
Bedford, MA 01730-9143
800/422-7777, 617/275-5800,
fax 617/275-1115

GDT Softworks
4664 Lougheed Hwy., Suite 188,
Burnaby, BC, V5C 6B7, Canada
800/663-6222, 604/291-9121,
fax 604/291-9689
AL: gdt.mkt; CIS: 72137,3246

Genesis Technology Group
3860 Bay Center Pl.,
Hayward, CA 94545
800/538-8729, 510/782-4800,
fax 510/782-4842

Gessler Educational Software
55 W. 13th St.,
New York, NY 10011-7958
212/627-0099, fax 212/627-5948

Global Village Communication
685 E. Middlefield Rd., Bldg. B,
Mountain View, CA 94043
800/736-4821, 415/390-8200,
fax 415/390-8282,
BBS 415/390-8334
AOL: globalvill; AL: globalvillag;
CIS: 75300,3473

Gold Disk
3350 Scott Blvd., Bldg. 14,
Santa Clara, CA 95054
800/982-9888, 408/982-0200,
fax 408/982-0298

Golden Triangle Computers
11175 Flintkote Ave., Bldg. 2,
San Diego, CA 92121
800/326-1858, 619/587-0110,
fax 619/587-0303

Granite Digital
3101 Whipple Rd.,
Union City, CA 94587
510/471-6442, fax 510/471-6267

Graphic Imaginations-GIP
66-01 Burns St., Suite 3C,
Rego Park, NY 11374
718/575-8208, fax 718/544-6674
AOL: gip1

Graphic Simulations
1200 E. Collins, Suite 214,
Richardson, TX 75081
214/699-7400, fax 214/699-0972
AOL: graphic

Graphisoft
400 Oyster Point Blvd., Suite 429,
South San Francisco, CA 94080
800/344-3468, 415/737-8665,
fax 415/871-5481
AOL: graphisoft; AL: graphisoftus

Great Plains Software
1701 SW 38th St.,
Fargo, ND 58103
800/456-0025, 701/281-0550,
fax 701/281-3700

Great Wave Software
5353 Scotts Valley Dr.,
Scotts Valley, CA 95066
408/438-1990, fax 408/438-7171

Grolier Electronic Publishing
Sherman Turnpike,
Danbury, CT 06816
800/285-4534, 203/797-3530,
fax 203/797-3835

Gryphon Software
7220 Trade St., Suite 120,
San Diego, CA 92121
800/795-0981, 619/536-8815,
fax 619/536-8932
AOL: gryphonsw; AL: gryphon;
CIS: 73140,3010

Handcraftedfonts
P.O. Box 14013,
Philadelphia, PA 19122
215/634-0634 (also fax)

Hayes Microcomputer Products
P.O. Box 105203,
Atlanta, GA 30348-5203
800/254-2937, 404/840-9200,
fax 404/441-1238

Heizer Software
1941 Oak Park Blvd., Suite 30,
P.O. Box 232019,
Pleasant Hill, CA 94523
800/888-7667, 510/943-7667,
fax 510/943-6882

Helix Technologies
744 Pinecrest Dr.,
Prospect Heights, IL 60070
800/364-3549, 708/465-0242,
fax 708/465-0252

Hewlett-Packard
Direct Marketing, P.O. Box 58059,
MS: 511L-SJ,
Santa Clara, CA 95051-8059
800/752-0900, 208/323-2551,
fax 800/333-1917 or
208/344-4809

Highlighted Data
4350 N. Fairfax Dr., Suite 450,
Arlington, VA 22203
703/516-9211, fax 703/516-9216

High Tide Software
2112A McKinley Ave.,
Berkeley, CA 94703
800/878-8433, 510/704-9927,
fax 510/704-9933

Hoffmann Software
P.O. Box 1375,
Lodi, CA 95241-1375
209/369-8586

HSC Software
1661 Lincoln Blvd., Suite 101,
Santa Monica, CA 90404
310/392-8441, fax 310/392-6015
AOL: cool tools

HyperGlot Software
P.O. Box 10746,
5108-D Kingston Pike,
Knoxville, TN 37939-0746
800/726-5087, 615/558-8270,
fax 615/588-6569

Hypro Technologies
8557 Higuera St.,
Culver City, CA 90232
310/473-0328, fax 310/822-8123

I

IdeaFisher Systems
2222 Martin St., Suite 110,
Irvine, CA 92715
800/289-4332, 714/474-8111,
fax 714/757-2896

Ideaform
908 E. Briggs Ave., P.O. Box 1540,
Fairfield, IA 52556
800/779-7256, 515/472-7256

IDG Books
155 Bovet Rd., Suite 310,
San Mateo, CA 94402
800/762-2974, 415/312-0600,
fax 415/358-1260

Image Club Graphics
729 24th Ave. SE, Calgary, AB,
T2G 5K8, Canada
800/387-9193, 403/262-8008,
fax 403/261-7013
AOL: imageclub; AL: cda0573;
CIS: 72560,2323

Image Smith
1313 Sepulveda Blvd.,
Torrance, CA 90501
800/876-6679, 310/325-1359,
fax 310/539-9784

Imaja
P.O. Box 6386, Albany, CA 94706
510/526-4621, fax 510/559-9571

IMG Publishing
3862 Grace Lane,
Glenview, IL 60025
708/486-0636, fax 312/850-0430
AOL: imgames; CIS: 71554,2761

Infogrip
1145 Eugenia Pl., Suite 201,
Carpinteria, CA 93013
800/397-0921, 805/566-1049,
fax 805/566-1079

Inline Software
800 W. Cummings Park,
Suite 4500, Woburn, MA 01801
800/453-7671, 617/935-1515,
fax 617/938-8353
AOL and AL: inline;
CIS: 75300,2014

Innovative Data Design
1820 Arnold Industrial Way, Suite L,
Concord, CA 94520
510/680-6818, fax 510/680-1165

Insignia Solutions
1300 Charleston Rd.,
Mountain View, CA 94043
800/848-7677, 415/694-7600,
fax 415/694-3705

Inspiration Software
2920 SW Dolph Ct., Suite 3,
Portland, OR 97219
800/877-4292, 503/245-9011,
fax 503/246-4292

Intellimation
Dept. GAPI, P.O. Box 1922,
Santa Barbara, CA 93116
800/346-8355, 805/968-2291,
fax 805/968-8899

Interactive Ventures
1380 Corporate Center Curve,
Suite 305, Eagan, MN 55121
800/937-6463, 612/686-0779,
fax 612/686-0721

InterCon Systems
950 Herndon Pkwy., Suite 420,
Herndon, VA 22070
703/709-5500, fax 703/709-5555

International Typeface Corp. (ITC)
866 Second Ave.,
New York, NY 10017
800/634-9325, 212/371-0699,
fax 212/752-4752

InterOptica Publishing
300 Montgomery St., Suite 201,
San Francisco, CA 94104
800/634-9325; 415/788-8788,
fax 415/788-8886

Interpress Technologies
250 West 49th St., Suite 202,
New York, NY 10019
212/245-2700, fax 212/245-2784

Intuit
2650 E. Elvira Rd., Suite 100,
Tucson, AZ 85706
602/295-3110, fax 800/756-1040
or 602/295-3015
CIS: go intuit

Iomega
1821 W. 4000 S., Roy, UT 84067
800/456-5522, 801/778-1000,
fax 801/778-3748

ISIS International
14270 Dickens St., Suite 6,
Sherman Oaks, CA 91423-4196
818/788-4747, fax 818/501-0653
AOL: isis intl

ISSI Data Products
22122 20th Ave. SE, Suite 152,
Bothell, WA 98021
800/962-0668, 206/343-7283,
fax 206/483-4806

J

Jabra
9191 Towne Centre Dr., Suite 330,
San Diego, CA 92122
800/327-2230, 619/622-0764,
fax 619/622-0353

James Engineering
6329 Fairmount Ave.,
El Cerrito, CA 94530
510/525-7350, fax 510/525-5740

JetFill
10815 Seaboard Loop,
Houston, TX 77099
800/695-4538, 713/933-1900,
fax 713/933-1909

Joe Huber and Associates
3907 Santa Clara Dr.,
Greenwood, IN 46142
317/888-9989

Johnson Books
1880 S. 57th Ct.,
Boulder, CO 80301
800/258-5830, 303/443-9766,
fax 303/443-1679

Jump Development Group
1228 Malvern Ave.,
Pittsburgh, PA 15217
412/681-2692, fax 412/681-2163

K

Kensington Microware
2855 Campus Dr.,
San Mateo, CA 94403
800/535-4242, 415/572-2700,
fax 415/572-9675

Kent-Marsh
3260 Sul Ross, Kent-Marsh Bldg.,
Houston, TX 77098
800/325-3587, 713/522-5625,
fax 713/522-8965

Key Tronic
P.O. Box 14687,
Spokane, WA 99213
800/262-6006, 509/928-8000,
fax 509/927-5224

Killer Tracks
6534 Sunset Blvd.,
Hollywood, CA 90028
800/877-0078, 213/957-4455,
fax 213/957-4470

Kinesis
915 118th Ave. SE,
Bellevue, WA 98005-3855
800/454-6374, 206/455-9220,
fax 206/455-9233

Kiwi Software
6546 Pardall Rd.,
Santa Barbara, CA 93117-4842
800/321-5494, 805/685-4031,
fax 805/968-1932

Korg
89 Frost St., Westbury, NY 11590
516/333-9100

Kurta
3007 E. Chambers St.,
Phoenix, AZ 85040
800/445-8782, 602/276-5533,
fax 602/276-9007

L

Labtec
11010 N.E. 37th Circle, Suite 110,
Vancouver, WA 98682
206/896-2000, fax 206/896-2020

La Cie
8700 SW Creekside Pl.,
Beaverton, OR 97005
800/999-1455, 503/520-9000,
fax 503/520-9100

Lanston Type
1340 E. Pender St.,
Vancouver, BC, V5L 1V8, Canada
800/663-8760, 604/253-0815,
fax 604/255-2601

LaserMaster
7156 Shady Oak Rd.,
Eden Prairie, MN 55344
800/950-6868, 612/944-9330,
fax 612/944-0522

Lazy Dog Foundry
275 E. 4th St., St. Paul, MN 55101
800/876-9807, 612/291-0306,
fax 612/291-0481

Leader Technologies
4590 MacArthur Blvd., Suite 550,
Newport Beach, CA 92660
800/922-1787, 714/757-1787,
fax 714/757-1777

The Learning Company
6493 Kaiser Dr.,
Fremont, CA 94555
800/852-2255, 510/792-2101,
fax 510/792-9628

Learning Services
P.O. Box 10636,
Eugene, OR 97440-2636
800/877-9378, 503/744-0883,
fax 503/484-7499

Learning Tomorrow
One E. Main St.,
Bloomsburg, PA 17815
800/722-1978, 717/387-8270,
fax 717/458-4075

Leister Productions
P.O. Box 289,
Mechanicsburg, PA 17055
717/697-1378, fax 717/697-4373

Letraset USA
40 Eisenhower Dr.,
Paramus, NJ 07653
800/343-8973, 201/845-6100,
fax 201/845-5351

Lexmark International
740 New Circle Rd.,
Lexington, KY 40511
800/358-5835, 606/232-2000,
fax 606/232-2380

Liberty Systems
375-A Saratoga Ave.,
San Jose, CA 95129-1339
408/983-1127, fax 408/243-2885

Lifestyle Software Group
63 Orange St.,
Saint Augustine, FL 32084
800/289-1157, 904/825-0220,
fax 904/825-0223

Light Source Computer Images
17 E. Sir Francis Drake Blvd.,
Suite 100, Larkspur, CA 94939
800/231-7226, 415/925-4200,
fax 415/461-8011
AL: lightsource

Lind Electronic Design
6414 Cambridge St.,
Minneapolis, MN 55426
800/659-5956, 612/927-6303,
fax 612/927-7740

Lingo Fun
P.O. Box 486,
Westerville, OH 43081
800/745-8258, 614/882-8258,
fax 614/882-2390

Linguist's Software
P.O. Box 580, Edmonds, WA 98020
206/775-1130, fax 206/771-5911

Linotype-Hell
425 Oser Ave.,
Hauppauge, NY 11788
800/842-9721, 516/434-2000,
fax 516/434-2706

LivingSoft
711-700 Pine Acre Rd.,
Janesville, CA 96114
800/626-1262, 916/253-2700,
fax 916/253-2703

The LLB Company
300 120th Ave. NE, Bldg. 1,
Suite 200, Bellevue, WA 98005
800/848-8967, 206/454-7258,
fax 206/454-7302

Logical Solutions
2124 University Ave., Suite 102,
Saint Paul, MN 55114
612/659-2495, fax 612/659-2498

Logitech
6505 Kaiser Dr.,
Fremont, CA 94555
800/231-7717, 510/795-8500,
fax 510/792-8901

Lucas Management Systems
12701 Fair Lakes Circle, Suite 350,
Fairfax, VA 22033
800/477-6648, 703/222-1111,
fax 703/222-8203

Lundin Laboratories
7071 Orchard Lake Rd., Suite 235,
West Bloomfield, MI 48322
800/426-8426, 810/851-8282,
fax 810/851-8294

Lyriq International
1701 Highland Ave., Suite 4,
Cheshire, CT 06410
800/433-4464, 203/250-2070,
fax 203/250-2072

M

MacConnection
14 Mill St., P.O. Box 178,
Marlow, NH 03456-9987
800/800-2222, 603/446-7711,
fax 603/446-7791

MacHome Journal
544 Second St.,
San Francisco, CA 94107
editorial 415/957-1911,
subscriptions 800/800-6542

Macintosh Accounting Consortium
1550 Dell Ave., Suite D,
Campbell, CA 95008
408/366-8330, fax 408/364-1662
AL: macacct

MacKay Associates
6439 Boxelder Dr.,
Lincoln, NE 68506
402/486-3550

Mackie Designs
20205 144th Ave. NE,
Woodinvile, WA 98072
800/258-6883, 206/487-4333,
fax 206/487-4337,
BBS 206/488-4586
CIS: go mackie

MacMall
2645 Maricopa St.,
Torrance, CA 90503-5144
800/222-2808, 310/787-4500,
fax 310/222-5800

MacPeak Research
3701 Bee Cave Rd.,
Austin, TX 78746
512/327-3211, fax 512/327-9553

Macromedia
600 Townsend St.,
San Francisco, CA 94103
800/945-4061, 415/252-2000,
fax 415/626-0554

MacToolkit
1234 Sixth St., Suite 204,
Santa Monica, CA 90401
310/395-4242, fax 310/393-7747

MacUser
950 Tower Lane, 18th floor,
Foster City, CA 94404
editorial 415/378-5600,
subscriptions 800/627-2247,
303/447-9330, fax 303/443-5080
CIS: go macuser or 72511,422;
MCI: 584-5561

MacVONK
940 Sixth Ave. SW, 11th Floor,
Calgary, AB, T2P 3T1, Canada
403/232-6545, fax 403/232-6425

MacWarehouse
P.O. Box 3013, 1720 Oak St.,
Lakewood, NJ 08701-3013
800/255-6227, 908/370-4779,
fax 908/905-9279,
BBS 203/855-1155
CIS: go mw

MacWEEK
301 Howard Street, 15th Floor,
San Francisco, CA 94105
editorial 415/243-3500,
subscriptions 609/786-8230,
fax 415/243-3651
CIS: go macweek; MCI: 323-1203

Macworld
501 Second St.,
San Francisco, CA 94107
editorial 415/243-0505,
subscriptions 800/288-6848 or
303/447-9330, fax 415/442-0766
AOL: macworld; AL: macworld1;
CIS: 70370,702

The Mac Zone
17422 N.E. Union Hill Rd.,
Redmond, WA 98052
800/248-0800, 206/883-3088,
fax 206/881-3421

Mainstay
591-A Constitution Ave.,
Camarillo, CA 93012
805/484-9400, fax 805/484-9428
CIS: 76004,1525

Management Science Associates
530 William Penn Pl., Suite 329,
Pittsburgh, PA 15219
800/366-4622, 412/471-7170,
fax 412/471-7173

Manhattan Graphics
250 E. Hartsdale Ave.,
Hartsdale, NY 10530
800/572-6533, 914/725-2048,
fax 914/725-2450

Mannesmann Tally
8301 S. 180th St., Kent, WA 98032
800/843-1347, 206/251-5524,
fax 206/251-5520

Manzanita Software Systems
2130 Professional Dr., Suite 150,
Roseville, CA 95661-3751
800/447-5700, 916/781-3880,
fax 916/781-3814

Maris Multimedia
99 Mounsell St., London E1 8AX,
United Kingdom
44/71/488-1566
CIS: 100136,2705

Mark of the Unicorn
1280 Massachusetts Ave.,
Cambridge, MA 02138
617/576-2760, fax 617/576-3609

Mark/Space Softworks
111 W. Saint John, Suite 238,
San Jose, CA 95113
800/799-4737, 408/293-7299,
fax 408/293-7298,
BBS 408/293-7290

Mastersoft
8737 E. Via de Commercio,
Scottsdale, AZ 85258
800/624-6107, 601/948-4888,
fax 602/948-8261

Mathemæsthetics
P.O. Box 298,
Boulder, CO 80306-0298
303/440-0707, fax 303/440-0504

Maxis
2 Theatre Square,
Orinda, CA 94563-3346
800/336-2947, 510/254-9700,
fax 510/253-3736,
BBS 510/254-3869
AL: d4459; CIS: go gambpub

MBS Technologies
4017 Washington Rd., Suite 4000,
McMurray, PA 15317
800/860-8700, 412/941-9076,
fax 412/941-7076

MECA Software
55 Walls Dr.,
Fairfield, CT 06430-0912
800/820-7458, 203/255-1441,
fax 800/944-6300 or
203/255-6300

MECC
6160 Summit Dr. N.,
Minneapolis, MN 55430
800/685-6322, 612/569-1500,
fax 612/569-1551

Media Design Interactive
The Old Hop Kiln, 1 Long Garden
Walk, Farnham, Surrey GU9 7HP,
United Kingdom
44/252/737-630,
fax 44/252/710-948

Medina Software
P.O. Box 521917,
Longwood, FL 32752
407/260-1676, fax 407/260-1636

Metro ImageBase
18623 Ventura Blvd., Suite 210,
Tarzana, CA 91356
800/525-1552, 818/881-1997,
fax 818/881-4557

MiBAC Music Software
P.O. Box 468,
Northfield, MN 55057
507/645-5851, fax 507/645-2377
AL: mibac; CIS: 71621,2025

Micro Format
830-3 Seton Ct.,
Wheeling, IL 60090
800/333-0549, 708/520-4699,
fax 708/520-0197

MicroFrontier
3401 101st St., Suite E,
Des Moines, IA 50322
800/388-8109, 515/270-8109,
fax 515/278-6828
AOL and AL: mfrontier;
CIS: 72662,1123

Microlytics
2 Tobey Village Office Park,
Pittsford, NY 14534
800/828-6293, 716/248-9150,
fax 716/248-3868

MicroMachines
7625 Hayvenhurst Ave., Suite 30,
Van Nuys, CA 91406
800/248-4001, 818/901-1700,
fax 818/901-1729

MicroMac Technology
27111 Aliso Creek Rd., Suite 145,
Aliso Viejo, CA 92656-3364
714/362-1000, fax 714/362-5428

MicroMat Computer Systems
7075 Redwood Blvd.,
Novato, CA 94945-4136
800/829-6227, 415/898-6227,
fax 415/897-3901

MicroNet Technology
80 Technology, Irvine, CA 92718
800/800-3475, 714/453-6000,
fax 714/453-6001

Micro Planning International
3801 E. Florida Ave., Suite 601,
Denver, CO 80210
303/757-2216, fax 303/757-2047

MicroProse Software
180 Lakefront Dr.,
Hunt Valley, MD 21030
800/879-7529, 410/771-1151,
fax 410/771-1174

Microsoft
One Microsoft Way,
Redmond, WA 98052-6399
800/426-9400, 206/882-8080,
fax 206/936-7329

Microspot
12380 Saratoga-Sunnyvale Rd.,
Suite 6, Saratoga, CA 95070
800/622-7568, 408/253-2000,
fax 408/253-2055

Microtech International
158 Commerce St.,
East Haven, CT 06512
800/626-4276, 203/468-6223,
fax 203/468-6466

Miramar Systems
121 Gray Ave., Suite 200B,
Santa Barbara, CA 93101
800/862-2526, 805/966-2432,
fax 805/965-1824

Mirror Technologies
5198 W. 76th St.,
Edina, MN 55439
800/654-5294, 612/832-5622,
fax 612/832-5709

Mobius Technologies
5835 Doyle St.,
Emeryville, CA 94608
800/800-4334, 510/654-0556,
fax 510/654-2834

Momentum
7 Waterfront Plaza,
500 Ala Moana Blvd., Suite 400,
Honolulu, HI 96813
808/543-6426, fax 808/522-9490

Monotype Typography
150 S. Wacker Dr., Suite 2630,
Chicago, IL 60606
800/666-6897, 312/855-1440,
fax 312/855-9475
AL: monotype

Motion Works
524 Second St.,
San Francisco, CA 94107
800/800-8476, 415/541-9333,
fax 415/541-0555
AL: mw.usa

Multi-Ad Services
1720 W. Detweiller Dr.,
Peoria, IL 61615-1695
800/447-1950, 309/692-1530,
fax 309/692-5444

Multicom Publishing
1100 Olive Way, Suite 1250,
Seattle, WA 98101
206/622-5530, fax 206/622-4380

MultiEducator
244 North Ave.,
New Rochelle, NY 10801
800/866-6434, 914/235-4340,
fax 914/235-4367

N

Nautilus CD
7001 Discovery Blvd.,
Dublin, OH 43017
800/637-3472, 614/382-3322,
fax 614/761-4110

NEC Technologies
1255 Michael Dr.,
Wood Dale, IL 60191
800/388-8888, 708/860-9500,
fax 800/366-0476 or
708/860-5812

Neil Media
2010 Stockbridge Ave.,
Redwood City, CA 94061-4131
415/369-6345, fax 415/369-4789
AOL: neilmedia; AL: neil.media;
CIS: 72630,3070

Neon Software
3685 Mount Diablo Blvd.,
Suite 203,
Lafayette, CA 94549-3723
800/334-6366, 510/283-9771,
fax 510/283-6507
AL: neon.sw

Newer Technology
7803 E. Osie St., Suite 105,
Wichita, KS 67207
800/678-3726, 316/685-4904,
fax 316/685-9368

NewGen Systems
17550 Newhope St.,
Fountain Valley, CA 92708
800/756-0556, 714/641-8600,
fax 714/641-2800

NewMedia
901 Mariner's Island Blvd.,
Suite 365, San Mateo, CA 94404
editorial 415/573-5170,
subscriptions 609/786-4430,
fax 415/573-5131

New World Computing
P.O. Box 4302,
Hollywood, CA 90078
800/325-8898, 818/889-5650,
fax 818/889-5682

New York Mac User's Group
873 Broadway,
New York, NY 10003
212/473-1600, fax 212/473-1745,
BBS 212/473-1967
AOL: nymug

Night Diamonds Software
P.O. Box 1608,
Huntington Beach, CA 92647
714/842-2492, fax 714/847-1106

Ninga Software
736 Eighth Ave. SW, Suite 330,
Calgary, AB, T2P 1H4, Canada
800/265-5555, 403/265-6611,
fax 403/265-5760

Nisus Software
107 S. Cedros Ave.,
Solana Beach, CA 92075
800/922-2993, 619/481-1477,
fax 619/481-6154

No Hands Software
1301 Shoreway Rd., Suite 220,
Belmont, CA 94002
800/598-3821, 415/802-5800,
fax 415/593-6868
AOL and AL: nohands;
CIS: 74740,2142

Nolo Press
950 Parker St., Berkeley, CA 94710
800/992-6656, 510/549-1976,
fax 510/548-5902

NoRad
1160 E. Sandhill Ave,
Carson, CA 90746
800/262-3260, 310/605-0808,
fax 310/605-5051

Nova Development
23801 Calabasas Rd., Suite 2005,
Calabasas, CA 91302-1547
800/395-6682, 818/591-9600,
fax 818/591-8885

Novell
122 E. 1700 South,
Provo, UT 84606-6194
800/453-1267, 801/429-7000,
fax 800/733-9673 or
512/346-8380

Now Software
921 S.W. Washington St.,
Suite 500,
Portland, OR 97205-2823
800/237-2078, 503/274-2800,
fax 503/274-0670
CIS: 71541,170

Nutridata Software
P.O. Box 769,
Wappingers Falls, NY 12590
800/922-2988, 914/298-1308

OBjectic Systems
P.O. Box 161,
Carmel, IN 46032-9998
800/859-9543, 317/898-4017
AL: d2321

Olduvai
9200 S. Dadeland Blvd., Suite 725,
Miami, FL 33156
800/822-0772, 305/670-1112,
fax 305/670-1992

ON Technology
One Cambridge Center,
Cambridge, MA 02142
800/548-8871, 617/374-1400,
fax 617/374-1433

Opcode Systems
3950 Fabian Way, Suite 100,
Palo Alto, CA 94303
800/557-2633, 415/856-3333,
fax 415/856-3332
AOL and AL: opcode;
CIS: go midiaven

Optical Access International
500 W. Cummings Park,
Suite 3250, Woburn, MA 01801
800/433-5133, 617/937-3910,
fax 617/937-3950

Optical Data
30 Technology Dr.,
Warren, NJ 07059
800/524-2481, 908/668-0022,
fax 908/755-0577

Optima Technology
17526 Von Karman,
Irvine, CA 92714
714/476-0515, fax 714/476-0613

Optimum Resource
5 Hiltech Lane,
Hilton Head, SC 29926
800/327-1473, 803/689-8000,
fax 803/689-8008

Orange Cherry/New Media Schoolhouse
P.O. Box 390,
Pound Ridge, NY 10576
800/672-6002, 914/764-4104,
fax 914/764-0104

Orange Micro
1400 N. Lakeview Ave.,
Anaheim, CA 92807
714/779-2772, fax 714/779-9332

Osborn/McGraw-Hill
2600 Tenth St.,
Berkeley, CA 94710-2586
800/227-0900, 510/549-6600,
fax 510/549-6603

OSC
480 Potrero Ave.,
San Francisco, CA 94110
800/343-3325, 415/252-0460,
fax 415/252-0560

Oxford University Press
200 Madison Ave.,
New York, NY 10016
800/334-4249, 212/679-7300
ext. 7127, fax 212/725-2972

P

Page Studio Graphics
3175 N. Price Rd., Suite 1050,
Chandler, AZ 85224
602/839-2763 (also fax)

Palo Alto Software
2641 Columbia St.,
Eugene, OR 97403
800/229-7526, 503/683-6162,
fax 503/683-6250

Panamax
150 Mitchell Blvd.,
San Rafael, CA 94903
800/472-5555, 415/499-3900,
fax 415/472-5540

Pantone
590 Commerce Blvd.,
Carlstadt, NJ 07072
800/222-1149, 201/935-5500,
fax 201/896-0242

PaperDirect
P.O. Box 618, 205 Chubb Ave.,
Lyndhurst, NJ 07071-0618
800/272-7377, 201/507-1996,
fax 201/507-0817

Paramount Interactive
700 Hansen Way,
Palo Alto, CA 94304
800/821-1177, 415/812-8200,
fax 415/813-8055

Parsoft Publishing
P.O. Box 1240, Wylie, TX 75098
615/883-2444

Passport Designs
100 Stone Pine Rd.,
Half Moon Bay, CA 94019
800/443-3210, 415/726-0280,
fax 415/726-2254
AOL and AL: passport;
CIS: 71333, 1433

Peachpit Press
2414 Sixth St., Berkeley, CA 94710
800/283-9444, 510/548-4393,
fax 510/548-5991
AOL: macbible

Peachtree Software
1505-C Pavilion Pl.,
Norcross, GA 30093
800/247-3224, 404/564-5800,
fax 404/564-5888

Peirce Software
719 Hibiscus Pl., Suite 301,
San Jose, CA 95117
800/828-6554, 408/244-6554,
fax 408/244-6882

Penelope Craft Programs
P.O. Box 1204,
Maywood, NJ 07607
201/368-8379

Penton Overseas
2470 Impala Dr.,
Carlsbad, CA 92008
800/748-5804, 619/431-0060,
fax 619/431-8110

PG Music
266 Elmwood Ave., Suite 111,
Buffalo, NY 14222
800/268-6272, 905/528-2368,
fax 905/628-2541
CIS: go midiaven

PhotoDisc
2013 4th Ave., 4th Floor,
Seattle, WA 98121
800/528-3472, 206/441-9355,
fax 206/441-9379

Pinnacle Micro
19 Technology, Irvine, CA 92718
800/553-7070, 714/727-3300,
fax 714/727-1913

Pioneer New Media Technologies
DMSD Division, 2265 E. 220th St.,
Long Beach, CA 90810
800/444-6784, 310/952-2111,
fax 310/952-2100

Pixar
1001 W. Cutting Blvd.,
Richmond, CA 94804
800/888-9856, 510/236-4000,
fax 510/236-0388
AOL: pixartech; AL: pixarmktg

Pixel City
2995 Woodside Rd., Suite 400,
Woodside, CA 94062
415/367-0808

Pixel Resources
P.O. Box 921848,
Norcross, GA 30092-7848
800/851-1427, 404/449-4947,
fax 404/449-3789
AOL: pixel resources; AL: pixl

PKWare
9025 N. Deerwood Dr.,
Brown Deer, WI 53223
414/354-8699, fax 414/354-8559

Peripheral Land (PLI)
47421 Bayside Pkwy.,
Fremont, CA 94538
800/288-8754, 510/657-2211,
fax 510/683-9713

Plextor
4255 Burton Dr.,
Santa Clara, CA 95054
800/886-3935, 408/980-1838,
fax 408/986-1010

Portfolio Software
Goodwin Baker Bldg., 1 Millet St.,
Richmond, VT 05477
800/729-3966, 802/434-4000,
fax 802/434-7000
tech support 802/434-6300
AOL: portsales; AL: portfolio;
CIS: 75300,520

Postcraft International
27811 Avenue Hopkins, Suite 6,
Valencia, CA 91355
805/257-1797, fax 805/257-1759

PrairieSoft
P.O. Box 65820,
West Des Moines, IA 50265
515/225-3720, fax 515/225-2422

Precision Type
47 Mall Dr.,
Commack, NY 11725-5703
800/248-3668, 516/864-0167,
fax 516/543-5721

Prima Publishing
3875 Atherton Rd.,
Rocklin, CA 95765
800/255-8989, 916/632-4400,
fax 916/632-4405

Prodigy
445 Hamilton Ave.,
White Plains, NY 10601
800/776-3449, 914/993-8000

Prometheus Products
9524 S.W. Tualatin-Sherwood Rd.,
Tualatin, OR 97062
800/477-3473, 503/692-9600,
fax 503/691-1101

Prosonus
2820 Honolulu Ave.,
Verdugo, CA 91046
800/999-6191, 818/766-5221,
fax 818/248-9417

ProVue Development
15180 Transistor Lane,
Huntington Beach, CA 92649
800/966-7878, 714/892-8199,
fax 714/893-4899

Psygnosis
675 Massachusetts Ave.,
Cambridge, MA 02139
800/438-7794, 617/497-7794,
fax 617/497-6759

Publish
501 Second St.,
San Francisco, CA 94107
editorial 415/243-0600,
subscriptions 800/685-3435 or
615/377-3322, fax 415/495-2354
AL: publish.mag; CIS: 76127,205;
MCI: publish

QMS
One Magnum Pass,
Mobile, AL 36618
800/631-2692, 205/633-4300,
fax 205/633-0116
Internet: info@qms.com

Quadra Interactive
701 Palomar Airport Rd., 3rd Floor,
Carlsbad, CA 92009
619/931-4755, fax 619/931-0660,
BBS 619/431-9138

Qualcomm
6455 Lusk Blvd.,
San Diego, CA 92121
800/238-3672, 619/587-1121,
fax 619/452-9096

Qualitas Trading Co.
2029 Durant Ave.,
Berkeley, CA 94704
510/848-8080, fax 510/848-8009

Quanta Press
1313 Fifth St. SE, Suite 223A,
Minneapolis, MN 55414
612/379-3956, fax 612/623-4570

Quark
1800 Grant St., Denver, CO 80203
800/788-7835, 303/894-8888,
fax 303/894-3395

Que Software (McMillan Publishing)
201 W. 103 St.,
Indianapolis, IN 46290
800/992-0244, 317/581-3500,
fax 800/448-3804

Queue
338 Commerce Dr.,
Fairfield, CT 06430
800/232-2224, 203/335-0906,
fax 203/336-2481

R

Radius
1710 Fortune Dr.,
San Jose, CA 95131
800/227-2795, 408/434-1010,
fax 408/434-0770

Rae Technology
19672 Stevens Creek Blvd.,
Suite 195, Cupertino, CA 95014
408/725-2850, fax 408/725-2855

Random House Reference & Electronic Publishing
201 E. 50th St.,
New York, NY 10022
800/733-3000, 410/848-2436,
fax 212/572-8700

RasterOps
2500 Walsh Ave.,
Santa Clara, CA 95051
800/729-2656, 408/562-4200,
fax 408/562-4065
AOL and AL: rasterhelp

Ray Dream
1804 N. Shoreline Blvd.
Mountain View, CA 94043
800/846-0111, 415/960-0768,
fax 415/960-1198
AOL: rdreamtech; AL: ray.dream

Reactor
445 W. Erie, Chicago, IL 60610
312/573-0800, fax 312/573-0891

Redgate Communications
660 Beachland Blvd.,
Vero Beach, FL 32963
800/333-8760, 401/231-6904,
fax 407/231-6847

REEVEsoft
P.O. Box 1884, Clemson, SC 29633
803/654-7378

ResNova Software
5011 Argosy Dr., Suite 13,
Huntington Beach, CA 92649
714/379-9000; fax 714/379-9014

Richard Carlton Consulting
P.O. Box 73484, Davis, CA 95617
916/753-0561

Richard Young Products
508 S. Military Trail,
Deerfield Beach, FL 33442
800/828-9949, 305/426-8100,
fax 305/421-4654

Rocky Mountain Computer Outfitters
P.O. Box 7850, Kalispell, MT 59901
800/249-0009, 406/758-8000,
fax 800/881-3090
AOL: outfitters; CIS: 76635,660

Roland
7200 Dominion Circle,
Los Angeles, CA 90040
213/685-5141, fax 213/722-0911

RT Computer Graphics
602 San Juan De Rio,
Rio Rancho, NM 87124-1146
800/891-1600, 505/891-1600,
fax 505/891-1350

S

ScanCo
P.O. Box 3217,
Redmond, WA 98073
800/722-6263, 206/481-5434,
fax 206/485-1255

Scholastic Software
P.O. Box 7502,
Jefferson City, MO 65102
800/541-5513, 314/636-5271,
fax 314/635-5881

Scitor
393 Vintage Park Dr., Suite 140,
Foster City, CA 94404
415/570-7700, fax 415/570-7807

Second Wave
2525 Wallingwood Dr., Bldg. 13,
Austin, TX 78746
512/329-9283, fax 512/329-9299

Seikosha America
10 Industrial Ave.,
Mahwah, NJ 07430
800/338-2609, 201/327-7227,
fax 201/818-9135

Shakespeare on Disc
P.O. Box 299,
Clinton Corners, NY 12514
914/266-5705, fax 914/876-6918

Sharp Electronics
Sharp Plaza, Box F1,
Mahwah, NJ 07430-2135
800/526-0522, 201/529-9593,
fax 201/529-9637

Sheppard Company
60 Thoreau St., Suite 187,
Concord, MA 01742-9116
508/287-0055

ShirtPocket Software
P.O. Box 40666, Mesa, AZ 85274
602/966-7667, fax 602/894-9136

Shiva
One Cambridge Center,
Cambridge, MA 02142
800/458-3550, 617/252-6300,
fax 800/370-6917 or
617/252-6852

Shreve Systems
1200 Marshall St.,
Shreveport, LA 71101
800/227-3971, 318/424-9791, fax
318/424-9771

Sigma Designs
46501 Landing Pkwy.,
Fremont, CA 94538
800/845-8086, 510/770-0100,
fax 510/770-2640

Signature Software
489 North 8th St., Suite 201,
Hood River, OR 97031
800/925-8840, 503/386-3221,
fax 503/386-3229
Internet: sigsoft.netcom.com

SketchTech
43 Main St. SE, Suite 410,
Minneapolis, MN 55414
800/379-3729, 612/379-1435,
fax 612/331-4962
AOL: leeanderso; AL: d2266

SoftArc
100 Allstate Pkwy.,
Markham, ON, L3R 6H3, Canada
905/415-7000, 905/415-7171

Softek Design
P.O. Box 2100, Telluride, CO 81435
303/728-5252, fax 303/728-6767

SoftKey International
201 Broadway,
Cambridge, MA 02139
800/227-5609, 617/494-1200,
fax 617/494-0067

Software Architects
19102 N. Creek Pkwy., Suite 101,
Bothell, WA 98011-8005
206/487-0122, fax 206/487-0467

The Software Toolworks
60 Leveroni Ct., Novato, CA 94949
800/234-3088, 415/883-3000,
fax 415/883-3303
AOL: toolworks

Software Ventures
2907 Claremont Ave.,
Berkeley, CA 94705
510/644-3232, fax 510/848-0885

Soho Computer Furniture
729 Boylston St., Suite 400,
Boston, MA 02116
617/266-4004, fax 617/266-4003

Sonnet Technologies
18004 Sky Park Circle, Suite 260,
Irvine, CA 92714-6428
800/945-3668, 714/261-2800,
fax 714/261-2461

Sony Electronics
Computer Peripheral Products,
3300 Zanker Rd.,
San Jose, CA 95134
800/352-7669, 408/432-0190,
fax 408/955-5171

Sound Source Unlimited
2985 E. Hillcrest Dr., Suite A,
Westlake Village, CA 91362
800/877-4778, 805/494-9996,
fax 805/495-0016,
BBS 805/373-8589

Spectral Innovations
1885 Lundy Ave., Suite 208,
San Jose, CA 95131
408/955-0366, fax 408/955-0370
AL: macdsp

Spectra Systems
2001 Westside Pkwy., Suite 125,
Alpharetta, GA 30201
404/410-7803, fax 404/410-7815

Spectrum HoloByte
2490 Mariner Square Loop,
Alameda, CA 94501
800/695-4263, 510/522-3584,
fax 510/522-3587,
BBS 510/522-8909
AOL: spectrum; CIS: go gambpub

Specular International
479 West St.,
Amherst, MA 01002-2904
800/433-7732, 413/253-3100,
fax 413/253-0540
AOL and AL: specular;
CIS: go multiven

Spider Island Software
4790 Irvine Blvd., Suite 105-347,
Irvine, CA 92720
714/669-9260, fax 714/669-1383

Stac Electronics
5993 Avenida Encinas,
Carlsbad, CA 92008
800/522-7822, 619/431-7474,
fax 619/431-9616

Star Micronics America
420 Lexington Ave., Suite 2702-25,
New York, NY 10170
800/447-4700, 212/986-6770,
fax 212/661-5838

StarNine Technologies
2550 9th St., Berkeley, CA 94710
510/548-0391, fax 510/548-0393

StarPlay Productions
P.O. Box 217,
Greeley, CO 80632-0217
800/203-2503, 303/339-7016,
fax 303/330-7553

StarPress Multimedia
303 Sacramento St., 2nd Floor,
San Francisco, CA 94111
415/274-8383, fax 415/291-0225

Steinberg
17700 Raymer St., Suite 1001,
Northridge, CA 91325
818/993-4091, fax 818/701-7452
CIS: Go midicven

Stevens Creek Software
21346 Rumford Dr.,
Cupertino, CA 95014
800/823-4279, 408/725-0424,
fax 408/725-0424
AL: stevenscreek

STF Technologies
P.O. Box 81, Concordia, MO 64020
800/880-1922, 816/463-2021,
fax 816/463-7958,
BBS 816/463-1131

Storm Technology
1861 Landings Dr.,
Mountain View, CA 94043
800/275-5734, 415/691-6600,
fax 415/691-9825
AL: stormtech; CIS: 73060,3227

Strata
2 W. Saint George Blvd., Suite
2100, Saint George, UT 84770
800/678-7282, 801/628-5218,
fax 801/628-9756
AOL: strata 3d; AL: strata3d

Sumeria
329 Bryant St., Suite 3D,
San Francisco, CA 94107
800/478-6374, 415/904-0800,
fax 415/904-0888

Summagraphics
9020 Capital of Texas Hwy. N.,
Suite 400, Austin, TX 78759
800/337-8662, 512/835-0900,
fax 512/345-9509

SuperMac Technology
215 Moffett Park Dr.,
Sunnyvale, CA 94089
800/334-3005, 408/541-6100,
fax 800/541-7680 or
408/541-6150
AOL: supermac; AL: smt.tech;
CIS: 76004,2330

Supra
7101 Supra Dr. SW,
Albany, OR 97321
800/727-8772, 503/967-2410,
fax 503/967-2401

Survivor Software
11222 La Cienega Blvd., Suite 450,
Inglewood, CA 90304
800/369-4691, 310/410-9527,
fax 310/338-1406

Symantec
175 W. Broadway,
Eugene, OR 97401
800/441-7234, 503/345-3322,
fax 503/334-7400
CIS: go symantec

Synergy Software
2457 Perkiomen Ave.,
Reading, PA 19606
800/876-8376, 215/779-0522,
fax 215/370-0548
AL: d2296

SyQuest Technology
47071 Bayside Pkwy.,
Fremont, CA 94538
800/245-2278, 510/226-4000,
fax 510/226-4100

Systems Control
P.O. Box 788, North U.S. 2,
Iron Mountain, MI 49801
800/451-6866, 906/774-8000,
fax 906/779-4217

T

Tanager Software
1933 Davis St., Suite 208,
San Leandro, CA 94577
800/841-2020, 510/430-0900,
fax 510/430-0917

Technöggin
1018 Delta Ave., Suite 303,
Cincinnati, OH 45208
800/305-7936, 513/321-1777,
fax 513/321-2348
AL: technoggin

Technology Concepts
9524 SW Tualatin-Sherwood Rd.,
Tualatin, OR 97062
800/477-3473, 503/692-9600,
fax 503/691-1101

Technology Works (TechWorks)
4030 Braker Lane W., Suite 350,
Austin, TX 78759
800/688-7466, 512/794-8533,
fax 512/794-8520

TechPool Studios
1463 Warrensville Center Rd.,
Cleveland, OH 44121-2676
800/543-3278, 216/291-1922,
fax 216/382-1915

Teknosys
3923 Coconut Palm Dr., Suite 111,
Tampa, FL 33619
800/873-3494, 813/620-3494,
fax 813/620-4039

Tektronix
P.O. Box 1000, MS 63-630,
Wilsonville, OR 97070-1000
800/835-6100, 503/682-7377,
fax 503/682-7450

TeleAdapt
51 E. Campbell Ave.,
Campbell, CA 95008
408/370-5105, fax 408/370-5110
CIS: 100111,2713

TeleTypesetting
311 Harvard St.,
Brookline, MA 02146
617/734-9700, fax 617/734-3974

Temporal Acuity Products
300 120th Ave. NE, Bldg. 1,
Suite 200, Bellevue, WA 98005
800/426-2673, 206/462-1007,
fax 206/462-1057
CIS: Go midibven

Terrace Software
P.O. Box 271, Medford, MA 02155
617/396-0382

Texas Instruments
P.O. Box 202230,
Austin, TX 78720-2230
800/527-3500, 512/794-5970,
fax 512/250-7329

Thought I Could
107 University Pl., Suite 4D,
New York, NY 10003
212/673-9724, fax 212/260-1194
CIS: 75056,1733

3G Graphics
114 Second Ave. S., Suite 104,
Edmonds, WA 98020
800/456-0234, 206/774-3518,
fax 206/771-8975

ThrustMaster
10150 SW Nimbus Ave.,
Portland, OR 97223-4337
503/639-3200, fax 503/620-8094
AOL: thrustmaster;
CIS: 76520,3325

Thunderware
P.O. Box 1299, Orinda, CA 94563
510/254-6581, fax 510/254-3047

timebox
P.O. Box 3060, Station D,
Ottawa, ON, K1P 6H6, Canada
613/236-8969, fax 613/236-9232

Time Warner Interactive Group
2210 W. Olive Ave.,
Burbank, CA 91506
800/593-6334, 818/955-9999,
fax 818/955-6499

Timeworks
625 Academy Dr.,
Northbrook, IL 60062
800/535-9497, 708/559-1300,
fax 708/559-1399
AOL: timeworks; CIS: go timeworks

T/Maker Company
1390 Villa St.,
Mountain View, CA 94041
800/395-0195, 415/962-0195,
fax 415/962-0201

Toshiba America
9740 Irvine Blvd., P.O. Box 19724,
Irvine, CA 92713
800/456-3475, 714/583-3000, fax
714/583-3140

Totem Graphics
6200-F Capitol Blvd.,
Tumwater, WA 98501
206/352-1851, fax 206/352-2554

Trace Research and Development Center
University of Wisconsin, S-151
Waisman Center, 1500 Highland
Ave., Madison, WI 53705-2280
608/263-5408, fax 608/262-8848

Transoft
1150 Coast Village Rd., Suite H,
Santa Barbara, CA 93108
800/949-6463, 805/565-5200,
fax 805/565-5208

Treacyfaces
P.O. Box 26036,
West Haven, CT 06516
203/389-7037, fax 203/389-7039

TrialMaker Software
5 Keniston Rd.,
Lynnfield, MA 01940
617/334-3367

Tribe Computer Works
960 Atlantic Ave., Suite 101,
Alameda, CA 94501
800/778-7423, 510/814-3900,
fax 510/814-3980

Trilobyte Software
6982 Devon Dr.,
Middletown, OH 45044
513/777-6641, fax 513/779-7760

Tuesday Software
215 Via Sevilla,
Santa Barbara, CA 93109
800/945-7889, 805/962-7889,
fax 805/564-8955

Tut Systems
2446 Estand Way,
Pleasant Hill, CA 94523
800/998-4888, 510/682-6510,
fax 510/682-4125

U

UMAX Technologies
3353 Gateway Blvd.,
Fremont, CA 94538
800/562-0311, 510/651-8883,
fax 510/651-8834

Upstill Software
1442A Walnut St.,
Berkeley, CA 94709
800/568-3696, 510/486-0761,
fax 510/486-0762
AL: cookware; CIS: 70521,1264

U.S. Robotics
8100 N. McCormick Blvd.,
Skokie, IL 60076
708/982-5010, fax 708/982-5235

URW America
4 Manchester St.,
Manchester, NH 03060
603/882-7445, fax 603/882-7210

UserLand Software
400 Seaport Ct.,
Redwood City, CA 94063
415/369-6600, fax 415/369-6618
CIS: go userland

The Valis Group
2270 Paradise Dr.,
Tiburon, CA 94920
800/825-4704, 415/435-5404,
fax 415/435-9862

Varcon Systems
10509 San Diego Mission Rd.,
Suite K, San Diego, CA 92108
619/563-6700, fax 619/563-1986
AOL and AL: varcon;
CIS: 76350,3036

Velocity Development
4 Embarcadero, Suite 3100,
San Francisco, CA 94111
800/856-2489, 415/776-8000,
fax 415/776-8099
AL: velocity

Ventana Press
P.O. Box 2468,
Chapel Hill, NC 27515
800/743-5369, 919/942-0220,
fax 919/942-1140

Ventura Educational Systems
910 Ramona Ave., Suite E,
Grover Beach, CA 93433
800/336-1022, 805/473-7383,
fax 805/473-7382

Viacom New Media
648 S. Wheeling Rd.,
Wheeling, IL 60090
800/877-4266, 708/520-4440,
fax 708/459-7456

Viacrypt
2104 W. Corea Ave.,
Phoenix, AZ 85029
800/536-2664, 602/944-0773,
fax 602/943-2601

VideoFusion
1722 Indian Wood Circle, Suite H,
Maumee, OH 43537
800/638-5253, 419/891-1090,
fax 419/891-9673
AL: videofusion

Visual Information Development (VIDI)
136 W. Olive Ave.,
Monrovia, CA 91016
818/358-3936, fax 818/358-4766

Virgin Games
18061 Fitch Ave., Irvine, CA 92714
800/874-4607, 714/833-8710,
fax 714/833-8717,
BBS 714/833-3305

Virginia Systems
5509 W. Bay Ct.,
Midlothian, VA 23112
804/739-3200, fax 804/739-8376

Virtus
117 Edinburgh S., Suite 204,
Cary, NC 27511
800/847-8871, 919/467-9700,
fax 919/460-4530
AOL and AL: virtus;
CIS: 75300,3251

Visatex
1745 Dell Ave.,
Campbell, CA 95008
800/722-3729, 408/866-6562,
fax 408/866-6598

Visionary Software
1820 S.W. Vermont, Suite A,
Portland, OR 97219-1945
800/877-1832, 503/246-6200,
fax 503/452-1198

Vividus
378 Cambridge Ave., Suite I,
Palo Alto, CA 94306
415/321-2221, fax 415/321-2282
AL: cornish1

Voudette
Village Station, Box 24935,
Los Angeles, CA 90024
310/474-7142, fax 310/474-7516

The Voyager Company
578 Broadway, Suite 406,
New York, NY 10012
800/446-2001, 212/431-5199,
fax 212/431-5799
AL: voyager

VST Power Systems
1620 Sudbury Rd., Suite 3,
Concord, MA 01742
508/287-4600, fax 508/287-4068

W

Wacom Technology
501 S.E. Columbia Shores Blvd.,
Suite 300, Vancouver, WA 98661
800/922-6613, 206/750-8882,
fax 206/750-8924

Wayzata Technology
2515 E. Highway 2,
Grand Rapids, MN 55744
800/735-7321, 218/326-0597,
fax 218/326-0598,
BBS 218/326-2939

Welcom Software Technology
15995 N. Barkers Landing,
Suite 275, Houston, TX 77079
800/274-4978, 713/558-0514,
fax 713/584-7828

Wintergreen Software
P.O. Box 15899,
New Orleans, LA 70175-5899
800/321-9479, 504/866-8658,
fax 504/866-8710

Wired
544 Second St.,
San Francisco, CA 94107-1427
subscriptions 800/769-4733,
415/904-0660, fax 415/904-0669
Internet: editor@wired.com, subscriptions@wired.com

WordPerfect
1555 N. Technology Way,
Orem, UT 84057
800/451-5151, 801/225-5000,
fax 801/222-5077,
BBS 801/225-4414

Working Software
P.O. Box 1844,
Santa Cruz, CA 95061-1844
800/229-9675, 408/423-5696,
fax 408/423-5699
AOL: workingsw; CIS: 76004,2072

Working Solutionz Software
2191 Rosencrans St.,
Simi Valley, CA 93065
805/522-2170, fax 805/527-7787

Xante
P.O. Box 16526,
Mobile, AL 36616-0526
800/926-8839, 205/476-8189,
fax 205/476-9421

Xaos Tools
600 Townsend St., Suite 270-E,
San Francisco, CA 94103
800/289-9267, 415/487-7000,
fax 415/558-9886
AOL: xaos tools; AL: d7093

XChange
P.O. Box 270578,
Fort Collins, CO 80527
800/788-7557, 303/229-0656,
fax 303/229-9773
CIS: go dtpven
x height
Font Ho

Xyvision
101 Edgewater Dr.,
Wakefield, MA 01880-1291
617/245-4100, fax 617/246-6209

Yamaha
Consumer Products Division,
P.O. Box 6600,
Buena Park, CA 90622
714/522-9937, fax 714/228-3913

YARC Systems
975 Business Center Circle,
Newbury Park, CA 91320
800/275-9272, 805/499-9444,
fax 805/499-4048
AOL and AL: yarc

Z

Zedcor
4500 E. Speedway, Suite 22,
Tucson, AZ 85712-5305
800/482-4567, 602/881-8101,
fax 602/881-1841
AOL and AL: zedcor

Zyxel
4920 E. La Palma Ave.,
Anaheim, CA 92807
800/255-4101, 714/693-0808,
fax 714/693-0705

Glossary

This glossary contains definitions for commonly used Macintosh terms (plus a few extras). For explanations of terms and products related to a specific subject, such as fonts or networking, see the relevant chapter or locate them through the Index.

When a word that's defined below occurs in the definition of another term, we usually put it in italics so you know you can look it up (but we don't always do that for common terms such as *file* and *software*). Words are alphabetized as if spaces and hyphens didn't exist; thus *database* comes before *data fork*, and *e-mail* falls between *ELF radiation* and *emulation*.

A

accelerator board A *card* containing a faster *processors*, more *memory*, or other electronic wizardry that speeds up a particular aspect of the computer's operation. The three main types are *CPU* accelerators, which speed up the Mac's overall operation; graphics accelerators (or accelerated *video cards*), which provide faster screen redraws; and *DSP* cards, which ramp up the processor-intensive operations common to graphics programs.

active window The currently selected *window*, where the next *command* (or anything you type) will be applied. The active window is always on top of overlapping windows, its *title bar* has a visible title and stripes, and its *scroll bars* are active.

adapter Electronic circuitry that adapts a device (such as a *monitor*, *printer*, or *network* cable) so that it's compatible with the Mac. An adapter can be a *card* (such as an *Ethernet* adapter) or a cable (such as the one required to attach a PowerBook to a desktop Mac in *SCSI disk mode*).

ADB Apple Desktop Bus, the standard *bus* for connecting *input devices* such as keyboards and mice to all Macs from the SE onward. ADB connections are different from those on the Plus and earlier Macs.

AIFF Audio interchange file format, the standard *file format* for sound files.

alert box A box that pops on screen, announced by one or more beeps, to give you information or a warning. Alert boxes don't require any information, but you may have to click a *button* such as OK or Cancel. Also called a message box. Compare *dialog box*.

alias A duplicate file *icon* (about 2K in size) that serves as a remote control for opening a *file*, *folder*, or *disk*. You can put an alias anywhere—on the *desktop*, in a folder, or on the *menu*—and it will find and open the original item when you *double-click* it or select it from the menu.

animation program Software that adds motion to images created in *paint*, *draw*, *presentation*, and 3-D *graphics* programs.

anti-aliasing A technique for smoothing the rough edges (the infamous *jaggies*) of *bit-mapped graphics*, usually by blurring the edges.

Apple events A System 7 feature that allows one *application* to invoke the features of another (on a single Mac or across a *network*) by sending it a *command* called an Apple event. It's the technology behind *AppleScript* and most *hot links*, and is part of Apple's overall scheme for interapplication communication (*IAC*), which also includes *OpenDoc*.

Apple Guide An *interactive* help system built into System 7.5. You tell Apple Guide what you want to do, and it shows you how to do it by walking you through the process.

** (Apple) menu** The *menu* at the left end of the *menu bar* in the *Finder* and within most applications. In System 7 you can make any *file*, *folder*, or *hard disk* appear on the menu by adding it (or its *alias*) to the Apple Menu Items folder; in System 6 the menu only gives you access to *desk accessories* and *control panels*.

ApplePrice The price that Apple believes one of its products will be sold for. Unlike list prices given by other companies, the ApplePrice is usually pretty close to the *street price*.

AppleScript Apple's *scripting language* (distributed as a system *extension*) that lets you write *scripts* to automate common tasks. Some *applications* incorporate AppleScript support, allowing you to create and run scripts within those programs.

AppleShare 1. A *Chooser extension* that lets you access shared files on networked Macs or AppleShare file servers. 2. Software that turns a Mac with a *hard disk* into a centralized file *server*, enabling other Macs on the *network* to access its files.

AppleTalk The *network protocols* built into every Mac. The Mac uses AppleTalk to talk to *laser printers* and other Macs connected to it via a cabling scheme such as *LocalTalk* or *Ethernet*. Compare *TCP/IP*.

application *Software* that does relatively complex tasks and that lets you create and modify *documents*. Common application types include *word processors*, *spreadsheets*, *database managers*, and graphics programs. Most *programs* are called applications, unless they're *utilities* or *system software*.

application heap The portion of a Mac's *memory* used by *applications*. Compare *system heap*.

Application menu In System 7, the *menu* at the right end of the *menu bar* that lets you switch between *programs* (and lets you hide the *windows* of programs you're not currently using). The menu's *icon* changes to match whichever program is currently active.

ARA AppleTalk Remote Access, a *protocol* (and product) that provides system-level support for dial-in (*modem*) connections to an *AppleTalk network*. With ARA, you can call your desktop Mac from a PowerBook and remotely access all the available services—*files*, *printers*, *servers*, *e-mail*, etc.

archive A copy of a *file* (often created with a compression utility) that's stored on a separate *disk* for safekeeping or as a *backup*.

ASCII The American Standard Code for Information Interchange is a system for referring to letters, numbers, and common symbols by code numbers (*A* is 65, for example). This widely used *file format* is useful for transferring files between Macs and PCs. On the Mac, ASCII files are often called *text files*. Pronounced "as-key."

authoring program Software for creating *interactive* software such as presentations, training materials, and games. It typically combines features found in *presentation programs* with a *scripting language*.

A/UX A version of *Unix* designed by Apple for use on the Mac. Pronounced as separate letters.

B

background printing A feature provided by the *system software* (accessed via the *Chooser*) and by *print spoolers* that lets you keep using the Mac while it's sending *documents* to the *printer* "in the background."

backing up Copying some or all of the files on your Mac to different *disks* or tape, so you won't lose the information if the original versions are damaged, lost, or stolen. The copied files are called backups.

balloon help When you point to items on the screen, this System 7 feature pops up cartoon-like message balloons to explain them. You turn it on or off from the *Help menu*.

bandwidth The amount of information that can travel between two points in a given time. The "broader" the bandwidth, the faster the data flows. Commonly used to describe how fast data can travel over a *bus*, or from *disk* into *memory*, or from one *modem* to another.

baud rate A measure of the speed at which a *modem* sends and receives bits of data. Technically, baud is not the correct term for transmission speed (except in ancient 300-baud modems); you should say *bps* (bits per second) instead.

bay See *storage bay*.

BBS Bulletin board service, a noncommercial dial-up service usually run by a *user group* or software company. By dialing up a BBS with your *modem*, you can exchange messages with other users (or the *sysop*) and *download* (or *upload*) software. A BBS has fewer features than a commerical *on-line service*, but it's usually free (except for the phone call).

beta version A prerelease version of a *program*, which is still getting the *bugs* worked out.

Bézier curve A type of curve used in *draw programs* that consists of mathematically defined line segments connected by control points. By adjusting the points, you can create complex shapes.

bit Short for binary digit, this is the smallest unit of information the computer can work with. It can represent only one of two things: yes or no, on or off, 0 or 1 (as it's expressed in the binary numbers used by computers). The computer usually groups bits together into bigger chunks such as *bytes*, *kilobytes*, and so forth.

bit depth The number of *bits* of the Mac's *memory* assigned to each *pixel* on the screen or each sample point on a *scanner*. One bit is just black and white; 8 bits gives you 256 colors or shades of gray; 16 bits supplies 65,536 colors; and 24 bits per pixel provides over 16.7 million colors.

bit map An image made up of dots (or *pixels*).

bit-mapped font A font in which each character is made up of a pattern (map) of dots. To display it correctly, you must have a separate set of character maps for each size (10 point, 12 point, and so on)—otherwise, you'll have a bad case of the *jaggies*. Also called a fixed-size or *screen font*. Compare *outline font*.

bit-mapped graphic An image made up of dots (*bits*) rather than discrete objects. Typically produced by *paint*, *image-editing*, and 3-D *graphics* programs. Sometimes called a raster image; compare *object-oriented graphic*.

board A piece of fiberglass or pressboard on which *chips* and other electronic parts are mounted. The connections between the chips are normally printed with metallic ink, so it's called a printed circuit (or PC) board. The main board in a computer is called the logic board or *motherboard*. A board that plugs into an *expansion slot* is called an add-in board or *card*.

bomb Another word for *crash*. Bombs are usually heralded by an *alert box* with a picture of a bomb, indicating you must restart the Mac. Compare *hang*.

Boolean operator Words such as *and*, *or*, and *not* that you place between text strings to refine a search. For example, you could search a *database* for "men *and* cook *or* clean *but not* married." Also see *wildcard*.

boot blocks Parts of a Mac's *startup disk* that are hold information about the *System file* and the *Finder*. When you start up the Mac, it checks this area for a pointer toward a valid *System Folder*.

booting Starting up a computer, which loads the *system software* into *memory*. (The idea is that the computer is "pulling itself up by its own bootstraps.") Restarting the computer is called rebooting or a warm boot.

bps Bits per second, the correct way to express the data-transfer speed of a *modem*. Today's modems generally range from 9,600 bps to 28,800 bps; compression can increase the effective *throughput* to higher levels. Compare *baud rate*.

buffer An area of *memory* set aside for the storage of transient data. On the Mac it's called the *disk cache*, but other devices, such as *printers* and *modems*, also have buffers, which allow them to process data more quickly.

bug A mistake, or unexpected occurrence, in a piece of software (or, less commonly, in a piece of hardware). Bugs often cause the Mac to *hang* or *crash*.

bulletin board See *BBS*.

bus A path over which electronic impulses (data) travel between various computer *devices*. Examples include the Apple Desktop Bus *(ADB)*, which connects keyboards and mice to the Mac, and the *SCSI* bus, which connects *hard disks* and other *peripherals*.

button An outlined area in a *dialog box* that you *click* on to choose, confirm, or cancel a *command*. Common buttons include OK, Cancel, Open, Save, and Apply. Also see *default button*, *checkbox*, and *radio button*.

byte Eight *bits*. A byte typically represents one character (letter, number, or other symbol) on the screen.

cache See *disk cache*.

cache card A *card* that speeds up the Mac by supplying a small amount of high-speed *memory* (called static RAM, or *SRAM*) that the *processor* can use to quickly store and retrieve data while it's working.

CAD Computer-aided design, a category of high-end *draw programs* used by engineers, architects, and designers. Pronounced "cad."

card A kind of *board* that has connectors on its edges, so you can plug it directly into an *expansion slot* on the Mac. Cards add functionality, such as *24-bit color* or an *accelerator*. Also called an add-in board.

carpal tunnel syndrome A nerve problem that causes pain, numbness, or tingling in the hands (and often in the forearms). Advanced cases can cause permanent nerve damage. It's one type of repetitive stress injury.

cdev Control panel device, the System 6 name for a *control panel*.

CD-ROM Compact disk, read-only memory. A type of *storage* device that looks just like an audio CD (in fact, you can play audio CDs on a CD-ROM *drive*) and stores as much data as a large *hard disk* (600MB or so), making it a popular means of distributing *fonts*, photos, electronic encyclopedias, games, and *multimedia* offerings. As the name indicates, however, you can't save or change files on a CD-ROM, only read them. Pronounced "see-dee rom."

checkbox A *button* that works as a *toggle*—that is, you turn an option on by *clicking* once in the empty checkbox (an *x* will appear), and click again to turn it off. Unlike *radio buttons*, any or all of a group of checkboxes can be on at once.

chimes of doom A heart-stopping sequence of chords played during startup (instead of the usual *boing*) when a serious problem prevents the Mac from completing the startup procedure. You'll usually also see the *Sad Mac*.

chip The most essential electronic component of a computer: a tiny piece of silicon (about the size of a baby's fingernail) with an electronic circuit embedded in it. The Mac's *processor* and *memory* (*RAM* and *ROM*) are chips, which are normally mounted on *boards* or *SIMMs*.

Chooser A *desk accessory* that displays which *printers* and, on a *network*, which file *servers* and shared folders are available to you. You select a printer or other item by clicking on its *icon*. The Chooser is also where you turn *background printing* and *AppleTalk* on and off.

Chooser extension An *extension* that displays an *icon* in the *Chooser* dialog box. It's what enables the Mac to communicate (through its *modem* and *printer ports*) with *networks* and with devices such as *printers* and *modems*. Two common Chooser extensions are the LaserWriter *driver* and *AppleShare*.

CISC Complex instruction set computing; pronounced "sisk." The *processor* design used in the 68000-series chips found in all Macs except the Power Macs. Compare *RISC*.

clicking Pressing and immediately releasing the *mouse* button. To *click on* something is to position the *pointer* over it and then click.

clip art Precreated graphics—from simple line art to full-color photographs—that you can use, royalty-free, in publications and presentations. Also called clip media.

Clipboard A temporary storage area in the Mac's *memory* that holds what you last cut or copied. *Pasting* inserts its contents into a *document*. Some programs have a *menu* item that lets you see what's in the Clipboard.

clock rate A measure of the performance of a computer's *CPU* (or *processor*). The CPU's operations are synchronized to a quartz crystal that pulses millions of times each second. The rapidity of these pulses—measured in *megahertz*—is the clock rate (or speed).

close box A small box at the left end of the *title bar* in the *active window*. Clicking it closes the window. Compare *size box* and *zoom box*.

code The actual statements or instructions (written in a programming language) that make up a piece of *software*.

color management Any of several approaches—including Apple's ColorSync *extension*—that attempts to provide a consistent match between the image colors you see on screen (or that are input from a *scanner*) and those that are printed on paper.

command The generic name for anything you tell the Mac to do. Commands are usually listed on *menus* or are invoked using *keyboard shortcuts*.

commercial software Programs sold for profit in stores or by mail order, with the purchaser paying before taking possession. Compare *shareware*, *freeware*, and *public-domain software*.

communications program Software that enables you to send and receive information through a *modem*.

compact Mac An all-in-one Mac such as the Classic II, SE, or Plus, which have a 9-inch monitor built into the same box as the *CPU*. Compare *modular Mac* and *portable Mac*.

compatible Said of *software* and/or *hardware* that work together correctly (that is, without *crashes* or other problems). Also refers to *PCs* made by other companies that work just like IBM PCs.

configuration 1. The components that make up a computer system (which model of Mac and what *peripherals*). 2. The physical arrangement of those components (what's placed where). 3. The software settings that enable two computer components to talk to each other (as in configuring *communications software* to work with a *modem*).

contact manager A *database* program that keeps track of the names, addresses, phone numbers, and so forth of your personal and business contacts. TouchBASE is one example of this genre, which is part of a larger software category called *PIMs*.

control panel In System 7, a control panel (lowercase) is a *utility* that lets you adjust basic parameters such as the speaker volume, *desktop* pattern, date and time, and so on. Control panels are kept in a folder called Control Panels (capitalized, plural); one way to open it is by selecting Control Panels from the *menu*. In System 6, control panels are called *cdevs*, and they're accessed through the Control Panel (capitalized, singular) command on the menu.

Control Strip A collapsible *palette* that comes with current PowerBooks and provides convenient, on screen access to features such as battery charge, sleep mode, sound volume, *AppleTalk*, file sharing, and the PowerBook *control panel*.

coprocessor A *chip* designed specifically to handle a particular task, such as math calculations or displaying graphics on-screen. A coprocessor is faster at its specialized function than the main *processor* is, and it relieves the processor of some work. A coprocessor can reside on the *motherboard* (an *FPU* is one example) or be part of an *expansion card*, as with an *accelerator*.

copy protection Any of the various annoying schemes that companies employ to prevent the unauthorized (and illegal) copying of their software.

cps Characters per second. Used to describe the speed of *inkjet* and *dot-matrix printers*.

CPU Central processing unit, the brains of the computer. The CPU interprets and executes the actual computing tasks; one measure of its performance is the *clock rate*. In the Mac, the entire CPU resides in the *processor* chip, which is located on the *motherboard*. Sometimes people (including us) use *CPU* as another word for the processor, motherboard, or the entire computer.

crash A problem (often caused by a *bug*) that causes a *program*, or the entire *operating system*, to unexpectedly stop working. If a program crashes, you sometimes can recover with the *force quit* command, but you often have to restart the Mac. Also see *bomb* and *hang*.

creator The four-letter code that a *file* uses to tell the *Finder* which program "owns" it. It distinguishes a *document* created with Microsoft Word (MSWD) from one created with MacWrite Pro (MWPR), for example, so that the correct file *icon* appears and the correct *application* is launched when you *double-click* on the icon. Compare *file type*.

cross-platform Refers to *software* (or anything else) that will work on more than one *platform* (type of computer).

CRT Cathode ray tube, the display technology used in virtually all desktop computer *monitors* and television sets. Portable computers typically use an LCD (liquid-crystal display).

cursor There's really no such thing as a cursor on the Mac (it's used on more primitive computers), but people often say *cursor* when they mean *pointer*.

D

DA The common name for a *desk accessory*; pronounced "dee-ay."

daisy chain A *hardware* configuration in which devices are connected to each other (via cables) in a linear series. Typically used to describe a *network* setup (such as the *nodes* on a *LocalTalk* network) or the arrangement of *SCSI devices* attached to your Mac.

DAT Digital audio tape, the most common type of tape backup. See *backing up*.

data The generic name for anything you input to a computer, or anything it outputs to you. It's the plural of datum, a single piece of information.

database A file created by a *database manager* that contains a collection of information organized into records, each of which contains labeled categories (called fields). It's sort of like an electronic Rolodex, or a set of 3- by 5-inch cards.

database manager A program that lets you create a *database*, enter data, and then search, *sort*, and output it. There are several categories of database managers, including flat-file, relational, and *contact managers*. Also called a database engine, database management system (DBMS), or simply (and confusingly) a database.

data fork The part of a Mac *file* that holds user-created data, such as text and graphics. *Documents* always have a data fork; *applications* sometimes do. Compare *resource fork*.

daughterboard A *board* that attaches to (rides piggyback on) another board, such as the *motherboard* or an *expansion card*. For example, you can often add a daughtercard containing additional *memory* to an *accelerator card*.

DAV slot A special *expansion slot* on the AV Macs that gives direct access to their digital-processing hardware. DAV stands for digital audio video.

default The option that will be used unless you change it. It often refers to preset parameters such as the margins in a *word processor* or the volume in the Sound *control panel*. Also see *default button*.

default button In a *dialog box*, the *button* with a heavy border that's activated when you hit [Return] or [Enter].

demo version A sample copy of *commercial software* (and sometimes *shareware*) that has limited capabilities (usually you can't save or print) but allows you to see how the program works.

desk accessory A mini-application (such as the Alarm Clock) that's normally accessed from the *menu*. In System 6 that's the only way to get to them, but in System 7 they can be kept anywhere. Desk accessories usually open only one *document* at a time and quit automatically when you close their *window*. Commonly called DAs.

desktop What you see on screen when you're in the *Finder:* the *menu bar*, background pattern, *Trash*, disk *icons*, *files*, *folders*, and so forth. It's the Mac's version of home base.

Desktop file An invisible file on every *disk* that stores data such as *icons*, the size and location of *windows*, and the information available with the Get Info command. There's one desktop file in System 6, two in System 7. Compare *directory*.

desktop publishing The process of designing printed documents (brochures, newsletters, magazines, books, etc.)—often using a *page layout program*—on a personal computer.

device Another word for *hardware*.

dialog box A box that appears on the screen (often after you issue a *command*) and requests information or a decision. Compare *alert box* and *window*.

DIF Data interchange format, a standard *file format* for *databases* (and sometimes *spreadsheets*). It preserves field names and data but not formulas or text *formatting*. Compare *SYLK*.

digitize To turn something from the real (analog) world into digital data on a computer. You might use a *scanner* to digitize pictures or text, a sound digitizer to record music or a human voice, or a video-digitizing board to input video from a VCR or camcorder. Also see *sampling*.

dimmed When something, such as a *menu* item, is dimmed (gray) on the Mac's screen, it means that you can't currently access it. When you eject a *disk*, its *icon* is dimmed, as are all *windows* and icons associated with it.

direct memory access A *chip* that handles data transfers between *memory* and various devices (*hard disks*, *floppy disk* drives, and anything connected to the Mac's *ports*), freeing up the main *processor* for other tasks. The AV Macs and Power Macs have a DMA chip.

directory An invisible *file* on every *disk* that keeps track of the name, size, and location of all other files. If this critical file becomes damaged, you can lose access to your data. Compare *Desktop file*.

disk A thin round platter on which computer *data* is stored in either *magnetic* or *optical* form. Although the disk is circular, its case is usually rectangular. The main types are *floppy disks*, *hard disks*, and *CD-ROMs*.

disk cache An area of *RAM* reserved for data recently read from *disk*, which allows the *processor* to quickly retrieve it if it's needed again. You adjust the cache's size in the Memory *control panel* (96K or 128K is usually optimal). In System 6 it's called the RAM cache. Also see *cache card* and *RAM disk*.

disk drive See *drive*.

display Another word for screen or *monitor*.

display card A *card* that controls an external *monitor*. Also called a *video card*.

display port A *port* where you can plug in a *monitor*. They were formerly called *video ports*, but some Macs now have ports for connecting to camcorders, TVs, and VCRs, which are also called video ports.

dock 1. (noun) A piece of *hardware* that attaches to a PowerBook Duo and gives it desktop-Mac features (such as a floppy disk drive, *ports*, and *expansion slots*). 2. (verb) To connect a PowerBook to a desktop Mac in *SCSI disk mode*.

document The *file* that you create and modify with an *application*. Examples are a letter, a drawing, and a mailing list.

dogcow His name is Clarus, and he appears in the Page Setup *dialog box* (File menu). The dogcow demonstrates the options (like Flip Vertical) by acting them out when you *select* them. Clarus says "Moof!"

DOS Pronounced "dahss," it refers to MS-DOS or PC-DOS, the (disk) *operating systems* used on IBM personal computers and *compatible* machines.

dot-matrix printer An impact *printer*, such as Apple's ImageWriter II, that forms images from a pattern of dots, which are created by an array of pins striking an inked ribbon against the paper.

double-clicking Positioning the *pointer* and quickly *clicking* the *mouse* button twice without moving the mouse. You double-click to open *applications* and *documents* (when the *pointer* is an arrow) and to *select* entire words (when the pointer is an *I-beam*).

double-sided disk A double-density *floppy disk* that stores information on both surfaces (top and bottom) and can hold 800K of data. Compare *single-sided disk* and *high-density disk*.

download 1. To retrieve a file from another computer using a *modem*. For instance, you might download some *shareware* from an *on-line service*. Opposite of *upload*. 2. To send a *font* or *PostScript file* from the Mac to a *printer*. In general, any font installed on your Mac is a downloadable font, and downloading can be done automatically or manually. Compare *resident font*.

dpi Dots per inch, a measure of the *resolution* of a *printer*, *scanner*, or *monitor*. It refers to the number of dots in a one-inch line. The more dots per inch, the higher the resolution.

drag To move the *pointer* while holding down the *mouse* button. Depending on the situation, dragging can move an object, *select* an area (indicated by a *selection rectangle*), or move you down a *menu*.

drag and drop 1. In System 7, a method of opening a *document* from the *Finder* by *dragging* its *icon* over an *application* icon (which will become *highlighted* if it can open the file) and releasing the *mouse* button. 2. In System 7.5, a *system enhancement* that lets you move or copy text and graphics between documents (and/or the *desktop*) simply by dragging the *selected* item to the new location, without going through the *Clipboard*. 3. The ability, either through the Drag and Drop extension or through a program's own capabilities, to move an item in a document by dragging it to the new location.

DRAM Dynamic random access memory, commonly called *RAM*.

draw program Software that lets you create finely detailed illustrations and saves them as *object-oriented graphics*. Some draw programs are based on *PostScript*, and there are specialized applications for charting and *CAD*. Compare *paint program*.

drive A motorized *device* that reads information from, and writes information onto, *disks* or tapes. The main types are *floppy disk* drives and *hard disk* drives, but there are also drives for *CD-ROMs*, *removable media*, and tape.

driver A piece of *software* that tells the Mac how to operate an external *device*, such as a *printer*, *hard disk*, *CD-ROM* drive, or *scanner*. For instance, you can't print unless you have a printer driver (such as the LaserWriter file) installed in the Extensions folder inside the *System Folder*. Hard disk drivers are invisible files that are loaded into *memory* when you start the Mac, while scanner drivers are usually *plug-ins* accessed from within a particular *application*.

DSP Digital signal processor, a *coprocessor* that specializes in heavy-duty number crunching, making it ideal for speeding up the *processor*-intensive operations associated with graphics, video, and audio programs. The AV Macs have a built-in DSP *chip*, or you can buy DSP *cards* for things like Photoshop acceleration and *JPEG* compression.

dumb quotes Straight quotation marks (and apostrophes) like those found on a typewriter. They look like this: " '. They're a big faux pas on a computer unless you're referring to feet, inches, hours, or minutes. Compare *smart quotes*.

DXF Drawing interchange format, a standard *file format* for 3-D *graphics* and *CAD* programs.

dye-sublimation printer A *printer* that creates images by heating special pigments that become gaseous (sublime) and then diffuse into the paper's special coating. Also called dye-diffusion or continuous-tone printers.

E

edutainment A combination of the words *education* and *entertainment*, it usually refers to children's software that provides educational value in an entertaining way—for example, by using games, animations, and sounds.

8-bit color See *bit depth*.

ELF radiation Extremely low frequency electromagnetic radiation (between 60 Hz and 75 Hz), which is generated by computer *monitors* and other electrical devices (including hair dryers). Compare *VLF radiation*.

e-mail Electronic mail—private messages sent between users on different computers, either over a *network* or via a *modem* connection to an *on-line service* or *BBS*.

emulation A way to allow *software* to run on a *processor* it was not designed for. When you run an *application* written for a *68K* processor (such as the Quadra) on a Power Mac (which has a *PowerPC* chip), it runs in emulation mode (which is slower). Emulation mode requires an emulator, a piece of software that imitates the native processor. For example, the Power Macs have a 68LC040 emulator built into their *ROM* chips and can come with SoftWindows, an emulator that lets you run *PC* programs. Compare *native*.

Enabler See *System Enabler*.

encryption Scrambling the data in a *file* to prevent unauthorized access. Accessing the information requires a password.

Energy Star A government program that requires all computer equipment the Feds buy to drop its power consumption below 30 watts when it's not being used. Most manufacturers are redesigning their products to meet this energy-saving standard.

EPS Encapsulated PostScript, a standard *file format* for high-resolution *PostScript* illustrations. It usually has two parts: the PostScript code (which tells the *printer* how to print the graphic) and a *PICT* image (for on-screen previews).

ergonomics The study of the relationship between people and their work environment. Working ergonomically means minimizing work-related health threats and setting up a comfortable, efficient workplace.

Ethernet A *network* cabling scheme for *AppleTalk* networks (as well as other types of networks) that's much faster than *LocalTalk*. Ethernet support is built into some Macs (otherwise you must install an Ethernet *card*), and it can be used with a variety of wiring systems.

expansion card See *card*.

expansion slot A connector inside the Mac where you can plug in a *card* that adds capabilities such as *acceleration* or *24-bit color*. The number and types of slots vary among Macs; the main types are *NuBus*, *processor direct (PDS)*, *DAV*, and (soon) *PCI*.

export To *save* data from one *application* in a *file format* that another program can *import* or *open*. Some programs have an Export *command* that's separate from their Save command.

extension Software (including many popular commercial *utilities*) that extends the system's capabilities by, say, enabling it to display QuickTime movies or use a particular type of *printer*. There are two main types: system extensions (*QuickTime*, *AppleScript*, and so on) and *Chooser extensions* (such as printer *drivers* and *AppleShare*). Extensions in the Extensions folder in the active *System Folder* are automatically *loaded* into *memory* when the Mac starts up. (Some extensions are also *control panels*.) Called an *init* in System 6.

extension manager A *utility* that lets you control which *extensions* are active (*loaded*) when the Mac starts up.

F

fat binary The name given to software that contains *code* for both *68K* and *PowerPC* processors. A fat-binary *application* automatically uses whichever type of code is appropriate for the Mac it's running on.

fax modem A type of *modem* that can send (and, in most cases, receive) faxes in addition to transferring data files. Unlike regular fax machines, fax modems can't send printed documents—only disk files.

FDHD Refers to the 1.4MB *SuperDrive* that comes with current Macs. FDHD stands for floppy disk, high density, and it's pronounced "fud-hud."

file A collection of information on a disk, usually a *document* or a *program*, that's lumped together and called by one name. Mac files usually consist of a *resource fork* and a *data fork*.

file format The structure that the data for a particular *document* is stored in (e.g., ASCII, RTF, PICT, TIFF). Most applications can save documents in one or more standard formats as well as their *native* format. Also see *file type*.

file server See *server*.

file-transfer protocol A set of conventions for determining how files will be packaged, sent, and verified over telephone lines. An ftp (such as Zmodem or Kermit) is independent of the computer, *modem*, and *communications software*.

file type The four-letter code that identifies the nature of a *file* to the *Finder*. All *applications* have the file type APPL; *text files* have the code TEXT; and many graphics are *PICT* (the same as their *file format*). Compare *creator*.

filter A piece of software that an *application* uses for *file-format* conversion or special effects. PageMaker, for example, has a filter that lets it import Microsoft Word files, while Photoshop has dozens of filters for effects such as image blurring. Filters can be part of the main application or external programs called *plug-ins*, as with Claris's *XTND* system.

Finder The basic *program* that generates the *desktop* and lets you access and manage *files* and *disks*. Together with the *System file* and the *ROMs*, it makes up the Mac's *operating system*. There are Finder substitutes, such as Apple's At Ease, that perform the same basic tasks (and usually give you other capabilities as well).

FireWire Apple's new *interface* standard for connecting *peripherals* to the Mac. It will be phased in over the next few years, gradually replacing the current *SCSI* standard.

floating-point processor A *coprocessor* (or part of the main *processor*) that handles sophisticated calculations, such as those used in *spreadsheets*, *CAD*, and scientific programs. The chip, called an *FPU* (floating point unit), is built into the 68040 (but not 68LC040) and *PowerPC* chips. On Macs with earlier processors, the FPU is a separate chip (that you buy separately) called a *math coprocessor*.

floppy disk A 3.5-inch removable *disk* that's flexible (although it's usually protected by a hard plastic case). Also called a diskette; compare *hard disk*.

floptical A technology for *removable media* that stores data magnetically but uses optical techniques to position the *read/write head*. Floptical disks, which resemble *floppy disks*, currently hold up to 21MB. Also see *magneto-optical*.

folder A grouping of *files* and/or other folders that's represented by a folder-shaped *icon* on the *desktop*. (Its equivalent on DOS machines is a subdirectory.) Also see *HFS*.

font The software that creates a *typeface* on the Mac. In olden (precomputer) times, it referred to a single size and style of a typeface, such as 9-point Times Italic.

font family A group of typefaces that's designed to work together. A typical family (say, Palatino) has four members: regular, bold, italic, and bold italic.

footprint The amount of space a piece of *hardware* takes up on your desk (and its dimensions).

force quit A System 7 feature that lets you return safely to the *Finder* (usually) when a program *hangs* or *crashes*. The command is [⌘] [Option] [Esc]. You lose unsaved work in the crashed application, but you'll be able to save work in other programs before restarting the Mac.

format See *file format*.

formatting 1. In a *word processor*, all the information above and beyond plain text that's added to a *document*. It includes character *styles* (bold, italic), spacing, indents, tabs, tables, and so forth. 2. Another word for *initializing* a *disk*.

FPU Floating-point unit, a specialized math *coprocessor*. See *floating-point processor*.

fragmentation A condition in which parts of a *file* are stored in different locations on a *disk*. When a file is fragmented, the drive's *read/write head* has to jump from place to place to read the data; if many files are fragmented, it can slow the drive's *performance*.

freeware Software that may be freely copied and used, but the copyright for which is retained by the author, who usually forbids you to alter or sell the program. Compare *public domain software* and *shareware*.

GeoPort A special type of *printer port* or *modem port* that can serve as a built-in *modem*, *fax modem*, speakerphone, and answering machine.

gigabyte A measure of computer *memory*, *disk* space, and the like that's equal to 1,024 *megabytes* (1,073,741,824 *bytes*), or about 179 million words. Sometimes a gigabyte is treated as an even billion bytes (*giga-* means *billion*), but that's almost 74 million bytes short. Abbreviated *G*, *GB*, or *gig*. Compare *kilobyte* and *megabyte*.

graphics tablet An *input device* that lets you draw with a stylus (pen) on a flat piece of plastic. You can make more precise movements than with a *mouse*, making it a great adjunct to *draw* and *paint programs*, particularly if the stylus is pressure-sensitive. Also called a digitizing or pressure-sensitive tablet.

grayscale Anything that contains shades of gray as well as black and white, such as a grayscale *monitor*, which typically displays 256 grays.

GUI Graphical user interface; see *user interface*.

GX font An *outline font*, in either *PostScript* or *TrueType* format, that takes advantage of *QuickDraw GX*. GX fonts can have larger character sets and can include special programming that lets the fonts decide for themselves when to use alternate characters (such as ligatures) or include other special features.

H

halftone A way of converting (*rasterizing*) a *grayscale* or color image (a photograph, say) into a pattern of dots for output on a *printer* or *imagesetter*.

handshaking The process computers and *modems* go through in order to establish a connection and agree on the speed and *protocols* for data transmission.

hang A *crash* where the Mac ignores input from the *mouse* and keyboard. You can sometimes escape with the *force quit* command; otherwise you must restart the Mac. Also called a freeze. Compare *bomb*.

hard disk A rigid (usually nonremovable) *disk*, and/or the *drive* that houses it. Actually, hard disks usually have several disks (or platters), and they store much more data and access it more quickly than *floppy disks* do. Also called a hard drive or hard disk drive.

hardware The parts of your computer system you can bump into—physical components such as *hard disks*, *printers*, *modems*, *scanners*, *cards*, keyboards, mice, and the Mac itself. Compare *software*.

header 1. Identifying text (such as the date or page number) that appears at the top of each *document* page (vs. the footer, which is at the bottom). 2. The part of a document's *code* that tells a program how to interpret its contents; the header defines the *file format*, for example.

Help menu The *menu* near the right end of the *menu bar* that lets you turn *Balloon Help* on and off and, in System 7.5, access *Apple Guide*. (Its title is a question mark inside a balloon.) In some programs, you can also use it to access *on-line* help.

HFS Hierarchical file system, the Mac's method of organizing *files* on a *disk*, in which files and *folders* can be nested (contained) within other folders.

hierarchical menu A *menu* that has *submenus* (indicated by arrows) attached to it.

high-density disk A *floppy disk* that can store 1.4MB of data when used on a Mac with a *SuperDrive*. Compare *single-sided disk* and *double-sided disk*.

highlight To make something stand out from its background in order to show that it's *selected* or active. The Mac usually handles this by reversing the colors (for example, switching black and white) or, in the case of text, by placing a colored bar over the words.

hot link A special "live" link between *applications* that lets you *select* an element in a *document* (say, an illustration in PageMaker) and, using a special key combination, open it directly into the program that created it (such as FreeHand). You can make changes to the element, then return to the original document and instantly see those changes.

hypertext A text-linking strategy that lets you jump between related information in a *document* by clicking on a *button* or *highlighted* word. *On-line* help systems often use hypertext links, as do some programs designed for the electronic distribution of documents (see, e.g., *PDD*).

I

IAC Interapplication communication, an underlying technology in System 7 whereby one *application* can send a message to another, either to exchange information or to make something happen. *Apple events* and *OpenDoc* are two implementations of IAC.

I-beam The shape (Ɪ) the *pointer* normally takes when it's dealing with text. You use the I-beam to create an *insertion point* or to *select* a range of text. Also called the *text tool.*

icon The little picture that represents a *file*, *folder*, *disk*, or tool. It's a key component of the Mac's *user interface*. Click it once to select it; *double-click* it to open a file, folder, or disk.

image-editing program Software that lets you alter existing images, such as photographs captured with a *scanner*, and saves them as *bit-mapped graphics*. Compare *paint program.*

imagesetter A high-quality (usually *PostScript*) *printer* that can output pages (on paper or film) at *resolutions* of 1,200 *dpi* or greater. They're usually found at *service bureaus*.

impact printer See *dot-matrix printer*.

import To bring data into a *document* from another document, often generated by a different *application*. For instance, you can import text and graphics into a *page layout program*, or import *spreadsheet* data into a *word processor*. This data sharing is made possible by the applications' support of common *file formats*. Compare *open*.

init What an *extension* is called in System 6. It's short for initialization program and pronounced "in-it."

initializing Setting up a *disk* (any kind) to receive information. When a disk is initialized, its magnetic media is divided into tracks and sectors, and a *directory* and *Desktop file* are created. Also called *formatting*.

inkjet printer A *printer* that forms text and images out of little dots created by tiny jets of ink.

input device Anything you use to directly input information to the computer: a *mouse*, keyboard, *trackball*, *graphics tablet*, joystick—even a *scanner* or digital camera. Also see *pointing device*.

insertion point The place in a *document* or *dialog box* where the next keystroke will add or delete text. The insertion point is represented by a blinking vertical line and is placed by *clicking* with the *I-beam* pointer.

Installer A *utility* that copies *system software* or an *application* from *floppy disks* or a *CD-ROM* to your *hard disk*. An Installer may also decompress the new files, remove obsolete files, place *extensions* and *control panels* in their proper folders, and/or create new folders.

integrated software A single *application* that includes several types of basic programs, such as a *word processor*, *spreadsheet*, *database manager*, *draw*, *paint*, and (often) *communications*.

interactive Said of software (particularly *multimedia*) that gives you some control over what's going on. You might click *buttons* to play a movie or jump to a different point in a presentation, or type in questions or answers that cause the program to respond in different ways. System 7.5's *Apple Guide* is an interactive help system.

interchange format A *file format* that's supported by most programs of a certain type (such as *word processors* or *paint programs*), allowing you to exchange files among them. *ASCII* is the standard interchange format for text, for example, while *PICT* and *TIFF* are common graphics formats. Compare *native*.

interface See *user interface*.

Internet A worldwide super-network that links thousands of individual *networks* and *on-line services*. You can gain access to the Internet—and its millions of users and thousands of newsgroups (discussion forums), *databases*, directories, and other digital goodies—if your computer is on one of the corporate, government, or university networks the Internet connects, or if you have an account with an Internet service provider. You also can send *e-mail* across the Internet from almost any on-line service.

J

jaggies The blocky, stair-stepped look common to *bit-mapped graphics* and *bit-mapped fonts*. *Anti-aliasing* can minimize this effect.

JPEG A sophisticated technique (it's not really a *file format*, per se) for *compressing* full-color *bit-mapped graphics*, such as photographs. It stands for Joint Photographic Experts Group.

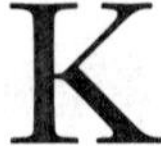

K An abbreviation for *kilobyte*, as in "an 800K file."

keyboard shortcut A combination of keystrokes (almost always involving [⌘] and often [Shift], [Option], and/or [Control] as well) that executes a *command* without you having to choose it from a *menu*. Also called a key combination or keyboard equivalent.

kilobyte A measure of computer *memory*, *disk* space, *document* size, and the like that's equal to 1,024 *bytes*, or about 170 words. Abbreviated *K*. Compare *megabyte* and *gigabyte*.

L

label One of seven descriptive names and colors that you can attach to *files* and *folders* using the Label *menu* in the *Finder*. You can sort files and folders by label to group related files and folders together (to do so, choose By Label from the View menu). To change the names and colors of labels, use the Labels *control panel*.

LAN Local area network, a *network* that's physically connected (via cables) and confined to a relatively small area, like one office or one building. Often just called a network. Compare *WAN*.

laserdisc A 12-inch disk that's similar to an audio CD but holds visual images (such as high-quality movies) as well as music. Some laserdisc players can be hooked up to the Mac. Also called a videodisc.

laser printer A *printer* that creates images by drawing them on a metal drum with a laser. An ink powder, called toner, sticks to the imaged portion of the drum and is then transferred and fused to the paper (as with a photocopying machine). Apple established the popularity of *PostScript*-based laser printers with its LaserWriter line.

LaserWriter 35 The standard set of 35 *resident fonts* that most *PostScript laser printers* have built into their *ROM*. So named because they first appeared in Apple's LaserWriter Plus.

launch *Open* (start) an *application*, that is, *load* it into *memory* from a *disk*.

Launcher A *control panel* that arranges the *icons* of selected *applications* and *documents* in a special *window*. To open a file, you click once on its icon.

list box A box with *scroll bars* that appears within a *dialog box* and lists things—*files*, *fonts*, or whatever.

list view One of five text-based ways—Name, Size, Kind, Label, and Date—that you can view a *folder's* contents in the *Finder*. In System 7, these are also called outline views because they can display a folder's contents in outline form, without opening another *window*.

load Get something ready to use. It can mean install (as in loading new *fonts*) or open (as in loading *extensions* into *memory* when the Mac starts up).

LocalTalk This refers to the networking *hardware* built into the Mac as well as to Apple's cabling scheme for connecting Macs on a *network*. Compare *PhoneNet* and *Ethernet*.

lock To prevent a *file* or *disk* from being changed. You can lock (or unlock) a file or *floppy disk* by clicking the Locked *checkbox* in its Get Info window. You also can lock a floppy disk by moving the plastic tab in the upper-left corner of its back side so that you can see through the little square hole. Locked disks are also called write-protected.

logic board See *motherboard*.

log on Establish a connection to a *server*, *BBS*, or *on-line service*, usually by entering a user name (or identification number) and a password. Disconnecting is called logging off.

M

MacBinary A format for transferring Mac files over a *modem* or to another type of computer that ensures that all component parts (including the *data fork*, *resource fork*, and *icons*) stay together, so that you wind up with a usable file. Virtually all file-transfer and *communications programs* support MacBinary.

macro A user-defined *keyboard shortcut* that executes a series of *commands*. Macros are easy to create; all you need is a macro *utility* to record your keystrokes and *mouse* clicks. If you want to automate complex tasks, however, you'll probably need a *scripting language*.

magneto-optical A technology for *removable media* that combines magnetic and optical techniques. MO disks resemble *floppy disks*, but in terms of capacity and speed they're more like *hard disks*. Also called erasable-optical disks.

mail merge The merging of *database* information (such as names and addresses) with a letter *template* in a *word processor*, in order to create personalized letters.

marquee The rectangle of moving dots (called "marching ants") that surrounds a *selected* area in some programs.

marching ants See *marquee*.

math coprocessor Another name for *floating-point processor*.

MB An abbreviation for *megabyte*.

media 1. The physical component of a *floppy disk*, *hard disk*, cartridge, tape, or *CD-ROM* that stores computer data. The main storage strategies are *magnetic* and *optical*. 2. The various ways of communicating, including print, video, and audio. See *multimedia*.

megabyte A measure of computer *memory*, *disk* space, *application* size, and the like that's equal to 1,024K (1,048,576 *bytes*) or about 175,000 words. Abbreviated *MB* or *meg*. Compare *kilobyte* and *gigabyte*.

megahertz A million cycles (occurrences, alterations, pulses) per second. Used to describe the speed at which a computer's *processor* (or *CPU*) operates. A 25-MHz processor can handle 25 million operations per second.

memory In general, another word for dynamic *RAM*, the *chips* where the Mac stores *system software*, programs, and data you are currently using. Other kinds of memory you may encounter are parameter RAM *(PRAM)*, video RAM (*VRAM*), and static RAM (*SRAM*). Most computer memory is volatile, that is, its contents are lost when the computer shuts down. Also see *ROM*.

menu A list of *commands*. To *select* one, *drag* down the menu until the desired command is *highlighted*, then release the *mouse* button. (If a command is unavailable, it will be *dimmed*.) Also see *pop-up menu*, *pull-down menu*, and *submenu*.

menu bar The horizontal strip across the top of the screen that contains the *menu* titles.

MHz An abbreviation for *megahertz*.

microprocessor See *processor*.

MIDI Musical instrument digital interface, a technology that enables a computer to record and play musical performances. The MIDI standard provides a common language and *interface* so that the Mac and the electronic instruments and software can reliably connect and communicate with one another. Pronounced "middy."

modem A piece of *hardware* that lets computers talk to each other over telephone lines (you also need a *communications program*). The modem translates back and forth between the computer's digital data and the sounds carried over the phone lines. (The word is a contraction of modulator/demodulator.) Also see *fax modem*.

modem port A *serial port* on the Mac's back panel that's ordinarily used for attaching a *modem*. You also can use the port to attach other serial devices, such as a *graphics tablet* or *inkjet printer*. Compare *printer port* and *GeoPort*.

modifier key A key that modifies the effect of the character key being pressed. In most Mac *applications*, for example, [⌘][S] saves the *document* you're working on. The standard keyboard has five modifier keys: [Shift], [Option], [⌘], [Control], and [Caps Lock].

modular Mac A desktop Mac whose *monitor* isn't built into the same box as the *CPU*. Most Macs sold today are modular, except for the PowerBooks and 500-series Performas and LCs. Compare *compact Mac* and *portable Mac*.

monitor The piece of *hardware* that contains the screen that you look at while you work. It's also called a *display* or *CRT* and can be *monochrome* (black and white), *grayscale*, or color. You connect it to the Mac's *display port* or to a *video card*.

monochrome Anything that contains just one color (and shades thereof). A monochrome *monitor*, for example, is either black and white (black is the color, white is the background) or *grayscale*.

MooV The *file format* for *QuickTime* movies. It can include video, audio, and animations.

morphing A special effect used in graphics, video, and animation that produces a smooth transformation of one shape into another, such as a pop star turning into a panther.

motherboard The heart, soul, and brains of the Mac. This plastic *board* resembles a miniature city, but its buildings are actually *chips* for things like the *processor*, *RAM*, and *ROM*, and the tiny roads connecting them are circuit traces. Also called the logic board. There are no fatherboards or sonboards, but check out *daughterboard*.

mount Make a *storage* device available as an *icon* on the *desktop*. The Mac can't access a disk until it's mounted on the desktop; to dismount a disk, you *drag* its icon to the *Trash*.

mouse The standard *pointing device* supplied with every Mac. Moving the mouse causes the on-screen *pointer* to move in the same direction.

MultiFinder A System 6 program that allows several *applications*, including the *Finder*, to be open at the same time. (This capability is built into System 7.)

multimedia Any presentation or program that combines several *media*, such as graphics, sound, video, animation, and/or text. Multimedia is everywhere these days—business presentations, *CD-ROM* games, educational software, and training systems—and it's often *interactive*.

multiscan monitor A *monitor* that can operate at different *resolutions* and scanning frequencies, allowing you to use it with a variety of computers. An important concept on the PC side of things, but less relevant in the Mac world. Most monitors are now multiscan units (older Apple monitors are not). Also (incorrectly) called MultiSync monitors (a brand name used by NEC).

multitasking Said of a computer that can do more than one thing at a time, such as *sorting* a *database* and recalculating a *spreadsheet*. The Mac isn't a true multitasking machine (yet).

multiuser Said of an *operating system* (such as *Unix*), *application*, or piece of *hardware* that can be used by more than one person at one time.

N

nanosecond A billionth of a second. Used to measure the speed of *memory (RAM)* chips, among other things. Abbreviated *ns*.

native 1. Said of software that's written specifically to run on a particular *processor*. For example, a program optimized for a *68K* processor runs in native mode on a Quadra, but it runs in *emulation* mode (which is slower) on a *PowerPC*-based Power Mac. 2. The *file format* in which an *application* normally saves its *documents*. The native format is generally readable only by that application (other programs can sometimes translate it using *filters*). Compare *interchange format*.

network In general, a group of computers set up to communicate with one another. Your network can be a small system that's physically connected by cables (a *LAN*), or you can connect separate networks together to form larger networks (called *WANs*). The *Internet*, for example, is made up of thousands of individual networks.

node Any *device* that's directly connected to a *network*. This usually includes computers, *printers*, and file *servers*.

NuBus slot A type of *expansion slot* within the Mac where you can attach NuBus *cards* that add capabilities such as *acceleration* or *24-bit color*. The number of NuBus slots varies among Mac models; you can often identify them by their slot covers on the Mac's back panel.

null modem cable A *serial port* cable that lets you connect a Mac directly to another computer, such as a *PC*, for direct data transfers.

object-oriented graphic An image made up of individual, mathematically defined objects, rather than a collection of *bits*. Typically created by *draw programs*, which are based on either *PostScript* or *QuickDraw*. Also called a vector graphic; compare *bit-mapped graphic*.

OCR Optical character recognition, a technology that lets you scan a printed page (with a *scanner*) and convert it into text *document* that you can edit in a *word processor*. Some OCR software also works with files received by a *fax modem*.

OEM Original equipment manufacturer, a company that produces a product that isn't sold on its own but instead is incorporated into another company's product. For example, Quantum is an OEM that makes hard disks sold under different names by other companies. Sometimes OEM is used as a verb: "Quantum OEMs disk drives for Apple."

on-line Actively connected to other computers or devices. You're on-line when you've *logged on* to a *network*, *BBS*, or *on-line service*. A device such as a *printer* is on-line when it's turned on and accessible to the Mac. (It can even refer to software: An on-line help system is one you can call up in your software, as opposed to opening a manual.) If you're not on-line, then you're off-line.

on-line service A commercial service that (for a price) provides goodies such as *e-mail*, discussion forums, tech support, software libraries, news, weather reports, stock prices, plane reservations, even electronic shopping malls. To access one, you need a *modem*. Popular on-line services include America Online, CompuServe, and eWorld. Compare *BBS* and *Internet*.

open 1. Start up an *application* and/or make a *document* visible on the screen, that is, load its contents into *memory* from a *disk*. Compare *import* and *save*. 2. Expand a *folder* or *disk* into a *window* by *double-clicking* on its *icon*. Also see *drag and drop*.

OpenDoc A *system enhancement* that lets you use several *applications* to work on different types of data within a single *document* (called a compound document because of the multiple formats it contains).

operating system The basic *software* that runs the computer itself. On the Mac, it consists of the *System file*, the *ROMs*, the *Finder*, and related *system software*. Often called the OS ("oh-ess") or just the system.

outline font A font in which each character's shape is stored as a mathematical outline. It can be scaled to any size with no loss of quality and will print at the highest available resolution. *PostScript*, *TrueType*, and *GX fonts* are outline-font formats. Also called a scalable font; compare *bit-mapped font*.

P

page layout program Software designed to combine text and graphics on a virtual page, giving you extensive control over the design and typography. The cornerstone of *desktop publishing*.

Paint A nearly obsolete *file format* (*file type* PNTG) that holds low-resolution black-and-white *bit-mapped graphics*. Compare *TIFF*.

paint program Software that lets you create digital paintings from scratch and saves them as *bit-mapped graphics*. Compare *image-editing program* and *draw program*.

palette A floating *window* within an *application* that sits above open *documents* so that you can easily access its contents. It can contain tools, *buttons*, colors, styles, or whatever is appropriate to the program. Also called windoids.

parallel port A type of *port* that transmits data in parallel—several bits side by side. The Mac doesn't have parallel ports, but they are common *printer interfaces* on *PCs*.

parameter RAM See *PRAM*.

partition A section of a *hard disk* that's *formatted* so the Mac will treat it as a separate disk. Partitioning can reduce wasted space and make file management easier, especially on a large disk. Also called a volume.

paste To insert something into a *document* from the *Clipboard* by choosing Paste from the Edit *menu* (or typing ⌘V).

patch A small piece of *code* added to an existing program to enhance *performance* or fix a *bug*.

PC Personal computer. While the Mac is, of course, a PC, the term refers almost exclusively to those *other* computers: IBM PCs and their *compatibles*.

PCI Peripheral component interconnect, a new kind of *expansion slot* that will appear on Mac models beginning in late 1994. The current slot types are *NuBus* and *PDS*.

PCMCIA A standard format for credit-card-size *expansion cards*, used to add features to 500-series PowerBooks, hand-held computers, and (in the future) desktop computers. The unpronounceable acronym stands for Personal Computer Memory Card International Association, but an easier mnemonic is People Can't Memorize Computer Industry Acronyms.

PDD Portable digital document, a *file format* introduced with *QuickDraw GX*. A *document* saved as a PDD file can be viewed and printed accurately on any Mac that has QuickDraw GX (or System 7.5), even if that Mac doesn't have the file's original *application* or *fonts*.

PDS See *processor-direct slot*.

peer-to-peer A *network* setup that allows every Mac to both offer and access network resources, such as shared files, without requiring a centralized *AppleShare server*.

performance In computer parlance: speed. (How well your computer actually performs, however, is based on much more than its raw speed.)

peripheral A piece of *hardware* that's outside (peripheral to) the main computer. In practice, it usually refers to external hardware—such as disk *drives*, *printers*, and *scanners*—sold by a *third party*.

PhoneNet A popular implementation of *LocalTalk* cabling that uses ordinary telephone wire to connect *devices* on an *AppleTalk network*.

Photo CD A technology developed by Eastman Kodak for scanning and storing photographs on *CD-ROM*. Many film developers will turn a roll of 35mm film into high-quality digital photos that you can access using a Photo CD–*compatible* CD-ROM *drive*.

PICS A standard *file format* for *animation* files.

PICT A standard *file format* for graphics files. It can contain both *object-oriented* and *bit-mapped* graphics and is the standard format for graphics that are cut or copied to the *Clipboard*.

PIM Personal information manager. Used to describe programs that keep track of information you need to conduct day-to-day personal business. They usually offer some combination of an address book (or *contact manager*), calendar and scheduling, and to-do lists.

piracy Copying *commercial software* (or *shareware*) without permission and without paying for it. Also called theft.

pixel One of the little points of light that make up the picture on a computer (or TV) screen. (The name is short for picture element.) The more pixels there are in a given area—that is, the smaller and closer together they are—the higher the *resolution*. Often, pixels are simply called dots.

PlainTalk A voice-related *system enhancement* that has two parts. Text-to-speech enables *applications* that support it to read text aloud. Voice recognition works in conjunction with *AppleScript* to let you control the Mac with spoken *commands*.

platform Usually refers to a particular type of computer running a particular *operating system*. The Mac is one platform, a *PC* running *Windows* is another, and a *Unix* machine is still another. Also see *cross-platform*.

plug-in A *software* module that adds capabilities to an *application*. Pop a plug-in file into the appropriate folder, and the program will sprout new features.

PMMU Paged memory management unit, the *chip* that makes *virtual memory* possible (provided the appropriate software is installed). Its functions are built into the 68030, 68040, and *PowerPC processors*.

pointer The little icon that moves on the screen when you move the *mouse* (or other *pointing device*). Its most common shapes are the arrow (↖), the *I-beam* (I), and the *wristwatch* (⌚). It takes on other shapes and names—such as the lasso (ℓ)—in other applications.

pointing device A *mouse*, *trackball*, or other *input device* that moves the *pointer* on screen.

pop-up menu A *menu*, typically found in a *dialog box* or *palette*, that pops up (or down or to the side) when you press the *mouse* button on its title (a box with a drop shadow around it). Compare *pull-down menu*.

port Computerese for a socket (or jack) where you plug in a cable to connect *devices* together. Most Macs have an *ADB* port, a *SCSI* port, a *display port*, a *printer port*, a *modem port*, and so forth.

portable Mac A smallish, (relatively) lightweight Mac, such as a PowerBook or the Portable, that includes the *CPU*, *monitor*, and keyboard in a single, fold-up unit. Compare *compact Mac* and *modular Mac.*

PostScript A programming language developed by Adobe that's designed to describe, in precise detail, how the text and graphics on a printed page should look. It's often referred to as a page description language and is used on many types of *printers* and *imagesetters*. Compare *QuickDraw*.

PostScript font An *outline font* format defined in *PostScript*. With *system software* versions before 7.5, PostScript fonts (also called *printer fonts*) must be used in conjunction with *bitmapped fonts* (the *screen fonts*). Compare *TrueType font.*

PowerPC A type of *processor* chip, based on powerful *RISC* technology and made by IBM and Motorola. Apple introduced PowerPC chips with the Power Macs and plans to phase out the *68K* processors used in other Macs.

PRAM Parameter RAM (pronounced "pee-ram"), a small portion of the Mac's *RAM* set aside to hold basic information such as the date and time, speaker volume, desktop pattern, and key-board and *mouse* settings. PRAM is powered by a battery, so it doesn't lose the settings when you shut down. Sometimes, however, the PRAM data gets corrupted, causing crashes or other problems. That's where *zapping the PRAM* comes in.

preferences The user-adjustable features of a *program*. Many programs create separate Preferences (or Prefs) files, which are usually stored in the *System Folder*.

presentation program Software that lets you combine text, charts, and illustrations—and, if you wish, animation, video, and sound—into electronic slide shows or *multimedia* presentations. You also can output the results to 35mm slides or videotape.

printer A *device* that takes the text and graphics sent from the Mac and puts them on a piece of paper. Most are computers in their own right, with *CPUs* and *memory*. The range of printer types includes *laser*, *inkjet*, *dot-matrix*, *thermal-fusion*, *dye-sublimation*, and *imagesetters*.

printer driver See *driver*.

printer font Another name for a *PostScript font*, which is an *outline font* designed to be used by *printers*. For screen display, you use a companion *screen font*.

printer port A *serial port* on the Mac's back panel that lets you connect to a *printer* or *LocalTalk network*. Compare *modem port* and *GeoPort*.

PrintMonitor A *print spooler* that comes with the *system software;* it shows you which files are printing as background tasks.

print spooler Software that intercepts a *document* on its way to the *printer*, temporarily storing it on *disk* until the printer is ready for it. It feeds the printer while you continue to work, providing *background printing*. System 7 has a built-in spooler, *PrintMonitor;* you can also buy a spooler *utility*.

processor The all-important *chip* that contains the computer's brains, or *CPU*. Sometimes called a microprocessor, it's located on the *motherboard*. Also see *coprocessor*.

processor-direct slot A type of *expansion slot* that connects to the *CPU* directly, rather than via a *bus* as with *NuBus* slots. Abbreviated *PDS*.

program Another word for *software*.

programmer's switch A small piece of plastic that comes with your Mac. It contains the reset button (which lets you restart the Mac in virtually any situation) and the interrupt button (used mainly by programmers). Also see *force quit*.

protocol A set of standardized rules for exchanging information between computers over a *network* or *modem* connection. For example, *AppleTalk* is a networking protocol, and Zmodem is a *file-transfer protocol* used in *telecommunications*. Protocols generally specify the data format, timing, sequencing, and error checking of data transmissions.

public domain software Software that has no copyright or fee, which means you can copy, use, and—unlike *freeware*—even alter and sell it. Compare *shareware* and *commercial software*.

Publish and Subscribe A data-linking strategy built into System 7 that's sometimes called "live cut and paste." You can *select* and *publish* (make available) data in one *document*, then *subscribe* (create a link) to it from one or more other documents. Whenever you change the original information, all the copies are automatically updated.

pull-down menu The kind of *menu* you find on the *menu bar*. It pops down when you click on its title; to keep it extended, you hold down the *mouse* button. Compare *pop-up menu*.

QuickDraw The Mac's *native* graphics language, which tells it how to draw everything on the screen: text, images, *dialog boxes*, *menus*, *icons*, you name it. QuickDraw, which is built into the Mac's *ROM*, is also responsible for producing *PICT* graphics and for outputting text and images to non-PostScript *printers*. Compare *PostScript*.

QuickDraw GX A *system enhancement* that makes big improvements in the way the Mac handles printing, graphics, *fonts*, and exchanges of formatted files between Macs.

QuickDraw printer A non-*PostScript printer*, which relies on the Mac's *QuickDraw* language to tell it how to print text and images.

QuickTime Apple's technology for recording and playing back time-based data (video, animation, and sound). Physically, QuickTime is an *extension* that provides a standard *user interface*, a special *file format* (*MooV*), and compression (movies can be huge).

quitting Leaving a *program* and returning to the *Finder* (or its equivalent).

R

radio button One in a group of buttons of which only one can be on at a time (like the presets on a car radio). When you *select* one radio button, the others are automatically deselected. Compare *checkbox*.

RAM Random access memory, the *chips* in a desktop Mac that contain most of its *memory*. RAM is the most common type of computer memory, and it's where the Mac stores *system software*, programs, and data you are currently using. It's formally called dynamic RAM (*DRAM*) because it's volatile, that is, the contents are lost when you turn off the Mac (or *crash*). It's pronounced "ram" and measured in *megabytes*. Compare *PRAM*, *SRAM*, *VRAM*, and *ROM*.

RAM cache See *disk cache*.

RAM disk It's not a *disk* at all, but rather a portion of *memory* set aside to act as a temporary disk. The Mac sees it as a hard disk, but because *RAM* is faster, the files and programs stored on it will run faster. (You get to decide how big the RAM disk is and what files it contains.) It's especially useful in PowerBooks because the Mac won't waste battery power spinning up the hard disk if the needed data is on the RAM disk.

rasterizing The process of converting the outlines of an *object-oriented graphic* or *font* into the *bit map* (a pattern of dots or *pixels*) required for display on a *monitor* or output on a *printer*. In printers, this step is usually handled by a *RIP*.

readme file A disk *document* that accompanies software and gives you information that's either very important or was left out of the printed manual.

read-only Refers to something you can view and print but not write (save changes) to. *Locked* files or disks are read-only, as are *CD-ROMs*.

read/write head The part of a *drive* mechanism that actually deposits information on (writes) and extracts information from (reads) the *disk*.

reboot See *booting*.

removable media Technically, any storage *media* (including *floppy disks*) that you can insert into and remove from the Mac or an external *drive*. In common usage, it usually refers to SyQuest and Bernoulli cartridges and *magneto-optical* and *floptical* disks.

rendering The process of drawing the final image in some graphics programs (such as 3-D graphics), which includes applying the specified colors, textures, shadows, movements, and so forth and outputting the image at the specified *resolution*.

resident font A *font* that's built into a printer's *ROM* (or stored on an attached *hard disk*), so it's always available for printing. Compare *download*.

resolution In general, this refers to how sharp and clear an image looks on screen or on paper, and how much detail you can see. It's usually determined by the number of dots (or *pixels*) per square inch—the more there are, the higher the resolution—and is used to describe *printers*, *monitors*, and *scanners*.

resource A piece of *code* with a specific purpose that's found in the *System file*, a *suitcase file*, or an *application*. Examples include *icons*, *fonts*, sounds, and keyboard layouts. Resources aren't usually separate files, but they can be (as with fonts and some sounds).

resource fork The part of a Mac *file* that holds program-specific *resources* such as *menus*, *dialog boxes*, sounds, *icons*, and *formatting* instructions. *Applications* always have a resource fork. Compare *data fork*.

RGB monitor A generic name for a color *monitor*, which uses three separate signals—red, green, and blue—to create the screen image.

RIP Raster image processor, a piece of hardware or software that converts (*rasterizes*) *object-oriented graphics* and *fonts* into the *bit maps* required for output on a *printer* or *imagesetter*.

RISC Reduced instruction set computing; pronounced "risk." A type of *processor* design that uses a relatively small set of instructions for faster operation. The *PowerPC* chip in the Power Macs is based on RISC technology. Compare *CISC*.

ROM Read-only memory; rhymes with *mom*. ROM is permanent *memory* that's programmed on a *chip* (called the RAM chip) and can't be altered. It contains parts of the *system software* responsible for very basic things, such as starting up and drawing images on the screen. Compare *RAM*.

RTF Rich text format, a *file format* for text files that includes *formatting* instructions. Also called interchange format.

run-time player A limited version of an *application*, such as a *database manager* or *presentation program*, that lets you access a *database* or play back a presentation, but not modify it or create new ones. You often can freely distribute the run-time player with *documents*, so that others can use them without having to install the full program.

S

Sad Mac The glum Mac face that appears on screen (accompanied by the *chimes of doom*) when the Mac can't start up due to a serious problem with its *hardware* or *system software*. When everything is OK, the Happy Mac appears during startup.

sampling Taking audio snapshots (called samples) of a sound wave (such as music or a voice) at regular intervals and turning them into a digital recording on the computer. The number of samples taken per second is called the sampling rate. Also see *digitize*.

save To transfer information (usually a *document*) from *memory* to a *disk*. Compare *open*.

scanner A *device* that converts images (such as photographs) into digital form so that they can be stored and manipulated on computers. When used in conjunction with *OCR* software, a scanner can convert a page of text into an editable *document*.

Scrapbook A *desk accessory* where you can permanently store material (text, graphics, sounds, movies) and then easily access it from within any program.

screen font Another name for a *bit-mapped font*. Screen fonts are required for the on-screen display of *PostScript fonts*. With *TrueType fonts*, they're often supplied to speed up the screen display of common type sizes.

screensaver A *utility* that temporarily replaces the current screen image with a blank screen or an amusing/attractive/silly moving image. It's designed to prevent a static image from being permanently burned into the screen phosphor.

script A series of *commands* (saved as a file) that automates everyday tasks, such as file backups, or adds capabilities to a program or presentation. A script is, in essence, a simple *program* that you write using a *scripting language*. Also see *macro*.

scripting language A simple programming language, such as *AppleScript* or HyperCard's HyperTalk, that you use to create *scripts*.

scroll bar The rectangular strip that appears on the right and/or bottom edges of a *window* when there's more information than is currently displayed. You can *click* in its gray area and/or use the scroll arrows and scroll box (thumb) to move the window's contents.

scrolling Moving through the contents of a *window* or *list box* in order to see things not currently displayed. It's normally done with the *scroll bar*.

SCSI Small computer systems interface; pronounced "scuzzy." The standard interface for con-necting *peripherals* to the Mac. You can attach up to seven *SCSI devices* to your Mac in a *daisy chain*. SCSI *ports* have been built into all Macs (except dockless Duos) since 1986. Compare *FireWire*.

SCSI device A *peripheral* that you connect to the Mac via a SCSI *port*. Examples include *hard disks*, *CD-ROM drives*, tape *backup* units, *scanners*, and some personal *printers*.

SCSI disk mode A way of connecting a PowerBook to a desktop Mac so the PowerBook behaves as if it were an external *hard disk*, allowing you to swap files back and forth. It's supported by most PowerBook models, but you need a special *adapter* cable.

SCSI ID The number assigned to a *SCSI device* so the Mac can distinguish it from other SCSI devices. Each device must have a unique number in the range from 0 to 6 (most peripherals let you change the ID with a switch or dial); the Mac itself is number 7. Also called the SCSI address.

select To choose something (text, graphic, object, region) that you want to change. You do this by *clicking* on an object or button, Shift-*clicking* on several objects, or *dragging* across an area. The chosen area (the selection) is either *highlighted* or surrounded by a *marquee*. Selecting by itself doesn't change anything, it just tells the Mac what you want to be affected by the next *command* or action. You deselect something by clicking elsewhere.

selection rectangle The dotted box that appears (in the *Finder* and many *applications*) when you *click* on an empty spot and *drag*. When you release the *mouse* button, the box disappears (or becomes a *marquee*) and everything within it is *selected*.

serial port A type of *port* that transmits data serially, one bit after another. The Mac's *modem* and *printer ports* are serial ports. Compare *parallel port*.

server A computer that provides shared, centralized resources—such as files, *e-mail*, *databases*, *modems*, and *printers*—to other computers on a *network*. *Server* can also refer to the software, such as *AppleShare*, that runs on such a computer. Compare *peer-to-peer*.

service bureau A business that can output your *documents* on specialized (read: expensive) equipment such as *laser* and *dye-sublimation printers*, large-format color printers, and *imagesetters*. Most service bureaus also let you rent time on computers, send faxes, and do photocopying.

sfil The standard *file format* for System 7 sound *resources*, which are stored in the *System file* and appear in the Sound *control panel*. To hear one, *double-click* on its *icon*.

shareware Software that you can try before you buy. Like *freeware* and *public domain software*, it's distributed on the honor system, usually through *on-line services*, *BBSs*, and *user groups*. You're allowed to try it out and give copies to others, but if you want to keep using it, you must pay the (usually nominal) registration fee. Compare *commercial software*.

Shift-click To hold down the Shift key while *clicking* the *mouse* button. Shift-clicking lets you *select* multiple objects or large amounts of text, depending on the program.

SIMM Single in-line memory module, a small card that holds *memory* chips. To add more *RAM* to your Mac, you buy SIMMs and plug them into *slots* on the *motherboard*. Pronounced "sim."

single-sided disk An older type of double-density *floppy disk* that stores just 400K of data on one surface. Compare *double-sided disk* and *high-density disk*.

68K Shorthand for Motorola's 68000 series of *processor* chips—the 68000, 68020, 68030, 68040, and 68LC040—used in every Mac model prior to 1994. (In this case, the *K* stands for *thousand*, not for *kilobyte*.) Also called the 680x0 series. They're gradually being replaced by *PowerPC* chips.

size box A small box found in the bottom-right corner of most *active windows*. *Clicking* and *dragging* it lets you change the window's size and shape. Compare *close box* and *zoom box*.

slot See *expansion slot*.

smart quotes True (curly) quotation marks that should be used for professional-looking text. They look like this: " '. Most fonts have them as Option characters. Compare *dumb quotes*.

snd The *resource* responsible for making the sounds you hear in programs and HyperCard *stacks*. In System 7, system sounds are *sfil* resources.

sneakernet A *file-sharing* strategy that uses hand-carried *disks* as the exchange *media*. Transfer speed depends on the efficiency of your footwear.

software The instructions that tell a computer what to do. It takes many forms, from an *application* on a disk to the *code* in a Mac's *ROM*. Also called *programs* or, redundantly, *software programs*. Compare *hardware*.

sort To order *selected* information (in a *database*, say, or a *word processing* document) by one or more criteria, such as alphabetically.

spreadsheet program Software that processes number-related information, allowing you to apply calculations and formulas to data that's organized in rows and columns of cells. Its documents are sometimes called worksheets.

SRAM Static RAM, a speedy but expensive form of *memory* found in *cache cards*. It boosts the Mac's performance by reducing the time the *processor* spends waiting for data from the slower dynamic *RAM*.

stack A *document* created by HyperCard.

startup disk The *disk* containing the *System file* and *Finder* that the Mac is currently using (which is usually the disk it started up from). If you have several disks *mounted* at the same time, you can designate which will be the startup disk using the Startup Disk *control panel*.

stationery A feature of System 7 (and some *applications*) that lets you create *templates*—*documents* that, when *double-clicked*, open an exact duplicate of themselves, leaving the original untouched. In System 7, you can turn most documents into stationery by clicking the Stationery Pad *checkbox* in their Get Info window.

storage Any type of *media* that you can store files on, including a *hard disk*, *floppy disk*, SyQuest cartridge, *magneto-optical* disk, or *DAT* tape.

storage bay A space inside the Mac where you can install additional disk *drives*. There are two sizes: 3.5-inch (the standard size for floppy disk drives, hard disks, and some cartridge drives) and 5.25-inch (*CD-ROM* drives, some hard disks, and cartridge drives).

street price The average price that a product sells for through mail order or dealers. It's usually significantly less than a company's official list price. Also see *ApplePrice*.

style In a word processor, a piece of *formatting* that's applied to text. A character style is an attribute—such as *font* and size, and whether it's bold or italic—that only affects individual letters. A paragraph style also includes information such as line spacing, indents, and tab settings.

style sheet A collection of character and paragraph *styles* that has a name, allowing you to quickly apply several *formatting* changes at once.

submarining An unsettling effect sometimes found on *passive-matrix* PowerBook screens: If you move the *pointer* too fast, it disappears until you stop moving it.

submenu The secondary *menu* that appears next to an existing menu when you choose a *command* name that has a small, right-pointing arrow.

suitcase A *file* that stores *fonts*, sounds, or *desk accessories*; its *icon* looks like a little suitcase. In System 7, suitcases operate like *folders*: You can *double-click* on them to open a *window* showing their contents, and *drag* items into and out of them. In System 6, you move items into and out of a suitcase file with Font/DA Mover.

SuperDrive The 1.4MB *floppy disk drive* that comes with all current Macs. It can read and write *single-sided* (400K) disks, *double-sided* (800K) disks, and *high-density* (1.4MB) disks. With the appropriate software, it can also read 3.5-inch disks from *PCs* and Apple II machines. It used to be called the *FDHD* (floppy disk, high-density) drive.

support 1. Help with *hardware* or *software* problems, usually in the form of advice from the technical support staff at the company that sold you the product. 2. To say that a piece of hardware or software *supports* something means that it works with it, or enables it to work. For example, System 7 supports *TrueType fonts*, while System 6 doesn't (normally).

surge protector A device that protects computer equipment from being damaged by variations in electrical current.

SYLK Symbolic link format, a standard *file format* for *spreadsheets* (and sometimes *databases*). It preserves formulas and text *formatting* as well as data. Compare *DIF.*

sysop A person who manages a *BBS* or moderates a forum (discussion group) on an *on-line service*. Short for system operator and pronounced "siss-op."

system 1. A computer setup. 2. Short for *operating system.*

System Enabler A file in the *System Folder* that makes the Mac *compatible* with the current version of the *system software* (starting with System 7.1). Different Mac models have different Enablers.

system enhancement A program (often an *extension*) that extends the capabilities of the *system software*, such as *AppleScript*, *QuickDraw GX*, or *QuickTime*. Some work in the background, adding features (such as movies) to *applications*, while others, such as At Ease and PowerTalk, are stand-alone programs that you can access directly.

System file The program the Mac uses to start itself and to provide certain basic information to all *applications*. Together with the *Finder* and *ROM*, it makes up the Mac's *operating system*.

System Folder The all-important *folder* on a Mac *disk* that contains the *System file*, *Finder*, and other *system software*. Only disks with a System Folder can be *startup disks*.

system heap The portion of a Mac's *memory* reserved for the *system software*. Compare *application heap*.

system software A catchall term for the basic programs that make the Mac work. It creates the *desktop*, provides universal *commands* such as Open, Save, and Cut, and includes features such as the *Clipboard*. Part of the system software is in *ROM*, and the rest is on disk in the *System Folder*, including the *Finder*, *System file*, *Chooser*, *control panels*, *extensions*, and *fonts*.

T

TCP/IP The network *protocols* used on the *Internet* and on many *multiplatform networks* (especially those with *Unix* machines). It stands for transmission control protocol/internet protocol. The Mac can speak TCP/IP using the MacTCP *extension*. Compare *AppleTalk*.

tear-off Refers to a *menu* (or *palette*) that you can detach from the main menu (or main palette) and move around on the screen like a palette. A tear-off menu/palette stays fully extended and remains in front of open *document* windows.

telecommunications The transfer of information between computers over telephone lines. Just plug in a *modem*, fire up some *communications software*, and you can make contact with the office computer, an *on-line service*, a *BBS*, or the *Internet*.

template A master *document* that you can use repeatedly without altering the original contents. Many *applications* provide templates (and/or let you create them); when opened, they actually create a duplicate copy, which you can modify as needed and save under a different name. System 7 has a template feature called *stationery*.

terminator A small *device* that eliminates echoes and other unwanted electrical signals from a *SCSI* bus or *network*. In a SCSI chain, it usually plugs into the SCSI port of the last device in the chain.

text box An area, usually in a *dialog box*, where you insert text. Also called a text field.

text editor A simple, no-frills *word processor* that works with plain *ASCII* text.

text file An *ASCII* file—just characters, no formatting.

text tool Another name for the *I-beam* pointer.

thermal-wax transfer printer A *printer* that creates images using tiny heated elements that push rolls of plastic film against a page, bonding a waxy ink to the paper. Also called heat-fusion or thermal-fusion printers.

third party You are the first party, Apple (the maker of your computer) is the second party, and the companies that make *hardware* and *software* for the Mac are third parties. It also refers to companies that make add-on software for major *applications*—for example, a *plug-in* for Adobe Photoshop (the second party in this case).

32-bit addressing A method of handling *memory* in System7 that enables most Macs to work with as much *RAM* as the machine can hold. Without it Macs have 24-bit addressing, which limits total RAM to 8MB.

32-bit clean A phrase used to describe *software* (including what's in *ROM*) that's written to work correctly (that is, without crashing) with 32-bit addressing. A few older Macs, such as the SE/30, aren't 32-bit clean and are said to have "dirty ROMs."

32-bit color Color that uses 32-bits to store each pixel's color value. Like *24-bit color* (see *bit depth*), it offers 16.7 million colors; the extra 8 bits per pixel don't offer more colors; they're reserved for special operations such as masking.

throughput The rate at which data can be transferred between two computers or other devices. With *modems*, it refers to the number of bits exchanged per second (see *bps*).

TIFF Tag image file format, the standard *file format* for high-resolution *bit-mapped graphics*, including those generated by most *scanners*.

tile 1. To arrange *windows* side by side, as if they were floor tiles. 2. To print an oversized image across several pieces of paper (which can then be taped together). 3. To repeat a pattern or texture across an image in a graphics program.

title bar The horizontal strip across the top of a *window* that contains its name. When the window is active, its title bar has horizontal stripes, a *zoom box*, and a *close box*. To move a window, you *drag* it by the title bar.

toggle A feature that changes its status (on or off) each time you use it. For example, the common type styles (bold, italic, etc.) are toggles, because the first time you choose them they turn on, and the next time they turn off. Other toggles include *checkboxes* and certain *menu* items (e.g., Show Ruler and Hide Ruler).

toolbox 1. A special *palette* containing *buttons* and tools that floats above a *document* for easy access. Also called a tool palette, unless it's a toolbar (a ribbon across the top of the screen). 2. The Toolbox is a collection of predefined software routines (*code*) built into the Mac's *ROM* that performs basic tasks such as drawing *dialog boxes* and displaying *menus*.

trackball A *pointing device* that resembles an upside-down *mouse*. Instead of sliding a mouse across the desk, you roll a ball in a stationary holder.

trackpad The touch-sensitive *pointing device* built into late-model PowerBooks. Instead of moving about the screen by rolling a *trackball*, you run a fingertip across the trackpad.

Trash The *icon* on the *desktop* into which you put *files* to be deleted; they aren't actually deleted, however, until you choose Empty Trash from the Special *menu*. You can also eject a *floppy disk* or dismount a *hard disk* (or *AppleShare* volume) by *dragging* its icon to the Trash.

TrueType An *outline font* format developed by Apple and supported by System 7. Unlike *PostScript fonts*, a single TrueType font file works for both the screen and any *printer*.

Tune-Ups Free utilities from Apple that fix bugs and enhance features of System 7.0 and 7.0.1. For System 7.1, they're called System Updates.

24-bit color See *bit depth*.

Type 1 font The primary format for *PostScript fonts*, developed by Adobe Systems.

typeface A collection of letters, numbers, punctuation marks, and symbols with an identifiable and consistent design. A typeface, such as Helvetica or Times, can include many different weights (light, semibold, bold, etc.) and styles (regular, italic, etc.). Compare *font*.

U

Undo The Mac's most beloved command (⌘Z), it lets you, well, *undo* the last thing you did in a program. Undo is often a *toggle*, so you can flip back and forth between two versions of something, and the cool programs have multiple undo, allowing you to go back more than one step.

Unix This *multiuser, multitasking, multiplatform operating system* was developed by Bell Labs and is pronounced "you-nix." Apple's implementation of Unix is called *A/UX*.

upload Send a *file* to another computer using a *modem*. Opposite of *download*.

user group A bunch of people who get together to share help and advice about their computers and software. Mac-specific user groups are often called MUGs, the largest of which are BMUG and the Boston Computer Society.

user interface The way a computer (or a *program*) interacts with the user. For example, the Mac's interface uses graphical elements—*icons, windows, buttons, menus, dialog boxes*—which is why it's called a graphical user interface, or GUI (pronounced "gooey").

utility A small program that enhances the *system software* or an *application*. *Screensavers*, spelling checkers, file finders, *extension managers*, and compression programs are all utilities.

V

vaporware A product that a company keeps promising to deliver but never does (or at least is very, very late in shipping).

VAR Value-added reseller, a person or company that buys hardware and software, packages it all together, and sells it to you as a complete system. A VAR will discuss your needs, make the buying decisions, install the system, train you, and provide support. For a price, of course.

vector graphics Another term for *object-oriented graphics*.

video card 1. A *card* that controls an external *monitor*. It can include features such as *24-bit color* and/or a graphics *accelerator*. 2. A card that *digitizes* the video signal from a TV, VCR, or camcorder. Also called a digitizing board or a digitizer.

video editor Software that lets you create and edit *QuickTime* movies, record video and audio (with the appropriate *digitizing* hardware), and output the movies in various formats.

video port 1. A *port* where you can attach an external *monitor*. Now called the *display port*. 2. A port where you can attach a VCR, camcorder, or TV. Video-in ports let you *digitize* the video signal coming from one of these devices, and video-out ports send digital data to them.

virtual memory A System 7 strategy that expands the available *memory* by treating vacant space on a *hard disk* as if it were *RAM*.

virus A program that replicates itself from one *file* or *disk* to another without your consent. They are spread through *floppy disks*, *networks*, and *on-line services* and can go undetected (unless you have an antiviral *utility*) until something goes wrong. Some viruses deliberately destroy data, and even those designed to be "benign" can cause *crashes*, slowdowns, and file corruption.

VLF radiation Very low frequency electromagnetic radiation (between 10KHz and 30KHz), which is emitted by the *CRTs* in *monitors* and televisions. Compare *ELF radiation*.

voice recognition The ability of the Mac to interpret and execute spoken *commands* (and even, with the right *software*, to take dictation). *PlainTalk* is one implementation.

VRAM Video *RAM*, a type of *memory* dedicated to handling the image displayed on a *monitor*. VRAM is built into many Macs, and it also comes on *display cards*.

W

WAN Wide-area network, a *network* that spans geographically separated areas, usually by using *modems* and dedicated, high-speed telephone lines. Compare *LAN*.

wildcard A character (usually * or *?*) that can stand for one or more unknown characters during a search. Searching for some text or a file using *Mac** would find *Macintosh*, *MacUser*, and *macadamia*.

window A rectangular frame on the Mac's screen that has a *title bar* and *scroll bars*. *Disks* and *folders* open into windows, and *documents* appear in windows when you're working on them. Compare *dialog box*.

Windows Microsoft *software* that adds a Mac-like graphical *user interface* to *PCs*.

word processor Software that lets you enter, edit, and *format* text. Not only that, but it also provides goodies such as spelling checkers, outlining, tables, footnotes, and tables of contents.

wristrest A little cushion that provides support for the wrists and helps prevent repetitive stress injury.

wristwatch The *icon* the *pointer* normally turns into while you wait for the Mac to do something.

WYSIWYG What you see is what you get—that is, the image you see on screen matches what will print on paper. Pronounced "wizzy-wig."

Z

zoom box A small box at the right end of the *title bar* in most *active windows*. Clicking it expands the window to display all the contents; clicking again restores the previous size and shape. Compare *close box* and *size box*.

Index

In this index, numbers and symbols are alphabetized as if spelled out. For example, *32-bit addressing* comes after *thin-wire Ethernet*, and *menu* is alphabetized as *Apple menu*. Also, all terms are alphabetized as if spaces and hyphens didn't exit, so, for example, *Kid Desk* comes before *KidPix*.

A

B

C

D

E

F

G

H

I

L

N

O

P

Q

R

S

T

U

V

W

Y

Z

More from Peachpit Press

Order Form

to order, call:

(800) 283-9444 or (510) 548-4393 or (510) 548-5991 (fax)

Qty	Title	Price	Total
	The Macintosh Bible CD-ROM	$25.00	
	The Macintosh Bible, 5th Edition	$30.00	
	The Macintosh Bible Book/CD-ROM Combo	$42.00	
		Subtotal	
		8.25% Tax (CA only)	
		Shipping	
		TOTAL	

Shipping	First Item	Each Additional
UPS Ground	$ 4	$ 1
UPS Blue	$ 8	$ 2
Canada	$ 6	$ 4
Overseas	$14	$14

Name

Company

Address

City State Zip

Phone Fax

❑ Check enclosed ❑ Visa ❑ MasterCard ❑ AMEX

Company purchase order #

Credit card Exp. Date

What other books would you like us to publish?

Please tell us what you thought of this book:

Peachpit Press, Inc. • 2414 Sixth Street • Berkeley, CA • 94710

More Raves from Readers...

Marvelous, Funny, Witty, Entertaining, Functional, Directional and Extremely Informative.

Shelly Frederick, Portland OR

Killer book...I use it often, and it makes me look really smart to my co-workers. (Wait, that didn't sound right, did it?) Thanks a million for writing it.

Jeffrey Smith, Melbourne FL

Excellent! Great! Fab! Spiffy! Dandy! Just Awful Darn Good!

Ray Batts, Wyoming MI

Now if I could only find such an intelligent, entertaining, practical, and well-written guide to programming my VCR! Keep up the excellent work.

A.J. Stone III, Centreville, VA

It's like having Technical Support at your finger tips, instead of waiting for someone to call you back while they look up the answer.

Katrina Birling, Neenah WI

Good before, during and after a meal.

Warren Hansen, Evanston IL

This is the BEST Mac book I have ever read. It reviews nearly every aspect of the computer, and gives very good tips and hints! Keep up the good work.

Roberto Martinez, Hempstead NY

Should be packed in every Macintosh box!

Dave Brocklebank, B.C. Canada

Finally someone out there who really does want us to know what is going on. Thank you.

Sarah Pennell, Sydney, Australia

What User Groups Said About Previous Editions

Unlike most reference works, which will put you to sleep in under three minutes, this one will keep you awake as you read over its pages and end up taking sides in the saucy banter of its editors.

Jean Mickelson, Madison Macintosh Users Group

I can honestly say that if there is only one book you can afford to buy, then, without the slightest doubt, you must own *The Macintosh Bible*.

Access (Louisville Computer Society)

The authors take the time and trouble to explain things clearly, avoiding the jargon found in many computer books.

Jim Alley, Newsletter of the Savannah Macintosh Users Group

No matter who you are, you'll find a wealth of useful information that would take an eternity to garner from other sources. A must buy.

Dave Wojtowicz, Columbia ApplePi

**Probably the best investment a new Mac user can make.
Buy this book!**

Mac International

Contains almost everything you've wanted to know about the Mac but didn't know who to ask.

Apple Library Users Group Newsletter

Each page is loaded with at least one or two gems of real help. This is one volume that no one—but no one—can take out of my home.

Max Rogel, Palm Beach MacBytes

The Macintosh Bible Doesn't End Here

Most computer books are out of date a few months after they're published. But not *The Macintosh Bible.* To keep the information in it current, a free update is included in the price. The update is 30 pages long, filled with new tips, tricks, shortcuts, and product reviews. It will be mailed to you at our expense in the Summer of 1995. For those registering their *Macintosh Bible* after that date, your update will be mailed out within one month of our receiving your registration card.

If you bought this book directly from us, you're already registered, and you'll get your update automatically. If you bought the book somewhere else, or ordered it from us but have moved since then, just fill out the card below and send it in.

To order other books and products, call us at 800/283-9444 or 510/548-4393, or fax us at 510/548-5991.

Order Card for Free Update to the Macintosh Bible

Please print clearly. Thanks.

Name ______________________________

Address ______________________________

____

City ______________________________

State/Zip/Country ______________________________

____

Please tell us what you think of this book (if you like—it's not required):

☐ Check here if you'd rather not receive information from other Mac-related companies.

Mail This Card to Receive Your Free Update Booklet

SEE OTHER SIDE FOR DETAILS

Place Stamp Here

Peachpit Press
2414 Sixth Street
Berkeley, CA 94710